Martti Nissinen
Prophetic Divination

Beihefte zur Zeitschrift für die alttestamentliche Wissenschaft

Volume 494

Martti Nissinen

Prophetic Divination

Essays in Ancient Near Eastern Prophecy

DE GRUYTER

ISBN 978-3-11-076413-0
e-ISBN (PDF) 978-3-11-046776-5
e-ISBN (EPUB) 978-3-11-046766-6
ISSN 0934-2575

Library of Congress Control Number: 2019937568

Bibliographic information published by the Deutsche Nationalbibliothek
The Deutsche Nationalbibliothek lists this publication in the Deutsche Nationalbibliografie; detailed bibliographic data are available on the Internet at http://dnb.dnb.de.

This volume is text- and page-identical with the hardback published in 2019.
Printing and binding: CPI books GmbH, Leck

www.degruyter.com

For Simo Parpola

Preface

The thirty-two essays collected in this volume document my research on the phenomenon of prophetic divination over the time span of a quarter of a century. The volume includes most of my articles on prophecy published in English or German, except for those I reworked for the book *Ancient Prophecy: Ancient Near Eastern, Biblical, and Greek Perspectives* (Oxford: Oxford University Press, 2017). The essays have not been updated, save the cases where my original text contains obvious mistakes, or where exceptionally important new information has caught my attention. The bibliographies, however, have been standardized, and the references to cuneiform sources have, where necessary, been changed to refer to the newest available text editions.

I would like to thank Reinhard G. Kratz, editor of the BZAW series, for the initiative for publishing this volume, as well as the de Gruyter staff, especially Albrecht Döhnert, Sophie Wagenhofer, Aaron Sanborn-Overby and Anett Rehner, for their highly professional work on the manuscript. Cordial thanks are due to Marika Pulkkinen, who has prepared the indexes while finishing the manuscript of her own doctoral dissertation. For the past six years, I have had the privilege of being the director of the Academy of Finland Center of Excellence "Changes in Sacred Texts and Traditions" (CSTT), a wonderful, diverse, and open-minded community of biblical, assyriological, and archaeological scholarship at the University of Helsinki. I thank each and every CSTT member for making my daily work a pleasure. And Maarit, my fiancée: thank you for your love and care!

Colleagues and friends from whom I have learned over the decades are too many to be mentioned here. There is one person, however, to whom I owe more than to any other scholar: Simo Parpola, who introduced me to the world of the cuneiform, who taught me the Assyrian prophetic texts years before their publication, and who is the co-author of one of the essays included in this book. This book is dedicated to him with much gratitude.

DOI 10.1515/9783110466546-001

List of Original Publications

I would like to thank the following publication houses for granting the permission of reprinting the previously published articles as indicated in the following list of original publications: Bloomsbury, Brill, EOS Verlag, Finnish Exegetical Society, Finnish Oriental Society, Kohlhammer, Oriental Institute of the University of Chicago, Palgrave Macmillan, Peeters, Penn State University Press, Society of Biblical Literature, Ugarit-Verlag, and Vandenhoeck & Ruprecht.

"Die Relevanz der neuassyrischen Prophetie für die alttestamentliche Forschung," in *Mesopotamica – Ugaritica – Biblica*, FS K. Bergerhof (ed. M. Dietrich and O. Loretz; AOAT 232, Kevelaer, Germany: Butzon & Bercker; Neukirchen-Vluyn: Neukirchener, 1993) 217–58.

"Falsche Prophetie in neuassyrischer und deuteronomistischer Darstellung," in *Das Deuteronomium und seine Querbeziehungen* (ed. T. Veijola; PFES 62; Helsinki: Finnische Exegetische Gesellschaft and Göttingen: Vandenhoeck & Ruprecht, 1996) 172–95.

"The Socioreligious Role of the Neo-Assyrian Prophets," in *Prophecy in Its Ancient Near Eastern Context: Mesopotamian, Biblical, and Arabian Perspectives* (ed. id.; SBLSymS 13; Atlanta, Ga.: Society of Biblical Literature, 2000) 89–114.

"City as Lofty as Heaven: Arbela and Other Cities in Neo-Assyrian Prophecy," in *'Every City Shall Be Forsaken': Urbanism and Prophecy in Ancient Israel and the Near East* (ed. L. L. Grabbe and R. D. Haak; JSOTSup 330; Sheffield: Sheffield Academic Press, 2001) 172–209.

"A Prophetic Riot in Seleucid Babylonia," in *'Wer darf hinaufsteigen zum Berg YHWHs?' Beiträge zu Prophetie und Poesie des Alten Testaments, Festschrift für Sigurður Örn Steingrimsson zum 70. Geburtstag* (ed. H. Irsigler; Arbeiten zu Text und Sprache im Alten Testament 72; St Ottilien: EOS Verlag, 2002a) 62–74.

"Prophets and the Divine Council," in *Kein Land für sich allein: Studien zum Kulturkontakt in Kanaan, Israel/Palästina und Ebirnâri für Manfred Weippert zum 65. Geburtstag* (ed. U. Hübner and E. A. Knauf; OBO 186; Fribourg and Göttingen: Academic Press Fribourg and Vandenhoeck & Ruprecht, 2002) 4–19.

"Das kritische Potential in der altorientalischen Prophetie," in *Propheten in Mari, Assyrien und Israel* (ed. M. Köckert and M. Nissinen; FRLANT 201; Göttingen: Vandenhoeck & Ruprecht, 2003) 1–32.

"Fear Not: A Study on an Ancient Near Eastern Phrase," in *The Changing Face of Form Criticism for the Twenty-First Century* (ed. M. A. Sweeney and E. Ben Zvi; Grand Rapids, Mich.: Eerdmans, 2003) 122–61

"Neither Prophecies nor Apocalypses: The Akkadian Literary Predictive Texts," in *Knowing the End from the Beginning: The Prophetic, the Apocalyptic and their Relationships* (ed. L. L. Grabbe and R. D. Haak; JSPSup 46; London: T & T Clark, 2003) 134–48.

(with S. Parpola) "Marduk's Return and Reconciliation in a Prophetic Letter from Arbela," in *Verbum et calamus: Semitic and Related Studies in Honour of the Sixtieth Birthday of Professor Tapani Harviainen* (ed. H. Juusola, J. Laulainen, and H. Palva; StOr 99; Helsinki: Finnish Oriental Society, 2004) 199–219.

DOI 10.1515/9783110466546-002

“What Is Prophecy? An Ancient Near Eastern Perspective,” in *Inspired Speech: Prophecy in the Ancient Near East*, FS H. B. Huffmon (ed. J. Kaltner and L. Stulman; JSOTSup 372; London: T & T Clark, 2004) 17–37.

“The Dubious Image of Prophecy”, in *Prophets, Prophecy, and Prophetic Texts in Second Temple Judaism* (eds. M. H. Floyd and R. D. Haak; LHBOTS 427; New York / London: T & T Clark, 2006) 26–41.

“From Holy War to Holy Peace: Biblical Alternatives to Belligerent Rhetoric,” in *Isaiah’s Vision of Peace in Biblical and Modern International Relations: Swords into Plowshares* (ed. R. Cohen and R. Westbrook; Culture and Religion in International Relations. New York: Palgrave Macmillan 2008) 181–97.

“Das Problem der Prophetenschüler,” in *Houses Full of All Good Things*, GS T. Veijola (ed. J. Pakkala and id.; PFES 95; Helsinki: Finnish Exegetical Society, 2008) 337–53.

“Transmitting Divine Mysteries: The Prophetic Role of Wisdom Teachers in the Dead Sea Scrolls,” in *Scripture in Transition: Essays on Septuagint, Hebrew Bible, and Dead Sea Scrolls in Honour of Raija Sollamo* (ed. A. Voitila and J. Jokiranta; JSJSup 126; Leiden: Brill, 2008) 513–33.

“Reflections on the ‘Historical-Critical’ Method: Historical Criticism and Critical Historicism,” in *Method Matters*, FS D. L. Petersen (ed. J. M. LeMon and K. H. Richards; SBLRBS 56; Atlanta, Ga.: Society of Biblical Literature, 2009) 479–504.

“The Historical Dilemma of Biblical Prophetic Studies,” *in Prophecy in the Book of Jeremiah* (ed. H. M. Barstad and R. G. Kratz; BZAW 388; Berlin: de Gruyter, 2009) 103–20.

“Wisdom as Mediatrix in Sirach 24: Ben Sira, Love Lyrics, and Prophecy,” in *Of God(s), Trees, Kings, and Scholars*, FS S. Parpola (ed. M. Luukko, S. Svärd, and R. Mattila; StOr 106; Helsinki: Finnish Oriental Society 2009) 377–90.

“Pesharim as Divination: Qumran Exegesis, Omen Interpretation and Literary Prophecy,” in *Prophecy after the Prophets: The Contribution of the Dead Sea Scrolls to the Understanding of Biblical and Extra-Biblical Prophecy* (ed. K. de Troyer and A. Lange; CBET 52; Leuven: Peeters, 2009) 43–60.

“Biblical Prophecy from a Near Eastern Perspective: The Cases of Kingship and Divine Possession,” in *Congress Volume, Ljubljana 2007* (ed. A. Lemaire; VTSup 133; Leiden: Brill, 2010) 441–68.

“Prophecy and Omen Divination: Two Sides of the Same Coin,” in *Divination and the Interpretation of Signs in the Ancient World* (ed. A. Annus; Oriental Institute Seminars 6; Chicago: Oriental Institute, 2010) 341–51

“Comparing Prophetic Sources: Principles and a Test Case,” in *Prophecy and the Prophets in Ancient Israel* (ed. J. Day ; LHBOTS 531; London: T & T Clark, 2010): 3–24

“The Exiled Gods of Babylon in Neo-Assyrian Prophecy,” in *The Concept of Exile in Ancient Israel and Its Historical Contexts* (ed. E. Ben Zvi and C. Levin; BZAW 404; Berlin: de Gruyter 2010) 27–38.

“Prophecy as Construct: Ancient and Modern,” in *“Thus Speaks Ishtar of Arbela”: Prophecy in Israel, Assyria and Egypt in the Neo-Assyrian Period* (ed. R. P. Gordon and H. M. Barstad; Winona Lake, Ind.: Eisenbrauns, 2013) 11–35.

“The Prophet and the Augur at Tušḫan, 611 B.C.,” in *Literature as Politics, Politics as Literature: Essays on the Ancient Near East in Honor of Peter Machinist* (ed. D. S. Vanderhooft and A. Winitzer; Winona Lake, Ind.: Eisenbrauns 2013) 329–337.

"Prophets and Prophecy in Joshua–Kings: A Near Eastern Perspective," in *Israelite Prophecy and the Deuteronomistic History: Portrait, Reality, and the Formation of History* *(ed. M. R. Jacobs and R. F. Person; SBLAIL 14. Atlanta: Society of Biblical Literature 2013) 103–128.

"Since When Do Prophets Write?," in *In the Footsteps of Sherlock Holmes: Studies in the Biblical Text in Honour of Anneli Aejmelaeus* (ed. K. de Troyer, T. M. Law and M. Liljeström; CBET 72. Leuven: Peeters 2014) 585–606.

"Sacred Springs and Liminal Rivers: Water and Prophecy in the Ancient Eastern Mediterranean," in *Thinking of Water in Late Persian/Early Hellenistic Period in Judah* (ed. E. Ben Zvi and C. Levin; BZAW 461; Berlin: Walter de Gruyter 2014) 29–48.

"Oracles at Qumran? Traces of Inspired Speakers in the Dead Sea Scrolls," in *Crossing Imaginary Boundaries: The Dead Sea Scrolls in the Context of Second Temple Judaism* (ed. M. S. Pajunen and H. Tervanotko; PFES 108. Helsinki: Finnish Exegetical Society, 2015) 165–181.

"(How) Does the Book of Ezekiel Reveal Its Babylonian Background?" *WO* 45 (2015) 85–98.

"The Book of Hosea and the Last Days of the Northern Kingdom: The Methodological Problem," in *The Last Days of the Kingdom of Israel* (ed. S. Hasegawa, C. Levin, and K. Radner; BZAW 511. Berlin: Walter de Gruyter, 2018) 369–382.

"Non-Male Prophets in Ancient Near Eastern Sources," in *Prophets* (ed. I. Fischer; Bible and Women 1.2.; Atlanta: SBL Press), forthcoming.

List of Abbreviations

4 R	H. C. Rawlinson, The Cuneiform Inscriptions of Western Asia. Vol 4. London: Trustees of the British Museum, 1875.
A.	Tablet signature of texts from Mari
AAA	*Annals of Archaeology and Anthropology*
AASF	Annales Academiae scientiarum fennicae
AB	Anchor Bible
AbB	F. R. Kraus, ed., *Altbabylonische Briefe in Umschrift und Übersetzung* (Leiden: Brill, 1964)
ABD	D. N. Freedman, ed., *The Anchor Bible Dictionary* (6 vols., New York: Doubleday, 1992)
ABL	R. F. Harper, *Assyrian and Babylonian Letters* (Chicago: University of Chicago Press, 1892–1914).
AD	A. J. Sachs and H. Hunger, *Astronomical Diaries and Related Texts from Babylonia.* Vols 1–3 (Vienna: Verlag der Österreichischen Akademie der Wissenschaften, 1988–96)
ADPV	Abhandlungen des Deutschen Palastina-Vereins
AfO	*Archiv für Orientforschung*
AfO.B	Archiv für Orientforschung, Beiheft
AHw	W. von Soden, *Akkadisches Handwörterbuch* (3 vols., Wiesbaden: Harrassowitz)
AJS Review	*Association for Jewish Studies Review*
AJSL	*American Journal of Semitic Languages and Literatures*
ALASP	Abhandlungen zur Literatur Alt-Syren-Palästinas und Mesopotamiens
AMT	R. C. Thompson, *Assyrian Medical Texts* (Oxford: Clarendon Press, 1923)
AnBib	Analecta Biblica
ANEM	Ancient Near East Monographs/Monografías sobre el Antiguo Cercano Oriente
ANES	Ancient Near Eastern Studies
ANET	James B. Pritchard, ed. *Ancient Near Eastern Texts Relating to the Old Testament.* (3rd ed., Princeton: Princeton University Press, 1969)
AO	Tablets in the collections of Musée du Louvre
AOAT	Alter Orient und Altes Testament
AoF	*Altorientalische Forschungen*
AOS	American Oriental Series
ARM	Archives royales de Mari
ARRIM	Annual Review of the Royal Inscriptions of Mesopotamia Project, Toronto
AS	Assyriological Studies
ASJ	*Acta Sumerologica* (Japan)
ATD	Das Alte Testament Deutsch
ATD.A	Das Alte Testament Deutsch: Apokryphen
AThANT	Abhandlungen zur Theologie des Alten und Neuen Testaments
AzTh	Arbeiten zur Theologie
BaF	Baghdader Forschungen

DOI 10.1515/9783110466546-003

BAK	H. Hunger, *Babylonische und assyrische Kolophone* (AOAT 2; Kevelaer: Butzon & Bercker and Neukirchen-Vluyn: Neukirchener, 1968)
BaM.B	Baghdader Mitteilungen: Beihefte
BASOR	*Bulletin of the American Schools of Oriental Research*
BBB	Bonner biblische Beiträge
BBET	Beiträge zur biblischen Exegese und Theologie
BBR	H. Zimmern, *Beiträge zur Kenntnis der babylonischen Religion* (Leipzig: Hinrichs, 1896)
BCSMS	*Bulletin of the Canadian Society for Mesopotamian Studies*
BEATAJ	Beiträge zur Erforschung des Alten Testaments und des antiken Judentums
BETL	Bibliotheca ephemeridum theologicarum lovaniensium
BEvT	Beiträge zur Evangelischen Theologie
BiBe	Biblische Beiträge
Bib	*Biblica*
BibInt	*Biblical Interpretation*
BibSem	The Biblical Seminar
BIOSCS	*Bulletin of the International Organization of Septuagint and Cognate Studies*
BKAT	Biblischer Kommentar, Altes Testament
BN	*Biblische Notizen*
BO	*Bibliotheca orientalis*
BThSt	Biblisch-theologische Studien
BTZ	*Berliner Theologische Zeitschrift*
BWANT	Beiträge zur Wissenschaft vom Alten und Neuen Testament
BWL	W. G. Lambert, *Babylonian Wisdom Literature* (Oxford: Clarendon Press, 1960; repr. Winona Lake, Ind., 1996)
BZ	*Biblische Zeitschrift*
BZAW	Beihefte zur Zeitschrift für die alttestamentliche Wissenschaft
CAD	*Chicago Assyrian Dictionary*
CAH	Cambridge Ancient History
CAI	W. E. Aufrecht, *A Corpus of Ammonite Inscriptions* (Lewiston, N.Y.: Edwin Mellen, 1989)
CANE	J. M. Sasson, ed., *Civilizations of the Ancient Near East* (4 vols., New York: Scribner's, 1995)
CBET	Contributions to Biblical Exegesis and Theology
CB.OT	Coniectanea Biblica: Old Testament Series
CBQ	*Catholic Biblical Quarterly*
CDA	J. Black, A. George, and N. Postgate, *A Concise Dictionary of Akkadian* (2nd ed., Wiesbaden: Harrassowitz, 2000)
CHANE	Culture and History of the Ancient Near East
COS	William W. Hallo and K. Lawson Younger Jr., eds. *The Context of Scripture*. 4 vols. (Leiden: Brill, 1997–2016).
CQS	Companion to the Qumran Scrolls
CRB	Cahiers de la Revue Biblique
CRRAI	Comptes rendus de la Rencontre Assyriologique Internationale
CT	*Cuneiform Texts from Babylonian Tablets in the British Museum*
CTH	Catalogue des textes hittites
CTN	Cuneiform Texts from Nimrud

CUSAS	Cornell University Studies in Assyriology and Sumerology
DA	A Boissier, *Documents assyriens rélatifs au présages* (Paris: Bouillon, 1894)
DDD^2	*Dictionary of Deities and Demons in the Bible.* Edited by K. van der Toorn, B. Becking, and P. W. van der Horst. Second edition (Leiden: Brill, 1995)
DJD	Discoveries in the Judean Desert
DMOA	Documenta et Monumenta Orientis Antiqui
DSD	*Dead Sea Discoveries*
DSSR	The Dead Sea Scrolls Reader
EBR	*Encyclopedia of the Bible and Its Reception*
EDSS	L. H. Schiffman and J. VanderKam, eds., *Encyclopedia of Dead Sea Scrolls* (2 vols., Oxford: Oxford University Press, 2000)
EHS.T	Europäische Hochschulschriften, Reihe 23: Theologie
EPRO	Etudes préliminaires aux religions orientales dans l'empire romain
ErIsr	*Eretz-Israel*
EVO	*Egitto e Vicino Oriente*
EvT	*Evangelische Theologie*
ExpTim	*Expository Times*
FAT	Forschungen zum Alten Testament
FCB	Feminist Companion to the Bible
FLP	Tablets in the collections of the Free Library of Pennsylvania
FM	Florilegium Marianum
FOTL	Forms of the Old Testament Literature
FRLANT	Forschungen zur Religion und Literatur des Alten und Neuen Testaments
GBS	Guides to Biblical Scholarship
Gilg.	The Epic of Gilgameš
HAR	*Hebrew Annual Review*
HAT	Handbuch zum Alten Testament
HBD	*HarperCollins Bible Dictionary*
HBM	Hebrew Bible Monographs
HBS	Herders biblische Studien
HdO	Handbuch der Orientalistik
HeBAI	*Hebrew Bible and Ancient Israel*
Hen	*Henoch*
HKM	S. Alp, *Hethitische Keilschrifttafeln aus Maşat-Höyük* (Ankara: Türk Tarih Kurumu Basımevi, 1991)
HR	*History of Religions*
HSAO	Heidelberger Studien zum alten Orient
HSM	Harvard Semitic Monographs
HSS	Harvard Semitic Studies
HTKAT	Herders theologischer Kommentar zum Alten Testament
HTR	*Harvard Theological Review*
HUCA	*Hebrew Union College Annual*
ICC	The International Critical Commentary
IEJ	*Israel Exploration Journal*
JAJSup	The Journal of Ancient Judaism Supplements
JANESCU	*Journal of the Ancient Near Eastern Society of Columbia University*
JAOS	*Journal of the American Oriental Society*

JARG	*Jahrbuch für Anthropologie und Religionsgeschichte*
JBL	*Journal of Biblical Literature*
JBTh	*Jahrbuch für biblische Theologie*
JCS	*Journal of Cuneiform Studies*
JEOL	*Journal of the Near Eastern Society "Ex Oriente Lux"*
JES	*Journal of Ecumenical Studies*
JHS	*Journal of Hellenic Studies*
JNES	*Journal of Near Eastern Studies*
JNSL	*Journal of Northwest Semitic Languages*
JRAS	*Journal of the Royal Asiatic Society*
JSJ	*Journal for the Study of Judaism*
JSJSup	Supplements to the Journal for the Study of Judaism
JSNTSup	Journal for the Study of the New Testament: Supplement Series
JSOT	*Journal for the Study of the Old Testament*
JSOTSup	Journal for the Study of the Old Testament: Supplement Series
JSP	*Journal for the Study of the Pseudepigrapha*
JSPSup	Journal for the Study of the Pseudepigrapha: Supplement Series
JTS	*Journal of Theological Studies*
K	Tablets in the collections of the British Museum
KAI	Herbert Donner and Wolfgang Röllig, *Kanaanäische und aramäische Inschriften.* 3 vols. Wiesbaden: Harrassowitz, ^{3}1971–76.
KAR	E. Ebeling, *Keilschrifttexte aus Assur religiösen Inhalts* (Leipzig 1919–23)
KAT	Kommentar zum Alten Testament
KBo	Keilschrifttexte aus Boghazköi
KHC	Kurzer Hand-Kommentar zum Alten Testament
KTU	M. Dietrich, O. Loretz, and J. Sanmartín, *Die keilalphabetischen Texte aus Ugarit, Ras Ibn Hani und anderen Orten* (Münster: Ugarit-Verlag, ^{3}2013)
KuT	Tablet signature of Kuşaklı texts
LAOS	Leipziger altorientalische Studien
LAS	S. Parpola, *Letters from Assyrian Scholars to the Kings Esarhaddon and Assurbanipal* (2 vols. AOAT 5/1–2; Kevelaer and Neukirchen-Vluyn: Butzon & Bercker and Neukirchener Verlag, 1970/1983).
LAPO	Littératures anciennes du Proche-Orient
LDSS	Library of the Dead Sea Scrolls
LeDiv	Lectio divina
LHBOTS	The Library of Hebrew Bible/Old Testament Studies
LKA	E. Ebeling, *Literarische Keilschrifttexte aus Assur* (Berlin: Akademie-Verlag, 1953)
LSJ	H. G. Liddell, R. Scott, and H. S. Jones, *A Greek-English Lexicon.* 9th ed. with revised supplement (Oxford: Oxford University Press, 1996)
LXX	The Septuagint
M.	Tablet signature of texts from Mari
MARI	*Mari: Annales de recherches interdisciplinaires*
MdB	Le Monde de la Bible
MDOG	*Mitteilungen der Deutschen Orient-Gesellschaft*
MDP	Mémoires de la délégation en Perse
MIO	Mitteilungen des Instituts für Orientforschung
MSL	Materialien zum sumerischen Lexikon/Materials for the Sumerian Lexicon

MT	Masoretic Text
NABU	*Nouvelles assyriologiques breves et utilitaires*
NBL	*Neues Bibel-Lexikon*
ND	Field numbers of texts excavated at Nimrud (Calah)
NEB.AT	Neue Echter Bibel: Altes Testament
NedTT	*Nederlands Theologische Tijdschrift*
NICOT	New International Commentary to the Old Testament
NRSV	The New Revised Standard Version
OAC	Orientis Antiqui Collectio
OBO	Orbis biblicus et orientalis
OEAGR	*Oxford Encyclopedia of Ancient Greece and Rome*
OECT	Oxford Editions of Cuneiform Inscriptions
OIP	Oriental Institute Publications
OLA	Orientalia Lovaniensia Analecta
Or	*Orientalia*
OTL	Old Testament Library
OTS	Oudtestamentische Studiën
PDRI	Publications of the Diaspora Research Institute
PBS	Publications of the Babylonian Section, Harvard University
PFES	Publications of the Finnish Exegetical Society
PIHANS	Publications de l'Institut historique-archéologique néerlandais de Stamboul
PNA	*The Prosography of the Neo-Assyrian Empire.* Vol. 1 edited by K. Radner; vols. 2 and 3 edited by H. D. Baker. Helsinki: The Neo-Assyrian Text Corpus Project, 1998–2002.
PRU	Palais royal d'Ugarit
PSBA	Proceedings of the Society of Biblical Archaeology
PTMS	Princeton Theological Monograph Series
PW	*A. F. Paulys Realencyclopädie der classischen Altertumswissenschaft.* New edition edited by G. Wissowa. 49 vols. (Munich)
QC	*The Qumran Chronicle*
RA	*Revue d'assyriologie et d'archéologie orientale*
RAcc	F. Thureau-Dangin, *Rituels Accadiens* (Paris: Leroux, 1921)
RB	*Revue biblique*
REA	*Revue des études anciennes*
RevQ	*Revue de Qumran*
RGRW	Religions in the Graeco-Roman World
RHR	*Revue d'histoire des religions*
RIMB	The Royal Inscriptions of Mesopotamia, Babylonian Periods
RINAP	Royal Inscriptions of the Neo-Assyrian Period
RlA	*Reallexikon der Assyriologie*
RS	Field numbers of tablets excavated at Ras Shamra
RVV	Religionsgeschichtliche Versuche und Vorarbeiten
SAA	State Archives of Assyria
SAAB	*State Archives of Assyria Bulletin*
SAACT	State Archives of Assyria Cuneiform Texts
SAAS	State Archives of Assyria Studies
SAMD	Studies in Ancient Magic and Divination

SANER	Studies in Ancient Near Eastern Records
SAT	Schriften des Alten Testaments
SB	Standard Babylonian
SBB	Stuttgarter biblische Beiträge
SBH	G. A. Reisner, *Sumerisch-babylonische Hymnen nach Thontafeln griechischer Zeit* (Berlin: Spemann, 1896)
SBLAB	Society of Biblical Literature Academia Biblica
SBLAIL	Society of Biblical Literature Ancient Israel and its Literature
SBLDS	Society of Biblical Literature Dissertation Series
SBLEJL	Society of Biblical Literature Early Judaism and its Literature
SBLGPBS	Society of Biblical Literature Global Perspectives on Biblical Scholarship
SBLMS	Society of Biblical Literature Monograph Series
SBLRBS	Society of Biblical Literature Resources for Biblical Study
SBLSBS	Society of Biblical Literature Sources for Biblical Study
SBLSS	Society of Biblical Literature Semeia Studies
SBLSymS	Society of Biblical Literature Symposium Series
SBLWAW	Society of Biblical Literature Writings from the Ancient World
SBLWGRW	Society of Biblical Literature Writings from the Graeco-Roman World
SBS	Stuttgarter Bibelstudien
SDSRL	Studies in the Dead Sea Scrolls and Related Literature
SEL	Studi epigrafici e linguistici sul Vicino Oriente Antico
SEÅ	Svensk Exegetisk Årsbok
SHANE	Studies in the History of the Ancient New East
SHCANE	Studies in the History and Culture of the Ancient Near East
SJOT	*Scandinavian Journal of the Old Testament*
SOTSMS	Society for Old Testament Study: Monograph Series
SpTU	*Spätbabylonische Texte aus Uruk*
SSN	Studia Semitica Neerlandica
STDJ	Studies on the Texts of the Desert of Judah
SThZ	*Schweizerische theologische Zeitschrift*
STK	*Svensk teologisk kvartalskrift*
StOr	*Studia Orientalia*
StPSM	Studia Pohl: Series Major
StUNT	Studien zur Umwelt des Neuen Testaments
SVTP	Studia in Veteris Testamenti pseudepigraphica
T.	Tablet signature of texts from Mari
TB	Theologische Bücherei
TBN	Themes in Biblical Narrative
TCL	Textes cunéiformes. Musée du Louvre
TCS	Texts from Cuneiform Sources
TDOT	G. J. Botterweck and H. Ringgren, eds., *Theological Dictionary of the Old Testament* (16 vols., Grand Rapids, Mich.: Eerdmans, 1974–2018)
TDP	R. Labat, *Traité akkadien de diagnostics et pronostics médicaux* (Paris: Académie internationale d'histoire des sciences, 1951)
THAT	E. Jenni and C. Westermann, eds., *Theologisches Handwörterbuch zum Alten Testament* (2 vols., Munich: Kaiser, 1971)
ThQ	*Theologische Quartalschrift*

ThWAT	G. J. Botterweck, H. Ringgren, and Heinz-Josef Fabry, eds., *Theologisches Wörterbuch zum Alten Testament* (9 vols., Stuttgart: Kohlhammer, 1973–2015)
ThZ	*Theologische Zeitschrift*
ThLZ	*Theologische Literaturzeitung*
ThWNT	G. Kittel, ed., *Theologisches Wörterbuch zum Neuen Testament* (10 vols., Stuttgart: Kohlhammer, 1933–1979)
TRu	*Theologische Rundschau*
TSAJ	Texte und Studien zum antiken Judentum
TUAT	*Texte aus der Umwelt des Alten Testaments*
UBL	Ugaritisch-biblische Literatur
UCOP	University of Cambridge Oriental Publications
UF	*Ugarit-Forschungen*
UTB	Uni-Taschenbücher
VAB	Vorderasiatische Bibliothek
VAT	Tablet signature of Staatlichen Museen zu Berlin
VF	*Verkündigung und Forschung*
VS	Vorderasiatische Schriftdenkmäler der Staatlichen Museen zu Berlin
W	Field numbers of tablets excavated at Warka (Uruk)
WBC	Word Biblical Commentary
WMANT	Wissenschaftliche Monographien zum Alten und Neuen Testament
WO	*Die Welt des Orients*
VS	Vorderasiatische Schriftdenkmäler der Königlichen/Staatlichen Museen zu Berlin
VT	*Vetus Testamentum*
VTSup	Supplements to Vetus Testamentum
WMANT	Wissenschaftliche Monographien zum Alten und Neuen Testament
WTJ	*Westminster Theological Journal*
WUNT	Wissenschaftliche Untersuchungen zum Neuen Testament
YOS	Yale Oriental Series, Texts
ZA	*Zeitschrift für Assyriologie*
ZABR	*Zeitschrift fur altorientalische und biblische Rechtsgeschichte*
ZAW	*Zeitschrift für die alttestamentliche Wissenschaft*
ZBK.AT	Zürcher Bibelkommentar: Altes Testament
ZThK	*Zeitschrift für Theologie und Kirche*
ZTT	Tablets from Ziyaret Tepe

Table of Contents

Preface — 7

List of Original Publications — 9

List of Abbreviations — 13

Part One: **Prophecy in Theory**

Prophecy as Construct, Ancient and Modern — 3

Reflections on the "Historical-Critical" Method: Historical Criticism and Critical Historicism — 29

What is Prophecy? An Ancient Near Eastern Perspective — 53

Prophecy and Omen Divination: Two Sides of the Same Coin — 75

Neither Prophecies nor Apocalypses: The Akkadian Literary Predictive Texts — 87

Part Two: **Prophecy in the Ancient Near East**

The Socioreligious Role of the Neo-Assyrian Prophets — 103

Non-Male Prophets in Ancient Near Eastern Sources — 127

The Prophet and the Augur at Tušḫan, 611 BCE — 153

Das kritische Potential in der altorientalischen Prophetie — 163

Fear Not: A Study on an Ancient Near Eastern Phrase — 195

The Exiled Gods of Babylon in Neo-Assyrian Prophecy — 233

Marduk's Return and Reconciliation in a Prophetic Letter from Arbela (with Simo Parpola) —— 245

City as Lofty as Heaven: Arbela and Other Cities in Neo-Assyrian Prophecy —— 267

A Prophetic Riot in Babylonia, 133 BCE —— 301

Part Three: **Biblical Prophecy in Ancient Near Eastern Context**

Die Relevanz der neuassyrischen Prophetie für die alttestamentliche Forschung —— 315

Biblical Prophecy from a Near Eastern Perspective: The Cases of Kingship and Divine Possession —— 351

Comparing Prophetic Sources: Principles and a Test Case —— 377

From Holy War to Holy Peace: Biblical Alternatives to Belligerent Rhetoric —— 397

Falsche Prophetie in neuassyrischer und deuteronomistischer Darstellung —— 419

Sacred Springs and Liminal Rivers: Water and Prophecy in the Ancient Eastern Mediterranean —— 441

Prophets and the Divine Council —— 461

Wisdom as Mediatrix in Sirach 24: Ben Sira, Love Lyrics, and Prophecy —— 479

Part Four: **Prophecy in the Hebrew Bible**

The Historical Dilemma of Biblical Prophetic Studies —— 499

Since When Do Prophets Write? —— 517

Prophets and Prophecy in Joshua–Kings: A Near Eastern Perspective — 539

Das Problem der Prophetenschüler — 563

The Dubious Image of Prophecy — 577

(How) Does the Book of Ezekiel Reveal Its Babylonian Context? — 597

The Book of Hosea and the Last Days of the Northern Kingdom: The Methodological Problem — 613

Part Five: **Prophecy in the Dead Sea Scrolls**

Transmitting Divine Mysteries: The Prophetic Role of Wisdom Teachers in the Dead Sea Scrolls — 631

Oracles at Qumran? Traces of Inspired Speakers in the Dead Sea Scrolls — 651

Pesharim as Divination: Qumran Exegesis, Omen Interpretation and Literary Prophecy — 663

Bibliography — 681

Index of Names — 751

Index of modern authors — 759

Index of Ancient Near Eastern Sources — 761

Index of Biblical References — 767

Part One: **Prophecy in Theory**

Prophecy as Construct, Ancient and Modern

Why Social Construction?

Prophecy, according to the prevailing view, is another form of religious mediation, or divination, the purpose of which is to transmit allegedly divine knowledge to human society. Like many other forms of divination, prophecy is a cross-cultural phenomenon found globally and independently in different times and cultures.[1] As such, prophecy belongs to the features shared by humanity at large as a type of universal human intuition, without any particular culture being able to claim it for itself. As argued by cognitive scientists of religion, the need for religious mediation emerges as a part of the human capacity to understand agency and intentionality involving counterintuitive agents (gods, spirits, and the like) and their representatives (shamans, prophets, etc.). Divination, hence, belongs to the recurrent patterns of understanding supernatural agency. Such patterns exist in different cultures and share common elements whether or not they are communicated through cultural contacts.[2]

At the same time, prophecy is a socially and historically contingent phenomenon. Its phenotypes and descriptions vary from culture to culture. Social construction comes into play whenever prophecy is conceptualized as a distinct category, practice, or institution. As socioreligious and political agents, people called prophets execute distinctive and culture-specific roles within the social and ideological structure, identity, and narrative of any given society depending on the societal interpretation and appreciation of different types of religious mediation.

In the wake of social constructionism, virtually everything has been said to be socially constructed; however, if everything is social construction, then social construction becomes everything, and the whole concept ultimately amounts to nothing. In his book *The Social Construction of What?* Ian Hacking calls for greater precision in the social construction discussion: what is it that we say is social-

1 See, e.g., T. W. Overholt, *Prophecy in Cross-Cultural Perspective: A Source-Book for Biblical Research* (SBLSBS 17; Atlanta, Ga.: Society for Biblical Literature, 1986); L. L. Grabbe, "Ancient Near Eastern Prophecy from an Anthropological Perspective," in *Prophecy in Its Ancient Near Eastern Context: Mesopotamian, Biblical, and Arabian Perspectives* (ed. M. Nissinen; SBLSymS 13; Atlanta, Ga.: Society of Biblical Literature, 2000) 13–32.

2 See, e.g., I. Pyysiäinen, *Supernatural Agents: Why We Believe in Souls, Gods, and Buddhas* (New York: Oxford University Press, 2009).

DOI 10.1515/9783110466546-004

ly constructed? According to him, the starting point is that "the existence or character of *X* is not determined by the nature of things. *X* is not inevitable. *X* was brought into existence or shaped by social events, forces, history, all of which could well have been different." Many, though not all, constructionists also claim that "*X* is quite bad as it is" and "[w]e would be much better off if *X* were done away with, or at least radically transformed"; but this need not necessarily be the case.[3] What is constructed is first and foremost the *idea* of *X* according to which people and things are classified. Hacking uses women refugees as one of his examples, saying that *X* in this case does not refer to individual women. "No, the *X* refers first of all to the woman refugee as a kind of person, the classification itself, and the matrix within which the classification works. In consequence of being so classified, individual women and their experiences of themselves are changed by being so classified."[4] That such an idea is not inevitable can be demonstrated by showing the contingent historical determinants of the process by which it came into being.[5]

In this essay, I attempt to demonstrate that prophecy as a distinct practice, concept, and category is not an inevitable phenomenon determined by the "nature of things" but, indeed, the product of socially contingent historical processes. If the socially constructed *X* is prophecy, neither the individual prophet nor universal human intuition of divine-human communication is referred to, but instead the kind of people, the classification itself, and the matrix within which it works.

While religious mediation can be found all over the world and can be understood as belonging to the basic architecture of human perception of supernatural agency, the concept of prophecy only makes sense when inhabiting a social setting. We cannot even say what prophecy is all about before we arrive at some kind of mutual agreement about the meaning of the word which, in fact, has different meanings in colloquial and scholarly languages and in different social contexts.[6] Prophecy exists if there is an understanding about what it means and how it can be recognized; prophets exist if there is a community acknowledging their existence and providing certain people and practices with such a

3 I. Hacking, *The Social Construction of What?* (Cambridge, Mass.: Harvard University Press, 1999) 6–7.

4 Ibid., 11.

5 Ibid., 38.

6 For an attempt at a definition of the concept of prophecy, see M. Nissinen, "What Is Prophecy? An Ancient Near Eastern Perspective," in *Inspired Speech: Prophecy in the Ancient Near East. Essays in Honor of Herbert B. Huffmon* (ed. J. Kaltner and L. Stulman; JSOTSup 372; London: T. & T. Clark, 2004) 17–37 (= pp. 53–73 in this volume).

label; hence, prophecy is an idea needed, defined, and maintained by human communities that provide the matrix within which the idea works.[7]

As Hacking argues, ideas and classifications do not emerge in a vacuum but, rather, within a social matrix surrounding them. Religious mediation as such belongs to the specific ways humans understand the world, and can be seen as the product of the human mind in the first place rather than of a particular social setting. However, there is an interdependence between the mental and the extramental. Ilkka Pyysiäinen writes: "Supernatural agent representations are mental concepts, ideas, images, and beliefs; texts, paintings, works of art, uttered words, and so on, are extramental, public representations expressing mental representations. Public representations also trigger mental representations."[8] In other words, the human intuition about gods communicating with humans is a mental representation, while the conceptualization of an institution or a phenomenon *as* prophecy is a public representation—or should we say "construct"?—based on the mental representation. To classify certain people *as* prophets, again, is impossible without this underlying construct. Such constructs are to a high degree contingent on social and historical processes, and the same can be said of everything that is stated about prophecy and prophets in a given historical context.

To say that prophecy is a construct, therefore, does not deprive the phenomenon thus designated of its historical veracity. On the contrary, it is precisely the social contingency that makes the construct inseparable from historical conditions.[9] As long as there have been communities acknowledging the idea that gods communicate with humans and equally acknowledging certain people as intermediaries of the divine knowledge, prophecy (the concept as well as the practice) has been an element of historical reality.

With regard to its global and historical dimensionality, prophecy is a polygonal construct. When talking about constructs of prophecy, we have to ask ourselves what we think is being constructed: individuals as "prophets," the category of "prophecy," a literary genre with the same name, all this, or something else? Another question to be asked is: Whose constructions are we talking about? Those of academics or religious authorities? Ancient or modern?

---

7 This has been pointed out already by R. R. Wilson, *Prophecy and Society in Ancient Israel* (Philadelphia, Pa.: Fortress, 1980) 28–32.

8 Pyysiäinen, *Supernatural Agents*, 53.

9 Cf., e.g., F. W. Dobbs-Allsopp, "Rethinking Historical Criticism," *BibInt* 7 (1999) 235–71, esp. 270.

Ancient and Modern Constructs of Prophecy

Past realities—assuming that there is such a thing as historical factuality and real people involved in it—can only be handled by way of interpretation and reconstruction.[10] Our constructs of prophecy are, necessarily, interpretation of ancient texts whose constructs are designed for purposes different from modern concerns. Therefore, constructs of prophecy in ancient texts must be distinguished from modern academic constructs resting upon them. At the same time, however, we have to accept that identifying constructs of prophecy in ancient texts presupposes an idea of what prophecy is, which, again, is a modern construct.

Am I getting overly complicated? What I want to say is that when we as scholars talk about ancient prophecy, we should identify ourselves as subjects of the social and historical processes, as a part of the matrix within which the constructs of prophecy take shape. Prophecy, as it appears in academic studies and textbooks, certainly reflects historical factuality, but it is nevertheless given form by the scholars who wrote those studies and textbooks. Rather than having an independent existence, it always inhabits a setting in a scholarly agenda, be that a "Theology of the Old Testament," a "History of Ancient Near Eastern Religion," or another matrix within which the idea of prophecy has a meaning.

Ancient constructs of prophecy appear in the sources in different ways. It is evident that some texts actively introduce a certain image of prophets and prophecy. In these cases, the construct of prophecy is part and parcel of the message of the text and the ideology propagated by it.[11] Sometimes, again, the image of a prophet is implied rather than intended; but even in these cases, ideological constructs are often involved.[12]

Modern constructs of ancient prophecy are always intended ones, at least if they are the result of a scholarly analysis. In scholarship, prophets are not simply historical personalities discovered by historical critical research, but are, at the same time, products of the scholars' creative minds and, as such, intellectual constructs. In fact, the modern creations can be considered heirs of their ancient precursors: prophets already appear as intellectual constructs in the prophetic

---

10 Further reflections of mine on this matter can be found in M. Nissinen, "Reflections on the 'Historical-Critical' Method: Historical Criticism and Critical Historicism," in *Method Matters*, FS D. L. Petersen (ed. J. M. LeMon and K. H. Richards; SBL Resources for Biblical Study 56; Atlanta, Ga.: Society of Biblical Literature, 2009) 479–504 (= pp. 29–52 in this volume).

11 Cf., e.g., M. Dijkstra, "'I Am Neither a Prophet nor a Prophet's Pupil': Amos 7:9–17 as the Presentation of a Prophet like Moses," in *The Elusive Prophet: The Prophet as a Historical Person, Literary Character, and Anonymous Artist* (ed. J. C. de Moor; OtSt 45; Leiden: Brill, 2001) 105–28.

12 Cf. the discussion on the Neo-Assyrian letter SAA 10 109 below.

books of the Hebrew Bible[13] and in their subsequent learned interpretations in, for instance, the Dead Sea Scrolls.[14]

The academic constructs of prophecy necessarily reflect the diversity of the sources, which hitherto have been roughly divided into two groups: biblical and extra-biblical. This division has a lot of weight, not only because of the distinctive literary and historical character of the canonized biblical text and the more or less haphazard variety of Near Eastern textual evidence, but also because of the history of research.

As an academic pursuit, the study of biblical prophecy has a long history, preceded by an even longer Jewish and Christian interpretative tradition. As a biblical concept, prophecy is contextualized in Jewish and Christian theology and religion, and more or less internalized by scholars influenced by this matrix, irrespective of their personal commitment to it. Prophecy, therefore, is not just an object of study but a significant constituent of cultural memory and provider of identity.

The academic study of biblical prophecy, for its part, is deeply rooted in nineteenth-century scholarship whose brilliant representatives, such as Julius Wellhausen and Bernhard Duhm, were the founding fathers of the scholarly image of what was later to be called the "classical prophecy" of ancient Israel; their contributions will be discussed below. When we turn to the study of "extra-biblical prophecy" (I would rather abandon this term, because it lumps together so much different material with the single common denominator of not being biblical, and replace it in the present context with "ancient Near Eastern" or "ancient Eastern Mediterranean" prophecy), the situation is totally different. The texts documenting prophecy in the ancient Eastern Mediterranean are not a constituent of any modern scholar's religious tradition. They do form part of our cultural heritage but not of our cultural memory (by "us," I am referring to the community of biblical and ancient Near Eastern scholars). Therefore, prophecy outside the Bible still frequently plays the role of "the other" in studies of ancient prophecy.

---

13 Cf., e.g., D. Edelman, "From Prophets to Prophetic Books: The Fixing of the Divine Word," in *The Production of Prophecy: Constructing Prophecy and Prophets in Yehud* (ed. D. Edelman and E. Ben Zvi; London: Equinox, 2009) 29–54.

14 See A. P. Jassen, *Mediating the Divine: Prophecy and Revelation in the Dead Sea Scrolls and Second Temple Judaism* (STDJ 68; Leiden: Brill, 2007); id., "The Presentation of the Ancient Prophets as Lawgivers at Qumran," *JBL* 127 (2008) 307–37; cf. M. Nissinen, "Transmitting Divine Mysteries: The Prophetic Role of Wisdom Teachers in the Dead Sea Scrolls," in *Scripture in Transition: Essays on Septuagint, Hebrew Bible, and Dead Sea Scrolls in Honour of Raija Sollamo* (ed. A. Voitila and J. Jokiranta; JSJSup 126; Leiden: Brill, 2008) 513–33 (= pp. 631–49 in this volume).

The Near Eastern texts have been the object of active study for only a short period, and their ideology is probably not internalized by many researchers, not to mention anyone outside the academic community. To this should be added that, in scholarship, the big picture of ancient Eastern Mediterranean prophecy is still in the making; in fact, scholars are only beginning to perceive (or "construct") the picture. While Mesopotamian and biblical prophecy have already been perceived as belonging to the same picture for quite some time, the discussion on the relationship between ancient Near Eastern prophecy and Greek oracle is still at an initial stage.[15]

I would now like to demonstrate the historical contingency of the constructs of prophecy and to deliberate on the questions "Social construction of what?" and "Whose constructs are they anyway?" using two very different examples: the constructs of prophecy (1) in the seventh-century B.C.E. Assyrian texts; and (2) in twentieth-century C.E. biblical scholarship.

The Assyrian Construct of Prophecy

The Neo-Assyrian sources provide us with a twofold documentation of prophecy. On the one hand, we have prophetic oracles at our disposal that have been intentionally written down on clay tablets and stored in the state archives, sometimes even reedited in small collections.[16] On the other hand, prophets and prophecy feature in non-prophetic texts of various kinds: letters, administrative documents, word-lists, and royal inscriptions.[17]

---

15 See, however, the important contributions of W. Burkert, *The Orientalizing Revolution: Near Eastern Influence on Greek Culture in the Early Archaic Age* (trans. W. Burkert and M. E. Pinder; Cambridge, Mass.: Harvard University Press, 1992); M. A. Flower, *The Seer in Ancient Greece* (Berkeley, CA: The University of California Press, 2008); A. Lange, "Literary Prophecy and Oracle Collection: A Comparison between Judah and Greece in Persian Times," in *Prophets, Prophecy and Prophetic Texts in Second Temple Judaism* (ed. M. H. Floyd and R. D. Haak; LHBOTS 427; New York: T. & T. Clark, 2006) 248–75; id., "Greek Seers and Israelite-Jewish Prophets," *VT* 57 (2007) 461–82; A. C. Hagedorn, "Looking at Foreigners in Biblical and Greek Prophecy," *VT* 57 (2007) 432–48; H. B. Huffmon, "The Oracular Process: Delphi and the Near East," *VT* 57 (2007) 449–60; N. Marinatos, "The Role of the Queen in Minoan Prophecy Rituals," in *Images and Prophecy in the Ancient Eastern Mediterranean* (ed. M. Nissinen and C. E. Carter; FRLANT 233; Göttingen: Vandenhoeck & Ruprecht, 2009) 86–94.

16 S. Parpola, *Assyrian Prophecies* (SAA 9; Helsinki: Helsinki University Press, 1997).

17 M. Nissinen, *References to Prophecy in Neo-Assyrian Sources* (SAAS 7; Helsinki: The Neo-Assyrian Text Corpus Project, 1998).

Especially the prophetic oracles, but also the royal inscriptions, introduce an image of prophecy that can easily be classified as an intended construct, which presents the prophets as mouthpieces of deities who essentially proclaim the state religion and ideology.[18] According to this image, the Assyrian prophets not only appear as channels of the divine legitimation of the king's rule and proclaimers of his special relationship to the divine world, but also as sources of the *Herrschaftswissen* necessary for exercising his power according to the divine will.[19] The prophets are presented as stern supporters of the king and his rule. However, the prophet's personality is not an issue here, since the prophets do not express their own opinions but utter divine words. Accordingly, what we find in the Assyrian prophetic oracles and inscriptions is the construct of *prophecy* as a channel of divine knowledge rather than of the *prophets* as individual agents.

The foremost constituents of the Assyrian construct of prophecy as represented by the prophetic oracles and inscriptions can be summarized under the following four rubrics.

(1) *The role of the prophets as mouthpieces of the divine word*, mostly (though not exclusively) spoken by the goddess Ištar.[20] The colophons mentioning the name and origin of the prophet usually imply that the prophets belong to the temples of Ištar in different cities, more often than not in Arbela. The colophon "By the mouth of Sinqiša-amur, a woman from Arbela" not only informs the reader about the name and gender of the prophet but also affiliates her with the city of Arbela—and not just the city but probably also with the temple of Ištar at Arbela called Egašankalamma, providing the oracle with an accredited background.

In the Assyrian religion, Ištar is the deity who pronounces the divine knowledge deriving from the divine council.[21] According to Simo Parpola, the Assyrian

---

18 See Parpola, *Assyrian Prophecies*, xviii – xliv.

19 See B. Pongratz-Leisten, *Herrschaftswissen in Mesopotamien: Formen der Kommunikation zwischen Gott und König im 2. und 1. Jahrtausend v. Chr.* (SAAS 10; Helsinki: The Neo-Assyrian Text Corpus Project, 1999).

20 Ištar speaks in different manifestations, usually as Ištar of Arbela or as Mullissu (i. e., Ištar of Nineveh), but also as Urkittu (i. e., Ištar of Uruk, SAA 9 2.6). Other deities speaking in the Assyrian prophecies include Aššur (SAA 9 3.2 and 3.3), Nabû (SAA 9 1.4), Bel (i. e., Marduk, SAA 9 1.4), and the goddesses of the Esaggil temple (SAA 9 2.1).

21 For the concept of the divine council and the role of the prophets and divination within it, see A. Lenzi, *Secrecy and the Gods: Secret Knowledge in Ancient Mesopotamia and Biblical Israel* (SAAS 19; Helsinki: The Neo-Assyrian Text Corpus Project, 2008) 50 – 62; cf. M. Nissinen, "Prophets and the Divine Council," in *Kein Land für sich allein: Studien zum Kulturkontakt in Kanaan, Israel/Palästina und Ebirnâri für Manfred Weippert zum 65. Geburtstag* (ed. U. Hübner and

assembly of the gods actually represents different aspects and manifestations of Aššur, the main and the only God, with Ištar representing his motherly aspect whose relation to the king is especially intimate.[22] The idea of Ištar as the mouthpiece of the divine council is expressed in a nutshell in an oracle from Ešnunna, which precedes the Neo-Assyrian oracles by some eleven centuries but formulates the idea more accurately than any individual Assyrian text:

> The secrets of the gods are placed before me. Because you constantly pronounce my name with your mouth, I constantly disclose the secrets of the gods to you.[23]

The Assyrian prophecies are fully in accord with this idea. In the Assyrian construct of prophecy, the prophets are perceived as mouthpieces of the divine council rather than of individual deities—or, if one prefers, of the one and only god manifest in his/her different aspects.[24]

(2) *The legitimacy of the royal succession.* The prominence of this element in the Assyrian construct of prophecy is understandable since, in the cases of both Esarhaddon and Assurbanipal, their designation as crown princes and their subsequent enthronements did not follow an incontestable procedure.[25] Close attention, therefore, is drawn to the legitimacy of these procedures. In the collection of prophecies spoken during the civil war between Esarhaddon and his brothers and shortly thereafter (that is, in 681–80 B.C.E.), the legitimacy of the royal succession and the complete undoing of the king's adversaries is a recurring theme, as for instance:

> I am Ištar of [Arbela]! Esarhaddon, king of A[ssyria]! In Assur, Ninev[eh], Calah and Arbe[la] I will give endle[ss] days and everlast[ing] years to Esarhaddon, my king. I am yo[ur] great midwife, I am your excellent wet nurse. For endless days and everlasting years I have established your throne under the great heavens.

E. A. Knauf; OBO 186; Freiburg: Universitätsverlag/Göttingen: Vandenhoeck & Ruprecht, 2002) 4–19 (= pp. 461–77 in this volume).

22 Parpola, *Assyrian Prophecies*, xxvi–xxxi.

23 FLP 1674; see M. deJong Ellis, "The Goddess Kititum Speaks to King Ibalpiel: Oracle Texts from Ishchali," *MARI* 5 (1987) 235–66, esp. p. 40.

24 Thus Parpola, *Assyrian Prophecies*, xxi; for discussion on the concept of monotheism, see the contributions of J. Baines, H. S. Versnel, S. A. Geller, S. Parpola, and B. N. Porter in *One God or Many? Concepts of Divinity in the Ancient World* (ed. B. N. Porter; Transactions of the Casco Bay Assyriological Institute 1; Chebeaque Island, ME: Casco Bay Assyriological Institute, 2000).

25 See, e.g., Nissinen, *References to Prophecy*, 14–30, 156–59; M. J. de Jong, *Isaiah among the Ancient Near Eastern Prophets: A Comparative Study of the Earliest Stages of the Isaiah Tradition and the Neo-Assyrian Prophecies* (VTSup 117; Leiden: Brill, 2007) 251–64, 266–70.

(...) Esarhaddon, legitimate heir, son of Mullissu! With a sharp dagger in my hand I will put an end to your enemies.

(...) Esarhaddon, leg[itimate] heir, son of Mul[lissu]! [I] keep thinking of [you], I have loved you great[ly]! I hold you by yo[ur] curl in the great heavens.[26]

An essentially similar message was later proclaimed to Assurbanipal, the crown prince designate (ca. 672 B.C.E.):

This is the word of Queen Mullissu: Fear not, Assurbanipal! Until I have done and given to you what I promised, until [yo]u yourself exercise kingship over the descendants of the bearded courtiers and over the successors of the eunuchs, [I will take ca]re of you in the Palace of Succession.

(...) You whose mother is Mullissu, fear not! You whose nurse is the Lady of Arbela, fear not! Like a nurse I will carry you on my hip. I will put you, a pomegranate, between my breasts.[27]

As these quotations demonstrate, the intimate relationship of the king or crown prince with Ištar is inseparable from the idea of the king's rule and his position as the point where heaven and earth meet, as expressed in the image of the goddess holding the king by his curl. The maternal imagery used of Ištar highlights Esarhaddon's and Assurbanipal's special relationship with the goddess, through which their communication with the divine world was secured. Prophecy was one of the principal means of communicating this divine knowledge which brought the king into a familial relationship with the heavenly world.[28]

(3) *The world dominion of the Assyrian king.* According to the Assyrian royal ideology, the king was not only the king of Assyria but a global ruler (*šar kiššati*) before whom every knee should bend. Not only are the enemies of the king vanquished but the whole world is given to him to rule:

[Lis]ten carefully, O Assyrians! [The king] has vanquished his enemy! [From] sun[set to] sun[ris]e, [from] sun[ris]e [to] sun[se]t [you]r [king] has trodden his enemy underfoot! I will destroy [Meli]d, [... I will de]stroy. I will deliver the Cimmerians into his hands, the land of Ellipi I will set on fire. Aššur has given him the whole world. From the place where the sun rises to where it sets there is no king to set beside him; he is bright like sunshine![29]

26 SAA 9 1.6 iii 7′–22′; iv 5–10, 20–29.

27 SAA 9 7:2–6; rev. 6–8.

28 See B. Pongratz-Leisten, "When the Gods Are Speaking: Toward Defining the Interface between Monotheism and Polytheism," in *Propheten in Mari, Assyrien und Israel* (ed. M. Köckert and M. Nissinen; FRLANT 201; Göttingen: Vandenhoeck & Ruprecht, 2003) 132–68, esp. 155–62.

29 SAA 9 3.2 i 27–ii 7.

Proclaiming the world dominion of the Assyrian king is an essential part of the Assyrian construct of prophecy. The oracles are permeated with belligerent language, but they also acknowledge peaceful encounters of the Assyrian king with kings who have submitted themselves to him. Despite their often well-deserved and self-proclaimed reputation as merciless invaders,[30] the Assyrians actually strove for peace in countries they subjugated, resorting to violence only when the supremacy of the Assyrian king was contested.[31] Mullissu says to Assurbanipal:

> [The king]s of the countries say to one another: "[Come, let us] go to Assurbanipal! The king has witnesses. [Whatever the god]s decreed to our fathers and forefathers, [now] let [hi]m pass judgment between us!" Mullissu has said: [You shall reig]n over [the king]s of the countries! You shall show them their boundaries; you shall determine the [ro]ads they take.[32]

As the voice of the Assyrian idea of the divine world order, prophecy transmits the *Herrschaftswissen* needed by the ruler. At the same time, it also makes divine knowledge accessible to the community as a whole and, thus, serves as a significant element in the maintenance of the symbolic universe legitimating the institutional order.[33]

(4) *Neo-Assyrian Theology.* It is quite revealing that the first comprehensive reconstruction of Neo-Assyrian theology was written by Simo Parpola as an introduction to the volume SAA 9 which includes the prophetic oracles.[34] It seems indeed that constitutive elements of the Neo-Assyrian religious ideas appear in a nutshell in the prophecies addressed to Kings Esarhaddon and Assurbanipal. In fact, all the above-mentioned elements of the Assyrian construct of prophecy are an integral part of the Neo-Assyrian religion and theology, a central constituent of which is the king's crucial position in the divine world order and

---

30 See, e.g., T. J. Lewis, "'You Have Heard What the Kings of Assyria Have Done': Disarmament Passages vis-à-vis Assyrian Rhetoric of Intimidation," in *Isaiah's Vision of Peace in Biblical and Modern International Relations: Swords into Plowshares* (ed. R. Cohen and R. Westbrook; Culture and Religion in International Relations; New York: Palgrave MacMillan, 2008) 75–100.

31 Thus F. M. Fales, "On *Pax Assyriaca* in the Eighth–Seventh Centuries BCE and Its Implications," in Cohen and Westbrook (ed.), *Isaiah's Vision of Peace*, 17–35; cf. id., *Guerre et paix en Assyrie: Religion et impérialisme* (Paris: Cerf, 2010).

32 SAA 9 7:8–13.

33 For legitimation and universe maintenance, see P. L. Berger and T. Luckmann, *The Social Construction of Reality: A Treatise in Sociology of Knowledge* (New York: Anchor Books, 1989 [orig. 1966]) 92–128.

34 Parpola, *Assyrian Prophecies*, xviii–xliv.

his relation to the heavenly realm.[35] In addition to this, the prophecies underscore the crucial position of Ištar as the divine mediator (in Parpola's terms, "Holy Spirit").[36] One of the recurrent specific theological topics arising from contemporaneous royal concerns is the idea of reconciliation, as expressed in, among other texts, the letter of the priest Aššur-ḫamatu'a to Assurbanipal:

> I [am] the Lord. I have entered (and) made peace with Mu[ll]issu. Assurbanipal, king of Assyria, whom she raised: Fear not! [I] am the Lord. I have remitted Assurbanipal to you in a country of truth. Him together with his country, I have remitted to you.[37]

This prophetic oracle quoted in the letter presents Marduk, "the Lord," as the head of the Babylonian gods against whom the Assyrian kings had sinned when the city of Babylon was destroyed by Sennacherib, the king of Assyria, in 689 B.C.E. The goddess Mullissu, for her part, stands there on behalf of Assurbanipal and Assyria. The role of the intermediary is here given to Mullissu (that is, Ištar of Nineveh), probably because it is Mullissu, as the spouse of the principal god Aššur, who stands in for all Assyrian gods and the king. She assumes the role of intercessor for the sinner-king before the divine council, whereupon Marduk speaks to her and she receives the declaration of mercy and reconciliation belonging to Assurbanipal and Assyria as a whole.[38]

It is by no means surprising that the intended construct of Assyrian prophecy can be found in texts intentionally produced with the purpose of preserving them in the state archives. These texts were used and reused for the king's purposes: collections of individual oracles were compiled, and, in all probability, the archival copies of prophecies served as textual sources for royal inscriptions. They were meant to provide evidence of the divine knowledge concerning the rule of Kings Esarhaddon and Assurbanipal, hence they probably corresponded to the king's and his officials' idea of true prophecy. Moreover, the prophecies do not just preach the royal ideology in a general manner but emerge from specific, critical moments in Esarhaddon's and Assurbanipal's career, such as civil wars and investitures of crown princes. This is the matrix within which the idea of

---

35 Ibid., xxxvi–xliv.

36 Ibid., xxvi–xxxvi.

37 SAA 13 139:1–9.

38 For this text and the idea of reconciliation, see M. Nissinen and S. Parpola, "Marduk's Return and Reconciliation in a Prophetic Letter from Arbela," in *Verbum et calamus: Semitic and Related Studies in Honour of the Sixtieth Birthday of Professor Tapani Harviainen* (ed. H. Juusola, J. Laulainen, and H. Palva; StudOr 99; Helsinki: Finnish Oriental Society, 2004) 199–219 (= pp. 245–65 in this volume); for a different historical explanation, see de Jong, *Isaiah among the Ancient Near Eastern Prophets*, 279–82.

prophecy is constructed in the Assyrian oracles; here, if anywhere, we have to do with constructs contingent on social and historical processes.

In view of the uniform and well-designed construct of Assyrian prophecy available in the oracles and inscriptions, it is informative to read other Assyrian texts in which prophets and prophecy sometimes appear in a somewhat different light. Several features of the "official" image of the prophets can be found in these texts as well; for instance, in the letter where the banishment of an anonymous person is recommended with words that closely resemble the extant prophetic texts;[39] or in another letter reporting the prophecy proclaimed to the substitute king at Akkad.[40]

Even the famous letter of Bel-ušezib, SAA 10 109, reveals that the Babylonian astrologer was well aware of the role of divination in the royal ideology.[41] But this letter also reveals something in the image of the prophets that is more difficult to harmonize with the prophetic image of the oracles and inscriptions, since this text deals with prophets as individuals, not with prophecy as a concept. In another letter, Bel-ušezib has no difficulty in quoting a word of Marduk that is best explained as a prophetic oracle; hence prophecy as such is not the target of his criticism.[42] In SAA 10 109, however, he is disheartened because Esarhaddon, after his victorious civil war, had granted an audience to male and female prophets instead of himself. That prophets were commonly regarded as diviners becomes clear, for example, from the inscriptions listing prophetic messages (*šipir maḫḫê*) together with other divinatory procedures,[43] as well as from the document from Tušḫan, according to which copper was delivered to

39 SAA 10 284; see S. Parpola, *Letters from Assyrian Scholars to the Kings Esarhaddon and Assurbanipal, Part II: Commentary and Appendices* (AOAT 5/2; Kevelaer: Butzon and Bercker; Neukirchen-Vluyn: Neukirchener Verlag, 1983) 208; Nissinen, *References to Prophecy*, 102–5.

40 SAA 10 352; see Parpola, *Letters from Assyrian Scholars*, 270–72; Nissinen, *References to Prophecy*, 68–77; de Jong, *Isaiah among the Ancient Near Eastern Prophets*, 304–5.

41 See Nissinen, *References to Prophecy*, 89–95; de Jong, *Isaiah among the Ancient Near Eastern Prophets*, 256–58.

42 SAA 10 111 rev. 23–26: "Bel has said: 'May Esarhaddon, king of Assyria, be seated on his throne like Marduk-šapik-zeri! I will deliver all the countries into his hands!'"

43 Esarhaddon Nin A ii 5–7: "Favourable omens in the sky and earth came to me. Oracles of prophets, messages of the gods and Ištar, were constantly sent to me and they encouraged my heart"; Esarhaddon Ass A ii 12: "Prophetic oracles concerning the establishment of the foundation of my priestly throne until far-off days were conveyed to me incessantly and regularly. Good omens kept occurring to me in dreams and speech omens concerning the establishment of my throne and the long life of my rule"; see E. Leichty, *The Royal Inscriptions of Esarhaddon, King of Assyria (680–669 BC)* (RINAP 4; Winona Lake, Ind.: Eisenbrauns, 2011) 14, 121, 124.

a prophet and an augur at the same time.[44] In Bel-ušezib's letter, the astrologer's grievance against the king's summons implies a ranking of professionals in divination invisible in the prophetic texts. Apparent suspicion towards prophetic utterances is also expressed by the temple administrator who refuses to obey the prophetic word and send the royal throne of the temple from Assur to Akkad until the word comes from the king himself.[45]

Even more dramatic deviations from the official image of prophecy are suggested by the paragraph of the Succession Treaty of Esarhaddon requiring a report of every derogatory word against Assurbanipal, the crown prince designate, even if they were expressed by prophets:

> If you hear an evil, ill, and ugly word that is mendacious and harmful to Assurbanipal, the great crown prince of the Palace of Succession, son of Esarhaddon, king of Assyria, your lord, may it come from the mouth of his enemy, from the mouth of his ally, from the mouth of his brothers, uncles, cousins, or his family, descendants of his father, or from the mouth of your brothers, sons, or daughters, or from the mouth of a prophet, an ecstatic, or an inquirer of divine words, or from the mouth of any human being at all, you must not conceal it but come and tell it to Assurbanipal, the great crown prince of the Palace of Succession, son of Esarhaddon, king of Assyria.[46]

That this was to be taken as a serious obligation is confirmed by the correspondence of Nabû-reḫtu-uṣur, an official who does exactly what the treaty binds him to do and reports on a prophecy uttered by a slave girl, according to which the progeny of Sennacherib (that is, both Esarhaddon and Assurbanipal) will be destroyed:

> A slave girl of Bel-aḫu-uṣur [...] upon [...] on the ou[tski]rts of H[arran]; since Sivan she has been enraptured and speaks a good word about him: "This is the word of Nusku: The kingship is for Sasî! I will destroy the name and seed of Sennacherib."[47]

44 ZTT 25; see S. Parpola, "Cuneiform Texts from Ziyaret Tepe (Tušḫan), 2002–2003," *SAAB* 17 (2008) 1–113, esp. 98–100.

45 SAA 13 37; see Parpola, *Letters from Assyrian Scholars*, 329; Nissinen, *References to Prophecy*, 78–81.

46 SAA 2 6 § 10; see Nissinen, *References to Prophecy*, 156–62; E. Otto, *Das Deuteronomium: Politische Theologie und Rechtsreform in Juda und Assyrien* (BZAW 284; Berlin: de Gruyter, 1999) 57–64.

47 SAA 16 59; see Nissinen, *References to Prophecy*, 108–54, and the discussion on the historical background of the letter in S. W. Holloway, *Aššur Is King! Aššur Is King! Religion in the Exercise of Power in the Neo-Assyrian Empire* (CHANE 10; Leiden: Brill, 2002) 410–12; de Jong, *Isaiah among the Ancient Near Eastern Prophets*, 271–74.

Nothing could be more diametrically opposed to the construct of Assyrian prophecy represented by the oracles, and advocated even by Nabû-reḫtu-uṣur himself, who, necessarily, considers the words of the slave girl a pseudoprophecy.

The polished appearance of the Assyrian oracles is the result of a process of preservation, transmission, and reuse, which gives rise to a construct of prophecy well matched with the reason and motivation of the process itself, representing an orthodox royal perspective.[48] However, the Assyrian sources provide us not only with an intended, "official" construct of prophecy but also with glimpses of reality that tell a different story. In view of the somewhat discrepant images of prophecy in non-prophetic sources, should we now conclude that the uniform construct of prophecy in the prophetic oracles and inscriptions is less reliable, if not false altogether, because it is to be regarded as an ideological product promoted by royal interests? This is hardly the case, since the Assyrian sources other than prophetic oracles and inscriptions do not really represent an alternative ideology, let alone a non-ideological point of view, but simply provide us with additional information. The ancient sources never convey an accurate and authentic reflection of the past, and there is no ideology-free zone where the modern scholar could be confident about the "truthfulness" of the information discernible from the sources. Zainab Bahrani is certainly right when she maintains that "[t]o disentangle ancient ideology's message from the truth of the past is no easy matter. We cannot point out ancient ideology as falsehood in opposition to our own truthful reconstructions of the past. What this amounts to is an unstated argument for a (very ideological) binary of self and other, ancient and modern."[49]

Assyrian constructs of prophecy are certainly ideological representations, in and through which the Assyrian state ideology exists, and these representations also serve as sources of the historical image of Assyrian prophecy. The dependence of modern constructs on ancient ones could not be more obvious, and, as Bahrani notes, it is difficult to avoid mimetic ("emic") reading, that is, repeating the ancient text's ideology, however critical ("etic") a stance on it we may try to maintain. "The reverse, thinking of ideology as a false image, is also derived from the same belief in the mimetic process. It is simply the other side of the coin."[50] What we have is an image, constructed *and* real.

---

48 See de Jong, *Isaiah among the Ancient Near Eastern Prophets*, 439–41.

49 Z. Bahrani, *Rituals of War: The Body and Violence in Mesopotamia* (New York: Zone Books, 2008) 71.

50 Ibid., 73–74.

Constructs of Prophecy in Biblical Scholarship

The previous section concerning the Assyrian construct of prophecy is, inevitably, my metaconstruct of the image provided by the available sources. When it comes to the construct of prophecy in biblical scholarship, it is of necessity the Hebrew Bible that sets the agenda. The scholarly construct can only be a metaconstruct emerging from the representations of the restricted textual material created by the people to whom we owe the availability of the biblical evidence. Just as in the case of Assyria, the metaconstruct cannot do without a certain amount of mimesis, however misleading this may be said to be from the historical point of view.

While mimetic reading of Assyrian texts may be considered an impediment to a reliable reconstruction of the past, mimetic reading of the prophetic books and other texts in the Hebrew Bible is actively encouraged in Jewish and Christian theology, because these texts are constituents of the Holy Book of Jews and Christians. Indeed, many books with the title "Theology of the Old Testament" consciously attempt a faithful representation of the theology of the biblical texts. This does not necessarily make them bad books—during its long history, this approach to the Bible has produced highly sophisticated and intellectual readings of the biblical text, as can be confirmed by a scholar whose basic reading as a student of theology included books written by, say, Gerhard von Rad, Walther Zimmerli, or Timo Veijola.[51] It would be all too simple to reduce the traditional divide between the genres "Theology of the Old Testament" and "History of Israelite/Ancient Near Eastern Religion"[52] to the dichotomy between mimetic

---

51 G. von Rad, *Theologie des Alten Testaments*, vol. 1: *Die Theologie der geschichtlichen Überlieferungen Israels* (Munich: Kaiser, ²1958); id., *Theologie des Alten Testaments, Band II: Die Theologie der prophetischen Überlieferungen Israels* (Munich: Kaiser, ²1960); W. Zimmerli, *Grundzüge der alttestamentlichen Theologie* (Theologische Wissenschaft 3; Stuttgart: Kohlhammer, ³1978); T. Veijola, "Depression als menschliche und biblische Erfahrung," in id., *Offenbarung und Anfechtung: Hermeneutisch-theologische Studien zum Alten Testament* (ed. W. Dietrich and M. Marttila; BibS[N] 89; Neukirchen-Vluyn: Neukirchener, 2007) 158–90; id., *Leben nach der Weisung: Exegetisch-historische Studien zum Alten Testament* (ed. W. Dietrich in collaboration with M. Marttila; FRLANT 224; Göttingen: Vandenhoeck & Ruprecht, 2008).

52 See the contributions to the theme issue *JBTh* 10 (1995; 2nd ed. 2001) with the title "Religionsgeschichte Israels oder Theologie des Alten Testaments," especially R. Albertz, "Religionsgeschichte Israels statt Theologie des Alten Testaments! Plädoyer für eine forschungsgeschichtliche Umorientierung" (pp. 3–24); I. Kalimi, "Religionsgeschichte Israels oder Theologie des Alten Testaments: Das jüdische Interesse an der biblischen Theologie" (pp. 45–68); F. Crüsemann, "Religionsgeschichte oder Theologie? Elementare Überlegungen zu einer falschen Alternative" (pp. 69–77); N. P. Lemche, "Warum die Theologie des Alten Testaments einen Irrweg

and objective (or emic and etic) readings, claiming that "Theologies" represent the former while "Histories" pursue the latter. Given the available sources, the ideal of objectivity easily leads to what David Clines calls a genetic fallacy.[53]

The binary of self and other reveals itself in the fact that, to my knowledge, no one has hitherto published a book entitled "Theology of the Assyrian Literature." There is no reason why such a book could not be written (in fact, the long introduction to Simo Parpola's publication of Assyrian prophecies would well deserve this title[54]), but the specialists on Assyrian literature have been conspicuously disinclined to do so—perhaps because the word "theology" for many implies a kind of mimetic reading alien to "true" historical analysis.

On the other hand, the dividing line between "theology" and "ideology" still seems to follow the course of the boundary of the self and the other.[55]

To be sure, there is a breathtaking number of studies of prophecy in the Hebrew Bible that do not present themselves as simply echoing the text's ideology but, on the contrary, strive for a critical reading, whether for the sake of historical reconstruction (the traditional approach still very much alive) or ideological criticism (which has been practised for a shorter period of time). These studies result in different constructs of prophecy, depending on whether they intend to draw an historical picture of ancient prophets in Israel and Judah or whether they focus on the literary images available in the biblical text. The problem, however, is that the distinction between the historical and the literary prophet is not always quite clear, and the reader of scholarly studies in biblical prophetic literature may time and again find her- or himself wondering whether "the prophet" in a given essay refers to the reconstructed historical person, the literary persona, or both at the same time. When the author of any given quotation from prophetic books is called "the prophet," the authors of the prophetic books are personalized in a way that gives the concept of authorship of these literary works a specific character.

Traditionally, prophetic studies focused on the reconstruction of the historical prophet. The rigid literary analysis of the biblical prophetic books initiated by the 19th century exegetes taught several generations of biblical scholars to make a distinction between the authentic and the secondary, in order to be

---

darstellt" (pp. 79–92); M.-T. Wacker, "'Religionsgeschichte Israels' oder 'Theologie des Alten Testaments'—(k)eine Alternative? Anmerkungen aus feministischexegetischer Sicht" (pp. 129–55).

53 D. J. A. Clines, "Historical Criticism: Are Its Days Numbered?" *Teologinen Aikakauskirja* 114 (2009) 542–58, esp. 546–47.

54 Cf. above, n. 34.

55 For discussion on "ideology," see, e.g., J. Barr, *History and Ideology in the Old Testament: Biblical Studies at the End of a Millennium* (Oxford: Oxford University Press, 2000) 102–40.

able to skim off the secondary layers superimposed upon the genuinely prophetic words, the *ipsissima verba*. The scholarly construct of ancient Israelite prophecy was strongly oriented towards the personal achievements of the great prophets, actually creating a canon within the canon, consisting of the prophets who enjoyed the highest appreciation of the scholars. Although the *ipsissima verba* approach has been deemed antiquated for quite some time, the aftermath of *Literarkritik* is still visible in the way that the ideal type of a biblical prophet is constructed on the basis of texts deemed to go back to the historical prophets or their alleged disciples. This is no longer a mimetic reading of the biblical text as a whole, but of carefully selected passages.

As an example of a recent, traditional, and sympathetic construct of Israelite prophecy, I have chosen a passage from a recent Hebrew Bible textbook—a very good one—edited by the late Erich Zenger (1939–2010) who himself authored the chapter on prophecy.[56] In Zenger's view, the "basic forms of the prophetic speech"[57] imply a "prophetic self-identification" consisting of the following four points:

1. The prophet is a mediator of the divine word, which he delivers unsolicited and without compromises.
2. The prophet has a charisma which enables him to express his relentlessly critical attitude towards contemporary society.
3. The prophet makes his appearance before the public, addressing his words to the king, the leaders of society, the priests of the temple of Jerusalem, as well as the people as a whole.
4. The prophet is essentially a critic, visionary, and "protestant," whose only legitimation is his immediacy to God, and, as a "protestant," he (or the book named after him) is necessarily opposed to office and institution.[58]

---

56 E. Zenger (ed.), *Einleitung in das Alte Testament* (Stuttgart: Kohlhammer, [7]2008) 417–26.
57 This echoes Claus Westermann's influential study, *Grundformen prophetischer Rede* (BEvT 31; Munich: Kaiser, 1960; [5]1978).
58 My English paraphrase of Zenger in Zenger (ed.), *Einleitung in das Alte Testament*, 423: "(1) Der Prophet ist Überbringer bzw. Bote ihm zuteil gewordener konkreter Gottesworte, die er ungefragt und kompromißlos übermitteln muß. (2) In der Inspiration und in der Kraft des ihm zugekommenen Gotteswortes hat der Prophet das Charisma der scharfen Gegenwartsanalyse bzw. der schonungslosen Gegenwartskritik. (3) Der Prophet sucht die Öffentlichkeit für das ihm übermittelte Gotteswort. Seine Adressaten sind der König, die führenden Kreise von Staat und Gesellschaft, die Priester am Jerusalemer Tempel, aber auch das ganze Volk. (4) Der Prophet ist von seinem Grundimpetus her Kritiker, Visionär und 'Protestant', dessen einzige Legitimation seine Gottunmittelbarkeit ist. Als 'Protestant' ist er (bzw. das nach ihm genannte Buch) die notwendige Gegeninstanz zum Amt und zur Institution."

It becomes immediately clear from the same textbook that this construct does not apply to all prophets mentioned in the Hebrew Bible. Not all prophets, not even the biblical ones, deliver their messages unsolicited; their attitude towards their society is not always relentlessly critical; they are not necessarily opposed to office and institution; and they are not always male. The textbook acknowledges the existence of ancient Near Eastern prophecy[59] and finds in the Hebrew Bible prophetic groups, cultic prophets, court prophets, and literary prophets alongside the "free, oppositional individual prophets."[60] It is clearly the last-mentioned group, however, that enjoys the status of "classical" prophets, represented by a few prophetic figures, first and foremost by Isaiah, Jeremiah, Hosea, Amos, and Micah, and perhaps Ezekiel—and not the whole books attributed to these characters, for that matter, but only the sections that are assumed to go back to the historical persons who gave their names to the books.

Reading the Hebrew Bible could well produce different constructs of the historical image(s) of prophecy in the ancient kingdoms of Israel and Judah. For instance, oracles against nations[61] could with good reason be introduced as the quintessence of biblical prophecy; at least they occupy a substantial portion of the biblical text. Isaiah would qualify as a court prophet as easily as Ezekiel would deserve to be called a cultic prophet, not to mention Haggai, Zechariah, and Malachi who seldom appear in the group picture of the great "classical" prophets. However, even today, Amos and Isaiah, rather than Joel, Haggai, or Micaiah ben Imlah, tend to be presented as archetypes of a true Israelite prophet, and much scholarly attention is paid to the historical figures of the archetypal prophets.

It strikes the eye that only Zenger's point (3) concerns the prophetic phenomenon in general, while the other points include attributes that would probably not apply by and large to prophetic figures in the Hebrew Bible or elsewhere. Social criticism and anti-ritualism are often regarded as core features of biblical prophecy, and, indeed, these are recurrent topics in the biblical prophetic books.[62] Nevertheless, these topics dominate the scene mainly because they

---

59 Ibid., 423–25.

60 Ibid., 418–20.

61 E.g., Isaiah 13–23; 25:10–12; 34:5–15; 58; Jeremiah 46–51; Ezekiel 25–32; Amos 1:1–2:3; Obadiah 1–15; Nahum; Zeph 2:4–15; Zech 9:1–8.

62 For social criticism, see, e.g., Isa 3:13–15; 5:8–23; 10: 1–4; Ezek 18:10–13; Hos 4:1–3; Amos 2:6–8; 4:1–3; 5:7–12; 8:4–8; Mic 2:1–5; 3:9–12; 6:9–12; 7:1–4; Hab 2:5–17. Passages interpreted as reflecting an anti-ritualistic bias include Isa 1:11–17; 58; 66; Jer 7:22; Hos 6:4–6; Amos 5:21–24; Mic 6:6–8; Zech 7:5–10.

are constantly underlined and introduced as the first things everyone should know about biblical prophecy. One can also fairly easily read between the lines that, from the point of view of the scholarly community, the construct of the free, oppositional individuals represents the "self," while that of the cultic prophets and the court prophets, including their ancient Near Eastern counterparts, belongs to the realm of the "other."

It goes without saying that the scholarly construct described above rests upon a small portion of the huge corpus of biblical texts where prophecy features in one way or another. As such, this construct carries forward the legacy of nineteenth-century biblical scholarship in which the primacy of the few preexilic prophets is deeply rooted. The persistence of this legacy is astonishing, since it has maintained its popularity, not only in biblical scholarship but also in preaching and teaching, as well as in popular media, down to the present day.[63] Julius Wellhausen is often presented as the foremost architect of the nineteenth-century construct of prophecy, and, indeed, it was the idea of *lex post prophetas*, adopted by Wellhausen from Karl Heinrich Graf, that gave the prophets a crucial position in the emergence of the distinctively Israelite religion.[64] But even Wellhausen had predecessors profoundly influenced by German idealism. The idealistic anthropology that enabled combining the function of religious mediation with brilliant religious individuals (*Genieästhetik*) can already be found in Heinrich Ewald's *Die Propheten des Alten Bundes*.[65] On the other hand, the "ethical monotheism" of the prophets was advocated by Abraham Kuenen, Well-

---

63 K. Schmid, "Klassische und nachklassische Deutungen der alttestamentlichen Prophetie," *Zeitschrift für neuere Theologiegeschichte* 3 (1996) 225–50, esp. 225: "Zu den wenigen Ergebnissen der alttestamentlichen Wissenschaft, die in Kirche und Öffentlichkeit nahezu ohne Abstriche rezipiert worden sind, gehört die Bestimmung des Wesens der alttestamentlichen Prophetie, wie es die historisch-kritische Forschung seit dem 19. Jahrhundert beschrieben hat"; cf. id., "Hintere Propheten (Nebiim)," in *Grundinformation Altes Testament: Eine Einführung in Literatur, Religion und Geschichte des Alten Testaments* (ed. J. C. Gertz; UTB 2745; Göttingen: Vandenhoeck & Ruprecht, 2006) 303–401, esp. 307.

64 J. Wellhausen, *Prolegomena zur Geschichte Israels* (Berlin: Reimer, ^{3}1886). Wellhausen gave credit to Graf for this idea; see id., *Geschichte Israels*, vol. 1 (Berlin: Reimer, 1878), esp. 4.

65 See H. Ewald, *Die Propheten des Alten Bundes: Zweite Ausgabe in drei Bänden, Vol. 1* (Göttingen: Vandenhoeck & Ruprecht, 1867); the first edition of this work was published in 1840. According to Schmid, "Klassische und nachklassische Deutungen der alttestamentlichen Prophetie," 233: "Heinrich Ewald markiert zunächst deswegen den Beginn der neueren Prophetenforschung, weil er das Phänomen der Prophetie konsequent idealistisch gedeutet hat und mit dieser Sicht den Grundstein des klassischen Prophetenbildes gelegt hat." For Ewald's position in the German theology and philosophy of his time, see R. Smend, "Heinrich Ewalds biblische Theologie: Hinweis auf ein vergessenes Buch," in *Epochen der Bibelkritik: Gesammelte Studien*, vol. 3 (ed. id.; Munich: Kaiser, 1991) 155–67.

hausen's Dutch discussion partner, a sworn anti-supernaturalist, according to whom the prophets "were not concerned at all about facts already laid down in the future; their concern was the moral behaviour of men and women, which ought to accord with the divine righteousness and justice."[66]

For Wellhausen, following in the wake of Ewald, the prophets were inspired individuals through whom God spontaneously communicated with people.[67] However, Wellhausen's prophets were no religious fanatics, nor even revolutionaries, but were deeply rooted in history and tradition and were aware of the "moral evidence," an absolute subjective conviction of the right moral behaviour, which they inherited from their tradition.[68]

It was probably Wellhausen's individualism, the product of the philosophical atmosphere of his time,[69] that gave the strongest impetus to the further development of the scholarly construct of prophecy. Wellhausen, however, did not ascribe to the prophetic individuals such a decisive role in the history of Israelite religion as did his contemporary Bernhard Duhm, whom Wellhausen criticized for exaggerating the importance of the prophets at the expense of priests.[70] While not regarding the prophets as dependent on the Torah, Wellhausen saw them in a sympathetic continuum with the Torah, representing the same ideas that contributed to its emergence. Duhm, again, while accepting the idea of *lex post prophetas*, gave the prophets the credit for bringing about a sea change in the Israelite religion—indeed, a complete revolution that constituted the beginning of the "real Israelite religion."[71] Duhm—much like Ewald but unlike

---

66 R. Smend, *From Astruc to Zimmerli: Old Testament Scholarship in Three Centuries* (trans. M. Kohl; Tübingen: Mohr Siebeck, 2007), 84, characterizing Abraham Kuenen's *De Profeten en de Profetie onder Israël: Historisch-dogmatische Studie*, 2 vols. (Leiden: Engels, 1875).

67 Wellhausen, *Prolegomena zur Geschichte Israels*, 416: "Das gehört zum Begriffe des prophetischen, der echten Offenbarung, dass Jahve, über alle ordnungsmässige Vermittelung hinweg, sich dem *Individuum* mitteilt, dem Berufenen, in welchem der geheimnisvolle und unzergliederbare Rapport energisch wird, worin die Gottheit mit dem Menschen steht."

68 Ibid.; see also Schmid, "Klassische und nachklassische Deutungen der alttestamentlichen Prophetie," 236–37.

69 For Wellhausen's individualism, see L. Perlitt, *Vatke und Wellhausen: Geschichtsphilosophische Voraussetzungen und historiographische Motive für die Darstellung der Religion und Geschichte Israels durch Wilhelm Vatke und Julius Wellhausen* (BZAW 94; Berlin: Töpelmann, 1965) 213–15. See also R. Smend, *Julius Wellhausen: Ein Bahnbrecher in drei Disziplinen* (Themen 84; Munich: Carl Friedrich von Siemens Stiftung, 2004) 53–58, who highlights the religious nature of Wellhausen's individualism.

70 J. Wellhausen, review of B. Duhm, *Die Theologie der Propheten als Grundlage für die innere Entwicklungsgeschichte der israelitischen Tradition* (Bonn: Marcus, 1875), in *Jahrbuch für Deutsche Theologie* 21 (1876) 152–58, esp. 157.

71 Duhm, *Die Theologie der Propheten*, 17.

Wellhausen—stressed the psychological and even ecstatic factors in the activity of the prophets,[72] thus adding a strong psychological element to Wellhausen's individualism. In addition, Duhm contributed decisively to the *Literarkritik* of the prophetic books, the purpose of which was to reveal the original words of the prophets blurred by later editors, for whom Duhm did not have much appreciation.[73] In his late work *Israels Propheten*, published no less than four decades after *Die Theologie der Propheten*, Duhm had sharpened the literary-historical image of the prophets and had grown away from earlier theological concepts.[74] What remained unchanged, however, was his conviction of the key role of the prophets, "die Männer des ewig Neuen," in the evolution of Israel's religion.[75]

Wellhausen and Duhm deserve to be called the principal architects of the scholarly idea of people called prophets, that is, a type of person classified as such within a threefold matrix: (1) the text of the Hebrew Bible, which was used exclusively as the source for constructing the prophetic image; (2) the history of Israelite religion, which was likewise reconstructed from the biblical text, and in which the prophets were found to appear as a significant factor; and (3) German idealism that enabled combining the divinely inspired medium of divine agency with an individual of great moral and theological stature. This construct was not based on a "mimetic" reading of the Hebrew Bible as a whole in the premodern spirit of a verbal inspiration but, rather, on a systematic selection of texts deemed to represent the genuine prophetic voice.

A fortunate combination of scholarly criticism, morality, and spirituality, the construct of prophecy built upon the foundation laid by Wellhausen and Duhm turned out to be immensely successful. This essay is too short to tell the whole story of what happened between the founding fathers and the recent textbook presented here as an example of the *Nachleben* of this construct. Three factors that influenced the development of this construct should not, however, go unmentioned:

---

72 Ibid., 34; cf. also G. Hölscher, *Die Profeten* (Leipzig: Hinrichs, 1914).

73 Cf., e.g., B. Duhm, *Das Buch Jeremia* (KHC 11; Tübingen: Mohr Siebeck, 1901) xviii–xix.

74 Cf. Smend, *From Astruc to Zimmerli*, 115.

75 B. Duhm, *Israels Propheten* (Tübingen: Mohr Siebeck, 1916; ^{2}1922) 8. Duhm saw a sharp contrast between the prophets and their followers: "Die großen Propheten des achten bis sechsten Jahrhunderts hatten ihre Jünger und Anhänger gehabt, die die Früchte ihrer schöpferischen Wirksamkeit in die eigenen Scheunen sammelten und als Gesetzgeber, Lehrer und Apokalyptiker das Volk viel mächtiger beherrschten als ihre Meister. *Diese ewig Mittelmäßigen* trachteten immer nach Abschluß und Ruhe; sie hielten sich, wie Jeremia sagt, für weise und *wollten nichts Neues*, keinen störenden Fortschritt. Der Fluß der israelitischen Geschichte hatte sein Meer erreicht, ein stilles Binnenmeer" (ibid.; emphases mine).

(1) The rise of form criticism, which paid attention to the forms of literature in biblical texts as well as the socioreligious matrix underlying them (*Sitz im Leben*). This did not necessarily affect the climactic position of the "classical" prophets, who were still discussed as a class *sui generis*,[76] but the form-critical view broadened the traditional perspective. The quest for the *Sitz im Leben* increased the sensitivity of scholars to prophecy as a socioreligious phenomenon not directly derivable from the biblical texts, whose literary forms are not necessarily of prophetic origin and should, therefore, be discussed separately from the phenomenon itself.[77]

(2) The dialectical theology which emphasized the Barthian idea of revelation *senkrecht von oben* and the irreconcilable dissimilarity between the human and the divine. This did not mean abandoning the prevailing construct of a true Israelite prophet, but it created tension between the continuity and discontinuity of the prophets with regard to their socioreligious contexts. This can be seen in the work of Gerhard von Rad who, in the first volume of his *Theologie des Alten Testaments*, placed much emphasis on the discontinuity,[78] but refined his view in the second volume devoted to the prophets, in which he interpreted them in line with developing historical circumstances.[79] For von Rad, history, in fact, became a crucial constituent of the divine-human communication.[80] This, however, resulted in a tradition-historical view of the prophets within the Israelite and biblical context,[81] rather than viewing prophecy as an historical, cross-cultural phenomenon, which von Rad mostly ignored.

---

76 Cf., e. g., H. Greßmann, "Die Aufgaben der alttestamentlichen Forschung," *ZAW* 24 (1930) 1–33, esp. 32.

77 See, especially, H. Gunkel, "Einleitungen," in *Die großen Propheten übersetzt und erklärt* (ed. H. Schmidt; SAT II/2; Göttingen: Vandenhoeck & Ruprecht, 1915) xi–lxxii. Gunkel presents his long introduction to the prophets in two parts, "Die geheimen Erfahrungen der Propheten," and "Die Propheten als Schriftsteller und Dichter." Importantly, he stresses that "*die meisten der genannten Gattungen nicht ursprünglich prophetisch sind*" (p. il; emphasis original).

78 Von Rad, *Theologie des Alten Testaments*, 1:133–34.

79 Idem, *Theologie des Alten Testaments*, 2:17–19.

80 Cf. Schmid, "Klassische und nachklassische Deutungen der alttestamentlichen Prophetie," 246: "Erstaunlicherweise ist bei von Rad gerade die Betonung der Geschichte im Gegenüber zur Schöpfung ein mittelbares Erbe der dialektischen Theologie, zeigte sie doch, daß Gott sich der Welt in ganz anderer Weise als in ihren eigenen Ordnungen, nämlich in der Geschichte zeigt."

81 C. R. Seitz, "Prophecy and Tradition-History: The Achievement of Gerhard von Rad and Beyond," in *Prophetie in Israel*, GS G. von Rad (ed. I. Fischer, K. Schmid, and H. G. M. Williamson; Altes Testament und Moderne 11; Münster: LIT, 2003) 29–52, esp. 46: "For von Rad, the primary context of interpretation was *the prophet in relationship to traditions*, on the one hand, and *the*

(3) The ideological climate of the post-World War II period, culminating in the student revolts in 1968.[82] The traditional construct of the prophets received a new political dimension in the interpretation of the 1960s generation, for whom the free, oppositional individual prophets served as an important model as independent anti-institutionalists. Interestingly, the critical attitude to authorities and the emphasis on human rights and equality not only buttressed the traditional construct of prophecy, but also gave a strong impetus to the subsequent feminist and postmodern discourses. A genuine and elegant representative of this generation was, without doubt, Erich Zenger, the author of the above-described example of the modern scholarly construct of prophecy.[83]

Despite its amazing ability to respond to the needs of different intellectual frameworks, the construct of the true prophet as a brave and independent individual and a religious mastermind has been undergoing a deconstruction for quite some time. Critical voices against the traditional construct of prophecy have been increasingly raised during the past decades,[84] and it is the conviction of most of today's scholars that the biblical constructs of prophecy, in all their complexity, go back to the production of the prophetic books of the Hebrew Bible and their literary history rather than to individual historical characters.[85] Moreover, the increasing awareness of prophecy as an ancient Eastern Mediter-

---

individual prophet in relation to events of his day, on the other, as God inspired his (the prophet's) particular take on these" (emphases original).

82 For the social and intellectual background of the 1968 events from a global perspective, see N. Frei, *1968: Jugendrevolte und globaler Protest* (Munich: Deutscher Taschenbuch Verlag, 2008).

83 As one of Zenger's students wrote in the preface to his *Festschrift:* "Als er 1972 junger Professor geworden war, mußte er sich gegen das Mißtrauen der 68er behaupten: 'Trau keinem über dreißig!'" (F.-L. Hossfeld, "Vorwort," in *Vom Sinai zum Horeb: Stationen alttestamentlicher Glaubensgeschichte* [ed. F.-L. Hossfeld; Würzburg: Echter, 1989], esp. 7); see also Zenger's portrait in S. Schroer, "Erich Zenger," in *Wer knackt den Kode: Meilensteine der Bibelforschung* (ed. T. Staubli; Düsseldorf: Patmos, 2009) 127–28.

84 To take just one example: D. J. A. Clines, "Metacommenting Amos," in *Of Prophets' Visions and the Wisdom of Sages*, FS R. N. Whybray (ed. H. A. McKay and D. J. A. Clines; JSOTSup 162; Sheffield: JSOT Press, 1993) 142–60.

85 See R. G. Kratz, "Probleme der Prophetenforschung," in *Prophetenstudien: Kleine Schriften II* (ed. id.; FAT 74; Tübingen: Mohr Siebeck, 2011) 3–17; cf. Schmid, "Klassische und nachklassische Deutungen der alttestamentlichen Prophetie," 249: "Die Komplexität der Prophetenbücher erklärt sich nicht durch die Komplexität der prophetischen Einzelpersönlichkeit, sondern durch die Komplexität der auf der erstmaligen schriftlichen Fixierung ihrer ursprünglichen Verkündigung fußenden innerbiblischen Literaturgeschichte." For most recent contributions on this complexity, see, e.g., the articles published in Edelman and Ben Zvi (eds.), *The Production of Prophecy*, and in *Constructs of Prophecy in Former and Latter Prophets and Other Texts* (ed. L. L. Grabbe and M. Nissinen; ANEM 4; Atlanta, Ga.: Society of Biblical Literature, 2011).

ranean phenomenon has caused a growing number of scholars to view biblical prophets, even the "classical" ones, as representatives of a broader, crosscultural phenomenon.[86]

Conclusion

In this essay, I hope that I have been able to demonstrate that the notion of a construct of prophecy, rather than being just another unnecessary offshoot of an all-encompassing social constructionism, is meaningful in understanding both ancient prophecy and modern scholarship. The social construction discussion typically emerges when the inevitability of something that is taken for granted is being questioned. There was a time when prophecy was referred to as a matter of course, when the scholarly category of prophecy was virtually equated with the historical phenomenon. Today, there is a growing awareness of prophecy as something that cannot be talked about at all except as an historical and literary phenomenon that is not self-evident but needs to be defined; that does not arise inevitably but needs to be constructed by any given community for historically contingent purposes.

Every time someone is referred to as a prophet, the reference is made to a representative of a type of person, presupposing a classification that determines the characteristics of that particular type, as well as a conceptual framework within which the classification is valid. Prophecy, therefore, is an idea needed, defined, and maintained by human communities that provide the matrix without which the idea of prophecy would not make sense. Whoever would create a construct of prophecy cannot help but make choices, arbitrating between issues deemed central or marginal, fundamental or non-essential. One of the most important scholarly choices to be made is the matrix within which the idea of prophecy is constructed. Changing the matrix will also change the construct.

In view of my reconstructions of the constructs of prophecy in Assyria and in modern scholarship, the reader might ask whether my treatment makes these constructs another *X* that is "quite bad as it is" and should rather be done away with. This is not my intention. I realize that any given construct, ancient or modern, highlights some aspects of the historical phenomenon while hiding others. This is simply what happens when mental concepts of communication with supernatural agents turn into public representations that are meant to be understood and shared by a religious or scholarly community.

---

86 E.g., de Jong, *Isaiah among the Ancient Near Eastern Prophets.*

What was being constructed in the Assyrian official image of prophecy was not the concept of prophecy as such but, rather, the role of divine-human communication, or divination, within the matrix of the royal ideology. It was thanks to the construct of the Assyrian king and the establishment of the Assyrian society that we have sources at our disposal, on the basis of which it becomes possible to recognize and analyse the construct. The dependence of modern scholars on the sources written by the very architects of the Assyrian construct of prophecy makes the scholarly reconstruction a kind of "mimetic" enterprise, however critically we attempt to read our sources.

In the case of biblical scholarship, it is much more difficult to give a simple answer to the questions about what is being constructed, and whose constructions are at issue. The biblical texts are much too wild and diverse to be tamed into a single and coherent image of prophecy, and biblical scholars cannot be said to have advocated a uniform ideology either, even though the scholarly agenda created in the late nineteenth century (that is, the quest for the original sayings of the prophets and their positioning in the history of Israelite religion) still provides the general matrix for scholarly constructs of prophecy. It is clear, however, that, unlike the Assyrians who did not develop a concept for prophecy separate from divination in general, the biblical texts often sharply distinguish prophecy from other kinds of divination. Biblical scholars have followed suit, intentionally conceptualizing prophecy as an historical and theological category. As a part of the story of biblical scholarship, prophecy does not merely serve as another interesting aspect of religious mediation shared by humanity at large. Rather, the constructs of prophecy reflect and represent the modern understanding of the shared knowledge of modern Western cultural identity.

Reflections on the "Historical-Critical" Method: Historical Criticism and Critical Historicism

"Die Liebe ist hier wie bei jeder Interpretation die beste Lehrmeisterin des Forschers."[1] (Hugo Greßmann)

Lamenting Historical Criticism?

Historical criticism, once considered the one and only legitimate scholarly method of investigating the biblical text, toward the end of the second millennium has been deprived of its status as *the* academic approach to the Bible. Itself a product of history and the so-called Enlightenment in particular, historical criticism is undergoing a redefinition under the influence of the post-Enlightenment mood of the emerging third millennium. It has never been a fixed and unaltered entity, though; Hugo Greßmann maintained already in 1924 that, while there is a unanimity to some degree about historical understanding being the actual purpose of Old Testament studies, a living scholarship will always produce new ways of attaining such understanding.[2] Greßmann was right, even though he could hardly imagine the course historical scholarship would take along with the "linguistic turn," that is, the idea that reality is constituted by language, which dismisses the ideal of historical objectivity not only as unreachable but as entirely impossible.[3] Moreover, the heterogeneous set of approaches coined

1 "Here, as with each interpretation, love is the best teacher of the researcher." H. Greßmann, "Die Aufgaben der alttestamentlichen Forschung," *ZAW* 42 (1924) 1–33, esp. 12.

2 Ibid., 1: "Bis zu einem gewissen Grade sind die Aufgaben der alttestamentlichen Forschung natürlich immer dieselben und haben alle nur ein einziges Ziel: das geschichtliche Verständnis des AT. Und noch kann man mit demselben Recht das Gegenteil behaupten: Wo die Wissenschaft in lebendigem Fluß bleibt, da wechseln die Aufgaben mit jedem Forschergeschlecht, weil sich neben den alten neue Wege zeigen, die demselben Ziel zuführen wollen." For Greßmann, this meant, among other things, the movement from source criticism to ancient Near Eastern studies: "Auf das literarkritische ist das vorderorientalische Zeitalter gefolgt" (8–9).

3 For the challenge of "linguistic turn" and postmodernism in historical studies, see, e.g., P. Novick, *That Noble Dream: The "Objectivity Question" and the American Historical Profession* (Cambridge: Cambridge University Press, 1988); G. G. Iggers, *Geschichtswissenschaft im 20. Jahrhundert: Ein kritischer Überblick im internationalen Zusammenhang* (Göttingen: Vandenhoeck & Ruprecht, 1993); id., *Historiography in the Twentieth Century: From Scientific Objectivity to the*

DOI 10.1515/9783110466546-005

as postmodernism has by its very elusiveness put the traditional self-image of historical criticism as an objective and disinterested scholarly pursuit in a melting pot.

The postmodern contention that there is no reality outside the text itself has challenged biblical criticism, as historical studies in general, throughout the latter part of the twentieth century. Since the radical antihistoricism of some postmodernist and poststructuralist theories attempts to render history as an awkward endeavor leading to an epistemological impasse, it has, therefore, not attracted the majority of (biblical) historians. As a result, new ways of formulating the task of historical criticism, refuting the objectivist and foundationalist assumptions, have been developed. Many scholars who would not carry the torch of postmodernism, at least not in its most radical appearance, are ready to admit that the challenge of postmodernism has forced historians to interrogate their methods of interpretation and encounter their own subjectivity.[4] Historical approaches inspired by poststructuralist theories, such as the New Historicism,[5] which turns away from theory and moves back toward the social contexts of the production of the texts, have been welcomed by a fair number of biblical critics, especially those whose research focuses on the biblical text itself as a historical product.[6]

Reading the biblical text as a literary product of history is one thing, while reconstructing history on its basis is another. Historical methodology has been a matter of controversy also in recent discussions concerning the possibility of reconstruction of past events using the biblical text as a historical source. The

---

Postmodern Challenge (Hanover, N. H.: Wesleyan University Press, 1997); P. Zagorin, "History, the Referent, and Narrative: Reflections on Postmodernism Now," *History and Theory* 38 (1999): 1–24; Hans-Jürgen Goertz, *Unsichere Geschichte: Zur Theorie historischer Referentialität* (Stuttgart: Philipp Reclam, 2001), 11–31; Elizabeth A. Clark, *History, Theory, Text: Historians and the Linguistic Turn* (Cambridge: Harvard University Press, 2004).

4 See, e.g., R. J. Evans, *In Defence of History* (London: Granta, 1997), 248.

5 For New Historicism, see, e.g., G. Henz-Piazza, *The New Historicism* (GBS; Minneapolis, Minn.: Fortress, 2002); and the contributions collected in H. Aram Veeser, ed., *The New Historicism* (New York: Routledge, 1989), especially those of Stephen Greenblatt ("Towards a Poetic of Culture," 1–14), Louis Montrose ("Professing the Renaissance: The Poetics and Politics of Culture," 15–36), and Hayden White ("New Historicism: A Comment," 293–302).

6 See, e.g., the issue on New Historicism in *BibInt* 5/4 (1997), with contributions by Stephen D. Moore, Robert P. Carroll, Harold C. Washington, Yvonne Sherwood, Clive Marsh, Susan Lochrie Graham, and H. Aram Veeser; see also F. W. Dobbs-Allsopp, "Rethinking Historical Criticism," *BibInt* 7 (1999) 235–71.

issues of writing the history of Israel[7] and chronology of the late Iron Age Palestine[8] have stirred heated debates among biblical scholars and archaeologists, produced a significant number of publications, and guaranteed big audiences for sessions where the debates have taken place, not to mention the public interest evident on television and in the press more generally.

No less than three decades ago, Leander Keck asked whether the historical-critical method would survive.[9] When David Clines presented an outspokenly critical review of historical criticism in Helsinki in 2007 with the title "Historical Criticism: Are Its Days Numbered?"[10] his answer was rather in the negative: historical biblical studies still seem to be well alive and going strong. Thus, in the absence of the corpse, there seems to be no reason for lamenting historical biblical criticism. This, however, should not grant its practitioners the luxury of resting on their laurels—at least not if the designation "critical" is supposed to do any justice to its meaning. Far from being in a state of endangerment, historical biblical studies should not let themselves be lulled into the idea that "the postmodernist challenge will eventually go away,"[11] thus missing the opportunity of selfcritical reflection.

---

7 That is, the debate prompted by, e.g., N. P. Lemche, *Early Israel: Anthropological and Historical Studies on the Israelite Society before the Monarchy* (VTSup 37; Leiden: Brill, 1985); idem, *The Old Testament between Theology and History: A Critical Survey* (Louisville, Ky.: Westminster John Knox, 2008); T. L. Thompson, *Early History of the Israelite People: From the Written and Archaeological Sources* (SHANE 4; Leiden: Brill, 1992); P. R. Davies, *In Search of "Ancient Israel"* (JSOTSup 148; Sheffield: Sheffield Academic Press, 1992); id., *The Origins of Biblical Israel* (LHBOTS 485; London: T&T Clark, 2007); id., *Memories of Ancient Israel: An Introduction to Biblical History – Ancient and Modern* (Louisville, Ky.: Westminster John Knox, 2008); see also the counterreactions by, e.g., W. G. Dever, *What Did the Biblical Writers Know and When Did They Know It? What Archaeology Can Tell Us about the Reality of Ancient Israel* (Grand Rapids, Mich.: Eerdmans, 2001); I. V. Provan, P. Long, and T. Longman, *A Biblical History of Israel* (Louisville, Ky.: Westminster John Knox, 2003); J. Bruun Kofoed, *Text and History: Historiography and the Study of Biblical Texts* (Winona Lake, Ind.: Eisenbrauns, 2005). For an overview of this discussion, see T. Krüger, "Theoretische und methodische Probleme der Geschichte des alten Israel in der neueren Diskussion," *VF* 53 (2008) 4–22.

8 That is, the low chronology suggested by Israel Finkelstein; see, e.g., "High or Low: Megiddo and Rehov," in *The Bible and Radiocarbon Dating: Archaeology, Text, and Science* (ed. T. E. Levy and T. Higham; London: Equinox, 2005), 302–9; and the criticism of A. Mazar, "The Debate over the Chronology of the Iron Age in the Southern Levant: Its History, the Current Situation, and a Suggested Resolution," in Levy and Higham, *The Bible and Radiocarbon Dating* (2005) 15–30.

9 L. E. Keck, "Will the Historical-Critical Method Survive? Some Observations," in *Orientation by Disorientation*, FS W. A. Beardslee (ed. R. A. Spencer; Pittsburgh: Pickwick, 1980) 115–27.

10 D. J. A. Clines, "Historical Criticism: Are Its Days Numbered?," *Teologinen Aikakauskirja* 114 (2009) 542–58.

11 Zagorin, "History, the Referent, and Narrative," 2.

"Historical-critical method" may not be the best possible designation for what it conventionally represents. Not all biblical studies placed under this heading are specifically historical, whereas studies that come forward as historical cannot always be considered critical. It is also worth asking whether all this should be called hypothesis, approach, or orientation but not a "method,"[12] which sounds more like a technical procedure than an interpretive intellectual pursuit. A further difficulty with the designation "historical-critical method" is its implied reference to a certain *Methodenkanon* of biblical studies—that is, the compound of textual criticism, source criticism, form criticism, and redaction criticism—which no longer constitutes the full agenda of historical biblical criticism. Nevertheless, taken as such, both "historical" and "critical" are genuinely descriptive of a broad range of approaches to the biblical text; therefore, it suggests itself to reflect their meaning and significance—indeed, their necessity—in the landscape of contemporary biblical studies.

I want to begin my reflections with a personal note. That biblical studies ought to be driven by a historical interest is far less self-evident today than it was at the University of Helsinki in the early 1980s, when I took my basic courses in biblical studies (or "exegetics," as the discipline was called) under the guidance of such well-known masters of historical criticism as Heikki Räisänen, the "fair-player" who programmatically transgresses the boundaries of biblical canon and theology,[13] and Timo Veijola, whose approach was as pointedly historical as it was theological—and, toward the sudden end of his life, increasingly canonical.[14] "New" methodologies, even though no longer new, played a minor role in my scholarly uppringing, although I came to witness my teachers' opening up toward the challenges coming from outside of the conventional *Methodenkanon.*[15] Instead of new methodologies, my scope was broadened toward ancient

---

12 See J. Barton, *The Nature of Biblical Criticism* (Louisville, Ky.: Westminster John Knox, 2007) 31–68.

13 See H. Räisänen, *Beyond New Testament Theology: A Story and a Programme* (London: SCM, 2000); for Räisänen's program, see also the articles collected in *Moving beyond New Testament Theology? Essays in Conversation with Heikki Räisänen* (ed. T. Penner and C. Vander Stichele; PFES 88; Helsinki: Finnish Exegetical Society, 2005).

14 See, e.g., T. Veijola, *Leben nach der Weisung: Exegetisch-historische Studien zum Alten Testament* (FRLANT 224; Göttingen: Vandenhoeck & Ruprecht, 2008); id., "Text, Wissenschaft und Glaube: Überlegungen eines Alttestamentlers zur Lösung des Grundproblems der biblischen Hermeneutik," *JBTh* 15 (2000) 313–39.

15 E.g., H. Räisänen, "Biblical Critics in the Global Village," in *Reading the Bible in the Global Village: Helsinki* (ed. id.; SBLGPBS 6; Atlanta, Ga.: Society of Biblical Literature, 2000) 9–28; id., "Matthew in Bibliodrama," in *Neutestamentliche Exegese im Dialog: Hermeneutik—Wirkungsgeschichte—Matthäusevangelium*, FS U. Luz (ed. P. Lampe, M. Mayordomo, and M. Sato; Neukir-

Near Eastern texts—and not primarily as the "context of Scripture," for that matter—when I continued my studies with Oswald Loretz the Ugaritologist[16] and Simo Parpola the Assyriologist, both known as rigid and enthusiastic philologists whose interest has never been restricted to their narrowly defined fields of scholarship. Later on, I became interested in gender studies (needless to say, mainly from a historical perspective) and learned valuable lessons of archaeological practice in the excavations of the Iron Age city of Kinneret.[17]

I relate all this, not to demonstrate any sense of a sovereign stewardship of the field, but to show where I come from and how proud I am to be the student of my teachers—and, at the same time, to give the reader an idea about where the limits of my own objectivity may be found, what kind of subjectivity I am accountable for, and where my blindspots might be found.[18]

Why Historical? The Necessity of Historical Criticism

Why *historical*? To me, the question of the necessity of historical criticism implies not so much a need for an apology, let alone a reactionary defense of historical biblical studies against inimical incursions of postmodernism, as a reflection of my own work. Therefore, I would not like to frame the question as a binary opposition between historical criticism and its postmodern/poststructuralist/post-Enlightenment critics. The historical/nonhistorical divide does not appear to me as particularly useful in describing the current methodological agenda of

---

chen-Vluyn: Neukirchener, 2008) 183–95; T. Veijola, "Depression als menschliche und biblische Erfahrung," in *Offenbarung und Anfechtung: Hermeneutisch-theologische Studien zum Alten Testament* (ed. W. Dietrich and M. Marttila; BibS[N] 89; Neukirchen-Vluyn: Neukirchener, 2007) 158–90.

16 I am happy to be listed among his students by Mark S. Smith, *Untold Stories: The Bible and Ugaritic Studies in the Twentieth Century* (Peabody, Mass.: Hendrickson, 2001), 44, even though there is very little I have done in the field of Ugaritic studies.

17 For the excavations at Kinneret, see J. Pakkala, S. Munger, and J. Zangenberg, *Kinneret Regional Project: Tel Kinrot Excavations* (Proceedings of the Finnish Institute in the Middle East, Report 2/2004; Vantaa: The Finnish Institute in the Middle East, 2004); available at www.kinneret-excavations.org.

18 This paper is written while enjoying the William D. Loughlin Membership at the Institute for Advanced Study in Princeton, New Jersey. I would like to express my heartfelt thanks to my colleagues in Princeton who have read the manuscript with a critical eye: Pamela Barmash, David Moon, and Peter Holquist, co-members at the Institute, and especially F. W. "Chip" Dobbs-Allsopp at the Princeton Theological Seminary. The remaining blindspots are all mine, not theirs.

biblical criticism. Whether one understands historical criticism mainly as a literary paradigm or sees its aim in historical reconstruction, what matters is *the relatedness and otherness between the critic and the source*, ancient or modern, the interplay between times and spaces in the hermeneutical process, in which "scholars should seek to understand the differing cultural and moral views of past and present societies—and to recognize the limited and often provincial quality of their own."[19] I have learned a lot from scholars who are persuaded by approaches other than historical but who are still familiar with the traditional historical-critical practice,[20] and I hope to be able to make this visible in what follows.

Having reached the point where historical criticism has been taken down from its pedestal of objectivity and the relativity of the historical knowledge is acknowledged, it is time to formulate the question positively: Why is historical criticism necessary, anyway? The following points are neither exhaustive nor presented in any particular order but represent my idea of why historical criticism should be praticed in the present-day social reality as I perceive it as a male, white, Finnish, Lutheran, heterosexual, and middle-aged member of the guild of biblical and ancient Near Eastern scholars.[21]

(1) Because it helps us to understand our own time and culture. Historical criticism can be seen as the (grand)mother or the midwife of most critical approaches to the Bible that have come to the fore in the twentieth century, at the very least in the sense that nonhistorical biblical studies have often emerged as a rebellion against the hegemony of the dominant paradigm. One could say that, for the purposes of the present-day society, it is more important to teach how this text is read and used today,[22] but even the present day is history tomorrow, and remembering the past is an important constituent element in perceiving the present.[23]

---

19 Clark, *History, Theory, Text*, 157.

20 In particular, I would like to mention Clines, "Historical Criticism."

21 Greatly startled by Elisabeth Schüssler Fiorenza's fierce criticism against Räisänen's attempt to read the Bible in the global village ("Defending the Center, Trivializing the Margins," in Räisänen, *Reading the Bible in the Global Village*, 29–48), I would like to emphasize that, having this background, it is not a conscious part of my scholarly agenda to partisan the case of the center over against the margins, to prefer Finnish for foreign, or to bolster heteronormativity or male dominance. If I am caught in the very act of doing so, I can only plead guilty, with explanation: I consciously strive for distancing myself from such positions.

22 See David J. A. Clines, *The Bible in the Modern World* (Sheffield: Sheffield Academic Press, 1997).

23 For the concept of cultural memory, see especially J. Assmann, *Religion and Cultural Memory: Ten Studies* (trans. R. Livingstone; Stanford, Calif.: Stanford University Press, 2006); trans. of *Re-*

While not being more foundational than other approaches, historical criticism is necessary to develop an understanding that the phenomena of the present world are the result of historical developments. As Dobbs-Allsopp poignantly remarks, "By studying the past we learn that the direction which history takes is contingent rather than absolute.... This knowledge of the contingency in the past can then make us aware of the changeability of the present."[24] Therefore, the interest of historical criticism is not only and narrowly antiquarian but ultimately hermeneutical.[25]

(2) Because historical questions require historical criticism. To have a job properly done, appropriate tools have to be used;[26] cutting the lawn with an axe simply does not work. Historical questions require historical criticism, but not all relevant questions are historical. There are significant areas of biblical scholarship where historical issues are of little or no relevance. Theological and lingustic studies, even though usually done under the label of the historical-critical method, need not be primarily concerned with historical issues, let alone methods related to literary criticism, such as rhetorical or reader-response criticism, or those related to ideological criticism, such as cultural or postcolonial criticism, or many other approaches, such as psychological reading of the Bible. The relevance of different approaches should always be interrogated, but the worst one can do is to resort to historical criticism in order to avoid important but discomforting issues raised by, say, feminist or postcolonial approaches, by declaring them irrelevant because they are not historical (and, by implication, not critical either)—which is not true. There is a historical dimension even to studies that deal with contemporary issues.

---

ligion und kulturelles Gedächtnis: Zehn Studien (Munich: Beck, [3]2007); for an application of this concept in biblical studies, see Davies, *Memories of Ancient Israel*, 105–23.

24 Dobbs-Allsopp, "Rethinking Historical Criticism" 270.

25 R. P. Carroll, "Poststructuralist Approaches: New Historicism and Postmodernism," in *The Cambridge Companion to Biblical Interpretation* (ed. J. Barton; Cambridge: Cambridge University Press, 1998), 50–66, esp. 57: "Yet both the categories of history and literature when used in relation to the Bible are equally in need of interpretation, so the old-fashioned category of hermeneutics remains as ever the fundamentally necessary approach to any reading of the Bible (whatever the intellectual basis of that approach)." See also H.-J. Goertz, *Umgang mit Geschichte: Eine Einführung in die Geschichtstheorie* (Rowohlts Enzyklopädie; Reinbek bei Hamburg: Rowohlt, 1995), 105–17.

26 See the editors' introductory essay, "Mastering the Tools or Retooling the Masters: The Legacy of Historical-Critical Discourse," in *Her Master's Tools? Feminist and Postcolonial Engagements of Historical-Critical Discourse* (ed. C. Vander Stichele and T. Penner; SBLGPBS 9; Atlanta, Ga.: Society of Biblical Literature, 2005), 1–29.

Biblical studies are done in time and space and are, therefore, always related to communities and readerships in history, ancient or modern. Indeed, many of the practitioners of, say, feminist and postcolonial studies necessarily work on historical themes that are not necessarily inspired by postmodernism. Colonialism, if anything, is a historical phenomenon;[27] reception criticism can be characterized as "a reader-response criticism cast on a historical plane";[28] the study of the modern construction of gender is greatly indebted to the Foucauldian concept of the "history of sexuality";[29] feminist criticism is often deconstruction and/or interpretation of ideologies of the past.[30]

(3) Because the Bible is a representative of ancient Near Eastern literature. As important as it is to understand the role of the Bible as a book that is printed, sold, read, and imposed upon in the present-day world in countless languages and different contexts, it is also necessary to appreciate its otherness as an ancient text produced in a world alien to us. Biblical studies need to be pursued in interaction and mutual appreciation with archaeology, Assyriology, Egyptology, Semitic philology, studies in classical antiquity, history of religion, and other fields of scholarship in which the relatedness and otherness between the critic and source has a historical dimension. This is important, both to be able to recognize the cultural situatedness of the producers of the biblical texts and to prevent the "biblical world," whether historical or literary, to become a virtual world on its own terms. Moreover, colleagues in these fields deserve to have discussion partners among biblical scholars who understand their language. As a matter of fact, many biblical scholars have expertise not only in biblical texts but also in one or more of the above-mentioned areas.

(4) Because historical criticism serves the public. This easily entices the biblical scholar to enjoy the rare opportunity of basking in the spotlight of publicity, but it is nevertheless vitally important that biblical scholars realize their responsibility for informing the public about their scholarship, often sponsored by taxpayers who have the right to know how public funds are spent. A typical situation for a biblical critic to be approached by mass media is when public attention is captured by sensational news concerning a newly discovered or publicized text or artifact. Historical critics render a good service by providing the general public with informed and critical, even media-savvy, assessments of the object in

---

27 For an attempt at "historical-critical postcolonialism," see J. W. Marshall, "Postcolonialism and the Practice of History," in Vander Stichele and Penner, *Her Master's Tools*, 93–108.

28 Clines, "Historical Criticism," n. 10.

29 M. Foucault, *The History of Sexuality*, 3 vols. (trans. R. Hurley; New York: Vintage, 1988–90).

30 See E. Fuchs, "The History of Women in Ancient Israel: Theory, Method, and the Book of Ruth," in Vander Stichele and Penner, *Her Master's Tools*, 211–31.

question.[31] The media are often on the move for goal-oriented answers of the type "... and the Bible is thus (not) true." Thus, is the task of the historical critic to refute uncritical historizing, to relativize biblicist or antibiblicist claims to the truth or untruth of the biblical text, to point out the potential exploitation of scholarship as continuation of politics,[32] and to assess critically the significance (or lack thereof) of the matter at issue for contemporary concerns, not retiring behind the screen of purportedly disinterested detachment. Doing so, the scholar fulfills his or her duty as a responsible citizen, which brings us to the next point.

(5) Because it is politically relevant. As the self-image of "objectivity" of biblical scholarship has turned out to be false, "to acknowledge that the critic is inextricably bound to and influenced by his or her own cultural-historical context is by default to acknowledge that the critic's interpretations and reconstructions of texts from the past must have relevance in the present as well."[33] This acknowledgement inevitably means that the different historical reconstructions and their alleged relevance cannot be presented as a historically ascertained truth. Their relevance is always at issue and has to be evaluated against the background of contemporary concerns. This becomes very clear when one compares the contrasting strategies of assessing the present-day relevance of the historical knowledge of same-sex eroticism in two recent books written by two biblical historians coming from similar academic background but different traditions of biblical interpretation[34] and their critical reception from the point of view of, for example, gender theories[35] and historical scholarship.[36]

31 E.g., the Nag Hammadi specialists who have ably and elegantly responded to the public interest in assessing the significance of the Gospel of Judas for audiences domestic (A. Marjanen and I. Dunderberg, *Juudaksen evankeliumi* [Helsinki: WSOY, 2006]) and international (E. Pagels and K. L. King, *Reading Judas: The Gospel of Judas and the Shaping of Christianity* [New York: Viking, 2007]).

32 See especially R. P. Carroll, "Clio and Canons: In Search of a Cultural Poetics of the Hebrew Bible," *BibInt* 5 (1997) 300–323, esp. 308–15.

33 Dobbs-Allsopp, "Rethinking Historical Criticism," 255.

34 I.e., the "pro-gay" M. Nissinen, *Homoeroticism in the Biblical World: A Historical Perspective* (trans. K. Stjerna; Minneapolis, Minn.: Fortress, 1998); and the "antigay" R. A. J. Gagnon, *The Bible and Homosexual Practice: Texts and Hermeneutics* (Nashville, Tenn.: Abingdon, 2001).

35 E.g., K. Stone, "Homosexuality and the Bible or Queer Reading? A Response to Martti Nissinen," *Theology and Sexuality* 7 (2001) 107–18; A. Heacock, "Wrongly Framed? The 'David and Jonathan Narrative' and the Writing of Biblical Homosexuality [sic]" *The Bible and Critical Theory* 3/2 (2007) 1–22.

36 Cf. the contrary opinions of J.-F. Nardelli, *Homosexuality and Liminality in the Gilgameš and Samuel* (Amsterdam: Hakkert, 2007); and M. Zehnder, "Observations on the Relationship between David and Jonathan and the Debate on Homosexuality," *WTJ* 69 (2007) 127–74.

(6) Because it is relevant for theology and for religious communities. Historical critics have often been seen as hostile toward faith-based readings of the Bible, which, therefore, should be reclaimed for the church.[37] In contrast to this, however, some would regard most of the contemporary biblical scholarship as theological practice under the camouflage of historical criticism.[38]

The relationship between historical criticism and theology is a complex one and is understood in a variety of ways. Many would opt for "history of Israelite religion" instead of "theology of the Old/New Testament,"[39] while others would consider both categories to be legitimate but methodologically incompatible,[40] and yet others take the antithesis to be mistaken altogether.[41] Evidently, the discussion is impaired by different sensitivities of the scholars toward the concept of "theology" and the equally different meanings they give to it. When reading biblical texts as historical literary products, it can be reasonably argued that texts communicating religious experiences always have a theological horizon that deserves to be understood as a part of the historian's encounter with the text.[42] On the other hand, it is equally justified to argue that, when biblical texts are used as a source of information on ancient history, this should not be influenced by any kind of theological recontextualization, ancient or modern.[43]

Now if "theology" in itself implies a confessional bias, the biblical critic should indeed be on the alert about what he or she is doing. In those academic

---

37 See C. E. Braaten and R. W. Jenson (eds.), *Reclaiming the Bible for the Church* (Edinburgh: T&T Clark, 1996).

38 See Barton, *The Nature of Biblical Criticism*, 167–71, referring to D. J. A. Clines, *Interested Parties: The Ideology of the Writers and Readers of the Hebrew Bible* (Sheffield: Sheffield Academic Press, 1995); P. R. Davies, *Whose Bible Is It Anyway?* (Sheffield: Sheffield Academic Press, 1995; London: T&T Clark, ^{2}2004); F. Segovia, *Decolonizing Biblical Studies: A View from the Margins* (Maryknoll, N.Y.: Orbis, 2000); and J. Berlinerblau, "The Unspeakable in Biblical Scholarship," *SBL Forum* (2006); online: http://www.sbl-site.org/publications/article.aspx?articleId=503.

39 So, in different ways, e.g., R. Albertz, "Religionsgeschichte Israels statt Theologie des Alten Testaments!" *JBTh* 10 (1995) 3–24; N. Peter Lemche, "Warum die Theologie des Alten Testaments einen Irrweg darstellt," *JBTh* 10 (1995) 79–92; id., *The Old Testament between Theology and History* (Louisville, Ky.: Westminster John Knox, 2008); Räisänen, *Beyond New Testament Theology.*

40 E.g., I. Kalimi, "Religionsgeschichte Israels oder Theologie des Alten Testaments: Das jüdische Interesse an der biblischen Theologie," *JBTh* 10 (1995) 45–68.

41 E.g., F. Crüsemann, "Religionsgeschichte oder Theologie? Elementare Überlegungen zu einer falschen Alternative," *JBTh* 10 (1995) 69–77.

42 This point has most recently been made by S. Byrskog, "När gamla texter talar: Om att tolka det förgångna," *STK* 84 (2008) 49–57, esp. 55; see also Veijola, "Text, Wissenschaft und Glaube."

43 So most recently E. Pfoh, "Más allá del círculo hermenéutico: El pasado de Israel entre la teología del Antiguo Testamento y la historia de Palestina," *Revista Bíblica* 69 (2007) 65–82.

settings, however, where biblical studies are housed in faculties of theology together with church history, systematic theology, practical theology, and even religious studies, biblical scholars *are* theologians by virtue of their education, and this title does not imply that their study is driven by a confessional commitment. What is (or at least should be) practiced as "theology" in these contexts is critical study of religious texts, traditions, and communities in conversation and cooperation with other disciplines in a mutually understandable language and methodology.[44] In this interdisciplinary enterprise, historical criticism of the Bible is a necessary discussion partner, and the benefit is mutual: much of the work of biblical critics is analyzing how the theological discourse works in their sources. On the other hand, historical critics can help to recognize what kind of transformations of meaning take place when theologians, ancient or modern, recontextualize texts that are already de- and recontextualized in the biblical canon.[45]

(7) Because it is fun. I am not joking. Few of us would do historical studies out of mere responsibility or sheer boredom. Many of us are simply fascinated by history, but this fascination ridicules all disciplined explanations, all objectivity, hence the epigraphic motto of this article, and hence the lack of a footnote at this point.

Why Critical? Toward a Critical Historicism

If the quest for an objective—that is, a single and complete—description of the full and authentic past is to be rejected as a foundationalist project that neither does justice to the multiple perspectives of the sources nor to the present-day diversity of relevant research questions, what kind of historical approach could still be called *critical*? I attempt an approach I would like to call "critical historicism" by reflecting upon the following four topics.

History Is Relatedness

Both the historian and the sources are historically situated, hence history is a relation between historically contingent representations of reality at both ends.

44 This, I believe, is close to the "critical theology" advocated by Barton, *The Nature of Biblical Criticism*, 185.
45 See Carroll, "Clio and Canons," 316.

Therefore, historical criticism requires a "wholehearted embrace of historical contingency, both with respect to the texts which are the object of study and to the people who are doing the studying."[46] The situatedness of the historian means that all study is done and all questions asked within a social, academic, and personal context, which is always reflected by the researcher's list of priorities and the hierarchy of relevant questions. The situatedness of the objects of study, again, means that, while being socially determined products of their own environment, they at the same time contribute to constructing their own time and culture instead of merely presenting photographic snapshots of it.

History, whether ancient or contemporary, is all about distance, otherness, and interpretation. There is an inevitable temporal and cultural distance between the historian and the past, between the context of the researcher and that of the source. Coping with this distance requires the establishment of a relation that is possible only when the otherness of the source in relation to the historian is recognized. Historical scholarship has been well aware of the *historicity of texts*, that is, their cultural specificity and social embeddedness. What may not have been fully acknowledged is the *textuality of history*, that is, that the past is accessible to us only through the mediation of textual remains, themselves subject to subsequent textual mediations.[47]

The otherness also means that the historian remains an outsider; where there is no direct access to the object of study, the only way to make sense of it is interpretation. In spite of the distance between the historian and the source, the objects of study "can never be wholly other from the interpreting self over against which they stand."[48] To come to terms with a textualized history in spite of the inevitable distance with the source and otherness it reflects, the text must be taken up into the researcher's consciousness, which, again, is historically situated, socially determined, personal, and subjective. But the very textuality of the source means that it has an existence independent of the reader. The distance between the text and the reader remains there; the otherness cannot be chased away.[49]

---

46 Dobbs-Allsopp, "Rethinking Historical Criticism," 241.

47 The reciprocal concern between the historicity of the texts and the textuality of history is introduced by Montrose, "Professing the Renaissance," 20; so also White, "New Historicism: A Comment," 297: "every approach to the study of the past presupposes or entails some version of a textualist theory of historical reality of some kind."

48 Lee Patterson, *Negotiating the Past: The Historical Understanding of Medieval Literature* (Madison, Wisc.: University of Wisconsin Press, 1987), 42.

49 See Dobbs-Allsopp, "Rethinking Historical Criticism," 265.

History Is a Construction

The slogan "wie es eigentlich gewesen" (how things really were) seems to be all that is remembered of Leopold von Ranke, one of the founding fathers of modern historiography, to whom all historical studies owe much of their source-based critical approach.[50] Von Ranke's ghost is usually conjured up as a caricature of the idea of historical objectivity,[51] "that noble dream" that was challenged long before postmodernism.[52] Very few (biblical) historians would stand up to defend a naïve objectivity today, yet there is a certain "reluctance among practicing historians to give up the idea that there is some connection between what they write and past reality."[53] This attitude could be called "reasonable objectivity,"[54] which acknowledges the otherness of the text and its world in relation to the world and experience of the reader. It is the referential illusion, that is, the idea of a direct referentiality between the source and historical factuality, that should be at issue rather than the straw man of objectivity,[55] for if the modern historians are subjective, so were the authors of written sources.

History is not a sequence of past events that the historian discovers but the intellectual construction that the historian creates on the basis of the available

---

50 See G. G. Iggers and J. M. Powell (eds.), *Leopold von Ranke and the Shaping of the Historical Discipline* (Syracuse, N.Y.: Syracuse University Press, 1990).

51 In fact, von Ranke's paradigm was not based on a strictly positivistic attitude but an aesthetic and religious experience of the past. "Ranke *did* insist on critical method, but unless his reasons for doing so and the creative-imaginative way in which he pursued critical research is taken into account, the 'paradigm' remains a mere shadow of Ranke's thought" (J. D. Braw, "Vision as Revision: Ranke and the Beginning of Modern History," *History and Theory* 46/4 [2007] 45–60, esp. 59, emphasis original).

52 See Novick, *That Noble Dream*; G. G. Iggers, "The Crisis of the Rankean Paradigm in the Nineteenth Century" in Iggers and Powell, *Leopold von Ranke*, 170–79; Clark, *History, Theory, Text*, 9–17.

53 L. L. Grabbe, *Ancient Israel: What Do We Know and How Do We Know It?* (New York: T&T Clark, 2007), 29.

54 Barton, *The Nature of Biblical Criticism*, 49; cf. E.-A. Knauf, "From History to Interpretation," in *The Fabric of History: Texts, Artifact and Israel's Past* (ed. D. V. Edelman; JSOTSup 127; Sheffield: Sheffield Academic Press, 1991), 26–64, esp. 30–31: "The difference between an objective, scientific history and a nonscientific history is not that the scientific historian is without presuppositions. The difference is that in scientific history the theory is as disputable as the facts are; the presuppositions are conceived to be debatable to the same extent that any statement derived from them is." See also Krüger, "Theoretische und methodische Probleme," 18–22.

55 See Goertz, *Unsichere Geschichte*, 15.

evidence; every history is the creative product of the human mind.[56] It is only the historian's creative (and ultimately subjective) process of collecting, selecting, arranging, contextualizing, and interpreting the available sources that gives a meaning to the pluriform historical data. This process makes the historical narrative possible—a narrative that is not a neutral description of past events but something that "serves to impose coherence, continuity, and closure on the messiness of life and of the historian's sources."[57] This means that historical studies of any kind, including biblical studies, are not likely to produce assured results; moreover, there is no more room for the "genetic fallacy," that is, the quest for "original" meanings as potentially superior to secondary interpretations.[58] Nevertheless, inquiring into the history of the emergence of texts and other cultural products (or, for instance, one's own mind) is often illuminating, even though the claim to provide a full and definitive explanation is, without any doubt, a fallacy.

The most immediate relation is not between the historian and the past but between the historian and the sources. The sources, again, disallow access to a full and authentic past. This is because the sources, too, are constructions of their authors and tell in the first place how they perceived and represented the things they describe. While referring to past events, the sources do not imply a direct link to the past. Especially in narrative sources, the past is a constituent in the construct of "cultural memory"[59] that does not simply represent the past but also provides identity. This, in fact, applies to modern historiography as well—especially if the sources form a significant part of the modern cultural memory, as is the case in biblical studies.[60] Memory is not an archive of information of the past but a part of the cognitive system that adapts present ex-

---

56 See Knauf, "From History to Interpretation," 26–27; and Goertz, *Umgang mit Geschichte*, 103–4, who underscores the importance of a "disciplined fantasy" in history writing.

57 Clark, *History, Theory, Text*, 86, referring to the theorists who emphasized the imaginary and ideological nature of the historical narrative; see, e.g., H. V. White, *Metahistory: The Historical Imagination in Nineteenth-Century Europe* (Baltimore, Md.: Johns Hopkins University Press, 1973); id., *Tropics of Discourse: Essays in Cultural Criticism* (Baltimore, Md.: Johns Hopkins University Press, 1978); id., *The Content of the Form: Narrative Discourse and Historical Representation* (Baltimore, Md.: Johns Hopkins University Press, 1987).

58 The "genetic fallacy" and the absence of assured results are among the weaknesses David Clines has found in historical criticism; see "Historical Criticism."

59 See above, n. 25.

60 See P. R. Davies, "The History of Ancient Israel and Judah," *ExpTim* 119 (2007) 15–21, esp. 19–20.

periences to previous ones and, hence, a prominent constituent of our construction of reality.[61]

The primary question, thus, cannot be what really happened but what kind of secondary reconstructions of the past are enabled by the primary reconstructions of the past, that is, the available set of sources. This inevitably restricts the scope of relevant research questions, the relevance of which, again, is dependent on the agenda of the researcher and the academic community where he or she is situated. The question to be asked is what degree of plausibility can be given to these reconstructions (or, rather, reconfigurations) with regard to the questions they attempt to answer.

By establishing a relation between a modern concept and ancient documents—prophecy and homosexuality come to my mind because of my own occupation with these concepts—we already start building our construction of history. This construction work begins when the historian decides which questions can be considered relevant and makes a choice between available objects of study. It is far from self-evident what is meant with the concept of "prophecy," hence the historian must decide what he or she means with it, since there is no single word inherent in the ancient Near Eastern texts that would be adequate for scholarly purposes. To quote myself, "[t]he definition is necessary first and foremost as an aid of communication between people who work on different fields with cognate materials. It should not be understood as a static image of truth; rather, it should be seen from the point of view of the sociology of knowledge as a methodical process that emerges from concrete needs of the scholarly community and develops along with its application."[62] The definition of "prophecy" is not an independent entity but a methodological tool necessary for constructing the image of the ancient phenomenon thus defined. "Homosexuality," again, is a term that has been used since the very late nineteenth century only, and it is not very useful when we try to construct the image of same-sex interaction in the ancient world. But it is certainly a concept inherent in the world and language of the modern historical critic, who must decide whether the study of ancient same-sex eroticism should be driven by modern concerns, and, if not, whether it is possible at all to create a "neutral" image of ancient homoeroticism without positioning oneself somehow in the contemporary discus-

61 See Goertz, *Unsichere Geschichte, 96.*

62 Martti Nissinen, "What Is Prophecy: An Ancient Near Eastern Perspective," in *Inspired Speech: Prophecy in the Ancient Near East, Essays in Honor of Herbert B. Huffmon* (ed. John Kaltner and Louis Stulman; JSOTSup 378; London: T & T Clark, 2004), 17–37, esp. 20 (= p. 56 in this volume).

sion. This, I think, is a good example of the otherness of the object of study, which, nevertheless, cannot be totally other from the interpreting self.

History Is Interpretation

The situatedness of the historical critic, at least if internalized to any degree, naturally leads to situations where the academic "objective" detachment is impossible, if not irresponsible, with regard to issues that concern people's lives in the contemporary social reality. This makes the so-called "advocacy readings" such as feminist, postcolonial, or queer readings necessary and natural. There is no reason why a historical critic could not practice such readings, as if they were inherently alien to historical criticism; as we have seen, there is a historical aspect to these readings, too. It is true that one should avoid "the deliberate overriding of proper historical judgement by promoting a particular point of view because it suits certain needs beyond academic interpretation and reconstruction of history,"[63] and a good deal of criticism is in place when the academic interpretation is designed to serve nonacademic needs. But whose needs are the academic needs anyway? The voices from the margins that remind the (historical) critics of the consequences of their own situatedness may help the historian to look in the mirror.[64] They also revive the question: For whom is the scholarship written, if not exclusively for fellow academics?[65]

One prominent aspect of many biblical historians' situatedness is their present or former context in religious communities; it is true, after all, that the majority of biblical scholars are somehow religiously affiliated. Many Christian and Jewish scholars take part in the life of religious communities as laypersons or as ordained ministers. It does not follow from this by any logical necessity that their scholarship is religiously motivated or that it is of inferior quality. Scholars have different commitments, and claims that a *religious* commitment in particular prevents the historian from being critical sounds like invoking the phantom of "objectivity" again. Since "[n]o-one is really 'disinterested'; everyone has an axe to

63 L. L. Grabbe, *Ezra-Nehemiah* (Old Testament Readings; London: Routledge, 1998), 6.
64 See R. S. Sugirtharajah, "Critics, Tools, and the Global Arena," in Räisänen, *Reading the Bible in the Global Village*, 49–60.
65 On the moral and political responsibility of the historian, see Knauf, "From History to Interpretation," 32–33; for the need of dialogue with participating communitites and the wider implications of scholarship from the point of view of archaeology, see Ian Hodder, *Archaeology beyond Dialogue* (Foundations of Archaeological Inquiry; Salt Lake City: University of Utah Press, 2003).

grind,"[66] a nonbeliever (so-called) is not necessarily better equipped as a biblical critic than a believer (so-called).[67] It is exactly at this point the distance and the otherness between the source and the historian must be acknowledged; otherwise, we end up cutting the lawn of history with our own axes, which would only result in bad scholarship.

If history is all about interpretation, what is it that we are supposed to understand? When reading texts written in human language, we interpret culturally constructed signs that are inevitably historical regardless of their age, immersed in time and place, contextualized in particular societies, and determined by their cultural memory and ideology. To understand these signs, the historian has to acknowledge the distance, otherness, and relation between her or him and the source and, in Lee Patterson's words, to refuse to "reduce difference and opposition to sameness by collapsing together subject and object."[68] This collapse easily happens if the otherness of the sources is forgotten and they are fused together with the historian's mindset to fuel his or her favorite ideas, be they motivated by religious commitment, a particular theory, or anything else. This, I believe, can be avoided by recognizing the correlations and discrepancies between the *textual worlds, symbolic worlds*, and *real worlds* of the texts and their interpreters.[69] The text, ostensibly the same regardless of the time when it is read, has multiple contexts, ancient as well as modern.[70] Any reconstruction of the past begins with making a difference between the symbolic world (or cultural specificity, or ideology) and the real world (or social embeddedness, or social reality) of each source and the researcher. This requires sensitivity toward the purpose, function, context, and ideology of the variety of texts and artifacts.

---

66 Barton, *The Nature of Biblical Criticism*, 13.

67 For the issue of faith-commitment and biblical criticism, see J. Barr, "Evaluation, Commitment, and Objectivity in Biblical Theology," in Räisänen, *Reading the Bible in the Global Village*, 127–52; Barton, *The Nature of Biblical Criticism*, 173–75. For a nonbeliever perspective, see J. Berlinerblau, *The Secular Bible: Why Nonbelievers Must Take Religion Seriously* (New York: Cambridge University Press, 2005).

68 Patterson, *Negotiating the Past*, 72. Dobbs-Allsopp ("Rethinking Historical Criticism," 252) writes: "Critical historicism wants to ally a poststructuralist reading strategy with the historicist respect for the other and belief that the cultural and social milieu in which past literary works originated is likely to be relevant for understanding those works."

69 This three-world model is developed by Kari Syreeni; see "Wonderlands: A Beginner's Guide to Three Worlds," *SEA* 64 (1999): 33–46.

70 Carroll, "Clio and Canons," 312: "The Bible is not just a book read and revered by thousands [sic!] of generations of Jews and Christians. It is deeply formative of belief and behaviour in its readers .... It is also a book read into and out of whatever cultural context the readers may find themselves situated in at any time of reading."

Historical Factuality Exists

The very idea of a sociohistorical contextualization inevitably presupposes that the textual world is not entirely self-contained but reflects past social realities. There is such a thing as a historical factuality and real people involved in it (and dinosaurs, for that matter); this cannot be eliminated by any theory.[71] This does not deprive history of its constructedness. On the contrary, the extremely fragmentary set of available sources from antiquity (not only texts but also archaeological remains) and the difficulty of determining the actual historical context of most of the biblical writings should convince every historical critic of the Bible of the impossibility of reaching the full and authentic past.[72] A sherd of ancient pottery is not a construction of the modern mind (unless it is a forgery, of course), but every theory built upon it is.

It is more evident today than ever before that no serious historical criticism of the Bible can be done without the data provided by archaeology and ancient Near Eastern texts[73]—which, however, cannot be used as "hard data" over against the biased presentation of the Bible but as culture-specific products that require exactly the same degree of criticism as the biblical texts. Even archaeological evidence requires the same critical process of interpretation as textual sources, hence archaeology is a scholarly construct to the very same extent as text-based history, involving the issues of understanding, construction, and ideology.[74] As Elizabeth Bloch-Smith notes, "Biblical Israel is an ancient literary construct given form more than 2000 years ago, while historical/archaeological Israel is a modern construct, a composite picture grounded in material remains, informed through biblical testimony, and fleshed out through insights produced by the social sciences."[75]

The present-day exploitation of archaeology of the southern Levant, Palestine, or Israel will convince anyone that there are interested parties with distinct

---

71 See Iggers, *Historiography in the Twentieth Century*, 119.

72 See Carroll, "Prophecy and Society," in *The World of Ancient Israel: Sociological, Anthropological and Political Perspectives* (ed. R. E. Clements; Cambridge: Cambridge University Press, 1989), 203–25.

73 So already Greßmann, "Die Aufgaben der alttestamentlichen Forschung," 11, 15.

74 See C. Renfrew and P. Bahn, *Archaeology: Theories, Methods and Praxis* (London: Thames & Hudson, [4]2004), 405–34; M. Shanks and I. Hodder, "Processual, Postprocessual and Interpretive Archaeologies," in *Interpreting Archaeology: Finding Meaning in the Past* (ed. Ian Hodder et al.; London: Routledge) 3–29.

75 E. Bloch-Smith, "Bible, Archaeology, and the Social Sciences: The Next Generation," in *The Hebrew Bible: New Insights and Scholarship* (ed. F. E. Greenspahn; New York: New York University Press, 2008) 24–42, esp. 37.

ideologies involved in interpreting the archaeological data. This is also true in fields such as Assyriology, Egyptology, or Ugaritic studies, where the situatedness of the scholars can be seen either in an outspoken intention of using the Near Eastern evidence to buttress the "reliability" of the Bible[76] or in more subtle ways of endorsing the historical accuracy of the Bible via interpretation of Near Eastern sources.

The limits of historical reconstruction correspond to the availability of evidence, on the one hand, and to the nature of sources, on the other hand. The perspective to the past opens itself differently depending on what kind of source is used as the gateway to the past. Sometimes the texts or artifacts are close enough to the events they describe to be interpreted as reflecting certain aspects of historical factuality (primary sources), while in other cases, there is a significant gap between the event and the sources that come to us through several recontextualizations (secondary sources).[77] An economical document such as a contract or a decree of expenditures; the pottery collected from an archaeological site; a letter written to the king by an official; a royal inscription; or a biblical prophetic book—all these are culture-specific products that are related to their past contexts each in their own way. Economical texts, without being overtly ideological, speak volumes about the structure and hierarchy of the society, distribution of wealth, and the agency of women; pottery is indicative of the construction of the social world of its users. Royal inscriptions, again, while retelling events of political history from the ruling king's point of view, are primarily to be read as representations of the royal ideology.

The biblical texts have gone through several de- and recontextualizations during their long history of emergence and interpretation and, therefore, virtually always fall into the category of secondary sources. A biblical text cannot simply be accepted as a historically accurate source unless it is proved wrong; rather, every reconstruction based on it must be argued for.[78] It is the historian's task to find out which purposes the texts once served and which kind of questions they are supposed to answer now, being on the alert for his or her own preferences in transferring meanings from sources to the construction of history.[79] This implies both the hermeneutical question of what the text meant and

---

76 E.g., K. A. Kitchen, *On the Reliability of the Old Testament* (Grand Rapids, Mich.: Eerdmans, 2003).

77 See Grabbe, *Ancient Israel*, 35.

78 Ibid., 35–36.

79 For the risk of illegitimate transfers of meaning, see Carroll, "Prophecy and Society," 206–9.

what it means[80] (supposing that texts continue to have meanings to their readers) and the search for the "interested parties" and their ideologies,[81] ancient and modern (supposing that there are no value-free meanings of a text).

Historical factuality exists; something has really happened in the past, and there are texts and artifacts that allow us to see glimpses of the past, "whose very disappearance authorizes the historian's work."[82] "What actually happened" becomes a legitimate question again when the naïve referentialism is abandoned, the constructed nature of knowledge is acknowledged, and the answer to that question in each case is given in awareness that, as far as historical factuality can be reached, every attempt to communicate it is interpretation.

Case Study: Prophecy

I have never considered myself a man of theory, so it has been an exciting effort to formulate the above thoughts on historical criticism in a way that would satisfy those more experienced in theoretical reflection. To convince at least myself —and, I hope, also David Petersen, a true historical critic to whom this *Versuch* is dedicated with much pleasure—that there is a correlation between my epistemological cogitations and source-based work, I close this essay with a case study of my own field of study, ancient Near Eastern prophecy.[83]

The sources on which our knowledge of the phenomenon of prophecy is based are well known: two textual corpora from eighteenth-century B.C.E. Mari and seventh-century B.C.E. Assyria, supplemented by miscellaneous cuneiform and West Semitic texts from different times and places, representing a variety of textual genres.[84] The Hebrew Bible, however, is the text where the issue of prophecy is more prominent than anywhere else and which is also important as a historical source, albeit a very different one from the other ancient sources.

---

80 This dichotomy was coined by Krister Stendahl; see his comments in "Dethroning Biblical Imperialism in Theology," in Räisänen, *Reading the Bible in the Global Village*, 61–66.

81 See Clines, *Interested Parties*.

82 Clark, *History, Theory, Text*, 156.

83 This section is based on a lecture given at the University of Lausanne on 17 October 2008 on the occasion of the colloquium "Les rédactions des livres prophétiques de la Bible hébraïque" organized by Thomas Römer and Jean-Daniel Macchi. I take this opportunity to thank the organizers as well as the co-lecturers Dominique Charpin and George Brooke for a most rewarding discussion.

84 The sources are collected in M. Nissinen, with contributions by C.-L. Seow, R. K. Ritner, and H. Craig Melchert *Prophets and Prophecy in the Ancient Near East* (SBLWAW 41; Atlanta, Ga.: Society of Biblical Literature, 2nd ed. 2019).

The difference between the Near Eastern sources and the Hebrew Bible lies mainly in the textual transmission. In the former, the information about prophets and prophecy is embedded in written oracles, letters, administrative documents, and so on, written usually by officials of the king or a temple and filed away in archives where they have been found by archaeologists of our times. In these cases, the chronological and cultural distance between the source and the event is usually not very long. The Hebrew Bible, again, is a collection of canonized writings that derive from different times and have been selected, edited, collected, and transmitted by several generations of scribes mostly in the time of the Second Temple of Jerusalem, that is, in the Persian and Hellenistic periods from the sixth until the second century B.C.E.

In both cases, all the information that we can gain of prophets and prophecy is dependent on the type of textual transmission. There is no direct access to the prophets as historical personalities; even the first-hand documents of their appearances come to us only to the extent the scribal filters between us and them allows us to perceive. Especially in the case of the Bible, this means that to identify the symbolic world or social embeddedness of, say, a prophetic book, the historical critic has to dig through countless layers of interpretation and recontextualization.

In the Hebrew Bible, texts concerned with prophets or prophecy are included in two different kinds of literature: the narrative and the prophetic books. The prophetic appearances narrated in the books of Samuel and Kings, not to mention Chronicles, are precarious evidence with regard to actual prophetic activities in the kingdoms of Judah and Israel. This is not only because of the significant chronological gap between the stories and the time they describe, but also because these narratives primarily function within their present literary contexts and may be multilayered or fictitious altogether, serving the ends of their editors. Therefore, our principal question should concern the *constructs* of prophecy in these texts, since it is only through the dark glass of these multiple and often deconstructable constructs that we have access to the eventual historical factualities that may be dimly visible as building material of these constructs.

If anything, the narratives in the Former Prophets and in Chronicles show what their authors and editors, predominantly living in the Second Temple communities, took for granted with regard to prophets and their activities in the times that these literary compositions describe (which is not necessarily compatible with the image they have of the prophets in their own time). It is reasonable to assume that a part of the image of the ancient prophets in these writings is based on older documents and thus contain indirect information of the prophetic goings-on in the ninth-seventh centuries B.C.E.; however, it is equally clear that all this material is reread and adapted to a secondary context. In other words, the primary context of, say, the stories about Elijah and Elisha (1 Kgs 17–2 Kgs 9) is their present literary context within the composition scholars call the Deuteronomistic History. They are not first-hand evidence of prophecy in the kingdom of Israel in the ninth century, even though they are still often used as if they were.

The prophetic books of the Hebrew Bible represent yet another kind of literature, which presents itself for the most part as divine words transmitted by the prophets to whom each book is ascribed, that is, the so-called writing prophets. However, the prophetic books are not primarily the work of these prophets but scribal compilations with a long editorial history. The books are likely to contain passages originating from written records based on actual prophetic performances, and there has been a more serious concentration on the "original" writer here than in any other part of the Hebrew Bible. The authors of the prophetic books are personalized to a higher degree than any other books of the Hebrew Bible. The very issue of the *ipsissima verba* of the prophets concerns exclusively the prophetic books (who would break a lance for the *ipsissima verba* of David or Job?), hence the whole concept of authorship is discussed differently from other books of the Hebrew Bible.

In their present contexts, however, even the passages that might go back to prophetic words once pronounced by the mouth of Isaiah, Jeremiah, Amos, and Hosea are completely decontextualized. They are edited from the point of view of communities that have read and reused them according to their own needs and preferences, creating their own constructs of prophets and prophecy. Reading the books of the "classical" prophets as providing direct historical data from the eighth and seventh centuries often means forgetting that "[t]exts are not photographs of social reality but are imaginative creations of their writers."[85] This easily introduces a procedural error of transferring meanings from texts to a historical reality, which may lead to serious misconceptions, not only of the prophets as persons, but of prophecy as an ancient phenomenon.

Does the situation get any different when we move to the evidence of prophecy in nonbiblical texts? To a certain extent, yes. Most of the texts of archaeological provenance, such as letters and administrative texts, do not usually have a long editorial history behind them and are, therefore, of less interpretive nature than the biblical texts. But the bad news is that even here we are entirely dependent on scribal control: the interests of the writers of these texts and the officials who have selected the material to be included in the archives—not to

85 Carroll, "Prophecy and Society," 207.

mention the accidental nature of archaeological finds. Therefore, the ancient Near Eastern texts are no photographs of social reality either.

To what extent this picture concurs with historical factualities must be judged with regard to the nature of the sources, their purposes and eventual biases.[86] The purpose of, say, a food-ration list is primarily administrative, for example, to keep record of how much barley had been delivered to whom.[87] Misleading records are unlikely to have ended up in the archives, so if prophets are mentioned among recipients of food rations, it is as good as certain that they actually were there. In the letters, the interest of the letter-writer plays a more significant role: when a temple official gives an account of a prophecy he has either witnessed or otherwise become aware of, he may manipulate the contents of the prophecy to correspond to his own purposes of citing it.[88] The problem is that the fragmentary condition and uneven distribution of the sources disallows us from seeing the whole picture. Why did some prophecies end up in archives, while the vast majority of them did not? Why are most prophecies known to us concerned with royal affairs, while the perspective of a private citizen is almost totally lacking? While we can be rather confident that many details in the general picture of the social reality of prophecy in the ancient Near East are not far from the historical reality, it is also possible that the picture is unproportional and that many local variations are not visible at all. Details that we do know may not be the most important details that we *should* know.

All that said, it is also true that every text is written by someone somewhere; thus, not reading them as photographs of social reality does not mean that they do not tell anything at all about the past. Texts are not isolated from the world in which they are written and interpreted, even though we have to be careful not to make straightforward moves from text to history and engage in illegitimate transfers of meaning. The point is that the information discernible from each text, bib-

---

86 I fully subscribe to the principles of historical reconstruction as presented by Grabbe, *Ancient Israel*, 35–36.

87 E. g., the Middle-Assyrian list VS 19 1 i 37–39 (Nissinen, *Prophets and Prophecy*, no. 123): "Ten homers four seah five liters of barley for Aššur-apla-iddina on the second day, for the food rations of the prophets, prophetesses and the *assinnus* of the Ištar temple."

88 This may be the reason why one prophet wanted a scribe to write a letter to the king from his own dictation: "Atamrum, prophet of Šamaš, came to me and spoke to me as follows: 'Send me a discreet scribe! I will have him write down the message which Šamaš has sent me for the king'" (ARM 26 414:29–33; Nissinen, *Prophets and Prophecy*, no. 48). The letter of the prophet is probably known to us (ARM 26 194; Nissinen, *Prophets and Prophecy*, no. 4); see D. Charpin, "Prophètes et rois dans le Proche-Orient amorrite: Nouvelles données, nouvelles perspectives," in *Florilegium Marianum 6*, FS A. Parrot (Mémoires de NABU 7; Paris: Societe pour l'Etude du Proche-Orient Ancien, 2002) 7–38, esp. 29–31.

lical or extrabiblical, depends on its writer and on its purpose (as far as these can be known), on its temporal distance from what it describes, on its genre and on the process of transmission.[89]

When drawing the picture of prophets in the ancient Near East, we should begin by paying attention to the constructs of prophecy within the sources we have at our disposal. If we can observe a similar construct occurring in different contexts, we can assume that it is shared by more than one writer and serves more than one episodic purpose. These observations are like pieces of a puzzle: when they fit together, they contribute to constructing a bigger picture that, as such, is not a photograph of historical reality but an interpretation of it, not the full and authentic past but fragments of different constructs of the past.

---

89 See Grabbe, *Ancient Israel*, 220.

What is Prophecy? An Ancient Near Eastern Perspective

Why the Question?

Herbert B. Huffmon is acknowledged as an outstanding expert in matters related to prophecy. In this paper, dedicated to him with much pleasure, I attempt at answering the question of what prophecy actually is—or, to put it more humbly, how I would like to understand the word and the underlying concept as a biblical and ancient Near Eastern scholar. The word "prophecy" is deeply rooted in the vocabulary of religious communities, but it also belongs to the academic language. However, Old and New Testament scholars may have varying nuances or even different meanings in using this word, not to speak about Classicists, Egyptologists and Assyriologists, many of whom are reluctant to mention the word "prophecy" at all because of the theological connotations and value judgments attached to it. Hence, the question "What is prophecy?" immediately provokes further questions.

Should the use of the word "prophecy" be restricted to theological discourse because of its roots in religious speech? This is hardly possible, because there is no unanimous understanding of the realm of "theology". On the other hand, there is no reason to create an idiosyncratic language which would make theology, whatever it means, incommensurable with other disciplines.

Should the word "prophecy", then, refer exclusively to the sources and phenomena related to religions which use it as a part of their own tradition, that is, Judaism, Christianity, and Islam? This would mean enclosing the term with a confessional wall, which would jeopardize its placement in a broader religious and socio-cultural context.

What if we take a historically or theologically influential phenomenon—in other words, Israelite or biblical prophecy—as a criterion and judge the "prophetic" nature of other sources and phenomena by this standard? This approach has the obvious disadvantage of using one specific tradition (usually one's own) as a yardstick which represents the genuine and proper form of prophecy, and making the comparative material appear as an under- or overdeveloped distortion of the chosen paragon. Thus far, the study of prophecy has been predominantly Bible-centered. This can be explained by the fact that this field of study is occupied by biblical scholars in first place, and many of them may be interested in the history and religion of the ancient Near East as the "context

DOI 10.1515/9783110466546-006

of scripture"[1] rather than in its own right. But even more importantly, an independent view of ancient Near Eastern prophecy has been impeded by the paucity of evidence. Therefore, even today, every new piece of prophecy, however small, is hailed as a welcome addition to the frustratingly incomplete picture.

Obviously, the concept of prophecy cannot be restricted to Christian, Jewish, and Islamic sources and societies. However, a broader understanding of prophecy does not make the term any simpler to cope with. What are the criteria for recognizing prophecy in sources in which this word is not inherent? Do we call a text prophecy because of its content or its religio-historical origin? Why do we call some people prophets and others not?

It is not easy to adapt a religious concept to scholarly language. The question "What is prophecy?" has implications for the sociology of science, implying the need to neutralize the traditional theological concept in a way that makes it applicable to scholarly use. Answering the question is necessary to enable interdisciplinary communication and to remove semantic misunderstandings between scholars who should be able to recognize related phenomena in different cultures irrespective of their education and religious background.

I start my own attempt at answering the question "What is prophecy?" with a survey of meanings of the word-family "prophecy". Second, I will add some viewpoints to the problem of the definition of prophecy, which is still very much under discussion. Third, I will present an overview of the sources recognizable as prophetic according to the revisited definition and, finally, I will offer some thoughts on the ideological conceptualization of prophecy in the Hebrew Bible.

The Word-Family "Prophecy"

First of all, "prophecy" is a word of the English language, the meaning of which is a matter of mutual agreement by the community that uses this word. The dictionary of English that I use every day, *Oxford Advanced Learners Dictionary of Current English*, doubtless reflects the semantics of current English correctly

1 *The Context of Scripture* is the title of the new three-volume collection of translations of ancient Near Eastern documents (W. W. Hallo and K. L. Younger [eds.], *The Context of Scripture*, Vols. 1–3; leiden: Brill, 1997, 2000, and 2002 = *COS* 1–3). The title of this collection has been criticized, all the more because many of the texts included are by no means associated with biblical texts or history; see, e. g., the review of O. Loretz in *UF* 28 (1996): 791–93. On the other hand, it is highly surprising that the major corpora of ancient Near Eastern prophetic texts (i. e., those of Mari and Assyria) are entirely excluded from the collection.

and authoritatively when it defines the noun "prophecy" as "a statement that sth will happen in the future, especially one made by sb with religious or magic powers", and the verb "prophesy" as "to say what will happen in the future (done in the past using religious or magic powers)". A "prophet" is "a person who claims to know what will happen in the future".[2] According to this dictionary, hence, the English-speaking community lays emphasis on the aspect of foretelling the future, using the word "prophecy" of a predictive activity of any kind. The first idea that an average English speaker associates with a prophet is obviously prognostication, and even academic scholars sometimes label their sources as prophecies, if they include predictions of the future. Why, then, are the scholars who work with biblical and ancient Near Eastern sources usually not quite happy with this understanding of prophecy? Why is the future-oriented definition of prophecy, which doubtless reflects an actual development in the semantics of the English language, not as good as any other definition?

To be sure, the same dictionary gives two further explanations for the word "prophet" in which the future plays no role at all. According to these explanations, a "prophet", in Christian, Jewish, and Muslim religions, is "a person sent by God to teach the people and give them messages from God". Furthermore, a "prophet (of sth)" is equated with "a person who teaches and supports a new idea, theory, etc.". These explanations insinuate that behind the future-oriented everyday meaning of "prophecy" there is a phenomenon, the main characteristic of which is speaking to people and transmitting messages, divine messages in particular. Indeed, the very concept of prophecy is deeply rooted in the biblical tradition where it is intertwined with the notion of an alleged divine-human communication, in which a human person, the so-called "prophet", acts as the mouthpiece of God. The same notion with respective activity is to be found also in the ancient Mediterranean environment of the writings of the Bible; in fact, different languages have inherited this word-family from Classical Greek, in which the respective word-family *prophētēs* denotes a comparable activity. According to Liddell and Scott"s *Greek-English Lexicon*, *prophēteia* is equivalent to the "gift of interpreting the will of gods" and *prophēteuō* to being an "interpreter of the gods", whereas *prophētēs* is "one who speaks for a God and interprets his will to man", or, generally, an "interpreter". This dictionary also specifies the meanings of the word-family in the New Testament, where it reflects especially

---

2 *Oxford Advanced Learner's Dictionary of Current English* (ed. S. Wehmeier; Oxford: Oxford University Press, ^{6}2000) 1016. The reader will note that a survey of German, French or, say, Finnish dictionaries will provide similar results.

the "gift of expounding scripture, speaking and preaching", and not only that, but also predicting future events.[3]

The meanings of words in modern languages cannot be determined by their use in ancient times, of course, but on the other hand, the reading of ancient sources should not be blurred by modern semantics. It becomes evident from the Classical Greek data that the primary idea expressed by "prophecy" was the interpretation of the divine will rather than prognostication which, nevertheless, was connected with prophecy as early as in the New Testament. The use of the word-family "prophecy" in modern languages owes its use first and foremost to the Bible—primarily to the Septuagint, but also to the New Testament and early Christian literature. When the translators of the Septuagint needed a Greek equivalent for the Hebrew *nābî'*, they chose a word denoting a person who speaks for God and interprets the divine will. Obviously, in their view, *prophētēs* rendered an idea that was close enough to what they thought a *nābî'* was. In modern scholarship, wherever the meaning of "prophecy" is specified, it is mostly understood along the same lines.

If the word "prophecy", then, can be agreed to denote primarily the activity of transmitting and interpreting the divine will, it can be used as a general concept of related activities in the ancient and the modern worlds, independently of its biblical roots and religious affiliations.[4] This requires further specification regarding the concrete activities that can be adequately designated as prophecy; in other words, a definition of prophecy is needed to make the word applicable to different contexts. The definition is necessary first and foremost as an aid of communication between people who work in different fields with cognate materials. It should not be understood as a static image of truth; rather, it should be seen from the point of view of the sociology of knowledge as a methodical process that emerges from concrete needs of the scholarly community and develops along with its application.

---

3 *LSJ:* 1539–40; cf. W. Bauer, *Griechisch-Deutsches Wörterbuch zu den Schriften des Neuen Testaments und der frühchristlichen Literatur* (ed. K. and B. Aland; Berlin and New York: de Gruyter, ^{6}1988) 1447–49; and, for the use of the word-family in Classical Greek, M. C. van der Kolf, "Prophetes," in *PW* 45 (1957) 797–814; and H. Krämer, "προφήτης κτλ. A: Die Wortgruppe in der Profangräzität," *TWNT* 6 (1959) 783–95.

4 For an anthropological, cross-cultural perspective, see T. W. Overholt, *Prophecy in Cross-Cultural Perspective: A Source-Book for Biblical Research* (SBLSBS 17; Atlanta, Ga.: Society for Biblical Literature, 1986); and L. L. Grabbe, "Ancient Near Eastern Prophecy from an Anthropological Perspective," in *Prophecy in Its Ancient Near Eastern Context: Mesopotamian, Biblical, and Arabian Perspectives* (ed. M. Nissinen; SBLSymS 13; Atlanta, Ga.: Society of Biblical Literature, 2000) 13–32.

A Definition of Prophecy and Some Qualifications

If the definition of prophecy is understood as a process rather than an entity, it is feasible to start working with an existing definition that already enjoys wide acceptance without a claim to being the final truth. Such a definition has been formulated by Manfred Weippert, according to whom prophecy is present when a person

(a) through a cognitive experience (a vision, an auditory experience, an audio-visual appearance, a dream or the like) becomes the subject of the revelation of a deity, or several deities and, in addition,

(b) is conscious of being commissioned by the deity or deities in question to convey the revelation in a verbal form (as a "prophecy" or a "prophetic speech"), or through nonverbal communicative acts ("symbolic acts"), to a third party who constitutes the actual addressee of the message.[5]

Essentially, the definition of Weippert refers to a process of divine-human communication consisting of the following four components:

1. the divine sender of the message;
2. the message (the "revelation");
3. the transmitter of the message (the prophet); and
4. the recipient of the message.

This exposition corresponds to the prevailing views in understanding prophecy as intermediation; according to an understanding shared by an increasing number of scholars, there can be no prophecy without God (or a deity), no prophecy without a message and audience, and, finally, no prophecy without a prophet.[6] All these components are present in the definition of Weippert, which is rather broad, as it should be to avoid confining prophecy to any particular characteristics that may be common but not universally applicable, such as the spontane-

5 M. Weippert, "Prophetie im Alten Orient," *NBL* 3 (1997) 197 (translation mine).

6 Prophecy is seen primarily as intermediation by the majority of scholars who have recently discussed the issue of definition; cf., e. g., T. W. Overholt, *Channels of Prophecy: The Social Dynamics of Prophetic Activity* (Minneapolis, Minn.: Fortress Press, 1989); H. B. Huffmon, "Ancient Near Eastern Prophecy," in *ABD* 5 (1992) 477–82; H. Barstad, "No Prophets? Recent Developments in Biblical Prophetic Research and Ancient Near Eastern Prophecy," *JSOT* 57 (1993) 46; L. L. Grabbe, *Priests, Prophets, Diviners, Sages: A Socio-Historical Study of Religious Specialists in Ancient Israel* (Valley Forge, Pa.: Trinity Press International, 1995) 107; D. L. Petersen, "Defining Prophecy and Prophetic Literature," in Nissinen (ed.), *Prophecy in Its Ancient Near Eastern Context* (2000) 33–44.

ity of prophecy,[7] ecstatic or charismatic qualities,[8] or the use of specific literary forms.[9] This does not mean that the definition is above criticism. David L. Petersen has criticized it for emphasizing too much the personal experience as a distinctive mark of prophecy.[10] In addition, I think the notion of "consciousness" needs clarification in connection with allegedly divine messages, the divine origin of which cannot be controlled by anyone, not even by the prophet her- or himself. Moreover, it may be asked whether it is sufficient to describe prophecy as one-way communication from the deity to the recipient, without reference to the social environment of this communication. A few qualifications are therefore necessary.

Prophecy and Divination

My first remark concerns the relationship of prophecy and divination. In contrast to the once influential idea of a substantial qualitative difference between prophecy and divination (i.e. consulting the divine world by various means), there is a growing tendency in the present-day study of biblical and ancient Near Eastern prophecy to consider prophecy an integral part of divination, rather than being in conflict with it in general terms.[11] This does not exclude individual clashes between prophets and diviners; what matters is that the social function of prophecy by and large has not been found to be different from that of divination. In the ancient Near East, in so far as we are correctly informed by the extant documents, the primary function of all divination was the so-called *Herrschafts-*

---

7 This aspect has been emphasized by A. Malamat, *Mari and the Bible* (SHCANE 12; Leiden: Brill, 1998) 61.

8 For Max Weber's concept of prophets as charismatic leaders, see J. Blenkinsopp, *Sage, Priest, Prophet: Religious and Intellectual Leadership in Ancient Israel* (Louisville, Ky.: Westminster/John Knox Press, 1995) 115–19; and R. E. Clements, "Max Weber, Charisma and Biblical Prophecy," in Gitay (ed.), *Prophecy and Prophets* (1997) 89–108.

9 This criterion is criticized by D. L. Petersen, "Rethinking the Nature of Prophetic Literature," in Gitay (ed.), *Prophecy and Prophets* (1997) 23–40.

10 Petersen, "Defining Prophecy and Prophetic Literature," 39–41.

11 See, e.g., M. deJong Ellis, "Observations on Mesopotamian Oracles and Prophetic Texts: Literary and Historiographic Considerations," *JCS* 41 (1989) 144–46; Overholt, *Channels*, 140–47; Barstad "No Prophets? Recent Developments in Biblical Prophetic Research and Ancient Near Eastern Prophecy," 47–48; Grabbe, *Priests*, 150–51; J. C., VanderKam, "Prophecy and Apocalyptics in the Ancient Near East," *CANE* 3 (1995) 2083; E. Cancik-Kirschbaum, "Prophetismus und Divination: Ein Blick auf die keilschriftlichen Quellen," in *Propheten in Mari, Assyrien und Israel* (ed. M. Köckert and M. Nissinen; FRLANT 201; Göttingen, Vandenhoeck & Ruprecht, 2003) 33–53.

wissen, that is, the conviction of the identity, capacity and legitimacy of the ruler and the justification and limitations of his (or, less frequently, her) power, based on the communication between the ruler and the god(s).[12]

I am totally in favor of seeing prophecy as one form of divination; nonetheless, I find it necessary to distinguish between different methods of becoming informed of what is believed to be the divine will.[13] If classified as a form of divination, prophecy, together with dreams and visions, clearly belongs to the non-inductive type, which does not presuppose exhaustive studies in the traditional omen literature and experience in observing material objects like celestial bodies and the entrails of animals. This is not to say that no learned techniques would have been required of a prophet, only that they were of a totally different kind than those employed by the practitioners of inductive divination, particularly by astrologers, haruspices or exorcists. The skills or aptitudes of prophets, visionaries and dreamers served the purpose of reaching a state of mind in which it was believed to be possible to become directly conversant with the divine will. Usually this seems to have presupposed an altered state of consciousness, but the ways of attaining the required condition may have been more or less frantic.[14]

The prophets very often claim to have received the divine message in a dream or a vision. In many cases it is virtually impossible to distinguish between prophecy and other visionary or oneiromantic activity, but the difference should nonetheless be recognized; not every visionary or dreamer can be called prophet. To be qualified as a prophecy, the dream or vision should contain a divine message to be transmitted and, if need be, interpreted; however, such dreams and visions can be seen by anybody. In practical terms it is not always possible to determine whether a particular dreamer is a prophet, especially if the source in question does not otherwise imply her/his prophetic role.

---

12 The concept of *Herrschaftswissen* is introduced by B. Pongratz-Leisten, *Herrschaftswissen in Mesopotamien: Formen der Kommunikation zwischen Gott und König im 2. und 1. Jahrtausend v. Chr.* (SAAS 10; Helsinki: The Neo-Assyrian Text Corpus Project, 1999), who incorporates in it all kinds of Mesopotamian divination: astrology, extispicy, prophetic oracles, dreams and the "correspondence" between gods and kings.

13 For this distinction, see also Cancik-Kirschbaum, "Prophetismus und Divination: Ein Blick auf die keilschriftlichen Quellen," 44–51.

14 For an assessment of the question of prophetic ecstasy, see Grabbe, *Priests*, 108–12.

Prophecy and Society

Second, the designation "prophet" not only refers to the position of a person in the process of communication but also implies a social role and function which distinguishes the person thus designated from other members of the society, no matter what kind of vocation may be understood to lie behind this role. Polymorphous as the image of a prophet in different times and documents is, it is not advisable to presume a particular institutional background, distinctive behavior or mode of expression as a precondition of prophecy.[15] What makes a prophet different from others is that he or she is believed to have the capacity of acting as the mouthpiece of God, in whatever manner or position.

In practical terms this special faculty very often—virtually always in the ancient Near East—means that prophets are attached to the temples of the deities whose words they transmit. As members of temple communities, they were set apart from the rest of the community; some of them (especially the ones with undefinable gender role that are known from both Mari and Assyria), belong to people whose condition of "otherness" is incompatible with the way of life of an average citizen.[16] The role of prophets also differs clearly from that of the practitioners of inductive divination, that is, scholars who were well versed in scholarly tradition and whose social esteem, at least in Mesopotamian societies, seems to have been generally higher than that of the prophets. At Mari, the messages of the prophets were transferred to the king by go-betweens, which indicates that the relation of the prophets to the king was not as direct as that of the scholars with whom the king maintained intensive contact.[17] From the

---

15 See Petersen, "Rethinking the Nature of Prophetic Literature," 27–30; "Defining Prophecy and Prophetic Literature," 33–37; cf. also Blenkinsopp, *Sage*, 123–29.

16 For the socioreligious role of the Assyrian prophets, see M. Nissinen, "The Socioreligious Role of the Neo-Assyrian Prophets," in id. (ed.) 2000: 89–114.

17 This is not to say that direct contacts between prophets and the king would have been excluded; cf. D. Charpin, "Prophètes et rois dans le Proche-Orient amorrite," in Lemaire (ed.), *Prophètes et rois* (2001) 34–41; and id., "Prophètes et rois dans le Proche-Orient amorrite: Nouvelles données, nouvelles perspectives," in *Florilegium Marianum 6*, FS A. Parrot (ed. id./J.-M. Durand; Mémoires de NABU 7; Paris: Societe pour l'Etude du Proche-Orient Ancien, 2002) 16–22. For the roles of the prophets *vis-à-vis* scholars at Mari, see J.-M. Durand, "La religión en Siria durante la época de los reinos amorreos según la documentación de Mari," in *Mitología y religión del Oriente Antiguo*, vol 2/1: *Semitas occidentales (Ebla, Mari)* (ed. P. Mander, and J.-M. Durand; Estudios Orientales 8; Sabadell: AUSA, 1995) 405–8; J. M. Sasson, "About 'Mari and the Bible'," *RA* 92 (1998) 116–19; for the same in Assyria, see S. Parpola, *Letters from Assyrian and Babylonian Scholars* (SAA 10; Helsinki: Helsinki University Press, 1993) xvii–xxvii; id., *Assyrian Prophecies* (SAA 9; Helsinki: Helsinki University Press, 1997) xlvii–xlviii;

point of view of gender, it is worth noting that there are a considerable number of women among ancient Near Eastern prophets but none among scholars, which also indicates a difference in social location.

Prophetic activity does not necessarily exclude other roles in society; the social position of the prophet may vary according to the integration of the prophetic role into the society as a whole. The often-made dichotomy between free, charismatic prophets and the so-called cultic or court prophets should no longer be upheld as a fundamental, generally applicable distinction, even though the solitary prophetic dissident, independent of human authorities and institutions, still appears as a paragon of prophecy even in scholarly literature. This prototype of a prophet is certainly based on a biblical model (e.g. Amos in Amos 7:14–15), but this may not quite tally with the historical facts. Moreover, the contraposition of free and institutional prophets correlates too much with ideas on "true" and "false" prophecy, which are confessional labels inconsistent with any general definition of prophecy.[18]

The distinction between "true" and "false" prophecy is nonetheless significant to the addressees of the prophetic message who ultimately decide whether or not the words of a prophet should be listened to. The social dynamic of the prophetic process of communication[19] is substantially characterized by the faith-based divine component. The acceptability of prophecy depends on the social acknowledgment of the speaking deity and the prophet; therefore, prophetic communication cannot be just one-way correspondence from a deity to humans but interacts perforce with the social hierarchy and belief systems of any given community. The prophets and the addressees are not the only participants in

---

M. Nissinen, *References to Prophecy in Neo-Assyrian Sources* (SAAS 7; Helsinki: The Neo-Assyrian Text Corpus Project, 1998) 167–69; id., "The Socioreligious Role of the Neo-Assyrian Prophets," 107–11.

18 See H. B. Huffmon, "The Origins of Prophecy," in *Magnalia Dei: The Mighty Acts of God*, FS G. E. Wright (ed. F. M. Cross, W. E. Lemke and P. D. Miller; Garden City, NY: Doubleday, 1976) 183–84; R. J. Coggins, "Prophecy: True and False," in *Of Prophets' Visions and the Wisdom of Sages*, FS R. N. Whybray (ed. H. A. McKay and D. J. A. Clines; JSOTSup 162; Sheffield: Sheffield Academic Press, 1993) 93; M. Nissinen, "Falsche Prophetie in neuassyrischer und deuteronomistischer Darstellung," in T. Veijola (ed.), *Das Deuteronomium und seine Querbeziehungen* (Schriften der Finnischen Exegetischen Gesellschaft 62; Helsinki: Finnische Exegetische Gesellschaft and Göttingen: Vandenhoeck & Ruprecht, 1996) 193–95 (= pp. 419–40 in the present volume). I hasten to add that prophecy has never been a value-free concept and an image of a prophet can never consist of "pure facts" alone; even a scholarly definition of a "prophet" is inevitably a construct of the academic community in spite of the attempt at using it regardless of confessional prerequisites.

19 Cf. Overholt, *Channels of Prophecy*, 17–25.

this process; it involves also other intermediaries that may be needed to transfer the prophetic message, interpreters of the prophetic words, scribes and archivists who take care of their writing and depositing, authorities who control the prophetic activity, and so on—not to forget public reactions which may substantially determine the viability of prophecies. All these factors, depending on the structures of the society, may stop the prophetic process or support it.

Prophecy and Prediction

Third, if intermediation is seen as the primary quality of prophecy, the eventual predictive aspect is subordinate to this quality. To be sure, the predictive meaning of the word "prophecy" in everyday language is not without foundation in ancient sources. Prophecies are very commonly orientated toward the future in one way or another. Rather than being downright descriptions of future events, however, the predictive element grows from the position of the present situation in the divine plan, as disclosed by the prophecy.[20] Hence, a prophetic prediction, as prophecy in general, fulfils the function of divine-human communication. In so far as this communication is about the future, as it frequently is, prophecies may include predictions, but not every prediction is a prophecy.

Consequently, the question arises whether texts which are predictive without showing any sign of the idea of divine-human communication and intermediation can be called prophecy in light of the meaning defined above. Some Akkadian[21] and Egyptian[22] predictive texts demonstrate the prophetic process only

20 L. L. Grabbe, "Poets, Scribes, or Preachers? The Reality of Prophecy in the Second Temple Period," in Grabbe and Haak (eds.), *Knowing the End from the Beginning* (2003) 192–215, 194: "Prophets claimed to proclaim messages of God about his plans, but this inevitably included the future. Prediction was not all there was to prophecy by any means, but it was certainly there."

21 The so-called Akkadian prophecies or Akkadian apocalypses, including the Marduk Prophecy, the Šulgi Prophecy, the Uruk Prophecy, the Dynastic Prophecy, and the two texts that simply bear the titles Text A and Text B. For an overview of these texts, see A. K. Grayson, *Babylonian Historical-Literary Texts* (Toronto Semitic Texts and Studies 3; Toronto, Ont./Buffalo, Ohio: University of Toronto Press, 1975) 13–22; deJong Ellis, "Observations on Mesopotamian Oracles and Prophetic Texts: Literary and Historiographic Considerations," 146–57; J. C. VanderKam, "Prophecy and Apocalyptics in the Ancient Near East," 2091–94 and cf. the translations in *COS* 1: 480–82 (by T. Longman) and *Prophéties et oracles*, vol. 1: *Dans le Proche-Orient ancien* (Supplément au Cahier Evangile 88; Paris: Cerf, 1994) 98–114 (by Philippe Talon). For the definitional problem, see also M. Nissinen, "City as Lofty as Heaven: Arbela and Other Cities in Neo-Assyrian Prophecy," in L. L. Grabbe and R. D. Haak (eds.), *"Every City Shall Be Forsaken": Urban-*

vaguely if at all, even though they sometimes have been labeled as prophecy precisely because they are predictions. As literature, these texts represent a genre clearly different from other ancient Near Eastern prophetic sources.[23] This does not set them entirely apart from prophecies, though.[24] While removing the definitional and terminological confusion caused by different uses of "prophecy", it should not be forgotten that the Akkadian literary predictive texts (also called Akkadian apocalypses) are literary offshoots of divination. Without actually being prophecy in the above defined meaning, they represent learned interpretation and application of divinatory sources in a way well comparable with literary interpretations of prophetic sources, which constitute my last qualification to the definition of prophecy.

Literary Interpretation of Prophecy

It may be discussed whether the literary reinterpretation, or *Fortschreibung*, of prophetic messages can still be called "prophecy" at all. In strictly phenomenological terms, the subsequent literary interpretation of prophecy, liable to alter or invent prophetic words and figures, could no longer bear this designation. The questions arise mainly from the Hebrew Bible; in extrabiblical sources, the temporal distance between the prophetic performance and the written record is usually not very long, hence the literary and interpretative process behind them is

ism and Prophecy in Ancient Israel and the Near East (JSOTSup 330; Sheffield: Sheffield Academic Press, 2001) 172–209.

22 For example, the Prophecies of Neferti, the Admonitions of Ipuwer, the Demotic Chronicle, the Prophecy of the Lamb (for these and other relevant texts, see the articles collected in A. Blasius and B. U. Schipper, *Apokalyptik und Ägypten: Eine kritische Analyse der relevanten Texte aus dem griechisch-römischen Ägypten* [OLA 107; Leuven: Peeters, 2002]); cf. the translations in M. Lichtheim, *Ancient Egyptian Literature: A Book of Readings*. I. *The Old and Middle Kingdoms* (3 vols.; Berkeley: University of California Press, 1973) 139–84; *COS* 1: 93–110 (by Nili Shupak) and *Prophéties et oracles*, vol. 2: *En Égypte et en Grèce* (Supplément au Cahier Evangile 88–89; Paris: Cerf, 1994) 6–30 (by Didier Devauchelle). For discussion of these texts as "prophecy", see N. Shupak "Egyptian 'Prophecy' and Biblical Prophecy: Did the Phenomenon of Prophecy, in Biblical Sense, Exist in Ancient Egypt?" *JEOL* 31 (1989–90) 1–40; and B. U. Schipper, "'Apokalyptik,' 'Messianismus,' 'Prophetie': Eine Begriffsbestimmung," in Blasius and Schipper (eds.), *Apokalyptik und Ägypten*, 21–40.

23 See M. Weippert, "Aspekte israelitischer Prophetie im Lichte verwandter Erscheinungen des Alten Orients," in Ad bene et fideliter seminandum, FS Karlheinz Deller (ed. G. Mauer and U. Magen; AOAT 220; Kevelaer: Butzon & Bercker; Neukirchen-Vluyn: Neukirchener Verlag, 1988) 287–319, 291–94.

24 Cf. Grabbe, *Priests, Prophets, Diviners, Sages*, 94.

nothing when compared with the formation of the biblical prophetic books that took centuries.

However, the Neo-Assyrian collections of prophetic oracles do testify to the reuse of prophecies in new historical situations, and prophetic words are also used in literary contexts, either as quotations from written sources or as freely invented paraphrases.[25] This evidence, without being voluminous, is enough to donstrate that the prophetic process of communication did not necessarily cease when the message reached its destination, but could be continued by subsequent hands. Hence, a definition of prophecy should not *a priori* exclude the literary products that emerged from the scribal interpretations of prophetic words. Rather, these should be considered secondary prolongation of the prophetic communicational process.

Prophetic Records from the Ancient Near East

Any definition of prophecy is a scholarly construct that can only be formulated in interaction with sources that are considered to represent the prophetic phenomenon in one way or another. Definitions are needed to delimit the relevant source material, but, on the other hand, the sources may compel us to rethink the definition. Therefore, answering the question "What is prophecy?" is a process that should not be paralyzed by unyielding and over-exact definitions. On the other hand, an inventory of ancient Near Eastern prophetic sources should not be understood as the formation of an extrabiblical canon, but rather as a provisional assessment of the present state of knowledge.

There exists a wide spectrum of ancient Near Eastern sources that either reflect the prophetic process of communication sketched above or mention a prophetic designation like the Hebrew *nābî'*, or the Akkadian *raggimu*, *maḫḫû*/*muḫḫûm* or *āpilum*.[26] At present, the updated list of documents that meet these requirements constitutes a group of over 170 individual texts, consisting basically of two kinds of sources: oracles of deities in written form, and references in documents of different kinds—letters, inscriptions, administrative records

25 See Nissinen, "Spoken, Written, Quoted, and Invented," 263–68.

26 For the prophetic designations, see J.-M. Durand, *Archives épistolaires de Mari 1/1* (ARM 26/1; Paris: Editions Recherche sur les Civilisations, 1988), esp. 386–96; id., *Mitología*, 322–34 (Mari); Parpola, *Assyrian Prophecies*, xlv–xlvii (Assyria).

and religious texts—that mention prophets, quote their sayings, or speak of their activities.[27] This source material can be divided in six groups:

1. The largest corpus of prophetic records comes from eighteenth-century Mari, comprising fifty letters with prophetic quotations.[28] These letters, which are virtually always addressed to King Zimri-Lim (c. 1775–1761 BCE),[29] report on prophecies delivered in the city of Mari, elsewhere in the kingdom, or even outside its borders. In addition, the Mari corpus includes a handful of documents other than letters that mention prophets (*āpilum/āpiltum, muḫḫûm/muḫḫūtum*): two ritual texts,[30] several administrative documents,[31] a report of crimes[32] and a literary text, the so-called "Epic of Zimri-Lim".[33]

---

27 For an extensive collection of translations and normalized transcriptions of the sources, see M. Nissinen (ed.), with contributions by C.-L. Seow, R. K. Ritner, and H. C. Melchert, *Prophets and Prophecy in the Ancient Near East* (SBLWAW 41; Atlanta, Ga.: Society of Biblical Literature, 2nd ed., 2019); translations for most texts are also included in *Prophéties et oracles*, vol. 1 (1994). A brief overview of the sources can be found in Weippert, "Aspekte israelitischer Prophetie," 287–319; id., "Prophetie im Alten Orient"; and Huffmon, "Ancient Near Eastern Prophecy." Additional source material has been discussed, for example, in H. B. Huffmon, "The Expansion of Prophecy in the Mari Archives: New Texts, New Readings, New Information," in Gitay (ed.), *Prophecy and Prophets* (1997) 7–22; id., "A Company of Prophets: Mari, Assyria, Israel," in Nissinen (ed.), *Prophecy in Its Ancient Near Eastern Context* (2000) 47–70; K. van der Toorn, "Mesopotamian Prophecy between Immanence and Transcendence: A Comparison of Old Babylonian and Neo-Assyrian Prophecy," in Nissinen (ed.), *Prophecy in Its Ancient Near Eastern Context* (2000) 70–87; M. Nissinen, "Spoken, Written, Quoted and Invented: Orality and Writtenness in Ancient Near Eastern Prophecy," in Ben Zvi and Floyd (eds.), *Writings and Speech in Israelite and Ancient Near Eastern Prophecy* (2000) 235–71; id., "The Socioreligious Role of the Neo-Assyrian Prophets" (= pp. 103–26 in this volume); id., "A Prophetic Riot in Babylonia, 133 BCE" (= pp. 301–11 in this volume); id., "Prophets and the Divine Council" (= pp. 461–77 in this volume)

28 Most of the relevant letters are included in the edition of Durand (*Archives*, 377–482); for a full list, see Appendix, nos. 1–50b. An extensive collection of transliterations and translations of the Mari texts has been published in J. J. M. Roberts, *The Bible and the Ancient Near East: Collected Essays* (Winona Lake, Ind.: Eisenbrauns, 2002) 157–253.

29 Two letters, FM 6 1 and ARM 26 223, can now be dated to the time of Zimri-Lim's predecessor, Yasmaḫ-Addu; see Charpin, "Prophètes et rois dans le Proche-Orient amorrite: Nouvelles données, nouvelles perspectives," 33–38.

30 FM 3 2 (Ritual of Ištar, Text 2); FM 3 3 (Ritual of Ištar, Text 3); see J. M. Durand and M. Guichard, "Les rituels de Mari," in Charpin and Durand (eds.), *Florilegium marianum 3* (1997) 19–78.

31 See Appendix, nos. 53–63, 65a.

32 M. 9717; see F. van Koppen, "Seized by the Royal Order: The Households of Sammêtar and Other Magnates at Mari," in Charpin and Durand (eds.), *Florilegium marianum 3* (1997) 356–57.

33 M. Guichard, *Florilegium Marianum 14: L'Épopée de Zimrī-Lîm* (Mémoires de NABU 16; Paris: SEPOA, 2014). The relevant excerpt of this text is quoted also in Durand, *Archives*, 393.

2. The prophetic activity in the Old Babylonian period was not restricted to Mari. This is demonstrated by two oracles of the goddess Kititum (Ištar) to Ibalpiel II, a contemporary of Zimri-Lim and the ruler of the Kingdom of Ešnunna that was located northeast of Babylonia.[34]

3. The second largest corpus of ancient Near Eastern prophecy derives from seventh-century Nineveh.[35] This Neo-Assyrian corpus comprises eleven clay tablets, including 29 individual prophetic oracles addressed to Kings Esarhaddon (681–669 BCE) and Assurbanipal (668–627 BCE), who ruled the Assyrian empire during the time Manasseh and Josiah were kings of Judah in Jerusalem; hence, the Neo-Assyrian prophets roughly coincide with the "classical" prophets of the Hebrew Bible.

Apart from the oracles, there are more than twenty Neo-Assyrian texts—inscriptions, letters, administrative documents, cultic texts and a treaty—alluding in one way or another to prophets (*raggimu/raggintu, maḫḫû/maḫḫutu*) or their sayings, and giving an impression of how prophecy was utilized and valued in Neo-Assyrian society.[36]

4. The Mesopotamian documentation of prophecy is supplemented by a random collection of individual texts from different ages and different geographical areas that is classified as prophecy because of reference to a human intermediary transmitting divine messages, or because the texts include prophetic designations. The temporal and geographic distribution of these odd pieces of prophecy is surprisingly wide, ranging from the twenty-first[37] to second[38] centuries BCE

34 FLP 1674 and 2064; see the edition of M. deJong Ellis, "The Goddess Kititum Speaks to King Ibalpiel: Oracle Texts from Ishchali," *MARI* 5 (1987) 235–66. Even an administrative document from Ešnunna (OECT 13 263) mentions prophets in the temple of Kititum; see S. Viaggio, "Sull'-amministrazione del tempio di Ištar Kitītum a Ishjali." *EVO* 29 (2006) 185–217.

35 SAA 9; see the edition of Parpola, *Assyrian Prophecies*; cf. M. Weippert, "Assyrische Prophetien der Zeit Asarhaddons und Assurbanipals," in *Assyrian Royal Inscriptions: New Horizons in Literary, Ideological and Historical Analysis* (ed. F. M. Fales; Orientis Antiqui Collectio 17; Roma: Istituto per l'Oriente, 1981) 71–115; id., ""König, fürchte dich nicht!" Assyrische Prophetie im 7. Jahrhundert v.Chr.," *Or* 71 (2002) 1–54.

36 Many of these are analyzed in Nissinen, *References*. For additional material, see Appendix, nos. 103, 110–114, 118–118j.

37 The letter of the King of Ur to Ur-Lisi (TCS 1 369; see P. Michalowski, *Letters from Early Mesopotamia* [SBLWAW 3; Atlanta, Ga.: Scholars Press, 1993] 55) mentions a *maḫḫû*.

38 The Late Babylonian astronomical diary concerning the year 133 BCE reports a prophetic appearance; see the edition in A. J. Sachs and H. Hunger, *Astronomical Diaries and Related Texts from Babylonia*, vol. 3: *Diaries from 164 B.C. to 61 B.C.* (Österreichische Akademie der Wissenschaften, Philologisch-historische Klasse, Denkschriften 247; Wien: Österreichische Akademie der Wissenschaften, 1996) 216–19; cf. Nissinen "A Prophetic Riot in Babylonia, 133 BCE" (= pp. 301–11 in this volume).

and covering considerable parts of the ancient Near East. The texts represent different genres, including letters,[39] administrative texts,[40] literary texts,[41] rituals,[42] lexical lists[43] and omens.[44]

There are also some borderline cases in which the reference to prophecy is still to be substantiated, notably the two Hittite fourteenth-century plague prayers with a possible reference to prophets among other practitioners of divination,[45] the references to persons called *munabbi'ātu* in administrative lists from thirteenth-century Emar,[46] as well as the three texts from Nuzi and one Middle-Babylonian omen from Assur mentioning people called *āpilum*.[47]

5. A few important documents testify to the existence of prophecy even in the West Semitic milieu.[48] The oldest of them is the Egyptian Report of Wenamon referring to a prophetic appearance in Byblos in the eleventh century.[49] The later sources are written in different forms of Aramaic, namely the inscription of Zakkur, king of Hamath (c. 800 BCE), who in his distress receives an encouraging oracle from Baal-Šamayin through prophets ([*b*]*yd ḥzyn w byd 'ddn*),[50] the inscription of Deir 'Alla from c. 700 BC reporting a vision of Balaam, the "visionary

---

39 See Appendix, nos. 119, 121, 135k.

40 See Appendix, nos. 123, 130 – 33, 135c–j.

41 See Appendix, nos. 122 (the Middle Babylonian "Righteous Sufferer" text from Ugarit) and 135p (a fragment of the fifth tablet of the Gilgameš Epic).

42 See Appendix, nos. 133, 135o.

43 See Appendix, nos. 120, 124 – 26, 135 l–n, 135q.

44 See Appendix, nos. 127 – 29.

45 *CTH* 378; cf. M. Weippert, "Aspekte israelitischer Prophetie im Lichte verwandter Erscheinungen des Alten Orients," 297 – 99 and the translation in *COS* 1: 156 – 60 (Gary Beckman) and in I. Singer, *Hittite Prayers* (SBLWAW 11; Atlanta, Ga.: Society of Biblical Literature, 2002) 56 – 69.

46 Emar 373; 379; 383; 406; cf. D. E. Fleming, "*nābû* and *munabbiātu:* Two New Syrian Religious Personnel," *JAOS* 113 (1993) 175 – 83.

47 Nuzi: HSS 13 152.16; 14 149.6 and 14 215.16; Babylonia: *KAR* 460.16; cf. B. Lion, "Les mentions de 'prophètes' dans la seconde moitié du IIᵉ millémaire av. J.-C.," *RA* 94 (2000) 21 – 32.

48 On West Semitic prophetic texts, see Weippert, "Aspekte israelitischer Prophetie im Lichte verwandter Erscheinungen des Alten Orients," 300 – 302; A. Lemaire, "Oracles, politique et littérature dans les royaumes araméens et transjordaniens (IXᵉ – VIIIᵉ s. av. n.è.)," in *Oracles et prophéties dans l'antiquité* (ed. J.-G. Heintz; Paris: De Boccard, 1997) 171 – 93; id., "Prophètes et rois dans les inscriptions ouest-sémitiques (IXᵉ – VIᵉ siècle av. J. C.)," in id. (ed.), *Prophètes et rois* (2001) 85 – 115.

49 Text: A. H. Gardiner, *Late Egyptian Stories* (Bibliotheca Aegyptiana 1; Brussels: La fondation égyptologique reine Élisabeth, 1932) 61 – 76; translation: M. Lichtheim in *COS* 1: 89 – 93 and R. K. Ritner in Nissinen (ed.), *Prophets and Prophecy* (no. 142).

50 Text: *KAI* 202; translation: A. Millard in *COS* 2: 155 and C.-L. Seow in Nissinen (ed.), *Prophets and Prophecy* (no. 137).

of the gods" (*ḥzh 'lhn*),[51] and the roughly contemporary Ammonite Citadel inscription with an oracle of the god Milkom.[52] Finally, Papyrus Amherst 63, an Aramaic text in Demotic script, probably includes a prophetic passage.[53]

6. A Luwian inscription from the late tenth/early ninth century BCE includes a demand of a person belonging to a god (*masanami-*) to erect a statue to the god Tarhunza.[54]

7. Prophecy is even documented in Iron Age Palestine by two or three Lachish ostraca from the late seventh century that mention the word *nb'*[55]—and, without doubt, also by the Hebrew Bible which allegedly contains prophetic words and references to prophecy from the pre-exilic period down to late postexilic times.

In spite of the surprisingly high number of individual extra-biblical texts listed above, it must be admitted that the evidence for prophecy in the ancient Near East is haphazard and uneven, the share of the texts from places other than Mari or (Neo-)Assyria being about one-eighth at best. The vast chronological and geographical distribution of the bits and pieces supplementing the source material from Mari and Assyria is nevertheless impressive, documenting prophetic activity of some kind in different parts of the ancient Near East through the centuries and thus witnessing to an established tradition. Only Egypt is missing from this list; apart from the Report of Wenamon, no Egyptian texts have thus far been identified as prophecy (that is, according to our definition; there are a few texts that have borne this label because they contain predictions of future events[56]). What can be learned from the wide distribution and meager amount of the documents is that it seems to have been a rarity that prophecy was ever written down. This is why we are dependent on the tip of the iceberg that occa-

---

51 Text: J. Hoftijzer and G. van der Kooij, *Aramaic Texts from Deir 'Alla* (DMOA 19; Leiden: Brill, 1976); translation: B. A. Levine in *COS* 2: 140–45 and C.-L. Seow in Nissinen, *Prophets and Prophecy* (no. 138).

52 Text: *CAI* 59; translation: W. E. Aufrecht in *COS* 2: 139 and C.-L. Seow in Nissinen, *Prophets and Prophecy* (no. 136).

53 Translation: R. C. Steiner in *COS* 1: 309–27; the relevant passage (col. vi, ll. 12–18) is treated on p. 313. For a new publication, see K. van der Toorn, *Papyrus Amherst 63* (AOAT 448; Münster: Ugarit-Verlag, 2018).

54 Tell Ahmar 6 §§17–26; see J. D. Hawkins, "The Inscription," in Guy Bunnens, *A New Luwian Stele and the Cult of the Storm-God at Til-Barsib-Masuwari* (Publications de la Mission archéologique de l'Université de Liège en Syrie, Tell Ahmar 2; Leuven: Peeters, 2006) and H. C. Melchert in Nissinen, *Prophets and Prophecy* (no. 143).

55 That is, ostraca 3, 16, and possibly 6; text: *HAE* 412–19, 425–27, 433–34; translation: D. Pardee in *COS* 3: 79–81 and C.-L. Seow in Nissinen, *Prophets and Prophecy* (nos. 139–41).

56 Cf. n. 20.

sionally peeks out from the ocean of the ancient Near Eastern source material. But even these bits and pieces are important because they show that prophecy indeed is attested all over the ancient Near East and thus can be regarded as an established tradition and institution among other forms of divination.

With regard to the Hebrew Bible, the question arises whether everything that is written in the so-called prophetic books should be called prophecy, and, if not, whether or not it is possible to separate the prophetic from the non-prophetic in these writings. These questions are notoriously difficult to address and are open to a methodological debate about the possibility of identifying the "authentic" voice of the prophets, or at least the oldest strata of the prophetic books. This inevitably leads us to our fourth topic, the interpretation of meanings imposed on prophecy in the Hebrew Bible.

Ancient Near Eastern Prophecy—Ancient Hebrew Prophecy—Biblical Prophecy

The ancient Near Eastern records of prophecy have turned out to be indispensable for understanding not only the prophetic phenomenon in general, but also the cultural and conceptual preconditions of prophecy in the Bible. Mainly because of its long and complicated literary history, the Hebrew Bible constitutes a document very different from other ancient Near Eastern prophetic sources. Not only does the interpretative process of the prophetic books of the Hebrew Bible prevent an immediate access to the historical phenomenon of Israelite and Judaean prophecy, it has produced a great deal of fiction as well.

There is no need to contrast extra-biblical "facts" with biblical "fiction", though.[57] It cannot be said that there is no ideology or theology, or even fiction, connected with prophecy in extra-biblical sources. That prophecy could be used as an effective tool for political purposes becomes extremely clear from the documents of Mari and Nineveh. The residual documents of Old Babylonian and Neo-Assyrian prophecy have likewise been preserved only to the extent that they have occasionally been written down and handed down to posterity. This was not done as a matter of routine, but for specific reasons. At Mari as well as in Nineveh, the interpretation of prophecy and the attitudes toward prophets were governed by political, social and personal needs and preferences, hence the viability of prophecy was determined by its ideological expedience.

57 Cf. H. Ringgren, "Israelite Prophecy: Fact or Fiction?," in *Congress Volume Jerusalem 1986* (ed. J. A. Emerton; VTSup 40; Leiden: Brill), 204–10; Barstad, "No Prophets?"

The *ipsissima verba*, that is, the actual spoken words of individual prophets, are as impossible to find in ancient Near Eastern sources as in the Bible. A written prophecy is always scribal work, and it is ultimately beyond our knowledge to determine to what extent the scribe would, or could, transmit the exact wording of the prophecy. The development from oral performance to written record happened under material restrictions and linguistic constraints, and the path from the prophet to the recipient may have been a complicated one.[58] Moreover, the ancient Near Eastern sources include quotations that may be purely literary imitations of prophetic language rather than actually proclaimed prophecies. In this respect, the ancient Near Eastern sources for prophecy are no less enigmatic than the writings of the Hebrew Bible.

Obviously, the problem of *ipsissima verba* emerges from the need to separate the "original" prophecy from "secondary" additions and interpretations. However, it does not seem to have been the primary task of the scribes to conserve the words uttered by the prophets in pristine condition but, rather, to make the messages viable and communicable. A prophecy makes no sense if it does not meet with any response in the audience; hence, it must be intelligible to the addressees.[59] This brings us back to the social dynamic of prophecy, which is not just words from the mouth of the prophet but a process, all components of which are relevant. A prophecy means nothing unless it is understood, interpreted and applied in a specific socio-religious and linguistic environment, whereby interpretation is not a matter of perverting the original words but making the message significant.

What makes the Hebrew Bible a special case is the creative exegetical reinterpretation of prophecy and its application in varying social and ideological circumstances of the Second Temple (both Persian and Hellenistic) period. Admittedly, the Neo-Assyrian sources do reveal the beginnings of a comparable development, but nowhere in the ancient Near Eastern literature are we able to find such an interpretative process lasting for centuries, during which prophe-

---

58 See J. M., Sasson, "Water beneath Straw: Adventures of a Prophetic Phrase in the Mari Archives," in *Solving Riddles and Untying Knots*, FS J. C. Greenfield (ed. Z. Zevit, S. Gitin and M. Sokoloff; Winona Lake, Ind.: Eisenbrauns, 1995) 607; K. van der Toorn, "From the Oral to the Written: The Case of Old Babylonian Prophecy," in Ben Zvi and Floyd (eds.), *Writings and Speech in Israelite and Ancient Near Eastern Prophecy* (2000) 219–34; Nissinen, "Spoken, Written, Quoted and Invented"; cf. Charpin, "Prophètes et rois dans le Proche-Orient amorrite," 31–33; id., "Prophètes et rois dans le Proche-Orient amorrite: Nouvelles données, nouvelles perspectives," 14–16 who reckons with more precise transcriptions of orally delivered prophetic words.

59 Cf. Van der Toorn, From the Oral the the Written," 232–34.

cy was virtually transformed into exegesis and gradually developed into a theological concept.[60]

The biblical conceptualization of prophecy goes hand in hand with the change in the image of the prophet observable in the Hebrew Bible. As a consequence of the religio-political upheavals of the seventh and sixth centuries BCE (the Assyrian hegemony, the destruction of Jerusalem, the Babylonian exile and the rebuilding of the temple), prophecy, among other things, was assessed from a new perspective. Undoubtedly, prophecy continued to exist in the Second Temple period; however, the somewhat wild and precarious quality of prophecy, the real origin of which is beyond any human control, had to be disciplined to meet the requirements of the authoritative theology, or theologies, of that period. It is by no means exceptional as such that prophecy was supposed to conform to the ideology of prevailing religious and political authorities; in Assyria, for example, the prophets were presumed to promote the imperial royal ideology, and it was highly inappropriate to prophesy against the king or the crown prince. In the postexilic Judaean community, again, the Torah became the precept of prophecy, and Moses, the mediator of the Torah, the model for prophets (Deut. 18:15–22).[61]

As a result of the sixth-century socio-religious changes, the image of a prophet underwent a transformation from diviner into preacher. This transformation happened in a creative literary process in which the prophetic inspiration lived on in the work of the scribes.[62] As heirs of Moses and the prophets,[63] the scribes ultimately structured the image, the history and the canon of biblical prophecy and caused not only the image of the prophets, but prophecy itself

---

60 The conceptualization of prophecy is reflected by the word *nĕbûʾâ* in late biblical (Neh. 6:1; 2 Chron. 9:29; 15.8; Sir. 44:3), Qumran and Mishnaic Hebrew; for this term, see A. Hurvitz, "Can Biblical Texts Be Dated Linguistically? Chronological Perspectives in the Historical Study of Biblical Hebrew," in *Congress Volume, Oslo 1998* (ed. A. Lemaire and M. Sæbø; VTSup 53; Leiden: Brill, 2000) 151–52.

61 Cf., e.g., Blenkinsopp, *Sage*, 163–65; and M. Köckert, "Zum literargeschichtlichen Ort des Prophetengesetzes Dtn 18 zwischen dem Jeremiabuch und Dtn 13," in *Liebe und Gebot: Studien zum Deuteronomium*, FS Lothar Perlitt (ed. R. G. Kratz and H. Spieckermann; FRLANT 190; Göttingen: Vandenhoeck & Ruprecht, 2000) 98–100.

62 In German, this phenomenon has been called "prophetische Prophetenauslegung" (O. H. Steck, *Die Prophetenbücher und ihr theologisches Zeugnis* [Tübingen: J. C. B. Mohr, 1996]) or "schriftgelehrte Prophetie" (W. Lau, *Schriftgelehrte Prophetie in Jes 56–66* [BZAW 225; Berlin: de Gruyter, 1994]).

63 For the succession of Moses, the prophets and the scribes, see T. Veijola, *Moses Erben: Studien zum Dekalog, zum Deuteronomismus und zum Schriftgelehrtentum* (BWANT 149; Stuttgart: Kohlhammer, 2000) 216–18.

to become a literary phenomenon and a part of a symbolic universe where different types of religious tradition—Torah, prophecy and wisdom—were joined together as aspects of the scholarly construct of revelation.[64] The literary prophecy also provided the principal channel of expression for the growing eschatological tendency of the Second Temple period, which caused the biblical prophetic literature to become an eschatological composition and paved the way for later apocalypticism.

Since the bloom of literary prophecy eclipses the concrete manifestations of prophecy, it is difficult to know what actually happened to prophetic activity in the Second Temple period. Even without the assumption of the total cessation of prophecy,[65] it seems that the traditional kind of transmission of divine messages declined and became socially marginalized, as implied, for example, by Zech. 13:2–6.[66]

Because of the process described above, the word "prophecy", being used of the concrete phenomenon as well as of its literary interpretation, has an ambiguous character. The pre-exilic Israelite and Judaean prophecy is represented only to the extent that the exilic and postexilic editors of the Hebrew writings have considered it worthy of reinterpreting. In their present form, the prophetic books of the Hebrew Bible document in the first place how earlier prophecy was chosen, edited, interpreted and rewritten to serve the ends of the editors and to correspond with their idea of prophecy and its significance. This inevitably distorts the picture of pre-exilic prophets and their activities, but even the nature of the postexilic prophecy remains faint in concrete terms.

To overcome the difficulties resulting from this ambiguity, it might be helpful to draw a distinction between *ancient Hebrew prophecy* on one hand and *biblical prophecy* on the other. According to this distinction presented here as a working hypothesis, ancient Hebrew prophecy (or: ancient Israelite prophecy, but this designation has the disadvantage of being connected with problems concerning the concept of "ancient Israel") describes the concrete transmission of the divine word in the Hebrew language in ancient Palestine by persons that qualify as prophets, that is, a phenomenon belonging to the context of ancient Near East-

---

64 For the theology of revelation as a scholarly construct in Second Temple Judaism, see K. van der Toorn, "Sources in Heaven: Revelation as a Scholarly Construct in Second Temple Judaism," in Hübner and Knauf (eds.), *Kein Land für sich allein* (2002) 265–77.

65 For contrasting views of whether prophecy actually ceased in the Second Temple period, see F. Greenspahn, "Why Prophecy Ceased?," *JBL* 108 (1989) 37–49; and B. D. Sommer, "Did Prophecy Cease? Evaluating a Reevaluation," *JBL* 115 (1996) 31–47.

66 Cf. D. L. Petersen, *Zechariah 9–14 and Malachi: A Commentary* (OTL; Lousville, Ly.: Westminster John Knox, 1995), 128.

ern prophecy. Biblical prophecy, for its part, is no longer a representative of the "authentic" prophetic phenomenon, but a part of a literary, intertextual system, interwoven with the development of the formation of the Hebrew canon consisting of Torah, Prophets and Writings. In other words, biblical prophecy means prophecy as interpreted by those who created the writings that gradually took the shape of what we call the Hebrew Bible. Within this context, all prophecy in these writings belongs to the category of biblical prophecy, which, however, is historically and literally rooted in ancient Hebrew prophecy. Textual remnants of the latter are likely to be found, if not from deep under the Near Eastern ground, then from the bowels of the biblical text. However, the methodological problem concerning their identification in the latter remains to be solved.

Prophecy and Omen Divination: Two Sides of the Same Coin

Divination is a system of knowledge and belief that serves the purpose of the maintenance of the symbolic universe[1] in a society sharing the conviction that things happening on earth are not coincidental but managed by superhuman agents, reflecting decisions made in the world of gods or spirits. The phenomenon of divination is known from all over the world, including the ancient eastern Mediterranean cultures where it had a fundamental socioreligious significance. "For most Greeks there was no such thing as 'coincidence,'"[2] and the same can be said of ancient Mesopotamians and the Levantine peoples, whose divinatory practices are well documented.[3]

---

1 For the concepts of "symbolic universe" and "universe-maintenance," see P. L. Berger and T. Luckmann, *The Social Construction of Reality: A Treatise in Sociology of Knowledge* (New York: Anchor Books, 1989 [= 1967]) 109–12.

2 M. A. Flower, *The Seer in Ancient Greece* (Berkeley, Calif.: University of California Press, 2008) 108.

3 For recent discussion on divination, in addition to the contributions in the present volume, see J.-G. Heintz (ed.), *Oracles et prophéties dans l'antiquité. Actes du Colloque de Strasbourg, 15–17 Juin 1995* (Université des sciences humaines de Strasbourg, Travaux du Centre de recherche sur le Proche-Orient et la Grèce antiques 15; Paris: de Boccard, 1997) [eastern Mediterranean world]; U. Koch-Westenholz, *Mesopotamian Astrology: An Introduction to Babylonian and Assyrian Celestial Divination* (CNI Publications 19; Copenhagen: Museum Tusculanum Press, 1995); B. Pongratz-Leisten, *Herrschaftswissen in Mesopotamien: Formen der Kommunikation zwischen Gott und König im 2. und 1. Jahrtausend v. Chr.* (SAAS 10; Helsinki: The Neo-Assyrian Text Corpus Project, 1999); A. Guinan, "A Severed Head Laughed: Stories of Divinatory Interpretation," in *Magic and Divination in the Ancient World* (ed. L. Ciraolo and J. Seidel; Ancient Magic and Divination 2; Groningen: Styx, 2002) 7–40; E. Cancik-Kirschbaum, "Prophetismus und Divination: Ein Blick auf die keilschriftlichen Quellen," in *Propheten in Mari, Assyria und Israel* (ed. M. Köckert and M. Nissinen; FRLANT 201; Göttingen: Vandenhoeck & Ruprecht, 2003) 33–53; F. Rochberg, *The Heavenly Writing: Divination, Horoscopy, and Astronomy in Mesopotamian Culture* (Cambridge: Cambridge University Press, 2004) [Mesopotamia]; E. Eidinow, *Oracles, Curses, and Risk among the Ancient Greeks* (Oxford: Oxford University Press, 2007); Flower, *The Seer*; S. I. Johnston, *Ancient Greek Divination* (Blackwell Ancient Religions; Chichester: Wiley-Blackwell, 2008) [Greece]; M. Dietrich and O. Loretz, *Mantik in Ugarit: Keilalphabetische Texte der Opferschau, Omensammlungen, Nekromantie* (ALASP 3; Münster: Ugarit-Verlag, 1990) [Ugarit]; F. H. Cryer, *Divination in Ancient Israel and Its Near Eastern Environment: A Socio-Historical Investigation* (JSOTSup 142; Sheffield: JSOTPress, 1994); A. Jeffers, *Magic and Divination in Ancient Palestine and Syria* (Studies in the History and Culture of the Ancient Near East 8; Leiden: Brill, 1996) [Hebrew Bible]; and D. E. Aune, "'Magic' in Early Christianity and Its Ancient Mediterranean Context: A Survey of Some Recent Scholarship," in *Ancient Christianity and "Magic"/Il cris-*

DOI 10.1515/9783110466546-007

The need for divination is triggered by uncertainty, and its purpose is to become conversant with superhuman knowledge in order to "elicit answers (that is, oracles) to questions beyond the range of ordinary human understanding."[4] Divination tends to be future-oriented, not necessarily in the sense of foretelling future events, but as a method of tackling the anxiety about the insecurity of life and coping with the risk brought about by human ignorance.[5] The rationale behind divination is the belief that a necessary amount of superhuman knowledge is available to humans, especially to those acknowledged by the society as diviners by virtue of their background, education, or behavior. The role of the diviner is essentially that of an intermediary between the human and superhuman worlds.

When mapping different methods of divination, it is customary to break them down into two categories: (1) inductive methods that involve systematization of signs and omens by observing physical objects (extispicy, astrology, bird divination, etc.); and (2) non-inductive or intuitive ones, such as dreams, visions, and prophecy. In the first category, the emphasis is on the cognitive process, while inspiration or possession are seen as typical of the second category.

The distinction between technical and non-technical divination is often traced back to Plato's *Phaedrus* (244a–245a), where Socrates makes the difference between the divinely inspired knowledge based on *mania* "madness" and the divinatory *tekhnē* based on observation and calculation, strongly in favor of the former as a source of divine knowledge: according to his reasoning, *mania* is divinely inspired and therefore superior to a sane mind (*sōphrosynē*), which is only of human origin. Plato's discussion on divination is known by Cicero (*De divinatione* 1.1.1–3) who addresses its significance for philosophical inquiry into the relationship of divine and human worlds, and thus can be considered another harbinger of the modern concept of divination.[6]

Moreover, and perhaps even more fundamentally, the dichotomy of prophecy and divination goes back to the Hebrew Bible, where prophecy is the privileged way of God's communication with humans, while other forms of divination are generally condemned (e. g., Lev 20:6; Deut 18:9–14; Isa 8:19). To be sure, div-

---

tianesimo antico e la "magia" (ed. T. Nicklas and T. J. Kraus; Annali di storia dell'esegesi 24/2; Bologna: Edizioni Dehoniane, 2007) 229–94 [early Christianity].

4 B. Tedlock, "Divination as a Way of Knowing: Embodiment, Visualisation, Narrative, and Interpretation," *Folklore* 112 (2001) 189.

5 For the concept of "risk," see Eidinow, *Oracles*, 13–25.

6 See J. Jacobs, "Traces of the Omen Series *Šumma izbu* in Cicero, *De divinatione*," in *Divination and Interpretation of Signs in the Ancient World* (ed. A. Annus; The Oriental Institute oft he University of Chicago Oriental Institute Seminars 6; Chicago: The Oriental Institute, 2010) 317–39.

ination is not censured altogether: dreams, for instance, do not seem to be denounced, and the divinatory apparatus called urim and thummim is part of the high priest's sacred breastplate (Exod 28:30; Lev 8:8). The elevated status of prophecy is not challenged anywhere in the biblical and early Jewish tradition, however, despite the fact that, for example, the use of Mesopotamian astrology is abundantly evidenced by the Dead Sea Scrolls and the Talmud.[7]

Plato's alleged value judgments and, especially, the outspoken antagonism toward divination in the Jewish and Christian Bible are probably the main reason why the rather depreciating word "superstition" is often used of omen divination, seldom of prophecy. Today, however, many biblical, ancient Near Eastern, and Classical scholars (and I find myself certainly among them) would agree that prophecy should not be contrapositioned with divination but should be seen as one form of it.[8] In my language, the word "prophecy" basically stands for the transmission of allegedly divine knowledge by non-technical means.[9] This definition, based on the technical/non-technical divide, works quite well with regard to biblical and ancient Near Eastern texts, but fluctuates somewhat when applied to Greek sources, as it seems that the Greek seers or prophets could sometimes divine in both ways.[10]

As a scholarly concept, "prophecy" does not cover exactly the semantic field of any divinatory vocabulary in ancient sources, where an exact counterpart to it cannot be found. In Greek, for example, the titles *prophētēs* and *mantis* are used of practitioners of divination of both types,[11] which suggests that the Greeks, Socrates notwithstanding, did not necessarily classify divination according to the technical/non-technical divide. Ancient texts were not written with our definitions in mind, and applying our terminology to ancient cultures and source materials often requires certain terminological flexibility. Anthropological evi-

---

7 See, for example, M. Albani, "Horoscopes in the Qumran Scrolls," in *The Dead Sea Scrolls after Fifty Years: A Comprehensive Assessment*, vol. 2 (ed. P. W. Flint and J. C. VanderKam; Leiden: Brill, 1999) 279–330; J. Ben-Dov and W. Horowitz, "The Babylonian Lunar Three in Calendrical Scrolls from Qumran," *ZA* 95 (2005) 104–20; M. J. Geller, "Deconstructing Talmudic Magic," in *Magic and the Classical Tradition*, ed. C. Burnett and W. F. Ryan; Warburg Institute Colloquia 7; London: The Warburg Institute, 2006) 1–18.

8 Cf. L. L. Grabbe, *Priests, Prophets, Diviners, Sages: A Socio-Historical Study of Religious Specialists in Ancient Israel* (Valley Forge, Pa.: Trinity Press International, 1995) 139–41; A. M. Kitz, "Prophecy as Divination," *CBQ* 65 (2003) 22–42; Cancik-Kirschbaum, "Prophetismus und Divination."

9 M. Nissinen, "What Is Prophecy? An Ancient Near Eastern Perspective," 20–25 (= pp. 57–64 in this volume).

10 Cf. Flower, *The Seer*, 84–91.

11 See ibid., 217–18.

dence of divination points to the same direction: inductive, intuitive, and interpretative techniques easily overlap.[12] Nevertheless, the difference between divinatory techniques remains, leaving the boundaries between prophecy (as defined above) and omen divination as represented by ancient eastern Mediterranean sources worth exploring.

I would like to approach the issue of prophecy and divination with the help of two claims: (1) that prophecy and omen divination are not the same thing, and (2) that they nevertheless belong firmly to the same symbolic universe, that is, to a shared conceptual, intellectual, and ideological world.

Why a Distinction Should be Made Between Prophecy and Omen Divination

To put it simply, the distinction between prophecy and omen divination should be made because most prophets probably had nothing to do with livers of sacrificial animals or with the observation of the movements of stars; to all appearances, prophecy was not a "science" by any definition. There are no traces of features that Seth Richardson found characteristic of extispicy: systematic organization of phenomena, causal association to other repeatable phenomena, creation of extensible theoretical categories, and empirical method in the employment of observation.[13] The prophets were not versed in secret lore in written form, most of them were probably illiterate,[14] and their education and initiation (of which our knowledge is virtually nonexistent[15]) must have been of totally different kind than that of the practitioners of extispicy, astrology, or exorcism.

This is not to say that the prophets were not familiar with the religious language of their communities, or that they had no techniques of accomplishing

---

12 As, for example, the Zulu diviner described by Tedlock ("Divination as a Way of Knowing," 193), who divined through the spirits (intuitive divination), with bones (inductive divination), and with the head (interpretation).

13 S. F. C. Richardson, "On Seeing and Believing: Liver Divination and the Era of Warring States (II)," in Annus (ed.), *Divination and Interpretation of Signs*, 225–66.

14 An illustrative example of this is the letter from Mari (ARM 26 414), in which a prophet has a scribe write down a message to the king; the letter in question has been preserved (ARM 26 194); see D. Charpin, "Prophètes et rois dans le Proche-Orient amorrite: Nouvelles données, nouvelles perspectives," in *Florilegium marianum 6*, FS A. Parrot (ed. D. Charpin and J.-M. Durand; Mémoires de NABU 7; Paris: SEPOA, 2002) 14–15, 29–31.

15 The biblical "call narratives" hide rather than reveal the process of becoming a prophet in ancient Israel and Judah.

their divinatory task. Prophetic oracles were predominantly verbal messages that were believed to be of divine origin, and the language used in them indicates a thorough knowledge of the oral/aural repertoire of the religious communities within which they were produced. The specific techniques of the prophets probably had to do with achieving the altered state of consciousness that enabled them to act as mouthpieces of the divine; heuristic examples of how such techniques of mediation between human and superhuman worlds could have worked are provided by shamanistic rites.[16] The prophetic messages were more often than not accompanied by a characteristic behavior that served as their identity-marker and a cultural signifier that made it possible for the audience to acknowledge their performances as prophetic.[17] Such behavior was evidently not expected of haruspices or astrologers.

Another feature that sets the prophets apart from the diviners of the scholarly type is their social location. While the prophets regularly communicate with kings in our sources, whether Mesopotamian, West Semitic, biblical, or Greek, they usually seem not to have belonged to the innermost circle of the kings who mostly were informed of their sayings through go-betweens. Prophets were clearly not part of the *ummānūtu*. This is not to say that the prophets represented a marginalized group or that their political agency was insignificant; however, the communication between the kings and the prophets is clearly not as intensive as that between kings and the scholars who maintained a regular correspondence with each other both at Mari and in Assyria.[18] As a matter of fact, it is the Hebrew Bible where the prophets and kings get together more often

---

16 See A.-L. Siikala, "The Siberian Shaman's Technique of Ecstasy," in *Studies on Shamanism* (ed. ead. and M. Hoppál; Ethnologica Uralica 2; Helsinki: Finnish Anthropological Society; Budapest: Akadémiai Kiadó, 1992) 26–40. For the interface of shamanism and prophecy, see H. B. Huffmon, "The *assinnum* as Prophet: Shamans at Mari?" in *Nomades et sédentaires dans le Proche-Orient ancien* (ed. C. Nicolle; Amurru 3; Paris: Éditions Recherche sur les Civilisations, 2004) 241–47.

17 For a stereotypical prophetic behavior, see R. R. Wilson, *Prophecy and Society in Ancient Israel* (Philadelphia, Pa.: Fortress Press, 1980) 33–42; Grabbe, *Priests*, 108–12; R. D. Nelson, "Priestly Purity and Prophetic Lunacy: Hosea 1:2–3 and 9:7," in *The Priests in the Prophets: The Portrayal of Priests, Prophets, and Other Religious Specialists in the Latter Prophets* (ed. L. L. Grabbe and A. O. Bellis; JSOTSup 408; London: T & T Clark, 2004) 115–33.

18 Cf. J. M. Sasson, "The Posting of Letters with Divine Messages," in *Florilegium Marianum 2*, FS M. Birot (ed. D. Charpin and J.-M. Durand; Mémoires de NABU 3; Paris: SEPOA, 1994) 299–316; and, with the assumption of a more intensive contact between the prophets and the king, D. Charpin, "Prophètes et rois dans le Proche-Orient amorrite," in *Prophètes et rois: Bible et Proche-Orient* (ed. A. Lemaire; Paris: Cerf, 2001) 34–37.

than anywhere else, the recurrent problems in their mutual appreciation notwithstanding.

Moreover, prophets seem to come from different backgrounds. There were probably persons whose role as a *mahhû*, *raggimu*, *nābîʾ*, *ḥōzê*, *prophētēs*, or *promantis* was more or less permanent, but we also encounter slave girls uttering prophecies,[19] as well as gender-neutral persons called *assinnu*, who feature as prophets several times.[20] The typical venue for prophetic performances is the temple, which suggests that the persons who assumed the prophetic role were more or less closely affiliated with temples, either as members of their personnel or otherwise belonging to the worshipping community. The temples of Annunitum at Mari and Dagan at Terqa, those of Ištar in Arbela and Aššur in Assur, temples of Apollo at Delphi and Didyma, and the temple of Jerusalem are well-known centers of prophetic activity, and the image of a prophet, whether biblical, Near Eastern, or Greek, virtually always shows a temple as the backdrop. This is something that cannot be said of practitioners of extispicy, at least when it comes to the second millennium and later.[21]

In Assyria in particular, prophecy was deeply rooted in the worship of Ištar, and it is probable that the Assyrian prophets were mainly recruited from her devotees.[22] This may, at least in part, explain an intriguing difference in the gestalt of the prophets in contrast with Mesopotamian omen diviners: the prophetic role was open to all sexes: women, men, and the genderless *assinnus*. In Greece, however, the gender distinction was less strict, since there were female seers who also practised technical divination.[23]

A final difference between prophecy and omen divination is that prophecy is basically an oral performance that neither presupposed written texts nor necessarily ever took a written form. This becomes quite evident when we compare the

---

19 E.g., ARM 26 214; SAA 16 59.

20 ARM 26 197; 212; 213; cf. the Assyrian prophets whose gender is ambiguous in SAA 9 1.1; 1.4; 1.5. For the *assinnu* and other Mesopotamian gender-neutral persons, see Huffmon, "The *assinnum* as Prophet"; S. Teppo, "Sacred Marriage and the Devotees of Ištar," in *Sacred Marriages: The Divine-Human Sexual Metaphor from Sumer to Early Christianity* (ed. M. Nissinen and R. Uro; Winona Lake, Ind.: Eisenbrauns, 2008) 75–92; U. Gabbay, "The Akkadian Word for 'Third Gender': The kalû (gala) Once Again," in *Proceedings of the 51st Rencontre Assyriologique Internationale Held at the Oriental Institute of the University of Chicago, July 18–22, 2005* (ed. R. D. Biggs, J. Myers, and M. T. Roth; Studies in Ancient Oriental Civilizations 62; Chicago, Ill.: The Oriental Institute, 2008) 49–56.

21 Cf. Richardson, "On Seeing and Believing".

22 S. Parpola, *Assyrian Prophecies* (SAA 9; Helsinki: Helsinki University Press, 1997) xlvii–xlviii.

23 Flower, *The Seer*, 211–15.

scanty number of written prophetic oracles available to us with the cornucopia of omen compendia and other divinatory texts.

But the very fact that prophecy actually *was* written down, however exceptional this might have been, is the point where the difference between prophecy and omen divination begins to reduce. Namely, when prophecy was written down, it became a document available to scholarly application; for example, the Assyrian scribes could use the prophecies in the archives of Nineveh as sources of their scribal works.[24] The Hebrew Bible, again, reflects a process of the written prophecy becoming literary prophecy through centuries of scribal exegesis especially in Second Temple Judaism.[25] The literary conglomerate of biblical prophecy can, therefore, not be straightforwardly equated with ancient Israelite or Judahite prophecy.

The literarization of prophecy resulted in an authoritative set of texts that were acknowledged as prophecy and used as a basis for further exegesis. This development begins already within the Hebrew Bible and continues in later Second Temple Judaism as demonstrated, for example by the literary phenomenon of the "rewritten Bible,"[26] and by the Dead Sea Scrolls.[27]

It is here that the power of the text with an "esoteric inner coherence"[28] brings prophecy very close to the realm of omen divination. By way of their textuality, even historical events could be interpreted as signs.[29] Especially in the

---

24 The best example of this is Esarhaddon's Nin A inscription, which demonstrably draws on the prophecies uttered on occasion of Esarhaddon's enthronement; see Parpola, *Assyrian Prophecies*, lxxii–lxxiii.

25 See, for example, M. H. Floyd, "The Production of Prophetic Books in the Early Second Temple Period," in *Prophets, Prophecy, and Prophetic Texts in Second Temple Judaism* (ed. id. and R. D. Haak; LHBOTS 427; London: T & T Clark, 2006) 276–97.

26 See the contributions in A. Laato and J. van Ruiten (eds.), *Rewritten Bible Reconsidered: Proceedings of the Conference in Karkku, Finland, August 24–26, 2006* (Studies in Rewritten Bible 1; Turku: Åbo Akademi Press; Winona Lake, Ind.: Eisenbrauns, 2008).

27 See A. P. Jassen, "The Presentation of Ancient Prophets as Lawgivers at Qumran," *JBL* 127 (2008) 307–37; and id., "Prophets and Prophecy in the Qumran Community," *AJS Review* 37 (2008) 299–334.

28 E. Frahm, "Reading the Tablet, the Exta, and the Body: The Hermeneutics of Cuneiform Signs in Babylonian and Assyrian Text in *Divination and Interpretation of Signs* (ed. A. Annus; Oriental Institute Seminars 6; Chicago: Oriental Institute, 2010) 93–141 (96).

29 J. Scurlock, "Prophecy as a Form of Divination, Divination as a Form of Prophecy," in Annus (ed.), *Divination and Interpretation of Signs*, 277–316 (282–83).

Qumran Pesharim, quotations from the prophetic books are used in a way reminiscent of the interpretation of omens.[30]

When prophecy once was written down, it enabled, in Scott Noegel's words, "the exegetical process as an act of performative power that legitimates and promotes the cosmological and ideological systems upon which divination is based."[31] This leads us to my second point:

Why Prophecy and Omen Divination Belong to the Same Symbolic Universe

All differences notwithstanding, it would be wrong to separate prophecy from omen divination in a way that suggests a fundamental disparity in their conceptual, intellectual, and ideological basis. On the contrary, I would like to argue that prophecy and omen divination represent different ways of attaining the same goal, that is, becoming conversant with the divine knowledge and judgment. According to Avi Winitzer, "extispicy, or divination in general, is nothing less than a source of revelation; its product is tantamount to the divinely revealed word";[32] without doubt, the same is true for prophecy. Just as extispicy reports are not to be seen as predictions in the first place but rather as divine judgments,[33] prophecy is not primarily foretelling the future (even though it can be predictive) but proclaiming the divine will at each particular moment, either to an individual or, as is more often than not the case, to the king and through him the whole kingdom.

From a cognitive point of view, represented in this volume by Ulla Koch, prophecy, like any other form of divination, can be seen as a system of making sense of the world, dealing with social or cognitive uncertainty, obtaining other-

---

30 Cf. M. Nissinen, "Pesharim as Divination: Qumran Exegesis, Omen Interpretation and Literary Prophecy," in *On Prophecy in the Dead Sea Scrolls and in the Hebrew Bible* (ed. K. De Troyer and A. Lange; Leuven: Peeters, 2009] 43–60 (= pp. 663–80 in this volume).

31 S. B. Noegel, "'Sign, Sign, Everywhere a Sign': Script, Power, and Interpretation in the Ancient Near East," in Annus (ed.), *Divination and Interpretation of Signs*, 143–62 (143).

32 A. Winitzer, "The Divine Presence and Its Interpretation in Early Mesopotamian Divination," in Annus (ed.), *Divination and Interpretation of Signs*, 177–97 (181); cf. A. Lange, "Interpretation als Offenbarung: Zum Verhältnis von Schriftauslegung und Offenbarung," in *Wisdom and Apocalypticism in the Dead Sea Scrolls and in the Biblical Tradition* (ed. F. García Martínez; BETL 168; Leuven: Peeters, 2003) 17–33.

33 F. Rochberg, "'If P, then Q': Form and Reasoning in Babylonian Divination," in Annus (ed.), *Divination and Interpretation of Signs*, 19–27.

wise inaccessible information and "to get things done, to make things right and to keep them that way."[34]Koch's criteria for a successful divination, that is, the appropriate signs, the strategic social information, and the credibility of the process including the neutrality of the diviner and an acknowledged superhuman agent, are well applicable to the prophetic process of communication; the prophetic process, as such, is usually not *based* on signs, but signs are nevertheless mentioned in prophecies.[35]

Especially in the royal context, divination was the medium through which the king was kept informed of his location within the divinely sanctioned order of the divine favors and obligations and the origin and legitimacy of his rule; this is what Beate Pongratz-Leisten aptly calls *Herrschaftswissen.*[36] It is through divination that the king is revealed "the secrets of the gods," that is, the decisions of the divine council usually proclaimed by the goddess Ištar, such as in the oracle from Ešnunna:

> O king Ibalpiel, thus says Kititum: The secrets of the gods (*niṣrētum ša ili*) are placed before me. Because you constantly pronounce my name with your mouth, I constantly disclose the secrets of the gods to you.[37]

This text, among many others, demonstrates that the prophets and other diviners function as intermediaries and channels of communication for the divine knowledge necessary for the king and country to live in safety and receive divine advice in times of crisis and uncertainty.

Cynthia Jean has provided us with several illuminating cases of the royal use of divination, and the examples could be multiplied.[38] The entire divinatory apparatus was at the king's disposal, and from his point of view it did not matter

---

34 U. S. Koch, "Three Strikes and You're Out! A View on Cognitive Theory and the First-Millennium Extispicy Ritual," in Annus (ed.), *Divination and Interpretation of Signs*, 43–59 (44). Cf. the cognitive approach to the biblical polemic against divination in G. Levy, "The Biblical Polemic against Divination in Light of the Domestication of Folk Psychology" [available at www.csr-arc.com/view.php?arc=6].

35 ARM 26 207:4; 212: 1′; 237:5; 240:4; Isa. 7:11; 8:18; 19:20; 38:7, 22; Jer. 44:29; Ezek. 4:3; 20:12, 20.

36 Pongratz-Leisten, *Herrschaftswissen.*

37 FLP 1674: 3–8; M. deJong Ellis, "The Goddess Kititum Speaks to King Ibalpiel: Oracle Texts from Ishchali," *MARI* 5 (1987) 240.

38 C. Jean, "Divination and Oracles at the Neo-Assyrian Palace: The Importance of Signs In Royal Ideology," in Annus (ed.), *Divination and Interpretation of Signs*, 267–75. Cf. the thorough documentation of the royal-divine communication in Pongratz-Leisten, *Herrschaftswissen*; and ead., "When Gods Are Speaking: Toward Defining the Interface between Polytheism and Monotheism," in *Propheten in Mari, Assyria und Israel* (ed. M. Köckert and M. Nissinen; FRLANT 201; Göttingen: Vandenhoeck & Ruprecht, 2003) 132–68.

whether the divine word came from the mouth of the prophet or an *ummānu*, provided, of course, that these persons were proved to be of accredited background.[39]

The communicative aspect of divination is highlighted by several studies. The human intermediary, the diviner or the prophet, was indeed seen as a member in the imagined chain of divine-human communication, who was there to transmit the divine knowledge. Whatever intellectual capacity was required of the diviner, it was not the diviner's knowledge and wisdom that was handed over to the people but the "secrets of gods" entrusted to him. The mouth of the diviner or prophet was speaking, not words of his or her own but of divine origin.

The role of the diviners as mediators is indicated by the Akkadian phrase *ša pî* "from the mouth": the oral tradition of scholars is referred to as *ša pî ummānī*,[40] the colophons of Assyrian prophecies indicate the speaker with the phrase "*ša pî* man/woman NN from the city X."[41] In a similar vein, the Pythia was the spokesperson (*prophētis*) of Apollo[42] who, in turn, was the *prophētēs* of his father, Zeus;[43] and in the Hebrew Bible, a standard phrase is that the word (*dābār*) of YHWH "came" to the prophet. Hence, the diviner or the prophet was literally a mouthpiece, whose personality, in theory, did not affect the knowledge to be transmitted: "Your great divinity, Šamaš, knows, I, your slave, a diviner, do not know."[44]

Such a "neutral" transmission of messages of superhuman origin was unthinkable without being influenced or inspired, even possessed, by the divine. Prophets, as we saw, were recognized by their characteristic behavior indicating the altered state of consciousness required of anyone speaking divine words; but even in extispicy, the aspect of divine presence is significant.[45] In the words of Alan Lenzi: "the diviner experienced the presence of the divine assembly itself, which had gathered around the victim to write their judgments in the organs of

---

39 This may be one of the reasons why the prophet's name and domicile are mentioned in the colophons of the Neo-Assyrian oracles. Even in the letters from Mari, the origin of the prophecy, if not necessarily the name of the prophet, is usually indicated.

40 See Jean, "Divination and Oracles," and cf. SAA 10 8.

41 See Parpola, *Assyrian Prophecies*, lxiii.

42 Thus Plato, *Phaedrus* 244b; Euripides, *Ion* 321, 1322.

43 Thus Aeschylus, *Eumenides* 17–19; cf. Johnston, *Ancient Greek Divination*, 51; Flower, *The Seer*, 86.

44 W. G. Lambert, *Babylonian Oracle Questions* (Winona Lake, Ind.: Eisenbrauns, 2007): 18:18 and passim.

45 See Winitzer, "Divine Presence."

the animal."[46] While the diviners hardly performed extispicy in an altered state of consciousness comparable to that of the prophets, the credibility of the process required them to be neutral agents inspired by the superhuman agent.[47]

In final analysis, even Plato, whose distinction between inspired and technical divination has been so influential in dividing diviners into technical and inspired ones, recognizes the divine inspiration of the "technical" diviners. In his dialogue with Ion, Socrates juxtaposes the diviners with the poets inspired by the Muses while arguing for the divine origin of poetry (*Ion* 534c–d):

> For not by art does the poet sing, but by power divine; had he learned by rules of art, he would have known how to speak not of one theme only, but of all; and therefore God takes away reason from poets, and uses them as his ministers, as he also uses the pronouncers of oracles and holy prophets (*khrēsmōdois kai tois mantesi tois theiois*), in order that we who hear them may know them to be speaking not of themselves, who utter these priceless words while bereft of reason (*nous mē parestin*), but that God himself is the speaker, and that through them he is addressing us.

---

46 A. Lenzi, *Secrecy and the Gods: Secret Knowledge in Ancient Mesopotamia and Biblical Israel* (SAAS 19; Helsinki: Neo-Assyrian Text Corpus Project, 2008) 55.
47 Flower, *The Seer*, 91.

Neither Prophecies nor Apocalypses: The Akkadian Literary Predictive Texts

The Texts

"Literary predictive texts" is a category proposed by Maria deJong Ellis[1] for a group of Akkadian texts also known as "Akkadian prophecies" or "Akkadian apocalypses". The group comprises the following six texts, of which I use the conventional titles:

1. Text A,[2]
2. Text B,[3]
3. Text C, or the Šulgi Prophecy,[4]
4. Text D, or the Marduk Prophecy,[5]
5. the Uruk Prophecy,[6]
6. the Dynastic Prophecy.[7]

These texts are discussed together[8] because they share a number of distinctive features. They are all post-event predictions (*vaticinia ex eventu*), describing

---

1 M. deJong Ellis, "Observations on Mesopotamian Oracles and Prophetic Texts: Literary and Historiographic Considerations," *JCS* 41 (1989) 127–86, esp. 146–48.

2 *KAR* 421; cf. A. K. Grayson and W. G. Lambert, "Akkadian Prophecies," *JCS* 18 (1964) 7–30, esp. 12–16.

3 Ibid., 16–19. Re-edited with new manuscripts in R. D. Biggs, "More Babylonian 'Prophecies'," *Iraq* 29 (1967) 117–32; cf. the new fragment in id., "Babylonian Prophecies, Astrology, and a New Source for 'Prophecy Text B'," in *Language, Literature, and History: Philological and Historical Studies Presented to Erica Reiner* (ed. F. Rochberg-Halton; AOS 67; New Haven, Conn.: American Oriental Society, 1987) 1–14.

4 Grayson and Lambert, "Akkadian Prophecies," 19–21; re-edited in R. Borger, "Gott Marduk und Gott-König Šulgi als Propheten: Zwei Prophetische Texte," *BO* 28 (1971) 3–24, esp. 14–15, 20–21.

5 Grayson and Lambert, "Akkadian Prophecies," 21–23; re-edited in Borger, "Gott Marduk und Gott-König Šulgi als Propheten," 5–13, 16–20.

6 H. Hunger, *Spätbabylonische Texte aus Uruk*, vol. 1 (Ausgrabungen der Deutschen Forschungsgemeinschaft in Uruk-Warka 9; Berlin: Gebr. Mann, 1976), esp. 21–23; cf. H. Hunger and S. A. Kaufman, "A New Akkadian Prophecy Text," *JAOS* 95 (1975) 371–75.

7 A. K. Grayson, *Babylonian Historical-Literary Texts* (Toronto Semitic Texts and Studies 3; Toronto and Buffalo: University of Toronto Press, 1975), esp. 24–37.

8 The most comprehensive analysis of the texts as a group (excluding Text B) in M. Neujahr, *Predicting the Past in the Ancient Near East: Mantic Historiography in Ancient Mesopotamia,*

DOI 10.1515/9783110466546-008

the reigns of successive kings and characterizing them in positive or negative terms. Their purpose is, evidently, to "justify a current idea or institution or to forecast future doom for a hated enemy".[9] The kings, usually introduced with the phrase "a king (or "prince", *rubû*) will arise", are anonymous and references to them vague enough to yield different interpretations, but the implied reader is probably supposed to catch the intended meaning. With the exception of Texts A and B, the ends of which have not been preserved, the succession of kings culminates in an ideal ruler, a just king, who defeats the enemies, restores the temples, and provides well-being for the land.

With regard to date and provenance, the group falls clearly into two parts. The extant manuscripts of Texts A–D come from Neo-Assyrian archives; fragments of Text B also from Nippur. Seemingly dealing with late-second-millennium kings, the texts have been dated accordingly,[10] but they are equally comprehensible against the background of Neo-Assyrian concerns.[11] On the other hand, the Uruk Prophecy and the Dynastic Prophecy are of Late Babylonian origin,

---

Judah, and in the Mediterranean World (Brown Judaic Studies 354; Providence, R. I.: Broen University, 2012); cf. T. I. Longman *Fictional Akkadian Autobiography: A Generic and Comparative Study* (Winona Lake, IN: Eisenbrauns, 1991) 131–90. For shorter overviews, see J.-G. Heintz, "Note sur les origines de l'apocalyptique judaïque à la lumière des 'prophéties akkadiennes'," in *L'Apocalyptique* (ed. F. Raphael et al.; Etudes d'histoire des religions 3; Paris: Paul Geuthner, 1977) 71–87; R. R. Wilson, *Prophecy and Society in Ancient Israel* (Philadelphia: Fortress Press, 1980), esp. 119–23; H. Ringgren, "Akkadian Apocalypses," in *Apocalypticism in the Mediterranean World and the Near East: Proceedings of the International Colloquium on Apocalypticism, Uppsala, August 12–17, 1979* (ed. D. Hellholm; Tübingen: Mohr Siebeck, 1983) 379–86; J. van Seters, *In Search of History: Historiography in the Ancient World and the Origin of Biblical History* (New Haven, Conn. and London: Yale University Press, 1983), esp. 96–99; J. C. VanderKam, "Prophecy and Apocalyptics in the Ancient Near East," in *CANE* 3 (ed. J. M. Sasson; New York: Scribner, 1995) 2083–94, esp. 2091–94; R. J. Clifford, "The Roots of Apocalypticism in Near Eastern Myth," in *The Encyclopedia of Apocalypticism*, vol. 1: *The Origins of Apocalypticism in Judaism and Christianity* (ed. J. J. Collins; New York: Continuum, 1998) 3–38, esp. 12–14).

9 A. K. Grayson, "Assyria and Babylonia," *Or* 49 (1980) 140–94, esp. 183.

10 The identification of the kings in Text A with the late-second-millennium kings of the Second Isin Dynasty by W. W. Hallo ("Akkadian Apocalypses," *IEJ* 16 [1966] 231–42, esp. 235–39), is rejected by W. G. Lambert (*The Background of Jewish Apocalyptic* [The Ethel M. Wood Lecture delivered before the University of London on 22 February 1977; London: The Athlone Press, 1978], esp. 18 n. 13) but followed by Longman (*Fictional Akkadian Autobiography*, 154–62). The dating of the Marduk and Šulgi Prophecies to the same period by Borger ("Gott Marduk und Gott-König Šulgi als Propheten," 21–23), is generally accepted. Text B is virtually undatable.

11 See W. Mayer, "Der babylonische Feldzug Tukulti-Ninurtas I. von Assyrien," *SEL* 5 (1988) 143–61, esp. 154–57.

clearly reflecting the political history of the Hellenistic era.[12] Whether the texts represent a text class of their own remains a matter of dispute. Text B is often dissociated from the group as differing too much from the others,[13] but there are differences between the remaining texts as well. The sequences of rulers and their reigns do not follow a set pattern. The Marduk and Šulgi Prophecies, belonging to the same series,[14] are written in the first person in a style akin to royal autobiographies, while the others are written in the third person. Unlike the Late Babylonian texts, the Neo-Assyrian compositions include mythological elements, especially the Marduk and Šulgi Prophecies, which are cast as being spoken before the divine council.[15]

A further question is the relation of the texts to other genres in cuneiform literature. It was observed long ago that they owe much to astrological omen literature, especially Text B which, in fact, is composed of omen apodoses and has exact parallels in astrological texts.[16] Text A is also full of related associations, and, at least to some extent, this is true for the other texts as well.[17] Since the literary predictive texts cannot be shown to go back to concrete divinatory activities of any kind, it is likely that the relationship between them and astrological omens is a literary one. Evidently, the authors of the literary predictive texts used

---

12 For the Seleucid date of the Dynastic Prophecy, see Grayson (*Babylonian Historical-Literary Texts*, 24–27). As to the Uruk Prophecy, Hunger and Kaufman ("A New Akkadian Prophecy Text") identified the tenth king who returns the gods and renews the city of Uruk with Nebuchadnezzar II (605–562). Alternative proposals have been made by Lambert (*The Background of Jewish Apocalyptic*, 10–12) (Nabopolassar) and J. A. Goldstein ("The Historical Setting of the Uruk Prophecy," *JNES* 47 (1988) 43–46) (Merodach-Baladan II). The setting proposed by Hunger and Kaufman is substantiated by P.-A. Beaulieu ("The Historical Background of the Uruk Prophecy," in *The Tablet and the Scroll*, FS W. W. Hallo [ed. M. E. Cohen, D. C. Snell and D. B. Weisberg; Bethesda, MD: CDL Press, 1993] 41–52), who dates the text to the first half of the third century BCE.

13 Thus, e.g., W. G. Lambert ("History and the Gods: A Review Article," *Or* 39 [1970] 170–77, esp. 175–76); Borger ("Gott Marduk und Gott-König Šulgi als Propheten," 23); Grayson (*Babylonian Historical-Literary Texts*, 15) and many others. Cf. however, R. D. Biggs, "Mesopotamia," *JCS* 37 (1985) 86–90; "Babylonian Prophecies, Astrology"; and "The Babylonian Prophecies," *Bulletin of the Canadian Society for Mesopotamian Studies* 23 (1992) 17–20, esp. 19.

14 This is indicated by the catch-line 'I am Šulgi at the end of the Marduk Prophecy (Borger, "Gott Marduk und Gott-König Šulgi als Propheten," 13 iv 16).

15 See Longman, *Fictional Akkadian Autobiography*, 183.

16 As noted by B. Pongratz-Leisten (*Herrschaftswissen in Mesopotamien: Formen der Kommunikation zwischen Gott und König im 2. und 1. Jahrtausend v. Chr.* [SAAS 10; Helsinki: The Neo-Assyrian Text Corpus Project, 1999], esp. 53), SAA 8 459 r. 5–6 corresponds to Text B, line 16 and SAA 8 459 r. 29 to Text B, line 29.

17 See Biggs, "Mesopotamia"; "Babylonian Prophecies, Astrology".

topoi and phraseology typical of omen literature to lend credibility for their reconstruction of the succession of events, cast in the form of prediction. The pattern for the chronological reconstruction, again, seems to come from chronographic literature, as represented, for instance, by the Weidner Chronicle,[18] Chronicle P,[19] and the Late Babylonian chronicle *SpTU* 1 2.[20] This literature provides a model for the periodization of events according to the reigns of successive kings, while the so-called pseudo-autobiographies[21] epitomize the first-person account employed in the Marduk and Šulgi Prophecies.

The Genre Trouble

Texts A-D were published by A. K. Grayson and W. G. Lambert in 1964 under the title "Akkadian prophecies"[22] and have persistently borne this designation ever since, even though it has not been welcomed with unanimous approval. Soon after their publication, W. W. Hallo proposed to rename the texts "Akkadian apocalypses",[23] eliciting a response in many studies to come. Both designations are still in use, though the use of different labels does not necessarily indicate major disagreements in the literary or historical interpretation of the texts. All studies that I am aware of agree that they are post-event predictions with a more or less specific, though not always unambiguous, historical setting and purpose. The issue is rather, how these texts relate to other sources that are called prophecies or apocalypses, that is, whether or not the Akkadian texts fit into conventional categories.

Before going into the reasons for the use or non-use of "prophecies" or "apocalypses" as designations of the Akkadian texts, it is worth noting that these words have been used with a conspicuous dissatisfaction, often appearing

---

18 A. K. Grayson, *Assyrian and Babylonian Chronicles* (TCS 5; Locust Valley, N. Y.: J. J. Augustin, 1975), esp. 145–51; for the new edition, see F. N. H. Al-Rawi, "Tablets from the Sippar Library I. The 'Weidner Chronicle': A Suppostitious Royal Letter Concerning a Vision," *Iraq* 52 (1990) 1–13.
19 Grayson, *Assyrian and Babylonian Chronicles*, 170–77; cf. Mayer, "Der babylonische Feldzug Tukulti-Ninurtas I. von Assyrien," 153–57.
20 Hunger, *Spätbabylonische Texte aus Uruk*, 19–20; cf. Beaulieu, "The Historical Background of the Uruk Prophecy," 50.
21 For these, see H. D. Galter, "Probleme historisch-lehrhafter Dichtung in Mesopotamien," in *Keilschriftliche Literaturen: Ausgewählte Vorträge der XXXII. Rencontre Assyriologique International, Münster, 8.–12.7.1985* (ed. K. Hecker and W. Sommerfeld; Berliner Beiträge zum Vorderen Orient 6; Berlin: Dietrich Reimer, 1986), 71–79, and Longman, *Fictional Akkadian Autobiography*.
22 Grayson and Lambert, "Akkadian Prophecies," 7.
23 Hallo, "Akkadian Apocalypses," 240.

in quotation marks, as if the texts thus designated were no unadulterated representatives of the respective text classes. In classifications of Akkadian literature, they have been treated as a subgenre of "historical-literary texts"[24] or "pseudoautobiographies",[25] using "prophecy" or "apocalypse" as descriptive headings rather than genre specifications. Suggestions have been made to give them up altogether, most notably by Ellis who prefers to avoid confusion by calling them "literary predictive texts".[26] Ellis's contribution is important in raising the question of whether the texts have been forcibly adapted to conventional genres into which they simply do not fit.

Some critical scholars have underscored that the texts do not necessarily form a single literary genre at all.[27] Moreover, it should not be forgotten that prophecy and apocalypticism are ultimately modern categories anachronistically applied to ancient documents in which this classification is inherent only to some extent or not at all. It is necessary to realize that as names of literary genres, prophecy and apocalypse are constructs of academic society, created to fulfill its needs. Such labels, rather than reflecting how things actually were, demonstrate how we want to make them fit the big puzzle we are trying to solve; in other words, definitions of prophecy and apocalypticism are constructions that create rather than describe reality. There is nothing wrong with this, though. We need terminology to work with and we also need to agree how to use it, recognizing the hidden presumptions that may steer our choice of words.[28] Therefore, it is quite sensible to survey the frontiers between and around prophecy and apocalypticism, even though it may be appropriate to speak of them as objectivized fictions rather than universally existing entities.

It is also true that prophecy and apocalypticism are not just artificial constructions without any historical basis. The terminology involving the Greek word families *prophēteia* and *apokalypsis* dates back to ancient times, even though these words were introduced only after the respective phenomena had

---

24 Grayson, *Babylonian Historical-Literary Texts*, 4–9; "Assyria and Babylonia," 182–88.

25 Longman, *Fictional Akkadian Autobiography*, 163–90. Longman interprets even the third-person accounts in Text A and in the Uruk Prophecy and the Dynastic Prophecy as autobiographies.

26 M. deJong Ellis, "Observations on Mesopotamian Oracles and Prophetic Texts: Literary and Historiographic Considerations," *JCS* 41 (1989) 127–86, esp. 148.

27 E.g., S. A. Kaufman, "Prediction, Prophecy, and Apocalypse in the Light of New Akkadian Texts," in *Proceedings of the Sixth World Congress of Jewish Studies*, vol. 1 (ed. A. Shinan; Jerusalem: World Union of Jewish Studies, 1977) 221–28, esp. 225–26 and van Seters, *In Search of History*, 99. Cf. Ellis's analysis of the scholarly development of this text class and her deliberations on their classification and genre labelling ("Observations on Mesopotamian Oracles and Prophetic Texts," 148–65).

28 Cf. ibid., 132–33.

been in existence for centuries.[29] Modern anachronisms may, hence, be based on ancient anachronisms, but this does not invalidate the fact that the phenomena, more or less successfully designated with the words "prophecy" and "apocalypticism", indisputably existed.

Why Not Prophecies?

When Grayson and Lambert published Texts A-D, they introduced them as "prophecies", thus abandoning earlier labels (e. g. "*narû*-literature"),[30] but without giving explicit reasons for the use of this designation. No conclusive arguments can be found in subsequent studies either, but it becomes obvious that the word is chosen because the texts predict, or pretend to predict, future events, and the word 'prophecy' is understood as a synonym of "prediction".[31]

The equation of prophecy with prediction has often been deemed ill-advised, however. As Hallo instantly remarked, prediction is not the principal business of biblical prophecy,[32] and even some extra-biblical texts are called prophecies for reasons other than their predictive quality. According to a widely accepted definition, a prophet is primarily an intermediary who transmits allegedly divine messages to human recipients.[33]

Prophecy, hence, is understood as a process of communication, involving a divine speaker and a message (that may or may not include predictions) to be

---

29 For *apokalypsis*, see M. Smith ("On the History of ΑΠΟΚΑΛΥΠΤΩ and ΑΠΟΚΑΛΥΨΙΣ," in Apocalypticism in the Mediterranean World and the Near East: Proceedings of the International Colloquium on Apocalypticism, Uppsala, August 12–17, 1979 [ed. D. Hellholm; Tübingen: Mohr Siebeck, 1983] 9–20), according to whom apocalypses carried this title from the very late first or early second century CE onwards.

30 Grayson and Lambert, "Akkadian Prophecies," 8. The designation "*narû*-literature" comes from H. G. Güterbock, "Die historische Tradition und ihre literarische Gestaltung bei Babyloniern und Hethitern bis 1200," *ZA* 42 (1934) 1–91, esp. 19–21.

31 Thus Biggs, "More Babylonian 'Prophecies'," 118: 'The rest of the main text [B] consists only of line after line of predications (i. e., omen apodoses), whence the characterization of the text as a prophecy'.

32 Hallo, "Akkadian Apocalypses," 233–34.

33 The transmission as the principal quality of prophecy has been emphasized by, e. g., H. B. Huffmon, "Ancient Near Eastern Prophecy," *ABD* 5 (1992) 477–82 (esp. 477); M. Weippert, "Prophetie im Alten Orient," *NBL* 3 (1997) 196–200 (esp. 197); M. Nissinen, *References to Prophecy in Neo-Assyrian Sources* (SAAS 7; Helsinki: The Neo-Assyrian Text Corpus Project, 1998), 5; and D. L. Petersen, "Defining Prophecy and Prophetic Literature," in *Prophecy in its Ancient Near Eastern Context: Mesopotamian, Biblical, and Arabian Perspectives* (ed. M. Nissinen; SBLSymS 13; Atlanta, Ga.: Society of Biblical Literature, 2000) 33–44, esp. 44.

delivered to a recipient or recipients by the prophet. This is also a basic meaning of the word family profeteia (*prophēteia*) in Classical Greek[34]—a word that the translators of the Septuagint chose as the principal reading of the Hebrew word family *(nābî')*, laying the foundations of our terminology. But the activity thus designated is not restricted to biblical environments. It is well known from all over the ancient Near East, as demonstrated by the prophecies quoted in Mari letters,[35] the oracles from Ešnunna,[36] the Neo-Assyrian oracles to Esarhaddon and Assurbanipal,[37] and some West Semitic equivalents, such as the Deir 'Alla inscription[38] and the oracle quoted in the Zakkur Inscription.[39]

Therefore, characterizing the literary predictive texts as prophecies is problematic not only, or even primarily, from the biblical point of view but also because there are texts that, while belonging to a clearly distinct genre, bear this designation on other—and better—grounds. Nobody denies the dissimilarity of, say, the Neo-Assyrian prophetic oracles and the contemporaneous literary predictive Texts A–D, but the attempts to make the distinction on a terminological level have led to confusing results. For instance, Grayson named "Akkadian oracles" the texts that today are usually known as "Assyrian prophecies", whereas he used the name "Akkadian prophecies" for literary predictive texts.[40] The German language yields the designations "Prophetien" (prophecies) and "Prophezeiungen" (predictions) respectively.[41]

The main difference between the texts is that the Akkadian literary predictive texts are literary from the beginning and, thus, clearly distinct from the Mesopotamian oracles. The literary predictive texts are not the product of a process of communication ensuing from an oral performance. The Marduk and Šulgi Prophecies do have a divine or deified speaker, but other components of the pro-

---

34 See *LSJ* 1539.

35 J.-M. Durand, *Archives épistolaires de Mari I/1* (ARM 26/1; Paris: Éditions Recherches sur les Civilisations, 1988), esp. 421–82.

36 M. deJong Ellis, "The Goddess Kititum Speaks to King Ibalpiel: Oracle Texts from Ishchali," MARI 5 (1987) 235–66.

37 S. Parpola, *Assyrian Prophecies* (SAA 9; Helsinki: Helsinki University Press, 1997).

38 J. Hoftijzer and G. van der Kooij, *Aramaic Texts from Deir 'Alla* (DMOA 19; Leiden: Brill, 1976).

39 *KAI* 202; see the translation and discussion in H. Donner and W. Röllig, *Kanaanäische und aramäische Inschriften*, vol. 2: *Kommentar* (Wiesbaden: Harrassowitz, [3]1973), esp. 204–11.

40 Grayson, *Babylonian Historical-Literary Texts*, 13–15.

41 Cf. M. Weippert, "Assyrische Prophetien der Zeit Asarhaddons und Assurbanipals," in *Assyrian Royal Inscriptions: New Horizons in Literary, Ideological, and Historical Analysis* (ed. F. M. Fales; Orientis Antiqui Collectio 17; Rome: Istituto per L'Oriente, 1981) 71–115, esp. 71–72; cf. W. Röllig, "Literatur § 4: Überblick über die akkadische Literatur," *RLA* 7 (1987/90) 48–66, esp. 65.

phetic process are not conclusive.[42] There is no intermediary, that is, prophet, involved, and the texts are not written in the form of a message addressed to a particular person or people. In other words: the literary predictive texts do not fit the construction of prophecy based on the idea of communication and intermediation.

Even when it comes to the written appearance, the literary predictive texts diverge considerably from the prophecies from Mari and Nineveh, both in terms of form and language. Rather than consisting of short oracles, originally written down individually on small tablets, they introduce long sequences of texts that form original units and can only have been authored by scribes well versed in scholarly tradition. On the other hand, the language of the literary predictive texts seems to draw from the repertoire of omen literature[43] and chronographic texts,[44] whereas the language of the prophecies—at least in the case of Assyria—owes much to royal and cultic poetry and mystical literature.[45]

The terminological distinction should not, however, lead to a total separation of the sources. As Lester Grabbe has emphasized, the fact that the literary predictive texts are literary does not set them categorically apart from prophecies, which in the Hebrew Bible (and probably in some extra-biblical sources as well) are often purely literary creations.[46] The prophetic process of communication was continued on a scribal and interpretative level throughout the Second Temple period down to Hellenistic times, so that the literary interpretation of written Hebrew prophecy not only surpassed oral communication of divine messages,[47] but also took on an increasingly future-oriented and eschatological tone.[48]

---

42 The deified king Šulgi presents himself, admittedly, as a mediator of the divine council, but, rather than appearing as a prophet, he assumes the role of a privy, similar to that of Ištar in the Ešnunna oracle (FLP 1674; see Ellis, "The Goddess Kititum Speaks to King Ibalpiel," 256).

43 See Biggs, "Mesopotamia"; "Babylonian Prophecies, Astrology"; Ellis, "Observations on Mesopotamian Oracles and Prophetic Texts," 159.

44 See Beaulieu, "The Historical Background of the Uruk Prophecy," 50; Ellis "Observations on Mesopotamian Oracles and Prophetic Texts," 160.

45 See Parpola, *Assyrian Prophecies*, xlvii–xlviii; Nissinen, "The Socioreligious Role of the Neo-Assyrian Prophets," in *Prophecy in its Ancient Near Eastern Context: Mesopotamian, Biblical, and Arabian Perspectives* (ed. id.; SBLSymS 13; Atlanta, Ga.: Society of Biblical Literature, 2000) 89–114 (esp. 97–98) (= pp. 103–26 in this volume).

46 L. L. Grabbe, *Priests, Prophets, Diviners, Sages: A Socio-Historical Study of Religious Specialists in Ancient Israel* (Valley Forge, Pa.: Trinity Press International, 1995), 94.

47 Cf. the respective statements of J. Barton, *Oracles of God: Perceptions of Ancient Prophecy in Israel after the Exile* (London: Darton, Longman & Todd, 1986), 197: "Indeed, it is tempting to say that the gift of interpreting prophecies is a *higher* gift than that required to deliver them in the

An unmistakable affinity between biblical prophecy and the literary predictive texts is the expectation of the ideal king and the *Heilszeit* under his rule. The comparison between the literary predictive texts and some messianic oracles of the Hebrew Bible, for example Jer 23:5–6 and Zech 6:12–13, reveals enough common elements to demonstrate a similar kind of expectation of a beatific time in a more or less distant future, characterized by well-being of the land, defeat of its enemies and perfect maintenance of the temples under the reign of a just and righteous king.[49]

The Akkadian literary predictive texts do not even pretend to trace their origin back to spoken prophecy. Nevertheless, they sometimes make common cause with prophecies, when it comes to the "concern to indicate correct and legitimate action".[50] The best example of such concern is the restoration of temples. The reestablishment of the cult of Marduk and other gods of Babylon after the destruction by Sennacherib in 689 was vehemently propagated by Assyrian prophetic oracles,[51] and the use of the Marduk Prophecy and the Šulgi Prophecy in the Neo-Assyrian period evidently had the same objective. Indeed, the question arises whether these texts, disguised as predictions from early times, were actually composed in that period to undermine the contemporary religio-political propaganda.[52]

---

first place"; and S. A. Geller, *Sacred Enigmas: Literary Religion in the Hebrew Bible* (London and New York: Routledge, 1996), 111: "Past seers, who have become sacred text, are canonical; future ones are to be viewed with such caution as to preclude any respect for them... Living prophecy is demoted to a phenomenon of popular religion, the source of vulgar fancies and passions of the moment, which are to be controlled and, one suspects, excluded."

48 For this development, see, e.g., O. Kaiser, *Der Gott des Alten Testaments: Theologie des Alten Testaments*, vol. 1: *Grundlegung* (Uni-Taschenbücher 1747; Göttingen: Vandenhoeck & Ruprecht, 1993), 231–62.

49 For this aspect from the perspective of the Uruk Prophecy, see P. Höffken, "Heilszeitherrschererwartung im babylonischen Raum: Überlegungen im Anschluß an W 22 307.7," *WO* 9 (1977) 57–71; Beaulieu, "The Historical Background of the Uruk Prophecy," 51.

50 Ellis, "Observations on Mesopotamian Oracles and Prophetic Texts," 178.

51 See M. Nissinen, "City as Lofty as Heaven: Arbela and Other Cities in Neo-Assyrian Prophecy," in *'Every City Shall Be Forsaken': Urbanism and Prophecy in Ancient Israel and the Near East* (ed. L. L. Grabbe and R. D. Haak; JSOTSup 330; Sheffield: Sheffield Academic Press, 2001) 172–309, esp. 195–201 (= pp. 267–300 in this volume).

52 Cf. Mayer, "Der babylonische Feldzug Tukulti-Ninurtas I. von Assyrien," 157; id., *Politik und Kriegskunst der Assyrer* (ALASP 9; Münster: Ugarit-Verlag, 1995), 230.

Why Not Apocalypses?

While "prophecy" turns out to be loaded with problems as a designation for the Akkadian literary predictive texts, there are plenty of features that suggest a relation with apocalypses, particularly with those of historical type. Especially the "king-will-arise" pattern is palpably similar to Dan 8:23–25 and 11:3–45. This led Lambert to conclude that Babylonian material was consciously adapted by the author of the book of Daniel,[53] and many others acknowledge the relevance of the literary predictive texts to apocalyptic literature even without the assumption of a direct dependence.[54]

Some would take the literary predictive texts as belonging to an early stage in the development of apocalypticism, while others find it sufficient to talk about them as providing "some of the stones out of which the structure of apocalypticism is built up".[55]

In addition to the "king-will-arise" pattern, the commonalities include the post-factum prediction, the periodization of the past as a sequence of kings whose reigns are either good or bad, anonymity and vague historical allusions, and the utilization of mantic wisdom. Even the esoteric element (cf. Dan 12:10) is there: the Dynastic Prophecy is the only one that certainly has a "secrecy colophon", according to which it may be shown to an initiated audience only,[56] but the intentionally ambiguous form of expression in other texts as well suggests that a certain interpretative apparatus is required of the implied reader-

---

53 Lambert, *The Background of Jewish Apocalyptic*, 13–17; similarly already Hallo ("Akkadian Apocalypses"), Heintz ("Note sur les origines de l'apocalyptique judaïque") and recently E. C. Lucas ("Daniel: Resolving the Enigma," *VT* 50 [2000] 66–80, esp. 73–76). Unfortunately, the dissertation of Lucas, "Akkadian Prophecies, Omens and Myths as Background for Daniel Chapters 7–12" (unpublished PhD Dissertation, University of Liverpool, 1989) was not accessible to me.

54 E.g., Grayson, *Babylonian Historical-Literary Texts*, 20–22; "Assyria and Babylonia," 184; J. D. Thomas, "Jewish Apocalyptic and the Comparative Method," in *Scripture in Context: Essays on the Comparative Method* (ed. C. D. Evans, W. W. Hallo, and J. B. White; PTMS 34; Pittsburgh, Pa.: Pickwick, 1980) 245–62, esp. 256; Longman, *Fictional Akkadian Autobiography*, 167–78; Beaulieu, "The Historical Background of the Uruk Prophecy," 50–51; Clifford, "The Roots of Apocalypticism in Near Eastern Myth," 12; VanderKam, "Prophecy and Apocalyptics in the Ancient Near East," 2094; J. J. Collins, *The Apocalyptic Imagination: An Introduction to Jewish Apocalyptic Literature* (Grand Rapids, Mich.: Eerdmans, ^{2}1998), 26–29, 96–98. Cf. the reservations of Kaufman, "Prediction, Prophecy, and Apocalypse," 225–27; Goldstein, "The Historical Setting of the Uruk Prophecy," 44; Biggs, "The Babylonian Prophecies," 18.

55 Ringgren, "Akkadian Apocalypses," 386.

56 Cf. Grayson, *Babylonian Historical-Literary Texts*, 36 iv 7–9; Lucas, "Daniel: Resolving the Enigma," 74–75.

ship. Sometimes the texts share certain features with apocalypses but not necessarily with each other. For instance, the two predictions formulated in the first person give the impression of being revelations of Marduk as the head and Šulgi as the privy of the divine council;[57] other texts do not include such heavenly scenes.

All this demonstrates conclusively that the authors of the Akkadian literary predictive texts drew on a reservoir of chronographic and divinatory material and literary devices similar to that utilized by the apocalyptic authors. Does this, however, provide sufficient reason to call them apocalypses? Most studies give a negative answer, mainly because of a different eschatology.[58] While the apocalyptic scenario includes a cosmic threat, a cataclysmic end of this world as a result of a divine judgment, the literary predictive texts contemplate a this-worldly future under an ideal but mundane ruler. In the Marduk Prophecy and the Šulgi Prophecy there is hardly any eschatology at all, since they predict a good king to appear in the near future. In the Neo-Assyrian environment this king would have been identified with the present ruler, Esarhaddon or Assurbanipal.

If the transcendent eschatology which involves divine judgment and retribution beyond the bounds of time is to be seen as a fundamental element of the worldview of apocalypticism and apocalyptic literature, then it is clear that the Akkadian literary predictive texts cannot be appropriately labeled apocalypses. Nevertheless, it deserves attention that the Uruk Prophecy and the Dynastic Prophecy, deriving from the third century BCE, belong to the Hellenistic milieu and are neither chronologically nor culturally too distant from emergent apocalypticism. Without assuming any genealogies or common concrete goals between apocalypses and literary predictive texts, it is easy to recognize similar methods and objectives of an intellectual scribal work on both sides. Many of these—periodization, pseudepigraphy, post-event prediction—are in accord with Hellenistic motifs, reflecting the change of sociopolitical circumstances in the Near East;[59] similar ideas and conceptions are observable also in a number of contemporary Egyptian texts also sometimes called "apocalypses".[60]

---

57 Cf. Longman, *Fictional Akkadian Autobiography*, 182–83.

58 E.g., Lambert, "History and the Gods," 176–77; Borger, "Gott Marduk und Gott-König Šulgi als Propheten," 24; Kaufman, "Prediction, Prophecy, and Apocalypse," 226; Clifford, "The Roots of Apocalypticism in Near Eastern Myth," 14.

59 Cf. Collins, *The Apocalyptic Imagination*, 33–37; Beaulieu, "The Historical Background of the Uruk Prophecy," 51–52.

60 For these texts (The Demotic Chronicle, The Lamb to Bocchoris, The Potter's Oracle, The Admonitions of Ipuwer, The Prophecies of Neferti, etc.), see Wilson, *Prophecy and Society*, 124–28;

What Difference Does It Make?—Conclusion

While both "prophecy" and "apocalypse" have shown themselves inadequate as a common designation for the group of Akkadian texts, Maria deJong Ellis's suggestion to call them "literary predictive texts" is ingenious and satisfactory for further use, especially because it is a correct description of the main characteristics of the texts without forcing them into a fixed literary genre. Moreover, the two keywords of this title—"literary" and "predictive"—associate the texts with both prophecies and apocalypses.

Being neither prophecies nor apocalypses according to our definitions, the Akkadian literary predictive texts share important features with both—especially, and interestingly, two things that prophecies and apocalypses have in common. The first is the orientation towards the future, which in the course of time became an essential quality of biblical prophetic literature. While apocalypses go further in their eschatology, bringing this world to a cataclysmic end, both biblical prophecies and the Akkadian literary predictive texts contemplate a beatific future under an ideal king's rule. Secondly, all three forms of literature build upon earlier literary tradition (omens, prophecies, chronographic and wisdom literature), manifesting the intellectual contribution of the anonymous scribes. It is precisely the increasingly literary and predictive quality of biblical prophecy that creates the association between the texts. The literalization, "sapientialization"[61] and eschatologization of the biblical prophecy, especially when it comes to texts that are characterized as "proto-apocalyptic",[62] paves the way for the apocalyptic mode of expression, blurring the muchdebated borderline between prophecy and apocalypticism.

The Hellenistic era is clearly the cultural and historical point of convergence, where biblical prophecy, emergent apocalypticism and the Akkadian literary pre-

J. G. Griffiths, "Apocalyptic in the Hellenistic Era," in *Apocalypticism in the Mediterranean World and the Near East: Proceedings of the International Colloquium on Apocalypticism, Uppsala, August 12–17, 1979* (ed. D. Hellholm; Tübingen: Mohr Siebeck, 1983) 273–93; D. Devauchelle, "Les prophéties en Egypte ancienne," in *Prophéties et oracles*, vol. 2: *En Égypte et en Grèce* (ed. J. Asurmendi, D. Devauchelle, R. Lebrun, A. Motte, and C. Perrot; Supplément au Cahier Evangile 89; Paris: Cerf, 1994) 6–30.

61 For the "sapientialization" of prophecy, see M. Sæbø, "Old Testament Apocalyptic and its Relation to Prophecy and Wisdom: The View of Gerhard von Rad Reconsidered," in *In the Last Days: On Jewish and Christian Apocalyptic and its Period*, FS B. Otzen (ed. K. Jeppesen, K. Nielsen, and B. Rosendal; Arhus: Aarhus University Press, 1994) 78–91, esp. 85–91.

62 See S. L. Cook, *Prophecy and Apocalypticism: The Postexilic Social Setting* (Minneapolis, Minn.: Fortress Press, 1995).

dictive tradition are observable in the same historical milieu. We may talk about stones of the same building, or, rather, stones from the same quarry belonging to different buildings. The texts demonstrate that at that time, both Jewish and Babylonian learned circles made sense of their present sociopolitical circumstances by means of rereading and literary interpretation of divinatory and chronographic literature under the influence of their respective traditions and the "Hellenistic mood".

Part Two: **Prophecy in the Ancient Near East**

The Socioreligious Role of the Neo-Assyrian Prophets

The Neo-Assyrian Evidence for Prophets and Prophecy

The Neo-Assyrian evidence for prophecy consists of documents of two kinds: the twenty-nine oracles included in the eleven tablets published recently by Simo Parpola,[1] and the haphazard collection of miscellaneous sources consisting of about thirty texts—inscriptions, letters, administrative documents, cultic and literary texts, and a treaty—that allude in one way or another to prophets or their sayings, most of which are included in my monograph devoted to these sources.[2] Neo-Assyrian documentation of prophecy provides essential insight into the role and image of the prophets as religious specialists and members of the community, and is relevant to our understanding of ancient Near Eastern prophecy as well as of Neo-Assyrian society and religion.

The Assyrian Prophets: *maḫḫû* and *raggimu*

Basic aspects of the socioreligious role of the Assyrian prophets can be learned from the Neo-Assyrian words for "prophet," *maḫḫû/maḫḫūtu* and *raggimu/raggintu*.[3] The word *maḫḫû/maḫḫūtu* is equal to *muḫḫûm/muḫḫūtum* ([MÍ.]LÚ.GUB.BA), which is one of the most common prophetic designations at

---

1 S. Parpola, *Assyrian Prophecies* (SAA 9; Helsinki: Helsinki University Press, 1997).
2 M. Nissinen, *Ancient Prophecy: Near Eastern, Biblical, and Greek Perspectives* (Oxford: Oxford University Press, 2017); cf. id., *References to Prophecy in Neo-Assyrian Sources* (SAAS 7; Helsinki: Neo-Assyrian Text Corpus Project, 1998), including analyses of the following texts: Esarhaddon Nin. A I 84 – ii 11; Ass. A I 31 – ii 26; Assurbanipal A ii 126 – iii 26; B v 46 – vi 16; T ii 7 – 24; SAA 2 6 § 10; SAA 7 9; SAA 10 109; 111; 284; 294; 352; SAA 13 37 (= *LAS* 317); SAA 16 59; 60; 61. For additional texts, see Appendix, nos. 103, 110 – 14, 118 – 118j.
3 See Parpola, *Assyrian Prophecies*, xlv – xlvii, with footnotes 212 – 36 (pp. cii – civ); B. Pongratz-Leisten, *Herrschaftswissen in Mesopotamien: Formen der Kommunikation zwischen Gott und König im 2. und 1. Jahrtausend v.Chr* (SAAS 10; Helsinki: Neo-Assyrian Text Corpus Project, 1999) 59 – 60.

DOI 10.1515/9783110466546-009

Mari[4] and attested elsewhere in various sources, such as omen collections, lexical texts, and administrative documents, from Ur III through the Old Babylonian and Middle Assyrian periods to the Neo-Babylonian.[5] While the use of *maḫḫû/maḫḫūtu* in Neo-Assyrian sources is virtually restricted to cultic texts and formal inscriptions,[6] the second designation, *raggimu/raggintu*, appears in administrative texts, personal letters, and colophons of the extant prophecies.[7] This implies that *raggimu/raggintu* was in fact the colloquial equivalent of *maḫḫû/maḫḫūtu*, which was probably no longer in use in the seventh century.

Both designations are derived from verbs denoting behavior: *maḫḫû* from *maḫû*, "to become crazy, to go into a frenzy,"[8] and *raggimu* from *ragāmu*, "to cry out, to proclaim." One might ask whether etymologies, notoriously treacherous in defining words, tell anything about the comportment of the prophets. Fortunately, we do not depend on etymology alone when tracing the image of the Mesopotamian prophets with this vocabulary. The verbs in question use their literal meanings when prophetic activities are described.[9] In Mari documents,

4 The word *muḫḫûm* is attested in RM 21 333:34, 43; ARM 22 167:8; ARM 23 446:9, 19; ARM 25 142:13; ARM 26 202:15; 206:5; 215:15; 220:16; 221:19; 221bis:12, 20, 27; 227:9; 243:7, 13; ARM 27 32:7; A. 1249b+: 2; A. 3165 ii 22; s. ii 3; A. 4676:5; *muḫḫūtum* in ARM 22 326:9; ARM 26 200:5, 21; 201:9, 15; 237:22; A. 1249b+:6; see J.-M. Durand, *Archives Épistolaires de Mari I/1* (ARM 26; Paris: Éditions Recherche sur les Civilisations, 1988), esp. 386–88, 398.

5 *muḫḫûm*: TCS 1 369:5 (Ur III); MDP 10 7:6, 9; MDP 18 171:14 (Old Babylonian); VS 19 1 i 38 (Middle Assyrian); OECT 1 plate 21:38; YOS 6 18:1, 7, 8, 10; YOS 7 135:6 (Neo-Babylonian); *CT* 38 4:81; Sm 332 r. 5 (Šumma alu); *TDP* 4:30 (Sagig); *DA* 211 r. 12; *MSL* 12 101–2:213; 132:117–18; 158:23; *muḫḫūtum:* TCL 10 39:11 (Old Babylonian); VS 19 1 i 38 (Middle Assyrian); *CT* 38 4:81 (Šumma alu); *MSL* 12 158:23. See Parpola, *Assyrian Prophecies*, xlv–vi, ciii, nn. 221, 222, 223, 228.

6 Absolute forms are only attested in the ritual texts (SAA 3 34:28; W. Farber, *Beschwörungsrituale an Ištar und Dumuzi: Attī Ištar ša harmaša Dumuzi* [Veröffentlichungen der Orientalischen Kommission 30; Wiesbaden: Franz Steiner, 1977] 140–42:31, 59), in the Succession Treaty of Esarhaddon (SAA 2 6 § 10:117) and in the decree of expenditures from the year 809 (SAA 12 69:29), whereas the royal inscriptions repeatedly use the compound *šipir maḫḫê*, "prophetic messages" (Esarhaddon Nin A ii 6; Ass A ii 12; Assurbanipal B v 95 [= C vi 127]; T ii 16 [= C i 61]).

7 *raggimu*: SAA 2 6 § 10:116; SAA 7 9 r. i 23; SAA 9 3.5 iv 31; [6 r. 11]; SAA 10 109:9; 294 r. 31; *raggintu:* SAA 9 7:1; 10 s. 2; SAA 10 109:9; 352:23, r. 1; SAA 13 37:7.

8 Rather than allophones of a noun of *parrās* pattern (*GAG* §55o, s. 62), *muḫḫûm* and *maḫḫû* are the Babylonian and Assyrian variants of a D-stem verbal adjective (Parpola, *Assyrian Prophecies*, ciii, n. 219). This makes unnecessary the assumption of a semantic contamination of two different words (H. Wohl, "The Problem of the *maḫḫû*," *JANESCU* 3 [1970–71]: 112–18).

9 There are plenty of nonprophetical attestations of both words; cf. 4 R 28:59: *ṣehru imaḫḫi rabû imaḫḫi*, "the small and the great alike go into a frenzy" (cf. Joel 3:1); *BWL* 38:21: *ana ša imḫû bēlšu imšû*, "Like one who has gone mad and forgotten his lord"; Esarhaddon Nin A i 41–42: *arkānu aḫḫēja immaḫûma mimma ša eli ilāni u amelūti lā ṭāba ēpušūma*, "Afterward my brothers

maḫû (N stem) indicates the condition in which the prophets receive and transmit divine words:

> *ina bīt Annunītim* UD.3.KAM *Šēlebum immaḫḫu umma Annunītumma* ...
> In the temple of Annunitum, on the 3rd day, Šelebum went into a frenzy and said: "Thus says Annunitum: (...)"[10]
>
> *Aḫātum amat Dagan-Malik immaḫḫima kī' am iqbi* ...
>
> Aḫatum, a slave girl of Dagan-Malik, went into a frenzy
> and spoke: (...)[11]
>
> [*ūmīšum*]*a Irra-gamil* [*imma*]*ḫêm* [*umma š*]*ūma* ...
> [On that day] Irra-gamil [went into a fr]enzy. [This is what] he said: (...)[12]

Interestingly enough, in a ritual text from Mari, the prophet is said to be deprived of his capacity to prophesy if he maintains an unaltered state of mind:

> *šumma ina rēš war*[*ḫim*] *muḫḫûm ištaqa*[*lma*] *an*[*a*] *maḫḫē'i*[*m*] *ul i*[*reddû*] ...
> If by the end of the mo[nth] the *muhhûm* maintains his equilibrium] and is not a[ble] t[o] prophes[y] (...)[13]

In Neo-Assyrian sources, again, the verb *ragāmu* is regularly used of prophetic performance:

> *Tašmētu-ēreš* [*raggimu annītu ina lib*]*bi Arbail irt*[*ugum*]
> Tašmetu-ereš, the [prophet], prop[hesied this i]n Arbela.[14]
>
> [*a*]*sseme mā pānāt nēpēšē annūti ragginti tartugūmu*
> *ana Damqî mār šatammi taqṭi*[*bi m*]*ā* ...
> [I] have heard that, before these rituals, a prophetess had prophesied, saying to Damqî, the son of the chief administrator: "(...)"[15]

---

went out of their senses doing everything that is displeasing to the gods and mankind." For a non-prophetical occurrence of *ragāmu*, see SAA 13 157:24: *mā Nabû-abu-da''in nuhatimmu irtugum*, "Then Nabû-abu-da''in, the cook, cried out."

10 ARM 26 213:5–7.

11 ARM 26 214:6–7.

12 ARM 26 222:12–14.

13 A. 3165 ii 21–23 (Ritual of Ištar, text 2); for the restoration and translation, see Durand, *Archives*, 386–87; J.-M. Durand and M. Guichard, "Les rituels de Mari," in D. Charpin and J.-M. Durand (eds.) 19–78, esp. 54, 58.

14 SAA 9 6 r. 11–12. The title of Tašmetu-ereš follows the professional determinative LÚ, which is partially broken but clearly visible (see the photograph in Parpola, *Assyrian Prophecies*, plate viii); however, the title itself is totally broken away.

15 SAA 10 352:22–25.

> *Mullissu-abu-uṣri raggintu ša kuzippī ša šarri ana māt Akkadî tūbilūni [ina] bēt ili tar-tug[u]m ...*
>
> Mullissu-abu-uṣri, the prophetess who conveyed the king's clothes to the land of Akkad, prophesied [in] the temple: (...)[16]

As demonstrated by the above examples, both *maḫû* and *ragāmu* tend to introduce direct divine speech, which indicates that, semantically, they encompass both aspects of the oral performance of the prophet, that is, the distinct behavior and the act of speech. In the Hebrew Bible, prophetic performance is expressed with derivatives of the root *nb'*, which means proclamation of divine words, often implying an appearance in an altered state of mind and, hence, providing a semantic equivalent of *maḫû* and *ragāmu.*[17]

In addition to the prophetic designations, the behavior and social location of the Assyrian prophets can be contextualized by comparison with related groups of people and their behaviors. It is revealing that in lexical lists as well as cultic and administrative texts, *raggimu* and *maḫḫû* are consistently associated with people like *zabbu* 'frenzied one', *kalû* 'chanter', *munambû* 'lamentation singer', *lallaru* 'wailer', *assinnu* and *kurgarrû* 'man-woman'—all devotees of Ištar with appearance and conduct different from the average citizen. For example:

la-bar	=	*kalû*	"chanter"
gala.maḫ	=	*kalamāḫu* (šu-*ḫu*)	"chief chanter"
i-lu-di	=	*munambû*	"lamentation singer"
i-lu-a-li	=	*lallaru*	"wailer"
lú.gub-ba	=	*maḫḫû*	"prophet"
lú.ní-zu-ub	=	*zabbu*	"frenzied one"
kur-gar-ra	=	*kurgarrû* (šu-*u*)	"man-woman"
ur-sal	=	*assinnu*	"man-woman"
lú.giš.bala-šu-du_7	=	*nāš pilaqqi*	"carrier of spindel"[18]

16 SAA 13 37:7–10.

17 E.g., Num 11:24–30; 1 Sam 10:10–13; 19:20; 1 Kgs 18:29; 22:10; Joel 3:1. In the semantics of Biblical Hebrew, however, use of the word family *nb'* is restricted to prophetic activities.

18 *MSL* 12 102–3:209–17 (M. Civil et al., *The Series lū = ša and Related Texts* [MSL 12; Rome: Pontificium Institutum Biblicum, 1969], 102–3); the designation *nāš pilaqqi* is equal to *assinnu* and *kurgarrû*. Cf. the decree of expenditures from Mari (ARM 21 333:42–44 = ARM 23 446:18–20): 1 *ṣubātum išārum Jadīda lillatum 1 ṣubātum išārum Ea-maṣi muhhû Itūr-Mēr* 1 *ṣubâtum išārum Šarrum-dāri nārum*, "one ordinary garment for Yadida 'the crazy woman,' one ordinary garment for Ea-maṣi, prophet of Itur-Mer, one ordinary garment for Šarrum-dari, the chanter." Note that the prophet is mentioned in association with a woman, whose tide *lillatum* probably designates ecstatic behavior, and with a chanter comparable to *kalû*.

aštakkan kurummāti ana zabbī zabbāti maḫḫê u maḫḫûti
I have placed breads for the frenzied men and women, for prophets and prophetesses.[19]

10 *emār* 4 *sât* 5 *qa Aššūr-apla-iddina ina* UD.2.KÁM *ana kurummat maḫḫu'ē maḫḫu'āte u* LÚ.SAL.MEŠ *ša bēt Iltār*
10 homers 4 seah 5 liters (of barley) for Aššur-apla-iddina on the 2nd day, for the food rations of the prophets, prophetesses, and the *assinnu's* (?) of the Ištar temple (of Kar-Tukulti-Ninurta).[20]

The uncertain gender of some Assyrian prophets—especially Bayâ, whose gender even the scribe of the tablet SAA 9 1 could not decide[21]—creates a link to the *assinnu* and the *kurgarrû*, whose gender role the goddess had changed permanently;[22] this is not surprising given that two of the Mari prophets, Šelebum and Ili-ḫaznaya, are explicitly designated as *assinnu.*[23] On the other hand, an established connection exists between prophets and the seers and visionaries called *šabrû* and *šā'ilu*, whose expertise is closely related to that of the prophets. The only Neo-Assyrian occurrence[24] of *šā'ilu* (*amat ili*) occurs in the Succession Treaty of Esarhaddon, where it is listed together with *raggimu* and *maḫḫû* and may, rather than designating a specific role or profession, be a general appellation for practitioners of different kinds of noninductive divination.[25] The *šabrû*, equated with *raggimu* in a lexical list[26] and appearing in close connection with both

19 Farber, *Beschwörungsrituale*, 142:59; cf. 140:31.
20 VS 19 1 i 37–39 (H. Freydank, "Zwei Verpflegungstexte aus Kār-Tukultī-Ninurta," *AoF* 1 [1974] 55–89, esp. 60). The reading *assinnu* is based on Freydank's copy, which shows clear traces of the sign SAL (= MÍ) between the signs LÚ and MEŠ (H. Freydank, *Mittelassyrische Rechtsurkunden und Verwaltungstexte* [Vorderasiatische Schriftdenkmäler 19; Berlin: Akademie-Verlag, 1976], plate 1).
21 SAA 9 1.4 ii 40 gives the name incongruously as MÍ.*ba-ia-a* DUMU URU.*arba-il*, "the woman Bayâ, son of Arbela." The name has both male and female occurrences in Neo-Assyrian sources (see M. Nissinen and M.-C. Perroudon, "Bāia," *PNA* 1/2 [1999] 253). In the case of Issar-la-tašiyaṭ, the masculine and divine determinatives [md] are written over the originally written MÍ (SAA 9 1.1 i 28); it is not clear whether this is an error of the scribe or indicates uncertainty about the gender of the prophet.
22 For *assinnu* and *kurgarrû*, see, e.g., G. Leick, *Sex and Eroticism in Mesopotamian Literature* (London and New York: Routledge, 1994), esp.157–69; M. Nissinen, *Homoeroticism in the Biblical World: A Historical Perspective* (trans. K. Stjerna; Minneapolis: Fortress Press, 1998), esp. 28–36.
23 ARM 26 197:4; 198:3; 213:6; M. 11299:8 (Šelebum); 212:5; M. 11299:13 (Ili-ḫaznaya). See Durand, *Archives*, 399.
24 I.e., besides the entry in the lexical list in *MSL* 12 233:33, where [LÚ.*ša-i*]-*lu* appears as a category of its own.
25 SAA 2 6 §10:117; cf. Nissinen, *References*, 160–61.
26 *MSL* 12 226:134: lû.šabra (PA.AL) = ŠU-*u*= *rag-gi*-[*mu*].

maḫḫû and *zabbu* in other texts,[27] is a visionary whose realm apparently consists of dreams and their interpretation.[28] A dream of a *šabrû* with many affinities with prophecy is reported in Assurbanipal's Prism B, following the quotation of an oracle that is best explained as prophetic.[29]

The outcome of the etymological and lexical examination is that the Assyrian prophets were proclaimers of divine words who formed part of the community of devotees of Ištar. They found their nearest colleagues among practitioners of non-inductive divination and among people whose more or less frenzied behavior, eventually perceived as odd by the majority of the population, corresponded to their role in the worship of the goddess.

The Prophets and the Goddess

The determinative factor in the socioreligious role of the Assyrian prophets is without doubt their affiliation with the goddess Ištar and worship of her.[30] Prophets act as mouthpieces of that goddess in her various manifestations; in Neo-Assyrian texts, Mullissu cannot be separated from Ištar as a divine being.[31] The prophets also live under the aegis of the goddess. Their association

---

27 *CT* 38 4 81–82: *šumma ina* URU LÚ.GUB.BA.MEŠ MIN (= *ma-ʾ-du*) [...] *šumma ina* URU MÍ.GUB.-BA.MEŠ MIN [...], "If there are many prophets in the city, [...]; if there are many prophetesses in the city, [...]; 87–88: *šumma ina* URU *šab ru*.MEŠ MIN [...] *šumma ina* URU *šab-ra-tu*$_4$ MIN [...], "If there are many frenzied men in the city, [...], if there are many frenzied women in the city, [...]"; *LKA* 29d ii 2: *zabbu liqbâkkima šabrû lišannakki*, "Let the *zabbu* tell you, the *šabrû* repeat it to you."

28 For *šabrû*, see *CAD* Š/1 15; Huffmon, "Ancient Near Eastern Prophecy," 5:480; Parpola, *Assyrian Prophecies*, xlvi–xlvii; Nissinen, *References*, 56.

29 Assurbanipal B v 49–76; see M. Weippert, "Assyrische Prophetien der Zeit Asarhaddons und Assurbanipals," in *Assyrian Royal Inscriptions: New Horizons in Literary, Ideological, and Historical Analysis* (ed. F. M. Fales; OAC 17; Rome: Istituto per l'Oriente, 1981), 71–115, esp. 97–98; Nissinen, *References*, 53–54; Pongratz-Leisten, *Herrschaftswissen*, 120–22.

30 As to the following, see the detailed documentation of Parpola, *Assyrian Prophecies*, xlvii–xlviii, with footnotes on pp. civ–cvi.

31 See B. Menzel, *Assyrische Tempel: Untersuchungen zu Kult, Administration und Personal* (Studia Pohl, Series Major 10/1; Rome: Biblical Institute Press, 1981), esp. 64–65, 116; M. Weippert, "Die Bildsprache der neuassyrischen Prophetie," in *Beiträge zur prophetischen Bildsprache in Israel und Assyrien* (ed. H. Weippert, K. Seybold, and M. Weippert; OBO 64; Freiburg, Switzerland: Universitätsverlag; Göttingen: Vandenhoeck & Ruprecht, 1985) 55–93, esp. 64; cf. SAA 3 7:11–12; SAA 9 2.4 ii 30; SAA 9 7 r. 6; and especially SAA 9 9, in which Mullissu and Lady (Ištar) of Arbela speak in the first-person singular as one divine being. Mullissu also appears as the one speaking in SAA 9 1.5 iii 4; SAA 9 5:3; and SAA 9 7:2, 12.

with other devotees of Ištar in the above-mentioned lexical lists and cultic texts, as well as their mention as recipients of food rations in the Ištar temple of the Middle Assyrian period, shows this fact conclusively. The prophets' permanent attachment to the temples is further documented by one oracle of the corpus, spoken by a votaress (*šēlūtu*) donated to the goddess by the king.[32] Many prophets have names related to the ideology of Ištar worship. These probably are not birth names but given when the prophetic role was assumed.[33]

As proclaimers of the word of Ištar, the prophets acted *as* Ištar. The primary role of the prophets as intermediaries between the divine and the human spheres reflects the role of Ištar/Mullissu as the mediator between the gods and the king, as demonstrated by a prophetic oracle and a letter containing a report of a prophetic utterance:

ina puḫur ilāni kalāmi aqṭibi balāṭaka
dannā rittāja lā urammâka ina pān ilāni
naggalapāja ḫarruddā ittanaššāka ana kāša
ina š[apt]ēja ētanarriš balāṭaka [...]

In the assembly of all the gods I have spoken for your life.
My arms are strong and will not cast you off before the gods.
My shoulders are always ready to carry you, you in particular.
I keep desiring your life with my l[ip]s [...][34]

[*anākū*] *Bēl ētarba issi Mu*[*ll*] *issu asillim*
Aššūr-bāni-apli šar māt Aššūr ša turabbīni [*l*]*ā tapallaḫ*
[*anā*] *ku Bēl artēanki Aššūr-bāni-apli ina māti ša kēnu šû adi mātīšu artēanki*

[I] am Bel, I have entered and made peace with Mullissu.
Assurbanipal, king of Assyria whom she raised: Fear not!
I am Bel, I have remitted Assurbanipal to you in a country of truth. Him together with his country I have remitted to you.[35]

---

32 SAA 9 1.7. Moreover, it is possible that the fragment SAA 13 148 is a remainder of another votaress's prophecy report: [...]-*ia* [...] *šēlūtu* [*ša*] *Issār* [*ša*] *Arbail ši*[*pirt*]*i* [*ann*]*ītu ana š*[*arri bēlīja* ...] *Issār* [...], "[...-]ya, votaress [of] Ištar [of] Arbela [reported] [th]is mes[sag]e for the ki[ng, my lord]: '[...] Ištar [...]'" It is not clear, however, whether this votaress had actually uttered the divine word in question, or just reports it to the king; cf. Parpola, *Assyrian Prophecies*, lxxvii; Whiting, introduction to S. W. Cole, and P. Machinist, *Letters from Priests to the Kings Esarhaddon and Assurbanipal* (SAA 13; Helsinki: Helsinki University Press, 1998).

33 E.g., *Ilūssa-āmur*, "I have seen her divinity"; *Issār-bēlī-da''ini*, "Ištar, strengthen my lord!"; *Issār-lā-tašiyaṭ*, "Do not neglect Ištar!"; *Sinqīša-āmur*, "I have seen her distress"; see Parpola, *Assyrian Prophecies*, il – lii.

34 SAA 9 9:16 – 20; cf. the similar language used in SAA 3 13.

35 SAA 13 139:1 – 9; cf. pp. 245 – 65 in this volume. The source in question is the letter of Aššur-ḫamatu'a, who begins with the word of Bel and attaches additional information. Hence, the let-

While the first quotation presents the goddess(es)[36] as intercessor(s) before the divine council, the second is the word of Bel, who declares his reconciliation with Assurbanipal upon the intercession of Mullissu who, for her part, stands on behalf of the king. Hence, the prophetic message appears as the earthly representation and counterpart of the divine intermediation of the goddess in the heavenly council. The prophet, impersonating the goddess, is the channel through which the benefit of her intercession, the divine reconciliation, is bestowed upon the king.

The closest textual parallels with Neo-Assyrian prophecies are found among poetry, hymns, and mystical works pertaining to the cult of different deities, but especially to that of Ištar. These show the prophets' familiarity with this literature and the associated cultic performances. In addition to the mythological compositions like Adapa and Gilgameš,[37] the royal and cultic poetry collected in SAA 3 provides an abundance of affinities with prophecy, especially

1. in hymns and prayers of Assurbanipal,[38] especially in the Dialogue between Assurbanipal and Nabû (SAA 3 13), which is both substantially and historically closely related to SAA 9 9 and was probably written by the same hand;[39]
2. in the letters from gods (or responses to *Gottesbriefe*), which are not prophecy as such, but employ confusingly similar language;[40]

---

ter gives an account of a prophetic appearance without being a report of prophecy in the strict sense.

36 The divine "I" in this oracle is spoken by Ištar and Mullissu as one divine being; cf. above, n. 36.

37 See Parpola, *Assyrian Prophecies*, cv, n. 246.

38 SAA 3 1; 2; 3; 7; 12; 13.

39 See Parpola, *Assyrian Prophecies*, lxxi. This text is often discussed together with the prophecies; cf. M. Dijkstra, *Gods voorstelling: Predikatieve expressie van zelfopenbaring in oudoosterse teksten en Deutero-Jesaja* (Dissertationes Neerlandicae, Series Theologica 2; Kampen: Kok, 1980), esp. 147–48; Weippert, "Assyrische Prophetien"; id., "Bildsprache"; M. Nissinen, "Die Relevanz der neuassyrischen Prophetie für die alttestamentliche Forschung," in *Mesopotamica—Ugaritica—Biblica: Festschrift für Kurt Bergerhof* (ed. M. Dietrich and O. Loretz; AOAT 232, Kevelaer, Germany: Butzon & Bercker; Neukirchen-Vluyn: Neukirchener, 1993) 217–58 (= pp. 315–50 in this volume). Pongratz-Leisten (*Herrschaftswissen*, 75) puts forward the idea that SAA 3 13 is a literary creation inspired by the prophecies ("eine literarische Kreation in Anlehnung an die Gattung der Prophetensprüche").

40 SAA 3 44–47; cf. Dijkstra, *Gods voorstelling*, 145–69; Weippert, "Assyrische Prophetien," 72, 112; A. Livingstone, *Court Poetry and Literary Miscellanea* (SAA 3; Helsinki: Helsinki University Press, 1989). For the "correspondence" of Assurbanipal with Aššur, see the comprehensive analysis in Pongratz-Leisten, *Herrschaftswissen*, 240–65.

3. in mystical works like SAA 3 37 and 39;[41] and
4. in the love lyrics of Nabû and Tašmetu (SAA 3 14).[42]

An open question is to what extent the literary parallels between prophecies and cultic literature go back to the scribes by whom the prophecy reports were formulated; in any case, similar use of language in both types of sources is not just a stylistic matter but the vehicle for expression of an essentially similar ideology.

Among the cult centers of Ištar, Arbela is by far the most important source of prophecy. If the letter of the temple official Nabû-reši-išši reporting an appearance of a prophetess was sent from Arbela, as suggested by the letter's greeting formula,[43] it only proves the assumption, probable anyway, that prophecies were uttered in the temple of Ištar of Arbela. Seven out of fifteen prophets known by personal names are Arbela-based: Aḫat-abiša (SAA 9 1.8), Bayâ (SAA 9 1.4; [2.2]), Dunnaša-amur (SAA 9 9 and 10), Issar-la-tašiyaṭ (SAA 9 1.1), La-dagil-ili (SAA 9 1.10; 2.3 and 3), Sinqiša-amur (SAA 9 1.2; [2.5]), and Tašmetu-ereš (SAA 9 6). The words of Ištar of Arbela were proclaimed even by prophets elsewhere;[44] a special devotion to that city is expressed by the prophetess Remutti-Allati, who comes from Dara-aḫuya, an unidentifiable locality "in the mountains" (*birti šaddâni*), proclaiming the words "Arbela rejoices!"[45]

The dominance of Ištar of Arbela does not, however, prevent the prophets from proclaiming the words of other deities. To all appearances, the prophet La-dagil-ili speaks on behalf of both Aššur and Ištar in the collection SAA 9 3,[46] and a short oracle of the prophet(ess) Bayâ (SAA 9 1.4) includes self-predications of three deities, Bel, Ištar, and Nabû. While most of the prophets, as devotees of Ištar, represent the motherly aspect of the divine, manifested as nursing the king and as fighting for him,[47] it is convenient for a prophet to act as the mouthpiece of Aššur when it comes to the covenant between the king and the main god

---

41 Cf. Parpola, *Assyrian Prophecies*, c, n. 175; cv, n. 248.

42 See M. Nissinen, "Love Lyrics of Nabû and Tašmetu: An Assyrian Song of Songs?" in "*Und Mose schrieb dieses Lied auf": Studien zum Alten Testament und zum Alten Orient*, FS Oswald Loretz (ed. M. Dietrich and I. Kottsieper; AOAT 250; Münster: Ugarit-Verlag, 1998) 585–634, esp. 602, n. 75; 608, n. 103; 613, n. 131; 614, n. 138.

43 SAA 13 144:1–9; cf. the note of Karen Radner in Cole and Machinist, *Letters*, 116.

44 SAA 9 2.4: Urkittu-šarrat from Calah.

45 SAA 9 1.3 ii 12.

46 See Nissinen, "Spoken, Written, Quoted, and Invented."

47 E.g., SAA 9 1.6 iii 15–22, iv 5–10; SAA 9 2.5 iii 29–34; SAA 9 7:14–r. 11; cf. SAA 3 13 r. 6–10. See Weippert, "Bildsprache," 62–64; Nissinen, "Relevanz," 242–47.

of Assyria.[48] Furthermore, when a Babylonian scholar quotes prophecy, he presents it as the words of Bel, that is, Marduk of Babylon,[49] and when affairs of the city of Harran are concerned, the Harranean deities Nikkal and Nusku speak.[50] All this implies a functional or aspectual, rather than "polytheistic," concept of God, which enabled the prophets to speak the words of the appropriate manifestation of the divine in a given situation. Accordingly, the Assyrian prophets were not divided into competing groups advocating specific deities, and their basic role as devotees of Ištar by no means prevented them from acting in temples of other gods.

As a matter of fact, the presence of prophets in temples other than those of Ištar is well documented. Adad-aḫu-iddina writes the king about an appearance of the prophetess Mullissu-abu-uṣri in the temple in which he is employed—most probably Ešarra, the Aššur temple in Assur[51]—and in a decree for the maintenance of the same temple from the year 809, prophetesses (*maḫḫâtu*) are mentioned in a paragraph concerning the "divine council" (*puḫur ilāni*).[52] When it comes to the Babylonian *akītu*-ritual, a prophet (*maḫḫû*) appears in a genuinely prophetic function as a "bringer of news" (*mupassiru*) to Zarpanitu, the spouse of Marduk, in the so-called Marduk Ordeal text.[53] Everything points to the conclu-

48 The oracle in SAA 9 3.3 ii 10–25 is followed by a double ritual instruction (lines 26–32). It is not compulsory to interpret the oracle as the document of the covenant, as I and many others have done (Nissinen, *References*, 28). It is clear that *annû šulmu ša ina pān ṣalme*, "This is the oracle of peace (placed) before the statue" (line 26), refers to the tablet on which the prophecy is written. However, the continuation *ṭuppi adê anniu ša Aššūr ... ina pān šarri errab*, "This covenant tablet of Aššur enters the king's presence" (lines 27–28), does not necessarily refer to the same tablet; see Pongratz-Leisten, *Herrschaftswissen*, 77–80.

49 SAA 10 111; see Nissinen, *References*, 96–101.

50 SAA 16 59; 60; see Nissinen, *References*, 122.

51 SAA 13 37 (= *LAS* 317); see S. Parpola, *Letters from Assyrian Scholars to the Kings Esarhaddon and Assurbanipal, Part II: Commentary and Appendices* (AOAT 5/2; Kevelaer, Germany: Butzon & Bercker; Neukirchen-Vluyn: Neukirchener, 1983), esp. 329; Nissinen, *References*, 78–81; Pongratz-Leisten, *Herrschaftswissen*, 83–84.

52 SAA 12 69:27–31; cf. L. Kataja and R. M. Whiting, Grants, Decrees, and Gifts of the Neo-Assyrian Period (SAA 12; Helsinki: Helsinki University Press, 1995). The divine council plays an important role in SAA 9 9:16: *ina puḫur ilāni kalāmi aqṭibi balāṭaka*, "In the assembly of all the gods I have spoken for your life"; cf. SAA 3 13:26: *pîya ammiu ša ṭābu iktanarrabka ina puḫur ilāni rabûti*, "My pleasant mouth shall ever bless you in the assembly of the great gods." The letter of Aššur-ḫamatu'a (SAA 13 139) contains an oracle in which Bel reconciles with Mullissu, who has interceded on behalf of Assurbanipal, presumably before the divine council; see above.

53 SAA 3 34:28 (= SAA 3 35:31): *maḫḫû ša ina pān Bēlet-Bābili illakūni mupassiru šû ana irtīša ibakki illak*, "The prophet who goes before the Lady of Babylon is a bringer of news; weeping he goes toward her." For this text (and for reservations about calling it the "Marduk Ordeal"), see

sion that while the Ištar worship in Arbela was undoubtedly the nerve center of prophecy, the network of prophets extended to other cities, where they represented their patroness even in temples of other deities.

The special devotion of Assyrian prophets to Ištar is compatible with the significance of the goddesses, often manifestations of Ištar, in the prophetic documents from Ešnunna (Kititum)[54] and Mari (Annunitum, Ištar of Bišra, Diritum, Belet-ekallim, Belet-biri, Ḫišamitum, Ninḫursag).[55] There is, however, no overall dedication of the prophets to the goddess in Mari documents, in which the role of male deities (Dagan, Šamaš, Adad, Itur-Mer, Nergal, Ea, Abba)[56] in prophecies is clearly more manifest than in Assyria. Moreover, while the prophets in the Neo-Assyrian sources are never called "*raggintu* of Ištar" or the like, the Mari prophets tend to be associated with a specific deity, for example, Lupaḫum, *āpilum* of Dagan.[57] This probably demonstrates the prophet's attachment to the temple of a particular god, which as such does not exclude proclaiming the words of other deities, even though this appears to be exceptional at Mari.[58]

The reason for the different significance of the goddess in these two corpora may be sought primarily in the special role of Ištar in the amalgamation of As-

---

T. Frymer-Kensky, "The Tribulations of Marduk: The So-Called 'Marduk Ordeal Text,'" *JAOS* 103 (1983) 131–41.

54 FLP 1674 and 2064; see M. deJong Ellis, "The Goddess Kititum Speaks to King Ibalpiel: Oracle Texts from Ishchali," *MARI* 5 (1987) 235–66.

55 Annunitum: ARM 22 326; 26 198; 212; 213; 214; 237; Ištar of Bišra: ARM 26 237; Diritum: ARM 26 199; 208; Belet-ekallim: ARM 26 209; 211 (?); 237; 240; Belet-biri: ARM 26 238; Ḫišamitum: ARM 26 195; Ninḫursag: ARM 22 167 (cf. A. 4676); 26 219. Note especially the role of the prophets in the rituals of Ištar (A. 3165; A. 1249b+); cf. Durand and Guichard, "Rituels de Mari."

56 Dagan: ARM 25 15; 26 196; 197; 199; 202; 205; 209; 210; 215; 220; 221; 223; 232; 233; A. 3796; M. 11436; T. 82; Šamaš: ARM 26 194; 414; Adad: ARM 25 142; A 1121+; 1968; Itur-Mer: ARM 21 333; 23 446; 26 236; Nergal: ARM 21 333; 23 446 (26 222?): Ea: ARM 26 208; Abba: ARM 26 227.

57 ARM 26 199:5; A. 3796:4–5; M. 11436:4. There are plenty of similar cases: Qišatum, *āpilum* of Dagan (ARM 25 15:9); Išhi-Dagan, *āpilum* of Dagan of Ṣubatum (T. 82:3–4); *āpilum* of Dagan of Tuttul (ARM 26 209:6); *āpilum* of Belet-ekallim (ARM 26 209:15); Qišti-Diritim, *āpilum* of Diritum (ARM 26 208:5–6); *āpilum* of Šamaš (ARM 26 194:2); Atamrum, *āpilum* of Šamaš (ARM 26 414:29–30); *āpilum* of Ninḫursag (ARM 26 219:5); *āpilum* of Marduk (ARM 26 371:9); Abiya, *āpilum* of Adad (A. 1968:3); Annu-tabni, *muḫḫūtum* of Annunitum (ARM 22 326:9–10); *muḫḫûm* of Dagan (ARM 26 220:16–17; 221:9; 243:13 [pl.]); Irra-gamil, *muḫḫûm* of Nergal (ARM 21 333:34 = ARM 23 446:9); Ea-maṣi, *muḫḫûm* of Itur-Mer (ARM 21 333:43 = ARM 23 446:19); Ea-mudammiq, *muḫḫûm* of Ninḫursag (ARM 22 167:8; A. 4676:5–6); *muḫḫûm* of Adad (ARM 25 142:13); *muḫḫûm* of Ami of Ḫubšalum (ARM 27 32:7); Ili-ḫaznaya, *assinnu* of Annunitum (ARM 26 212:5–6).

58 In addition to the word of his patron god Dagan, Lupaḫum seems to deliver an oracle of the goddess Diritum in ARM 26 199:29–40. Moreover, Iddin-ili, the priest (*šangûm*) of Itur-Mer, reports a dream of his in which he receives a word of Belet-biri (ARM 26 238).

syrian imperial ideology with Assyrian religion, which reached a climax in the Sargonid era.[59] However, the sparse documentation shows the elementary connection of prophecy and the cult of Ištar in her various manifestations in different parts of Mesopotamia throughout the ages, which speaks against the much-debated theory of Mesopotamian prophecy as a product of Western influence.[60] Without speculating on the "origin" of prophecy in cultural and geographic terms, if there is an origin, one might note the prominent role of male deities in the few West Semitic documents of prophecy and other oracular activity,[61] and ask whether the relatively lesser prominence of the goddess in the prophetic documents of Mari is due to socioreligious circumstances and traditions different from those of imperial Assyria.

The Prophets and the King

Apart from the biblical narratives about prophets having an immediate communication with the kings of Israel or Judah—which may have happened less often than one would have expected[62]—at least one ancient Near Eastern source hints

---

59 See Parpola, *Assyrian Prophecies*, xxxvi–xliv.

60 This theory, put forward by H. Tadmor, "The Aramaization of Assyria: Aspects of Western Impact," in *Mesopotamien und seine Nachbarn: Politische und kulturelle Wechselbeziehungen im Alten Vorderasien vom 4. bis 1. Jahrtausend v. Chr* (ed. H.-J. Nissen and J. Renger; Berliner Beiträge zum Vorderen Orient 1; Berlin: Dietrich Reimer, 1982), 449–70, esp. 458, and supported by, e.g., M. Hutter, *Religionen in der Umwelt des Alten Testaments I: Babylonier, Syrer, Perser* (Studienbücher Theologie 4/1; Stuttgart: Kohlhammer, 1996), 107, and A. Malamat, "The Cultural Impact of the West (Syria-Palestine) on Mesopotamia in the Old Babylonian Period," *AoF* 24 (1997) 310–19, esp. 315–17, has been objected to by, e.g., A. Millard, "La prophétie et l'écriture—Israël, Aram, Assyrie," *RHR* 202 (1985) 125–44, esp. 133–34, and most emphatically and conclusively by Parpola, *Assyrian Prophecies*, xiv. Cf. also Pongratz-Leisten, *Herrschaftswissen*, 49–51.

61 E.g., the Zakkur Inscription, the Deir ʿAlla Inscription, the Ammonite Citadel Inscription, etc.; cf. A. Lemaire, "Oracles, politique et littérature dans les royaumes araméens et transjordaniens (IXe–VIIIe s. av. n.è.)," in *Oracles et prophéties dans l'antiquité: Actes du Colloque de Strasbourg, 15–17 Juin 1995* (ed. J.-G. Heintz; Université des sciences humaines de Strasbourg, Travaux du Centre de recherche sur le Proche-Orient et la Grèce antiques 15; Paris: De Boccard, 1997) 171–93.

62 These encounters happen between the anonymous prophet and Jeroboam (1 Kgs 13:1–10); Elijah and Ahab (1 Kgs 18:16–20, 41); Micaiah and Ahab/Jehoshaphat (1 Kgs 22:1–28); Elijah and Ahaziah (2 Kgs 1); Elisha and Ben-Hadad, king of Damascus (2 Kgs 8:7–15); Isaiah and Ahaz (Isa 7); Isaiah and Hezekiah (Isa 37–39 = 2 Kgs 19–20) and Jeremiah and Zedekiah (Jer 34:1–7; 37:17–21; 38:14–28). Jeremiah 21; 36; 37:1–10 are not direct encounters, and, in Jer 22, the prophet is ordered by God to go to the king, but the encounter never takes place.

at such encounters, namely the letter of the well-known Babylonian astrologer Bel-ušezib to the king Esarhaddon. Bel-ušezib wonders why Esarhaddon, following his coronation, has summoned "prophets and prophetesses" (*raggimānu raggimātu*) instead of him and in spite of the services he has provided for Esarhaddon during the civil war preceding his rise to power.[63]

This reference is unique in ancient Near Eastern sources, and Bel-ušezib's tone expresses his astonishment and jealousy, as if it were exceptional for prophets to be honored by the king's summons. It is not certain that this reference indicates a face-to-face rendezvous between the prophets and the king. The "summoning" (*rēšu našû*) primarily means employing: the life of a scholar depended on the king's use of his services, and Bel-ušezib is furious because Esarhaddon, at the beginning of his rule, has made use of the prophets' services before consulting the skilled and loyal Babylonian astrologer.

The Mari archives provide, to the best of my knowledge, no record of a situation in which a prophet met the king in person; at best, the prophet proclaimed at the gate of the palace, as the anonymous prophet of Marduk in Babylon, delivering a message to the Assyrian king Išme-Dagan, who had received asylum from Hammurabi, king of Babylon.[64] The meager evidence does not allow conclusions about whether direct encounters between the prophets and the king really took place at Mari, and if so, how often, but the existing sources give the impression that while King Zimri-Lim maintained close contact with practitioners of extispicy,[65] he was less active in consulting prophets. Even dreamers and visionaries seem to have communicated their messages more directly to the king than the prophets, whose words were usually conveyed to him by officials from different parts of the kingdom or by women of the court, especially by Queen Šibtu and other royal women (Addu-duri, Inib-šina).[66] Even in Assyria, the kings did not carry on a correspondence with the prophets; however, the transmission of prophetic messages differed from that in Mari. In Assyria, prophecies apparently were seldom reported in letters of court officials,

---

63 SAA 10 109:8–16; cf. Nissinen, *References*, 89–95. For Bel-ušezib and his correspondence, see M. Dietrich, *Die Aramäer Südbabyloniens in der Sargonidenzeit (700–648)* (AOAT 7; Kevelaer, Germany: Butzon & Bercker; Neukirchen-Vluyn: Neukirchener, 1970), 62–68.

64 ARM 26 371; see D. Charpin, "Le contexte historique et géographique des prophéties dans les textes retrouvés à Mari," *BCSMS* 23 (1992) 21–31, esp. p. 28–29.

65 See Pongratz-Leisten, *Herrschaftswissen*, 137–54.

66 For the transmission of prophecies at Mari, see J. M. Sasson, "The Posting of Letters with Divine Messages," in *Florilegium Marianum II, Mémorial M. Birot* (Mémoires de NABU 3; Paris: SEPOA, 1994) 299–316; K. van der Toorn, "Old Babylonian Prophecy between the Oral and the Written," *JNSL* 24 (1998) 55–70.

but they were transmitted to the king in reports, the contents of which were limited to the oracle proper. In some cases, these reports were deposited in the royal archives.[67] This implies a higher esteem for prophecies, which, in this procedure, were considered on a par with astrological and extispicy reports.

Both the oracles proper and the references to them in the royal inscriptions make it plain that the Assyrian kings, at least Esarhaddon and Assurbanipal, like Zimri-Lim, received prophecies during their military campaigns. There may even have been prophets at the front,[68] but prophecies uttered elsewhere and transmitted to the king by a third party are better documented. The best examples are the pertinent letters of Queen Šibtu of Mari[69] and the Assyrian prophecies formally addressed to Naqia, the king's mother (SAA 9 1.7; 1.8; 5).

Female intermediaries, whether at Mari or in Assyria, commonly transmitted words of female prophets. The female-through-female communication was not exclusive, though, since the royal women of Mari—Šibtu, Inib-šina, Addu-duri, and others—report appearances of male persons as well,[70] and male officials, both at Mari and in Assyria, give accounts of female prophets.[71] It is noteworthy, however, that three out of four known personal names of Mari prophetesses are transmitted by female writers,[72] and that both oracles to Naqia in which the

67 For this procedure, see Nissinen, "Spoken, Written, Quoted, and Invented."

68 This is suggested by accounts of kings in the royal inscriptions having received prophecies during battles, as well as by the lodging list of mostly high officials that also includes the prophet Quqî (SAA 7 9 r. i 23). One might ask whether the prophecy of Remutti-Allati, spoken "in the middle of the mountains" (SAA 9 1.3), was uttered on the battlefield.

69 ARM 26 207; 208; 211; 212; 213; 214; 236; for the correspondence of Šibtu, see W. H. Ph. Römer, *Frauenbriefe über Religion, Politik und Privatleben in Māri: Untersuchungen zu G. Dossin, Archives Royales de Mari X (Paris, 1967)* (AOAT 12; Kevelaer, Germany: Butzon & Bercker; Neukirchen-Vluyn: Neukirchener, 1971); P. Artzi and A. Malamat, "The Correspondence of Šibtu, Queen of Mari in *ARM* X," *Or* 40 (1971) 75–89 (reprinted in A. Malamat, *Mari and the Bible* [SHANE 12; Leiden: Brill, 1998] 175–91); Sasson, "Posting," 303–8.

70 Šibtu: ARM 26 208 (Qišti-Diritim); Addu-duri: ARM 26 195 (Iṣi-aḫu); 237 (Dadâ); 238 (Iddin-Ili).

71 Mari: ARM 26 201: Baḫdi-Lim (*muḫḫūtum*); ARM 26 210: Kibri-Dagan (*awiltum aššat awīlim*); ARM 26 199: Sammetar (*qammatum*); ARM 26 200: Aḫum (Ḫubatum *muḫḫūtum*). Assyria: SAA 10 352: Mar-Issar (*raggintu*); SAA 13 37: Adad-aḫu-iddina (Mullissu-abu-uṣri *raggintu*); SAA 13 144: Nabû-reši-išši (name unknown, female).

72 I.e., Aḫatum the slave girl (ARM 26 214: Šibtu), Kakka-lidi (ARM 26 236: Šibtu), and Innibana the *āpiltum* (ARM 26 204: Inib-šina); only the name of Ḫubatum the *muḫḫūtum* is reported by a male writer (ARM 26 200: Aḫum). Note also that the names of the *assinnus* Šelebum (ARM 26 197: Inib-šina; 213: Šibtu) and Ili-ḫaznaya (ARM 26 212: Šibtu) are mentioned by women only (the writer of ARM 26 198 is unknown).

name of the prophet is extant are spoken by female prophets.[73] This evidence suggests that the royal women were in closer contact with prophetesses than the male persons of the court. In the case of Naqia, the relationship with the prophetesses may be based on personal contacts with the personnel of Ištar temples, all the more probable since many prophecies and other texts refer to the nursing of the Assyrian princes "in the lap" of the goddess, which probably has a concrete point of reference in entrusting the royal infants to the temples of Ištar.[74]

This only adds to the evidence that the worship of Ištar was the primary setting for the Assyrian prophets' socioreligious role, within which even the connection between the prophets and the king was established. The position of the prophets as servants of the goddess entitled them to communication with the king; on the other hand, it also enabled them to express demands to the king and even to criticize his comportment. Even though, ideologically, there should have been no discrepancy between the king's decisions and the divine will, the king was a human being, liable to commit offenses against the divine world. Hence, the potential for a conflict between the god and the king, forcefully actualized in the biblical prophecy, existed even in Assyria. Esarhaddon, for instance, was explicitly reminded at his coronation of his obligations to Ištar (SAA 9 3.5 iii 18–37). Even though this prophecy deals with cultic matters reminiscent of similar demands in Mari letters[75] and, for example, of Mal 1:11–14, no distinction should be made between "cultic" and "social" criticism, since perfection is required of the king in both respects. The lack of social demands in the extant Neo-Assyrian prophecies[76] does not mean that the social offenses of the

---

73 I.e., SAA 9 1.7 (Issar-beli-da''ini) and 1.8 (Aḫat-abiša); in SAA 9 5, the name, if indicated, is destroyed. In addition, the king's mother is mentioned in SAA 9 2.1 i 13 and 2.6 iv 28 (?).

74 E. g., SAA 9 7 r. 6: *ša Mullissu ummašūni lā tapallaḫ ša Bēlet Arbail tārīssūni lā tapallah,* "You whose mother is Mullissu, have no fear! You whose nurse is Lady of Arbela, have no fear!"; SAA 3 13 r. 6–8: *ṣehru atta Aššūr-bāni-apli ša umašširūka ina muḫḫi Šarrat Nīnua lakû atta Aššūr-bāni-apli ša ašbaka ina burki Šarrat Nīnua,* "You were a child, Assurbanipal, when I left you with the Queen of Nineveh; you were a baby, Assurbanipal, when you sat in the lap of the Queen of Nineveh!" For entrusting the Assyrian princes to temples of Ištar, and for further references, see Parpola, *Assyrian Prophecies,* xxxix–xl; ic–c, nn. 174–77.

75 E.g., ARM 26 215:15–21: *muḫḫûm pān Dagan [i]tbīma kī'am iqbi u[m]māmi šūma admati mê zakūtim ul ašatti ana bēlīka šupurma u mê zakūtim lišqenni,* "A prophet arose before Dagan and spoke: 'How long shall I not be able to drink pure water? Write to your lord that he would provide me with pure water!'"

76 The archives of Mari contain traces of such prophetic demands, especially in the letters of Nur-Sîn from Aleppo (FM 7 38 and 39), for which see Sasson, "Posting," 314–16; J.-G. Heintz, "Des textes sémitiques anciens à la Bible hébraïque: Un comparatisme légitime?" in *Le comparatisme en histoire des religions* (ed. F. Bœspflug and F. Dunand; Paris: Cerf, 1997) 127–56,

king, according to the prevailing standards, were not of concern to the goddess and her servants.

That Neo-Assyrian prophecies have been preserved only from the time of Esarhaddon and Assurbanipal raises the question whether these kings were the only ones to promote prophecy, to the extent that their words were not only filed in the archives but also quoted by the scribes who authored their inscriptions.[77] The existing sources indeed give the impression that the activity of prophets, while not restricted to this period, enjoyed a higher social esteem during the reigns of Esarhaddon and Assurbanipal than ever before in Assyria. The extant documents from the time of the previous Sargonid kings include no mention of prophets, nor do documents from earlier periods provide information about prophets' existence, except for a couple of Middle and Neo-Assyrian decrees of expenditures in which prophets are listed among recipients of food rations.[78] If this argument *ex silentio* is consistent with reality, it may be assumed that, while the prophets were there all the time, the kings valued them differently at different times.

However, there is more than one side to the matter. The overwhelming majority of the material in the Assyrian archives derives from the reigns of Esarhaddon and Assurbanipal, while the percentage of sources from the time of earlier Sargonid kings is modest indeed. In fact, the archives of Nineveh and Mari are by far the most abundant Mesopotamian archives, and it may not be a pure coincidence that it is in these two sets of sources that the extant Mesopotamian prophecies are to be found. That these huge archives include just a few prophetic documents from the decades prior to their destruction indicates that, if prophetic reports were written and even stored, they were normally not meant for long-term preservation.[79] Hence, the small quantity of prophecy in the existing sources is not an accurate indicator of the significance of prophecy, any more than

---

esp. 136–50; H. B. Huffmon, "The Expansion of Prophecy in the Mari Archives: New Texts, New Readings, New Information," in *Prophecy and Prophets: The Diversity of Contemporary Issues in Scholarship* (ed. Y. Gitay; SBL Semeia Studies; Atlanta: Scholars Press, 1997), 7–22, esp. 16–17; Malamat, *Mari and the Bible*, 151–56.

77 It is conceivable that the prophecies of SAA 9 1 and 3 were used by the author(s) of Esarhaddon's Nin A inscription (see Weippert, "Assyrische Prophetien," 93–95; Parpola, *Assyrian Prophecies*, lxviii–lxi; Nissinen, *References*, 30–31), and at least some of the prophetic quotations in the inscriptions of Assurbanipal may be cited from written sources (see Nissinen, *References*, 58–61).

78 SAA 12 69; VS 19 1; see above.

79 Tablets with a single prophetic oracle are attested form Ešnunna (FLP 1674; 2064) and Assyria (SAA 9 7–11), but not from Mari; archival copies of collections of oracles are only known from Assyria. Cf. Nissinen, "Spoken, Written, Quoted, and Invented."

the total lack of letters from the time of Sennacherib implies that he had no correspondence.

While the silence of the sources yields only ambiguous interpretations, two arguments in favor of the special appreciation of prophecy by the kings Esarhaddon and Assurbanipal remain. First, only Esarhaddon apparently had prophecies recopied and compiled in collections, consciously preserving them for posterity. Second, the inscriptions of Tiglath-Pileser III, Sargon II, and Sennacherib in all their comprehensiveness make no mention of prophets. While the Sargonid kings in general—and not only Esarhaddon, traditionally regarded as especially "superstitious"—showed a remarkable interest in omens of different kinds,[80] it is clear that Esarhaddon and Assurbanipal in their inscriptions refer to divination, including prophecy, more than their predecessors. But even under their reigns, the scholars—haruspices, astrologers, exorcists—are better represented in the sources than the prophets.

The Prophets and Other Diviners

It is typical of the Neo-Assyrian royal inscriptions that prophecies (*šipir maḫḫê*) are mentioned together with other forms of divination. The Nin A inscription of Esarhaddon, calling prophecies "messages of the gods and the goddess" (*našparti ilāni u Ištar;* Nin A ii 6), equates them with "favorable omens in the sky and on earth." In the Ass A inscription, prophecies appear together with astrological omens and dreams, as well as with *egerrû*-oracles (Ass A ii 12–22), which, at least at Mari, are more or less equivalent to prophecies.[81] Likewise, an inscription of Assurbanipal bundles "good omens, dreams, *egerrû*-oracles, and prophetic messages" (B v 95). These lists of divinatory methods are reminiscent not only of 1 Sam 28:6, in which King Saul, before turning to a necromancer, is said to have tried dreams, Urim, and prophets, but also of the Hittite prayers in which

80 See F. M. Fales and G. B. Lanfranchi, "The Impact of Oracular Material on the Political Utterances and Political Action in the Royal Inscriptions of the Sargonid Dynasty," in J.-G. Heintz (ed.), *Oracles et prophéties dans l'antiquité*, 99–114. Note also the "anti-divinatory" attitude of one of the editions (E) of Esarhaddon's Babylon inscription; see M. Cogan, "Omens and Ideology in the Babylon Inscription of Esarhaddon," in *History, Historiography, and Interpretation: Studies in Biblical and Cuneiform Literatures* (ed. H. Tadmor and M. Weinfeld; Jerusalem: Magnes Press; Leiden: Brill, 1983) 76–87.

81 For *egerrû* at Mari, see ARM 26 196:8–10; 207:4–11; 244:11–14; cf. Durand, *Archives*, 385; S. A. L. Butler, *Mesopotamian Conceptions of Dreams and Dream Rituals* (AOAT 258; Münster: Ugarit-Verlag, 1998), 151–57.

the king seeks relief from plagues by different divinatory means, eventually including prophecy of some kind.[82]

Listing techniques of divination implies that difference among them was acknowledged; even prophecy stands in its own right. However, the means prophets used for receiving divine messages were not exclusively "prophetic," that is, typical of the prophets only. There were other ecstatics besides prophets; visions and dreams could be experienced by other people as well; and, in many cases, the difference between prophetic and other noninductive divination, or "possession divination," is extremely difficult to define. On the other hand, the inductive methods of divination required specialized studies and could be practiced only by experts whose methods did not considerably overlap. Astrologers observed celestial phenomena while haruspices interpreted viscera of sacrificial animals, never vice versa. However, their respective expertises were complementary, and scholarly cooperation evidently existed.[83] What united the scholars of different kinds (astrologers, haruspices, and exorcists) was their scholarship, the profound knowledge of traditional literature, and a high level of literacy—qualities that are not prerequisites to noninductive divinatory skills, which may not include literary activity at all.

Hence, if we want to divide divination into subcategories, the basis of division cannot be the difference between prophecy and all other kinds of divination. The dividing lines should be drawn between different techniques of divination; there are also differences between the social roles of the techniques' practitioners. The Assyrian prophets are a class distinct from the scholars, differing in gender, social standing and politics.

First, the majority of the Assyrian prophets known to us are women, while the female representation among the scholars is virtyally nonexistent.

Second, as noted earlier, prophets, unlike scholars, do not write letters to the king; if their words are written, they are transmitted to the king in reports written by professional scribes.[84]

---

82 See O. R. Gurney, "Hittite Prayers of Mursili II," *AAA* 27 (1940): 26–27 (*KUB* 24 3 ii 19–22 = *KUB* 24 4 i 10–12); A. Goetze, *Die Pestgebete des Muršiliš* (Kleinasiatische Forschungen 1; Weimar, 1927–30) 218–19 (Pestgebet 2 §10); and cf. A. Kammenhuber, *Orakelpraxis, Träume und Vorzeichenschau bei den Hethitern* (Hethitische Texte 7; Heidelberg: Winter, 1976) 119–33; M. Weippert, "Aspekte israelitischer Prophetie im Lichte verwandter Erscheinungen des Alten Orients," in *Ad bene et fideliter seminandum*, FS K. Deller (ed. G. Mauer and U. Magen; AOAT 220; Kevelaer, Germany: Butzon & Bercker; Neukirchen-Vluyn: Neukirchener, 1988) 287–319, esp. 297–99.
83 See S. Parpola, "Mesopotamian Astrology and Astronomy as Domains of the Mesopotamian 'Wisdom,'" in *Die Rolle der Astronomie in den Kulturen Mesopotamiens* (ed. H. D. Galter; Grazer Morgenländische Studien 3; Graz, Austria: Universitätsbibliothek, 1993) 47–59, esp. 51–52.
84 See Nissinen, "Spoken, Written, Quoted, and Invented."

Third, while scholars transmitted received tradition as successors of the mythical, antediluvian sages,[85] prophets acted as direct mouthpieces of gods; both roles were the result of education and training in a specific environment.

Fourth, prophets do not take part in political counseling in the way of the scholars; they do not form part of the king's closest advisory body and were not members of the political elite, or the "magnates" (LÚ.GAL.MEŠ).[86] This does not prevent them, by the medium of oracles, from being actively involved in political decision making, but unlike the scholars they do not seem to be in the position of making practical suggestions. Scholars sometimes make suggestions on the grounds of prophetic oracles,[87] but more often on the basis of their learned observations and political instinct.

In Assyria, the roles of scholar and prophet are not interchangeable. The inductive and non-inductive methods of divination are never mixed, although, in a literary context, the outcome of divination may sometimes be described in a way that resembles prophecy.[88] However, when dreams and visions are reported, for example, in inscriptions, the source seems immaterial to the author, and it is often impossible to decide whether the dream or vision in question should be defined as prophetic.[89] Visionaries like the *šabrû* and the *šāʾilu* are virtually

---

85 See S. Parpola, *Letters from Assyrian and Babylonian Scholars* (SAA 10; Helsinki: Helsinki University Press, 1993), xvii–xxiv.

86 For the officials belonging to this class, see R. Mattila, *The King's Magnates: A Study of the Highest Officials of the Neo-Assyrian Empire* (SAAS 11; Helsinki: Neo-Assyrian Text Corpus Project, 2000); S. Parpola, "The Assyrian Cabinet," in *Vom Alten Orient zum Alten Testament*, FS W. von Soden (ed. M. Dietrich and O. Loretz; AOAT 240; Kevelaer, Germany: Butzon & Bercker; Neukirchen-Vluyn: Neukirchener, 1995) 379–401.

87 As Bel-ušezib does in SAA 10 111 and Nabû-nadin-šumi in SAA 10 284; see Nissinen, *References*, 96–105.

88 E.g., Esarhaddon Nin A i 61–62: *alik lā kalâta idāka nittallakma ninâra gārēka,* "Go ahead, do not hold back! We walk by your side, we annihilate your enemies!" These words are called *šīr takilti*, "oracle of encouragement," which refers to extispicy; see Nissinen, *References*, 33–34; Pongratz-Leisten, *Herrschaftswissen*, 84–85.

89 For a similar situation at Mari, see Sasson, "Posting," 300. Many Mari letters conventionally included in the "prophetic" corpus are, in fact, dream reports (e.g., ARM 26 233; 234; 235; 236; 238; 239; 240; and other letters classified under the title "Les rêves" in Durand, *Archives*, 465–82), and it is often difficult to decide whether they should be qualified as prophetic dreams, if the dreamer her/himself is not designated explicitly as a prophet; for an attempt to differentiate between prophecies and (non-prophetic) dreams in Mari letters, see I. Nakata, "Two Remarks on the So-Called Prophetic Texts from Mari," *Acta Sumerologica* 4 (1982) 143–48. As to Mari dreams in general, see J. M. Sasson, "Mari Dreams," *JAOS* 103 (1983) 283–93; Pongratz-Leisten, *Herrschaftswissen*, 107–11.

equated with prophets in Neo-Assyrian texts, and the dreams of *šabrûs* recorded in the prisms of Assurbanipal are reported in language that could also be used by the Assyrian prophets.

What makes the prophets distinctive from others in Neo-Assyrian society is their attachment to the worship of Ištar and to the respective socioreligious role, comparable to that of other devotees like the *assinnu* and *kurgarrû,* whose gender role was permanently changed by the goddess. The prophets may not have been generally characterized by a specific gender role, although indications to that effect exist (see above); in any case, the association of *maḫḫû* and *raggimu* with other ecstatics and the connotation of frantic behavior suggest that to be a prophet required a role and way of life distinctive from that of an average Assyrian citizen. Like the representatives of the "third gender," the prophets impersonated the goddess—at least functionally, if not in their outer appearance. This explains the prominent role of women in prophecy without making it solely an *affaire de femmes:* the goddess who is able to take the role of both sexes can be impersonated by female and male persons alike.

All this is not to say that the purpose of prophecy would have been different from that of divination in general. The difference is qualitative rather than functional; all branches of divination share a common ideological and theological basis. In Assyrian imperial ideology, there should not have been any discrepancy among prophets, scholars, and other diviners who worked for a common goal, for example, during the war of Esarhaddon against his brothers.[90] The legitimation of all divination was based on the idea that gods indeed communicate with humans and that the decisions of the heavenly world affect earthly circumstances. There were different channels, however, through which the divine will was brought to humans' attention, as well as different human beings who were qualified to take care of the logistics.

Conclusions

Given the state of publication up to 1998, it was understandable that Neo-Assyrian prophetic documents had not had a decisive role in the study of prophecy, even though their value to comparative studies was often acknowledged.[91]

90 SAA 9 1.8 and SAA 10 109:8–15 show that the queen mother Naqia consulted prophets (Aḫat-abiša) as well as scholars (Bel-ušezib and probably the exorcist Dadâ) during the expatriation of Esarhaddon.

91 Apart from the few works by H. B. Huffmon, M. Weippert, and others dedicated to the Neo-Assyrian prophetic sources (see the bibliography, including works dated before 1997, in Parpola,

Now, having the extant documentation published in an easily accessible form, the time is ripe for a full-scale assessment of the implications of the Neo-Assyrian sources for the understanding of prophecy, both in Mesopotamia[92] and in general; in this essay, this work has been attempted from the point of view of the socioreligious role of the Assyrian prophets.

The Neo-Assyrian sources we have at our disposal—both the actual prophetic oracles and other texts—make prophets appear as practitioners of one branch of noninductive divination, whose characteristic role as devotees of Ištar also brought them into a close relationship with the king. Apart from the Neo-Assyrian sources, prophetic oracles and documents concerning the appearance of prophets (*maḫḫû/muḫḫûm*) show, in all their sparsity, that prophecy in Mesopotamia was not just an accidental and temporary phenomenon, imported from somewhere else in the Neo-Assyrian era, but that prophets were there all the time. If the worship of Ištar may be claimed as "genuinely" Mesopotamian, this claim certainly applies to prophecy.

Regarding the Assyrian prophets' socioreligious role and its implications for the image of the prophet in the ancient Near East, the Neo- Assyrian sources reinforce the elementary connection of prophecy with temples and the royal court, known from the sources from Mari and Ešnunna, as well as from the Hebrew Bible. However, the image of the Assyrian prophet sketched above turns out to be different from the widespread idea of prophecy, based largely on biblical material and interpreted within the symbolic world of modern scholarship; the following presentation of the prophet's image, as opposed to the image of the priest, appeared in a recent reconstruction of ancient Israelite society:

> Prophets claim to have been individually called by a deity, that is, their vocation is customarily not inherited or taught, as is the case for priests. Prophets tend not to be associated with institutions. And prophets are less concerned than priests with maintaining the status quo; that is, they are usually more involved in promoting dynamic social change as innovators and reformers.[93]

Assyrian Prophecies, cix–cxii), see, e.g., R. R. Wilson, *Prophecy and Society in Ancient Israel* (Philadelphia: Fortress Press, 1980), 111–19; J. L. Sicre, *Profetismo en Israel: El profeta, los profetas, el mensaje* (Estella, Spain: Verbo divino, 1992), 238–40; L. L. Grabbe, *Priests, Prophets, Diviners, Sages: A Socio-historical Study of Religious Specialists in Ancient Israel* (Valley Forge, Pa.: Trinity Press International, 1995), 91–92.

92 For a comprehensive treatment of the Mesopotamian oracular sources, including the prophetic sources, see Pongratz-Leisten, *Herrschaftswissen*, 47–95 (for Assyrian sources, esp. 74–95).

93 P. McNutt, *Reconstructing the Society of Ancient Israel* (Library of Ancient Israel; London: SPCK; Louisville: Westminster John Knox Press, 1999), 179. Note that the author herself also ac-

This hardly matches the picture of the prophets of Mari or Assyria, who were associated with institutions, in the framework of which their expertise was taught and learned, and who—at least on the basis of the extant sources—were apparently not the first to promote social change. If there were prophets like those described above, no documentation of their activity has been preserved. Moreover, the idea of prophecy as quoted is problematic even in view of the Hebrew Bible. The idea of antagonism between the prophet and the priest may be wrong—Jeremiah, for example, is introduced as *min hak-kōhănîm*, that is, a priest (Jer 1:1).[94] Furthermore, the Hebrew Bible is explicit about associating the prophets with the temple of Jerusalem or other cult places, even in cases in which the prophet takes a critical attitude toward the official cult. For example, the biblical figures of Jeremiah or Ezekiel are unthinkable without the temple of Jerusalem in the background, not to mention Haggai and Zechariah and their ultimatums on reconstruction of the Second Temple. There are innovators, reformers, and promoters of dynamic social change among the biblical prophets, but one might ask about the breadth of evidence for this kind of prophecy and to what extent it goes back to historical circumstances. In other words, to what extent does "biblical prophecy"—prophecy as depicted in the final form of the Hebrew Bible—correspond to "ancient Israelite prophecy," the concrete historical phenomenon? The prophetic literature of the Hebrew Bible is the result of centuries of selecting, editing, and interpreting, and can give only a partial and somewhat distorted view of the phenomenon.[95] It is widely accepted today that the biblical prophetic figures represent an amalgamation of subsequent generations' interpretations,[96]

---

knowledges different types of prophets: "Presumably, prophets who upheld the status quo (and thus were not associated with types of movements described here) would have been supported by those in power, and peripheral prophets, who were critical of the status quo, by those who wanted some kind of a change" (180–81).

94 See, e.g., R. P. Carroll, *The Book of Jeremiah: A Commentary* (OTL; London: SCM, 1986), 90–91. Even if *min hak-hōhănîm* should be understood as a reference to Jeremiah's father Hilkiah and not to himself (thus W. McKane, *A Critical and Exegetical Commentary on Jeremiah* [vol. 1; ICC; Edinburgh: T. & T. Clark, 1986], 1), it does not change the socioreligious background of Jeremiah as being from priestly circles.

95 See Grabbe, *Priests, Prophets, Diviners, Sages*, 117: "The impression is frequently given that the OT prophets were primarily social critics and ethicists. This is based partly on a failure to consider the contents of the prophetic books as a whole and partly on a failure to recognize that the contents of prophetic books are not necessarily the product of prophets. That is, in the course of transmission and editing of the tradition, the contents of the prophetic books may well be to a significant extent the product of scribes, priests, and sages."

96 For Jeremiah, see Carroll, *Jeremiah*, 55–64; for Ezekiel, see K.-F. Pohlmann, *Das Buch des Propheten Hesekiel (Ezechiel): Kapitel 1–19* (ATD 22/1; Göttingen: Vandenhoeck & Ruprecht, 1996), 40–41; for Amos, see C. Levin, "Das Amosbuch der Anawim," *ZTK* 94 (1997) 407–36;

behind and among which the historical figures of the prophets must be sought—if there is a methodology, or methodologies, that enable this quest.

While it may be a hopeless task to reconstruct historical personalities from the biblical prophetic texts—even redaction criticism can only identify strands of material, from different ages, that remain ultimately anonymous—comparative studies are helpful in outlining ancient Israelite prophecy and the roles of the prophets, provided that each source is studied in its own right and hasty conclusions are avoided.[97] From the comparative point of view, the Neo-Assyrian prophetic sources are no doubt prominent: not only do they derive from the height of Assyrian political and cultural influence, acknowledged as a key period in the literary and ideological formation of the Hebrew Bible,[98] they also demonstrate textual, metaphorical, and ideological affinities with prophetic and other biblical texts.[99] These texts, together with similar texts in other ancient Near Eastern prophetic sources, make interpretation of ancient Israelite/Judean prophecy as an indigenous phenomenon unwarranted.[100] While it is unsound methodology to maintain that conclusions from the Assyrian evidence apply to ancient Israelite society, so that the image of the Israelite/Judean prophets could be drawn

---

for the problem in general, see, e.g., O. H. Steck, *Die Prophetenbücher und ihr theologisches Zeugnis: Wege der Nachfrage und Fährten zur Antwort* (Tübingen: Mohr, 1996).

97 For comparative attempts of different kinds, see, e.g., O. Loretz, "Die Entstehung des Amos-Buches im Licht der Prophetien aus Māri, Assur, Ishchali und der Ugarit-Texte: Paradigmenwechsel in der Prophetenforschung," *UF* 24 (1992) 179–215; H. M. Barstad, "No Prophets? Recent Developments in Biblical Prophetic Research and Ancient Near Eastern Prophecy," *JSOT* 57 (1993) 39–60 (reprinted in *The Prophets: A Sheffield Reader* [ed. Philip R. Davies; Biblical Seminar 42; Sheffield: Sheffield Academic Press, 1996] 106–26); Heintz, "Des textes sémitiques anciens à la Bible hébraïque."

98 See, e.g., E. Otto, "Die besiegten Sieger: Von der Macht und Ohnmacht der Ideen in der Geschichte am Beispiel der neuassyrischen Großreichspolitik," *BZ* 43 (1999) 180–203.

99 See Weippert, "Assyrische Prophetien," 104–11; Nissinen, "Relevanz," 225–53; Parpola, *Assyrian Prophecies*, passim.

100 *Pace* R. R. Wilson, "Prophet," *HBD* (1996) 884–89, esp. 886: "[T]here is no biblical evidence to indicate that Israel recognized prophecy as an import. In addition, anthropological studies of prophetic phenomena show that prophecy can arise spontaneously in any society when the necessary social and religious conditions are present. There is therefore no reason to assume that prophets could not have appeared in Israel without outside cultural influence." While the chronological and geographical distribution of ancient Near Eastern prophecy raises the question whether prophecy anywhere in the ancient Near East can be considered a foreign import, it also speaks for prophecy's cultural communicability rather than for unique and isolated phenomena.

from the Assyrian model,[101] it is also true that Neo-Assyrian prophetic sources provide, chronologically, the most immediate point of comparison for the biblical prophetic literature. They also provide the closest historical and phenomenological analogy to ancient Israelite/Judean prophecy.

101 See the just warnings of J. Blenkinsopp, *Sage, Priest, Prophet: Religious and Intellectual Leadership in Ancient Israel* (Library of Ancient Israel; Louisville: Westminster John Knox Press, 1995), 6–7.

Non-Male Prophets in Ancient Near Eastern Sources

1 Non-Male Prophecy in the Ancient Near East

Prophecy is, and was, a gender-inclusive phenomenon. Both women and men, even trans- or intersexed persons, can be found among people who act as intermediaries between the human and divine world. According to anthropological and textual evidence, this is true for the modern times as well as for the distant past.[1] Among different types of religious agency, prophecy appears as the one that is perhaps the least gender-specific, typically not discriminating between the subjects of prophetic activity on the basis of gender. Without claiming that this has been true always and everywhere, the non-gender-specific pattern occurs often enough in the sources to make it a distinct feature of prophetic divination.

What can we know, then, about ancient prophecy, and how can we know it? Whoever wants to study the prophetic phenomenon in the ancient Near East has to content her/himself with the fact that the sources documenting ancient prophecy are few and far between. The Hebrew Bible notwithstanding, most of the available texts documenting prophecy derive from two sources, the Old Babylonian Mari and the Neo-Assyrian Nineveh; other than that, we have only scattered texts from different times and places, giving only a very restricted view on prophecy in other historical contexts.[2] Written by scribes other than the prophets themselves, the texts are always secondary to the prophetic performances. They represent different genres, each of which yields but a narrow and genre-specific view of the prophets and the historical scene of their activity. On the other hand,

1 For anthropological evidence, see Lester L. Grabbe, "Her Outdoors: An Anthropological Perspective on Female Prophets and Prophecy," in *Prophets Male and Female: Gender and Prophecy in the Hebrew Bible, the Eastern Mediterranean, and the Ancient Near East* (ed. Corrine L. Carvalho and Jonathan Stökl; SBLAIL 15; Atlanta: Society of Biblical Literature, 2013), 11–25; Kirsi Stjerna, "Finnish Sleep-Preachers: An Example of Women's Spiritual Power," *Nova religio* 5 (2001): 102–20; Thomas W. Overholt, *Prophecy in Cross-Cultural Perspective: A Sourcebook for Biblical Researchers* (SBLSBS 17; Atlanta: Scholars Press, 1986).

2 The available evidence is collected in Martti Nissinen, *Prophets and Prophecy in the Ancient Near East*, with contributions by Choon-Leong Seow, Robert K. Ritner, and H. Craig Melchert. 2nd ed. (SBLWAW 41; Atlanta: Society of Biblical Literature, 2019). Henceforth, "no." (plus number) refers to the texts included in this collection and, at the same time, to the appendix of the present volume.

DOI 10.1515/9783110466546-010

the wide variety of genres also makes it possible to view prophets and prohecy from different angles. In addition, the temporal range and geographical distribution of the sources demonstrate the permanence of the prophetic phenomenon as a part of ancient Near Eastern divination through millennia. The gender aspect of prophetic activity varies according to culture-specific patterns and preconditions.

This article, based on original sources and an increasing number of studies in non-male prophetic activity in the ancient Near East,[3] aims at a full inventory of female and other non-male subjects of prophetic activity in ancient Near Eastern sources. The evidence can be divided in three sets of sources: (1) Old Babylonian texts, mostly from the 18th century BCE kingdom of Mari; (2) Assyrian texts, predominantly from the 7th century BCE archives of Nineveh; and (3) the Hebrew Bible, the pertinent passages of which are difficult to date, but presumably derive from eighth through fourth centuries BCE.

Other ancient documents of prophecy from the Near East, written in languages other than Akkadian or Hebrew,[4] do not mention non-male prophets. However, female prophecy was a permanent feature of Greek oracular practice in later periods, represented by the well-known female prophets of Apollo at Delphi and Didyma, as well as the priestesses of Dodona.[5] Even the New Testament ac-

---

3 E.g., Susan Ackerman, "Why Is Miriam Also among the Prophets (And Is Zipporah among the Priests?)," *JBL* 121 (2002): 47–80; Irmtraud Fischer, *Gotteskünderinnen: Zu einer geschlechtsfairen Deutung des Phänomens der Prophetie und der Prophetinnen in der Hebräischen Bibel* (Stuttgart: Kohlhammer, 2002); Wilda C. Gafney, *Daughters of Miriam: Women Prophets in Ancient Israel* (Minneapolis: Fortress Press, 2008); Hugh G. M. Williamson, "Prophetesses in the Hebrew Bible," in *Prophecy and Prophets in Ancient Israel: Proceedings of the Oxford Old Testament Seminar* (ed. John Day; LHBOTS 531; London: T & T Clark, 2010), 65–80; Jonathan Stökl, "Female Prophets in the Ancient Near East," ibid., 47–61; id. "Gender 'Ambiguity' in Ancient Near Eastern Prophecy: A Reassessment of the Data behind a Popular Theory," in Stökl and Carvalho (eds.), *Prophets Male and Female*, 59–80; Hanna Tervanotko, "Speaking in Dreams: The Figure of Miriam and Prophecy," ibid., 147–68; Esther J. Hamori, "Childless Female Diviners in the Bible and Beyond," ibid., 161–91; ead. *Women's Divination in Biblical Literature: Prophecy, Necromancy, and Other Arts of Knowledge* (The Anchor Yale Bible Reference Library; New Haven: Yale University Press, 2015); Martti Nissinen, *Ancient Prophecy: Near Eastern, Biblical, and Greek Perspectives* (Oxford: Oxford University Press, 2017), 297–325.

4 I.e., the Zakkur Stela (no. 137), the Deir Alla inscription (no. 138), the Amman Citadel Inscription (no. 136), the Til Barsip Stela (no. 143), and the Lachish Letters (nos. 139–41).

5 For the female prophets of Apollo, see, e.g., Lisa Maurizio, "Anthropology and Spirit Possession: A Reconsideration of the Pythia's Role at Delphi," *JHS* 115 (1995): 69–86; Michael A. Flower, *The Seer in Ancient Greece* (Berkeley: University of California Press, 2008), 211–39; Antti Lampinen, "Θεῷ μεμελημένε Φοίβῳ: Oracular Functionaries at Claros and Didyma in the Imperial Period," in *Studies in Ancient Oracle and Divination* (ed. Mika Kajava; Acta Instituti Romani

knowledges female prophecy,[6] and female prophets played a prominent role in early Montanism.[7] Even though Greek-language sources fall out of the scope of this article, it is important to recognize that non-male prophecy is not typical of Near Eastern cultures but belongs to a wider Eastern Mediterranean tradition.

Genrewise, the main part of the Old Babylonian evidence consists of ca. 20 letters belonging to the correspondence of King Zimri-Lim of Mari, plus a couple of administrative documents from Mari and Larsa, a text pertaining to the ritual of Ištar at Mari, and a lexical list. The Assyrian documents comprise a dozen of written oracles attributed to non-male prophets, half-a-dozen letters to King Esarhaddon of Assyria, and a few Middle Assyrian and Neo-Assyrian administrative documents, omen texts and lexical lists. The narrative texts of the Hebrew Bible mention four women in the books of Exodus, Judges, 2 Kings, 2 Chronicles, and Nehemiah, as well as an anonymous female prophet in the book of Isaiah, and an anonymous group of women who are said to have prophesied in the book of Ezekiel. The historical information obtainable from the available source texts is essentially related on the textual genre. The written oracles as well as the royal correspondence from Mari and Assyria proveide primary evidence documenting the recording of prophetic performances according to the preference and interpretation of contemporary writers. The administrative and ritual texts provide first-hand evidence of the presence of (non-male) prophets in Mesopotamian temples, and the lexical lists indicate how (non-male) prophets were associated with socio-religious groups. The biblical passages mentioning non-male subjects of prophetic activity are embedded in secondary literary contexts and, therefore, historically more distant from the circumstances they refer to. They can be read as documents of interpretation and alleged impact of prophetic activity set in the more or less distant past, in some cases even yielding valuable historical information.

Non-male persons involved in prophetic activity can be recognized in the sources in two ways. First, the Akkadian and Hebrew languages use certain specific designations for prophetic activity and its practitioners. Secondly, even without carrying any prophetic or other title, people can be acknowledged as

---

Finlandiae 40; Rome: Institutum Romanum Finlandiae, 2013), 49–88; Nissinen, *Ancient Prophecy*, 25–27; 130–37, 191–200; 224–42.

6 The female prophet Hannah is mentioned in Luke 2:36–38, and the daughters of Philip are said to have had the gift of prophecy (Acts 21:9).

7 See Antti Marjanen, "Female Prophets among Montanists," in Stökl and Carvalho (eds.), *Prophets Male and Female*, 127–43.

subjects of prophetc activity if they do what prophets do, that is, transmit divine messages without using inductive methods.[8]

2 Non-Male Prophets in Old Babylonian Sources

2.1 *muḫḫūtum* and *āpiltum*

The Old Babylonian texts written in the Akkadian language have two different designations used exclusively of female prophets. Both correspond to a masculine noun used of male prophets. The most common among them is derived from the verb *maḫû*, denoting frenzied behavior. The Old Babylonian form *muḫḫūtum* appears in a lexical list as an equivalent of the Sumerian mí-lú-gub-ba; this entry follows the corresponding male designation *muḫḫûm*, Sumerian lú-gub-ba (no. 120). Both entries appear in the vicinity of designations of male and female people with ecstatic behavior (*zabbu*, *zabbatu*). The other designation, *āpiltum*, is the feminine equivalent of the much more common *āpilum*, derived from the verb *apālum* and denoting something like "interpreter" or "spokesperson."[9]

The women carrying the title *muḫḫūtum* are without exception presented as prophets of female deities. A ritual text pertaining to the ritual of Ištar, a major annual celebration of the city of Mari, mentions female prophets (pl. *muḫḫâtum*) among the performers of the ritual (no. 52).[10] An anonymous woman is listed among recipients of silver in a document from the Babylonian city of Larsa from the time of King Rim-Sîn I (early eighteenth century BCE). This woman, designated as a *muḫḫūtum* (mí.lú.gub.ba) of Inanna of Zabala, receives half-a-shekel of silver (no. 135 g). Another, poorly known manifestation of Ištar, Ištar of Bišra, also speaks through a *muḫ*[*ḫūtum*]. This is reported by Ḫammi-šagiš to his father, the official Šu-nuḫra-Ḫalu. Judged from the few words that have been preserved, the divine message is about divine protection (no. 50b).[11]

---

8 For the definition of prophecy as non-inductive (or non-tehnical) method of divination, that is, acquiring divine knowledge, see Manfred Weippert, *Götterwort in Menschenmund: Studien zur Prophetie in Assyrien, Israel und Juda* (FRLANT 252; Göttingen: Vandenhoeck & Ruprecht, 2014), 231–32; Jonathan Stökl, *Prophecy in the Ancient Near East: A Philological and Sociological Comparison* (CHANE 56; Leiden: Brill, 2012), 7–11; Nissinen, *Ancient Prophecy*, 19–23.

9 See Paolo Merlo, "*āpilum* of Mari: A Reappraisal," *UF* 36 (2004): 323–32; Stökl, *Prophecy in the Ancient Near East*, 43.

10 Another text pertaining to the same ritual mentions a male prophet in a similar role (no. 51).

11 Ištar of Bišra appears also in no. 42; for this deity, see Jean-Marie Durand, "La religion à l'époque amorrite d'après les archives de Mari," in *Mythologie et religion des sémites occiden-*

The rest of the women carrying the title *muḫḫūtum* are affiliated with Annunitum, an Ištar-like goddess who had a prominent temple at Mari.[12] Annu-tabni, a *muḫḫūtum* of Annunitum, is awarded with some pieces of clothing by the court official Mukannišum in an administrative document from Mari (no. 58, lines 6–10):

> One *uṭublum* garment of second quality and two woven turbans for Annu-tabni, female prophet of Annunitum.

Two letters from Mari may refer to one and the same *muḫḫūtum*. The official Baḫdi-Lim tells about the hair and the garment fringe of a *muḫḫūtum* brought to him by Aḫum, a priest of the temple of Annunitum in the city of Mari (no. 11). A prophet's hair and a fringe of a garment were sometimes attached to the letter to represent the prophet when the trustworthiness of the prophetic words were tested against another method of divination.[13] Baḫdi-Lim is also attaching the "tablet of Aḫum" which may, in fact, be the letter in which Aḫum himself reports two oracles delivered by Ḫubatum, the *muḫḫūtum*, relating to Zimri-Lim's victory over the Yaminite tribes (no. 10).[14] Addu-duri, Zimri-Lim's mother, writes to the king about an ominous dream of her own, also quoting an anonymous *muḫḫūtum* who had arisen in the temple of Annunitum and delivered the goddess's warning against going on campaign (no. 42, lines 21–26):

> Another matter: a female prophet arose in the temple of Annunitum and spoke: "Zimri-Lim, do not go on campaign! Stay in Mari, and I shall continue to answer.

Addu-duri, too, attaches a hair and a fringe of a garment – not of the prophet, however, but of her own (no. 42).

The other designation, *āpiltum*, is attested only twice. One woman carrying this title is introduced by her name: Inib-šina, sister of King Zimri-Lim, reports an oracle prononunced by Innibana the *āpiltum*. The wording of the divine mes-

---

taux, Vol. 1: *Ebla, Mari* (ed. Gregorio del Olmo Lete; OLA 162; Leuven: Peeters, 2008), 163–631; 249, 270, 288.

12 For Annunitum, see Spencer L. Allen, *The Splintered Divine: A Study of Ištar, Baal, and Yahweh Divine Names and Divine Multiplicity in the Ancient Near East* (SANER 5; Berlin: de Gruyter, 2015), 192–97.

13 Cf., e.g., Esther J. Hamori, "Gender and the Verification of Prophecy at Mari," *WO* 42 (2012): 1–22.

14 For Zimri-Lim's wars agains the Yaminites, see Dominique Charpin and Nele Ziegler, *Florilegium marianum 5: Mari et le Proche-Orient à l'époque amorrite, Essai d'histoire politique* (Mémoires de NABU 6; Paris: SEPOA, 2003), 190–91, 194–95.

sage is badly damaged, but it seems to warn the king about moving and acting too freely when his enemies are "circling about his borders" (no. 14). The other occurrence of the word is in the letter of Nur-Sîn, Zimri-Lim's representative in the kingdom of Aleppo. Nur-Sîn does not refer to any particular person but refers to prophets as an undefined group (no. 1, lines 34–45):

> Previously, when I was still residing in Mari, I would convey every word sopken by a male or female prophet (*āpilum u āpiltum*) to my lord. Now, living in another land, would I not communicate to my lord what I hear and what they tell me? Should anything ever not be in order, let not my lord say: "Why have you not communicated to me the word which the prophet (*āpilum*) spoke to you when he was demanding your area?" Herewith I communicate it to my lord. My lord should know this.

Nur-Sîn, thus, wants to convince the king about his constant alertness to divine messages. The impersonal way the prophets are mentioned as a male-female assembly tells nothing specific about the women prophets but, rather, places them on a par with the male ones. In the same letter, Nur-Sîn quotes a male *āpilum* and an oracle pronounced by "prophets" (*āpilū*, masculine plural), which can be understood as a gender-inclusive reference.

The difference between the two designations, *muḫḫūtum* and *āpiltum*, is far from clear. The available evidence may suggest that the role of the male *muḫḫûm* was more temple-bound while the male *āpilum* was more mobile and could be employed by the royal court.[15] The rareness of the word *āpiltum* makes it difficult to know whether such a distinction can be made between the corresponding feminine designations as well. Nevertheless, it deserves attention that neiher of these two cases gives the female prophets any affiliation to a specific temple.

2.2 Women with Other than Prophetic Titles

Non-male persons acting as prophets may sometimes carry titles that are not specifically prophetic and may refer to a different role. In the letters of Mari, divine words are transmitted by a woman with the title *qammatum*. This title is used three times, probably referring to one and the same anonymous woman (nos. 7, 9, 13). She is called "*qammatum* of Dagan of Terqa," which associates her with Dagan and probably also with the major temple of this deity in the city of Terqa. The meaning of the title itself is unclear and does not necessarily

15 Cf. Durand, "La religion à l'époque amorrite," 420–23, 445–50; Stökl, *Prophecy in the Ancient Near East*, 43–49.

denote a prophetic function. The message of the *qammatum* was directed against making peace between the kingdoms of Mari and Ešnunna, and it is referred to by three different letter-writers, each quoting the proverb-like saying "beneath straw water runs" (*šapal tibnim mû illakū*) but otherwise giving a different wording to the oracle.[16] Both Inib-šina, the king's sister, and Sammetar, his high official, tell about the *qammatum* having come to them with her message. Both writers may refer to the same two-step event, since Sammetar says to have rewarded the woman with a garment and a nose-ring, after which she "delivered her instructions in the temple of Belet-ekallim to the high pr[iestess In]ib-šina" (no. 9, lines 51–54). Whatever these instructions (*wu"urtum*) may have been, and whatever the social position of the *qammatum* was, all this indicates that the divine word she transmitted was given serious consideration.

In addition to people introduced in texts with prophetic and other designations, female persons may appear as fulfilling a prophetic function without carrying any specific title. This is especially true for the letters from Mari, which report several divine messages transmitted by women whose role was not specifically prophetic. A dream of a titleless woman may be reported[17] or the female sender of a letter reports s dream seen by herself. Zunana reports to the king a revelation of Dagan in her dream concerning her servant girl (no. 37), and Addu-duri, Zimri-Lim's mother, reports two ominous dreams of her own, both concerning the safety of Zimri-Lim (nos. 42, 43). Some letter-writers report divine messages mediated by ordinary women. Kibri-Dagan tells about an anonymous "woman, a spouse of a free man" (*ištēn awīltum aššat awīlim*) who had claimed to have been sent by Dagan with a soothing message to Zimri-Lim predicting the fall of Hammurabi, king of Babylon (no. 20, lines 11–2′):

> Dagan has sent me. Write to your lord that he should not be anxious, and [neither] should the la[nd] be anxious. [Ha]mmurabi, [king o]f Babylon [...... is ru]shing to his complete undoing."

Queen Šibtu writes about the performance of Aḫatum, the servant girl (*ṣuḫartum*) of Dagan-malik in the temple of Annunitum, that had been reported to her by

16 I.e., Inib-šina (no. 7, lines 11–19), Sammetar (no. 9, lines 41–50), and Kanisan (no. 12, lines 7–16) who, in fact, quotes the oracle as words of a male prophet (*muḫḫûm*). This discrepancy may be due to the chain of communication: Kanisan writes what he had heard from his father who, for his part, had heard about the oracle from others, hence Kanisan did not necessarily know who the actual speaker was.

17 I.e., no. 41, the vision of Kakka-lidi, and no. 36, the dream of Ayala, an otherwise unknown woman.

Aḫum, the priest of the temple. The girl had gone into trance and delivered on oracle, in which the deity (presumably Annunitum) promises to deliver Zimri-Lim's enemy up to his hand in spite of his negligence towards the deity (no. 24).

2.3 *Assinnu*

One well-attested designation used of persons involved in prophetic activity is *assinnu*, which is known throughout the entire period of cuneiform writing, from the third through the first millennium BCE.[18] Together with another designation *kurgarrû*, the title *assinnu* is used of ritual performers closely affiliated with the worship of the goddess Ištar. They can be found performing in ritual dramas such as battle scenes, in purification rites, and in sickness rituals. They are mentioned receiving food rations together with male and female prophets in a texts from the Middle-Assyrian city of Kar-Tukulti-Ninurta (no. 123). This evidence does not present prophesying as the main occupation of the *assinnu*, even though persons thus designated could assume the prophetic role at least at Mari, as we shall shortly see. In lexical lists, the *assinnu* as well as the *kurgarrû* are regularly associated with prophets and other ecstatics, as well as people with various cultic functions, especially those related to lament and magic.[19] If the socio-religious location of the *assinnu* with that of prophets was as close as the lexical associations suggest, this may explain their involvement in the transmission of divine messages.

Why, then should the *assinnu* be discussed in the context of non-male prophetic agency? This is because the *assinnu*, without being a woman, does not fulfill the expectations of the traditional male performance either. The translations of the word include terminology such as "cult homosexual" and "male cult prostitute," and depending on the underlying gender theory (or the lack thereof), the *assinnu*'s have also been characterized as transvestites, hermaphrodites, and third-gender persons. The gender-ambivalent characteristics of the *assinnu*

18 The Sumerian equivalent saĝ-ur-saĝ is used already in Ur III period texts, and the latest occurrences of *assinnu* are to be found in texts belonging to the Arsacid period. See Saana Svärd and Martti Nissinen, "(Re)constructing the Image of the *Assinnu*," in *Studying Gender in the Ancient Near East* (eds. Saana Svärd and Agnès Garcia Ventura; Winona Lake: Eisenbrauns, 2018), 373–411.

19 See nos. 124, 126; for more examples, see Svärd and Nissinen, "(Re)constructing the Image of the *Assinnu*."

have also been contested.[20] While the sources are not informative enough to reveal any details of the sexual performance of the *assinnu*, there are consistent hints through the source material from different places and periods that the way the *assinnu* acted as sexual beings was somehow non-standard and related to Ištar's power of transgressing and transforming gender. They do not seem to have assumed the conventional male agency and function in the society, but are presented as people, whose masculinity was turned into femininity by Ištar herself.[21]

Two persons carrying the title *assinnu* are known by name in the documents from Mari. Queen Šibtu reports to Zimri-Lim, her husband, about a message Ili-ḫaznaya, *assinnu* of Annunitum, had transmitted in the temple of Annunitum. Almost the whole message is broken away, but what is left of it suggests that it concerned Babylon and its king Hammurabi (no. 22). The letters concerning Šelebum, the other *assinnu*, are better preserved. Inib-šina, Zimri-Lim's sister, refers to her previous message concerning an oracle delivered by Šelebum without quoting it, but since she goes on by reporting the above-quoted oracle of the *qammatum* concerning the peace with Ešnunna, one could assume that Šelebum had transmitted a divine word with related content. One of the letters of Šibtu is all about Šelebum, who had gone into trance in the temple of Annunitum and pronounced the following oracle (no. 23, lines 7–22):

> Thus says Annunitum: Zimri-Lim, you will be tested in a revolt! Protect yourself! Let your most favored servants whom you love surround you, and make them stay there to protect you! Do not go around on your own! As regards the people who would tes[t you]: those pe[ople] I deli[ver up] into your hands.

As much as Šelebum's services may have been appreciated by the king through the royal women, he himself gives a murky picture of his life. The writer of a letter (the names of the writer and the addressee are broken away) reports about Šelebum having come to him/her, complaining about his inadequate living conditions, eating porridge and living "amidst an abundance of shit and piss" (no. 8). The way he refers to his insufficient alimentation ("*idatum*-beer has been taken from Annunitum") gives the impression that he depended on the provisions of the temple.

---

20 Ilona Zsolnay, "The Misconstrued Role of the *assinnu* in Ancient Near Eastern Prophecy," in Stökl and Carvalho (eds.), *Prophets Male and Female*, 81–99; cf. also Stökl, "Gender 'Ambiguity' in Ancient Near Eastern Prophecy."

21 Thus the *Epic of Erra* 4:52–59; see Ilan Peled, "*assinnu* and *kurgarrû* Revisited," *JNES* 73 (2014): 283–97; 287–88.

3 Non-Male Prophets in Assyrian Sources

3.1 *maḫḫūtu*

The Assyrian word *maḫḫūtu* corresponds linguistically to the Old Babylonian *muḫḫūtum*, but has a different socio-lingustic profile. A Neo-Assyrian lexical list presents the word as an equivalent of the Sumerian mí-al-è-dè (no. 125, line 119). Even here, *maḫḫūtu* is grouped together with the male lú-al-è-dè = *maḫḫû* and the male and female ecstatics (*zabbu, zabbatu*), hence the list follows the Old Babylonian lexical tradition, probably also corresponding to the contemporary socio-religious practice. This may be deduced from the association of male and female prophets and male and female ecstatics in the ritual text pertaining to the ritual of Ištar and Dumuzi, performed on the twenty-eighth and twenty-ninth day of the month of Tammuz to a person seized by spirits or evil things. The ritual is performed in the presence of certain personnel including a male and a female prophet (*maḫḫû, maḫḫūtu*) and a male and a female ecstatic (*zabbu, zabbatu*) (no. 118, line 31).

In omen literature, *maḫḫūtu* is used three times in a quite interesting manner. The strong presence of prophets in a city, whether male or female, is introduced as an unfavorable omen in the series of city omens *Šumma ālu* (no. 129, lines 101–2):

> If there are many male prophets (*maḫḫû*) in a city, the city will fall.
>
> If there are many female prophets (*maḫḫātu*) in a city, the city will fall.

The omen list is structured in a way similar to the lexical lists, grouping together diviners (prophets, dreamers, haruspices, etc), cultic performers (musicians, dancers, *kurgarrû*), and people with different kinds of disabilities, such as limping men and women, "crazy" men and women, people with skin diseases, deaf and blind persons, and cripples. It is difficult to explain the logic of the omen list, according to which the city is well if there are many "crazy" people, red-skinned persons, and dancers, while prophets, like most other groups including wise men, musicians, and haruspices, appear as unfavorable omens. The only thing that diviners, cultic performers and disabled people seem to share is their liminal position between the human and divine worlds, either as intermediaries or as carriers of god-given signs in their bodies. In the birth omens of the series *Šumma izbu*, the idea is easier to grasp (no. 127):

> If an anomaly's right ear is cropped and inflated with wind: female prophets will' seize the land.
>
> If an anomaly's left ear is cropped and inflated with wind: the same happens to the land of the enemy.[22]

The idea here seems to be based on the left-right dichotomy.[23] The left side usually indicates a negative value, hence the presence of female prophets in the own country would be a favorable omen (right ear), while their appearance in the enemy's country (left ear) would be unfavorable for the own country. This logic could be applied even to the city omens, if the ominous "city" in them is a city belonging to an enemy.

In the above-mentioned texts—lexical lists, ritual texts and omens— the word *maḫḫūtu* are used in a generic sense. Only in two administrative documents this word is used to refer to specific individuals, both times in plural and without mentioning personal names. In a long Middle Assyrian list of food rations from Kar-Tukulti-Ninurta, barley is delivered to temple officials to be distributed among the temple personnel (no. 123):

> Ten homers four seah five liters for Aššur-apla-iddina on the second day for the food rations of the male and female prophets (*maḫḫu'ē maḫḫu'āte*) and the *assinnus* of the Ištar temple.

This text without doubt refers to persons who actually functioned in the temple of Ištar in the Middle Assyrian capital. It also indicates that the association of prophets with *assinnus*, which can be found many times in lexical lists, has a counterpart in the structure of the temple communities. The presence of female prophets in a major Assyrian temple becomes evident also in the Neo-Assyrian list of expenditures for ceremonies in the temple of Ešarra, that is, the temple of the Assyrian principal god Aššur in the city of Assur (no. 110):

> The expenditure for the divine council: [The c]onfectioner tak[es] 1 seah of honey, 5 liters of oil and 4 seahs [5 liters of sesame. The bakers take] 10 homers of barley for bread and 5 homers of wheat for *qa*[*dūtu*]-bread. The brewers tak[e] 1 homer 5 liters (of barley) for the presence of the female prophets. Total: 1 seah 4 liters of honey, 5 liters of oil, 4 seahs 5 liters of sesame, [11 homers 5 seahs of barley], 5 homers of wheat. All this [is the expenditure for the divine council].

---

22 The commentary to this omen (no. 128) clarifies that the word *maḫḫātu* means "possessed people" (*šēḫu*).

23 See Ann K. Guinan, "Left/Right Symbolism in Mesopotamian Divination," *SAAB* 10 (1996): 5–10.

This text is dated to the time of Adad-nirari III (year 809 BCE) and relates to various different cultic occasions in Ešarra. The ceremony in which the prophets are involved is the celebration of the divine council, which makes sense with regard to the intermediary function of the prophets. Since no male prophets are mentioned in this text pertaining to a specific ceremony, it may be concluded that only female prophets participated in it.

The use of *maḫḫūtu* in extant Neo-Assyrian texts is rather genre-specific, since it is to be found only in lexical and omen texts, and in administrative documents. Unless new evidence gives reason to conclude otherwise, this indicates that *maḫḫūtu* was not the word for a female prophet used in Neo-Assyrian vernacular but was rather an official and literary designation.

3.2 *raggintu*

The designation of a female prophet that belonged to Neo-Assyrian colloquial speech seems to have been *raggintu* rather than *maḫḫūtu*. Female prophets are called *raggintu* both in letters and in written oracles,[24] but not in literary texts or administrative documents. This word and its male equivalent *raggimu* are derived from the verb *ragāmu*, which means shouting and proclaiming. *Raggintu* is an exclusively Neo-Assyrian word[25] and can be understood as the standard title of a female prophet in this period.

Only two or three women carrying the title *raggintu* in the texts are known by their names. A poorly preserved tablet contains a fragmentary prophecy to Assurbanipal pronounced by Dunnaša-amur "the prophetess who pro[phesied...]" (no. 95). The title is written logographically as MÍ.GUB.BA, the pronunciation of which is (and was) up to the reader, but most probably should be read as *raggintu*.[26] Two other cases are clearer. An oracle report from the time of Assurbanipal is ascribed to the *raggintu* Mullissu-kabtat, whose name serves as the colophon in the very beginning of the tablet (no. 92). The tablet contains one or more prophe-

---

24 Letters: nos. 105, 109, 111; written oracles: nos. 92, 95.

25 The male word *raggimu* is also Neo-Assyrian, with the exception of one occurrence in a Late Babylonian lexical list (no. 135q).

26 Thus Simo Parpola, *Assyrian Prophecies* (SAA 9; Helsinki: Helsinki University Press, 1997), xlvi; cf. Stökl, *Prophecy in the Ancient Near East*, 152, who prefers to read the logogram as *maḫḫūtu*. The same woman is the speaker of no. 94; the title is broken, but she is probably introduced as [a woman of Arbe]la ([*mar'at Arba*]*il*).

cies[27] of Mullissu, that is, Ištar of Nineveh, addressed to Assurbanipal who appears to be still the crown pronce of Assyria, living in the Palace of Succession. The oracle assures the goddess's support to the kingship of Assurbanipal, his authority over his own courtiers and the kings of other countries, and the motherly care executed by the goddess (no. 92, lines r. 6–11):

> You whose mother is Mullissu, fear not! You whose nurse is the Lady of Arbela, fear not! Like a nurse I will carry you on my hip. I will put you, a pomegranate, between my breasts. At night I will be awake and guard you; throughout the day I will give you milk, at dawn I will hush you. Fear not, my calf whom I rear!

Another *raggintu* whose name is known is Mullissu-abu-uṣri, whose prophecy is the subject matter of a letter written to the king (Esarhaddon) by Adad-aḫu-iddina, a temple administrator probably functioning in the temple of Ešarra in the city of Assur. He tells that Mullissu-abu-uṣri, who had earlier conveyed the king's clothes to "the land of Akkad," had prophesied that even the throne should also be sent away (no. 111, lines 11–r. 9):

> The throne from the temple [...] Let the throne go! I will catch the enemies of my king with it!

The temple administrator is reluctant to rely on this prophecy and promises to act according to what the king orders. It is possible that both the king's clothes and the throne were meant to be used in the substitute king ritual that took place on occasion of the lunar eclipse in the newly re-established cult site of Akkad in the month of Tebet (X), 671 BCE.[28] Mar-Issar, Esarhaddon's emissary in Babylonia, gives an account of the burial of Damqî, the subsitute king, mentioning even the performances of a *raggintu* on this occasion (no. 109, lines 22–r. 4):

> [I] have heard that, before rituals, a female prophet had prophesied (*raggintu tartugum*), saying to Damqî, the son of the chief adminsitrator: "You will take over the kingship!" [Moreover], the female prophet had spoken to him in the assembly of the country: "I have revealed the thieving polecat of my lord and placed it in your hands."

---

27 The first part of the text (lines 2–11) may be quoted from an earlier oracle; see Weippert, *Götterwort in Menschenmund*, 120–21.

28 For this occasion and the letter, see Simo Parpola, *Letters of Assyrian Scholars to the Kings Esarhaddon and Assurbanipal, Part 2: Commentary and Appendices* (AOAT 5/2. Kevelaer: Butzon & Bercker and Neukirchen-Vluyn: Neukirchener Verlag, 1983), 176–77, 270–72; Martti Nissinen, *References to Prophecy in Neo-Assyrian Sources* (SAAS 7; Helsinki: Neo-Assyrian Text Corpus Project, 1998), 68–77.

The reception of divine words sounding like royal oracles (the name of the deity is not mentioned) would have served as the proof of the real kingship of the substitute king.

Anonymous *raggintu*'s are mentioned by the astrologer Bel-ušezib who writes to Esarhaddon soon after his rise to power, complaining about not haing been treated according to his merits by the newly entrhoned king. He wonders who the king had summoned male and female prophets (*raggimānu raggimātu*), but not Bel-ušezib who had told the omens of kingship to Esarhaddon and looked after his interests during the civil war, even if his own life was threatened (no. 105, lines 7–21).[29] Bel-ušezib's choice of words indicates that the renowned astrologer was demoralized about the king's favor towards people who in his eyes appeared as second-rank diviners.

3.3 Women without Title or with Other than Prophetic Titles

Prophetic titles are not used of all people who appear involved in prophetic activity in Neo-Assyrian sources. In some cases, the title of the prophet whose words are quoted is broken away, as in the fragmentary letter of Nabû-reši-išši, who says a female person to have "prophesied" (*tarrugum*), but her name and title, if originally mentioned, have not been preserved (no. 113, line r. 7).

Most Neo-Assyrian prophetic oracles name the prophet without, however, giving her or him any specifically prophetic title. The two collections of prophetic oracles, SAA 9 1 and 2, include sixteen individual oracles pronounced by ten different prophets whose names have been preserved. Five of them are presented as women (Sinqiša-amur, a woman from Arbela; Remut-Allati from Dara-aḫuya; Issar-beli-da''ini, a female votary of the king; Aḫat-abiša, a woman from Arbela; and Urkittu-šarrat, a woman from Calah), two are presented as men (La-dagil-ili, a man from Arbela; [Nabû]-ḫussanni, a man from Assur), and in three cases the gender is not clear; we shall discuss these cases below. The colophons of the individual oracles included in the collections follow a certain pattern, indicating the name, the place of origin, and the gender of the prophet, such as: "By the mouth of Aḫat-abiša, a woman from Arbela" (*ša pî Aḫat-abīša mar'at Arbail*). The prophetic title is left unmentioned, as if it was found superfluous in a colophon attached to a prophetic oracle. One could sensibly argue that these women were exactly the people who were called *raggintu* by contemporary Assyrians.

29 For this letter, see Nissinen, *References to Prophecy*, 89–95.

Non-male persons acting as prophets sometimes carry titles that refer to a role that is not specifically prophetic. In Neo-Assyrian sources there are a couple of cases where the prophetic word has been pronounced by a *šēlūtu*, a femaly votary belonging to the temple community.[30] This role does not as such entail prophetic activity. The votaries were women who were given to temples. Some of them were daughters or wives of high-ranking men, others are presented as the property of the temple. The cases are too few to define the agency of the *šēlūtu* more precisely, but the prophetic function of two votaries, Issar-beli-da''ini and the anonymous woman mentioned in a fragment of a letter indicates that women belonging to temple communities could assume a prophetic role even without being "officially" labelled as prophets (nos. 74, 114).

We have seen that the letters from Mari sometimes quote divine messages received by ordinary women. This is not common Neo-Assyrian texts; in fact, only one such letter can be quoted, written by Nabû-reḫtu-uṣur who reports a conspiracy to Esarhaddon. He tells about a slave girl (*amtu*) of Bel-aḫu-uṣur, who had pronounced an oracle of Nusku concerning Sasî, the person whom Nabû-reḫtu-uṣur believed to be among the main insurrectionists (no. 115, lines r. 2–5):

> A slave girl of Bel-aḫu-uṣur [...] upon [...] on the ou[tski]rts of H[arran]; since Sivan she has been enraptured and speaks a good word about him: "This is the word of Nusku: the kingship is for Sasî! I will destroy the name and seed of Sennacherib!"[31]

Even though an oracle like this was probably considered pseudoprophecy by Nabû-reḫtu-uṣur, he nevertheless feels obliged to report it and recommends the case to be examined by performing a ritual on the slave girl's account.

3.4 Prophets of Unclear Gender

The *assinnu*'s whose gender role was different from the conventional male performance, are known also from Neo-Assyrian sources. They are attested in differ-

30 See Saana Svärd, *Women's Roles in the Neo-Assyrian Era: Female Agency in the Empire* (Saarbrücken: VDM Verlag, 2008), 79–80.

31 See Nissinen, *References to Prophecy*, 108–53 and cf. the discussion in Steven W. Holloway, *Aššur Is King! Aššur Is King! Religion in the Exercise of Power in the Neo-Assyrian Empire* (CHANE 10. Leiden: Brill, 2003), 336–37, 410–14; Eckart Frahm, "Hochverrat in Assur," in *Assur-Forschungen: Arbeiten aus der Forschungsstelle "Edition literarischer Keilschrifttexte aus Assur" der Heidelberger Akademie der Wissenschaften* (eds. Stefan M. Maul and Nils P. Heeßel; Wiesbaden: Harrassowitz, 2010), 89–137.

ent types of texts—not only in lexical lists and omen texts but also in administrative and literary texts as well as in texts referring to rituals and cultic actions.[32] These documents demonstrate that the *assinnu*'s belonged to the Neo-Assyrian society, especially to communities worshipping Ištar.

As already mentioned above, the *assinnu*'s are listed together with male and female prophets receiving food rations in the Middle-Assyrian administrative text from Kar-Tukulti-Ninurta. No Neo-Assyrian document presenting an *assinnu* functioning as a prophet are known so far. However, there are three cases, all in the collection of ten oracles to Esarhaddon from the year 673 BCE (SAA 9 1) indicating that the gender of the prophet was not clear to the scribe who wrote the tablet. In the first case, the feminine determinative indicating the gender of Issar-la-tašiyaṭ has been erased and replaced by a masculine one by the scribe (no. 68). This may simply be an error of the scribe who has corrected his own mistake; if not, it may reflect the uncertainty of the scribe about the gender of the prophet. In two other cases, the same scribe has knowingly given ambiguous information on the gender of the prophet. The prophet Bayâ is introduced as "a man" from Arbela whose name nevertheless has a feminine determinative (no. 71: MÍ.*ba-ia-a* DUMU URU.*arba-ìl*).[33] The name of Ilussa-amur has a feminine determinative, but the domicile is given with a masculine gentilic *Libbālā*[*yu*] instead of *Libbālītu* (no. 72: MÍ.DINGIR-*sa—a-mu*[*ur*] URU.ŠÀ—URU-*a*-[*a*]). The problem regarding the gender of these persons has been interpreted as their belonging to the people representing the "third gender" or undefinable sex. Since this cannot be shown by gender-specific determinatives, it has been indicated by using intentionally contradictory designations.[34]

Some scholars have warned against laying too much weight on these three cases, either explaining all of them as scribal errors or suspecting that they are resting on "modern reconstruction of gender ambiguity."[35] In my view, the way this professional scribe writes the names (at least in the cases of Bayâ and Ilussa-amur) is ambiguous enough to reflect the ambiguity confronted by the scribe himself. This, of course, does not turn all prophets into genderwise ambiguous

---

32 See the appendix of Svärd and Nissinen, "(Re)constructing the Image of the *Assinnu*."

33 The same prophet is probably the speaker on no. 79 as well, but the determinative is broken away (see Parpola, *Assyrian Prophecies*, il).

34 Parpola, *Assyrian Prophecies*, il–l; Saana Teppo (Svärd), "Sacred Marriage and the Devotees of Ištar," in *Sacred Marriages: The Divine-Human Sexual Metaphor from Sumer to Early Christianity* (eds. Martti Nissinen and Risto Uro; Winona Lake: Eisenbrauns, 2008), 75–92.

35 Thus Stökl "Gender 'Ambiguity' in Ancient Near Eastern Prophecy," 78. Weippert, *Götterwort in Menschenmund*, 187–88 interprets the incongruities as scribal errors.

persons, but increases the probability that such persons, like the *assinnu*, could assume the prophetic function.

4 Female Prophets in the Hebrew Bible

Biblical Hebrew knows one designation for a female prophet. The word *nĕbîʾâ* is the female equivalent of the standard Hebrew word for a male prophet, *nābîʾ*. The feminine word has six occurrences in the Hebrew Bible (Exod 15:20; Judg 4:4; 2 Kgs 22:14; Isa 8:3; Neh 6:14; 2 Chron 34:22); in addition, the verb *hitnabbêʾ* used of prophesying is used of women who "prophesy (*mitnabbĕʾîm*) out of their own hearts" in Ezek 13:17.

Beginning with the last of the female prophewts in biblical chronology, Nehemiah mentions in his memoire Noadiah the *nĕbîʾâ* and "the rest of the prophets who wanted to make me afraid" (Neh. 6:14) together with his archenemies Tobiah and Sanballat.[36] Nothing more is told about this woman,[37] but it is noteworthy that she is the only prophet presented as a contemporary in Ezra-Nehemiah; all other prophets are figures of the past.[38] Earlier in the same chapter, Nehemiah tells to have been accused of putting up prophets to proclaim him king of Jerusalem, which he vehemently denies and takes this as pure intimidation (Neh 6:5–9). The text gives the impression that there was prophetic activity in Jerusalem that was not favorable to Nehemiah's mission, Noadiah being among his opponents perhaps even as the leader of the group of prophets. Noadiah and the other prophets, perhaps both male and female, may be taken as continuing the prophetic tradition in Jerusalem, the legitimacy of which which was called into question during the reorganization of the worship of the Second Temple. Nothing is said about Noadiah's prophetic activity, but her role is presented as emphatically political.

---

36 On Noadiah, see Robert P. Carroll, "Coopting the Prophets: Nehemiah and Noadiah," in *Priests, Prophets and Scribes: Essays on the Formation and Heritage of Second Temple Judaism in Honour of Joseph Blenkinsopp* (eds. Eugene Ulrich et al.; JSOTSup 149; Sheffield: Sheffield Academic Press, 1992), 87–99; Fischer, *Gotteskünderinnen*, 255–73; Martti Nissinen, "The Dubious Image of Prophecy," in *Prophets, Prophecy, and Prophetic Texts in Second Temple Judaism* (eds. Michael H. Floyd and Robert D. Haak; LHBOTS 427; London: T & T Clark, 2006), 26–41 (= pp. 577–96 in this volume); 30–35; Gafney, *Daughters of Miriam*, 111–14; Williamson, "Prophetesses in the Hebrew Bible," 65–67; Hamori, *Women's Divination*, 186–88.

37 In the Septuagint, Noadiah is presented as a male person (2 Esd 16:14: τῷ Νωαδια τῷ προφήτῃ).

38 I.e., Haggai and Zechariah in Ezra 5:1–2; 6:14 and anonymous prophets in the past in Ezra 9:11; Neh 9:26, 30, 32.

The female prophet mentioned in the book of Isaiah[39] collaborates with the prophet Isaiah who is told by God to take a tablet and write on it the name Maher-shalal-hash-baz. Isaiah tells that he "went to the prophetess (*wā-'eqrab 'el-han-nĕbî'â*), and she conceived and bore a son" who is then given the name written on the tablet; the ominous name "Pillage hastens, looting speeds" predicts that "the wealth of Damascus and the spoil of Samaria will be carried away by the king of Assyria" (Isa 8:1–4). The mother of the child is anonymous but her designation bears a definite article. The woman is not called Isaiah's wife; what matters more than the marital configuration is that the woman who gives birth to the child with the God-given ominous name is actually called a prophet in the narrative set in the mouth of Isaiah. She is not presented as speaking divine words;[40] giving birth to the child is her oracle. Unlike Gomer, the woman who bore children with likewise portentous names for the prophet Hosea (Hos 1:2–9), she is recognized as a prophet and her agency is on equal terms with that of Isaiah. She participates in the ominous chain of events including the inscription of the name by Isaiah, the sexual intercourse between the two, the parturition of the son by herself, and the fulfilment of the prophecy by God. The female prophet is first and foremost a narrative character, hardly revealing anything about the family life of historical prophets but demonstrates the (gendered) use of prophecy in a religio-political narrative.

Another religio-political narrative employing a female prophet is 2 Kgs 22:3–20, which tells about the "Book of Law" (*seper hat-tôrâ*) found during the restoration works in the temple of Jerusalem. Hilkiah the high priest and Shaphan the scribe bring the scroll to the notice of King Josiah who sends them together with three royal officials to inquire God about the scroll. The men go to Huldah, the wife of Shallum, keeper of the warderobe, and she delivers an oracle to Josiah, according to which God's wrath has kindled against Jerusalem and its temple and he will bring a disaster upon them. Josiah himself, however, will not see the disaster but will be gathered to his ancestors in peace.[41]

---

39 On her, see, e.g., Ernst Axel Knauf, "Vom Prophetinnenwort zum Prophetenbuch: Jesaja 8,3f im Kontext von Jesaja 6,1–8,16," *lectio difficilior* 2/2000 (www.lectio.unibe.ch); Fischer, *Gotteskünderinnen*, 189–220; Gafney, *Daughters of Miriam*, 103–7; Williamson, "Prophetesses in the Hebrew Bible," 74–76; Hamori, *Women's Divination*, 160–66.

40 Unless Isa 8:3–4 is not originally an oracle spoken by her, as suggested by Knauf, "Vom Prophetinnenwort zum Prophetenbuch."

41 On Huldah, see, e.g., Lowell K. Handy, "The Role of Huldah in Josiah's Cult Reform," *ZAW* 106 (1994): 40–53; Renita J. Weems, "Huldah, the Prophet: Reading a (Deuteronomistic) Woman's Identity," in *A God So Near: Essays on Old Testament Theology in Honor of Patrick D. Miller* (eds. B. A. Strawn and N. R. Bowen; Winona Lake, Ind.: Eisenbrauns, 2003), 321–39; Fischer, *Gotteskünderinnen*, 158–88; Gafney, *Daughters of Miriam*, 94–103; Williamson, "Prophetesses

Whether or not the character of Huldah is based on a historical personality, in the world of the narrative she is a central agent in the event that, according to 2 Kings 22–23 eventually leads to a religious reform carried out by Josiah; in 2 Chron 34 the reform precedes Huldah's oracle. In both narratives, the most authoritative delegation representing both the temple and the royal court is sent to Huldah, even though there were other prophets in Jerusalem (cf. 2 Kgs 23:2). She carries the title *nĕbîʾâ* but is presented through her husband's profession which may create a link between her and the temple or court, depending on whose warderobe Shallum was keeping. That she lives in the new quarter of Jerusalem may be mentioned to create a certain distance between her and the temple and court institutions. The words pronounced by Huldah have a distinct Deuteronomistic character, and the whole story can be seen as fulfilling the Deuteronomic ideals about a king consulting and observing the Torah (Deut 17:18–20), mediated by a prophet raised up by God (Deut 18:15–22).[42] Obviously, such a role could be attributed to a woman, and it is noteworthy that both the first and the last prophets mentioned in Joshua–Kings, Deborah and Huldah, are women.

Deborah, who features in the narrative of the book of Judges (Judg 4–5), is a figure very different form her prophetic colleagues.[43] She bears the title *ʾiššâ nĕbîʾâ* (Judg 4:4), and she indeed pronounces divine words that sound like royal oracles of victory: "Up! For this is the day on which the Lord has given Sisera into your hand. The Lord is indeed going out before you" (Judg 4:14; cf. 4:6). Deborah's agency, however, is not limited to mediating divine messages, since she also acts as a judge: the first thing that is said about her is that she "used to sit under the palm of Deborah between Ramah and Bethel in the hill country

in the Hebrew Bible," 68–72; Hamori, *Women's Divination*, 148–59; Blaženka Scheuer, "Huldah: A Cunning Career Woman?," in *Prophecy and Prophets in Stories: Papers Read at the Fifth Meeting of the Edinburgh Prophecy Network* (eds. Bob Becking and Hans M. Barstad; OTS 65; Leiden: Brill, 2015), 104–23.

42 For the similarity of Huldah's oracle with the book of Jeremiah, see Thomas Römer, "From Prophet to Scribe: Jeremiah, Huldah, and the Invention of the Book," in *Writing the Bible: Scribes, Scribalism, and Script* (ed. Philip R. Davies and Thomas Römer; BibleWorld; Durham, NC: Acumen, 2013), 86–96; for the role of Huldah as a follower of Moses, Fischer, *Gotteskünderinnen*, 182–85.

43 On Deborah, see, e.g., Fischer, *Gotteskünderinnen*, 109–30; Gafney, *Daughters of Miriam*, 85–93; Yaakov S. Kupitz and Katell Berthelot, "Deborah and the Delphic Pythia: A New Interpretation of Judges 4:4–5," in *Images and Prophecy in the Ancient Eastern Mediterranean* (eds. Martti Nissinen and Charles E. Carter; FRLANT 233; Göttingen: Vandenhoeck & Ruprecht, 2009), 95–124; Williamson, "Prophetesses in the Hebrew Bible," 72–74; Hamori, *Women's Divination*, 82–93.

of Ephraim; and the Israelites came up to her for judgement" (Judg 4:5). The role of judge can, for sure, be understood as another divinatory function, invoking the image of the Delphic Pythia sitting on her tripod.[44] At the same time it highlights Deborah's position as one of the judges who led the people of Israel before the establishment of the monarchy. Deborah's leadership is even of military nature, as she plays a crucial role in the war of Barak against Jabin, king of Canaan, and his commander Sisera. It deserves attention that she is called "a mother of Israel" in this military context (Judg 5:7), which may highlight her divinatory role as the mediator of divine ion. On top of all this, she is also presented as a musician, intoning a song of victory together with Barak: "Awake, awake, Deborah! Awake, awake, utter a song!" (Judg 5:12).

The multiple roles of Deborah are interesting from the point of view of both prophecy and gender. Her divinatory role goes beyond the conventional functions of prophecy, especially when it comes to military leadership; on the other hand, both judging and music can be understood as means of divine-human communication. The way the figure of Deborah combines divinatory and leadership functions can be compared to the equally manifold job descriptions of Moses and Samuel.[45] In the biblical narrative, such an amalgamation of divinatory roles seems to belong to the time when there was no king—and also no prophets of the conventional type. On the other hand, Deborah is but another example of a formidable female figure in Joshua–Kings. The narrative in Judges 4, indeed, rests on the action of two powerful women, Deborah and Jael.[46]

The first woman called prophet in the Hebrew Bible is Miriam, the sister of Aaron.[47] She is first introduced when the troops of Pharaoh have gone into the sea and the Israelites have marched on dry ground to the other side. Miriam bears the title *nĕbîʾâ*, and what she does is that she takes up a drum and sings to the people a song of victory: "Sing to the Lord, for he has triumphed gloriously; horse and rider he has thrown into the sea" (Exod 15:20). While music is undeniably a way of divine-human communication, one may ask whether this

---

44 See Kupitz and Berthelot, "Deborah and the Delphic Pythia."

45 Hamori, *Women's Divination*, 88–89.

46 See Ora Brison, "Jael, *'eshet heber* the Kenite: A Diviner?," in *Joshua and Judges* (eds. Athalya Brenner and Gale A. Yee; Texts @ Contexts; Minneapolis: Fortress Press, 2013), 139–60.

47 On Miriam, see, e.g., Ursula Rapp, *Mirjam: Eine feministisch-rhetorische Lektüre der Mirjamtexte in der hebräischen Bibel* (BZAW 317; Berlin: de Gruyter, 2002); Susan Ackerman, "Why Is Miriam Also among the Prophets?"; Rainer Kessler, "Miriam and the Prophecy of the Persian Period," in *Prophets and Daniel* (ed. Athalya Brenner; A Feminist Companion to the Bible, Second Series 8; Sheffield: Sheffield Academic Press, 2001), 77–86; Fischer, *Gotteskünderinnen*, 64–94; Gafney, *Daughters of Miriam*, 76–85; Tervanotko, "Speaking in Dreams"; Hamori, *Women's Divination*, 61–81.

song is enough to qualify Miriam as a prophet, but there is another text which clearly implies that she was recognized as such. Numbers 12 tells about a conflict between Miriam and Moses, and the story is essentially about prophetic authority. Miriam and Aaron oppose the marriage of Moses and come to him asking: "Has the Lord spoken only through Moses? Has he not spoken through us also?" (Num 12:2)—as if the reader was reminded of Mic 6:4, where Moses, Aaron, and Miriam appear together as the ones who lead the people out of Egypt.[48] Miriam (but not Aaron) becomes punished with disease because of questioning the authority of Moses. Miriam's prophetic role is not denied; what matters more is the authority of Moses to whom God speaks face to face, and who is, therefore, superior to any other prophet (Num 12:6 – 8). The narrative indicates that Miriam is "remembered in connection to her role as a prophet, if in a deeply conflicted fashion."[49] The remembrance of Miriam as involved in divine-human communication continues in Hellenistic Jewish literature in works such as Visions of Amram and Pseudo-Philo.[50]

Finally, a group of women is presented in Ezek 13:17 – 23 as "the daughters of your people, who prophesy out of their own imagination" (13:17: *bĕnôt ʿammĕkā ham-mitnabbĕʾôt mil-libbĕhen*). Ezekiel is told to prophesy (*nibbāʾ*) to them, pronouncing divine condemnation to the practice of these women, described as sewing bands on wrists and making veils for the heads in order to entrap human lives. Despite the difficulties in translating the Hebrew vocabulary, the activity designated as "prophesying" (*hitnabbēʾ*) does not seem to refer to the transmission of divine words as in the case of the just-condemned male prophets (13:1 – 16) but, rather, to a different kind of divination. Entrapping "lives" (*nĕpāšôt*) has been interpreted, for instance, as necromancy.[51] In the concluding verse the women are supposed to hear that they will no longer "see false visions nor practise divination" (13:23: *šāwʾ lōʾ teḥĕzênâ wĕ-qesem lōʾ tiqsamnâ ʿôd*), which complements the image of the women with two more divinatory terms. The divinatory agency of the women condemned in Ezekiel 13 is described in quasi-pre-

48 Therefore, Kessler, "Miriam and the Prophecy of the Persian Period," reads Numeri 12 as a countertext to Mic 6:4. Rapp, *Mirjam*, 178 – 93, suggests that the advocacy of Miriam's prophetic role goes back to the same circles of the Persian period that even Noadiah represented.

49 Hamori, *Women's Divination*, 81.

50 See Tervanotko, "The Figure of Miriam and Prophecy."

51 Thus Hamori, *Women's Divination*, 167 – 83, and Jonathan Stökl, "The מתנבאות of Ezekiel 13 Reconsidered," *JBL* 132 (2013): 61 – 76, whereas Nancy R. Bowen ("The Daughters of Your People: Female Prophets in Ezekiel 13:17 – 23," *JBL* 118 [1999]: 417 – 33) associates the activity of the women with medical and ritual aspects of childbirth.

cise but vague terms—perhaps intentionally so as a part of enemy rhetoric relying on negative stereotypes.[52]

What matters from the point of view of prophecy in Ezek 13:17–23 is that the use of the verbal root *nb'* overlaps with other divinatory vocabulary in the description of the activity of the women. This challenges our customary definition of prophecy and makes the women operate at the crossroads of prophecy and other kinds of divination—or, perhaps, at the interface of divination and magic, if divination is understood as acquisition of superhuman knowledge, while magic is supposed to bring about a change in the patient's life; in this case, the *nĕpāšôt* manipulated by the women.

5 Comparison

The survey of non-male subjects of prophetic activity demonstrates the presence and impact of women and people with unconventional gender performance in all major source materials of ancient Near Eastern prophecy. Space permits only a brief comparison of the sources by way of conclusion.[53]

Female prophets feature most prominently in Neo-Assyrian texts, in which two-thirds of the prophets known to us are women. This reflects the strong connection of prophecy with the worship of Ištar, the goddess who disclosed the secrets of gods to humans. Even though the prophets of Ištar are not exclusively women, virtually all non-male prophets speak her words, as far as the divine speaker discernable.[54] Non-male prophets have a strong presence even in the documents from Mari, but their share in these sources is about one-third. All but three non-male subjects of prophetic activity in Mari documents, as far as this can be known, are connected with Annunitum or Ištar, while male prophets at Mari appear speak the words of both male and female deities. While there is no universal gender correspondence between prophets and deities, the correlation between female deities and non-male prophets is palpable both at Mari and in Assyria.

Both in Assyrian and Old Babylonian sources, non-male prophets not only pronounce words of female deities but are also somehow linked to their temples.

52 I am indebted to Patrik Jansson for this perspective.

53 For a more profound analysis, see Nissinen, *Ancient Prophecy*, 297–325, 346–48.

54 That is, Ištar or one of her manifestations, among whom I count even Annunitum. Exceptions to this rule include the *qammatum* of Dagan of Terqa (nos. 7, 9), Zunana, who reports the revelation of Dagan in her dream (no. 37), Kakka-lidi, who had a vision of Itur-Mer (no. 41), and the slave-girl in the region of Harran, who spoke the words of Nusku (no. 115).

The only female prophet known from Old Babylonian sources other than Mari documents is the anonymous *muḫḫūtum* affiliated with the temple of Inanna in Zabala, which was one of the major Babylonian centers of her worship. In the kingdom of Mari, all women bearing the title *muḫḫūtum* as well as the two *assinnu*'s pronounce the words of Annunitum or Ištar or perform in their temples. The case with the only known *āpiltum* is unclear because of the damages of the tablet. It is noteworthy that none of the three women who mediate the words of Dagan, the *qammatum* form Terqa, Zunana, and the "spouse of a free man," bear a standard prophetic title, neither does Kakka-lidi, whose vision in the temple of the male god Itur-Mer is reported by Queen Šibtu (no. 41).

In Assyria, the link between non-male prophets and the goddess Ištar, either in the form of Ištar of Arbela or Mullissu, is ubiquitous. Egašankalamma, her temple in Arbela, is the most important centre of Neo-Assyrian prophecy in the sources known to us.[55] Female prophets can also be found in Ešarra, the temple of Aššur in the city of Assur, where the divine council was celebrated in the presence of female prophets (no. 110), and which is the probable base of Mullissu-abu-uṣri (no. 111) and Ilussa-amur (no. 72). One woman, Urkittu-šarrat, comes from Calah, where the was a prominent temple of Ištar, there called the Lady of Kidmuri. The only non-male prophets mediating words of male deities are the slave-girl who speaks the words of Nusku in the outskirts of Harran (no. 115), and Bayâ who speaks in the name of Bel and Nabû in addition to Ištar (no. 71).

In addition to the strong link between female deities and non-male prophets, it is typical of the letters from Mari that the words spoken by non-male prophets are reported to Zimri-Lim by his closest women: his wife Šibtu, his sister Inib-šina, and his mother Addu-duri.[56] Even male persons quote words of female prophets in Mari correspondence,[57] but reports of performances of male prophets written by women are very few.[58] This suggests a closer connection of the royal women of Mari with non-male prophets than with male ones. In Assyrian letters, all references to non-male prophets have written by male persons.[59] This, of

---

55 See Martti Nissinen, "Ištar of Arbela," in *Ancient Arbela: Pre-Islamic History of Erbil* (ed. Raija Mattila, Zidan Bradosty, and Jessica Giraud; Syria Supplement Series; Beirut: Institute Français en Proche-Orient, forthcoming).

56 Šibtu: nos. 17, 22, 23, 24, 41; Inib-šina: nos. 7, 14; Addu-duri: nos. 35, 42; cf. Zunana (no. 37), Šimatum (no. 44), and Timlû (no. 45), who report their own dreams.

57 I.e., Nur-Sîn (no. 1), Sammetar (no. 9), Aḫum (no. 10), Baḫdi-Lim (no. 11), Kibri-Dagan (no. 20), Itur-Ašdu (no. 27), and Ḫammi-šagiš (no. 50b).

58 I.e., Addu-duri (nos. 5, 43) and Šibtu (nos. 17, 18, 21).

59 I.e., Bel-ušezib (no. 105), Mar-Issar (no. 109), Nabû-reši-išši (no. 113), and Nabû-reḫtu-uṣur (no. 115).

course, is due to the lack of female writers in Assyrian correspondence and tells nothing about the relationship between prophets and women. The fact that Naqia, the queen mother, is addressed in many extant prophetic oracles[60] suggests a strong link between her and the prophets of Ištar of Arbela.

The divinatory agency of non-male prophets is related to political and religious institutions and their authority. Deriving from royal archives, both of the two main corpora of sources are strongly occupied with in royal concerns; especially in Assyria, the prophets regardless of their gender appear as orthodox proclaimers of the state ideology.[61] In this respect, the agency of non-male prophets is not different from that of male prophets. Direct contacts between rulers and prophets, whether male or non-male, are not reported, which does not exclude the possibility that the ruler was witnessing prophetic performances, for instance in rituals where they took place, such as the ritual of Ištar at Mari. However, the king was typically not approached by the prophets themselves. The words spoken by non-male prophets are without exception brought to the king's notice by his officials, temple administrators, or family members.

Throughout the Mesopotamian source material it becomes clear that non-male prophets had an established position in temple communities. As mediators of divine knowledge, non-male prophets enjoyed the same appreciation as male ones—at least in theory, since the words mediated by prophets regardless of their person and gender were divine words.[62] In practical terms, however, a certain gender bias becomes evident in the divinatory practice at Mari, where the messages transmitted by non-male prophets were more often checked against another method of divination using the hair and the fringe of the garment attached to the letter by the writer.[63]

What makes the sources from the Levant genderwise different from those from Mari and Assyria is the prevalence of male prophets. Non-male prophets are only known from the Hebrew Bible, where the share of women among prophets mentioned by name is only about one-tenth. The drastically smaller number of female prophets in the Hebrew Bible compared with Mari or, especially, Assyria, may go back to historical circumstances, since all the few Levantine texts at

60 Oracles addressed to Naqia include the following: no. 74 (probably Ištar of Arbela, female votary Issar-bel-da''ini), no. 75 (Ištar of Arbela, female prophet Aḫat-abiša), no. 78 (goddesses of Esaggil, male prophet [Nabû]-ḫussanni), no. 83 (Ištar of Uruk, unknown prophet), and no. 90 (Ištar of Arbela, unknown prophet).

61 See Parpola, *Assyrian Prophecies*, xxxvi–xliv.

62 For discussion on the religious agency of women, see Nissinen, *Ancient Prophecy*, 304–14.

63 See Hamori, "Gender and the Verification of Prophecy at Mari"; for a comparable case in Assyria, cf. no. 115.

our disposal represent the male god/male prophet pattern. However, the meager amount of sources prevents definitive conclusions concerning the gender ratio of Levantine prophets. Defining the socioreligious status of female prophets in "ancient Israel," whether in the monarchical or post-monarchical period, is equally difficult with the available texts in hand.

The Hebrew Bible does not yield a coherent presentation of female prophets. The biblical presentation shares some important features with the patterns known from cuneiform sources. The position of Huldah in particular is in every respect comparable to her Mesopotamian colleagues in relation to kings and religio-political power.[64] None of the female prophets of the Hebrew Bible are presented as being employed by either the temple or the royal court, but the temple of Jerusalem provides itself as the natural base of Noadiah, and perhaps the same can be said of Huldah, especially if the occupation of her husband is understood as being affiliated to the temple. The conflict between Miriam and Moses in Numbers 12, as well as the laconic reference to Noadiah by Nehemiah may reflect power struggles in the Persian period, implying a relatively strong claims of women for religious authority.

On the other hand, some female subjects of prophetic activity in the Hebrew Bible appear in roles that do not conform very well to the image of non-male prophecy in the cuneiform sources. The distribution of divinatory roles and the interface of divination and magic are far less absolute as they appear to be in Mesopotamian tradition. Biblical diviners—women in particular—may mediate divine words, but they also engage in other activities. This raises the question of who of them should be labelled as "prophets" anyway.[65] The women accused of "prophesying out of their own hearts" in Ezek 13:17–23 are described in terms of divination or magic rather different from what is unually understood as prophecy. Some narrative characters, such as Deborah and Miriam, assume multiple divinatory and leadership roles which, because of their legendary nature, are difficult to conform with any kind of historical practice. For this reason, it is also difficult to know exactly how prophetic divination in Judah or Yehud differed from the one documented in the sources from Mari and Assyria.

Knowledge of ancient prophecy comes to us through several filters created partly by the whim of chance, partly by ancient scribes and archivists who

---

64 See, e.g., Handy, "The Role of Huldah in Josiah's Cult Reform."

65 See Hamori, *Women's Divination*, who discusses also Rebekah, Rachel, Hannah, the necromancer of En-Dor, The "wise woman" of 2 Sam 14 and 20, and the women in the vision of Joel 3; cf. Fischer, *Gotteskünderinnen*, who includes the women mentioned in Exod 38:8, the woman of En-Dor, and the women of Joel 3; and Gafney, *Daughters of Miriam*, who discusses the women of Joel 3 and the daughters of Heman in 1 Chron 25:5–6.

long ago determined what we are able to see today. In the case of the Hebrew Bible, due to the long process of textual transmission, the distance between the text and the historical divinatory practice is significantly larger than in the cuneiform sources. In the Hebrew Bible, female prophets appear in narratives embedded in contexts that dissociate the prophetic figures from their historical environments, unless the prophets are narrative characters from the first beginning. The image of biblical prophecy is the construct of biblical writers who may have had ideological reasons for dimishing the role of women without, however, erasing it altogether. The ideological bias, however, is not typical of Hebrew Bible only. The selection of the prophecies that were written down and preserved for posterity was far from being a a bias-free process. The Assyrian construct of prophecy reflects the royal ideology propagated in temples of Ištar, and this may partly explain the prevalence of the non-male prophets of Ištar in the extant Assyrian sources. The ancient Near Eastern sources, thus, provide us with authentic but biased glimpses into the ancient divinatory practice, without ever showing the full picture. Much remains undisclosed, but it becomes clear that prophecy was not jus a man's profession.

The Prophet and the Augur at Tušḫan, 611 BCE

A New Prophetic Text

Our knowledge of Mesopotamian prophecy is based on written evidence derived mainly from two sources and periods: the seventh-century state archives of the Assyrian Empire at Nineveh and the eighteenth-century archives from the city of Mari. These materials, supplemented by additional Near Eastern texts dating from Old Babylonian through Hellenistic times, make it possible to draw a fairly comprehensive picture of Mesopotamian prophecy. The available evidence has now been collected in the second edition of a volume to which Peter Machinist invaluably contributed his knowledge of the Mesopotamian texts and sharp editorial eye.[1] Although this anthology was comprehensive at the time of its publication, undoubtedly a bulk of similar such materials still remains hidden beneath Near Eastern soil. One can realistically expect new evidence to come to light in future archaeological excavations. In this vein, it is my pleasure to discuss here, in Peter's honor, one such cuneiform text, recently published by Simo Parpola,[2] which introduces the most recent addition to the evidence of divinatory activity in Mesopotamia.

ZTT 25[3] is a short administrative text belonging to the archive of 28 cuneiform tablets unearthed in 2002 at Ziyaret Tepe, on the upper course of the Tigris River in southeastern Turkey, east of the modern city of Diyarbakır. The site has been identified as the ancient city of Tušḫan, well known from Neo-Assyrian documents.[4] The probable date of the archive is most intriguing. On the basis of the eponyms preserved in the aforementioned tablets, along with the fact that the building in which the archive was found had been destroyed by fire, it is extremely likely that the archive not only predates the destruction of Tušḫan by

1 M. Nissinen, with contributions by C. L. Seow, R. K. Ritner, and H. Craig Melchert, *Prophets and Prophecy in the Ancient Near East* (2nd ed.; SBLWAW 41; Atlanta: SBL Press, 2019). Peter Machinist was the volume editor of both editions of this book, and his work has left traces on every page of the book.

2 S. Parpola, "Cuneiform Texts from Ziyaret Tepe (Tušḫan), 2002–2003," *SAAB* 17 (2008) 1–113.

3 Ibid., 98–100 and pl. xxii.

4 For the identification, see ibid., 25–27.

DOI 10.1515/9783110466546-011

the Babylonians in Tammuz (IV), 611 B.C.,[5] but that it also postdates the fall of Nineveh in Ab (V), 612 B.C.[6] If so, this would mean that the texts from Ziyaret Tepe document the very last year of what remained of the Assyrian empire, in a city destined for imminent destruction.

ZTT 25: Text and Translation

Despite its brevity and poor state of preservation, ZTT 25 turns out to be a surprisingly informative piece of evidence concerning divination in the Assyrian empire and in the ancient Near East in general. The text reads as follows:

[1]6 *manâ* [2]*ra[gg]im[u]* (⸢LÚ⸣.GU[B].B[A]) [3]*ina abu[lli]*
[4]1 *manû [er]û* [5]*dā[gi]l [iṣṣū]ri*
[6][1 (?)] *manû ana bēt [ili]*
[7][2 (?) *m]anâ ana* [...]
blank space
[8]*gi[mir]* 10 *manâ*

[1]6 minas (of copper to) [2]the pro[p]he[t] [3]at the [city] gate.
[4]1 mina of c[oppe]r (to) [5]the au[gu]r.
[6][1 (?)] mina to the house [of the god].
[7][2 (?) m]inas to [...].
blank space
[8]T[otal], 10 minas.

What is immediately striking in this text is its documentation of the payment of a substantial amount of copper[7] to representatives of two kinds of divination: prophecy and augury. In view of the probable historical background of the Ziyaret Tepe texts, the reason why diviners were consulted is not difficult to fathom. The fall of Nineveh and the march of the Babylonian troops northwards along the course of the Tigris did not bode well for Tušḫan; on the contrary, the attack of the inimical forces was clearly on the horizon. A military threat, whether viewed from the perspective of the ones attacking or those being attacked, con-

5 The crucial passage in the Fall of Nineveh Chronicle has been restored by Parpola as follows: – – [*ina* KUR]*—aš-šur šal-ṭa-niš* [DU.ME URU].MEŠ *šá* KUR. ⸢*du-uš*⸣*-ḫa-a[n x x x] u* KUR.*šu-[ub-š]e?-a ik-šu-ud*"– – [He marched about] imperiously [in Assy]ria and conquered the [citie]s of T[u]šḫa[n, ...] and Šu[*br*]*ia*" (Parpola, "Cuneiform Texts from Ziyaret Tepe," 14 n. 12; see also A. K. Grayson, Assyrian and Babylonian Chronicles [TCS 5; Locust Valley, NY: Augustin, 1975], 95 lines 54–55).
6 For the date, see Parpola, "Cuneiform Texts from Ziyaret Tepe," 12–14.
7 The badly damaged sign URUDU is restored by Parpola from the traces at the top and the end of the break.

stituted a situation in which oracles were typically consulted. At Tušḫan, as elsewhere, diviners seem to have been readily available to mediate such knowledge.

Two Types of Diviners

Of the two types of diviners mentioned in the tablet,[8] prophets are known from Neo-Assyrian prophetic oracles and other sources.[9] In lexical lists, the logographic designation LÚ.GUB.BA appearing here corresponds to Akkadian *muḫḫûm*/*maḫḫû*,[10] though in Neo-Assyrian times it may actually have been spoken as *raggimu*,[11] the colloquial Neo-Assyrian term for "prophet." Prophets appear in several Assyrian cities, more often than not in connection with Ištar's temples and worship. Thus the finding of a prophet in a major city of the empire's northern regions does not come as a great surprise.

Augurs also appear in Neo-Assyrian sources—no less frequently, in fact, than prophets, even though much less research has been devoted to them.[12] The term *dāgil iṣṣūri* is exclusively Neo-Assyrian, with its earliest attestations found in late eighth-century documents from Calah. Augurs tend to appear in reputable company. In the texts from Calah they are mentioned among recipients of wine, along with scholars and diviners of different types.[13] In later times, they appear

---

8 For prophecy as another type of divination, see E. Cancik-Kirschbaum, "Prophetismus und Divination: Ein Blick auf die keilschriftlichen Quellen," in *Prophetie in Mari, Assyrien und Israel* (ed. M. Köckert and M. Nissinen; FRLANT 201; Göttingen: Vandenhoeck & Ruprecht, 2003) 33–53; M. Nissinen, "Prophecy and Omen Divination: Two Sides of the Same Coin," in *Divination and the Interpretation of Signs in the Ancient World* (ed. A. Annus; Oriental Institute Seminars 6; Chicago: Oriental Institute, 2010) 341–51 (= pp. 75–85 in this volume).

9 See S. Parpola, *Assyrian Prophecies* (SAA 9; Helsinki: Helsinki University Press, 1997); M. Nissinen, *References to Prophecy in Neo-Assyrian Sources* (SAAS 7; Helsinki: Neo-Assyrian Text Corpus Project, 1998).

10 lú-gub-ba = *maḫḫû* (*MSL* 12 4:212, 213); cf. Old Babylonian: lú-gub-ba = *muḫḫûm* / mí-lú-gub-ba = *muḫḫūt*[*um*] (*MSL* 12 5:22, 23–24).

11 Parpola, *Assyrian Prophecies*, xlvi.

12 For augurs in Assyria, see especially K. Radner, "The Assyrian King and His Scholars: The Syro-Anatolian and the Egyptian Schools," in *Of God(s), Trees, Kings, and Scholars*, FS S. Parpola (ed. M. Luukko et al.; StudOr 106; Helsinki: Finnish Oriental Society, 2009) 221–38, esp. 231–38, which features far more on the *dāgil iṣṣūri* than the data assembled in *CAD* D 25.

13 For example, CTN 1 3 + 3 145 lines i 3–6, iv 5; CTN 1 14 lines 3–5; cf. CTN 1 6 lines 20, 22–23; CTN 1 8 lines 35–36, where diviners are mentioned. For these texts, see F. M. Fales, "A Fresh Look at the Nimrud Wine Lists," in *Drinking in Ancient Societies: History and Culture of Drinks in the Ancient Near East* (ed. L. Milano; History of the Ancient Near East/Studies 6; Padova: S.A.R.G.O.N., 1994) 361–80.

in various contexts and situations: listed alongside Egyptian scribes and dream interpreters in an administrative document;[14] concluding a treaty with the king together with scribes, haruspices, exorcists, and physicians;[15] borrowing 1.5 minas of silver;[16] complaining about someone who has allegedly deprived them of their possessions;[17] and mentioned in connection with the visit of the king of Hamath.[18] The inclusion of augurs in a treaty together with scholars implies a similar status, which is never the case with prophets, whose audience with the Assyrian king brought insult to at least one astrologer.[19] Augurs also seem to have valuable possessions at their disposal.

In the texts from Ziyaret Tepe, another augur is attested: Šumu-lēšir, who is said to be from Šubria (ZTT 4 e. 6–7; cf. ZTT 2 line 3; 5 rev. 5).[20] This corresponds nicely to the fact that augurs from Šubria in eastern Anatolia were to be found in different Assyrian cities in the Neo-Assyrian period—and not only from Šubria but also from the Anatolian Commagene (Akk. *Kummuḫḫu*) and from the Syrian city of Hamath.[21] Hence, the appearance of an augur at Tušḫan, a city at the crossroads of Mesopotamian and Anatolian cultures and within a stone's throw of Šubria, makes perfect sense.

Augury was probably external to the Mesopotamian heartland as a form of divination, and may have spread from Anatolia to both Mesopotamia and Rome.[22] It was one of the more prominent methods of Hittite divination along

---

14 F. M. Fales and J. N. Postgate, *Imperial Administrative Records, Part I: Palace and Temple Administration* (SAA 7; Helsinki: Helsinki University Press, 1992) 1 iii 11.

15 S. Parpola, *Letters from Assyrian and Babylonian Scholars* (SAA 10; Helsinki: Helsinki University Press, 1993) 7 lines 6–14.

16 T. Kwasman and S. Parpola, *Legal Transactions of the Royal Court of Nineveh, Part I: Tiglath-Pileser III through Esarhaddon* (SAA 6; Helsinki: Helsinki University Press, 1991) 317 line 2.

17 G. B. Lanfranchi and S. Parpola, *The Correspondence of Sargon II, Part II: Letters from the Northern and Northeastern Provinces* (SAA 5; Helsinki: Helsinki University Press, 1990) 163.

18 M. Luukko and G. Van Buylaere, *The Political Correspondence of Esarhaddon* (SAA 16; Helsinki: Helsinki University Press, 2002) 8 line 7.

19 Parpola, *Assyrian Prophecies*, 109 line 9.

20 See Parpola, "Cuneiform Texts from Ziyaret Tepe," 43.

21 See Radner, "The Assyrian King and His Scholars," 235–36.

22 See B. J. Collins, *Hittites and Their World* (Archaeology and Biblical Studies 7; Atlanta: Society of Biblical Literature, 2007) 166–69; see also J.-M. Durand, "La divination par les oiseaux," *MARI* 8 (1997) 273–82. For Hittite divination, see G. M. Beckman, "The Tongue is a Bridge: Communication between Humans and Gods in Hittite Anatolia," *ArOr* 67 (1999) 519–34; T. van den Hout, "Bemerkungen zu älteren hethitischen Orakeltexten," in *Kulturgeschichten: Altorientalische Studien für Volkert Haas zum 65. Geburtstag* (ed. T. Richter et al.; Saarbrücken: Saarbrückener Druckerei und Verlag, 2001) 423–40; R. H. Beal, "Hittite Oracles," in *Magic and Divination in the Ancient World* (ed. L. Ciraolo and J. Seidel; Leiden: Brill, 2002) 57–81.

with dreams, extispicy, and, perhaps, prophecy.[23] Evidence of its practice is attested in several Hittite sources. In one letter, for example, three augurs are described writing a letter to the queen; in another, the outcome of bird divination concerning a military attack is reported to the king; and in yet other missives we learn that dreams and oracles were counterchecked by means of augury.[24] Augurs, among other diviners, also are also referred to in prayers.[25] Augury, together with extispicy, belongs to the most prominent forms of divination in the Greek,[26] Etruscan,[27] and Roman[28] cultures, and it may well have its origin in Anatolia.

Since the Tušḫan archive dates to a dramatic moment immediately following the fall of Nineveh, we find divination functioning in a very typical context. To be sure, diviners were certainly consulted in various matters, not only in times of crisis. Nonetheless, since the primary function of divination, sociologically speaking, is to help people cope with the insecurities inevitably brought about by human ignorance,[29] political upheavals and military attacks were doubtless the principal occasions when available specialists were consulted.

---

23 Whether prophecy was part of Hittite divination is somewhat unclear. However, some expressions may be best interpreted as referring to prophets; for example, in King Mursili's second plague prayer to the storm god: "[Or] if people have been dying because of some other reason, then let me either see it in a dream, or let it be established through an oracle, or let a man of god declare it" (CTH 378.II § 11; no. 11 in I. Singer, *Hittite Prayers* [SBLWAW 11; Atlanta: Society of Biblical Literature, 2002] 60); the "man of god" could perhaps be seen as fulfilling a prophetic function.

24 KBo 15.28 = no. 3 in H. A. Hoffner, Jr., *Letters from the Hittite Kingdom* (SBLWAW 15; Atlanta: Society of Biblical Literature, 2009) 84–85; *HKM* 47 = no. 50 in ibid., 178–81; KuT 50 and KuT 49 = nos. 92 and 93 in ibid., 262–67.

25 CTH 376.A § 7 = no. 8 in Singer, *Hittite Prayers*, 52; CTH 382 § 11 = no. 19 in ibid., 84.

26 See S. I. Johnston, *Ancient Greek Divination* (Blackwell Ancient Religions; Chichester: Wiley-Blackwell, 2008) 128–30.

27 See, for example, J.-R. Jannot, *Religion in Ancient Etruria* (trans. J. Whitehead; Madison: University of Wisconsin Press, 2005) 27–29, who, without discussing Near Eastern evidence, thinks that the "observation of the flight of birds, although it ultimately became a Roman specialty, was probably Etruscan in origin" (p. 29); N. Thomson de Grummond, "Prophets and Priests," in *The Religion of the Etruscans* (ed. N. Thomson de Grummond and E. Simon; Austin: University of Texas Press, 2006) 41–42.

28 See M. Beard, J. North, and S. Price, *Religions of Rome: A Sourcebook* (2 vols.; Cambridge: Cambridge University Press, 1998) 2:171–72; note that the bird diviners lend their name, *augures*, to upper-class politicians who had nothing to do with observing birds (Cicero *Div.* 2.33, 70: *non enim sumus ii nos augures qui avium reliquorumve observatione futura dicamus*).

29 For the idea and function of divination, see the articles collected in A. Annus (ed.), *Divination and the Interpretation of Signs in the Ancient World* (Oriental Institute Seminars 6; Chicago: Oriental Institute, 2010); see also W. Burkert, "Signs, Commands, and Knowledge: Ancient Divination between Enigma and Epiphany," in *Mantikê: Studies in Ancient Divination* (ed. S. I. John-

ZTT 25 appears to provide important evidence for technical and intuitive divination being consulted side by side by the same patrons. It is interesting to note that the Tušḫan documents do not mention the firstranking diviners like haruspices and astrologers but, rather, prophets and augurs whose services were utilized in 611 B.C. Considering the proximity of the city with the Anatolian culture, the presence of the augur is quite natural, and since Ištar of Nineveh was the patron deity of Tušḫan and the city probably boasted a temple of Ištar,[30] the prophetic performance is nothing unexpected either.

Rewarding Diviners

According to the document at hand, a total of ten minas of copper was delivered: six to the prophet, one to the augur, one (?) to a temple, and yet another two (?) to an unknown recipient. That prophets and other diviners were paid for their services is well attested from all over the ancient eastern Mediterranean. While this fact sometimes elicited accusations of greed—in the Hebrew Bible (Mic 3:5, 11), for example, and also in Greek sources[31]—most diviners doubtless lived by their divinatory skills; there was nothing principally wrong with this.[32] The best evidence comes from Mari, where prophets could demand a reimbursement for their services and would be rewarded accordingly: "She demanded a *laḫarûm*-garment and a nose-ring, and I ga[ve them to] her," writes the majordomo Sammetar to King Zimri-Lim about an anonymous female prophet at Terqa.[33] Another prophet mentioned in the same letter, Lupaḫum,[34] appears as receiving a donkey in one

ston and P. T. Struck; RGRW 155; Leiden: Brill, 2005) 29–49; M. A. Flower, *The Seer in Ancient Greece* (Berkeley: University of California Press, 2008) 72–80.

30 See Parpola, "Cuneiform Texts from Ziyaret Tepe," 24–25, 72–73.

31 For example, Creon in Sophocles' *Antigone* 1055: "The entire race of seers is fond of silver"; for similar accusations, see Flower, *The Seer in Ancient Greece*, 135–36.

32 See J. Bowden, "Oracles for Sale," in *Herodotus and His World: Essays from a Conference in Memory of George Forrest* (ed. P. Derow and R. Parker; Oxford: Oxford University Press, 2003) 256–74. For the distress of a scholar who had fallen out of the favor of the king and, therefore, lost his income, see S. Parpola, "The Forlorn Scholar," in *Language, Literature, and History: Philological and Historical Studies Presented to Erica Reiner* (ed. F. Rochberg-Halton; AOS 67; New Haven: American Oriental Society, 1987) 257–78.

33 ARM 26 199: 51–52; see Nissinen, *Prophets and Prophecy in the Ancient Near East*, 31 no. 9.

34 ARM 26 199 lines 5–40.

document and a shekel of silver in another.[35] Prophets also receive garments,[36] rings,[37] and sometimes even lances of bronze.[38]

The reward given to the prophet at Tušḫan far exceeds the amounts reported as compensation in other extant sources. Karen Radner has estimated that in Neo-Assyrian times, the purchasing power of one mina of copper corresponded to one shekel of silver or bronze, ten homers of barley, or one or two camels;[39] hence the six minas mentioned in ZTT 25 made a small fortune. Assuming these amounts reflect remuneration for services rendered, an interesting question is why the prophet in this text received six times the amount that was given to the augur. Although an answer to this question must remain in the realm of speculation, it is possible that this generous bequest resulted from the divine message's content and the prophet's ability to inspire his audience with confidence in the desperate situation. It is also possible that the augur was needed only to double-check the prophet's original message.

The Possible Contents of the Divine Messages

Whatever the explanation, the significant expenditure of copper reflects the urgency of the situation and the patrons' appreciation of the diviners, the prophet in particular. The outcome of the augury would probably have been a negative reply to a question like: "Will the enemy attack Tušḫan and destroy it?"[40] The actual contents of the prophecy may have resembled the oracles proclaimed to

35 A. 3796 and M. 11436; see Nissinen, *Prophets and Prophecy in the Ancient Near East*, 83 no. 53, 89 no. 62.

36 As evident in the ARM 26 199 passage quoted above (and n. 37); also ARM 9 22 line 14; 21 333 lines 34, 43; 22 167 line 8; 22 326 lines 6–9; see Nissinen, *Prophets and Prophecy in the Ancient Near East*, 84–87 nos. 54–56, 58.

37 ARM 25 142 lines 12–15 and T. 82 (made of silver); see Nissinen, *Prophets and Prophecy in the Ancient Near East*, 89–90 nos. 61, 63.

38 ARM 25 15 lines 7–9: "Two lances of bronze for Qišatum, prophet of Dagan"; see Nissinen, *Prophets and Prophecy in the Ancient Near East*, 88 no. 60.

39 See K. Radner, *Die neuassyrischen Privatrechtsurkunden als Quelle für Mensch und Umwelt* (SAAS 6; Helsinki: Neo-Assyrian Text Corpus Project, 1997) 248; ead., "Money in the Neo-Assyrian Empire," in *Trade and Finance in Ancient Mesopotamia* (ed. J. G. Dercksen; MOS Studies 1; Leiden: NINO, 1999) 127–57, esp. 156.

40 Compare, for example, the outcome of augury in the Hittite letter *HKM* 47 lines 15–19: "We thoroughly investigated by augury the matter of (Your Majesty's planned attack on) the town Takkašta, and we obtained an answer. Regarding the campaign we said (i.e., predicted?) as follows: 'His Majesty will (successfully) attack Takkašta and reap its crops as well'" (translation from Hoffner, *Letters from the Hittite Kingdom*, 180).

Esarhaddon when his kingship was at stake: "Is there an enemy that has attacked you, while I have kept silent? The future shall be like the past!"[41] In any case, it is difficult to imagine that it anticipated the utter destruction that was about to follow. Both the prophet and the augur must have fulfilled their function, the otherwise invaluable information: how "to get things done, to make things right and to keep them that way."[42]

The extant Neo-Assyrian prophetic oracles are typically addressed to the king of Assyria. Yet this possibility is difficult to imagine in the present case, considering the historical moment when the oracle was pronounced. Oracles spoken to Esarhaddon in his absence in Nineveh during the 680 B.C. civil war between him and his brothers, as well as those addressed to Zimri-Lim while the latter was not in Mari, show conclusively that kings did not need to be present when prophecies were proclaimed to them. If Sîn-šarru-iškun, Assyria's last actual king, was still alive at the time of this oracle's pronunciation, he could well have been its addressee. However, we do not know of his fate after Nineveh's fall; whether he committed suicide, was murdered or executed, or just disappeared, is not recorded in any extant Assyrian source.[43] In the quite probable case that he was killed, the prophecies may have been proclaimed to the city as a collective, or, alternatively, to an important functionary in the city. Alternatively, the recipient of the oracle could have been Aššur-uballiṭ II, who may still have been active in the region of Tušḫan by the time of its pronouncement.

The Proclamation Situation

That the copper was distributed at the city gate probably implies a public occasion. According to Parpola, "[i]f it was a fee for a solicited prophetic oracle, a plausible occasion would have been a great public gathering outside the city wall, just before an imminent battle against the invading Babylonian army."[44]

---

41 Parpola, *Assyrian Prophecies*, 1.4 ii 34–37.

42 U. S. Koch, "Three Strikes and You're Out! A View on Cognitive Theory and the First-Millennium Extispicy Ritual," in Annus (ed.), *Divination and the Interpretation of Signs*, 43–59, esp. 44.

43 For the sources, see J. R. Novotny, "Sîn-šarru-iškun," *PNA* 3/1 (2002) 1143–45; cf. also H. Schaudig, "Sîn-šarru-iškun," *RlA* 12 (2009–11) 522–24.

44 Parpola, "Cuneiform Texts from Ziyaret Tepe," 99. A gate as the venue of a prophetic performance is documented in a letter from Mari that gives account of an incident at Babylon: "A prophet of Marduk stood at the gate of the palace, proclaiming incessantly: 'Išme-Dagan will not escape the hand of Marduk. That hand will tie together a sheaf and he will be caught in it.' This is what he kept proclaiming at the gate of the palace. [Nobo]dy said anything to

It is feasible, albeit not certain, that the divinatory acts took place on this occasion. The prophecy could also have been spoken in the temple. The one mina of copper designated for the "house [of the god]" connects the diviners with a possible ritual context in a temple, probably the above-mentioned temple of Ištar, which provides a natural context for prophecy. It is noteworthy that the tablet is written by the scribe who also wrote tablets ZTT 12 and 13 relating to a festival arranged in the *akītu* temple of Tušḫan in Sivan (III), 611 B.C. Parpola plausibly suggests that "a festival was arranged at that time in the *akītu* house to secure the support of the goddess for the impending battle."[45]

The same festival would have provided a venue for the divinatory acts for which the prophet and the augur were rewarded. The gathering at the city gate may have been part of the same festival, the timing of which may be explained with the urgent situation.[46] Within weeks, Tušḫan was destroyed. We may never know whether the prophet and the augur survived to enjoy their newly acquired riches.

---

him." (ARM 26 371 lines 9–17; translation from Nissinen, *Prophets and Prophecy in the Ancient Near East*, 73 no. 47).

45 Parpola, "Cuneiform Texts from Ziyaret Tepe," 100. For the *akītu* temple mentioned in ZTT 12 and 13, see ibid., 72–73.

46 The traditional, agricultural *akītu* took place in Nisannu (I) and Tishri (VII); however, the date of the Assyrian military *akītu*, which was of a more occasional nature, did not follow this rule; see A. Annus, *The God Ninurta in the Mythology and Royal Ideology of Ancient Mesopotamia* (SAAS 14; Helsinki: Neo-Assyrian Text Corpus Project, 2002) 90–94. For *akītu* in general, see J. Bidmead, *The* Akītu *Festival: Religious Continuity and Royal Legitimation in Mesopotamia* (Piscataway, NY: Gorgias, 2002); B. Pongratz-Leisten, Ina šulmi īrub: *Die kulttopographische und ideologische Programmatik der* akītu-*Prozession in Babylonien und Assyrien im 1. Jahrtausend v. Chr.* (Baghdader Forschungen 16; Mainz: Philipp von Zabern, 1994); ead., "Akitu," *EBR* 1 (2009) 694–97.

Das kritische Potential in der altorientalischen Prophetie

I. Fehlt der außerbiblischen Prophetie ein kritisches Potential?

Die altorientalischen Texte prophetischen Inhalts sind bisher gewöhnlich aus biblischer Perspektive untersucht worden, entweder um die altisraelitische Prophetie in ihrem religionsgeschichtlichen Kontext erscheinen zu lassen oder um die Besonderheit der biblischen Prophetie besser beleuchten zu können. Die vorrangig biblische Perspektive auf die altorientalische Prophetie ist einerseits darin begründet, dass der Begriff „Prophetie" aus historischen Gründen zunächst zum Vokabular der Bibelwissenschaftler(innen) und Theolog(inn)en gehört hat, andererseits aber auch darin, dass die bis zum Ende des vergangenen Jahrhunderts vorgelegten Zeugnisse der altorientalischen Prophetie an Zahl bescheiden und zeitlich wie geographisch begrenzt gewesen sind. Die bibelzentrische Betrachtungsweise hat nicht nur den Nachteil, dass dabei meistens nur diejenigen Aspekte der altorientalischen Texte betont werden, die dem Vergleich mit den biblischen Texten dienlich sind. Die außerbiblischen Quellen werden auch oft nach biblisch-theologischen Kriterien bewertet, wobei das Urteil meist zugunsten der biblischen Prophetie gesprochen wird.[1] Die höhere Wertschätzung der biblischen Prophetie ist wiederum eng verbunden mit der Idee des von den großen biblischen Schriftpropheten angeregten ethischen Monotheismus, der angeblich diese Propheten qualitativ von ihrer religiösen Umwelt radikal unterscheidet und auf ein höheres, geistiges Niveau erhebt.[2]

Die Forschungslage hat sich aber insofern verändert, als uns heute eine beträchtliche Zahl an bisher unbekannten Quellen zur Verfügung steht: die prophetischen Korpora aus Mari und Assyrien und eine ganze Reihe von einzelnen

---

1 Zur Kritik der bibelzentrischen Fragestellung s. z.B. M. deJong Ellis, „Observations on Mesopotamian Oracles and Prophetic Texts: Literary and Historiographic Considerations," *JCS* 41 (1989) 127–86, esp. 132–33; J. M. Sasson, „About 'Mari and the Bible'," *RA* 92 (1998) 97–123.

2 Zum Erbe dieser Idee in der Prophetenforschung s. O. Loretz, „Die Entstehung des Amos-Buches im Licht der Prophetien aus Māri, Assur, Ishchali und der Ugarit-Texte: Paradigmenwechsel in der Prophetenforschung," *UF* 24 (1992) 179–215, esp. 198–208.

DOI 10.1515/9783110466546-012

Zeugnissen aus verschiedenen Teilen des Alten Orients.[3] Dies ermöglicht besser denn je die Betrachtung der biblischen Prophetie als Teil eines altorientalischen Phänomens, wie auch eine eigenständige Bewertung des außerbiblischen Materials. Dabei sind natürlich Unterschiede zu erwarten, nicht nur zwischen biblischer und außerbiblischer Prophetie, sondern zwischen den prophetischen Korpora überhaupt.[4] In mancher Hinsicht bleibt die Eigentümlichkeit der biblischen Prophetie unbestreitbar. Vor allem der literarische Prozess, dessen Ergebnis die prophetischen Bücher der Hebräischen Bibel sind, hat im Alten Orient keine Parallele;[5] wobei freilich die Anfänge eines vergleichbaren Prozesses in Assyrien nicht übersehen werden dürfen.[6]

Den größten Unterschied hat man im angeblichen Fehlen des kritischen Potentials in der außerbiblischen Prophetie gesehen. Es wird oft behauptet, die altorientalische Prophetie außerhalb des Kanons der Hebräischen Bibel sei Heilsprophetie schlechthin; ihr fehle die für die großen biblischen Propheten typische ethisch-theologisch motivierte Herrschafts- und Gesellschaftskritik. Als Beispiel für diese Auffassung sei hier ein Abschnitt aus einer der neuesten Einleitungen in das Alte Testament zitiert. Nachdem die historischen Gemeinsamkeiten der altorientalischen und israelitischen Prophetie anerkannt worden sind, werden die Unterschiede wie folgt dargestellt:[7]

> Vor dem Hintergrund der altorientalischen Prophetie erhalten die oppositionellen Einzelpropheten Israels ein noch schärferes Profil. Vergleichbare radikale Konflikte zwischen Propheten und König bzw. Staat gibt es in altorientalischen Texten bislang nicht. In den wenigen Fällen, in denen dort Kritik geäußert wird, bezieht diese sich auf den Kult, aber nicht auf gesellschaftliche und ethische Fragestellungen. Ebenso fehlt die massive Gerichtsansage,

3 Das gesamte Material is übersetzt in M. Nissinen, mit Beiträgen von C.-L. Seow, R. K. Ritner und H. C. Melchert, *Prophets and Prophecy in the Ancient Near East* (2. Auflage; SBLWAW 41; Atlanta: SBL Press, 2019).

4 Zu den theologischen Unterschieden zwischen Mariprophetie und assyrischer Prophetie s. K. van der Toorn, „Mesopotamian Prophecy between Immanence and Transcendence: A Comparison of Old Babylonian and Neo-Assyrian Prophecy," in *Prophecy in Its Ancient Near Eastern Context: Mesopotamian, Biblical, and Arabian Perspectives* (ed. M. Nissinen; SBLSymS 13; Atlanta Ga.: Society of Biblical Literature, 2000) 70 – 87.

5 Dies betont J. Jeremias, „Das Proprium der alttestamentlichen Prophetie," *ThLZ* 119 (1994) 483 – 94.

6 Vgl. Nissinen, „Spoken, Written, Quoted and Invented: Orality and Writtenness in Ancient Near Eastern Prophecy," in *Writings and Speech in Israelite and Ancient Near Eastern Prophecy* (ed. E. Ben Zvi and M. H. Floyd; SBLSymS 10; Atlanta: Society of Biblical Literature, 2000) 253 – 54, 257 – 58.

7 E. Zenger, et al. (eds.), *Einleitung in das Alte Testament* (ed. C. Frevel; Stuttgart: Kohlhammer, ^{8}2012), 518.

die das Proprium der vorexilischen (Schrift-)Propheten Israels ist. Daß den altorientalischen Propheten das Schicksal des Volkes am Herzen lag, wie dies in Israel der Fall war, ist nirgends zu erkennen.

Das hier von der altorientalischen Prophetie gezeichnete Bild ist nicht aus der Luft gegriffen, sondern gründet sich auf die neueste Forschung, und zwar vor allem auf die von Manfred Weippert und mir selbst vertretenen Ansichten.[8] Es bedarf aber insofern einer Korrektur, als inzwischen Texte bekannt geworden sind, in denen die altorientalischen Propheten durchaus kritisch ihre Stimme erheben.[9] Da es allerdings noch an eingehenden Studien zu diesem Thema fehlt, empfiehlt es sich, einige einschlägige Texte probeweise ins Auge zu fassen. Ich gebe zu, dass ich mich dabei an das alte Schema halte: Ein Bibelwissenschaftler untersucht altorientalische Quellen, um ein aus der biblischen Fragestellung entstandenes Problem zu lösen. Ich hoffe aber, zugleich einen wichtigen Aspekt der altorientalischen Prophetie von innen beleuchten und dabei an einen Themenkreis anschließen zu können, der mit dem Verhältnis von Prophetie und Herrschaft im

8 M. Weippert, „Aspekte israelitischer Prophetie im Lichte verwandter Erscheinungen des Alten Orients," in *Ad bene et fideliter seminandum*, FS Karlheinz Deller (ed. G. Mauer and U. Magen; AOAT 220; Kevelaer: Butzon & Bercker; Neukirchen-Vluyn: Neukirchener Verlag, 1988) 287–319; M. Nissinen, „Die Relevanz der neuassyrischen Prophetie für die alttestamentliche Forschung," in *Mesopotamica – Ugaritica – Biblica*, FS K. Bergerhof (ed. M. Dietrich and O. Loretz; AOAT 232, Kevelaer, Germany: Butzon & Bercker; Neukirchen-Vluyn: Neukirchener, 1993) 217–58 (= S. 419–40 in dem vorliegenden Band).

9 L. L. Grabbe, *Priests, Prophets, Diviners, Sages: A Socio-Historical Study of Religious Specialists in Ancient Israel* (Valley Forge, Pa.: Trinity Press International, 1995), 89, listet mehrere Texte aus Mari auf und kommt zu der Schlussfolgerung: „The OT prophets are not alone in criticizing and admonishing the ruler and even bringing bad news" (vgl. auch S. 92); vgl. auch R. P. Gordon, „From Mari to Moses: Prophecy at Mari and in Ancient Israel," in *Of Prophets' Visions and the Wisdom of Sages*, FS R. N. Whybray (ed. H. A. McKay and D. J. A. Clines; JSOTSup 162; Sheffield: JSOT Press, 1993) 63–79, esp. 76–78; H. B. Huffmon, „The Expansion of Prophecy in the Mari Archives: New Texts, New Readings, New Information," in *Prophecy and Prophets: The Diversity of Contemporary Issues in Scholarship* (ed. Y. Gitay; SBL Semeia Studies; Atlanta, Ga.: Society of Biblical Literature, 1997) 7–22, esp. 17–18; id., „A Company of Prophets: Mari, Assyria, Israel," in *Prophecy in Its Ancient Near Eastern Context: Mesopotamian, Biblical, and Arabian Perspectives* (ed. M. Nissinen; SBLSymS 13; Atlanta, Ga.: Society of Biblical Literature, 2000) 47–70, esp. 54–55; H. M. Barstad, „Den gammeltestamentliga profetismen belyst ved paralleller fra Mari," *TTK* 72 (2001) 51–67, esp. 62–63. Schon R. R. Wilson, *Prophecy and Society in Ancient Israel* (Philadelphia, Pa.: Fortress, 1980), 110, machte die folgende Bemerkung zu den Propheten von Mari aufgrund der damals bekannten Quellen: „Their utterances were intended to bring about changes in the social and religious establishments, particularly by improving the lot of the gods and cults which the intermediaries represented. Most of their messages were innovative and designed to bring about changes in existing conditions."

Allgemeinen zu tun hat. Deswegen untersuche ich die außerbiblischen Texte, ohne auf ihre biblischen Parallelen einzugehen. Ich verzichte auf den Vergleich, um das altorientalische Material für sich erscheinen zu lassen. Das bedeutet aber nicht, der Vergleich sei uninteressant oder gar unnötig.

Im Folgenden werden die wichtigsten Texte gesammelt, in denen ein mesopotamischer König – zunächst Zimri-Lim von Mari (1774–1760 v.Chr.) oder Asarhaddon von Assyrien (681–669 v.Chr.) – wegen seines Verhaltens oder seiner Handlungen von Propheten kritisiert wird. Unter Kritik verstehe ich neben dem direkten Urteil auch Warnungen und Forderungen, die Fehltritte des Königs oder Nachlässigkeiten in seiner Tätigkeit implizit zum Ausdruck bringen.

II. König, Tempel und Tempelbewohner

Wie aus den mesopotamischen Königsinschriften aller Zeiten sehr deutlich zu ersehen ist, gehörte die Betreuung der Tempel und des Kultes zu den wichtigsten Pflichten eines mesopotamischen Königs.[10] Tempelbau und -restauration war eine fromme Aufgabe, die nur mit göttlicher Einwilligung und Förderung durchgeführt werden durfte. Der Kontakt zur Gottheit wurde unter anderem auch von Propheten vermittelt,[11] weshalb es nicht überrascht, dass die in den prophetischen Quellen enthaltene Kritik sich oft gegen Nachlässigkeiten in der Pflege der Götter und ihrer Tempel richtet. Am mildesten erscheint der Vorwurf der Nachlässigkeit, wenn er mit einer Heilsprophetie verbunden ist, wie in der von der Königin Šibtu übermittelten Prophetie von Aḫatum (ARM 26 214):[12]

> *ana bēlīja qibīma umma Šibtu amatkāma / ina bīt Annunītim ša libbi ālim Aḫātum ṣuḫarat Dagan-Malik immaḫḫima kīam iqbi ummāmi / Zimri-Lim u šumma atta mišâtanni anāku elīka aḫabbuṣ / nakrīka ana qātīka umalla / u awīlī šarrāqīja aṣabbatma ana karāš Bēlet-ekallim akammissunūti / ina ŝanîm ūmim Aḫūm sangûm ṭēmam annêm šārtam u s[i]ssiktam ublamma / ana bēlīja ašpuram šārtam u sissiktam aknukamma ana ṣēr bēlīja uštābilam*

10 S. etwa J. N. Postgate, *Early Mesopotamia: Society and Economy at the Dawn of History* (London: Routledge, 1992), 262–66.

11 Vgl. M. Nissinen, *References to Prophecy in Neo-Assyrian Sources* (SAAS 7; Helsinki: The Neo-Assyrian Text Corpus Project, 1998), esp. 35–42.

12 J.-M. Durand, *Archives épistolaires de Mari 1/1* (ARM 26/1; Paris: Editions Recherche sur les Civilisations, 1988), 442–43; Übersetzung auch id., *Les documents épistolaires du palais de Mari*, vol. 3 (Littératures anciennes du Proche-Orient 18; Paris: Cerf, 2000), 316; M. Dietrich, „Prophetenbriefe aus Mari," in *TUAT* 2/1 (1986) 83–93, esp. 93.

Sprich zu meinem Herrn: Folgendermaßen Šibtu, deine Dienerin: / Im Tempel der Annunitum, der innerhalb der Stadt gelegen ist,[13] kam Aḫatum, die Dienerin von Dagan-Malik, ins Rasen und sprach folgendermaßen: / „Zimri-Lim, auch wenn du mich vernachlässigt hast, werde ich um deinetwillen massakrieren![14] / Ich werde deinen Feind dir in deine Hände überantworten und die Leute, die mich bestohlen[15] haben, werde ich ergreifen und zum Lager[16] von Belet-ekallim zusammenbringen." / Am nächsten Tag brachte der Priester Aḫum diese Nachricht zusammen mit dem Haarschopf und dem Gewandsaum zu mir. / Ich habe jetzt meinem Herrn geschrieben, dass er den Haarschopf und den Gewandsaum versiegeln und zu meinem Herrn bringen lassen soll.

Die Prophetin sammelt glühende Kohlen auf dem Haupt des Königs im Auftrag der Göttin, die verspricht, für den König trotz seiner Fahrlässigkeit in die Bresche zu springen. Der unverhohlene Tadel ist geschickt mit dem göttlichen Zuspruch verknüpft, zugleich wird dem König aber deutlich gemacht, dass der Tempel von Annunitum Verlust erlitten hat; die Göttin ist „bestohlen" worden. Zwar wird die Göttin selbst dafür sorgen, dass die Schuldigen zur Rechenschaft gezogen werden, aber sie erinnert den König deutlich an seine Pflichten. Es ist wohl nicht von ungefähr, dass die Königin von dem Priester Aḫum auf die Prophezeiung aufmerksam gemacht wurde. Der Priester handelt hier als Übermittler im Interesse des Tempels, indem er die Nachricht zusammen mit den üblichen Verifizie-

---

13 Es gab einen Tempel von Annunitum auch außerhalb der Stadtmauer; s. ARM 26 229:6 – 7, und vgl. J.-M. Durand, „L'Organisation de l'espace dans le palais de Mari: Le témoignage des textes," in *Le système palatial en Orient, en Grèce et à Rome: Actes du colloque de Strasbourg 19 – 22 Juin 1985, Université des sciences humaines de Strasbourg* (ed. E. Lévy; Travaux du Centre de recherche sur le Proche-Orient et la Grèce antiques 9; Leiden: Brill 1987) 39 – 110, esp. 91.

14 Nach der Kollation von Durand, *Archives épistolaires de Mari*, 443, ist *a-ḫa-ab-bu-uṣ*$_4$ zu lesen. Frühere Übersetzungen setzen die Lesung *a-ḫa-ab-bu-ub* voraus, z. B. Dietrich, „Prophetenbriefe aus Mari", 93: „… so werde ich doch (liebevoll) über dich flüstern"; vgl. W. L. Moran, „New Evidence from Mari on the History of Prophecy," *Bib* 50 (1969) 15 – 56, esp. 31, und *CAD* Ḫ 2 – 3 sub *ḫabābu* B.

15 Zu dieser Übersetzung s. P.-R. Berger, „Einige Bemerkungen zu Friedrich Ellermeier: Prophetie in Mari und Israel (Herzberg, 1968)," *UF* 1 (1969), 209.

16 Übersetzung unsicher; das „Lager" geht auf G. Dossin, „Sur le prophétisme a Mari," in *La divination en Mésopotamie ancienne et dans les régions voisines* (CRRAI 14; Paris: Presses universitaires de France, 1966) 77 – 86, esp. 82, zurück; so auch Durand, *Archives épistolaires de Mari*, 443. Anders Dietrich, „Prophetenbriefe aus Mari", 93: „zur Vernichtung durch Belet-ekallim" (*karāšu* II; s. AHw 448 und vgl. Moran, „New Evidence from Mari," 31) und W. von Soden, „Einige Bemerkungen zu den von Fr. Ellermeier in 'Prophetie in Mari und Israel' erstmalig bearbeiteten Briefen aus ARM 10," *UF* 1 (1969) 198: „im Bauch der Belet-ekallim"; dem letztgenannten Vorschlag, angeblich gestützt von einer unpublizierten Parallele, folgt inzwischen auch J.-M. Durand, „Les 'déclarations prophétiques' dans les lettres de Mari," in *Prophéties et oracles*, vol. 1: *Dans le Proche-Orient ancien* (Supplément au Cahier Evangile 88; Paris: Cerf, 1994) 8 – 78, esp. 70: „pour le ventre de Bêlet-Ekallim".

rungsmitteln, Haarschopf und Gewandsaum *(šārtum u sissiktum)*,[17] zur Königin bringt.

Um des Tempels Vorteil geht es auch einem neuassyrischen Tempelverwalter namens Nabû-reši-išši in seinem Brief, in dem er dem König vom Auftreten einer Prophetin berichtet (SAA 13 144 r. 7 – s. 1):[18]

tarrugu[*m*] *mā atâ* GIŠ.*ni*-[...] *qablu* ... *ana muṣurāja tādin*
mā pān šarri qibia lūsaḫḫirū lidnūni
mā gabbi nuḫšu [...]-*šu addana*

[...] sie prophezeite: „Warum ist das [...]-Holz, der Hain (und) ...[19] den Ägyptern gegeben? Sprich in Anwesenheit des Königs, dass sie mir zurückgegeben werden sollen, und ich werde seinem [...] allen Reichtum geben."

Die hier sprechende Gottheit ist möglicherweise Ištar von Arbela, die durch den Mund der Prophetin ihr Vermögen zurückverlangt. Der abgebrochene Teil des Textes hat vielleicht Angaben über die Verkündigungssituation enthalten; man gewinnt den Eindruck, als sei die Prophetie in Anwesenheit von Nabû-reši-išši gesprochen worden, oder als hätte er selbst das Orakel eingeholt. Seine Rolle als Briefverfasser darf nicht übersehen werden, denn es handelt sich offensichtlich um Eigentum des Tempels, für das er zuständig ist. Die Prophetie ermöglicht es ihm, die Forderung nach der Rückgabe des Eigentums der Göttin in den Mund zu legen und damit seine eigene kritische Haltung gegenüber dem König zu verschleiern.

Schroffer äußert sich ein Prophet *(muḫḫûm)* in einem Brief des Lanasûm, des Vertreters von Zimri-Lim in Tuttul, der zuerst von einer gut ausgefallenen Opfermahlzeit berichtet, dann aber wie folgt fortsetzt (ARM 26 215:15 – 25):[20]

u muḫḫûm pān Dagan [*i*]*tbīma kīam iqbi u*[*m*]*māmi šūma / admati mê zakūtim ul ašatti / ana bēlīka šupurma u mê zakūtim lišqenni / inanna anumma etqam ša qaqqadīšu u sissiktašu ana ṣēr bēlīja ušābilam / bēlī l*[*i*]*zakki*

17 Zu diesen s. Durand, *Archives épistolaires de Mari*, 40; id., „La religión en Siria durante la época de los reinos amorreos según la documentación de Mari," in *Mitología y religión del Oriente Antiguo*, vol 2/1: *Semitas occidentales (Ebla, Mari)* (ed. id. and P. Mander; Estudios Orientales 8; Sabadell: AUSA, 1995) 125 – 533, esp. 361.

18 S. W. Cole and P. Machinist, *Letters from Priests to the Kings Esarhaddon and Assurbanipal* (SAA 13; Helsinki: Helsinki University Press, 1998), esp. 116 – 17. Zu diesem Brief s. auch Nissinen, „Spoken, Written Quoted and Invented," 259 – 60.

19 Mit den Zeichen *li-du-x* (Z. r. 9) ist nichts anzufangen.

20 Durand, *Archives épistolaires de Mari*, 443 – 44; vgl. id., „La cité-état d'Imâr à l'époque des rois de Mari," *MARI* 6 (1990) 39 – 92, esp. 51, 58.

> Ein Prophet ist vor Dagan aufgestanden und hat wie folgt gesprochen: / „Wie lange noch werde ich kein reines Wasser zu trinken bekommen? / Schreibe deinem Herrn, er möge mir reines Wasser zu trinken geben!" / Ich habe nun eine Locke von seinem Haupt[21] und seinen Gewandsaum meinem Herrn bringen lassen. / Mein Herr soll ein Reinigungsopfer darbringen.

Das Aufstehen des Propheten vor Dagan bedeutet, dass der Prophet sich vor die Gottesstatue setzt, um als Sprachrohr des Gottes zu wirken; es spricht also der Gott, dem es an reinem Wasser mangelt.[22] Folglich handelt es sich um Opfergaben für den Gott, nicht um Nahrung für den Propheten. Auch hier muss aber die Rolle des Briefschreibers beachtet werden. Er mildert die Kritik an den unvollkommenen Opfern des Königs durch gute Nachrichten von einem vollkommenen Opfermahl, macht aber zugleich deutlich, dass der König bei der Betreuung des Dagan-Tempels, wohl in Tuttul, seine Pflichten nicht ganz erfüllt hat. Lanasûm sendet nicht nur die Verifizierungsmittel des Orakels, sondern fügt auch seine eigene Mahnung zum Reinigungsopfer hinzu.[23]

In den oben behandelten Briefen kommt die Rolle des Tempelpersonals in der Übermittlung der Prophetenworte anschaulich zum Ausdruck. Die Priester und Behörden wahrten die Interessen der Tempel und des dazugehörigen Personals. Da auch die Propheten in der Regel zum Tempelpersonal gehörten[24] und ihr Lebensstandard demnach wahrscheinlich im Wesentlichen auf dem Wohlstand des Tempels beruhte,[25] entsprachen die Erinnerungen an die mangelhaften Opfer-

---

21 Das Wort *etqum*, anstelle des gewöhnlichen *šārtum*, könnte auf die außergewöhnlich wilde Behaarung des Propheten hinweisen; dasselbe Wort ist im Gilgameš-Epos in Bezug auf Enkidu benutzt (I ii 37). Vgl. Gordon, „From Mari to Moses," 68–69.

22 S. van der Toorn, „Mesopotamian Prophecy," 82.

23 Vgl. J. M. Sasson, „The Posting of Letters with Divine Messages," in *Florilegium Marianum 2*, FS M. Birot (ed. D. Charpin and J.-M. Durand; Mémoires de NABU 3; Paris: SEPOA, 1994) 299–316, esp. 311.

24 Dies war sowohl in Mari als auch in Assyrien der Fall; vgl. Durand, „La religion en Siria," 455–58 und M. Nissinen, „The Socioreligious Role of the Neo-Assyrian Prophets," in *Prophecy in Its Ancient Near Eastern Context: Mesopotamian, Biblical, and Arabian Perspectives* (ed. id.; SBLSymS 13; Atlanta, Ga.: Society of Biblical Literature, 2000) 89–114, esp. 90–102 (= S. 103–26 in dem vorliegenden Band).

25 Zumindest in Mari wurden die Propheten manchmal für ihre Orakel gebührend bezahlt, aber es geht in diesen Fällen offenbar eher um einmalige Zuwendungen als um ein sicheres Einkommen; z. B. ARM 25 142:12–15: *1 ḫullu kaspim ana muḫḫîm ša Addu inūma têrtam ana šarrim iddinu* „ein silberner *ḫullum*-Ring für den Propheten von Adad, als er ein Orakel an den König lieferte." Des weiteren s. A. 3796; A. 4676; ARM 9 22:14; ARM 21 333:43 = ARM 23 446:19; ARM 22 167 r. 8; 326:6–10; ARM 25 15:7–9; M. 11436; T. 82 ix 2–4; s. Durand, *Archives épistolaires de Mari*, 380–81.

gaben auch ihren persönlichen Interessen. Dies demonstriert anschaulich ein Brief, der den König von der kümmerlichen Lage eines Propheten in Kenntnis setzt (ARM 26 198:3–14):[26]

> *Šēlebu[m illikamma] kīam iqbi umma šūma / šikāram idatam itti Annu[nītim īkimū] / inūma ana išātim qē[mam aḫšiḫū] u ina mušīḫtim bab[assam] kīma qēmim iddin[ūnim] / ina pānīja aṭṭu[lma] / šinīšu ištu adi nak[rim] akšudu inanna šal[šīšu] / bītam ušba u anāku m[ā]di[š] zê u šīnāti wašbāku u [qa]nâm t[i]minim(?) akka[l]*
>
> Šelebu[m kam zu mir] und sprach wie folgt: / „Man hat das *idatum*-Bier[27] von Annu[nitum weggenommen]. / Als [ich Me]hl für das Feuer[28] [verlangte], gaben [sie mir] Br[ei](?) in einem Topf[29] anstelle des Mehls. / [Also] musste ich mich selbst versorgen.[30] / Seitdem bin ich zweimal in das Fein[des(land)?[31]] gegangen, und jetzt zum dritt[en Mal]. / Sie wohnt in dem Tempel, ich aber wohne inmitten einer Fülle von Scheiße und Pisse und esse das *timinum*-Rohr[32].

Trotz mancher Schwierigkeiten, diesen Text zu übersetzen und zu verstehen, wird deutlich, dass der *assinnu* Šelebum, der aus anderen Texten als Prophet gut bekannt ist,[33] verlassen daliegt. Er ernährt sich von den Einkünften des Tempels der Annunitum, hat sich aber mit Wenigem begnügen müssen, offenbar wegen verminderter Abgaben für den Tempel. Zudem ist er aus irgendwelchen Gründen zum dritten Mal weggeschickt worden und lebt in unmenschlichen Verhältnissen, denen seine kargen Worte deutlich Ausdruck verleihen. Der Brief gilt als Zeugnis

---

26 Ibid., 425; vgl. auch Barstad, „Den gammeltestamentliga profetismen," 63. Ob dieser Text, wie Durand annimmt, mit dem identisch ist, den Inib-šina, die Schwester des Königs, in ARM 26 197 erwähnt, ist völlig unklar; vgl. S. B. Parker, „Official Attitudes toward Prophecy at Mari and in Israel," *VT* 43 (1993) 50–68, esp. 54 Anm. 15.

27 Zu diesem Bier s. M. Birot, *Textes administratifs de la salle 5 du palais (2e partie)* (ARM 12; Paris: Editions Recherche sur les Civilisations, 1964) 13.

28 Elliptische Ausdrucksweise für: „um Brot zu backen."

29 Zu *mušīḫtum* als Variante von *mašīḫum*, s. Durand, *Archives épistolaires de Mari*, 425.

30 Eine mutmaßliche Übersetzung von *ina pāni naṭālum*, lit. etwa „vor sich anschauen."

31 Ob tatsächlich ein fremdes Land gemeint ist oder eher eine Umgebung, in der Šelebum sich fremd vorkommt, ist fraglich.

32 Ein unbekanntes Wort, das wohl ein zu menschlicher Nahrung untaugliches Surrogat bezeichnet.

33 Vgl. ARM 26 197:4–5: *ina p[ā]nītim Šēlebum assinnu têrtam iddi[na]mma ašpurakkum* „Vor einiger Zeit hat der *assinnu* Šelebum mir ein Orakel übermittelt, und ich habe dir (darüber) geschrieben"; ARM 26 213:5–7: *ina bīt Annunītim* UD.3.KAM *Šēlebum immaḫḫu umma Annunītumma* „Im Tempel von Annunitum kam Šelebum vorgestern ins Rasen und sagte: 'So spricht Annunitum ....'" Ein weiterer *assinnu* namens Ili-ḫaznaja ist in ARM 26 212 als Prophet bezeugt; eine Überlassungsurkunde zeigt, dass auch er zum Personal des Annunitum-Tempels gehörte (M. 11299); s. Durand, *Archives épistolaires de Mari*, 399.

dafür, dass die Auslieferungen des Königs für die Tempel nicht nur rituelle Vorgänge waren und nicht nur den Göttern zugute kamen, sondern auch zum Lebensunterhalt der Tempelbewohner beitrugen, die alle Abzüge an ihrem eigenen Leibe verspürten.

Wenn auch die von den Propheten verkündeten Gottesworte im Prinzip keine Privatmeinungen waren, können sie doch nicht unabhängig vom konkreten Leben der Propheten betrachtet werden. Die Betreuung der Tempel war keine ausschließlich „kultische" Sache, sondern hatte auch eine soziale Dimension. Der Tempel war ein Symbol der gesellschaftlichen Identität und zugleich eine soziale Institution, die unter Umständen die Außenseiter und Unterprivilegierten der Gesellschaft in ihre Obhut nahm.[34] Zu diesen gehörten auch die *assinnu* wie Šelebum, die als Vertreter des „dritten Geschlechts" nur als Diener der Göttin gesellschaftlich gewürdigt wurden und deren Wohlstand demnach von dem des Tempels völlig abhängig war.[35] Somit hat die prophetische Kritik an der unvollkommenen Tempelpflege, wenn sie auch in den uns bekannten Fällen meist auf kultische Handlungen gerichtet ist, auch ein gesellschaftskritisches Potential.

Weitere Forderungen sind in zwei leider nur fragmentarisch erhaltenen Maribriefen zu finden. In Brief ARM 26 218[36] erhebt der unbekannte Schreiber gegen den König den Vorwurf, er habe ein auf göttlichen Befehl errichtetes Steindenkmal *(ḫumūsum)*[37] nicht gebührend mit Opfergaben und anderen Zuwendungen gewürdigt. In Brief ARM 26 219 wiederum meldet sich ein Prophet mit einer giftigen Botschaft der Göttin Ninḫursag (Z.4–10, 21–24):[38]

ūm nī[qe in]a bīt [N]inḫur[sagga] āpilum š[a Nin]ḫursagga it[bīma] kīam idbu[b um]māmi šū[ma] / ištiššu šinīšu u šalāšī[šu] pān Zim[ri-Lim] erištī ē[ri]šma u [m]i[mma] ul iddin[am ...] / [u]mma anāku[ma ...]

annêtim ā[pilum] idbub u anumma š[ārtam u sissiktam] ša āpilim ana bēlīja u[šābilam] / bēlī ša epēšīšu līpu[š ...]

Am Tag der Op[fer i]m Tempel von [N]inḫur[sag] ist ein Prophet v[on Nin]ḫursag aufge-[standen]. Er hat Folgendes gesprochen: / „Einmal, zweimal, sogar drei[mal] habe ich vor

34 S. Postgate, *Early Mesopotamia*, 135–36.

35 Zu Stellung und Funktion von *assinnu*, s. B. Groneberg, „Die sumerisch-akkadische Inanna/Ištar: Hermaphroditos?," *WO* 17 (1986) 25–46, esp. 33–41; G. Leick, *Sex and Eroticism in Mesopotamian Literature* (London and New York: Routledge, 1994), esp. 157–69; M. Nissinen, *Homoeroticism in the Biblical World: A Historical Perspective* (trans. K. Stjerna; Minneapolis, Minn.: Fortress, 1998), 28–36.

36 Durand, *Archives épistolaires de Mari*, 446–47.

37 Zu *ḫumūsum* s. Durand, „La religión en Siria," 297–98.

38 Durand, *Archives épistolaires de Mari*, 447–48.

Zim[ri-Lim] mein Verlangen geäußert, aber er hat mir nich[ts] gegeb[en ...] / Ich habe gesagt [...]

(Z. 11–20 schlecht erhalten)

Dies hat der P[rophet] gesprochen. Ich habe hiermit die Ha[arsträhne und den Gewandsaum] des Propheten meinem Herrn b[ringen lassen]. / Mein Herr möge tun, was er für das Beste hält.

Der Vorwurf wird ohne Umschweife vorgetragen, und die Überreste der zerstörten Zeilen lassen vermuten, dass der Brief weitere Anklagen enthielt. Auffallend ist allerdings die Stellung des Briefverfassers, der zwar Haarschopf und Gewandsaum des Propheten wegen der eventuellen Kontrolle des Prophetenorakels durch andere divinatorische Methoden schickt, seine eigene Meinung aber nicht ausspricht. Wir wissen nicht, wer den Brief verfasst hat. Aber die in ihm zum Ausdruck kommende distanzierte Haltung gegenüber der Prophetie weist darauf hin, dass der Verfasser nicht in erster Linie die Interessen des Ninḫursag-Tempels vertritt, andererseits aber die dreimalige Forderung der Göttin nicht stillschweigend übergehen kann.

Eine zornige Göttin[39] ist auch in einem neuassyrischen Prophetenorakel anzutreffen, und zwar im fünften Orakel der Sammeltafel SAA 9 3, auf der Prophetien zusammengestellt sind, die anlässlich der Thronbesteigung Asarhaddons gesprochen wurden. Dieser Prophetenspruch hat einen von den ihm vorangehenden Heilsorakeln *(šulmu)* ganz abweichenden Ton. Asarhaddon, dem soeben der Umkreis der vier Himmelsrichtungen gegeben worden ist (SAA 9 3.2), der mit dem assyrischen Hauptgott Assur einen Bund geschlossen hat (SAA 9 3.3) und dessen Vasallen eine kultische Mahlzeit als Zeichen ihrer Untertänigkeit eingenommen haben (SAA 9 3.4), erntet jetzt Vorwürfe wegen der Vernachlässigung der Göttin Ištar (SAA 9 3.5 iii 16–37):[40]

abat Issār ša Arbail ana Aššūr-aḫu-iddina šar māt Aššūr /
akī ša memmēni lā ēpašūni lā addinakkanni / mā 4 sippī ša māt Aššūr lā akpupâ lā addinakkâ /
nakarka lā akšūdu giṣṣiṣīka ajjābīka [akī gu]rṣipti lā alqūtu /
[att]a ana ajjāši mīnu taddina / [ak]āli ša qarīti l[aššu] ša ak lā bēt ili / a[kkall]i akālī akk[a]lli kāsī / mā ina pāni adaggal ēnu ina muḫḫi aktarar /
mā kettumma 1 sūt akāl aṣūdi l sūt massītu ša šikāri ṭābi ke ʾʾin / urqī akussu laššia ina pīa laškun lumalli kāsu ina muḫḫi lassi / lalâja lutirra

Wort der Ištar von Arbela an Asarhaddon, König von Assyrien: /
Als hätte ich nichts getan, dir nichts gegeben! / Habe ich nicht die vier Pfosten von Assyrien

39 Vgl. M.-C. Perroudon, „An Angry Goddess,“ *SAAB* 6 (1993) 41–44.

40 S. Parpola, *Assyrian Prophecies* (SAA 9; Helsinki: Helsinki University Press, 1997), esp. 25–26; Übersetzung auch K. Hecker, „Zukunftsdeutungen in akkadischen Texten,“ *TUAT* 2/1 (1986) 56–82, esp. 61.

gebeugt und dir gegeben? / Habe ich nicht deinen Feind besiegt? Habe ich deine Gegner, deine Widersacher nicht [wie Schmetter]linge eingesammelt? /
Was hast denn [d]u mir gegeben? / [Es gibt] k[ein B]rot für das *qarītu*-Bankett, als gäbe es keinen Tempel! / Mein Brot ist mir ve[rweige]rt, mein Becher ist mir verweigert. / Ich warte darauf, ich richte darauf die Augen. /
Wahrlich, stelle Brot auf in einer Schüssel von einem Seah, ein Trinkgefäß von einem Seah voll guten Bieres! / Ich will Gemüse und Suppe aufnehmen und an meinen Mund setzen, ich will den Becher füllen und daraus trinken! / Ich will meinen Reiz wiedergewinnen!

Die Göttin erinnert den neuen König mit deutlichen Worten daran, wem Lob und Dank für seine Thronbesteigung gebühren. Sie hat ihm die „vier Pfosten von Assyrien" – d.h. Assur, Ninive, Kalhu und Arbela, die das gesamte assyrische Kernland verkörpern[41] – gegeben, seine Feinde vernichtet und die Rebellen gefangen genommen (vgl. SAA 9 3.5 iv 22–30), und in dem vorangehenden Orakel bewirtet sie die Götter und die Vasallen beim Bundesmahl anlässlich der Thronbesteigung Asarhaddons. Nach alledem sitzt sie jetzt angeblich verlassen da, ohne Brot und Bier, möchte aber ihren Reiz, der wegen Asarhaddon in Verfall geraten ist, wiedergewinnen.

Der „Reiz" der Göttin hat eine Parallele in einer späteren Prophetie an Assurbanipal, die das Laufen der Göttin in der Steppe und auf den Bergen, wo das Unwetter ihre schöne Figur verdorben hat, schildert.[42] Es handelt sich um Anspielungen auf das Gilgameš-Epos,[43] die im Falle von Asarhaddon einen konkreten Bezugspunkt in seiner Exilierung als Kronprinz und in seinem Eilmarsch durch die Steppe gegen seine Brüder haben. Laut der Inschrift Asarhaddons war Ištar im Bruderkrieg an seine Seite getreten und hatte ihm zum Sieg verholfen.[44] Ihre Teilnahme an der Drangsal Asarhaddons wurde dadurch symbolisiert, dass

---

41 Vgl. Parpola, *Assyrian Prophecies*, 26 ad loc.; M. Nissinen, „City as Lofty as Heaven: Arbela and Other Cities in Neo-Assyrian Prophecy," in L. L. Grabbe and R. D. Haak (eds.), '*Every City Shall Be Forsaken': Urbanism and Prophecy in Ancient Israel and the Near East* (JSOTS 330; Sheffield: Sheffield Academic Press, 2001) 172–209, esp. 186–95 (= S. 267–300 in dem vorliegenden Band).

42 SAA 9 9:5–15.

43 Diese sind von Parpola, *Assyrian Prophecies*, 41 ad loc., angeführt; vgl. auch M. Weippert, „'König, fürchte dich nicht!' Assyrische Prophetie im 7. Jahrhundert v.Chr.," *Or* 71 (2002) 1–54, esp. 52–53.

44 E. Leichty, *The Royal Inscriptions of Esarhaddon, King of Assyria (680–669 BC)* (RINAP 4; Winona Lake, Ind.: Eisenbrauns, 2011), 13 (Nin A [§ 27] i 74–78): *Ištar bēlet qabli u tāḫāzi rā 'imat šangûtīja idāja tazzizma / qašassunu tašbir tāḫāzāšunu raksu tapṭurma / ina puḫrīšunu iqbû umma annû šarrāni / ina qibītīša ṣīrti idāja ittanasḫarū tebû arkīja* „Ištar, die Herrin des Kampfes und der Schlacht, die mein Priestertum liebt, trat auf meine Seite, zerbrach ihren Bogen und löste ihre Schlachtordnung auf. Da erscholl in ihrem Heer der Ruf: 'Dieser ist unser König!' Auf ihren erhabenen Befehl schlugen sie sich alle auf meine Seite und stellten sich hinter mich."

sich die Göttin während seiner Abwesenheit in den „Steppenpalast“, d.i. eine *akītu*-Kapelle außerhalb von Arbela in Milqia, zurückzog, um von dort dem triumphierenden Asarhaddon entgegen zu kommen.[45] Von ihren Anstrengungen erschöpft, befindet sich die Göttin jetzt wieder in ihrem Tempel und erwartet den Gegendienst Asarhaddons.

Wenn dieses Orakel tatsächlich im Kontext der Thronbesteigungsfeier verkündet worden und seine Anknüpfung an die anderen Orakel nicht rein redaktionell ist, wurde Asarhaddon gleich am ersten Tag seiner Regierung ein tüchtiger Verweis wegen Pflichtvergessenheit erteilt. Man kann fragen, ob es dabei wirklich um etwas schon Geschehenes geht; eher gewinnt man den Eindruck, dass der eben inthronisierte König sicherheitshalber wegen Versäumnissen getadelt wird, derer er noch gar nicht schuldig sein kann. Die Göttin, die sein Priestertum liebt,[46] erinnert ihn auf diese Weise an seine künftigen Pflichten, damit er sie nie vergisst.

Einen eindeutigen historischen Hintergrund hat hingegen ein Orakel des Propheten La-dagil-ili, auf den wahrscheinlich auch die zuletzt behandelte Prophetie zurückgeht. Die Sammeltafel SAA 9 2, in der Prophetien vom Anfang der Regierung Asarhaddons gesammelt sind, enthält das folgende Wort von Ištar an den König bezüglich der Götter von Babylon (SAA 9 2.3 ii 22–27):[47]

> *dibbīja annūti issu libbi Arbail ina bētānukka esip / ilāni ša Esaggil ina sēri lemni balli šarbubū / arḫiš 2 maqaluāti ina pānīšsunu lušēṣiū lillikū šulamka liqbiū*
>
> Nimm dir diese meine Worte aus Arbela zu Herzen: / Die Götter von Esaggil schmachten in einer üblen, chaotischen Wüste. / Sende eiligst zwei Brandopfer vor sie und lass ihnen deinen Friedensgruß sagen!

Der Wiederaufbau von Babylon mit dem zentralen Marduktempel Esaggil scheint auch im ersten und letzten Orakel dieser Sammeltafel (SAA 9 2.1 und 2.6) thematisiert zu sein, obschon der Text in beiden Fällen stark beschädigt ist. Die Sympathie der Propheten von Arbela für die babylonischen Götter ist bemerkenswert und hat eine theologisch-politische Motivation. Babylon lag ja, seitdem Sanherib die Stadt im Jahre 689 verwüstet hatte, in Trümmern, und Asarhaddon

45 Zur Kapelle in Milqia und den *akītu*-Prozessionen s. B. Menzel, *Assyrische Tempel*, vol. 1: *Untersuchungen zu Kult, Administration und Personal* (StPSM 10.1; Rome: Biblical Institute Press, 1981), esp. 113; B. Pongratz-Leisten, „The Interplay of Military Strategy and Cultic Practice in Assyrian Politics,“ in *Assyria 1995: Proceedings of the 10th Anniversary symposium of the Neo-Assyrian Texts Corpus Project, Helsinki September 7–11, 1995* (ed. S. Parpola and R. M. Whiting; Helsinki: The Neo-Assyrian Texts Corpus Project, 1997) 145–52, esp. 249–50; Nissinen, „City as Lofty as Heaven,“ 183–86.

46 Vgl. oben Anm. 44.

47 Parpola, *Assyrian Prophecies*, 16.

versuchte seine ganze Regierungszeit hindurch, die Ehrenschuld seines Vaters zu sühnen.[48] Diese Verpflichtung wurde ihm offenbar von Anfang an von den Propheten vorgehalten, die die Restauration als Zeichen der Versöhnung zwischen Himmel und Erde ansahen.[49] Demnach geht es in dem zitierten Orakel um viel mehr als um zwei Brandopfer, denn diese Opfer sind nur als erster Anstoß zur Rehabilitierung der Götter von Babylon und zugleich des ganzen Landes Babylon zu verstehen. Eine scheinbar „kultische" Forderung ist hier von großer politischer und theologischer Tragweite.

Wesentlich für die kultischen Pflichten des Königs ist, dass der assyrische König bei seiner Thronbesteigung auch die Rolle des (obersten) Priesters *(šangû)*[50] und folglich die Hauptverantwortung für die Pflege der Götter und Tempel übernahm. Er war auch der „perfekte Mensch" *(eṭlu gitmālu)*,[51] der als Repräsentant des gesamten Volkes in seinem Reich, wenn nicht der ganzen Menschheit, die göttlichen Ordnungen pünktlich befolgen musste. Da die Unvollkommenheit des Königs in dieser Hinsicht den göttlichen Zorn erregte, musste der König rechtzeitig vor der göttlichen Bestrafung gewarnt werden; und hierfür stand ihm der ganze divinatorische Apparat, darunter auch die Prophetie, zur Verfügung.[52] Als Vertreter der Divination waren die Propheten tatsächlich in der Lage, den König zu ermahnen und zu kritisieren. Die Propheten hatten an sich keine persönliche Autorität; denn ihre Kritik beruhte, zumindest im Prinzip, nicht auf ihren eigenen Meinungen. Sie galten als Verkünder des Gotteswortes. Gerade ihre Rolle als Sprachrohr der Götter ermöglichte es ihnen, direkte Mahnungen und Kritik auszusprechen, was aus dem Mund eines Bürgers und selbst eines Ratgebers absolut undenkbar gewesen wäre. Aus dieser Perspektive betrachtet, kann die

---

48 Zur ideologischen und theologischen Bedeutung des Wiederaufbaus von Babylon s. z. B. J. A. Brinkman, „Through a Glass Darkly: Esarhaddon's Retrospects on the Downfall of Babylon," *JAOS* 103 (1983) 35–42; B. N. Porter, *Images, Power, and Politics: Figurative Aspects of Esarhaddon's Babylonian Policy* (Philadelphia, Pa.: American Philosophical Society, 1993), esp. 77–153.

49 Näheres dazu bei Nissinen, „City as Lofty as Heaven," 195–201.

50 Zur Priestertitulatur des Königs s. M.-J. Seux, *Épithètes royales akkadiennes et sumériennes* (Paris: Letouzey et Ané, 1967), esp. 21, 287–88. Zu den kultischen Handlungen des Königs von Assyrien und seinem Verhältnis zu den Priestern s. Menzel, *Assyrische Tempel*, 157–74.

51 Zu diesem und ähnlichen Titeln s. Seux, *Épithètes royales*, 92; vgl. S. Parpola, „The Assyrian Tree of Life: Tracing the Origins of Jewish Monotheism and Greek Philosophy," *JNES* 52 (1993) 161–208, esp. 168.

52 Zur Stellung des Königs zwischen menschlicher und göttlicher Welt s. S. Parpola, *Letters from Assyrian and Babylonian Scholars* (SAA 10; Helsinki: Helsinki University Press, 1993), esp. xv–xvi; id., „Monotheism in Ancient Assyria," in *One God or Many? Concepts of Divinity in the Ancient World* (ed. B. N. Porter; Transactions of the Casco Bay Assyriological Institute 1; Casco Bay, Maine: Casco Bay Assyriological Institute, 2000) 165–209, esp. 190–192.

assyrische Prophetie grundsätzlich keine bloße Heilsprophetie sein, sondern enthält notwendig ein kritisches Potential, das sich auch als Unheilsprophetie verwirklichen konnte. Die uns bekannten assyrischen Prophetenorakel, die zunächst nur Heilsprophetie vertreten, vermitteln ein einseitiges Bild von der Wirklichkeit.

Insgesamt gilt es festzustellen, dass die Beachtung der kultischen Forderungen von der Rechtschaffenheit des Königs in anderen Dingen nicht zu trennen war.[53] Die prophetischen Forderungen zur kultischen Vollkommenheit in Assyrien wie auch in Mari sind mit der theologisch begründeten und göttlich sanktionierten Stellung des Königs im Verhältnis zu den Göttern und zu seinem Volk eng verbunden und dürfen nicht deswegen bagatellisiert werden, weil ihre Anliegen uns als wenig himmelstürmend erscheinen mögen.[54] In den folgenden Texten kommt das Idealbild des gerechten Königs noch deutlicher zum Vorschein.

III. König und Gerechtigkeit

Wenn auch die Forderungen bezüglich der Tempel nicht ohne den Bezug auf ihre gesellschaftlichen Dimensionen betrachtet werden können, so ist es doch in den altorientalischen prophetischen Quellen um direkte Mahnungen zur sozialen Gerechtigkeit relativ schlecht bestellt. Dass dieses Anliegen den Propheten nicht grundsätzlich fremd war, kann aber immerhin an einigen Beispielen aus der Marikorrespondenz demonstriert werden. Es geht in diesen Texten immer um die Urpflicht des Königs, eine gerechte Ordnung *(mīšarum)* in seinem Land zu schaffen.

53 Vgl. O. Kaiser, „Kult und Kultkritik im Alten Testament," in *„Und Mose schrieb dieses Lied auf": Studien zum Alten Testament und zum Alten Orient*, FS Oswald Loretz (ed. M. Dietrich and I. Kottsieper; AOAT 250; Münster: Ugarit-Verlag, 1998) 401–26, esp. 411–14, hier 413–14: „In der Regel ging man davon aus, daß die Bedingungen für die Annahme eines Opfers erfüllt waren, wenn die Opfervorschriften eingehalten wurden. (...) Andererseits war die Lauterkeit der das Opfer Darbringenden (Ps 15; 24,3–5) und der das Opfer Vollziehenden (Mal 1,6–2,9) die stillschweigende Voraussetzung für seine göttliche Annahme."

54 Jeremias übertreibt den „eklatanten und unübersehbaren Gegensatz zwischen der Prophetie in Mari und derjenigen in Israel" in dieser Hinsicht („Hier – in Mari – geht es um ein Paar Opfertiere mehr oder die Abgabe eines Stückes Land, dort – im Alten Testament – geht es um den Gehorsam des Königs gegenüber dem überlieferten Willen Gottes und seinen aktuellen Willenskundgebungen durch den Propheten" („Proprium," 487). Er führt diesen Unterschied aber nicht auf die Überlegenheit des biblischen Gottesbildes zurück, sondern hat seinen überlieferungsgeschichtlichen Grund richtig gesehen.

Um sich als gerechte Herrscher zu bewähren, hatten die mesopotamischen Könige die Möglichkeit, ein *(an)durārum*, d.h. eine Lastenbefreiung, zu promulgieren.[55] Dazu wird Zimri-Lim in Mari in einem Brief des Propheten *(āpilum)* von Šamaš aufgefordert, der im Namen des Gottes verschiedene Ansprüche an den König stellt (ARM 26 194).[56] Aus dem Brief geht deutlich hervor, dass Zimri-Lim vor kurzem seine Feinde besiegt hat.[57]

Jetzt verlangt der Gott, dass er einen Thron sowie seine Tochter zum Šamaš-Tempel von Sippar sendet (Z. 4–7). Auch soll er dem Adad von Aleppo sein Vorbehaltsgut *(asakkum)* überliefern (Z. 13–18) und dem Dagan ein bereits von einem anderen Propheten *(āpilum)* erwähntes Geschenk geben (Z. 19–23). Die Geschenke an die Hauptgötter von Mari, Aleppo und Sippar in Babylonien weisen nicht nur auf „eine weite geographische Ausdehnung der kultischen Aktivität“[58] hin, sondern symbolisieren den göttlich begründeten Machtanspruch des Zimri-Lim „vom Aufgang der Sonne bis zu ihrem Untergang“, wie im weiteren Verlauf des Briefes prophetisch verkündet wird. Dem Gott Nergal von Ḫubšalum, der auf seiner Seite gestanden hat, soll er einen Bronzedolch und andere Geschenke darbringen lassen, wie er es versprochen hat (Z. 24–31). Es handelt sich also um Gegendienste, die Zimri-Lim nach einem siegreichen Krieg für die göttliche wie menschliche Hilfe leisten soll. Mit dem illoyalen König Hammurabi von Kurdâ hat der Gott indessen andere Pläne (Z. 32–43):

> *u šanītam umma Šamašma / Ḫammurabi šar Kurdâ [s]arrātim ittīka i[dbub] / u qāssu ašar šanê[m š]aknat / qātka i[kaššassu] u ina libbi mātī[šu a]ndurāram tuwa[ššar] / u an[u]mma mātum k[alûša] ina qātīka nadna[t] / [k]īma ālam taṣab[batūma a]ndurāram tuwaššar [u akk]êm šarrūtka [d]ari[at]*

> Ferner, so spricht Šamaš: / „Hammurabi, König von Kurdâ, hat mit dir [be]trügerisch ges[prochen]. Er ist aber jetzt anderwär[ts be]schäftigt. / Deine Hand wird [ihn gefangen nehmen] und in [seinem] Land wirst du die Lastenbefreiung promu[lgieren]. / Jetzt ist das

55 Zu *mīšarum* und *andurārum* s. M. Weinfeld, „Sabbatical Year and Jubilee in the Pentateuchal Laws and their Ancient Near Eastern Background,“ in *The Law in the Bible and in its Environment* (ed. T. Veijola; PFES 51; Helsinki and Göttingen: Finnish Exegetical Society, 1990) 39–62; id., *Social Justice in Ancient Israel and in the Ancient Near East* (Publications of the Perry Foundation for Biblical Research in the Hebrew University of Jerusalem; Jerusalem: Magnes Press and Minneapolis, Minn.: Fortress Press, 1995), esp. 75–96; in bezug auf Mari s. D. Charpin, „L'*andurârum* à Mari,“ *MARI* 6 (1990) 253–70; Durand, „La religión en Siria,“ 526–28.

56 Durand, *Archives épistolaires de Mari*, 417–19; Übersetzung auch Durand, *Les documents épistolaires du palais de Mari*, 87–89.

57 Zum historischen Hintergrund dieses Briefes s. D. Charpin and J.-M. Durand, „La prise du pouvoir par Zimri-Lim,“ *MARI* 4 (1985) 297–343, esp. 332–33.

58 Huffmon, „The Expansion of Prophecy in the Mari Archives,“ 13.

g[anze] Land dir in deine Hände gegeb[en]. / Indem du die Stadt über[nimmst] und die Lastenbefreiung promulgierst, (erweist sich) dein Königtum [auf die]se Weise als ewig.

Da Hammurabi von Kurdâ offenbar noch nicht besiegt worden ist, liegt hier eine echte prophetische Verheißung vor: Zimri-Lim wird ihn entthronen. Der Sinn des *andurārum* ist darin zu sehen, dass Zimri-Lim zu Anfang seiner Herrschaft in Kurdâ eine gerechte Ordnung schaffen und sich somit als ein gerechter König erweisen werde. Darüber hinaus gibt die Prophetie den politischen Hoffnungen auf die Erweiterung des Machtbereichs von Zimri-Lim Ausdruck, die sich aber als vergeblich erweisen sollten; Zimri-Lim nahm Kurdâ nie ein.[59]

Ein entsprechender Anspruch, verbunden mit der kritischen Haltung gegenüber dem König, erscheint in zwei Briefen des Nur-Sîn, des Legaten Zimri-Lims in Alaḫtum, einem Verwaltungsgut von Mari im Gebiet des Königtums Jamḫad, dessen Hauptstadt Aleppo war. Der längere (und wohl auch jüngere) von ihnen, der die Tafelsignatur A. 1121 trägt, wurde von A. Lods und G. Dossin im Jahr 1950 veröffentlicht[60] und zählt zu den ersten Maribriefen, die überhaupt als Zeugnis für Prophetie anerkannt wurden. B. Lafont fügte 1984 die zweite Tafelhälfte A. 2731 hinzu und komplettierte damit den Brief,[61] dessen vollständiger Text jetzt in einer neuen Edition von J.-M. Durand vorliegt.[62] Der Anlass des Briefes FM 7 39 ist die Übergabe einer Opfergabe *(zukrum)*[63] an den Gott Adad von Aleppo und eine

59 Charpin, „L'*andurârum* à Mari," 268.

60 A. Lods and G. Dossin, „Une tablette inédite de Mari, intéressante pour l'histoire ancienne du prophetisme sémitique," in *Studies in Old Testament Prophecy,* FS T. H. Robinson (ed. H. H. Rowley; Edinburgh: T & T Clark, 1950) 103–10.

61 B. Lafont, „Le roi de Mari et les prophètes du dieu Adad," *RA* 78 (1984) 7–18. Der Text A. 2731 wurde von Dossin, „Sur le prophétisme à Mari," 78, veröffentlicht.

62 J.-M. Durand, *Florilegium marianum 7: Le culte d'Addu d'Alep et l'affaire d'Alahtum* (Mémoires de *NABU* 8; Paris: SEPOA, 2002), esp. 137–40. Übersetzung auch bei Durand, *Les documents épistolaires du palais de Mari,* 130–33 und Dietrich, „TUAT 2/1," 85–87.

63 Das Wort *zukrum* kommt nur hier vor und wird in *CAD* Z 153 „pasture-land (?)" und in *AHw* 1536 „männliches Gesinde" übersetzt; vgl. *CDA* 449: „male personnel". Da das Wort aber hier parallel mit *liātum* (line 9) „Vieh" (*CAD* L 218; AHw 557–58 sub *lītu)* erscheint, wird es häufig mit „Vieh" o.ä. übersetzt; so u.a. Dossin, „Sur le prophétisme á Mari," 78; Lafont, „Le roi de Mari," 11; Dietrich, „TUAT 2/1,", 85, und A. Malamat, *Mari and the Bible* (SHCANE 12; Leiden: Brill, 1998), esp. 108. Aufgrund des Gebrauchs von *zukrum* in Emar ist es aber inzwischen wahrscheinlich geworden, dass es sich um ein Opferritual handelt; s. D. E. Fleming, *Time at Emar: The Cultic Calendar and the Rituals from the Diviner's House* (Winona Lake, Ind.: Eisenbrauns, 2000), esp. 120–24; Durand, *Les documents épistolaires du palais de Mari,* 232–33; id., *Florilegium marianum 7,* 135–36.

Landschenkung *(niḫlatum)*[64] an Adad von Kallassu. Kallassu ist eine Örtlichkeit unweit von Alaḫtum, das Durand wiederum mit Alalaḫ gleichsetzt.[65]

Nur-Sîn behauptet, dem König diesbezüglich schon fünf Mal geschrieben zu haben, offenbar ohne Erfolg (Z. 1–12). Jetzt beruft sich Nur-Sîn schließlich auf ein durch Propheten *(āpilū)* übermitteltes Orakel *(têrtum)* von Adad, dem Herrn von Kallassu. In diesem Orakel erinnert Adad den König daran, dass er ihn auf den Thron seines Vaterhauses zurückgebracht hat, und droht an, dass er wieder wegnehmen kann, was er ihm gegeben hat, wenn der König ihm das Landgut nicht übereignen sollte. Wenn aber der König seinen Wunsch erfüllt, wird er ihm das Land vom Aufgang der Sonne bis zu ihrem Untergang geben (Z. 13–28). Zudem weiß Nur-Sîn zu berichten, dass ein Prophet das Gebiet von Alaḫtum als das geforderte Besitztum identifiziert hat (Z. 29–33).

Offensichtlich etwas verlegen, diese unerbittliche Forderung eines beträchtlichen Eigentums dem König übermitteln zu müssen, verweist Nur-Sîn darauf, dass er den König immer auf jedes ihm bekannte Prophetenorakel aufmerksam gemacht hat, früher in Mari und jetzt im Ausland, damit der König nicht sagen kann, Nur-Sîn habe seine Pflichten verletzt (Z.34–45). Zuletzt beruft er sich auf ein Orakel von Adad von Aleppo (Z.46–62):

> *[šanī]tam āpilum ša Addi bēl Ḫalab [itti Abu]-ḫalim illikamma kīam iqbêm ummāmi / ana bēlīka šupur / ummāmi Addu bēl Ḫalab ul anākū ša ina suḫātīja urabbûkama ana kussêm bit abīka uterrûk[a] / [m]imma ittīka ul err[i]š / inūma ḫablum u ḫabi[ltum] išassikkum izizma dī[n]šunu dīn / [a]nnītam ša ittīka errišū / annītam ša ašpurakkum teppešma ana awātīja taqâlma mātam ištu ṣ[ītiš]a ana erbīša u māt[ka matt]am anaddinakkum / [a]nnītam ā[pilum ša] Addi bēl Ḫalab maḫar A[b]u-ḫalim iqbêm annītam bēlī lū īde*

> [Fer]ner, ein Prophet von Adad, dem Herrn von Aleppo, kam [mit Abu]-ḫalim und sprach: / „Schreibe deinem Herrn Folgendes: / Bin ich nicht Adad, der Herr von Aleppo, der dich auf seinem Schoß großgezogen und di[ch] auf den Thron deines Vaterhauses zurückgebracht hat? / Ich wünsche nichts von dir! / Wenn aber ein Unterdrückter oder eine Unterd[rückte] an dich appelliert, stehe (ihnen zur Seite) und verschaffe ihnen Recht! / Nur dies wünsche ich von dir. / Wenn du das tust, was ich dir geschrieben habe, und auf mein Wort achtest, werde ich dir das Land vom Au[fgan]g der Sonne bis zu ihrem Untergang, [dein vergr]ößertes Land, geben." / Dies hat der Pr[ophet von] Adad, dem Herrn von Aleppo, vor Abu-ḫalim gesprochen. Mein Herr nehme dies zur Kenntnis!

---

64 Das Wort *niḫlatum* wird im Gefolge von A. Malamat, „History and Prophetic Vision in a Mari Letter," *ErIs* 5 (1958) 67–73, esp. 68, 70, (Hebr. vgl. id., *Mari and the Bible*, 109), mit „Landgut, Erbbesitz" (von *naḫālum* „erben" im Akkadischen von Mari, vgl. Ugar. *nḥl* und Hebr. *naḥălâ;* s. AHw 712, und vgl. *CDA* 253: „transferred property") übersetzt.

65 S. Durand, *Florilegium marianum 7,* 60–66.

Der Gott von Aleppo stellt sich als der Vater Zimri-Lims vor, der ihn auf den Thron seines irdischen Vaters Jaḫdun-Lim nach dem Interregnum des Jasmaḫ-Adad, des Marionettenherrschers des Šamši-Adad, des Königs von Assyrien, zurückgebracht hat. Dies mag überraschen, ist doch Adad von Aleppo für Zimri-Lim ein ausländischer Gott. Der Anspruch Adads gründet sich aber auf historische Umstände und politische Beziehungen zwischen Mari und Jamḫad.[66] Jarim-Lim, der König von Jamḫad und Zimri-Lims Schwiegervater, hatte ihm bei seiner Machtübernahme Hilfe geleistet,[67] und Hammurabi, der Nachfolger von Jarim-Lim, hatte ihm Alaḫtum abgetreten.[68] Dieses fordert Adad nun zurück, womit das Prophetenwort außenpolitische Bedeutung gewinnt.

Beide Orakel des Gottes Adad – auf deren biblische Parallelen schon mehrfach hingewiesen worden ist[69] – sind sich im Wortlaut weitgehend ähnlich.[70] Dies ist ein Hinweis darauf, dass die schriftliche Fassung auf Nur-Sîn selbst zurückgeht, zumal es angeblich um Äußerungen mehrerer Propheten geht. Jedoch sind die Orakel darin verschieden,[71] dass Nur-Sîn im zweiten Orakel auf eine Prophetie zurückgreift, die die Gerechtigkeit des Königs und die Rechte derer, die Unrecht erleiden, besonders hervorhebt. Weder das zitierte Gotteswort noch Nur-Sîn selbst machen deutlich, was damit konkret gemeint ist; im Prinzip könnte es sich durchaus um eine allgemeine ethische Forderung handeln. Allerdings berichten die Quellen, dass die Übernahme von Alaḫtum durch Zimri-Lim für die

---

66 Zu den geschichtlichen Hintergründen s. ibid., 59–60, 66–71; ferner Lafont, „Le roi de Mari," 14–18; H. Klengel, „Ḫalab – Mari – Babylon: Aspekte syrisch-mesopotamischer Beziehungen in altbabylonischer Zeit," in *De la Babylonie à la Syrie, en passant par Mari*, FS J.-R. Kupper (ed. Ö. Tunca; Liège: Université de Liège, 1990) 183–95; Malamat, *Mari and the Bible*, 112–14.

67 In A. 1153:8–10 legt Zimri-Lim die folgenden Worte in den Mund Jarim-Lims: *Zimri-Lim ana kussêšu anāku ušēri[bma] ša danānīšu u išdē kussê[šu du]nnūnim lūpuš* „Bin ich nicht derjenige, der Zimri-Lim dazu verholfen hat, seinen Thron wiederzugewinnen, und seine Macht und das Fundament seines Throns befestigt?"; s. G. Dossin, „Une opposition familiale," in: *La voix de l'opposition en Mésopotamie: Colloque organisé par l'institut des Hautes Études de Belgique 19 et 20 mars 1973*, (Bruxelles: Institut des hautes études de Belgique, 1973) 179–188, esp. 180–83; vgl. Malamat, *Mari and the Bible*, 113.

68 Dies wird in den Briefen A. 1257 (Durand, *Florilegium marianum 7*, 128–32), A. 1496 (ibid., 119–20) und A. 4445 (ibid., 161–64) berichtet. Vgl. die gründliche Analyse der diesbezüglichen Quellen ibid., 59–97.

69 Z. B. 2 Sam 7 (Malamat, *Mari and the Bible*, 106–21); Jer 22:1–5 (M. Anbar, „Aspect moral dans un discours 'prophetique' de Mari," *UF* 7 [1975] 517–18).

70 A. Schart, „Combining Prophetic Oracles in Mari Letters and Jeremiah 36," *JANES* 23 (1995) 75–93, esp. 83.

71 Schart (ibid., 83) vermutet, Nur-Sîn wolle seinen Brief mit einem angenehmeren Orakel abschließen, in dem die Forderungen nicht, wie im ersten Orakel, mit bedingungslosen *šumma*-Sätzen, sondern indikativisch ausgedrückt sind.

Landbesitzer in der Tat eine Katastrophe war: Sie mussten Alaḫtum verlassen, während die „Arbeiterklasse“ im Dienst der neuen Landesherren bleiben durfte; freilich wird dies in der Korrespondenz von Nur-Sîn nicht als Unrecht, sondern als eine normale Maßnahme dargestellt.[72] Andererseits hatte Gašera, die Königinmutter von Aleppo, in ihrem eigenen Interesse Einsprüche gegen vermeintliche Rechtsverletzungen in Alaḫtum erhoben, die Nur-Sîn und andere Beamte Zimri-Lims jedoch entschieden zurückwiesen.[73]

Man gewinnt den Eindruck, dass Nur-Sîn, der dem König angeblich schon zum fünften Mal schreibt, ihn mit der unangenehmen Forderung der Rückgabe des Eigentums in Alaḫtum bedrängen muss. Dabei versucht er, mit einem moralischen Argument aus dem Mund des Gottes auf den König einzuwirken, jedoch in der Weise, dass dieser schließlich selbst entscheiden muss, wem eigentlich Unrecht geschehen ist.

Das Anliegen von Nur-Sîn gewinnt Konturen, wenn wir den oben behandelten Brief mit einem anderen von ihm verfassten Schreiben (FM 7 38[74]) vergleichen, das kürzlich von Durand veröffentlicht worden ist. Dieser Brief gilt als ältester Beleg für das Chaosmotiv im Alten Orient.[75] Darüber hinaus ist der königsideologische Kontext der Prophetie unverkennbar. Nur-Sîn zitiert auch hier ein Prophetenwort in der Weise, dass die Prophetie selbst das Thema des Briefes ist und als Abfassungszweck dient:

ana bēlīja qibīma umma Nūr-Sîn waradkāma / Abīja āpilum ša Addi bēl Ḫala[b] illikamma kīam iqbêm / ummāmi Adduma mātam kalâša ana Jaḫdun-Lim addin u ina kakkēja māḫiram ul irši / jâtam īzibma mātam ša addinūšu[m] ana Šamšī-Addu ad[di]n / [...] Šamšī-Addu [...] [...ana kussêm bīt abīka] lut[ê]rka / ana k[ussêm bit abika] utêrka / kakk[ī] ša itti Têmtim amtaḫṣu addinakkum / šamnam ša namrīrūtīja apšuškāma / mamman ana pānīka ul izz[iz] /

---

72 Dazu Durand, *Florilegium marianum 7*, 77–79, mit den Briefen von Nur-Sîn A. 2635+M. 13597 (ibid., 99–102) und A. 1257 (ibid., 128–32);

73 Zum Konflikt mit Gašera s. ibid., 79–80. Davon berichten u. a. die Briefe A. 1257 (Nur-Sîn: ibid., 128–32) und A. 4445 (Šû-nuḫra-halu: ibid., 161–64).

74 J.-M. Durand, „Le mythologème du combat entre le dieu de l’orage at la mer en Mésopotamie,“ *MARI* 7 (1993) 41–61; id., *Florilegium marianum 7*, 134–35. Übersetzung auch Durand, *Les documents épistolaires du palais de Mari*, 83–84.

75 S. N. Wyatt, *Myths of Power: A Study of Royal Myth and Ideology in Ugaritic and Biblical Tradition* (UBL 13; Münster: Ugarit-Verlag, 1996), esp. 129–31; id., „Arms and the King: The Earliest Allusions to the *Chaoskampf* Motif and their Implications for the Interpretation of the Ugaritic and Biblical Traditions,“ in: *„Und Mose schrieb dieses Lied auf“: Studien zum Alten Testament und zum Alten Orient*, FS O. Loretz (ed. M. Dietrich and I. Kottsieper; AOAT 250; Münster: Ugarit-Verlag, 1998) 833–882, esp. 841–844; M. Bauks, „‘Chaos’ als Metapher für die Gefährdung der Weltordnung,“ in *Das biblische Weltbild und seine altorientalischen Kontexte* (ed. B. Janowski and B. Ego; FAT 32; Tübingen: Mohr Siebeck, 2001) 431–64, esp. 437–38.

[a]wātī ištēt šime inūma mamman ša dīnim išassik<kum> / ummāmi ḫ[abt]āku izizma / dīnšunu dīn [iša]riš ap[ulšu] / [an]nītam ša ittīka e[rrišu] /
inūma girram tu[ṣṣû b]alum têrtim lā tu[ṣṣi] / [i]nūma anāku ina têrtīj[a a]zza[zz]u girram taṣi / [š]umma [lā k]īamma bābam [lā] tuṣṣi /
annītam āpilum iqbêm / anum[ma šārat āpilim] u si[ssiktašu ana bēlīja uštābilam]

Sprich zu meinem Herrn: Folgendermaßen Nur-Sîn, dein Diener:
Abija, ein Prophet des Adad, des Herrn von Alep[po], kam zu mir und sprach so: „So spricht Adad: Ich habe das gesamte Land Jaḫdun-Lim gegeben. Dank meiner Waffen hat er keinen als seinesgleichen anerkannt. Trotzdem hat er mich verlassen, so habe ich das Land, das ich ihm gegeben habe, Šamši-Adad geg[ebe]n. [...] Šamši-Adad [...], [...auf den Thron deines Vaterhauses] will ich dich zurückbringen!" So habe ich dich auf den Th[ron deines Vaterhauses] zurückgebracht und dir die Waffe[n] gegeben, mit denen ich Tiamat bekämpfte. Ich habe dich mit dem Öl meines Glanzes gesalbt, niemand wird dir Widerstand leisten.
Nun höre ein einziges [W]ort von mir: Wenn sich jeder beliebige Mensch, um zu seinem Recht zu kommen, an <dich> wendet und sagt: ‚Mir ist Un[recht gescheh]en', stehe (ihm zur Seite) und verschaffe ihm Recht; gib [ihm eine ehr]liche An[twort]. [Nur di]es ver[lange] ich von dir! Wenn du in den Krieg zi[ehst], niemals tue es, [o]hne ein Orakel einzuholen. [W]enn ich [mich] in [meinem] Orakel offenbare, zieh ins Feld; [w]enn dies [nicht] geschieht, sollst du [nicht] zu dem Stadttor hinausgehen."
Dies hat der Prophet gesagt. [Ich habe] hie[rmit den Haarschopf des Propheten] und [seinen] Gew[andsaum zu meinem Herrn bringen lassen].

Wie Jack M. Sasson überzeugend dargelegt hat,[76] geht das hier zitierte Orakel wohl auf ein einst von dem Propheten gesprochenes Wort zurück und dient als Beispiel für das von Nur-Sîn selbst formulierte Orakel von Adad von Aleppo in FM 7 39. In dieser Prophetie kommt das Verhältnis zwischen Adad und Zimri-Lim besonders anschaulich zum Ausdruck. Das Orakel hat eine klare Struktur, die dem chronologischen Schema „einst – jetzt – danach" folgt.[77] Zimri-Lim wird zunächst an die Geschichte der Thronfolge in Mari erinnert, um deutlich zu machen, dass er Adad dafür zu danken hat, dass er überhaupt auf dem Thron seines Vaterhauses sitzt[78] Jetzt ist er aber zum König gesalbt,[79] und die mythischen Waffen, mit denen

76 Sasson, „The Posting of Letters," 314–16; vgl. auch id., „Mari and the Bible," 119–20.
77 Vgl. J.-G. Heintz, „Des textes sémitiques anciens à la Bible hébraïque: Un comparatisme légitime?" in *Le comparatisme en histoire des religions* (ed. F. Bœspflug and F. Dunand; Paris: Cerf, 1997) 127–56, esp. 138–39; cf. Bauks, „'Chaos' als Metapher," 437.
78 Zur Rolle des Gottes Adad im politischen Geschichtsbild von Mari, s. Durand, „La religión en Siria," 365–68.
79 Dies ist wohl der einzige außerbiblische Beleg für die Salbung eines Königs; vgl. Wyatt, „Arms and the King," 843, bemerkt dazu: „This most distinctive of Israelite and Judahite Rites is now given a pedigree going back a millennium."

die Chaosmächte bekämpft worden sind,[80] wurden ihm als Zeichen der Legitimierung seiner Herrschaft überreicht.[81] Was der Gott nun von ihm verlangt, ist einerseits die Gerechtigkeit gegenüber den Menschen in seinem Machtbereich und andererseits die Orakeleinholung als Zeichen seines Gehorsams gegenüber der göttlichen Welt. Besser könnten die Beziehung zwischen himmlischem und irdischem Königtum und die Stellung des Königs zwischen den beiden Welten als Hüter der Weltordnung kaum zum Ausdruck kommen.[82] Auch die Rolle der Prophetie in der Propagierung dieser Ideologie ist hier besonders anschaulich.

Der Spruch von Abija erweckt den Eindruck eines Krönungsorakels,[83] obschon der Brief sicherlich später geschrieben worden ist; die Korrespondenz von Nur-Sîn stammt aus Aleppo, er selbst war aber früher, als Zimri-Lim schon regierte, in Mari angestellt gewesen (FM 7 39:34). Zudem weist die Beifügung der üblichen Identifikationsmittel darauf hin, dass Nur-Sîn ein von dem Propheten soeben überbrachtes Orakel und nicht etwa einen alten, in schriftlicher Form aufbewahrten, Prophetenspruch zitiert. Trotzdem greift das Orakel inhaltlich auf die grundlegenden Pflichten Zimri-Lims zurück, die ihm bei seiner Thronbesteigung aufgebürdet wurden. An und für sich ist das Orakel ein stilgerechtes Beispiel für Heilsprophetie, jedoch schließt sein ideologisch-moralisches Anliegen zugleich ein kritisches Potential ein. Das Zitieren eines solchen Orakels macht es Nur-Sîn möglich, den König zugleich auf seine gottgegebenen Pflichten – und implizit auch auf seine Pflichtvergessenheit – aufmerksam zu machen.

---

80 Zum Kampf des Wettergottes Adad und dessen altorientalischen und biblischen Parallelen s. H. Klengel, „Der Wettergott von Halab," *JCS* 19 (1965) 87–93; P. Bordreuil and D. Pardee, „Le combat de *Ba'lu* avec *Yammu* après les textes ougaritiques," *MARI* 7 (1993) 63–70; Heintz, „Des textes sémitiques,"; P. Fronzaroli, „Les combats de Haddad dans les textes d'Ébla," *MARI* 8 (1997) 283–290; Wyatt, „Arms and the King"; M. Köckert, „Die Theophanie des Wettergottes Jahwe in Psalm 18," in *Kulturgeschichten*, FS V. Haas (ed. T. Richter, D. Prechel, and J. Klinger; Saarbrücken: Saarbrücker Druckerei und Verlag, 2001) 209–26.

81 Dass es sich um konkrete Gegenstände handelt, zeigt A. 1858 (Durand, „Le mythologème du combat," 53; id., *Florilegium marianum 7*, 15): *ana bēlīja qi*[*bī*]*ma umma Sūmu-ila waradkāma / kakkē ša Addi ša Ḫalab ikšudūnimma / ina bīt Dagan ina Terqa kalêkšunūti / ana kīma bēlī išapparam lūpuš* „Sprich zu meinem Herrn: Folgendermaßen Sumu-ila, dein Diener: / Die Waffen von Adad von Aleppo sind angekommen. / Ich behalte sie im Tempel von Dagan in Terqa / bis daß mein Herr mir schreibt, wie (mit ihnen) vorgegangen werden soll." Vgl. Wyatt, *Myths of Power*, 130; id., „Arms and the King," 843–44; van der Toorn, „Mesopotamian Prophecy," 58.

82 Vgl. Bauks, „'Chaos' als Metapher," 460–61; ferner S. M. Maul, „Der assyrische König: Hüter der Weltordnung," in, *Priests and Officials in the Ancient Near East: Papers of the Second Colloquium on the Ancient Near East – The City and its Life* (ed. K. Watanabe; Heidelberg: Winter, 1999) 201–14.

83 Vgl. Heintz, „Des textes sémitiques," 146–50; Wyatt, „Arms and the King,"841; Bauks, „'Chaos' als Metapher," 449.

Darüber hinaus hat Herbert B. Huffmon darauf hingewiesen, dass die Aufgabe des Königs, die Sache der Unterdrückten zu führen, in dem Adad-Orakel ganz ähnlich ausgedrückt ist wie in dem fast zeitgleichen Epilog des Kodex Hammurabi.[84] Das gleiche Ideal ist schon in den Gesetzen von Ur-Nammu (2111–2094 v. Chr.)[85] zu finden; das Eintreten für die Unterdrückten gilt als eine der wichtigsten Pflichten des mesopotamischen Königs. Die Prophetie von Abija erweist sich demnach als durchaus „gesetzesgemäß" und zeigt, dass die Verbindung von Prophetie und Gesetz kein ausschließlich biblischer Sachverhalt ist.

Die oben behandelten Briefe aus dem 18. Jahrhundert sind die einzigen uns bekannten prophetischen Dokumente, in denen der Anspruch auf soziale Gerechtigkeit unumwunden zur Sprache kommt. In der neuassyrischen Prophetie fehlen entsprechende Mahnungen ganz, was aber grundsätzlich nicht so gedeutet werden darf, als sei die Gerechtigkeit dem assyrischen König gleichgültig gewesen. Im Gegenteil: Die Sorge für das Wohl der Armen und Unterdrückten gehört bekanntlich als fester Bestandteil zum Idealbild des Königs als *šar kitti u mīšari* „König von Recht und Gerechtigkeit" überall in Mesopotamien zu allen Zeiten, wie aus den literarischen Quellen – vom Gesetz des Ur-Nammu, dem Kodex Hammurabi und etwa dem neubabylonischen Fürstenspiegel[86] bis hin zu den

84 Huffmon, „ A Company of Prophets," 54–55; vgl. Kodex Hammurabi, Epilog, Z. xlvii 59–78, xlviii 3–47: „Damit der Starke den Schwachen nicht schädigt, um der Waise und der Witwe zu ihrem Recht zu verhelfen, habe ich in Babel, der Stadt, deren Haupt Anu und Enlil erhoben haben, in Esaggil, dem Tempel, dessen Grundfesten wie Himmel und Erde fest sind, um dem Lande Recht zu schaffen, um die Entscheidung(en) des Landes zu fällen, um den Geschädigten Recht zu verschaffen, meine überaus wertvollen Worte auf (m)eine Stele geschrieben und vor meiner Statue (namens) 'König der Gerechtigkeiten' aufgestellt." ... „Ein geschädigter Bürger, der eine Rechtssache bekommt, möge vor meine Statue (namens) 'König der Gerechtigkeiten' treten, meine beschriftete Stele möge er lesen, meine Stele möge die Rechtssache ihm klären, seinen Richterspruch möge er ersehen, sein Herz möge er aufatmen lassen (und sagen): 'Hammurapi, der Herr, der wie ein leiblicher Vater für die Leute da ist, hat auf das Wort seines Herrn Marduk hin sich bemüht, den Wunsch Marduks oben und unten erreicht, das Herz seines Herrn Marduk erfreut und Wohlergehen für die Leute auf ewig bestimmt und dem Lande zu seinem Recht verholfen' – dies möge er sagen und vor meinem Herrn Marduk und meiner Herrin Zarpanitu von ganzem Herzen mich segnen" (Übersetzung von R. Borger in *TUAT* 1/1, 76).

85 Prolog, Z. 162–170: „Den Waisen überantwortete ich keineswegs dem Reichen, die Witwe überantwortete ich keineswegs dem Mächtigen, den ‚Mann von 1 Scheqel' überantwortete ich keineswegs dem ‚Manne von 1 Rinde'" (Übersetzung von W. H. P. Römer in *TUAT* 1/1, 19).

86 W. G. Lambert, *Babylonian Wisdom Literature* (Oxford: Clarendon Press, 1960; repr. Winona Lake, Ind.: Eisenbrauns, 1996), esp. 112–15. Der Text beginnt mit den Worten (Z. 1–3): *šarru ana dīni lā iqūl nišīšu inneššâ mātšu innammi / ana dīn mātīšu lā iqūl Ēa šar šīmāti šīmtašu ušannima aḫīta irteneddīšu* „Wenn der König nicht Recht ausübt, wird sein Volk in Verwirrung geraten und sein Land verwüstet. / Wenn er nicht Recht seines Landes ausübt, wird Ea, der Herr des Schicksals, sein Schicksal ändern und das Unglück ihn stets verfolgen lassen."

literarischen Prophezeiungen der hellenistischen Zeit[87] – deutlich wird.[88] Die neuassyrischen Könige bildeten in dieser Hinsicht sicherlich keine Ausnahme. Da zudem die „kultischen“ und gesellschaftlichen Pflichten des Königs nicht voneinander zu trennen sind und die Propheten am besten geeignet waren, den König durch Gotteswort an seine Pflichten zu erinnern, gibt es keinen Grund, warum das kritische Potential der altorientalischen Prophetie sich nicht auch in Gesellschaftskritik niederschlagen sollte. Den beiden Briefen des Nur-Sîn ist es zu danken, dass dieses Argument nicht ganz *e silentio* gezogen werden muss. Dass die assyrischen Quellen nichts davon berichten, wird verständlich, wenn man den Abfassungs- und Archivierungszweck der schriftlichen Zeugnisse bedenkt. Die assyrischen Prophetensprüche wurden im Archiv abgelegt, vor allem als Beweis der Legitimität des Königtums von Asarhaddon bzw. Assurbanipal sowie ihrer Sonderstellung als erwählte Kronprinzen und Könige, die in einem besonderen Verhältnis zu Ištar (und zu ihren Propheten) standen.[89] Diesem Zweck aber dienten die kritischen Äußerungen nicht.

IV. Der König und seine Gegner

Die Unheilsprophetie ist kein unbekanntes Phänomen im Alten Orient. Abgesehen von der prophetischen Vision einer kosmischen Katastrophe in dem Text aus Deir ʻAlla, der teilweise der biblischen Unheilsprophetie sehr nahe kommt,[90] richtet sie sich aber in der Regel gegen Fremde, d.h. im Fall von Mari gegen Ešnunna,[91] Elam,[92] Ekallatum[93] oder Babylon[94] (bzw. deren Könige) sowie gegen

---

87 D.h. die „literary predictive texts,“ die auch akkadische Prophetien oder Apokalypsen genannt werden; s. dazu deJong Ellis, „Observations on Mesopotamian Oracles.“

88 S. Weinfeld, *Social Justice*, 45–74.

89 S. Parpola, *Assyrian Prophecies*, xxxvi–xliv; Nissinen, „Die Relevanz der neuassyrischen Prophetie,“ 230–32.

90 Vgl. etwa M. Weippert and H. Weippert, Der „Bileam“-Text von *Tell Der ʿAllā* und das Alte Testament, in M. Weippert, *Jahwe und die anderen Götter: Studien zur Religionsgeschichte des antiken Israel in ihrem syrisch-palästinischen Kontext*, Tübingen: Mohr Siebeck, 1997, 163–188, (Übersetzung nach: The Balaam Text from *Deir ʿAllā* and the Study of the Old Testament, in: J. Hoftijzer / G. van der Kooij [Hg.], *The Balaam Text from Deir'Alla Re-evaluated: Proceedings of the International Symposium held at Leiden, 21–24 August 1989*, Leiden: Brill, 1991, 151–184).

91 ARM 26 196; 197; 199.

92 ARM 26 208; vgl. den Gottesbrief ARM 26 192 und den Traum ARM 26 228.

93 ARM 26 207; 371; vgl. ARM 26 196 r. 9.

94 ARM 26 209; 210; 212; 371.

die jaminitischen Stämme,[95] und im Fall von Assyrien gegen Elam,[96] Ellipi[97] und die Kimmerier.[98]

Unbedingte Unheilsverkündigung gegen den eigenen Herrscher ist in den außerbiblischen Quellen sehr selten, fehlt aber nicht völlig. Zwei assyrische Quellen zeigen eindeutig, dass man mit Prophetie gegen den König nicht nur im Prinzip rechnen musste, sondern dass sie auch explizit geäußert wurde. Diese Texte habe ich schon anderweitig behandelt,[99] weshalb hier auf sie nur kurz hingewiesen werden soll. Unter den Paragraphen des großen Thronnachfolgevertrags von Asarhaddon, die dazu verpflichten, dem König jeden Ausdruck der Untreue anzuzeigen, befindet sich einer, in dem sich diese Meldepflicht auf ein „unanständiges, ungutes oder unschönes Wort" in Bezug auf den Kronprinzen Assurbanipal aus dem Munde von *raggimu, maḫḫû oder šā 'ilu amat ili* – d. h. von den Spezialisten der nicht-induktiven Divination – bezieht (SAA 2 6 § 10, Z. 108–122). Der Vertrag geht also allen Ernstes davon aus, dass jemand von der göttlichen Autorität des Prophetenwortes im Dienst der politischen Gegner des Königs Gebrauch machen kann, was nicht nur eine relativ hohe politische Wertschätzung der Prophetie voraussetzt, sondern auch darauf hindeutet, dass nicht alle Prophetie unter der direkten Kontrolle des Königs stand. Anschaulich wird dies in den Briefen von Nabû-rehtu-uṣur an Asarhaddon, in denen der Briefverfasser der in dem Vertrag vorausgesetzten Pflicht nachkommt, indem er eine Dienerin des Bel-aḫu-uṣur anzeigt. Diese Frau hatte angeblich am Stadtrand von Harran[100] ein Orakel des Gottes Nusku gesprochen, dem zufolge die Dynastie Sanheribs vernichtet werden und das Königtum an einen gewissen Sasî übergehen sollte (SAA 16 59 r. 4–5). In diesem Fall wurde Prophetie zugunsten einer allerdings rechtzeitig unterdrückten Verschwörung benutzt, was viel über die politische Verwendbarkeit der Prophetie aussagt.

---

95 ARM 26 199; 200; 233.

96 SAA 9 7:14; SAA 9 8.

97 SAA 9 3.2 ii 2.

98 SAA 9 3.2 ii 1; SAA 9 7:14.

99 M. Nissinen, „Falsche Prophetie in neuassyrischer und deuteronomistischer Darstellung," in *Das Deuteronomium und seine Querbeziehungen* (ed. T. Veijola; Schriften der Finnischen Exegetischen Gesellschaft 62; Helsinki: Finnische Exegetische Gesellschaft and Göttingen: Vandenhoeck & Ruprecht, 1996) 172–95, (S. 419–40 des vorliegenden Bandes; vgl. engl. id., „Prophecy against the King in Neo-Assyrian Sources," in *„Lasset uns Brücken bauen ...": Collected Communications to the 15th Congress of the IOSOT* [ed. K.-D. Schunk and M. Augustin; Frankfurt a.M.: Peter Lang, 1998] 157–70); id., *References to Prophecy*, 108–62.

100 Das heißt wahrscheinlich in dem „am Stadtrand von Harran" aufgerichteten Zederntempel, in dem Asarhaddon auf seinem Weg nach Ägypten gekrönt wurde; vgl. SAA 10 174:10–16 (Übersetzung auch bei Hecker, „Zukunftsdeutungen in akkadischen Texten," 79–80).

Aus Mari ist uns kein Prophetenspruch gegen den eigenen König bekannt, wohl aber Prophetie, die zu Zimri-Lims Außenpolitik kritisch Stellung nimmt, wie schon am Beispiel einiger oben behandelter Texte deutlich geworden ist. Darüber hinaus soll noch in aller Kürze auf einige weitere, bereits gut erforschte Briefe hingewiesen werden, in denen Äußerungen eines prophetischen Missfallens an den politischen Vorhaben Zimri-Lims erhalten geblieben sind.

In dem Maribrief, in dem die Forschung zum ersten Mal Prophetie erkannt hat (ARM 26 233),[101] erstattet der Statthalter Itur-Ašdu Bericht über einen Traum eines gewissen Malik-Dagan.[102] Diesem Mann sei auf seinem Wege von Saggaratum nach Mari in einem Traum eine Offenbarung von Dagan zuteil geworden, in welcher der Gott fragt, ob die Jaminiten[103] mit der mit ihnen zusammengestoßenen Truppe Zimri-Lims zu einem friedlichen Übereinkommen gelangt sind. Auf die verneinende Antwort Malik-Dagans hin wundert sich Dagan, warum keine Boten von Zimri-Lim vor ihn getreten sind, um ihm einen vollständigen Lagebericht *(ṭēmum gamrum)*[104] vorzulegen; andernfalls hätte er ihm die Jaminiten schon längst übergeben. Dagan sendet den Mann zu Zimri-Lim, damit dieser seine Boten mit dem vollständigen Bericht zu ihm schicke; dann werde der Gott die Jaminiten „in einem Fischerkorb zappeln lassen" (Z. 16–39). Auch dieses Gotteswort spielt mit dem Schema „einst – jetzt – danach" (vgl. oben FM 7 38).[105] Die Fragen Dagans sind wohl rhetorisch zu verstehen: Der Gott weiß, dass die Jaminiten mit der Truppe Zimri-Lims zu keinem friedlichen Übereinkommen gelangt sind, will aber Zimri-Lim seine Pflichtvergessenheit rückblickend vorhalten.[106] Jetzt wird der König aufgefordert, seinen Bericht vorzulegen, ohne den das am Ende der Got-

101 Durand, *Archives épistolaires de Mari*, 473–76; Übersetzung in id., *Les documents épistolaires du palais de Mari*, 78–83; Dietrich, „Prophetenbriefe aus Mari," 91–92. Erstveröffentlichung: G. Dossin, „Une révélation du dieu Dagan à Terqa," *RA* 42 (1948) 125–34.

102 Es geht hier ausdrücklich um einen Traumbericht, der nicht ohne Weiteres als Prophetie bezeichnet werden kann, weil Malik-Dagan keinen prophetischen Titel trägt; immerhin bekommt er den prophetischen Auftrag, Zimri-Lim das Wort des Dagan zu überbringen; vgl. Durand, „La religión en Siria," 317.

103 Die Jaminiten („Söhne der rechten Seite") wohnten südwestlich von Mari, während die Sim'aliten („Söhne der linken Seite,") zu denen auch Zimri-Lim gehörte, von der anderen Seite des Euphrat stammten. S. dazu D. Charpin and J.-M. Durand, „'Fils de Sim'al': Les origines tribales des Rois de Mari," *RA* 80 (1986) 141–83.

104 Der Ausdruck *ṭēmum gamrum* bezeichnet hier einen detaillierten Zwischenbericht über einen noch unvollendeten Krieg; s. B. Pongratz-Leisten, *Herrschaftswissen in Mesopotamien: Formen der Kommunikation zwischen Gott und König im 2. und 1. Jahrtausend v. Chr.* (SAAS 10; Helsinki: The Neo-Assyrian Text Corpus Project, 1999), esp. 204–7.

105 Vgl. A. Schmitt, *Prophetischer Gottesbescheid in Mari und Israel* (BWANT 6/14; Stuttgart: Kohlhammer, 1982) 22–23.

106 Vgl. J. M. Sasson, „Mari Dreams," *JAOS* 103 (1983) 283–93, esp. 290–91.

tesrede verkündete bedingte Heilswort keine Erfüllung finden wird. Man gewinnt den Eindruck, dass Dagan seine Worte in seinem Tempel und nicht auf dem Feld erteilt,[107] weshalb die Einholung des Orakels als Zeichen des königlichen Gehorsams unbedingt im Dagan-Tempel erfolgen muss. Hinter diesem theologischen Argument ist auch ein Bedürfnis des Tempels in Terqa oder aber auch der Provinzverwaltung zu spüren, über die gegenwärtige politische Lage informiert zu werden. Zimri-Lim musste in seinen ersten Regierungsjahren an mehreren Fronten kämpfen, weshalb seine Regierung keineswegs gesichert war. Seine Kriegsführung an sich wird nicht kritisiert.

Ein paar Jahre später schreibt der Majordomus Sammetar dem König, ein Prophet *(āpilum)* von Dagan namens Lupaḫum habe ihm Folgendes vorgetragen (ARM 26 199:30 – 39):[108]

> *as[s]urri šarrum balum ilim šalim ana awīl [Eš]nunna napištašu ilappat / kīma ša ina pānītim inūma m[ār]ē Jamīna urdūnimma ina Saggarātim ušbū u ana šarrim aqbû umma anākūma / ḫârî ša mārē Jamīna lā taqaṭṭal / ina ḫuburrê qinnātīšunu aṭarrassunūti u nārum ugammarakkum / [in]anna balum i[la]m iš[a]llu n[apiš]tašu lā ilappat*
>
> Vielleicht wird der König, ohne ein Orakel einzuholen, einen Eid mit dem Mann aus [Eš]nunna schwören![109] / Früher, als die Jaminiten zu mir kamen und sich in Saggaratum niederließen, sprach ich zu dem König: / „Schließ keinen Vertrag[110] mit den Jaminiten! / Ich werde sie zu ihren zerstreuten Nestern treiben[111], und der Fluss wird ihnen, dir zugute, ein Ende machen." / Nun sollte er keinen Eid ohne Gott(eswort) schwören.

Am nächsten Tag sei eine *qammatum* von Dagan von Terqa zu ihm gekommen und habe Folgendes gesagt (ARM 26 199:44 – 50):

> *šapal tibnim mû il[lakū] / ana salīmim ištanapp[arūnikkum] ilūšunu iṭarradū[nikkum] / u šāram šanêmma ina libbīšunu ikappudū / šarrum balum ilam išallu napištašu lā ilappat*
>
> Unter dem Stroh fl[ießt] Wasser! / Sie senden [dir] ständig Friedensangebote, sogar ihre Götter senden sie [dir], / in ihren Herzen haben sie aber andere Pläne. / Der König sollte keinen Eid ohne Gott(esbescheid) schwören!

Lupaḫum vergleicht die gegenwärtige Lage mit der Situation zur Zeit des Briefes von Itur-Ašdu. Damals waren die Jaminiten bis nach Saggaratum vorgedrungen,

---

107 Vgl. van der Toorn, *Mesopotamian Prophecy*, 80 – 82.

108 Durand, *Archives épistolaires des Mari*, 426 – 29; Übersetzung in id., *Les documents épistolaires du palais de Mari*.

109 Der Ausdruck *napištam lapātum* (wörtlich: „den Hals berühren") deutet wohl auf eine symbolische Handlung bei Vertragsabschluss hin.

110 Zum Ausdruck *ḫâram qaṭālum* (wörtlich: „Eselhengst töten") vgl. Anm. 109.

111 Zu dieser Übersetzung vgl. Durand, *Archives épistolaires des Mari*, 427 – 28.

Zimri-Lim aber hatte mit ihnen keinen Frieden geschlossen, sondern sie besiegt und ihre Stammesführer getötet.[112] Der Sieg Zimri-Lims sei damals durch Einholung eines Orakels gesichert geworden, und dasselbe Verfahren sollte der König nach Aussage des Propheten jetzt wiederholen, da der damalige Alliierte der Jaminiten, Ibalpiel II., der König von Ešnunna, jetzt einen Vertrag mit Zimri-Lim schließen wolle. Zimri-Lim hatte gegen ihn schon längst gekämpft, und in seinem sechsten Regierungsjahr (ZL 4' = 1770/69) fing er an, nach Friedensmöglichkeiten zu suchen.[113] Er stieß aber auf Widerstand bei einigen Propheten oder zumindest bei den Leuten, die in ihren Briefen entsprechende Prophetensprüche zitierten. Unter ihnen waren sehr einflussreiche Persönlichkeiten, und zwar nicht nur der „Ministerpräsident" Sammetar, sondern auch Inib-šina, die Schwester und politische Beraterin des Königs.

Auch sie zitiert den Spruch der *qammatum*, in abweichendem Wortlaut, aber sachlicher Übereinstimmung mit dem Brief Sammetars (ARM 26 197:11–24):[114]

> *[u]mma šīma /salīmātum ša awīl Ešn[unna] dāṣtumma /šapal tibnim mû illakū / u ana šētim ša ukaṣṣaru akammissu / ālšu uḫallaq u makkuršu a ištu aqdami šulputam ušalp[a]t / annītam iqbêm / inanna pagarka uṣur / balum têrtim ana libbi ālim lā terru[b]*
>
> Dies hat sie gesagt: „Die Friedenserklärungen des Mannes von Ešn[unna] sind falsch. / Unter dem Stroh fließt Wasser! / Ich werde ihn in einem Netz, das ich knüpfen werde, einfangen. / Seine Stadt will ich zerstören, und seinen Besitz, der seit den alten Zeiten nicht ruiniert war, werde ich ruinieren." / Dies hat sie zu mir gesprochen. / Nun sieh dich vor! / Ohne ein Orakel tritt nicht in die Stadt ein!

Das Sprichwort „Unter dem Stroh fließt Wasser" wird auch in einem dritten Brief wiedergegeben, den Kanisan aufgrund dessen schrieb, was er von seinem Vater gehört hatte. In diesem Fall stammt der Spruch angeblich von einem männlichen Propheten *(muḫḫûm)* (ARM 26 202):[115]

---

112 Dies geschah in seinem dritten Regierungsjahr 1773/72 (ZL 1'); das nächste Jahr (ZL 2') wurde nach diesem Ereignis benannt; zur Chronologie von Mari vgl. Charpin and Durand, „La prise du pouvoir," 304–8; M. Anbar, *Les tribus amurrites de Mari* (OBO 108; OBO 162; Fribourg and Göttingen: Academic Press Fribourg and Vandenhoeck & Ruprecht, 1991), esp. 30–37.

113 Zu den historischen Begebenheiten s. D. Charpin, „Un traité entre Zimri-Lim de Mari et Ibâl-pî-El II d'Ešnunna," in *Marchands, Diplomates et Empereurs*, FS P. Garelli, (ed. id. and F. Joannès; Paris: Éditions Recherche sur les Civilisations, 1991) 139–66; s. auch id., „Le contexte historique et géographique des prophéties dans les textes retrouvés à Mari," *BCSMS* 23 (1992) 21–31, esp. 22–23; Anbar, *Les tribus amurrites de Mari*, 62–63.

114 Durand, *Archives épistolaires des Mari*, 424; Übersetzung in id., *Les documents épistolaires du palais de Mari*, 403–40; Dietrich, „Prophetenbriefe aus Mari," 88.

115 Durand, *Archives épistolaires des Mari*, 431.

abī Kib[r]ī-D[agan] ana Māri [išpuram umma] šūma / awātim [ša ina bīt Dagan] in[n]epšā [ešme k]īam i[dbubūnim u]mmāmi / ša[pal tibnim] mû ill[akū] / illikma ilum ša bē[l]ij[a] awīlê ajjābīšu ana qātīšu umalli / inann[a] muḫḫû[m k]īma pānānu[mm]a irṭub ši[t]assam / annītam Kib[rī-Dag]an išpur[am] / bēlī ana šu[lmīšu têr]ētim šūpušim [....]

Mein Vater Kibri-D[agan hat mir] in Mari [folgendermaßen geschrieben]: / „[Ich habe gehört] welche Worte [in dem Tempel von Dagan] geäußert worden sind; so [haben sie zu mir] ges[prochen]: / ‚Un[ter dem Stroh] fli[eßt] Wasser! / Der Gott mei[nes] Herrn ist gekommen, er hat seine Feinde ihm in die Hände übergeben.‘ / Jetzt, wie auch früher, brach der Prophet in ständige Proklamation aus.“ /
So hat Kib[ri-Dag]an geschrieben. / Mein Herr möge zu [seinen eigenen] Gun[sten Ora]kel einholen [...]

Ešnunna wird in diesem Brief nicht genannt, doch handelt es sich in allen drei Fällen wahrscheinlich um die gleiche Situation, wenn nicht um ein und denselben prophetischen Auftritt,[116] von dem Kanisan auf Umwegen gehört hatte und vielleicht nicht mehr wusste, von wem das Orakel eigentlich gesprochen worden war. Das Sprichwort ist in allen drei Briefen wörtlich zitiert, wird aber jeweils mit verschiedenen Worten ausgelegt, was wohl darauf hindeutet, dass wir es zunächst mit den Ansichten der Briefverfasser zu tun haben, wobei die Prophetie dazu dient, den König davon zu überzeugen, dass mit Ešnunna kein Bund zu schließen ist. Die Friedensunterhandlungen Zimri-Lims werden unter Berufung auf Prophetie indirekt kritisiert, was darauf hindeutet, dass die Propheten (Lupaḫum und die *qammatum*) tatsächlich dagegen waren. Besonders augenfällig ist die Art und Weise, wie die Stellungnahme Lupaḫums in dem Brief Sammetars geschildert wird: Der Prophet scheint nicht Gottesworte, sondern seine eigene Meinung zu äußern, was im Kontext der altorientalischen Prophetie ganz eigenartig ist.[117] Die prophetischen Stellungnahmen sind ohne Zweifel deshalb zitiert, weil die Briefverfasser der gleichen Meinung sind; alle drei betonen die Bedeutung der Orakeleinholung, womit wohl nicht nur Prophetie, sondern auch andere Divinationsarten gemeint sind.

Die politischen Schlussfolgerungen werden schließlich Zimri-Lim anheim gestellt, und wir wissen, dass er den prophetisch untermauerten Rat seines inneren Kreises nicht befolgte, sondern tatsächlich einen Vertrag mit Ešnunna schloss. Der Text des Vertrags ist erhalten geblieben und macht zusammen mit der Korrespondenz des Unterhändlers Isḫi-Dagan deutlich, dass Zimri-Lim in

116 S. Parker, „Official Attitudes toward Prophecy," 57–60; J. M. Sasson, „Water beneath Straw: Adventures of a Prophetic Phrase in the Mari Archives," in *Solving Riddles and Untying Knots*, FS J. C. Greenfield (ed. Z. Zevit, S. Gitin, and M. Sokoloff; Winona Lake, Ind.: Eisenbrauns, 1995) 599–608.

117 Vgl. ibid., 603.

diesem Vertrag dem Ibalpiel unterlegen war: Er nennt ihn seinen „Vater".[118] Die Korrespondenz um die Ešnunnafrage zeigt, dass der König die Kritik an seiner Politik, selbst wenn sie mit prophetischer Autorität ausgesprochen war, nicht immer beachtete, manchmal – zumindest vorläufig – zu seinem eigenen Vorteil: In wenigen Jahren (ZL 9' = 1765/64) gelang es Zimri-Lim, mehrere Stadtfürsten zu Vasallen zu machen und die Bedeutung von Ešnunna erheblich zu vermindern.[119]

V. Die Propheten als Vertreter des Herrschaftswissens

Die oben behandelten Dokumente aus Mari und Assyrien gelten als ein unwiderlegbarer Beweis dafür, dass die Propheten in diesen Gesellschaften in der Lage waren, die Unternehmungen des Königs kritisch zu beurteilen und ihm Vorwürfe wegen der Unvollkommenheit in der Erfüllung seiner Pflichten zu machen. Die altorientalische prophetische Kritik, sei sie nun milder oder schärfer ausgedrückt, ist theologisch in der Forderung begründet, dass der König dem Idealbild des frommen und gerechten Herrschers entsprechend handelt. Die Kritik ist immer gegen einen einzelnen König gerichtet und betrifft in der Regel seine Entscheidungen in einzelnen Situationen, nicht seine Person oder seine Legitimität.[120] Das kritische Potential der Prophetie führt in den uns bekannten Quellen nicht zu einer umfassenden Unheilsprophetie gegen das Königtum als Institution oder gegen die eigene Gesellschaft in ihrer Gesamtheit. Von SAA 16 59 abgesehen, richtet sich unbedingte Unheilsprophetie lediglich gegen Nachbarkönige und Fremdvölker. Voraussetzung für die prophetische Kritik war immerhin eine gewisse Distanz der Propheten zum König.[121] Diese Distanz war deshalb möglich, weil man selbstverständlich davon ausging, dass diese Menschen in ihrer prophetischen Rolle Gotteswort zu übermitteln vermochten. Vor dem Hintergrund des altorientalischen Orakelwesens erscheinen die Propheten als Vertreter derjenigen Institution, die Beate Pongratz-Leisten unter dem Begriff „Herrschaftswissen" behandelt.[122] Das

---

118 Zu den Quellen s. Charpin, „Un traité," passim.

119 S. Anbar, *Les tribus amurrites de Mari*, 65–68.

120 „Autrement dit: les prophéties étaient toujours favorables au roi, mais pas nécessairement à sa politique du moment" (D. Charpin, „Prophètes et rois dans le Proche-Orient amorrite," in *Prophètes et rois: Bible et Proche-Orient* [ed. A. Lemaire; Paris: Cerf, 2001] 21–53, esp. 49).

121 S. dazu E. Cancik-Kirschbaum, „Prophetismus und Divination: Ein Blick auf die keilschriftlichen Quellen," in *Propheten in Mari, Assyrien und Israel* (ed. M. Köckert und M. Nissinen; FRLANT 201; Göttingen: Vandenhoeck & Ruprecht, 2003) 33–53.

122 Pongratz-Leisten, *Herrschaftswissen in Mesopotamien*, 286–88.

Herrschaftswissen befähigt den König zum Machterwerb und Machterhalt und funktioniert nicht nur organisatorisch, sondern auch als Wissen zur Identitäts- und Herrschaftssicherung, wobei dem Spezialwissen der divinatorischen Techniken eine besondere Rolle zukommt. Über dieses Spezialwissen verfügt das gesamte Orakelwesen, und zwar nicht nur die induktive Divination wie Astrologie und Eingeweideschau, sondern auch Träume und Prophetie, die Pongratz-Leisten als Formen des Herrschaftswissens eingehend erörtert.[123]

Als Vertreter des Herrschaftswissens waren die Propheten ein fester Bestandteil der Gesellschaft, die aus den konstitutiven Elementen Palast, Tempel und Haushalt bestand.[124] Das wohlwollende Verhältnis *(šulmu)* zwischen König und Göttern war dabei die Voraussetzung für die Stabilität der sozialen wie auch der kosmischen Struktur, und die Vertreter des Herrschaftswissens waren dafür verantwortlich, diese Stabilität durch die Kommunikation zwischen Gott und König aufrecht zu erhalten. Dies bedeutet natürlich, dass die Propheten wie auch die anderen Götterbefrager ohne Zweifel im Dienst des Herrschaftssystems standen, innerhalb dessen ihnen eine Rolle als Vertreter des Herrschaftswissens zukam. Eben in dieser Rolle waren sie aber auch geradezu dazu verpflichtet, den König zu mahnen, zu warnen und nötigenfalls auch zu kritisieren. Herrschaftswissen ermöglichte also Herrschaftskritik, die wohl nicht nur aus ideologischen, sondern auch aus praktischen Gründen angeregt wurde. Wie oft und in welcher Weise diese Kritik in konkreten Situationen ausgesprochen werden konnte, ist eine andere Frage, die aufgrund der uns zur Verfügung stehenden Quellen nur sehr lückenhaft beantwortet werden kann.

Da es demnach in der Natur der Sache liegt, dass zur altorientalischen Prophetie im Allgemeinen auch ein kritisches Potential gehörte, stellt sich die Frage, die uns zurück zur Hebräischen Bibel führt und auf die hier zum Schluss nur noch hingewiesen werden kann: Warum gewinnt dieses Potential in den Prophetenbüchern der hebräischen Bibel eine so viel herausragendere und umfassendere Gestalt?

Es mag sein, dass die neuere Forschung den sozialkritischen Aspekt der biblischen Prophetie aus ihrem eigenen Gegenwartsinteresse heraus mit solchem Nachdruck hervorgehoben hat, dass dadurch manche anderen Aspekte in den Schatten gestellt worden sind. Man kann aber nicht leugnen, dass die prophetische Kritik in der Bibel im Vergleich mit außerbiblischen Quellen nicht nur wesentlich umfangreicher ist, sondern auch inhaltlich ein schärferes und radikaleres Profil hat, besonders wenn sie als Bestandteil der Unheilsprophetie erscheint. In

123 Ibid., 47–127.

124 Zur mesopotamischen Gesellschaftsstruktur s. Postgate, *Early Mesopotamia*, 73–154.

dieser Hinsicht hat das am Anfang dieses Artikels aufgeführte Zitat nach wie vor manches für sich. Immerhin ist aus den mesopotamischen Quellen zu lernen, dass Kultkritik und Sozialkritik sehr viel enger beieinander liegen, als man gemeinhin annimmt. Ferner sollten die vermeintlichen „Konflikte zwischen Propheten und König bzw. Staat" hinterfragt werden, und zwar mit Rücksicht auf das Verhältnis zwischen Herrschaftswissen und Herrschaftskritik und dessen Einfluss auf die Entwicklung des Prophetenbildes im Werdegang der biblischen Prophetenbücher.

Das kritische Profil der biblischen Prophetie kann grundsätzlich auf die historische Entwicklung der Prophetie in Israel und Juda wie auch auf die Literargeschichte der Prophetenbücher zurückgehen. Man kann im Prinzip davon ausgehen, dass das herrschaftskritische Element von Hause aus zur politisch-religiösen Kultur Israels und Judas gehört und auch prophetischen Ausdruck gefunden hat; jedoch erschwert die Quellenlage Schlussfolgerungen darüber, wie diese Kritik in vorexilischer Zeit zur Sprache kam und inwieweit sie auf diejenigen zurückgeht, die in der Folgezeit das biblische Prophetenideal geprägt haben. Aufgrund der einzigen uns zur Verfügung stehenden Quelle, der hebräischen Bibel, ist man zu der Auffassung gekommen, die vornehmsten biblischen Vertreter der prophetischen Gesellschafts- und Herrschaftskritik – Amos, Hosea, Micha und Jesaja – hätten ihren unerhört scharfen Protest als Herolde einer gegenüber dem älteren Prophetentum neuen Art von „intellectual leadership" erhoben und zugleich den Samen für die zukünftige, weitgehend deuteronomistische Konstruktion der Schriftpropheten gelegt.[125] Da jedoch die biblische Prophetie ein unter exilisch-nachexilischen Umständen entstandenes literarisches Phänomen ist und die ältere altisraelitische Prophetie nur selektiv und fragmentarisch dokumentiert wurde, bleibt die Rolle dieser Persönlichkeiten, sofern sie historische Vorbilder haben, in ihrem historischen Kontext im Großen und Ganzen unklar. Deswegen darf die prophetische Kritik der hebräischen Bibel nicht nur vor dem

---

125 So J. Blenkinsopp, *Sage, Priest, Prophet: Religious and Intellectual Leadership in Ancient Israel* (Library of Ancient Israel; Louisville, Ky.: Westminster/John Knox Press, 1995), esp. 141–54; vgl. T. L. Fenton, „Israelite Prophecy: Characteristics of the First Protest Movement," in *The Elusive Prophet: The Prophet as a Historical Person, Literary Character and Anonymous Artist* (ed. J. C. de Moor; OTS 45; Leiden: Brill, 2001) 129–41. Das Problem ist mit der Frage verbunden, ob die vorexilischen Schriftpropheten überhaupt ursprünglich zu den *nĕbîʾîm* zählten oder ob diese Bezeichnung erst nachträglich auf sie übertragen wurde. S. dazu R. P. Carroll, „Poets not Prophets: A Response to 'Prophets through the Looking Glass,'" *JSOT* 27 (1983) 25–31; B. Vawter, „Were the Prophets *nābîʾs*?," *Bib* 66 (1985) 206–20; T. Fenton, „Deuteronomistic Advocacy of the *nābîʾ*: 1 Samuel ix 9 and Questions of Israelite Prophecy," *VT* 47 (1997) 23–42; F. J. Gonçalves, „Les 'prophètes écrivains' étaient-ils des נביאים?," in *The World of the Aramaeans*, vol. 1, FS P.-E. Dion (ed. P. M. M. Daviau, J.W. Wevers, and M. Weigl; JSOTS 324; Sheffield: Sheffield Academic Press, 2001) 144–85.

Hintergrund der israelitisch-judäischen Gesellschaft der vorexilischen Zeit, sondern muss auch und besonders im Hinblick auf die exilischen und nachexilischen Verhältnisse ausgelegt werden, die wohl nicht weniger Anlass zu Kritik gegeben haben.[126] Dabei büßen die altorientalischen prophetischen Zeugnisse nicht an Bedeutung ein, denn die den altorientalischen Quellen eigene Wechselwirkung von Herrschaftswissen und Herrschaftskritik muss auch in Bezug auf die biblischen Quellen erörtert werden, wenngleich die Herrschaftsstrukturen sich inzwischen mehrfach und radikal verändert haben. Denn nach wie vor ist „der Mut, die Dinge beim Namen zu nennen, in einer notwendigerweise durch Herrschaft und also auch Gewalt bestimmten Welt riskant und daher zu allen Zeiten einfacher prinzipiell als konkret anzutreffen",[127] und trotzdem hat es Männer und Frauen[128] gegeben, die es gewagt haben.

---

126 So am Beispiel des Amosbuches Loretz, „Die Entstehung des Amos-Buches," 208; vgl. C. Levin, „Das Amosbuch der Anawim," *ZTK* 94 (1997) 407–36; zum Problem im Allgemeinen s. R. P. Carroll, „Prophecy and Society," in *The World of Ancient Israel: Sociological, Anthropological and Political Perspectives* (ed. R. E. Clements; Cambridge: Cambridge University Press, 1989) 203–25.

127 Kaiser, „Kult und Kultkritik im Alten Testament," 414.

128 Man denke nur an den Konflikt der Prophetin Noadja mit Nehemia (Neh 6,14); vgl. dazu R. P. Carroll, „Coopting the Prophets: Nehemiah and Noadiah," in *Priests, Prophets and Scribes*, FS J. Blenkinsopp (ed. E. Ulrich, J. W. Wright, R. P. Carroll, and P. R. Davies; JSOTS 149, Sheffield: Sheffield Academic Press, 1992) 87–99.

Fear Not: A Study on an Ancient Near Eastern Phrase

A Brief History of Research

The identification of fixed formulaic expressions and the search for their sociocultural origin, or *Sitz im Leben*, is characteristic of traditional form criticism. In the study of the "basic forms of prophetic literature," fixed formulas have been taken as structural elements, the origin of which is not necessarily prophetic but can be traced back to nonprophetic contexts. The prime example of such a formula is "Thus says the Lord" *(kô ʾāmar YHWH),* the so-called *Botenformel.* In the biblical prophetic literature, this formula typically introduces divine speech, but its original context has been found in a profane communication situation, the transmission of a message from one person to another by an intermediary who forwards the message to the addressee, introducing it with the words "Thus says N." This form-critical observation was of permanent value for the study of prophecy, since it sustained the understanding of the role of the prophet as an intermediary and prophecy as communication.[1]

A more complicated case is presented by another well-known formula, "fear not" (*ʾal-tîrāʾ*, etc.). In the Hebrew Bible this phrase is often, though by no means exclusively, used in prophetic contexts, with a notable concentration in Second Isaiah.[2] Hugo Gressmann, a leading figure of the early days of form criticism, identified it as an element of revelatory oracular speech *(Offenbarungsrede)* common to ancient Near Eastern sources. In his literary analysis of Second Isaiah, published in 1914, he quoted several examples of oracles, known today as Assyrian prophecies,[3] to show the stereotyped character and the cheering and comforting function of the respective Akkadian phrase *lā tapallaḫ,* as well as its proximity to the divine self-identification "I am ... DN."[4] All this Gressmann saw was

1 See L. Köhler, *Deuterojesaja stilkritisch untersucht* (BZAW 37; Giessen: Töpelmann, 1923), 102–5; C. Westermann, *Grundformen prophetischer Rede* (BEvT 31; Munich: Kaiser, 1960; [5]1978), 70–82; ET: *Basic Forms of Prophetic Speech* (trans. H. C. White; repr. Louisville: Westminster/John Knox, 1991), 98–128.

2 Isa 40:9; 41:10, 13, 14; 43:1, 5; 44:2; 51:7; 54:4; cf. Isa 7:4; 8:12; 10:24; 35:4; 37:6; Jer 1:8; 10:5; 30:10; 42:11; 46:27, 28; Ezek 2:6; 3:9; Joel 2:21, 22; Zeph 3:16; Hag 2:5; Zech 8:13, 15; Dan 10:12, 19.

3 S. Parpola, *Assyrian Prophecies* (SAA 9; Helsinki: Helsinki University Press, 1997).

4 H. Gressmann, "Die literarische Analyse Deuterojesajas," *ZAW* 34 (1914) 254–97, esp. 287–90. The texts quoted are SAA 9 1.1; 1.4; 1.8.

DOI 10.1515/9783110466546-013

fully compatible with Second Isaiah, who, according to him, used the formula under "Babylonian" influence.[5]

Gressmann's idea of the Mesopotamian background of the "fear not" formula was soon refuted by Ludwig Köhler, who also related it with theophany but derived it from the numinous experience of the presence of the divine rather than from oracular practices.[6] Köhler's contribution met with little approval,[7] whereas the theory of Joachim Begrich, published fifteen years later in 1934, became all the more influential.[8] Begrich traced the Deutero-Isaianic "fear not" oracles back to a cultic context similar to that of the individual lament psalms *(Klagelieder des Einzelnen)*. He rested his argument on the observations of Hermann Gunkel,[9] according to whom the sudden change of mood from lament to consolation and encouragement, typical of these psalms, corresponds to the prayer of the individual and the subsequent divine answer spoken by the priest (cf. also Lam 3:57). Begrich considered this "priestly oracle of salvation" *(priesterliches Heilsorakel)* an established pattern, familiar to and consciously taken over by Second Isaiah, who adapted the prayers of the individual to his own purposes, addressing his people as a collective in singular form.

Begrich's theory of the priestly oracle was ingenious enough to become the most quoted explanation of the phrase "fear not" and the salvation oracles of Second Isaiah in decades to come, as demonstrated, for example, by studies devoted to the concept of the fear of God in the Hebrew Bible.[10] It did not remain

5 "Die Abhängigkeit des im Exil lebenden Deuterojesaja von babylonischen Vorbildern wird damit zur Gewissheit erhoben; denn wie will man dies in der israelitischen Literatur der Propheten bis dahin unerhörte Nebeneinander der Formeln 'Ich bin Jahwe' und 'Fürchte dich nicht' und ihre Verknüpfung mit dem Hymnenstil der ersten Person einleuchtender erklären als durch den Einfluss der babylonischen Orakelliteratur, in der gerade diese drei Erscheinungen von jeher zu beobachten sind?" (Gressmann, "Die literarische Analyse Deuterojesajas," 290).

6 L. Köhler, "Die Offenbarungsformel 'Fürchte dich nicht' im Alten Testament," *SThZ* 36 (1919) 33–39.

7 Cf., however, W. Pesch, "Zur Formgeschichte und Exegese von Lk 12,32," *Bib* 41 (1960) 25–40, esp. 26–31; *HAL* 413.

8 J. Begrich, "Das priesterliche Heilsorakel," *ZAW* 52 (1934) 81–92; repr. in *Gesammelte Studien zum Alten Testament* (ed. W. Zimmerli; TB 21; Munich: Kaiser, 1964) 217–31.

9 H. Gunkel, *Einleitung in die Psalmen: Die Gattungen der religiösen Lyrik Israels* (completed by J. Begrich; Göttingen: Vandenhoeck & Ruprecht, [4]1985), 246–47. Begrich does not mention F. Küchler, who made the same argument on similar grounds already in 1918 (F. Küchler, "Das priesterliche Orakel in Israel und Juda," in *Abhandlungen zur semitischen Religionsgeschickte und Sprachwissenschaft*, FS W. W. Grafen von Baudissin [ed. W. Frankenberg and F. Küchler; BZAW 33; Gießen: Töpelmann, 1918] 285–301).

10 S. Plath, *Furcht Gottes: Der Begriff* jr' *im Alten Testament* (AzTh 2/2; Stuttgart: Calwer, 1963), 119; J. Becker, *Gottesfurcht im Alten Testament* (AnBib 25; Rome: Pontifical Biblical Institute

unchallenged, though. More detailed form-critical investigations, performed by Walther Zimmerli, Claus Westermann, and others, substantially refined the analysis of the structural elements of the salvation oracle, whereby Begrich's idea of the priestly oracle was modified and enriched with new viewpoints and alternative patterns of the oracle of salvation.[11] Westermann, for example, did not question the priestly oracle as such, but he found it insufficient to explain the proclamation of Second Isaiah. He made a distinction between the oracle of salvation *(Heilszusage)* derived from cultic practices of priests, and the proclamation of salvation *(Heilsankündigung),* which he considered a purely prophetic function. The "fear not" oracles and their extrabiblical parallels he placed in the first category.[12]

Some scholars called into question Begrich's theory as a whole, for example, Edgar W. Conrad, who found the "priestly oracle of salvation" – both the *Gattung* and the *Sitz im Leben* – to be ill founded altogether and traced the "fear not" oracles of Second Isaiah back to two different genres, the war oracle and the patriarchal oracle.[13] In spite of the criticism, the priestly oracle held out quite well among other explanations of the "fear not" formula, as can be seen from relevant articles in theological dictionaries.[14]

Press, 1965), 52–53; L. Derousseaux, *La crainte de Dieu dans l'Ancien Testament: Royauté, Alliance, Sagesse dans les royaumes d'Israël et Juda. Recherches d'exégèse et d'histoire sur la racine yârê* (LD 63; Paris: Cerf, 1970), 97.

11 W. Zimmerli, "Ich bin Jahwe," in *Geschichte und Altes Testament*, FS A. Alt (BHT 16; Tübingen: Mohr, 1953) 179–209, esp. 193–203; repr. in id., *Gottes Offenbarung: Gesammelte Aufsätze* (TB 19; Munich: Kaiser, 1963) 11–40, esp. 24–34; C. Westermann, "Das Heilswort bei Deuterojesaja," *EvT* 24 (1964) 355–73 (summarized in id., *Forschung am Alten Testament* [TB 24; Munich: Kaiser, 1964], 117–24); cf. id., *Prophetische Heilsworte im Alten Testament* (FRLANT 145; Göttingen: Vandenhoeck & Ruprecht, 1987), 33–53; ET: *Prophetic Oracles of Salvation in the Old Testament* (trans. K. Crim; Louisville: Westminster/John Knox, 1991), 39–66; H.-E. von Waldow, "Anlass und Hintergrund der Verkündigung des Deuterojesaja" (diss.; Univ. of Bonn, 1953); H. Graf Reventlow, *Liturgie und prophetisches Ich bei Jeremia* (Gütersloh: Gütersloher Verlagshaus, 1963); A. Schoors, *I Am God Your Saviour: A Form-Critical Study of the Main Genres in Is. xl–lv* (VTSup 24; Leiden: Brill, 1973); R. F. Melugin, *The Formation of Isaiah 40–55* (BZAW 141; Berlin and New York: de Gruyter, 1976); J. M. Vincent, *Studien zur literarischen Eigenart und zur geistigen Heimat von Jesaja, Kapitel 40–55* (BBET 5; Frankfurt am Main: Lang, 1977).

12 Westermann, "Das Heilswort bei Deuterojesaja," passim; cf. idem, *Prophetische Heilsworte,* 35–36 (= *Prophetic Oracles,* 39–40).

13 E. W. Conrad, "Second Isaiah and the Priestly Oracle of Salvation," *ZAW* 93 (1981) 234–46; id., "The 'Fear Not' Oracles in Second Isaiah," *VT* 34 (1984) 129–52. For earlier criticism see, e.g., R. Kilian, "Ps 22 und das priesterliche Heilsorakel," *BZ* 12 (1968) 172–85; R. P. Merendino, "Literarkritisches, Gattungskritisches und Exegetisches zu Jes 41,8–16," *Bib* 53 (1972) 1–42.

14 H.-P. Stähli, "ירא *jr*ʾ fürchten," *THAT* 1 (1971) 765–78, esp. 772–73; G. Wanke, "φοβέω κτλ. B. φόβος und φοβέομαι im Alten Testament," *ThWNT* 9 (1973) 194–201, esp. 199; ET: *TDNT* 9:197–

The popularity of Begrich's theory is striking, considering that he himself wisely admitted that his evidence was indirect, presenting his theory modestly as a working hypothesis.[15] The hypothesis was well spoken and comprehensible enough to catch on with subsequent studies, but was it really comprehensive enough to make out a certain case for the priestly oracle, and did it even attempt an exhaustive explanation of the origin of the phrase "fear not"? The following points call for attention: (1) There is no single occurrence of the phrase in the individual lament psalms.[16] If the use of the salvation oracle in Second Isaiah is tied to these psalms,[17] the origin of "fear not" must be sought elsewhere. (2) Begrich's intention was primarily to demonstrate the existence of the priestly oracle, not the origin of the phrase "fear not." Apparently for this reason he confined himself to Second Isaiah, making no argument of the use of the phrase in other contexts. (3) The designation of the oracle as "priestly" rests solely on the implied assumption that it was spoken by a priest after the prayer of the individual. Here the argument is indirect indeed, since the relevant psalms – or Lam 3:57, or any other text where the phrase occurs – make no mention of any kind of a priest, whatever is concretely meant by this word. (4) The extrabiblical sources are completely ignored by Begrich, who refers to Gressmann's article only once to reproach him for the failure of identifying the alleged priestly context of Second Isaiah's use of the phrase.[18] Consequently, he fails to recognize the relevance of prophecy in defining the origins of the salvation oracle in Second Isaiah.

By the time Begrich wrote his article, the Assyrian oracles quoted by Gressmann had virtually fallen into oblivion. One can only speculate whether these

205, esp. 203; H. F. Fuhs, "יָרֵא *jāre'*," *ThWAT* 3 (1982) 869–93, esp. 884–85; ET: *TDOT* 6:290–315, esp. 305–6; cf. also W. Grimm and K. Dittert, *Deuterojesaja: Deutung – Wirkung – Gegenwart* (Calwer Bibelkommentare; Stuttgart: Calwer, 1990), 457–60.

15 "Da ein Beweis nach Lage der Dinge hier nur indirekt geführt werden kann, muss das Ergebnis, das sich dem Verfasser herausgestellt hat, hier notwendig kurz vorgenommen werden, freilich nur im Sinne einer Arbeitshypothese, die dem Leser das Ziel unserer Ausführungen deutlich machen soll und deren Recht allein von der Schlüssigkeit und Überzeugungskraft der Beweisführung abhängt" (Begrich, "Das priesterliche Heilsorakel," 81).

16 The only occurrence in the Psalter, Ps 49:17, hardly bears any relevance to the matter in hand: "Do not envy (*'al tîrā'*) a man who becomes rich."

17 "Dass Deuterojesaja gerade auf diese Gattung zukam, hat seinen entscheidenden Grund darin, dass er selbst aufs tiefste in seiner Frömmigkeit und in seinem Denken mit der Psalmenfrömmigkeit verbunden ist" (Begrich, "Das priesterliche Heilsorakel," 92).

18 "H. Gressmann hat (...) zwar die Formel richtig als zur Offenbarungsrede gehörig erkannt, jedoch den grösseren Zusammenhang nicht gesehen, aus dem sie Deuterojesaja entnommen hat" (Begrich, "Das priesterliche Heilsorakel," 83).

texts would have been taken more intensively into consideration had they been called prophecies instead of "oracles." In subsequent treatments they were quoted time and again for the sake of comparison, even by the critics of the priestly oracle theory, but this was done in discussion with Begrich and his followers, and the texts were not acknowledged as prophecies.[19] This is true even in the case of Philip B. Harner, whose contribution was important in rehabilitating Gressmann's argument of the oracular pattern common to the Mesopotamian texts and Second Isaiah, in expanding it with new relevant material, and in pointing out the royal focus of the Assyrian oracles, but who overlooked the prophetic nature of the extrabiblical evidence, taking it as an external confirmation of Begrich's theory.[20]

The first form-critical analysis that took full advantage of the extrabiblical material, including the Assyrian prophecies, was the dissertation of Meindert Dijkstra (1980), whereas the first comprehensive study of the Assyrian prophecies was published by Manfred Weippert in 1981.[21] Both Dijkstra and Weippert found the Assyrian prophecies most relevant parallels to the salvation oracles of Second Isaiah, but Weippert labeled these texts as "royal oracles" *(Königsorakel)* rather than priestly oracles, since they were addressed to the king and spoken by prophets rather than priests. Weippert questioned explicitly the viability of Begrich's theory of the priestly oracle as a mere commonplace in the traditio-historical analysis of Second Isaiah,[22] doubtless presenting the most forcefully argued alternative to it, especially from the point of view of prophecy in the ancient Near East. More recently, in a thorough comparison of the Neo-Assyrian prophecies and Second Isaiah, Weippert has reaffirmed that in Second Isaiah the prophetic royal oracle is employed, independently from the Neo-Assyrian prophecies but clinging to a common ancient Near Eastern tradition.[23]

---

19 E. g., Zimmerli, "Ich bin Jahwe," 194–95; Plath, *Furcht Gottes,* 121; Westermann, "Das Heilswort," 360–62; Merendino, "Literarkritisches," 29–31; Schoors, *I Am God,* 39–45.

20 P. B. Harner, "The Salvation Oracle in Second Isaiah," *JBL* 88 (1969) 418–34.

21 M. Dijkstra, *Gods voorstelling: Predikatieve expressie van zelfopenbaring in Oudoosterse teksten en Deutero-Jesaja* (Dissertationes Neerlandicae, Series Theologica 2; Kampen: Kok, 1980), esp. 136–70; M. Weippert, "Assyrische Prophetien der Zeit Asarhaddons und Assurbanipals," in *Assyrian Royal Inscriptions: New Horizons in Literary, Ideological, and Historical Analysis* (ed. F. M. Fales; Orientis Antiqui Collectio 17; Rome: Istituto per l'Oriente, 1981), 71–115; cf. id., "De herkomst van het heilsorakel voor Israël bij Deutero-Jesaja," *NedTT* 36 (1982) 1–11.

22 Weippert, "Assyrische Prophetien," 91–92, 108–11; cf. id., "De herkomst," 5.

23 M. Weippert, "'Ich bin Jahwe'—'Ich bin Ištar von Arbela.' Deuterojesaja im Lichte der neuassyrischen Prophetie," in *Prophetie und Psalmen.* FS Klaus Seybold (ed. Beat Huwyler, Hans-Peter Mathys, and Beat Weber; AOAT 280; Münster: Ugarit-Verlag, 2001), 31–59.

The form-critical study of the phrase "fear not" has been strongly connected with the study of Second Isaiah. However, there are plenty of biblical occurrences of "fear not" in other contexts, such as the patriarchal narratives (Gen 15:1; 21:17; 26:24; 46:3) and the Deuteronom(ist)ic literature (Deut 1:21; 7:18; Josh 8:1; 10:8; 11:6; etc.). Otto Kaiser, for instance, combined the salvation oracle with a fearsome theophany experience, not forgetting the Assyrian parallels.[24] Gerhard von Rad, in his classic study on the holy war in ancient Israel, listed "fear not" among the typical phraseology of holy war language, and several scholars after him accepted its belonging to this alleged institution.[25] Cognate expressions were found in a military context even in extrabiblical sources, such as the Mari letters and the Aramaic Zakkur inscription.[26] This not only suggested that

---

24 O. Kaiser, "Traditionsgeschichtliche Untersuchung von Genesis 15," *ZAW* 70 (1958) 107–26, esp. 111–13.

25 G. von Rad, *Der Heilige Krieg im alten Israel* (Zurich: Zwingli, 1951), 7–8; ET: *Holy War in Ancient Israel* (trans. M. J. Dawn; Grand Rapids: Eerdmans, 1991), 45, lists the following occurrences: Exod 14:13–14; Deut 20:3; Josh 8:1; 10:8, 25; 11:6; Judg 7:3; 1 Sam 23:16–17; 30:6; 2 Sam 10:12. J. Becker, *Gottesfurcht im Alten Testament* (AnBib 25; Rome: Pontifical Biblical Institute Press, 1965) 52, takes the war oracles as a secondary application of the priestly oracle of salvation, whereas L. Derousseaux, *La crainte de Dieu dans l'Ancien Testament: Royauté, Alliance, Sagesse dans les royaumes d'Israël et Juda. Recherches d'exégèse et d'histoire sur la racine yâré* (LD 63; Paris: Cerf, 1970) 97, on the other hand, sees the war oracle as the primary context of the formula; similarly Merendino, "Literarkritisches."

26 On Mari see J.-G. Heintz, "Oracles prophétiques et 'guerre sainte' selon les archives royales de Mari et l'Ancien Testament," in *Congress Volume: Rome 1968* (VTSup 17; Leiden: Brill, 1969) 112–28, esp. 121–25. The texts quoted by Heintz are ARM 13 114 (= ARM 26 210): 11–14: *Dagan išpuranni šupur ana bēlīk[a l]ā iḫâš u mā[tum]ma [lā] iḫâš,* "Dagan has sent me. Write to your lord that he should not be anxious, and [neither] should the la[nd] be anxious"; and ARM 10 80 (= ARM 26 197) 26–27: *ana ramānīšu ištanarrar ana ramānīka la taštanarra*[*r*]. The translation of the last text is uncertain. According to the suggestion of Durand, the verb *šarārum* means here "to shine brilliantly" (J.-M. Durand, *Archives épistolaires de Mari I/1* [ARM 26/1; Paris: Éditions Recherche sur les Civilisations, 1988], 424); hence the translation, "I have heard people saying: 'He is always distinguishing himself.' Do not try to distinguish yourself!" The alleged stereotyped character of the "fear not" formula in Mari letters was immediately refuted by P.-E. Dion, who found the evidence too narrow to sustain Heintz's argument (P.-E. Dion, "The 'Fear Not' Formula and Holy War," *CBQ* 32 [1970] 565–70), whereas Heintz's examples of the so-called Übergabeformel "I [the god] deliver the enemies into your [the king's] hand" (Heintz, "Oracles prophétiques," 125–29), were found to rest on more solid ground (Dion, "Fear Not," 569–70). Cf. below, n. 93. On Zakkur see J. F. Ross, "Prophecy in Hamath, Israel, and Mari," *HTR* 63 (1970) 1–28, esp. 8–9; cf. H.-J. Zobel, "Das Gebet um Abwendung der Not und seine Erhörung in den Klageliedern des Alten Testaments und in der Inschrift des Königs Zakir von Hamath," *VT* 21 (1971) 91–99, who found here another representative of Begrich's priestly oracle.

the holy war ideology was not restricted to ancient Israel[27] but also that the alleged priestly oracle was not the only *Sitz im Leben* of the formulaic use of the expression "fear not."

More recently, Karel van der Toorn has demonstrated the prophetic contribution to the ancient Near Eastern ideology of war with ample evidence of what he called the "oracle of victory," including the Assyrian "fear not" oracles.[28] The contribution of van der Toorn, like that of Weippert, is significant in illuminating the issue from both the ancient Near Eastern and the Hebrew prophetic point of view.

In today's discourse the currency given to traditional form-critical issues is substantially decreased, and the quest for a single, definable *Sitz im Leben* of fixed formulas seems to be obsolescent. In the case of "fear not," little has happened during the past two decades. In spite of the criticism, Begrich's theory is still quoted often, and little attention is paid to his complete ignoring of the extrabiblical sources and his failure to recognize the prophetic component of the "priestly" oracle. If the Assyrian oracles are referred to as parallels at all,[29] this is done as a matter of routine, usually even without recognizing them as prophecies. With regard to our increased knowledge of ancient Near Eastern sources and the state of publication improved by the new edition of the Assyrian prophecies by Simo Parpola (SAA 9) as well as other sources from the Assyrian archives, the fundamental observations made already by Gressmann and improved by, for example, Weippert and van der Toorn deserve renewed attention and confirmation.

---

27 This was argued especially by M. Weippert, who used ample evidence from Assyria to demonstrate the broader context of the idea of divinely promoted warfare; see "'Heiliger Krieg' in Israel und Assyrien: Kritische Anmerkungen zu Gerhard von Rads Konzept des 'Heiligen Krieges im alten Israel,'" *ZAW* 84 (1972) 460–93. Cf. also M. Weinfeld, "Divine Intervention in War in Ancient Israel and in the Ancient Near East," in *History, Historiography and Interpretation: Studies in Biblical and Cuneiform Literatures* (ed. id. and H. Tadmor; Jerusalem: Magnes, 1983) 121–47; R. J. van der Spek, "Assyriology and History: A Comparative Study of War and Empire in Assyria, Athens, and Rome," in *The Tablet and the Scroll: Near Eastern Studies in Honor of William W. Hallo* (ed. M. E. Cohen, D. C. Snell, and D. B. Weisberg; Bethesda, Md.: CDL Press, 1993) 262–70; L. L. Rowlett, *Joshua and the Rhetoric of Violence: A New Historicist Analysis* (JSOTSup 226; Sheffield: Sheffield Academic Press, 1996).

28 K. van der Toorn, "L'Oracle de victoire comme expression prophétique au Proche-Orient ancien," *RB* 94 (1987) 63–97.

29 They are completely ignored by K. Baltzer, who in his new voluminous commentary on Second Isaiah (*Deutero-Iesaja* [KAT 10/2; Gütersloh: Gütersloher Verlagshaus, 1999]; ET: *Deutero-Isaiah: A Commentary* [Hermeneia; Minneapolis: Fortress, 2001]) neither discusses the Assyrian prophecies nor pays any special attention to the "fear not" formula.

On the other hand, the distribution of "fear not" in the ancient Near Eastern sources is wide and has hitherto not been fully investigated. There are numerous attestations of "fear not" in Akkadian *(lā tapallaḫ),* many of which have remained unexplored so far, and at least one in Old Aramaic (*ʾl tzḥl*).[30] Therefore, to find new facets to an old problem and to broaden the scope of the discussion, a study dedicated to the occurrences of this expression in ancient Near Eastern (mainly Mesopotamian) documents suggests itself.

Fear Not, but Fear: Semantic Viewpoints

The semantic field of verbs for fear, like Hebrew *yrʾ* or Akkadian *palāḫu,* is twofold, covering both "fear" in the sense of fright, horror, or anxiety, and "respect," denoting reverence, respectful behavior, obedience, or, especially in theological contexts, veneration.[31] Correspondingly, the object of fear is either any kind of threat or menace to the subject's safety, or an authority, human or divine. In the latter case, the fear is usually motivated by the superior position and the powers vested in the authority in question, as in the case of an obstinate governor: *ipallaḫ issu pān šarri išamme,* "He will become afraid of the king and obey."[32] In theological contexts "fear" is virtually synonymous to devotion and worship, or even to a proper way of life: *[p]alāḫ ilāni damāqu ullad [p]alāḫ Anunnakī balāṭu uttar,* "Fear of the gods creates kindness, fear of the Anunnaki returns life."[33] On the other hand, fear can be misplaced if it is motivated by improper authorities, as in Isa 57:11 (NEB):

---

30 See, e.g., Old Assyrian: *TCL* 19 47:10; Old Babylonian: *TCL* 1 23:15; 18 80:18; *PBS* 7 17:21; Middle Babylonian: *KBo* 1 13 r. 5; *BWL* 50:35; *PRU* 4 35:5; 36:32; Standard Babylonian: *Cuthaean Legend* 157; Neo-Assyrian/Babylonian: *Poem of Erra* iv 27; Assurbanipal Prism B v 46; OIP 114 98:20; SAA 3 13:24; SAA 9 1 i 5, 24, 30; ii 16, 33; iii 30; v 21; 2 i 13, 15; iii 17, 19, 29; iv 28, 30; 4:5; 7:2, r. 6, 11; SAA 10 171:14; 278 r. 7; 320:11; SAA 15 104 r. 17; 306:5; SAA 21 16 r. 3; 20:8; 38:16; 50 r. 9; 63:12; Late Babylonian: RAcc 144: 434. This list is based on *CAD* P (sub *palāḫu*) and the files of the Neo-Assyrian Text Corpus Project in Helsinki. I am indebted to Dr. Raija Mattila and Prof. Simo Parpola for making these resources accessible to me. For Old Aramaic see *KAI* 202 A 13.

31 For Hebrew consult the dictionaries and cf. Becker, *Gottesfurcht;* Stähli, *THAT* 1; Fuhs, *ThWAT* 3; for Aramaic cf. Dan 6:27, etc.; for Akkadian, see *AHw* 2:812–13.

32 SAA 10 285 r. 3–4; see S. Parpola, *Letters from Assyrian and Babylonian Scholars* (SAA 10; Helsinki: Helsinki Univ. Press, 1993), 221.

33 SAA 10 188 r. 9–10; see Parpola, *Letters from Assyrian and Babylonian Scholars*, 155; and cf. Prov 1:7: *yirʾat YHWH rēʾšît daʿat,* "Fear of the Lord is the beginning of knowledge; 9:10: *tĕḥillat ḥokmâ yirʾat YHWH,* "Fear of the Lord is the beginning of wisdom"; 14:27: *yirʾat YHWH mĕqôr ḥayyîm,* "Fear of the Lord is the source of life"; etc.

Whom do you fear so much *(dāʾagtā wattîrĕʾî),* that you should be false,
that you never remembered me or gave me a thought?
Did I not hold my peace and seem not to see,
while you showed no fear of me *(wĕʾôtî lōʾ tîrāʾî)?*[34]

Due to the semantic variability, expressions for fear, or lack thereof, denote different attitudes. For this reason not every prohibitive construction involving a verb for "fear" can be taken as a specimen of a fixed formula. In private discourse, such expressions may occur in contexts where a person is forbidden to obey inappropriate authorities, or to show loyalty to wrong directions, as in a Neo-Babylonian letter from Nippur:

> *[a]na muḫḫi mīni nasīk Ubūlu umma šum ili šū[l]ā Bāniya ul tapallaḫ*
>
> [O]n wh[at] account is the sheikh of the Ubulu tribe saying: "Sw[ea]r an oath by god to me that you will not fear Baniya"?[35]

A similar expression may be used when reproaching a person with disrespectful behavior or negligence, as in the Old Babylonian letter of King Ammiditana to a Sippar merchant:

> *ana mīnim šipāt enzim nēmettaka ana Bābili lā tušābilam/ana epēšim annîm kî lā taplaḫ/ kīma ṭuppi annia[m] tammar[u] šipāt enzim nēmettaka ana Bābili šūbilam*
>
> Why have you not sent the goat's wool, your duty, to Babylon?/How could you not be afraid to act like that?/As soon as you see this tablet, send goat's wool, your duty, to me to Babylon![36]

In this case *la taplaḫ* is used as a fixed phrase,[37] not as a prohibitive, however, but corresponding to the phrase "how dare you!" A similar shade of meaning is expressed as a prohibition in the passage of the *Poem of Erra*, where the governor of Babylon becomes enraged and incites the leader of the army to outrageous crimes:

---

34 For a prohibition against fearing, i. e., venerating, other gods, see also Judg 6:10; 2 Kgs 17:34–39; Jer 10:5.

35 OIP 114 98:16–20; see S. W. Cole, *Nippur IV: The Early Neo-Babylonian Governor's Archive from Nippur* (OIP 114; Chicago: Oriental Institute, 1996), 205.

36 A. Ungnad, *Babylonische Briefe aus der Zeit der Hammurapi-Dynastie* (VAB 6; Leipzig: Hinrichs, 1914), no. 82:14–22 (p. 74).

37 Cf. the same phrase in ibid., no. 71 (p. 64): *ana mīnim adi inanna puḫādī nēmettaka ana ekallim lā ublam/ana epēšim annîm kî lā tapla[ḫ]*, "Why have you not sent the lambs to the palace up to now?/How could you not be afrai[d] to act like that?"

ana āli šâšu ša ašapparūka atta amēlu
ila lā tapallaḫ lā taddar amē[la]
ṣeḫra u rabâ ištēniš šumitma
eniq šīzib šerra lā tezziba ayyamma
nakma būšē Bābili lašallal atta

You are the man whom I shall send to that city!
You shall respect neither god nor man.
Put young and old alike to death.
You shall not leave any child, even if he still sucks milk.
You shall pillage the accumulated wealth of Babylon.[38]

The lack of fear implies here extreme arrogance, impiety, and moral corruption, which sets this and similar[39] occurrences of the phrase "fear not" apart from its use in expressions of encouragement and comfort, which are the main context of the use of this phrase and the principal source material of this essay. Nevertheless, the semantic ambiguity of the concept of fear is not without implications for understanding the phrase "fear not."

Mayer I. Gruber has pointed out the difference between justified "fear" and unjustified "anxiety."[40] While the individual, for the sake of her or his own safety, should have fear in front of a legitimate authority, royal or divine, he or she should not be anxious when confronting anything that should not be feared. This becomes crystal clear in texts to be quoted below, in which the one to be feared – the god(dess) or the king – tells the one(s) addressed not to be anxious about people or things that must not be feared. Hence "fear not" is never a demand not to revere the speaker but an exhortation to show fearlessness before illegitimate powers and to give up unjustified anxiety, which causes a state of paralysis and inability to act.[41] As such, it can appropriately be called an "encouraging formula" (*Ermutigungsformel*).[42]

38 *Erra* iv 26–30; see L. Cagni, *L'Epopea di Erra* (Studi Semitici 3; Rome: Istituto di Studi del Vicino Oriente, 1969), 136–37. Translation from S. Dalley, *Myths from Mesopotamia: Creation, The Flood, Gilgamesh and Others* (Oxford: Oxford Univ. Press, 1989), 303–4.

39 Cf. Luke 18:2: "There was once a judge who did not fear God and did not care about people *(ton theon mē phoboumenos kai anthrōpon mē entrepomenos)*."

40 M. I. Gruber, "Fear, Anxiety and Reverence in Akkadian, Biblical Hebrew and Other North-West Semitic Languages," *VT* 40 (1990) 411–22.

41 Cf. SAA 9 1.1 i 25: "Fear not! You are paralyzed, but I, in the midst of wailing, will get up and sit down." See also Gruber, "Fear," 416–17, who points out the parallelism between Akk. *palāḫu*, "to fear," and *nīd aḫi*, "throwing down of the arm" (E. Leichty, *The Royal Inscriptions of Esarhaddon, King of Assyria (680–669 BC)* [RINAP 4; Winona Lake, Ind.: Eisenbrauns, 2011], 125 iii 43), and the corresponding Heb. *yr*ʾ and *rph ydyim* (Zeph 3:16).

42 See Weippert, "Ich bin Jahwe," 37.

However, "fear not" refers not only to earthly powers. The close proximity of the formula to the divine self-identification "I am Ištar of Arbela" (etc.) alone suggests that it is by the same token intended as a "soothing formula" *(Beschwichtigungsformel)*, easing the frightening experience of the revelation of the divine.[43] In the Hebrew Bible, this is conclusive from Exod 20:18–21 (NEB):

> When all the people saw how it thundered and the lightning flashed, when they heard the trumpet sound and saw the mountain smoking, they trembled *(way-yar' hāʿām way-yānūʿû)* and stood at a distance. "Speak to us yourself," they said to Moses, "and we will listen; but if God speaks to us, we shall die." Moses answered, "Do not be afraid *('al-tîrā'û)*. God has come only to test you, so that the fear of him *(yir'ātô)* may remain with you and keep you from sin." So the people stood at a distance, while Moses approached the dark cloud where God was.

Thus God should be feared, but the divine presence should not cause anxiety. In theophany the distance between God and humans, characterized as "fear," becomes apparent and must be reduced for the moment when God speaks to humans.

Private Discourse

In private correspondence "fear not" points to different kinds of fearlessness, depending on the object or the reason of fear. At its mildest, it is said or written by one person to another without any specific threat in mind and regardless of these persons' positions in relation to each other. In these cases "fear not" equals "don't worry" and may be taken as belonging to colloquial communication between humans, as it appears in two Old Babylonian letters:

> *[k]īma Nūr-Ilabrat a Gemūtum tušakkali anāku īde/mimma lā tapallaḫi/*
> *a[n]āku šalmāku u awīlum šalim/u šunātūa [m]ādiš [d]amqā*

> I know how you support Nur-Ilabrat and Gemutum./Fear [fem.] nothing!/
> I am well, the gentleman[44] is well,/and my dreams are very good.[45]

---

43 Thus Weippert, "Assyrische Prophetien," 78–79. Cf. already Köhler, "Offenbarungsformel"; and Kaiser, "Traditionsgeschichtliche Untersuchung," 111–13.

44 In spite of the singular forms, two persons appear as the senders of the letter (l. 3; both names are broken). The "gentleman" may refer to the other writer, or, if the actual writer is a woman, to her husband.

45 *PBS* 7 17: 21–25; see M. Stol, *Letters from Collections in Philadelphia, Chicago and Berkeley* (AbB 11; Leiden: Brill, 1986), 10–11.

u mimma lā tapallaḫā/šulumkunu šuprānimma libbī linūḫ

Fear [pl.] nothing!/Your well-being convinces me that I can be with a peaceful mind.[46]

In both cases these wishes follow the subject matter of the letter as a kind of a personal appendix, independent of the actual message. Without naming any specific cause of anxiety, the writers simply want to assure that all is well with them, and express their conviction, based on dreams or personal knowledge, that the same holds true for the addressee.

A similarly phrased word of encouragement is uttered by another Old Babylonian writer who urges the addressee to go before his gods without fear:

ana maḫar Zababa u Ištār alāka mimma lā tapallaḫ

Do not be at all afraid to enter before Zababa and Ištar![47]

It is not clear whether the encounter with the deities is enough to frighten the addressee or whether the writer has something more specific in mind. The letter ends here, and if the writer hints at any particular need of the addressee to go to Zababa and Ištar,[48] for example, to consult them through a diviner in a personal distress, this is hidden between the lines.

An Old Assyrian letter from Anatolia is a little more explicit, since the verb *palāḫu* clearly implies the addressee's concern for the logistics of an important message:

minima lā tapallaḫ miššum têrtaka ana Burušḫattim mātima la illikam

Do not be at all afraid that your message would not reach Burušhattum![49]

---

46 Lit. "Your well-being [or: your greeting] announces to me that my heart should calm down," *TCL* 1 23:14–18; see Ungnad, *Babylonische Briefe*, no. 129, pp. 106–9.

47 *TCL* 18 80:15–18; see the copy in G. Dossin, *Lettres de la première dynastie babylonienne II* (TCL 18; Paris: Geuthner, 1934), pl. 47. I owe the reading of the first divine name as Zababa to W. Sommerfeld, *Der Aufstieg Marduks: Die Stellung Marduks in der babylonischen Religion des zweiten Jahrtausends v. Chr.* (AOAT 213; Kevelaer: Butzon & Bercker; Neukirchen-Vluyn: Neukirchener Verlag, 1982), 119 n. 2.

48 These particular deities are probably chosen as gods of the city of Kiš, where the addressee is supposed to live; thus Sommerfeld, *Der Aufstieg Marduks*, 119.

49 *TCL* 19 47:10–15; see the copy in J. Lewy, *Tablettes cappadociennes, troisième série, première partie* (TCL 19; Paris: Geuthner, 1935), pl. 44. For Burušhattum (Hitt. Purushattum), see S. Aro, "Tabal: Zur Geschichte und materiellen Kultur des zentralanatolischen Hochplateaus von 1200 bis 600 v.Chr." (Ph.D. diss., Univ. of Helsinki, 1998), 53.

In the above examples, the potential sources of anxiety, whether or not specified, belong to the sphere of private life, and *mimma lā tapallaḫ* (etc.) is used in discourse between humans, in which the social standing of the persons involved plays no role. These texts also provide the oldest attestations of the phrase that I know and speak for a primary use of "fear not" in colloquial speech concerning everyday cares. A similar use of analogous expressions is well known, not only from the Hebrew Bible (e.g., *ʾal-tîrĕʾî* in Gen 35:17; Ruth 3:11; *ʾal-tîrāʾû* in Gen 43:23), but probably from countless languages and literatures independent of one another. This context is too broad to be defined as *Sitz im Leben*, since the use of "fear not" cannot be shown to be restricted to any specific situations or forms of speech or literature.

Royal Discourse

Letters to the King

When used in communication between humans in Neo-Assyrian and Neo-Babylonian sources, the phrase "fear not" occurs in royal correspondence, where the anxieties of the private life and the fear of the royal authority overlap. An unknown officer of Sargon II reports to the king what he has said to another, likewise unknown person:

> *ittalka iqṭibīya m[ā ...]/dibbi ṭābū issīy[a idubbub mā] atâ Nāṣib-ilu kî an[nie .../libbu] assakanšu nūk lā ta[pallaḫ ...] ekalli lallik*
>
> He came and said to me: "[... ...]."/[He spoke] kindly with m[e but said]: "Why [does] Naṣib-ilu [...] in this ma[nner]?"/I encouraged him, saying: "F[ear] not! I will go to the palace [and ...]"[50]

The writer is obviously in the position to say a good word for his friend in front of the king. When he claims to have told his friend not to fear, he is anticipating a similar word from the mouth of the king, accompanied by actions that should remove all concern about what the certain Naṣib-ilu had done to the writer's comrade.

If "fear not" is said to the king himself, it is phrased differently: instead of *lā tapallaḫ*, the writers use the more courteous form *šarru (lū) lā ipallaḫ*, "the king should not be afraid," which reflects the unequal status of the correspondents.

---

50 SAA 15 104 r. 14–18: see A. Fuchs and S. Parpola, *The Correspondence of Sargon II, Part III: Letters from Babylonia and Eastern Provinces* (SAA 15; Helsinki: Helsinki Univ. Press, 2001), 71.

In both of the cases at hand, the cause of worry is mentioned explicitly. The chief exorcist Nabû-nadin-šumi allays the king's fears caused by an untoward portent:

> *u ina muḫḫi itti annīti šarru bēlī [issi lib]bīšu lū [l]ā idabbub/Bēl u Nabû ammar ittu šētuqi maṣû ana šarri bēlīya ušettuqū/šarru bēlī lū lā ipallaḫ*
>
> The king, my lord, should not be worried about this portent./Bel and Nabû can make a portent pass by, and they will make it bypass the king, my lord./The king, my lord, should not be afraid.[51]

Similarly, Urad-Nanaya, the physician, soothes the feelings of the father of a sick child:

> *šulmu adanniš ana Aššūr-mukīn-palū'a/ḫunṭu anniu ša šanīšu šalšīšu [i]ṣbatušūni šarru lā ipallaḫ/sa[kik]kûšu šulmu tariṣ/šulmu šū*
>
> Aššur-mukin-pale'a is doing very well./The king should not be afraid of this fever which has two or three times seized him;/his pulse is normal and sound;/he is well.[52]

Functionally, the use of "fear not" in these letters is similar to the previously mentioned occurrences in Old Babylonian correspondence. The cause of anxiety has to do with the king's personal safety or private life, and the writers base their assurances on their own conviction and expertise.

The Royal Word

The exhortation not to fear becomes a significantly different tone when it is spoken by the king himself. In such cases the use of the phrase is inseparable from the position of the king as the supreme authority. In the Hebrew Bible a royal word of this kind is spoken, for example, by David to Mephibosheth (Meribaal) in 2 Sam 9:7 (NEB):

> David said: "Do not be afraid (*'al tîrā'*); I mean to show you kindness for your father Jonathan's sake, and I will give you back the whole estate of your grandfather Saul; you shall have a place for yourself at my table."[53]

---

51 SAA 10 278:12 – r. 7; see Parpola, *Letters from Assyrian and Babylonian Scholars*, 217.

52 SAA 10 320:7 – 12; see ibid., 258. Aššur-mukin-pale'a was the son of King Esarhaddon, probably born shortly after his enthronement, who seems to have been in poor health as a child; see K. Radner, Aššūr-mukīn-palē'a, *PNA* 1/I (1998) 197 – 98.

53 For 2 Sam 9 see T. Veijola, "David und Meribaal," in *David: Gesammelte Studien zu den Davidüberlieferungen des Alten Testaments* (PFES 52; Helsinki: Finnish Exegetical Society; Göttingen: Vandenhoeck & Ruprecht, 1990) 58 – 83 (= *RB* 85 [1978] 338 – 61), according to whom this

According to the story, Mephibosheth could count on this royal promise, which for him meant a permanent change in his social status.

An opposite experience can be found in the letter of an unknown astrologer who is worried about his employment in the service of the king of Assyria:

> *mīnū ḫiṭṭūa šarru itti ummānīšu rēšā ul išši/šarru iqtabi umma lā tapallaḫ umma rēška anašši/u la libbi kî ēlû adi muḫḫi enna šarru rēšā ul išši*
>
> What is my fault that the ting has not summoned me with his scholars?/The king said: Have no fear, I will summon you./But when I departed from there, up to now the king has not summoned me.[54]

The writer expresses openly the concern for his future, totally dependent on the king's favor. He also makes dear that, in spite of the king's assurances, he still has every reason to fear, because his life is in the hands of the king who has failed to keep his promise. The words *lā tapallaḫ* mean here more than neighborly consolation or encouragement; they are royal words coming from the one who himself is to be feared and whose "fear not" should inspire one with particular confidence in powers vested in him. In other words, the people have only the king to fear; otherwise they have nothing to fear. This is what the king himself affirms to his subjects, for instance, in SAA 21 50:

> [..... *taš*]*puranni mā šēpēka niṣbat/mā palḫāni issu pān šagalûti ša māt Aššūr/issu pān turrūte ša kutalli ana Elamti/ūmâ kî ša taqbianni ina pān Bēl-iqīša alkāni/kaqquru bēt tar-a''imāni lušaṣbitkunu/ina libbi šībâ urdānīya attunu bīrtu ša* LÚ.*r*[*u*] *iṣṣi Bēl-iqīša uṣrā/ina libbi ilānīja attama šumma anāku ušaggalukkanūni šumma ana kutalli usaḫḫarukkanūni ana Elamti/assaprakkunu lā tapallaḫā* [......]
>
> [...... *Concerning what* you w]rote: "We wish to grasp your feet, we are afraid of getting deported by Assyria and of being exposed to Elam" — now, in accordance with what you said, come before Bel-iqiša and let him settle you in a territory that you like./Stay there as my servants and guard the fortress of ... with Bel-iqiša!/I swear by my gods that I shall not deport you and not expose you to Elam./I am writing to you: have no fear! [......][55]

Assuming that Bel-iqiša is identical to the leader of the Gambulu tribe inhabiting the area between Babylonia and Elam, this letter reflects the politically delicate

---

speech of David is the turning point of the story (pp. 70–71). Cf. also Joseph's words to his brothers in Gen 50:21: "Do not be afraid *('al-tîrā'û).* I will provide for you and your dependents."

54 For SAA 10 171:11–17 see Parpola, *Letters from Assyrian and Babylonian Scholars,* 131. The name of the writer of the letter is broken away. The same concern is expressed by the astrologer Bel-ušezib in SAA 10 109; see M. Nissinen, *References to Prophecy in Neo-Assyrian Sources* (SAAS 7; Helsinki: Neo-Assyrian Text Corpus Project, 1998), 89–95.

55 SAA 21 50:2–r. 9.

status of the Gambuleans between Elam and Assyria/Babylonia.[56] Bel-iqiša had submitted to Esarhaddon, who treated him favorably and who, having concluded a treaty with Urtaku, king of Elam, in the year 674, was on good terms also with Elam.[57] The letter may be read as the answer of the new king Assurbanipal to some Gambuleans who were concerned about their status after the transfer of power, which always meant a redistribution of royal favors. In this context "fear not" is a royal promise of loyalty toward people whose submission has been accepted. The letter was certainly written before Urtaku and his allies, Bel-iqiša among them, probably in the year 664, unexpectedly invaded Babylonia, thus breaking up their loyalty to Assyria with fatal consequences.[58]

In the correspondence of Assurbanipal, the phrase "fear not" occurs repeatedly, always in letters written by the king to his subjects or vassals. With the probable exception of SAA 21 50 quoted above, their dates are close to the time of the revolt of his brother Šamaš-šumu-ukin, the subordinate ruler of Babylonia, with whom he was at war from 652 to 648. Not surprisingly, the king's exhortation not to fear calls for perseverance and loyalty in the ever changing conjunctures of war. In a letter dated to the 5th of Tishri (VII), 652 and concerning men of two Babylonian cities, Cutha and Surmarrati, Assurbanipal says to Zakir and Kabtiya[59] that they should not be afraid (SAA 21 16). The letter is too badly broken to yield a solid interpretation, but if is imaginable that the addressees of the letter held a responsible, probably military position in or near Cutha, a strategically important city, which fell into the hands of Šamaš-šumu-ukin less than a year later.[60]

A better-preserved message from the king is presented by SAA 21 38:

---

56 See H. D. Baker, "Bēl-iqīša," *PNA* 1/II (1999) 315–16; G. Frame, *Babylonia 689–627 b.c.: A Political History* (Uitgaven van het Nederlands Historisch-Archaeologisch Instituut te Istanbul 69; Istanbul: Nederlands Historisch-Archaeologisch Instituut, 1992), 81, 111, 118–20.

57 Cf. E. Leichty, *The Royal Inscriptions of Esarhaddon, King of Assyria (680–669 BC)* (RINAP 4; Winona Lake, Ind.: Eisenbrauns, 2011), 18 iii 71–83; cf. M. W. Waters, *A Survey of Neo-Elamite History* (SAAS 12; Helsinki: Neo-Assyrian Text Corpus Project, 2000), 42–45.

58 For the unsuccessful invasion of Urtaku, supported by Bel-iqiša, Nabû-šumu-ereš, the governor of Nippur, and Marduk-šumu-ibni, a Babylonian general of Urtaku, see J. Novotny and J. Jeffers, *The Royal Inscriptions of Ashurbanipal (668–631 BC), Aššur-etel-ilāni (630–627 BC), and Sîn-šarra-iškun (626–612 BC), Kings of Assyria,* Part 1 (RINAP 5/1; University Park, Pa.: Eisenbrauns, 2018), 66–67 iv 15–60; and cf. Frame, *Babylonia,* 118–21; Waters, *Survey,* 45–47.

59 For this person, see H. D. Baker, "Kabtia," *PNA* 2/I (2000) 594. Probably the same person writes in another letter (*ABL* 202) about Babylonians taking a loyalty oath.

60 See Frame, *Babylonia,* 144, 146.

ana Sîn-tabni-uṣur/ina muḫḫi Sîn-šarra-uṣur ša ta[qbûni] mā annūri nik[lu] inakkil/samku ina mu[ḫḫīja] ikarrar/lā t[apallaḫ]/mīnu ḫappu anniu ina muḫḫīka iqabbi/anāku lā uddâ ša [...] *u taddanūni x* [*x maṣṣartī*] *taṣṣurūni* [...] *u tasmûni mī*[*nu ḫīṭu*]/*u tablaṭanni ina muḫḫi bēt bē-l*[*ēka*]/*šû mīnu iqabbi ina muḫḫīka u ina libbimma anāku atâ ašamme/lā tapallaḫ tuāršu/ napšatka ibašši ina pānīya/u ina muḫḫi alākīka ša taqbûni mā rabūti iktallûni/šalaš šanāti tattitiz maṣṣartu tattaṣar zikirka ina pānīya tuddammiq/ūmâ simān taqāni ša māti/maṣṣar-taka tuk*[*tīn*] *tettiqa tallaka/ūlâ itiz maṣṣartaka uṣur adi mātu ta*[*tqanūni*]/*u ina ūmēšu tallaka pānīya ḫaddute tammar* [...] *u tasaḫḫur ina šal*[*imte*] *tallak*

To Sîn-tabni-uṣur:/Concerning Sîn-šarra-uṣur about whom you s[aid]: Now then, he is devising a scheme/and *spreading rumors* against me/have no f]ear]!/What can this *fool*[61] say against you?/Don't I know what you [*do*] and deliver, *h*[*ow*] you have kept [my watch...]ed, ... ed *without bl*[*ame*],/and lived for the house of [your] lord[s]?/What could he say against you? And in the middle of it, why should I listen to it?/Do not fear his return!/Your life is with me!/As to your coming about which you said: "The magnates have held me back,"/it is the third year now that you have stood by and kept my watch, making yourself a good name in my presence./Now, at the moment that the country is getting safe, you could move on to come, having estab[lished] your guard./Alternatively, stay there and keep [your] wat[ch] until the country has been put up in order;/then you can come, see [my] beaming [face], and return in safe[ty].[62]

Both Sîn-tabni-uṣur and Sîn-šarra-uṣur were sons of Nikkal-iddina, governor of the city of Ur, which most of the time was "a bastion of pro-Assyrian sentiment in southern Babylonia, an area whose tribal groups frequently provided support for rebel movements."[63] Sîn-šarra-uṣur followed his brother Sîn-balassu-iqbi as the governor of Ur, probably just before Šamaš-šumu-ukin rose up in arms and with his consent, whereas Assurbanipal would have supported Sîn-tabni-uṣur.[64] The letter quoted here is not the only one to give the impression that Sîn-tabni-uṣur was given preference over Sîn-šarra-uṣur by Assurbanipal, who, after having consulted diviners, replaced Sîn-šarra-uṣur by his brother at some turn during the war – in 650 at the latest but probably earlier.[65] Since the king gives Sîn-tabni-uṣur the credit for keeping guard of the city for three years without release and now gives him permission to leave the city, the letter is certainly written after Ur was relieved by Assurbanipal in 650, but not necessarily before the war was over. As in SAA 21 37, the king encourages the governor,

61 Lit. perhaps: "stinker."

62 SAA 21 38: 1 – r. 15.

63 Frame, *Babylonia,* 101.

64 See J.-M. Durand, "Note à propos de la date d'*ABL* 290," *RA* 75 (1981) 181 – 85; cf. Frame, *Babylonia,* 126.

65 The word *samku* is probably derived from *samāku,* "to cover up," and may here refer to secrets or malicious gossips.

giving his word that he will not believe the bad rumors circulated by Sîn-šarra-uṣur. Having once been pardoned by the king in spite of having submitted to the enemy during a famine in the city,[66] Sîn-tabni-uṣur would have had every reason to trust in this royal word.

Due to the damaged state of the tablet, the historical background of SAA 21 20 is not explicit in the extant wording of the letter. To all appearances, it is written to the inhabitants of a city, threatened by the forces of someone who is himself shut up in another city and surrounded by the army of the author of the letter. This leaves little doubt that the person in question is Šamaš-šumu-ukin and that Assurbanipal has authored the letter during the siege of Babylon in the years 650 – 648:

> [……] *u attunu atâ kî anniu tāmurāni ša duāki lā tadūkā ša ṣabāte lā taṣbatā/ša illikūninni šunû ina muḫḫīkunu maʾdū/ūmâ lā tapallaḫā/maṣṣartu ša bēt ilānīya uṣrā/šû gabbīšuma ina libbi āli esir u emūqīya labiūšu/ūmâ bēt mār šiprīšu tammarāni/ša duāki tadūkā ša ṣabāte ṣabtā* [……]
>
> [……] But you [pl.], when you saw this, why did you not kill those who were to be killed and seize those who were to be seized?/Certainly (the troops) who came were not more numerous than you!/Now fear not, but guard my temples!/He is shut up in the city with all his forces, and my army is surrounding him./Now wherever you see a messenger of his, kill those who are to be killed and seize those who are to be seized! [……][67]

Again, the king pronounces his *lā tapallaḫā* to people whom he knows or believes to be in an emergency, demanding loyalty. It seems that the addressees have lent an ear to messages from the adversary and not offered enough resistance, but the king is willing to forgive this, if they remain loyal to him even under the threat of an aggressor. The king himself seems not to be operating near the city in question, so he cannot promise any military backup but only assure that the enemy will soon be slain. In this context fearlessness requires faith without seeing (cf. Isa 7:4, 9), supposing the people's confidence in the king's sovereignty, which is ultimately of divine origin; hence the king's "fear not" can be trusted as if it were a divine word. In Assurbanipal's letters, this phrase always has political overtones: it reminds the addressees of their position and connotes a demand for fidelity to the king.

---

66 In the letter *ABL* 1274, the citizens of Ur assure the loyalty of their governor in spite of the fact that he had no other option than to surrender because of starvation; cf. Frame, *Babylonia*, 166.
67 SAA 21 20: 3′–14′ (for transcription and translation, see n. 55 above). A fragment of a royal order with similar content has been preserved in SAA 15 306: 2–6 (Fuchs and Parpola, *Correspondence of Sargon II, Part III*, 192): [...] "the fort sho[uld be ……] it [should] be watched over; and [……] fetc[h] for your watch […… Fear [not], be con[fident! ...] Gua[rd] this [fo]rt!"

King to King

The turbulences of the Šamaš-šumu-ukin revolt affected not only Babylonia but also Elam, whose rulers changed at a brisk pace, and so did their loyalties to Assyria.[68] A prime example is provided by Tammaritu II, who ruled 651–649 after having killed his predecessor and uncle Humban-nikaš II, a puppet of Assyria who before his short rule had been granted asylum by Assurbanipal, but who went over to Šamaš-šumu-ukin when the revolt began. Tammaritu remained on Šamaš-šumu-ukin's side, but when he, in turn, was toppled by Indabibi, he survived by fleeing to Assyria.[69] Assurbanipal protected Tammaritu who even dwelt in his palace.[70] There are discordant records concerning Assurbanipal's relation to Indabibi,[71] who ruled only until the next year. (648). He was killed by the Elamites who put Humban-haltaš III on the throne. By this time Babylon fell and the war was over, but Assurbanipal soon attacked Elam, forcing Humban-haltaš to flee, and giving Tammaritu a second chance.[72] The long letter from Assurbanipal to Tammaritu, SAA 21 63, probably dates from this period of time, since it mentions the names Humban-haltaš (Ass. Ummanaldasi, l. r. 5) and Nabû-bel-šumati (l. 15), the right hand of Šamaš-šumu-ukin who was protected by Humban-haltaš after the fall of Babylon. The context of the phrase "fear not" (*lā tapallaḫ*, l. 12) is broken, but the remaining text suggests an account concerning the threat constituted by people from Raši, the area between Elam and northern Babylonia, and the coming of Assurbanipal's troops to assistance:

> *[ṭuppi Aššur-bāni-apli] šar [māt Aššūr] a[na Tamma]rītu šar Elamti šulmu ana yāši lū šulmu a[na kāša]/ina muḫḫi emūqī annūti ša* [...] *lā immagāni* [...]*/ina muḫḫi Rāšāja* [...] *ša ina kutallīkunu* [...] *ina muḫḫi kabbusi ša māti/šū* [...] *ūmâ issi māt Aššūr urru adi* [...] *ittalkū u ammaka* [...] *ušamḫirūni/ulâ* [... *i*]*zzazū lā tapallaḫ* [... ...]
>
> [A tablet of Assurbanipal], king [of Assyria], t[o Tamma]ritu, king of Elam: I am well, may [you, too], be well./Concerning these troops that [*were* ...] *they were* not [...] in vain!/As to

68 For an overview of the complicated circumstances in Elam during the years 652–645, see Waters, *Survey*, 62–80.

69 Novotny and Jeffers, *The Royal Inscriptions of Assurbanipal*, 75–76 vii 43–76.

70 Ibid., 76 vii 55–60.

71 Prism B vii 61–76, completed by the time Indabibi gained power, tells about his assurances of goodwill and peace (Novotny and Jeffers, *The Royal Inscriptions of Ashurbanipal*, 76), and in the letter SAA 21 60, Assurbanipal calls Indabibi his "brother." However, Prism C ix 11–52, compiled two or three years later, gives a less harmonious impression of the Assyrian-Elamite relations at that time (ibid., 133–34). See Waters, *Survey*, 66.

72 Ibid., 245–47 (Prism A iv 110 – v 35 40). Waters, *Survey*, 69–70, dates the campaign either to 648 or 657; the month of Sivan (III) is given in the inscription.

> the Rašeans, [...] who [...] in your back [...] to subjugate the country:/they have now ... from Assyria and gone as far as [...] and [...] there. [The ... who] have done correspondingly,/or [... are s]taying [...]./Fear not! [... ...][73]

A better-preserved part from the conclusion of the letter probably refers to a treaty between Assurbanipal and Tammaritu:

> *ša abu ana mar'i lā eppašūni anāku [ētapaš] attannakka/atta [...] ḫussa ṭābāte annā[te ...] epuš dilip šallimanni/u [adê] ša ina pān ilāni ša šamê u kaq[qiri ...] utammûkāni [...]*
>
> What even a father has not done for a son, I have [done] and given to you!/As for you, remember [this], unremittingly strive to return to me these [*many*] favors,/and [*keep*] the [treaty] that I have made you swear before [*all*] the gods of heaven and earth![74]

Both the encouraging "fear not" and the reference to a treaty suggest that Assurbanipal was quite serious about Tammaritu's renewed rulership. Whatever his political plans were, they did not work out, though. Tammaritu's second tenure in Elam lasted only a few months, after which he was captured and brought back to Assyria; he is mentioned later among other captured vassals who were forced to pull Assurbanipal's carriage.[75] Presumably, he failed to return to the great king his favors, hence the divine-royal "fear not" was no longer in force.

Assurbanipal's correspondence with his vassal has an earlier counterpart in the letter of the Hittite king Šuppiluliuma to Niqmadu II, king of Ugarit, dating to the first half of the fourteenth century.[76] At that time, Šuppiluliuma was confronted by a coalition of Syrian kings supported by Mitanni. King Niqmadu of Ugarit, rather than joining this anti-Hittite league, chose to conclude a treaty with Šuppiluliuma, which in concrete terms meant vassalage under the Hittite king.[77] The letter begins with the following words:

> *umma Šamši šarri rabî ana Niqmanda qibima/enūma Nuḫaš u Mugi[š] ittīya nakrūma/u atta Niqmandu lā tapallaḫšunu itti ramānīka lū putqu-dāta/kî ša ultu maḫirî abbūka itti Ḫatti šalmū u lā nakrū/anumma atta Niqmandu lū akannama/itti nakrīya lū nakrāta itti šalāmīya lū šalmāta/u šumma atta Niqmandu amāte annâti ša šarri rabî bēlīka tašamme u tanaṣṣaršina/u šarrumma tammar dumqa ša šarru rabû bēlka udammiqakku*

---

73 SAA 21 63: 1–12 (for transcription and translation, see n. 55 above).

74 Ibid., r. 19–24.

75 Novotny and Jeffers, *The Royal Inscriptions of Ashurbanipal*, 261 (Prism A x 6–39); cf. Waters, *Survey*, 72.

76 RS 17.132; see J. Nougayrol, *PRU IV: Textes accadiens des archives sud* (Mission de Ras Shamra 9; Paris: Imprimerie nationale and Librairie C. Klincksieck, 1956), 35–37.

77 For the treaty, see ibid., 37–48; cf. M. Dietrich and O. Loretz, "Der Vertrag zwischen Šuppiluliuma und Niqmadu," *WO* 3 (1966) 206–45.

> Thus the Sun, the great king; speak to Niqmadu: Nuhašše and Muki[š] are now at war with me./You, Niqmadu: Do not be afraid of them, trust in yourself!/As your fathers before were my allies and not enemies,/let it now be the same way with you, Niqmadu:/may you be the enemy of my enemies and the ally of my allies!/And if you, Niqmadu, listen to these words of the great king, your lord, take heed of them,/you, king, will see the good deeds that the great king, your lord, will do to you.[78]

After having urged Niqmadu to remain faithful and to trust in his word,[79] Šuppiluliuma writes:

> *u šumma šarrānu gabbūšunu ṣābī mimma ana ḫabāti ša mātīka umaššarū/u atta Niqmandu lā tapallaḫšunu/ḫamutta mār šiprāka ana muḫḫīya šupramma lillikka*
>
> And if all those kings send any troops to plunder your country,/you, Niqmadu, be not afraid of them,/but send immediately a messenger of yours to me![80]

No reader will miss the paternalistic tone of this letter, very similar to the language Assurbanipal or any Assyrian king would use when writing to their vassals. While animating Niqmadu to self-reliance, he makes clear that he himself is the one who is to be feared, not the kings involved in anti-Hittite undertakings. Again, one is reminded of the biblical exhortations not to be afraid of the enemy, spoken by God (Num 21:34; Deut 3:2) or by Moses or Joshua (Exod 14:13; Num 14:9; Deut 1:29; 3:22; Josh 10:25). It has been noted that Šuppiluliuma speaks in his letter like a god.[81] Indeed, the great king seems to relate to his vassal as gods do to him, just as, for example, Assurbanipal relates to Gyges, king of Lydia, who allegedly sent his messenger *(mār šipri)* to tell him about a dream of his concerning his obeisance to Assurbanipal's sovereignty.[82]

A certain kind of king-to-king communication is represented also by the "Cuthaean Legend of Naram-Sîn," a tale preserved in several manuscripts of the Old Babylonian and Standard Babylonian (Neo-Assyrian) recensions.[83] In this fictional autobiography, Naram-Sîn, the legendary king of Akkad, narrates in first

78 Nougayrol, *PRU* 4:35–36, ll. 1–18.

79 Ibid., 36, ll. 28–29: *Niqmandu ina arki ūmi amāte ša šarri rabî bēlīka taqâp*, "Niqmadu, from day to day trust in the word of the great king, your lord!"

80 Ibid., 36, ll. 30–34.

81 H. Wildberger, "'Glauben' im Alten Testament," *ZTK* 65 (1968) 129–59, esp. 136; cf. Dion, "Fear Not," 566.

82 Novotny and Jeffers, *The Royal Inscriptions of Ashurbanipal*, 237 (Prism A ii 95–110), 50 vi 14–25 (Prism E2); cf. M. Cogan and H. Tadmor, "Gyges and Assurbanipal: A Study in Literary Transmission," *Or* 46 (1977) 65–85; Nissinen, *References to Prophecy*, 57–58.

83 See J. G. Westenholz, *Legends of the Kings of Akkad: The Texts* (Winona Lake, Ind.: Eisenbrauns, 1997), 263–331.

person about his battle against hordes of heavenly creatures that entirely devastate his forces. According to the Standard Babylonian recension, Naram-Sîn finally gains a victory, but is not allowed to annihilate the enemy. The recension concludes with an admonition to a future ruler, the message of which is that he should live in peace, taking good care of everyday pursuits and not engage in violent enterprises:

> *atta mannu lū iššakku u rubû lū mimma šanāma*
> *ša ilānu inambûšu šarrūta ippuš ...*
> *narâ annâ amurma ša pī narê annâ šimēma*
> *lā tessiḫḫu lā tenniššu*
> *lā tapallaḫ lā tatarrur*
> *išdāka lū kīna*
>
> You, whoever you are, be it governor or prince or anyone else,
> Whom the gods will call to perform kingship. ...
> Read this stele! Hearken unto the words of this stele!
> Be not bewildered! Be not confused!
> Be not afraid! Do not tremble!
> Let your foundations be firm![84]

One cannot help comparing *lā tapallaḫ la tatarrur* with the structurally similar Deuteronomistic phrase, "Do not be afraid, do not be discouraged" *(ʾal/lōʾ tîrâ wĕʾal/lōʾ tēḥāt),* especially when said by Moses to his follower Joshua (Deut 31:8), or to the Israelites (Deut 1:21; cf. God to Joshua, Josh 8:1; Joshua to the people, Josh 10:25). The setting is different in that Joshua and the Israelites are called up to fight, whereas the follower of Naram-Sîn is urged not to engage in war.[85] Fearlessness appears in the Cuthaean Legend among qualities of a peaceful leadership, which gives "fear not" a tone rather different from its use in military contexts. There is no fundamental ideological clash, however, since the very message of the Cuthaean Legend is essentially convergent with the general idea of divine warfare, advocated by the Deuteronomists as well, in which the role of the humans is auxiliary at best. This ideology becomes a pronounced form when "fear not" is used in divine discourse.

---

84 Lines 149–50, 154–58; see Westenholz, *Legends*, 326–27.
85 Cf. Rowlett, *Joshua*, 100.

Divine Discourse

Ludlul bēl nēmeqi

The oldest attestation of *lā tapallaḫ* in divine discourse is probably to be found in *Ludlul bēl nēmeqi*, or The Poem of the Righteous Sufferer.[86] This literary work is conventionally dated to the Kassite period (i. e., 15th-12th centuries), although the extant manuscripts are all Neo-Assyrian/Babylonian.[87] The implied author, having described his miseries (illness, loss of his formerly esteemed position and futile endeavors to find relief), tells in the third tablet of the poem about a series of dreams that finally promised well. In the first dream, "a remarkable young man of extraordinary physique" appears, but the text is too fragmentary to reveal what he says to the sufferer. In the second dream, he becomes cleansed by another remarkable young man, whereas in the third dream a female being speaks to him:

ašlušma šuttu anaṭ[ṭal] ina šutti aṭṭulu mūšīt[īya]
ištē[t] batūltu banû zī[mūšu]/nišiš x x x iliš ma[šlat]
šarrat nišī [... ...]/īrubamma itta[šba ... ...]
qibâ aḫulapī [... ...]/lā tapallaḫ iqbâ
mimmu šutta īṭul [... ...]
iqbima aḫulapī magal šum[ruṣma]
ayyumma ša ina šāt mūši ibnû bī[ra]

A third time I sa[w] a dream, in [my] nightly dream I saw
A certain young woman of shining countenance],/ ... like a human being, eq[ual] to a god,
A queen of the peoples [... ...]./She entered and [sat down], [... ...]
"Speak my deliverance [... ...]!"/"Fear not," she said, [... ...]
Whatever of a dream one has seen [... ...]
She spoke my deliverance: "Most wre[tched] is he,
Whoever he is, the one who saw the nightly vision."[88]

---

86 W. G. Lambert, *Babylonian Wisdom Literature* (Oxford: Oxford Univ. Press, 1960; repr. Winona Lake, Ind.: Eisenbrauns, 1996), 21–62; cf. the translation of Benjamin R. Foster, "The Poem of the Righteous Sufferer," *COS* 1:486–92 (no. 1.153). Note also *KBo* 1 13, a somewhat later Middle Babylonian text from Anatolia, in which *lā tapallaḫ* occurs in a broken context. The text is too badly broken to be interpreted; cf. the transliteration and translation of Sommerfeld, *Der Aufstieg Marduks*, 198–99. According to him, the text may be part of an otherwise unknown mythological narrative or a historical-literary poem (p. 197).

87 See Lambert, *Babylonian Wisdom Literature*, 29.

88 Tablet iii, ll. 29–38; see Lambert, *Babylonian Wisdom Literature*, 48–51 (cf. the correction on p. 345); Foster, "Poem," 490.

The speech of the female dream goddess, best described as an oracle of salvation,[89] anticipates the fourth and final dream, in which a diviner speaks an oracle of Marduk, the supreme god, who then releases the sufferer from his distress; the diviner (*mašmaššu*) assumes a remarkably prophetic role, holding a tablet in his hands and saying: "Marduk has sent me" (*Mardukma išpuranni;* iii 41–42). The climax of the story, the turn for the better, is marked with oracular experiences, in which the exhortation "fear not" is embedded in a divinatory context.

Ištar to Assurbanipal

In Assurbanipal's letters "fear not" is reminiscent of words of Moses, who encourages the people not to be afraid in face of the enemy because the divine force behind them is greater (e.g., Exod 14:13; Deut 1:29; 3:22; 20:1; 31:6; cf. also Neh 4:8 [Eng. 4:14]). But they also remind one of divine words, which according to Assurbanipal's own account were spoken to him by Ištar in a critical situation. Since several manuscripts of *Ludlul bēl nēmeqi* belonged to Assurbanipal's library, it is not far-fetched to assume that the above quoted section has influenced the following passage, which even repeats the word order *lā tapallaḫ iqbâ:*

> *inḫēya šunūḫūti Ištār išmēma lā tapallaḫ iqbâ/ušarḫiṣanni libbu/ana nīš qātēka ša taššâ ēnāka imlâ dimtu artaši rēmu*
>
> Ištar heard my desperate sighs and said to me: "Have no fear!"/She made my heart confident (saying):/"Because of the hand-lifting prayer you said, your eyes being filled with tears, I have mercy upon you."[90]

Assurbanipal's tears were caused by the surprise attack of Teumman, king of Elam, in 653, after which he claims to have uttered a long prayer with the above quoted divine reaction. The answer of the goddess implies an essentially similar role division as in Assurbanipal's letters, only the king now assumes the role of the distressed whereas the goddess plays the part of the sovereign. Like the Gambuleans in SAA 21 50, Assurbanipal begs his superior for help, and the goddess utters the queenly "fear not" to her "son" who has shown his fidelity to her, just as he himself pacifies his faithful servant Sîn-tabni-usur in SAA 21 38.

---

89 Cf. Harner, "Salvation Oracle," 422.
90 Novotny and Jeffers, *The Royal Inscriptions of Ashurbanipal*, 69 (Prism B v 45–48).

In a dream expanding this answer, Ištar promises to take care of the warfare, telling the king to relax.[91] Without directly corresponding to the message of Assurbanipal in SAA 21 20, the dream renders a similar idea: the people should not be frightened, but trust in the one who alone should be feared. But the dream, being a divine message, says more: whereas Assurbanipal tells the people to "kill the one to be killed and seize the one to be seized," Ištar urges the king to make merry and leave all fighting to her. This statement represents hyperbolically the idea that reserves all warfare to divine intervention. The "quietist" aspect of the ideology of divine warfare can be found already in Mari prophecies, but it is also observable in the Cuthaean legend, in the Hebrew Bible, and, as we shall see, in Neo-Assyrian prophecies.[92]

The inscription of Assurbanipal is noteworthy in two further respects. First, "fear not" is presented in a formulaic manner. In the clause *lā tapallaḫ iqbâ*, the word order makes the words *lā tapallaḫ* the object of the verb *qabû* rather than a direct speech, which indicates a formulaic use of words perceived as a fixed compound. Second, "fear not" is part of a divine speech, an oracle of salvation presumably transmitted by a prophet.[93] This brings us to the use of the phrase in the Neo-Assyrian prophetic oracles.

"Fear not" in Prophecy

More than in any other extant source, *lā tapallaḫ* is used in Neo-Assyrian prophecies (SAA 9), where it has nineteen occurrences in twelve different oracles; this makes up approximately half of the attestations of the phrase that I am aware of. Hence it is not by chance that these texts, if any, are mentioned as parallels

91 Ibid., 100–101 (Prism B v 49–76).

92 On Mari see, e.g., ARM 26 237:22–26: *muḫḫūtum ina bīt Annunītim [i]tbêma/ummāmi Zimri-Lim ana gerrim lā tallak/ina Māri šibma u anākūma ātanappal*, "A *muḫḫūtum* arose in the temple of Annunitum and spoke:/'Zimri-Lim, do not go on campaign!/Stay in Mari, and I shall continue to answer.'" The word "quietism" is used by W. L. Moran with regard to this text in "New Evidence from Mari on the History of Prophecy," *Bib* 50 (1969) 15–56, esp. 40. At Mari there are no attestations of *lā tapallaḫ*, but the idea of fearlessness in a threatening situation is certainly there; of the two texts brought into discussion by Heintz, "Oracles prophétiques," 121–25, ARM 26 210 is still conclusive in spite of Dion's criticism (cf. above, n. 26); here I concur with Rowlett, *Joshua*, 98. For the OT see esp. Exod 14:13–14 (NEB): "'Have no fear *(ʾal tîrāʾû)*,' Moses answered, 'stand firm and see the deliverance that the Lord will bring you this day. ... The Lord will fight for you so hold your peace.'"

93 See Weippert, "Assyrische Prophetien," 97–98; Parpola, *Assyrian Prophecies*, xlvi–xlvii; Nissinen, *References to Prophecy*, 53–54.

of biblical "fear not" oracles. Furthermore, even the assumption of a fixed formula with a definable *Sitz im Leben* may be appropriate with regard to these oracles. The density of the phrase allows manifold observations of the place and function of *lā tapallaḫ* in divine discourse.

1. Any reader of the Assyrian prophecies will notice at first glance that "fear not" often assumes a structural function as the opening or closing formula, just as it does in Second Isaiah.[94] Quoting this phrase is one of the most frequent ways to begin an oracle. In these cases it is always combined with the name of the addressee, for example: *Aššūr-aḫu-iddina lā tapallaḫ,* "Esarhaddon, fear not!"[95] and once preceded by the name of the prophet and the speaking deity: *Mullissu-kabtat raggintu/[m]ā abat šarrati Mullissu šî/mā lā tapallaḫ Aššūr-bāni-apli,* "Thus the prophetess Mullissu-kabtat:/This is the word of Queen Mullissu:/Fear not, Assurbanipal!"[96] In a few cases "fear not" is placed at the end of the oracle as a closing formula, for example, in the same oracle as above: *atta lā tapallaḫ mūrī ša anāku urabbûni,* "Fear not, you, my calf whom I rear."[97]

Another typical and formulaic feature in several Assyrian prophecies is the divine self-identification *anāku Issār ša Arbail,* "I am Ištar of Arbela" (etc.), again corresponding to *ʾānî YHWH,* "I am Yahweh" (etc.), in Second Isaiah.[98] It is used independently of "fear not," but in the oracles of the collection SAA 9 1, both formulas tend to appear close to each other.[99] Even in the other tablets of the

---

94 See Parpola, *Assyrian Prophecies,* lxvi; Weippert, "Ich bin Jahwe," 37–41. For the OT see Isa 41:14; 43:1; 44:2 (opening formula); 41:13 (closing formula).

95 SAA 9 2.5 iii 19; cf. SAA 9 1.1 i 4–5 [*Aššūr-aḫu-*]*iddina šar mātāti* [*lā t*]*apallaḫ,* "[Esarh]addon, king of the lands, [f]ear [not]!"; SAA 9 1.2 i 30: *šar māt Aššūr lā tapallaḫ,* "King of Assyria, fear not!"; SAA 9 1.4 ii 16: *la tapallaḫ Aššūr-aḫu-iddina,* "Fear not, Esarhaddon!"; SAA 9 2.2 i 15: [*lā tapa*]*llaḫ Aššūr-aḫu-iddina,* "[Fe]ar [not], Esarhaddon." Moreover, in SAA 9 1.8 v 21 the actual oracle to Esarhaddon begins with *šarru lā tapallaḫ,* "O King, fear not!"

96 SAA 9 7:1–2.

97 SAA 9 7 r. 11; cf. SAA 9 2.1 i 13: [*lā tapa*]*lliḫi ummi šarri,* "[Fe]ar [not], mother of the king!"; SAA 9 2.4 iii 17: *lā tapallaḫ ina ṣilli Aššūr-aḫu-iddina šar māt Aššūr,* "Fear not! Esarhaddon is in my protection."

98 See Parpola, *Assyrian Prophecies,* lxv; Weippert, "Ich bin Jahwe," 42–49. For the OT see Isa 41:13; 43:3 (close to *ʾal tîrāʾ*); cf. 42:6, 8; 43:11, 15; 44:24; 45:3, 5, 7, 18, 21; 48:17; 49:23, 26; cf. *ʾānōkî ʾēl,* "I am God," Isa 43:12; 45:3; 46:9.

99 SAA 9 1.1 i 18, 20–21; 1.4 ii 30; 1.6 iii 7: *anāku Issār ša Arbail,* "I am Ištar of Arbela"; cf. SAA 9 1.1 i 11–12; 1.2 i 36 (?): *Bēlet rabītu anāku anāku Issār ša Arbail,* "I am the great Lady, I am Ištar of Arbela"; 1.8 v 12: *anāku Bēlet Arbail,* "I am the Lady of Arbela." Only in SAA 9 1.4 does the self-identification involve other divine names: *anāku Bēl,* "I am Bel" (ii 17); *anāku Nabû,* "I am Nabû" (ii 38).

corpus, where the formulaic self-identification of this type is not attested,[100] the divine *anāku* always accompanies the exhortation "fear not,"[101] marking the divine discourse and leaving the addressee with no uncertainty about who the speaker is.

As a structural element framing the oracles, "fear not" is used in a genuinely formulaic way. Besides the semantic content of the phrase as such and its immediate surroundings, it connotes more: it functions as a signifier of a prophecy, encapsulating the whole substance of the following or preceding oracle. In fact, when used together with the divine self-predication and the name of the addressee (cf. above, SAA 9 7:1–2), "fear not" alone is enough to constitute a prophecy. Nevertheless, it always has a context from which it becomes a specific tone: encouragement before the enemy, promises for future support, or the special relationship of the king to the goddess.

2. The Neo-Assyrian prophecies have sometimes been classified as "war oracles" because of the frequent divine encouragements concerning the king's encounter with his enemies.[102] Inadequate though it is to maintain that Assyrian prophecy in its entirety would fall under this kind of a *Gattung* (not every Assyrian prophecy has to do with war), enemies are a recurring theme in the oracles, some of which are actually spoken in critical situations. This is especially true for the collection SAA 9 1, the oracles of which derive from the time when Esarhaddon was expatriated and at war against his brothers before his victory and enthronement.[103] The first — and most frequently quoted — prophecy of this collection serves as a prime example of "fear not" proclaimed in the midst of a battle:

> *[Aššūr-aḫu-]iddina šar mātāti [lā t]apallaḫ/[a]yyu šāru ša idibakkāni aqappušu lā aksupūni/ nakarūtēka kî šahšūri ša Simāni ina pān šēpēka ittangararrū/*
> *Bēlet rabītu anāku anāku Issār ša Arbail ša nakarūtēka ina pān šēpēka akkarrūni/ayyūte dibbīja ša aqqabakanni ina muḫḫi lā tazzizūni/*
> *anāku Issār ša Arbail nakarūtēka ukāṣa addanakka/anāku Issār ša Arbail ina pānātūka ina kutallīka allāka/*
> *lā tapallaḫ atta ina libbi muggi anāku ina libbi ū'a atabbi uššab*
>
> [Esarh]addon, king of the lands, fear [not]!/What is the wind that has attacked you, whose wings I have not broken?/Like ripe apples your enemies will roll before your feet./

100 Save SAA 9 3.3 ii 24–25: *lēmurū lūna''idūni akī Aššur bēl ilāni anākūni*, "Let them see it and praise me, for I am Aššur, lord of the gods!" and, provided that the restoration is correct, SAA 9 2.3 i 36–38: [*anāku B*]*ēlet Arbail* [*Aššūr-aḫu-iddina šar*] *māt Aššūr* [*lā tapallaḫ*], "[I am the L]ady of Arbela! [Esarhaddon, king] of Assyria, [fear not!]."
101 Cf. the oracles SAA 9 2.1; 2.2; 2.4; 2.5; SAA 9 4; SAA 9 7.
102 Cf. Stähli, *THAT* 1:773; Rowlett, *Joshua*, 116–19.
103 For the historical background, see Nissinen, *References to Prophecy*, 14–34.

I am the great Lady, I am Ištar of Arbela who will throw your enemies before your feet./
Have I spoken to you any words that you could not rely upon?/
I am Ištar of Arbela, I will flay your enemies and deliver them up to you./I am Ištar of Arbela, I go before you and behind you./
Fear not! You are paralyzed, but I, in the midst of wailing, will get up and sit down.[104]

The well-structured and highly stylistic interplay of "fear not" and the divine self-identification has a single focus: the divine intervention at the critical moment when Esarhaddon is "paralyzed," that is, unable to act (and not yet even a king!).[105] This makes the oracle, as well as other "fear not" oracles in SAA 9 1,[106] a full-fledged representative of the ideology of divine warfare: the "getting up" and "sitting down" seem to express the whole action of the goddess, who rises to the king's rescue, fights for him, and finally returns to her place. Even Naqia, Esarhaddon's mother, who did her best for her son (and against his brothers) during the war,[107] received a prophetic assurance that the Lady of warfare and battle will have the last word:

anāku Bēlet Arbail/ana ummi šarri kî taḫḫurīninni mā/ša imitti ša šumēli ina sūnīki tassakni/
mā īyû ṣīt libbīja ṣēru tussarpidi/
ūmâ šarru lā tapallaḫ/šarrūtu ikkû danānu ikkûma

I am the Lady of Arbela!/To the king's mother, since you implored me, saying:/"The one on the right and the other on the left you have placed in your lap./My own offspring you expelled to roam the steppe!"/
Now, king, fear not!/Yours is the kingdom, yours is the power![108]

The use of "fear not" in this prophecy deserves attention not only as a response to a prayer, for which see below, but also as the beginning of the actual oracle, which is addressed directly to Esarhaddon, though physically delivered to his mother, who received prophecies on behalf of her son during his absence (cf.

104 SAA 9 1.1 i 4–27.
105 Parpola, *Assyrian Prophecies*, 5, comments: "The king is here pictured as a baby crying violently (to the point of paralysis) in its distress, the goddess as mother rushing to help it."
106 Cf. SAA 9 1.2 i 30–32: *šar māt Aššūr lā tapallaḫ/nakru ša šar māt Aššūr ana ṭabaḫḫi addana*, "King of Assyria, fear not! The enemy of the king of Assyria I will lead to the slaughter"; SAA 9 1.6 iii 30–iv 4: *lā tapallaḫ šarru/aqtibak lā aslīk*[*a*]*/utakki*[*lka*] *lā ubāš*[*ka*]*/nāru ina tuqunni ušēbar*[*ka*], "Fear not, king! I have spoken to you, I have not let yo[u] down!/I have inspi[red you] with confidence, I have not caused [you] to come to shame!/I will lead [you] safely across the River."
107 For her see Nissinen, *References to Prophecy*, 22–24; S. C. Melville, *The Role of Naqia/Zakutu in Sargonid Politics* (SAAS 9; Helsinki: Neo-Assyrian Text Corpus Project, 1999).
108 SAA 9 1.8 v 12–23.

SAA 9 1.7; SAA 9 5). Later on, when Esarhaddon was ruling in Nineveh, she herself, in turn, was encouraged by the same words in prophecies addressed to her son; this indicates the importance of her political role as well as her close relationship to the prophets:

> *Aššūr-aḫu-iddina šar māt Aššūr/[nakarūtēka] usappak [ina šēpēya] ukabbas/[lā tapa]lliḫi ummi šarri*
>
> Esarhaddon, king of Assyria!/I will catch [your enemies] and trample them [under my foot]./[Fe]ar not, mother of the king![109]

3. The previous prophecy begins the collection SAA 9 2, which is composed of oracles from the beginning of Esarhaddon's rule. In this collection, too, "fear not" is repeated frequently, however, in an atmosphere different from the momentous tone of the SAA 9 1 prophecies. These oracles are not true "war oracles," since the war is over, and the oracles orient toward the future, assuring the divine support and protection:

> *[lā tapal]laḫ Aššūr-aḫu-iddina/[akī m]allāḫi damqi ina kāri ṭābi [eleppu uk]alla/akī ša pānīti [lū ina u]rkīti/ina batbattīka [asaḫḫu]r maṣṣartaka anaṣṣar*
>
> [Fe]ar not, Esarhaddon!/[Like] a skilled [p]ilot [I will s]teer [the ship] for a good harbor./[Let the f]uture be like the past!/[I will circl]e around you, I will stand guard for you.[110]

The enemies are now looked upon from the perspective of the safety of the king and his prosperous future, guaranteed by reconciliation of heaven and earth (SAA 9 2.3 ii 1–5, etc.). Because of the shift of perspective into the future, even the neighboring states are envisioned as potential adversaries rather than an actual menace:

> *atta lū qālāka Aššūr-aḫu-iddina/ṣīrāni Elamāya Mannāya abīar/Urarṭāya šiṭrīšu abarrim/igib ša Mugalli ubattaq/mannu ēdu mannu ḫablu/lā tapallaḫ ina ṣilli Aššūr-aḫu-iddina šar māt Aššūr*
>
> You, Esarhaddon, keep silent!/I will select the emissaries of the Elamite king and the Mannean king,/I will seal the messages of the Urartean king,/I will cut off the heel[111] of Mugallu.[112]/Who is now lonely, who is now wronged?/Fear not! Esarhaddon is in my protection.[113]

---

109 SAA 9 2.1 i 10–13; cf. SAA 9 2.6 iv 28, where the preserved [*l*]*ā tapalliḫi* is probably addressed to Naqia.

110 SAA 9 2.2 i 15–19.

111 I interpret the word in the same meaning as *eqbu*, "heel."

112 Mugallu was the king of Melid in Anatolia.

113 SAA 9 2.4 iii 12–17.

The "quietist" idea of the divine warfare thus is in force even when there is no actual military situation, and the change of perspective does not alter the fundamental ideology behind the "fear not" exhortation.

4. One of the central aspects of Begrich's theory of the priestly oracle was that the salvation oracle is spoken in response to the prayer of a person in distress.[114] Two such cases have indeed been discussed in this article. Both the inscription of Assurbanipal reporting his request for help in a military situation and the subsequent answer of Ištar, and the prophecy in response to the plea of Naqia, the queen mother,[115] not only explicitly mention that the prayers have been uttered but even quote their words.

Another well-known example is the Aramaic inscription of Zakkur, king of Hamath, who reports to have received a response from his patron deity Baʿalšamayim through prophetic intermediaries. After describing how he was besieged in the city of Hazrak by seventeen kings, he says:

> *w'š' ydy 'l bʿlš[my]m wyʿnny bʿlšmy[n/w ymll] bʿlšmym 'ly [b]yd ḥzyn wbyd ʿddn [wy'mr 'ly] bʿlšmym/'l tzḥl ky 'nh hm/[ktk w'nh 'q]m ʿmk/w'nh 'ḥṣlk mn kl [mlky' 'l zy] mḥ'w ʿlyk mṣr*
>
> I lifted my hands to Baʿalša[mayi]m, and Baʿalšamayim anwered me./Baʿalšamayim [spoke] to me [thr]ough seers and messengers[116] [and] Baʿalšamayim [said]:/"Fear not! I have made [you] king [and I will st]and by [you]./I will rescue you from all [these kings who] have laid a siege against you!"[117]

This reminds one not only of the previously quoted inscription of Assurbanipal, but also of Esarhaddon's report on his rise to power, where he, having heard about his rebelling brothers' evil deeds, claims to have prayed with raised hands to the great gods with the following response: *alik lā kalâta idāka nittallakma ninâra gārêka,* "Go ahead, do not hold back! We go by your side, we an-

114 Begrich, "Das priesterliche Heilsorakel," 82–85.

115 See, respectively, Novotny and Jeffers, *The Royal Inscriptions of Ashurbanipal*, 68–69 (Prism B v 16–48); SAA 9 1.8.

116 For the interpretation of the word *ʿddn,* see Ross, "Prophecy," 4–8.

117 *KAI* 202 A 11–15. For this text see also Ross, "Prophecy"; Zobel, "Das Gebet"; S. B. Parker, *Studies in Scripture and Inscriptions: Comparative Studies on Narratives in Northwest Semitic Inscriptions and the Hebrew Bible* (New York and Oxford: Oxford Univ. Press, 1997), 106–12; A. Lemaire, "Oracles, politique et littérature dans les royaumes araméens et transjordaniens (IXe–VIIIe s. av. n.è.)," in *Oracles et prophéties dans l'antiquité. Actes du Colloque de Strasbourg 15–17 Juin 1995* (ed. J.-G. Heintz; Université des sciences humaines de Strasbourg, Travaux du Centre de recherche sur le Proche-Orient et la Grèce antiques 15; Paris: De Boccard, 1997), 171–93, esp. 172–75.

nihilate your enemies."[118] This oracle of encouragement *(šīr takilti)* is probably the result of extispicy, and hence no prophecy, but the report echoes the prophecy SAA 9 3.3;[119] neither source employs the phrase "fear not," but the setting is essentially the same as in inscriptions of Zakkur and Assurbanipal. Furthermore, a comparable situation – Assurbanipal's war against Šamaš-šumu-ukin – is to be found behind the Dialogue of Assurbanipal and Nabû,[120] in which the king's prayers alternate with divine responses. Even *lā tapallaḫ* appears once, in the answer of Nabû mediated by a ghost or a dream god *(zaqīqu):*[121] *lā tapallaḫ Aššūr-bāni-apli ... pīya ammiu ša īābu iktanarrabka ina puḫur ilāni rabūti,* "Fear not, Assurbanipal! ... My pleasant mouth shall ever bless you in the assembly of the great gods."

These documents can be quoted in support of one essential aspect in Begrich's theory of the priestly oracle; as a matter of fact, they express the divine response to the prayer much more explicitly than the biblical lamentation psalms do.[122] However, the priestly component of the salvation oracle remains no less vague than in Begrich's argumentation. In Esarhaddon's inscription, the *šīr takilti* probably comes from a diviner; whether the *bārû* should be called "priest" is a matter of definition. In the Zakkur inscription, as well as in SAA 9 1.8, the oracle is clearly prophetic. Who, then, is imagined to mediate the divine responses in the Dialogue of Assurbanipal and Nabû? First, one should remember that the text is a poetic construction and need not to be understood as an exact report of any actual "dialogue between the king and the god." However, it is probable that Assurbanipal, in his distress during the Šamaš-šumu-ukin war, prayed to the goddess in her temple more than once, and was certainly also provided with divine words in response. The dialogue SAA 3 13 may constitute a poetic compilation reflecting such situations, and it is evident that the language used by the scribe is essentially the same that the same scribe used for prophetic words in SAA 9 9.[123]

5. In several cases the exhortation not to fear is accompanied with the reconciliation of Assyria and its king with gods – an idea unseparable from the spe-

---

118 Leichty, *The Royal Inscriptions of Esarhaddon*, 13 i 61–62.

119 See Nissinen, *References to Prophecy*, 24–28.

120 See Parpola, *Assyrian Prophecies*, lxxi.

121 SAA 3 13:24, 26; cf. the appearance of the dream goddess in *Ludlul bēl nēmeqi*.

122 Cf. Westermann, "Das Heilswort bei Deuterojesaja," 360–61, with a reference to SAA 3 13; and Zobel, "Das Gebet," 98, with regard to the Zakkur inscription.

123 See B. Pongratz-Leisten, *Herrschaftswissen in Mesopotamien: Formen der Kommunikation zwischen Gott und König im 2. und 1.Jahrtausend v.Chr.* (SAAS 10; Helsinki: Neo-Assyrian Text Corpus Protect, 1999), 75.

cial relationship of the king with Ištar/Mullissu. In the case of SAA 9 2.5, the reconciliation of the exiled gods of Babylon, much propagated by the prophets,[124] is presented as an analogy to, if not the prerequisite of, the stabilization of Assyria and Esarhaddon's rule:

> *Aššūr-aḫu-iddina lā tapallaḫ/māt Aššūr utaqqan/ilāni zenûti* [*is*]*si māt Aššūr ušal*[*l*]*am*
>
> Esarhaddon, fear not!/I will put Assyria in order,/I will reconcile the angry gods [wi]th Assyria.[125]

The divine speaker, even though not indicated, is doubtless Ištar, who enacts the reconciliation also in SAA 9 1.4, where the prophet(ess?) Bayâ acts as the mouthpiece of three different deities. In this oracle, which proclaims the legitimacy of the kingship of Esarhaddon from his very birth, Ištar assumes the role of the mediator between the king and the gods, all incorporated in Aššur.[126] By the same token, she assures Esarhaddon that she took him in her custody already when he was a child:

> *anāku Issār ša Arbail Aššūr issīka ussallim/ṣeḫerāka attaṣakka/lā tapallaḫ na''idanni*
>
> I am Ištar of Arbela. I have reconciled Aššūr with you./I already carried you when you were a baby./Fear not, praise me![127]

Both aspects, the stabilization of the country and the reconciliation with gods, arc combined in the letter of Aššur-ḫamatu'a, priest of the temple of Ištar in Arbela, to Assurbanipal:

> [*anāku*] *Bēl ētarba issi Mu*[*ll*]*issu assilim/Aššūr-bāni-apli šar māt Aššūr ša turabbīni* [*l*]*ā tapallaḫ/*[*anā*]*ku Bēl artēanki/Aššūr-bāni-apli ina māti ša kēnu/kēni šû adi mātīšu artēanki*

124 See M. Nissinen, "City is Lofty as Heaven: Arbela and Other Cities in Neo-Assyrian Prophecy," in "*Every City Shall Be Forsaken*": *Urbanism and prophecy in Ancient Israel and the Near East* (ed. L. L. Grabbe and R. D. Haak; JSOTSup 330; Sheffield: Sheffield Academic Press, 2001), 170–207, esp. 193–200 (= pp. 267–300 in this volume).

125 SAA 9 2–5 iii 19–20.

126 For Aššur as the totality ot gods, see S. Parpola, "Monotheism in Ancient Assyria," in *One God or Many? Concepts of Divinity in the Ancient World* (ed. B. N. Porter; Transactions of the Casco Bay Assyriological Institute 1; Casco Bay, Maine: Casco Bay Assyriological Institute, 2000) 165–209, esp. 168–73.

127 SAA 9 1.4 ii 30–33.

[I] am Bel, I have entered and made peace with Mullissu./Assurbanipal, king of Assyria, whom she raised: Fear not!/I am Bel, I have remitted Assurbanipal to you (fem.) in a country of truth. Him together with his country I have remitted to you.[128]

The letter rather atypically begins with an oracle, this time presented as the word of Bel, or Marduk, the supreme god of Babylonia who in this letter seems to take the position Aššur has in the previously quoted oracle; this may indicate that the "country of truth" is Babylonia. The role division between Bel, Mullissu, and Assurbanipal calls for attention. The triangle Bel-Mullissu-Assurbanipal fully corresponds here to Aššur-Ištar-Esarhaddon in SAA 9 1.4. Bel, presumably presented as the head of the divine council, is speaking to the king and to the goddess simultaneously. "Fear not" is addressed to the king; however, Bel reconciles with the goddess and has mercy on her, who stands there on behalf of the king and country. Hence the words *lā tapallaḫ* come to the king through the mediation of the goddess who "raised" him. The same idea can be found in the prophecy SAA 9 9 (where *lā tapallaḫ* is not attested), as well as in the Dialogue of Assurbanipal and Nabû (SAA 3 13), in which the phrase "fear not" is used in the context of Assurbanipal's struggle before the divine council, and followed by the idea of him as the child of Mullissu (queen of Nineveh).[129]

The special relationship of the king with the goddess finds multiple expressions in prophecies, and even the phrase "fear not" is repeatedly embedded in this context, as the following two examples demonstrate:

ša Mullissu ummašūni lā tapallaḫ
ša Bēlet Arbail tārīssūni lā tapallaḫ ...
atta lā tapallaḫ mūrī ša anāku urabbûni

You whose mother is Mullissu, fear not!
You whose nurse is the Lady of Arbela, fear not! ...
Fear not, you, my calf whom I rear.[130]

anāku abūka ummaka/birti agappīya urtabbīka nēmalka ammar/lā tapallaḫ Aššūr-aḫu-iddina/birti izirîya ammātēya ašakkanka/ina libbi ū'a nakarūti ša šarrīya aka[šša]d/māt Aššūr utaqqan šarr[ūtu ša] šamê utaqqa[n ...]

I am your father and mother./I brought you up between my wings, I will see how you prosper./Fear not, Esarhaddon!/I will place you between my arm and forearm./In the midst of

128 SAA 13 139:1–9.

129 See, respectively, SAA 3 13:24–26 (see the quotation above); SAA 3 13 r. 6–7: *ṣeḫru atta Aššūr-bāni-apli ša umašširūka ina muḫḫi šarrat Nīnua/lakû atta ša ašbāka ina burki šarrat Nīnua*, "You were a child, Assurbanipal, when I left you with the queen of Nineveh,/you were a baby, Assurbanipal, when you sat in the lap of the queen of Nineveh."

130 SAA 7 r. 6, 11 and SAA 9 2.5 iii 29–34.

distress, I will va[nqu]ish the enemies of my king./I will put Assyria in order, I will put the king[dom of] heaven in orde[r ...]

The position of Ištar/Mullissu as the one who puts both Assyria and the kingdom of heaven in order conflates with her role as the mother of the king and intercessor before the divine council. Moreover, the role of Mullissu as the spouse of Aššur makes her the principal intercessor on behalf of the king and humankind.[131] Her "fear not" to the king is based on the conviction that the divine council will decide in his favor. On the other hand, the position of the king as the child of the goddess makes him a partly divine figure, through whom the people participate in divine favors.[132] Hence, when the king himself says "fear not" to his subjects or vassals, as Assurbanipal does in the above-discussed letters, he does so with divine authority, passing down the very word spoken to himself by the gods.

6. The last example of the use of "fear not" as an element of prophetic language is the Late Babylonian ritual text from Hellenistic Uruk.[133] The text is a compilation of hymns, prayers, and ritual acts to be performed before Bel (Marduk) by *šešgallu*, the high priest of Uruk, on the occasion of the New Year Festival from the 2nd through the 5th of the month of Nisan (I). At a certain point of the ritual, the king enters the presence of Bel and, stripped of his royal insignia by the high priest, affirms his faithfulness in performing his duties.[134] The divine response follows after a lacuna of a few lines:

lā tapallaḫ [...] *ša Bēl iqṭabi* [...] *Bēl ikribka* [*ilteme* ...] *ušarbi bēlūtka* [...] *ušaqqa šarrūtka* [...]/*ina ūm eššēši epu*[*š* ...] *ina pīt bābi ubbib qāt*[*ka* ...] *urri u mūši lū* [...]/*ša Bābili ālšu* [...] *ša Esaggil bīss*[*u* ...] *ša mārē Bābili ṣāb kidin*[*nīšu* ...]/*Bēl ikarrabku* [... *an*]*a dāri*[*š*] *uḫallaq nakarku ušamqat zāmânku*/*enūma iqbû šarru kabāt appi ginûšu i*[*ppuš*]/*ḫaṭṭa kippata miṭṭa agâ ušeṣṣima ana šarri* [*inamdin*]/*lēt šarri imaḫḫaṣ enūma lēssu* [*imḫaṣ*]/*šumma dimātūšu illik Bēl sal*[*im*]/*šumma dimātūšu lā illakā Bēl ezzi*[*z*] *nakru itebbamma išakkan miqissu*

131 This was a central idea in rituals of divine love, in this case in the love ritual *(quršu)* of Mullissu; see M. Nissinen, "Akkadian Rituals and Poetry of Divine Love," in *Mythology and Mythologies* (ed. R. M. Whiting; Melammu Symposia 2; Helsinki: Neo-Assyrian Text Corpus Project, 2001) 93–136, esp. 95–97.

132 See Parpola, *Assyrian Prophecies*, xxxvi–xlvi; id., "Monotheism," 192–95.

133 F. Thureau-Dangin, *Rituels accadiens* (Paris: Ernest Leroux, 1921), 129–46; cf. Harner, "Salvation Oracle," 421; van der Toorn, "L'Oracle," 93; id., "Mesopotamian Prophecy Between Immanence and Transcendence: A Comparison of Old Babylonian and Neo-Assyrian Prophecy," in *Prophecy in Its Ancient Near Eastern Context: Mesopotamian, Biblical, and Arabian Perspectives* (ed. M. Nissinen; SBLSymS 13; Atlanta: SBL, 2000) 71–87, esp. 77.

134 Thureau-Dangin, *Rituels accadiens*, 144, ll. 415–27.

> "Fear not! [...] of Bel has said [...] Bel [has heard] your prayer [...] He has enlarged your rule [...] He will exalt your kingship [...]!/On the day of the *eššēšu* festival, do [...]! Upon the opening of the gate, purify [your] hands [...]! May [...] day and night! [You], whose city Babylon is, [...], whose temple Esaggil is, [...], whose [...] the people of Babylon, the privileged citizens are: Bel will bless you [... fo]r eve[r]! He will destroy your enemy, he will annihilate your adversary!"/When he [the high priest] has spoken this, the king p[erforms] his regular offering in a dignified manner./He (the high priest) takes the scepter, the ring, the divine weapon, and the crown and [gives] them to the king./He slaps the face of the king./If, when he [slaps] his face, his (the king's) tears flow, Bel is favor[able]; if his tears do not flow, Bel is angr[y], and an enemy will rise and cause his downhill.[135]

Although the oracle resembles the extant prophetic oracles known to us, it is not spoken by a prophet but by the high priest, the central figure of the ritual who here assumes a divinatory role. The oracle is not an independent, much less a spontaneous uttering, but an integral part of liturgy, which goes on with offerings of the king, to whom his royal insignia are returned, and with an act of divination, which is a kind of final test of Bel's acceptance of his rule. The oracle provides itself as an example of a reuse of prophecy[136] in a liturgy, in which the ideological heritage of Mesopotamian kingship is carried on under the rule of Seleucid kings.[137] The function of "fear not" remains unaltered: it begins an oracle of salvation, compressing its contents in a nutshell. In this case the oracle is indeed spoken by a priest, but clearly designed after a prophetic model.

"Fear Not" in the Hebrew Bible: Reinterpretation of the Royal Ideology

In Assyrian prophecy, as we have seen, "fear not" is more than an encouraging or soothing formula; it is a signifier of the position of the king as the point of convergence between heaven and earth. As such, this formula belongs firmly to the language of the Assyrian royal ideology as a sign of the divine acceptance of the king's rule. The inventory of the phrase "fear not" shows that, whenever part of the divine discourse, it is seldom uttered to anyone else than to kings and other royal figures in Mesopotamia. This holds good even for the few non-Mesopotamian documents, the letter of Šuppiluliuma and the inscription of Zakkur.

---

135 Ibid., 144–43, ll. 434–52.

136 It is called "frozen" prophecy by van der Toorn, "Mesopotamian Prophecy," 77.

137 One is tempted to ask whether the Seleucid kings actually attended the New Year rituals at Uruk at all, and if not, who represented them.

In Second Isaiah Israel or Jacob typically appears as the addressee of prophecies very similar to those spoken to kings of Assyria, which, as demonstrated by Weippert, present a reinterpretation of the traditional ancient Near Eastern royal oracle.[138] This makes it worthwhile to ask whether the royal focus of the ancient Near Eastern use of the phrase "fear not" could be compared to the state of affairs elsewhere in the Hebrew Bible. The private discourse notwithstanding, the phrase occurs either (1) in direct divine speech, (2) in divine words transmitted by an intermediary, or (3) in the mouth of an authority who speaks to the people as a collective.

1. When God says "fear not" directly to a person, the addressee is sometimes a prophet like Jeremiah (Jer 1:8), Ezekiel (Ezek 2:6, 3:9), or Daniel (Dan 10:12, 19), who is encouraged not to be anxious before the opponents of the divine word he is commissioned to speak.[139] Otherwise this happens either to patriarchal figures in the narratives of Genesis (Abraham: Gen 15:1; Hagar: 21:17; Isaac: 26:24; Jacob: 46:3), or to Moses (Num 21:34; Deut 3:2) and Joshua (Josh 8:1; 10:8; 11:6) in Deuteronomistic texts. In both cases, as Edgar W. Conrad has shown, the divine words bear close resemblance with regard to both form and content to the "fear not" oracles in Second Isaiah.[140] However, Second Isaiah hardly combines two existing genres employing the "fear not" formula as Conrad argues; it is more likely that both the patriarchal oracles and the war oracles, like Second Isaiah, owe their use to the ancient Near Eastern royal pattern, here applied to patriarchs as corporate personalities or to divinely authorized leaders like Moses and Joshua.

2. In several cases "fear not" is part of a divine word transmitted by an intermediary, sometimes an angel but mostly a prophet; this is in line with the assumption that the phrase is part and parcel of prophetic, rather than priestly, discourse. It is addressed either to the people (Isa 8:12; 10:24; Jer 42:11; Zech 8:13, 15; 2 Chr 20:15, 17)[141] or to its leaders (angel to Gideon: Judg 6:23; Isaiah to Ahaz: Isa 7:4; Isaiah to Hezekiah: 2 Kgs 19:6//Isa 37:6; Haggai to Zerubbabel: Hag 2:5). The only "ordinary" people to receive the divine "fear not" are the widow of Zarephath

---

138 Weippert, "Assyrische Prophetien," 108–11; id., "De herkomst," passim; id., "Ich bin Jahwe," 49–51. See Isa 41:10, 13, 14; 43:1, 5; 44:2; cf. Jer 30:10; 46:27–28, the close affiliation to Second Isaiah of which has been noticed (see W. McKane, *A Critical and Exegetical Commentary on Jeremiah*, vol. 2 [ICC; Edinburgh: T&T Clark, 1996], 762, 1137). In Isa 54:4 the addressee is Jerusalem; cf. Zeph 3:16.

139 This applies even to Elijah, to whom the divine word is spoken by an angel in 2 Kgs 1:15.

140 Conrad, "Fear Not," passim.

141 Here the Levite Jahaziel assumes the role of a prophet.

(1 Kgs 17:13) and the disciple of Elisha (2 Kgs 6:16); in both cases the word is spoken by prophetic figures, Elijah and Elisha, respectively.

3. In some cases leaders of people like Samuel (1 Sam 12:20), David (2 Sam 9:7; 1 Chr 22:13; 28:20), or Nehemiah (4:8 [Eng. 4:14]) say "fear not" to the people without explicitly presenting it as a divine word. Especially in the cases of Moses (Exod 14:13; 20:20; Deut 1:21, 29; 3:22; 7:18; 20:1; 31:6, 8) and Joshua (Num 14:9; Josh 10:25) it is evident, however, that they do it under divine authority, and the words they speak essentially correspond to oracles spoken directly by God or through intermediaries.[142] In the case of Moses, this is compatible with his role as a prophet and intermediator between God and the people.[143]

The short survey of the occurrences of "fear not" in the Hebrew Bible pays no attention to the relative chronology and the ideological affiliation of the texts, and hence is too brief to explain exhaustively the various aspects of this phrase in biblical environments. I hope, however, to have provided some support for the argument that *ʾal-tîrāʾ* and *lā tapallaḫ* are historically, ideologically, and institutionally related, and the formulaic use of the phrase is essentially rooted in the institutions of kingship and prophecy.

Conclusion

On the basis of the above analysis, I contend that "fear not" is a standard expression in the ancient Near East, with a clear emphasis on the Neo-Assyrian period and in an oracular, especially prophetic, context.

Like the prophetic *Botenformel*, "Thus says the Lord," which can be traced to a profane communication situation, the phrase "fear not" can be found in human and in divine speech alike in the ancient Near Eastern sources. In private discourse, which probably constitutes the primary context of its use, it cannot be called a formula with a clearly definable *Sitz im Leben*.

The institutionalized, formulaic use of "fear not" as an encouraging and soothing formula is dearly connected with divine speech, usually transmitted by prophets, predominantly to royal figures or leaders of the people. In Assyrian

142 In Deut 20:3 the delivering of the "fear not" oracle is interestingly delegated to a priest; the oracle itself, however, is a full-fledged representative of the "war oracle" to be found in the mouth of God or Moses elsewhere in Deuteronomy.

143 See L. Perlitt, "Mose als Prophet," *EvT* 31 (1971) 588–608 (repr. in id., *Deuteronomium-Studien* [FAT 8; Tübingen: Mohr Siebeck, 1994] 1–19); Timo Veijola, *Moses Erben: Studien zum Dekalog, zum Deuteronomismus und zum Schriftgelehrtentum* (BWANT 149; Stuttgart: Kohlhammer, 2000), 216–18.

prophecy the formula signifies the position of the king between heaven and earth: even in the mouth of the king, "fear not" is uttered by the supreme authority whose word is regarded equal to the divine word from the point of view of the addressee. In the Hebrew Bible, too, the use of "fear not" has a clear emphasis on the leaders of the people (patriarchs, Moses, Joshua, kings, etc.), or on the people as a collective, which is typical to the reinterpretation of the royal ideology in Second Isaiah. Both ancient Near Eastern and biblical sources hence point to the origin of the "fear not" formula in the institutions of kingship and prophecy.

The phrase "fear not" can be spoken in response to a prayer, but there are only a few ambiguous signs of priestly use of the phrase; hence Begrich's theory of the priestly oracle finds little support in the ancient Near Eastern sources, and also the allegedly indigenous origin of the biblical "fear not" oracles becomes improbable. On the other hand, and in support of the previous work of Gressmann and his followers, the ancient Near Eastern, especially prophetic, background of "fear not" is amply demonstrated.

The Exiled Gods of Babylon in Neo-Assyrian Prophecy

> Take to heart these words of mine from Arbela:
> The gods of Esaggil are languishing in an evil, chaotic wilderness.[1]

These words of Ištar, attributed to the prophet La-dagil-ili, were probably spoken in the temple of Ištar in the Assyrian city of Arbela in the very beginning of the reign of King Esarhaddon of Assyria, that is, in the year 681 or 680 BCE. They have been preserved to us on a clay tablet probably compiled shortly thereafter and containing six prophetic oracles (SAA 9 2).[2] These very prophecies may well be alluded to in Esarhaddon's inscription composed in early 679 BCE and related to his enthronement in the year 680 (Assur A), according to which prophetic oracles, in addition to dreams and speech omens, concerning the establishment of the foundation of Esarhaddon's throne were incessantly conveyed to him when he ascended the throne.[3] That the oracle collection was assembled from individual prophecies and preserved in the state archives of the Assyrian empire at Nineveh is an indication of the significance of the prophecies even the moment after they were uttered.

The central theme of both the inscription Assur A and the prophetic oracles compiled in SAA 9 2 is "the stabilization of the king's rule, the relenting of the gods and the restoration of the cosmic harmony."[4] Such a proclamation was urgently needed after the turmoil of the civil war that preceded Esarhaddon's rise to power, shaking the foundations of Assyrian kingship and reflected in the prophetic oracles proclaimed before his enthronement (SAA 9 1).[5] In addition, the collection of the prophetic oracles plays another melody that makes a counter-

1 SAA 9 2.3 ii 22–27; see S. Parpola, *Assyrian Prophecies* (SAA 9; Helsinki: Helsinki University Press, 1997), 16; translation from M. Nissinen, with contributions by C. L. Seow, R. K. Ritner, and H. C. Melchert, *Prophets and Prophecy in the Ancient Near East* (SBLWAW 41; Atlanta: 2nd ed.; Atlanta: SBL Press, 2019), no. 80.

2 The tablet probably dates to the year 679 BCE; see Parpola, *Assyrian Prophecies*, lxix.

3 E. Leichty, *The Royal Inscriptions of Esarhaddon, King of Assyria (680–669 BC)* (RINAP 4; Winona Lake, Ind.: Eisenbrauns, 2011), 121, 124 ii 12–26: "Prophetic oracles concerning the establishment of the foundation of my priestly throne until far-off days were conveyed to me incessantly and regularly" (translation from Nissinen, *Prophets and Prophecy in the Ancient Near East*, no. 98).

4 Parpola, *Assyrian Prophecies*, lxix.

5 For the historical background of the oracle collection SAA 9 1, see Parpola, *Assyrian Prophecies*, lxviii–lxix;: M. Nissinen, *References to Prophecy in Neo-Assyrian Sources* (SAAS 7; Helsinki: The Neo-Assyrian Text Corpus Project, 1998), 15–30.

DOI 10.1515/9783110466546-014

point to the *cantus firmus* of the stabilization of the throne: at least four of the six oracles (SAA 9 2.1, 2.3, 2.5 and 2.6) mention the city of Babylon, its main temple Esaggil, and other Babylonian gods in a most favorable tone.[6] The goddesses of Esaggil introduce themselves already in the first, introductory oracle of the collection,[7] and the last one is spoken in the name of Urkittu, that is, the manifestation of Ištar in the city of Uruk.[8] The gods of Esaggil are mentioned in the third oracle,[9] and the proclaimer of the fourth oracle is called Urkittu-šarrat, "Urkittu is Queen," even though she comes from the Assyrian city of Calah.[10] All this makes a Babylonia significant issue in the collection of prophecies, and this is hardly a coincidence.

According to the above quotation, the gods of Esaggil are "languishing in an evil, chaotic wilderness." This figurative expression refers to the historical fact that the gods were banished from the temple which was ruined a decade earlier by Sennacherib, the father and predecessor of Esarhaddon, who, as is well known, conquered and destroyed the whole city in the year 689.[11]

The emphatic concern for Babylon and its gods is eye-catching in prophecies concerning the establishment of the rule of the king of Assyria. Why did the As-

---

6 Cf. M. Nissinen, "City as Lofty as Heaven: Arbela and Other Cities in Neo-Assyrian Prophecy," in *"Every City Shall Be Forsaken": Urbanism and Prophecy in Ancient Israel and the Near East* (ed. L. L. Grabbe and R. B. Haak; JSOTSup 330; Sheffield: Sheffield Academic Press, 2001) 172–209, (195–201)) (= pp. 267–300 in this volume).

7 SAA 9 2.1 i 8–9 (Parpola, *Assyrian Prophecies*, 14): *a-ni-nu* ᵈIŠTAR.MEŠ [*x x x x i*]*na* É.SAG.ÍL "We are the goddesses [… … i]n Esaggil."

8 SAA 9 2.6 iv 8 (Parpola, *Assyrian Prophecies*, 18): [*a-na-ku* ᵈ*ur-k*]*i-tú na-id-a-ni* "[I am Urk]ittu, praise me!"

9 SAA 9 2.3 ii 24 (Parpola, *Assyrian Prophecies*, 16): DINGIR.MEŠ *ša* É.SAG.ÍL *ina* EDIN.ḪUL *bal-li* "The gods of Esaggil are languishing in an evil, chaotic wilderness."

10 SAA 9 2.4 iii 18 (Parpola, *Assyrian Prophecies*, 17): TA* *pi-i* MÍ.*ur-kit-tu—šar-rat* URU.*kal-hi.tú* "From the mouth of the woman Urkittu-šarrat from Calah."

11 For the sources, see E. Frahm, *Einleitung in die Sanherib-Inschriften* (AfO Beiheft 26; Wien, Institut für Orientalistik, 1997), T 122, pp. 151–54 (the Bawian inscription; cf. D. D. Luckenbill, *The Annals of Sennacherib* [OIP 2; Chicago, Ill.: University of Chicago Press, 1924], 78–85); cf. T 18, pp. 106–7; T 139, pp. 173–74 (the Bit Akiti inscription = Luckenbill, *Annals of Sennacherib*, 135–39). For Sennacherib's destruction of Babylon, see, e.g., L. D. Levine, "Sennacherib's Southern Front: 704–689 B.C.," *JCS* 34 (1982) 28–69, esp. 50–51, 53–55; J. A. Brinkman, *Prelude to Empire: Babylonian Society and Politics, 747–626 B.C.* (Occasional Publications of the Babylonian Fund 7; Philadelphia: Babylonian Fund, University Museum, 1984), 67–70; H. D. Galter, "Die Zerstörung Babylons durch Sanherib," in *Studia Orientalia memoriae Jussi Aro dedicata* (ed. H. Halén; StOr 55/5; Helsinki: Finnish Oriental Society,1984) 161–73; G. Frame, *Babylonia 689–627 B.C.: A Political History* (Istanbul: Nederlands Historisch-Archaeologisch Instituut te Istanbul, 1992), 52–63; S. W. Holloway, *Aššur is King! Aššur is King! Religion in the Exercise of Power in the Neo-Assyrian Empire* (CHANE 10; Leiden: Brill, 2002), 354–55.

syrian prophets from Arbela, Assur, and Calah make the case of the Babylonian gods their own, demanding their wellbeing as mouthpieces of the Ištars of Arbela and Nineveh,[12] or even speaking *as* goddesses of Esaggil?[13] With regard to pertinent historical data and other textual material, this question is not difficult to answer.

"The Evil, Chaotic Wilderness"

The story of the exile of the Babylonian gods begins a few years before Sennacherib's destruction of Babylon in 689. The sources[14] indicate that when Sennacherib took action against the tribe of Bit-Yakin and its Elamite supporters in the year 694, he seized the gods of Bit-Yakin from the deported tribesmen.[15] The same year, the god of the city of Der called Anu-rabû (or Ištaran) was deported to Assyria.[16] In 693, Sennacherib plundered the gods of the cities of Uruk and Larsa.[17] The later correspondence indicates that six statues of Babylonian gods had been brought to Assyria between the years 694 and 689; these may include the above-mentioned gods of the Bit-Yakinites.[18]

The plundering of the gods of Babylonian cities and tribes was an unambiguous sign of humiliation and a demonstration of the authority of King Sennacherib in Babylonia. The temples of the city of Babylon still seem to have been provided for by Sennacherib in the late 690's,[19] however, this was but a

---

12 Cf. SAA 9 2.4 ii 30 (Parpola, *Assyrian Prophecies*, 16): *a-bat* ^{d}15 *šá* URU.*arba-ìl a-bat šarra-ti* ^{d}NIN.LÍL "The word of Ištar of Arbela, the word of Queen Mullissu"; note that Mullissu is equalled to Ištar of Nineveh, and the speaker of the oracle is a prophetess from Calah.

13 SAA 9 2.1 i 8–9; cf. above, note 7.

14 See especially Holloway, *Aššur is King!*, 138–39, 353–54.

15 Frahm, *Einleitung in die Sanherib-Inschriften*, T 16, pp. 102–5 ("Taylor Prism"; cf. Luckenbill, *Annals of Sennacherib*, 23–47), T 25–27, pp. 113–16 (the "Smith Bulls"; cf. Luckenbill, *Annals of Sennacherib*, 76–77, 117–24); cf. H. D. Galter, L. D. Levine and J. E. Reade, "The Colossi of Sennacherib's Palace and Their Inscriptions," *ARRIM* 4 (1986) 28–30.

16 Leichty, *The Royal Inscriptions of Esarhaddon*, 108:94; A. K. Grayson, *Assyrian and Babylonian Chronicles* (TCS 5; Locust Valley, N.Y.: Augustin, 1975), 128:1; cf. Brinkman, *Prelude to Empire*, 69 n. 329.

17 Frahm, *Einleitung in die Sanherib-Inschriften*, T 64, pp. 137–38 (cf. Luckenbill, *Annals of Sennacherib*, 153–53); Grayson, *Assyrian and Babylonian Chronicles*, 78–79 ii 48–iii 3; cf. Brinkman, *Prelude to Empire*, 62 n. 299; Frame, *Babylonia*, 76.

18 SAA 13 190; cf. S. Cole and P. Machinist, *Letters from Priests to the Kings Esarhaddon and Assurbanipal* (SAA 13; Helsinki: Helsinki University Press, 1999), xii.

19 An inscription of Sennacherib can be found on paving stones from Marduk's processional road leading to Esaggil predating 689 BCE; cf. Frahm, *Einleitung in die Sanherib-Inschriften*,

prelude to the destruction of Babylon in the year 689, of which Sennacherib gives a terrifying account in his Bawian inscription.[20] In addition to a graphic and detailed description of the plundering and devastation of the city, he tells how "his people" (rather than he himself) seized and smashed the gods who dwelled there; the smashing of the gods is mentioned even in the Bit Akiti inscription.[21] On the other hand, the gods Adad and Šala of the Assyrian city of Ekallate were returned to their original place; these statues had allegedly been deported to Babylon 418 years earlier by the Babylonian king Marduk-nadin-aḫḫe.[22]

Sennacherib's account of the destruction of Babylon is exaggerated in many respects; nevertheless, while many details remain suspicious, a serious destruction of the city can be regarded as a historical fact,[23] and the same can be said of the exile of the Babylonian gods. As the prophetic oracles alone indicate, not all the gods of Babylon were smashed but, rather, plundered and brought to Assyria. The first and foremost among them was Marduk, the supreme god of Babylon and the principal deity of the Esaggil temple, whose statue likewise ended up in Assyria.[24] The expatriation of Marduk is not reported by Sennacherib, but there is ample evidence of Marduk's sojourn in the Assyrian capital; for instance, the chronicles report that Bel (that is, Marduk) stayed twenty years in Assur, therefore the *akītu* festival could not take place in Babylon.[25]

As much as the destruction of Babylon was a ruthless military countermeasure to the offenses of the rebelling Babylonians against the Assyrian imperial authority, in the written records it is presented as a symbolic action manifesting the

---

T 167, pp. 191–92 = RIMB B.6.23.1 (G. Frame, *Rulers of Babylonia from the Second Dynasty of Isin to the End of Assyrian Domination (1157–612 BC)* [RIMB 2; Toronto: University of Toronto Press, 1995], 154). Furthermore, Sennacherib claims to have given gifts to Bel and Zarpanitu, the main divine couple of Esaggil, in 694 BCE; cf. Frahm, ibid., T. 174:10–11, p. 207. See Holloway, *Aššur is King!*, 242, 310, 357.

20 See n. 11 and cf. G. W. Vera Chamaza, *Die Omnipotenz Aššurs: Entwicklungen in der Aššur-Theologie unter der Sargoniden Sargon II, Sanherib und Asarhaddon* (AOAT 295; Münster: Ugarit-Verlag, 2002), 314–16 (no. 75).

21 Luckenbill, *Annals of Sennacherib*, 137:37; cf. Galter, "Die Zerstörung Babylons durch Sanherib," 167–70; Vera Chamaza, *Die Omnipotenz Aššurs*, 313–14 (no. 74); Holloway, *Aššur is King!*, 356.

22 Luckenbill, *Annals of Sennacherib*, 83:48–50; Vera Chamaza, *Die Omnipotenz Aššurs*, 315; cf. Brinkman, *Prelude to Empire*, 67 n. 317; Holloway, *Aššur is King!*, 149.

23 For discussion of the extent of the damage, see B. N. Porter, *Images, Power, and Politics: Figurative Aspects of Esarhaddon's Babylonian Policy* (Philadelphia: American Philosophical Society, 1993), 46–50; Frame, *Babylonia*, 55–56.

24 See Vera Chamaza, *Die Omnipotenz Aššurs*, 95–99, who convincingly argues that the statue of Marduk was not destroyed but brought to Assyria.

25 Grayson, *Assyrian and Babylonian Chronicles*, 127:32; 131:1–4.

supremacy of Assyria. The story of the eradication of the Babylonian capital is mirrored by Sennacherib's account of the construction of the Assyrian capital, Nineveh,[26] and the same function is fulfilled by piling up the dust of Babylon in the *akītu* house of Dilmun near the city of Assur.[27] This symbolism reflects a reversal of the cosmic order: the obliteration of the temples of Babylon made it impossible to celebrate the New Year's *akītu* festival in Babylon, hence it was now celebrated in Assyria—on top of the dust of the destroyed city. In the words of Steven Holloway, "the reduction of Babylon to chaotic mud is evocative of the political theology of *Enūma eliš*, thereby transferring the locus of the New Year's celebration from the realm of Ti'amat to victorious Assur."[28]

"Let Your Greeting of Peace Be Pronounced to Them"

While the political and cosmic reversal brought about by Sennacherib was certainly an unambiguous demonstration of political and ideological supremacy of Assyria over Babylonia, it was not without political, economical, and ideological problems. Assyria could not afford to keep Babylonia as a desolated, hostile backyard. Apart from problems caused by the ruined economy and chaotic administration, the religious and ideological basis of the whole procedure did not remain unquestioned; obviously, Sennacherib's demonstration of power went too far, and it was the task of Esarhaddon, his son and successor, to make reparations for his father's sins.

As a matter of fact, there are a few signs of the restoration of local cults in Babylonia already in Sennacherib's last years, first and foremost the return of the gods plundered from Uruk in 693 BCE to their own city in 681.[29] Moreover, in a letter addressed to Esarhaddon, an unknown person from Uruk refers to himself and his brothers as having been "shaven," that is, consecrated, by Sennacherib, probably to serve Eanna, the main temple of Uruk.[30] However, it was only Esar-

---

26 See Galter, "Die Zerstörung Babylons durch Sanherib," 168–69.

27 Thus according to the Bit Akiti inscription (Luckenbill, *Annals of Sennacherib*, 137–38:38–47; Vera Chamaza, *Die Omnipotenz Aššurs*, 313); see Holloway, *Aššur is King!*, 356.

28 Ibid.

29 Grayson, *Assyrian and Babylonian Chronicles*, 81 iii 29; cf. Brinkman, *Prelude to Empire*, 62 n. 299, 70 n. 334; Frame, *Babylonia*, 59–60; Holloway, *Aššur is King!*, 278, 357.

30 SAA 18 82:18–20 (F. Reynolds, *The Babylonian Correspondence of Esarhaddon and Letters to Assurbanipal and Sin-šarru-iškun from Northern and Central Babylonia* [SAA 18; Helsinki: Helsin-

haddon who attempted programmatically a full-scale restoration of Babylon and its temples, to which he had been urged already before his accession. One of his trusted astrologers, the Babylonian Bel-ušezib, claims to have told him the "omen of kingship" when Esarhaddon as crown prince was sent away from Nineveh because of his brothers' rebellion.[31] The meaning of the omen had been the following: "Esarhaddon will restore Babylon (and) reestablish Esaggil."[32] Another early voice raised for the gods of Babylon is the prophecy of La-dagil-ili from his first regnal year worth quoting here again:[33]

> Take to heart these words of mine from Arbela:
> The gods of Esaggil are languishing in an evil, chaotic wilderness.
> Let two burnt offerings be sent before them at once;
> Let your greeting of peace be pronounced to them.

Esarhaddon indeed took these words to heart: In the light of the written records, the rebuilding of Babylon and the repatriation of its gods were among his major concerns. The repeated claims of Esarhaddon to have repaired various Babylonian temples from the very beginning of his reign are grandiloquent enough to be characterized as "ideologically revealing but historical nonsense."[34] Nevertheless, he seemed to have made a serious effort to take care of the exiled gods of Babylonia, to rebuild their temples[35] and, when possible, to repatriate them.[36] According to Esarhaddon's own account, this could only happen after receiving the "firm positive answer" (*annu kēnu*) of the gods, that is, an "oracle of encouragement" (*šîr tikilti*) as the result of extispicy, or another kind of divine message, including prophecy.[37] This may indicate that the prophecies concerning

---

ki University Press, 2003], 64). Holloway, *Aššur is King!*, 358, identifies the author with Aḫḫe-šaya, the priest of Eanna and commandant of Uruk.

31 SAA 10 109 (S. Parpola, *Letters from Assyrian and Babylonian Scholars* [SAA 10; Helsinki: Helsinki University Press, 1993], 86–88); for this letter, see Nissinen, *References to Prophecy*, 89–95.

32 SAA 10 109: 13–15 (Parpola, *Letters from Assyrian and Babylonian Scholars*, 87).

33 SAA 9 2.3 ii 22–27 (Parpola, *Assyrian Prophecies*, 16).

34 Holloway, *Aššur is King!*, 361.

35 For Esarhaddon's building projects in Babylonia, see Porter, *Images, Power, and Politics*, 41–66.

36 For the case of Marduk, see Porter, ibid., 137–48.

37 Cf. Leichty, *The Royal Inscriptions of Esarhaddon*, 107: 72–79; Vera Chamaza, *Die Omnipotenz Aššurs*, 480 (no. 208): "Before the judgment of Šamaš and Adad I prostrated myself with reverence. Upon their firm decision I commissioned haruspices (to inquire) about entering the *bīt mummi*. I performed an extispicy concerning Assur, Babylon and Nineveh, as well as the masters who should perform the task and get to know the secret lore. I shared the task (between the ha-

Babylon were not just spontaneous utterances of random pro-Babylonian prophets but solicited by the king, who from the very beginning assumed the cultic patronage of Babylonia as an important constituent of his royal image.

The inscriptions of Esarhaddon—the AsBbE inscription in particular—sometimes present his good intentions as accomplished projects,[38] but it becomes evident from the royal correspondence that many restoration works were actually going on in different parts of Babylonia during his reign, for example, in Uruk, Nippur, Borsippa, Der, Dur-Šarruken, and Cutha, as well as in Akkad, where the age-old cult was reestablished when the gods of Akkad were returned from their exile in Elam in the year 674.[39] The biggest effort, of course, was the rebuilding of the city of Babylon and its temples, including the administrative organization of Esaggil which seems to have been established even before the temple was restored. To all appearances, the restoration works started already in the year 680 and were continued throughout Esarhaddon's reign.[40] The correspondence of Esarhaddon (especially the letters SAA 13 161–185) yields a lot of information on details of these restoration works and helps to evaluate the often idealistic picture given by the inscriptions.

By the time of the proclamation of the prophecy of La-dagil-ili, the gods of Esaggil were still in Assyria, hence the divine word proclaimed by the prophet is to be read as a strong plea for their official recognition and veneration while still sojourning in the "evil, chaotic wilderness." This included the restoration of the statues which were probably in a state of dereliction after their removal from Babylonian cities. The Assyrian records do not provide us with any information of whether offerings were brought to the gods of Esaggil, but, according to Esarhaddon's own account, their statues were "properly born" (*kēniš immaldūma*), that is, restored in the worship (*bīt mummu*[41]) of Ešarra, the main temple of

ruspices) one by one. The oracles were unanimous and (the gods) gave me a firm positive answer (*annu kēnu*). In Assur, the city of the government, the residence of the father of the gods of Assur, they told me to enter the *bīt mummi* and determined the names of the masters who should perform the task. Upon oracle(s) of encouragement and well-being (*šīr tikilti šalmūte*) they ordered the performing of this task, saying: 'Bring quickly the ... of the storehouse, do not give up and do not incline your ear to anything else!' I trusted in their firm positive and unchanging answer (*annāšun kēnu lā mušpēlu*) and my heart was confident."

38 Leichty, *The Royal Inscriptions of Esarhaddon*, 136–137: 33–49; cf. Porter, *Images, Power, and Politics*, 145.

39 See the table in Holloway, *Aššur is King!*, 243–47 (Table 5).

40 See Vera Chamaza, *Die Omnipotenz Aššurs*, 178–85.

41 For *bīt mummi*, see A. Berlejung, *Die Theologie der Bilder: Herstellung und Einweihung von Kultbildern in Mesopotamien und die alttestamentliche Bilderpolemik* (OBO 162; Freiburg, Schweiz: Universitätsverlag and Göttingen: Vandenhoeck & Ruprecht, 1998), 89–93.

the city of Assur.[42] The prophetic word, as we can see, was not proclaimed in vain.

"I Will Reconcile the Angry Gods with Assyria"

As long as the gods of Esaggil were exiled, there was an imbalance between cosmic powers, and this threatened the security of Assyria and its king, hence the following prophecy to Esarhaddon:

> Esarhaddon fear not! I will protect Assyria, I will reconcile the angry gods with Assyria.[43]

According to this prophecy, the anger of these gods constituted a threat to Assyria. As usual, the "fear not" formula introduces a promise for the king:[44] Ištar presents herself as the divine patroness of the country, placing herself between Assyria and the "angry gods" and promising to bring about reconciliation. These lines are excerpted from the beginning of the oracle of Sinqiša-amur,[45] the preserved part of which neither thematizes issues related to Babylonia nor mentions Babylonian gods directly; however, there is no doubt that the "angry gods" who need to be reconciled with Assyria should be identified with the exiled gods of Babylon or, more precisely, those of the Esaggil temple.[46]

The divine anger is often connected with the absence of gods from their temples. In Neo-Assyrian and Neo-Babylonian documents there are many instances of temples that had been abandoned by their patron deities; for instance, the temple of Kidmuri in Calah and the temple of Eanna in Uruk were both abandoned by the local manifestation of Ištar who had left her temple in anger.[47]

---

42 Leichty, *The Royal Inscriptions of Esarhaddon*, 108: 87; Vera Chamaza, *Die Omnipotenz Aššurs*, 480. That the statues were "properly born" rather refers to their restoration than making new statues in replacement of earlier destroyed ones; cf. Vera Chamaza, ibid., 217: "im Grunde genommen haben wir es nicht mit der Konsekration einer neuerschaffenen Marduk-Statue zu tun, sondern mit einer 'Wiedereinweihung' der von Sanherib entweihten Marduk-Statue. Es ist also anzunehmen, daß diese Ritual nur zur Überwindung jener Profanierung dient, damit die heiligen Götterstatuen wieder kultfähig werden."
43 SAA 9 2.5 iii 19–20 (Parpola, *Assyrian Prophecies*, 17).
44 Cf. M. Nissinen, "Fear Not: A Study on an Ancient Near Eastern Phrase," in *The Changing Face of Form Criticism for the Twenty-First Century* (ed. M. A. Sweeney and E. Ben Zvi; Grand Rapids, Mich.: Eerdmans, 2003), 122–61, (148–57) (= pp. 195–232 in this volume).
45 For the identification of the prophet, see Parpola, *Assyrian Prophecies*, lii.
46 As I have argued earlier in Nissinen, "City as Lofty as Heaven," 198–99.
47 Cf. Nissinen, *References to Prophecy*, 37–42.

In the Babylon inscription of Esarhaddon, it is the anger of Marduk that caused the city of Babylon to be destroyed, the cosmic "balance" (lit. "controversy," *mithurtu*) to be shaken, the people to flee the city, and the gods to leave their sanctuaries.[48] The destruction of the city and the desolation of the temples finds a theological explanation: the devastation is caused by the voluntary and infuriated alienation of the god from her/his people.

However, the divine alienation was not the last word. All texts mentioned above, in which the divine alienation plays a role, report the rebuilding of the temples and reinstallation of their cults, hence the divine alienation is balanced by the divine reconciliation, which allows the gods to return to their temples. The divine alienation–divine reconciliation pattern is well known, not only from Mesopotamia, but also from the Hebrew Bible, the book of Ezekiel in particular.[49] This pattern is also manifest in Esarhaddon's Babylon inscription[50] which should be read as a post-event attempt to understand and interpret the past catastrophy; as such, it can be understood as a kind of tool for surviving the posttraumatic stress reaction caused by the catastrophy.

A similar therapeutic need may have prompted the "Sin of Sargon" text (SAA 3 33), which is disguised as Sennacherib's last will, urging Esarhaddon to make a statue of Marduk as a sign of the reconciliation of the Babylonian gods with Assyrian gods.[51] The disparagement of Marduk is in this text presented as a sin, allegedly caused by Sargon II, but actually referring to Sennacherib's brutal action against Babylon. This sin could be reconciled by the rehabilitation of Marduk, which in practical terms meant the restoration of the statue of the god and its repatriation.

Reconciliation, therefore, was not a purely theological idea, but had an important material aspect manifest in the Assyrian-Babylonian cultic geography and choreography; statues of gods, temples and their worship were an indispensable sign of the restored equilibrium between heaven and earth. Even the pro-

48 Leichty, *The Royal Inscriptions of Esarhaddon*, 245:10.

49 See D. Bodi, *The Book of Ezekiel and the Poem of Erra* (OBO 104; Fribourg: Universitätsverlag and Göttingen: Vandenhoeck & Ruprecht, 1991), 191–218; D. I. Block, "Divine Abandonment: Ezekiel's Adaptation of an ancient Near Eastern Motif," in *Perspectives on Ezekiel: Theology and Anthropology* (ed. M. S. Odell and J. T. Strong; SBLSymS 9; Atlanta: Society of Biblical Literature, 2000) 15–42.

50 See J. A. Brinkman, "Through a Glass Darkly: Esarhaddon's Retrospects on the Downfall of Babylon," *JAOS* 103 (1983) 35–42, esp. 40–42.

51 For this text, see H. Tadmor, B. Landsberger, and S. Parpola, "The Sin of Sargon and Sennacherib's Last Will," *SAAB* 3 (1989) 3–52.

phetic proclamation from early on had simultaneously a practical and ideological focus.

"I Have Entered and Made Peace with Mullissu"

Esarhaddon's reparative policy included, naturally, also the repatriation of the statues of the exiled gods of Babylonian sanctuaries. The repatriation of Marduk in particular was understood as a sacred duty. Following the restoration of the temple of Esaggil, the return of Marduk to his temple would reestablish the cosmic order and thus expiate the crime committed by Sennacherib. Esarhaddon made an unsuccessful attempt to bring the statue of Marduk back to Babylon in the year 669, but his son Assurbanipal was successful in accomplishing its repatriation a year later, in the month of Iyyar (II), 668.[52] The oracle queries from the month of Nisan (I) of this year indicate that even his brother, Šamaš-šumu-ukin, the crown prince of Babylonia, was involved in this project: "I ask you, Šamaš, great lord, whether Šamaš-šumu-ukin, son of Esarhaddon, king of Assyria, should within this year seize the hand of the great lord, [Marduk, i]n the Inner City, and lead Bel (to Babylon)."[53] This is natural, because Šamaš-šumu-ukin had been appointed the crown prince of Babylonia and, after his father's death, was considered the ruler of Babylonia. The actual power, however, was in Assurbanipal's hands.

Marduk's return is reflected in a letter sent to Assurbanipal soon after it happened:[54]

> I [am] the Lord. I have entered (and) made peace with Mu[ll]issu.
> Assurbanipal, king of Assyria, whom she raised: Fear not!
> [I] am the Lord. I have remitted Assurbanipal to you in a country of truth.
> Him together with his country, I have remitted to you.
> I left your city in peace and safety. Mercy (and) compassion
> [......] *(Break)*

"The Lord" speaking in this text, which to all appearances is a written version of a prophetic oracle uttered in the the temple of Ištar at Arbela and written down by the priest Aššur-ḫamatu'a, is none else than Marduk himself who has appa-

52 For details, see Vera Chamaza, *Die Omnipotenz Aššurs*, 210–27.

53 SAA 4 262 r. 6–8 (I. Starr, *Queries to the Sunged: Divination and Politics in Sargonid Assyria* [SAA 4; Helsinki: Helsinki University Press, 1990], 236).

54 SAA 13 139 (Cole and Machinist, *Letters from Priests to the Kings Esarhaddon and Assurbanipal*, 111).

rently entered his proper temple and now proclaims the reconciliation through the mouth of an anonymous prophet.[55] It is noteworthy that Marduk, while addressing Assurbanipal, is speaking first and foremost to Mullissu, that is, Ištar of Nineveh. This underlines the position of Ištar between the king and Marduk (or rather, the divine council of Esaggil) interceding on behalf of him and proclaiming the divine word to him. The prophets of Arbela were primarily prophets of Ištar; whether Ištar of Arbela or Mullissu is not an issue, since these two manifestations of the goddess tend to merge together in Assyrian prophecies.

The prophecy recorded in the letter of Aššur-ḫamatu'a reads like the fulfillment of the promise uttered in the earlier oracle quoted above. Marduk, and with him probably even the rest of the "angry gods" of Babylonia are now reconciled with Assyria. Marduk has made peace with Mullissu, and, as an act of mercy, remitted Assurbanipal to the godddess, his divine mother. This indicates a state of peace between Babylonia and Assyria as well as the restoration of the balance between heavenly powers.[56] On the mundane level, from the point of view of the Babylonians, "one of the most serious impediments to cooperation with the Assyrians was at last removed."[57]

When Esaggil was rebuilt and Marduk had returned to his temple, it was possible again to celebrate the *akītu* festival in its proper place. As an epilogue of Marduk's exile in Assyria, the banishment of Marduk is commemorated in a ritual commentary, the so-called "Marduk Ordeal" (SAA 3 34/35), probably to be associated with the first *akītu* in Esaggil after the return of the statue of Marduk in Babylon.[58] This text strongly commiserates with Marduk's tribulations when describing how he is beaten and sent to prison, a metaphor for his exile in Assyria. Even a prophet plays a role in this ritual as a "bringer of news" (*mupassiru*), who tells the Lady of Babylon (that is, Marduk's wife Zarpanitu) that his husband is being taken to captivity. This text has no happy ending, but it was not necessary either, since everybody knew that Marduk had returned home.

The exile of the Babylonian gods was the outcome of ruthless military action against Babylonia, the consequences of which became a heavy economic and

---

55 For this letter, see M. Nissinen and S. Parpola, "Marduk's Return and Reconciliation in a Prophetic Letter from Arbela," in *Verbum et calamus: Semitic and Related Studies in Honour of the Sixtieth Birthday of Professor Tapani Harviainen* (ed. H. Juusola, J. Laulainen, and H. Palva; StOr 99; Helsinki: Finnish Oriental Society, 2004) 199–219 (= pp. 245–65 in this volume).

56 See Nissinen and Parpola, "Marduk's Return and Reconciliation," 214–16.

57 Porter, *Images, Power, and Politics*, 148.

58 Thus T. Frymer-Kensky, "The Tribulations of Marduk: The So-called 'Marduk Ordeal Text,'" *JAOS* 103 (1983) 131–41 (140); cf. Frame, *Babylonia*, 58–59.

political burden to be carried by the Assyrians, whose victory turned out to be a Pyrrhic one. However, in the documents known to us, Sennacherib is never directly blamed for his policy, even though criticism against it is only slightly disguised in the "Sin of Sargon" text. Instead, the contemporary interpretation of the situation was outspokenly theological; it was not seen as the result of a political failure, rather, the exile of the gods was a voluntary action of the gods, motivated by divine anger against the people's wrong behavior. It was Marduk himself who took action against impious people, the punishment was upon the people, not upon the gods. Therefore, the corrective political action taken by Esarhaddon had to be religiously motivated as well.

While Sennacherib's destruction of Babylon and deportation of the gods was a symbolic act, so was the restoration of Babylonian temples and the repatriation of their gods; Sennacherib demonstrated the supremacy of Assyria and its gods–his son, the restitution of the cosmic order. Prophecy, like divination in general, was an important institution in reminding the king of the divine foundation of his kingship as well as of the responsibilities it entails. Together with scholars and temple officials, the prophets (or at least some of them) from Arbela, Assur, and Calah seem to have made the case of Babylonia their own. This kind of ideological interurbanism was more than merely an altruistic service to the suffering southern neighbor. It can be seen as an effort to overcome the rivalry between Assyria and Babylonia in favor of a common and uniform state ideology and single national image. At any rate, it indicates how seriously the Babylonian problem was taken and how important the reconciliation was considered. Exile was not just a matter of power politics. It was a matter of heaven and earth, its dimensions were both material and spiritual.

Marduk's Return and Reconciliation in a Prophetic Letter from Arbela (with Simo Parpola)

The repatriation of the statue of Marduk from Assyria to Babylonia, seriously attempted by Esarhaddon and finally achieved by his son, Assurbanipal, in the year 668 BCE, is a major event in Neo-Assyrian history. The letter of Aššur-ḫamatu'a to Assurbanipal (*ABL* 1249 = SAA 13 139)[1] is seldom mentioned among the sources related to this event.[2] In this study, dedicated with pleasure to our colleague and friend Tapani Harviainen, it is our purpose to demonstrate that this letter indeed provides a weighty insight into Marduk's return, especially from the ideological and theological point of view. The letter has not attracted the attention it deserves; save a few remarks in recent publications,[3] it has not been studied comprehensively before. This may be due to difficulties in reading

1 Edition: S. W. Cole and P. Machinist, *Letters from Priests to Kings Esarhaddon and Assurbanipal* (SAA 13; Helsinki: Helsinki University Press, 1999), 111; normalized transcription and translation also in M. Nissinen, with contributions by C. L. Seow, R. K.Ritner, and H. C. Melchert, *Prophets and Prophecy in the Ancient Near East* (SBLWAW 41; Atlanta: Society of Biblical Literature, 2nd ed.; Atlanta: SBL Press, 2019) no. 112. Earlier editions: E. G. Klauber, "Zur Politik und Kultur der Sargonidenzeit," *AJSL* 30 (1914) 233–87; L. Waterman, *Royal Correspondence of the Assyrian Empire*, vol. 2. (University of Michigan Studies, Humanistic Series 18; Ann Arbor: University of Michigan Press, 1930), 370–371.

2 For recent discussion on Marduk's return, see B. N. Porter, *Images, Power, and Politics: Figurative Aspects of Esarhaddon's Babylonian Policy* (Philadelphia: American Philosophical Society, 1993), 137–148; G. W. Vera Chamaza, *Die Omnipotenz Aššurs: Entwicklungen in der Aššur-Theologie unter der Sargoniden Sargon II., Sanherib und Asarhaddon* (AOAT 295; Münster: Ugarit-Verlag, 2002), 210–227.

3 S. Parpola, *Assyrian Prophecies* (SAA 9; Helsinki: Helsinki University Press, 1997), lxxvii; B. Pongratz-Leisten, *Herrschaftswissen in Mesopotamien: Formen der Kommunikation zwischen Gott und König im 2. und 1. Jahrtausend v.Chr* (SAAS 10; Helsinki: The Neo-Assyrian Text Corpus Project, 1999), 91; M. Nissinen, "Prophets and the Divine Council," in *Kein Land für sich allein: Studien zum Kulturkontakt in Kanaan, Israel/Palästina und Ebirnâri für Manfred Weippert zum 65. Geburtstag* (ed. U. Hübner and E. A. Knauf; OBO 186; Freiburg Schweiz: Universitätsverlag and Göttingen: Vandenhoeck & Ruprecht, 2002) 4–19, esp. p. 11–12 (= pp. 461–77 in this volume); id., "Fear Not: A Study on an Ancient Near Eastern Phrase," in *The Changing Face of Form Criticism for the Twenty-First Century* (ed. M. A. Sweeney and E. Ben Zvi; Grand Rapids, Mich.: Eerdmans, 2003) 122–161, esp. p. 155–156 (= pp. 195–232 in this volume); P. Villard, "Les prophéties à l'époque néo-assyrienne," in *Prophètes et Rois: Bible et Proche-Orient* (ed. A. Lemaire; Paris: Cerf, 2001) 55–84, esp. p. 71.

DOI 10.1515/9783110466546-015

and interpreting the text of the partly damaged and unconventionally designed tablet.

Text, Translation and Philological Notes[4]

Obv.	1	*⸢a!⸣-n[a!-ku]* EN *e!-⸢tar!⸣-ba!*	I *[am]* the Lord. I have entered
	2	TA* ^{d}NI[N.L]ÍL *a-si-l[i]m!*	(and) made peace with Mu*[ll]*issu.
	3	^{m}*aš-šur-DÙ-A* LUGAL KUR-AŠ	Assurbanipal, king of Assyria,
	4	*ša! tú-ra-bi-i-ni!*	whom she raised:
	5	*[l]a! ta-pa-làḫ*	Fear not!
	6	*[a-n]a!-ku!* EN *ar-te-an-ki*	*[I]* am the Lord. I have remitted
	7	$^{m!}$*aš-šur*-DÙ-A *ina* KUR *ša* GIN	Assurbanipal to you in a country of
	8	*šu-ú a-di* KUR-*šu*	truth. Him together with his country,
	9	*ar-te-an-ki*	I have remitted to you.
	10	*ina* [D]I!-*mu šal-lim-te*	I left your city in peace and safety.
	11	TA* URU-*ki at-tú-ṣi*	Mercy (and) compassion
	12	*⸢re!⸣-e!-mu! gim-lu*	[...]
	13	*[x x x x x] ⸢ni? x⸣*	(Break)
		(about four lines broken away)	
Rev.		(about four lines broken away)	
	1′	*⸢a!-na!* 15?⸣ EN *at-⸢ta!⸣-[ḫar?]*	I *appea*[*led*] and prayed to [*Ištar*]
	2′	*ú-sa-ri-ir-ri*	(and) the Lord, (and then)
	3′	^{md}PA-MAN-PAB LÚ*.⸢UŠ!⸣-*kib!-si*	sent Nabû-šarru-uṣur, a tracker
	4′	*ša mu-gi-ia a-sa-par*	of my *contingent*.
		(space of two lines)	
	5′	*a-na* LUGAL EN-*ia*	To the king, my lord:
	6′	ARAD-*ka* ^{m}*aš-šur-ḫa-mat-ia*	your servant, Aššur-ḫamatu'a.
	7′	*aš-šur* ^{d}15 *a-na* LUGAL	May Aššur and Ištar bless the king!
	8′	*lik-ru-ub-bu*	

Obv. 1. Cf. *a-na-ku* ^{d}EN "I am Bel," SAA 9 1 ii 17 (oracle to Esarhaddon from year 680). Note that in the present text, Bel is repeatedly written with the plain EN sign, omitting the divine determinative. This orthography is extremely rare in Neo-Assyrian texts: out of a total of more than 600 references to Bel, the

4 Exclamation marks in the transliteration indicate corrections to the *ABL* copy. Most of these have been verified through collation of the original by Parpola in 1966 and 1996, and were already included in the SAA edition by Cole and Machinist (1999), but some are new (see obv. 1, 4, 6, 13, rev. 1) and derive from a study of the photographs reproduced in Plate I and notes made earlier at the British Museum. Question marks indicate uncertain restorations and readings from photographs, not verified through collation. The notes take as their point of departure the SAA edition and the translation in Nissinen, *Prophets and Prophecy in the Ancient Near East*, 168.

determinative is otherwise omitted only in ten cases, viz. in six letters from the last years of Esarhaddon,[5] and in four legal documents dated between 638 and 627 BCE.[6] It is striking that all the six letters in question, written by scholars involved in the implementation of Esarhaddon's cultic reforms in Babylonia, appear to have been written between Adar 671 and Iyyar 670, the very time period during which the statue of Marduk commissioned by Esarhaddon was being fashioned in the temple workshops of Assur.[7] The omission of the determinative in these texts was certainly not accidental but reflects the Assyrian understanding of Bel Marduk as the divine lord *par excellence* – the heavenly paragon of the king of Assyria – conceived of as a hypostasis of the supreme god, Aššur. In line with this understanding, the determinative is usually also omitted in Neo-Assyrian personal names containing the theophoric element Bel,[8] but *never* in corresponding Babylonian names (which reflected the Babylonian understanding of Bel as the supreme god).[9]

Against this background, the omission of the determinative must have been deliberate in the present oracle as well. A further orthographic detail in the text likewise seems to convey a covert message to the reader (see note on obv. 3 below). While the present *written* version of the oracle presumably goes back to an oral original, these two orthographic details, though not part of the original prophecy, are certainly well in line with it, and both definitely added an important dimension to its ideological/political message. They connoted the theological subordination of Bel to Aššur, and hence the political subordination of Babylonia to Assyria.

---

5 SAA 10 53:13, 61:7, 69 r. 12, 298 r. 5, 352 r. 10, and 357 r. 4.

6 SAA 14 155 r.3, and A. Y. Ahmad, "The Archive of Aššur-mātu-taqqin," *Al-Rāfidān* 17 (1996) 207–288, nos. 2 r 6. 11 r. 6 and 30:10.

7 See the commentaries on SAA 10 69, 352 and 357 in *LAS* II (S. Parpola, *Letters from Assyrian Scholars to the Kings Esarhaddon and Assurbanipal, Part II: Commentary and Appendices* [AOAT 5/2; Kevelaer: Butzon & Bercker and Neukirchen-Vluyn: Neukirchener Verlag, 1983]). SAA 10 53, 61 and 298, which cannot be dated precisely, certainly also date from the same general time period; note that SAA 10 296, which refers to the same patient as SAA 10 298, dates from Adar 671. The involvement of Balasî and Nabû-aḫḫe-eriba in the reorganization of the Babylonian cult is attested in SAA 10 40–41; for Mar-Issar (the sender of SAA 10 252 and 357), see SAA 10 348–349, 353–359 and 365–368.

8 Out of 2052 attestations of Neo-Assyrian names with the element Bel, only 280 (about 10%) are written with the determinative.

9 The determinative was so essential to the Babylonian orthography of Bel that it coalesced with the EN sign into a ligature, $^{d+}$EN, which was exclusively used for writing the god's name in Neo-Babylonian, but never in Neo-Assyrian.

e-tar-ba: In contemporary texts, the verb *erābu* "to enter" served as a *terminus technicus* for the return of a divine statue to its temple.[10] Correspondingly, the verb *uṣû,* "to go/come out," occurring in obv. 11, was a technical term for the departure of a divine statue from its temple.[11] It is therefore virtually certain that *e-tar-ba* here refers to Bel's return to his (newly restored) temple in Babylon, Esaggil. This can be compared with Assurbanipal's inscription L^4 ii 29–33 quoting the king's prayer to Marduk in his first regnal year:

> Remember Babylon, which you destroyed in your anger, relent, and return to Esaggil, the palace of your lordship! Long enough have you abandoned your city and resided in a place unworthy of you. You are the highest of gods, Marduk! Command the journey to Babylon, may the entry *(erēb)* into Esaggil be effected by your holy, unalterable word!

On the other hand, Esaggil was also the place where the divine council *(puḫur ilāni)* met. It is referred to as the permanent seat of the council in *Enūma eliš*[12] and its cellas and chapels housed, in addition to Bel and Beltiya, all the major gods of the Babylonian pantheon as well. Thus, return to Esaggil in this case also meant return to the assembly of gods. Probably *e-tar-ba* was a *double entendre* to be understood in both ways in the present context[13]

2. *a-si-lim:* The basic stem of *salāmu* is otherwise not attested in prophetic oracles,[14] but in other Neo-Assyrian texts it always means "to make peace" in the political sense, often with the connotation of *voluntarily submitting* to the superior power of Assyria (cf. Arabic *aslama).*[15] This connotation was doubtless also

---

10 See B. Pongratz-Leisten, Ina šulmi īrub: *Die kulttopographische und ideologische Programmatik der akītu-Prozession in Babylonien und Assyrien im 1. Jahrtausend v. Chr.* (BaF 16; Mainz: Philipp von Zabern, 1994), 159–164, with many examples.

11 See ibid., 180–184 and note on obv. 11.

12 *Enūma eliš* vi 57–81.

13 Note that the inscription of Assurbanipal just quoted explicitly refers to a meeting of the gods after Marduk's arrival in Babylon (J. Novotny, *Selected Royal Inscriptions of Assurbanipal: L^3, L^4, LET, Prism I, Prism T, and Related Texts* (SAACT 10; Helsinki: The Neo-Assyrian Text Corpus Project, 2014), 79–98, r. iii 12–19).

14 The D-stem of the verb occurs several times in Neo-Assyrian prophetic oracles, referring to the *pacification* of gods angry with Assyria through the intercession of Ištar (see SAA 9 1 ii 31, 2 ii 3, 2 iii 20, and 2 iv 19). All these oracles date from the period of civil war and internal turmoil in Assyria following the murder of Sennacherib in 681 BCE. In addition, the verbal adjective *salmūti* occurs in two oracles, referring to *submissive* vassals brought to the king with their tribute, again by Ištar (SAA 9 1 ii 4 and 2 i 9).

15 E.g., *Muskāiu issēni issilim* "the Phrygian has made peace with us," SAA 1 1:38 and 47; note especially *adê issēni šuknu ma nissilim* "conclude a treaty with us, we have made/chosen peace," SAA 15 90 r. 19–20.

Plate I. ABL 1249 (83–1–18,361). Courtesy Trustees of the British Museum.

implicit in the present passage with Mullissu representing Assyria as the spouse of Aššur and the divine mother of Assurbanipal.[16] Accordingly, Bel's reconciliation with Mullissu *theologically* sanctioned Babylonia's permanent subordination to Assyria, a message already connoted by the spelling of the god's name.

3. The spelling KUR-AŠ for Assyria is rare outside Neo-Assyrian royal inscriptions and is otherwise found only in eight texts, a royal letter from about 671 BCE,[17] five oracle reports and a treaty from the time of the Šamaš-šumu-ukin rebellion (652–648 BCE),[18] and the so-called Zakutu treaty imposed by the queen mother on behalf of Assurbanipal immediately after Esarhaddon's death in late 669 BCE.[19] The occurrence of this rare spelling in these very texts does not seem accidental. KUR-AŠ is related to the logographic spelling of Aššur's name as DINGIR-AŠ, "the one and only god," which stressed the universal and undivided nature of Aššur's divinity.[20] Correspondingly, the spelling KUR-AŠ, whose logographic components meant "a single country," implied the basic unity of Assyria, which remained undivided despite the installation of Šamaš-šumu-ukin as the king of Babylon. In the present context, coming from the mouth of Bel, it effectively and irrevocably sanctioned Assyria's hegemony over Babylonia under Assurbanipal.

4. ***tú-ra-bi-i-ni*** is the preterite 2nd person fern. sg. subj. of *rabbû* "to raise, bring up," with elision of the subjunctive morpheme /u/ after the final *-i*, as in *taq-bi-ni* (pret. 3rd person fem. sg. subj. of *qabû* "to say"), SAA 16 2 r. 3.[21] The writing of the feminine prefix with *tú-* instead of *tu-* is somewhat unusual but not unparalleled; there are 31 other cases of the prefix written with *tú-* in the electronic corpus of Neo-Assyrian, and 85 further cases of *tú-* in word-initial position. See also note on obv. 11 below.

The sign *tú* is composed of three wedges only, whereas *tu* has as many as 8 wedges. Thus the use of *tú* here *could* indicate that the present text was composed and sent in a hurry. Writing Bel without the divine determinative, Assyria

16 On Mullissu as the divine mother and wet-nurse of the Assyrian king, see Parpola, *Assyrian Prophecies,* xxxvi–xlii. Note that in Assyrian theology, Mullissu was also the mother and wet-nurse of Bel (see ibid., c, nn. 175–176).

17 SAA 16 28 r. 7. The sender is Esarhaddon's daughter, who writes to her sister-in-law, the wife of Assurbanipal.

18 See SAA 2 9 (treaty), and SAA 4 280 r. 4, 287 r. 7; 290:21, r. 3; 293 r. 12; 297 r. 3; 302:1, 6, 8, 9.

19 SAA 2 8:2, 17, 21, 24; r. 4, 7, 9, 11, 14, 17, 26.

20 See S. Parpola, "Monotheism in Ancient Assyria," in *One God or Many? Concepts of Divinity in the Ancient World* (ed. B. N. Porter; Casco Bay, Maine: Casco Bay Assyriological Institute, 2000) 165–209.

21 In corresponding forms with object suffixes, however, the final *-i* was elided instead, cf. *tu-ra-bu-šú-ni,* SAA 3 34:33.

with the AŠ sign only, and *kettu* in obv. 7 logographically (see below) would also have saved some time. However, the gain would have been minimal – a matter of a few seconds only. It should also be noted that the scribe could have saved even more time in writing *šú* (two wedges) instead of *šu* (5 wedges), *u* (one wedge) instead of *ú* (7 wedges), MAN (two wedges) instead of LUGAL (12 wedges), *šá* (four wedges) instead of *sa* (7 wedges), and so on. Hence the explanation for the unusual spellings is almost certainly *not* be sought in the need for speed (which undoubtedly was there), but in the writing conventions and deliberate orthographic choices of the scribe.

6. The repetition of Bel's self-identification, the feminine suffixes in lines 6, 9 and 11, and the reference to Assurbanipal in the third person in line 8 imply that from this point on, the oracle was not addressed to Assurbanipal but to Mullissu. The oracle thus had two addressees, which is unusual but not unparalleled in the Assyrian prophecy corpus; cf. SAA 9 1.8, 2.1 and 2.6, all of which are addressed to Esarhaddon and his human mother (Naqia) in a way closely resembling the present text, with the prophet abruptly shifting his attention from one addressee to the other. Since Mullissu was the *divine* mother of the king, the parallelism with the present text is remarkable. On the Assyrian queens as images of Mullissu (corresponding to the notion of the king as an image of Bel), see *LAS* II p. XCVIII, n. 159.[22]

ar-te-an-ki is the perfect 1st person singular of *riāmu* (Bab. *rêmu),* with the standard Neo-Assyrian assimilation of the final *-m* to the feminine suffix. The verb is related to the noun *rēmu* "mercy," but although it did denote an act of mercy or grace, it did not simply mean "to have mercy upon"[23] but more technically "to grant/bestow" or "remit/excuse" (a thing requested or pleaded for).[24] It regularly takes *two* objects in Neo-Assyrian, a direct one denoting the thing granted or excused, and an indirect one denoting the beneficiary of the action,

---

22 The official seals of the Neo-Assyrian queens had a scorpion as their central motif. This motif symbolized the "bedroom" goddess Išḫara and applied to the queen in her mediating role, which she shared with the celestial queen, Mullissu; see S. Herbordt, "Neo-Assyrian Royal and Administrative Seals and their Use," in *Assyrien im Wandel der Zeiten* (ed. H. Waetzoldt and H. Hauptmann; CRRAI 39 = HSAO 6; Heidelberg: Heidelberger Orientverlag, 1997) 279–83, and B. N. Porter, "Beds, Sex, and Politics: The Return of Marduk's Bed to Babylon," in *Sex and Gender in the Ancient Near East* (ed. S. Parpola and R. M. Whiting; CRRAI 47; Helsinki: The Neo-Assyrian Text Corpus Project, 2002) 523–35.

23 Thus Nissinen, *Prophets and Prophecy in the Ancient Near East* (1st ed.), 168. "To have mercy upon" was expressed with the idiom *rēmu ina muḫḫi/ana X šakānu* in Neo-Assyrian, which corresponds to the idiom *rēmu ana X rašû* of the royal inscriptions (cf. n. 21 below).

24 Cf., KUG.UD *ša* Ú.MEŠ *be-lí li-ri-ma-a-ni* "may my lord remit me the silver for the plants," ND 3467 r. 11 f *(Iraq* 15 146).

expressed either with a pronominal suffix appended to the verb[25] or with a noun preceded by *ana.*[26] Accordingly, the suffix *-ki,* referring to Mullissu, here represents the *indirect* object of the verb, while Assurbanipal in the next line must be the direct object.[27] The underlying word order (verb followed by object) is unusual but by no means unknown in Neo-Assyrian,[28] and is attested several times in the Neo-Assyrian prophecy corpus.[29]

Consequently, the present passage must be understood as a *display of mercy* on the part of Bel, the divine king – an act consistent with his attribute *rēmānu/rēmēnû* "merciful"[30] – *in response to a plea* of Mullissu on behalf of her son (or, more exactly, in response to a prayer of Assurbanipal, which his "mother," as intercessor between king and god, had pleaded for in the divine council). As argued in more detail below, the issue at stake was the Babylonian policy of earlier Assyrian kings, particularly Sargon and Sennacherib, who by their actions had disrupted the cosmic harmony and thus committed mortal "sins." Since Assurbanipal was not personally culpable of these sins, the most appropriate translation of *riāmu* in the present context would probably be "to exonerate."

7. This line has been previously translated "Assurbanipal is in a country which is loyal,"[31] but this is impossible since, as just noted, Assurbanipal is the object of the preceding verb, while *šû* in the next line links up with *adi nišēšu* and hence cannot be taken as the predicate of the sentence (see note on obv. 8). Consequently, the words *ina* GIN *ša* GIN must be interpreted an adverbial phrase belonging to the preceding clause. Such phrases were normally

25 E.g., ÉŠ.QAR-*ka lu-ri-ma-ka* "I will excuse you from your dues," SAA 1 235:16 f; UDU.MEŠ-*ka lu-u-ri-ma-ka* "I will excuse you from your sheep," SAA 1 236 r. 8.

26 E.g., *an-ni-u gab-bu ša* PN ... *ina* TI-*šu a-na* PN DUMU-*šú i-ri-mu-u-ni* "all this is what PN had bestowed upon PN, his son, when still alive," ADD 779:7–10; *il-ku ša* RN ... *a-na* LÚ.EN.NAM *i-ri-mu-u-ni* "dues that Sargon, king of Assyria, has remitted to the governor," ADD 766:1.

27 Cf. *re-e-mu ar-ši-šú-ma* DUMU *ṣi-it-*ŠÀ-*bi-šú ú-tir-ma a-ri-im-šú* (var. *a-din-šú)* "I had mercy upon him (= the king of Tyre) and granted (var. gave) his son and offspring back to him," J. Novotny and J. Jeffers, *The Royal Inscriptions of Ashurbanipal (668–631 BC), Aššur-etel-ilāni (630–627 BC), and Sîn-šarra-iškun (626–612 BC), Kings of Assyria,* Part 1 (RINAP 5/1; University Park, Pa.: Eisenbrauns, 2018), 61 ii 56–57.

28 See *LAS* II p. 313 sub r. 2f for several examples; note also SAA 10 289 r. 12 *(issu aiaka ninaššia igrê),* NL 39 64 *(basi ašappara nišēšu);* SAA 21 38:16 *(lā tapallaḫ titāršu)*

29 SAA 9 1 ii 28 *(mutuḫ ēnēka* "lift up your eyes"), 2 ii 32 *(uḫayyāṭa lā kēnūti),* 3 r. iii 11 *(tamaššiā adê annûti)* and 14 *(tanaṣṣarā adê annûti).*

30 See *Enūma eliš* vii 27–30 and the evidence discussed in *LAS* II p. 58.

31 SAA 13 139; similarly Nissinen, *Prophets and Prophecy in the Ancient Near East* (1st ed.), 168: "Assurbanipal is in a country which remains loyal to him."

placed before the predicate in Neo-Assyrian, but they could occasionally also follow the verb.[32]

This conclusion makes it necessary to reconsider the interpretation of the logogram GIN. It cannot be taken to stand for the stative of the verb *kuānu* "to be true, loyal" *(*kēnatūni)*, as previously done, since it lacks the subjunctive ending *-ni* and phonetic complement(s) required by this interpretation.[33] On the other hand, taking it to stand for the adjective *kēnu* "true, honest" (the usual reading of the plain GIN sign in Neo-Assynan)[34] would not make any sense in the context. Accordingly, GIN probably stands here for *kettu* "truth, honesty,"[35] and the phrase GIN *ša* GIN, for *mātu ša ketti* "country of truth." This interpretation is supported by the fact that a similar phrase (*šipirtu ša ketti* "message of truth") is attested in a contemporary prophetic oracle (SAA 13 43 r. 7f). Even though the phrase "country of truth" as such is unparalleled in Assyrian sources, the concept itself is well attested in contemporary texts.[36]

8. The phrase ***šu-ú a-di*** **KUR-*šu*** "him together with his country" recalls the stock phrase *šu-ú a-di* UN.MEŠ-*šu* "he together with his people" (or "family, kin, magnates, men, army, helpers," etc.) referring to foreign kings and potentates in Sargonid royal inscriptions and letters. The present passage has a perfect

---

32 E.g., *tallakā ina ālānikunu* "you will go to your cities," SAA 9 3 iii 9; *nittitzi* [*ina*] *pānēšunu* "we stood before them," SAA 16 41:13. Close to 100 similar examples could be cited.

33 Cf, e.g., GIN-*ku-u-ni* = *kēnākūni* "(whether) I am loyal," SAA 21 155 r. 9. Logographically written forms of *kuānu* regularly required a phonetic complement (e.g., GIN-*an*) in Neo-Assyrian to avoid confusion with forms of *alāku* (e.g., DU-*ku*) written with the same sign. The subjunctive ending *-ni* is regularly written out in logographically written forms of *alāku*, e.g. DU-*a-ni* = *illakanni*, SAA 5 217 r. 12; DU-*u-ni-ni* = *illikūninni*, SAA 5 117:18.

34 E.g., *atta zēru* GIN *ša* RN "you are the true seed of Sennacherib," SAA 16 96 r. 1; RN ŠEŠ *la* GIN "Šamaš-šumu-ukin, the dishonest brother," SAA 4 282:18. For further examples, see *PNA* s.v. Aḫu-kēnu "the brother is true," Ilu-kēnu-uṣur "O god, protect the true one," and like names (Abu-kēnu, Aššūr-kēnu, Aššūr-kēnu-balliṭ, Aššūr-kēnu-īdi, Aššūr-kēnu-uṣur, Aššūr-lā-kēnu-ubâša, Ḫabil-kēnu, Ilu-kēnu, Ilu-kēnu-balliṭ, Inūrta-kēnu-īdi, Inūrta-kēnu-uṣur, Kēnu-lāmur, Kēnu-lēšir, etc.).

35 The usual Neo-Assyrian logogram for *kettu* was ZI (see *PNA* s.w. Aššūr-kettu-irâm, Aššūr-kettu-uṣur, Bēl-kettu-ēreš, Ilu-kettu-irâm, Ilu-kettu-uṣur, Nabû-išid-ketti, Nabû-kettu-irâm, Nabû-kettu-uṣur, and Nabû-rā'im-ketti), but the value GIN = *kettu* is attested in two names, Nabû-zēr-ketti-lēšir and Nabû-zēr-ketti-uṣur, which are regularly written ^{md}PA-NUMUN-GIN-GIŠ and ^{md}PA-NUMUN-GIN-PAB in Neo-Assyrian texts (sec *PNA* 2/II: 905–907). In Assyrian royal inscriptions and Neo-Babylonian texts, by contrast, Nabû-zēr-kitti-līšir is regularly written ^{md}AG-NUMUN-ZI-SI.SÁ or ^{md}PA-NUMUN-*kit-ti-li-šir*.

36 Cf., e.g., the following omen cited in 28 contemporary omen reports: "If the moon and sun are in balance, the land will become stable/honest *(mātu ikân)*. Reliable/truthful speech *(pû kīnu)* will be placed in the mouth of people" (for attestations see SAA 8, index s.v. *atmû)*. In these omens, "the land" refers to Assyria, as does "the country of truth" in the present oracle.

parallel in a letter of Sargon II, where *šūtu adi nišēšunu* following a personal name functions as the object of the verb *šēbulu* "to send."[37]

10. This line recalls the phraseology of reports on divine processions, cf. SAA 10 98:7–9, *aš-šur* ᵈNIN.LÍL *ina šul-me it-tu-ṣi-ú ina šá-li-in-ti e-tar-bu-u-ni* "Aššur and Mullissu left (the temple) in peace and (re-)entered it safely," and SAA 1 188:8-r.5: "Sin came out *(it-tu-ṣi-a)* and entered the *akītu* chapel; the king's sacrifices were performed in peace *(i-na* DI-ww); Sîn re-entered his temple and took his seat safely *(i-na ša-lim-ti)*."[38]

11. URU-***ki*** "your city" certainly refers to the city of Assur, where the statue of Bel commissioned by Esarhaddon was fashioned and from where it started its procession to Babylon in the first year of Assurbanipal.[39] As the spouse of Aššur, Mullissu resided in the Ešarra temple of Assur, next to the holy of holies of Aššur.[40] For ***at-tú-ṣi*** "I left" cf. note on obv. 1; the writing with *tu* (instead of *tu)* is unusual but not unparalleled.[41] The line as a whole is an allusion to Neo-Assyrian royal inscriptions, where departure from "Assur, my city" (URU-*ia aš-šur)* figures as a topos.[42]

12. This line alludes to a curse found in two treaties of Esarhaddon ("May Ištar, who dwells in Arbela, not show you mercy and compassion").[43] It is not excluded that following line is to be restored accordingly.[44]

Rev. 1. The first four signs are almost completely destroyed and the readings of the third and fourth signs are very conjectural, *a*ᶦ*-na*ᶦ at the beginning seems certain by comparison with rev. 5, where the tails of the verticals of *a* are similarly forked, and the Winkelhakens of *na* similarly placed. Between *na* and

---

37 PN *šu-tú a-du* UN.MEŠ-*šú* LÚ*.A-KIN-*ka a-du* UGU-*ḫi-ia lu-bi-la-šú-nu*, SAA 1 1 r. 28 f *(šūtu* and *adu* were free variants of *šû* and *adi* in Neo-Assyrian).

38 On the unusual gemination in *šal-lim-te* see S. Parpola, "The Forlorn Scholar," in *Language, Literature and History: Philological and Historical Studies Presented to Erica Reiner* (ed. F. Rochberg-Halton; AOS 67; New Haven, Conn.: American Oriental Society, 1987) 274–75. On the writing DI-*mu* (for expected DI-*me)* cf. E. Leichty, *The Omen Series Šumma izbu* (TCS 4; Locust Valley, N. Y.: Augustin, 1970) 28–29; it is also attested as a spelling for the genitive in SAA 1 187 r. 6; SAA 10 46:9; SAA 13 26:8; and NL 40 r. 6.

39 See E. Leichty, *The Royal Inscriptions of Esarhaddon, King of Assyria (680–669 BC)* (RINAP 4; Winona Lake, Ind.: Eisenbrauns, 2011), 108–9; Novotny, *Selected Royal Inscriptions*, 79 r. iii 2–11; SAA 4 262–64.

40 See G. van Driel, *The Cult of Aššur* (Assen 1969), 39–40.

41 Cf. *i-tú-ṣi*, SAA 1 111:9; SAA 5 223 r. 3, 227:18; NL 13 r. 3; *i-tú-ṣi-a*, NL 43:6, GPA 193 r. 10; *i-tú-ṣi-ú*, SAA 1 179 r. 19; *i-tú-ṣu-ni*, NL 14 r. 19; *i-tú-ṣu-u-ni*, SAA 15 53:7, 9.

42 E.g., *ul-tú* URU-*ia aš-šur at-tu-muš* "I departed from Assur, my city," Leichty, *The Royal Inscriptions of Esarhaddon*, 87:10. and passim in inscriptions of earlier kings.

43 *Issār āšibat Arbail re-e-mu gim-lu lū lā išakkan elīkun*, SAA 2 5 iv 2 and 6:459.

44 E.g., "[show] mercy and compassion [to ....]."

EN, where a divine name is required by the context, there is room for an 8 mm wide sign or sign group. This is too much for *aš-šur*, which measures 5 mm in obv. 3 and rev. 7, but exactly the width of ^{d}15 (= Ištar) in rev. 7. The head of a horizontal is visible on the left, and tails of a vertical and a pair of two verticals (the one on than right being very short) can be seen in the break exactly where the verticals of DINGIR and 15 should be by comparison with rev. 7. The reading ^{d}15 (which is be expected in the context, the sender being a priest of Ištar) thus seems possible. It is true that there seem to be two extra tails of verticals in the break, which do not fit this reading. However, similar extra tails of verticals, which are nothing but unintentional scratches, are also found elsewhere on the tablet (e.g., right in the next line, between *ú* and *sa*; see also PAB in rev. 3, TA* in obv. 4, and DI in obv. 10).

The incomplete verbal form at the end of the line could also be restored *at-t*[*a-lak*] "I went," *at-t*[*a-na*] "I gave," *at-t*[*a-saḫ*] "I sacrificed," or *at-t*[*a-ṣa*] "I brought (to)." However, a verb similar in meaning to *sarruru* "to pray" is suggested by the paragogic syllable in ***ú-sa-ri-ir-ri***, indicating iteration.[45] Cf. *upnīya apteti ilāni ussarrir* "I opened my fists and prayed to the gods," SAA 10 240 r.7; *tarruṣā qātāia ussarrīri ana urdi u anti* "my hands are stretched out, I have prayed to slave and slave-girl," SAA 3 12:16–17.

4. The word ***mu-gi*** is otherwise attested only in the military title *rab-muggi* "strategos," on which see *LAS* II (1983) p. 515, and K. Radner, *Die neuassyrischen Texte aus Tall Šēḫ Ḥamad* (BATSH 6/2, Berlin: Reimer 2002), 12–13. The laconic *a-sa-par* is an ellipsis for "I sent (to the king/palace)," cf., e.g., SAA 5 45:7 and 245 r. 2.

5–8. The presence of this address and blessing formula (as well as the vertical format of the tablet) marks the text as a letter, but placing the address at the end is abnormal and virtually unparalleled in Neo-Assyrian letters.[46] In other letters of Aššur-ḫamatu'a, the address is in its normal place at the beginning of the letter, so its exceptional placement in the present case must be related to the content of the text which, properly speaking, was not a letter but simply a tran-

---

45 See *LAS* II, p. 237 r. 1 and J. Hämeen-Anttila, *A Sketch of Neo-Assyrian Grammar* (SAAS 13; Helsinki: The Neo-Assyrian Text Corpus Project, 2000), 36. Cf. the frequent phrase *assa'al ūtaṣṣīṣi* "I inquired and investigated" (CAD Š/1 278a).

46 A full address and salutation formula closing a letter is found on the reverse of SAA 1 258, but it has been erased and replaced by an identical formula with additional sender information on the obverse. The Neo-Babylonian letter *ABL* 456 has an address and sender formula on the left side, but this merely duplicates information already given at the beginning of the letter. SAA 1 133 r. 10–13 similarly repeats information already given at the beginning of the letter. A blessing at the end is also found in another letter of Aššur-ḫamatu'a (SAA 13 140).

script of a prophecy, followed by a few explanatory comments. As such, it resembles Neo-Assyrian omen and extispicy reports, where the name of the reporting scholar was likewise given only at the end of the text.[47] Normally the relevant authorship indication (*ša* PN "from/by PN") was very brief and lacked address and blessing formulae, but there are a few exceptions. For example, the reports of Nabû'a of Assur (SAA 8 126 – 138) are regularly closed by the blessing, "May Nabû and Marduk bless the king."[48] A perfect parallel to the present text is provided by SAA 8 445, which has a full address and blessing formula on the reverse. None of these reports, however, have the vertical tablet format which the present text has in common with letters.

6. The final element of the sender's name is also written *ḫa-mat-ia* in SAA 13 138 (as against *ḫa-mat-**u-a*** in SAA 13 139 and 140).[49] However, SAA 13 138 differs orthographically from the present letter, which means that at least one of them was *certainly not* written by Aššur-ḫamatu'a personally.[50] Since the forms *ú-sa-ri-ir-ri* and *lik-ru-ub-bu* in rev. 2 and 8 can only be explained with reference to intonation, it is likely that the present letter *in its entirety* was written from dictation and hence not by Aššur-ḫamatu'a personally. Possibly all the letters signed by him were written down by different scribes.[51]

8. The form *lik-ru-ub-bu* (with geminated *b*) is unparalleled in Neo-Assyrian but recalls the unusual lengthening of penultimate vowels in comparable positions in Middle Assyrian laws,[52] and hence probably reflects a "pausal" intonation resulting from the abnormal placement of the blessing at the end of letter.[53] Similar "pausal" forms are sporadically attested in other Neo-Assyrian texts, too, e.g., [*le*]-*pu-**u-šu*** "they should do" at the end of SAA 10 76.[54]

---

47 See SAA 4 and 8.

48 In SAA 8 296 the authorship indication is followed by a blessing, which introduces a petition to the king.

49 A similar variation between final *-ia* and *-u-a* is also attested in the names Aššur-mukin-palê'a/palû'a (sec *PNA* 1/I: 192) and Šeru'a (cf. ^{d}*še-ru-wa-a* [*passim*], ^{d}*še-ru-u+a*, VTE pl.1:19; ^{d}*še-ru-ú-a*, KAR 214 i 10; ^{d}*še-ru-u$_8$-a*, STT 88:11; **še-ru-ia*, 3 R^2 66 i 9), and is probably to be explained orthographically rather than phonetically.

50 SAA 13 138 writes ^{d}*aš-šur*, ^{d}EN, LÚ, MAN, *šá/ša, šu-u, as-se-me/as-sap-ra*, where the present letter writes *aš-šur*, EN, LÚ*, LUGAL, *ša, šu-ú, a-si-lim/a-sa-par.*

51 The orthography of SAA 13 140 – 142 is in agreement with that of the present letter, which may mean that they were written by the same scribe, but the data are too limited to make it possible to reach final certainty about the matter.

52 Cf. *i-qar-ri-i-bu* (KAV 1 i *22), il-lu-ú-ku* (ii 71), *e-ep-pu-ú-šu-uš* (iii 13), *iṣ-ṣa-ab-bu-ú-tu* (iii 94), *e-pa-a-áš* (2 v 38), etc. (all at the end of a paragraph).

53 See provisionally Hämeen-Anttila, *A Sketch of Neo-Assyrian Grammar,* 30 and 35 – 36.

54 Cf. also SAA 5 233 r. 3, SAA 10 352 s. 1, SAA 13 62 r. 10, and NL 71:27 (all at the end of a letter).

Author, Structure, and the Writing Situation

The author of the letter, Aššur-ḫamatu'a, is only known from his correspondence, of which five letters (SAA 13 138–142) have been preserved.[55] In his letters he reports a theft of temple property (SAA 13 138) as well as the installation of two statues of the king on both sides of the goddess Ištar (SAA 13 140 and 141).[56] These letters present him as a priest or other high temple official of a temple of Ištar, without doubt in Arbela,[57] during the reign of Assurbanipal who is the addressee of the present letter.

The design of the letter SAA 13 139 is atypical and unique, not only among the correspondence of Aššur-ḫamatu'a, but within the Neo-Assyrian corpus in general. It begins with a divine self-presentation, followed by an oracle that covers the preserved part of the obverse. If this was all, the text could be classified either as an oracle report comparable to the prophecies SAA 9 7–11 or as a *šipirtu*[58] a letter from the god to the king devoid of authorship indications. On the reverse, however, the speaker changes: the writer himself gives a very brief account of his prayer to the deity and the sending of the letter; the destroyed lines may have contained a likewise brief note on how the oracle came to his notice. The formal greeting, which normally begins a letter, follows only after a blank space as a conclusion. The greeting itself is as tersely-worded as possible, omitting not only the usual wishes of well-being but even the epithet "my lord" in the concluding blessing formula.[59]

The cuneiform text is written by the hand of a competent scribe. A few linguistic and orthographic peculiarities strike the eye *(at-tú-ṣi,* line 11; *ú-sa-ri-ir- ri,* line r. 2; *lik-ru-ub-bu,* line r. 8), but they may be deliberate choices of the scribe, however, the scanty, almost curt, style of the personal notes of the writer, the placement of the greeting at the end, as well as the rather unusual note concerning the dispatch of the letter, give the impression that it was not written out the

55 Cf. K. Radner, "Aššur-ḫamātū'a," *PNA 1*/I: 186–87.

56 For these royal images, see I. J. Winter, "Art *in* Empire: The Royal Image and the Visual Dimensions of Assyrian Ideology," in *Assyria 1995: Proceedings of the 10th Anniversary Symposium of the Neo-Assyrian Text Corpus Project, Helsinki, September 7–11, 1995* (ed. S. Parpola and R. M. Whiting; Helsinki: The Neo-Assyrian Text Corpus Project, 1997) 359–81, esp. p. 376.

57 SAA 13 140 r. 2–5: [DINGIR.MEŠ] *a-ši-bu-te* [URU].*arba-il a-na* LUGAL EN-*ia lik-ru-bu* "May [the gods] who dwell in Arbela bless the king, my lord."

58 See Pongratz-Leisten, *Herrschaftswissen*, 226–32, 260–61.

59 The greeting in SAA 13 142: 1–5 is not much longer: *a-na* LUGAL E[N-*ia*] ARAD-*ka* [md]*a*[*š- šur—ḫa-mat-ia*] *aš-šur* [15] *a-na* LUG[AL EN-*ia*] *lik-r*[*u-bu*] "To the king, [my] l[ord]: your servant, A[š-šur-ḫamatu'a]. May Aššur and [Ištar] ble[ss the ki[ng, my lord]."

regular way. Evidently, the oracle was written down first, which indicates that Aššur-ḫamatu'a had it recorded immediately when it came to his knowledge. Whether he himself had been present when the oracle was uttered, or he was informed about its contents in due time (his consequent prayer to the god would speak for the first alternative), he wanted to forward it to the king as quickly as possible. Apparently, he added his comments right away on the reverse and gave the letter to the first person available, the tracker Nabû-šarru-uṣur,[60] to be conveyed to the king.

While the unusual appearance of the letter may, thus, be due to a hasty writing procedure, one should note that the oracle itself is very skillfully formulated and full of ideological subtleties. Hence, the letter itself may have been written quickly, but the text is too well thought out in every respect to be a hurried notation of what Aššur-ḫamatu'a heard a prophet speaking. If the oracle was requested by the king from the temple, Aššur-ḫamatu'a could probably anticipate the message of the oracle well enough to give it instantly a judicious and politically correct wording.

Historical Situation

The reason for writing the letter lies in the historical situation reflected by the divine words: Bel, i.e., Marduk, had departed from the city and entered another place. This probably refers to the departure of the statue of Marduk from Assur and its arrival at the Esaggil temple in Babylon at the beginning of Assurbanipal's reign.

In the year 689 BCE, as is well known, the city of Babylon was destroyed by Sennacherib, the gods of Babylon were expatriated and the statue of Marduk was brought to Assur. Esarhaddon, Sennacherib's son, changed course completely in his Babylonian policy. Throughout his reign, the rebuilding of the city and its temples and the repatriation of the gods of Babylon was his major concern, and he cannot be blamed for not having made every effort to send Marduk back home.

As a matter of fact, Esarhaddon did restore the statues of the gods of Babylon in the workshop (*bīt mummu*)[61] of Ešarra, the main temple of Aššur,[62]

---

60 Nabû-šarru-uṣur is a very common name in Assyria, but the tracker cannot be identified with any of his namesakes; see H. D. Baker, "Nabû-šarru-uṣur," *PNA* 2/II (2001) 877 (no. 39).

61 For *bīt mummu*, see A. Berlejung, *Die Theologie der Bilder: Herstellung und Einweihung von Kultbildern in Mesopotamien und die alttestamentliche Bilderpolemik* (OBO 162; Freiburg Schweiz: Universitätsverlag and Göttingen: Vandenhoeck & Ruprecht, 1998) 89–93.

where they were "born" anew.[63] In his AsBbE inscription, he even claims to have had them enter the city of Babylon.[64] Proleptic as this inscription is, it does not quite tally with historical fact; Marduk never made his way as far as to Babylon during Esarhaddon's reign. It is true that Esarhaddon indeed began the ceremonial river cruise of the statue of Marduk to Babylon in the month of Iyyar (II), 669 BCE. This attempt turned out to be unsuccessful, however: on the 18th of lyyar, as the procession had advanced as far as Labbanat, a locality on the river Tigris not far away from Babylon, a malportentous incident stopped its progress.[65]

Even though it is not mentioned in any extant source, it is evident that the procession with Marduk had to turn back and Babylon was never reached. No later than the next year, however, Assurbanipal was able to do what was left unfinished by his recently deceased father: the chronicles report that Marduk and the gods of Babylon left Assur and entered Babylon on the 24th of lyyar (II) of the year of the accession of Šamaš-šumu-ukin, i.e., 668 BCE.[66]

Theology of Reconciliation

The renewed journey of Marduk was not begun without divine consent, as the oracle queries concerning this event demonstrate.[67] These queries may have followed a standard procedure, though the extant queries from the Sargonid period deal otherwise with military, political, and medical matters rather than cultic issues. This alone indicates that the return of Marduk constituted a special case with significant political overtones which, in turn, are deeply connected with

---

62 Leichty, *The Royal Inscriptions of Esarhaddon*, 107–9:79–96.; cf. ibid., 167:1–7; 168:1–7; 169:1–6; Vera Chamaza, *Die Omnipotenz Aššurs*, 471–72, 479–82. For the making of the statues, see Berlejung, *Theologie der Bilder*, 158–71.

63 Leichty, *The Royal Inscriptions of Esarhaddon*, 108:87–88: *Bēl Bēltīa Bēlet Bābili Ēa Madâm ilāni rabûti qereb Ešarra bīt zārîšunu kēniš immaldūma išmuhū gattu* "Bel, Beltia, Belet-Babili, Ea and Madanu, the great gods, were properly born in Ešarra, the temple of their begetter, and their statues flourished."

64 Ibid., 137:42–49; cf. ibid., 113:1–13; 208 vii 5–11.

65 The incident at Labbanat is reported in the letter *LAS* 29 = SAA 10 24; see Parpola, *LAS* II, 32–35. For this journey, see also Vera Chamaza, *Die Omnipotenz Aššurs*, 210–20.

66 A. K. Grayson, *Assyrian and Babylonian Chronicles* (TCS 5; Locust Valley, N. Y.: J. J. Augustin 1975), 86: 34–36; 127: 35–36; 131: 5–6. This is also reported in Assurbanipal's inscriptions; see M. Streck, *Assurbanipal und die letzten assyrischen Könige bis zum Untergange Niniveh's* (VAB 7; Leipzig, Hinrichs, 1916), 236:10–11; Novotny, *Selected Royal Inscriptions*, ii 26–iii 30.

67 SAA 4 262–265; see I. Starr, *Queries to the Sungod: Divination and Politics in Sargonid Assyria* (SAA 4; Helsinki: Helsinki University Press, 1990), 236–40; cf. Vera Chamaza, *Die Omnipotenz Aššurs*, 484–487. One of these queries (SAA 4 262) is dated to the 23rd of Nisan (I), 668.

ideological and theological concerns arising from the events of the year 689 BCE.[68]

Until Sennacherib's destruction of Babylon, it had been the normal Assyrian ideology to view Assyria and Babylonia as sister nations – if not a single nation – under one ruler. Sennacherib's policy meant an abrupt reversal of this ideology, and this was regarded as a grave mistake in various circles, not only in Babylonia but also in Assyria. From the very beginning of his reign, Esarhaddon was goaded into the restoration of the city of Babylon and its temples and the rehabilitation of the Babylonian gods – directly by prophets and scholars[69] and indirectly by officials.[70] That Esarhaddon took this encouragement to his heart is reflected by his inscriptions concerning Babylonia[71] and especially in the "Sin of Sargon" text (SAA 3 33) which, disguised as Sennacherib's last will, urges Esarhaddon to make a statue of Marduk as a sign of the reconciliation of the gods of Babylonia with the gods of Assyria.[72] Importantly, this text makes the disparagement of Marduk a sin committed by Sargon when he broke "the treaty of the king of gods" (SAA 3 33 17–20), i.e., in historical terms, his treaty with Merodach-Baladan, King of Babylonia. This had caused an imbalance not only between Assyria and Babylonia and their respective gods, but also between heaven and earth. Only a reconciliation of the Assyrian king with the gods of Babylonia would return the cosmic harmony disturbed by the king's sin. The principal sign of reconciliation is the rehabilitation of Marduk, the principal god of Babylonia, as

---

68 For Esarhaddon's Babylonian policy, see J. A. Brinkman, "Through a Glass Darkly: Esarhaddon's Retrospects on the Downfall of Babylon," *JAOS* 103 (1983) 35–42; B. N. Porter, *Images, Power, and Politics*; G. Frame, *Babylonia 689–627 B.C.: A Political History* (Istanbul: Nederlands historisch-archaeologisch instituut, 1992), 64–101; M. Nissinen, "City as Lofty as Heaven: Arbela and Other Cities in Neo-Assyrian Prophecy," in *"Every City Shall Be Forsaken": Urbanism and Prophecy in Ancient Israel and the Near East* (ed. L. L. Grabbe and R. D. Haak; JSOTSup 330; Sheffield: Sheffield Academic Press, 2001) 172–209, esp. p. 195–201 (= pp. 267–300 in this volume); Vera Chamaza, *Die Omnipotenz Aššurs*, 168–237

69 Cf. the collection of prophecies SAA 9 2; see Parpola, *Assyrian Prophecies*, lxix–lxx; Nissinen, "City as Lofty as Heaven," 195–201. On the letter of the astrologer Bel-ušezib (SAA 10 109 r. 23–26), see S. Parpola, "The Murderer of Sennacherib," in *Death in Mesopotamia* (ed. B. Alster; Mesopotamia 8 (= CRRAI 26); Copenhagen: Akademisk Forlag, 1980) 171–82, esp. p. 179–80.

70 E.g., Ubaru, the governor of Babylon (SAA 18 14).

71 First and foremost the Babylon inscriptions; see Leichty, *The Royal Inscriptions of Esarhaddon*, 193–221, 231–37, 243–46 (RINAP 4 104–108, 114, 116); cf. the inscriptions mentioned in note 62.

72 See H. Tadmor, B. Landsberger and S. Parpola, "The Sin of Sargon and Sennacherib's Last Will," SAAB 3 (1989) 3–51.

quasi-equal[73] to Aššur, the supreme god of Assyria. This theology, then, was put into practice by repatriating the gods of Babylon.

This is what the prophecy recorded in the letter of Aššur-ḫamatu'a is all about. Assurbanipal did not need the priest from Arbela to tell him that Marduk had departed from Assur and entered Babylon; the king was certainly well enough informed of the practicalities of the ceremonial procession. What he needed was a message from Marduk himself affirming that the procedure had achieved its purpose and the "Sin of Sargon" had been expiated. Aššur-ḫamatu'a probably knew about Marduk's journey and was waiting to hear the oracle that may have been requested by the king from Egašankalamma, the temple of Ištar in Arbela which was the center of Assyrian prophecy. This was the most natural place to receive such oracles, since the goddess's demands for the rehabilitation of the Babylonian gods had been proclaimed there from the early days of Esarhaddon on.[74] In addition, Assurbanipal, like his father, had an especially devotional relation to this particular temple, calling himself the "product" of Emašmaš and Egašankalamma, i.e., the temples of Ištar in Nineveh and Arbela.[75]

The theology of reconciliation and the rehabilitation of Marduk, important as it is in the prophecy recorded in the letter of Aššur-ḫamatu'a, by no means abrogates the Assyrian hegemony over Babylonia, which is expressed in a subtle but unmistakable way all through the letter. The writing of Bel's name leaving EN without the divine determinative; the rare spelling KUR—AŠ glorifying Aššur's supremacy and the unity of Assyria; the use of the verb *salāmu* which indicates political submission; calling Assyria the "land of truth" – all this in the mouth of Bel is a weighty political message to the Babylonians about the divinely ordained distribution of power.

---

73 The plain EN sign alone indicates Bel's subordination to Aššur. Furthermore, Vera Chamaza, *Die Omnipotenz Aššurs*, 228–34, demonstrates that the role of Marduk remained subordinate to Aššur as his first-born son. The "equality" of the gods must be viewed not only against the absolute supremacy of Aššur in the Assyrian pantheon but also against the idea of Aššur as the totality of gods, whose different aspects are manifest in individual gods; see Parpola, "Monotheism in Ancient Assyria," 168–73.

74 E.g., SAA 9 2.3 ii 22–27: "Gather into your innards these words of mine from Arbela: The gods of Esaggil languish in the 'steppe' of mixed evil. Quickly let two burnt offerings be sent out to their presence, and let them go and announce your well-being!" Cf. M. Nissinen, "Das kritische Potential der altorientalischen Prophetie," in *Propheten in Mari, Assyrien und Israel* (ed. M. Köckert and M. Nissinen; FRLANT 201; Göttingen: Vandenhoeck & Ruprecht, 2003) 1–32, esp. p. 12–13 (= pp. 163–94 in this volume).

75 SAA 3 3:10; cf. Nissinen, "City as Lofty as Heaven," 180–83.

Mullissu as Intercessor Before the Divine Council

Bel's oracle begins with words that broaches the subject straight away: "I [am] the Lord. I have entered and made peace with Mu[ll]issu." This alone expresses the essential message of the whole text and, together with the subsequent address, would be enough to constitute a prophetic oracle. The following words are addressed directly to Assurbanipal using the formula "Fear not!" (Akk. *lā tapallaḫ),* which is typical of prophetic oracles throughout the ancient Near East and indicates a benevolent and encouraging encounter with the divine. More than once in Assyrian prophetic oracles, this formula is connected with the idea of reconciliation and the special relationship of the Assyrian king with the goddess Ištar/Mullissu.[76] While the prophecies usually express the outcome of the reconciliation with words denoting order and safety *(taqqunu),* this oracle of Bel is most emphatic about mercy and compassion *(riāmu/rêmu).*

The "entering" *(erābu)* of Bel is most naturally interpreted as meaning the arrival of his statue at the city of Babylon. However, the verb probably has a double meaning here, since *ētarba* can also refer to the god's entering into the scene where the words of reconciliation are spoken. Even though no other gods than Bel and Mullissu are mentioned in the extant part of the text, the oracle is cast as a heavenly scene which is best understood as the council of gods. This setting also explains why Mullissu is the one who is being reconciled, and why Bel, after having spoken his "fear not" to Assurbanipal, immediately turns to Mullissu and starts speaking to her.

The triad of Bel, Mullissu and Assurbanipal conforms exactly to the triangle of Aššur, Ištar and Esarhaddon in the prophetic oracle SAA 9 1.4 which also includes Bel, Nabû and "sixty great gods" as further members of the divine council.[77] Moreover, the situation is closely reminiscent of the prophecy SAA 9 9 in which Ištar and Mullissu, merged into one divine being, speak for Assurbanipal in front of the *puḫur ilāni,* as well as of the Dialogue of Assurbanipal and Nabû (SAA 3 13), in which Assurbanipal, presented as a child raised by the Queen of Nineveh (i. e., Mullissu), expresses the distress he feels about standing before the council of gods. Even in Assurbanipal's account of his war against Elam in the

76 See SAA 9 1.4 ii 30–33; 9 2.5 iii 19–20, 29–34; cf. Nissinen, "Fear Not," 154–57.
77 For this paragraph, see Nissinen, "Prophets and the Divine Council," 11–16.

year 653 BCE, Ištar of Arbela appears as the "counsellor of the gods" who speaks for the king in front of Aššur.[78]

In SAA 9 1.4 it is Aššur who is reconciled with Esarhaddon upon the intercession of Ištar whereas, in the present case, Marduk appears in the role of the head of the Babylonian gods against whom the Assyrian kings have sinned according to the "Sin of Sargon" theology. The goddess Mullissu, for her part, stands there on behalf of Assurbanipal and Assyria. The role of the intermediary is here given to Mullissu rather than to Ištar of Arbela probably because Mullissu, as the spouse of Aššur, stands in for the Assyrian gods and the king. As the one who nursed and raised Assurbanipal (SAA 3 13 r. 6–8), she assumes the role of intercessor for the sinner-king before the divine council (cf. SAA 9 9). Therefore, Bel speaks to her and she receives the declaration of mercy and reconciliation belonging to Assurbanipal and Assyria as a whole.

Reconciliation of Assyria – Redemption of Israel

The Assyrian theology of reconciliation is deserving of a thorough comparison with several aspects of biblical theology. In the present context, we content ourselves with a concluding remark on a topic worthy of a study of its own, namely the theology of redemption in Second Isaiah. As Manfred Weippert has demonstrated, this text bears more resemblance to Assyrian prophecy than any other part of the Hebrew Bible. Weippert has already pointed out several commonalities between Second Isaiah and Assyrian prophecy, e.g., the "Fear not" formula,[79] the divine self-presentation,[80] the maternal imagery,[81] and the divine love.[82] To these we would like to add the idea of the redemption, typical of Second Isaiah, in which the Redeemer (*gō'ēl*) is one of the commonest designations of God,[83] and the verb *g'l* is used several times[84] with the meaning of "restoring a disturbed divinely sanctioned order."[85]

---

78 Prism B v 36–42; J. Novotny and J. Jeffers, *The Royal Inscriptions of Ashurbanipal*, 69.

79 Isa 40:9; 41:10, 13, 14; 43:1, 5; 44:2; 51:7; 54:4.

80 Isa 41:4, 13, 17; 42:6, 8; 43:3, 15; 44:24; 45:5, 7, 18; 48:17; 49:23.

81 Isa 46:3–4; 44:1–2.

82 Isa 43:4; see M. Weippert, "De herkomst van het heilsorakel voor Israël bij Deutero-Jesaja," *NedTT* 36 (1982) 1–11; id., "'Ich bin Jahwe' – 'Ich bin Ištar von Arbela': Deuterojesaja im Lichte der neuassyrischen Prophetic," in *Prophetie und Psalmen*, FS Klaus Seybold (ed. B. Huwyler, H.-P. Mathys and B. Weber; AOAT 280; Münster: Ugarit-Verlag, 2001) 31–59. See also P. Merlo, "Profezia neoassira e oracoli di salvezza biblici: Motivazioni, forme e contenuti di un possibile confronto," *Rivista Biblica* 50 (2002) 129–52.

83 Isa 41:14; 43:14; 44:6, 24; 47:4; 48:17; 49:7, 26; 54:5, 8.

Even though redemption is not conceptually identical with reconciliation in general, the idea of redemption in Second Isaiah comes very close to the theology of reconciliation expressed in Assyrian prophecy and in the letter of Aššur-ḫamatu'a. A people has sinned against the divine will, which has caused the deity to forsake his temple.[86] Marduk abandoned Esaggil, YHWH the temple of Jerusalem – both prime symbols of the divine foundation of the city and the god-people relationship. After a period of divine wrath and absence, the time has come to speak tender words again and to proclaim to the people that their debt has been paid (cf. Isa 40:2). Isa 43:1–7, in particular, uses expressions well comparable to the prophetic words of Marduk in the letter of Aššur-ḫamatu'a; cf. verses 1, 4a: "These are words of YHWH who created you, Jacob, who formed you, Israel: Fear not, for I have redeemed you; I have called you by name, you are mine ... For you are precious in my eyes, you are honored, and I love you." The divine "fear not," creation/upbringing,[87] redemption/reconciliation, calling by name and the divine love – all these themes are common between the texts in which the divine and human role-casting is strikingly similar. In Second Isaiah, understandably, all divine functions are attributed to YHWH and the prophecy is addressed to Israel; this is typical of the Deutero-Isaianic interpretation of the ancient Near Eastern royal oracle.[88] While Isa 43:1–7, like many other sayings in Isa 40–55, evidently picks up themes known from other prophetic books of the Hebrew Bible,[89] the theology of redemption, so prominent in Second Isaiah, seems to find the nearest counterpart in Assyrian prophecy. This cannot be due to a direct influence of any extant Assyrian source on the anonymous author(s) of the words of Second Isaiah; regardless of the dating of individual passages in Isa 40–55, the Assyrian documents we have at our disposal were already buried with the city of Nineveh. Nevertheless, the cultural

---

84 Isa 43:1; 44:22–23; 48:20; 52:9.

85 J. Blenkinsopp, *Isaiah 40–55: A New Translation with Introduction and Commentary* (AB 19 A; New York: Doubleday, 2002), 111. For the verb *g'l* in Second Isaiah, see H. Ringgren, "*gā'al*," *TDOT* 2 (1975) 350–55, esp. p. 354–55; J. D. W. Watts, *Isaiah 34–66* (WBC 25; Waco, Tex.: Word Books, 1987) 106–107.

86 For the theme "divine alienation – devastation: divine reconciliation – reconstruction," see Brinkman, "Through a Glass Darkly," 40–41.

87 Assurbanipal is "raised" by Mullissu in SAA 13 139:4; in SAA 9 9 r. 2 however, he is called the "creation" of the hands of Mullissu and the Lady of Arbela *(binūt qātīšina)*.

88 See Weippert, "'Ich bin Jahwe' – 'Ich bin Ištar von Arbela,'" 49–51.

89 See H.-C. Schmitt, "Erlösung und Gericht: Jes 43,1–7 und sein literarischer und theologischer Kontext," in *Alttestamentlicher Glaube und biblische Theologie*, FS H.-D. Preuß (ed. J. Hausmann and H.-J. Zobel; Stuttgart: Kohlhammer, 1992) 120–31, esp. p. 128–30.

and ideological interaction between the people of Marduk and that of YHWH, however controversial, did not end with the fall of Nineveh.

City as Lofty as Heaven: Arbela and Other Cities in Neo-Assyrian Prophecy

1. Cities of God and King

> There is a river whose streams gladden the city of God,
> which the Most High has made his holy dwelling;
> God is in that city; she will not be overthrown,
> and he will help her at the break of the day (Ps. 46.4–5, NEB).

In the ancient Near Eastern and biblical literature, cities are more than just densely populated communities with a more or less hierarchical spatial and social differentiation through the distribution of work, economy, and power.[1] In the above quotation from a biblical psalm, the city is called the place "which the Most High has made his holy dwelling". As such, it appears as a theological or mythological, rather than a political or economical entity. The function of the city as the city of God transcends the limitations of everyday perception and justifies metaphors that violate concrete experience: the psalmist can make waters flow in Jerusalem[2] with no more difficulty than, say, John the visionary can envisage the holy city, new Jerusalem, coming down out of heaven adorned like a bride. In both cases, the city is presented as the dwelling of God among humans, a space of the divine presence where heaven touches earth and the divine blessing and protection, or even wrath, is bestowed upon people (Ps 46:5–8; Rev 21:1–4). Taken from the Hebrew Bible and the New Testament, these examples serve as an illustration of the symbolic, emblematic, and mythological function of the city of Jerusalem.[3] This function, however, is not re-

1 For a characterization of what may be called a city, see, e. g., V. Fritz, *The City in Ancient Israel* (BibSem 29; Sheffield: Sheffield Academic Press, 1995), 19; M. Van De Mieroop, *The Ancient Mesopotamian City* (Oxford: Clarendon Press, 1997), 36–37.

2 The "river", of course, is just one of the elements of ancient Near Eastern mythology reflected in Ps 46 (chaos-motif, El's throne "at the springs of the rivers" [*KTU* 1.17 vi 47] etc.), for which see, e. g., F. Stolz, *Strukturen und Figuren im Kult von Jerusalem* (BZAW 118; Berlin: W. de Gruyter, 1970), 163–67; P. C. Craigie, *Psalms 1–50* (WBC 19; Waco, TX: Word Books, 1983), 341–46; B. Janowski, *Rettungsgewissheit und Epiphanie des Heils: Das Motiv der Hilfe Gottes "am Morgen" im Alten Orient und im Alten Testament. Band I: Alter Orient* (WMANT 59; Neukirchen-Vluyn: Neukirchener Verlag, 1989), 185–87.

3 The symbolic role of Jerusalem, reflected, for instance, in the biblical Zion theology, has hitherto been the object of an intensive study; see, e. g., B. C. Ollenburger, *Zion, the City of the Great*

DOI 10.1515/9783110466546-016

stricted to biblical presentations of Jerusalem but is universally known from ancient Near Eastern sources and deserves attention alongside the geo-political and economic aspects of urbanism.

The idea of the city as the city of God, the "dwelling of the Most High" among humankind, was embodied in "Houses Most High", that is, in temples, in their rituals and personnel, which formed an essential part of the ancient Near Eastern urban society. Moreover, temples maintained a close contact with another significant dwelling: the palace, the residence of the king or his representative in the city. In Marc Van De Mieroop's words, "Temple and palace were basic urban institutions, and they were institutions that defined a city".[4]

The link between the temple and the palace is well motivated: the king could only rule with the divine consent and was obliged to establish the worship of the deities and take care of the property and staff of the temples.[5] Negligence in this respect was inexcusable, and the subsequent absence of the god and his or her cult from the city was a disaster.[6] On the other hand, the temple was the venue of royal festivities like enthronements and triumphs after victorious wars, which made the rituals occasions of the royal manifestations of power; even regular rituals could serve the purpose of demonstrating the king's rule.[7] Hence, the temple was an integral part of the organization of the city and state, a symbol of simultaneity of theology and politics and, due to its often considerable property, an important economical factor. Without doubt the temple was regarded as a sa-

King: A Theological Symbol of the Jerusalem Cult (JSOTSup 41; Sheffield: Sheffield Academic Press, 1987). For the amalgam of the political and symbolic aspects of the biblical presentation of Jerusalem, see, e.g., S. Talmon, "The Biblical Concept of Jerusalem," *JES* 8 (1971) 300–16; M. Weinfeld, "Jerusalem—a Political and Spiritual Capital," in *Capital Cities: Urban Planning and Spiritual Dimensions. Proceedings of the Symposium Held on May 27–29, 1996, Jerusalem, Israel* (ed. J. G. Westenholz; Bible Lands Museum Jerusalem Publications 2; Jerusalem: Bible Lands Museum, 1998) 15–40.

4 Van de Mieroop, *The Ancient Mesopotamian City,* 52.

5 For Assyria, see J. N. Postgate, *Early Mesopotamia: Society and Economy at the Dawn of History* (London: Routledge, 1992), 262–66; for Palestine, see G. Ahlström, *Royal Administration and National Religion in Ancient Palestine* (Leiden: Brill, 1982), 1–8; for Moab, B. Routledge, "Learning to Love the King: Urbanism and the State in Iron Age Moab," in *Aspects of Urbanism in Antiquity: From Mesopotamia to Crete* (ed. W. E. Aufrecht, N. A. Mirau, and S. W. Gauley; JSOTSup 244; Sheffield: Sheffield Academic Press, 1997) 130–44 (139–40).

6 See Van De Mieroop, *The Ancient Mesopotamian City,* 48, and cf. the discussion below on the "Sin of Sargon' and the absence of Marduk from Babylon.

7 See B. Pongratz-Leisten, "The Interplay of Military Strategy and Cultic Practice in Assyrian Politics," in *Assyria 1995: Proceedings of the 10th Anniversary symposium of the Neo-Assyrian Texts Carpus Project, Helsinki September 7–11, 1995* (ed. S. Parpola and R. M. Whiting; Helsinki: The Neo-Assyrian Texts Corpus Project, 1997) 145–52.

cred space in terms of purity and impurity, but it was not an isolated "religious" realm within the otherwise "secular" urbanspace—rather, the whole city could be seen as a "sacred landscape", a mythologized entity as the dwelling of God and king.[8] The fundamental association of the city, the god, and the king is observable already in the oldest records of urbanism from ancient Sumer and Egypt[9] and is probably a legacy of ancient, pre- urban societies.[10] The mythological and theological glorification of the city becomes apparent, for instance, in hymns addressed to a city and its temples,[11] and in the celebration of city walls which symbolized the frontier between the organized, divinely ruled city and the chaotic and demonic desert.[12]

Not every urban settlement was glorified as a city of God. Cities that were economical and political centers of states or districts usually also housed central temples, enjoying higher religious status than the more peripheral settlements. This was evident not only in Bronze Age city states which were comprised of but one city and its surroundings, but also in the Iron Age II territorial states of Syria-Palestine where the regional spatial hierarchy and urbanization developed hand in hand with state formation, and where there were only a limited number of urban centers and major places of worship.[13] In the empires of Mesopotamia, again, there was a more differentiated hierarchy of cities[14] and a greater diversity of religious traditions; several big cities boasted significant temples

8 See H. Cancik, "Rome as Sacred Landscape: Varro and the End of Republican Religion in Rome," *Visible Religion* 4–5 (1985–86) 250–65.

9 For cities, temples, and rulers in Sumer, see Postgate, *Early Mesopotamia*, 22–32; for Egypt, see C. Routledge, "Temple as the Center in Ancient Egyptian Urbanism," in Aufrecht, Mirau and Gauley (eds.), *Aspects of Urbanism in Antiquity*, 221–35.

10 I. M. Lapidus, "Cities and Societies: A Comparative Study of the Emergence of Urban Civilization in Mesopotamia and Greece," *Journal of Urban History* 21 (1986) 257–92 (285); cf. Cancik, "Rome as Sacred Landscape," 260: "Sacred landscape carries a materialized memory of society and is a phenomenon of 'long duration.'"

11 E.g., SAA 3 8 (Arbela), 9 (Uruk) and 10 (Assur); for older examples, see J. G. Westenholz, "The Theological Foundation of a City, the Capital City and Babylon," in id., *Capital Cities*, 43–54 (46–48).

12 For the visual and symbolic significance of the city wall, cf. Van De Mieroop, *The Ancient Mesopotamian City*, 73–76; B. Pongratz-Leisten, Ina šulmi īrub: *Die kulttopographische und ideologische Programmatik der* akītu-*Prozession in Babylonien und Assyrien im 1. Jahrtausend v. Chr.* (Baghdader Forschungen, 16; Mainz: Philipp von Zabern, 1994), 25–31.

13 For the urbanization in Israel/Judah, see Fritz, *The City in Ancient Israel*, for Moab, see Routledge, "Learning to Love the King."

14 For the settlement hierarchy, see M. Liverani, *Studies on the Annals of Ashurnasirpal II.*, vol. 2: *Topographical Analysis* (Quaderni di Geografica Storica 4; Rome: Centro Stampa d'Ateneo, 1992), 125–26, 131–32.

in which the worship of different deities had a long history: Marduk in Babylon, Aššur in Assur, Nabû in Borsippa, Sîn in Harran, Ninurta in Calah, Inanna/Ištar in Uruk, Akkad and Arbela, and so on. The multiplicity of local traditions was brought under one governmental and ideological umbrella by the centralized imperial administration, which could use the symbolic and theological significance of a city as a powerful tool in propagating imperial ideology.[15] On the symbolic and ideological level, the city manifested the presence of the God and the king, represented by temples, monuments, and local administration. The divine foundation of the city made it a symbol of convergence of the divine and human worlds and caused the name and the fame of the city to be meaningful not only to its inhabitants but to the whole empire.[16]

Hence, it is not enough to locate the ancient Near Eastern cities on the geographical and political map; seeing urbanism in a broader perspective requires locating the cities on the "mental maps" of their inhabitants as well. While there are plenty of studies of cities and urbanism in the ancient Near East and Eastern Mediterranean from the point of view of spatial and social organization and regional hierarchy,[17] the symbolic, theological, and ideological aspects of the ancient Near Eastern city still call for more attention.[18] This article is but a

15 Besides the royal rituals, the ideology was propagated by renaming cities and towns by names that contained an ideological message, e.g., the following names in Esarhaddon's list of toponyms included in his account of the campaign against Šubria (E. Leichty, *The Royal Inscriptions of Esarhaddon, King of Assyria (680–669 BC)* (RINAP 4; Winona Lake, Ind.: Eisenbrauns, 2011), 85–86 iv 14–22): *Aššūr-māssu-utīr,* "I have returned to Aššur his land'; *Aššūr-mannu-išannan,* "Who is like Aššur'; *Mušakšid-nakiri,* "The (divine) one who makes (the king) vanquish the enemies'; *Aššūr-inâr-garû'a,* "Aššur destroys my enemies' etc.; see B. Pongratz-Leisten, "Toponyme als Ausdruck assyrischen Herrschaftsanspruchs," in Ana šadî Labnāni lū allik: *Beiträge zu altorientalischen und mittelmeerischen Kulturen*, FS W. Röllig (ed. ead., H. Kühne and P. Xella; Kevelaer: Butzon & Bercker; Neukirchen–Vluyn: Neukirchener Verlag, 1997) 325–43.

16 See Westenholz, "The Theological Foundation of a City."

17 E.g., Fritz, *The City in Ancient Israel*; Postgate, *Early Mesopotamia,* 22–50, 73–87; Van De Mieroop, *The Ancient Mesopotamian City*; J. M. Wagstaff, "The Origin and Evolution of Towns: 4000 BC to AD 1900," in *The Changing Middle Eastern City* (ed. G. H. Blake and R. I. Lawless; London: Croon Helm, 1980) 11–33; Lapidus, "Cities and Societies," 257–92 and the articles in Aufrecht, Mirau and Gauley (eds.), *Aspects of Urbanism in Antiquity*; and Westenholz (ed.), *Capital Cities.*

18 These aspects have been studied recently by Pongratz-Leisten, Ina šulmi īrub, 18–19, 25–36; ead., "Toponyme als Ausdruck assyrischen Herrschaftsanspruchs"; Van De Mieroop, *The Ancient Mesopotamian City,* 42–61; Westenholz, "The Theological Foundation of the City"; I. Shaw, "Building a Sacred Capital: Akhenaten, El-Amarna and the "House of the King's Statue,'" in Westenholz (ed.), *Capital Cities,* 55–64; J. D. Hawkins, "Hattusa: Home to the Thousand Gods of Hatti," in Westenholz (ed.), *Capital Cities,* 65–82; Lapidus, "Cities and Societies," 282–85.

modest attempt at approaching these aspects, using the Neo-Assyrian documentation for prophecy as source material.

2. Arbela: Heaven without Equal

The idea of a divinely founded city at the intersection of the human and divine worlds is most gracefully presented in the Hymn to the City of Arbela:

> SAA 3 8:1–18
> *Arbail Arbail*
> *šamê ša lā šanāni Arbail āl nigūti Arbail*
> *āl isinnāti Arbail āl bēt ḫidāti Arbail*
> *aiak Arbail aštammu ṣīru ekurru šundulu parakku ṣīḫāti*
> *bāb Arbail šaqû māḫāzu*
> *āl tašīlāti Arbail mūšab ḫidāti Arbail*
> *Arbail bēt ṭēmi u milki rikis mātāti Arbail*
> *mukīn parṣī rūqūti Arbail*
> *kî šamê šaqi Arbail išdāšu kunnā kî ša[māmi]*
> *ša Arbail šaqā rēšīšu ištanannan* [...]
> *tamšīlšu Bābili šinnassu Aššūr*
> *māḫāzu ṣīru parak šimāti bāb šamê*
>
> *ana libbīšu errabū maddanāt mātāti*
> *Issār ina libbi ušbat Nanaia mārat Sîn* [...]
> *Irnīna šarissi ilāni issārtu bukurtu* [...]
>
> Arbela, O Arbela!
> Heaven without equal, Arbela! City of merry-making, Arbela!
> City of festivals, Arbela! City of the temple of jubilation, Arbela!
> Shrine of Arbela, lofty hostel, broad temple, sanctuary of delights!
> Gate of Arbela, the pinnacle of *holy to*[*wns*]!
> City of exultation, Arbela! Abode of jubilation, Arbela!
> Arbela, temple of reason and counsel! Bond of the lands, Arbela!
> Establisher of profound rites, Arbela!
> Arbela is as lofty as heaven. Its foundations are as firm as the heavens.
> The pinnacles of Arbela are lofty, it vies with [...]
> Its likeness is Babylon, it compares with Assur.
> O lofty sanctuary, shrine of fates, gate of heaven!
>
> Tribute from the lands enters into it.
> Ištar dwells there, Nanaya, the [...] daughter of Sîn,
> Irnina, the foremost of the gods, the first-born goddess [...]

In this hymn, the city of Arbela is the dwelling of the goddess Ištar in her various manifestations, associated with high spirits as well as with reason and counsel (*ṭēmu u milku*). Conspicuously enough, the city is called "heaven without equal". The whole city of Arbela is presented as a sanctuary, representing its tutelary goddess in a way that the very name of the city becomes a divine connotation. Besides the hymn, this can be seen in personal names with Arbela as the theophoric element: *Mannu-kī-Arbail*, "who is like Arbela"; *Arbail-ḫammat*, "Arbela is totality"; *Arbail-ilā'i*, "Arbela is my god"; *Arbail-šarrat*, "Arbela is queen"; *Arbail-šumu-iddina*, "Arbela has given a name"; *Arbail-lāmur*, "May I see Arbela"; *Arbailītu-bēltūni*, "the one from Arbela is our lady". These names clearly refer to Ištar of Arbela; even names like *Arbailāiu/Arbailītu* "the one (m./f.) from Arbela", do not refer to the place of domicile in the first place but are further expressions of the devotion to the goddess of this deified city, acknowledged all over Assyria.[19]

Such a plethora of theological and symbolic attributes cannot be assigned to whatever urban settlement, but it can well be expected of Arbela, which in the hymn parallels the capital cities of Babylonia and Assyria. Inhabited from the Sumerian era to our times,[20] Arbela owes much of its significance and long history of settlement to its strategic location. Situated at the western foothill of the Zagros mountains, Arbela is at the crossroads of traffic routes in the lowlands east of the Tigris and controls important passageways leading to the north and the northeast from the Assyrian heartland. Due to this favorable location, Arbela was a regional center[21] as well as a military base[22] and a seat of learning, hosting scribes and diviners.[23] More than anything, it was a prominent cult center. It was the dwelling of Ištar of Arbela—also called "the Lady of Arbela" (*bēlet Arbail*) or "Ištar who dwells in Arbela" (*Issār āšibat Arbail*)—who, especially in

---

19 Of the 35 known persons by the name *Arbailāiu*, and four by *Arbailītu*, nobody is referred to as coming from Arbela; see the respective entries by Raija Mattila and K. S. Schmidt in K. Radner (ed.), *The Prosopography of the Neo-Assyrian Empire*, I/1 (Helsinki: The Neo-Assyrian Text Corpus Project, 1998), 124–27. Similar name patterns with other divine names are well known: *Mannu-kī-Aššūr, Aššūr-ilā'i, Adad-šumu-iddina, Adad-bēlāni, Aššūr-lāmur* and so on; cf. *Mannu-kī-Libbāli, Mannu-kī-Nīnua* and other names with a name of a city in the place of the theophoric element.

20 A comprehensive history of Arbela has not been written hitherto, neither has the site been excavated; the center of the modern city of Erbil is built above the huge mound of 30 meters accumulation of settlement layers.

21 In the Neo-Assyrian era, Arbela was the center of the "district of Arbela" (*ḫalzu Arbail;* SAA 12 50:7; 71:5; 72 r.11 etc.), and its governor (*pāḫutu*) is mentioned on a par with governors of Nineveh and Dur-Šarruken in SAA 10 369.

22 For military activities in the Neo-Assyrian Arbela, cf. SAA 1 149; 155; SAA 5 141; 152.

23 The letters SAA 10 136–42, reporting astrological observations, are sent by "the decurion of Arbela' (*rab eširti ša ṭupšarrī ša Arbail*). The extant extispicy reports with indication that they are performed in Arbela are SAA 4 195; 300 and 324.

the time of Esarhaddon and Assurbanipal, had an established position among the Great Gods. She is one of the most frequently mentioned deities with hundreds of attestations in greetings of letters, inscriptions and other documents from their time, often together with her *alter ego*, Ištar of Nineveh/Mullissu. The temple of Ištar of Arbela, Egašankalamma, was one of the major temples in Assyria.[24] As the "shrine of the fates" and the "gate of heaven", it was the abode of traditional secret lore,[25] awesome festivities[26]—and prophecy.

Among the sources of prophecy, Arbela has no peer in Assyria; a brief look at the index of place names in the edition of the Neo-Assyrian prophetic texts reveals that the name of Arbela is mentioned more often than any other geographical name in this corpus.[27] Seven out of fifteen prophets known by personal names are Arbela-based:

> Aḫat-abiša, a woman from Arbela (*mar'at Arbail* SAA 9 1.8),
> Bayâ, a (wo)man[28] from Arbela (*mār Arbail* SAA 9 1.4; [2.2]),
> Dunnaša-amur,[29] a woman from Arbela ([*mar'at Arba*]*il* SAA 9 9; cf. 10),
> Issar-la-tašiyaṭ, a man from Arbela (*mār Arbail* SAA 9 1.1),
> La-dagil-ili, a man from Arbela (*mār Arbail* SAA 9 1.10; *Arbailāja* 2.3 and 3),
> Sinqiša-amur, a woman from Arbela (*mar'at Arbail* SAA 9 1.2; [2.5])
> Tašmetu-ereš "prophesied in Arbela" ([*ina lib*]*bi Arbail irt*[*ugum*] SAA 9 6).

In addition, the letter of Nabû-reši-išši (SAA 13 144) reports a prophecy delivered by a woman in a temple which to all appearances is located in Arbela.[30] On the

---

24 The temple, like the city, has not been excavated; for written sources, B. Menzel, *Assyrische Tempel*, vol. 1: *Untersuchungen zu Kult, Administration und Personal* (Studia Pohl Series Maior 10.1; Rome: Biblical Institute Press, 1981), 6–33; A. R. George, *House Most High: The Temples of Ancient Mesopotamia* (Mesopotamian Civilizations 5; Winona Lake, IN: Eisenbrauns, 1993), 90, #351.

25 The text SAA 3 38, "The Rites of Egašankalamma", is a further representative of the genre of mystical texts deriving from the Babylonian tradition (SAA 3 34–40), for which see A. Livingstone, *Mystical and Mythological Explanatory Works of Assyrian and Babylonian Scholars* (Oxford: Clarendon Press, 1986).

26 In addition to the above-quoted hymn, cf., e.g., the reference to a *qarītu* banquet of Ištar in SAA 13 147. For the *akītu* festivals, see below.

27 S. Parpola, *Assyrian Prophecies* (SAA 9; Helsinki: Helsinki University Press, 1997), 53.

28 For the uncertain gender of Bayâ, see Parpola, *Assyrian Prophecies*, il and the respective entry in *PNA* I/2 (1999) 253.

29 Possibly identical with Sinqiša-amur; cf. Parpola, *Assyrian Prophecies*, il–l and the respective entry in *PNA* I/2 (1999) 388.

30 This is discernible from the greeting formula typical of writers form Arbela as well as from the letter SAA 13 145 by the same writer. This letter mentions temple weavers which are known especially from Arbela (cf. SAA 13 186); see the notes of K. Radner in S. W. Cole and P. Machinist,

other hand, Ištar of Arbela is the one speaking in at least fourteen oracles of the prophetic corpus[31] and, in addition, in two prophecies quoted in the inscriptions of Assurbanipal.[32] Moreover, Lady of Arbela speaks through at least two prophets who come from outside of Arbela, namely, Urkittu-šarrat from Calah (SAA 9 2.4) and Remutti-Allati from Dara-aḫuya (SAA 9 1.3). This, along with the devotion to her in personal names, may be taken as a further indication of the veneration of Ištar of Arbela as a national, rather than a local manifestation of the divine.

The strong concentration on Arbela in the prophetic sources from the time of Esarhaddon and Assurbanipal corresponds with these kings' particular attachment for the city. Egašankalamma was well taken care of and decorated by both kings.[33] Esarhaddon visualized his enduring presence in this temple by letting his doubled image be placed on the right and left sides of Ištar.[34] Assurbanipal, too, presented the temple as the object of his special devotion. In the dialogue between him and Nabû, the god says the following to the king who is praying for his life in Emašmaš, the temple of Ištar of Nineveh:

SAA 3 13:16–18:
šīmtaka ša abnûni tattanaḫḫaranni mā
tuqnu bila ina Egašankalamma
napšatka ittanaḫḫaranni mā
balāssu urrik ša Aššūr-bāni-apli

Your fate, which I devised, incessantly prays to me thus:
"Bring safety into Egašankalamma!"
Your soul incessantly prays to me:
"Prolong the life of Assurbanipal!"

Letters from Priests to the Kings Esarhaddon and Assurbanipal (SAA 13; Helsinki: Helsinki University Press, 1999), 116–17.

31 I.e., SAA 9 1.1; 1.2; 1.4; 1.6; 1.8; 1.9; 1.10; SAA 9 2.3; 2.4; SAA 9 3.4; 3.5; SAA 9 5; SAA 9 6 and SAA 9 9. In addition, SAA 9 1.3 and 2.5 are to be understood as the words of Ištar of Arbela; furthermore, she appears together with Mullissu in SAA 9 7.

32 I.e., in his accounts of the campaigns against Mannea (Prism A iii 4–7) and Elam (Prism B v 45–48); see J. Novotny and J. Jeffers, *The Royal Inscriptions of Ashurbanipal (668–631 BC), Aššur-etel-ilāni (630–627 BC), and Sîn-šarra-iškun (626–612 BC), Kings of Assyria,* Part 1 (RINAP 5/1; University Park, Pa.: Eisenbrauns, 2018), 69, 239.

33 Esarhaddon: Leichty, *The Royal Inscriptions of Esarhaddon*, 155:8–11; Assurbanipal: Novotny and Jeffers, *The Royal Inscriptions of Ashurbanipal*, 216 (Prism T) ii 7–17.

34 This is reported in the letters of Aššur-ḫamatu'a (SAA 13 140 and 141); cf. I. J. Winter, "Art *in* Empire: The Royal Image and the Visual Dimensions of Assyrian Ideology," in Parpola and Whiting (eds.), *Assyria 1995*, 359–81 (376).

This prayer juxtaposes the "safety" of Egašankalamma and the life of Assurbanipal by means of a poetic parallelism, tying the fate of the king in with the stability of the temple. The idea of "safety" (*tuqnu*) implies both physical security and peace and reconciliation between heaven and earth, as is discernible from prophetic oracles of Ištar of Arbela, which frequently use the verb *taqqunu* ("to put in order") and its derivatives in a similar meaning.[35] Language reminiscent of prophecy can also be found in a document of a royal votive gift given for Egašankalamma by one of the kings "[for the preservation of] my [life], the lengthening of my days, the longevity of my kingship, and the destruction of my enemies, [...] and in Egašankalamma until distant days I [...]".[36] The damages of the text notwithstanding, the dependance of the reign of the king on the endurance of the temple is unmistakable.

Furthermore, Assurbanipal assures his regular attendance at Egašankalamma in his prayer addressed to the Lady of Arbela on account of the assault of Teumman, king of Elam, in the year 653.[37] Assurbanipal heard about Teumman when he was attending a festival of Ištar in Arbela, "her beloved city" (*āl narām libbīša*). Having received the message he, according to the inscription, burst into tears and uttered a long prayer to the goddess, whom he presents as his creator, as goddess of warfare, and as his intercessor before Aššur. Upon the prayer, he got a twofold answer from Ištar: first an encouraging oracle, probably a prophetic one, and still in the same night, a dream report of a dreamer (*šabrû*).[38] In the next month, "the month of the messages of the goddesses" (*šipir ištārāti*, i.e.

---

35 E.g., SAA 9 1.2 i 33–34: [*ina*] *bēt rēdūtēka* [*utaqq*]*anka* [*urabb*]*akka*, "[In] the Palace of Succession [I ke]ep you safe and [rai]se you"; 1.10 vi 22–26: *aklu taqnu takkal mê taqnūti tašatti ina libbi ekallīka tataqqun*, "You shall eat safe food, you shall drink safe water, you shall live in safety in your palace"; 2.5 iii 19–20: *māt Aššūr utaqqan ilāni zenûti* [*is*]*si māt Aššūr ušal*[*l*]*am*, "I will keep Assyria safe, I will reconcile the angry gods with Assyria"; 5:9: *tuqqun ana A*[*ššūr-aḫu-iddina šar māt Aššūr a*]*ddan*, "I will give security for [Esarhaddon, king of Assyria]"; cf. SAA 16 59 s.3 [*atta*] *tuqūnu ina ekallīka šībi*, "[As for you], stay in safety in your palace!". See M. Nissinen, *References to Prophecy in Neo-Assyrian Sources* (SAAS 7; Helsinki: The Neo-Assyrian Text Corpus Project, 1998), 153.

36 SAA 12 89:7: [*ana balāṭ napšātī*]*ya arāk ūmīya šulburu šarrūtīya sakāp nakrūtīya* [...] *qereb Egašankalamma ana ṣât ūmē*[...]; reconstruction according to the edition. For prophetic parallels, cf., e.g., SAA 9 1.2; 1.6; 2.3; 2.5.

37 Novotny and Jeffers, *The Royal Inscriptions of Ashurbanipal*, 69: 32–33: *anāku ašrēki aštene"i allika ana palāḫ ilūtīki u šullum parṣēki*, "I visit regularly your dwellings, I come to worship you and take care of your rituals".

38 Novotny and Jeffers, *The Royal Inscriptions of Ashurbanipal*, 69–70 v 45–72. The passage is discussed at length in P. Gerardi, "Assurbanipal's Elamite Campaigns: A Literary and Political Study" (Dissertation, University of Pennsylvania, 1987), 145–47; Nissinen, *References to Prophecy*, 53–56.

prophecies), he mobilized his troops and vanquished Teumman.[39] This lengthy passage in the inscription of Assurbanipal is revealing in many respects. Besides being emphatic about Arbela as the place of communication between the goddess and the king, it serves as an illustration of a typical situation in which prophecies were uttered and as a paragon of the ideology of holy war. Moreover, it provides a kind of compendium of Ištar theology, presenting the goddess as the creator and mother of the king in a language very similar to that of the prophecies.

In the final analysis, the reason for the prominence of the city of Arbela among the Assyrian cities and the appreciation of prophecy in that city must be sought from the distinctive relationship between the goddess and the king. Simo Parpola has emphasized that when Assurbanipal in his hymn to the Ištars of Arbela and Nineveh calls himself the "product of Emašmaš and Egašankalamma" (SAA 3 3:10; see below), he refers to his upbringing as the royal infant in the temples of Ištar in Nineveh and Arbela, and even the prophecies and related texts which present the goddess(es) as the wet nurse or the mother of the king[40] should be understood accordingly.[41] This practice is a concrete reflection of the old idea of the king as the creation of the gods, abundantly represented in inscriptions, hymns, and prophecies, but it goes even further: it is a simulation of what were imagined to be the heavenly circumstances: just like the Ištars of Nineveh and Arbela are the nurses of Marduk in the divine world (SAA 3 39:19–22), they are tending the king, "the Marduk of the people" (SAA 10 112 r. 31), in the human sphere. As far as the sources give the right impression, this practice was begun only with Esarhaddon whose mother Naqia obviously maintained a close contact with the prophets of Arbela.[42] Hence, Esarhaddon's and Assurbanipal's particular devotion to Arbela was due to the exceptionally intimate relationship they had with the Lady of Arbela and her cult. This explains much of the outstanding position of the city of Arbela in the sources from the period of Esarhaddon and Assurbanipal, and it also sheds light on the special appreciation of prophecy during their rule as a by-product of the increased significance of the institutions of the Ištar worship in Arbela.

---

39 Novotny and Jeffers, *The Royal Inscriptions of Ashurbanipal*, 70–71 v 73–vi 9.

40 SAA 9 1.6 iii 15–18; 2.5 iii 26–27; 7 r. 6–11; SAA 3 13 r. 6–8 etc.

41 Parpola, *Assyrian Prophecies*, xxxix–xl.

42 She is addressed several times in the prophetic oracles: SAA 1.7 v 8; 1.8 v 12–20; 2.1 i 13; 2.6 iv 28 (?); 5:4; cf. Nissinen, *References to Prophecy*, 22–24; S. C. Melville, *The Role of Naqia/Zakutu in Sargonid Politics* (SAAS 9; Helsinki: The Neo-Assyrian Text Corpus Project, 1999), 27–29.

3. The Palace of the Steppe in Milqia

In the vicinity of Arbela there was a locality which, though not represented by its name, is otherwise identifiable in the prophetic oracles. In the prophecy to the queen mother Naqia, Ištar of Arbela says that she will "go out to the Palace of the Steppe":

> SAA 9 5:8–9
> *ina ekal ṣēri u*[*ṣṣa* ...] *tuqqun ana A*[*ššūr-aḫu-iddina šar māt Aššūr a*]*ddan*
>
> I will [go] to the Palace of the Steppe [...] I will give protection for E[sarhaddon, king of Assyria],

In yet another oracle, the goddess sends an oracle to Esarhaddon from the steppe:

> SAA 9 1.9 v 27–30
> *Issār ša Arbail ana ṣēri tattūṣi šulmu ana mūrīša ana birit āli tassapra ana uṣê*[*ša* ...]
>
> Ištar of Arbela has left for the steppe. She has sent an oracle of peace to her calf[43] in the city. At [her] coming out [...]

Even though badly broken, the texts are revealing enough. The sojourning of the goddess in the steppe makes perfect sense, as Esarhaddon allegedly renewed an "*akītu*-house in the steppe, a house of festivals" (*bīt akīt ṣēri bīt nigūti*).[44] We know that in a locality called Milqia, situated not far away from Arbela, there was an *akītu*-house of Ištar of Arbela.[45] There are records of worship of Ištar of Arbela in Milqia from the time of Shalmaneser III,[46] and the references to

---

43 For the king as the "calf" of the goddess, see M. Nissinen, *Prophetie, Redaktion und Fortschreibung im Hoseabuch: Studien zum Werdegang eines Prophetenbuches im Lichte von Hos 4 und 11* (AOAT 231; Kevelaer: Butzon & Bercker; Neukirchen–Vluyn: Neukirchener Verlag, 1991), 290–94; Parpola, *Assyrian Prophecies*, xxxvi–xliv.

44 Leichty, *The Royal Inscriptions of Esarhaddon*, 117:20, 32.

45 For the sources, see Menzel, *Assyrische Tempel I*, 113; S. Parpola, *Neo-Assyrian Toponyms* (AOAT 6; Kevelaer: Butzon & Bercker; Neukirchen–Vluyn: Neukirchener Verlag, 1970), 248; George, *House Most High*, 87, #313.

46 I.e., the prayer *KAR* 98, in which Milqia is mentioned in a broken context and the Lady of Arbela is addressed among other deities (see Menzel, *Assyrische Tempel*, vol. 2: *Anmerkungen, Textbuch, Tabellen und Indices* [Studia Pohl, Series Maior 10.2; Rome: Biblical Institute Press, 1981], 111*, nos 1519–21), and the poetic account of his campaign to Urartu, which reaches its climax when the king enters a palace, arranges the festival of the Lady of Arbela in Milqia and, finally, performs a lion hunt in Assur (SAA 3 17 r. 27–30; provided that the readings are

works done in this locality in the correspondence of Sargon II may also deal with her shrine.[47] Assurbanipal mentions the "Palace of the Steppe, dwelling of Ištar" in Milqia and the accompanying *akītu*-house;[48] in general, the sources from the time of Esarhaddon and Assurbanipal give the best picture about what it was needed for. It appears that Ištar of Arbela, who in Milqia was called Šatru,[49] dwelt there during the absence of the king, in anticipation of a triumph after his returning from a victorious campaign. When the king arrived, the goddess left Milqia and, together with the king, entered the city of Arbela in a solemn procession.[50] The two prophetic references to the "(Palace of the) Steppe" are to be interpreted as references to the triumphal celebration after Esarhaddon had defeated his brothers. The first oracle (SAA 9 5) must have been proclaimed while Esarhaddon was still absent, since it is addressed to the queen mother who during the civil war received prophecies on behalf of her son.[51] The second oracle

---

correct); see E. Weissert, "Royal Hunt and Royal Triumph in a Prism Fragment of Ashurbanipal (82–5–22,2)", in Parpola and Whiting (eds.), *Assyria 1995*, 339–58 (348–49).

47 I.e., SAA 1 146, a letter of Šamaš-upaḫḫir concerning some city rulers (*bēl ālāni*) whom the king had ordered to work in Milqia, and SAA 1 147, a letter from these city rulers who complain that the work is a great burden on them. The nature of the king's work (*dullu šarri*) is not specified, but since virtually all other occurrences of Milqia are connected with this sanctuary or its festivals, it may be that the works have to do with it; there is a reference from this time to "washing" some clothing in Milqia which was needed in offering rituals (ND 2789:8–9; see the publication of B. Parker, "Administrative Tablets from the North-West Palace, Nimrud," *Iraq* 23 [1961] 15–67 [53] and the corrected reading of Menzel, *Assyrische Tempel*, 111*, nn. 1522–24). Moreover, Milqia is mentioned in the letter of Kišir-Aššur (SAA 1 125): "Upon my coming from Milqia to Dur-Šarruken, I was told that there had been an earthquake in Dur-Šarruken …".

48 J. Novotny, *Selected Royal Inscriptions of Assurbanipal: L^3, L^4, LET, Prism I, Prism T, and Related Texts* (SAACT 10; Helsinki: The Neo-Assyrian Text Corpus Project, 2014), 80: 6–7: *Milqia ekal ṣēri mūšab Issār anḫūssu uddiš bīt akīssu arṣip ālu ina gimirtīšu ušaklil*, "As for Milqia, I renovated the delapidated Palace of the Steppe, I reconstructed its *akītu*-house, I rebuilt the whole town."

49 With regard to the above-quoted passages of prophecy in connection with other sources it is evident that the name Šatru, pace Menzel, *Assyrische Tempel I*, 113, should not be disconnected from Ištar of Arbela.

50 This procession is described in SAA 13 149, probably following Esarhaddon's conquest of Egypt, and in Assurbanipal's report on his triumph after the defeat of Teumman, king of Elam (E. F. Weidner, "Assyrische Beschreibungen der Kriegs-Reliefs Aššurbânaplis," *AfO* 8 [1932/33] 175–203 [184:43–46]); see S. Parpola, *Letters from Assyrian Scholars to the Kings Esarhaddon and Assurbanipal*, vol. 2: *Commentary and Appendices* (AOAT 5.2; Kevelaer: Butzon & Bercker; Neukirchen–Vluyn: Neukirchener Verlag, 1983) 158–59, 192–93; Pongratz-Leisten, Ina šulmi īrub, 79–83; ead., "The Interplay of Military Strategy and Cultic Practice," 249–50; Weissert, "Royal Hunt and Royal Triumph," 347–50.

51 See Nissinen, *References to Prophecy*, 22–24.

(SAA 9 1.9) presupposes that the war is over, since the king is already in the city (of Nineveh or Arbela), awaiting the encounter with the goddess.

Milqia is not an independent case, but belongs together with the institutions of Arbela as a kind of ceremonial extension of the city. Milqia was probably no major urban settlement, neither could it be situated far away from Arbela. The designation of its main building as the "Palace of the Steppe" indicates that it was located outside the walls of the city of Arbela, symbolizing the world of chaos in the middle of which the goddess sojourned when the king was in the turmoils of war.[52] The procession from the "steppe" to the city after the victory, hence, visualized the victory over the powers of "evil, chaotic wilderness" (SAA 9 2.3 ii 24). The ceremonies in Arbela and Milqia illustrate how the concrete and symbolic aspects of urbanism fuse together, as Beate Pongratz-Leisten has pointed out.[53] The military significance of Arbela not only increased the mobility of people and goods enhancing financial investments and administration, it also made it necessary to make the presence of the king emphatically manifest and promote the cult of the patron goddess with whom the king had a special relationship.

4. The Doorjambs of Assyria: Assur, Nineveh and Calah

Besides Arbela, a whole range of Mesopotamian cities are explicitly or implicitly acknowledged in the Neo-Assyrian prophetic sources. The oracle of an unknown prophet in the oracle collection SAA 9 1 provides a good starting point for the survey, as it itemizes four major Assyrian cities as belonging to the sphere of Esarhaddon's reign:

SAA 9 1.6 iii 8–14
anāku Issār ša [Arbail] Aššūr-aḫu-iddina šar māt A[ššūr]

52 See Pongratz-Leisten, Ina šulmi īrub, 74–78.

53 Pongratz-Leisten has generalized a similar conclusion from the evidence from a group of strategically important Assyrian cities, including Arbela, Nineveh, Kilizi, Kurbail, and Harran ("The Interplay of Military Strategy and Cultic Practice," 251): "The paramount military role of these [strategically important] cities presupposed the support and the promotion of their respective patron-gods. (...) (A)t the moment when the city was rebuilt into a military garrison, the cult of the city god also experienced a special financial and theological promotion. (...) This promotion is quite understandable, considering the fact that the Assyrian king wanted to be helped and protected by the patron-god of a border garrison in close proximity to his enemies."

ina Libbi āli Nīnu[a] Kalḫa Arbai[l] ūmē arkūt[e] šanāte dārāt[e] ana Aššūr-aḫu-iddina šarrīja addanna

I am Ištar of [Arbela]! Esarhaddon, king of A[ssyria]!
In Assur, Ninev[eh], Calah and Arbe[la] I will give endle[ss] days and everlasti[ng] years to Esarhaddon, my king.

This neither restricts the rule of Esarhaddon only to the cities in question, nor is the list of cities a random choice of the prophet or the scribe. The four cities, Assur, Nineveh, Calah, and Arbela, are the most important urban centers in the Assyrian heartland,[54] each of them having a long history of settlement and religious tradition. In the royal poetry, these cities embody the idealized functions of the Assyrian city and state,[55] and the worship of Ištar, the main speaker of the Assyrian prophetic word, played a central role in all of them.[56] When Assur, Nineveh, Calah, and Arbela are mentioned together, they are not just a list of four cities but represent the whole *māt Aššūr*; hence, the "endless days and everlasting years" in these four cities epitomize Esarhaddon's eternal rule over all Assyria.[57] A similar idea is represented by another oracle which most probably refers to Assur, Nineveh, Calah, and Arbela as the "four doorjambs of Assyria":[58]

SAA 9 3.5 iii 16–22, iv 15–17
abat Issār ša Arbail ana Aššūr-aḫu-iddina šar māt Aššūr
akī ša memmēni lā ēpašūni lā addinakkanni
mā 4 sippī ša māt Aššūr lā akpup, lā addinakkâ nakarka lā akšūdu …
[ūm]â rīš Aššūr-aḫu-iddina
[4 sipp]ī ša māt Aššūr [aktapp]a attanakka [nakar]ka aktašad

54 Of the other cities in that region, only Dur-Šarruken, the capital of Sargon II, could rival Assur, Nineveh, Calah, and Arbela in size and significance, but it had lost its status as the capital to Nineveh and, being founded so late by Sargon II, lacked the venerable tradition the four cities had. It is never mentioned in the extant sources for prophecy.

55 In addition to the above quoted Hymn to the City of Arbela (SAA 3 8), cf. SAA 3 7 (Assurbanipal's Hymn to Ištar of Nineveh) and SAA 3 10 (Blessing for the City of Assur); it may be coincidental that no such hymn to Calah has been preserved. See A. Livingstone, *Court Poetry and Literary Miscellanea* (SAA 3; Helsinki, Helsinki University Press, 1989), xxv–xxvi.

56 For the the worship of Ištar in these cities, see Menzel, *Assyrische Tempel I*, 63–65, 70–74 (Assur); 114–18 (Nineveh); 102–3 (Calah).

57 Later in the same oracle, the mentioning of Assur and Arbela alone is enough to render the same idea: *Aššūr-aḫu-iddina ina Libbi āli ūmē arkūte šanāte dārāte addanakk[a] Aššūr-aḫu-iddina ina libbi Arbai[l] arītka deiqtu a[nāku]*, "Esarhaddon, in Assur I will give yo[u] endless days and everlasting years! Esarhaddon, in Arbe[la] I [will be] your good shield!" (SAA 9 1.6 iv 14–19).

58 Cf. Parpola, *Assyrian Prophecies*, 26 *ad loc.*

> Word of Ištar of Arbela to Esarhaddon, king of Assyria.
> As if I had not done or given to you anything! Did I not subdue and give
> to you the four doorjambs of Assyria? Did I not vanquish your enemy?...
> [Theref]ore, rejoice, Esarhaddon!
> [The four doorjamb]s of Assyria [I have subdu]ed and given to you! I have vanquished your [enemy]!

While the first of the passages quoted above is taken from a prophecy proclaimed during Esarhaddon"s war against his brothers,[59] presenting his rule as a prospective reality, the second belongs to the context of his enthronement, referring to the victory he gained over his enemies. The four cities represent here the "people of Assyria" (*nīšē māt Aššur*) who, according to the account of Esarhaddon's inscription, came before him and kissed his feet after the goddess had disrupted the ranks of the enemies.[60] The doorjamb (*sippu*) metaphor presents the cities as the doorways through which the newly enthroned king Esarhaddon enters his sphere of power, as entrances which the goddess, by vanquishing his enemies, has "subdued" and opened for him to come in.[61]

Of the four "doorjambs", Assur clearly comes second in importance after Arbela in the prophetic sources. As the ancient capital of Assyria and as the center of the worship of Aššur, the Assyrian supreme god,[62] Assur had a significance among Assyrian cities that exceeded its political weight. It was the city where the Assyrian kings were enthroned and buried, and its most outstanding temple, Ešarra, was the principal shrine of Aššur.[63] The earliest Neo-Assyrian evidence for prophecy in Assur is the mention of female prophets (*maḫḫâte*) in a list of expenditures for the maintenance of various ceremonies of Ešarra dated to the sixth day of Adar (XII) of the eponym year of Adad-nerari III (809).[64] Furthermore, Assur is given as the place of origin of two prophets from the time of Esarhaddon, [Nabû]-ḫussanni[65] (SAA 9 2.1) and Ilussa-amur[66] (SAA 9 1.5). The institu-

59 See Nissinen, *References to Prophecy*, 24–25.

60 Leichty, *The Royal Inscriptions of Esarhaddon*, 13–14: 74–81.

61 Cf. Ps 24:7 (NEB): "Lift up your heads, you gates, lift yourselves up, your everlasting doors, that the king of glory may come in."

62 For the role of Aššur as the universal god in Assyrian religion, see Parpola, *Prophecies*, xxi; id., "The Assyrian Tree of Life: Tracing the Origins of Jewish Monotheism and Greek Philosophy," *JNES* 52 (1993) 161–208 (205–206).

63 See Menzel, *Assyrische Tempel I*, 36–63; George, *Houses Most High*, 145, #1035.

64 SAA 12 69. The prophets are mentioned in a section concerning the "divine council" (lines 27–31).

65 For the restoration of the name, which could also be [Aššur]-ḫussanni, see Parpola, *Assyrian Prophecies*, li.

tional affiliation of these prophets is not indicated; Ešarra is not the only alternative, since there was a temple of Ištar in Assur as well. Ešarra, however, is the temple where the appearance of the prophetess Mullissu-abu-uṣri is reported by Adad-aḫu-iddina in his letter to the king (SAA 13 37). According to the preserved text of the fragmentary letter, this woman prophesied (*tartugum*) in the temple that the throne housed in that temple should be sent to Akkad for a substitute king ritual.[67] What makes Ešarra the most probable venue for this prophetic appearance, besides the structure of the blessing formula of the letter,[68] is that not just any throne was good enough to be used in that ritual, but it had to be the actual royal throne, the one on which Esarhaddon was seated when he was enthroned in Ešarra.

The enthronement of Esarhaddon at the end of the year 681 BCE is referred to at the beginning of the account of the construction of Ešarra in the inscription Assur A, written in 679 BCE.[69] Even prophetic messages (*šipir maḫḫê*) are mentioned among the signs of good portent (*ittāti dunqi*) coming from the different kinds of divination which enouraged the newly enthroned king.[70] This is not just a rhetorical note, since the prophecies proclaimed on that occasion by the prophet La-dagil-ili (from Arbela!) were collected and preserved for posterity in the collection SAA 9 3. The role of Ešarra and the city of Assur as the symbol of the Assyrian royal ideology becomes unmistakable in the introductory passage of this collection:

> SAA 9 3.1 i 9–15
> [*šulmu a*]*na šamê kaqqiri* [*šulm*]*u ana Ešarra* [*šulmu*] *ana Aššūr-aḫu-iddina šar māt Aššūr* [*šulm*]*u ša Aššūr-aḫu-iddina* [*iškun*]*ūni ina muḫḫi šēpē lillik* [*isinnu ina*] *Ešarra Aššūr issakan* [...] *ša Libbi āli*
>
> [Peace] with heaven and earth! [Peac]e with Ešarra! [Peace] with Esarhaddon, king of Assyria! May the [peac]e [establish]ed by Esarhaddon become stable and prosper![71] Esarhaddon has arranged [a banquet[72] in] Ešarra. [...] of Assur.

66 This name is otherwise attested only in a fragment of a list of provisions from Assur, *KAV* 121, in which together with other women she receives provisions.
67 For this letter and its historical background, see B. Landsberger, *Brief des Bischofs von Esagila an König Asarhaddon* (Mededelingen der Koninklijke Nederlandse Akademie van Wetenschappen, afd. Letterkunde, Nieuwe reeks 28/6; Amsterdam: Koninklijke Nederlandse Akademie van Wetenschappen, 1965), 49; Parpola, *Letters*, 329; Nissinen, *References to Prophecy*, 78–81.
68 SAA 13 37:4–6: "May Aššur, Mullissu, Nabû and Marduk bless the king, my lord"; cf. Parpola, *Letters*, 329.
69 For the inscription, cf. B. N. Porter, *Images, Power, and Politics: Figurative Aspects of Esarhaddon's Babylonian Policy* (Philadelphia: American Philosophical Society, 1993), 97–99.
70 Leichty, *The Royal Inscriptions of Esarhaddon*, 121, 124 i 9–ii 26.
71 Lit.: "go on its feet", or "get on to its feet".

Ešarra and the city of Assur are here represented as the space where the peace between heaven and earth is celebrated, where the *šulmu* established by Esarhaddon, the well-being based on cosmic harmony and personified by the king, becomes manifest. In the two prophetic oracles following the introductory passage, the *šulmu* is proclaimed in prophetic words and made material in the form of tablets which are placed first before the courtyard god Bel-Tarbaṣi (SAA 9 3.2 ii 8) and then before the Image (of Aššur), probably in the throne room where the king is seated (SAA 9 3.3 ii 26).

In the prophetic oracles, then, the city of Assur, together with its main temple, assumes a ceremonial role as the scene of events which are not only of paramount political importance but also symbolize the fundamentals of the Assyrian religion and royal ideology. It is hardly a matter of chance that in the prophetic oracles, the city is never called *(Āl) Aššūr* (URU-*aš-šur* or BAL.TIL.KI) but consistently referred to as *Libbi āli* (URU.ŠÀ—URU), the Inner City,[73] which, rather than just meaning the "city center", is a honorific designation which implies the message of the centrality of Assur as the dwelling of the Assyrian supreme god.

The role of the city of Assur in the prophetic oracles clearly overshadows that of the capital city of the empire, Nineveh. Even though there was an eminent temple of Ištar in Nineveh called Emašmaš,[74] no single prophet of the corpus comes from there, nor is the city of Nineveh indicated as the provenance of any prophecy quoted outside the prophetic corpus. This virtual silence, however, does not mean that there was no prophetic activity in Nineveh. In his retrospective account of his rise to power, Esarhaddon claims to have been encouraged by prophecies (*šipir maḫḫê*) which were constantly sent to him on occasion of his joyful entering into Nineveh and his ascending the throne of his father.[75] Whether originating from Nineveh or other places, such prophecies were certainly delivered (cf. SAA 9 1!) and read out in Nineveh. When the astrologer Bel-ušezib complains about the insufficient attention paid to him by the newly enthroned king, he refers to prophets and prophetesses that have been summoned by the

---

72 Thus according to the restoration of Parpola, *Assyrian Prophecies*, 22 *ad loc.* What follows is probably a description of a procession leading to Esarhaddon's enthronement.

73 SAA 9 1.5 iii 5; 1.6 iii 9; iv 1; 2.1 i 14; 3.1 i 15.

74 See Menzel, *Assyrische Tempel I*, 116–17; George, *House Most High*, 121–22, #742.

75 Leichty, *The Royal Inscriptions of Esarhaddon*, 14 i 87–ii 11: "In the month of Adar (XII), a favorable month, on the 8th day, the day of the festival of Nabû, I triumphantly entered Nineveh, the residence of my lordship, and happily ascended the throne of my father. The Southwind, the breeze of Ea, was blowing—the wind whose blowing portends well for exercising the kingship. Favorable omens in the sky and on earth came to me. Oracles of prophets, messages of the gods and the Goddess, were constantly sent to me and they encouraged my heart."

king instead of him (SAA 10 109:7–16). Provided that the king actually granted an audience to the prophets, and the "summoning" does not simply stand for employing, Nineveh provides itself as a natural site of this encounter. In these sources, however, Nineveh is merely the implied scene of events without any emphatically symbolic connotation.

The suspicious nonappearance of Nineveh in the prophetic oracles, save its inclusion in the group of the "four doorjambs" (SAA 9 1.6 iii 9) and its juxtaposition with Calah in a passage to be quoted below (SAA 9 2.4 iii 7–11) could be explained by the impression given by the texts that of the twin manifestations of Ištar, the dominance of Ištar of Arbela in prophecy is unquestionable, while Ištar of Nineveh never appears as the speaker in the prophetic oracles. However, this is not, in fact, the case. When the goddess speaks in a double apparition, it is always Mullissu who appears together with Ištar of Arbela (SAA 9 2.4 ii 30; 7 r. 6; 9 r.1), and Mullissu, on the other hand, is the wife of Aššur whose role wholly converges with that of Ištar of Nineveh. The pairing of Ištar of Arbela and Mullissu in the prophetic oracles corresponds to the juxtaposition of the Ištars of Arbela and Nineveh elsewhere.[76] This can be exemplified by the letter of the exorcist Nabû-nadin-šumi to the king, in which he recommends the banishment of a person by virtue of the (prophetic) words of the Ištars of Arbela and Nineveh;

SAA 10 284 r. 4–8
kî ša Issār ša N[īnua] Issār ša Arbail iqban[ni]
mā ša issi šarri bēlīn[i] lā kēnūni mā issu māt Aššūr ninassaḫšu

According to what Ištar of N[ineveh] and Ištar of Arbela have said: "Those who are disloyal to the king our lord, we shall extinguish from Assyria," he should indeed be banished from Assyria!

The divine words referred to by Nabû-nadin-šumi turn out to be a paraphrase of a prophetic oracle (SAA 9 2.4 ii 31–33),[77] in which the divine speakers are Ištar of Arbela and Mullissu. This not only speaks for the identification of Ištar of Nineveh and Mullissu but underlines the conclusion that the two goddesses are actually one. The same impression can be gathered from Assurbanipal's Hymn to the Ištars of Nineveh and Arbela:

---

76 Cf. Parpola, *Assyrian Prophecies*, xl, lxxi and note that the dialogue between Assurbanipal and Nabû (SAA 3 13), which is both historically and substantially very closely related to the prophecy SAA 9 9, takes place in Emašmaš, the Ištar temple of Nineveh, which is also called the dwelling of Mullissu (Leichty, *The Royal Inscriptions of Esarhaddon*, 116 r. 5: *Emašmaš atman Mullissi bēltīya*). In this dialogue, the motherly roles of Mullissu (lines 21–22) and the Queen of Nineveh (lines r. 2–8) fuse together.
77 See Nissinen, *References to Prophecy*, 102–105.

SAA 3 3:6–12.r. 14–16
zikir šaptēšina girru napḫu atmûšina kunnū ana dāriš
anāku Aššūr-bāni-apli bibil libbīšin zēr Aššūr rabû [ili]tti Nīnâ, binūt Emašmaš [u] Egašanka-lamma ša ultu libbi bīt rē[dūti ušar]bâ šarrūtī [ina p]îšina ell[i qab]û labār kussīja …

Bēlit-Nīnâ, ummu alittīya tašruka šarrūtu ša lā šanāni Bēlit Arbail bā[nī]tīya taqbâ balāṭī dārāte

A word from their lips is blazing fire! Their utterances are valid for ever!
I am Assurbanipal, their favorite, most valued seed of Assur, [offs]pring of Nineveh, product of Emašmaš [and] Egašankalamma, whose kingship they [made gr]eat even in the Palace of Succession], [In] their pure mouth is [spok]en the endurance of my throne …

The Lady of Nineveh, the mother who bore me, endowed me with unparalleled kingship; the Lady of Arbela, my creator, ordered everlasting life for me.

The language and imagery of this hymn is blatantly "prophetic", being in many ways parallel to the extant prophetic oracles.[78] Even though this is not a warrant for us to take the hymn as a specimen of prophecy from Nineveh (the language of prophecy common with this and many other forms of poetry rather explains itself by the background of prophecy in the worship of Ištar), expressions like "word from their lips" and "in their pure mouth" may be interpreted in terms of prophecy. No specific attention is paid to the city of Nineveh in this hymn,[79] except its being the "home" of the goddess and the location of her temple, Emašmaš.

Nineveh appears together with Calah as a potential hotbed of insurrection in an oracle belonging to the collection from the beginning of Esarhaddon's reign:

SAA 9 2.4 iii 7–14
akê akê ša ana […] ma'dūti ú-[[sa?]]-na-'u-[x-ni]
mā immati mātu nakkuru ibbašši mā ina Kalḫi Nīnua lū lā nūšab
atta lū qālāka Aššūr-aḫu-iddina ṣīrāni Elamāja Mannāja abīar Urarṭāja šiṭrīšu abarrim igib ša Mugalli ubattaq

78 E.g.: SAA 3 3:3 "who have no equal among the great gods", cf. SAA 9 9:3: "they are strongest among the gods"; SAA 3 3:13: "I knew no father or mother, I grew up in the lap of the goddesses", cf. SAA 9 2.5 iii 26–27: "I am your father and mother, I raised you between my wings"; SAA 3 3:14–15: "As a child the great gods guided me, going with me on the right and the left", cf. SAA 9 1.4 ii 20–24: "When your mother gave birth to you, sixty great gods stood with me and protected you. Sîn was at your right side, Šamaš at your left", and so on.
79 Cf. Assurbanipal's Hymn to Ištar of Nineveh (SAA 3 7), where the city does play a certain role.

> How, how to respond to those who ...[80] to many [people], saying: "Will the way of this country ever change? Let us not stay in Calah and Nineveh!"
> You, Esarhaddon, keep silent! I will select the emissaries of the Elamite king and the Mannean king, I will seal the messages of the Urartean king, I will cut off the heel[81] of Mugallu.[82]

In this case, the two cities do not seem to assume any emphatically symbolic or emblematic role. As the capital city, Nineveh is a natural choice as an example of a city where problems of domestic policy may surface, and Calah is given as the place of origin of the prophetess Urkittu-šarrat who delivered the oracle. The cities seem to appear as *pars pro toto*, as two examples of places where the previously mentioned "disloyal ones" (*lā kēnūti*, SAA 9 2.4 ii 29, 32) may show up, rather than being specifically pointed out as the main trouble spots. The same applies to the sample of foreign nations listed in the oracle, Elam, Mannea, Urartu, and Melid, which at the beginning of Esarhaddon's reign would not (yet) necessarily harass Assyria any more than other countries did.[83]

The fact that Urkittu-šarrat is designated as a *Kalḫītu* (SAA 9 2.4 iii 18) makes it evident that prophets were active in the city of Calah, where their natural base was the temple of the Lady of Kidmuri, the local manifestation of Ištar.[84] This temple was restored by Assurnasirpal II in the ninth century, and again by Assurbanipal who in his inscription gives an account of the re-establishment of the cult of the Lady of Kidmuri, which, according to this account, had meanwhile

---

80 The word is partly erased, partly broken and difficult to interpret. It could be explained as *ussana"ū[ni]*, an otherwise not attested Dtn-form of *ša'û* "run', but this verb does not occur in Neo-Assyrian.

81 The word is interpreted as *eqbu*, "heel' (see *AHw* 231).

82 Mugallu was the king of Melid in Anatolia; cf. SAA 4 1–12 and see S. Aro, "Tabal: Zur Geschichte und materiellen Kultur des zentralanatolischen Hochplateaus von 1200 bis 600 v.Chr" (Ph.D. diss., University of Helsinki, 1998), 149–53.

83 This is not to say that each of these nations would not have caused any trouble in the future. After less than half a decade, during the years 676–675 BCE, Esarhaddon took a campaign against both Mannea and Melid, while Elam raided northern Babylonia. Only the mention of Urartu is peculiar in this context, as Urartu was already defeated at the end of the eighth century by Sargon II and hardly constituted any serious threat in the time of Esarhaddon. Urartu might not refer only to the state with the same name but also to other powers that were active in the north, above all the Cimmerians who were allied with Ursâ, king of Urartu, against Šubria. For a historical overview, see A. K. Grayson, "Assyria: Sennacherib and Esarhaddon (704–669 B.C.)," *CAH*² 3/2 (1991) 103–41 (127–32).

84 For this temple, see Menzel, *Assyrische Tempel I*, 102–3; J. N. Postgate and J. Reade, "Kalhu," *RLA* 5 (1976–80) 303–23 (308–9); George, *House Most High*, 113, #645.

been in a state of dereliction.[85] While this may not quite have been the case (there are indications that Bet Kidmuri existed even in the time of Esarhaddon), it is conclusive that Assurbanipal indeed promoted the cult of the Lady of Kidmuri.[86] As the sources of inspiration, Assurbanipal mentions dreams and prophecies (*šipir maḫḫê*) that were constantly sent to him by the goddess "to make perfect her majestic divinity and glorify her precious rites".[87] Formulaic as this language is, it certainly reflects the concern of the prophets for the temple that employed them.

With regard to the "mental map" of the prophecies, the geographical scope of the prophecy of Urkittu-šarrat deserves attention. While the oracle proclaims the word of Ištar of Arbela and Nineveh (Mullissu), the prophetess comes from Calah and is probably affiliated to the temple of the Lady of Kidmuri. On the other hand, her name means "Urkittu is Queen", and even though the appellation Urkittu is indistinguishable from Mullissu in the Neo-Assyrian sources,[88] it carries the memory of the city of Uruk and its goddess. Together, the four manifestations of the goddess, associated with four cities, not only demonstrate the extension of Ištar's dominion but also the fundamental unity of the different manifestations of the goddess.

5. Babylon and the Gods of Esaggil

Among the cities acknowledged in the Neo-Assyrian sources for prophecy, a special attention is devoted to Babylon, the capital city of the sister nation. This

---

85 Novotny and Jeffers, *The Royal Inscriptions of Ashurbanipal*, 216 ii 7–24.

86 See Nissinen, *References to Prophecy*, 35–37. It is not altogether clear, though, in which city this happened, since both Calah and Nineveh housed a temple of the Lady of Kidmuri in the Neo-Assyrian era; for the Bet Kidmuri in Nineveh, see Menzel, *Assyrische Tempel I*, 121–22. In his long petition to Assurbanipal, the exorcist Urad-Gula claims to have arranged a banquet in Bet Kidmuri (SAA 10 294 r. 23)—whether in Calah or in Nineveh, can only be guessed. Moreover, it is unclear whether his visit to this temple had anything to do with his turning to a prophet, about which he tells later in the same letter (line r. 32).

87 J. Novotny and J. Jeffers, *The Royal Inscriptions of Ashurbanipal*, 216 ii 14–17: *ana šuklul ilūtīša ṣīrti šurruḫu mēsēša šūqurūti ina šutti šipir maḫḫê ištanappara kayyāna*, "To make perfect her majestic divinity and glorify her precious rites, (the Lady of Kidmuri) constantly sent me orders through dreams and prophetic messages." Note the affinity to the respective account of Esarhaddon's accession to throne in the Ass A inscription (above, n. 74).

88 Parpola, *Assyrian Prophecies*, lii; cf. especially SAA 3 13 r. 2: "May he who grasped the feet of the Queen of Nineveh not come to shame in the assembly of the great gods; may he who sits next to Urkittu not come to shame in the assembly of those who wish him ill!"

must be partly due to the prophetic tradition in Babylonia, documented at long intervals from Ur III[89] through Old Babylonian[90] and Neo-Babylonian[91] periods to the Hellenistic times.[92]

However, there are also timely reasons for the relevance of Babylonian matters in the Neo-Assyrian oracles.

To be sure, the name of the city of Babylon occurs in the Neo-Assyrian prophetic corpus only once in a broken context (SAA 9 2.6 iv 4). However, the gods of Esaggil, the temple of Marduk in Babylon and the principal place of worship in all Babylonia,[93] make an impressive appearance in the collection of prophecies from the beginning of Esarhaddon's reign (SAA 9 2). As the introductory oracle of the collection, the compilers have chosen that of [Nabû]-ḫussanni from Assur, in which Ištar speaks in her various manifestations, including the goddesses of Esaggil:

SAA 9 2.1 i 5–12
[... *anāku*] *Banītu* [...] *utaqqan* [*kussiu ša Aššūr-aḫu*]-*iddina ukâna* [...]
anīnu ištarāti [... *i*]*na Esaggil* [...] *Aššūr-aḫu-iddina šar māt Aššūr*
[*nakarūtēka*] *usappak* [*ina šēpēya*] *ukabbas*

89 In TCS 1 369:5, a *muḫḫûm* of Innin of Giršu appears as the recipient of a barley ration; see E. Sollberger, *The Business and Administrative Correspondence under the Kings of Ur* (TCS 1; Locust Valley, NY: J.J. Augustin, 1966), 90.

90 The best document of prophecy in Old Babylonian Babylon is the letter of Yarim-Addu to Zimri-Lim, king of Mari (ARM 26 371) which reports the appearance of a prophet (*āpilum*) of Marduk at the gate of the royal palace in Babylon; see D. Charpin et al., *Archives épistolaires de Mari I/2* (ARM 26.2; Paris: Editions Recherche sur les Civilisations, 1988), 177–79. In addition, there are several occurences of *muḫḫûm* in Old Babylonian sources, e.g., MDP 18 171:14 *Ri-bi-i mu-ḫu-um*, "Ribī the prophet".

91 E.g., YOS 6 18 lists two persons designated as "sons" of prophets: $^{md+}$AG NUMUN GIN A ^{m}LÚ.GUB.BA "Nabû-zēru-ukīn son of the prophet" (lines 1, 7); ^{m}*remut* ^{d}EN A ^{m}LÚ.GUB.BA "Remūt-Bēl son of the prophet" (lines 8, 10). In these cases, the prophet is the ancestor of the family.

92 I.e., the Late Babylonian *akītu* ritual in which a high priest (*šešgallu*) utters an oracle of Bel closely akin to prophetic language (F. Thureau-Dangin, *Rituels accadiens* [Paris: Ernest Leroux, 1921], 144–45). This seems to witness a literary adaptation of prophecy in cultic literature; see K. van der Toorn, "L'oracle de victoire comme expression prophétique au Proche-Orient ancien," *RB* 94 (1987) 63–97 (93).

93 See George, *House Most High*, 139–40, #967.

> [... *I am*] Banitu,[94] [...] I will put in order. I will establish [the throne of Esarh]addon. [...]
> We are the goddesses [... i]n Esaggil! [...] Esarhaddon, king of Assyria!
> I will catch [your enemies] and trample them [under my foot].

The self-presentation of Ištar as the goddesses of Esaggil at the very outset of the collection speaks for itself, but the concern for Babylon becomes even more emphatic in the course of the text of the collection. The concluding sixth oracle obviously thematizes Babylon and Esaggil again, being partly presented as the word of Urkittu (Ištar of Uruk/Mullissu; SAA 9 2.6 iv 1–15); however, this prophecy is too fragmentary for a proper interpretation. In the third oracle from the mouth of La-dagil-ili from Arbela, Ištar of Arbela does not speak *as* the deities of Esaggil, but *for* them:

> SAA 9 2.3 ii 22–27
> *dibbīja annūti issu libbi Arbail ina bētānukka esip*
> *ilāni ša Esaggil ina ṣēri lemni balli šarbubū*
> *arḫiš 2 maqaluāti ina pānīšunu lušēṣiū lillikū šulamka liqbiū*
>
> Take to heart these words of mine from Arbela:
> The gods of Esaggil are languishing in an evil, chaotic wilderness.
> Let two burnt offerings be sent before them at once, let your greeting of peace be pronounced to them![95]

This appealing speech is intelligible when interpreted against the fact that Babylon still lay in ruins after its destruction by Sennacherib a decade earlier (689 BCE), after a whole cycle of Babylonian uprisings and the subsequent punitive campaigns. When Esarhaddon, after the victorious civil war against his brothers ascended the throne of his father, the situation in Babylonia was certainly the most urgent political problem he had to face. It was one of the principal efforts of Esarhaddon throughout his reign to establish a political control over the potentially rebellious Babylonia, and not only that, but a *modus vivendi* between Assyria and Babylonia, governed by an ideology of a single nation under one king.[96] This

94 Banitu is a designation of the creation goddess Belet-ili, here appearing as an aspect of Ištar; see Parpola, *Assyrian Prophecies*, xviii and cf. K. Deller, "STT 366: Deutungsversuch 1982," *Assur* 3 (1983), 139–53 (142–43).

95 This translation takes the people who take the offerings to the gods as the subject of the precatives *lillikū* and *liqbiū*; in this case "your well-being" (*šulamka*) means the king's greeting to the gods. If, on the other hand, the gods of Esaggil are to interpreted as the subject, then *šulamka* would be the oracle of salvation of these deities concerning Esarhaddon's well-being.

96 For the political history of Babylonia before and during the reign of Esarhaddon, see J. A. Brinkman, *Prelude to Empire: Babylonian Society and Politics, 747–626 B.C.* (Occasional Publications of the Babylonian Fund 7; Philadelphia: The University Museum, 1984), 67–84;

ideology was theologically motivated by the divine foundation of the city of Babylon[97] and the respective veneration of Marduk and other gods of Esaggil, whose harsh treatment by Sennacherib caused a guilty conscience later on, as the famous "Sin of Sargon" text (SAA 3 33) demonstrates. In this text, designed as a kind of testament of Sennacherib to his son, the death of Sargon on the battlefield is explained as a consequence of his insufficient veneration of the gods of Babylonia.[98] Esarhaddon is urged to make the statue of Marduk and finish what his father left unfinished: "Accept what I have explained to you, and reconcile [the gods of Babylonia] with your gods!" (SAA 3 33 r. 26 – 27.) This is perfectly in line with the above-quoted prophecy, as well as with the whole collection, the central theme of which is the consolidation of Esarhaddon's throne and the reconciliation between him and the divine world:

> SAA 9 5 iii 19 – 20
> *Aššūr-aḫu-iddina lā tapallaḫ*
> *māt Aššūr utaqqan ilāni zenûti [is]si māt Aššūr ušal[l]am*
>
> Esarhaddon, fear not!
> I will protect Assyria, I will reconcile the angry gods with Assyria.

Among the "angry gods" in question, the Babylonian ones certainly were the angriest. It is noteworthy that reconciliation, not only with the gods of Assyria but also with those of Babylonia, is presented as prerequisite of the safety and wellbeing of Assyria. This is beautifully exemplified by the fact that the prophets from Assur and Arbela seem to have been among the first proponents of this ideology.

The prophets were not alone, though, since similar ideas were also cherished by scholars who belonged to the closest board of the king's advisors. Bel-ušezib, the best known Babylonian scholar employed by Esarhaddon, repeatedly embeds a similar message in his letters. Soon after Esarhaddon's accession, he re-

---

G. Frame, *Babylonia 689 – 627 B.C.: A Political History* (Uitgaven van het Nederlands Historisch-Archaeologisch Instituut te Istanbul 69; Istanbul: Nederlands Historisch-Archaeologisch Instituut te Istanbul, 1992), 52 – 101; for the ideological dimensions of Esarhaddon's political efforts, see J. A. Brinkman, "Through a Glass Darkly: Esarhaddon's Retrospects on the Downfall of Babylon," *JAOS* 103 (1983) 35 – 42 and, most profoundly, Porter, *Images, Power, and Politics*, esp. 77 – 153.

97 See Westenholz, "The Theological Foundation of the City," 49 – 51.

98 See H. Tadmor, B. Landsberger and S. Parpola, "The Sin of Sargon and Sennacherib's Last Will", *SAAB* 3 (1989) 3 – 52. The ideological context of this text fits the time of Esarhaddon rather than that of Sennacherib; for this reason, Landsberger (p. 35) and Parpola (pp. 45 – 47) argue for a date of composition during Esarhaddon's reign.

minds the king of the sign of kingship, which he told to the queen mother Naqia and to an exorcist during Esarhaddon's expatriation at the time of the civil war preceding his rise to power. The meaning of the sign is the following: "Esarhaddon will rebuild Babylon and restore Esaggil" (SAA 10 109: 13–15).[99] In another letter a few years later, the same astrologer quotes words that to all appearances are of prophetic origin:

> SAA 10 111 r. 23–26
> *Bēl iqtabi umma akī Marduk-šapik-zēri Aššūr-aḫu-iddina šar māt*
> *Ašš[ūr] ina kussîšu lū ašib u māt[āti] gabbi ana qātēšu amanni*
>
> Bel has said: "May Esarhaddon, king of Ass[yria], be seated on his throne like Marduk-šapik-zeri, and I will deliver all the countr[ies] into his hands."

As well as presenting the divine speech as that of Marduk (Bel) of Babylon, the point is that Marduk-šapik-zeri was a king of Babylon four hundred years earlier (1081–1069 BCE), and his merits included the rebuilding of the fortifications of Babylon and the conclusion of an alliance with the contemporary Assyrian king, Aššur-bel-kala.[100] Presenting him as the paragon of a divinely favored king implies that nothing less is required of Esarhaddon.

Moreover, the theory and practice of the theology of reconciliation is amply represented also by the inscriptions of Esarhaddon that concentrate on his building projects in Babylonia. According to the Babylon inscription of Esarhaddon, the most programmatic text in favor of the reconstruction of Babylon, it was Marduk himself who together with the other gods abandoned Babylon in his anger at the negligent and treacherous people and relented only when Babylon and its temples were repaired and the gods brought back to where they belonged.[101]

According to the inscriptions, which are partly corroborated by archaeological evidence, the repatriation of the gods of Babylonia and the building of temples began at the very beginning of Esarhaddon's reign and continued ever

99 This is an application of an omen taken from the omen collection *Enūma Anu Enlil* (56) which he quotes in an abridged form later in the letter (SAA 10 109 r. 14–15); see S. Parpola, "The Murderer of Sennacherib," in *Death in Mesopotamia* (ed. B. Alster; Mesopotamia 8 (= CRRAI 26); Copenhagen: Akademisk Forlag, 1980) 171–82 (179–80).

100 See G. Frame, *Rulers of Babylonia from the Second Dynasty of Isin to the End of Assyrian Domination (1157–612 BC)* (RIMB 2; Toronto: University of Toronto Press, 1995), 45–49.

101 Leichty, *The Royal Inscriptions of Esarhaddon*, 196 i 34–ii 9; 203 i 37–ii 22; 212 i 10–ii 3; 236 i 19–ii 18; 244–45:7–9. For the "divine alienation—divine reconciliation" pattern, see Brinkman, "Through a Glass Darkly," 40–41; for the use of this pattern in prophecy, Nissinen, *References to Prophecy*, 38–41.

since.[102] In spite of all his efforts, however, Esarhaddon could not carry out the main objective of this project, the restoration of Esaggil. He attempted to reinstate the statue of Marduk in Esaggil in his last year (669), but an inauspicious event obstructed this enterprise.[103] The works on Esaggil were finally completed at the beginning of the reign of Assurbanipal who calls Esarhaddon "builder of Esaggil" and only claims to have completed what his father left unfinished.[104]

In addition to the prophecies, letters, and inscriptions, there is one document in which the fate of Babylon and her patron god Marduk is the central theme: the so-called Marduk Ordeal text, a commentary on a ritual in which Marduk is beaten and sent to prison (SAA 3 34/35). It has been argued with good reason that this text, rather than being anti-Babylonian propaganda, commiserates with the god and reflects the politics of the circles who never gave up the veneration of Marduk and promoted the rebuilding of Babylon and Esaggil.[105] As the *akītu* festival, for obvious reasons, did not take place in Babylon during the reigns of Sennacherib and Esarhaddon,[106] the ritual is most probably to be associated with the return of the statue of Marduk in Babylon at the beginning of Assurbanipal's reign.[107] In one passage of this text, even a prophet (*maḫḫû*) opens his mouth;

SAA 3 34:28–29/SAA 3 35:31
maḫḫû ša ina pān Bēlet-Bābili illakūni mupassiru šû ana irtīša ibakki
illak mā ana ḫursān ubbulūšu šî taṭarrad mā aḫūa aḫūa [...]

---

102 See Porter, *Images, Power, and Politics*, 41–75.

103 For the date, see Parpola, *Letters from Assyrian Scholars*, II, 32 (ad SAA 10 24). The fragment K 6048+8323 possibly refers to the same incident; see W. G. Lambert, "Esarhaddon's Attempt to Return Marduk to Babylon," in *Ad bene et fideliter seminandum: Festgabe für Karlheinz Deller* (ed. G. Mauer and U. Magen; AOAT 220; Kevelaer: Butzon & Bercker; Neukirchen–Vluyn: Neukirchener Verlag, 1988) 157–74. The return of the statue of Marduk and other gods is overoptimistically anticipated in the AsBbE inscription (Leichty, *The Royal Inscriptions of Esarhaddon*, 137:42–49).

104 M. Streck, *Assurbanipal und die letzten assyrischen Könige bis zum Untergange Niniveh's* (VAB 7; Leipzig: Hinrichs, 1916), 228:5 and 226:8–9.

105 So T. Frymer-Kensky, "The Tribulations of Marduk: The So-called 'Marduk Ordeal Text,'" *JAOS* 103 (1983) 131–41 (139–40); cf. Livingstone, *Mystical and Mythological Explanatory Works*, 236–53; Porter, *Images, Power, and Politics*, 139–40.

106 Thus the Esarhaddon and Akitu Chronicles; see A. K. Grayson, *Assyrian and Babylonian Chronicles* (TCS 5; Locust Valley, NY: J.J. Augustin, 1975), 127: 31–36, 131:1–8.

107 Frymer-Kensky, "The Tribulations of Marduk," 140.

> The prophet who goes before the Lady of Babylon is a bringer of news; weeping he goes toward her: "They are taking him (scil. Marduk) to the *ḫursān*[108]!" She sends (the prophet) away, saying: "My brother, my brother!" [...]

With regard to the proclamation of the Assyrian prophets on behalf of the gods of Esaggil, there is nothing surprising in the appearance of a prophet in a ritual like this, especially if the suggested historical background is correct. Whatever role the prophets may have played in *akītu* rituals in general, this particular case reflects their pro-Babylonian attitude. Along with the exorcists who are designated as "his people" (*nišīšu*) in the previous line,[109] the cultic commentary presents the prophets as sympathizers of Marduk, the maltreated lord of Babylon.

The failure to return Marduk to Esaggil notwithstanding, Esarhaddon took great pains with the rebuilding of Babylon, and the position assigned to the main god of Esaggil and Babylonia was conspicuously renowned in Assyria during his reign. Consistently with the reconciliation ideology, the veneration of Marduk, having suffered a serious decline in the time of Sennacherib, was again part of the public image of the king.[110] According to the written documents at our disposal, this development was enhanced by the joint efforts of the supporters of the reconciliation between Assyrian and Babylonia—prophets, diviners, and scribes.

6. Akkad as the Venue for the Substitute King Ritual

The Babylonian policy of Esarhaddon appears in a somewhat different light in the letters sent by his agent in Babylonia, Mar-Issar. For all his goodwill towards Babylonia, Esarhaddon had to keep his eyes open for any trace of insurrection among the Babylonians whose attitudes towards Assyria were often critical if not hostile after Sennacherib's destructive maneuvers, and Mar-Issar was in Bab-

108 This word is interpreted as meaning the river ordeal, but Frymer-Kensky ("The Tribulations of Marduk," 138–39) shows that it rather means the cosmic location where Marduk is held captive.

109 SAA 3 34:27/3 35:22: "The exorcists (LÚ.MAŠ.MAŠ.MEŠ) who go in front of him reciting an incantation, are his people (UN.MEŠ-*šu*); they [go] wailing in front of him"

110 See Porter, *Images, Power, and Politics*, 137–48 and cf. B. N. Porter, "What the Assyrians Thought the Babylonians Thought about the Relative Status of Nabû and Marduk in the Late Assyrian Period," in Parpola and Whiting (eds.), *Assyria 1995*, 253–60.

ylonia precisely for that reason. In his famous report on the burial of the substitute king in the city of Akkad in the year 671 BCE (SAA 10 352), Mar-Issar quotes two prophecies uttered by a prophetess in the course of the substitute king ritual, obviously in order to convince the king that the somewhat exceptional choice of the substitute king was the will of the gods: the person who died for the sake of the king was the son of the temple administrator (*šatammu*) of Akkad. He also tells that the inhabitants of Akkad as well as other Babylonians became nervous, obviously for the reason that the execution of the son of a high official reminded the Babylonians of their political situation.[111]

The role of the city of Akkad in the substitute king ritual is highly ceremonial. Akkad (Agade) was the ancient Sargonid capital of Babylonia in the second half of the third millennium, and its patroness, the Lady (Ištar) of Akkad, belonged to the prominent Babylonian manifestations of the goddess. Even though Akkad never achieved political importance after the Gutian invasion in the twenty-second century (it recovered for a while only in the Kassite period), it retained its symbolic value in mythological and religious literature as the center of the cult of Ištar.[112] It was Esarhaddon who, as a part of his rebuilding project in Babylonia, revived the city and returned Ištar and other gods of Akkad from Elam in the year 674 BCE.[113] The reason for the rebuilding of Akkad was doubtless its symbolic and religious significance as the ancient capital rather than its strategic or economical importance. The substitute king ritual was necessary because the lunar eclipse afflicted Babylonia, and by arranging it in Akkad Esarhaddon gave the city an exalted position. Very probably the substitute king ritual and the archaic "assembly of the country"[114] convoked on that occasion were one of the few major events that had taken place in the newly rebuilt city. By means of this event Esarhaddon not only paid homage to time-honored Babylonian traditions but also demonstrated and enacted his kingship over Babylonia.

---

111 For this letter and the role of prophecy in it, see Nissinen, *References to Prophecy*, 68–77.

112 The history of the city is summarized by G. J. P. McEwan, "Agade after the Gutian Destruction: The Afterlife of a Mesopotamian City," *AfO Beiheft* 19 (1982) 8–15.

113 Grayson, *Assyrian and Babylonian Chronicles*, 84:16–18; 126:21–22; cf. SAA 10 359 and Frame, *Babylonia*, 73–75.

114 The *puḫrum* is a well-known institution from the Early Dynastic and Old Babylonian periods; see Postgate, *Early Mesopotamia*, 80–81; Van De Mieroop, *The Ancient Mesopotamian City*, 121–28.

7. Pseudoprophecy in Harran, the City of the Moon God

The city of Harran enjoyed a remarkable political and religious status in the Neo-Assyrian era. The political and strategic significance of the city was related to its role as a trading center along several commercial routes between Mesopotamia, Syria-Palestine, and Asia Minor, whereas its religious prestige was based on the age-old tradition of the worship of Sîn, the Moon God, in Harran.[115] Since the ninth century, the city was part of the Assyrian empire, achieving a distinguished religio-political position especially in the time of Esarhaddon and Assurbanipal. Just as he did in Arbela, Esarhaddon demonstrated his special appreciation of Harran, his incessant devotion to the Moon God and his enduring presence in Harran by placing his doubled statue on the right and left sides and the images of his sons behind and in front of the image of Sîn.[116] Assurbanipal, for his part, rebuilt Eḫulḫul, the temple of Sîn, including the cella of Nusku called Emelamanna.[117]

Harran plays an important role in the letters of Nabû-reḫtu-uṣur, who warns the king about an alleged conspiracy that has an outpost in that city (SAA 16 59–61). He is informed about the scheming of a certain Sasî and his accomplices for the overthrow of Esarhaddon that culminated in a (pseudo)prophecy uttered by a "slave girl" of Bel-aḫu-uṣur from Harran. This woman had allegedly spoken "in the neighborhood of Harran" words of the god Nusku, according to which the dynasty of Sennacherib will be destroyed and Sasî will be the king (SAA 16 59 r. 2–5). Even though Nabû-rehtu-uṣur did not know that the whole episode was probably due to an intentional misleading,[118] the way he connects the

115 See T. M. Green, *The City of the Moon God: Religious Traditions of Harran* (Religions in the Graeco-Roman World 114; Leiden: Brill, 1992); E. Lipiński, *Studies in Aramaic Inscriptions and Onomastics* (OLA 57; Leuven: Peeters, 1994), 171–92; S. W. Holloway, "Harran: Cultic Geography in the Neo-Assyrian Empire and its Implications for Sennacherib's 'Letter to Hezekiah' in 2 Kings," in *The Pitcher is Broken*, FS G. W. Ahlström (ed. id. and L. K. Handy; JSOTSup 190; Sheffield: Sheffield Academic Press, 1995) 276–314. For the symbolic and figurative meanings of the moon-god of Harran, see C. Uehlinger, "Figurative Policy, Propaganda und Prophetie," in *Congress Volume Cambridge 1995* (ed. J. A. Emerton; VTSup 66; Leiden: Brill, 1997) 297–349 (315–23).

116 SAA 10 13; cf. Winter, "Art *in* Empire," 376.

117 J. Novotny and J. Jeffers, *The Royal Inscriptions of Ashurbanipal*, 115 i 76–85; for the sources, see also George, *House Most High*, 99, #470, and 123, #764.

118 Sasî was probably Esarhaddon's agent among the conspirators and kept the king up to date about what was happening; see Nissinen, *References to Prophecy*, 108–53.

prophecy against the king with the city of Harran deserves attention. First, while referring to the word of Mullissu in SAA 16 60, he is consistent in quoting words of Nikkal against the words claimed to be those of Nusku in SAA 16 59.[119] This is because Nikkal and Nusku were the wife and the son of Sîn, and the cult of this divine family was centered in Harran;[120] indeed, Sîn, Nusku, and Nikkal turn out to be the Harranean equivalent of the triad Bel, Nabû, and Ištar/Mullissu, to which Nabû-reḫtu-uṣur shows himself to be devoted in the greetings of his three letters (SAA 16 59:2–3; SAA 16 60:2–3; SAA 16 61:2–3) and which appears as the triune divine speaker in the prophecy of Bayâ (SAA 9 1.4).

The designation of Sîn as "the Lord of Harran" (*bēl Ḫarrān*), very common, for example, in personal names all over the empire,[121] manifests the fundamental affinity of the god and the city; even in Nineveh, his temple is called "the house of the Lord of Harran" (*bīt bēl Ḫarrān*). This temple was the venue of the false extispicy which the kidnapped scholar Kudurru was forced to perform with the series of the temple of Nusku in hand and which certainly was part of the same conspiracy Nabû-reḫtu-uṣur was concerned about (SAA 10 179).[122] Remarkably, the god and the city belong together, with the political and symbolic aspects of the city interwoven, no matter what kind of undertaking is in process. Likewise, in the letter of Nabû-reḫtu-uṣur, the city of Harran is not only represented by its name but also by its gods; events that take place in Harran are interpreted by him as affecting the gods who have chosen the city as their dwelling, and vice versa.

An interesting aspect of the religio-political eminence of the city of Harran reveals itself in the fact that the oracle of Nusku against the king was proclaimed, not within the city, but "on the outskirts" of Harran (*ina q[an]ni ša Ḫarrān]*). The same expression occurs in a letter in which Marduk-šumu-uṣur re-

---

119 SAA 16 59:8: *dabābu ša Nikkal ū[da ...]* "I k[now] the words of Nikkal"; ibid., line 12–13: *[ina li]bbi dabābi Nik[kal annie] lā taši[aṭ...]* "Do not disrega[rd these] words of Ni[kkal!...]"; cf. SAA 16 60:8–9: *dabābu anniu ša Mullissu [šû šarru bēlī] ina libbi lū lā i[šīaṭ]* "This is the word of Mullissu; [the king, my lord,] should not be ne[glectful] about it."

120 For the worship of these deities in Harran, see Green, *The City of the Moon God*, 19–43; id., "The Presence of the Goddess in Harran," in *Cybele, Attis and Related Cults*, FS M. J. Vermaseren (ed. E. N. Lane; Religions in the Graeco-Roman World 131; Leiden: Brill, 1996) 87–100; Holloway, "Harran: Cultic Geography in the Neo-Assyrian Empire," 287–91.

121 *Bēl-Ḫarrān-bēlu-uṣur*, "O Lord of Harran, protect the lord"; *Bēl-Ḫarrān dūrī* "Lord of Harran is my protective wall"; *Bēl-Ḫarrān-issē'a*, "Lord of Harran is with me"; *Bēl-Ḫarrān-šaddû'a*, "Lord of Harran is my mountain"; *Bēl-Ḫarrān-šarru-uṣur*, "O Lord of Harran, protect the king" etc.; see the respective entries by P. Villard, K. Radner and H. D. Baker in *PNA* I/2 (1999) 300–304.

122 See Nissinen, *References to Prophecy*, 133–35.

minds Assurbanipal about the temple of cedar, built "on the outskirts" of Harran to be the scene of a royal ceremony when Esarhaddon was on his way to conquer Egypt in Nisan (I), 671 BCE. In this ceremony, Esarhaddon was crowned in the presence of Sîn and Nusku and a (prophetic?) oracle was spoken to him: "You will go and conquer the world with it!" (SAA 10 174: 10–16). This "act of propaganda staged as a symbolic act"[123] was a formidable demonstration of the presence of the king and the gods of Harran—but why outside Harran and not in the city itself? It seems that the temple of cedar was built "on the outskirts" of Harran just as the *akītu*-houses, like the one in Milqia, were often situated outside the city walls. A sanctuary outside the city not only symbolized the dwelling of the god outside her/his proper place, but also enabled a triumphal procession from the realm of chaos into the city. The function of the *akītu*-processions was to celebrate the re-establishment of order, to visualize the power and presence of the king and to inspire the people with confidence. Even though such a triumphal procession is not mentioned with regard to the ceremony in the temple of cedar (which may or may not be identical with the otherwise attested *akītu*-house of Harran[124]), the function of this ceremony is largely the same as that of the *akītu*. Moreover, it is conceivable that the oracle of Nusku against the king was proclaimed nowhere else than in this particular spot only less than a year after the coronation ceremony took place. The symbolic effect of the "prophetic" message, diametrically opposed to the idea of the ceremony, even though it was most probably nothing but political bluff, was certainly great enough to arouse general indignation among the people in Harran and elsewhere who were loyal to the king—and turn their attention away from what was really happening. Whoever engineered this event, could not have used better the symbolic value of Harran as the city of god and king for his purposes.

8. Dara-aḫuya in the Middle of the Mountains

The remaining locality appearing in the Neo-Assyrian sources for prophecy[125] is Dara-aḫuya, which is mentioned in the authorship note of the shortest of the extant oracles of the prophetic corpus:

---

123 Uehlinger, "Figurative Policy, Propaganda und Prophetie," 317.

124 For the *akītu*-ceremony in Harran, for which there is evidence from about the same time (SAA 10 338), see Pongratz-Leisten. "The Interplay of Military Strategy and Cultic Practice," 248.

125 I exclude Tyre, because it is mentioned only in the colophon of one tablet: Nis[an] 18, eponymy of Bel-šadu'a, governor of Tyre (SAA 9 9 r. 6).

SAA 9 1.3 ii 11–15
rīšāk issi Aššūr-aḫu-iddina šarrīya
rīši Arbail

ša pî Rēmūt-Allati ša Dāra-aḫūja ša birti šaddâni

I rejoice over Esarhaddon, my king!
Arbela rejoices!

By the mouth of the woman Remut-Allati from Dara-aḫuya in the middle of the mountains.

There are several interesting features in this tiny piece of prophecy. First, the formulation "my king" implies that the speaker is a divine one. Moreover, even without a self-identification, it is beyond doubt that the speaker is Ištar of Arbela; the unmistakable poetic parallelism alone suggests what we have already learned, namely, that the goddess and the city are virtually one: the goddess rejoices, ergo, Arbela rejoices! The language of the prophecy sounds like a quotation from the Hymn to the city of Arbela.[126] Thirdly, in spite of the Arbela-centered message, the place of origin of the prophetess Remut-Allati and her oracle is indicated to be elsewhere, in a town (URU) called Dara-aḫuya which should be looked for "in the middle of the mountains".

This prophecy includes the only attestation of the name Dara-aḫuya which not only means that the settlement in question can hardly be a major one, but also makes its localization difficult. A village in the vicinity of Arbela (which is not far away from the mountains) may suggest itself; however, there is another possible explanation. Since all the oracles of the collection SAA 9 1 belong to the context of Esarhaddon's war against his brothers and seem to be arranged according to a loose chronology,[127] it is plausible to think that the prophecy of Remut-Allati is an oracle of encouragement, received during the war as a foretaste of the coming victory. The placement of the oracle in the collection may, of course, be purely redactional; however, it does not exclude the possibility that the prophecy was actually spoken somewhere "out there" when Esarhaddon and his troops were on the move towards Nineveh. The indefinite determining of the position of Dara-aḫuya "in the middle of mountains" may intentionally hint

126 SAA 3 8 r. 18–22: *Arbail rīša* [...] *nīšī iriššū* [...] *Bēltu rīšat* [...] *irīša bēt* [...] *ekurru kuzbu za"un* [...] *Bēltu ša bīti ša Arbail irīša libb*[*aša*...], "Arbela rejoices! The people rejoice [...] The Lady rejoices [...] The house of [...] rejoices! The temple is adorned with attractiveness [...] the Lady of the House of Arbela rejoices, [her] heart [...].'

127 In SAA 9 1.2 Esarhaddon appears as a crown prince, and SAA 9 1.4 to 1.8 give the impression of having been received in the turmoils of war, whereas SAA 1.9 and 10 presuppose that the war is over.

at the period when Esarhaddon was "roaming the steppe", outside the safe urban space and exposed to the powers of disorder. If this is true, the prophecy of Remut-Allati may be taken as another specimen of the encouraging divine messages Esarhaddon later claimed to have received constantly at that time in response to his prayers.[128] Dara-aḫuya, on the other hand, may be nothing but an intermediary station without any special relevance for the issue of prophecy and cities.

9. Conclusion

Urbanism is not a major issue in Neo-Assyrian prophecy. The social and economic aspects of urbanism are never thematized in the prophetic sources which reveal little of the social setting of the prophets in the cities, and even less of the place of the prophets outside them. According to the extant indications of the place of origin of a prophet or a prophetic oracle, the Assyrian prophets appear as urban-dwellers, but this is because the primary context of prophetic activity is the temple of the god(dess), and the temple, on the other hand, is an urban institution.

To be sure, cities are mentioned as places where people live, where certain events take place and where, for instance, insurrections may arise. Only cities, and with the exception of Dara-aḫuya, only the most prominent ones, are mentioned as domiciles of prophets or as places of prophetic performances. Likewise, the place names that appear in the prophetic oracles or in connection with prophecy in other sources, belong without exception to the major cities of the Assyrian empire, all of them housing a temple of Ištar or one of her manifestations. This is well in line with the institutional affiliation of the prophets to the temples of pre-eminent Assyrian cities, among which Arbela clearly assumed an outstanding position as the cradle of prophecy.

However, the cities are not mentioned merely as geographical locations of prophetic performances, and this is what makes it relevant to study the role of the cities in Assyrian prophecy. In the sources pertinent to prophecy, cities are, in fact, meaningful as ideological rather than spatial entities. Cities represent something that concerns and embraces the whole empire: they are embodiments of the divine presence[129] and the king's reign, manifestations of the fundamental unity of god, king, and people. Especially cities like Arbela, Assur,

128 Leichty, *The Royal Inscriptions of Esarhaddon*, 14 ii 5–6.

129 Or, as in the case of Babylon, divine absence, which is only the other side of the same coin.

Babylon, and Harran are dwellings of the divine, being themselves representations of their tutelary deities—Ištar, Aššur, Marduk, and Sîn—and proclaiming their glory. By the same token, in the framework of the imperial ideology, the cities are representations of the royal power, places in which the omnipresence of the king, chosen by the gods, is manifested by means of images, rituals, hymns, and divine words. In the final analysis, hence, the aspect of urbanism in Assyrian prophecy is best interpreted from the point of view of the prophets' symbolic universe, reflecting their theological and ideological, albeit socially conditioned conception of the reality.[130]

130 For the hermeneutical applicability of the concept of "symbolic universe" introduced by P. L. Berger and T. Luckmann (*The Social Construction of Reality: A Treatise in the Sociology of Knowledge* [Garden City, NY: Doubleday, 1966]), see K. Syreeni, "Wonderlands: A Beginner's Guide to Three Worlds," *SEÅ* 64 (1999) 33–46.

A Prophetic Riot in Babylonia, 133 BCE[1]

The Babylonian astronomical diaries from 652 down to 61 BCE[2] are anything but exciting reading. For the most part, they consist of meteorological and astrological reports, without much commentary on the viability of this meticulously collected information. Occasionally, however, the long and wearisome lists of observations of planets and weather are supplemented by short memoranda of events that have been found worth memorializing in the diaries. More often than not, these deal with offerings or military achievements of kings, enemies or Babylonian administrators. Among these rather laconic records, there is one special case reporting at unusual length on a certain Boatman who allegedly creates a pandemonium in Babylon and Borsippa, the principal cities of Babylonia, incurring the hatred of the local religious authorities. This account has inspired the editor, Hermann Hunger, to the following comment: "Obviously this very interesting tablet, reporting about religious and other upheavals, needs to be studied in depth."[3] Giuseppe Del Monte, who has written a monograph on the astronomical diaries from the Hellenistic era, notes the prophetic role of the protagonist of this account, as well as its relevance to the history of contemporary Judaism.[4] Indeed, the text may be welcomed as a valuable, though enigmatic, document of prophetic activity from an era less abundant in prophetic sources.

The passage in question belongs to the diary AD 3 No. -132 dealing with the events of the year 133 BCE. It is preserved in a longer version in manuscript B

1 The original title of this essay was "A Prophetic Riot in Seleucid Babylonia". I thank Bert van der Spek for pointing out that in 133 BCE, Babylonia, in fact, was under Parthian rule, not under the Seleucids; see R. J. van der Spek, *"Ik ben een boodschapper van Nanaia!": Een Babylonische profeet als teken des tijds (133 voor Christus)*. Amsterdam: Vrije Universiteit Amsterdam, 2014.

2 A. J. Sachs and H. Hunger, *Astronomical Diaries and Related Texts from Babylonia*, vol. 1–3 (Österreichische Akademie der Wissenschaften, Philosophisch-historische Klasse, Denkschriften 195, 210, 247; Wien: Österreichische Akademie der Wissenschaften, 1988–96).

3 Sachs and Hunger, *Astronomical Diaries* 3, 218. For an in-depth study, see now van der Spek, *"Ik ben een boodschapper van Nanaia!"*.

4 G. F. del Monte, *Testi dalla Babylonia Ellenistica*, vol. 1: *Testi Cronografici* (Studi Ellenistici 9; Pisa and Roma: Istituti editoriali e poligrafici intemazionali, 1997), 126: "Il curioso ed interessantissimo episodio del profeta-marinaio ehe annuncia la venuta di un 'dio potente che colpisce i vostri dèi', considerato un pazzo dall'*establishment* religioso di Borsippa ma che raccoglie grande consenso fra la gente comune, e che andrà inquadrato verisimilmente fra i fermenti del giudaismo della seconda metà del Il secolo a.e.v. (nella Babilonia esisteva sicuramente a quest'epoca una forte comunità giudaica, anche se le fonti locali ne tacciono), non mancherà di suscitare una messe di interventi da parte degli specialisti."

DOI 10.1515/9783110466546-017

(lines r. 25–36 + lower, left and upper edge)[5] and a shorter in manuscript C (lines 26–34).[6] Both versions are presented below in normalized transcription and translation. The transcriptions are based on the transliterations of the edition of Hunger, but I owe a great deal also to Simo Parpola who collated the transliterations with the photographs included in the same edition, suggested new readings and checked my translation.[7]

Texts

AD 3 B r. 25–u. e. 5

[r 25] *arḫu šuātu iltēn mār Mallāḫi ittaṣb[atamm]a* [26]*ṭēnzu išnima*
iltēn parakku birīt bīt Sîn bīt Egišnugal abulli [Marduk ...][27] *nadû*
nindabû ana muḫḫi iškunma
ṭēmu ṭābu ana niši iqbi umma Bēl ana Bābili īrub
[nišū][28] *zikarū u sinnišāti illikūnimma*
nindabû ana muḫḫi parakki šuāti iškunū
ana tarṣa [p]arakki šuāti[29] *īkulū ištû iḫammū iruššū*
2 kulūlū ḫi-ba-ṣu-x-x ana parakki šu[āti]
[30]UD.11.KÁM x 2 LÚ.X.MEŠ *ṣīrūtu x x x* X.MEŠ *našûnimma*
x X.MEŠ *ultu nišē (?) māti ana [...]*
[mār Mallaḫi][31] *ṭemu ana nišī šunūtu iqbi*
um<ma> Nanāya ana Barsip ana Ezida īterub
ḫanṭiš mār Mallāḫi šu[āti] [32]*u nišū ša ittīšu*
ana Barsip illikūnimma mārē Barsip ana pānīšunu iḫtamû iḫtadû
dalāti abulli [33]*ana pānīšunu iptetû*
mār Mallāḫi u nišū [...] [34]*īpulū umma* [d]*x [...]* [35]*kulūlū šuāti [...]* [36]*[...] Nanāya [...]*
[lo e 2]*[...* [3] *...] x x x x ina narkabti iškunū*
mār Mallāḫi šuāti x x x x x [4]*[...] x x x ina Bābili Barsip u* X.MEŠ *[...]*
[5]*[... inn]ammir u rigimšu ina sūqāti u berēti išemmû* [6]*[...]x x x x [...]*
[l e 1] *[umma mār] šip[r]i ša Nanāya a[nāku] ana muḫḫi ilu dannu māḫiṣu ilīkunu šaprāku*
kiništ[u] bīt ilī šuāti ana mār [Mallāḫi ...] [2]*īpulū*

5 Sachs and Hunger, *Astronomical Diaries* 3, 216–19 with plates 218–19 (copy) and 220 (photograph).

6 Sachs and Hunger, *Astronomical Diaries* 3, 224–25 with plate 221 (photograph).

7 Thanks are also due to R. M. Whiting for correcting my English, for bibliographical tips and for discussion.

iḫsā ana [arki]kunu tūrā ana ālānīkunu
ālu ana ḫubti u šillat lā tanamdā
ilī kīma ālu šillat lā tušēṣâ [...]
[3]*[mār Mallāḫi] īpulšunūtu umma mār [šip]ri ša Nanāya anākūma*
ālu ana ḫubti u šillat ul anamdin
kīma qāt ili dannu māḫiṣu ana Ezida UR [...]
[4]*[kiništu] bīt ilī šuāti ana nišī ša it[ti mār Mallāḫi] šuāti īpulū*
ša amat šābibannu lā tašemmânu
[šēzib]ā napšatkunu[5]*[uṣr]ā ramānīkunu*[...]
nišū šanūtu qabêššunu ul imḫurū x iqbû$^{u\ e}$ *umma*
[...][2] *ana Ezida* [...] *ilu dannu māḫiṣ[u* ... [4] ...] *mār Mallāḫi* [...] *šuāt[i...]*
(remaining lines unintelligible)

(r. 25) In that month, a man belonging to the Boatman family became s[eiz]ed[8] and went into frenzy. A dais which lies between the temple of Sîn, Egišnugal, and the gate [of Marduk[9] ...] (27) He placed a food offering upon it and delivered a good message to the people: "Bel has entered Babylon!" The [people[10]], men and women alike, came and placed food offerings on that dais and, opposite to that dais, ate and drank, rejoiced[11] and made merry. Two *luxuriant*[12] crowns ... th[at] dais.

(30) On the 11th day, two high-ranking *persons* were brought ... and ... from *the people*[13] of the land to [... *Boatman*][14] delivered a message to these people: "Nanaya has entered Borsippa and Ezida!" Instantly, th[at] Boatman and the people with him went to Borsippa. The citizens of Borsippa rejoiced[15] and exulted in their presence and happily opened the *doors of the city gate*[16] in front of them. Boatman and the people [...]. They answered: "The god these crowns ... [...] Nanaya [...]" [...] placed [...] in a chariot.

---

8 Reading *it-taṣ-b[a-ta-am-m]a*; cf., however, van der Spek, *"Ik ben een boodschapper van Nanaia!"*, 11 n. 32.
9 Cf. del Monte, *Testi dalla Babylonia Ellenistica*, 125 n. 224.
10 Reading LÚ.[UN.MEŠ] with ibid., 124.
11 The word *i-ḫa-am-mu-ú* is derived from *ḫamû*, which is equivalent to *ḫadû* "to rejoice." van der Spek, *"Ik ben een boodschapper van Nanaia!"*, 11 n. 36 derives the word from *ḫamû* B "to become confident."
12 Possible reading: *ḫi-ba-ṣu-ú-tú*!.
13 Reading UN.MEŠ.
14 Restoring [MÁ.LAḪ$_4$] at the end of line r. 30.
15 Cf. above, n. 9.
16 Adopting the uncertain reading GIŠ.IG.MEŠ KÁ.GAL; cf. del Monte, *Testi dalla Babylonia Ellenistica*, 124 n. 223.

(lower edge 3) That Boatman [...] in Babylon and Borsippa and [... he ap]-peared, on the streets and squares they listened to his proclamation[17] [...]

(left edge 1) "[I am] a mes[senger] of Nanaya![18] I have been sent on behalf of the strong, hitting god,[19] your God." The council of that temple responded to [that] Boatman [*and to the people with him*], saying: "Retreat back, return to your cities! Do not deliver up the city to loot and plunder! Do not let the gods of the city be carried off as spoils! [...]" (left edge 3) [*Boatman*][20] responded, saying: "I am a [mes]senger of Nanaya, I will not let the city fall prey to plunderers! As the hand of the strong, hitting god [...s] to Ezida [...]"

[The council] of that temple responded to the people who were wi[th] that [Boatman]: "Do not listen to the words of that fanatic[21]! [*Save*] your lives, [*protect*] yourselves! [...]" The other people did not take up their words but said: "[...] to Ezida [...] the strong, hitting god [...] Boatman [...]"

(rest too fragmentary for translation)

AD 3 C 26–33

[26]*arḫu šuātu iltēn mār Mallāḫi parakkū ina birit abulli Marduk u* [...]
[27][...] *sinnišāti ana libbi ipḫurā u kusāpu ina libbi īkulā*
UD.11.[KAM ... [28] ...] *ṣīrūtu ultu Bābili u ultu ālāni šanûtu u* [...]
[29][... *ul*]*tu Barsip mār Mallāḫi šuāti ina niše ṣīr*[*ūti* ...]
[30][...].*MEŠ nišē ultu āli x x x x x x* [...]
[31][...]-*tu ina libbīsunu idūkū u* [...]
[32][...] *ina Bābili u Barsip*[*... 33 ... šipi*]*štu ša a*[*na* ...]
(rest destroyed)

(26) In that month, a man belonging to the Boatman family [...] the daises in the gate of Marduk and [...] women assembled in it and ate bread there.

(27) On the 11th day, [...] high-ranking [...]s from Babylon and from other[22] cities and [... fr]om Borsippa. That Boatman with the high-ranking people

17 Possible reading: *ri-gim-šú.*
18 Reading [*um-ma* LÚ.DUMU] *šip*-[*r*]*i šá na-na-a-a a*-[*na-ku*]; cf. left edge 3.
19 For the translation of *ilu dannu māḫiṣu,* see below.
20 Restoring [MÁ.LAḪ$_4$] at the beginning of left edge 3.
21 The word *šābibannu* "hothead" is derived from *šabābu* "to glow". Cf. van der Spek, *"Ik ben een boodschapper van Nanaia!"*, 13 n. 42: "profeet" (< *šabābu* B).
22 Reading *šá-nu-ú-tú* with del Monte, *Testi dalla Babylonia Ellenistica*, 127.

(30) [...]s the people from the city [...] they killed in their midst and [... the mes]sage that [was to be sent] t[o ...]

(rest destroyed)

Commentary

The diary of the seventh month of the year 133 BCE of our chronology begins, as usual, with astronomical observations (lines B 30 – r. 17), followed by short notes on the rising of the river level (r. 17–18), on the plundering of a harbor by an enemy (r. 18–20), on the undertakings of Pilinus, the general of Babylonia (r. 21–23) and on the reading of some leather documents of King Arsaces to the Babylonians (r. 23–25). The rest of the report consists of the unusually long account of the appearance of a person called "Boatman". The designation *mār Mallāḫi* (LÚ.DUMU MÁ.LAH$_4$), lit. "son of a boatman", is a Late Babylonian eponymous name which by no means indicates that he himself is a sailor of any kind but rather that he belongs to the descendants of a boatman who has given the name for the whole family;[23] analogously, some people are called "son of Prophet" *(mār Maḫḫē*/A ^{m}LÚ.GUB.BA) in Neo-Babylonian documents.[24]

The first thing that is told of Boatman is that he became seized and "changed his consciousness"[25], that is, went into a frenzy. This not only refers to the general nature of his performance, but also gives the first hint at his prophetic role, which in Mesopotamia is regularly connected with frantic behavior, as can be seen from the derivation of the word *muḫḫûm/maḫḫû* from the verb *maḫû* "to go into a frenzy".[26] In this frantic state of mind, he went to a dais in a public place, placed a food offering upon it and started proclaiming an *euangelion (ṭemu ṭābu)* about the entering of Bel (Marduk) to Babylon. With regard to

---

23 A person with the same eponym name is attested in the Neo-Babylonian contract VS 4 95:11: $^{md+}$AG-GIN-NUMUN A LÚ. MÁ.LAH$_2$, "Nabû-mukīn-zēru son of Boatman".

24 YOS 6 18:$^{md+}$ AG-NUMUM-GIN A ^{m}LÚ.GUB.BA "Nabû-zēru-ukīn son of Prophet" (lines 1, 7); ^{m}*re-mut-*^{d}EN A ^{m}LÚ.GUB.BA "Remūt-Bēl son of Prophet" (lines 8, 10); YOS 7 135: ^{m}SIG$_5$-*he-el* A ^{m}LÚ.GUB.BA "Damiq-Bēl son of Prophet" (line 6). For the eponymous names, see G. Frame, *Babylonia 689 – 627 B.C.: A Political History* (Uitgaven van het Nederlands Historisch-Archaeologisch Instituut te Istanbul 49; Istanbul: Nederlands Historisch-Archaeologisch Instituut te Istanbul, 1992), 34.

25 The expression used here is *ṭēmu šanû* "change the reason".

26 Cf. M. Nissinen, "The Socioreligious Role of the Neo-Assyrian Prophets", in *Prophecy in Its Ancient Near Eastern Context: Mesopotamian, Biblical, and Arabian Perspectives* (ed. id.; SBL Symposium Series 13; Atlanta, Ga.: Society of Biblical Literature, 2000) 89 – 114, 90 – 93 (= pp. 103 – 26 in this volume).

the date of his appearance, this message may indicate that the appearance of Boatman coincided with the *akītu*-festival of Marduk which is attested in Babylon in the seventh month (Tishri); this festival corresponded to the better known New Year festival in the first month (Nisan).[27] The only reason why Marduk would have left the city is the procession of the god from his *akītu*-house outside the city, passing through the Ištar gate into the inner city and symbolizing the victory of order over chaos.[28] If this is the scenario within which Boatman made his first appearance, it is important to note how he contextualized his message by integrating his performance into a public festival, which included enough merrymaking and probably made the people attentive to any kind of private show with a joyful message.

The dais at which he delivered his speech was located somewhere between the monumental center of Babylon and the Marduk gate in the Eastern wall of the city.[29] It seemed to be equipped with two (mural) crowns *(kulūlu)*, which indicates the dedication of the dais to a goddess. In Assyria, the mural crown was the symbol of queens as images of the Queen of Heaven (Ištar/Mullissu). In Hellenistic times, it is the symbol of Cybele, an earth and mother goddess with connections to Ištar, and of Tyche as the personification and patroness of a city, perhaps best exemplified by the Tyche of Antioch.[30] On the occasion reported in our text, the crown is associated with Nanaya, the Babylonian equivalent of Ištar and the city goddess of Borsippa, which is the scene of the following events.

---

27 Cf. B. Pongratz-Leisten, "The Interplay of Military Strategy and Cultic Practice in Assyrian Politics," in *Assyria 1995: Proceedings of the 10th Anniversary Symposium of the Neo-Assyrian Text Corpus Project, Helsinki, September 7–11, 1995* (ed. S. Parpola and R. M. Whiting; Helsinki: The Neo-Assyrian Text Corpus Project, 1997), 246, For the correspondence between the Nisan and Tishri festivals, see S. Parpola, *Letters from Assyrian Scholars to the Kings Esarhaddon and Assurbanipal*, vol. 2: *Commentary and Appendices* (AOAT 5/2, Kevelaer Neukirchen-Vluyn: Neukirchener Verlag, 1983), 186–87 and cf. SAA 8 165:5–r. 1: "Adar (XII) and Elul (VI) are beginning of the year, as Nisan (1) and Tishri (VII) are at the beginning of the year."

28 See Pongratz-Leisten, "The Interplay of Military Strategy and Cultic Practice in Assyrian Politics," 251–52.

29 Egišnugal was the temple of Sîn at Babylon; see A. R. George, *House Most High: The Temples of Ancient Mesopotamia* (Mesopotamian Civilizations 5; Winona Lake, IN: Eisenbrauns, 1993), 114.

30 On the mural crown, see M. Hörig, *Dea Syria: Studien zur religiösen Tradition der Fruchtbarkeitsgöttin in Vorderasien* (AOAT 208; Kevelaer Neukirchen-Vluyn: Neukirchener Verlag, 1979), 129–197. The following work was, unfortunately, not accessible to me: D. Metzler, "Mural Crowns in the Ancient Near East and Greece", in *An Obsession with Fortune: Tyche in Greek and Roman Art* (ed. S. B. Matheson; Catalogue for the Exhibition held at the Yale University Art Gallery, 1 September–31 December, 1994; New Haven: Yale University Press, 1994).

On the 11th day of the seventh month, so goes the story, two persons belonging to the high society of Babylon (*ṣīrūtu*/LÚ.MAḪ.MEŠ) joined Boatman's audience which also attracted some "people of the land". Now Boatman proclaimed a new message: "Nanaya has entered Borsippa and Ezida!" Again, his proclamation is placed in the context of local festivities; it has an exact parallel in the diary of the preceding sixth month (line B 29): "In that month, (this message) was in the mouth of people big and small: 'Nanaya has entered Borsippa and Ezida!'"[31] By analogy to the similar expression concerning Bel, one would expect that this likewise refers to a procession of Nanaya to Ezida, the main temple of her spouse Nabû.[32] There are no records of such an *akītu* of Nanaya; Neo- and Late Babylonian love rituals of different divine couples arc attested in the seventh month in Babylonian cities,[33] but the Late Babylonian love ritual of Nanaya and Nabû in Borsippa took place in the second month, not in the sixth or in the seventh.[34] However, there is Neo-Assyrian evidence of a procession of Nabû, Nanaya's spouse, to Babylon in the sixth month,[35] and it is not out of the question that Nanaya followed her husband, even though this is not explicitly stated. Obviously, they also had to return to Borsippa. which may have taken place in the seventh month.

If a similar procession of Nabû and Nanaya took place in Borsippa in the Late Babylonian era, it would provide the cultic context for Boatman's proclamation. Otherwise we have to conclude that Boatman and his audience arranged the procession of Nanaya by themselves. They made the trip of ca. 20 km from

---

31 Sachs and Hunger, *Astronomical Diaries* 3, 214.

32 For Ezida, see George, *House Most High*, 159 – 60.

33 First and foremost the ritual of Anu and Antu in Uruk (F. Thureau-Dangin, *Rituels akkadiens* [Paris: Ernest Leroux, 1921]); possibly also a ritual of Šamaš and Aya in Sippar; see M. Nissinen, "Akkadian Rituals and Poetry of Divine Love," in *Mythology and Mythologies: Methodological Approaches to Intercultural Influences* (ed. R. M. Whiting; Melammu Symposia 2; Helsinki: The Neo-Assyrian Text Corpus Project, 2001) 93 – 136, 106 – 109.

34 *SBH* 8 ii 12ff.; see Nissinen, "Akkadian Rituals and Poetry of Divine Love," 99 – 101. Only the unpublished Aramaic text in Demotic script (Papyrus Amherst 63) gives account of a ritual of love between Nanaya and her beloved in the seventh month. This ritual belongs to the New Year festival of an Aramaic-speaking population in Upper Egypt, originally coming from the area between Babylonia and Elam. See the translation and notes in R. C. Steiner, "The Aramaic Text in Demotic Script," in *The Context of Scripture*, vol. 1: *Canonical Compositions from the Biblical World* (ed. W. W. Hallo and K. L. Younger; Leiden: Brill, 1997) 309 – 27; and cf. Nissinen, "Akkadian Rituals and Poetry of Divine Love," 101 – 102.

35 SAA 10 357:8 – r. 6: "As to what the king, my lord, wrote to me: 'The month Elul (VI) is intercalary; do not perform the ceremonies this month' – Ammu-salam entered Babylon on the evening of the 6th day; the god Nabû had come before him. on the 3rd. The gate was kept open before Bel and Nabû on the 4th, the 5th and the 6th, and sacrifices were performed."

Babylon to Borsippa and took the emblems of the goddess, the mural crowns, with them to symbolize her entering the city. At the city gate, they were given a warm welcome by the citizens of Borsippa who, like the people in Babylon, joined their exultation. The text that apparently describes the events in Borsippa is mostly destroyed; the preserved part of the text mentions the mural crowns (r. 35) as well as a chariot (lo. e. 3), probably needed for a procession.

The text gives the impression that Boatman's performances took place amid a blaze of publicity. His voice was heard on streets and squares of Babylon and Borsippa, attracting much attention. But what was the substance of his proclamation? According to the story, Boatman presented himself as a messenger, i.e., prophet of Nanaya ([*mār*] *šip*[*r*]*i ša Nanāya a*[*nāku*]) which is in line with the cultic performances he had been promoting in Borsippa. This was not the whole truth, however, since he maintained to have been sent on behalf of another divine being, as though Nanaya and her worship were nothing but a reflection of an even greater divinity called "the strong god, the hitting god, your god(s)" *(ilu dannu māḫiṣu ilīkunu).* This god has no name drawn from the Babylonian pantheon, but he is introduced as "your god(s)" to the Babylonians. Syntactically, the plural form *ilīkunu* (DINGIR.MEŠ) has no other antecedent than the singular *ilu* (DINGIR), which means that the plural expression has a singular meaning, similar to Hebrew *'ĕlōhêkem.* The message of Boatman, hence, seems to be a kind of monotheistic declaration. As the prophet of Nanaya he is ultimately speaking on behalf the "strong, hitting god", manifest in Nanaya and all other gods of Babylon.[36]

Giuseppe del Monte interprets the text differently, translating "I am sent on behalf of a strong god that hits your gods!"[37] This would mean that Boatman's god would beat the Babylonian gods, showing himself as superior to them. The translation renders a logical idea in view of the fierce reaction of the religious authorities. It turns out to be unlikely, however, because the compound *ilu dannu māḫiṣu* appears again in 1. e. 3 without being followed by any noun,[38] and the participle *māḫiṣu* "hitting" is not in the construct state, as the

---

36 Cf. S. Parpola, *Assyrian Prophecies* (SAA 9; Helsinki: Helsinki University Press, 1997), xxi–xxxvi; and id., "Monotheism in Ancient Assyria," in *One God or Many? Concepts of Divinity in the Ancient World* (ed. B. N. Porter; Transactions of the Casco Bay Assyrio!ogical Institute 1; Casco Bay, Maine: Casco Bay Assyriological Institute, 2000) 165–209, 168–173 on the Assyrian concept of Aššur as the totality of gods.

37 Del Monte, *Testi dalla Babylonia Ellenistica*, 126: "io sono inviato a proposito del dio potente ehe colpisce i vostri dèi!" Cf. van der Spek, *"Ik ben een boodschapper van Nanaia!"*, 13, 15–16: "een Sterke God, de Vernietiger (van) uw god(en)."

38 Cf. the comment of H. Hunger in Sachs and Hunger, *Astronomical Diaries* 3, 221.

translation would require. Furthermore, the repeated self-identification of Boatman as a messenger of Nanaya sounds odd if the "strong, hitting god" is divorced from the goddess altogether.

What, then, is meant with the unique divine epithet *māḫiṣu?* The verb *maḫāṣu*, in addition to its basic meaning "to hit, strike, beat", has a plethora of secondary meanings,[39] and without a more detailed context it is extremely difficult to arrive at a precise meaning. When used of gods, the verb usually refers to their destructive powers, diseases, etc.[40] The participle *māḫiṣu*, again, means "beater, striker", but also "weaver" and, what may be the most relevant meaning here, "hunter" or "archer".[41] This reminds one of the well-known figure of the arrow-shooting god, depicted on a Neo-Assyrian cylinder seal (Fig. 1) and presenting a mythological scene of a god vanquishing his monstruous enemy. This picture is usually understood as showing Ninurta or Adad pursuing Anzu or Asakku.[42] Simo Parpola interprets it in terms of a more sophisticated theology, integrating different functions or aspects of divinity. In his reading, the god who shoots the arrow is Enlil/Marduk, the arrow represents his son Ninurta/Nabû and the bow Ištar/Mullissu, respectively. The monster as the target of the arrow is "the world as a place of sin, darkness and death".[43] This interpretation corresponds well with the idea of the "hitting god" as the supreme god or divinity *per se*.

If this was the message of Boatman, however, he was gravely, if not intentionally, misunderstood by the temple council of Ezida. The favorable response from the audience suggests that his proclamation met with general approval among the citizens of Borsippa, whereas the religious authorities felt themselves threatened. In their interpretation, Boatman's tidings of the "strong, hitting god" had fatal consequences for the city and its gods. "Retreat back, return to your cities!", they told the people. "Do not deliver up the city to loot and plunder! Do not let the gods of the city be carried off as spoils!" The reaction is massive in proportion to the private performance of a single prophet whose message, judged from the sympathy of the public, was benevolent rather than menacing. It is difficult to see anything in Boatman's proclamation forecasting "loot and plunder". This seems rather like an exaggerated counterblast of the temple authorities, who may have interpreted the appearance of Boatman as an incitement

39 Cf. *CAD* M/1, 71–84.

40 See *CAD* M/1, 75–76.

41 See *CAD* M/1, 102; *CDA* 190–191.

42 So, e.g., J. Black and A. Green, *Gods, Demons and Symbols of Ancient Mesopotamia: An Illustrated Dictionary* (ill. T. Rickards; London: British Museum Press, 1992), 14.

43 Parpola, "Monotheism in Ancient Assyria," 201.

Figure 1: A god pursuing a monster depicted on a Neo-Assyrian cylinder seal. From J. Black & A. Green 1992, 14.

to defy law and order constituted by the government. In addition, they seem to have been offended on behalf of their gods and took Boatman's propagation of the "strong, hitting god" as a manifestation of a dangerous heresy. For them, Boatman obviously appeared as a prophet enticing the people to follow a god "whom neither you nor your fathers have known" (cf. Deut 13:1–11).

Boatman obviously tried to convince the temple council of himself as a true prophet with good intentions and sound theology. This was ignored by the authorities who, rather than entering into theological conversations with Boatman, called him a fanatic or hothead, thus belittling his person and depriving him of credibility. Some people in the audience were not satisfied with the attitude of the temple council, however, but made a loud protest against its reaction. The quotation of their speech, written on the upper edge of the tablet, is badly damaged, but the readable words include Ezida, "strong, hitting god" and Boatman's name, indicating a defense of him and his message. The response of the temple council, if there was any, is broken away, and the reader is left in the dark about Boatman's fate. The remains of the shorter version in manuscript C, however, include the words *ina libbīšunu idūkū* "they killed in their midst", which in all their curtness allude clearly enough to the developing of the argumentation into a riot that cost some people, if not Boatman himself, their lives. To have been included in the sparingly chosen events recorded in the astronomical diaries, this upheaval cannot have been a minor one.

The account of the prophetic riot in Seleucid Babylonia opens up vistas for further studies that go beyond the bounds of this article. At least three topics deserve to be taken into consideration:

1) As transmitter of divine messages, Boatman assumes a clearly prophetic role. The episode provides a significant piece of evidence of prophetic activity the in 2nd century BCE. a dark age in the history of ancient Near Eastern prophecy.

2) The theology of the "strong, hitting god" should be investigated with regard to its Assyrian precursors as identified by Parpola, without forgetting the eventual communication with contemporary Judaism, one of the intellectual centers of which was nowhere else than in Babylonia, as Del Monte rightly notes.

3) The episode is interesting also from a sociological point of view, involving a charismatic, solitary prophet, an enthusiastic response from the people in the streets and squares, and the stem resistance of religious authorities who resorted to extreme alarmism, disparaging comments and, finally, to force and violence, thus demonstrating the vulnerability of their power. All this reminds one of the somewhat later but much better known appearance of a prophet from Nazareth in Jerusalem.

In conclusion of this brief contribution in honor of my senior Icelandic colleague, Prof. Sigurður Örn Steingrímsson, I can only repeat the wish of Hermann Hunger: this text should be studied in depth!

Part Three: **Biblical Prophecy in Ancient Near Eastern Context**

Die Relevanz der neuassyrischen Prophetie für die alttestamentliche Forschung

1. Die neuassyrische Prophetie

1.1. Einführung

Im Vergleich zu der im Laufe von vier Jahrzehnten angewachsenen respektablen Menge der Literatur über die prophetischen Briefe aus dem westmesopotamischen Mari aus dem achtzehnten Jh. v. Chr.[1] haben die mit ebenso guten Gründen als Prophetie geltenden neuassyrischen Orakel aus dem siebten Jahrhundert v. Chr. bisher nur vereinzelt Beachtung gefunden. Das „Aschenputteldasein" dieser Orakel[2] sollte eigentlich schon Verwunderung erregen angesichts der Tatsache, daß die Texte bereits seit rund einem Jahrhundert veröffentlicht sind und vor allem weil sie aus der Epoche stammen, in der die israelitische Prophetie der herkömmlichen Auffassung nach ihre Blütezeit erlebte.

Im Rahmen der biblischen Chronologie würden die an die assyrischen Könige Asarhaddon (681–669) und Assurbanipal (669–629) adressierten Worte in der Zeit zwischen Jesaja und Jeremia ihren Platz finden. Schon von dieser Tatsache her entsteht die Erwartung, daß das zeitgenössische assyrische Material zum Verständnis der alttestamentlichen Prophetie einen willkommenen Beitrag leisten könnte. Denkt man dazu noch an die gerade in jenem Jahrhundert vorherrschende politisch-kulturelle Hegemonie des assyrischen Imperiums, von deren Einfluß das Alte Testament ein vielfaches Zeugnis ablegt, so wird man weiter davon ausgehen dürfen, daß Sprache und Gedankenwelt der neuassyrischen prophetischen Orakel nicht nur in den Prophetenbüchern, sondern auch anderswo im Alten Testament Parallelen finden.

---

1 Vgl. dazu die Bibliographien bei E. Noort, *Untersuchungen zum Gottesbescheid in Mari: Die „Mariprophetie" in der alttestamentlichen Forschung* (AOAT 202; Kevelaer: Butzon & Bercker; Neukirchen-Vluyn: Neukirchener Verlag, 1977), esp. 111–32; A. Malamat, „A Forerunner of Biblical Prophecy: The Mari Documents," in *Ancient Israelite Religion*, FS F. M. Cross (ed. P. D. Miller Jr., P. D. Hanson, and S. D. McBride; Philadelphia, Pa.: Fortress Press, 1987) 33–52, esp. 47–48; M. deJong Ellis, „Observations on Mesopotamian Oracles and Prophetic Texts: Literary and Historiographic Considerations," *JCS* 41 (1989) 127–86, esp.134–35.

2 Eine zutreffende Beurteilung von M. Weippert, „Die Bildsprache der neuassyrischen Prophetie," in *Beiträge zur prophetischen Bildsprache in Israel und Assyrien* (ed. H. Weippert, K. Seybold, and M. Weippert; OBO 64; Fribourg and Göttingen: Academic Press Fribourg and Vandenhoeck & Ruprecht, 1985) 55–93, esp. 56.

DOI 10.1515/9783110466546-018

Die Saumseligkeit der Alttestamentler bei der Heranziehung der neuassyrischen Prophetie findet ihre natürliche Erklärung in der schwierigen Zugänglichkeit des Textmaterials. Außer in den Übersetzungen einiger Texte in Sammelwerken[3] und Einzeluntersuchungen[4] finden sich die Texte verstreut in Textausgaben, oft nur in Keilschrift ohne Übersetzung und Kommentar. Eine systematische Untersuchung der Texte verdanken wir bisher zunächst Manfred Weippert, dessen Artikel den Grund für die weitere Forschung gelegt hat.[5]

Die im Stillstand lebende Forschung wird sich aber hoffentlich bald aufraffen, und zwar aufgrund dessen, daß das Material zum ersten Mal in einer einzigen Textausgabe zur Verfügung stehen wird. Das neuassyrische prophetische Korpus wird nämlich von Simo Parpola im Rahmen des Projektes „State Archives of Assyria" etwa gleichzeitig mit dem vorliegenden Aufsatz veröffentlicht (SAA 9).[6] Da die durch den verwickelten Publikationsstand verursachten Schwierigkeiten mit dieser Gesamtausgabe der Vergangenheit angehören, ist es an der Zeit, dieses interessante Material aus alttestamentlicher Sicht gebührend zu bewerten. Bevor wir uns aber in die Texte und deren biblische Parallelen vertiefen, ist eine Erklärung für die Abgrenzung des Materials sowie für seine Bezeichnung als Prophetie nötig.

3 R. H. Pfeiffer, „Akkadian Oracles and Prophecies," *ANET*[2] (1955) 449–52; R. D. Biggs, „Akkadian Oracles and Prophecies," *ANET*[3] (1969) 604–5; und zuletzt K. Hecker, „Zukunftsdeutungen in akkadischen Texten," *TUAT* 2/1 (1986) 56–82; des weiteren s. Weippert „Die Bildsprache der neuassyrischen Prophetie," 56; M. Nissinen, *Prophetie, Redaktion und Fortschreibung im Hoseabuch: Studien zum Werdegang eines Prophetenbuches im Lichte von Hos 4 und 11* (AOAT 231; Kevelaer: Butzon & Bercker; Neukirchen-Vluyn: Neukirchener Verlag, 1991), esp. 405–6.

4 Genannt seien T. Ishida, *The Royal Dynasties in Ancient Israel: A Study on the Formation and Development of Royal-Dynastic Ideology* (BZAW 142; Berlin/New York: De Gruyter, 1977), 90–92, 115–16; H. Spieckermann, *Juda unter Assur in der Sargonidenzeit* (FRLANT 129; Göttingen: Vandenhoeck & Ruprecht, 1982), esp. 295–303.

5 Als gründlichste Übersicht über Form, Inhalt und geschichtlichen Hintergrund der Texte gilt M. Weippert, „Assyrische Prophetien der Zeit Asarhaddons und Assurbanipals," in *Assyrian Royal Inscriptions: New Horizons in Literary, Ideological and Historical Analysis* (ed. F. M. Fales; Orientis Antiqui Collectio 17; Roma: Istituto per l'Oriente, 1981) 71–115; vgl. auch id., „'Heiliger Krieg' in Israel und Assyrien: Kritische Anmerkungen zu Gerhard von Rads Konzept des 'Heiligen Krieges im alten Israel,'" *ZAW* 84 (1972) 460–93, esp. 473–74, 481–82; id., „De herkomst van het heilsorakel voor Israël bij Deutero-Jesaja," *NedTT* 36 (1982) 1–11; id., „Die Bildsprache der neuassyrischen Prophetie," passim; id., „Aspekte israelitischer Prophetie im Lichte verwandter Erscheinungen des Alten Orients," in *Ad bene et fideliter seminandum*, FS Karlheinz Deller (ed. G. Mauer and U. Magen; AOAT 220; Kevelaer: Butzon & Bercker; Neukirchen-Vluyn: Neukirchener Verlag, 1988) 287–319, esp. 302–5.

6 Dieser Artikel hätte nicht verwirklicht werden können ohne die Hilfe von Prof. Simo Parpola, der mir die noch unveröffentlichten Probeabzüge der Textausgabe sowie Photographien des Urtextes zur Verfügung gestellt hat. Ihm möchte ich dafür an dieser Stelle herzlich danken.

1.2. Abgrenzung des Materials und seine Bezeichnung als Prophetie

Der gründlichen Präsentation des betreffenden Textmaterials durch M. Weippert[7] ist zu danken, daß hier nur einige Grunddaten – die freilich in Einzelheiten von denen von Weippert abweichen – vorgestellt zu werden brauchen. Das Korpus der neuassyrische Prophetie besteht aus zehn Tontafeln (SAA 9 1–9; SAA 3 13),[8] die sich ursprünglich in den neuassyrischen Staatsarchiven befanden und heute in der Koyunjik-Sammlung des Britischen Museums aufbewahrt werden. Die Tafeln enthalten insgesamt achtundzwanzig Einzelorakel, von denen ein Viertel auf einer ursprünglichen Einzeltafel erhalten geblieben ist – zwei von ihnen (SAA 9 4 und 6) allerdings schwer beschädigt.[9] Von den restlichen einundzwanzig Orakeln sind zehn auf der Tafel SAA 9 1, sechs auf SAA 9 2 und fünf auf SAA 9 3 überliefert, jeweils aneinandergereiht und durch einen Strich voneinander getrennt.[10] Die drei

---

7 Weippert, „Assyrische Prophetien der Zeit Asarhaddons und Assurbanipals," passim; s. besonders die Tabellen S. 112–15. Vgl. auch Weippert, „Die Bildsprache der neuassyrischen Prophetie," 55–58.

8 Ein Verzeichnis der Texte mit Angaben über Museumsnummer und Erstveröffentlichung sowie mit ausgewählten Übersetzungen befindet sich im Anhang meiner Dissertation (Nissinen, *Prophetie, Redaktion und Fortschreibung im Hoseabuch*, 405–6). Die Numerierung und die Transliteration der Texte folgt der Gesamtausgabe von S. Parpola (SAA 9). Da die endgültige Fassung dieser Ausgabe mir während der Vorbereitung dieses Aufsatzes noch nicht zur Verfügung stand, sind kleinere Abweichungen möglich. Der Text SAA 3 13 stellt insofern einen Grenzfall dar, als er als einen unmittelbaren, ohne Übermittlung einer prophetischen Persönlichkeit aufgeführten Dialog des Königs Assurbanipal mit dem Gott Nabû darstellt. Da der Text der Hand des gleichen Schreibers wie SAA 9 9 entstammt, den gleichen geschichtlichen Hintergrund hat und zudem vielfache sprachliche und inhaltliche Berührungen mit den eigentlichen Prophetensprüchen aufweist, ist seine Miteinbeziehung in diese Gruppe jedoch als begründet anzusehen.

9 Die Fragmente SAA 9 4 (= 83–1–18, 839) und SAA 9 6 (= 91–5–9, 106 + 91–5–9, 109) fehlen bei Weippert, der seinerseits („Die Bildsprache der neuassyrischen Prophetie," 56 Anm. 6; vgl. id., „Aspekte israelitischer Prophetie im Lichte verwandter Erscheinungen des Alten Orients," 302 Anm. 36) dazu noch drei Fragmente zählt: SAA 9 11 (= CT 53, 219); SAA 9 10 (83–1–18, 726 = CT 53, 946) und SAA 13 148 (= K 10865 = CT 53,413). Es handelt sich um winzige Bruchstücke, deren Zugehörigkeit zu den prophetischen Texten zunächst nur im Hinblick auf gewisse Prophetenbezeichnungen möglich ist (vgl. unten Anm. 39–40).

10 Die Zählung der Einzelorakel ist wegen der Beschädigungen der Tafeln nicht ganz sicher; vgl. die etwas abweichende Zählung von Weippert, „Assyrische Prophetien der Zeit Asarhaddons und Assurbanipals," 112, der auch SAA 9 7 (K 883) und SAA 3 13 (K 1285) als Sammeltafel behandelt, wohl aber zu unrecht. Denn mit SAA 9 7:12 dürfte kein neues Orakel einsetzen (so ibid., 72 Anm. 5), da die Z. 12–13 gerade die Thematik der Z. 8–11 fortsetzt (Assurbanipals Macht über die Könige der Fremdvölker) und zudem der sonst immer verwendete Trennungsstrich fehlt. Demgegenüber ist SAA 3, 13 wegen der dialogischen Struktur *trotz* der Striche als eine Einheit zu verstehen. Die drei

Sammeltafeln legen ein Zeugnis davon ab, daß die neuassyrischen Könige es für notwendig hielten, die prophetischen Orakel sammeln, kopieren und archivieren zu lassen. Warum dies so geschah, wird weiter unten näher erörtert.

Die Abgrenzung des Materials erfolgt anhand bestimmter Kriterien.[11] Das Attribut 'neuassyrisch' impliziert, daß die Texte aus der Epoche des neuassyrischen Imperiums datieren und daß die von ihnen vertretene Sprachform das Neuassyrische ist.[12] Ferner weisen die Texte einige gemeinsame Charakteristika auf, durch die sie sich von der übrigen Omen- und Orakelliteratur unterscheiden. Erstens sind sie alle direkte Gottesrede an eine Einzelperson oder an ein breiteres Publikum, übermittelt von einer meist namentlich genannten Persönlichkeit.[13] Zudem weisen alle Texte mehr oder weniger eindeutig auf geschichtliche Ereignisse hin. Zweitens sind sie mit keiner induktiven Methode wie etwa der Opferschau oder der Astrologie verbunden, sondern verstehen sich ausschließlich als unmittelbarer, nicht-technischer Gottesbescheid.

Die schriftliche Hinterlassenschaft des alten Mesopotamien läßt diese Art von Divination als ganz spärlich erscheinen, indem sie außer in den neuassyrischen Orakeln zunächst nur in Mari zu beobachten ist.[14] Trotzdem berechtigen die oben genannten distinktiven Züge eine Behandlung der Texte als ein zusammenhängendes Korpus, wofür sich der Begriff 'Prophetie' als eine geeignete Bezeichnung anbietet.

In bezug auf außerbiblische Texte hat man die Bezeichnung 'Prophetie' allerdings insofern für problematisch gehalten, als sie das Anliegen der christlich-jüdischen Theologie zum Ausdruck bringt und von der Bibel her sekundär auf außerbiblische Zusammenhänge übertragen worden ist. Sieht man die Referenz des Begriffs 'Prophetie' als rein biblisch, so hält man gern seine Anwendung in Verbindung mit mesopotamischen Texten für irreführend. So ist jüngst Maria

---

Sammeltafeln K 2647+Rm 2.99; K 6064 und Rm 2.236 (jetzt SAA 3 44; 45; 46), die einige Berührungen mit den prophetischen Orakeln aufweisen, aber eher als Antworten auf Gottesbriefe zu verstehen sind, werden auch von Weippert (ibid., 72, 112) in diesem Zusammenhang nicht behandelt.

11 Vgl. auch ibid., 71–72.

12 Das Orakel SAA 9 7 bildet eine partielle Ausnahme, indem seine Sprache eher als assyrisierendes Neubabylonisch als Neuassyrisch zu charakterisieren ist.

13 Ausnahme: SAA 3 13 (vgl. oben Anm. 8).

14 Zu ähnlichen Charakteristika der Mariprophetie vgl. Malamat, „A Forerunner of Biblical Prophecy," 34–35. Bezeichnend für die Quellenlage ist, daß wir schon aus der Zeit des Asarhaddon und Assurbanipal 354 Orakelanfragen kennen, die die Opferschau voraussetzen (I. Starr, *Queries to the Sungod: Divination and Politics in Sargonid Assyria* [SAA 4; Helsinki: Helsinki University Press, 1990]), während die prophetischen Briefe aus Mari etwa 0,3 % von dem insgesamt ca. 150.000 Texte umfassenden Korpus ausmachen.

deJong Ellis gegen die Kategorisierung gewisser akkadischer Texte als 'Prophetie' aufgetreten.[15] Andererseits sind die vielfachen Unterschiede zwischen dem biblischen und dem mesopotamischen Material auch von den Exegeten betont worden, indem etwa Ed Noort den Begriff in bezug auf die Orakel aus Mari in Gänsefüßchen gesetzt hat.[16]

Die in vielen Punkten begründete Kritik an der Anwendung des Begriffs 'Prophetie' hat zugleich auch ihre Probleme. Wird auf seinen Gebrauch außerhalb der Bibel kategorisch verzichtet, so liegt die Gefahr eines doppelten Fehltritts nahe: einerseits bleibt die alttestamentliche Prophetie von verwandten Erscheinungen im Alten Orient in einem eigenen biblischen Ghetto isoliert und wird hermetisch als ein spezifisch israelitisch-jüdisches Phänomen betrachtet; andererseits wird die weitgehend mit den alttestamentlichen Prophetenbüchern (oder mit deren „echten" Teilen) gleichgesetzte israelitische Prophetie als eine allzu einheitliche und problemlose Größe gegenüber dem bunten Spektrum altorientalischer Divination angesehen.

Als ein Element jüdisch-christlich-islamischer Theologie kann die Rede über 'Prophetie' auch in bezug auf das Alte Testament als anachronistisch angesehen werden. Können wir aber darin Übereinkommen, diesen traditionellen Begriff in einem bestimmten Sinne auf *die orakelhafte Übermittlung eines unmittelbaren, durch kein technisches Mittel erfolgten Gottesbescheids* zu beziehen, wird es doch wohl berechtigt sein, ihn als Oberbegriff für eine besondere Form der altorientalischen Orakelinstitution zu gebrauchen. Dieser Bestimmung schließt sich gut die Definition von Weippert an, nach der ein(e) Prophet(in) eine Person männlichen oder weiblichen Geschlechts ist, „die 1. in einem kognitiven Erlebnis, einer Vision, einer Audition, einem Traum o.ä., der Offenbarung einer Gottheit oder mehrerer Gottheiten teilhaftig wird, und 2. sich durch die betreffende(n) Gottheil(en) beauftragt weiß, die Offenbarung in sprachlicher oder metasprachlicher Fassung an einen Dritten, den eigentlichen Adressaten, zu übermitteln."[17]

---

15 Vgl. Ellis, „Observations on Mesopotamian Oracles and Prophetic Texts," 132–33, 146–47. Ellis erkennt dabei die Gefahr, daß ein Begriff wie 'Prophetie' allzu sehr mit den religiös-kulturellen Voraussetzungen und den Werturteilen des Auslegers verbunden ist: „We must also attempt to avoid imposing on the source value judgments conditioned by our own religious beliefs or those of our heritage" (S. 132).

16 Nach Noort, *Untersuchungen zum Gottesbescheid in Mari*, 92 (vgl. S. 109) darf „in Mari von einem einheitlichen Phänomen 'Prophetie', das zu der Prophetie in Israel in Beziehung gesetzt werden kann und als deren Vorgeschichte dargestellt werden kann, nicht gesprochen werden." Zum Problem der Definition des Begriffs 'Prophetie' hat Noort (ibid., 9–34) einen wichtigen Beitrag geleistet.

17 Weippert, „Aspekte israelitischer Prophetie im Lichte verwandter Erscheinungen des Alten Orients," 289–90.

Angesichts dessen ist die terminologische Kritik von Ellis insofern als völlig adäquat anzusehen, als es um Texte geht, die den oben formulierten Voraussetzungen nicht entsprechen. In der Tat richtet Ellis ihre Spitze ausdrücklich gegen die Anwendung des Begriffs 'Prophetie' bezüglich der seit den sechziger Jahren „Akkadian prophecies"[18] oder aber auch „Apokalypsen" genannten Texte, die zukünftige Begebenheiten auf politischem Gebiet weissagen.[19] Es handelt sich größtenteils um *vaticinia ex eventu* mit einer bestimmten politischen Absicht, ohne daß ein Offenbarungserlebnis oder ein Übermittlungsauftrag überhaupt zur Sprache kommt. Deswegen trifft die von Ellis vorgeschlagene Bezeichnung 'literary predictive texts'[20] für sie ausgezeichnet zu, während die von ihr 'oracular reports' genannte Gruppe auf das hinauskommt, was wir als 'Prophetie' bezeichnen wollen.

1.3. Das Problem des Ursprungs der neuassyrischen Prophetie

Aus der Tatsache, daß von der altorientalischen Prophetie in dem oben definierten Sinne außer dem Alten Testament zunächst nur zwei Textkorpora, Mari und Ninive, mit einem zeitlichen Unterschied von einem Jahrtausend zur Verfügung stehen,[21] erhebt sich die Frage, warum sie so wenige Spuren hinterlassen hat. Da

---

18 So A. K. Grayson and W. G. Lambert, „Akkadian Prophecies," *JCS* 18 (1964) 7–30, die vier Texte (A–D) unter diesem Titel anführen. Später hat Grayson (*Babylonian Historical-Literary Texts* [Toronto Semitic Texts and Studies 3; Toronto/Buffalo: University of Toronto Press, 1975], esp. 13–23) die Gruppe dadurch modifiziert, daß er den Text B ausfallen läßt und zwei weitere Texte mit einbezieht, so daß jetzt fünf Texte zur Diskussion stehen: 1) Der Assur-Text *KAR* 421 (= Text A); 2) Die Autobiographie von Marduk (= Text D), mit der 3) die Autobiographie von dem vergöttlichten König Šulgi zusammengefügt worden ist (= Text C; zu den beiden letztgenannten vgl. R. Borger, „Gott Marduk und Gott-König Šhulgi als Propheten: Zwei Prophetische Texte," *BO* 28 [1971] 3–24; Hecker, „Zukunftsdeutungen in akkadischen Texten," 65–68); 4) die neubabylonische „Uruk-Prophetie" (dazu H. Hunger and S. A. Kaufman, „A New Akkadian Prophecy Text," *JAOS* 95 [1975] 371–75; Hecker, „Zukunftsdeutungen in akkadischen Texten," 69–70) und 5) die „dynastische Chronik" aus der Seleukidischen Zeit (dazu Grayson *Babylonian Historical-Literary Texts*, 24–37).

19 Zu diesen Texten und zu den Problemen ihrer Kategorisierung s. den ausführlichen Überblick über die Forschungsgeschichte bei Ellis, „Observations on Mesopotamian Oracles and Prophetic Texts," 146–57 und auch Weippert, „Aspekte israelitischer Prophetie im Lichte verwandter Erscheinungen des Alten Orients," 291–94 mit Literatur.

20 Ellis, „Observations on Mesopotamian Oracles and Prophetic Texts," 148; vgl. Weippert, „Aspekte israelitischer Prophetie im Lichte verwandter Erscheinungen des Alten Orients," 294.

21 Das sonstige relevante Material hat Weippert (ibid., 297–302) zusammengefaßt. Neben einem hethitischen Gebet Muršilis II. (14. Jh.) und dem Reisebericht des Ägypters Wenamun (11. Jh.), in denen jeweils der hethitische Ausdruck **šiuniyant-* und der ägyptische *'dd '3* mit Vorbehalt als

hier weitgehend nur *e silentio* argumentiert werden kann, muß eine verläßliche Antwort darauf noch unterbleiben; trotzdem sei es erlaubt, einige Vermutungen anhand des vorhandenen Materials anzustellen.

Die plausibelste Erklärung dürfte vorläufig davon ausgehen, daß die Prophetie in erster Linie mündlich vorgebracht und nur unter außergewöhnlichen Umständen schriftlich überliefert bzw. archiviert wurde. Die Zufälligkeit der Überlieferung zeigt sich in dem spärlichen Vorkommen prophetischer Zitate in neuassyrischen Briefen und Königsinschriften sowie in der aramäischen Zakkur-Inschrift (*KAI* 202).[22] Bezüglich der Prophetie in Mari und im Alten Testament hat man den gemeinsamen Zug notiert, daß die Prophetie besonders durch Krisensituationen hervorgerufen wurde,[23] und das gleiche gilt, wie unten gezeigt wird, auch für die neuassyrische Prophetie, in der es darauf ankam, die verwickelten Machtinteressen innerhalb des neuassyrischen Reichs mit göttlichem Wort zu regeln. Dies bot zugleich den Anlaß dafür, die Orakel in schriftlicher Form als Beweis des göttlichen Beifalls für die siegreiche Partei aufzubewahren.

Das Vorkommen der Prophetie einmal in der im westlichen Mesopotamien liegenden Stadt Mari und dann im neuassyrischen Imperium, das schon unter einem starken aramäischen Einfluß lebte, hat die Annahme veranlaßt, es ginge im Ganzen um ein westsemitisches, zeitweilig von Syrien her in mesopotamisches Gebiet eingeströmtes Phänomen. Nach Wolfram von Soden zum Beispiel sieht es so aus, „als hätte nach 750 eine prophetische Bewegung, die für uns zuerst in Israel faßbar wird, zeitweise große Teile Vorderasiens erfaßt."[24] Allerdings wird

---

Bezeichnungen eines Gottbegeisterten des prophetischen Typs deuten lassen, kommen zunächst einige aramäische Texte aus dem 9. Jh. zur Frage, und zwar die Zakkur-Inschrift *KAI* 202 samt dem bekannten Bileam-Text aus Deir ʿAlla (vgl. dazu die umfassende Bibliographie bei Weippert, ibid., 301–2). Dazu kommt aber noch ein wichtiges Stück, nämlich das von Ellis 1987 veröffentlichte Kititum-Orakel aus Iščali (18. Jh.); s. dazu unten.

22 Vgl. etwa *LAS* 213:4–8; 280:22–r4; 317:7–r9 (vgl. jeweils Parpola 1983, *Letters from Assyrian Scholars to the Kings Esarhaddon and Assurbanipal, vol. 2: Commentary and Appendices* [AOAT 5/2; Kevelaer: Butzon and Bercker; Neukirchen-Vluyn: Neukirchener Verlag, 1983] 208, 271, 329); E. Leichty, *The Royal Inscriptions of Esarhaddon, King of Assyria (680–669 BC)* (RINAP 4; Winona Lake, Ind.: Eisenbrauns, 2011), 14 ii 5–67; 124 ii 12–17. (vgl. Spieckermann, *Juda unter Assur in der Sargonidenzeit*, 295–96). Zur Zakkur-Inschrift vgl. unten Kap. 2.5.

23 Malamat, „A Forerunner of Biblical Prophecy," 42: „The crisis factor was certainly one of the principal forces engendering prophetic manifestations both in Mari and in Israel." Vgl. auch Noort, *Untersuchungen zum Gottesbescheid in Mari*, 90–91.

24 W. von Soden, „Aramäische Wörter in neuassyrischen und neu- and spätbabylonischen Texten: Ein Vorbericht III," *Orientalia* Nova Series 46 (1977) 183–97, esp. 187; ähnlich mit Vorbehalt H. Tadmor, „History and Ideology in the Assyrian Royal Inscriptions," in Fales (ed.), *Assyrian Royal Inscriptions*, 13–33, esp. 29; Weippert, „Assyrische Prophetien der Zeit Asarhaddons und Assurbanipals," 104; id., „Die Bildsprache der neuassyrischen Prophetie," 86; vgl. A. L. Oppenheim,

die Beweisführung dieser Vermutung schon dadurch erschwert, daß sie gänzlich auf dem vorhandenen geringen Material beruht, dessen Existenz als eine Glückssache anzusehen ist. Geradezu unwahrscheinlich wird sie aber durch die von Ellis unlängst veröffentlichten Orakel von der Göttin Kititum, einer lokalen Manifestation der Ištar, an den König Ibalpiel II. von Ešnunna (FLP 1674; 2064). Es handelt sich um mit den Mari-Briefen zeitgenössische und mit diesen in vielfacher Hinsicht vergleichbare Dokumente, die mit guten Gründen als Zeugnisse prophetischer Tätigkeit betrachtet werden dürfen.[25] Kann man also im Falle der Mari-Prophetie noch mit einer westlichen Provenienz rechnen, so wird dies wesentlich schwieriger im Falle eines aus dem Gebiet von Ešnunna, d. h. aus dem Tal von Diyala östlich von Tigris stammenden Textes.

Stellen wir nun die neuassyrischen und biblischen Texte zwecks Vergleichs nebeneinander, so ist wegen der vielen offenen Fragen Vorsicht geboten gegenüber jeglichen Versuchen, literarische Verhältnisse zwischen den Texten zu konstruieren. Anstatt der Genealogien müssen wir uns also noch mit Analogien begnügen. Aber von der Warte aus, daß die zeitgenössischen assyrischen Quellen als Dokumente der unmittelbaren Umwelt des Alten Testaments überhaupt unser Verständnis der atl. Texte fördern können, erscheint die Motivation zur Parallelisierung geboten. Es ist das vorrangige Ziel dieses Aufsatzes, zu zeigen, in wel-

---

Ancient Mesopotamia: Portrait of a Dead Civilization (Chicago and London: The University of Chicago Press, ^{2}1977), esp. 221–22; Ishida, *The Royal Dynasties in Ancient Israel*, 92; Spieckermann, *Juda unter Assur in der Sargonidenzeit*, 302.

25 Dazu grundlegend M. deJong Ellis, „The Goddess Kititum Speaks to King Ibalpiel: Oracle Texts from Ishchali," *MARI* 5 (1987) 235–66, esp. 251–56 (vgl. auch ead., „Observations on Mesopotamian Oracles and Prophetic Texts," 138–40). Im Orakel FLP 2064 sind außer einigen vereinzelten Wörtern nur die zwei ersten Zeilen erhalten geblieben (vgl. die Photographie und Abschrift bei Ellis, „The Goddess Kititum Speaks to King Ibalpiel," 239), die in beiden Texten identisch sind: LUGAL *I-ba-al-pi-el um-ma* ^{d}*Ki-ti-tum-ma* „O König Ibalpiel, so (spricht) Kititum." Dagegen ist FLP 1674 vollständig erhalten. Die Göttin Kititum entschleiert dem König die Geheimnisse der Götter, deren zentrale Aussage der ökonomische Wohlstand und die Legitimität der Herrschaft des Königs sind. Dieser letztgenannte Aspekt wird folgendermaßen in Worte gekleidet (Transliteration und Übersetzung von Ellis, „The Goddess Kititum Speaks to King Ibalpiel," 240, 258; vgl. Kommentar S. 261, 265): *i-na mi-il-ki ša* DINGIR.MEŠ *i-na ši-ip-ṭì ša An-nim ma-tum a-na be-li-im na-ad-na-at-ku-um* „At the advice of gods, (and) by the command of Anu, the country is given you to rule" (FLP 1674, Z. 9–13). – *iš-di* GIŠ.GU.ZA-*ka a-na-ku* ^{d}*Ki-ti-tum ú-da-na-an la-ma-⌜sa⌝-[am] ⌜na⌝-ṣé-er-tam aš-ta-ak-na-ak-⌜kum⌝* „I, Kititum, will strengthen the foundations of your throne. I have established a protective spirit for you" (FLP 1674, Z. 22–25). Daraus entsteht eine Verbindung mit den neuassyrischen prophetischen Orakeln, die dadurch noch verstärkt wird, daß der König nach der Aussage der Kititum in ihrer besonderen Obhut steht; zu *lamassu* als göttlich-immanentes weibliches Schutzwesen neben dem maskulinen *šēdu* vgl. Oppenheim, *Ancient Mesopotamia*, 199–206; Ellis, „The Goddess Kititum Speaks to King Ibalpiel," 265.

chen Punkten die Parallelität der Textkorpora am deutlichsten wahrnehmbar ist und wo die zentralen Probleme des Vergleichs liegen. Es gilt zu betonen, daß hier lediglich provisorische Bemerkungen gemacht werden, die noch zu prüfen sind und noch keine tiefgehenden Schlußfolgerungen erlauben.

2. Zentrale Themen der neuassyrischen Prophetie und ihre alttestamentlichen Parallelen

2.1. Rollenverteilung und geschichtlicher Hintergrund der neuassyrischen Orakel

Ein neuassyrischer Prophetenspruch nennt immer namentlich sowohl den Adressaten als auch die sich zu Wort meldende Gottheit, in der Regel auch die das Wort vermittelnde Person; so z. B. in dem Orakel SAA 9 7, das mit folgenden Worten einsetzt:

Beispiel 1: SAA 9 7:1–2

Mullissu-kabtat raggintu	(Spruch der) Prophetin Mullissu-kabtat:
[*m*]*ā abat šarrati Mullissu šī*	Wort der Königin Mullissu:
mā lā tapallaḫ Aššūr-bani-apli	Fürchte dich nicht, Assurbanipal!

In den Sammeltafeln SAA 9 1 und 2 schließt jeder einzelne Spruch mit einer Mitteilung über den/die Prophet(inn)en und dessen/deren Heimat etwa in der Form „Aus dem Munde des Issar-la-tašijat, eines Manns aus Arbela“.[26] In den Einzeltafeln sind diese Angaben oft den Beschädigungen der Tafel zum Opfer gefallen, doch ist in SAA 9 6 und 9 ein Kolophon mit Namen, im letzteren Falle sogar mit Datum erhalten geblieben. Leider lassen sich sowohl die Namen als auch das Datum nur mit Schwierigkeiten deuten.[27]

---

26 SAA 9 1.1:28 f.: *ša pi-i* [md]15–*la–ta-ši-ia-aṭ* DUMU URU.*arba-ìl.* Ob Ištar-lā-tašīјaṭ in der Tat ein Mann oder eine Frau gewesen ist (vgl. Weippert, „Assyrische Prophetien der Zeit Asarhaddons und Assurbanipals,“ 83; Spieckermann, *Juda unter Assur in der Sargonidenzeit*, 298), muß ohne letztendliche Bestätigung bleiben, denn der das männliche Personendeterminativ darstellende senkrechte Keil ist deutlich über einem ursprünglichen weiblichen Determinativ MÍ geschrieben. Nach DUMU sind ebenfalls, wenn auch weniger deutlich, Reste von dem Zeichen MÍ zu spüren. Der Kopist hat offenbar zuerst automatisch an eine Frau gedacht, dann aber sofort seinen Fehler erkannt und korrigiert.

27 SAA 9 6 s. 1–2: [[m]][[d]] LÁL[?]—KAM-*eš* ⌈LÚ⌉[*ra-gi-mu ina* Š]À URU.*arba-ìl ir-t*[*u-gu-um*]. Daß es sich um einen Propheten männlichen Geschlechts handelt, geht aus der relativ sicher erkennbaren Verbalform (Gt Prät. Sg. 3. M. von *ragāmu* ‘schreien’) hervor. Der Name ist nicht mit Sicherheit zu

Die uns bekannten Prophetennamen sind meist stark symbolisch (*Ištar-lā-tašījaṭ* 'Ištar ist nicht nachlässig' bzw. 'Vernachlässige Ištar nicht!'[28]; *Sinqīša-āmur* 'Ich habe ihre Bedrängnis gesehen'[29]; *Ilūssa-āmur* 'Ich habe ihre Göttlichkeit gesehen'[30]; *Mullissu-kabtat* 'Mullissu ist groß'[31]; *Urkittu-šarrat* 'Urkittu ist Königin'[32]) und hängen offensichtlich mit dem Prophetenauftrag der betreffenden Person zusammen. Von den erhaltenen zwölf Namen gehören mindestens sieben, möglicherweise sogar neun zu Frauen,[33] was deutlich darauf hinweist, daß der prophetische Gottesbescheid in Assyrien sehr häufig Sache der Frauen war. Ähnliches gilt, wenn auch in geringerem Maße, auch für die einschlägigen Mari-Briefe,[34] wogegen die alttestamentliche Überlieferung mit ihren fünf Belegen für *něbî'â* (Mirjam Ex 15:20; Debora Ri 4:4; Hulda 2 Kön 22:14 || 2 Chr 34:22; die Frau des

rekonstruieren; Simo Parpola hat den Namen als Tašmetu (LÁL) -ēreš (KAM) 'Tašmetu hat verlangt' vorgeschlagen. SAA 9 9 r. 4–6: *ša* KA ^{MÍ}KAL-*šá–a-mur* [0] ITI.⸢BARAG⸣ UD.18.KÁM *lim-mu* ^{m}EN–KUR-*u*-a LÚ.GAR.KUR *Ṣur-ri*. Das Datum wäre nach dieser Lesung 18. Nisan 650 v. Chr. Zum Problem der Lesung vgl. Weippert, „Assyrische Prophetien der Zeit Asarhaddons und Assurbanipals," 73–74; Nissinen, *Prophetie, Redaktion und Fortschreibung im Hoseabuch*, 282–83.

28 SAA 9 1.1:28'.

29 SAA 9 1.2 ii 9'.

30 SAA 9 1.5:5'.

31 SAA 9 7:1.

32 SAA 9 2.4 iii 18'.

33 Es gibt zwei Grenzfälle, von denen der des Ištar-lā-tašīјaṭ schon oben in Anm. 27 behandelt worden ist. Schwieriger ist die Lage bei der widersprüchlichen Angabe des Namens Bajâ in SAA 9 1.4:40': *ša pi-i* ^{MÍ}*ba-ia-a* DUMU URU.*arba-ìl*. Entweder ist das Determinativ MÍ ein Fehler, oder aber fehlt es nach DUMU. Wenn das sprachlich sehr nahestehende Orakel SAA 9 2.2 der gleichen Person zugeschrieben werden kann, so würde es sich wegen der mask. Nisbe-Form *arbailāja* (vgl. dazu *GAG* 56p S. 69 f.) um einen Mann handeln; SAA 9 2.2:35' lautet: [*x x x x x*]-⸢*a*⸣ URU.*arba-ìl*-⸢*a.a*⸣. Andererseits kennen wir aber auch einen eindeutig femininen Beleg des gleichen Namens (MÍ.*ba-ia-a*) in einer Liste des Tempelpersonals in Huzirina (Sultantepe) aus dem 5. Jh. v. Chr.; s. O. R. Gurney and P. Hulin, *The Sultantepe Tablets II* (Occasional Publications of the British Institute of Archaeology at Ankara 7; London: The British Institute of Archaeology at Ankara, 1964), esp. Nr. 406 r. 10' (Hinweis S. Parpola). Unter diesen Umständen muß das Geschlecht von Bajâ noch offenbleiben. Die Tabelle von Weippert, „Assyrische Prophetien der Zeit Asarhaddons und Assurbanipals," 113 ist zu ergänzen durch den oben (Anm. 28) genannten Mann Tašmētu-ēreš aus Arbela, wozu mit der Möglichkeit zu rechnen ist, daß der Prophetinnenname ^{MÍ}KAL-*šá–a-mur* (vgl. oben Anm. 28) mit Sinqīša-āmur (SAA 9 1.2:9'; 2.5?) identisch ist; vgl. dazu Nissinen, *Prophetie, Redaktion und Fortschreibung im Hoseabuch*, 283.

34 Vgl. Malamat, „A Forerunner of Biblical Prophecy," 43–44, sowie die Tabelle bei K. Koch, „Die Briefe 'prophetischen' Inhalts aus Mari: Bemerkungen zu Gattung und Sitz im Leben," *UF* 4 (1972) 53–77, esp. 76, die mindestens sechs Fälle zeigt, in denen die göttliche Botschaft aus dem Munde einer Prophetin (*muḫḫūtum, āpiltum* oder *qabâtum*) genommen worden ist.

Jesaja Jes 8:3; Noadja Neh 6:14) den weiblichen Prophetismus eher als eine Marginalerscheinung erscheinen läßt.[35]

Wie oben schon festgestellt, gibt es im Akkadischen ebensowenig wie in den anderen semitischen Sprachen (einschl. des Hebräischen!) einen einheitlichen Begriff für die von uns als 'Prophetie' bezeichnete Tätigkeit. In unseren neuassyrischen Orakeln scheint immerhin das Verb *ragāmu* 'rufen, schreien' mit seinen Derivaten ein Terminus technicus für die Übermittlung des unmittelbaren Gottesbescheids zu sein, denn es gibt unter den namentlich genannten Personen eine *raggintu*[36] und einen *raggimu*,[37] wozu das Verb in den wenigen erhaltenen Reste von SAA 9 6 nicht weniger als dreimal (Z. 16, 18, 22) vorkommt. Darüber hinaus ist auch die in Mari gewöhnliche Bezeichnung *maḫḫû* 'Ekstatiker' in den zeitgenössischen Königsinschriften belegt.[38] Dagegen enthält das Epitheton *šēlūtu ša šarri* 'Tempeloblatin' der Issar-bel-da"ini[39] keinen spezifischen Hinweis auf prophetische Tätigkeit.

Als Heimatort der Prophet(inn)en werden außer einer sonst unbekannten Siedlung namens Dāra-aḫūja, die angeblich „zwischen den Bergen" liegt,[40] die Städte des assyrischen Kerngebiets mitgeteilt: aus Assur kommen zwei Orakel

---

35 Von diesen hat eigentlich nur Hulda einen deutlich prophetischen Auftrag inne; vgl. Spieckermann, *Juda unter Assur in der Sargonidenzeit*, 302.

36 SAA 9 7:1: Mullissu-kabtat.

37 SAA 9 3.5 iv 31. Die Reste des vorangehenden Prophetennamens weisen vielleicht auf Lā-dāgil-ili hin, denn das letzte Zeichen des Namens ist teilweise erhalten und ist relativ sicher als DINGIR zu lesen; ihm entstammen auch die Orakel SAA 9 1.10 und 2.3.

38 In dem Altbabylonischen von Mari erscheint das Wort in der Form *muḫḫū(tu)m* und stellt neben dem in Ninive fehlenden *āpil(t)um* 'Beantworter(in)' das gewöhnlichste Prophetenepitheton dar. Vgl. Koch, „Die Briefe 'prophetischen' Inhalts aus Mari," 76; Noort, *Untersuchungen zum Gottesbild in Mari*, 69–75; und Malamat, „A Forerunner of Biblical Prophecy," 38–39. – Weippert, „Die Bildsprache der neuassyrischen Prophetie," 57; und id., „Aspekte israelitischer Prophetie im Lichte verwandter Erscheinungen des Alten Orients," 303 belegt eine *maḫḫūtu* auch in den prophetischen Texten und dürfte damit auf das Vorkommen einer ^{MÍ}GUB.BA in SAA 9 10 (CT 53, 946 = 83-1-18, 726), l. s. 2 hinweisen. Dieses Fragment zählt zu den zusätzlichen drei Texten, die Weippert („Die Bildsprache der neuassyrischen Prophetie," 56, Anm. 6; „Aspekte israelitischer Prophetie im Lichte verwandter Erscheinungen des Alten Orients," Anm. 36) zum prophetischen Korpus rechnet.

39 SAA 9 1.7:11. Weippert („Die Bildsprache der neuassyrischen Prophetie," 57; id., „Aspekte israelitischer Prophetie im Lichte verwandter Erscheinungen des Alten Orients," 303) weiß von einer zweiten *šēlūtu* zu berichten; gemeint ist offenbar die Erwähnung einer *šēlūtu ša Issār* in dem Fragment SAA 13 148 (CT 53,413 = K 10865) Z. 2, ein weiteres Stück, das von Weippert in das prophetische Material mit einbezogen wurde. Da allerdings *šēlūtu* keine spezifisch prophetische Bezeichnung ist, ist die Zugehörigkeit dieses Fragments zu unserem Textkorpus, wie Weippert auch feststellt, nicht sicher.

40 SAA 9 1.3:15': URU.*da-ra-a-ḫu-u-ia ša bir-ti* KUR.MEŠ-*ni*.

(SAA 9 1.5; 2.1) und aus Kalḫu eins (SAA 9 2.4). Als Sitz der Prophetie überragt allerdings eine Stadt den anderen weit, und zwar Arbela, das herausragende Zentrum der Ištarverehrung.[41] Aus Arbela stammen sechs von den uns bekannten zwölf Prophet(inn)en, und zudem wahrscheinlich noch drei Orakel von unbekannten Personen (SAA 9 1.6; 1.9; 5).

Die starke Konzentration auf Arbela hängt augenfällig mit der Tatsache zusammen, daß Ištar in den Orakeln auch sonst als die redende Gottheit dominiert in dem Maße, daß sie sogar in einigen Orakeln spricht, die einen anderen Ausgangsort angeben (SAA 9 1.3; 2.4). Dies deutet darauf hin, daß die neuassyrische Prophetie, zumindest in der uns überlieferten Form, in Verbindung steht mit dem Kult der Ištar.

Die andere Göttin, die in den neuassyrischen Prophetensprüchen häufig erscheint, ist Mullissu (^{d}NIN.LÍL), ursprünglich Gemahlin Enlils, im assyrischen Pantheon aber die des Hauptgottes Aššur.[42] In den Prophetien pflegen freilich die Rollen und Repliken der Ištar und Mullissu derart zu verschmelzen, daß es nicht immer ganz deutlich wird, um welche von den beiden Göttinnen es sich eigentlich handelt – in der Tat gewinnt man den Eindruck, „daß hier die beiden Göttinnen vor den Ohren des Hörers bzw. vor den Augen des Lesers zu einer einzigen verschmelzen, wie ja auch Mullissu und Ištar von Nineve in neuassyrischer Zeit gelegentlich identifiziert worden sind“.[43] Deswegen wäre es vielleicht angebracht, Mullissu in der Prophetie als eine von den zahlreichen Erscheinungsformen Ištars zu betrachten. Neben Ištar von Arbela (*Ištar ša Arbail*) kommen in der Prophetie auch Hypostasen wie *šarrat Nīnua* (Königin von Ninive),[44] *Urkittu* (Ištar von Uruk)[45] und *Bānītu*[46] vor, und es ist durchaus möglich, daß mehrere von ihnen zugleich erscheinen, wie der Ausspruch *a-ni-nu* ^{d}*iš-tar*-MEŠ [*x x x i*]*na é-sag-íl* „Wir sind die Göttinnen („Ištars“)... in Esangil“ (SAA 9 2.1:8’f.) zeigt.[47]

41 S. dazu B. Menzel, *Assyrische Tempel*, vol. 1: *Untersuchungen zu Kult, Administration und Personal* (StPSM 10.1; Rome: Biblical Institute Press, 1981), esp. 6–10.

42 Vgl. ibid., 63–64. Mullissu (< **munliltu*) ist eine feminine Emesal-Form des Namens Enlil.

43 Weippert, „Die Bildsprache der neuassyrischen Prophetie,“ 64; vgl. Menzel, *Assyrische Tempel*, 64–65, 116.

44 SAA 3 13 r. 2, 6 f.

45 Außer im Namen der Prophetin Urkittu-šarrat (SAA 9 2.4:18’), die interessanterweise aus Kalḫu stammt, wird Urkittu in SAA 3 13 r. 3 erwähnt.

46 SAA 9 2.1:5’.

47 Der Begriff *ištaru* bedeutet zwar im allgemeinen ‘Göttin’ als die weibliche Entsprechung von *ilu* ‘Gott’ (vgl. Oppenheim, *Ancient Mesopotamia*, 199–206). Da Ištar in unserem Zusammenhang als *die* Göttin gilt und in den folgenden Orakeln sonst ausschließlich das Wort hat, ist es denkbar, daß die *ištarāti* des babylonischen Marduk-Tempels sich als ihre Erscheinungsformen verstehen.

Die anderen Gottheiten melden sich in den prophetischen Orakeln wesentlich seltener. In den drei ersten Orakeln der Sammeltafel SAA 9 3, die mit dem Thronbesteigungsfest des Asarhaddon im Aššur-Tempel Ešarra im Jahre 681 zusammenhängen,[48] spielt immerhin Aššur eine bedeutende Rolle als der, der die ganze Welt dem König Asarhaddon gegeben[49] und seine Feinde und Rivalen vernichtet hat. In den beiden folgenden Orakeln (SAA 9 3.4–5) wird aber das Wort wieder Ištar von Arbela überlassen, die als Gastgeberin des den Vasallenkönigen bereiteten Bundesmahls redet. Nabû hat seine Hauptrolle als Dialogpartner Assurbanipals in SAA 3 13, und erscheint als „Herr des Griffels" (*bēl qarṭuppi*) in SAA 9 1.4 zusammen mit Bel (Marduk) und Ištar von Arbela. Daß in einem Orakel drei Gottheiten sprechen, ist ein interessantes Phänomen, das nicht so zu verstehen sein dürfte, daß je eine Gottheit an ihrem Platze auftritt – vielmehr handelt es sich um Aspekte eines übergeordneten göttlichen Wesens, wie es auch oben bei den *ištarāti* von Esangil der Fall war.

Die Empfänger der göttlichen Botschaft gehören stets zur königlichen Familie. In den meisten Fällen sind die Orakel an die Könige Asarhaddon oder Assurbanipal adressiert, dem letztgenannten zumindest einmal (SAA 9 7) als dem Kronprinzen. In den uns erhaltenen Orakeln verdient die Rolle der Königinmutter Naqija (Zakutu) Beachtung, vor allem weil die an sie gerichteten Orakel (SAA 9 1.8; 2.1; 5[50]) einen wichtigen Hinweis auf den Anlaß und geschichtlichen Hintergrund der uns bekannten Texte geben.

Naqija, deren Name[51] auf deren aramäischen Ursprung hindeutet, war die Mutter Asarhaddons und wirkte in den Wirren der Thronnachfolge Sanheribs besonders aktiv zugunsten ihres Sohns. Es war gerade Naqija, der Asarhaddon seine Ernennung zum Kronprinzen verdankte. Diese keineswegs eindeutige Vorrangstellung Asarhaddons erregte eine solche Mißgunst bei seinen Brüdern, daß diese ihn in die Verbannung trieben, ihren Vater Sanherib ermordeten und versuchten, im assyrischen Reich zur Macht zu gelangen. Erst in der Folge eines Bürgerkriegs gelang es Asarhaddon, im Jahre 681 das Land seiner Herrschaft

48 SAA 9 3.1:14 läßt sich vielleicht folgendermaßen ergänzen: [*i-sin-nu ina*] *é-šar-ra* ᵈ*aš-šur is-sa-kan* „[Eine Feier] in Ešarra hat Aššur veranstaltet." Zur Datierung vgl. auch Weippert, „Assyrische Prophetien der Zeit Asarhaddons und Assurbanipals," 95.

49 SAA 9 3.2 ii 3–6: *kippat erbettim Aššūr ittannaššu issu bēt inappaḫanni bēt irabbūni šarru miḫiršu laššu* „Den Erdkreis hat Aššur ihm gegeben. Vom Aufgang (der Sonne) bis zu (ihrem) Niedergang ist ihm kein König gleich" (vgl. etwa Ps 113:3; Jes 45:6; Mal 1:11).

50 Daß Naqija die Empfängerin von SAA 9 5 ist, wird wahrscheinlich durch die feminine Form des Befehls *qablīki ruksī* „Gürte deine Lenden" (Z. 4).

51 *Zakūtu* ist eine akkadische Übersetzung des Namens *Naqīja*, der ähnlich wie hebr. *nāqî* 'rein, schuldlos' bedeutet. Zur Person und Bedeutung von Naqija s. H. Lewy, „Nitokris – Naqî'a," *JNES* 11 (1952) 264–86.

einzuverleiben. Die Rebellion der Brüder und die Machtbefugnis Asarhaddons, die von Naqija mit Kräften gestützt wurde, spiegelt sich in mehreren Orakeln eindeutig wider, wie unten näher gezeigt wird.

Einige Jahrzehnte später befand sich auch Assurbanipal in ähnlicher Lage, nachdem sein Bruder Šamaš-šumu-ukin, der nach dem Testament Asarhaddons nach dessen Tod über Babylonien regierte, sich im Jahre 652 mit Unterstützung der Elamiter empörte, so daß auch Assurbanipal dazu gezwungen war, sein Königtum in einem Bruderkrieg zu verteidigen.[52] So sind mit den „Feinden" (*nakarūti*), deren Vernichtung fast in jedem Orakel prophezeit wird, sehr oft, wenn nicht sogar in meisten Fällen, die rebellierenden Königsbrüder samt ihren Truppen gemeint, obgleich wohl auch ausländische Angreifer, vor allem die Elamiter und Kimmerier, mehrmals genannt werden.[53] Ein Orakel (SAA 9 8) konzentriert sich gänzlich auf Elam. Daß die einheimischen Gegner jedoch als Feinde des Königs in der Prophetie vorherrschen, hängt damit zusammen, daß die Zerstörung der Feinde einen Teilaspekt des einen zentralen Themas darstellt, und zwar der Legitimität des Königtums von Asarhaddon bzw. Assurbanipal.

2.2. Thronfolge und Königsideologie

Daß die prophetischen Orakel an Asarhaddon und Assurbanipal mit den oben beschriebenen Thronwirren in Verbindung stehen, ist in vielen Fällen offensichtlich. In diesem Zusammenhang ist auch der Anlaß zur Sammlung und Archivierung der Orakel zu suchen, denn die beiden Könige haben sozusagen schwarz auf weiß göttliche Garantie für ihr Königtum verlangt, um ihre Machtbefugnis legitimieren zu können. Daraus erklärt sich, daß die Propheten nicht müde werden, ein ums andere Mal zu wiederholen, daß Asarhaddon bzw. Assurbanipal und keiner sonst der von den Göttern erwählte König sei. Dies wird aufs deutlichste z. B. in einer Prophetie an die Königinmutter Naqija geäußert:

Beispiel 2: SAA 9 1.8:

52 Auch Assurbanipal war dabei auf die Unterstützung Naqijas angewiesen; vgl. Lewy, „Nitokris – Naqî'a," 1952, 280 – 283.

53 Vgl. SAA 9 3.2 ii 1 f.: [KUR.]*gi-mir-a.a ina* ŠU!-*šú a-*⌈*šá*⌉*-kan* ⌈*i*⌉*-šá-tu ina* KUR.*el-li-pi um-ma-ad* „Die Kimmerier werde ich in seine Hände übergeben, das Land von Ellipi werde ich in Brand stecken." – SAA 9 7:14: *ki-i* KUR.NIM.KI KUR.*gi-mir-a a-*⌈*gam*⌉*-mar* „Wie Elam, so werde ich die Kimmerier vernichten."

anāku bēlit Arbail / ana ummi šarri kī taḫḫurīninni / mā ša imitti ša šumēli ina sūniki tassakni / mā īyû ṣit libbīja ṣēru tussarpidi / ūmâ šarru lā tapallaḫ / šarrūtu ikkû danānu ikkūma ša pī Aḫāt-abīša mārat Arbail

Ich bin die Herrin von Arbela! / An die Königinmutter, weil du dich mir zuwandtest / und sagtest: „Den von rechts (und) den von links hast du in deinen Schoß gelegt, / meinen eigenen Sproß hast du aber in der Steppe herumlaufen lassen", / (sage ich): Nun, König, fürchte dich nicht! / Das Königtum ist dein, die Macht ist dein!
Aus dem Munde der Aḫat-Abiša, einer Frau aus Arbela.

Aus dieser Prophetie läßt sich entnehmen, daß Naqija während der Verbannung Asarhaddons an Ištar appelliert hatte, weil die Brüder, die nicht Naqijas Söhne waren, sich als überlegen erwiesen hatten und somit in den Augen der Königinmutter auf dem Schoß der Herrin von Arbela saßen. Die Prophetin übermittelt dazu eine Beteuerung der Ištar, daß das Königtum Asarhaddon und nicht seinen Brüdern gehörte. Ferner geht aus dieser Prophetie hervor, daß Naqija die Orakel an Asarhaddon empfing, als dieser des Landes verwiesen war, was viel über ihre politische Gewichtigkeit aussagt.

Die Legitimität der Thronfolge wird auch dadurch unterstrichen, daß Asarhaddon als *aplu kēnu* „rechter Erbe" bezeichnet wird, dessen Macht Ištar bis in unbegrenzte Zukunft bestätigt:

Beispiel 3: SAA 9 1.6 iii 7'–22'; iii 30'–iv 10; iv 20–25

anāku Issār ša [Arbail] / Aššūr-aḫu-iddina šar māt Aš[šūr] / ina Libbāli Nīnua Kalḫa Arbail ūmē arkūt[e] šanāte dārāt[e] ana Aššūr-aḫu-iddina šarrīy[a] adanna / sabsubtaka rabītu anāku mušeniq!-ta-ka de'iqtu anāku / ša ūmē arkūte šanāte dārāte kussīka ina šapal šamê rabûte uktin ...
lā tapallaḫ šarru / aqṭibak lā aslik[a] / utakki[lka] lā ubāš[ka] / nāru ina tuqunni ušēbar[ka] / Aššūr-aḫu-iddina aplu kēnu mār Mullissi / ḫangaru akku ina qātēya nakarūtēka uqatta ... Aššūr-aḫu-iddina aplu kēnu mār Mullissi / ḫissat[ka] ḫassā[ku] artāmk[a] adan[niš]

Ich bin Ištar von Arbela! / Asarhaddon, König von Assyrien: / In Assur, Ninive, Kalḫu und Arbela werde ich lange Tage, dauernde Jahre meinem König Asarhaddon geben. / Ich bin deine große Hebamme, ich bin deine gute Amme. / Für lange Tage, dauernde Jahre habe ich deinen Thron unter dem großen Himmel befestigt ...
Fürchte dich nicht, König! / Ich habe zu dir gesprochen und habe dich nicht getäuscht. / Ich habe dich ermutigt und werde dich nicht zuschanden machen. / Ich bringe dich in Sicherheit über den Fluß hinüber. / Asarhaddon, legitimer Erbe, Sohn der Mullissu! / Mit einem schneidenden Dolch[54] in meinen Händen vernichte ich deine Feinde ...
Asarhaddon, legitimer Erbe, Sohn der Mullissu! / Ich denke an dich, ich liebe dich sehr.

54 Das Wort *ḫangaru* dürfte sich aus dem syr. *ḥang^{e}rā* ‘Dolch’ erklären (vgl. von Soden, „Aramäische Wörter: Vorbericht III," 187), während *akku* als Verbaladjektiv von *akāku* (*ekēku*)

In diesem Text begegnen mehrere Elemente, die zur Grundstruktur der assyrischen Königsideologie gehören und die auch zahlreiche Berührungspunkte mit dem Alten Testament aufweisen. Man denke nur an den Königspsalm Ps 21, in dem zuerst (Vss. 2–8) die von Jahwe gegebene Macht und Pracht des „Königs" samt seiner langen Regierung, dann (Vss. 9–13) die Vernichtung seiner Feinde beschrieben werden.[55]

Der akkadische Ausdruck *ūmē arkūte šanāte dārāte* „lange Tage, dauernde Jahre", der in Ps 21:5 *'ōrek yāmîm 'ôlām wā-'ēd* eine hebräische Entsprechung hat, bedeutet zunächst langes Leben und dauerhafte Regierung des betreffenden Königs. Dem liegt aber der echt dynastische Gedanke nicht fern, der schon durch den Titel *aplu kēnu* zum Ausdruck kommt und in einer Prophetie mit klaren Worten geäußert wird: *ina libbi ekallīka tataqqun mara'ka mar mar'īka šarrūtu ina burki ša Inurta uppaš* „Du wirst sicher in deinem Palast wohnen, dein Sohn und dein Enkel werden im Schoß von Ninurta als Könige herrschen" (SAA 9 1.10:27–29; vgl. SAA 9 2.3:II:11'-14'). Daraus wird ersichtlich, daß die Dynastie im familiären Sinne keine fremde Idee im neuassyrischen Reich war.[56]

Unter Berufung auf die Natanweissagung 2 Sam 7:4–17 hat man geradewegs auf die Ähnlichkeiten der mesopotamischen prophetischen Aussagen mit der jerusalemischen dynastischen Königsideologie hinweisen können.[57] Die ge-

---

'kratzen' (vgl. *AHw* 193) verstanden werden kann; anders von Soden (ibd., 184), der *akku* (= *aggu* 'grimmig, zornig') auf das aram. *'akk^{e}ṯā* 'Zorn' und *'akk^{e}ṯānā* 'zornig' bezieht.

55 Zu diesem Psalm vgl. O. Loretz, *Die Königspsalmen: Die altorientalisch-kanaanäische Königsideologie in jüdischer Sicht*, vol. 1: *Ps 20, 21, 72, 101 und 144: Mit einem Beitrag von I. Kottsieper zu Papyrus Amherst* (UBL 6; Münster: Ugarit-Verlag, 1988), esp. 77–102. Ob der König in der heutigen Gestalt des Psalms als ein wirklich regierender König oder als ein Kollektivbegriff für das Volk Israels zu verstehen sei, hängt davon ab, ob man den Psalm als einen vorexilischen Ritualtext oder als eine nachexilische Kompilation betrachten will. Diese Gegenüberstellung ist aber insofern falsch, als der Psalm seinen ursprünglichen Sitz im Leben wirklich im Rahmen des vorexilischen Königskults hat, später aber durch Kommentierung und Neusemantisierung in einem kollektiven Sinne umgedeutet wurde. Daß der Assoziationshintergrund des Psalms die altorientalische Königsideologie ist, ist öfters vermutet worden und dürfte keinem Zweifel unterliegen.

56 Somit gegen Ellis, „Observations on Mesopotamian Oracles and Prophetic Texts," 175, die in den mesopotamischen Orakeln keinen dynastischen Aspekt findet: „What *is* absent in Mesopotamian speculative thought, although it certainly existed in political practice, is the idea of a 'dynasty' in a familial sense. A Mesopotamian 'dynasty' is in the first instance a line of rulers based in a single capital. That capital — and hence the line of rulers— is sanctioned by the presence and cooperation of the deity."

57 Zu den Parallelen in der Mariprophetie vgl. A. Malamat, „A Mari Prophecy and Nathan's Dynastic Oracle," *Prophecy*, FS G. Fohrer (ed. J. A. Emerton; BZAW 150. Berlin/New York: De Gruyter, 1980) 68–82; zu den in der neuassyrischen Prophetie vgl. Ishida, *The Royal Dynasties in*

meinsamen Züge sind in der Tat unmißverständlich: nicht nur wird dem König die Fortdauer seiner Dynastie versprochen (2 Sam 7:12 f.16 vgl. Ps 89:5, 30, 37 f.), sondern er wird auch Sohn Gottes genannt (2 Sam 7:14 vgl. Ps 2:7; 89:27–30; Jes 9:5).[58] Fragt man nach dem Charakter und Ursprung dieser Affinität, so darf man nicht vergessen, daß 2 Sam 7 in der jetzt vorliegenden Gestalt einen durchaus deuteronomistischen Text darstellt, dessen Gedanken nicht einfach auf die Königszeit Judas zurückgeführt werden können.[59] Daß dem Kapitel ein vorexilisches Königsorakel zugrundeliegt, ist allgemein anerkannt worden, aber über den Umfang dieses Orakels gehen die Meinungen auseinander.[60] Aller Wahrscheinlichkeit nach gehören jedoch die Schlüsselaussagen in Vss. 12 und 14, d. h. die Gottessohnschaft des Königs und die Verheißung des Nachkommens, zum ältesten Bestand des Textes, den aber die deuteronomistischen Redaktoren nachher stark erweitert haben.

Die Natanweissagung bietet indes ein gutes Beispiel für eine exilisch-nachexilische Fortschreibung der vorexilischen jerusalemischen Königsideologie, und

---

Ancient Israel, 90–92; Weippert, „Assyrische Prophetien der Zeit Asarhaddons und Assurbanipals," 105–6.

58 Ishida, *The Royal Dynasties in Ancient Israel*, 91–92 führt nicht weniger als sechzehn Zitate aus SAA 9 1, 2 und 3 an, die, ohne die Themen von 2 Sam 7 immer ganz genau zu treffen, doch die Verwandtschaft der Ideen und Ausdrücke sehr anschaulich zum Ausdruck bringen. Die Sohnschaft des Gottes und der dynastische Gedanke sind auch in einem prophetischen Text aus Mari (FM 7 39) zu belegen; vgl. Malamat, „A Mari Prophecy and Nathan's Dynastic Oracle," 79–80.

59 So jedoch Ishida, *The Royal Dynasties in Ancient Israel*, 82, der die Einheitlichkeit des ganzen Kapitels sowie dessen Datierung in die davidisch-salomonische Zeit ohne eingehende Argumentation voraussetzt. Malamat, „A Mari Prophecy and Nathan's Dynastic Oracle," 78 gibt die Mehrschichtigkeit des Textes zu, hält sie aber für unbedeutend in diesem Zusammenhang: „Suffice it here to say that the prophecy *per se* comes from the period of the United Monarchy, with a Davidic nucleus and an adaptation under Solomon." Dies entspricht der Auffassung von T. N. D. Mettinger, *King and Messiah: The Civil and Sacral Legitimation of the Israelite Kings* (CB.OT 8; Lund: CWK Gleerup, 1976), esp. 62 von der Datierung und Redaktion des Orakels (s. u. Anm. 61).

60 Weippert, „Assyrische Prophetien der Zeit Asarhaddons und Assurbanipals," 105, gibt ohne Begründung eine Rekonstruktion, nach der das Orakel aus den Vss. 8 f., 11ab, 12. 14a, 15a, 16 besteht. Von den detaillierten Versuchen, das vordtr. Orakel herauszuarbeiten, seien hier Mettinger, *King and Messiah*; und T. Veijola, *Verheißung in der Krise: Studien zur Literatur und Theologie der Exilszeit anhand des 89. Psalms* (AASF B 220; Helsinki: Suomalainen tiedeakatemia, 1982) genannt. Mettinger (vgl. S. 62–63) identifiziert das ursprüngliche Orakel mit einem davidischen Kern aus der Zeit von Salomo in den Vss. 1a, 2–7, 12–14a, 16*, 17, das nach dem Tod Salomos eine dynastische Redaktion (Vss. 8–9, 11b, 14b–15, 16*, 18–22a, 27–29) und schließlich eine dtr. Redaktion (Vss. 1b, 10–11a, 22b–26) erfahren habe. Demgegenüber findet Veijola (vgl. S. 62) vordtr. Material nur in den Vss. 1a, 2–4.5 (ohne *'l 'br*), 8a (ohne *l'bry*), 9a.12.14 f., während der erste dtr. Redaktor DtrH den Text durch die Vss. 11b, 13, 16, 18–21, 27aβγb –29 und der spätere Redaktor DtrN durch 8a (*l'bry*), 8, 9b–11a, 22–27aa erweitert habe.

ähnliches gilt ohne Zweifel auch für viele andere einschlägige Texte des Alten Testaments, wie etwa für die Königspsalmen. Dies mahnt zur Vorsicht gegenüber der Annahme, daß alles, was über einen König geäußert wird, als solches den vorexilischen Verhältnissen entspreche. Demgegenüber wird es möglich, zu betrachten, wie die ursprünglich der Königsinstitution angehörenden Konzeptionen in dem königslosen Milieu nach der Zerstörung Jerusalems weiterleben.

Als Beispiel dafür gelten die Gedanken von göttlicher Liebe und Erwählung, die sowohl in assyrischen als auch in biblischen Texten eine bedeutende Rolle spielen. Wie der oben zitierte Text zeigt, ist die Liebe einer Gottheit zu einem König eine für die neuassyrische Prophetie typische Idee, die die exklusive Beziehung zum Ausdruck bringt, die zwischen Gottheit und König aufgrund der Initiative des erstgenannten besteht. Diese exklusive göttliche Liebe bedeutet vor allem, daß der genannte König und kein anderer von der Gottheit erwählt worden ist, um als deren „Sohn" das Königtum auszuüben. Der Erwählungsgedanke hat zwar im Blick auf die neuassyrischen Bruderkriege einen ganz konkreten Bezug, gehört aber auch sonst als fester Bestandteil zur mesopotamischen Königsideologie.

Im Alten Testament begegnen wir der Liebes- und Erwählungstheologie vor allem in der deuteronomistischen Literatur. Im Deuteronomium kommen die semantischen Felder von *'hb* und *bḥr* einander sehr nahe, indem die Liebe als Grund der Erwählung gilt (Dtn 4:37; 7:6 – 8; 10:15).[61] Als Objekt der Verben erscheint aber kein König, sondern das *Volk* Israel. Hier haben wir es mit einer typisch deuteronomistischen Projektion zu tun, wobei das Volk an die Stelle des Königs tritt und zum unmittelbaren Empfänger der göttlichen Verheißungen wird. Diese Kollektivierung bzw. „Demokratisierung" der Königsideologie versteht sich am besten in einer Situation, wo das Königtum als konkrete Institution untergegangen war. Die königlichen Verheißungen Jahwes verloren in dieser Situation zwar nicht ihre Gültigkeit, aber die „Gnaden Davids" (Jes 55:3) mußten jetzt auf das ganze Volk bezogen werden. Dies hinderte natürlich weder am Reden von den vergangenen Königen als den individuellen Empfängern der göttlichen Gaben noch an der Erwartung einer einzelnen messianischen Gestalt. So kann Jahwe fortwährend Salomo lieben (2 Sam 12:24) wie auch David als Erwählter Jahwes (Ps 89:4, 20) und als wiederbelebter König (Ez 34:23 f.; 37:24 f.) gilt.

Die Erwählungstheologie herrscht ferner in deuterojesajanischen Orakeln, deren Motive und Bildersprache in vielfacher Hinsicht an die neuassyrische Prophetie erinnern, wie Manfred Weippert deutlich gezeigt hat (Jes 41:8 – 18;

61 Vgl. etwa R. Lauha, *Psychophysischer Sprachgebrauch im Alten Testament: Eine struktursemantische Analyse von לב, נפש und רוח*, vol. 1: *Emotionen* (AASF B Diss 35; Helsinki: Suomalainen tiedeakatemia, 1983), esp. 174.

43:1–4; 44:1–5; 45:1–7; 48:12–15).[62] Daß hier gerade das Königsorakel eher als das „priesterliche Heilsorakel" als Vorlage gedient hat,[63] machen die zahlreichen und nahen Berührungen mit den neuassyrischen Königsorakeln in der Tat wahrscheinlich. Stimmt die Theorie von Weippert, nach der der Hintergrund dieser Orakel in der vorexilischen judäischen Königsprophetie zu suchen sei,[64] so haben die Propheten in Jerusalem ihre Königsideologie und die damit verbundene Sprache mit ihren assyrischen Kollegen *mutatis mutandis* weitgehend gemein gehabt. Diese sehr erwägenswerte Annahme schließt jedoch die Möglichkeit nicht aus, daß die deuterojesajanischen Aussagen auch Einflüsse aufweisen, die erst in der Exilszeit aufgenommen worden sind.

Auf jeden Fall gelten die deuterojesajanischen Texte als ein erhellendes Beispiel für die Entwicklung und Funktion der Königsprophetie in der Exilszeit. Der unmittelbar an Kyros gerichtete Spruch Jes 45:1–7 hat seine Funktion als Königsprophetie noch bewahrt,[65] während diejenigen Orakel, die von Israel/Jakob reden, in ihrem Gedankeninhalt und in der Metaphorik in keiner Hinsicht davon abweichen, so daß auch hier tatsächlich von einer Kollektivierung der Königsprophetie gesprochen werden kann. Da die davidische Dynastie im Deuterojesaja (mit Ausnahme von 55:3) jedoch kein Thema ist, haben wir es hier mit einem anderen Assoziationshintergrund zu tun als in der deuteronomistischen Literatur.

Die Selbstvorstellung *anāku Ištar ša Arbail* zählt zu den charakteristischen Merkmalen der neuassyrischen Prophetie[66] (vgl. oben Beispiel 2) und hat die für Deuterojesaja ebenso charakteristische biblische Entsprechung „Ich bin Jahwe" z. B. in der Kyros-Prophetie (Jes 45:5). Diese Parallelität ruft nicht nur die Annahme eines prophetischen Sitzes im Leben dieser Formel hervor, sondern zeigt auch deutlich das Moment, wo sich ihre biblische Funktion von der assyrischen unterscheidet. Im Falle des Deuterojesaja ist nämlich neu die Fortsetzung „außer mir gibt es keinen Gott" (Jes 45:5; vgl. 43:11; 45:21; Hos 13:4 und den Dekalogprolog!). Durch diese Betonung wird die Formel zum monotheistischen Manifest, das in Verbindung mit Kyros geradezu missionarische Dimensionen gewinnt.

---

62 Vgl. Weippert, „Assyrische Prophetien der Zeit Asarhaddons und Assurbanipals," 108–11; id., „De herkomst van het heilsorakel voor Israël bij Deutero-Jesaja," passim.

63 Weippert, „Assyrische Prophetien der Zeit Asarhaddons und Assurbanipals," 110; id., „Aspekte israelitischer Prophetie im Lichte verwandter Erscheinungen des Alten Orients," 312–13.

64 Weippert, „De herkomst van het heilsorakel voor Israël bij Deutero-Jesaja," 10–11.

65 Vgl. Weippert, „Assyrische Prophetien der Zeit Asarhaddons und Assurbanipals," 109–10.

66 Vgl. oben Beispiel 3 und s. Weippert, „Assyrische Prophetien der Zeit Asarhaddons und Assurbanipals," 77–78.

2.3. Der Bundesgedanke

Wie oben schon festgestellt, sind in der Prophetie mit den „Feinden“ nicht nur die rivalisierenden Thronprätendenten, sondern auch die auswärtigen Völker und Könige genannt. Es wird z. B. prophezeit, wie die besiegten und eingejochten Feinde Asarhaddon Tribut zahlen,[67] oder wie die Könige der Länder ihre Grenzen und Schicksale der Entscheidung des Kronprinzen Assurbanipal überlassen.[68] Das assyrische Imperium erlebte unter Asarhaddon und Assurbanipal eine Blütezeit, deren Beständigkeit aber andauernd bedroht war wegen der wiederkehrenden Bruderkriege, die große politische und militärische Kraftreserven in Anspruch nahmen. Deswegen war es neben den innenpolitischen Bedürfnissen der beiden Könige, die Legitimität ihres Throns zu rechtfertigen, auch notwendig, den zahlreichen Vasallenkönigen klarzustellen, wer der Herr des Imperiums eigentlich sei. Hier knüpft die neuassyrische Prophetie an den mit der Vertragsinstitution zusammenhängenden Sprachgebrauch an, wie aus dem folgenden Beispiel sehr deutlich zu ersehen ist. Es handelt sich um ein Orakel, dessen Sitz im Leben wahrscheinlich ein für die Vasallenkönige bereitetes Gastmahl anläßlich der Erneuerung des jeweiligen Vertrags bei der Thronbesteigung Asarhaddons ist:[69]

Beispiel 4: SAA 9 3.4 iii 2–15

mê ṣarṣāri tassiqīšunu / massītu ša sūti mê ṣarṣāri tumtalli tattannaššunu / mā taqabbiā ina libbīkunu mā Issār pāqtu šī / mā tallakā ina ālānīkunu nagiānīkunu / kusāpu takkalā tamaššiā adê annūti / mā issu libbi mê annūti tašattiā / taḫassasāni tanaṣṣarā adê annūti / ša ina muḫḫi Aššūr-aḫu-iddina aškunūni

---

67 SAA 9 2.5:23–25: *nakarūti ina sigarāti salmūti ina maddanāti ina pān šēpēšu ubbala* „Die Feinde im Joch, die Friedensstifter mit Tribut werde ich unter seine Füßen bringen“; vgl. SAA 9 1.2 ii 3–5.

68 SAA 9 7:12 f.: [^{d}NIN.L]ÍL *taq-ṭi-bi ma-a* [LUGAL.ME]Š *šá* KUR.KUR [*ta-pi-a*]*l ta-ḫu-ma-a-ni tu-kal-lam-*⸢*šu-nu*⸣ [KA]SKAL. MEŠ *ina* GÌR.2-*šu-nu* GAR-*an* „[Mulli]ssu sagte: [Du wirst über die Kön]ige der Länder [herrsch]en, du wirst ihnen (ihre) Grenzen zeigen und den Weg (unter) ihren Füßen.“

69 Vgl. Spieckermann, *Juda unter Assur in der Sargonidenzeit*, 300. Dagegen führt Ishida, *The Royal Dynasties in Ancient Israel*, 115–16 diesen Text als Beispiel für einen Vertrag zwischen dem König und das Volk an. Allerdings weist die Rede von den „Städten und Bezirken“ eher auf die Vasallenkönige hin, während mit den „Göttern meiner Väter und meiner Brüder“ (SAA 9 3.4:II:35: DINGIR.MEŠ AD.MEŠ *-ia* ⸢ŠEŠ.MEŠ⸣*-ia*) wohl die bei dem Vasallenvertrag als Zeugen stehenden Götter gemeint sind. Das Orakel wird bei Ishida fälschlich mit dem vorangehenden Orakel über *ṭuppi adê* (s. dazu unten) verbunden; im Original sind sie mit einem Strich voneinander getrennt. Vielleicht aus diesem Grund hat Ishida auch den eigentlichen Anlaß des Bundesrituals verkannt.

> Du gabst ihnen *ṣarṣāru*-Wasser[70] zu trinken, / ein Gefäß von einem Seah fülltest du mit *ṣarṣāru*-Wasser und gabst ihnen / (und sagtest): „Ihr sagt in euren Herzen: ‘Ištar ist (doch) machtlos![71]’ / (Dann) geht ihr in eure Städte und eure Bezirke, / eßt Brot und vergeßt diesen Vertrag. / (Wenn) ihr (aber) von diesem Wasser trinkt, / werdet ihr euch (wieder) erinnern und diesen Vertrag bewahren, / den ich für Asarhaddon geschlossen habe.“

Wer religionsgeschichtliches Vergleichsmaterial für das bundestheologische Moment des neutestamentlichen Herrenmahls (Mk 14:24parr; 1 Kor 11:25) sucht, wird hier eine interessante Belegstelle finden. Was das Alte Testament betrifft, so liegt die Relevanz dieser Prophetie im Wesentlichen darin, daß hier die gleichen Redewendungen erscheinen, die wir nicht nur aus zeitgenössischen assyrischen Staatsverträgen und Königsinschriften, sondern auch in hebräischer Sprache aus dem Alten Testament gut kennen. Dieser Sprachgebrauch wird im oben zitierten Text durch den Begriff *adê* und die damit zusammenhängenden Verben *mašû, ḫasāsu* und *naṣāru* erkennbar.[72] Im Alten Testament wirkt die bundestheologische Terminologie, die besonders in der Nähe der deuteronomistischen Kreise reichlich sprießt, wie eine Adaptation der Wendungen der akkadischen Vertragssprache:

Verb:	*mašû* ‘vergessen’	*škḥ* ‘vergessen’
	haṭû ‘sündigen’	*ḥṭ’* ‘sündigen’
	etāqu ‘übertreten’	*‘br* ‘übertreten’
	mêšu ‘verachten’	*‘zb* ‘verlassen’
		m’s ‘verwerfen’
	ḫasāsu ‘sich erinnern’	*zkr* ‘sich erinnern’
	naṣāru ‘bewahren’	*nṣr* ‘befolgen’
		šmr ‘bewahren’
Objekt:	*adê* ‘Vertrag’	*‘dwt* ‘Bundesbestimmungen’
	ṭābtu ‘Güte (= Vertrag)’	*ṭwb(h)* ‘Güte’

70 Das umstrittene Wort *ṣarṣāru* (‘Grille’ oder ‘Schlange’? Vgl. AHw 1086; CAD Ṣ 115) kommt in einem ähnlichen Zusammenhang in einer Šurpu-Beschwörung (iii 62; R. Reiner, *Šurpu: A Collection of Sumerian and Akkadian Incantations* [AfO.B 11; Osnabrück: Biblio, 1970], esp. 21) vor, in der ein Eid „beim Trinken aus *ṣarṣāru*“ (*māmīt ina ṣarṣāri mê šatû*) erwähnt wird. Diese Aussage läßt an irgendeinen Krug denken (Hecker, „Zukunftsdeutungen in akkadischen Texten,“ 61: „Wasser aus Weihwasserkrug“) und gilt als Hinweis dafür, daß es sich um ein spezielles Getränk handelt, das bei einer Vereidigungszeremonie getrunken wird.

71 Das Wort *pāqtu* ist von *piāqu* ‘eng sein’ (AHw 865) abgeleitet.

72 Vgl. die von É. Lipiński, *Le poème royal du Psaume lxxxix 1–5.20–38* (CRB 6; Paris: Gabalda, 1967), esp. 74f. aufgeführten Beispiele aus den Inschriften Assurbanipals.

māmītu 'Eid'	*bryt* 'Bund'
	twrh 'Tora'
	Jahwe selbst

Im Hinblick darauf, daß die judäischen Könige tatsächlich Vertragspartner des assyrischen Großkönigs waren, ist es kein Wunder, daß die damaligen hochpolitischen Klischees sich auch im palästinischen Raum verbreiteten, zumal die Verträge zweifelsohne auch in die Sprache des Vasallen übertragen wurden. Daß die atl. bundestheologische Sprache aber zudem auch eine innere Entwicklung erfahren hat, geht aus den Objekten hervor. Als Objekt der akkadischen Verben erscheint immer der Vertrag, ausgedrückt mit dem Terminus technicus *adê* oder der naheliegenden Begriffe *ṭābtu* oder *māmītu*. Im hebräischen begegnen wir demgegenüber neben *bĕrît* und *'ēdût* auch die Tora oder kurzerhand Jahwe selbst als Objekt der Bundesverben.[73]

In diesem Punkt kommt die grundsätzliche Umwandlung der assyrischen Vertragsideologie zum israelitischen Bundestheologie besonders anschaulich zum Vorschein. Ein assyrischer *adê* beruht auf dem Prinzip der Gegenseitigkeit der Kontrahenten, die grundsätzlich als gleichwertig betrachtet werden, obschon der assyrische Großkönig doch in Wirklichkeit die Oberhand behält.[74] Als Zeugen des Vertrags, und gegebenenfalls als Vollstrecker seiner Sanktionen, stehen die Götter beider Parteien.[75] Wenden wir uns der alttestamentlichen Konzeption des Bundes (*bĕrît*) zwischen Jahwe und Israel zu, so können wir sofort bemerken, daß Jahwe in diesem Modell mehrere Funktionen gleichzeitig zukommt. Hat er nämlich selbst die Rolle des überlegenen Kontrahenten inne, so bringt er mit gleicher Souverä-

73 Näheres zu den akkadischen Belegen und zu dem dtr. Charakter des alttestamentlichen Sprachgebrauchs s. Nissinen, *Prophetie, Redaktion und Fortschreibung im Hoseabuch*, 180–86. Zu dem dort nicht behandelten Verb *mêšu* 'verachten' vgl. etwa SAA 4 280 r. 1–4, wo sowohl die Königsideologie als auch der Vertragsgedanke schön zum Ausdruck kommen: (Übersetzung nach Starr, *Queries to the Sungod*, 263): „Nabû-bel-šimate, the Sealander, who did not keep the favor (*lā nāṣir ṭābtu*) of Assurbanipal, king of Assyria, your creature (*binūt qātēka*), his lord, who invoked your great name lightly, and disregarded it (*imēšū*) haughtily..." Zu *'ēdût* vgl. T. Veijola, „Zu Ableitung und Bedeutung von *hē'īd* I im Hebräischen," *UF* 8 (1976) 343–51.

74 Zu der Semantik und den konkreten Bezügen des Begriffs *adê* s. S. Parpola, „Neo-Assyrian Treaties from the Royal Archives of Nineveh," *JCS* 39 (1987) 161–89, esp. 180–83, nach dem *adê* die Bezeichnung für einen solennen, verbindlichen Vertrag ist. Es ist zu beachten, daß *adê* nicht bloß einen Treueid bezeichnet, sondern zwei Parteien voraussetzt, die im Prinzip gleiche Rechte und gleiche Pflichten haben. Daß die uns bekannten Verträge ausschließlich zwischen Großmacht und Kleinstaaten geschlossen worden sind, hat natürlich zur Folge, daß sich die grundsätzliche Parität der Parteien nicht ganz verwirklicht.

75 Vgl. etwa S. Parpola and K. Watanabe, *Neo-Assyrian Treaties and Loyalty Oaths* (SAA 2; Helsinki: Helsinki University Press, 1988), xxxvii.

nität auch die Strafe für jeglichen Vertragsbruch zur Ausführung, wie z. B. aus Hos 4:1–10; 12:3 oder aus Ps 89:35–46 ersichtlich wird.[76] Damit hat Jahwe sowohl die Rolle des Großkönigs als auch die der göttlichen Zeugen für sich in Anspruch genommen. Wir haben es hier mit einer theologisch-monotheistischen Modifikation der politischen Vertragsideologie zu tun, in der die Assimilation der ursprünglich getrennten Aufgaben in der Person Jahwes die natürlichste Lösung war – spätestens seitdem es in Jerusalem keinen König mehr gab! Mag die Idee von dem Königtum Jahwes auch auf älteren Vorstellungen beruhen, so konnte sich dieser Gedanke in der Exilszeit voll entfalten bis hin zu einer Theokratie, in der der König als Zwischenglied nicht mehr nötig war.

Die alttestamentliche Modifikation wird erklärlich einerseits dadurch, daß der König in Assyrien sowie wahrscheinlich auch in Israel als eine Art korporative Personlichkeit verstanden wurde, d. h. zugleich als Gottessohn und als Repräsentant seines Volkes vor den Göttern, so daß die ihm geschenkten göttlichen Gaben durch ihn dem ganzen Volk zugute kamen. Vor diesem Hintergrund läßt sich nicht nur die Kollektivierung der Königsideologie, sondern auch die Tatsache verstehen, daß in dem *bĕrît* das Volk sich selbst repräsentieren kann – ein altorientalischer Vertrag wurde doch grundsätzlich zwischen *Königen* geschlossen!

Andererseits verdient Beachtung, daß Ištar in der oben zitierten Prophetie für Asarhaddon als Einsetzer von *adê*, also in einem Sinne als Partei und nicht nur als Zeuge auftritt. Diese assyrische Art von „Bundestheologie" erklärt sich durch das vorangehende Orakel auf der gleichen Tafel (SAA 9 3.3), in dem *adê* mit der Prophetie gleichgesetzt wird.[77] Das Orakel wurde im Aššur-Tempel Ešarra, wohl auf dem Thronbesteigungsfest Asarhaddons,[78] vorgetragen als Beweis dafür, daß der Sieg Asarhaddons über seine Feinde auf göttlichem Willen beruhte. Die Tafel, auf der das Orakel geschrieben war, wird als Vertragsurkunde (*ṭuppi adê*) bezeichnet, die in feierlicher Prozession vor dem König getragen und ihm vorgelesen

76 Daß mit dem „Zeugen in den Wolken" in Ps 89:38 Jahwe selbst gemeint ist, hat T. Veijola, „Davidverheißung und Staatsvertrag: Beobachtungen zum Einfluß altorientalischer Staatsverträge auf die biblische Sprache am Beispiel von Psalm 89," *ZAW* 95 (1983) 9–31, esp. 20–22 (vgl. id., „The Witness in the Clouds: Ps 89:38," *JBL* 197 [1988] 413–17, esp. 416–17) gezeigt. Zur doppelten Rolle Jahwes vgl. ferner P. Buis, *La notion d'Alliance dans l'Ancien Testament* (LeDiv 88; Paris: Cerf, 1976), 121; K. Nielsen, *Yahweh as Prosecutor and Judge: A Investigation of the Prophetic Lawsuit (Rîb-Pattern)* (JSOTS 9; Sheffield: JSOT, 1978), 74.

77 Zu diesem Orakel (vgl. oben Anm. 70) s. Parpola, „Neo-Assyrian Treaties from the Royal Archives of Nineveh," 181 und Ellis, „Observations on Mesopotamian Oracles and Prophetic Texts," 144.

78 Vgl. Weippert, „Assyrische Prophetien der Zeit Asarhaddons und Assurbanipals," 95. Einen ähnlichen Hintergrund für das Kititum-Orakel FLP 1674 schlägt Ellis, „Observations on Mesopotamian Oracles and Prophetic Texts," 140 vor.

wurde.[79] Das von dem Propheten vermittelte Gotteswort gilt seitens der Gottheit als eine verbindliche Zusage (*šulmu* 'Heilsorakel, Verheißung') der Vernichtung der Feinde.

Aus diesem Orakel ist zu entnehmen, daß auch das Verhältnis von Gott und König in Assyrien als ein *adê* verstanden wurde. Im Alten Testament haben wir eine ähnliche Konstellation vor uns in der Rede vom „Bund" (*bĕrît*) zwischen Jahwe und David, besonders wie er im Ps 89 zur Sprache kommt.[80] Stimmt die Datierung dieses Psalms in seiner heutigen Gestalt in die deuteronomistische Kreise der späten Exilszeit,[81] so handelt er von einem historischen König in einer geschichtlichen Stunde, als das Königtum in Israel schon untergegangen war. Damit stoßen wir wieder einmal auf die „Demokratisierung" der Königsideologie, der wir in anderer Form schon bei Dtjes begegneten: Der Bund zwischen Jahwe und David wird *de facto* zum Bund zwischen Jahwe und dem Volk Israel.[82] Ps 89 ist ein anschauliches Beispiel für die schmiegsame Übertragung königlicher Sprachfiguren auf die kollektive Ebene, indem in ihm die ursprünglich der Königsideologie entstammenden Epitheta wie *'ebed* 'Knecht' (V. 4, 21, 40), *bāḥîr* 'Erwählte' (V. 4, 20), *māšîăḥ* 'Gesalbte' (V. 39, 52) und *bĕkôr* 'Erstgeborene' (V. 28) so verwendet werden, daß sie unbefangen auf das Volk bezogen werden können. Zugleich ermöglicht sich auch die Rede von einem „ewigen Bund" (*bĕrît 'ôlām* 2 Sam 23:5 u. a.),[83] das sich nicht auf die Lebzeit eines einzigen Königs beschränkt, wie es bei dem assyrischen *adê* doch der Fall ist.[84] Das Zwischenglied zwischen

---

79 Z. 32: *ina pān šarri isassiū*. Daß das Verb *šasû* (ass. *sasû*) vom Vorlesen eines Briefs verwendet wird, zeigt ein Brief von Aššur-Le'i an Sargon (SAA 5 218:14' – r. 1): *egirāte ša Nabû-ḫamātū'a ina Nīnua pān šarri bēlīja ussēriba issisiū* „I have forwarded the letters of Nabu-ḫamatua to Nineveh, and they will have read them to the king (by now)" (G. B. Lanfranchi and S. Parpola, *The Correspondence of Sargon II*, vol. 2: *Letters from the Northern and Northeastern Provinces* [SAA 5; Helsinki: Helsinki University Press, 1990], esp. 156). Dies benötigt auch die Anwesenheit des Königs in dem Ritual (gegen Weippert, „Assyrische Prophetien der Zeit Asarhaddons und Assurbanipals," 95).

80 Zu den Parallelen des Psalms in den altorientalischen Vertragstexten vgl. Lipiński, *Le poème royal du Psaume lxxxix*, 1–5.20–38, sowie die kritische Bewertung seiner Untersuchung mit zusätzlichem Material bei Veijola, „Davidverheißung und Staatsvertrag."

81 Vgl. Veijola, *Verheißung in der Krise*, 117–18.

82 Vgl. ibid., 173–75.

83 S. dazu Veijola, *Verheißung in der Krise*, 67–69.

84 Vgl. Ellis, „Observations on Mesopotamian Oracles and Prophetic Texts," 176–77: „The concept of 'covenant' is thus emphatically attested, but there is no idea of a long-term 'Covenant.' There is a treaty, but it is dependent on adherence to the treaty terms by the human partner and only implicitly relies on patterns of interaction established in the past. It is *not* a promise of eternal election and support." Freilich begegnen wir doch auch in der neuassyrischen Prophetie einer Ausdehnung der Zeitperspektive ins Unbestimmte, indem die Dauer der Regierung des Königs für

Jahwe und dem Volk, der König, kann in dieser übertragenen Königsideologie weiterleben entweder als reine Sprachfigur für das Volk oder aber auch als eine konkret verstandene Messiasgestalt.

Die neuassyrische Prophetie verschärft das Bild von der assyrischen Königsideologie, das wir schon aus anderen zeitgenössischen Dokumenten relativ gut kennen. Daß der jerusalemische Gedanke über das Verhältnis von Gott, König und Volk in mehreren Punkten damit übereinstimmt hat, lassen die alttestamentlichen Hinweise erkennen, wenn auch die Königsideologie in ihnen zunächst nur in einer übertragenen Form erscheint. Die Kollektivierung der Königsverheißungen wird doch erst möglich, wenn sie einmal einem konkreten Individuum gegolten haben. Ob die jerusalemische Königsideologie aber schon von alters her mit einem Begriff wie *bĕrît* in Verbindung stand, ist nicht klar und bedarf näherer Untersuchung.

2.4. Gott als Mutter und Kriegsheld

In den Augen des modernen Lesers erscheint das Gottesbild der neuassyrischen Prophetie mit seinen ebenso stark betonten mütterlichen und militanten Zügen als drastisch zwiespältig. Einerseits wird die Göttin Ištar/Mullissu als Mutter oder Amme gezeichnet, die das königliche Kind liebt, schützt und betreut:[85]

Beispiel 5: SAA 9 7:20 – 25

mā ša Mullissu ummašūni lā tapallah̬ / ša bēlat Arbail tārīssūni lā tapallah̬ / mā kī tārīti ina muh̬h̬i giššīya anaššīka / mā armannu ina bīrit tulêya ašakkanka / ša mūšīya ērāk anaṣṣarka / ša kal ūme h̬ilpaka addan / ...... / mā atta lā tapallah̬ mūrī ša anāku urabbûni

(Du,) dessen Mutter Mullissu ist, fürchte dich nicht! / (Du,) dessen Amme die Herrin von Arbela ist, fürchte dich nicht! / Wie eine Amme nehme ich dich auf meinen Schoß, / als einen Granatapfel setze ich dich zwischen meine Brüste. / Des Nachts wache ich und beschütze dich, / jeden Tag gebe ich dir Milch, /......[86] / Du, fürchte dich nicht, mein Kalb, das ich aufziehe!

ūmē arkūte šanāte dārāte versprochen wird (vgl. oben Beispiel 3), was semantisch wohl das gleiche besagt wie hebr. *ʿad ʿôlām*. Dies hängt mit der oben behandelten dynastischen Problematik zusammen.

85 Zu den Mutter- und Ammenbildern in der neuassyrischen Prophetie grundlegend Weippert, „Die Bildsprache der neuassyrischen Prophetie," 71 – 78; einiges dazu auch bei Nissinen, *Prophetie, Redaktion und Fortschreibung im Hoseabuch*, 276 – 90.

86 Der Text *ša kallamāri unnānika uṣur uṣur uppaška* läßt sich nicht mit Sicherheit übersetzen, weil die Bedeutung von *unnānu* unbekannt ist. Vgl. die Übersetzungen von Weippert, „Die Bildsprache der neuassyrischen Prophetie," 62 und Hecker, „Zukunftsdeutungen in akkadischen

Ein Text wie dieser kann vorzüglich illustriert werden mit reichlichem Bildmaterial aus dem ganzen altorientalischen Gebiet, gehört doch die stillende Mutter zu den am weitesten verbreiteten altorientalischen Bildmotiven und ist auch im ikonographischen Nachlaß des neuassyrischen Reichs gut vertreten.[87] Es geht dabei in der Regel um keine beliebige Mutter-Kind-Konstellation, sondern eben um eine Göttin mit einem Gotteskind oder einem König.[88] An den gleichen Motivkreis schließt sich auch die Bezeichnung des Königs als Jungvieh (*mūru*) an, denn auch die säugende Kuh ist ein gewöhnliches ikonographisches Motiv im altorientalischen Raum[89] und kann das Verhältnis von Göttin und König ebenso zum Ausdruck bringen wie das Mutter-Kind-Motiv.

Andererseits sind die Orakel stets auch von einer grimmigen Aggressivität geprägt, indem wiederholt beschrieben wird, wie den Feinden des Königs der Garaus gemacht wird. Finden wir uns in den Inhalt der oben beschriebenen, als *šulmu* und *adê* bezeichneten Prophetie (SAA 9 3.3) hinein, so stellt es sich heraus, daß die zentrale Aussage des Heilsorakels gerade die soeben geschehene Vertilgung der Konspiranten ist:

Beispiel 6: SAA 9 3.3:10–25

annûrig sarsarrāni annūti ussadbibūka ussēṣūnikka iltibûka / atta pīka taptitia mā anina Aššūr / anāku killaka asseme / issu libbi abul šamê attaqallalla / lakrur išātu lušākilšunu / atta ina bīrtuššunu tazzaz / issu pānīka attiši / ana šadê ussēlīšunu / abnāti aqqullu ina muḫḫīšunu azzunun / nakarūtēka uḫtattip dāmēšunu nāru umtalli / lēmurū lūna"idūni akī Aššūr bēl ilāni anākūni

Als eben diese Rebellen[90] gegen dich intrigierten, dich hinaustrieben und umzingelten,[91] / öffnetest du deinen Mund: „Bitte, Aššur!" / Ich hörte deine Klage. / Von dem Himmelstor her

Texten," 63, die von dem Wort *unnīnu* 'Gebet' ausgehen: „Jeden Morgen merke ich mir deine Gebete, merke (sie) mir und erfülle (sie) dir"; „Früh am Morgen führe ich — merke (es) dir, merke (es) dir — deine Bitten für dich aus."

87 Dazu umfassend U. Winter, *Frau und Göttin: Exegetische und ikonographische Studien zum weiblichen Gottesbild im Alten Israel und in dessen Umwelt* (OBO 53; Fribourg and Göttingen: Academic Press Fribourg and Vandenhoeck & Ruprecht, 1983), esp. 118–19, 387–93.

88 S. ibid., 132–34, 388.

89 Dazu vor allem O. Keel, *Das Böcklein in der Milch seiner Mutter und verwandtes: Im Lichte eines altorientalischen Bildmotivs* (OBO 33; Fribourg and Göttingen: Academic Press Fribourg and Vandenhoeck & Ruprecht, 1980), esp. 46–141; vgl. Winter, *Frau und Göttin*, 404–13.

90 Zu *sarsar(r)ānu* 'Rebell', 'Möchtegern-König' (< *sarru*; in der bab. Ortographie mit š geschrieben) vgl. Weippert, „'Heiliger Krieg' in Israel und Assyrien," 481.

91 Von *lawû* 'umzingeln'; ibid., 481 leitet von *la'ābu/le'ēbu* ab.

wurde ich zur brennenden Glut,[92] / damit ich ein Feuer anzündete und es sie fressen ließ. / Du standest in ihrer Mitte, / aber ich nahm sie weg von dir, / trieb sie ins Gebirge / und ließ Glutsteine auf sie regnen. / Ich schlachtete deine Feinde, füllte mit ihrem Blut den Fluß. / Man möge es sehen und mich preisen, daß ich Aššur bin, der Herr der Götter!

Als redende Gottheit hat in diesem Orakel zwar Aššur das Wort, aber auch Ištar begnügt sich nicht mit ihrer Rolle als Mutter und Amme, sondern schließt zugleich ausgeprägt militante Züge in sich:

Beispiel 7: SAA 9 1.1:6 – 14

ayyu šāru ša idibakkāni / aqappušu lā aksupūni / nakarūtēka kī šaḫšūri ša simāni ina pān šēpēka ittangararrū / bēltu rabītu anāku / anāku Issār ša Arbail / ša nakarūtēka ina pān šēpēka akkarrūni

Welcher ist der Wind, der sich gegen dich erhoben hat,[93] / dessen Flügel ich nicht abgeschnitten hätte? / Deine Feinde werden wie Äpfel des Monats Siman vor deinen Füßen umherrollen. / Ich bin Ištar von Arbela, / die ich deine Feinde vor deinen Füßen niederwerfe.

Die scheinbare Verschmelzung der Rollen Ištars als Amme und Kriegerin hat ihren Grund dort, wo die Motivation der uns bekannten neuassyrischen Prophetensprüche auch sonst zu suchen ist, d. h. in der Legitimation des Königtums von Asarhaddon bzw. Assurbanipal. Steht die Liebes- und Kriegsgöttin Ištar als *fortuna imperatoris* in einem persönlichen, exklusiven Liebesverhältnis zu dem König,[94] so ist es natürlich, daß sie ihrem Liebling über die Schwierigkeiten hinweghilft, die seiner Machtbefugnis im Wege stehen. Demnach übernimmt die Göttin die Verantwortung für die Vernichtung der Feinde, während der König auf ihrem Schoß gut aufgehoben ist:

Beispiel 8: SAA 3 13 r. 2 – 10

ša iṣbatu ana šēpē šarrat Nīnua lā ilūad ina puḫur ilāni rabūti / ša ina qanni Urkittu kammus lā ilūad ina puḫur ḫaddânūtēšu / ina puḫur ḫaddânūtēya lā tumaššaranni Nabû / ina puḫur bēl ṣassīya lā tumaššara napšātīya

Wer die Füße der Königin von Ninive ergriffen hat, möge nicht in der Versammlung der großen Götter zuschanden weiden! / Wer an der Seite der Urkittu weilt, möge nicht zuschanden werden in der Versammlung seiner Gegner! / Verlasse mich nicht in der Ver-

92 Das Wort *an/qqullu* bedeutet Himmelsglut (vgl. AHw 54); hier handelt es sich wahrscheinlich um ein davon abgeleitetes denominales Verbum. Zur Form vgl. *ittangararrū* in SAA 9 1.1:10' (unten Beispiel 7). Die folgenden Prekativsätze sind in einem finalen Sinne zu verstehen.

93 Von *tabû* (= *tebû*); zu dieser von S. Parpola vorgeschlagenen Ableitung vgl. Nissinen, *Prophetie, Redaktion und Fortschreibung im Hoseabuch*, 120.

94 Vgl. dazu Oppenheim, *Ancient Mesopotamia*, 205, 207

sammlung meiner Gegner, Nabû! / Verlasse mein Leben nicht in der Versammlung meiner Widersacher!

ṣeḫru atta Aššūr-bāni-apli ša umašširūka ina muḫḫi šarrat Nīnua / lakû atta Aššūr-bāni-apli ša ašbāka ina burki šarrat Nīnua / erbi zīzēša ina pīka šaknā / šina tenniq šina taḫallap ana pānīka / ḫaddânūtēka Aššūr-bāni-apli kī sīpi ina pān mê išu"ū / kī burbillāti ša pān šatti untatarruqū ina pān šēpēka / tazzaz Aššūr-bāni-apli ina tarṣi ilāni rabûti tuna"ad Nabû

Klein warst du, Assurbanipal, als ich dich der Königin von Ninive überließ. / Ein Kindlein warst du, als du auf dem Schoß der Königin von Ninive saßest / Ihre vier Brüste sind in deinen Mund gesteckt: / An zweien saugst du, aus zweien melkst du auf dein Gesicht. / Deine Gegner, Assurbanipal, werden wie Pollen (?)[95] über der Wasserfläche fliegen, / wie *burbillātu*-Insekten im Frühling werden sie vor deinen Füßen zerrieben. / Du, Assurbanipal wirst vor den großen Göttern stehen und Nabû preisen.

Was das Alte Testament betrifft, so finden sich dort kriegerische Züge des Gottesbilds im Überfluß und bedürfen hier keiner besonderen Präsentation. Beachtenswert sind dagegen die an Zahl geringen, aber vielsagenden Stellen, wo deutlich feminine Metaphern Jahwe zugeeignet werden: „Siehe, ich breite aus bei ihr den Frieden wie einen Strom... Ihre Kinder sollen auf dem Arme getragen werden, und auf den Knien wird man sie liebkosen. Ich will euch trösten, wie einen seine Mutter tröstet ..." (Jes 66:12 f.) — „Hab ich denn all das Volk empfangen oder geboren, daß du mir sagen könntest: Trag es in deinen Armen, wie eine Amme ein Kind trägt ..." (Num 11:12).[96] Bezüglich von Hos 11 spricht man herkömmlich von der Vaterliebe Jahwes, aber auch in diesem Fall weist die stark an die assyrische Prophetie erinnernde Bildersprache doch eher auf die Mutter-Kind-Konstellation hin:[97] „Als Israel ein Knabe war, liebte ich es, aus Ägypten rief ich meinen Sohn ... Ich habe Ephraim laufen geholfen, ich nahm sie (ihn) auf meine Arme... Ich neigte mich zu ihm und gab zu essen" (Hos 11:1, 3, 4).

Diese Beispiele vermögen schon die zahlreichen gemeinsamen Punkte in der mütterlichen Metaphorik der neuassyrischen Prophetie und des Alten Testaments zu veranschaulichen. In beiden Fällen ist die feminine Rede von der Gottheit mit

---

95 *AHw* 1036 – 37: 'eine Getreideart'; A. Livingstone, *Court Poetry and Literary Miscellanea* (SAA 3; Helsinki: Helsinki University Press, 1989), 147: 'pollen (?)'.

96 Der Sprecher hier ist zwar Mose, aber dieser von ihm erhobene Vorwurf impliziert wohl, daß gerade Jahwe als die Mutter des Volkes gilt. Das Verb *yld* könnte zwar auch ein männliches Subjekt haben, aber mit einem vorangehenden *hrh* ist dies nicht wahrscheinlich. Denn diese beiden Verben in dieser Reihenfolge bilden einen Gesamtausdruck für die Geburt eines Kindes.

97 Der mütterliche Aspekt des Gottesbilds in Hos 11 ist von H. Schüngel-Straumann, „Gott als Mutter in Hosea 11," *ThQ* 166 (1986) 119 – 34, nachdrücklich betont worden; zur Kritik und Weiterführung ihrer These sowie zu den Verbindungen mit den assyrischen Orakeln vgl. Nissinen, *Prophetie, Redaktion und Fortschreibung im Hoseabuch*, 268 – 94.

einem Themenkomplex verbunden, dessen Grundidee, die göttliche Liebe zu einem Kind, das als Sohn der Gottheit vorgestellt werden kann, mit der Schilderung von mütterlichen Tätigkeiten wie Tragen, Füttern und Großziehen zur Sprache gebracht wird. Es gilt wieder einmal wahrzunehmen, daß die assyrischen Texte ausschließlich vom *König* reden, während in den biblischen Beispielen immer das *Volk* Gegenstand der göttlichen Fürsorge ist.

Die Stellen, die Jahwe als Mutter oder Amme darstellen, berechtigen an sich keine Rede von Jahwe als Frau oder Göttin, denn das Thema ist dabei kaum die Geschlechtlichkeit Gottes, sondern die göttlichen Handlungen, die mit einer vielfältigen Bildersprache zum Ausdruck gebracht werden können.[98] Im Falle von Jahwe wird die feminine Rede auch dadurch verständlich, daß der einzige Gott der alttestamentlichen Überlieferung wegen seines Ausschließlichkeitsanspruchs die weiblichen Gottheiten (Ašera, Aštarte) verdrängen, zugleich aber deren Funktionen absorbieren mußte.

Ferner verdient Beachtung, daß mit der Zweiteilung in „männliche" und „weibliche" Eigenschaften leicht eine anachronistische Dichotomie hergestellt wird. Die Rollen der Amme und Kriegsführerin assimilieren sich ungezwungen in Ištar und können in ein und derselben Prophetie fließend wechseln. Dies mag auf den ersten Blick befremdend wirken, aber hier haben wir es mit einem Problem des modernen Lesers zu tun. Die assyrischen Prophet(inn)en haben diese göttlichen Aufgaben wohl kaum als widersprüchlich empfunden, denn es geht nicht in erster Linie um eine Theorie über das Wesen der Götter, sondern um ihre Tätigkeiten im Verhältnis zu den Menschen. Aus der zärtlichen Pflege des Kindes und der blutigen Vertilgung derjenigen, die seine Geborgenheit bedrohen, entsteht eine untrennbare funktionelle Einheit mit dem Zweck, die Stellung des königlichen „Kindes" als des legitimen Erben zu beweisen. Die Bildersprache hat also kaum einen ontologischen, sondern eher einen *funktionellen* Bezug, was selbst die Rede von Ištar oder Jahwe als Vater und Mutter zugleich ermöglicht.[99]

98 Vgl. Schüngel-Straumann, „Gott als Mutter in Hosea 11," 133: „'Gott als Mutter' kann darum genauso die prophetische bzw. biblische Gotteserfahrung ausdrücken wie 'Gott als Vater', wenn man sich bewußt bleibt, daß *beides* Bilder sind, die in ihrer jeweiligen Ganzheit nicht beabsichtigen, den andern Teil auszuschließen. Das göttliche zeigt sich mit verschiedenen Gesichtern, wobei je nach den Umständen einmal das väterliche, dann das mütterliche Angesicht Gottes hilfreicher erscheint." Entsprechend spricht Winter, *Frau und Göttin*, 674 von einem „Gott jenseits der Geschlechtlichkeit."

99 SAA 9 2.5:26': *anāku abūka ummaka* „Ich bin dein Vater und deine Mutter." Der Name der redenden Gottheit ist durch Beschädigung der Tafel leider weggefallen, aber die sprachliche Ähnlichkeit mit der Ištar-Prophetie SAA 9 1.2 legt die Vermutung nahe, daß auch hier Ištar spricht. Vgl. Dtn 32:18: „Den Fels, der dich gezeugt hat, hast du außer acht gelassen und hast vergessen den

2.5. Die Formel „Fürchte dich nicht!"

Im engen Zusammenhang mit der göttlichen Aufgabe, den König zu beschützen und seinen Kriegserfolg zu garantieren, steht die in der neuassyrischen Prophetie sehr gebräuchliche Formel „Fürchte dich nicht" (*lā tapallaḫ*),[100] der fast immer das Versprechen des göttlichen Beistands und der Vernichtung der Feinde folgt:

Beispiel 9: SAA 9 1.2:30'-34'

šar māt Aššūr lā tapallaḫ / nakru ša šar māt Aššūr ana ṭabaḫḫi addana / [ina libbi] bīt rēdūtēka [utaqq]anka

König von Assyrien, fürchte dich nicht! Dem Feind des Königs von Assyrien liefere ich eine Schlacht. / Dich lasse ich in deinem Thronfolgepalast sicher weilen.

Eine entsprechende Formel ist auch aus aramäischem Gebiet bekannt, und zwar aus der vom Ende des neunten Jh. stammenden Zakkur-Inschrift *KAI* 202, in der berichtet wird, wie der von Feinden belagerte König von Hamat und Lu'aš an seinen Gott Ba'l-šamain appelliert und der Gott ihm durch den Mund der Propheten ein Orakel über die Errettung des Königs vor seinen Feinden erteilt. Das Zitat des prophetischen Wortes (Z. A 13) setzt dabei gerade mit der Formel „Fürchte dich nicht" (*'l tzḥl*) ein.[101]

Schließlich können wir wahrnehmen, daß die alttestamentliche Formel *'al tîrā'* immer wieder in einem vergleichbaren Zusammenhang vorkommt, besonders in den Büchern Dtn und Jos, wo Jahwe Mose oder Josua ermutigt, dem übermächtigen Feind tapfer entgegenzutreten, und verspricht, den Feind in ihre Hände zu geben (Dtn 3:2 usw.; Jos 10:8 usw.). Ferner ist die Formel den deuterojesajanischen. Orakeln, deren nahe Verwandtschaft mit der neuassyrischen Prophetie schon deutlich geworden ist, besonders eigen: „Du sollst mein Knecht sein: ich erwähle dich und verwerfe dich nicht! Fürchte dich nicht, ich bin mit dir, weiche nicht, denn ich bin dein Gott. Ich stärke dich, helfe dir auf... Siehe, zu Spott und zuschanden sollen werden alle, die dich hassen! Sie sollen werden wie nichts, und

---

Gott, der dich geboren hat." Da das Verb *yld* hier dem *ḥyl* pol. 'kreißend hervorbringen, gebären' vorangeht, hat es offenbar hier anders als in Num 11:12 ein männliches Subjekt.

100 SAA 9 1.1:5': 1.2 i 30'; 1.4:16'; 1.8:21; 2.1:13'; 2.2:16'; 2.5:19'; 4:5'; 7:2; SAA 3 13:24; vgl. oben Beispiele 1, 2, 3 und 5.

101 Zu diesem Text s. J. F. Ross, „Prophecy in Hamath, Israel, and Mari," *HThR* 63 (1970) 1–28, esp. 1–11; H.-J. Zobel, „Das Gebet um Abwendung der Not und seine Erhörung in den Klageliedern des Alten Testaments und in der Inschrift des Königs Zakir von Hamath," *VT* 21 (1971) 91–99; Weippert, „Assyrische Prophetien der Zeit Asarhaddons und Assurbanipals," 102f.; 1988, 300–301; Nissinen, *Prophetie, Redaktion und Fortschreibung im Hoseabuch*, 144–45.

die Leute, die mit dir hadern, sollen umkommen" (Jes 41:9 – 11; vgl. 43:1, 5; 44:2; 54:4; vgl. auch oben Beispiel 8!).

Aufgrund dieses Materials erscheint es berechtigt, den Sitz im Leben der Formel „Fürchte dich nicht" eher in der prophetischen als in der priesterlichen Verkündigung zu suchen.[102] Die Aussage der Formel ist dabei, daß die Gottheit dem König/Volk beisteht und ihm den Sieg bringt, und zwar ohne Verdienst des menschlichen Kämpfers: „Jahwe wird für euch streiten und ihr werdet stille sein" (Ex 14:14) – „Du, Asarhaddon, sei still!" (SAA 9 2.4 iii 11' *atta lū qālāka Aššūr-aḫu-iddina*).[103]

3. Die neuassyrische Prophetie und das Prophetenbild des Alten Testaments

Bei der Gegenüberstellung der neuassyrischen Prophetie und des Alten Testaments könnte man von der Erwartung ausgehen, daß das wichtigste atl. Vergleichsmaterial in den Prophetenbüchern, und zwar vor allem in ihren als „echt" zu definierenden Teilen zu finden wäre. Die oben angeführten Beispiele zeigen jedoch, daß nicht so sehr die Prophetenbücher, sondern vielmehr die Geschichtsbücher und die Psalmen immer wieder Parallelen bieten. Innerhalb des Prophetenkanons tritt der (nach)exilische Mittelteil des Jesajabuches (Jes 40 – 55) in den Vordergrund, während die vorexilischen „klassischen" Propheten so gut wie schweigen.

Diese Beobachtung gibt Anlaß zu vielerlei Überlegungen. Einerseits wird die auch sonst wahrscheinliche Vermutung bestärkt, daß die Prophetie auch in anderen Teilen des Alten Testaments Spuren hinterlassen habe. Andererseits

102 Die Formel „Fürchte dich nicht" gehört als fester Bestandteil zu dem von Begrich postulierten „priesterlichen Heilsorakel"; vgl. J. Begrich, „Das priesterliche Heilsorakel," *ZAW* 52 (1934) 81 – 92, esp. 85 – 86; zu der Formel s. auch. S. 195 – 232 in dem vorliegenden Band.

103 Vgl. einerseits 1 Sam 17:45 – 47; Hos 1:7; Ps 20:8 usw.; andererseits den von Weippert, „'Heiliger Krieg' in Israel und Assyrien" 483 zitierten Hymnus von Assurbanipal an die Ištars von Ninive und Arbela (SAA 3 3 r. 4 – 6): *ul [ina danā]nīya ul ina danāni qaštīya ina em[uq x x x x u] danāni ištarātīya mātāti lā* ⌈*ma*⌉*-[g]i-ri-ia ušakniša ana nīr Aššūr* „Nicht [durch] meine [eig]ene [Kraft], nicht durch die Stärke meines Bogens, (sondern) durch die Kraft [meiner Götter und] die Stärke meiner Göttinnen beugte ich die Länder, die mir nicht Gehorsam leisteten, unter das Joch Aššurs." Die hier anzutreffende Kriegsideologie gehört engstens zusammen mit der Diskussion über die von von Rad aufgestellte Konzeption des „heiligen Krieges," wozu, wie Weippert („'Heiliger Krieg' in Israel und Assyrien") gezeigt hat, die neuassyrischen Prophetien, Hymnen und Gottesbriefe einen wichtigen Beitrag leisten. Vor allem zeigen sie, daß der von Gott berechtigte und betreute Krieg eine gemeinorientalische Erscheinung ist, von der kein „profaner" Krieg unterschieden werden kann.

braucht man nicht unbedingt damit zu rechnen, daß die biblische Parallele eines neuassyrischen Prophetenworts auch immer ein Stück authentischer Prophetie sein muß. Was z. B. die Königs- und Bundesideologie angeht, so können die Texte auch gut ohne das Vorzeichen 'Prophetie' nebeneinandergestellt werden. Und es kann kein Zufall sein, daß diese wesentlichen Themen der neuassyrischen Prophetie ihre nächsten biblischen Parallelen in den exilisch—nachexilischen, überwiegend deuteronomistischen Texten finden.

Die Verteilung der Parallelen auf die verschiedenen Teile des Alten Testaments ist ferner ein Zeichen für die unterschiedliche Überlieferungsgeschichte der neuassyrischen resp. israelitischen Prophetie. Sind uns die assyrischen Orakel in den im Archiv abgelegten Originaltafeln erhalten, so kennen wir die israelitische Prophetie nur als eine Komponente eines gewaltigen Redaktionsprozesses. Die assyrische Prophetie wurde niemals zum Gegenstand eines solchen interpretativen Wiedergebrauchs und vermag deshalb ein unmittelbareres Bild von dem prophetischen Phänomen zu übermitteln als das Alte Testament, in dem die Prophetie sich von ihren konkreten Erscheinungsformen schon entfernt hat und zu einem theologischen Begriff geworden ist.

Im Studium des Alten Testament hat man die durch die Distanz der eigentlichen Prophetie von der endgültigen Textgestalt entstandenen Schwierigkeiten dadurch zu überwinden versucht, daß die „echten" Worte der Propheten aus dem späteren Zuwachs herausgearbeitet worden sind. Trotz dieses an sich richtigen Bestrebens ist eine Beschreibung der „Geschichte der israelitischen Prophetie" nur von den Voraussetzungen her möglich gewesen, die die Redaktoren der alttestamentlichen Texte vorher bestimmt haben. Ihnen verdanken wir sowohl die Auswahl als auch den theologischen Interpretationshorizont der uns überlieferten Texte. Dies wiederum mahnt zur Vorsicht davor, die den Propheten Amos, Hosea, Jesaja, Micha und Jeremia zugeschriebenen Bücher als ein vollständiges Bild der israelitischen Prophetie des achten und siebten Jahrhunderts zu betrachten.

Will man sich also mit der vorexilischen israelitischen Prophetie vertraut machen, so wäre es äußerst hilfreich, eine von dem Redaktionsprozeß des Alten Testaments unabhängige Perspektive zu finden, die die Voraussetzungen der im Alten Testament überlieferten Texte von außen beleuchten kann. In Frage kommen dabei zunächst Parallelen, die deutliche Analogien zu den atl. Texten zeigen und zeitlich wie geographisch nicht allzu weit entfernt liegen. Die neuassyrische Prophetie entspricht diesen Voraussetzungen und vermag deswegen die verlangte Perspektive innerhalb methodisch gebührender Grenzen zu bieten.

Ein voreiliger Optimismus in dieser Hinsicht wird dadurch gezügelt, daß sich die augenfälligsten alttestamentlichen Parallelen der neuassyrischen Prophetie außer in dem Deuterojesaja größtenteils anderswo als in den Prophetenbüchern befinden. Die Bindung der Prophetie an das Königtum erinnert zwar an Konfrontationen zwischen einem israelitischen König und einem Prophet, aber in diesen Fällen handelt es sich meist um ausgesprochen konfliktbeladene Begegnungen, in denen der Prophet dem König gegenübersteht. Die ethisch-theologische Unheilsverkündigung der alttestamentlichen Prophetengestalten findet indes keine Entsprechung in der neuassyrischen Prophetie, in der der König fast ausnahmslos mit positivem Ton angeredet wird.[104] Schlimmstenfalls wird Asarhaddon der Vorwurf ungenügenden Vertrauens zu Ištar von Arbela gemacht,[105] oder er wird wegen mangelhafter Opfergaben getadelt.[106] Der Vorwurf führt allerdings zu keinem negativen Schluß, sondern zu einer erneuten Beteuerung der Zuverlässigkeit der göttlichen Botschaft[107] oder zu kultischen Anweisungen.[108]

Bei alledem dürfen wir aber nicht übersehen, daß das Alte Testament selbst mehrfach Hinweise darauf gibt, daß die „klassischen" Unheilspropheten der Überlieferung nicht der ganzen Wahrheit der israelitischen Prophetie entsprechen. Von dem Buch Jeremia gewinnt man den Eindruck, als wäre der Prophet Jeremia vielmehr ein eigentümlicher Sonderfall gewesen unter den anderen Propheten, deren Botschaft das „Friede! Friede!" war (Jer 6:14). Diesen Propheten kam es darauf an, das Volk aufzumuntern, die politischen Strukturen zu festigen und die Machthaber zu unterstützen. Von der grimmigen Polemik Jeremias her (vgl. Jer 23:9–32 u.a.) kann man sich vorstellen, daß gerade diese Art von Prophetismus in Jerusalem gang und gäbe war, während die Vertreter der gegenteiligen Ansicht eher eine sowohl von dem Volk als auch von dem Establishment gehaßte Ausnahme darstellten. Außer Jeremia wird nur der Prophet Uria genannt (Jer 26:20–24), der von Jojakim getötet wurde, während Jeremia selbst zuweilen in den Stock gelegt wurde (Jer 20:2) und ständig um sein Leben bangen mußte.

Die Konstellation eines „wahren" Propheten gegen eine Unmenge von „falschen" Propheten, die sich auch in den Büchern Micha (2:6–11; 3:5–8) und Ezechiel (13) findet, spitzt sich zu in dem Fall von Elia, des Gegenspielers von einer Schar von achthundertfünfzig kanaanäischen Propheten (1 Kön 18), sowie in dem des Micha ben Jimla, der unter vierhundert israelitischen Kollegen als Un-

104 Zur ähnlichen Einstellung der Mari-Prophetie zum König vgl. Malamat, „A Forerunner of Biblical Prophecy," 42.

105 SAA 9 1.10:7–12: *dabābu pāniu ša aqabakanni ina muḫḫi lā tazzīzi / ūmâ ina muḫḫi urkî tazzazma* „Konntest du dich etwa nicht auf das frühere Wort, das ich dir sprach, verlassen? / Auf das neuerliche kannst du dich jetzt verlassen!" (vgl. Weippert, „Aspekte israelitischer Prophetie im Lichte verwandter Erscheinungen des Alten Orients," 317; ähnlich SAA 9 1.1:6'f.15'–17'; 1.2 ii 2'f.; 1.4:34'–36').

106 SAA 9 3.5 iii 27–29: *ša ak lā bēt ili a[kkall]i akālī akk[a]lli kāsī* „Als ob es keinen Tempel gäbe, ist mein Opferbrot einbehalten, ist mein Opfertrank einbehalten."

107 SAA 9 1.1: 11'–15'.18'–27'; 1.2 ii 3'–8'; 1.4: 37'.

108 SAA 9 3.5 iii 32–37.

glücksprophet auftritt, als Josafat und Ahab, die Könige von Israel und Juda, des göttlichen Ratschlusses bezüglich eines Feldzugs nach Ramoth-Gilead bedürfen (1 Kön 22:1–28). Sowohl die Befragungssituation als auch die von der Mehrheit der Propheten gegebene Antwort entspricht dem, was auch in der neuassyrischen Prophetie wiederholt zum Ausdruck kommt.[109]

Die schematische Gegenüberstellung von „wahrer" und „falscher" Prophetie, in der die letztgenannte immer mit überlegenen Kräften auftritt, gibt Anlaß zu Bedenken gegen die historische Glaubwürdigkeit der atl. Erzählungen, die doch ein ausgesprochenes theologisches Ziel haben und grundsätzlich nicht als Augenzeugenberichte zu betrachten sind. Andererseits darf man aber auch fragen, ob diese Konstellation einmal als erzählerisches Motiv glaubhaft sein konnte, ohne irgendwie den realen Verhältnissen zu entsprechen. Dürfen wir nun jedenfalls damit rechnen, daß die dem Hof freundliche, optimistische Prophetie im vorexilischen Israel/Juda ähnlich wie in Assyrien in reichem Maße existiert hat,[110] so erhebt sich die Frage, warum im Alten Testament der von einer Minorität vertretene kritische Typ als die „wahre" Prophetie vorherrscht, während im Staatsarchiv von Ninive ausschließlich positive Prophetie aufbewahrt wurde.

Die Antwort muß ohne Zweifel von der Motivation ausgehen, die Texte überhaupt zu archivieren, zu kopieren und zu interpretieren. Wie oben festgestellt, wurden die prophetischen Orakel in Assyrien deswegen im Archiv abgelegt, weil das Königtum Asarhaddons und Assurbanipals der göttlichen Legitimation schmerzlich bedurfte. Von dieser Notwendigkeit aus kamen natürlich nur die für diese Könige günstigen Orakel in Frage. Von einer andersartigen Prophetie sind keine Dokumente erhalten geblieben, obgleich man wohl damit rechnen kann, daß auch die rivalisierenden Thronprätendenten ihren Anspruch durch das prophetische Wort untermauert haben.[111]

---

109 In einer Inschrift Asarhaddons wird berichtet, daß die Götter von mehreren Opferschauern (*bārû*) gleichzeitig befragt wurden, und die Entscheidung erst getroffen wurde, wenn die Weisungen „wie aus einem Munde" (*kī pî ištēn indaḫarāma*; Leichty, *The Royal Inscriptions of Esarhaddon*, 107:75) miteinander übereinstimmten. M. Weinfeld, „Ancient Near Eastern Patterns in Prophetic Literature," *VT* 27 (1977) 178–95, esp. 184–85, macht darauf aufmerksam, daß in der Micha-Erzählung die Worte der Propheten in ähnlicher Weise einstimmig (1 Kön 22,13; wörtl. „mit einem Munde" *pê 'eḥad*) günstig für den König sind. Da aber der Gottesbescheid in der assyrischen Inschrift eben nicht auf Prophetie, sondern auf Eingeweideschau erfolgt, dürfte hier wohl keine unmittelbare Parallele vorliegen.

110 Vgl. die Überlegungen bei Weippert, „Aspekte israelitischer Prophetie im Lichte verwandter Erscheinungen des Alten Orients," 308–10.

111 Darauf weist der große Asarhaddon-Vertrag mit klaren Worten hin, indem es befohlen wird, jedes böse Wort über Assurbanipal ihm sofort bekanntzugeben. Unter den potentiellen Verleumdern des Assurbanipal werden auch Propheten (*raggimu, maḫḫû, šā'ilu*) genannt: *šumma*

Im Alten Testament zeigt sich dagegen eine andere Motivation, die etwa aus der Kritik an den „falschen“ Propheten in Ez 13 ersichtlich wird: „Meine Hand soll über die Propheten kommen, die Trug reden und Lügen wahrsagen ... Weil sie mein Volk verführen und sagen: ‘Friede!’, wo doch kein Friede ist, und weil sie, wenn das Volk sich eine Wand baut, sie mit Kalk übertünchen, so sprich zu den Tünchern, die mit Kalk tünchen: ‘Die Wand wird einfallen!’... Hier ist weder Wand noch Tüncher — das sind die Propheten Israels, die Jerusalem wahrsagen und predigen ‘Friede!’, wo doch kein Friede ist, spricht Herr Jahwe“ (Ez 13:9aα, 10 – 11a, 15b-16).

Als Kriterium der Prophetie dürfte, außer der eventuellen (im Alten Testament nicht belegten) Überprüfung durch ein technisches Orakel,[112] nur die geschichtliche Verifikation der Botschaft zur Verfügung gestanden haben (vgl. Dtn 18:20 – 22; Jer 28:9). Das oben angeführte Zitat aus dem Buch Ezechiel zeigt, daß die optimistische Heilsprophetie sich angesichts der Erfahrungen der Exilszeit als Betrug erwiesen hatte und ihre Verkünder, wie groß ihre Schar auch gewesen sein mochte, für Pseudopropheten gehalten wurden (vgl. Thr 2:14).

Als verläßlich bewährte sich also nur die Prophetie, die zur Bewältigung der mit der politischen Katastrophe verbundenen theologischen Krise beitragen konnte. Deswegen wurde gerade die Unheilsprophetie zum Gegenstand der massiven Nachinterpretation, deren Ertrag uns vor Augen steht. Auch die Heilsprophetie blieb zwar in übertragener Funktion in den „demokratisierten“ Königsorakeln in Jes 40 – 55 am Leben — offenbar weil sich das in ihnen angekündigte Ende des Exils sodann als wahr erwies, womit das Verifikationskriterium erfüllt wurde.

Hand in Hand mit der seit der Exilszeit getriebenen Interpretation der Unheilsprophetie verstärkt sich die Auffassung von den Propheten als Prediger, die das Volk ständig mahnen, auf seinen bösen Wegen umzukehren und an den Geboten Jahwes festzuhalten (vgl. 2 Kön 17:13 u. a.). Dieses ausgesprochen deuteronomistische Ideal hat sowohl das biblische Prophetenbild als auch die alt-

---

abutu lā ṭābtu lā de’iqtu la bānītu ina nuḫḫi Aššūr-bāni-apli ... lu ina pī raggime maḫḫê šā’ili amat ili ... tašammāni tupazzarāni lā tallakāninni ana Aššūr-bāni-apli ... lā taqabbāni „Solltet ihr ein böses, unschönes oder ungebührendes Wort über Assurbanipal, ... sei es aus dem Munde eines Rufers, eines Ekstatikers oder eines Orakelbefragers, ... hören, so dürftet ihr es nicht geheimhalten, sondern ihr müßt kommen und es Assurbanipal ... berichten“ (SAA 2 6 10:108 f, 116 f, 119 f, 122).

112 Dies scheint in Mari üblich gewesen zu sein; darüber hinaus wurde dem prophetischen Brief oft Locke und Gewandsaum (*šārtum u sissiktum*) des/der Prophet(inn)en als Pfand beigefügt; vgl. dazu Koch, „Die Briefe ‘prophetischen’ Inhalts aus Mari,“ 72 – 74; Noort, *Untersuchungen zum Gottesbescheid in Mari*, 84 – 86; Weippert, „Aspekte israelitischer Prophetie im Lichte verwandter Erscheinungen des Alten Orients,“ 315; Ellis, „Observations on Mesopotamian Oracles and Prophetic Texts,“ 136.

testamentliche Wissenschaft tief beeinflußt, indem es noch häufig als Grundhaltung der sogenannten „klassischen" Prophetie gebilligt wird. Inwiefern diese Auffassung den Verhältnissen im vorexilischen Israel/Juda entspricht oder das Anliegen der nachexilischen Theologie zum Ausdruck bringt, gilt noch als eine großenteils unbeantwortete Frage.

Biblical Prophecy from a Near Eastern Perspective: The Cases of Kingship and Divine Possession

What do we mean when we talk about prophets and prophecy? The question is relevant because prophecy is not a self-evident phenomenon that could be observed independently by any interested individual, but rather a construct, the meaning of which must be decided by those who participate in its formation – in our case, the scholarly community. The concept of prophecy has biblical roots: it is an integral part of the long-developed language of biblical scholarship, which has resulted in the status of biblical prophets as the model of prophecy in general. Today, however, the increasing availability of extrabiblical Near Eastern texts related to what is called prophecy has begun to challenge the primacy of the Bible, inspiring a growing number of more or less comparative studies on prophecy in nonbiblical – whether Mesopotamian, West Semitic, or Greek – documents.[1] In fact, the extrabiblical application of the concept of prophecy has been surprisingly easy, which may (and should) raise the question whether the biblical concept has all too carelessly been imported to contexts where its use is not hereditary, and how much confusion this may have caused that we are not yet even aware of. This actualizes the questions of definition and the choice of perspective.

Serious attempts have been made to define prophecy in a way that facilitates mutual understanding in the scholarly discussion, and not without avail. Today, the basis of any definition is commonly seen in intermediation as the principal function of prophecy, and this is also my conviction.[2] However, the wide-

1 A comprehensive anthology of texts documenting prophecy in the ancient Near East, together with a comprehensive bibliography, is available in M. Nissinen, with contributions by C.-L. Seow, R. K. Ritner, and H. Craig Melchert, *Prophets and Prophecy in the Ancient Near East* (2nd edition; SBLWAW 41; Atlanta: Society of Biblical Literature, 2019). This work is henceforth referred to as SBLWAW 41 with text numbers.

2 For a classic formulation of this definition, see M. Weippert, "Prophetie im Alten Orient," *NBL* 3 (1997)196 – 200; for qualifications and critique, see, e.g., D. L. Petersen, "Defining Prophecy and Prophetic Literature," in *Prophecy in Its Ancient Near Eastern Context: Mesopotamian, Biblical, and Arabian Perspectives* (ed. M. Nissinen; SBLSymS 13, Atlanta: Society of Biblical Literature, 2000), 33 – 44; M. Nissinen, "What Is Prophecy? An Ancient Near Eastern Perspective," in *Inspired Speech: Prophecy in the Ancient Near East, Essays in Honor of Herbert B. Huffmon* (ed. J. Kaltner and L. Stulman; JSOTS 378; London: T. & T. Clark, 2004) 17 – 37 (= p. 53 – 73 in this volume).

DOI 10.1515/9783110466546-019

spread agreement on this fundamental issue leaves room for a number of further questions, for example: Is there a continuity or discontinuity between oral/aural prophecy and prophetic writings? What is the relationship between prophecy and (other kinds of) divination? How does the concept of prophecy function when moved outside the conventional biblical or Jewish-Christian framework? Should the Israelite, or biblical, or Jewish prophecy be considered a class of its own after all? Is it justified to apply the same concept to related phenomena and sources which may turn out to be distinct in several respects? How are different kinds of source materials to be evaluated as evidence of prophecy, whether in a historical, ideological, or phenomenological sense? It is far beyond the scope of this paper to give an answer to all these highly relevant questions, but I try to keep them in mind when looking at biblical prophecy from a Near Eastern perspective, with the purpose of examining whether there are enough relevant points of comparison to justify the cross-cultural application of the concept of prophecy, despite its biblical origin, in the ancient Near Eastern context.

The Near Eastern prophetic texts have often played an ancillary role as a comparative material to the study of biblical prophecy; yet the attention paid to the selection of pertinent texts is greatly unproportional with regard to its relatively small size in comparison with the ocean of other divinatory texts from the ancient Near East. On the other hand, the documentation of prophecy constitutes a corpus of over 170 individual texts, well comparable in size and substance to the biblical prophetic books. Its haphazard nature notwithstanding, this documentation yields a fairly comprehensive picture of the prophetic phenomenon in Mesopotamia and in the Levant. The sources originate from different places and periods of time, enabling the appreciation of prophecy as an integral and permanent part of the socioreligious landscape of Western Asia. Therefore, it makes sense to take a look at biblical prophecy from the perspective of the Near Eastern prophetic phenomena as represented by the available documents, setting the agenda according to the aspects that appear to be recurrent in the available documentation and looking for cognate features in biblical literature.

Comparative studies often suffer from a certain imbalance, especially if the so-called "parallels" are given a secondary role, using them first and foremost to support theories concerning the actual target of interest, that is, the biblical texts. Ancient Near Eastern texts may, for instance, be used as a means of controlling the authenticity and historical accuracy of biblical prophetic texts, or they can be presented as hard evidence against attempts at dehistoricizing the biblical prophets or dismantling the prophetic books.[3] The uncritical use of parallels is the most notorious feature of comparative studies that, especially if they follow a prescribed agenda, often leads to unjustified generalizations and unreliable results.

To avoid the shortcomings of "parallelomania,"[4] we could, of course, argue for an *Eigenbegrifflichkeit* of biblical prophecy, examining biblical prophecy as a self-sustaining system and resorting to the comparative material only in cases where the biblical corpus cannot explain itself. Taking this approach, however, would not help us to examine the cross-cultural applicability of the concept of prophecy; rather, it would lead to an ethnocentric point of view that impedes rather than facilitates the contextualization of biblical prophecy. Therefore, I think, we are better advised to read the Hebrew Bible as another representative of ancient Near Eastern literature, approaching biblical prophecy as a variation of the general phenomenon of transmitting allegedly divine knowledge. Such an approach has been taken in recent studies dealing with prophecy in the Hebrew Bible from a religio-historical and sociological point of view.[5]

With "biblical prophecy" – as distinct from "ancient Hebrew prophecy" – I mean prophecy as the literary construct that we have in front of our eyes when reading the Hebrew Bible.[6] Consequently, in this paper, I am reading the Hebrew Bible as a corpus of literature that represents its own characteristic images of prophets and prophecy – images that are multifarious and sometimes contradictory. This means that I am not comparing Near Eastern documents primarily with the so-called "classical prophets" and their supposed words and deeds, prioritizing their lifetime as a privileged period of Israelite prophecy; neither am I making a qualitative difference between the prophetic and historical books of the Hebrew Bible as documents of prophecy. Instead, I take the Hebrew Bible as a text, in which everything that is said about the prophets in one way or

---

3 This, I am afraid, is what happens in works with an apologetic tendency, e.g., in K. A. Kitchen, *On the Reliability of the Old Testament* (Grand Rapids: Eerdmans, 2003), 373–420.

4 The justified warnings of S. Sandmel, "Parallelomania," *JBL* 81 (1962) 1–13, are still worth heeding.

5 E.g., J. Blenkinsopp, *Sage, Priest, Prophet: Religious and Intellectual Leadership in Ancient Israel* (Library of Ancient Israel; Louisville, Ky.: Westminster/John Knox Press, 1995), 115–65; L. L. Grabbe, *Priests, Prophets, Diviners, Sages: A Socio-Historical Study of Religious Specialists in Ancient Israel* (Valley Forge, Pa.: Trinity Press International, 1995), 66–118; P. D. Miller, *The Religion of Ancient Israel* (Library of Ancient Israel; Louisville, Ky.: Westminster John Knox, 2000), 174–89; cf. already R. R. Wilson, *Prophecy and Society in Ancient Israel* (Philadelphia, Pa.: Fortress, 1980); T. W. Overholt, *Channels of Prophecy: The Social Dynamics of Prophetic Activity* (Minneapolis: Fortress Press, 1989).

6 For this distinction, see Nissinen, "What Is Prophecy?", 28–31.

another serves the ends of the texts' authors and editors and their communities, irrespective of the origin of individual stories or oracles. At this stage of the investigation, I will not pay primary attention to the dating of individual biblical texts. In general, however, I assume that the books of the Hebrew Bible as we have them are the product of a long editorial process that did not end before the late Persian or Hellenistic period. I would be the last person to undermine the search for prophecy as a historical phenomenon in the kingdoms of Israel and Judah, or the importance of diachronic historical analyses of prophecy and the prophetic books in the Hebrew Bible. However, when looking at the biblical text from a Near Eastern perspective, I consider it necessary to take the first look from a distance, paying but marginal attention to the literary history of the biblical writings.

Instead of attempting a full-scale comparison of biblical and extrabiblical texts, I have chosen two rather different topics that can be seen as typical of the prophetic phenomenon in the Near Eastern documents, assessing their significance for the biblical construct of prophecy. The cases discussed are 1) the relation of prophets to kings, and 2) the network of prophecy, music, lament, and divine possession. It is my main objective to bring the documents into dialogue with each other. Due to the limited space, but also because of the synchronic approach which needs to be completed by diachronical analyses at a later stage, my explanations and conclusions will remain brief, tentative, and thus liable to criticism.

I. Prophets and Kings

The elementary affiliation between the institutions of prophecy and kingship is amply documented all over the Near Eastern sources available to us. Royal concerns are dealt with in the majority of the extant prophetic oracles which almost without exception are addressed to a king, most often to Zimri-Lim of Mari[7] and Esarhaddon and Assurbanipal of Assyria,[8] but also to Ibalpiel of Ešnunna,[9] Zak-

7 Most of the letters citing prophetic oracles are published in J.-M. Durand, *Archives épistolaires de Mari I/1* (ARM 26/1; Paris: Editions Recherche sur les Civilisations, 1988); these and a number of additional documents can be found in SBLWAW 41, nos. 1–65b.

8 The Assyrian oracles are to be found in S. Parpola, *Assyrian Prophecies* (SAA 9; Helsinki: The Neo-Assyrian Text Corpus Project, 1997); other Neo-Assyrian documents are discussed in M. Nissinen, *References to Prophecy in Neo-Assyrian Sources* (SAAS 7; Helsinki: The Neo-Assyrian Text Corpus Project, 1998); cf. SBLWAW 41, nos. 68–118j.

kur of Hamath,[10] and the ruler of Byblos.[11] Even Greek oracles, notably the Pythia of Delphi, were regularly consulted by kings, such as Croesus of Lydia.[12] Without actually being part of the court personnel but rather belonging to temples and other cult places, prophets evidently belonged to the divinatory apparatus consulted by ancient Near Eastern rulers. But how important was their role compared with different types of diviners in general?

The fragmentary set of sources available provides us only with a rather short list of kings receiving prophetic messages. This may give the impression that the prophets, for most of the time, did not play a significant role, at least when it comes to royal issues. There may be some truth in this impression, but it must be balanced against the provenance of the extant oracles, the lion's share of which comes from two major archives, Mari and Nineveh. Taken together, the bits and pieces of our documentation attest to a geographically and chronologically widespread institution that was readily available to kings, at least in Mesopotamia and in the West Semitic world. In the Old Babylonian period, for instance, Zimri-Lim of Mari was not the only king to be addressed by prophets. A couple of prophecies to an earlier king of Mari, Yasmaḫ-Addu, have been preserved,[13] his rival and ally Ibalpiel of Ešnunna received prophetic oracles,[14] and the letters from Mari inform us of prophecies uttered in different places, from Aleppo to Babylon.[15] Of the few West Semitic prophetic documents, only the Zakkur stele says explicitly that the king of Hamath had received prophetic oracles,

---

9 The two oracles from Ešnunna are published in M. deJong Ellis, "The Goddess Kititum Speaks to King Ibalpiel: Oracle Texts from Ishchali," *MARI* 5 (1987) 235–66; cf. SBLWAW 41, nos. 66–67.
10 *KAI* 202; cf. the translation of Choon-Leong Seow in SBLWAW 41, no. 137.
11 See A. H. Gardiner, *Late Egyptian Stories* (Bibliotheca Aegyptiana 1; Brussels: La fondation égyptologique reine Élisabeth, 1932), 61–76; cf. the translation of Robert K. Ritner in SBLWAW 41, no. 142.
12 See V. Rosenberger, *Griechische Orakel: Eine Kulturgeshichte* (Darmstadt: Wissenschaftliche Buchgesellschaft, 2001), 160–65. For the role of the Delphic oracle in Athenian democracy, see H. Bowden, *Classical Athens and the Delphic Oracle: Divination and Democracy* (Cambridge, UK: Cambridge University Press 2005).
13 I.e., A. 3760 and ARM 26 223 (cf. SBLWAW 41, nos. 3 and 34); for an edition and the dating of these texts, see D. Charpin, "Prophètes et rois dans le Proche-Orient amorrite: Nouvelles données, nouvelles perspectives", in *Florilegium marianum 6: Recueil d'études à la mémoire d'André Parrot* (ed. id. and J.-M. Durand; Mémoires de *NABU* 7; Paris: SEPOA, 2002) 7–38, esp. 34–37.
14 Cf. above, note 10.
15 In addition to cities within Zimri-Lim's reign, such as Terqa, Tuttul, Saggaratum, and Qaṭṭunan, there are letters containing prophetic oracles from Aleppo (FM 7 39 and FM 7 38; cf. SBLWAW 41, nos. 1 and 2), Babylon (ARM 26 371; cf. SBLWAW 41, no. 47), and Andarig (ARM 26 414; cf. SBLWAW 41, no. 48).

but even other texts, such as the Mesha stele[16] and the Amman citadel inscription,[17] may be quoted as indirect evidence of the kings of Moab and Ammon receiving prophetic oracles.[18]

The fact that Esarhaddon and Assurbanipal were the only Neo-Assyrian kings not only to record prophetic oracles in their archives but to even mention them in their inscriptions, is probably indicative of their special predilection for prophecy.[19] That these kings seem to have been more inclined than their predecessors to lend their ears to prophets does not, however, warrant the conclusion that prophecy was a West Semitic import that only sporadically reached Mesopotamian courts.[20] Prophets were there all the time, even though their political relevance and their role among the diviners consulted by the royal court may have varied depending on the king, country, and period of time.

The institutional affiliation between prophecy and kingship is quite natural when seen in the context of kingship and divination in general. Among other diviners, the prophets were representatives of the *Herrschaftswissen*, that is, they were one of the media through which the king was kept informed of the divine favors and obligations and the origin and legitimacy of his rule.[21] This was the ideological foundation of their activity and the basis of their acknowlegdment by the royal court. The words of those prophets who were regarded as mouthpieces of deities (not all of them were) were appreciated accordingly. The prophets did not address the king as themselves but in the name of the deity, which gave

---

16 *KAI* 181; cf. A. Lemaire, "Notes d'épigraphie nord-ouest sémitique," *Syria* 64 (1987) 205–16, esp. 210–14.

17 See W. E. Aufrecht, *A Corpus of Ammonite Inscriptions* (Ancient Near Eastern Texts and Studies 4; Lewiston, N.Y.: Edwin Mellen, 1989), 154–63 (no. 59); cf. SBLWAW 41, no. 136; A. Lemaire, "Oracles, politique et littérature dans les royaumes araméens et transjordaniens (IXᵉ–VIIIᵉ s. av. n.è.)," in *Oracles et prophéties dans l'antiquité* (ed. J.-G. Heintz; Travaux du Centre de recherche sur le Proche-Orient et la Grèce antiques 15; Paris, 1997) 171–93, esp. 180–81.

18 Thus A. Lemaire, "Prophètes et rois dans les inscriptions ouest-sémitiques (IXᵉ–VIᵉ siecle av. J.-C.)," in *Prophètes et rois: Bible et Proche-Orient* (ed. id.; Lectio divina, hors série; Paris: Cerf, 2001) 85–115, esp. 101–11.

19 Cf. my earlier deliberations in M. Nissinen, "City as Lofty as Heaven: Arbela and Other Cities in Neo-Assyrian Prophecy," in *"Every City Shall Be Forsaken": Urbanism and Prophecy in Ancient Israel and the Near East* (ed. L. L. Grabbe and R. D. Haak; JSOTS 330; Sheffield: Sheffield Academic Press, 2001) 172–209, esp. 180–83 (= pp. 267–300 in this volume).

20 The Western provenance of prophecy has been assumed by A. Malamat, "The Cultural Impact of the West (Syria-Palestine) on Mesopotamia in the Old Babylonian Period," *AoF* 24 (1997) 310–19.

21 See B. Pongratz-Leisten, *Herrschaftswissen in Mesopotamien: Formen der Kommunikation zwischen Gott und König im 2. und 1. Jahrtausend v. Chr.* (SAAS 10; Helsinki: The Neo-Assyrian Text Corpus Project, 1999).

them the opportunity of speaking to the king as the gods do, not using the courtly phraseology that other diviners were obliged to use in their letters, but beginning the message with formulas like the "Word of Ištar of Arbela."[22] From this position, they were entitled to address the king in different ways – not always favorably, as is most often the case, but also in a critical tone.[23] To use traditional form critical categories, the ancient Near Eastern prophecies do not just include *Heilsworte* but also *Mahnworte* and *Gerichtsworte*; in other words, the prophecies communicate words of support and instruction as well as those of warning, indictment, and judgment.[24] Even though only a relatively small number of sources represent the categories of indictment and judgment, they should not be overlooked. The distribution of these categories in the extant documents does not necessarily reflect the actual variety of prophetic proclamation.

As important as the prophets were regarded by the ancient Near Eastern kings, or at least some of them, there are few records of direct contacts between kings and prophets. The demoralized comment of the astrologer Bel-ušezib on the prophets and prophetesses Esarhaddon had summoned instead of himself[25] may be taken as an expression of professional jealousy, but it also implies that this was an unusual thing for the king to do. The kings of Mari, according to the existing evidence, were informed about prophecies mostly by go-betweens,[26] and the Assyrian kings received prophecies in the form of written reports.[27] How often the kings were present in situations where prophecies were uttered is very difficult to conclude. We may assume that Esarhaddon was there when the prophecies concerning his kingship were spoken on the occasion of his

22 SAA 9 2.4 ii 30; 3.4 ii 33; 3.5 iii 16; 5:1; 7:2.

23 For prophetical criticism in the Near Eastern documents, see M. Nissinen, "Das kritische Potential in der altorientalischen Prophetie," in: M. Köckert and M. Nissinen (eds.), *Propheten in Mari, Assyrien und Israel* (FRLANT 201; Göttingen, 2003) 1–32 (= pp. 163–94 in this volume).

24 Cf. the useful table in J. H. Walton, *Ancient Near Eastern Thought and the Old Testament: Introducing the Conceptual World of the Hebrew Bible* (Grand Rapids, Mich.: Eerdmans, 2006), 245–47.

25 SAA 10 109; cf. Nissinen, *References to Prophecy*, 89–95.

26 See J. M. Sasson, "The Posting of Letters with Divine Messages," in *Florilegium marianum 2: Recueil d'études à la mémoire de Maurice Birot* (ed. D. Charpin and J.-M. Durand; Mémoires de *NABU* 3; Paris: SEPOA, 1994) 299–316.

27 For the report format, see K. Radner, "The Relation Between Format and Content of Neo-Assyrian Texts," in *Niniveh 612 BC: The Glory and Fall of the Assyrian Empire* (ed. R. Matilla; Catalogue of the 10th Anniversary Exhibition of the Neo-Assyrian Text Corpus Project; Helsinki, 1995) 63–78, esp. 72–74.

own enthronement ritual,[28] and the king of Mari was expected to take part in the ritual of Ištar where even the prophets were performing.[29]

That the kings heard prophets speaking, perhaps on a regular basis, does not, however, mean that they had personal contacts with prophets in the same way they communicated with their trusted astrologers, haruspices, and exorcists. The available documentation yields the impression that, while prophecies were appreciated as divine words, the kings did not maintain personal relationships with prophets. They do deliver messages from deities to kings, but the kings are seldom found in direct consultations with them,[30] nor do the prophets feature as advisors to the king in the same way as the scholars, whose relationship with the king is often a personal one, and many of whom – unlike the prophets – are familiar to us as persons, thanks to their intensive correspondence with the kings. Among the Near Eastern prophets, there is no one who would stand out as a personality of whom we know anything but some basic data like the name, the domicile, and the title.

Turning now to the Hebrew Bible, it is easy to notice that the communication between prophets and kings is taken as a matter of course. Kings of Israel and Judah, from the first to the last, regularly receive divine words spoken by people designated as prophets. Many times this happens on their own initiative; kings who actively seek the services of prophets include Saul who looked after Samuel (1 Sam 9), himself joined a prophetic band (1 Sam 10:9–12), and later turned to prophets, albeit without avail (1 Sam 28:6); Jeroboam on the occasions of the destruction of the altar at Bethel and the sickness of his son (1 Kgs 13:6–10; 14:1–18); Ahab who needs an oracle concerning his joint campaign with Jehoshaphath against Ramoth-Gilead (1 Kgs 22; 2 Chr 18); Ahasiah, having fallen through a window in his upper chamber (2 Kgs 1); Jehoram, Jehoshaphath, and the king of Edom facing difficulties during their campaign against Moab (2 Kgs 3:9–20); Ben-Hadad, the sick king of Damascus (2 Kgs 8:7–15); Joash at the deathbed of the prophet Elisha (2 Kgs 13:14–19); Hezekiah, intimidated by Sennacherib (2 Kgs 19:1–34; Isa 37:1–35; cf. 2 Chr 32:20); Josiah, scandalized by the newly found law book (2 Kgs 22:3–20; 2 Chr 34:19–28); Zedekiah, facing the threat

---

28 See the five prophecies included in SAA 9 3 (Parpola, *Assyrian Prophecies*, lxiv, 22–27; cf. SBLWAW 41, nos. 84–88).

29 FM 3 2 and 3 3; see J.-M. Durand and M. Guichard, "Les rituels de Mari," in *Florilegium marianum 3: Recueil d'études à la mémoire de Marie-Thérèse Barrelet* (ed. D. Charpin and J.-M. Durand; Mémoires de *NABU* 4; Paris: SEPOA, 1997) 19–78, esp. 52–63, 72–75.

30 Cf., however, D. Charpin, "Prophètes et rois dans le Proche-Orient amorrite," in Lemaire (ed.), *Prophètes et rois*, 21–53, esp. 34–37, who interprets a part of the evidence in favor of more direct contacts between prophets and the king than, e.g., J. M. Sasson (see above, n. 26).

of Nebuchadnezzar (Jer 21:1–10; 37:3–10; 38:14–26). When there was no longer a king, the elders of Israel approached Ezekiel (Ez 8:1; 14:1; 20:1).

Equally as often, the biblical prophets deliver unsolicited oracles to kings, addressing them directly or indirectly: Nathan (2 Sam 7:4–17; 12:1–14; 1 Chr 17:3–15) and Gad (1 Sam 22:5; 2 Sam 24:11–19; 1 Chr 21:9–19) to David; Ahiah to Jeroboam (1 Kgs 11:29–39); Shemaiah to Rehoboam (1 Kgs 12:22–24; 2 Chr 12:5–8); Azariah son of Oded (2 Chr 15:1–7) and Hanani (2 Chr 16:7–10) to Asa; Jehu son of Hanani to Baasha (1 Kgs 16:1–7) and to Jehoshaphath (2 Chr 19:1–3); Jahaziel son of Zechariah (2 Chr 20:14–17) and Eliezer son of Dodavah (2 Chr 20:37) to Jehoshaphath; Elijah to Ahab (1 Kgs 18; 21:17–29) and to Jehoram of Israel (in a letter; 2 Chr 21:12–15); anonymous prophets to Ahab (1 Kgs 20:13–14, 22, 39–43); the anonymous "son of a prophet" to Jehu (2 Kgs 9:1–13); two anonymous prophets to Amaziah (2 Chr 25:7–10, 15–16); Oded to Ahaz (2 Chr 28:9–11); Isaiah to Ahaz (Isa 7:10–25) and to Hezekiah (2 Kgs 20:1–11), not to mention Cyrus (Isa 45:1–7); Jeremiah to the kings of neighboring kingdoms (Jer 27:2–11), to Josiah, Jehoiachim and Jehoiachin (Jer 22:10–19, 24–30), and to Zedekiah (Jer 32:3–5; 34:1–7); Hosea to the royal house (Hos 5:1); Amos to Jeroboam (Am 7:10–11) – and, by analogy, Haggai to Zerubbabel (Hag 2:20–23) and, possibly, Noadiah to Nehemiah (Neh 6:14).

Viewed from the Near Eastern perspective, the patterns of communication between prophets and kings seem rather familiar. Irrespective of the historicity of each encounter, which in many – if not most – cases is doubtful, the array of kings receiving prophetic messages demonstrates that the biblical writers regarded the communication between prophets and kings as standard procedure. Like the kings of Mari and Assyria, the biblical kings turn to prophets in critical situations, and the prophets deliver oracles of support, instruction, warning, indictment, and judgment to the kings. The sayings of the prophets relate to political, cultic, and private matters, their activity is intensified in times of crises, and they proclaim judgment over foreign nations. Like in the ancient Near East, prophets are involved in the investiture of new kings (1 Sam 9–10; 16:1–13; 1 Kgs 1:32–40; 19:15–16; 2 Kgs 8:13; 9:1–13; cf. Hag 2:20–23),[31] and they keep

---

31 The Assyrian cases of prophetic involvement in the investiture of kings include the enthronement of Esarhaddon (SAA 9 3) and the substitute king ritual reported in SAA 10 352; see Nissinen, *References to Prophecy*, 25–30, 68–77. At Mari, letter FM 7 38 (cf. SBLWAW 41, no. 2) may refer to an original enthronement oracle; see J.-G. Heintz, "Des textes sémitiques anciens à la Bible hébraïque: Un comparatisme légitime?," in *Le comparatisme en histoire des religions: pour un état de la question* (ed. F. Bœspflug and F. Dunand; Paris: Cerf, 1997) 127–56, esp. 146–50. Lemaire, "Prophètes et rois dans les inscriptions ouest-sémitiques," 86–93, points out the similarity between lines 4–5 of the Tel Dan stela where Hasael, the son of Ben Hadad

the kings informed of their duties, legitimacy and the ideological and theological basis of their power. By and large, the function of prophets as specialists in the *Herrschaftswissen* in the Hebrew Bible corresponds to that in the ancient Near East in general.

All these fundamental similarities between the images of prophets and kings in the Hebrew Bible and other Near Eastern sources should be appreciated at their full value, but some significant differences must also be noted. The relationship between kings and prophets seems rather more immediate in the Hebrew Bible. The list of encounters between prophets and kings, to which even Daniel's communication with Nebuchadnezzar, Belshazzar and Darius (Dan 1–6) should be added, is much longer than can be assembled from the entire Near Eastern documentation. Sometimes biblical kings, like the king of Mari, are only indirectly informed of prophecies (Josiah in 2 Kgs 22; Jehoiachim in Jer 36; the king of Nineveh in Jon 3), but much more often the communication between prophets and kings in the Hebrew Bible is direct and personal. Jeremiah, with his antagonistic messages, faces some problems at times in this respect, but there are prophets – Elijah, for instance (1 Kgs 21:17–24) – who seem to have no difficulties in approaching the king personally in spite of their aggressive proclamations against him. Indeed, prophets like Nathan (2 Sam 7:4–17; 12:1–14) and Isaiah (Isa 7) conform to the conventional picture of "court prophets" better than their Near Eastern colleagues of whom this term is (often derogatorily) used.

Actually, the role of some prophets comes closer to that of the Mesopotamian scholars: not only do they perform divinatory acts that in Mesopotamia would belong to the realm of the exorcists (2 Kgs 20:1–11//Isa 38:1–8, 21–22), but they also appear as active agents in political decision-making, having a direct access to the king (1 Kgs 1:11–31; 2 Kgs 19:1–7//Isa 37:1–7; Isa 7; Jer 38:14–28). All this makes the role of biblical prophets vis-à-vis the kings more prominent and independent than can be deduced from any Near Eastern source.

To this can be added that, while the portrait of some of the biblical prophets remains quite as faint as that of the Near Eastern prophets in general, many prophets in the Hebrew Bible stand out as the main characters in the stories written about them. The Hebrew Bible does not provide us with too many details of the life and deeds of Obadiah, Nahum, Habakkuk, or Zephaniah, but a great deal more is said about figures like Isaiah, Jeremiah, Ezekiel, and Hosea, whose personalities, theologies, biographies, and psychopathologies have, therefore, been the subject of intensive research. However, the increasing awareness of the diffi-

---

says: "[and] Hadad made [m]e king," and 2 Kgs 8:13, where Elisha the prophet proclaims that the God of Israel will make him king of Aram.

culties in reaching historical persons behind the texts has turned scholarly attention from the prophets as historical personalities to the prophetic books as scribal works and the development of the prophetic tradition in the Second Temple period when the scribal enterprise, for the most part, took place.[32] This highlights the difference between the Hebrew Bible and the Near Eastern documents, which include several reports on prophetic performances; these, however, are to be found in letters written to the king, not in literary compositions like the stories about prophets included in biblical books. In general, the Near Eastern documentation consists of mostly contemporary reports on prophecies delivered to the king himself, while the Hebrew Bible tells stories about the encounters of kings and prophets in a secondary literary setting.

Moreover, and partly because of this difference in documentation, the ideological junctures of prophecy and kingship are much more complex in the Hebrew Bible than in other Near Eastern documents. Ideological neutrality can hardly be said to belong to prophecy anywhere; in a way, prophets mostly appear as stern supporters of the dominant ideology of each textual corpus, whether biblical or nonbiblical. The difference is that, while the Near Eastern sources, as a rule, themselves represent the royal ideology of the kingdom they come from, whether Mari, Assyria, or Hamath, the biblical texts present a more tangled case.

There are enough traces of the "classical" Near Eastern royal ideology in the Hebrew Bible to make it probable that the type of royal prophecy amply documented in Near Eastern sources also existed in Jerusalem. These include the oracle of Nathan in 2 Sam 7[33] and Haggai's oracle to Zerubbabel (Hag 2:21–23),[34] as

---

32 See, e.g., E. Ben Zvi, "The Prophetic Book: A Key Form of Prophetic Literature," in *The Changing Face of Form Criticism for the Twenty-First Century* (ed. E. Ben Zvi and M. A. Sweeney; Grand Rapids, Mich.: Eerdmans, 2003) 276–97; U. Becker, "Die Wiederentdeckung des Prophetenbuches: Tendenzen und Aufgaben der gegenwärtigen Prophetenforschung," *BTZ* 21 (2004) 30–60; M. H. Floyd, "The Production of Prophetic Books in the Early Second Temple Period," in *Prophets, Prophecy, and Prophetic Texts in Second Temple Judaism* (ed. id. and R. D. Haak; LHBOTS 427; New York and London: T & T Clark, 2006) 276–97; K. van der Toorn, *Scribal Culture and the Making of the Hebrew Bible* (Cambridge, Mass.: Harvard University Press, 2007), 173–204.

33 For a recent analysis, see, e.g., P. Kasari, *Nathan's Promise in 2 Samuel 7 and Related Texts* (PFES 97; Helsinki: The Finnish Exegetical Society, 2009), who finds the original royal oracle to David in 2 Sam 7:1a, 2–5a, 8aβbα*, 9a, 12aαβb, 14a, 15a, 17.

34 These verses, in my view, reflect the tradition of Near Eastern royal prophecy irrespective of whether Zerubbabel was actually designated here as a king or even a messiah. Being supportive of the ruling elite under the leadership of Zerubbabel, "[i]t advocates the perpetuation of Israelite institutions and traditions within the context of accommodation to the realities of Persian rule" (J. Kessler, *The Book of Haggai: Prophecy and Society in Early Persian Yehud* [VTSup 91; Lei-

well as royal psalms that may have their background in prophetic activity (Ps 2; 21; 45; 110).[35] Especially in Second Isaiah, many passages resemble the Neo-Assyrian oracles and are likely to utililize language and ideas inherited from traditional royal prophecy.[36]

On the other hand, the harsh antagonism of many biblical prophets towards kings and kingship is virtually unparalleled in Near Eastern sources, where the king can certainly be criticized,[37] but the criticism never goes as far as to declare the end of the ruling dynasty of the country (cf. 1 Kgs 14:10 – 11; 16:2 – 4; Jer 22:30; Am 7:9, 17) – except for one case, reported by Nabû-reḫtu-uṣur to Esarhaddon as a pseudoprophecy proclaiming the destruction of the seed of Sennacherib (SAA 16 59).[38] This important piece of evidence shows that even in Assyria, prophecy could be used by oppositional circles against the ruling king, which is not surprising as such. What is noteworthy is that such a document, thanks to the solicitous servant of the king, has been preserved in the Assyrian state archives, where the point of view of the adversaries of the kings is poorly represented. This raises the question about the origin and motivation of the prophetic opposition against biblical kings.

It is evident that the lion's share of biblical texts dealing with kings and prophets do not grow out of the official royal ideology but from a distinct ideological soil, fertilized by oppositional, sometimes theocratic-antimonarchical – and, to a great extent, *post*monarchical ideas. The perspective of the biblical books is neither that of the kings nor that of the prophets, but that of a third party not directly involved in the encounters of kings and prophets but looking at them, and manufacturing them, from a distance, for purposes nourished by other than royal or prophetic concerns. This is not to say that no historical evidence of such encounters can be deduced from the Hebrew Bible; a careful diachronic scrutiny may well be able to reveal some authentic cases that actually took place in the kingdoms of Israel and Judah, and the comparative evidence may be helpful in recognizing them. Nevertheless, it remains a problem whether

den: Brill, 2002], 279), hence being functionally equivalent with ancient Near Eastern prophecy in general.

35 For traces of prophetic activity in the Psalms, see J. Hilber, *Cultic Prophecy in the Psalms* (BZAW 352; Berlin and New York: W. de Gruyter, 2005), 76 – 217.

36 See M. Weippert, "'Ich bin Jahwe' – 'Ich bin Ištar of Arbela': Deuterojesaja im Lichte der neuassyrischen Prophetie," in *Prophetie und Psalmen*, FS K. Seybold (ed. B. Huwyler, H.-P. Mathys, and B. Weber; AOAT 280; Münster: Ugarit-Verlag, 2001) 31 – 59.

37 See Nissinen, "Das kritische Potential in der altorientalischen Prophetie."

38 See M. Luukko and G. van Buylaere, *The Political Correspondence of Esarhaddon* (SAA 16; Helsinki: Helsinki University Press, 2002), 52 – 53; cf. Nissinen, *References to Prophecy*, 108 – 53.

the fragmentary evidence found in the biblical texts, edited by the Second Temple scribes according to their ideological preferences, is enough to enable a reliable historical reconstruction of the relationship between the prophets and the kings.

From a historical point of view, the fierce opposition to kings and kingship in the Hebrew Bible may be quite as disproportional as the virtual lack thereof in other Near Eastern documents. For the editors of the biblical books, the end of the monarchy was as much a reality as was the monarchy's endurance for the scribes of Assyria and Mari, and this certainly had an effect on the general tone of the documents we have at our disposal. On both sides, we are dependent on incomplete evidence representing biased views, and this makes the comparison a cumbersome task.

All difficulties notwithstanding, there is enough evidence to warrant the conviction that, in the kingdoms of Judah and Israel, the institutions of prophecy and kingship were affiliated in more or less the same way as is documented by texts from other parts of the Near East. The historical and ideological role of prophets as specialists in *Herrschaftswissen* and, thus, an essential part of the royal divinatory apparatus is presupposed by the biblical texts regardless of their dating. This is true especially for texts that describe the kings and their activities, that is, the Deuteronomistic History[39] and, in particular, the Chronicles,[40] where the communication between prophets and kings is depicted as more intensive than anywhere else, not to mention the book of Daniel. Hence, even texts of late origin follow the ancient Near Eastern pattern in reinforcing the fundamental affinity of the institutions of prophecy and kingship.

However, there are also intriguing differences between the images of prophets and kings in biblical and extrabiblical texts – first and foremost the active and, at times, aggressive engagement of the biblical prophets on the one hand, and their divinatory (and even non-divinatory) functions atypical of other Near Eastern prophets on the other. The roles of biblical prophets are mani-

---

39 For the significance of prophets and prophecy in the Deuteronomistic History, see, e.g., W. Dietrich, "Prophetie im deuteronomistischen Geschichtswerk," in *The Future of the Deuteronomistic History* (ed. T. Römer; BETL 147; Leuven: Peeters, 2000) 47–65; cf. also E. Ben Zvi, "'The Prophets' – References to Generic Prophets and their Role in the Construction of the Image of 'Prophets of the Old' within the Postmonarchic Readership/s of the Book of Kings," *ZAW* 116 (2004) 555–67. See also pp. 539–62 in this volume.

40 See W. M. Schniedewind, *The Word of God in Transition: From Prophet to Exegete in the Second Temple Period* (JSOTS 197; Sheffield: Sheffield Academic Press, 1995); Y. Amit, "The Role of Prophecy and Prophets in the Chronicler's World," in Floyd and Haak (ed.), *Prophets, Prophecy and Prophetic Texts in Second Temple Judaism*, 80–101.

fold and should not be forced into a harmonized image. There may be historical and sociological reasons for the variety of the roles of biblical prophets. In Mesopotamia, there was a clear division between scholars and prophets, but an overlap of roles is more likely in less differentiated societies like those of Judah and Israel; for example, the priestly lineage of Jeremiah (Jer 1:1) and Ezekiel (Ez 1:3), if historical, probably had implications for their social role and educational background. To a great extent, however, this diversity is without doubt the product of the creativity of the authors and editors of the biblical texts, and some part of it may be due to a secondary "prophetization" of characters like Samuel[41] or, in a different vein, *'anšê 'ĕlohîm* like Elijah or Elisha. It must be borne in mind that most methods of divination other than prophecy are condemned by the biblical writers, especially the Deuteronomists to who we owe many of the biblical encounters between prophets and kings. While the existence of the diviners is acknowledged, kings turning to them appear in a dubious light, and the word of God never comes through their activities. In terms of this ideology, there is little room for diviners other than prophets who make the king conversant with the divine will.

II. Prophecy, Music, Lament, and Divine Possession

Prophecy and Music

Why music? It may strike one as surprising to take up this issue in comparative studies on prophecy. However, I hope to be able to demonstrate that music indeed does appear as worthy of consideration with regard to biblical and ancient Near Eastern prophecy, especially when it is connected with two other issues relevant for prophecy, namely lament and divine possession.

In the Hebrew Bible, music is several times associated with prophecy. Two of the five biblical prophetesses are said to strike up a song. Miriam, explicitly designated as a *nĕbî'â*, takes a drum and, followed by women who dance and beat the drums, she intunes the song: "Sing to the Lord, for he is highly exalted; The horse and his rider he has hurled into the sea" (Ex 15:20 – 21). Deborah sings her

41 Cf. W. Dietrich, "Samuel – ein Prophet?," *Sacra Scripta* 5 (2007) 11 – 26, who finds no less than seven facets in the biblical image of Samuel: priest (which probably was the office of the historical Samuel), prophet, military liberator, tribal leader, kingmaker, advisor of kings and opponent to kings.

famous song together with Barak son of Abinoam (Judg 5:2–31), although she is not called prophetess here but in another context (Judg 4:4). Two prophets are associated with love songs: Isaiah sings one himself (Isa 5:1–2), and Ezekiel's caricature among his people is "no more than one who sings love songs with a beautiful voice and plays an instrument well" (Ez 33:32). Moreover, Saul falls into a frenzy when the band of prophets comes prophesying (*mitnabbĕ'îm*) down from the *bamah* of Gebah, accompanied by harps, drums, flutes and lyres (1 Sam 10:5). Elisha calls for a harp player, and when the musician is playing his instrument, the hand of God comes upon Elisha – that is, he goes into a trance (cf. Ez 1:3, 22 8:1, etc.) – and he gives a prophecy sought by the kings of Israel and Judah (2 Kgs 3:13–20). Finally, the descendants of Asaph, Heman and Jedutun are commissioned to prophesy (*hannibbĕ'îm* Q), that is, to sing (*šîr*), with lyres, harps and cymbals while performing the temple service; men who had learned this skill are said to be no fewer in number than two hundred and eighty-eight (1 Chr 25:1–7).

These few instances do not turn the prophets into musicians, but they are not purely coincidental either, and they have not gone unnoticed by scholars.[42] It has been suggested that the association between prophecy and music has a "Canaanite" background,[43] and whether or not we want to approach the issue from the point of view of the Canaanites vs. Israelites divide, it makes sense to take a look at Near Eastern evidence that indeed corroborates the association between prophecy and music.

At Mari, the ritual of Ištar was the annual highpoint of the ritual calendar. According to two texts describing this royal ceremony,[44] even prophets and prophetesses feature prominently in it, together with musicians. According to one of these texts (FM 3 2), when the king enters the temple and takes his position, the musicians first strike up "ma-é-ur-re-men," a Sumerian canonical city lamentation. After this, the prophet is supposed to prophesy and another canonical lamentation, "ú-ru am-ma-da-ru-bí,"[45] is sung if he is able to fulfill his task. If he, however, 'maintains his equilibrium" (*ištaqal*), that is, fails to achieve the

42 Cf., e.g., Blenkinsopp, *Sage, Priest, Prophet*, 131; Schniedewind, *The Word of God in Transition*, 173; Miller, *The Religion of Ancient Israel*, 185; cf. the comparative material presented in A. Haldar, *Associations of Cult Prophets among the Ancient Semites* (Uppsala: Almqvist & Wiksell, 1945), 118–120.

43 Thus, e.g., W. F. Albright, *Yahweh and the Gods of Canaan: A Historical Analysis of Two Contrasting Faiths* (London: Athlone Press, 1968), 187–89.

44 FM 3 2 and 3 3 (cf. SBLWAW 41 nos. 51–52); see Durand and Guichard, "Les rituels de Mari."

45 Cf. N. Wasserman and U. Gabbay, "Literatures In Contact: The Balag Úru àm-ma-ir-ra-bi and Its Akkadian Translation UET 6/2, 403," *JCS* 57 (2006) 69–84.

altered state of mind necessary for prophesying, the music is not performed and the musicians can go. In the other text (FM 3 3), the female prophets and the musicians come before the goddess, and there is, again, an interplay between prophesying and lamentation, but the text is too poorly preserved to yield a clear idea of what actually happens. According to a possible reading, if the prophetesses are not able to prophesy, the musicians cover for them by singing a lamentation. In both cases, prophecy coincides with lamentation, which may be taken as an indication of the presumed contents of the prophecy.

A further connection between prophets and musicians is suggested by a document from Mari, which itemizes garments given to two prophets (*muḫḫûm*), two chanters (*nārum*), one *lillatum* (literally "crazy woman"; the title probably indicates ecstatic behavior) and two further persons without titles.[46] There is a marked correspondence between this document and the lexical lists, both Old Babylonian and Neo-Assyrian,[47] that associate prophets (*muḫḫûm/muḫḫūtum, maḫḫû/maḫḫûtu, raggimu/raggintu*) with chanters (*kalû, kalamāḫu*) and lamentation singers (*munambû, lallaru*) on one hand, and with frenzied people (*zabbu/zabbatu*) on the other. Even the gender-neutral people called *assinnu* and *kurgarrû* are included in the same lists and tend to appear together with prophets in other texts, too. This is quite natural: some of these people are known as prophets,[48] and they also perform in rituals of Ištar, especially in frantic dance and battle scenes, carrying bladed weapons, possibly used for self-mutilation; hence the designations *nāš pilaqqi* "carrier of spindel" and *ša kakka našû* "sword-man" in lexical lists.

Music was certainly not the one and only precondition of achieving the prophetic state of mind, but it seems to have been a source of inspiration and one of the elements coexisting with the prophetic activity, at least in a cultic setting. Altogether, the prophets, musicians, and other presenters make up a cultic ensemble with different but partly overlapping roles belonging to the same performative context. This substantiates the performative nature of ancient Near Eastern prophecy, of which even the biblical writers seem to have been well aware, de-

---

46 ARM 21 333 (cf. SBLWAW 41, no. 55); see J.-M. Durand, *Textes administratifs des salles 134 et 160 du Palais de Mari* (ARM 21; Paris: Editions Recherche sur les Civilisations, 1983), 442–49.
47 The lists include *MSL* 12 5.22 (Old Babylonian); 4.212; 4.222 and 6.2 (Neo-Assyrian) (cf. SBLWAW 41 nos. 120, 124, 125, and 126); see M. Civil et al., *The Series* lú = ša *and Related Texts* (MSL 12; Rome: Pontificium Institutum Biblicum, 1969), 102–3, 132, 225–26, 158.
48 I.e., the *assinnus* Šelebum (ARM 26 197, 198, and 213; cf. SBLWAW 41, nos. 7, 8, and 23) and Ili-ḫaznaya (ARM 26 212; cf. SBLWAW 41, no. 22); cf. the three Assyrian prophets whose gender is unclear, Issar-la-tašiyaṭ (SAA 9 1.1 i 28; cf. SBLWAW 41, no. 68), Bayâ (SAA 9 1.4 ii 40; cf. SBLWAW 41, no. 71) and Ilussa-amur (SAA 9 1.5 iii 5–6; cf. SBLWAW 41, no. 72).

spite the biblical (and scholarly) tendencies to dissociate "true" Israelite prophecy from this context.

Prophecy and Lament

The sources are regrettably unspecific about actual manifestations of the interplay of prophecy and music, and the same must be said of prophecy and lament. The relationship is evident, yet difficult to define in detail since there are not many texts in which prophets are explicitly said to perform a lament or to be involved in related acts. The oracles of prophets from Mari and Assyria never actually represent the genre of lamentation, so we have to content ourselves with the above-mentioned ritual texts in which prophets play a role related to lamenting. In addition to the ritual of Ištar at Mari, a prophet is mentioned in the Neo-Assyrian Marduk Ordeal text, where he goes weeping before the Lady of Babylon (that is, the goddess Zarpanitu), bringing her the bad news of the captivity of her husband Marduk.[49]

The behavior of Balaam the seer in the Deir ʿAlla inscription is also reminiscent of lamenting: "When Balaam arose on the morrow, (his) hand [was slack], (his) right hand [hung] low. [He fasted continually] in his chamber, he could not [sleep], and he wept continually" (Comb. I:3–4).[50] What follows, however, is not a lamentation, but an oracle of doom.

Prophets and prophetesses (*maḫḫû* and *maḫḫūtu*) also feature in a ritual that takes place on the 29th day of the month of Tammuz, "when Ištar makes the people of the land wail over Dumuzi, her beloved," to be performed for a person seized by the spirit of a dead person, a demon, or any other evil thing.[51] The ritual involves substantial food offerings, and also some music, to judge from the wind instruments dedicated to Dumuzi. The only thing that is said about the role of the prophets in this ritual is that they are there together with "shepherd boys of Dumuzi" – that is, cult functionaries who intercede on behalf of the sick one – and a frenzied man and woman (*zabbu* and *zabbatu*). The prophets receive a few

---

49 SAA 3 34:28–29 (cf. SBLWAW 41, no. 103); for this text, see T. Frymer-Kensky, "The Tribulations of Marduk: The So-called 'Marduk Ordeal Text,'" *JAOS* 103 (1982) 131–41.

50 J. Hoftijzer and G. van der Kooij, *Aramaic Texts from Deir ʿAlla* (DMOA 19; Leiden: Brill, 1976). Translation according to Choon-Leong Seow in Nissinen, *Prophets and Prophecy in the Ancient Near East*, 210–11 (SBLWAW 41, no. 138).

51 K 2001+; see W. Farber, *Beschwörungsrituale an Ištar und Dumuzi:* Attī Ištar ša harmaša Dumuzi (Veröffentlichungen der Orientalischen Kommission 30; Wiesbaden: Harrassowitz, 1977), 128–62 (cf. SBLWAW 41, no. 118).

pieces of bread and are present when the sick person begins to recite his prayer to Ištar. The performative role of the prophets and ecstatics must be extracted by reading between the lines, but it is probably to mediate the healing power of the goddess and to intercede on behalf of the sick person. This scenery inevitably brings to mind the prophet Isaiah with his fig-cakes at the sickbed of King Hezekiah (2 Kgs 20:1–7), as well as the "songs of the stricken"[52] belonging to the songs composed by King David "through prophecy" (*nĕbûʾa*) according to the great Psalms scroll from Qumran (11Q5 XXVII, 9–10).

The bonding of prophets with lamentation singers in Near Eastern documents finds no exact parallel in the Hebrew Bible since there is no class of cultic functionaries in the temple of Jerusalem equal to the Mesopotamian so-called "lamentation priests." Nevertheless, in the Hebrew Bible, prophecy and lament appear to belong together even more closely than in extrabiblical documents. Chronicles, again, give us the most outspoken evidence of this association by making the prophet Jeremiah the author of the lamentation on Josiah (2 Chr 35:25) and probably inspiring the later tradition of Jeremiah as the author of the book of Lamentations (*B. Bat.* 15a, etc.). Jeremiah, of course, is known as the foremost lamentation singer, unrivaled by anyone but King David the psalmist, by virtue of the book under his name that contains a whole series of laments, often labelled "confessions." Other prophets, too, are presented as uttering lamentations (for instance, Ez 19; 21:11; Am 5:1–3; Jon 2:3–10; Mic 1:8; Hab 1:2–4, 12–17; 2:1; 3:1), and the people are urged to lament by the prophets (Isa 13:6; 14:31; 32:9–14; Jer 6:26; 9:19; Ez 30:2; Joel 1:5–14).

On the whole, the frequency of laments and lament-like poems in the prophetic books of the Hebrew Bible creates a fundamental connection between these two institutions in the conceptual world of the biblical writers. This is not to say anything about the actual origin of the biblical lamentations which, for the most part, are likely to be scribal products with little or no relation to prophetic performances. Evidently, poems like the psalms of Jonah (Jon 2:3–10) or Habakkuk (Hab 3) derive from a reservoir of Hebrew poetry utilized by the au-

52 Provided that this is the correct translation of *pēgûʿîm*; thus, e.g., J. A. Sanders, *The Psalms Scroll of Qumran Cave 11 (11QPs*[a]*)* (DJD 4; Oxford: Clarendon, 1965); cf. J. P. M. van der Ploeg, "Un petit rouleau de psaumes apocryphes (11QpsAp[a])," in *Das frühe Christentum in seiner Umwelt*, FS K. G. Kuhn (ed. G. Jeremias et al.; Göttingen: Vandenhoeck & Ruprecht, 1971) 128–39. For an alternative, calendrical interpretation "intercalary days", see M. Chuytin, "The Redaction of the Qumranic and the Traditional Book of Psalms as Calendar," *RevQ* 63 (1994) 367–97. I am indebted to Mika Pajunen and Torleif Elgvin for having drawn my attention to the problem of the translation of the word.

thors or editors of the respective prophetic books,[53] but it is also thinkable that books like Hosea[54] and Amos[55] include material that originates from actual lamentations after the fall of the Northern Kingdom, whether or not originally uttered by the prophets. What matters from the comparative point of view is that the association of prophecy and lament, well known from the ancient Near East, is acknowledged by the biblical writers for whom it seems to have been a matter of course. In fact, much like in the case of kingship, they have intensified the case to the point that ultimately turns the socioreligious phenomenon of lamenting prophets into a literary construct.

Prophecy and Divine Possession

That ecstasy (*ek-stasis*) – or, if we prefer, possession[56] – was understood as the state of mind required for prophetic inspiration in the ancient Near East, was already suggested in the classic study of Gustaf Hölscher, *Die Profeten*,[57] albeit

---

53 On the psalm of Jonah, cf, e. g., J. Jeremias, *Die Propheten Joel, Obadja, Jona, Micha* (ATD 24/3; Göttingen: Vandenhoeck & Ruprecht, 2007), 91; on the psalm of Habakkuk, cf., e. g., L. Perlitt, *Die Propheten Nahum, Habakuk, Zephanja* (ATD 25/1; Göttingen: Vandenhoeck & Ruprecht, 2004), 82–83.

54 Cf. M. Nissinen, *Prophetie, Redaktion und Fortschreibung im Hoseabuch: Studien zum Werdegang eines Prophetenbuches im Lichte von Hos 4 und 11* (AOAT 231; Kevelaer: Butzon & Bercker; Neukirchen-Vluyn: Neukirchener Verlag, 1991), 308–12, 339–40.

55 Cf. R. G. Kratz, "Die Worte des Amos von Tekoa," in Köckert and Nissinen (eds.), *Propheten in Mari, Assyrien und Israel*, 54–89, esp. 74–76, 80–82.

56 There is no space here for an appropriate discussion of terminology concerning different ways of being possessed or achieving an altered state of mind; R. R. Wilson, for example, makes a difference between trance as a *"psycho-physiological state marked by dissociation"*, whereas possession is a *"cultural theory that explains how contact takes place between the supernatural and natural worlds"* (*Prophecy and Society in Ancient Israel*, 33–34; italics original). For further discusson on the issue of prophecy and ecstasy in recent times, see, e. g., S. B. Parker, "Possession Trance and Prophecy in Pre-Exilic Israel," *VT* 28 (1978) 271–85; Wilson, *Prophecy and Society in Ancient Israel*, 33–42; G. André, "Ecstatic Prophecy in the Old Testament," in *Religious Ecstasy: Based on Papers Read at the Symposium on Religious Ecstasy Held at Abo, Finland, on the 26th–28th of August 1981* (ed. N. G. Holm; Stockholm: Almqvist & Wiksell, 1982) 187–200; Grabbe, *Priests, Prophets, Diviners, Sages*, 108–12; Blenkinsopp, *Sage, Priest, Prophet*, 134–38; T. L. Fenton, "Deuteronomistic Advocacy of the *nābîʾ*: 1 Samuel ix 9 and Questions of Israelite Prophecy," *VT* 47 (1997) 23–42, esp. 31–34; id., "Israelite Prophecy: Characteristics of the First Protest Movement," in *The Elusive Prophet: The Prophet as a Historical Person, Literary Character and Anonymous Artist* (ed. J. C. de Moor; OTS 45; Leiden: Brill, 2001) 129–41, esp. 131–33.

57 G. Hölscher, *Die Profeten* (Leipzig: Hinrichs, 1914).

with minimal contemporary evidence consisting mainly of the story of Elijah and the prophets of Baal on Mount Carmel (1 Kgs 18) and the Egyptian narrative of Wenamun, who gives an account of a "great seer" who becomes ecstatic and delivers an oracle of the god Amon on his behalf to the prince of Byblos.[58] Today, this conviction, shared by a number of scholars since Hölscher,[59] can be confirmed with substantial evidence from Mesopotamia, including the texts quoted above.

The standard prophetic designations *muḫḫûm/muḫḫūtum* and *maḫḫû/maḫḫūtu* are derived from the Akkadian verb *maḫû* "to become crazy, to go into a frenzy,"[60] and this verb is used when referring to prophetic performances. Unfortunately, there are no descriptions of what actually happened on these occasions and how the prophetic ecstasy was achieved. Theoretically, one might suspect that *immaḫḫu*[61] is nothing more than a customary introduction to prophetic speech that has lost its original reference to frenzied behavior. That this is not the case, however, is confirmed by a Neo-Assyrian commentary on the birth omens in *Šumma izbu*, in which the *maḫḫû* are equated with *šēḫānu* "possessed men."[62] Additionally, the above-quoted ritual text from Mari presupposes that the prophetic performance is not successful if the prophet "maintains his equilibrium." On the whole, the god- or spirit-possessed element is likely to have been part of the performative context of ancient Near Eastern prophecy, and the same is probably true for ancient Greek (even though the alleged frenzy of the Pythia has come under suspicion)[63] and Arabian prophecy.[64]

The possessive aspect of prophetic activity is strongly suggested by the Hebrew Bible, too, and there is no need to view this kind of prophecy as an early

---

58 For this text, cf. above, n. 12.

59 Cf., e.g., T. H. Robinson, *Prophecy and the Prophets in Ancient Israel* (London: Duckworth, 1923, ^{2}1953); A. Jepsen, *NABI: Soziologische Studien zur alttestamentlichen Literatur und Religionsgeschichte* (Munich: Beck, 1934); J. Lindblom, *Profetismen i Israel* (Stockholm: Svenska kyrkans diakonistyrelsen, 1934); ET; *Prophecy in Ancient Israel* (Oxford: Blackwell, 1963, ^{2}1973).

60 See *CAD* M/1, pp. 115–16.

61 Cf. ARM 26 213:5–7; 214:6–7; 222:12–14 (SBLWAW 41, nos. 22, 23, and 33, respectively).

62 K 1913: 365d–e (cf. SBLWAW 41, no. 128); see E. Leichty, *The Omen Series Šumma izbu* (TCS 4; Locust Valley, N.Y.: Augustin, 1970), 230–31.

63 On ecstasy and oracles in Greece, see W. Burkert, *Greek Religion* (trans. J. Raffan; Cambridge, Mass.: Harvard University Press, 1985), 109–18; for the Pythia, see, e.g., Rosenberger, *Griechische Orakel*, 48–58.

64 For the Arabian *kāhin* prophets, see J. Hämeen-Anttila, "Arabian Prophecy," in *Prophecy in Its Ancient Near Eastern Context: Mesopotamian, Biblical, and Arabian Perspectives* (ed. M. Nissinen; SBLSymS 13; Atlanta, Ga.: Society of Biblical Literature, 2000) 115–46, esp. 124: "[w]e are told next to nothing of the *kāhins'* possible ecstatic techniques ... In any case, the *kāhin* must have been a shamanlike visionary who forced his familiar spirit to descend upon him."

phenomenon influenced by the so-called "Canaanites."[65] Attempts to make a distinction between the "sober" ecstasy of the biblical prophets and the more frantic, or "orgiastic," ecstasy elsewhere are arbitrary at best.[66] Different types of ecstasy can certainly be recognized and differences between biblical and other accounts can be shown, but no general dividing line between biblical and extrabiblical prophets can be drawn in this respect.

Not only the self-lacerating prophets of Baal (1 Kgs 18:28; cf. *Ugaritica* 5 162:11),[67] but also many prophets of Yahweh engage in ecstatic behavior in the Hebrew Bible, making spirit journeys and seeing heavenly things (2 Kgs 5:26; 6:17; Ez 3:12–15; 8; 11; 37:1–14; 40–48; cf. Paul in 2 Cor 12:1–5). In fact, like in the Near East, presence in the divine council is required of a true prophet (1 Kgs 22:19–23; Isaiah 6; Jer 23:16–22; Am 3:7),[68] and seeing visions, which is one of the basic methods of obtaining a prophetic message (cf. Ez 1; 10; Am 7:1–9; 8:1–3; 9:1–4; Zech 1–6), requires an altered state of mind. No qualitative difference can be made between biblical and extrabiblical, or Israelite and non-Israelite, prophets: "[i]f Ezekiel does not have ecstatic experiences, then we have no criteria to judge that *anyone* of antiquity had such experiences."[69]

Another aspect of the divine possession of the prophets is also their God-given privilege to indulge in extravagant behavior like Isaiah's going naked for three years (Isa 20:1–6), Ezekiel's unusual carryings-on (Ez 4–6; 12; 24:15–27), Jeremiah's celibacy (Jer 16:1–9), and Hosea's marriage with the woman of bad reputation (Hos 1). "Symbolic acts" like these are not so well known from ancient Near Eastern documents – what comes to mind is the prophet eating raw lamb in

65 Thus Hölscher, *Die Profeten*, and A. Jepsen, *NABI: Soziologische Studien zur alttestamentlichen Literatur und Religionsgeschichte* (Munich: Beck'sche Verlagsbuchhandlung, 1934); cf. J. Lindblom, "Zur Frage des kanaanäischen Ursprungs des altisraelitischen Prophetismus," in *Von Ugarit nach Qumran*, FS O. Eissfeldt (ed. J. Hempel and L. Rost; Berlin: Töpelmann, 1958) 89–104.

66 I agree with Lester Grabbe, according to whom such distinctions "seem nothing but willful attempts to bolster a partisan view of the 'classical' Israelite prophets" (*Priests, Prophets, Diviners, Sages*, 110); Grabbe hereby criticizes the views of André, "Ecstatic Prophecy in the Old Testament," and Parker, "Possession Trance and Prophecy in Pre-Exilic Israel."

67 Cf. J. J. M. Roberts, "A New Parallel to 1 Kings 18:28–29," *JBL* 89 (1970) 76–77 (repr. in id., *The Bible and the Ancient Near East: Collected Essays* [Winona Lake, Ind., 2002] 102–3).

68 Cf. M. Nissinen, "Prophets and the Divine Council", in: U. Hübner and E.A. Knauf (eds.), *Kein Land für sich allein: Studien zum Kulturkontakt in Kanaan, Israel/Palästina und Ebirnâri für Manfred Weippert zum 65. Geburtstag* (OBO 186; Freiburg Schweiz and Göttingen, 2002), pp. 1–19 (= pp. 461–77 in this volume).

69 Grabbe, *Priests, Prophets, Diviners, Sages*, 110.

front of the city gate in a letter from Mari[70] – and they have usually not been classified as instances of ecstasy. Nevertheless, they certainly imply a mental condition that in modern times might cause the person in question to be sent to a lunatic asylum; for contemporaries, however, they were meant to signify divine possession.

Regardless of its etymology, which is probably not related to ecstatic behavior,[71] the use of the derivatives of the Hebrew root *nb'* often implies an altered state of mind,[72] corresponding to the Akkadian words *maḫû* and its derivatives, the equation of which with "possession" renders exactly the same idea as the words of Samuel to Saul preparing him to meet the prophets of Gebah: "The Spirit of the Lord will come upon you, and you will prophesy with them; and you will be changed into a different person" (1 Sam 10:6). Saul's frenzy is accompanied by music, perhaps the same way as the musicians of Mari responded to the performances of the prophets. On the other hand, the prophesying of the Levitical singers is equated with their songs of praise to God, accompanied by musical instruments (1 Chr 25:1, 3, 6, 7). While the case of Saul seems to be presented by the narrator as something no longer belonging to the implied reader's world (cf. 1 Sam 9:12), the Chronicler's association of music, prophecy and temple cult not only corresponds to the Near Eastern evidence but suggests that prophetic inspiration was part and parcel of the cultic performance even in the Second Temple of Jerusalem.[73]

Whether or not connected with musical or other performative elements, the state of being possessed by the spirit (*in-spiratio*) is presented as the precondition for prophesying even elsewhere in the Bible, from Moses and his elders (Num 11:24–30) to Third Isaiah (Isa 61:1), Ezekiel (Ez 2:2, etc.), Hosea (Hos 9:7), Joel (3:1–2), Micha (Mic 3:8), Jesus (Luke 4:14–20) – and beyond: in the great Psalms scroll from Qumran, King David the musician (cf. 11Q5 XXVIII, 4 [= Ps 151:2]) is said to have composed his works "through prophecy" (*nĕbû'â*)

70 ARM 26 206:5–24 (cf. SBLWAW 41, no. 16); for this text, see, e.g., J.-G. Heintz, "La 'fin' des prophètes bibliques? Nouvelles théories et documents sémitiques anciens," in id. (ed.), *Oracles et prophéties dans l'antiquité*, 195–214, esp. 202–12.

71 For recent studies on the etymology of Hebrew *nābî'* and Akkadian *nabûm*, see D. E. Fleming, "The Etymological Origins of the Hebrew *nābî'*: The One Who Invokes God," *CBQ* 55 (1993) 217–24; Fenton, "Deuteronomistic Advocacy of the *nābî'*," 34–36 ("speaker").

72 Cf. Num 11:24–30; 1 Sam 10:5–6, 10, 13; 18:10; 19:20, 21, 23–24; 1 Kgs 18:29; 22:10; cf. also the designation *mĕšugga'* "mad" in 2 Kgs 9:11; Jer 29:26; Hos 9:7.

73 For prophecy, music, and inspiration in Chronicles, see Schniedewind, *The Word of God in Transition*, 170–88.

under the influence of "a discerning and enlightened spirit" from God (11Q5 XXVII, 4, 11).

Divine possession did not always result in extraordinary activity, though. It seems that the ecstatic element of prophecy became problematic along with the scribalization of prophecy and the prophetic ideal during the Second Temple period at the latest.[74] This is indicated by a few defamatory statements about prophets (Hos 9:7–9; Zech 13:2–6; cf. Jer 29:26), implying a dubious attitude towards the traditional image, social role and performative culture of the prophets, including ecstatic or otherwise extraordinary comportment.[75] When the authoritative prophetic role was taken over by scribes and wisdom teachers, this happened greatly at the expense of the traditional performative culture, which was more or less driven into the margins of the society. The word of God was now written down, and the primary prophetic tasks were its study and interpretation. But even this was not done without the inspiration coming from God.

Philo of Alexandria would hardly have spoken of prophets possessed by God (*theophorētos, Spec.* 1:65), or explained his own experience with a state of divine possession (*hypo katokhēs entheou*) and "corybantic frenzy" (*korybantia; Migr.* 34–35), without having been familiar with the tradition of prophetic spirit possession, whether through Plato, or his Jewish education, or both.[76] Philo's description of his experience shows, among other things, that there is no reason to make a sharp universal distinction between ecstatic experience and being filled with the spirit of wisdom. As prophecy became more and more equated with the study and interpretation of the Scriptures, this became a spirit-driven enterprise: "I will again pour out doctrine like prophecy, and bequeath it to future generations," says Ben Sira (Sir 24:33),[77] who understood the task of the wise man to be the study of the Law, the prophecies and the sayings of famous men (39:1–3). "If

74 Fenton, "Israelite Prophecy," reckons with a "new prophecy" in Israel and Judah that distances itself from the "old" prophetic frenzy: "The new prophets transform the role of the ancient Near Eastern prophet, modifying or reacting against his traditional function and behaviour" (139); cf. also Blenkinsopp, *Sage, Priest, Prophet*, 138–154. The problem is whether this transformation of prophecy can really be traced hack to pre-exilic prophetic figures or whether it is essentially a later development.

75 Cf. M. Nissinen, "The Dubious Image of Prophecy," in Floyd and Haak (eds.), *Prophets, Prophecy, and Prophetic Texts in Second Temple Judaism*, 26–41 (= pp. 577–96 in this volume).

76 See J. R. Levison, "Philo's Personal Experience and the Persistence of Prophecy," in Floyd and Haak (eds.), *Prophets, Prophecy, and Prophetic Texts in Second Temple Judaism*, 194–209, esp. 197–202.

77 Ben Sira's view of prophecy has been recently analyzed by P. C. Beentjes, "Prophets and Prophecy in the Book of Ben Sira," in Floyd and Haak (eds.), *Prophets, Prophecy, and Prophetic Texts in Second Temple Judaism*, 135–50.

it is the will of the great Lord, he will be filled with a spirit of intelligence; then he will pour out wise sayings of his own and give thanks to the Lord in prayer" (39:6). This, too, is spirit possession, now happening in the *bêt midrāš* of the scribe rather than as a part of a cultic performance. Hence, we arrive at inspiration by learning, teaching, and research, which even for today's audience may be more acceptable, or at least more familiar, than the traditional type of prophetic frenzy.

A different trajectory of traditional prophetic tradition can be seen in the strong prophetic-charismatic element in the activity of John the Baptist and his ilk (Mk 1:6; cf. Zech 13:4), and also in early Christianity. Even music is not absent from the picture: Paul associates music with glossolaly and prophetic revelation (1 Cor 14:7, 15, 26), and according to the Letter to the Ephesians, Christians should not be intoxicated by wine but filled by the Spirit, singing psalms, hymns, and spiritual songs (Eph 5:18–20; cf. Col 3:16). Without being explicitly about prophecy, this passage is reminiscent of the Levite singers prophesying by means of music and singing "thanks and praise to the Lord" in 1 Chr 25:1–7.

Given the nature of the documentation, it is not easy to draw a coherent picture of prophecy, music, lament and divine possession in the ancient Near East. By and large, however, while details remain vague, the recurrent association of these four elements in various text types from different periods of time suggests that the whole network is not purely coincidental. Mesopotamian lexical lists show that their compilers associated prophets with ecstatics and lamentation singers; the outlay of garments from Mari has prophets appearing together with musicians as recipients of royal gifts; and in the ritual text from Mari, the whole band plays together. All this supports the understanding that prophecy in the ancient Near East indeed belonged to the same performative context with ecstatic actions, music, and lament. The Hebrew Bible, again, gives a clear impression that things were not different in the world of the authors and editors of the biblical texts, regardless of their dating. The God-possessed behavior of the prophets, a salient feature of ancient Near Eastern prophecy, may not always enjoy the undivided appreciation of biblical writers – or biblical scholars – but it is acknowledged and usually not condemned. Lament is brought into a closer contact with prophecy in the Bible than anywhere else in Near Eastern sources, and the prophetic performance is sometimes even accompanied by music.

Conclusion

The above survey of two chosen aspects supports the view that what we call prophecy, that is, the kind of divination that involves a nontechnical transmission of divine knowledge, is a genuinely cross-cultural phenomenon within the ancient Near Eastern context. Arriving at this conclusion should no longer come as a hair-raising surprise to anyone; rather, it confirms what has already been the conviction of many scholars for a century. However, it seems like the Near Eastern substratum of prophecy has not yet quite attracted the attention it deserves. There are still more than enough studies on biblical or Israelite prophecy uninterested in its wider cultural context, as well as presentations of Near Eastern religions that leave the issue of prophecy untouched. Today, having a substantial documentation at our disposal, the time is ripe for a fuller contextualization of biblical prophecy as well as for a general appreciation of prophecy as a permanent and significant factor in the history of Near Eastern religion.

The second conclusion to be drawn is that the Hebrew Bible is not only an invaluable source for but also a characeristic representative of the prophetic phenomenon – just one among others, however, not the paragon by which the prophetic quality of other sources should be defined or evaluated. In view of the above survey, there is no need to view the common elements between biblical and Near Eastern prophecy as "Canaanite" or otherwise foreign influences, alien to the genuine "Israelite" prophecy. The evidence rather suggests a local variation of the prophetic phenomenon common to the ancient Near East, or better, to the Eastern Mediterranean world.

This is not to programmatically exclude indigenous features in biblical prophecy, and this brings me to the third conclusion concerning the nature of the sources. As pointed out before, we cannot compare prophets with prophets but only texts with other texts. Whether biblical or nonbiblical, the extant documents are never neutral reports on prophetic activities but tendentious and often haphazard glimpses that come to us through several filters consisting of the authors, editors, archivists and interpreters of the texts. Therefore, historical conclusions concerning the factuality of the events reported by the sources are often difficult to draw. On the other hand, it is also interesting and rewarding to observe who writes what and why, as far as this can be discerned from the texts – for example, how certain features of prophecy, like the biblical prophets' engagement in lamentations, are highlighted by the biblical writers, or how the communication between prophets and kings becomes more intensive, but also develops a distinctive character when we move from the Deuteronomistic History to the Chronicles.

An important distinctive feature of the Hebrew Bible is its nature as a canonized corpus of literature, written over several centuries. Being what it is, the Hebrew Bible testifies to a formidable aspect in the history of prophecy that is not documented anywhere else in the ancient Eastern Mediterranean cultural sphere. The very emergence of the biblical corpus has produced the type of prophecy here labelled as "biblical prophecy," and thereby contributed to an unprecedented understanding of prophecy as inspired interpretation of authoritative texts, which also led to new ways of experiencing what it means to be possessed by the spirit.

Comparing Prophetic Sources: Principles and a Test Case

1 Ancient Near Eastern Prophecy as the Context of Biblical Prophecy

1.1 Prophetic Studies in Transition

Increasing knowledge of ancient Near Eastern prophetic texts has during the last couple of decades led to a growing awareness of prophecy in the ancient kingdoms of Israel and Judah as an integral rather than antagonistic factor in the Near Eastern socio-religious milieu. Thanks to the much-improved documentation, it can be seen today better than ever that the biblical text demonstrates the Near Eastern cultural roots of prophecy in Israel and Judah in multiple ways. On the other hand, however, the biblical text also introduces features of prophecy difficult to explain on the basis of the common Near Eastern background.[1] Hence, the age-old question of comparability of the biblical text with other Near Eastern material inescapably raises itself, with high expectations. Given this propitious research situation, it is my purpose in this essay to outline some methodological principles of such comparison, as well as to present a test case which I hope to be helpful in clarifying these principles.

The selection of ancient Near Eastern documents of prophecy that we have at our disposal at the beginning of the third millennium CE is well known already and need not be described here in detail; suffice it to repeat the common knowledge that there are two corpora of Mesopotamian prophetic documents, one found in the archives of the Old Babylonian state of Mari from the eighteenth century BCE,[2] and another in the archives of the Neo-Assyrian empire in Nineveh

1 For a more thorough discussion, see M. Nissinen, "Biblical Prophecy from a Near Eastern Perspective: The Cases of Kingship and Divine Possession," in *Congress Volume, Ljubljana 2007* (ed. A. Lemaire; VTSup 133; Leiden: Brill, 2010) 441–68 (= pp. 351–75 in this volume).

2 J.-M. Durand, *Archives épistolaires de Mari I.1* (ARM 26/1; Paris, Éditions Recherce sur les Civilisations, 1988). A few pertinent texts (ARM 26 371, 372 and 414) were published by F. Joannès in D. Charpin, F. Joannès, S. Lackenbacher, and B. Lafont, *Archives èpistolaires de Mari 1/2* (ARM 26/2; Paris: Editions Recherche sur les Civilisations, 1988).

DOI 10.1515/9783110466546-020

from the seventh century BCE,[3] and so roughly contemporary with important biblical prophetic figures such as Isaiah and Jeremiah. In addition to these, there is scattered evidence of prophecy in different parts of Mesopotamia from the twenty-first to the second century BCE, as well as a few telling examples of prophecy in the West Semitic milieu, temporally and geographically close to the kingdoms of Israel and Judah.[4] All this evidence comprises more than 170 individual texts which make up a literature well comparable in size to the biblical corpus of prophetic books.[5]

The ancient Near Eastern selection of prophetic documents, however, should not be viewed as a kind of extra-biblical prophetic canon. Its composition may vary according to different criteria of defining a text as "prophetic", and it can quite realistically be expected to grow when new documents are found or previously known texts are recognized as evidence of prophecy.[6] In fact, the Neo-Assyrian oracles, published by Simo Parpola in 1998, began to be seriously considered as prophecy only in the late 1960s, in spite of the fact that some of them were already recognized as such by the end of the nineteenth century.[7] Even the documentation from Mari has been expanded by several important texts since Jean-Marie Durand's edition of 1988.[8] The newest document mentioning

---

3 S. Parpola, *Assyrian Prophecies* (SAA 9; Helsinki: HelsinkiUniversity Press, 1997). Cf. also M. Nissinen, *References to Prophecy in Neo-Assyrian Sources* (SAAS 7; Helsinki: The Neo-Assyrian Text Corpus Project, 1998).

4 See Martti Nissinen, with contributions by C.-L. Seow, R. K. Ritner, and H. Craig Melchert, *Prophets and Prophecy in the Ancient Near East* (2nd edition, SBLWAW 41; Atlanta: Society of Biblical Literature, 2019),

5 Hence I do not quite share the opinion of D. W. Rooke ("Prophecy," in *The Oxford Handbook of Biblical Studies* [ed. J. W. Rogerson and J. M. Lieu; Oxford: Oxford University Press, 2006] 385–96, 392), according to whom "[t]he major problem with attempted comparisons between Israelite and other types of ancient Near Eastern prophecy is the very small amount of information that is available about the other types".

6 For example, the Old Babylonian letter containing a message from Ištar, possibly sent by a prophet to a deputy of the king of Uruk (W19900, 1 = SBLWAW 41 135a; see B. Pongratz-Leisten, "When the Gods Are Speaking: Toward Defining the Interface between Polytheism and Monotheism," in M. Köckert and M. Nissinen [eds.], *Propheten in Mari, Assyrien und Israel* [FRLANT 201; Göttingen: Vandenhoeck & Ruprecht, 2003], 132–68, 155–56).

7 For the early history of their research, see Parpola, *Assyrian Prophecies*, xiii–xiv.

8 For additional texts, see, for example, H. B. Huffmon, "The Expansion of Prophecy in the Mari Archives: New Texts, New Readings, New Information," in *Prophecy and Prophets: The Diversity of Contemporary Issues in Scholarship* (ed. Y. Gitay; SBL Semeia Studies; Atlanta: Society of Biblical Literature, 1997) 7–22; J. J. M. Roberts, *The Bible and the Ancient Near East* (Winona Lake, IN: Eisenbrauns, 2002), 157–253; D. Charpin, "Prophètes et rois dans le Proche-Orient amorrite: Nouvelles données, nouvelles perspectives," in *Florilegium marianum 6*, FS A. Parrot (ed. id. and J.-M. Durand; Mémoires de NABU 7; Paris: SEPOA, 2002) 7–38.

a prophet was recently found in an archive excavated at Ziyaret Tepe.[9] All this evidence justifies the statement that we are only beginning to recognize fully something that was suggested long ago by critical scholars but which was difficult to substantiate: that biblical prophecy is but a part—though a distinctive and in many ways unique part—of a larger picture. The next step following this observation is to ask why it is necessary. What do we know now that we did not know before? What kind of changes does this knowledge bring about in our view of biblical prophecy, or prophecy in general?

1.2 The Perils and Advantages of Comparative Studies

Comparative studies, with all their perils and advantages, are a natural consequence of asking the aforementioned questions. In most cases this means comparison between the Bible and extra-biblical documents, which is a worthwhile but dangerous enterprise—worthwhile because it serves the purpose of viewing the biblical text in its cultural context, and dangerous because it easily leads to sweeping generalizations or to a goal-directed exploitation of ancient Near Eastern sources to justify Bible-based and sometimes questionable claims. If the prophets from Mesopotamia and Syria are seen primarily as forerunners of the biblical prophets and the ancient Near East as the "context of Scripture", it is difficult to change the Bible-centred perspective into a more comprehensive view of prophecy as an ancient Near Eastern phenomenon, documented by sources, the general significance of which is not dependent on their applicability to biblical studies.

We should never forget to ask: "Why am I doing this?", "What do I actually want to know?" Scholars are often blamed for importing hidden agendas into discussion—both those labelled as "revisionists" and others with a conspicuous predilection for early datings. Indeed, probably every scholar works under presuppositions that may be difficult to render explicit to the scholarly community, sometimes even to oneself.

Let me try to answer these questions for my own part. I am not particularly "in search of pre-exilic Israel", even though I have learned a lot from a volume with this title that I am happy to quote in this essay.[10] I am keenly interested in the history of the kingdoms of Israel and Judah, and I would love to know more about prophecy as practised in those kingdoms. However, I do not think that the

9 S. Parpola, "Cuneiform Texts from Ziyaret Tepe (Tušḫan) 2002–2003," *SAAB* 17 (2008): 1–113.
10 J. Day (ed.), *In Search of Pre-Exilic Israel* (JSOTSup 406; London: T & T Clark, 2004).

pre-exilic period has an intrinsic value, and I do not consider pre-exilic sources more valuable than post-exilic ones. I do not exclude the possibility that some texts of the Hebrew Bible can be best explained against pre-exilic circumstances, but I am also open to readings of prophetic passages from the point of view of post-monarchical concerns. Moreover, I would like to ask what kind of comparisons could be made without precise knowledge of the age and historical context of the texts and how this might enhance our understanding of ancient prophecy.

A further challenge to comparative studies is related to the diversity of the ancient Near Eastern sources for prophecy, including the Hebrew Bible. There are many ways of documenting prophecy; hence it must be carefully considered what kind of historical information is obtainable from each source, be it a written oracle,[11] an entry appearing in a word-list,[12] a legal document,[13] a letter reporting a prophetic appearance,[14] a paraphrase of prophetic words in a literary context,[15] or a prophetic book, a genre known only from the Hebrew Bible. It is a major methodological challenge to determine how each individual piece of this multifarious documentation contributes to drawing the larger picture.

Whether biblical or extra-biblical, the available set of sources our knowledge is extracted from does not yield a full picture of the prophetic phenomenon at any historical moment. The selection of documents at our disposal, which are virtually always *texts*, is the result of a huge process, beginning sometimes with the spoken word of a prophet, sometimes with the pen or stylus of a scribe, and ending with a publication, whether a printed version of the Bible or a scholarly edition of an ancient text with an archaeological provenance. This process is random on one hand and systematic on the other. It is random because the discovery of ancient documents is unavoidably a matter of chance. Whether it is the result of sheer coincidence like Qumran or Nag Hammadi, or the result of responsible archaeological work, it is quite certain that not everything has been found

11 For example, the Assyrian oracles published in SAA 9 (Parpola, *Assyrian Prophecies*).

12 For example, the lexical lists MSL 12 4.212 and 4.222 (M. Civil et al., *The Series lú = ša and Related Texts* [MSL 12; Rome: Pontificium Institutum Biblicum, 1969], 103, 132).

13 For example, the donation of a silver ring to a prophet (ARM 25 142; see J.-M. Durand, *Archives épistolaires de Mari 1/1* [ARM 26/1; Paris: Editions Recherche sur les Civilisations, 1988], 380–81).

14 For example, the letter of Mar-Issar to Esarhaddon reporting a prophecy uttered on the occasion of the substitute king ritual at Akkad (SAA 10 352; see S. Parpola, *Letters from Assyrian and Babylonian Scholars* [SAA 10; Helsinki: Helsinki University Press, 1993], 228–29).

15 For example, the quotation of words of Ištar to Assurbanipal concerning his Mannean campaign (Prism A iii 4–10; see J. Novotny and J. Jeffers, *The Royal Inscriptions of Ashurbanipal (668–631 BC), Aššur-etel-ilāni (630–627 BC), and Sîn-šarra-iškun (626–612 BC), Kings of Assyria*, Part 1 (RINAP 5/1; University Park, Pa.: Eisenbrauns, 2018), 239).

so far, and so our picture remains incomplete. The systematic element comes into play with the fact that we are entirely dependent on the scribes who decided which prophecies were considered worth writing down, the archivists and librarians who selected the material they wanted to keep in their collections, and the editors of the biblical books who created the image and ideology of the prophets in the Hebrew Bible. What we see is the outcome of this process, the reconstruction of which is a matter of careful methodological consideration.

Comparing ancient Near Eastern prophecy with ancient Hebrew prophecy is an especially demanding task. With the exception of two or three letters from Lachish which mention prophets,[16] there is nothing outside the Hebrew Bible that informs us about the prophetic phenomenon in ancient Israel and Judah in the monarchical or even in the Persian period. The Hebrew Bible, again, is a literary composition unparalleled by any ancient Near Eastern document, and, therefore, presents a particular challenge to comparison, especially if it aims at historical reconstruction. Since this requires a fair amount of knowledge of the historical context of the sources, one of the most important tasks in historical comparison is the dating of the sources.

1.3 The Problem of Dating

Anyone familiar with the critical study of the Bible knows how arduous a task the dating of the prophetic texts (or any text) of the Hebrew Bible can be, and how many divergent opinions, based on different methodological approaches, have been introduced into the discussion. In practical terms, anyone who wants to compare biblical and extra-biblical prophetic sources must face a question akin to the following: "How can one prove that anything comes from the eighth rather than, say, the fifth century BCE?" Hugh Williamson has recently discussed this question, admitting that "in the case of texts which are demonstrably more than 2000 years old, nothing can be 'proved'", and suggests some relevant methodical ways of establishing reasonable probabilities.[17] This is certainly true for biblical texts, but it must be added that the extra-biblical material which is even older, can, as will be demonstrated below, often be dated rather precisely. When it comes to the Bible, however, we can no longer choose

16 That is, the Lachish ostraca 3 and 16 (see C.-L. Seow, "West Semitic Sources," in Nissinen, Prophets and Prophecy, nos. 139 and 141); some scholars reconstruct to word *h*[*nb'*], even in ostracon 6, line 5, but this reading is primarily inspired by Jer. 38:4.

17 H. G. M. Williamson, ""In Search of the Pre-Exilic Isaiah," in Day (ed.), *In Search of Pre-Exilic Israel*, 181–206, esp. p. 182–83.

from two alternatives regarding the authorship of a given verse in the prophetic books—that is, the assumption of the authorship of the prophet to which the book is ascribed until the contrary is proved, or *vice versa*. The situation is far more complex than that. Every dating, early and late alike, has to be, if not "proved", then at least corroborated with positive arguments, the more convincing the better.

It goes without saying that one and the same biblical passage can be interpreted against the background of different periods of time. To use the book of Amos as an example of recent scholarship, there is an intriguing reading of it as a late post-exilic book reflecting the concerns of the pious poor, the *ʿănāwîn*, of the third century BCE.[18] On the other hand, there are also attempts to give an early date even to those passages of the book that are traditionally regarded as later additions, such as the last verses of the book in ch. 9.[19] Both views are based on sophisticated argumentation, the validity of which is a matter of dispute. The worst we can do is to resort to the kind of circular reasoning which makes the social crisis of the eighth century BCE and the social criticism in the book of Amos dependent on each other. As Walter Houston puts it, "we cannot date any specific text in these books [*scil.* Isaiah, Amos and Micah] to the eighth century simply on the grounds of its subject matter. But there *was* a social crisis in the eighth century."[20] It is up to scholarly insight to decide to what extent a given text originally has to do with this or another crisis.

It is most fortunate that many of the ancient Near Eastern prophetic sources can rather easily be located in history. In fact, the two major corpora of prophetic texts, those from Mari and Assyria, can be dated fairly accurately without major problems. Almost all prophetic texts from Mari date from the time of King Zimri-Lim, who reigned a decade and a half from c. 1774 to c. 1760 BCE.[21] Thanks to the efforts of Mari scholars, we are now able to reconstruct the events of this period with greater precision than ever, which often yields an individual prophetic document a more or less certain historical background. A good example of

---

18 C. Levin, "Das Amosbuch der Anawim," *ZTK* 94 (1997): 407–36.

19 M. A. Sweeney, "The Dystopianization of Utopian Prophetic Literature: The Case of Amos 9:11–15," in *Utopia and Dystopia in Prophetic Literature* (ed. E. Ben Zvi; PFES 92; Helsinki: Finnish Exegetical Society, 2006), 175–85.

20 W. Houston, "Was There a Social Crisis in the Eighth Century?," in Day (ed.), *In Search of Pre-Exilic Israel*, 130–49, esp. p. 147; emphasis original.

21 For a historical overview of this period, see D. Charpin, "Histoire politique du Proche-Orient amorrite (2002–1595)," in *Mesopotamien: Die altbabylonische Zeit* (ed. id., D. O. Edzard and M. Stol; OBO 160/4; Fribourg: Academic Press; Göttingen: Vandenhoeck & Ruprecht, 2004) 25–480, 192–316.

this are the letters of Nur-Sîn to Zimri-Lim (FM 7 38 and 39) that are connected with Zimri-Lim's affairs in Alalakh in the mid-1760s BCE.[22] The extant Assyrian prophecies, again, are all addressed to Kings Esarhaddon (681–669 BCE) and Assurbanipal (668–627 BCE). One of them has a date written in the colophon,[23] and most of them are well understandable against the background of three historical events: the civil war preceding Esarhaddon's rise to power and his enthronement (681–680 BCE); the appointment of Assurbanipal as the crown prince of Assyria (672 BCE); and the revolt of his brother, Šamaš-šumu-ukin (652–648 BCE).[24] Even other prophetic sources sometimes bear exact dates, as is the case with the astronomical diary reporting a prophetic appearance in Babylonia in the month of Tishri, 133 BCE.[25]

When it comes to the Hebrew Bible, the situation is totally different. This difficulty is due to what the (Hebrew) Bible is: a canonized composition of texts of different age as the result of a centuries-long editorial process. Hard evidence of this process is available to us from a very late period only, and the earliest text-critical evidence shows that by the beginning of the Common Era the text of this composition was still not completely fixed. Since it is presumable that this composition includes a fair amount of text material that is older, the methodological question arises how to identify and date the textual evidence embedded in the late composition that in all likelihood dates from earlier periods. I repeat this common knowledge in order to demonstrate how different the sources are that we have at hand when we start comparing biblical texts with ancient Near Eastern documents.

With regard to source criticism, the main difference between biblical and other ancient Near Eastern documents lies in the process of transmission. The chronological distance between the Near Eastern prophetic documents and their presumable origin in the oral performance of the prophets varies from a few days to a decade, whereas in the case of the biblical prophetic texts as we have them, we have to reckon with centuries. The editorial processes were prob-

22 See J.-M. Durand, *Florilegium Marianum 7: Le Culte d'Addu d'Alep et l'affaire d'Alahtum* (Mémoires de NABU 8; Paris: SEPOA, 2002), 59–97, 134–40.

23 SAA 9 9 r. 6–7; see Parpola, *Assyrian Prophecies*, 41.

24 For the dates of the Assyrian oracles, see ibid., lxviii–lxxi.

25 *AD* 3-132B and -132C; see A. J. Sachs and H. Hunger, *Astronomical Diaries and Related Texts from Babylonia*, vol. 3: *Diaries from 164 B.C. to 61 B.C.* (Österreichische Akademie der Wissenschaften, Philosophisch-historische Klasse, Denkschriften 247; Vienna: Österreichische Akademie der Wissenschaften, 1996), 216–19, 224–25, and cf. M. Nissinen, "A Prophetic Riot in Seleucid Babylonia," in *"Wer darf hinaufsteigen zum Berg JHWH's": Beiträge zu Prophetie und Poesie des Alten Testaments*, FS S. Ö. Steingrímsson (ed. H. Irsigler; ATSAT 72; St Ottilien: EOS, 2002) 63–74 (= pp. 301–11 in this volume).

ably similar in the beginning: there were scribes who wrote down their versions of the prophecies according to their own discretion, and archivists who decided what they wanted to file away in their archives. Moreover, the compilation of collections of oracles probably required taking some documents and leaving the others. All this creates a distance between the spoken and the written word, which cannot be presumed to be identical. The so-called *ipsissima verba* remain unreachable in both cases.[26]

What makes the Hebrew Bible different from any other ancient Near Eastern source is the length, the depth and the purpose of the editorial activity that turned prophecy into literature. There is evidence of the beginnings of editorial activity in the Assyrian documents that reinterpret prophetic words to new audiences, transcending specific historical situations.[27] However, the huge scribal prolongation of the prophetic process of communication in post-monarchical Yehud, triggered by the radical socio-religious and political crisis inflicted by the loss of the Temple and kingship and the change in demographic status and worldview, is without parallel in the Near East. Written prophetic documents from the Near East can usually be considered an interpretation of the spoken word of a prophet or of a previously written text. And yet, only in the Hebrew Bible do we have prophetic books which are "by definition reinterpretive documents, whose writers reapply patterns of divine–human interaction discerned in one particular historical context to another later historical context" in such a way that, "in final analysis the prophetic viewpoint expressed in a prophetic book owes more to the writer than to the original prophet".[28] The scribal activity producing literary prophecy may not be the "proprium" of biblical prophecy as such,[29] but the literary process that designed the genre of the prophetic book and

---

26 Cf. K. van der Toorn, "From the Oral to the Written: The Case of the Old Babylonian Prophecy," in *Writings and Speech in Israelite and Ancient Near Eastern Prophecy* (ed. E. Ben Zvi and M. H. Floyd; SBL Symposium Series 10; Atlanta: Society of Biblical Literature, 2000) 219–34, 228–33; M. Nissinen, "How Prophecy Became Literature," *SJOT* 19 (2005) 153–72.

27 The collection SAA 9 1 was probably compiled around 672 BCE from oracles proclaimed in 681 and/or 680 BCE (see Parpola, *Assyrian Prophecies*, lxviii–lxx). The purpose of the original prophecies was to support Esarhaddon's rise to power, which was on shaky grounds because of the civil war. The investiture of Assurbanipal as crown prince in 672 made it necessary to remind the Assyrians of the divine election of Esarhaddon a decade earlier.

28 M. H. Floyd, "The Production of Prophetic Books in the Early Second Temple Period," in Floyd and Haak (ed.), *Prophets, Prophecy, and Prophetic Texts in Second Temple Judaism* (LHBOTS 427; New York and London: T & T Clark, 2006), 276–97, esp. p. 290.

29 This conviction of J. Jeremias ("Das Proprium der alttestamentlichen Prophetie," *ThLZ* 119 [1994] 483–94) has recently been challenged by A. Lange ("Literary Prophecy and Oracle Collection: A Comparison between Judah and Greece in Persian Times," in *Prophets, Prophecy,*

gave the concept of prophecy a new meaning[30]— indeed, *created* the concept of prophecy as we have inherited it, whether as scholars, or as believing Jews, Christians or Muslims—is certainly unparalleled in the ancient Near East, at least to the best of our present knowledge.

1.4 What Is Being Compared?

As a consequence of the above reflections, I would like to suggest that, whenever involved in comparative studies in prophecy, we should try to be consistent in comparing sources, not prophets.[31] We cannot claim to be able to compare the prophet Amos of Tekoa with the prophet Bayâ of Arbela, since it is highly improbable that we have any access to historical personalities called by these names in a few particular texts. What can we do, then? Obviously, we can read the book bearing the name of the prophet Amos and the Assyrian oracle collections that include prophecies allegedly uttered by Bayâ, and make all kinds of observations.

---

and Prophetic Texts in Second Temple Judaism [ed. M. H. Floyd and R. D. Haak; LHBOTS 427; New York: T & T Clark International, 2006] 248–75) on the basis of ancient Near Eastern texts and, above all, Greek oracle collections.

30 The crucial impact of the literary process of the prophetic books on the biblical image of prophets and prophecy has been highlighted by many scholars from different perspectives; for more recent contributions, see, for example, E. Ben Zvi, "The Prophetic Book: A Key Form of Prophetic Literature," in *The Changing Face of Form Criticism for the Twenty-First Century* (ed. id. and M. A. Sweeney; Grand Rapids, Mich.: Eerdmans, 2003) 276–97; R. G. Kratz, "Das Neue in der Prophetie des Alten Testaments," in *Prophetie in Israel: Beiträge des Symposiums "Das Alte Testament und die Kultur der Moderne"*, GS G. von Rad (ed. I. Fischer, K. Schmid, and H. G. M. Williamson; Altes Testament und Moderne 11; Münster: LIT, 2003) 1–22; C. Levin, "Das Wort Jahwes an Jeremia: Zur ältesten Redaktion der jeremianischen Sammlung," *ZTK* 101 (2004) 257–80; M. H. Floyd, "The Production of Prophetic Books in the Early Second Temple Period," in Floyd and Haak (eds.), *Prophets, Prophecy, and Prophetic Texts*, 276–97; K. van der Toom, *Scribal Culture and the Making of the Hebrew Bible* (Cambridge, MA: Harvard University Press, 2007), 173–204.

31 Rooke ("Prophecy," 392) is right in her contention that "the safest comparison is at the level of the texts rather than at the level of what kind of activity might have produced the texts"; equally right is H. M. Barstad ("*Comparare necesse est?* Ancient Israelite and Ancient Near Eastern Prophecy in a Comparative Perspective," in *Prophecy in Its Ancient Near Eastern Context: Mesopotamian, Biblical, and Arabian Perspectives* [ed. M. Nissinen; SBL Symposium Series 13; Atlanta: Society of Biblical Literature, 2000] 3–11, 9): "When we compare biblical 'prophecy' with 'prophecy' in other texts or cultures it is always our own views of prophecy that we compare". All this, of course, does not mean that the socio-religious background of the texts should be dropped from the agenda of the comparative enterprise altogether.

Let us take the biographical notes on each prophet as an example. Bayâ appears as the speaker of two oracles belonging to two different oracle collections,[32] and all information available to us concerning this prophet is written in the standard colophons following the text of the oracle on each tablet. This prophet is said to come from Arbela, which doubtless refers to the prophet's affiliation with the temple of Ištar in Arbela, the cradle of Neo-Assyrian prophecy.[33] The oracle is said to be delivered "by the mouth" of the prophet, referring to an oral performance probably written down by someone else. The gender of this prophet is ambiguous because the name is written with a female determinative (MÍ), even though the prophet is said to be a "son" (DUMU) of Arbela. Unless this ambiguity is due to a slip of the scribe,[34] the prophet may belong to those devotees of Ištar who were considered neither men nor women, and represented a "third gender" as a sign of the power of the goddess over human gender and as mythological reminiscences of the goddess's journey to the Netherworld.[35] All this information—the oral performance, the religious affiliation and even the ambiguous gender of the prophet—makes perfect sense in view of what is known about the historical background of the sources in the early seventh-century Assyria; the original oracles probably date form the years 680 – 679.[36]

In the case of Amos, we learn from the first verse of the book (Amos 1:1) that this man, who is said to be one of the sheep-farmers (*nōqĕdîm*) of Tekoa, a village in Judah, "saw" (*ḥzh*) words (this probably implies that he was believed to have received them in visions) concerning Israel during the reigns of Uzziah, king of Judah, and Jeroboam, king of Israel, "two years before the earthquake". In another context (Amos 7:10 – 17), in accordance with the introductory verse, he is called "seer" (*ḥōzeh*) by Amaziah, the priest of Bethel, who had written about him to King Jeroboam and now tells him to go back to Judah and prophesy (*hinnābēʾ*) there instead of Bethel, the king's sanctuary and a royal palace. Amos denies belonging to the prophetic guild: "I am no prophet, nor am I a prophet's son", and claims to be "a herdsman and a dresser of sycomorefigs", who was told by God to prophesy against Israel. The introductory verse (Amos 1:1) seem-

32 That is, SAA 9 1.4 and 2.2; see Parpola, *Assyrian Prophecies*, 6, 14 – 15.

33 Cf. M. Nissinen, "City as Lofty as Heaven: Arbela and Other Cities in Neo-Assyrian Prophecy," in *'Every City Shall Be Forsaken": Urbanism and Prophecy in Ancient Israel and the Near East* (ed. L. L. Grabbe and R. D. Haak; JSOTSup 330; Sheffield: Sheffield Academic Press, 2001) 172 – 209, 176 – 83 (= pp. 267 – 300 in this volume).

34 Thus M. Weippert, "'König, fürchte dich nicht!': Assyrische Prophetie im 7. Jahrhundert v.Chr.," *Or* 71 (2002) 1 – 54, 34.

35 Thus Parpola, *Assyrian Prophecies*, xxxiv, il.

36 See ibid., lxviii – lxix.

ingly provides the reader with information similar to the colophons of the Assyrian oracles: name, provenance, the type of transmission of divine words and the date (which may originally have belonged to the Assyrian tablets, the ends of which, with the exception of one tablet, are broken away). However, the case of Amos is more problematic since there is a certain discrepancy between the beginning of the book, where Amos is presented as the one who "sees" divine words, and in Amos 7:14, where he vehemently rejects the designation "seer" given to him, not only by Amaziah the priest, but implicitly also by the introductory verse of the book. Moreover, unlike the case of Bayâ, the social role of Amos is rather difficult to fathom, at least if we look at it from an ancient Near Eastern point of view: a farmer, presumably without any kind of literary education or affiliation to any religious institution, reciting, if not writing, sophisticated Hebrew poetry and confronting religious authorities outside his homeland.[37] The built-in dissonance in the image of Amos as a non-prophet fulfilling divinatory functions may not surprise us if we look at it from the point of view of the biblical prophetic ideal refined by two centuries of biblical scholarship, according to which Amos, the free spirit and social critic, is the paragon of a true prophet. But Amos does appear as a curiousity when seen from the perspective of our present knowledge of prophetic social roles in the ancient Near East. Moreover, the dissonance between the information given by Amos 1:1 and 7:14 raises questions concerning the unity of the literary product we call the book of Amos.

To be sure, the incongruities within the book of Amos have for a long time been subject to diachronic analyses of the editorial history of the book, attributing much if not all biographical material to the pre- or postexilic editors of the book: hence the information given by it on the prophet Amos should be understood as part of a strategy by later writers to address their own ideas to their readers. Whether or not this is true in the case of Amos 7:10–17 (as I think it is),[38] the case of the book of Amos as a whole serves as an example of the differ-

---

37 This oddity has been pointed out by Ł. Niesiołowski-Spanò ("Biblical Prophet Amos: A Simple, Poor Shepherd from Judah?" in *Εὐεργεσίας χάριν*, FS B. Bravo and E. Wipszycka [ed. T. Derda, J. Urbanik, and M. Węcowski; The Journal of Juristic Papyrology, Supplement 1; Warsaw: Sumptibus auctorum, 2002] 211–17), who denies that Amos is depicted as a "simple, poor shepherd from Judah".

38 Concurring with many other scholars, I am convinced that Amos 7:10–17 is placed secondarily in its present context and dates from a later period, not reporting actual words and deeds of the prophet Amos; for more recent studies on the passage, see, among others, H. G. M. Williamson, "The Prophet and the Plumb-Line: A Redaction-Critical Study of Amos 7," in *The Place Is Too Small for Us: The Israelite Prophets in Recent Scholarship* (ed. R. P. Gordon; Sources for Biblical and Theological Study 5; Winona Lake, IN: Eisenbrauns, 1995) 453–77; J. Werlitz, "Amos und sein Biograph: Zur Entstehung und Intention der Prophetenerzählung Am 7,10–17," *BZ*

ence between the literary history of the prophetic books of the Bible and the remaining ancient Near Eastern documentation. The sources represent different genres. Comprising a variety of genres of literature—divine words, poetry, narrative sections and so on—as the result of a long editorial process, a prophetic book certainly can and should be used as a historical source, but it cannot be applied to historical reconstruction in the same way as the Assyrian oracle collections, the editorial process of which is considerably shorter. The genre of a prophetic book is only known from the Bible, where its function is to transcend the message of ancient prophets for new audiences, not to conserve the "original" word of the prophet.[39]

This is not to say that the texts attributed to Amos and Bayâ cannot be compared with each other at all. "Future shall be like the past", says the prophet Bayâ in both oracles attributed to him/her (SAA 9 1.4 ii 37 and 2.2 i 17–18),[40] meaning that there will always be divine support for the rule of King Esarhaddon. This is in apparent contradiction to Amos 5:2: "She has fallen to rise no more, the virgin Israel", which proclaims the opposite to Israel. We can ask, however, whether both derive from the same Near Eastern prophetic tradition of proclaiming blessing to one's own king and destruction to the enemy, although in the case of Amos with reversed roles. A similar correspondence can be observed between Bayâ's word—"Esarhaddon, king of Assyria! I will vanquish yo[ur enemies]" (SAA 9 2.2 i 22)—and the prophecy (*vaticinium ex eventu*) of Amos to King Jeroboam—"Your land shall be divided by a measuringline, and you yourself shall die in an unclean country" (Amos 7:14). The two oracles seem to be two sides of the same coin, a coin which has the king's image on it.

Whenever two texts are compared, we can make obsevations of the vocabulary, literary form, ideology and theology of the texts, consider them from the point of view of their literary contexts and their editorial history, and examine what they inform us about various aspects of what we call prophecy. It deserves attention that the relationship between Amaziah, Amos and Jeroboam corresponds well with what we know about the relationship between priests, prophets and kings in the ancient Near Eastern documents in general, priests reporting

---

NF 44 (2000) 233–51; and cf. L. Schmidt, "Die Amazja-Erzählung (Am 7,10–17) und der historische Amos," *ZAW* 119 (2007) 221–35, who admits that the passage is a later insertion, yet early enough to be used as indirect evidence for the historical Amos.

39 For the prophetic book as a genre, see Ben Zvi, "The Prophetic Book"; Floyd, "The Production of Prophetic Books."

40 The wordings of the two oracles of Bayâ differ slightly, yielding, however, an almost identical translation: *urkīūte lū kî pānīūte* (SAA 9 1.4 ii 37), "the future shall be like the past"—*akī ša pānīti* [*lū ina u*]*rkīti* (SAA 9 2.2 i 17–18), "[let the f]uture be like the past".

prophetic messages to the king and exercising control over prophetic activity.[41] Quite certainly, we can also attempt a sketching out of the historical background and "*geistige Heimat*" of the texts. To take Amos and Bayâ again as examples, this is considerably easier in the oracle of Bayâ, which can be dated rather firmly; in the case of the book of Amos, we must ponder several alternatives depending on the dating of each part of the book.

In any case, placing the sources side by side for the sake of comparison requires a sense of what is being compared. As stated above, different texts yield different information. In some cases—for instance, in administrative documents—the sources inform us rather directly about prophets, while in others they tell more about the purposes of their writers than the prophetic phenomenon in its own right. Most often—as is the case, for instance, in the letters reporting prophetic performances at Mari and in Assyria—the sources must be read in both ways: the letters certainly give us some indispensable information about prophetic activities in their time, but this information is totally dependent on the point of view of the writers and their audiences.[42]

To be able to make a difference between different levels of the perception of prophecy in the Hebrew Bible, I have introduced the distinction between *biblical prophecy*, meaning prophecy as it is supposed to be understood by the readers of the biblical texts, and *ancient Hebrew prophecy*, referring to the historical phenomenon of prophecy in the kingdoms of Israel and Judah and in the Persian province of Yehud.[43] Biblical prophecy we have in front of our eyes; ancient Hebrew prophecy can only be reconstructed from the biblical text with more or less probability with the help of exegetical methods—including the comparative method. For comparative studies this means that the primary counterparts of comparison are extra-biblical documents and the biblical text, that is, ancient Near Eastern prophecy and biblical prophecy. To what extent it is possible to compare ancient Hebrew prophecy with ancient Near Eastern prophecy is anoth-

---

41 This has recently been convincingly shown by J. B. Couey ("Amos vii 10–17 and Royal Attitudes toward Prophecy in the Ancient Near East," *VT* 53 [2008] 300–14), who surveys a number of similar instances in Near Eastern sources and concludes: "The evidence strongly suggests, then, that priests in ancient Israel and Judah functioned as royal officials, loyal to the king and responsible for monitoring prophetic activity on his behalf" (313–14).

42 Cf. van der Toorn, "From the Oral to the Written," 225–28.

43 See M. Nissinen, "What Is Prophecy? An Ancient Near Eastern Perspective", in *Inspired Speech: Prophecy in the Ancient Near East*, FS H. B. Huffmon (ed. J. Kaltner and L. Stulman; JSOTSup 378; London: T&T Clark International, 2004) 17–37, 31 (= pp. 53–73 in this volume); id., "How Prophecy Became Literature," 166–67.

er question that involves all the difficulties of historical reconstruction described above.

Not everything depends on dating when texts are compared. As the above example from Amos 7:10 – 17 shows, much of the comparison can be done without dating, assuming that both sources present themselves as authentic representatives of ancient Near Eastern literature and prophetic tradition, each in its own way. Dating becomes significant if we wish to establish literary or, at least, cultural dependencies between the documents—for instance, between Neo-Assyrian prophecies and Second Isaiah.[44] Such dependencies, however, are not the absolute prerequisite for drawing the larger picture of ancient Near Eastern prophecy. In most cases, dependencies between source materials from the ancient Near East cannot be demonstrated, but it is nevertheless possible to increase our understanding of prophecy by observing similarities and distinctive features in prophetic sources from different times and places. The result is not a tree-like diagram we may be used to striving for, but rather a pizzalike collage that shows different kinds of family resemblances between source materials which are more or less historically connected. All these sources belong to the Near Eastern cultural sphere, which unites them anyway, but the comparison can be extended to prophecy as a global phenomenon.

Despite all the caveats mentioned so far, the comparative study of ancient Near Eastern prophecy should not be regarded as a desperate attempt altogether. We do have at our disposal a sizable, even though uneven, source material that makes comparison possible, especially when supplemented by relevant non-prophetic extra-biblical and biblical sources that help to contextualize the prophetic documents. Hence, comparison between the biblical and extra-biblical sources is a worthwhile and legitimate enterprise if it is undertaken with steady awareness of *what* is being compared for what purpose. Personally—and I am talking as a biblical scholar—I have more or less eschewed this comparison, primarily because I have felt a need to study each set of sources independently of biblical concerns. Now I will venture to sketch out some commonalities and differences between the biblical and ancient Near Eastern sources, using divination as a test case.

---

44 Cf. M. Weippert, "'Ich bin Jahwe' – 'Ich bin Ištar von Arbela': Deuterojesaja im Lichte der neuassyrischen Prophetie," in *Prophetie und Psalmen*, FS K. Seybold (ed. B. Huwyler, H.-P. Mathys and B. Weber; AOAT 280; Münster: Ugarit-Verlag, 2001) 31–59.

2 The Test Case: Prophecy as Divination

2.1 The Role of Divination in the Ancient Near East

In ancient Near Eastern studies, prophecy (if this word is used) is usually regarded as a sub-type of divination. In other words, prophets are seen as further representatives of the institution, the purpose of which is to make the people, the king in particular, conversant with the divine will in a variety of ways.[45] I fully subscribe to this view, though I would like to emphasize the distinctive characteristics of different divinatory practices: in prophecy, the divine word is allegedly received intuitively, probably in an altered state of mind, and this clearly sets prophecy apart from astrology or extispicy, which are based on observations of physical objects and their scholarly interpretation. This difference is visible also in the social location of diviners of different kinds: at least in the Mesopotamian society, "academics" such as haruspices, astrologers or exorcists assumed social roles clearly different from prophets, who were not affiliated with literary and scribal education but rather belonged to the context of worship.[46]

What unites different divinatory practices is their function in guiding the decision-making in society by means of revealing the divine will. This is much more than mere fortune-telling or predicting the future. Prophets, like other diviners, act as instruments of divine encouragement and warning, and they are typically consulted in situations of war and political crises. A telling example of this is the newest available document of prophecy, an outlay of copper found in Ziyaret Tepe (ancient Tušḫan) and dating from the year 611 BCE, that is, from the very last days of the Assyrian empire after the fall of Nineveh.[47] Just before the battle against the invading Babylonian army, both an augur (*dāgil iṣṣūri*) and a prophet

45 For the interface of prophecy and divination, see, for example, H. M. Barstad, "Prophecy in the Book of Jeremiah and the Historical Prophet," in *Sense and Sensitivity*, FS R. Carroll (ed. A. G. Hunter and P. R. Davies; JSOTSup 348; Sheffield: Sheffield Academic Press, 2002) 87–100, 87–89; E. Cancik-Kirschbaum, "Prophetismus und Divination: Ein Blick auf die keilschriftlichen Quellen," in Köckert and Nissinen (eds.) *Propheten in Mari, Assyrien und Israel*, 33–53; Pongratz-Leisten, "When the Gods Are Speaking"; A. M. Kitz, "Prophecy as Divination," *CBQ* 65 (2003) 122–24.

46 Cf. Parpola, *Assyrian Prophecies*, xlvii–xlviii; M. Nissinen, "The Socioreligious Role of the Neo-Assyrian Prophets," in id. (ed.) *Prophecy in Its Ancient Near Eastern Context*, Mesopotamian, Biblical, and Arabian Perspectives (ed. id.; SBLSymS 13; Atlanta, Ga.: Society of Biblical Literature, 2000) 89–114, 95–102 (= pp. 103–26 in the present volume).

47 Parpola, "Cuneiform Texts from Ziyaret Tepe."

(*raggimu*) have been paid for their services. The substantial amount of six minas of copper given to the prophet is noteworthy regardless of whether he ever survived the fall of the city to be able to enjoy his riches. Furthermore, the use of two distinctive methods of divination deserves attention: the city in distress needed every divine instruction they could get.

Even though the king was not the only employer of diviners and prophets, the societal function of divination is fundamentally associated with the institution of kingship. The position of the ancient Near Eastern king as the link between the divine and human worlds also made him the prime recipient of prophetic and other oracles. Divination was the medium through which the king was kept informed of the divine favours and obligations and the origin and legitimacy of his rule; this is what Beate Pongratz-Leisten calls *Herrschaftswissen* in her important monograph *Herrschaftswissen im alten Mesopotamien.*[48] It is especially through prophets that the "the secrets of the gods", that is, the decisions of the heavenly council usually proclaimed by the goddess Ištar, were revealed to the king.[49] Hence the prophets function as intermediaries and channels of communication for the divine knowledge necessary for the king and country to live in safety and receive divine advice in times of crisis and uncertainty.

2.2 Divination and Prophecy in the Hebrew Bible

Much of this is easily observable in the Hebrew Bible, where prophets appear as proclaming the word of Yahweh to kings and authorities, often in political or religious crises; if not more, this shows that the authors and editors of the prophetic and historical books of the Hebrew Bible were well aware of the function of prophecy as *Herrschaftswissen.* A telling example of this is the decisive role of the prophetess Huldah in introducing the *sēper hat-tôrâ* as the constitution of the religious reform of King Josiah, as reported by the Deuteronomists in 2 Kgs

48 B. Pongratz-Leisten, *Herrschaftswissen im alten Mesopotamien: Formen der Kommunikationzwischen Gott und König im 2. Und 1. Jahrtausend v. Chr.* (SAAS 10: Helsinki: The Neo-Assyrian Text Corpus Project, 1999).

49 Cf. the oracle from Ešnunna (FLP 1674: 1–8; cf. Nissinen, *Prophets and Prophecy in the Ancient Near East*, no. 66): "O king Ibalpiel, thus says Kititum: The secrets of the gods (*niṣrētum ša ilī*) are placed before me. Because you constantly pronounce my name with your mouth, I constantly disclose the secrets of the gods to you."

22:14–20.[50] Moreover, prophets such as Isaiah and Jeremiah, as well as several prophets mentioned in the Deuteronomistic History, not to forget Chronicles, are repeatedly brought to a direct contact with the kings—more than is observable in any prophetic document from Mesopotamia.[51] Whether we have to do with a late reconstruction or description of actual events, all this points to the conclusion that (1) prophecy as an institution had a significant divinatory function in the politics of the Judaean kings when the kingdom still existed, and (2) this function of prophecy was remembered long after the collapse of the institution of kingship in Jerusalem. When it comes to prophecy in relation to other forms of divination, the Hebrew Bible takes a different stance. That prophecy is understood as a sort of divination is acknowledged, for example, in 1 Samuel 28, where Saul tries to inquire of God by means of dreams, Urim and prophets (v. 6), and finally resorts to a necromancer. The existence of astrologers, necromancers and other people bearing somewhat unclear designations, including *qōsēm, mĕʿônēn, mĕnaḥēš, mĕkaššēp, yiddĕônî*, and so on,[52] is also acknowledged, but their activities are either condemned or ridiculed. While prophecy is not presented in the Hebrew Bible as the only legitimate way of receiving knowledge of the divine will (dreams, for instance, are not rejected as such, and the Urim and Thummim belong to the priestly equipment without criticism of their use), the prophet clearly enjoys an elevated position. This is obviously the reason for the sharp distinction between prophecy and divination with the respective positive and negative value judgments in modern scholarship until recent days. Since the nineteenth century, scholars have appreciated the prophets as champions of "ethical monotheism" (which is primarily a modern rather than biblical construction[53]), while divination has been the paragon of a less-devel-

---

50 For the original function of the newly found book as a divine oracle and its redactional reinterpretation as a law-book, see J. Ben-Dov, "Writing as Oracle and as Law: New Contexts for the Book-Find of King Josiah," *JBL* 127 (2008) 223–39.

51 A more thorough survey of the encounters between prophets and kings in the Hebrew Bible is available in Nissinen, "Biblical Prophecy from a Near Eastern Perspective" (pp. 351–75 in this volume). See also the articles included in A. Lemaire (ed.), *Prophètes et rois: Bible et Proche-Orient* (Lectio divina, hors série; Paris: Cerf, 2001).

52 For these and other prophetic role labels, see, for example, J. Blenkinsopp, *Sage, Priest, Prophet: Religious and Intellectual Leadership in Ancient Israel* (Library of Ancient Israel; Louisville, KY: Westminster John Knox, 1995), 123–29.

53 Cf. O. Loretz ("Die Entstehung des Amos-Buches im Licht der Prophetien aus Māri, Assur, Ishchali und der Ugarit-Texte: Paradigmenwechsel in der Prophetenforschung," *UF* 24 [1992] 179–215, 185) with regard to the traditional interpretation of Amos: "Im Grunde steht dieser Typ der Amos-Forschung uneingestanden und unbewußt unter dem Diktat der Vergangenheit,

oped, irrational superstition. In the context of the Hebrew Bible, however, the distinction is not motivated by a universal ethical rule, but a particular, authoritative set of instructions, the Torah, governed by a particular idea of the relationship of God and his people mediated by Moses, the paragon of a prophet (Deut 18:15–22). This is not to say that every prophetic text in the Hebrew Bible originally reflects this idea, but this is certainly how the "Prophets" as a part of the composition (or "canon", if we prefer) of the Hebrew Bible wishes to be read.

2.3 Literary Prophecy as Scribal Divination

With regard to prophecy and divination, it is interesting to observe what happened to prophecy when the kingdom of Judah collapsed and the people had to manage the consequences of this crisis—first, the so-called exilic period or the "Templeless age"[54] when the ruling class was deported to Babylonia; and then, after a few decades, the attempts at building a new Temple and establishing a new community of worshippers of Yahweh. There was a fundamental change in the concept, practice and social context of prophecy during this long and troublesome period, extending from the first occupation of Jerusalem in 598 BCE well into the time of Nehemiah in mid-fifth century BCE. We may observe two parallel developments presupposing each other: on the one hand, the decline and marginalization (but not disappearance) of the traditional type of prophecy as oral delivery of divine messages; and on the other hand, the rise of the literary interpretation of written prophecies which becomes the preferred and authoritative sort of divination in the Second Temple community.

One of the consequences of the destruction of the monarchy and social institutions in the early sixth century BCE was that prophecy became divorced from its socio-religious context as a royal institution, thereby losing its traditional function and setting. Prophecy did not disappear in the post-monarchical period; such figures as Haggai and Zechariah bear witness to the contrary, and enough traces of prophetic activity can be extracted from the text of the Hebrew Bible to demonstrate that prophecy of the traditional type never died away com-

---

gekettet an die Vorstellungen, die seit dem letzten Jahrhundert mit den Thesen *lex post prophetas* und *ethischer Monotheismus* umschrieben werden."

54 This term is preferred by J. Middlemas, *The Templeless Age: An Introduction to the History, Literature, and Theology of the "Exile"* (Louisville, KY: Westminster John Knox, 2007), 1–6.

pletely, even though it seems to have been driven into the margins of society.[55] However, there was an alternative kind of prophetic practice, and this was assumed by the scribal circles who were responsible for transmitting the holy tradition in general and the prophetic tradition in particular. The management of the divination as *Herrschaftswissen* was now essentially a scribal enterprise. The scribes, in the words of Michael Floyd, "kept records of prophetic activity, cultivating among themselves forms of prophecy that were expressed in writing and selectively recording forms of prophecy that were not."[56] It should be noted that this was probably the role of the scribes even before the post-monarchical period. However, the way the scribes developed "the theory and practice of prophetic divination as conducted with reference to the current worldview" (*ibid.*) was now different because of the changes in the worldview. To use a distinction introduced by Armin Lange, *written prophecy*, meaning written records of orally delivered prophetic messages, was largely, if not entirely, replaced by *literary prophecy*, that is, literature that reinterprets earlier written records of prophecy, transcending the original proclamation situations and recontextualizing them in other contexts.[57]

The authoritative concept of prophecy, separated from other forms of divination and elevated above them, was in the post-monarchical period inspired by the figures of the past and introduced by the scribes who took care of the intermediation of the prophetic tradition, producing prophetic books by relying on earlier written records and reinterpreting them, thereby assuming the personae of the past prophets.[58] As Joachim Schaper has noticed with reference to Ezekiel, the textualization and "sacerdotalization" of prophecy ultimately led to the "death of the prophet" as the intermediary of divine knowledge. "In Ezek 1:28bβ – 3:15, writing is no longer the *documentary medium* of prophetic discourse but its *material prerequisite*."[59]

It was only the formation and subsequent authorization of prophetic literature that led to a full appreciation of literary prophecy, that is, the prophetic

---

55 See, for example, L. L. Grabbe, "Poets, Scribes or Preachers? The Reality of Prophecy in the Second Temple Period," in *Knowing the End from the Beginning: The Prophetic, the Apocalyptic and their Relationships* (ed. id. and R. D. Haak; JSPSup 46; London: T&T Clark International, 2003) 192 – 215; M. Nissinen, "The Dubious Image of Prophecy," in Floyd and Haak (eds.) 2006: 26 – 41 (= pp. 577 – 96 in this volume).

56 Floyd, "The Production of Prophetic Books," 285.

57 Lange, "Literary Prophecy and Oracle Collection," 249 – 50.

58 Cf. Floyd, "The Production of Prophetic Books," 285 – 92.

59 J. Schaper, "The Death of the Prophet: The Transition from the Spoken to the Written Word of God in the Book of Ezekiel," in Floyd and Haak (eds.), *Prophets, Prophecy, and Prophetic Texts in Second Temple Judaism*, 63 – 79, esp. p. 79; emphases original.

books, as prophecy *par excellence*. This, again, highlighted the importance of the interpretation of the prophetic books in a way that gave the scholars and teachers of wisdom as authorized interpreters of the prophetic word a quasi-prophetic role. This can be seen very clearly, for instance, in Ben Sira (cf. Sir 24:33; 39:6)[60] and in the Dead Sea Scrolls.[61] Interestingly, prophetic and scholarly roles merge together in a way that leads to a reconceptualization of prophecy.

Returning, in conclusion, to the comparative view, it is easy to note that none of the ancient Near Eastern documents reflects a development comparable to the one described above that took place in Yehud. This by no means prevents the comparison between the sources—it only requires alertness to the critical points of the comparative analysis. The conceptual distinctions that have been made above might be helpful in acknowledging the nature of the sources being compared: that of biblical prophecy and ancient Hebrew prophecy on the one hand, and that of written prophecy and literary prophecy on the other. To use the example of Bayâ and Amos again, the oracles of Bayâ are an illustrative specimen of written prophecy, whereas the book of Amos, as a prophetic book, clearly belongs to the category of literary prophecy.

The institution of divination offers itself as a particularly rewarding test case, because it highlights an aspect of Near Eastern prophecy that appears to be significant in the biblical texts regardless of their dating, demonstrating the function of prophecy as *Herrschaftswissen* in early and late texts alike. Moreover, the comparative view also helps us to see where Second Temple Judaism takes a course of its own with regard to the concept and practice of prophecy.

---

60 Cf. P. C. Beentjes, "Prophets and Prophecy in the Book of Ben Sira," in Floyd and Haak (eds.), *Prophets, Prophecy, and Prophetic Texts in Second Temple Judaism*, 135–50.

61 For this aspect of prophecy in the Dead Sea Scrolls, cf. the contributions by G. J. Brooke, "Prophecy and Prophets in the Dead Sea Scrolls: Looking Backwards and Forwards," in Floyd and Haak (eds.), *Prophets, Prophecy, and Prophetic Texts in Second Temple Judaism*, 151–65; and A. P. Jassen, "The Presentation of Ancient Prophets as Lawgivers at Qumran," *JBL* 127 (2008) 307–37; cf. also M. Nissinen, "Transmitting Divine Mysteries: The Prophetic Role of Wisdom Teachers in the Dead Sea Scrolls," in *Scripture in Transition: Essays on Septuagint, Hebrew Bible, and Dead Sea Scrolls in Honour of Raija Sollamo* (ed. A. Voitila and J. Jokiranta; JSJSup, 126; Leiden: Brill, 2008) 513–33 (= pp. 631–49 in this volume).

From Holy War to Holy Peace: Biblical Alternatives to Belligerent Rhetoric

Does Religion Kill?

Does religion kill? In the post-cold war world, this question is asked by many who feel haunted by a new sense of insecurity caused by acts of extreme violence performed in the name of God. Many people would not hesitate to answer in the affirmative: There are enough rituals, sacred texts, divine beings, and human authorities in different religions that not only accept killing but also give straightforward orders to kill when sacred things are at stake. Others would maintain that the prime mover of violence should not be sought in religion but in the human condition: Human beings, due to the complexity of their mutual relations, commit violent acts irrespective of their religiosity, while religion is often utilized as the ultimate justification for violence. In other words, religion does not kill, but people use it to justify their violent pursuits. If these are the alternatives, I would rather opt for the second stance. However, I find it necessary, not only to identify elements that make religion a source of conflict and arc used in justifying violence and warfare, but also to look for sensible alternatives.

It is not my intention to contemplate the philosophical, psychological, or theological problems of violence and religion.[1] Instead, I take a sociohistorical approach to the issue from the points of view of both holy war and trust, first presenting examples of the rhetoric of holy war from the ancient Near East, and then considering a trust-based hermeneutical alternative to this rhetoric. In concluding, I will discuss Isaiah 2:2–4 and Micah 4:1–5, from this perspective.

Throughout history, war and violence have been justified as divinely authorized means of punishing evil, but this does not automatically make religion the reason for conflicts or even the principal motive for them. The long-lasting crisis in the Middle East, for instance, has been characterized not primarily as a religious conflict but as "an accumulation of conflicts deriving from secular power politics, the unsolved heritage of colonialism, internal tensions and the super-

1 For a philosophical approach to this problem, see R. Girard, *Violence and the Sacred* (Baltimore: Johns Hopkins University Press, 1977); for psychological approaches, see the articles in *The Destructive Power of Religion: Violence in Judaism, Christianity, and Islam*, Vol. 1, *Sacred Scriptures, Ideology, and Violence* (ed. R. Ellens; Westport, Conn.: Praeger, 2004).

DOI 10.1515/9783110466546-021

powers' cynical aspirations to power and control in the area."[2] In spite of this, many of those deeply involved in this complex of sociopolitical problems do not hesitate to interpret them in religious terms. In a disillusioned political situation, religion gives a coherent explanation for the state of affairs, as well as a simple, often dualistic, precept to follow. The element of violence is frequently there, even though it does not necessarily belong to such a precept. The so-called fundamentalists, that is, groups and individuals who have absolutized their own beliefs and aims and the ways of pursuing them, are typically seen as carrying the torch of religion in justifying violent acts; however, not everything that is called "fundamentalism" is violent or motivated by religion.

Should we then, after all, conclude that religion kills? At least it is evident that pursuing ideal conditions expressed in the language of religion may lead to extremely violent ways of action sanctioned within the same language. Hence the title of a recent book by Charles Kimball, *When Religion Becomes Evil*,[3] not only alludes to the political concept of the "axis of evil" but also reflects the lamentable fact that religious traditions indeed are susceptible to becoming catalysts in policies that lead to extreme suffering. Kimball gives five major warning signs that tend to precede any instance of religiously sanctioned evil: absolute truth claims, blind obedience, establishing the "ideal" time, the end justifies any means, and declaring holy war.

I would agree with Kimball that these are signs of corruption in religion that can be prevented by authentic faith,[4] although I am convinced that, due to multiple understandings of what should be called, "authentic" faith in any given tradition, it is more than difficult to make a difference between corrupted and authentic forms of religious commitments, let alone declare any form of religion as "evil." It belongs to the "ambivalence of the sacred," inherent in every culture and religion, that violence and religion are interwoven in a way that makes it difficult to think of a religion free of all elements of violence.[5] These elements are

2 My translation of Dr. Pertti Multanen, a Finnish specialist in Near Eastern politics "Nouseeko Lähi-idän kriisi uskonnoista" ["Does the Crisis in the Middle East Arise from Religions?"], in *Vanhan aatamin kuoletus: Herännäiskirjoituksia vuodelta 2004* (ed. U. Karjalainen; Lapua: Herättäjä-Yhdistys, 2004), 79–95, esp. 94.

3 C. Kimball, *When Religion Becomes Evil* (San Francisco: Harper San Francisco, 2002).

4 Ibid., 186–87: "The complicity of religious persuasions in global conflicts today is undeniable, but understanding this complicity requires that we clearly grasp the difference between what we have called corrupt forms of religious commitment and the authentic forms that offer hope."

5 See R. S. Appleby, *The Ambivalence of the Sacred: Religion, Violence, and Reconciliation* (Oxford: Rowman & Littlefield, 2000); cf. S. M. Thomas, *The Global Resurgence of Religion and the*

not, however, uncontrollable fatalities but something that can be identified, understood, and controlled from inside the religious tradition. Therefore, I find it a meaningful hermeneutical task and, indeed, my responsibility as a representative of a religious tradition to look for an "antidote to violence and extremism"[6] in religious practice. This will bring me to Isaiah 2:2–4 and Micah 4:1–5, but let me first concentrate on Kimball's fifth warning sign, declaring holy war, as it includes elements of each of the four preceding warning signs.

Divine Wars in the Ancient Near East

The unholy alliance of religion and war belongs to the history of humanity at large; all corners of the world at any given time have seen rulers who wage war in the name of their gods. The idea of holy war, which I define as a war sanctioned by religion, is also to be found at the roots of the Jewish-Christian-Islamic world, that is, in the ancient Near East, where it was known everywhere. There is ample evidence to prove this, including the Hebrew Bible, which tells about Israelites, the people of God, righting against their idolatrous enemies. The elements of biblical holy war, as delineated by Gerhard von Rad in his classic work *Der heilige Krieg im alten Israel,*[7] included consecrating the soldiers, the weapons, and the whole camp to their holy functions; the holiness of the warfare is manifested in the absolute ritual purity of the soldiers and their whole equipment. Before going off to war, it was important to make sacrifices to God, who delivered confirmation of the war in the form of an oracle, such as "God has put the enemy in your hands." After this the war was started, and since God was the actual fighter and commander, the number and strength of the Israelite troops were insignificant. The wars were God's wars and the enemies God's enemies, hence Israel was not supposed to fear but to trust in the power of God. Israel gained victory over its enemies, who lost heart when God struck them with horror. The spoils were consecrated to God; all the people, the cattle as well as the plundered goods belonged to God. When the war was over, the Israelites went to their homes.

Transformation of International Relations: The Struggle for the Soul of the Twenty-First Century (New York: Palgrave MacMillan, 2005), 13–14.

6 Kimball, *When Religion Becomes Evil,* 187.

7 G. von Rad, *Der heilige Krieg im alten Israel* (AThANT 20; Zürich: Zwingli Verlag, 1951); trans. and ed. by M. J. Dawn as *Holy War in Ancient Israel* (Grand Rapids, Mich.: Eerdmans, 1991).

Gerhard von Rad's theory of biblical holy war[8] should be viewed with three critical viewpoints in mind: (1) It is based on a selection of elements collected from the Pentateuch and the Deuteronomistic History, while the prophetic books of the Hebrew Bible would provide different ideas, as represented, for example, by our theme texts; (2) It is an unhistorical theological construction, which was not necessarily ever put into effect. The pertinent texts were written centuries after the events they report, hence the texts describing the idea and practice of the holy war reveal the ideology of their authors rather than historical facts;[9] in practice, the people of Israel and Judah would have had little possibility of waging such wars; (3) However, the biblical writers did not invent the idea of holy war out of their own heads. The reconstruction by von Rad is hermetically biblical, which led him to look for the origin of the biblical holy war in the pre-state amphictyony of the Israelite tribes. However, as was conclusively shown by Manfred Weippert,[10] the idea of a divinely sanctioned war can be found in a vast array of ancient Near Eastern documents, and its presence in the Hebrew Bible only demonstrates the affinity of the biblical writers for their historical environment. The wars of Israel's neighbors, like the Arameans and the Moabites, were wars of their gods, to say nothing of the Assyrians, whose literary records—royal inscriptions, prophecies, oracle queries, and even royal poetry—include ample evidence of the ideology, propaganda, and practice of divinely sanctioned wars.[11]

One of the most telling sources describing Assyrian holy war ideology is without doubt Prism B of Assurbanipal, king of Assyria (668–627 BCE). This royal inscription, written in 649, not only offers a vivid glimpse of Assyrian warfare in general, but it can also be compared with holy war rhetoric both in the Hebrew Bible and in the present day. In a long section of the inscription,[12] Assurbanipal gives an account of his war against Elam in 653.

---

8 Cf. the introductory essay of B. C. Ollenburger, "Gerhard von Rad's Theory of Holy War," in von Rad, *Holy War in Ancient Israel*, 1–33.

9 Cf., e. g., V. Fritz, *Die Entstehung Israels im 12. und 11. Jahrhundert v. Chr.* (Biblische Enzyklopädie 2; Stuttgart: Kohlhammer, 1996), 127.

10 M. Weippert, "'Heiliger Krieg' in Israel und Assyrien: Kritische Anmerkungen zu Gerhard von Rad's Konzept des 'Heiligen Krieges im alten Israel,'" *ZAW* 84 (1972) 460–93.

11 Cf. T. J. Lewis, "'You Have Heard What the Kings of Assyria Have Done': Disarmament Passages vis-à-vis Assyrian Rhetoric of Intimidation," in *Isaiah's Vision of Peace in Biblical and Modern International Relations: Swords into Plowshares* (ed. R. Cohen and R. Westbrook; New York: Palgrave MacMillan, 2008), 75–100; F. M. Fales, "On *Pax Assyriaca* in the Eighth-Seventh Centuries BCE and Its Implications," ibid., 17–35.

12 Lines iv 15–vi 9; see J. Novotny and J. Jeffers, *The Royal Inscriptions of Ashurbanipal (668–631 BC), Aššur-etel-ilāni (630–627 BC), and Sîn-šarra-iškun (626–612 BC), Kings of Assy-*

Elam, the southeastern neighbor of the Assyrian empire, located in the southwestern part of today's Iran, was a political rival of Assyria throughout the first half of the seventh century. Esarhaddon, Assurbanipal's father, had in 674 established peaceful relations with Urtaku, king of Elam, who, however, only a decade later invaded Babylonia, the southern part of the Assyrian empire. In the subsequent combat, Urtaku was killed and Assurbanipal beat off the Elamites and their Babylonian allies, while a usurper called Teumman seized the throne of Elam. Urtaku's three sons, together with sixty members of the Elamite royal family, escaped the "murders of Teumman" to Assyria.[13] The presence of the Elamite establishment in Assyria inevitably presented a political threat to Teumman, who sent two envoys to Assurbanipal, demanding that he send the Elamite princes back to Elam. Upset by the defiance of Teumman, whom he calls "image of a demon," Assurbanipal had the envoys detained. Even the heavens reacted: Sîn, the moon god, delivered bad omens to Teumman and struck him with a disease that paralyzed his lips and made his eyes squint, but Teumman would not take back his impudent words; on the contrary, he promised not to give up until he ate dinner in the center of Nineveh, the capital of Assyria.[14]

Teumman was not just swaggering; he assembled his troops against Assyria. Assurbanipal recounts that, while worshipping the goddess Ištar in her holy city of Arbela (modern Erbil, the capital of the Iraqi Kurdistan), he heard about the assault of Teumman, "whose power of discernment Ištar had confused." War was inevitable, and the *casus belli* is presented in the inscription in a humble prayer of Assurbanipal, the pious king, whose rule was divinely ordained. The supreme god Aššur himself wanted Assurbanipal to become king, hence Assurbanipal fulfilled a god-given task and the gods were with him. Ištar, the counselor of gods and the intermediary between the king and the gods, was the intercessor of Assurbanipal. She approached Aššur, speaking good words for Assurbanipal before him, so that he, raising his pure eyes, wished Assurbanipal

---

ria, Part 1 (RINAP 5/1; University Park, Pa.: Eisenbrauns, 2018), 66 – 71. For a transcription of the Akkadian text and an English translation, see M. Nissinen, with Contributions by C. L. Seow, R. K. Ritner, and H. C. Melchert, Prophets and Prophecy in the Ancient Near East (2nd ed.; Atlanta, Ga.: SBL Press, 2019), no. 101. For the pertinent passage of the inscription, see also M. Nissinen, *References to Prophecy in Neo-Assyrian Sources* (SAAS 7; Helsinki: The Neo-Assyrian Text Corpus Project, 1998), 43 – 61.

13 Novotny and Jeffers, *Royal Inscriptions of Ashurbanipal*, 66 – 68 (Prism B iv 15 – 79). For an analysis of the events in this period in the history of Elam, see M. W. Waters, *A Survey of Neo-Elamite History* (SAAS 12; Helsinki: The Neo-Assyrian Text Corpus Project, 2000), 42 – 55.

14 Novotny and Jeffers, *Royal Inscriptions of Ashurbanipal*, 68 (Prism B iv 80 – v 9); A. Livingstone, *Court Poetry and Literary Miscallanea* (SAA 3; Helsinki: Helsinki University Press, 1988), 67 (SAA 3 31:11 – 13).

to be the king. At war, Ištar was the initiator and supreme warrior. If she was ready for war, Assurbanipal could not but follow.[15]

The attack of Teumman, of course, had to be repelled. Assurbanipal maintains that Teumman had started the war without any provocation on the part of Assyria. He gives a heartrending description of how his ardent worship was interrupted by the news of Teumman's attack, and how deep an emotional shock it was to him. The wickedness of the ungodly and demonic king of Elam is especially emphasized. Teumman plays the ideological role of the enemy typical of the Assyrian royal inscriptions: He is the archetypal corrupted enemy who did not revere gods and the sovereignty of the king of Assyria.[16] Therefore, having caused grief to gods and the king alike, he was to be destroyed.

The king had no right to go to war without divine consent, hence warfare was always preceded by an oracle query, hundreds of which have been preserved.[17] In fact, the oracular institution was an organic part of political action.[18] Usually the divine answer was obtained by means of an extispicy ritual; however, in the present case, it comes through the mouths of a prophet and a dreamer, following upon the king's prayer:

> Ištar heard my desperate sighs and said to me: "Fear not!" She made my heart confident, saying: "Because of the prayer you said with your hand lifted up, your eyes being filled with tears, I have compassion for you." The very same night as I implored her, a visionary lay down and had a dream. When he woke up, he reported to me the nocturnal vision shown to him by Ištar: "Ištar who dwells in Arbela entered, having quivers hanging from her right and left and holding a bow in her hand. She had drawn a sharp-pointed sword, ready for battle. You stood before her and she spoke to you like a mother who gave birth to you. Ištar, the highest of the gods, called to you and gave you the following order: 'You are prepared for war, and I am ready to carry out my plans.' You said to her: 'Wherever you go, I will go with you!' But the Lady of Ladies answered you: 'You stay here in your place! Eat food, drink beer, make merry and praise my godhead, until 1 go

---

15 Novotny and Jeffers, *Royal Inscriptions of Ashurbanipal*, 68–69 (Prism B v 10–45).

16 See F. M. Fales, "The Enemy in Assyrian Royal Inscriptions: the 'Moral Judgement,'" in *Mesopotamien und seine Nachbarn: Politische und kulturelle Wechselbeziehungen im Alten Vorderasien vom 4. bis 1. Jahrtausend v. Chr.* (ed. H.-J. Nissen and J. Renger; BBVO 1; Berlin: Reimer, 1982), 425–35.

17 See I. Starr, *Queries to the Sungod: Divination and Politics in Sargonid Assyria* (SAA 4; Helsinki: Helsinki University Press, 1990).

18 See F. M. Fales and G. B. Lanfranchi, "The Impact of Oracular Material on the Political Utterances and Political Action in the Royal Inscriptions of the Sargonid Dynasty," in *Oracles et Prophéties dans l'antiquité: Actes du colloque de Strasbourg15–17 juin 1995* (ed. J.G. Heintz; Université des sciences humaines de Strasbourg, Travaux du Centre re recherche sur le Proche-Orient et la Grèce antiques 15; Paris: Boccard, 1997), 99–114.

> to accomplish that task, making you to attain your heart's desire. You shall not make a wry face, your feet shall not tremble, you shall not even wipe away the sweat in the tumult of war!' She sheltered you in her sweet embrace; she protected your entire body. Fire flashed in her face, and she went raging away, directing her anger against Teumman, king of Elam, who had made her furious."[19]

Ištar, thus, is tender mother and cruel warrior at the same time. The king is safe in her bosom—woe to Teumman who intimidated the king and made the goddess furious! The inscription makes it more than clear that wars were motivated by divine will, not for political or economical reasons. It is the goddess who fights; the king and other humans are mere instruments in her hands.

Upon the divine command, then, Assurbanipal mobilized his troops and took the straightest route against Teumman, whose pitiful attempts to flout the divine will and Assyrian troops were doomed to fail. The Elamites became horror-stricken, while Assurbanipal was encouraged by the great gods "with good omens, dreams, speech omens and prophetic messages." At their command Assurbanipal filled the outskirts of Susa, the capital of Elam, with corpses "as if with thorn and thistle," cutting off Teumman's head in front of his troops.[20]

Assurbanipal's war against Teumman was depicted on the wall relief of his palace.[21] The final scene is set in a garden with Teumman's head fastened to one of the trees. Assurbanipal, who has now attained his heart's desire, is reclining on a divan, facing his queen with a bowl and a flower in his hands. The holy war was over, the demon was defeated.

The booty that the gods wanted the hands of the Assyrians to grasp does not seem very impressive—Assurbanipal says he carried off "chariots, wagons, horses, mules, harnessed animals and trappings he for war"[22]—but the outcome of the war had political significance, as the status of Elam as a sovereign state was now over.[23] Elam was dismembered and given to the princes who had escaped the "murders of Teumman" to Assyria. Neutralizing Elam, however, did not succeed completely. Even though the Elamites were no longer capable of direct resistance to Assyria, they took part in the war that broke out between Assurba-

---

19 Novotny and Jeffers, *Royal Inscriptions of Ashurbanipal*, 69–70 (Prism B v 45–72).

20 Ibid., 70–71 (Prism B v 73–vi 9).

21 See J. M. Russell, *The Writing on the Wall: Studies in the Architectural Contexts of Late Assyrian Palace Inscriptions* (Mesopotamian Civilizarions 9; Winona Lake, Ind.: Eisenbrauns, 1999), 154–99; for the pictures, see also J. Reade, *Assyrian Sculpture* (London: British Museum Press, 1998), 80–91.

22 Novotny and Jeffers, *Royal Inscriptions of Ashurbanipal*, 71 (Prism B vi 3–4).

23 Cf. R. Mattila, "The Political Status of Elam after 653 B. C. according to *ABL* 839," *SAAB* 1 (1987) 27–30.

nipal and his brother Šamaš-šumu-ukin, the ruler of Babylonia, only a few years later. Supporting the rebellious brother, they caused much trouble to Assurbanipal without, however, being able to revive the Elamite kingdom.[24]

The religious tone of Assurbanipal's inscription, combined with the extreme cruelty with which enemies are treated, could be said to be typical of the Assyrians, whose culture, according to a widespread conception, was brutal and militant. This portrait certainly arises from the biblical image of Assyrians as invaders and suppressors of people, and this is partly due to the image promulgated by the Assyrians themselves.[25] The awe-inspiring propaganda was but one tool in Assyria's rise to supremacy in the Near East; the Assyrians—unlike, say, the Israelites or the Arameans—indeed had the opportunity of putting the common idea of holy war into practice. It is interesting to note that, along wich the expansion of the Assyrian empire during the Sargonid dynasty in the eighth and seventh centuries, the divine legitimation of war plays an increasingly important role in the self-presentation of the Assyrian kings in their inscriptions. Mario Fales and Giovanni Lanfranchi conclude that "the Sargonid kings tried to project throughout their royal inscriptions the image of a sovereign who follows the will of gods attentively, and not least by means of exact quotes of their favorable omens."[26] Assurbanipal, too, is most emphatic about his reliance on the divine legitimation of his actions, which in his case, according to his own testimony, was based on a personal initiation into scribal lore.[27]

Some readers may have recognized a certain likeness between Assurbanipal's discourse and the descriptions in the Hebrew Bible, but relevant points of comparison can be found even in today's world. The inscription of Assurbanipal, together with the Hebrew Bible and other ancient Near Eastern documents, has enough commonalities with modern belligerent rhetoric to demonstrate that the concept of the struggle between good and evil has ancient roots. Assyria, Judaism, Islam, and Christianity belong historically to the same building, and hence it is not surprising that similar structures of belligerent rhetoric are still used in Christianity and Judaism, as well as in Islam.

Charles Kimball's warning signs of religion becoming "evil" are not difficult to find in King Assurbanipal's belligerent rhetoric. For example, establishing the

---

24 See Waters, *A Survey of Neo-Elamite History*, 64–80.

25 See, e.g., P. Machinist, "Assyria and Its Image in First Isaiah," *JAOS* 103 (1983) 719–37; Lewis, "'You Have Heard What the Kings of Assyria Have Done.'"

26 Fales and Lanfranchi, "The Impact of Oracular Material," 114.

27 J. Novotny, *Selected Royal Inscriptions of Assurbanipal: L^3, L^4, LET, Prism I, Prism T, and Related Texts* (SAACT 10; Helsinki: The Neo-Assyrian Text Corpus Project, 2014), 77, 96 (inscription L^4 i 18–23).

"ideal" time is clearly pursued by him. In the Assyrian royal ideology, this meant the absolute hegemony of the Assyrian empire in the whole world known to him; the Assyrian king had titles such as "king of the world" *(šar kiššati)* and "king of the four regions of the world" *(šar kibrât erbetti)*[28]—designations that were meant to be taken literally and achieved by any thinkable means, first and foremost by wars, which were essentially presented as wars of the gods against their enemies.

In the holy war rhetoric, ancient and modern alike, the prerequisite for the establishment of the ideal world is the destruction of evil, which unavoidably legitimizes the use of violence. The end, therefore, justifies the violent means of pursuing the ideal world. In the real world, however, violence generates violence, and religion, sanctioning war against evil, becomes the catalyst of evil. Sooner or later, this screams for alternative ways of coping with the complicated system of identities, loyalties, and power relationships in international society.

From Holy War to Trust

Religious traditions and their sacred writings are a powerful tool in sanctioning violence and war. At the same time, the very same traditions and writings include an abundance of "abiding truths and principles that provide the first antidote to violence and extremism,"[29] in favor of peace and nonviolence. While I hesitate to declare as "corruption" every single element of violence in any given religious tradition that, I am afraid, cannot be purified of violence altogether, I am certainly in favor of the search in these traditions for elements that have the potential for leading the way to peace and reconciliation.

The responsibility for the interpretation, implementation, and transformation of religious traditions and their sacred texts is always on people who contribute to the development of their traditions. This is the responsibility of teachers and academics who, to a greater extent than people in general, should be aware of the constructive and destructive powers inherent in their traditions; it is also the responsibility of religious communities and their leaders who influence the members' attitudes and actions. Finally, it is the responsibility of the international community, which cannot champion the case of one single tradi-

28 Cf. M.-J. Seux, *Épithètes royales akkadiennes et sumeriennes* (Paris: Letouzey et Ané, 1967), 13–14, 305–12.
29 Kimball, *When Religion Becomes Evil*, 187.

tion, to learn to appreciate difference and dialogue in spite of the often-violent resistance.

The significance of religions in developing this appreciation cannot be underestimated. As Rabbi Jonathan Sacks puts it in his book *The Dignity of Difference,* "If religion is not part of a solution, it will certainly be part of the problem."[30] Sacks' book is a strong plea for intercultural and interreligious tolerance, respect, and responsibility in a world that is threatened with a "clash of civilizations"[31] and that is run by the market economy, the rule of which is often harsh and unconcerned with people's living conditions. Sacks' chief points—responsibility, morality, justice, education, equality, and environmental sustainability—are not new as such; what I find significant in his book is the emphasis on the role of religions in promoting and sustaining these fundamental values.

In the ideological world of the cold war period, religion appeared as an obsolete, fading phenomenon. The secularization of culture and politics has led to an idea of religion as a body of privately held ideas rather than a community of people who share much more than a set of beliefs with each other. The present world situation, however, indicates clearly enough that religions have not lost their vitality—on the contrary, as Scott Thomas has noted, the twenty-first century began in a spirit of a global resurgence of religion: "The postmodern world is turning out to be a post-secular world as well."[32] Therefore, ignoring the role of religions in the global community would be a serious political mistake. The so-called Western secularism should not make us blind to the fact that the majority of the human population base their identities on the foundation of their religious traditions, which are regarded holy and inviolable. Whether this leads to a "clash of civilizations" essentially depends on the ability of the international community to recognize and appreciate different faith-based identities.

Being, thus, a decisive factor in the formation of identities, religions may also contribute to conflicts. The disillusionment with modernization as being virtually equal to Westernization, as well as the failure of the market economy to produce equality and welfare, may result in a new "struggle for authenticity" in the non-Western world,[33] a reassertion of what is believed to be an authentic

30 J. Sacks, *The Dignity of Difference: How to Avoid the Clash of Civilizations* (rev. ed., London and New York: Continuum, 2003), 9.

31 S. Huntington, *The Clash of Civilizations and the Remaking of World Order* (New York: Simon & Schuster 1996).

32 Thomas, *The Global Resurgence of Religion,* 19–45 (quotation from p. 45).

33 Ibid., 41–42.

identity as opposed to the alleged Western import. This easily creates mutual mistrust at the global as well as individual levels. In the words of Jonathan Sacks, "Identity divides. The very process of creating an 'Us' involves creating 'Them'— the people not like us."[34] This also means that identities are not inborn qualities of people and societies but are formed by interaction and interdependency.

The rhetoric of holy war follows the logic of separation and mistrust: "They" have to be subdued or destroyed to protect "Us" and everything "We" stand for. Sacks challenges this logic by envisioning a covenantal relationship that affirms the dignity of difference and can be the basis of cooperation without dominance and submission; the concept is rooted in the theology of the covenant (Heb. *bĕrît)* in the Hebrew Bible.[35] Covenantal relationships are sustained by trust: "Covenant is the use of language to create a bond of trust through the word given, the word received, the word honoured in mutual fidelity."[36] As the result of—and, indeed, as a prerequisite for—covenant, trust works diametrically against the ideology of holy war. Trust is possible only if "They" are known and their difference appreciated.

The concept of trust that underlies Sacks' vision is a much-discussed issue in the social and economic sciences of the 1990s. His connection of trust to covenantal relationships is reminiscent of the definition of Francis Fukuyama: "Trust arises when a community shares a set of moral values in such a way as to create expectations of regular and honest behavior."[37] This is what Adam Seligman, who has developed the concept further, would call confidence rather than trust. Seligman makes a distinction between "confidence" in institutions and "trust" in people; trust, in his theory, is a phenomenon fundamentally tied to modern ideas of the individual and modern forms of the division of labor and respective social roles and agencies.[38] Moreover, Seligman separates trust from faith, which he sees as an "ontological trust beyond the world of social action."[39] Trust, in Seligman's terms, is the counterpart of and solution to risk as

---

34 Sacks, *The Dignity of Difference*, 10.
35 Ibid., 148–54, 192–209.
36 Ibid., 202.
37 F. Fukuyama, *Trust: The Social Virtues and the Creation of Prosperity* (London: Hamish Hamilton, 1995), 153.
38 A. Seligman, *The Problem of Trust* (Princeton, N.J.: Princeton University Press, 1997), 6–9.
39 Ibid., 22: "Indeed, it is this act of ontological trust (which in fact bypasses all epistemological procedures of verification) that is at the heart of the Jewish tradition, represented at the revelation on Mount Sinai when the Israelites are reported to have accepted godly commandments with the phrase נעשה ונשמע [*sic*] *(n'asch v'nishmah,* we will do and we will listen)."

a constitutive aspect of life in modern society; risk emerges when the systemically based expectations, on which confidence is based, come to their limits.[40] Relevant to our discussion is Seligman's observation that the preconditions for this kind of trust are disappearing, which makes him ask whether "risk is not giving way to danger and the problems which were once encompassed by a calculus of trust and mistrust are not redefined by one of confidence or lack thereof."[41] Historically, this would mean that the short interlude of trust as the solution to an internally framed risk of a willful actor in modern society is giving way to the renewed need of confidence as a protection against an external danger in the late or postmodern world. A new aspect of danger has recently manifested itself in the form of unpredictable and unorganized terrorist acts, while confidence is being imposed by means of surveillance, control, and military activity. In this counterproductive development, confidence becomes the counterpart of and companion to mistrust.

The distinctions Seligman finds between trust, confidence, and faith are not directly applicable to the reading of ancient texts—biblical or other—because his concept of trust does not apply to texts written in the premodern period. He can also be justly criticized for overemphasizing the autonomy of the modern self; for undermining individual agency in the dynamics of premodern societies of which he seems to have a rather mechanical understanding; for depriving the word "trust" of much of its everyday meaning and splitting up the largely overlapping semantic fields of trust and confidence, a distinction which cannot even be worked out in many languages other than English; and so on. All this notwithstanding, the distinction between trust in people, system-based confidence, and faith (that is, trust in God) is good to keep in mind when we now turn to exploring the alternatives to belligerent rhetoric in the Hebrew Bible.

Faith, Trust, and Confidence: Isaiah 2:2–4 and Micah 4:1–5

In the Hebrew Bible, it is virtually impossible to make a distinction between expressions derived from Hebrew roots *ʾmn* (Hi.) and *bṭḥ* denoting trust, confidence, and faith. Nevertheless, it is interesting to compare the use of these words in the Hebrew Bible with the vocabulary of Seligman. With human objects, the verbs *heʾemîn* and *bāṭaḥ* occur in surprisingly negative contexts, often denot-

---

40 Seligman. *The Problem of Trust,* 63–65, 170.
41 Ibid., 172.

ing a false security, while with regard to God, they always have a positive meaning.[42] Humans are not to be relied on, and self-security is condemned; the only legitimate object of trust is God and His word. In Seligman's terms, then, trust in people is excluded, and there is little confidence in human institutions—only faith, the "ontological trust beyond the world of social action," remains. Even warfare is based on faith; the Israelites should not trust in their own power: "The Lord will fight for you, so hold your peace" (Exod. 14:14). This is reminiscent of the inscription of Assurbanipal quoted above, where Ištar tells him to stay in his place while she fights for him.[43] Thus, seen as opposed to confidence in human institutions, trust in God does not always appear as an antidote to violence; it can well be used as a part of the belligerent rhetoric. This has little to do with the trust-based covenantal relationships contemplated by Jonathan Sacks.

In the Hebrew Bible, though, there are alternative ways of trusting in God, which might correspond better to Sacks' idea of trust-based relationships. Especially in the book of Isaiah, the people are exhorted to trust in God, for example, in Isaiah 7:9: "Have firm faith, or you will not stand firm" *(ʾim lōʾ taʾămînû kî lōʾ tēʾāmēnû)*. The play with the root *ʾmn* conveys an idea very similar to what is expressed with the root *bṭḥ* in Isaiah 30:15: "In quiet confidence *(bĕ-hašqēt û-bĕ-biṭḥâ)* your strength will lie." In both cases, the Judeans are warned against engaging in military enterprises, which would only bring about a disaster, and encouraged to stay calm, putting their trust and faith in God. While these exhortations appear in political contexts, at least on the literary level, our theme texts, Isaiah 2:2–4 and Micah 4:1–5, contemplate trust in God as an enduring condition in a beatific future.[44] In this vision, trust in God creates an undisturbed confidence of people in each other, so that swords are beaten into plowshares and, according to the Micah version, everyone can sit under their own fig tree without fear.

The composition, date, and literary relationship of Isaiah 2:2–4 and Micah 4:1–5 are not the primary concern of this article; for a variety of reasons, I am

---

42 Cf. the observations of Alfred Jepsen in his articles, "אמן *ʾāman*," *TDOT* 1 (1974): 292–323, esp. 300–9; and "בטח *bāṭaḥ*," *TDOT 2* (1975): 88–94.

43 The same idea is expressed in an Assyrian prophetic oracle pronounced to Esarhaddon, Assurbanipal's father: "Do not trust in humans! Lift up your eyes and focus on me! I am Ištar of Arbela." See S. Parpola, *Assyrian Prophecies* (SAA 9; Helsinki: Helsinki University Press, 1997), 6: 27–30; cf. Nissinen, *Prophets and Prophecy*, no. 71.

44 Even though the Hebrew vocabulary of trust is not used in these passages, the peoples' trust in God is implied by their willingness to submit to God's instruction expressed in imperative and cohortative forms *lĕkû wĕ-naʿălê* and *wĕ-nēlĕkâ* (Isa 2:3, Mic 4:2).

inclined to concur with those who find both texts rather late redactional insertions into their present textual contexts, dating them to no earlier than the Persian period, that is, from the late sixth to fourth centuries BCE.[45] The questions which of the two texts came first, and whether both draw from the same source or are inserted into both books by the same redactor, cannot be properly discussed here.

There is a whole lot to be learned from our theme texts about the religion and identity of the community that produced them, probably in Jerusalem under Persian rule.

First, the community lived before the separation of religion and society. It had a religion-based identity, with God and Jerusalem, God's holy city, at its core. The texts demonstrably borrow from the language and ideology of the Zion Psalms (Pss. 46, 48, 66, 76, etc.),[46] which, on the other hand, cling to the Near Eastern tradition of hailing particular cities as embodiments of the divine presence and as manifestations of the fundamental unity of god, king, and people.[47] In the vision of Isaiah 2:2–4 and Micah 4:1–5, there is no (longer) room for a human political leader. Instead, the rule of the God of this community is absolute, Mount Zion is the center of the world, and the word of this God, Torah *(tôrah/dĕbar yhwh)*, is imposed upon all nations. It depends on the reader how much of the often-applauded universalism remains in these texts if they are read from this Zion-centered perspective, which is the ideological cornerstone of the composition of the book of Isaiah as a whole.[48]

Second, identity divides. Even this aspect is strongly present in our theme texts, which do not dissolve the difference between the community and other na-

---

45 For the Persian dating of Isa 2:2–4, sec M. A. Sweeney, *Isaiah 1–39 with an Introduction to Prophetic Literature* (FOTL 16; Grand Rapids, Mich.: Eerdmans, 1996), 98–99; J. Blenkinsopp, *Isaiah 1–39: A New Translation with Introduction and Commentary* (AB 19; New York: Doubleday, 2000), 190; for a postexilic date for Mic 4:1–5, see R. Kessler, *Micha* (HTKAT; Freiburg: Herder, 1999), 181–83; E. Ben-Zvi, *Micah* (FOTL 21B; Grand Rapids, Mich.: Eerdmans, 2000), 94–106; J. Wagenaar, *Judgement and Salvation: The Composition and Redaction of Micah 2–5* (VTSup 85; Leiden: Brill, 2001), 272.

46 See J. T. Willis, "Isaiah 2:2–5 and the Psalms of Zion," in *Writing and Reading the Scroll of Isaiah: Studies of an Interpretive Tradition*, Vol. 1 (eds. C. C. Broyles and C. A. Evans; VTSup 70/1; Leiden: Brill, 1997), 295–316.

47 See M. Nissinen, "City as Lofty as Heaven: Arbela and Other Cities in Neo-Assyrian Prophecy," in *"Every City Shall Be Forsaken": Urbanism and Prophecy in Ancient Israel and the Near East* (ed. L. L. Grabbe and R. D. Haak; JSOTSup 330, Sheffield: Sheffield Academic Press, 2001), 174–209 (= pp. 267–300 in this volume).

48 See A. Laato, *"About Zion I Will not Be Silent": The Book of Isaiah as an Ideological Unity* (CB.OT 44; Stockholm: Almqvist & Wiksell, 1998).

tions. In Micah 4:5, even the difference between the God of Israel and the gods of the nations is acknowledged in spite of the submission of the nations to the instruction issued from Zion: "All peoples may walk, each in the name of his God, but we will walk in the name of YHWH, our God, for ever and ever." One may ask whether this is believed to be true in the ideal future envisioned in the preceding verses or whether it only refers to the present situation of the intended readership.[49] In any case, the nations are not said to become one—on the contrary, God is there to judge between them. The result of this judgment is a peaceful modus vivendi of different identities that continue to exist.

Third, in contrast with many other texts, Israel appears here with the nations, not against them. The motif of the battle of the nations *(Völkerkampf)*, which can be found in many prophetic texts, including the books of Isaiah and Micah, as well as the Zion Psalms,[50] is transformed into the pilgrimage of the nations *(Völkerwallfahrt)* to Jerusalem.[51] The inversion of battle and pilgrimage corresponds to the beating of swords into plowshares. There are other texts that proclaim God's quelling of war and weapons (e.g., Ps 46:9; Isa 9:3–4),[52] but in the case of Isaiah 2:2–4 and Micah 4:1–5, the nations, upon divine instruction, do it themselves. The difference between "Us" and "Them" remains, after all, but it does not prevent the joint enterprise from becoming instructed by God. Holy war is no longer on the divine agenda. The nations are welcomed to Mount Zion, they are not excluded from receiving God's word, that is, Torah.[53] Hence, there prevails a confidence that surmounts the difference in identities and enables the communities to share the moral values in such a way that holy war is deleted from the agenda and replaced by a "holy peace."[54] A related,

---

49 Cf. Ben-Zvi, *Micah*, 101–2.

50 Cf, e.g., Isa 13:2–5; Mic 4:11–13; Joel 4:1–3, 9–12; Zech 12:2–9, 14:1–3; Ps 46, 48, 76.

51 Sec Wagenaar, *Judgement and Salvation*, 264–68.

52 Willis, "Isaiah 2:2–5 and the Psalms of Zion," 305.

53 It is disputed whether the word *tôrâ* here and in other parts of the book of Isaiah means the Mosaic Torah or whether it should be understood as a more open concept of a prophetic Torah; in favor of the latter alternative, cf. I. Fischer , "World Peace and 'Holy War'—Two Sides of the Same Theological Concept: "YHWH as Sole Divine Power" (A Canonical and Intertextual Reading of Isaiah 2:1–5, Joel 4:9–21, and Micah 4:1–5)," in Cohen and Westbrook (eds.), *Isaiah's Vision of Peace*, 151–65; ead., *Tora für Israel—Tora für die Völker* (SBS 164; Stuttgart: Katholisches Bibelwerk, 1995); R. Kessler, "Zwischen Tempel und Tora: Das Michabuch im Diskurs der Perserzeit," *BZ* 44 (2000) 21–36.

54 Interestingly, Francis Landy ("Torah and Anti-Torah: Isaiah 2:2–4 and 1:10–26," *BibInt* 11 [2003] 317–34) pays attention to the gender aspect of the divine instruction. In his view, the grammatically female *tôrâ* and the masculine *dĕbar-YHWH* complement each other in God's speech, which encompasses both genders. "The Torah, as a universal language, has a maternal quality; within its orbit, the nations abandon their phallic rivalries" (321).

probably later and even more outspoken, vision is to be found in Isa 19:19 – 25, in which Egypt and Assyria worship together, and God blesses them, saying, "Blessed be my people Egypt, Assyria my handiwork, Israel my inheritance."[55]

Fourth, the Micah version of the text includes a significant expansion of the ideas expressed in Isaiah 2:2 – 4.[56] On the one hand, it intensifies the scene of the divine arbitration: "He will judge between *many* peoples and arbiter among *mighty* nations *afar*" (Mic. 4:3), thus globalizing the scene even more than the Isaianic version. On the other hand, it individualizes the outcome of the divine arbitration by the famous image of each individual sitting without fear under his own vine and fig tree (Mic. 4:4). This sounds like a reflection of the Deureronomistic idealization of the time of Solomon in 1 Kings 5:5: "All through the days of Solomon, Judah and Israel dwelt in safety, each under his own vine and fig-tree, from Dan to Beersheba"; or even the Assyrian propaganda in the mouth of Rabshakeh, the chief officer of King Sennacherib: "Make peace with me and come out to me, and you may all eat from your own vines and fig-trees and drink water from your own cisterns"—with the significant difference, however, that no war and no earthly king is needed to bring about this ideal time, which is neither *Pax Salomonica* nor *Pax Assyriaca*, but a divinely established "holy peace."[57]

Privatization of the universal vision brings into play the aspect of personal safety based on trust in the "holy peace" established by God, turning the perspective from global, eschatological judgment to the privacy of the homes of the intended readership and thus generating an image of a world without fear. The blatantly unrealistic and ideological vision of the peoples streaming to Jerusalem becomes its ultimate motivation from the desire for peace in the everyday life of the community and its individual members. This, ultimately, is the word of God, the object and basis of trust: "For it was the Lord of Hosts who spoke" (Mic. 4:4).

It should not be forgotten that the texts present a vision of a world that did not exist in the everyday experience of their primary readership. People did not

55 Cf. the comments of Sacks, *The Dignity of Difference*, 204: "Some 2,700 years before Horace Kallen coined the term 'pluralism', Isaiah had given it religious meaning. God's world is diverse. The paths to salvation are many." While the hermeneutical potential of the text to this effect should not be denied, this kind of universalism prohably exceeds the understanding of the primary readership. For historical interpretations in different settings, see, e.g., Sweeney, *Isaiah 1–39*, 271 – 73 (time of Manasseh); Blenkinsopp, *Isaiah 1 – 39*, 317 – 20 (Hellenistic age, which, in my view, is more probable).

56 See J. Limburg, "Swords to Ploughshares: Text and Contexts," in Broyles and Evans (eds.), *Writing and Reading the Scroll of Isaiah*, 279 – 93, esp. 285 – 86.

57 Cf. Kessler, *Micha*, 186.

stream to Mount Zion, God's instruction did not reach the nations, swords were not beaten into plowshares, and there was every reason to be afraid of violence. Clearly, the texts present a fantasy of an ideal world not experienced by any of their readers. If the texts, then, ultimately manifest "euphoria in the postdisaster period,"[58] or "dreams of grandeur of the actually powerless,"[59] or, less triumphalistically understood, an expression of the simple and sincere hope of a small community for a safe environment, what was the starting point for such a vision in the real world? The texts presuppose that there was not enough faith in the intended readership to make the vision true. But was there no confidence either, or could the texts be placed against a historical background where confidence in human institutions would indeed have played a significant role?

The Life of a Small Nation: Desire for Peace

The life of a small nation sandwiched between superior powers, like Judah/Yehud or, say, Finland, is continuous walking on a tightrope. Political autonomy or independence does not remove the need to come to terms with major political actors with overwhelming military, economic, and political resources. These powers can be encountered in different ways, by military confrontation, by political passivity, or by entering into a contractual relationship and concluding a political treaty. Making a treaty or a contract requires a fair amount of mutual confidence, even in cases where there is no equality between parties and the inferior party is more or less forced to enter the treaty by the superior party. In Seligman's terms, this is confidence, not trust, based on systemically based expectations, and I think this distinction works here quite well. I take Finland, my home country, as an example.[60]

After World War II, Finland had, in addition to huge indemnities demanded by the Soviet Union, few options but to conclude the Treaty of Friendship, Cooperation and Mutual Assistance with its powerful eastern neighbor, a contract that remained in force from 1948 to 1992. Even though this treaty aroused expressions of political moralism in the West regarding so-called Finlandization, this arrangement prevented the worst from happening. The indemnities were paid to the last penny, which required the establishment of whole branches of industry in this formerly agricultural country. Politically, Finland never shared the fate of

58 Blenkinsopp, *Isaiah 1–39*, 190.

59 Ben-Zvi, *Micah*, 106.

60 For an overview of the history of Finland in the post-World War II period, see E. Jutikkala and K. Pirinen, *A History of Finland* (trans. by Paul Sjöblom; Helsinki: WSOY, 2003).

the Baltic and East European nations but remained a democratic society and experienced an era of unprecedented economic growth and prosperity in the decades following. The word "trust" was much misused in those days to describe the Finnish-Soviet relationship, but there was certainly a sufficient amount of confidence, if not in the Soviet Union as a political system, then in the personal relationships of the leaders of the states. Despite the political pressure and the latent but existing military threat, the post-World War II period was a peaceful and propitious time in Finland. The importance of the nineteenth- and early-twentieth-century construction of Finnish identity for this survival strategy, one of its basic constituents being Lutheran Christianity, cannot be underestimated.

The conditions in Finland in the twentieth century CE are, of course, not directly comparable with those in Judah/Yehud at the time when the books of Isaiah and Micah were written; yet I cannot resist the temptation to look at the political history of that small nation from this perspective. The rise of Assyria to political supremacy in the Near East is usually presented as an unparalleled political crisis, and the Assyrians themselves as oppressors without rival; both the Hebrew Bible and the propaganda of the Assyrians themselves have strongly contributed to this picture. However, it is hardly adequate to describe the Assyrian era as a period of perpetual oppression, calamity, and cultural persecution. True, the Assyrians took over political control in Syria-Palestine in 730s BCE, and countless lives were lost and many cities destroyed in the military campaigns of the Assyrian kings, especially in the Northern Kingdom. This was not the fate of Judah, however. King Ahaz of Judah paid his tribute to Assyria, which certainly put his solvency to the proof, but Judah was not invaded. Assyrian supremacy lasted for more than a century, and most of the time, in fact, there prevailed a modus vivendi between Judah and Assyria. It was broken by Hezekiah at a high price, but reestablished by his son Manasseh. In the Hebrew Bible, Hezekiah is the hero while Manasseh plays the role of the apostate, but this may largely be the hindsight of the Deuteronomists.[61] In practical terms, as far as the sources reveal, the long reign of Manasseh seems like a peaceful and relatively prosperous era, which can with good reason be called *Pax Assyriaca,* based on

61 Note, however, the rehabilitation of Manasseh by the Chronicler who makes him repent his sins after having been punished by God (2 Chr 33:9–13). For a recent comparison of the Deuteronomistic and Chronistic accounts of Manasseh, see M. A. Sweeney, "King Manasseh of Judah and the Problem of Theodicy in the Deuteronomistic History," in *Good Kings and Bad Kings* (ed. L. L. Grabbe; LHBOTS 393; London: T&T Clark, 2005), 264–78, esp. 268–72.

a contractual relationship *(adê)* between the superpower and the vassal state.[62] Even though Assyria was in a position to dictate the terms, it also protected allies who agreed to fulfill the often-harsh conditions of the treaty. For Judah, the tribute to Assyria was certainly a heavy economic burden, but it may also have speeded up economic development in the Judean hill country. As a matter of fact, political pressure from Assyria forced Judah to develop its political and economical infrastructure into a full-blown state, to be destroyed only by the Babylonians in 586.

In the Persian period, which I consider the most probable historical background for Isaiah 2:2–4 and Micah 4:1–5, the former kingdom of Judah was turned into the Persian province of Yehud, and there was no longer a contractual relationship between rulers of states. This political arrangement is never openly questioned in the Hebrew Bible. On the contrary, Cyrus is hailed in messianic terms in the second part of the book of Isaiah.[63] Ezra and Nehemiah were authorized by the Persians, and the jurisdiction of the province could hardly be established without the consent of the Persian king.[64] If there was discontent among the people in Yehud with Persian rule (and it is difficult to believe there was not any dissatisfaction at all!), it must be read between the lines.[65] This was the period when the religion of Israel took the rorm we know from the Hebrew Bible, and when the Hebrew Bible itself started to emerge as an authoritative collection of sacred writings. As much as can be interpreted from the meager and episodic sources from that period, life in Yehud was not extremely prosperous but relatively peaceful, without any major external military threat. Yehud was "a not-

---

62 For a historical analysis of the time of Manasseh, see E.-A. Knauf, "The Glorious Days of Manasseh," in Grabbe (ed.), *Good Kings and Bad Kings*, 164–88. For *Pax Assyriaca,* cf. Fales, "On *Pax Assyriaca* in the Eighth-Seventh Centuries BCE."

63 Cf. M. A. Sweeney, "Isaiah and Theodicy after the *Shoah*," in *Strange Fire: Reading the Bible after the Holocaust* (ed. Tod Linafelt; Sheffield: Sheffield Academic Press, 2000), 208–19, esp. 211: "Throughout Deutero-Isaiah, YHWH announces the coming of Cyrus and the restoration of Jerusalem as divine acts that demonstrate YHWH's sovereignty over all creation. In short, Deutero-Isaiah identifies YHWH with the imperial power of Persia ... Both Isa. 2.2–4 and 60–62 ... correspond well to the identification of YHWH's sovereignty with the rise of the Persian empire."

64 Even though this does not necessarily mean a direct imperial authorization of the Pentateuch by the Persians, I find it impossible to think that local laws could have been implemented without approval from the Persians; for recent discussion, see the articles in *Persia and Torah: The Theory of Imperial Authorization of the Pentateuch* (ed. J. W. Watts; SBLSymS 17; Atlanta: Society of Biblical Literature, 2001).

65 For eventual anti-Persian sentiments, cf. D. L. Smith-Christopher, *A Biblical Theology of Exile* (Overtures to Biblical Theology; Minneapolis: Fortress, 2002).

wealthy province in a rather out-of-the-way part of the empire."[66] This was not an ideal world, but there was enough confidence and hope to generate a vision of the future world of trust.

Epilogue

The rhetoric of holy war has a powerful function in legitimizing aspirations to power and dominion and convincing potential supporters of their justification; however, it never carries far enough and does not solve any single problem. Sooner or later there is a need to find solutions by means of negotiation and mutual agreements. True, these do not immediately bring about peace and prosperity, as the bargaining positions are seldom equal, but any ruling apparatus will find it necessary to listen to the other party. Force, violence, and economic superiority may guarantee the dominion of the stronger party for some time, but they also create profound mistrust and nourish terrorism and revolution, the detection and prevention of which requires colossal resources. This was as evident with the rule of Assurbanipal as it is with the more recent "war on terrorism." Establishing mutual confidence, on the other hand, frees these resources to purposes that can better serve people's needs.

There is no need to talk about trust, confidence, or faith, unless the uncertainty and unpredictability of life makes it unavoidable. Political upheavals, and even less dramatic events, demonstrate that being in full control of one's life is not possible for any society or individual, that crucial decisions concerning their lives are made elsewhere. Uncertainty needs to be tolerated, though, because every step toward the future requires orientation toward things hoped for but not seen. Uncertainty can be faced either with trust or with fear. Trust maintains the momentum and motivates those involved to face the risks and step toward the future. Fear, on the other hand, prevents movement, motivates the building of security structures, and gives reasons for aggressive activities against any given danger. Where there is no trust, or even confidence, there is mistrust, suspicion, insecurity, and paranoia. Where the security systems fail, trust may be tested to the utmost, and this situation calls for metatrust, or trust beyond trust that I would call trust in God, or faith. The role of religion in facing risk and danger is twofold. Religion can give rise to visions of peace and reconcilia-

66 L. L. Grabbe, *A History of the Jews and Judaism in the Second Temple Period*, Vol. 1: *Yehud: A History of the Persian Province of Judah* (Library of Second Temple Studies 47; London and New York: T & T Clark, 2004), 154.

tion, but it can also become "evil"; God can be invoked for the purposes of violent pursuits. The best antidote to this is sensitivity to religious traditions and their responsible interpretation.

Falsche Prophetie in neuassyrischer und deuteronomistischer Darstellung

I

Wie kann eine Prophetie als „falsch" erklärt und von einer „wahren" Prophetie unterschieden werden? Diese in verschiedenen Teilen des Alten Testaments aktuelle Frage hat seit langem auch die Alttestamentler geplagt, die sich mit den betreffenden Texten beschäftigt haben. Die oft dramatischen Auseinandersetzungen der Propheten Jeremia, Ezechiel und Micha mit den sogenannten falschen Propheten[1] sind wohlbekannt (Jer 6:13–15; 23:13–32; 27:14–17; 28; 29:8–9, 15, 21–23; Ez 13; Mi 3:5–12). Außerdem meldet sich die Frage in einer oder anderer Weise in den Geschichtsbüchern, z. B. im Falle von Elija (1 Reg 18) und Micha ben Jimla (1 Reg 22:1–28), sowohl auch im Deuteronomium, wo sie zweimal von einem grundsätzlichen Gesichtspunkt aus betrachtet wird (13:2–6; 18:15–22). Das Problem ist jedoch nicht ausgesprochen biblisch – im Grunde genommen ist es eigentlich zu erwarten, daß es in jeder Gemeinschaft auftaucht, in der die Prophetie, d. h. die menschliche Übermittlung einer angeblich göttlichen Botschaft, ein anerkanntes Phänomen ist. Es wird in diesem Aufsatz zu zeigen versucht, daß die „falsche" Prophetie zumindest auch im neuassyrischen Reich eine dringende Frage war, und daß sie dort wie im Alten Testament nicht nur ein rein theoretisches Dilemma darstellte, sondern ein erstrangiges politisches Risiko, das zu konkreten Maßnahmen Anlaß gab.

Um den Begriff Prophetie, dessen Gebrauch in außerbiblischen Zusammenhängen nicht unumstritten gewesen ist[2], zu rechtfertigen, dürfte es notwendig sein, zuerst zu verdeutlichen, was in dem vorliegenden Kontext damit ausgedrückt wird. Das Wort Prophetie bedeutet eine Übermittlung einer sprachlichen oder metasprachlichen Botschaft, die eine Person (ein Prophet oder eine Prophetin)

---

1 Das Epitheton stammt eigentlich nicht aus der hebräischen Bibel, sondern aus der Septuaginta (*pseudoprophētēs* Jer 6:13; 33:7, 8, 11, 16; 34:7; 35:1; 36:1, 8; Sach 13:2), aus jüdischen Schriften (*T. Jud.* 21:9; Philo, *Spec.* 4,51; Josephus, *B.J.* 6,285 u. ö.) und aus dem Neuen Testament (Mt 7:15; 24:11, 24; Mk 13:22; Lk 6:26; Apg 13:6; 2 Pt 2:1; 1 Jh 4:1; Apk 16:13; 19:20; 20:10).

2 Vgl. die dazu geäußerten Bedenken von E. Noort, *Untersuchungen zum Gottesbescheid in Mari: Die „Mariprophetie" in der alttestamentlichen Forschung* (AOAT 202; Kevelaer: Butzon & Bercker; Neukirchen-Vluyn: Neukirchener Verlag, 1977) 92. 109 und M. deJong Ellis, „Observations on Mesopotamian Oracles and Prophetic Texts: Literary and Historiographic Considerations," *JCS* 41 (1989) 127–86, 132–33, 146–47.

DOI 10.1515/9783110466546-022

ohne induktive Techniken angeblich von einer Gottheit empfängt, um sie an einen individuellen oder kollektiven Adressaten zu übermitteln[3]. Die konstitutiven Elemente der Prophetie sind demnach 1) die Gottheit als Sender der Botschaft, 2) das Orakel (oder die metasprachliche Handlung) als Substanz der Botschaft, 3) der Prophet als Vermittler der Botschaft und 4) der Adressat oder die Adressaten als Empfänger der Botschaft.

Das Problem bei der Identifizierung der „falschen" Prophetie liegt offen zutage: jede Botschaft mit einem prophetischen Anspruch kann die drei letzten Bedingungen erfüllen, aber von einer wahren Prophetie muß vorausgesetzt werden, daß auch und vor allem die erste Bedingung erfüllt wird, daß also die Botschaft tatsächlich von einer Gottheit stammt. Eben diese wichtigste Bedingung ist aber unkontrollierbar, denn ihre Erfüllung ist jenseits aller menschlichen Beobachtungsgabe. Der wahre Prophet ist der, der den Plan Gottes wirklich weiß (1 Reg 22:19 – 23) – aber wer hat denn wirklich im Rat des Herrn gestanden? Diese Frage ist im Jeremiabuch (Jer 23:18) wohl nicht rhetorisch, sondern in allem Ernst gemeint[4].

---

3 Dazu genauer M. Weippert, „Aspekte israelitischer Prophetie im Lichte verwandter Erscheinungen des Alten Orients," in *Ad bene et fideliter seminandum*, FS Karlheinz Deller (ed. G. Mauer and U. Magen; AOAT 220; Kevelaer: Butzon & Bercker; Neukirchen–Vluyn: Neukirchener Verlag, 1988) 287– 319, 289–90 und M. Nissinen, „Die Relevanz der neuassyrischen Prophetie für die alttestamentliche Forschung," in *Mesopotamica – Ugaritica – Biblica*, FS K. Bergerhof (ed. M. Dietrich and O. Loretz; AOAT 232, Kevelaer, Germany: Butzon & Bercker; Neukirchen-Vluyn: Neukirchener, 1993) 217-58, 221 (= S. 315 – 50 im vorliegenden Band). Vgl. auch die sehr ähnliche Definition von H. B. Huffmon, „The Origins of Prophecy," in *Magnalia Dei: The Mighty Acts of God*, FS G. E. Wright (ed. F. M. Cross, W. E. Lemke, and P.D. Miller; Garden City, N.Y.: Doubleday, 1976) 171 – 86, 172, nach der der Prophet eine Person ist, „who through non-technical means receives a clear and immediate message from a deity for transmission to a third party." Demnach ist es eben die Nicht-Benutzung induktiver Methoden (oder: Benutzung nicht-induktiver Methoden), die die Prophetie von anderen Formen des Gottesbescheids unterscheidet. Dies benötigt keine unüberbrückbare Kluft zwischen Prophetie und anderen divinatorischen Praktiken als Übermittlung göttlicher Botschaft; vgl. T. W. Overholt, *Channels of Prophecy: The Social Dynamics of Prophetie Activity* (Minneapolis, Minn.: Fortress Press, 1989), 140 – 47; L. L. Grabbe, *Priests, Prophets, Diviners, Sages: A Socio-Historical Study of Religious Specialists in Ancient Israel* (Valley Forge, Pa.: Trinity Press International, 1995), 139 – 41; F. H. Cryer, „Der Prophet und der Magier: Bemerkungen anhand einer überholten Diskussion," in *Prophetie und geschichtliche Wirklichkeit im alten Israel*, FS S. Herrmann (ed. R. Liwak und S. Wagner; Stuttgart: Kohlhammer, 1991) 79 – 88; idem, *Divination in Ancient Israel and its Near Eastern Environment* (JSOTS 142; Sheffield: Sheffield Academic Press, 1994), 325. Cryer rechnet freilich damit, daß auch die Propheten „technische" Divination praktiziert hätten, hat aber m. E. keinen überzeugenden Beweis dafür geliefert.

4 So auch H.-J. Hermisson, „Kriterien 'wahrer' und 'falscher' Prophetie im Alten Testament: Zur Auslegung von Jeremia 23,16 – 22 und Jeremia 28,8 – 9," *ZThK* 92 (1995) 121 – 39, 130, der freilich im

Im Alten Testament besteht kein Mangel an Kriterien der falschen Prophetie. Das Problem entsteht vielmehr daraus, daß aus den verschiedenen Einzelfällen keine handfeste Kriteriologie entsteht, die überall gelten würde. Das Thema ist schon gründlich behandelt worden in zahlreichen Studien[5], die insgesamt die Kontextbezogenheit einzelner Kriterien sowie deren Hinfälligkeit als allgemeingültige theoretische Regeln deutlich genug gezeigt haben. Als Beispiel möge der bekannte Konflikt des Propheten Jeremia mit dem Propheten Hananja dienen (Jer 28): Hier steht in der aktuellen Konfliktsituation nur Wort gegen Wort, ohne daß sich das eine oder das andere objektiv unumstritten als „wahr" oder „falsch" erweisen würde. Erst nachträglich wird es möglich, mittels des Erfüllungskriteriums (vgl. Dtn 18,21 f.) die Entscheidung zu treffen, und hier geht es nicht um heuristische Überlegungen, sondern um deuteronomistische[6] Theologie, die die Prophetie des Jeremia als „wahr" erscheinen läßt[7]. Das Beispiel macht an-

---

ursprünglichen Text keine Frage findet; zur Frage sei der Satz erst durch den redaktionellen Zusatz in V. 18b geworden.

5 Die neuesten Beiträge sind wohl Hermisson („Kriterien 'wahrer' und 'falscher' Prophetie"), Grabbe (*Priests, Prophets, Diviners, Sages*), 113 – 15 und R. J. Coggins, „Prophecy: True and False," in *Of Prophets' Visions and the Wisdom of Sages*, FS R. N. Whybray (ed. H. A. McKay and D. J. A. Clines; JSOTS 162; Sheffield: Sheffield Academic Press, 1993) 80 – 94. Aus der seit den 70er Jahren erschienenen Literatur seien die folgenden Werke genannt: J. L. Crenshaw, *Prophetic Conflict* (BZAW 124, Berlin: De Gruyter, 1971); F.-L. Hossfeld und I. Meyer, *Prophet gegen Prophet: Eine Analyse der alttestamentlichen Texte zum Thema: Wahre und falsche Prophetie* (BiBe NF 9; Fribourg: Schweizerisches Katholisches Bibelwerk, 1973); G. Münderlein, *Kriterien wahrer und falscher Prophetie: Entstehung und Bedeutung im Alten Testament* (EHS.T 33; Frankfurt a.M.: Peter Lang, 1974 [^{2}1979]); I. Meyer, *Jeremia und die falschen Propheten* (OBO 13; Freiburg: Universitätsverlag und Göttingen: Vandenhoeck & Ruprecht, 1977); B. O. Long, „Social Dimensions of Prophetie Conflict," *Semeia* 21 (1981) 31 – 53; J. Blenkinsopp, *A History of Prophecy in Israel* (rev. and enlarged ed.; Louisville, Ky.: Westminster/John Knox Press, 1996 [11984]), 184 – 88; R. P. Carroll, *From Chaos to Covenant: Prophecy in the Book of Jeremiah* (New York: Crossroad, 1981), 192 – 97; J. L. Sicre, *Profetismo en Israel: El profeta, los profetas, el mensaje* (Estella, Spain: Verbo divino, 1992), 145 – 48 (dort auch eine Bibliographie der überraschend zahlreichen spanischen Beiträge zum Thema).

6 Das zum Maßstab der wahren Prophetie erklärte Erfüllungskriterium in Jer 28:8 – 9 ist deuteronomistisch und setzt das Scheitern der Prophetie von Hananja selbstverständlich voraus; s. Hermisson („Kriterien 'wahrer' und 'falscher' Prophetie"), 134 – 37 und G. Wanke, *Untersuchungen zur sogenannten Baruchschrift* (BZAW 122; Berlin: De Gruyter, 1971), 19 – 36.

7 Vgl. R. P. Carroll, *The Book of Jeremiah: A Commentary* (OTL; London: SCM, 1986), 547 – 50 und grundsätzlich O. Kaiser, *Der Gott des Alten Testaments: Theologie des Alten Testaments*, vol. 1: *Grundlegung* (Uni-Taschenbücher 1747; Göttingen: Vandenhoeck & Ruprecht, 1993), 230: „Daß das in dem deuteronomistischen Prophetengesetz Dtn 18,9 – 22 benannte Kriterium der Erfüllung der Weissagung (V. 21 f.) sich lediglich bei der Beurteilung und Auswahl tradierter Prophetien, aber keineswegs in der aktuellen Konfliktsituation anwenden ließ, sagt einem die praktische Vernunft."

schaulich, daß sich kein prophetischer Konflikt, historisch oder literarisch, in einem freien ideologischen Raum abspielt, sondern Auseinandersetzungen lebendiger Menschen widerspiegelt. Dabei geht es nachdrücklich darum, was die Propheten *sagen*, d. h. um den *Inhalt* der Botschaft, von dessen Anerkennung auch die Wahrhaftigkeit bzw. Falschheit der Prophetie abhängig ist.

Diese Tatsache ist in der Tat im Dtn 13[8] emstgenommen und zu einem Grundsatz entwickelt worden. Hier wird es den Israeliten von Jahwe verboten, einem „Propheten oder Traumseher" (*nābî' 'ô ḥōlem ḥălôm*) zuzuhören, der unter ihnen ersteht (*yāqûm*), ein Zeichen oder Wunder ankündigt und sagt: „Laßt uns gehen und anderen Göttern dienen." Vielmehr muß er getötet werden wegen der „trügerischen Rede" *(dibber-sārâ),* weil er versucht hat, das Volk zur Apostasie zu führen. Selbst wenn das von ihm angekündigte Zeichen oder Wunder eintreffen sollte, ändert es nichts daran (Dtn 13:2–6). Auch die engsten Angehörigen und Freunde, „dein Bruder, Sohn deines Vaters oder Sohn deiner Mutter, oder dein Sohn oder deine Tochter, oder das Weib deines Busens, oder dein Freund, den du liebst wie dich selbst," (V. 7)[9] sowie alle möglichen Verführer in anderen Städten (Vss. 13–14) sollen gleichfalls getötet werden, sollte es sich heraussteilen *('emet nākôn had-dābār;* vgl. Dtn 17:4), daß sie das Volk zum Dienst an anderen Göttern verleitet haben.

Im Hinblick auf Dtn 18:20–22 und die Falschprophetenpolemik des Jeremiabuches ist das Kriterium von Dtn 13, der Ausschließlichkeitsanspruch Jahwes, unerhört eindeutig und klar[10]. Es fällt besonders auf, daß das Kriterium von Dtn 13 ausgesprochen inhaltlich ist und ganz und gar davon abhängt, was der „Prophet

8 Vgl. die neuesten Beiträge zu diesem Kapitel: P. E. Dion, „Deuteronomy 13: The Suppression of Alien Religious Propaganda in Israel during the Late Monarchical Era," in *Law and Ideology in Monarchic Israel* (ed. B. Halpern und D. W. Hobson; JSOTS 124; Sheffield: Sheffield University Press 1991) 147–216 und T. Veijola, „Wahrheit und Intoleranz nach Deuteronomium 13," *ZThK* 92 (1995) 287–314.

9 So nach der Übersetzung von LXX, die wohl von einer Vorlage übersetzt worden ist, die älter ist als der MT, in dem die Wörter „Sohn deines Vaters" fehlen. Hier folge ich A. Aejmelaeus, „Licence to Kill? Deut 13:10 and the Prerequisites of Textual Criticism," in *Verbum et Calamus: Semitic and Related Studies in Honour of the Sixtieth Birthday of Professor Tapani Harviainen* (eds. H. Juusola, J. Laulainen und H. Palva; StOr 99: Helsinki: Finnish Oriental Society, 2004), 1–22, gegen B. M. Levinson, „Textual Criticism, Assyriology, and the History of Interpretation: Deuteronomy 13:7a as a Text Case in Method," *JBL* 120 (2001): 211–43.

10 U. Rüterswörden, „Das Böse in der deuteronomischen Schultheologie," in *Das Deuteronomium und seine Querbeziehungen* (ed. T. Veijola; Schriften der Finnischen Exegetischen Gesellschaft 62; Helsinki: Finnische Exegetische Gesellschaft un Göttingen: Vandenhoeck & Ruprecht, 1996), 223–41, sieht hier eine bewußte Ergänzung von Dtn 18:20–22. Andererseits setzt Dtn 13 nach Veijola, „Wahrheit und Intoleranz nach Deuteronomium 13," 297–301 die Falschprophetenpolemik des Jeremiabuches und die dabei angewandten Kriterien bereits voraus.

oder Traumseher" *sagt*. Es wird überhaupt nicht spekuliert, ob er wirklich von Jahwe gesandt ist – das Gegenteil wird wohl vorausgesetzt[11], aber andererseits wird auch damit gerechnet, daß das von ihm versprochene Wunder eintrifft. Auch hier ist das inhaltliche Kriterium maßgebend: Jahwe „versucht euch, um zu erfahren, ob ihr ihn von ganzem Herzen und von ganzer Seele liebt" (V. 4), d.h. ob die Leute sich zu seiner Ausschließlichkeit bekennen. Daran sollen die Israeliten festhalten, unabhängig davon, was die Propheten sagen und von woher sie kommen.

Es wird im folgenden zu zeigen versucht, daß eben das inhaltliche Kriterium auch in den neuassyrischen Belegen für die falsche Prophetie von ausschlaggebender Bedeutung ist. In den uns bekannten prophetischen Orakeln an die Könige Asarhaddon und Assurbanipal (SAA 9) kommt die Frage nicht zur Sprache. Vielmehr ist der Beweis in zwei nicht-prophetischen Texten zu finden, von denen der erste gut, der zweite noch kaum bekannt ist. Es handelt sich 1) um den großen Thronnachfolgevertrag des Königs Asarhaddon anläßlich der Investitur seines Sohnes Assurbanipal zum Kronprinzentum im Jahre 672 (SAA 2 6), und 2) um den Brief eines gewissen Nabû-reḫtu-uṣur an Asarhaddon, in dem ein Aufruhrversuch vermutlich im Jahre 671/670 (s.u.) aufgedeckt wird (SAA 16 59).

II

Der zehnte Paragraph des Thronnachfolgevertrags von Asarhaddon[12] lautet folgendermaßen (SAA 2 6 § 10:108–22):

> Solltet ihr ein unanständiges, ungutes oder unschönes Wort, daß in bezug auf Assurbanipal, den großen Kronprinzen des Nachfolgepalastes, den Sohn von Asarhaddon, König von Assyrien, eures Herrn, nicht anständig und gut ist, hören, sei es aus dem Munde seines Feindes oder aus dem Munde seines Verbündeten oder aus dem Munde seines Bruders oder aus dem Munde seiner Onkel, seiner Vetter, seiner Familie, der Nachkommenschaft seines Vaterhauses, oder aus dem Mund eures Bruders, eurer Söhne, eurer Töchter, oder aus dem Munde *eines Propheten, eines Ekstatikers, eines Traumdeuters,* oder aus dem Munde jedes beliebigen

---

11 Man beachte, daß der „Prophet oder Traumseher" in Dtn 13,2 offenbar aus eigener Initiative „ersteht" *(yāqûm)*, während Jahwe in deuteronomistischen Texten die wahren Propheten „erstehen läßt" (*hēqîm*, Dtn 18:15, 18); vgl. Veijola, „Wahrheit und Intoleranz nach Deuteronomium 13," 294.

12 Zu diesem Text s. schon R. Frankena, „The Vassal-Treaties of Esarhaddon and the Dating of Deuteronomy," *OTS* 14 (1965) 122–54 und jetzt grundlegend K. Watanabe, *Die adê-Vereidigung anläßlich der Thronfolgeregelung Asarhaddons* (BaM.B 3; Berlin: Mann, 1987); S. Parpola und K. Watanabe, *Neo-Assyrian Treaties and Loyalty Oaths* (SAA 2; Helsinki: Helsinki University Press, 1988).

Menschen, so dürft ihr es nicht verheimlichen, sondern ihr sollt kommen und es dem Assurbanipal, dem großen Kronprinzen des Nachfolgepalastes, dem Sohn von Asarhaddon, König von Assyrien, anzeigen.

Dieser Paragraph stellt ein Beispiel für Vertragsbestimmungen dar, die dazu verpflichten, jeden Ausdruck der Untreue dem König zur Kenntnis zu bringen. Die meisten gut erhaltenen Verträge enthalten eine oder mehrere derartige Bestimmungen[13], deren Formulierung und Umfang variieren, die sich aber stets nach dem folgenden Schema richten: „Wenn ihr ein böses Wort aus dem Munde von (N. N.) hört, mußt ihr es (dem König) anzeigen."

Der Thronnachfolgevertrag des Asarhaddon ist bei weitem der größte unter den Verträgen, die uns zur Verfügung stehen, und in ihm befinden sich auch die ausführlichsten Kataloge von Menschen, die der Intrigen gegen den König verdächtig sein können. Unsere Aufmerksamkeit richtet sich vor allem darauf, daß der Vertrag in diesem Zusammenhang auch Fachleute der Götterbefragung erwähnt. Nicht nur die Gelehrten (*ummânī*), d. h. Spezialisten der Astrologie und Eingeweideschau, sind mit einbezogen (§ 6:79)[14], sondern auch *raggimu, maḫḫû* und *šāʾilu*. Es ist schwierig zu sagen, ob diese drei Titel auch drei distinkte Klassen von religiösen Experten mit jeweils charakteristischen Rollen und Techniken repräsentieren. Eine deutliche Unterscheidung zwischen ihnen läßt sich nur schwierig durchführen, so daß man mit einer bestimmten terminologischen Überschneidung rechnen muß[15]. Die drei Titel sind in einer Weise geordnet, die sie

---

13 SAA 2 3:2–4; SAA 2 4:4–7; SAA 2 6 §§ 6, 10–13, 57; SAA 2 8 r.2–27; SAA 2 9:6–9.12–16; SAA 2 13 iii 10–17; vgl. SAA 2 2 iii 23 ff.

14 Damit erübrigt sich die Frage von Cryer, *Divination*, 215: „It is interesting that Esarhaddon makes no such demand of his vassal's extispicy priests or astrologers; did he assume that they would remain loyal to their sovereign in any case, or did he simply assume that his own court diviners would keep him informed on that level of divination?"

15 Es fällt auf, daß der Gebrauch von *maḫḫû* in neuassyrischen Texten ausgesprochen literarisch ist. Das Wort kommt in literarischen Texten und in Königsinschriften vor, in denen es die in den Briefen übliche Bezeichnung *raggimu* geradezu zu ersetzen scheint (vgl. z. B. E. Leichty, *The Royal Inscriptions of Esarhaddon, King of Assyria (680–669 BC)* (RINAP 4; Winona Lake, Ind.: Eisenbrauns, 2011), 14 ii 6; 124 ii 12; J. Novotny and J. Jeffers, *The Royal Inscriptions of Ashurbanipal (668–631 BC), Aššur-etel-ilāni (630–627 BC), and Sîn-šarra-iškun (626–612 BC), Kings of Assyria*, Part 1 (RINAP 5/1; University Park, Pa.: Eisenbrauns, 2018), 71 (line v 88). Als Faustregel gilt, daß *maḫḫû* (oder *muḫḫû*, das gewöhnliche Prophetenepitheton in Mari; vgl. J.-M. Durand, *Archives épistolaires de Mari 1/1* [ARM 26/1; Paris: Editions Recherche sur les Civilisations, 1988], 386–388) in der neuassyrischen Zeit als Kultfunktionär-Ekstatiker erscheint (vgl. z. B. SAA 3 34:28), während *šāʾil(t)u* im allgemeinen – wenn auch nicht ausschließlich – mit der Traumdeutung zu tun hat (AHw 1133–34; vgl. A. L. Oppenheim, *The Interpretation of Dreams in the Ancient Near East: With a Translation of an Assyrian Dream-Book* (Transactions of the American Philosophical Society 46/3;

praktisch zu einer Zunft von Spezialisten in nicht-induktiven divinatorischen Methoden vereinigt[16].

Während der gesamte uns bekannte Korpus der neuassyrischen Prophetie königsfreundlich ist und jedes Orakel zur Legitimation und Untermauerung seines Königtums geäußert worden ist, rechnet der Thronnachfolgevertrag von Asarhaddon unbefangen damit, daß die Prophetie sich auch *gegen* den König wenden kann. Offenbar gab es Propheten, die weder bei dem König angestellt waren noch unter seiner unmittelbaren Kontrolle standen, und deswegen mußte sich der König stets von anderen über ihre Äußerungen informieren lassen, um das gesamte Potential zum Aufruhr unter seinen Untertanen eliminieren zu können. Die Propheten waren in der Lage, gegen den König im Namen einer göttlichen Autorität Aufruhr stiften zu können, und deshalb erscheint es als folgerichtig, daß sie in den Vertragsbestimmungen erwähnt sind, die die Pflicht, dem König alle böse Worte gegen ihn anzuzeigen, festsetzen.

Die im Hinblick auf andere Verträge einzigartige Erwähnung von Gelehrten und Propheten als potentiale Intriganten in dem großen Thronnachfolgevertrag des Asarhaddon könnte als Ausdruck der besonderen Vorliebe dieses Königs für sie gesehen werden. Bekanntlich schätzte ja Asarhaddon sowohl die Anweisungen der Gelehrten als auch das prophetische Wort sehr hoch, und konnte deswegen auch deren Gefährlichkeit als Werkzeug seiner Gegner erkennen. Dies kann wohl als möglich angesehen werden, aber daraus folgt nicht, daß das gleiche im Prinzip nicht auch von anderen Königen gesagt werden könnte. Daß der Fall von Asarhaddon besser dokumentiert ist, macht ihn keineswegs ratloser oder „abergläubiger" als die anderen Könige. Da von dem ganzen neuassyrischen Vertragswesen nur wenige Reste verschont geblieben sind, mag die Nicht-Erwähnung von Gelehrten und Propheten in den uns bekannten Verträgen ein reiner Zufall sein.

Es gilt hier besondere Aufmerksamkeit der Tatsache zu widmen, daß die Warnung vor betrügerischen Propheten ihren Weg auch in Dtn 13 gefunden hat, in einen Text also, der bekanntlich auch sonst eine beachtliche Ähnlichkeit mit

---

Philadelphia, Pa.: American Philosophical Society, 1956], 221; Cryer, *Divination*, 158). Die mir bekannten Belege von *raggim(t)u*, die alle neuassyrisch oder neubabylonisch sind, lassen seine/ihre Rolle einfach als Übermittler(in) göttlichen Wortes erscheinen (*raggim/ntu*: SAA 10 352:23.r.1; SAA 10 109:9; LAS 317:7; *raggimu*: MSL 12 226:134; SAA 2 6:116; SAA 7 9:23; SAA 9 3.5 iv 31; SAA 10 109:9; SAA 11 294 r.31).

16 Man beachte, daß im Hebräischen eine noch größere Vielfalt prophetisch-divinatorischer Bezeichnungen vorherrscht; die Wörter *nābîʾ*, *ḥōzê*, *rōʾê*, *ḥôlem*, *qōsem*, *ʿônen* und *kaššāp* sind zwar keine Synonyme, aber die exakte Rollenverteilung ist unklar; vgl. Kaiser, *Der Gott des Alten Testaments*, 213–19.

(neu)assyrischer Vertragssprache aufweist, weshalb mit Recht angenommen worden ist, daß seine Formulierungen tatsächlich diesem Sprachgebrauch entstammen[17].

Die wichtigsten gemeinsamen Züge zwischen Dtn 13 und dem Asarhaddon-Vertrag brauchen hier nur in aller Kürze zusammengefaßt zu werden:

1) Asarhaddon, der König von Assyrien, und Jahwe, der Gott Israels, befinden sich genau in der gleichen Position gegenüber den Menschen, mit denen der Vertrag (*adê*) oder der Bund (*bĕrît*) geschlossen ist[18].

2) Der „Prophet und Traumseher" (Dtn 13:2, 4, 6) ist ein zusammengesetzter Ausdruck, der exakt mit der Korporation von *raggimu, maḫḫû* und *šāʾilu* korrespondiert – man bemerke, daß *šāʾilu* im akkadischen besonders mit dem Traumorakel verbunden ist.

3) Der intime Kreis der betreffenden Menschen wird in beiden Texten in entsprechender Weise berücksichtigt.

4) Die Männer aus anderen Städten üben dieselbe verallgemeinernde Funktion aus wie das „wer auch immer" (*napḫar ṣalmāt qaqqadi mal bašû*) im Asarhaddon-Vertrag.

5) Die „trügerische Rede *(dibber-sārâ)* gegen Jahwe, euer Gott" ist eine direkte Parallele zu dem „unanständigen, unguten oder unschönen Wort in bezug auf Assurbanipal" (*abutu lā ṭābtu lā deʾiqtu lā banītu ina muḫḫi Aššūr-bāni-apli*) – oder etymologisch zu der „trügerischen und falschen Rede gegen Assurbanipal" (*dabāb surrāti u lā kēnāte ina muḫḫi Aššūr-bāni-apli*) in SAA 2 6 § 57:502–3.[19]

6) Das Verbot, den Betrügern „zuzuhören" (Dtn 13:4), hat Entsprechungen anderswo im Asarhaddon-Vertrag (SAA 2 6 § 18: 201–6; vgl. § 29:344).

---

17 Z. B. Dion, „Deuteronomy 13," 198–99; Veijola, „Wahrheit und Intoleranz nach Deuteronomium 13," 291, 293–94, 296, 298, 309; B. M. Levinson, „'But You shall surely kill him': The Text-Critical and Neo-Assyrian Evidence for MT Deut 13:20," in *Bundesdokument und Gesetz: Studien zum Deuteronomium* (ed. G. Braulik; HBS 4, Freiburg: Herder, 1995) 37–63. Zum Hintergrund der Bundesterminologie des Deuteronomiums in der altorientalischen Vertragsinstitution und besonders im Asarhaddon-Vertrag s. z.B. Frankena, „The Vassal-Treaties of Esarhaddon"; M. Weinfeld, *Deuteronomy and the Deuteronomic School* (Oxford: Clarendon, 1972), 91–100.

18 Daß das Wort *bĕrît* in Dtn 13 zwar nicht genannt wird, ändert nichts an der Tatsache, daß die Grundkonzeption dieses Textes ausgesprochen bundestheologisch ist; nach Veijola gehört die Grundschicht von Dtn 13 zu der von ihm herausgearbeiteten deuteronomistischen bundestheologischen Redaktion (DtrB) des Deuteronomiums; s. T. Veijola, „Bundestheologische Redaktion im Deuteronomium," in idem (ed.), *Das Deuteronomium und seine Querbeziehungen*, 242–76.

19 S. E. Jenni, „Dtn 19,16: *sarā* 'Falschheit'," in *Mélanges Bibliques et orientaux en l'honneur de M. Henri Cazelles* (ed. A. Caquot und M. Delcor; AOAT 212; Kevelaer: Butzon & Bercker und Neukirchen-Vluyn: Neukirchener Verlag, 1981), 201–11.

Der größte Unterschied zwischen den Texten besteht darin, daß der „Prophet, Ekstatiker oder Traumdeuter" im Asarhaddon-Vertrag nicht getötet, sondern nur angezeigt werden soll, während der „Prophet oder Traumseher" von Dtn 13 ohne weiteres sterben muß. Dies hängt wohl mit der hohen Wertschätzung der Prophetie in der deuteronomistischen Theologie[20] zusammen.

Was die Identifizierung der falschen Prophetie angeht, so besteht zwischen den Texten eine maßgebende Übereinstimmung: das inhaltliche Kriterium des prophetischen Wortes. Im Dtn 13 ist die Prophetie selbstverständlich falsch, wenn sie zum Fremdgötterdienst auffordert. Der Thronnachfolgevertrag Asarhaddons wiederum geht davon aus, daß wahre Prophetie auf keinen Fall gegen den König oder den Kronprinzen gerichtet sein kann. Es geht in beiden Fällen um Betrug gegen den Vertragspartner, und zwar gegen die stärkere Partei, der es frei steht, die Vertragsbestimmungen zu diktieren.

Es ist nicht schwierig zu sehen, wovon die zahlreichen Berührungspunkte von dem Deuteronomium und den neuassyrischen Verträgen ihren Ursprung herleiten: Das Königtum Juda wurde von Sanherib in der Zeit Hiskijas vasallisiert, dessen Sohn Manasse (ca. 687–642) Bundesgenosse von Asarhaddon und Assurbanipal war. Zweifelsohne hat er auch einen Vertrag mit dem Großkönig geschlossen, wozu auch andere Vasallenkönige verpflichtet waren[21]. Da die Verträge in den Sprachen der beiden beteiligten Parteien verfaßt wurden, machten sich die Judäer mit der neuassyrischen Vertragssprache vertraut. Das lange und relativ stabile Regime des loyalen Manasse war wohl überhaupt die Zeit, als die assyrische Staatsideologie ihre tiefsten Spuren in Israel hinterließ[22]. In der Folgezeit assimilierte sich das in der politischen Sphäre beheimatete sprachliche und

---

20 Vgl. Rüterswörden, „Das Böse," 238.

21 Manasse, König von Juda (^{m}*me-na-si-i šàr* URU.*ia-ú-di*; vgl. Var.), erscheint in der Liste von „transpotamischen" (*eber nāri* vgl. hebr. *'ēber han-nāhār* und aram. *'ăbar nāhărā'*) Königen, die Asarhaddon vasallisiert hatte, zusammen mit den Königen von Tyros, Edom, Moab, Gaza, Askalon, Ekron, Byblos, Arwad, Ammon und Asdod (E. Leichty, *The Royal Inscriptions of Esarhaddon*, 23 v 54–73). Diese Liste ist von Assurbanipal (Prisma C ii 27: ^{m}*mi-in-se-e* LUGAL KUR.*ia-ú-di*) so gut wie wörtlich übernommen worden (Novotny and Jeffers, *The Royal Inscriptions of Ashurbanipal*, 116).

22 Zur Zeit des Manasse in dieser Hinsicht s. M. Cogan, *Imperialism and Religion: Assyria, Israel and Judah in the Eighth and Seventh Centuries B.C.E.* (SBLMS 19; Missoula, Mt.: Scholars Press, 1974), 88–96; H. Spieckermann, *Juda unter Assur in der Sargonidenzeit* (FRLANT 129; Göttingen: Vandenhoeck & Ruprecht, 1982), 375–76. Man beachte, daß Cogan, der in *Imperialism and Religion*, 114 die Zeit des Manasse noch als „an age of unprecented abandonment of Israelite tradition" bezeichnet, neuerdings davor gewarnt hat, die Rolle der religionspolitischen Pression dabei zu übertreiben (idem, „Judah Under Assyrian Hegemony: A Re-examination of Imperialism and Religion," *JBL* 112 [1993] 403–14).

ideologische Modell zu einem konstitutiven Bestandteil eines theologischen Paradigmas, das nicht mehr von seinem Vorbild abhängig war, aber noch lange nach dem Untergang der mesopotamischen Großreiche im Werk der deuteronomistischen Theologen nachlebte. Damit ist weder gesagt, daß die alttestamentliche Bundestheologie restlos von den Assyrern übernommen worden sei[23], noch daß es sich um eine beabsichtigte bzw. zwangsläufige, auf einmal geschehene mechanische Entlehnung der assyrischen Ideen handele. Vielmehr muß man mit einer allmählichen, religiös-sozialen Akkulturation rechnen, die es ermöglichte, begriffliche und gedankliche Strukturen der neuassyrischen Vertragsinstitution der israelitischen Tradition anzupassen, als eigen anzunehmen und inhaltlich zu modifizieren.

Die vollinhaltliche Theologisierung der politischen Vertragsideologie und des damit zusammenhängenden Sprachgebrauchs ist sicher nicht aus dem Stegreif unterlaufen, ja kaum einmal möglich gewesen zu der Zeit, als die entsprechenden politischen Strukturen noch existierten. Die Ähnlichkeit zwischen dem Deuteronomium und den neuassyrischen Dokumenten besagt somit nicht, daß die Texte zur gleichen Zeit verfaßt wären[24], geschweige denn, daß etwa Dtn 13 von dem Asarhaddon-Vertrag unmittelbar abhängig sein müßte. Obschon in diesem Fall ohne Zweifel davon auszugehen ist, daß der Asarhaddon-Vertrag den *terminus post quem* für Dtn 13 bildet, besteht die Analogie zwischen den Texten ohne die Voraussetzung einer direkten Genealogie. Vielmehr haben wir es hier mit einem anschaulichen Beispiel für das deuteronomistische Nachleben der aus dem neuassyrischen Vertragswesen adaptierten Strukturen zu tun[25].

---

23 Z. B. C. Levin, *Die Verheißung des neuen Bundes in ihrem theologiegeschichtlichen Zusammenhang ausgelegt* (FRLANT 137; Göttingen: Vandenhoeck & Ruprecht, 1985), 125 – 127, sieht den israelitischen Königsvertrag als Vorbild der Bundestheologie an und mißt den außenpolitischen Verträgen nur eine beschränkte Bedeutung bei; vgl. dazu meine Ausführungen in *Prophetie, Redaktion und Fortschreibung im Hoseabuch: Studien zum Werdegang eines Prophetenbuches im Lichte von Hos 4 und 11* (AOAT 231; Kevelaer: Butzon & Bercker; Neukirchen–Vluyn: Neukirchener Verlag, 1991), 204–8, dort bes. Anm. 229.

24 So u. a. Dion, „Deuteronomy 13," 204–5, vgl. dagegen Veijola, „Wahrheit und Intoleranz nach Deuteronomium 13," 309–10.

25 Nach der Analyse von Veijola („Wahrheit und Intoleranz nach Deuteronomium 13") ist bereits der von den V. 2, 3*, 4 – , 9, 10aα, 11b – 14, 16a, 17aα^2, 18b, 19 gebildete Grundtext des Kapitels deuteronomistisch und nachexilisch. Auch Dion, „Deuteronomy 13," 192 rechnet mit einem deuteronomistischen Ursprung der Grundschicht (V. 2a, 3b, 4a*, 6a*b, 7*, 8 – 19; s. S. 167 – 75), die er immerhin in die Zeit des Joschija datiert (S. 196).

III

Daß die im Thronfolgevertrag Asarhaddons bestimmte Anzeigepflicht im neuassyrischen Reich nicht nur grundsätzlich galt, sondern ernstgenommen wurde und u. U. auch zu konkreten Maßnahmen führte, kommt in einem neuassyrischen Brief aus der Spätzeit Asarhaddons besonders anschaulich zutage. In seinem Brief SAA 16 59 (*ABL* 1217 + *CT* 53 118) bemüht sich Nabû-reḫtu-uṣur darum, dem König Asarhaddon zu zeigen, daß sein Mißtrauen gegenüber der Loyalität der Propheten nicht unbegründet sei. In diesem Brief wird eine Prophetie gegen Asarhaddon wörtlich zitiert und mit einer anderen Prophetie widerlegt. Darüber hinaus werden Intrigen einiger namentlich genannter Leute, die sich die falsche Prophetie zunutze machen wollten, aufgedeckt und Maßnahmen gegen sie vorgeschlagen. Auch zwei weitere Briefe von derselben Person, SAA 16 60 (*CT* 53 17 + *CT* 53 107) und SAA 16 61 (*CT* 53 938), sind zum gleichen historischen Kontext gehörig und enthalten zusätzliche Information[26].

Der erhalten gebliebene Text des Briefs SAA 16 59 lautet wie folgt (die deutsche Übersetzung gründet sich auf die Transliteration und englische Übersetzung des Urtextes von Prof. Simo Parpola, der sie mir freundlicherweise zur Verfügung gestellt hat):

> An den König, mei[nen] Herrn. Dein Diener Nabû-reḫtu-uṣur. Bel, Be[let, Nabû und Tašme]tu, Ištar von Ninive und Ištar von Arbela mögen dir lange Tage und immer[währende Jahre] verleihen!
>
> Diejenigen, die gegen die Güte deines Vaters und gegen den Vertrag deines Vaters und deinen (eigenen) Vertrag gesündigt haben, hat Nikkal [*aufgedeckt*]. Vernichte ihren Namen und Samen aus deinem Palast! Nach [...] wird sie/wirst du werfen. Die Mitwiss[er] von Sasî [mögen sofort sterben]!

26 Eine neue Edition ist in M. Luukko und G. Van Buylaere, *The Political Correspondence of Esarhaddon* (SAA 16; Helsinki: Helsinki University Press, 2002) veröffentlicht. Die in der *ABL*-Edition von R. F. Harper enthaltenen zahlreichen Fehler werden von L. Waterman, *Royal Correspondence of the Assyrian Empire*, vol. 2. (University of Michigan Studies, Humanistic Series 18; Ann Arbor: University of Michigan Press, 1930), 344 – 47 wiederholt, was seine Übersetzung großenteils unzuverlässig macht. Einige Zeilen des Briefs sind früher veröffentlicht worden von M. Dietrich, *Die Aramäer Südbabyloniens in der Sargonidenzeit (700 – 648)* (AOAT 7; Kevelaer, Germany: Butzon & Bercker; Neukirchen-Vluyn: Neukirchener, 1970), 160–61 (Z. r.3 – 5, 9 – 10; Nr. 58 – 59); id., „Prophetie in den Keilschrifttexten," *JARG* 1 (1973) 15 – 44, 39 (Z. 1 – 13, r. 2 – 5; nur Übersetzung) und S. Parpola, *Letters from Assyrian Scholars to the Kings Esarhaddon and Assurbanipal*, vol. 2: *Commentary and Appendices* (AOAT 5/2; Kevelaer: Butzon and Bercker / Neukirchen-Vluyn: Neukirchener Verlag, 1983), 239, Anm. 412, 417 (Z r. 4 – 5 und r. 2 – 3) und 464 (Z. r. 9 – 17; Nr. 59; nur Übersetzung).

Höre mich, o König, mein Herr! Ich w[eiß] das Wort von Nikkal: „[...] mögen sterben! [Rette] dein Leben und das Leben deiner Familie! [*Die Götter/die Göttinnen*] mögen dein Vater und deine Mutter sein, sie mögen aufhe[ben ...]! Richte dein Leben nicht zugrunde, laß das Königtum nicht aus deinen Händen [entgleiten]!"

Höre mich, o König, mein Herr! Vernachläs[sige dieses] Wort von Nik[kal] nicht! [...] x x [...] der Brief [...] (Rest zerstört)

[...] sind ständig vor ihm [...] ist in ihren Mund gelegt [...] die ganze Zeit über Sas[î ...] „Benimm dich gut vor dem König! Mögen sie machen mit Nabû-bel-[...] mit Ubru-Nabû [...] mit den Magnaten, d[ie ...] (Rest zerstört)

Vielleicht [...] mögen sie sich erkundigen. Eine Dienerin des Bel-aḫu-uṣur [hat] am Stadtrand von H[arran] üb[er ...]. Seit Simanu ist sie ... (?) und spricht darüber ein günstiges Wort: „So lautet das Wort von Nusku: Das Königtum gehört zu Sasî! Ich werde den Namen und Samen des Sanherib vernichten!"

Dein *rab mūgi* soll die Familie des Bel-aḫu-uṣur unter dem Tor des Tempels von Nabû verhören. Die *ša šēpi*, die die Dienerin nach/aus dem Haus von Sasî gebracht haben, sollen sie herbringen, und eine Eingeweideschau (?) über sie möge der König(?) [...] Bel-aḫu-uṣur soll aus Harran hingebracht werden. Nusku [...] Der Namen und Samen von Sasî, Bel-aḫu-uṣur und ihrer Mitwisser mögen zunichte werden! Bel und Nabû mögen den Namen und Samen des Königs, meines Herrn in die fernste Zukunft befestigen!

Mit Ardâ sollen sie folgendermaßen reden: „In der Nacht des 27. Tags, als der Schriftgelehrte Issar-nadin-apli an diesem bestimmten Moment zu [Sa]sî, dem Stadtoberhaupt, ging und mit dem Eunuch Awjanu [...] der Schriftgelehrte Issar-nadin-apli (und?) Nabû-eṭir dies [es ...] Was hat Sasî am 28. Tag bezüglich [...]? Hat Sasî am nächsten Tag mit dir und [...] geredet? Warum hast du nicht [angezeigt] was du gese[hen und gehört hast]?"

Der *rab mūgi* [soll ...] die Männer [...] Issar-[nadin]-apl[i ... Die Männer, d]ie mit ihnen und mit Sasî konspirieren [mögen sterben]! [...] Deine [Söh]ne und deine Onkel mögen dich beschützen! [...] möge deine [...] sammeln! [Du,] sei gut aufgehoben in deinem Palast [...] bis [... Die Männer mögen ster]ben! Rette dein Leben!

Trotz der zahlreichen Eigennamen und Zeitangaben bereitet die historische Interpretation dieses Briefs keine geringen Schwierigkeiten, und zwar nicht nur wegen seines fragmentarischen Zustands, sondern auch deswegen, weil der heutige Leser über die genannten Persönlichkeiten nicht mehr gut genug informiert ist, um ihre Stellungen und Rollen in dem berichteten Kontext problemlos zu verstehen. Der Anlaß des Schreibens ist allerdings klar. Es ergibt sich, daß jemand namens Sasî zusammen mit seinen Anhängern den Argwohn von Nabû-reḫtu-uṣur erregt hat. Dieser sonst unbekannte Mann[27] tut in seinen Briefen sein

27 Eine Person namens Nabû-reḫtu-uṣur, der als Zeuge in einem Kontrakt aus dem Jahre 679 (SAA 6 268:9) sowie in einem anderen aus dem Jahre 666 (SAA 6 314 r. 27) erscheint, mag mit dem Absender der Briefe identisch sein. Andere gleichnamige Personen, die aus späteren Zeiten bekannt sind (z. B. SAA 12 35:13 und 36:10), sind kaum mehr mit ihm identifizierbar; s. die Belege bei Parpola, *Letters from Assyrian Scholars*, 238, Anm. 408; H. D. Baker, „ Nabû-rēḫtu-uṣur," *PNA* 2/II (2001): 861–62.

Möglichstes, den König von der drohenden Lebensgefahr zu überzeugen und die angebliche Konspiration von Sasî und seinen Mitverschwörern aufzudecken. Er weiß Bescheid über die gegen Asarhaddon ausgesprochene Prophetie sowie über die heimlichen Versammlungen der mit Sasî liierten Leute. Auf Grund dieser und anderer zu seiner Kenntnis gebrachten Informationen[28] hat er die feste Überzeugung gewonnen, daß diese Leute dem König eine Falle gestellt haben und nur die beste Gelegenheit abwarten, den König zu ermorden[29]. Die Mahnungen „Rette dein Leben" (*napšatka šēzib*)[30] und „Diese Menschen mögen (sofort) sterben" ([*arḫiš*] *nīšī limūtū* o. ä.)[31] werden in seinen Briefen wie eine Zauberformel wiederholt[32].

Sasî und seine Anhänger erscheinen dem Verfasser als Leute, die „gegen die Güte deines Vaters und gegen den Vertrag deines Vaters und deinen eigenen Vertrag gesündigt haben". Diese Phrase, die Nabû-reḫtu-uṣur in allen seinen drei Briefen wiederholt[33], ist eine makellose Stilprobe der neuassyrischen Vertragssprache. Sowohl die Synonymität von *ṭābtu* „Güte" und *adê* „Vertrag" als auch das Verb *ḫaṭû* „sündigen" entsprechen genau der in den neuassyrischen Verträgen und anderen Dokumenten befindlichen Standardphraseologie[34] und gelten als unmißverständliche Merkmale der „geistigen Heimat" des Verfassers, der mit diesen Wendungen seine Untertänigkeit und politische Korrektheit zu zeigen vermag[35].

---

28 Laut SAA 16 60 und 61 hat Nabû-reḫtu-uṣur im Monat Arahsamna (VIII) eine „Vision" erlebt (*diglu adaggal*), die ihn offenbar auf die Konspiration aufmerksam gemacht hat. Darüber hinaus denunziert er in SAA 16 60 weitere damit verbundene Personen, über die er brieflich informiert worden ist.

29 So SAA 16 60 (*CT* 53 17) r.19–20: [ERIM.MEŠ? *š*]*a* ᵐ*sa-si-i šu-ub-tú ú*-[*se-ši-bu x x x*] „[Die Männer v]on Sasî haben eine Falle ge[stellt...]" Zu *šubtu* in der Bedeutung 'Falle' vgl. SAA 1 175:16; 244:9; SAA 5 33 r. 12.

30 SAA 16 59 s. 4; SAA 16 60 (*CT* 53 17) r. 10, 16, 19, s. 3.

31 SAA 16 59 (*ABL* 1217):9, r. 9–10, s. 1.4; SAA 16 60 (*CT* 53 17) r.10, 14, 15–16, 17.

32 In der Tat schreibt Nabû-reḫtu-uṣur in SAA 16 60 (*CT* 53 17) r.16: *egirtu annītu lū šiptu* „Dieser Brief sei eine Beschwörung."

33 SAA 16 59 (*ABL* 1217):-5.; SAA 16 60 (*CT* 53 17):5–6; SAA 16 61:4–6.

34 Vgl. Frankena, „The Vassal-Treaties of Esarhaddon," 134–37; Parpola und Watanabe, *Neo-Assyrian Treaties*, xvi–xxiii; Nissinen, „Die Relevanz der neuassyrischen Prophetie," 238 und ferner etwa M. Weinfeld, „Covenant Terminology in the Ancient Near East and its Influence on the West," *JAOS* 93 (1973) 190–99; M. Fox, „*Ṭôb* as a Covenant Terminology," *BASOR* 209 (1973) 41–42; I. Johag, „*ṭwb*: Terminus Technicus in Vertrags- und Bündnisformularen des Alten Orients und des Alten Testaments," in *Bausteine biblischer Theologie*, FS G. J. Botterweck, (ed. H.-J. Fabry; BBB 50; Köln: Hanstein, 1977) 3–23.

35 Vgl. z. B. den Brief von Urad-Nanaya an Asarhaddon SAA 10 316:19–r.4: „Wegen diese Wortes des Königs wurden diese Rechtsbrecher, die gegen die Güte (des Königs) konspirierten (*ina muḫḫi*

Die Vertragssprache ist in dem vorliegenden Brief aber kein bloßes ideologisches Kolorit, sondern ist in dem konkreten geschichtlichen Moment fest verankert. Die Untertanen des assyrischen Königs waren ja dazu verpflichtet, zuerst anläßlich der Einsetzung des Asarhaddon im Jahre 683 und dann der des Assurbanipal im Jahre 672 zum Kronprinzentum einen Treueid in Form eines Vertrags zu schwören. Die beiden Thronnachfolgeverträge sind erhalten geblieben und jetzt als SAA 2 3 bzw. SAA 2 6 veröffentlicht worden[36]. Es ist mehr als wahrscheinlich, daß gerade diese zwei Texte mit „dem Vertrag deines Vaters und deinem eigenen Vertrag" gemeint sind.

Allem Anschein nach kommt nun Nabû-reḫtu-uṣur mit seinen Briefen eben der Verpflichtung nach, die Aufruhrstifter anzuzeigen und ihre Pläne nichtig zu machen. In seinen beiden anderen Briefen betont er, daß er an den Vertrag des Königs gebunden ist („[Ich bin] ein Vertragspartner des Kö[nigs, meines Herrn]!"[37]), und zeigt, daß er seinerseits ihm die Treue bewahren will. Was er schreibt, stimmt so schön mit den Paragraphen des Thronnachfolgevertrags von Asarhaddon überein, daß man sich des Eindrucks nicht erwehren kann, daß die Bestimmungen dieses Vertrags ihm bekannt waren. Im allgemeinen geht es um die Pflichten, die im § 12 des Asarhaddon-Vertrags wie folgt ausgedrückt werden (SAA 2 6:130–146):

> Sollte irgeneiner in bezug auf Assurbanipal, den großen Kronprinzen des Nachfolgepalastes, den Sohn von Asarhaddon, König von Assyrien, eures Herrn, der zu seinen Gunsten einen Vertrag mit euch geschlossen hat (*ša ina muḫḫīšu adê issīkunu iškunūni*), euch Rebellion und Aufruhr (*sīḫu bārtu*), nämlich ihn zu tö[ten], ermorden oder zu verderben, vorschlagen, und ihr das aus dem Munde irgendeines hört, müßt ihr die Aufruhrstifter ergreifen und zu Assurbanipal, dem großen Kronprinzen des Nachfolgepalastes, bringen.
>
> Wenn ihr imstande seid, sie zu ergreifen und zu töten, müßt ihr sie ergreifen und töten und ihren Namen und Samen im Lande vernichten (*šumšunu zara'šunu ina māt lā tuḫallaqāni*). Wenn ihr aber nicht imstande seid, sie zu ergreifen und zu töten, müßt ihr Assurbanipal, den großen Kronprinzen des Nachfolgepalastes, informieren, euch auf seine Seite stellen und die Aufruhrstifter ergreifen und töten.

ṭābti idbubūni) und die, nachdem sie den Vertrag des Königs (*adê ša šarri*) zusammen mit seinen Dienern vor Aššur und den großen Göttern geschlossen hatten, gegen den Vertrag sündigten (*ina libbi adê iḫṭūni*), von Aššur und den großen Göttern gebunden und den Händen des Königs überliefert. Die Güte des Königs (*ṭābtu ša šarri*) holte sie ein."

36 Zur geschichtlichen Einordnung von SAA 2 3 s. S. Parpola, „Neo-Assyrian Treaties from the Royal Archives of Nineveh," *JCS* 39 (1987) 161–89, 164.180; Parpola und Watanabe, *Neo-Assyrian Treaties*, xxviii.

37 EN-*a-de-e šá* LU[GAL EN-*ia a-na-ku*] SAA 16 61:11; vgl. SAA 16 60 (*CT* 53 17):11.

Ganz offensichtlich erfüllt Nabû-reḫtu-uṣur in seinen Briefen diese Anzeigepflicht und denunziert etwas, was im § 19 desselben Vertrags mit folgenden Worten verboten worden ist (SAA 2 6:212 f.):

> Ihr dürft nicht eine Versammlung veranstalten, euch verschwören und einem aus eurer Mitte das Königtum geben.

Da es ihm offenbar unmöglich ist, selber die Aufruhrstifter zu ertappen und zu töten, informiert er den König über ihre geheimen Versammlungen, damit seine Offiziere dies tun. Es verdient Beachtung, daß die Vernichtung des „Namens und Samens", d. h. der Nachkommenschaft, die im Asarhaddon-Vertrag (im Gegensatz zu den anderen intakten Verträgen) unaufhörlich wiederholt wird[38], auch im Brief von Nabû-reḫtu-uṣur eine gängige Wendung ist: „Vernichte ihren Namen und Samen aus deinem Palast!" (*šumšunu zara'šunu issu libbi ekallīka ḫalliqi* ABL 1217:6[39]); „Der Name und Samen von Sasî, Bel-aḫu-uṣur und ihrer Mitwisser mögen zunichte werden! Bel und Nabû [mögen] den Namen und Samen des Königs, meines Herrn in die fernste [Zukunft bef]estigen!" (*šumu zar'u ša Sāsî ša Bēl-aḫu-uṣur ša nīšī ša issīšunu ūdūni liḫliq šumu zar'u ša šarri bēlīja Bēl Nabû ana ṣât* [*ūmē lū ki*]*nnū* SAA 16 59 r. 9–10).

Die Vernichtung der Vertragsbrecher wird verkündigt im Namen der Göttin Nikkal (ᵈNIN.GAL) – oder, im Falle von SAA 16 60 und 61, in dem der Göttin Mullissu (ᵈNIN.LÍL). In SAA 16 59 beteuert der Verfasser, daß er sich auf das Wort von Nikkal bezieht: „Höre mich, o König, mein Herr! Ich w[eiß] das Wort von Nikkal" (*anīnu šarru bēlī dabābu ša Nikkal ū*[*da*] Z. 8). Nach einigen Zeilen warnt er den König davor, mit „[diesem] Wort" von Nikkal/Mullissu nachlässig umgehen: „Höre mich, o König, mein Herr! Vernachlässige dieses] Wort von Nik[kal] nicht!" (*anīnu šarru bēlī* [*ina l*]*ibbi dabābi Ni*[*kkal annie*] *lā taši*[*aṭ*] Z. 12–13). Auch die beiden anderen Briefe von ihm enthalten eine entsprechende Warnung: „Dies ist das Wort von Mullissu. Möge [der König, mein Herr], es nicht vernachlässigen]!" (*dabābu anniu ša Mullissi* [*šū šarru bēlī*] *ina libbi lū lā i*[*šīaṭ*] SAA 16 60 (*CT* 53 17): 8–9. = SAA 16 61:8–9)[40]. Unmißverständlich wird hier auf ein soeben zitiertes, vermutlich prophetisches Orakel der betreffenden Göttin hingewiesen, dessen Substanz die Vernichtung der Vertragsbrecher und die Festigung der Herrschaft des Asarhaddon bildet.

---

38 SAA 2 6:140–41, 161, 255–56, 315, 435–36, 538–39, 543–44, 661.

39 Vgl. SAA 16 60 (*CT* 53 17):7–8; SAA 16 61:7–8: *šumšunu issu māt Aššūr issu libbi ekallīka tuḫallaqa.*

40 Vgl. SAA 16 60 (*CT* 53 107):12, wo offenbar ebenfalls ein Wort von Ištar zitiert wird; leider ist der Text hier fast völlig zerstört; ᵈ 15 *šá* NINA.KI *ma-a* [*x x x*] „Ištar von Ninive (sagt): [...]".

Es ist allerdings schwierig zu sagen, ob das Orakel von Nikkal/Mullissu jeweils wörtlich zitiert oder eher paraphrasiert worden ist. Die Erwähnung von Sasî in SAA 16 59 gehört kaum zum Wortlaut eines Orakels – zumindest wäre es untypisch für eine Prophetie, andere Einzelpersonen als Könige namentlich zu nennen[41]. Vielmehr drückt sie die Überzeugung des Verfassers aus, daß das Wort von Nikkal in bezug auf Sasî und seine Mitwisser interpretiert werden soll. Somit wendet er den im göttlichen Wort ausgedrückten allgemeinen Grundsatz („die Vertragsbrecher werden vernichtet") auf einen Einzelfall an.

Im Rahmen des vorliegenden Aufsatzes ist es von Bedeutung, daß die Untreue des Sasî in Gestalt eines angeblich prophetischen Orakels ans Licht kommt. Auf der Rückseite des Briefs (Z. r. 2–5) weiß Nabû-reḫtu-uṣur zu berichten, eine „Dienerin" (GÉME/*amtu*) eines gewissen Harranäer Bel-aḫu-uṣur sei am Stadtrand von Harran (*ina q*[*a-n*]*i šá*⸢URU⸣. K[ASKAL]) aufgetreten und habe ein Orakel des Gottes Nusku ausgesprochen, laut dem Sasî das Königtum übernehmen werde: „So lautet das Wort von Nusku: Das Königtum gehört Sasî! Ich werde den Namen und Samen des Sanherib vernichten!" (*abat Nusku šī šarrūtu ana Sāsî mā šumu zar'u ša Sîn-aḫḫē-rība uḫallaqa* SAA 16 59 r. 4–5). Die im zehnten Paragraphen des Asarhaddon-Vertrags anerkannte Realität, daß alle Propheten nicht zugunsten des Königs verkündigen, gewinnt somit eine konkrete Gestalt.

Der Verfasser erwidert die Prophetie mit einer anderen Prophetie. Das angebliche Orakel von Nusku ist dem früher zitierten Wort von Nikkal diametral gegenübergesetzt, und zwar ohne Zweifel unter der Voraussetzung, daß das Wort der „Dienerin" eine falsche Prophetie ist. Nabû-reḫtu-uṣur zieht die Möglichkeit kaum einmal in Erwägung, daß Nusku wirklich so etwas hätte sagen können. Er erklärt im Gegenteil, daß der „Name und Samen" von Sasî und seiner Mitverschwörer (von Nusku?) vernichtet werde, während der „Name und Samen" des Königs von Bel und Nabû für ewig gefestigt wird. Das am Anfang des Briefes zitierte Wort von Nikkal würde somit in Erfüllung gehen.

Daß Nabû-reḫtu-uṣur keinen Vorschlag macht, die „Dienerin" wegen ihres Spruchs kurzerhand zu töten, entspricht der Bestimmung des Asarhaddon-Vertrags (§ 10), die keine Tötung des Propheten usw., sondern nur die Anzeige voraussetzt. Anders verhält sich mit den Verschwörern, deren Vernichtung ihm § 12 gemäß selbstverständlich ist. Bemerkenswert ist indes auch, daß er vorschlägt, die „Dienerin" dem Urteil eines *dullu* (Z. r. 7; vermutlich einer Eingeweideschau[42])

41 In den uns bekannten prophetischen Orakeln (SAA 9) sind Asarhaddon und Assurbanipal die einzigen vorkommenden menschlichen Personennamen.

42 Vgl. SAA 10 313:6–12: *qallatu ša ina bēt Šamâ ša ina pānīja paqdatu ultu dulla ša attalû ibaššu ina muḫḫīša inneppuš* „(Was) die Sklavin des Hauses von Šamâ, die in meiner Obhut anvertraut wurde, (angeht): wenn die Zeit des Verfinsternisrituals gekommen ist, wird es über sie ausgeführt."

anheimzustellen. Beim ersten Anblick scheint hier der einzige neuassyrische Beleg für die Überprüfung der Prophetie durch andere Methoden der Götterbefragung[43] vorzuliegen, was den Eindruck macht, daß Nabû-reḫtu-uṣur immer noch schwanke, ob das Nusku-Orakel doch für echt zu halten sei. Im Kontext der neuassyrischen Königsideologie wäre es aber widersinnig, die Götter zu befragen, ob die Prophetie gegen den König wahr ist, d.h. ob das Königtum wirklich dem König gehört – ebensowenig hätte man fragen können, ob die Götter wirklich Götter seien. Vielmehr bezieht sich die vorgeschlagene Götterbefragung darauf, das Vorhandensein der angeblichen Verschwörung und die Rolle des Sasî in ihr zu bestätigen. Orakelbefragungen von dieser Art sind wohlbekannt (SAA 4 139–148)[44], und viele von ihnen handeln von den politischen Unruhen der Jahre 670/671[45]. Es ist ferner möglich, daß die Befragung der offenbar gewordenen Verbindung von Harran und Harranäern mit der Verschwörung gelten sollte.

Es ist sicher kein Zufall, daß eine Frau in der Gegend von Harran im Namen von Nusku auftritt, denn es war gerade Harran, wo diese Gottheit damals besonders verehrt wurde[46]. In der neuassyrischen Periode wurde Nusku als Sohn des Mondgottes Sîn betrachtet, der gerade der Hauptgott von Harran war und in neuassyrischer Periode auch in größerem Maßstab Bedeutung gewann[47]. Ferner

---

SAA 10 315: 17–19: *šumma ina pān šarri bēlīja maḫir bārāni dullu ina muḫḫi lēpušū* „Wenn es dem König, meinem Herrn, recht ist, so mögen die Opferschauer darüber eine Eingeweideschau durchführen."

43 Zu diesem Gebrauch in Mari vgl. etwa Noort, *Untersuchungen zum Gottesbescheid in Mari*, 84–86; Durand, *Archives épistolaires de Mari* 1/1, 409.

44 In den meisten Fällen sind in den Befragungen alle möglichen Menschen, die der Verschwörung verdächtig sein können, aufgezählt, aber in den wenigen erhalten gebliebenen Resten von SAA 4 143 scheint es sich um eine Einzelperson zu handeln.

45 Vgl. I. Starr, *Queries to the Sungod: Divination and Politics in Sargonid Assyria* (SAA 4; Helsinki: Helsinki University Press, 1990), lxiii.

46 Parpola, *Letters from Assyrian Scholars*, 11, 101; É. Lipiński, *Studies in Aramaic Inscriptions and Onomastics* (OLA 57; Leuven: Peeters, 1994), 184. Der Tempel von Nusku hieß É.ME.LAM.AN.NA, d.h. „Haus des himmlischen Glanzes."

47 Der Kult von Sîn und vielleicht auch der von Nikkal wurden wahrscheinlich schon in der Zeit des Naram-Sîn (ca. 2185–2149) von Ur nach Harran gebracht. É.ḪUL.ḪUL, der Sîn-Tempel von Harran, der auch eine Nusku-Kapelle einschloß, wurde von den neuassyrischen Königen aktiv gefördert; vgl. etwa J. Novotny, *Selected Royal Inscriptions of Assurbanipal: L^3, L^4, LET, Prism I, Prism T, and Related Texts* (SAACT 10; Helsinki: The Neo-Assyrian Text Corpus Project, 2014), 84 (lines r. 51–55); Streck, *Assurbanipal und die letzten assyrischen Könige*, 179:37–39. Zu den Kulten von Sîn, Nikkal und Nusku in Harran und deren Verbreitung in der neuassyrischen Periode s. Lipiński, *Studies in Aramaic Inscriptions*, 171–92; S.W. Holloway, „Harran: Cultic Geography in the Neo-Assyrian Empire and its Implications for Sennacherib's 'Letter to Hezekiah' in 2 Kings," in *The Pitcher is Broken*, FS G.W. Ahlström (ed. idem and L.K. Handy; JSOTSup 190; Sheffield: Sheffield Academic Press, 1995) 276–314.

ist es ganz folgerichtig, daß Nabû-reḫtu-uṣur sich gerade in diesem bestimmten Brief auf das Wort von Nikkal statt von Mullissu bezieht, denn diese Göttin war die Gemahlin von Sîn und wurde deswegen natürlich ebenfalls in Harran verehrt[48]. Nabû-reḫtu-uṣur stellt also das Wort der Harranäer Göttin dem angeblichen Orakel des Harranäer Gottes gegenüber.

Daß das Wort gegen Asarhaddon gerade „am Stadtrand von Harran" (*ina qanni ša Ḫ[arrān]*) ausgesprochen wurde, ist ebensowenig ein Zufall. Während seines ägyptischen Feldzugs im Jahr 671 hatte nämlich Asarhaddon gerade „am Stadtrand von Harran" eine Machtdemonstration veranstaltet, von der der Hauptexorzist Marduk-šumu-uṣur einige Jahre später (667) dem König Assurbanipal folgendermaßen berichtet (SAA 10 174:10–16)[49]:

> Als der Vater des Königs, meines Herrn, nach Ägypten gin[g], wurde am Stadtrand von Harran (*ina qa-an-ni* URU.KASKAL) ein Tempel aus Zedernholz geb[aut]. Sîn saß oberhalb eines Stabs mit zwei Kronen auf dem Haupt und Nusku stand vor ihm. Der Vater des Königs, meines Herrn, trat ein und setzte [die Krone(n)?] auf sein Haupt. (Es wurde ihm gesagt:) „Du wirst gehen und die Länder damit erobern!" [Er gi]ng und eroberte Ägypten. Die übrigen Länder, [die] sich (noch) nicht Assur und Sîn unterworfen haben, wird der König, der Herr der Könige, erobern.

Im Brief des Marduk-šumu-uṣur gilt dieses außerordentliche Ritual als ein Symbol der Weltherrschaft Asarhaddons und als ein günstiges Omen für Assurbanipal, der zu jener Zeit noch Ägypten beherrschte. In lokaler Hinsicht bedeutete aber das Ritual sowie der zu dessen Ausführung eingerichtete Zederntempel eine Manifestation der Anwesenheit des neuassyrischen Königs und seiner Herrschaft in Harran. Es leuchtet ein, daß die „Dienerin" mit ihrem Nusku-Orakel nirgendwo anders als an diesem bestimmten Ort aufgetreten sein soll; eine bessere Stätte hätten sich die Aufruhrstifter für ihren Zweck kaum vorstellen können. Eine prophetische Proklamation gegen Asarhaddon gerade dort, wo sich seine Gegenwart manifestierte, und zwar im Namen eines Gottes, der der oben beschriebene Zeichenhandlung kurz zuvor beigewohnt hatte, stellte eine offene Aufruhrverkündigung mit ungeheurem symbolischen Wert – und zugleich ein Majestätsverbrechen ersten Ranges – dar.

Damit ist auch ein wichtiger Anhaltspunkt für die Datierung des Briefes SAA 16 59 gewonnen, der sich mit anderen Quellen bestätigen läßt. Die Briefe des Nabû-reḫtu-uṣur, die jedenfalls zwischen den Jahren 672 und 669 verfaßt sein

48 Vgl. Streck, *Assurbanipal und die letzten assyrischen Könige*, 288:10.

49 Zur diesem Brief s. Parpola, *Letters from Assyrian Scholars*, 100; C. Uehlinger, „Figurative Policy, Propaganda und Prophetie," in *Congress Volume Cambridge 1995* (ed. J. A. Emerton; VTSup 66; Leiden: Brill, 1997) 297–349.

müssen[50], sind nämlich mit anderen Dokumenten in Verbindung zu bringen, die auf die eine oder andere Weise mit der im Frühjahr 670 aufgedeckten und unterdrückten Rebellion zu tun haben. Laut der Chroniken[51] richtete Asarhaddon in seinem elften Jahr „viele von seinen Magnaten" hin, wahrscheinlich schon im ersten Monat dieses Jahres[52]. Die Chroniken machen keine weitere Mitteilungen darüber, wer diese „Magnaten" waren und warum sie hingerichtet wurden. Es steht aber eine ganze Reihe von Dokumenten aus der betreffenden Zeitspanne zur Verfügung, die von einer Verschwörung gegen Asarhaddon handeln und die locker miteinander Zusammenhängen[53]. Auf Grund der Briefe von Nabû-reḫtu-uṣur und einiger anderer Dokumente liegt es nahe, daß die Eunuchen bei dem Aufruhr die Hauptakteure waren[54] und daß Harran dabei eine Rolle spielte[55], obschon Ninive wohl der wichtigste Schauplatz der Verschwörung war.

50 Eine frühere Datierung (vgl. Dietrich, *Die Aramäer*, 50 – 55) halte ich schon wegen der nahen Verbindungen der Briefe mit dem Asarhaddon-Vertrag für ausgeschlossen.

51 A. K. Grayson, *Assyrian and Babylonian Chronicles* (TCS 5; Locust Valley, NY: J.J. Augustin, 1975), 86:29; 127:27: MU.11.KÁM LUGAL (*ina*) KUR-*aš-šur* LÚ.GAL.MEŠ-*šu ma-du-tú ina* GIŠ.TUKUL *id-duk*.

52 Eine ungewöhliche Eponymdatierung eines Kontraktes aus Nisannu (I) 670 deutet an, daß das Eponymat dieses Jahres wegen politischer Unruhen noch nicht bestimmt worden ist: ITI.BARAG *lim-mu ša* EGIR ᵐITI.AB-⸢*a*⸣-[*a*] „Monat Nisannu (I), Eponym (desjenigen) nach Kanunayu." (SAA 6 286:11); vgl. M. T. Larsen, „Unusual Eponymy-Datings from Mari and Assyria," *RA* 68 (1974) 14 – 24, 22; Parpola, *Letters from Assyrian Scholars*, 238.

53 Außer der oben erwähnten Orakelbefragungen (SAA 4 139 – 147) sind die Briefe SAA 10 199 und 316 zu nennen (zum letztgenannten vgl. auch oben Anm. 34), in denen ein in das Frühjahr 670 datierbarer schwerer Anfall Asarhaddons mit einer vor kurzem unterdrückten Verschwörung in Verbindung gebracht wird (vgl. Parpola, *Letters from Assyrian Scholars*, 238).

54 Eunuchen werden verdächtigt in SAA 16 59 r.13; SAA 16 60 (*CT* 53 17) r .9, s. 3. Darüber hinaus berichten im Jahre 670 sowohl Šumu-iddina, *šatammu* von Babylon (TKSM 21/676; s. B. Landsberger, *Brief des Bischofs von Esagila an König Asarhaddon* [Mededelingen der Koninklijke Nederlandse Akademie van Wetenschappen, afd. Letterkunde, Nieuwe reeks 28/6; Amsterdam: Koninklijke Nederlandse Akademie van Wetenschappen, 1965]) als auch Mar-Issar, der Agent Asarhaddons in Babylonien (SAA 10 354; s. Parpola, *Letters from Assyrian Scholars*, 278) dem Asarhaddon über Eunuchen, die nach Babylonien geflohen sind. Den wichtigsten Beweis führt jedoch Kudurru, ein Babylonier, der in Assyrien als Geisel und Lehrling der Gelehrtheit weilt (vgl. SAA 10 160 r.13–14; SAA 11 156:14; SAA 16 17:7). Er rapportiert dem König brieflich (SAA 10 179), wie er im Monat Arahsamna (VIII) (vgl. SAA 16 60 (*CT* 53 17):10; SAA 16 61:10!) von hohen assyrischen Beamten aus seinem Gefängnis in den Tempel von Bel-Harran (d.h. Sîn) kidnappt war, damit er dort eine Opferschau ausführe, laut deren das Königtum dem Obereunuch gehöre (Z. r. 4 – 11). Unter den Mitwissern dieser Verschwörung wird u.a. „der Stadtoberhaupt" (LÚ.*šá*—UGU—URU) genannt (Z. 17); der Titel entspricht dem des Sasî in SAA 16 59 r. 12. Man beachte jedoch, daß laut dem Bericht von Kudurru die Eunuchen selbst nicht an dieser Sitzung teilnahmen.

Ob nun der von Nabû-reḫtu-uṣur verdächtigte Sasî wirklich zu den Verschwörern gehörte, ist schwierig zu schließen. Er wird zwar auch in anderen, meist namenlosen Briefen an den König aus verschiedenen Gründen verdächtig gemacht[56], aber in anderen Dokumenten erscheint er als ein hoher Beamter im Dienst des Königs ohne Schatten eines geringsten Argwohns[57]. Vielleicht war die in Harran zweifellos geschehene Ausrufung von Sasî zum König nur ein Scheinmanöver, um den Verdacht auf ihn statt auf die eigentlichen Hauptverschwörer zu lenken. Diese Vermutung wird vor allem durch die Tatsache hervorgerufen, daß ein Bürgermeister (*ḫazannu*) mit dem Namen Sasî als Zeuge eines Kontrakts noch im Jahre 666 erscheint – und zwar zusammen mit Nabû-reḫtu-uṣur und Issar-nadin-apli (SAA 6 314 r. 10, 24, 27)! Ob es sich in allen diesen Dokumenten wirklich um dieselben Personen handelt wie in den oben behandelten Briefen, ist natürlich nicht sicher, aber diese Möglichkeit ist auch keineswegs von der Hand zu weisen.

Die Briefe von Nabû-reḫtu-uṣur beweisen, daß nicht alle Prophetie in der neuassyrischen Reich königsfreundlich war – anders als die erhalten gebliebenen Orakel an und für sich andeuten würden. Die Prophetie konnte auch gegen ihn gerichtet sein, wie es bei dem oben zitierten Nusku-Orakel unbestreitbar der Fall war. Es ist indes kein Wunder, daß intakte prophetische Texte von dieser Art uns nicht mehr zur Verfügung stehen. Hätte so ein Orakel einmal eine schriftliche Gestalt gewonnen und wäre zur Kenntnis des Königs gelangt, so wäre es ohne weiteres von ihm oder von seinen Offizieren bei erster Gelegenheit zerstört worden – man erinnere sich nur an die Erzählung des Jeremiabuches (Jer 36:11–26), in der der König Jojakim die Schriftrolle des Propheten Jeremia ins Feuer wirft! Eben deswegen müssen wir uns mit wenigen und wahllosen Hinweisen aus zweiter Hand, wie dem Zitat in dem oben behandelten Brief, behelfen. Aber selbst die spärliche Evidenz legt genügend an den Tag, daß der assyrische König nicht mit einer ungeteilten Loyalität von der Seite der Propheten und anderer Spezialisten des Gottesbescheids rechnen konnte. Im Lichte von SAA 16 59 entspricht es also aller Erwartungen, daß die potentielle Untreue der Propheten im Thronnachfolgevertrag des Asarhaddon – und eventuell auch in anderen, uns nicht bekannten Verträgen – anerkannt wurde.

---

55 Harran wird auch in SAA 16 60 (CT 53 107) r. 5 innerhalb eines gebrochenen Briefzitates genannt: *kî annî q*[*ab*]*i mā ina Ḫarrāni* ... „Es wird ge[sa]gt, daß in Harran ...“ Darüber hinaus entsteht die Verbindung mit Harran durch die oben genannten Briefe SAA 10 174 und 179.

56 Z. B. SAA 16 69:8 – r. 1; SAA 16 65 r. 2; SAA 16 62 r .5; SAA 16 71:5. Im erstgenannten Beleg wird Sasî „Bürgermeister“ (*ḫazannu*) einer Stadt genannt, von deren Name leider nur wenige Reste erhalten geblieben sind (^{m}*sa-si-i* LÚ*.*ḫa-za-nu* [*ša*] ⌜URU⌝.⌜*x*⌝; Koll. S. Parpola; nach ihm kann das letzte Zeichen entweder NINA oder KASKAL sein).

57 SAA 10 176:12; 377 r.2; SAA 11 156:19; SAA 16 17:9.

Als ein konkretes Zeugnis historischer Vorgänge leistet der Brief SAA 16 59 einen wichtigen Beitrag zum Problem der falschen Prophetie. Vor allem hebt sich hier ebenso wie im Dtn 13 oder im Asarhaddon-Vertrag die Bedeutung des *inhaltlichen* Kriteriums hervor. Die Prophetie der „Dienerin" war falsch, weil sie gegen die Herrschaft des regierenden Königs gerichtet war. Andere Kriterien kommen nicht zur Sprache und waren wohl auch nicht nötig.

IV

Die Suche nach den Kriterien der wahren und falschen Prophetie ist kein modernes, nur den analytischen Geist der Moderne befriedigendes Unternehmen. Schon die Mitwelt der biblischen und altorientalischen Schriften kümmerte sich um diese Frage, und zwar nicht aus akademischen Gründen. Bei der Suche nach den Kriterien kamen dabei die Bedeutung und die Bedürfnisse der immanenten Elemente der Prophetie – des Propheten, der Botschaft und des/der Adressaten – mit Nachdruck zum Vorschein. Die oben behandelten Texte sind ausdrücklich darauf bedacht, was die Prophetie *verursacht* und wie sich ihre Folgen in der jeweiligen Gemeinschaft konkretisieren. Eben deswegen ist die Frage in unseren Texten nicht theoretisch, sondern aktuell, ja lebenswichtig.

Eine wahre Prophetie muß als ein echtes Gotteswort anerkannt werden, ansonsten verliert sie ihren Geltungsanspruch. Um als solche identifiziert werden zu können, muß es aber im Lichte der hier behandelten Texte auch bekannt oder zumindest definierbar sein, was eine Gottheit überhaupt sagen *kann*. Über das prophetische Wort muß es demnach Wahrheitskriterien geben, anhand deren eine Prophetie als wahrhaftig bzw. falsch eingeschätzt werden kann. Dies wird besonders deutlich in den Fällen, wo Gott selbst die Menschen mit einem Scheinwunder (Dtn 13:3–4) oder „Lügengeist" (*rûăḥ šeqer* 1 Reg 22:19 – 23) verblüfft, um ihre Treue zu erproben.

Es geht also um Grundsätze, die in der jeweiligen Gemeinschaft als konstitutiv und gottgegeben gelten und als solche unwiderruflich sind, sei es nun ein Prophet oder ein Engel vom Himmel (vgl. Gal 1:8), der anderes verkündigen würde. Diesen Grundsätzen sind auch die Kriterien der wahren und falschen Prophetie jeweils untergeordnet[58]. Als Kontrollinstanz dient im neuassyrischen Reich die vorherrschende Königsideologie, im Falle des Deuteronomiums dagegen das deutero-

58 Vgl. Huffmon, „The Origins of Prophecy," 184: „Prophecy thus has a precarious quality, as ultimately only internal and subjective confessional criteria can distinguish true and false prophecy." Schärfer äußert sich Carroll, *From Chaos to Covenant*, 474 zu Jer 23:25 – 32: „There is not criteriology here but ideology which determines truth or falsehood."

nomische Gesetz mit dem Hauptgebot[59] an seiner Spitze, vermittelt durch den Propheten Mose (Dtn 18:15)[60]. Dementsprechend kann die wahre Prophetie im neuassyrischen Reich nicht das Königtum Asarhaddons oder Assurbanipals bestreiten – ebensowenig wie im nachexilischen Israel den Ausschließlichkeitsanspruch Jahwes (Dtn 13) oder etwa in johannäischen Gemeinden die Inkarnation Christi (1 Jh 4:1–3).

Grundsätze von dieser Art müssen gemeinschaftlich anerkannt sein, um eine allgemeine Geltung zu gewinnen. Indes ist aber auch damit zu rechnen – und das Alte Testament ist das vornehmste Zeugnis darüber –, daß ihr Geltungsanspruch wegen politisch-religiöser Rivalitäten und Umstürze innerhalb einer Gemeinschaft immer wieder auch bestritten wird. Eben dies macht es geradezu unmöglich, eine allgemeingültige Kriteriologie der wahren und falschen Prophetie aufzustellen[61]. Die Falschheit bzw. Wahrhaftigkeit einer Prophetie erscheint in den Augen der politisch-religiösen Machthaber der judäischen Königszeit in einem wesentlich anderen Licht als in denen der nachexilischen deuteronomistischen oder priesterlichen Autoritäten; der Fall von Jeremia dient als ein anschauliches Beispiel dafür.

Es kommt nun schließlich darauf an, wer und mit welchem Recht die Macht besitzt, die Wahrheitskriterien zu bestimmen und zu sanktionieren. Damit gelangen wir zu der Frage von Prophetie und menschlicher Autorität, die sich bei der Analyse der oben behandelten Texte vordrängt, die im Rahmen des vorliegenden Aufsatzes jedoch nur für die weitere Diskussion aufgeworfen werden kann.

---

59 D. h. das des ausschließlichen Dienstes von Jahwe; vgl. Kaiser, *Der Gott des Alten Testaments*, 186, 189, 201.

60 Vgl. Hermisson, „Kriterien „wahrer“ und „falscher“ Prophetie,“ 136–37.

61 Vgl. Grabbe, *Priests, Prophets, Diviners, Sages*, 118 und Coggins, „Prophecy: True and False,“ 93: „Conclusions of this kind may seem unduly negative, but they may be necessary, for too often the issue of false prophecy has been approached as if it is an issue that could be resolved to everyone's satisfaction if only the right scholarly techniques were applied. To a far greater extent that such an approach allows, there are ideological factors to be taken into account – particularly the recognition of the need within the religious community to legitimate certain voices and to exclude others – factors that make objective assessment extremely elusive.“

Sacred Springs and Liminal Rivers: Water and Prophecy in the Ancient Eastern Mediterranean

Water is the absolute precondition for the existence of everything that grows, breaths, and moves. Every living creature is dependent on water, not only to sustain living organisms, but also for other important functions, such as cleaning and transportation. At the same time, water—not just the lack of water but water itself—may also bring about death, since all breathing creatures may drown in it, and flooding water may destroy the same life it has upheld and (re)generated.[1]

According to Thales of Miletus, the pre-Socratic Greek Philosopher, water was the first principle, generator, and nourisher of all things.[2] Thales's view may have been influenced not only by everyday experience, but also by the idea of the divine power of water—an idea "ubiquitous in religious history."[3] Being the source of both life and death, it is no wonder that divine attributes were given to water. Since water has an "infinitely mutable and thereby unpredictable" quality,[4] it was understood as the site and medium of supernatural agency. Consequently, water is often connected to magical, medical, and divinatory practices.[5] Even in prophecy, as this essay attempts to demonstrate, water

---

1 For the significance of water to human culture in general, see V. Strang, *The Meaning of Water* (Oxford: Berg, 2004).

2 Aristotle, *Metaphysics* 1.3, 983b; cf. Diogenes Laertius 1.27. See O. Keel, "Altägyptische und biblische Weltbilder, die Anfänge der vorsokratischen Philosophie und das Ἀρχή-Problem in späten biblischen Schriften," in *Das biblische Weltbild und seine altorientalischen Kontexte* (ed. B. Janowski and B. Ego; FAT 32; Tübingen: Mohr Siebeck, 2001) 27–63, esp. 36–40; M. Munn, "Earth and Water: The Foundations of Sovereignty in Ancient Thought," in *The Nature and Function of Water, Baths, Bathing and Hygiene from Antiquity through Renaissance* (ed. C. Kosso and A. Scott; Technology and Change in History 11; Leiden: Brill, 2009), 191–210, esp. 206.

3 Strang, *The Meaning of Water*, 85.

4 R. Taylor, "River Raptures: Containment and Control of Water in Greek and Roman Constructions of Identity," in Kosso and Scott (ed.), *The Nature and Function of Water, Baths, Bathing and Hygiene from Antiquity through Renaissance*, 21–42, esp. 30.

5 See, e.g., Taylor, "River Raptures," 30–31; Y. Erbil and A. Mouton, "Water in Ancient Anatolian Religions: An Archaeological and Philological Inquiry on the Hittite Evidence," *JNES* 71 (2012) 53–74; S. I. Johnston, *Ancient Greek Divination* (Blackwell Ancient Religions; Chichester: Wiley-Blackwell, 2008), 98–99; A. Jeffers, *Magic and Divination in Ancient Palestine and Syria* (SHCANE 8; Leiden: Brill, 1996), 160–66; M. J. Geller, "West Meets East: Early Greek and Babylonian Diagnosis," in *Magic and Rationality in Ancient Near Eastern and Graeco-Roman Medicine*

DOI 10.1515/9783110466546-023

occasionally features either as part of the oracular process, or as an ingredient of the prophetic message.

All three aforementioned qualities of water—that is: (1) the source of life and purity; (2) a medium for practical functions and supernatural agency; and (3) a destructive power—can be found in Mesopotamian, biblical, and Greek prophetic sources, albeit in different proportions depending on the nature of the source material. In the following essay, I will not refer to every single case in which water is mentioned in these source materials, but will focus on these three recurring topics.

1 Water as Source of Life and Purity

Water, for understandable reasons, is used globally as a metaphor for life, probably without any notable culture-specificity. For equally understandable reasons, in many contexts, including the prophetic ones, the life-giving quality of water is attributed to supernatural agency, if not presented as having a divine substance itself. This is the case in the book of Jeremiah, where God is presented as "the fountain of living water" (Jer 2:13; 17:13); this sounds like an apotheosis of the "fountain of life" that is found in Proverbs and Psalms (Ps 36:10; Prov 10:11; 13:14; 14:27; 16:22; cf. the "fountain of wisdom" Prov 18:4). The connotation of the "living" water (*mayim ḥayyîm*) is twofold: it combines the life-giving quality of water with its evolution from a natural source, as opposed to the still-standing water of an artificial cistern (Jer 2:13).[6] In Jer 17:13, forsaking God, the fountain of living water, is equated with death: "O hope of Israel! O Lord! All who forsake you shall be put to shame; those who turn away from you shall be recorded in the underworld, for they have forsaken the fountain of living water, the Lord."

The source of the living water is frequently located in the temple of Jerusalem (or the city of Jerusalem, which amounts to the same thing). Ps 46:5 reads: "There is a river whose streams make glad the city of God, the holy habitation of the Most High." This contrafactual image turns Jerusalem into a mythological fortress and paradise, in the midst of the chaos of roaring waters, trembling mountains, and raging nations.[7] The image is reinforced in Ezekiel's temple

(ed. H. F. J. Horstmanshoff, M. Stol, and C. R. van Tilburg; Studies in Ancient Medicine 27; Leiden: Brill, 2004), 24–25, 47–48, 51–52.

6 Cf. S. Herrmann, *Jeremia* (BKAT 12/2; Neukirchen-Vluyn: Neukirchener Verlag, 1990), 127–28.

7 See B. Ego, "Die Wasser der Gottesstadt: Zu einem Motiv der Zionstradition und seinen kosmologischen Implikationen," in Janowski and Ego (ed.), *Das biblische Weltbild und seine altori-*

vision in Ezekiel 47, in which water runs from below the threshold of the entrance to the temple, growing into a mighty stream that flows to every part of the land, nourishing trees that bear fresh fruit every month, "because the water for them flows from the sanctuary" (v. 12).[8] The water coming forth from the temple also becomes the source of eschatological prosperity in Joel 3:18 and Zech 14:8,[9] not to forget the book of Revelation, in which John is shown "the river of the water of life, bright as crystal, flowing from the throne of God and of the Lamb" (Rev 22:1). Between the branches of this river the tree of life grows (v. 2), turning the city into a paradise, a topic widely elaborated in apocalyptic literature.[10]

An interesting offshoot of this idea of the river flowing from a divine source can be found in the book of Ben Sira, in which Ben Sira identifies himself as a teacher, and as a rivulet from the stream of Lady Wisdom in Sir 24:30 – 34: "As for me, I was like a canal from a river, like a water channel into a garden. I said, 'I will water my garden and drench my flower-beds.' And lo, my canal became a river, and my river a sea. I will again make instruction shine forth like the dawn, and I will make it clear from far away. I will again pour out teaching like prophecy, and leave it to all future generations." This is, without doubt, the closest association made between prophecy and water in early Hellenistic Jewish literature, making the "source of the living water" also the source of prophecy, and turning water into a metaphor of wisdom and the Torah.[11] The water channel, once again, represents the teacher-prophet whose instruction is presented as watering the garden, that is, the people attentive to his teaching.

Forsaking the only source of the living water implies worshiping other deities, which implies impurity, at least in texts with a cultic concern. This high-

entalischen Kontexte, 361 – 89, esp. 363 – 69. Already Philo (*Somn.* 2:246) takes it for granted that "the writer here means, figuratively, to speak of some other city than the visible city of God."

8 Cf. D. Bodi, "The Double Current and the Tree of Healing in Ezekiel 47:1 – 12 in Light of Babylonian Iconography and Texts," *WO* 45 (2015) 22 – 37.

9 For a comparison of Ezek 47, Joel 3:18, and Zech 14:8, see C. L. Meyers and E. M. Meyers, *Zechariah 9 – 14: A New Translation with Introduction and Commentary* (AB 25C; New York: Doubleday, 1993), 435 – 36.

10 See D. E. Aune, *Revelation 17 – 22* (WBC 52C; Nashville: Thomas Nelson, 1998), 1175 – 78 for an abundance of references.

11 Cf. P. C. Beentjes, "What about Apocalypticism in the Book of Ben Sira," in *Congress Volume Helsinki 2010* (ed. M. Nissinen; VTSup 148; Leiden: Brill, 2012) 207 – 27, esp. 221 – 23; B. G. Wright, "Conflicted Boundaries: Ben Sira, Sage and Seer," ibid., 229 – 53, esp. 234 – 38; M. Nissinen, "Wisdom as Mediatrix in Sirach 24: Ben Sira, Love Lyrics, and Prophecy," in *Of God(s), Trees, Kings, and Scholars*, FS S. Parpola (ed. M. Luukko, S. Svärd, and R. Mattila; StOr 106; Helsinki: Finnish Oriental Society 2009) 377 – 90 (= pp. 479 – 95 in this volume).

lights another globally known quality of water: its healing and cleansing power, which can be seen as a corollary to its lifegiving capacity.[12] In Ezekiel, the restoration of the people of Israel also means their purification: "I will sprinkle clean water upon you, and you shall be clean from all your uncleannesses, and from all your idols I will cleanse you" (Ezek 36:25). In Zech 13:1, the eschatological day of salvation brings about the purification of the people: "On that day a fountain shall be opened for the house of David and the inhabitants of Jerusalem, to cleanse them from sin and impurity."

Ritual purity of priests and other cultic functionaries was of paramount importance everywhere in the ancient Eastern Mediterranean. Divination was commonly considered a ritual act, and therefore purity was required of diviners in Mesopotamia[13] as well as in Greece.[14] In biblical and Mesopotamian sources, however, the status of the prophets in terms of purity remains unclear. Prophetic performances do not seem to have been regarded as ritual acts in the Near East, and there are no records of purification practices preceding them; one Neo-Assyrian letter reports a prophetic performance *before* the *bīt rimki* rituals performed to the substitute king in Akkad,[15] but this says nothing about the purity of the female prophet in question. In the Hebrew Bible, the so-called calling vision of the prophet Isaiah includes the purification of the prophet's unclean lips, not with water, but by touching his lips with a piece of glowing coal (Isa 6:6–7). The background of this scene was probably the mouth-washing or mouth-opening rituals performed in the ancient Near East, but it is unclear whether it implies a general requirement of a prophets' purity.[16] The prophet Ezekiel is expressly told by God to cook unclean food as a sign of the impure state of the

---

12 See J. D. Lawrence, *Washing in Water: Trajectories of Ritual Bathing in the Hebrew Bible and Second Temple Literature* (SBLAB; Atlanta: Society of Biblical Literature, 2006).

13 See M. Guichard and L. Marti, "Purity in Ancient Mesopotamia: The Paleo-Babylonian and Neo-Assyrian Periods," in *Purity and the Forming of Religious Traditions in the Ancient Mediterranean World and Ancient Judaism* (ed. C. Frevel and C. Nihan; Dynamics in the History of Religion 3; Leiden: Brill, 2013) 47–113, esp. 80–81.

14 See S. I. Johnston, *Ancient Greek Divination*, 119–25; R. Parker, *Miasma: Pollution and Purification in Early Greek Religion* (Oxford: Clarendon Press, 1983), 226–29.

15 SAA 10 352; for this letter, see S. Parpola, *Letters from Assyrian Scholars to the Kings Esarhaddon and Assurbanipal*, vol. 2: *Commentary and Appendices* (AOAT 5/2; Kevelaer: Butzon & Bercker and Neukirchen-Vluyn: Neukirchener Verlag, 1983), 270–72; M. Nissinen, *References to Prophecy in Neo-Assyrian Sources* (SAAS 7; Helsinki: The Neo-Assyrian Text Corpus Project, 1998), 68–77.

16 V. Hurowitz, "Isaiah's Impure Lips and Their Purification in the Light of Akkadian Sources," *HUCA* 60 (1989) 39–89, suggests a background in the Mesopotamian mouth-washing ritual, and G. Y. Glazov, *The Bridling of the Tongue and the Opening of the Mouth in Biblical Prophecy* (JSOTSup 311; Sheffield: Sheffield Academic Press, 2001), 116–64, in the Egyptian mouth-opening ritual.

people exiled from Jerusalem, and he replies by saying that he has never eaten anything unclean (Ezek 4:9–17). This, however, indicates defiling Ezekiel's priestly, rather than prophetic, body.[17]

If the association between prophets and purity remains somewhat faint in Near Eastern texts, Greek sources leave no doubt about the significance of purity in the oracular process, at least when it comes to Delphi and Didyma, the two most significant oracle sites of the Hellenistic Greek world. The Pythia of Delphi, according to Plutarch, had to be unmarried and "virginal," because she served as Apollo's bride; the Pythia's "virginity" does not necessarily have sexual overtones but rather refers to her state of purity and freedom from bodily pollution in the first place.[18] The Pythia had to undergo ritual preparations for every oracular session. The sources tell of a purifying bath after dawn in the Castalian spring,[19] maybe also drinking from it. The inquirers of the oracle, too, had to be ritually purified before being brought to the Pythia to receive the word of Apollo, and the priests ensured that the day was auspicious for the consultation by presenting a goat to Apollo and sprinkling it with water. If the goat nodded its head, the sign was positive, and the goat was sacrificed.[20]

Also in the temple of Apollo at Didyma, the female prophet prepared herself for the reception of the words of the god.[21] Iamblichus, the third-century CE neoplatonist, writes about the bathing and the fasting of the prophetess in preparation for prophesying:[22]

> This is what is shown by the abundance of sacrifices, the established custom of the whole ritual, and everything that is performed with due piety prior to divination: also the baths of

---

17 Thus J. E. Lapsley, "Body Piercings: The Priestly Body and the 'Body' of the Temple in Ezekiel," *HeBAI* 1 (2012) 231–45, esp. 236–38; cf. M. S. Odell, "You Are What You Eat: Ezekiel and the Scroll," *JBL* 117 (1998) 229–48, according to whom the symbolic acts in Ezek 1–5 indicate a process duting which Ezekiel "must relinquish or, at least, adapt certain elements of his priestly identity before he can assume the role of a prophet" (248).

18 For the Pythia's sexual abstinence as a matter of ritual purity, see H. W. Parke and D. E. W. Wormell, *The Delphic Oracle*, vol. 1: *The History* (Oxford: Blackwell, 1956), 35; M. A. Flower, *The Seer in Ancient Greece* (Berkeley: University of California Press, 2008), 224–25; Johnston, *Ancient Greek Divination*, 42–43.

19 E.g., scholia on Euripides' *Phoenician Maidens*.

20 This reconstruction of events is based on Euripides, *Ion* 93, 419; *Phoen*. 224; Plutarch, *Moralia* 3:397a; 3:435b; see also Parke and Wormell, *The Delphic Oracle* 1, 19–45.

21 Cf. J. Fontenrose, *Didyma: Apollo's Oracle, Cult, and Companions* (Berkeley: University of California Press, 1988), 81–82.

22 Iamblichus, *De Myst*. 3.11 (127:11–13); see E. C. Clarke, J. M. Dillon, and J. P. Hershbell, *Iamblichus: De mysteriis: Translated with Introduction and Notes* (SBLWGRW 4; Atlanta: SBL, 2003), 148–49.

> the prophetess, her fasting for three whole days, abiding in the innermost sanctuaries, already possessed by light, and rejoicing in it for a long time.

The purifying function of water, thus, played an important role in the workings of the Greek oracle. Sacred springs were not always associated with divinatory power,[23] but many times they appear as a vector of transmitting divine knowledge.[24] In the most significant Greek oracle sites they served as the source of not only purity but also divine inspiration, as we shall see in the next chapter.

2 Water as Medium of Divine Agency

Water is used as a medium of supernatural agency in different kinds of divination, such as the Anatolian ichthyomancy (fish divination)[25] and the Mesopotamian and Greek lecanomancy (oil divination).[26] Such media are less common in prophecy, which is essentially a non-technical method of divination. Nevertheless, there is some evidence of water or drink being used as a part of the oracular process, either as a means of triggering the prophets' altered state of consciousness or as a constituent of a ritual act connected to prophesying–or as both, as is the case in Jewish mysticism. In the Hekhalot literature, water not only appears as a ritual precondition for divine revelation, but also as the site where the rev-

23 For example, the famous Sacred Spring at Corinth is not known as an oracle site. See G. D. R. Sanders, "The Sacred Spring: Landscape and Traditions," in *Corinth in Context: Comparative Studies on Religion and Society* (ed. S. J. Friesen, D. N. Schowalter, and J. C. Walters; Leiden: Brill, 2010) 365–89.

24 See, e.g., W. Burkert, "Olbia and Apollo of Didyma: A New Oracle Text," in *Apollo: Origins and Influences* (ed. J. Solomon; Tucson, Ariz.: The University of Arizona Press, 1994) 49–60, esp. 59; R. L. Bengisu, "Lydian Mount Karios," in *Cybele, Attis and Related Cults*, FS M. J. Vermaseren (ed. E. N. Lane; RGRW 131; Leiden: Brill, 1996) 1–36, esp. 9–10; J. Larson, *Greek Nymphs: Myth, Cult, Lore* (Oxford: Oxford University Press, 2001), 11–20. For later times, see G. R. Varner, *Sacred Wells: A Study in the History, Meaning, and Mythology of Holy Wells and Waters* (New York: Algora Publishing, ²2009); J. Rattue, *The Living Stream: Holy Wells in Historical Context* (Woodbridge: Boydell Press, 1995).

25 See D. Lefèvre-Novaro and A. Mouton, "Aux origins de l'ichthyomancie en Anatolie ancienne: sources archéologiques et textuelles," *Anatolica* 34 (2008) 7–51.

26 For sources of Mesopotamian lecanomancy, see G. Pettinato, *Die Ölwahrsagung bei den Babyloniern* (Studi Semitici 21–22; Roma: Istituto di studi del Vicino Oriente, 1966); for Greek and Roman lecanomancy, see D. Ogden, *Magic, Witchcraft and Ghosts in the Greek and Roman Worlds: A Sourcebook* (New York: Oxford University Press, 2002), 39–40; 205–6. Unfortunately, I have not been able to consult the recent study by N. Anor, *Reading the Oil Omens: A Study of Practice and Record of Mesopotamian Lecanomancy* (Jerusalem: Hebrew University, 2010).

elation takes place, and, most notably, as a medium for inducing the altered state of consciousness.[27] It is quite probable that the medieval Jewish mystics' predilection for water had its roots in the use of water as a medium of divine knowledge in the ancient Eastern Mediterranean.

We have just seen how the Hebrew Bible frequently locates the source of the living water in the temple of Jerusalem. Although in Jerusalem no actual source of water formed part of the architecture of the temple, many Greek sanctuaries were built around a natural well, as is true for some major sites of the Apollonian oracle where the water played a role in the oracular process. This, to be sure, was not the case at Delphi, where the Castalian spring was not located within the sanctuary itself but about 500 m east of its entrance. The inner sanctum (*adyton*) of the temple of Apollo at Delphi was built around the "navel of the earth," (*omphalos*[28]), where there was no source of water but there was, allegedly, a chasm exhaling vapors emerging from the ground. The tripod on which the Pythia sat and uttered the words of Apollo was located above the spot where the chasm was believed to produce the vapors that contributed to the altered state of mind of the female prophet.[29]

Unlike Delphi, the other two members of the "big three" locations of Apollonian prophecy, the temples at Didyma and Claros, were both constructed around a water source. At the heart of the temple of Apollo at Didyma there was a very large open-air *adyton*, within which there was a "little temple" (*naiskos*), as well as the sacred spring with an archaeologically attested spring chamber built around it.[30] It was probably a natural water source that had an important function in the oracular sessions which, therefore, took place in the *adyton*. Iamblichus reports that the female prophet of Didyma wet her feet in the water, probably of the sacred spring, and inhaled its vapors. This, according to him, enabled the prophet to "partake" of Apollo, that is, to become possessed by him:

---

27 See G. W. Dennis, "The Use of Water as a Medium for Altered States of Consciousness in Early Jewish Mysticism: A Cross-Disciplinary Analysis," *Anthropology of Consciousness* 19 (2008) 84–106.

28 See J. Kindt, "Omphalos," *Encyclopedia of Ancient History* (ed. R. S. Bagnall et al.; Wiley Blackwell, 2013), 4900–4901.

29 Thus Plutarch, *Moralia* 5:433c–d; Diodorus Siculus 16.26.1–6. For the problem of the chasm and the reality of the presence of gases, see J. Bowden, *Classical Athens and the Delphic Oracle: Divination and Democracy* (Cambridge: Cambridge University Press, 2005), 18–19.

30 For the architecture of the temple at Didyma, see Fontenrose, *Didyma*, 28–44; K. Tuchelt, *Branchidai–Didyma: Geschichte, Ausgrabung und Wiederentdeckung eines antiken Heiligtums, 1765–1900* (Antike Welt Sondernummer 22 [= Zaberns Bildbände zur Archäologie 3]; Mainz: von Zabern, 1991); A. M. Greaves, *Miletos: A History* (London: Routledge, 2002), 111–17.

> And as for the woman at Branchidai who gives oracles, it is either by holding the staff first given by a certain god that she is filled by the divine radiance; or else when sitting on the axle she predicts the future; or when dipping her feet or skirt in the water, or inhaling vapour from the water, at any rate, she receives (*dekhetai*) the god: prepared and made ready by any or all of these preliminaries for his reception from without, she partakes (*metalambanei*) the god.[31]

Iamblichus' terminology of "receiving" and "partaking" of the god corresponds to his idea of divine possession as a communion with the divine, in which the human consciousness is partly or wholly replaced with the divine consciousness: "For either the god possesses us, or we become wholly the god's property, or we exercise our activity in common with him. And sometimes we share in the god's lowest power, sometimes in his intermediate, and sometimes in his primary power. And sometimes there is a mere participation, sometimes a communion, and sometimes even a union."[32] Iamblichus relates that even the male prophet of Claros, through similar means as the female prophet of Didyma—fasting, seclusion, and drinking the water from the sacred spring—"has the inspiration of the god illuminating the pure sanctuary of his own soul, and providing for it an unhindered divine possession, and a perfect and unimpeded presence."[33] One could imagine that the communion with the divine took place without the help of any material media, and it is possible that Iamblichus gives a neoplatonic explanation to practices that were known to have existed at these oracle sites. Nevertheless, it deserves attention that Iamblichus also recognized the use of music in inducing the state of possession, the explanation being that "before it gave itself to the body, the soul heard the divine harmony."[34]

Even at Claros an underground *adyton* has been uncovered in excavations,[35] and ancient writers refer to a sacred spring that played an important role in producing oracles at this site. Iamblichus writes: "It is agreed by everyone that the oracle at Colophon prophesies by means of water. There is a spring in a subterranean chamber, and from it the prophet drinks on certain appointed nights,

---

31 Iamblichus, *De Myst.* 3.11 (127:4–9); see Clarke, Dillon, and Hershbell, *Iamblichus*, 148–49.
32 Iamblichus, *De Myst.* 3.5 (111:7–11); see Clarke, Dillon, and Hershbell, *Iamblichus*, 130–31; C. Addey, "Divine Possession and Divination in the Graeco-Roman World: The Evidence from Iamblichus's *On the Mysteries*," in *Spirit Possession and Trance: New Interdisciplinary Perspectives* (ed. B. E. Schmidt and L. Huskinson; London: Continuum, 2010), 171–85.
33 Iamblichus, *De Myst.* 3.11 (126:1–3); see Clarke, Dillon, and Hershbell, *Iamblichus*, 146–47.
34 Iamblichus, *De Myst.* 3.9 (120:3–10); see Clarke, Dillon, and Hershbell, *Iamblichus*, 140–41; Addey, "Divine Possession and Divination in the Graeco-Roman World," 177–78.
35 For the archaeology of Claros, see J. de la Genière, "Klaros: Bilan provisoire de dix campaignes de fouilles," *REA* 100 (1998) 235–56.

after performing many preliminary ceremonies, and after drinking, he delivers his oracles, no longer seen by the spectators present. That this water has oracular power is immediately obvious."[36] Even Pliny knows that "in the cave of Apollo at Claros at Colophon there is a pool, a draught from which causes marvelous oracular utterances to be produced, though the life of the drinkers is shortened."[37] Tacitus relates that the prophet at Claros was an illiterate man: "There, it is not a woman, as at Delphi, but a priest chosen from certain families, generally from Miletus, who ascertains simply the number and the names of the applicants. Then descending into a cave and drinking a draught from a secret spring, the man, who is commonly ignorant of letters and of poetry, utters a response in verse answering to the thoughts conceived in the mind of any inquirer."[38] Again, water functions as a medium of divine inspiration and knowledge—and even of poetic expression, as in the case of an anonymous boy as reported by Apuleius:

> I recall having read various things of the same kind in the philosopher Varro, a man of the most exact scholarship and erudition; one of them was that when the people of Tralles used magic to inquire about the outcome of the Mithridatic war, a boy gazing at a reflection of Mercury in water gave a prophecy of the future in a hundred and sixty lines of poetry.[39]

The oracles of Zeus were pronounced in the fourth major oracle site, Dodona, the best-known symbol of which was the sacred oak.[40] According to some ancient authors, the rustling of the tree's branches and leaves were interpreted by priests called *selloi*. Later texts name even more sources of prophetic inspiration, for instance, the sounds of Dodona's famous bronze cauldrons; these are associated with the prophetesses' activity by Clement of Alexandria and by Lucan.[41]

Even water is associated with Dodona prophecy in later sources, according to which, the "murmuring" of the spring flowing under the roots of the oak in-

36 Iamblichus, *De Myst.* 3.11 (124:8–12); see Clarke, Dillon, and Hershbell, *Iamblichus*, 144–147.
37 Pliny, *Nat. hist.* 2.232.
38 Tacitus, *Annales* 2.54.
39 Apuleius, Apologia 42.6. I thank Christopher Jones for drawing my attention to this text.
40 For the oracle of Dodona, see E. Eidinow, *Oracles, Curses, and Risk among the Ancient Greeks* (Oxford: Oxford University Press, 2007); B. Kowalzig, *Singing for the Gods: Performances of Myth and Ritual in Archaic and Classical Greece* (Oxford: Oxford University Press, 2007), 331–52; Johnston, *Ancient Greek Divination*, 60–72.
41 Clement of Alexandria, *Exhortation to the Greeks* 2.11; Lucan 6.425.

spired the female prophets to prophesy.[42] Archaeologically, no such spring has been found at Dodona; rather, the idea of a spring at Dodona is comparable to the inspirational springs at other famous oracle sites, and attests "both to the practice of embroidering great religious sites with additional, remarkable physical characteristics ... and to the tendency to transfer the traits of one oracle to another."[43]

The most reliable information concerning the connection between the sacred spring and prophecy comes from Didyma and Claros. In both cases, the sacred spring is at the heart of the sanctuary, where prophesying also takes place. The case of Delphi is different because it involves not water but vapors, but the idea is the same, that a substance conveys the divine spirit to the prophet, causing her to reach an altered state of consciousness and, thus, to be able to utter divine words. Even at Delphi, the water of the Castalian spring is necessary in the Pythia's preparations for receiving the divine word.

This kind of association of water and prophecy is known neither in the Hebrew Bible nor in any other ancient Near Eastern source. Nothing in these sources suggests that the "living water" available at temples ever played a role in the prophetic process of communication. This may partly be due to our lack of knowledge about how the oracular process in the Near East actually worked, but one should also note that Mesopotamian temples were not constructed around natural springs with which the prophetic activity inside could have been connected; the same can be said of the temple of Jerusalem, whose association with water belongs to an eschatological reality (see above).

There is one letter from Mari, though, suggesting that prophetic inspiration could have been triggered by means of drinking a liquid of some kind:[44]

---

42 Servius, Commentary on the *Aeneid* 3.446: *circa hoc templum quercus inmanis fuisse dicitur, ex cuius radicibus fons manabat, qui suo murmure instinctu deorum diversis oracula reddebat: quae murmura anus Pelias nomine interpretata hominibus disserebat.* Cf. Pliny, *Nat. Hist.* 2.228.

43 Johnston, *Ancient Greek Divination*, 66. For the archaeology of Dodona, see M. Dieterle, *Dodona: Religionsgeschichtliche und historische Untersuchungen zur Entstehung und Entwicklung des Zeus-Heiligtums* (Spudasmata 116; Hildesheim: Olms, 2007).

44 ARM 26 207 (= SBLWAW 41 17): 3–11; for interpretations of this text, see J.-M. Durand, "In vino veritas," *RA* 76 (1982) 43–50; C. Wilcke, "*ittātim ašqi aštāl:* Medien in Mari?," *RA* 77 (1983) 93; J. M. Sasson, "The Posting of Letters with Divine Messages," in *Florilegium Marianum 2*, FS M. Birot (ed. D. Charpin and J.-M. Durand; Mémoires de NABU 3; Paris: SEPOA, 1994) 299–316, esp. 307–8; M. Nissinen, "Prophetic Madness: Prophecy and Ecstasy in the Ancient Near East and in Greece," in *Raising Up a Faithful Exegete*, FS R. D. Nelson (ed. K. L. Noll and B. Schramm; Winona Lake, Ind.: Eisenbrauns, 2010) 3–29, esp. 15–16; D. Charpin, "Le prophétisme dans le Proche-Orient d'après les archives de Mari (xviiie siècle av. J.-C.)," in *Les recueils prophétiques de la Bible: Origines, milieux, et contexts proche-oriental* (ed. J.-D. Macchi et al.;

> Concerning the campaign my lord is planning, I gave drink to male and female persons to inquire about signs.[45] The oracle is extremely favorable to my lord. Likewise, I inquired of male and female persons about Išme-Dagan. The oracle is unfavorable to him.

The one writing to King Zimri-Lim here is Queen Šibtu, who, even in another letter,[46] reports using the same divinatory technique, which is as obscure as it is interesting. Šibtu does not explicate what kind of drink she provided the male and female persons with, or how and why it facilitated the oracular process; in fact, she only mentions the act of giving drink, not the liquid itself. In any case, the men and women in question are prompted, by drinking, to utter the inquired oracles. It seems that this method of soliciting oracles was somewhat unusual, since Šibtu anticipated an accusation that she had obtained the oracle in an inappropriate way: "Perhaps my lord would say this: 'She has made them speak by fraudulent means.'"[47]

In another letter from Mari, likewise sent by Queen Šibtu to her royal husband Zimri-Lim, the divine assembly under the leadership of Ea takes an oath by drinking water mixed with dirt taken from the door-jambs of Mari:[48]

Le monde de la Bible 64; Geneva: Labor et fides, 2012), 31–73, esp. 65; J. Stökl, *Prophecy in the Ancient Near East: A Philological and Sociological Comparison* (CHANE 56; Leiden: Brill, 2012) 49–50.

45 This translation of the Akkadian phrase *ittātim zikāram u šinništam ašqi* interprets the male and female persons themselves as signs in the same way a prophet appears in the *Epic of Zimri-Lim* (SBLWAW 41 64), line 139: "The hero of the land saw his sign, the prophet" (see Charpin, "Le prophétisme d'après les archives de Mari," 65). Sasson, "The Posting of Letters with Divine Messages," 308 translates "I gave male and female the signs to drink," assuming that the drink contains the signs to be interpreted.

46 ARM 26 212 (= SBLWAW 41 22): 1–2.

47 ARM 26 207 (= SBLWAW 41 17): 35–36.

48 ARM 26 208 (= SBLWAW 41 18): r.15–26. For this text, see C. Uehlinger, "Audienz in der Götterwelt: Anthropomorphismus und Soziomorphismus in der Ikonographie eines altsyrischen Zylindersiegels," *UF* 24 (1992) 339–59, esp. 351–52; J. M. Sasson, "Mari Apocalypticism Revisited," in *Immigration and Emigration within the Ancient Near East*, FS E. Lipiński (ed. K. van Lerberghe and A. Schoors; OLA 65; Leuven: Peeters, 1995) 285–98, esp. 286–87; M. Nissinen, "Prophets and the Divine Council," in *Kein Land für sich allein: Studien zum Kulturkontakt in Kanaan, Israel/Palästina und Ebirnâri für Manfred Weippert zum 65. Geburtstag* (ed. U. Hübner and E. A. Knauf; OBO 186; Fribourg: Universitätsverlag and Göttingen: Vandenhoeck & Ruprecht, 2002) 4–19, esp. 7–8 (= pp. 461–77 in this volume); D. Charpin and J.-M. Durand, "Des volontaires contre l'Élam," in *Literatur, Politik und Recht in Mesopotamien*, FS C. Wilcke (ed. W. Sallaberger, K. Volk, and A. Zgoll; Orientalia Biblica et Christiana 14; Wiesbaden: Harrassowitz, 2003) 63–76, esp. 74–75.

> Door-jamb dirt from the gate of Mari was brought and dissolved in water. The gods and goddesses drank it and Ea said to the gods: "Stand up, those of you who intend harm to the brickwork of Mari or to the protective guardian [of Mari]!" The gods and the goddesses [said]: "We intend no harm to the brickwork of Mari or to the protective guardian of Mari!"

The historical context of this vision of the prophet Qišti-Diritim, quoted by Šibtu in her letter, is the invasion of the Elamites in Zimri-Lim's tenth regnal year, and it can be read as a prophetic endorsement of his military actions against the Elamites, protecting them under a divine oath.

Another example of the function of water as the medium in oathtaking can be found in the oracle of Ištar of Arbela belonging to the collection of prophecies pronounced at the meal of the covenant, that was served on the terrace of the Ešarra temple at Assur[49], on the occasion of Esarhaddon's enthronement in in 680 BCE:[50]

> She gave them *ṣarṣāru* water to drink. She filled a pitcher of one seah with ṣarṣāru water, gave it to them and said: "You say to yourself: 'Ištar–she is small beer!' Then you go into your cities and your districts, eat your own bread and forget this covenant. But every time you drink this water you remember me and keep this covenant which I have made on behalf of Esarhaddon."

The text combines ritual actions with divine words and reads like a scribal compilation describing a ritual and the prophetic oracle pronounced during that ritual.[51] A specific kind of water, *mê ṣarṣāru*, serves as a reminder of the covenant. The meaning of the word *ṣarṣāru* is unclear,[52] but it is also used in an in-

---

49 The terrace of the Ešarra temple is mentioned as the scene of royal rituals in Assur; see S. Parpola, *Assyrian Prophecies* (SAA 9; Helsinki: Helsinki University Press, 1997), 25 (ad iii 2); G. van Driel, *The Cult of Aššur* (SSN 13; Assen: van Gorcum, 1969), 194.

50 SAA 9 3.4 (= SBLWAW 41 87) iii 3–15. For interpretations of this text, see Parpola, *Assyrian Prophecies*, xix–xx; E. Otto, *Das Deuteronomium: Politische Theologie und Rechtsreform in Juda und Assyrien* (BZAW 284; Berlin: de Gruyter, 1999), 80–84; M. Weippert, "'König, fürchte dich nicht!': Assyrische Prophetie im 7. Jahrhundert v.Chr.," *Or* 71 (2002) 1–54, esp. 15–19; Nissinen, "Prophets and the Divine Council," 14–15; M. J. de Jong, *Isaiah among the Ancient Near Eastern Prophets: A Comparative Study of the Earliest Stages of the Isaiah Tradition and the Neo-Assyrian Prophecies* (VTSup 117; Leiden: Brill, 2007), 409–11; Stökl, *Prophecy in the Ancient Near East*, 138–40.

51 Cf. de Jong, *Isaiah among the Ancient Near Eastern Prophets*, 411; Stökl, *Prophecy in the Ancient Near East*, 140.

52 Parpola, *Assyrian Prophecies*, 25, associates it with the rabbinic *ṣarṣūr*, which means a stone vessel used as a cooler (cf. *CAD* Ṣ 115 sub *ṣarṣaru* B).

cantation in which it also belongs to taking an oath by drinking water from *ṣarṣāru*.[53]

Here it is a prophet of Ištar who mediates divine words concerning the *adê* being made between the gods of Assyria and the vassal states, as well as between Esarhaddon and the vassal kings as the gods' earthly representatives. The oath is taken by gods and humans alike, the vassal kings participating in the meal of covenant, to which the gods are also invited by Ištar.[54] The specific water used for the oath-taking apparently functioned as a medium of divine agency, serving as a reminder, but also probably as the activator, of the covenant, hence fulfilling a function similar to the wine in Christian eucharist: "Whenever you drink it, do this for the remembrance of me" (cf. Mark 14:24; 1 Cor 11:25).

3 Water as Destructive Power

The flipside of the life-giving powers of water is its destructive force. The West Semitic and biblical mythology knows the Sea and the River as rivals and adversaries of benevolent divine powers.[55] In Ugaritic mythology, the chaotic and destructive aspect of Yam competes with the life-giving aspects of Baal.[56] Such a combat is even reflected in prophetic literature, for instance, in Hab 3:8: "Was your wrath against the rivers, O Lord? Or your anger against the rivers, or your rage against the sea, when you drove your horses, your chariots to victory?" In the book of Ezekiel, the oracles against Tyre (Ezekiel 27–28) repeatedly use the expression "in the heart of the seas" (*bĕ-lēb yāmîm*) for the site of both dominion (27:4) and destruction (27:25–27); the corresponding Akkadian phrase *ina qabal tâmtim* denotes the utmost end of the horizon and symbolizes the global dominion of the Assyrian king.[57]

53 Šurpu iii 62; see E. Reiner, *Šurpu: A Collection of Sumerian and Akkadian Incantations* (AfO Beiheft 11; Osnabrück: Biblio, 1970 [repr. 1956]), 21.

54 The tablet is broken here, but what remains can be read as Ištar's invitation to the gods (SAA 9 3.4 ii 35–36: DINGIR.MEŠ AD.MEŠ-*ia* ŠEŠ.MEŠ-*ia al-ka-ni ina* ŠÀ *a-d*[*e-e x x x x*] "Come, gods, my fathers and brothers! [*Enter*] the coven[ant ...]."

55 See, e.g., J. Day, *God's Conflict with the Dragon and the Sea: Echoes of a Canaanite Myth in the Old Testament* (UCOP 35; Cambridge: Cambridge University Press, 1985).

56 See P. Bordreuil and D. Pardee, "Le combat de *Ba'lu* avec *Yammu* après les textes ougaritiques," *MARI* 7 (1993) 63–70; cf. J.-M. Durand, "Le mythologème du combat entre le dieu de l'orage at la mer en Mésopotamie," *MARI* 7 (1993) 41–61.

57 See M. Lang and R. Rollinger, "Im Herzen der Meere und in der Mitte des Meeres: Das Buch Ezechiel und die in assyrischer Zeit fassbaren Vorstellungen von den Grenzen der Welt," in *In-*

Rivers in particular appear as liminal spaces that can bring about destruction as well as the act of salvation, through the crossing of them. The crossings of the Red Sea (Exod 14) and the river Jordan (Josh 3) are foundational events in biblical history, marking a transition from one status to another; the parting of waters by the prophets Elijah and Elisha in 2 Kgs 2:8, 14 is a clear reminiscent of this. Ancient Near Eastern kings, including Alexander the Great, repeatedly recorded crossings of rivers during their campaigns, presenting them not merely as technical operations, but as acts of royal skill and divine will.[58]

In Neo-Assyrian prophecy, rivers are part of the chaotic wilderness, full of all kinds of liminal spaces, that Ištar ranges through for the sake of the life of Assurbanipal, her beloved king:[59]

> Desiring your life I roam the steppe, continually crossing rivers and oceans, ranging mountains and alps. Continually crossing all rivers, I am finished off by droughts and showers. My charming figure they ravage; my body is exhausted and troubled for your sake.

This is reminiscent, not only of Gilgameš's roaming of the steppe after the death of Enkidu, but also of Esarhaddon's, Assurbanipal's father's, "roaming in the steppe"[60] while being expatriated during the civil war preceding his ascendance to the throne of Assyria.[61] Crossing rivers and oceans (*nārāti u tâmāti*), even "all rivers" (*nārāti kalīšina*), symbolizes the all-encompassing efforts of the goddess

---

terkulturalität in der Alten Welt: Vorderasien, Hellas, Ägypten und die vielfältigen Ebenen des Kontakts (ed. R. Rollinger et al.; Philippika 34; Wiesbaden: Harrassowitz, 2010) 207–64. The expression *qabal tâmtim* is used by the king of Tyre in Assurbanipal's annals, where he is said to dwell "in the heart of the sea" (Prism B ii 39 and parallels); see J. Novotny and J. Jeffers, *The Royal Inscriptions of Ashurbanipal (668–631 BC), Aššur-etel-ilāni (630–627 BC), and Sîn-šarra-iškun (626–612 BC), Kings of Assyria,* Part 1 (RINAP 5/1; University Park, Pa.: Eisenbrauns, 2018), 61.

58 See R. Rollinger, *Alexander und die großen Ströme: Die Flußüberquerungen im Lichte altorientalischer Pioniertechniken (Schwimmschläuche, Keleks und Pontonbrücken)* (Classica et Orientalia 7; Wiesbaden: Harrassowitz, 2013).

59 SAA 9 9 (= SBLWAW 41 94): 8–15.

60 Cf. SAA 9 1.8 (= SBLWAW 41 75) v 12–20: "I am the Lady of Arbela! To the king's mother since you implored me, saying: 'The one on the right and the other on the left you have placed in your lap. My own offspring you expelled to roam the steppe.'" This refers to Esarhaddon's two rebelling brothers.

61 For this text and the allusions to Gilgameš, see Parpola, *Assyrian Prophecies,* il–l, 41; de Jong, *Isaiah among the Ancient Near Eastern Prophets,* 405–8; C. Halton, "Allusions to the Stream of Tradition in Neo-Assyrian Oracles," *ANES* 46 (2009) 50–61, esp. 57–58.

to save Assurbanipal's life in the middle of the civil war, and convince the divine council (*puḫur ilāni*) about his kingship.[62]

The river already appears as the site of the enemies' destruction in a letter from Mari, in which the majordomo Sammetar reports the words of the prophet Lupaḫum:[63]

> As before, when the Yaminites came to me and settled in Saggaratum, I was the one who spoke to the king: "Do not make a treaty with the Yaminites! I shall drive the shepherds of their clans away to Ḫubur (*ina ḫu-bu-ur-re-e*), and the river will finish them off for you." Now then, he should not pledge himself without consulting God.

As the underworld river, Ḫubur[64] symbolizes the death of the Yaminites, but at the same time, it is also used as a pun on Habur, the tributary of the Euphrates within the area of the kingdom of Mari.[65] Lupaḫum's words present the prophecy concerning the defeat of the Yaminites as a "lesson that Zimri-Lim should be drawing from recent history"[66] in a situation where he has to decide whether to make a treaty with the king of Ešnunna.[67] The river is mentioned several times in the context of Esarhaddon's civil war and his eventual victory:[68]

> Fear not, king! I have spoken to you, I have not slandered you! I have inspired you with confidence, I have not caused you to come to shame! I will lead you safely across the River.

Similarly to the mention of Ḫubur/Habur in the Mari letter cited above, the prophetic reference to the river is both historical and mythological.

---

62 The tablet is dated to the year 650, when Assurbanipal was waging war against his brother Šamaš-šumu-ukin; see Nissinen, "Prophets and the Divine Council," 12–13. According to de Jong, the text "skillfully ties up the fate of Ashurbanipal and Šamaššum-ukin with that of Gilgameš and Enkidu. The Leitmotif of SAA 9 9 is the life of Ashurbanipal, which through the Gilgames-parallel mirrors the death of Šamaš-šum-ukin" (*Isaiah among the Ancient Near Eastern Prophets*, 408).

63 ARM 26 199 (= SBLWAW 41 9): 32–39.

64 See H. D. Galter, "Hubur," *DDD*^{2} (1999) 430–31.

65 See D. Charpin, "Prophètes et rois dans le Proche-Orient amorrite: Nouvelles données, nouvelles perspectives," in *Florilegium Marianum 6*, FS A. Parrot (ed. D. Charpin and J.-M. Durand; Mémoires de NABU 4; Paris: SEPOA, 2002) 7–38, esp. 25 n. 149.

66 J. M. Sasson, "Water beneath Straw: Adventures of a Prophetic Phrase in the Mari Archives," in *Solving Riddles and Untying Knots*, FS J. C. Greenfield (ed. Z. Zevit, S. Gitin, and M. Sokoloff; Winona Lake, Ind.: Eisenbrauns, 1995) 599–608, esp. 603.

67 For the historical circumstances, see Charpin, "Prophètes et rois dans le Proche-Orient amorrite," 22–25.

68 SAA 9 1.6 (= SBLWAW 41 73) iii 30 – iv 4.

The river probably represents mythical allusions[69], but is also a historical point of reference to Esarhaddon's victory over his brothers before his ascension to the Assyrian throne.[70] This is what Esarhaddon himself relates in his inscription:[71]

> I reached embankment of the Tigris and, upon the command of Sîn and Šamaš, the lords of the harbor, I let all my troops jump across the broad river Tigris, as if it were nothing but a ditch.

Again, the crossing of the river appears as a divinely ordered act of salvation which is not merely part of a military strategy, but constitutes a transition from one phase to another, in Esarhaddon's case: from the chaotic period of the civil war to the restoration of kingship. The river represents a dangerous liminal space to be traversed before the transition is completed. As in the case of Ḫubur/Habur in the letter from Mari, the river symbolizes the victory of the king and the destruction of his enemies:[72]

> As you were standing in their midst, I removed them from your presence, drove them up the mountain and rained fire and brimstone upon them. I slaughtered your enemies and filled the River with their blood.

The prophetic oracles and the royal inscriptions doubtlessly refer to historical events that accompanied Esarhaddon's rise to power, but both genres do it in a highly mythologized manner. The account of Esarhaddon's war against his brothers is replete with allusions to literary works that depict Ninurta's and Marduk's battles against their enemies (*Lugale, Enuma eliš*), equating the king to these gods and mythologizing his battles against his enemies.[73]

---

69 For the deification of the river Tigris, see B. Alster, "Tigris," *DDD*² (1999) 870–71.

70 Thus Parpola, *Assyrian Prophecies*, lxxiii, 8; Nissinen, *References to Prophecy in Neo-Assyrian Sources*, 25. For a different historical interpretation of the oracle SAA 9 1.6, see de Jong, *Isaiah among the Ancient Near Eastern Prophets*, 267–68, who dates it to the period preceding Esarhaddon's campaign to Egypt in 674 BCE.

71 Esarhaddon 1 (= Nineveh A = SBLWAW 41 97) i 84–86; see E. Leichty, *The Royal Inscriptions of Esarhaddon, King of Assyria (680–669 BC)* (RINAP 4; Winona Lake, Ind.: Eisenbrauns, 2011), 14.

72 SAA 9 3.3 (= SBLWAW 41 86) ii 18–23.

73 See A. Annus, *The God Ninurta in the Mythology and Royal Ideology of Ancient Mesopotamia* (SAAS 14; Helsinki: The Neo-Assyrian Text Corpus Project, 2002), 100; cf. de Jong, *Isaiah among the Ancient Near Eastern Prophets*, 259.

Finally, the river appears as the site of salvation and destruction in Assurbanipal's inscription about his war against Elam in 653 BCE. The *grande finale* of this war takes place at the river Ulaya before entering Susa, the Elamite capital:[74]

> Upon the command of Aššur and Marduk, the great gods, my lords, who encouraged me with good omens, dreams, speech omens, and prophetic messages, I defeated them in Tell Tuba. With their bodies I stuffed up Ulaya. With their corpses, as if with thorn and thistle, I filled the outskirts of Susa.

Just as the crossing of the Tigris was the final and decisive ordeal Esarhaddon had to go through before his rise to power, the crossing of Ulaya marks the divinely ordained victory of Assurbanipal over the Elamites. Again, the river brings about salvation to the king and destruction to his enemies. Filling the river with their corpses is an image of total destruction that is also shown in the relief depicting Assurbanipal's war against the Elamites (figure). The lower register of the relief, originally belonging to the North Palace of Nineveh, shows the river Ulaya literally stuffed up with the dead bodies of the enemies.[75]

Assurbanipal's relief is a prime example of a performative image that does not simply illustrate the events related in the inscription, as a visual copy of preexisting reality, but creates and renews that reality through the act of representation: "Representation was thought to make things happen, not simply to depict."[76] In fact, this is true not only for the relief but also for the inscription. Both the textual and pictorial media, rather than recording acts of eyewitnessing, carry an authoritative ideological interpretation of the recorded events.[77]

Even the river, whether textual or graphic, has a performative function. It is "real" in the sense that it has a historical and geographical point of reference, but it is also contextualized by the textual/iconographic ideological program. The river retains its mythological value as a liminal space where both salvation

---

74 Prism B v 87–92 (= SBLWAW 41 101). See Novotny and Jeffers, *The Royal Inscriptions of Ashurbanipal*, 71; for the historical circumstances, see Nissinen, *References to Prophecy in Neo-Assyrian Sources*, 46–51.

75 For these reliefs and the epigraphs attached to them, see J. M. Russell, *The Writing on the Wall: Studies in the Architectural Context of Late Assyrian Palace Inscriptions* (Mesopotamian Civilizations 9; Winona Lake, Ind.: Eisenbrauns, 1999), 156–99; Z. Bahrani, *Rituals of War: The Body and Violence in Mesopotamia* (New York: Zone Books, 2008), 23–55.

76 Bahrani, *Rituals of War*, 53.

77 See C. Uehlinger, "Neither Eyewitnesses, Nor Windows to the Past, but Valuable Testimony in its Own Right: Remarks on Iconography, Source Criticism and Ancient Data-Processing," in *Understanding the History of Ancient Israel* (ed. H. G. M. Williamson; Proceedings of the British Academy 143; Oxford: Oxford University Press, 2007), 173–228.

and destruction take place, and it is indexical in constantly renewing the permanent meaning of the event in the minds of the audience.

Figure 1: Assurbanipal's war against the Elamites

4 Conclusion

The significance of water for prophecy reveals itself in manifold ways in ancient Eastern Mediterranean prophetic texts and practices. As the source of life, water can be equated with a benevolent deity. It can also be seen as a metaphor for, or manifestation of, divine favor. As a medium, water can be used as a direct source of prophetic inspiration, and as an effective means of supernatural action, whether it is used for purification or as a constituent of a ritual act. As a destructive power, water can be associated with the realm of chaos and death.

No coherent "water ideology" can be found in sources of prophecy, be they taken from the Hebrew Bible, Mesopotamian texts, or Greek literature, but a few recurring topics can nevertheless be identified. In biblical prophecy, water appears as the source of life and purity. Greek writers, thanks to whom we are somewhat better informed about the details of the oracular process in major Greek oracle sites, tended to associate oracles with sacred springs and the preparatory purification rites that the prophets underwent before uttering their oracles. In the case of Didyma and Claros, water also played a role as the medium of the divine agency, making the prophets receptive to the divine word. In biblical and other Near Eastern texts, water does not appear as a part of the oracular process, except for two letters from Mari in which men and women are given a specific drink in order to obtain oracles. In addition, some Mesopotamian texts mention the function of water as a medium of supernatural agency in connection to taking an oath. Both the Hebrew Bible and Mesopotamian prophetic texts associate water with destructive mythological powers. Rivers in particular appear as liminal spaces, the crossing of which brings about destruction to enemies, and salvation for those under divine protection.

Prophets and the Divine Council

kî mî ʻāmad bĕ-sôd YHWH wĕ-yērē' wĕ-yišmaʻ 'et-dĕbārô
Who has stood in the council of Yahweh and seen and heard[1] his word?
(Jer 23:18)

The Council of God in the Hebrew Bible

There are two ways to explain the motto, quoted from the Book of Jeremiah. It can be read as a rhetorical question emphasizing the hidden intentions of God, who is beyond human perception and knowledge (cf. Job 5:18). As such, it is mostly explained as a wisdom gloss with the implied answer "nobody".[2] On the other hand, it has been understood as referring to the previously mentioned false prophets, of whom it is said later (Jer 23:22): "If they had stood in my council, they would have proclaimed my word to my people". If this is the correct interpretation, then the question in verse 18 is not rhetorical but quite serious, implying that true prophets indeed were believed to have access to the council of God, the decisions of which are the substance of their prophetic proclamation.[3] This paper is written in support of the second alternative, which I try to substantiate with some ancient Near Eastern evidence.

The council of God in the Hebrew Bible is no novelty; the occurrences are well known and need only be briefly listed here. The "council of Yahweh"

1 The word *yišmaʻ* may be a later addition, explaining the difficult expression "seeing YHWH'S word"; cf. W. McKane, *A Critical and Exegetical Commentary on Jeremiah*, vol. 1 (ICC; Edinburgh: T. & T. Clark, 1986), esp. 581.

2 Volz, P., *Der Prophet Jeremia* (KAT 10; Leipzig and Erlangen: Deichert, 1922), esp. 235; W. Rudolph, *Jeremia* (HAT 1/12; Tübingen: Mohr Siebeck, ^{3}1968), esp. 152–53 (gloss); W. Thiel, *Die deuteronomistische Redaktion von Jeremia 1–25* (WMANT 41; Neukirchen-Vluyn: Neukirchener Verlag, 1973), esp. 251; McKane, *Jeremiah*, 582. Cf. A. Auld, "Amos and Apocalyptic: Visions, Prophecy, Revelation," in *Storia e tradizioni di Israele*, FS J. A. Soggin (ed. D. Garrone and F. Israel; Brescia: Paideia, 1991) 1–15, 6: "It may well have been a prophetic or visionary commonplace to claim such experience. I wonder if it is not being implicitly objected that none of the prophets can dare to claim access to the divine privy council (or kitchen cabinet?)".

3 If H. J. Hermisson ("Kriterien "wahrer" und "falscher" Prophetie im Alten Testament: Zur Auslegung von Jeremia 23,16–22 und Jeremia 28,8–9," *ZThK* 92 [1995] 121–39), 126 is right in his assertion that the second half of verse 18 is a later addition, then the original text may not be a question at all. Hermisson translates: "Wahrlich: Wer im Rat Jahwes stand, der sehe und lasse hören (*w^{e}-yašmaʻ*) sein Wort!".

DOI 10.1515/9783110466546-024

(*sôd YHWH* Jer 23:18; Ps 25:14; cf. *sôdî* Jer 18:22; *sôd 'ĕlôăh* Job 15:8) and related expressions like "meeting of God" (*'ădat 'ēl* Ps 82:1) and "council/convocation of the Holy Ones" (*qĕhal/sôd qĕdōšîm* Ps 89:6, 8), as well as references to "sons of God" (*bĕnê 'ēlîm* Ps 29:1; 89:7; *bĕnê 'elyôn* Ps 82:6; *bĕnê ha-'ĕlōhîm* Job 1:6; 2:1)[4], "all gods" (*kol ĕlōhîm* Ps 97:7), or simply "gods" (*ĕlōhîm* Ps 82:1, 6), imply a notion of an assembly headed by Yahweh, which consists of divine beings and makes judicial decisions concerning terrestrial conditions.[5]

Even prophetic involvement in the divine council is well documented in the Hebrew Bible.[6] On several occasions, prophets appear to be present in the council of God and receive a commission to intermediate its decisions to the people. The vision of Micaiah son of Imlah reflects this idea (1 Kgs 22:19–22); Isaiah volunteers as the messenger of the divine council when God asks: "Whom shall I send? Who will go for us?" (Isa 6:8); the opening verses of Second Isaiah (Isa 40:1–8) imply a similar setting;[7] and in the Book of Amos it is affirmed that God does nothing without revealing his *sôd* to prophets, his servants (Am 3:7).[8] Moreover, in one of the visions of the prophet Zechariah (3:1–7) the

---

[4] Also Gen 6:2, 4, without the implication of a divine council; for the probable reading *bĕnê 'ēlîm* instead of the Masoretic *bĕnê yiśrā'ēl* in Deut 32:8, see *BHS*.

[5] For the divine council in the Hebrew Bible, see, e.g., H. Robinson, "The Council of Yahweh," *JTS* 45 (1944) 151–57; H.-J. Fabry, "*sôd*: Der himmlische Thronrat als ekklesiologisches Modell," in *Bausteine biblischer Theologie*, FS G. J. Botterweck (ed. id.; BBB 50; Köln/Bonn: Hanstein, 1977) 99–126, esp. 118–22; E. T. Mullen Jr., *The Divine Council in Canaanite and Early Hebrew Literature* (HSM 31; Chico, Calif.: Scholars Press, 1980), esp. 168–244; H. Niehr, *Der höchste Gott* (BZAW 190; Berlin: de Gruyter, 1990), esp. 78–94; H.-D. Neef, *Gottes himmlischer Thronrat: Hintergrund und Bedeutung von sôd JHWH im Alten Testament* (Arbeiten zur Theologie 79; Stuttgart: Calwer, 1994), esp. 13–17; S. B. Parker, "The Beginning of the Reign of God: Psalm 82 as Myth and Liturgy," *RB* 102 (1995) 532–59; id., "Council," *DDD*[2] (1999) 204–8; O. Loretz, "Rechtfertigung aus der Perspektive altorientalischer und alttestamentlicher juristischer Terminologie," *Teologinen Aikakauskirja* 105 (2000) 75–88, esp. 80–82.

[6] See E. C. Kingsbury, "The Prophets and the Council of Yahweh," *JBL* 83 (1964) 279–86; Mullen, *The Divine Council*, 215–26; M. E. Polley, "Hebrew Prophecy within the Council of Yahweh, Examined in its Ancient Near Eastern Setting," in *Scripture in Context: Essays in the Comparative Method* (ed. C. D. Evans, W. W. Hallo, and J. B. White; Pittsburgh Theological Monograph Series 34; Pittsburgh: Pickwick, 1980) 141–56; Neef, *Gottes himmlischer Thronrat*, 15–17.

[7] Cf. F. M. Cross, "Council of Yahweh in Second Isaiah," *JNES* 12 (1952) 274–78.

[8] The verse is a prosaic and generalizing, probably Deuteronomistic (or even later; Auld, "Amos and Apocalyptic," dates it close to the Book of Daniel), comment on the idea of prophetic warning in the poem 3:3–8; cf., e.g., J. Jeremias, *Der Prophet Amos* (ATD 24/2; Göttingen: Vandenhoeck & Ruprecht, 1995), esp. 36–37.

high priest Joshuah is present in the heavenly court[9], accused by "Satan" and defended by the angel (or envoy, *mal'āk)* of Yahweh.

It is also well known that the biblical notion of the council of God is built upon a common ancient Near Eastern concept of a divine council defining the destinies of both gods and humans. In more or less elaborate form, this concept[10] is familiar from Ugaritic, Aramaic, and Mesopotamian sources.[11] There is evidence that the judgements of the divine council were transmitted by means of divination[12], but it may be less commonly known that the concept of the council is also well represented in extrabiblical sources for prophecy from different times and places. When Theodore Mullen wrote his monograph *The Divine Council in Canaanite and Early Hebrew Literature* (1980), the lack of knowledge concerning pertinent sources made it possible to talk about "the unparalleled phenomenon of the classical prophets" and to maintain that the prophetic involvement in the divine council "constitutes a radical break with all other council traditions in the ancient Near East."[13] During the past two decades, however, our awareness of the evidence for prophets within the divine council has substantially increased, enabling us to investigate the role of the prohets in the divine council as a common ancient Near Eastern tradition.

---

9 H. Graf Reventlow, *Die Propheten Haggai, Sacharja und Maleachi* (ATD 25/2; Göttingen: Vandenhoeck & Ruprecht, 1993), 52: "Es handelt sich hier um keine Symbolvision, sondern um visionär geschaute Vorgänge im himmlischen Thronrat Jahwes".

10 For an overview of terminology in different Semitic languages, see Mullen, *The Divine Council*, 117–20.

11 See T. Jacobsen, "Primitive Democracy in Ancient Mesopotamia," *JNES* 2 (1943) 159–72; Fabry, "*sôd:* Der himmlische Thronrat als ekklesiologisches Modell," 99–118; Mullen, *The Divine Council*; Niehr, *Der höchste Gott*, 71–78; Neef, *Gottes himmlischer Thronrat*, 18–27; Parker, "Council."

12 See E. Cassin, "Note sur le 'puḫru(m)' des dieux," *La voix de l'opposition en Mésopotamie* (Colloque organisé par l'Institut des Hautes Etudes de Belgique, 19 et 20 mars 1973; Bruxelles: Institut des Hautes etudes de Belgique, 1973) 111–18, esp. 113 and, especially, the texts published by A. Goetze, "An Old Babylonian Prayer of the Divination Priest," *JCS* 22 (1968) 25–29 (YBC 5023) and I. Starr, *The Rituals of the Diviner* (Bibliotheca Mesopotamica 12; Malibu, CA: Undena, 1983), esp. 30–31 (HSM 7494:13–19 = Text A) with commentary, 56–59.

13 Mullen, *The Divine Council*, 283; cf. Polley, "Hebrew Prophecy within the Council of Yahweh," 149: "There are no parallel passages in Mesopotamian, Egyptian, or Ugaritic texts which present the prophet as called within the assembly of gods in order to speak forth the decision of the assembly. The texts which deal with prophetic vision of the council are unique to Hebrew thought".

The Deir ʿAlla Inscription

To begin with a text from the outskirts of the biblical landscape, thoroughly studied by Manfred Weippert to whom these lines are gratefully dedicated, the divine council plays a prominent role in the Balaam inscription from Transjordanian Deir ʿAlla [Tell Dēr ʿAllā], written in ca. 700 BCE[14]. The text is difficult to interpret, and there is no need to go deeper into the details here, since the notion of the divine council as such is non-controversial and already acknowledged by many scholars. It is clear from the preserved lines in the beginning that Balaam, the "seer of [the] gods" (*ḥzh ʾlhn*), has become conversant with a word of El transmitted by gods who approached him in a nocturnal visitation (comb. I lines 1–2)[15]:

> *wyʾ tw ʾlwh ʾlhn blylh [wy ʾmrw l]h kmš ʾl*
> *wy ʾmrw l[blʿ]m br bʿr kh*
>
> The gods came to him at night [and spoke to] him according to what El says.[16] This is what they spoke to [Balaa]m, son of Beor.

The following line is too enigmatic to reveal what the gods actually said.[17] In any case, as a consequence of the vision, Balaam is fasting and weeping, and when some other people want to know why he is doing this, he tells about a shocking decision of the council (*mwʿd*) of gods (comb. I lines 5–7):

> *šbw ʾḥwkm mh š[dyn...] wlkw rʿw pʿlt ʾlhn*
> *ʾl[h]n ʾtyḥdw wnṣbw šdyn mwʿd*
> *wʾmrw lš[mš] tpqy skry šmyn*
> *bʿbky šm ḥšk wʾl ngh*
>
> Sit down! I shall tell you what the Šadd[ayin have ...ed]. Come, see the works of the gods!
> The gods came together, the Šaddayin gathered together in an assembly.
> They said to Ša[mš][18]: "May you break the bolts of heaven,
> may there be darkness and not light in your clouds".

---

14 Editio princeps: J. Hoftijzer and G. van der Kooij, *Aramaic Texts from Deir ʿAlla* (DMOA 19; Leiden: Brill, 1976); cf. J. A. Hackett, *The Balaam Text from Deir ʿAlla* (HSM 31; Chico, Calif.: Scholars Press, 1984); M. Weippert, *Jahwe und die anderen Götter* (FAT 18; Tübingen: Mohr Siebeck, 1997).

15 I follow the transliteration and interpretation of Weippert, *Jahwe und die anderen Götter*, 165–69.

16 The word used here is *mšʾ* corresponding to Heb. *maśśāʾ* "utterance".

17 For different suggestions, see Weippert, *Jahwe und die anderen Götter*, 167 n. 15.

18 Or: Ša[gar]; see ibid., 179–80.

What follows is a description of a convulsion of nature well comparable with the prophetic oracles of doom in the Hebrew Bible, especially with those connecting the "Day of Yahweh" with darkness (Isa 13:10; Joel 2:2; Am 5:20), and, in a more general sense, also with Isaiah's calling vision (cf. Isa 6:11–13). The Balaam inscription is the only extrabiblical text reporting a prophetic oracle of doom coming from the divine council. The geographical, cultural, and probably ethnic vicinity of its composers to the Hebrew-speaking population on the other (and even on the same) side of the Jordan river[19] suggests that the idea of the prophet as the mouthpiece of the divine council derives from the same roots as the one to be found in the Hebrew Bible.

Letters from Mari

The Oath of the Gods in Favor of Mari

The tradition of the prophetic involvement in the divine council has its roots in the Old Babylonian period at the latest where it is documented independently by sources from Mari and Ešnunna. At Mari, two letters to King Zimri-Lim give account of a prophetic oracle in which the prophet witnesses a decision of a divine council and transmits its decisions to the king.[20] A letter of Queen Šibtu (ARM 26 208) reports a divine message transmitted by Qišti-Diritim, a prophet (*āpilum*) of the goddess Diritum (lines 1'-26')[21]:

> *umma [Ēama ...] kimt[um ...] nī[š ilim i niḫsus] / ašar m[û ibaššu] nīš ilim ni[ḫsus] / Asumêm iš[tassi] Asumûm arḫ[iš illik] awātam ana Ēa [iqbi] / ša Asumûm [iqbû] ul ešme / it[bīma Ēa] iqbi ummāmi / [kīma nīš ilim] nizakkarū rū[šam] u sippam ša bāb [Māri] lilqūnimma / nīš ilim [i niḫs]us / rūšam u sippam ša bā[b] Māri ilqūnimma ina mê imḫuḫūma / ilū u ilātum i[š]tê*

19 Cf. ibid., 187: "So ist eine polytheistische Inschrift aus einer Gegend, die nach dem Alten Testament eine israelitische Bevölkerung hatte, nicht von vornherein als nichtisraelitisch anzusehen. Die 'Nationalität' des 'Bileam'-Textes kann deshalb aufgrund innerer Kriterien nicht festgestellt werden". Cf. B. A. Levine, "The Deir ʿAlla Plaster Inscriptions," in *COS* 2: 140–45, esp. 141.

20 Cf. C. Uehlinger, "Audienz in der Götterwelt: Anthropomorphismus und Soziomorphismus in der Ikonographie eines altsyrischen Zylindersiegels," *UF* 24 (1992) 339–59, esp. 351–52; R. P. Gordon, "From Mari to Moses: Prophecy at Mari and in Ancient Israel," in *Of Prophets' Visions and the Wisdom of Sages*, FS R. N. Whybray (ed. H. A. McKay and D. J. A. Clines; JSOT.S 162; Sheffield: Sheffield Academic Press, 1993) 63–79, esp. 72; B. Pongratz-Leisten, *Herrschaftswissen in Mesopotamien: Formen der Kommunikation zwischen Gott und König im 2. und 1. Jahrtausend v. Chr.* (SAAS 10; Helsinki: The Neo-Assyrian Text Corpus Project, 1999), esp. 70–71.

21 J.-M. Durand, *Archives Épistolaires de Mari 1/1* (ARM 26/1; Paris: Editions Recherche sur les Civilisations, 1988), 437–38.

> *umma Ēama ana ilī / tibā ša ana libitti Māri u rābiṣ [Māri u]gallalū / [il]ū u ilāt[um iqbênim umm]āmi ana libitti [Mā]ri u rābiṣ Māri ul nugalla[l]*
>
> Thus says [Ea: "...] the family [... let us take] the oath! / Where [there is] wa[ter][22] we mi[nd][23] the oath". / He called the god Asumûm, and Asumûm [came] quick[ly, saying] a word to Ea / – what Asumûm [said], I did not hear. / [Ea] ro[se] and said: / "[Because] we shall declare [an oath], door-jamb di[rt][24] from the gate of [Mari] shall be taken to us, and [we shall mi]nd the oath". / Door-jamb dirt from the ga[te] of Mari was taken and dissolved in water. / The gods and the goddesses drank it and Ea said to the gods: / "Stand up,[25] those of you who intend harm to the brickwork of Mari or to the protective guardian [of Mari]!". / The gods and the goddesses [said]: "We intend no harm to the brickwork of [Ma]ri or to the protective guardian of Mari!".

This episode describes a session of a divine council headed by Ea who by divinatory means puts the gods and goddesses under oath not to intend harm to the city of Mari; this is compatible with the traditional role of Ea as the resourceful god of wisdom.[26] The role of the god Asumûm is somewhat unclear, but he seems to be a vizier of Ea[27] who intermediates between Ea and other deities.[28] The prophet's vision is incomplete in that he "did not hear" what Asumûm said to Ea, but the underlying thought may be that Ea wants to hear from Asumûm that the gods are ready to take the oath, or Asumûm gives instructions to perform the divinatory act connected with the oath. In any case, the prophet is able to transmit the message of this heavenly episode, the unanimous benevolence of the divine council towards Mari. Because of the break of the text preced-

---

22 Thus according the restoration of W. L. Moran, "New Evidence from Mari on the History of Prophecy," *Bib* 50 (1969) 15–56, esp. 50.

23 See W. Heimpel, "Minding an Oath," *NABU* (1999) 41, who makes a distinction between "declaring" (*zakārum*) and "minding" (*ḫasāsum*) an oath.

24 For this hendiatical translation, see J. M. Sasson, "Mari Apocalypticism Revisited," in *Immigration and Emigration within the Ancient Near East*, FS E. Lipiński (ed. K. van Lerberghe and A. Schoors; OLA 65; Leuven: Peeters, 1995) 285–98, esp. 286 n. 9.

25 Thus according to the interpretation of ibid., 286 n. 10, reading *ti-ba-a* and interpreting it as a contracted imperative 2. pl. of *tebûm* (for *tibiā*).

26 See Cassin, "Note sur le 'puḫru(m)' des dieux," 117. For Ea (Aya) in Syria, see J.-M. Durand, "La religión en Siria durante la época de los reinos amorreos según la documentatión de Mari," in *Mitología y religión del Oriente Antiguo*, vol. 2/1: *Semitas Occidentales (Ebla, Mari)* (ed. id. and P. Mander; Estudios Orientales 8; Sabadell: AUSA, 1995) 125–533, esp. 189–92; for the prominence of Ea, especially in association with the king's behavior, see V. Hurowitz, "Advice to a Prince: A Message from Ea," *SAAB* 12 (1998) 39–53.

27 Asumûm is probably identical with Usumu, the Janus-faced vizier of Ea, see Sasson, "Mari Apocalypticism Revisited," 155 n. 2; Durand, "La religión en Siria," 192.

28 Uehlinger, C., "Audienz in der Götterwelt," 351 is able to illustrate the text with a similar episode depicted on a contemporary cylinder seal.

ing this episode it is not, of course, entirely sure that it belongs to the prophecy of Qišti-Diritim. In view of the beginning of the prophetic quotation on the obverse, which combines well with the oath of the gods, however, this is quite probable. The very message of the letter of Šibtu appears to be the conviction acquired by divination that nothing will menace the king and country: "Nobody will r[ise] against the throne of Ma[ri]. It is Zimr[i-Lim] to whom the Upper Country[29] is giv[en]. [He will break] the lance of the El[amites]" (lines 9–13).

Judgement on the God of Ešnunna

In ARM 26 196, Šamaš-naṣir, governor of Terqa, gives account of a vision concerning a heavenly verdict of Dagan concerning another deity (lines 1'-14')[30]:

> *[ummāmi ana pānīya Tišpak lis]sû šipṭ[a]m luddin / Tišpak [i]ssûnimma ana Tišpak Dagan kī'am iqbi ummāmi / ištu Šinaḫ mātam tebīl inann[a] ūtka ittalkam ūtka kīma Ekallātim tamaḫḫar / annītam maḫar Dagan u Yakrub-El [i]q[b]i umma Ḫanatma / ana šipṭim ša taddinu aḫka lā tanaddin*
>
> "[Now, let them c]all [Tišpak before me] and I will pass judgment". / So they called on Tišpak, and Dagan said to Tišpak as follows: / "From Šinah(?)[31] you have reigned the land. Now your day has passed,[32] you will confront your day like Ekallatum". / This is what happened before Dagan, and Ikrub-El said[33]: "Hanat says: / 'Be not neglectful of the judgement that you passed'."

In the beginning of the letter, the writer refers to the request of Zimri-Lim, who was planning to set out on a campaign, to report whatever oracle occurs in the temple of God (*ig[e]rrûm ša ina bit illm i[ba]ššû*). Now Dagan, the principal god of Mari, passes a judgment over Tišpak, the god of Ešnunna. This is done in the presence of other gods, of whom Ikrub-El, a god of Terqa, and Ḫanat, a goddess of a city with the same name, take part in the discussion, reminding Dagan of his

---

29 For *ala'itum* in a meaning similar to (*mātum*) *elītum*, see Durand, *Archives Épistolaires de Mari 1/1*, 438.

30 Ibid., 422–23.

31 Thus according to the hypothetical reading of Sasson, "Mari Apocalypticism Revisited," 288 n. 13.

32 Cf. the expression *ūmūšu qerbū* (ARM 26 212:8'; see J.-G. Heintz, "Aux origines d'une expression biblique: *ūmūšu qerbū*, in A.R.M. X/6, 8'?," *VT* 21 [1971] 528–40).

33 Thus Sasson, "Mari Apocalypticism Revisited," 288; cf. K. van der Toorn, "A Prophetic Role-Play Mistaken for an Apocalyptic Vision: ARM 26/196," *NABU* (1998) 3, who translates "This he said before Dagan and Yakrub-Il", interpreting the verb *iqbi* as referring to a human speaker of the divine words, i.e., the prophet.

judgment. The verdict of Dagan clearly corresponds to Zimri-Lim's hoped-for victory over King Ibalpiel II of Ešnunna[34], whose god – and, through him, the king himself – is threatened with an end as sudden as that of Ekallatum.[35] The damage of the tablet does not allow us to conclude who the visionary was, but, since the king has obliged him to report every oracle he hears to be delivered in the temple of God, the vision presumably was delivered in the temple of Dagan in Terqa by a local prophet or other visionary.

Oracle from Ešnunna

Considering the historical message embedded in the vision reported by Šamaš-naṣir, it is interesting that even Zimri-Lim's adversary, King Ibalpiel II of Ešnunna, received prophetic messages, albeit with quite different content, about the decisions of the divine council, as the oracle of the goddess Kititum (Ištar) to Ibalpiel indisputably demonstrates (FLP 1674)[36]:

> *šarru Ibâl-pî-ēl umma Kitītumma / niṣrêtum ša ilāni maḫrīja šaknā / aššum zikrum ša šumīya ina pîka kayyānu niṣrēt ilāni aptanattiakkum / ina milki ša ilāni ina šipṭi ša Annim mātum ana bēlim nadnatkum / šīn mātim elītim u šaplītim tapaṭṭar / makkūr mātim elītim u šaplītim tebedde / maḫīrka ul imaṭṭi ayyim mātim ša qātka ikšudū / akal tanēḫtim ikā[niššum] / išdi kussîka anāku Kitītum / udannan lamassam naṣertam aštaknakkum [u]zunka libaššiam*
>
> O king Ibalpiel, thus says Kititum: / The secrets of the gods are placed before me. / Because you constantly pronounce my name with your mouth, I keep disclosing the secrets of the gods for you. / On the advice of the gods and by the command of Anu, the country is given you to rule. / You will ransom[37] the upper and lower country, / you will amass[38] the riches of the upper and lower country. / Your commerce will not diminish, there will be a perm [anent] food of peace[39] [for] any country that your hand keeps hold of. / I, Kititum, will

34 For historical circumstances, see D. Charpin, "Le contexte historique et géographique des prophéties dans les textes retrouvés à Mari," *BCSMS* 23 (1992) 21–31.

35 The reference to Ekallatum means Išme-Dagan, son of Šamši-Adad, king of Assyria, and brother of Yasmaḫ-Addu, the predecessor of Zimri-Lim on the throne of Mari, who was the king of Ekallatum.

36 See M. deJong Ellis, "The Goddess Kititum Speaks to King Ibalpiel: Oracle Texts from Ishchali," *MARI* 5 (1987) 235–66.

37 The reading (*ši-in* ... *ta-pa-ṭa₃-ar*) and translation of lines 14–15 according to ibid., 261–63, who interprets the "loosening of the sandals" (*šēnam paṭārum*) as an idiom.

38 If the word *tebedde* may be derived from *pedû* "to ransom/redeem" (ibid., 263), lines 16–17 form a parallelism with lines 14–15.

39 The expression *akal tanēḫtim* is not attested elsewhere but can be compared with, e.g., *aklu taqnu* and *mê taqnūti* in the Neo-Assyrian prophetic oracle SAA 9 1.10 vi 22–23.

strengthen the foundations of your throne, / I have established the protective spirit for you. May your [e]ar be attentive to me!

This text presents a (prophetic) oracle, probably written down on the occasion of Ibalpiel's accession to the throne.[40] It represents the type of a letter from a deity to the king called *šipirtu*, which contains only divine words without further authorship indications.[41] The message of the oracle is that the divine council has made a decision in Ibalpiel's favor. The decision made under the leadership of Anu, the supreme god, includes the extent of the reign of Ibalpiel, the foundation of his throne and the abundance of the country. The goddess Kititum presents herself as the one who is informed of the arbitrations of the gods and who has the task of transmitting them to the king: "I keep disclosing the secrets of the gods for you" (*niṣrēt ilāni aptanattiakkum*). The goddess has the role of the divine intermediary, who constantly communicates the "secrets of gods" to the king. She functions as the diviner of the gods, whereas the human diviner–a prophet or some other practitioner of divination—represents her and the whole divine council in pronouncing the desicion in human language to the human addressee.[42] There is no qualitative difference between prophecy and other kinds of divination here–on the contrary, as Robert P. Gordon notes, "[a]ccess to the divine council provides ... a point of substantial contact between divinatory and prophetic practice".[43]

40 Ellis, "The Goddess Kititum Speaks to King Ibalpiel," 250.

41 E.g., SAA 13 43 (= ABL 1369); see Pongratz-Leisten, *Herrschaftswissen in Mesopotamien*, 226–27, 260–62. I have classified the Ešnunna oracle among prophecies in report format in my earlier article (M. Nissinen, "Spoken, Written, Quoted and Invented: Orality and Writtenness in Ancient Near Eastern Prophecy," in *Writings and Speech in Israelite and Ancient Near Eastern Prophecy* [ed. E. Ben Zvi and M. Floyd; SBLSymS 10; Atlanta GA: Society of Biblical Literature, 2000] 235–71, esp. 242), whereas Pongratz-Leisten, *Herrschaftswissen in Mesopotamien*, 204 and L. L. Grabbe, "Ancient Near Eastern Prophecy from an Anthropological Perspective," in *Prophecy in Its Ancient Near Eastern Context: Mesopotamian, Biblical, and Arabian Perspectives* (ed. M. Nissinen; SBLSymS 13; Atlanta: Society of Biblical Literature, 2000) 13–32, esp. 24–25 would rather see the text as a letter from the goddess to the king. The lack of mention of the prophet may turn the scales in favor of a *šipirtu*.

42 For the interplay of celestial and terrestrial judicial roles in the Old Babylonian diviner's ritual, see Starr, *The Rituals of the Diviner*, 57–58; M. deJong Ellis, "Observations on Mesopotamian Oracles and Prophetic Texts: Literary and Historiographic Considerations," *JCS* 41 (1989) 127–86, esp. 139–40.

43 Gordon, "From Mari to Moses," 67.

Neo-Assyrian Texts

The Intercession of the Goddess for Assurbanipal

The position of the goddess in the divine council of Ešnunna is closely reminiscent of a similar pattern in Neo-Assyrian texts. In spite of the time-difference of more than a millennium, they provide us with an essentially uniform concept of the divine council and the roles of the goddess and the prophets in it. Let us start with a letter of Aššur-ḫamatu'a, a priest of the temple of Ištar in Arbela, to Assurbanipal (SAA 13 139)[44]:

> [*anāku*] *Bēl ētarba issi Mu*[*ll*]*issu assilim / Aššūr-bāni-apli šar māt Aššūr ša turabbīni /* [*l*]*ā tapallaḫ* [*anā*]*ku Bēl artēanki / Aššūr-bāni-apli ina māti ša kēnu / kēni šû adi mātīšu artēanki / ina šulmu šallimte issu ālīki attūṣi / rēmu gimlu* [...] (Break)
> *ana* [*Issār*] *Bēl atta*[*ḫar*] *usarriri / Nabû-šarru-uṣur rādi kibsi ša mūgīya assapar / ana šarri bēlīja urdaka Aššūr-ḫamātū'a / Aššūr Issār ana šarri likrubbu* (sic!)

> [I] am Bel, I have entered and made peace with Mullissu. Assurbanipal, king of Assyria whom she raised: Fear not! I am Bel, I have remitted Assurbanipal to you (f.)[45] in a country of truth. Him together with his country I hve remitted to you. I departed safely and securely from your city. Mercy and compassion [...] (Break)
> I implored and prayed to [*Ištar*] and Bel. Then I dispatched Nabû-šarru-uṣur, a tracker of my contingent (?). To the king, my lord, your servant Aššur-ḫamatu'a. May Aššur and Ištar bless the king.

The letter has a remarkable structure: it begins with the divine word, followed by some personal lines of the writer. About one third of the letter is broken away; this part may have included a note of how the divine word came to the writer's notice. The greeting is most untypically placed at the end of the letter. This structure makes the letter a representative of a format of its own. Being a letter with a greeting from the actual writer, it is not a report of prophecy which typically includes the words of the deity and indications of the prophet who transmitted them, but not of the person who wrote the tablet.[46] Neither does it conform to the *šipirtu* type, which contains only divine words without further qualifica-

---

44 S. W. Cole and P. Machinist, *Letters from Priests to the Kings Esarhaddon and Assurbanipal* (SAA 13; Helsinki: Helsinki University Press, 1999), esp. 111. For SAA 13 139, see pp. 245–65 in this volume.

45 The feminine suffix in *artēanki* indicates that Mullissu is addressed.

46 See S. Parpola, *Assyrian Prophecies* (SAA 9; Helsinki: Helsinki University Press, 1997), esp. liii–liv, lxii.

tions.[47] Presumably Aššur-ḫamatu'a had a prophetic performance, experienced by himself in the temple, written down and dispatched it to the king with Nabû-šarru-uṣur.

From the point of view of prophetic involvement in the divine council, the text is most rewarding, thanks to the clear role casting, which is slightly different form that in the Kititum oracle from Ešnunna, since it is Bel and not Mullissu who speaks to the king. Nevertheless, the role of the goddess as the intermediary becomes clear. Bel, i. e., Marduk, the supreme god of Babylonia, declares his reconciliation with Assurbanipal upon the intercession of Mullissu. She stands there on behalf of the king and receives Bel's declaration of mercy and reconciliation which, through her, belongs to Assurbanipal and the whole country. Bel's departure from "your city" – whatever city this might refer to – gives a hint at a specific historical situation, namely, the return of Marduk from the exile, caused by Sennacherib's destruction of Babylon in the year 689, to his temple some twenty years later, in the beginning of Assurbanipal's rule. Theologically speaking, the repatriation of Marduk and other gods was a sign of reconciliation of the gods who in their anger had abandoned the city.[48]

The divine council is not mentioned explicitly in the letter of Aššur-ḫamatu'a, but the language and the idea fully concurs with the the oracle of the female prophet Dunnaša-amur (SAA 9 9:16–21):

> *ina puḫur ilāni kalāmi aqṭibi balāṭaka / dannā rittāya lā urammāka ina pān ilāni / naggalapāya ḫarruddā ittanaššāka ana kāša / ina š[apt]ēya ētanarriš balāṭaka* [...] *balāṭaka balāṭtu tušattar*
>
> In the assembly of all the gods I have spoken for your life. / My arms are strong and will not cast you off before the gods. / My shoulders are always ready to carry you, you in particular. / I keep desiring your life with my l[ip]s [...] your life, you increase life.

Again, the goddess, who in this prophecy is Ištar and Mullissu in one person, intercedes on behalf of Assurbanipal, explicitly before the divine council (*puḫur ilāni*). The idea is that the prophetic message is the terrestrial counterpart of the divine intermediation of the Goddess in the divine council. The prophet does not speak on her own behalf but impersonates the goddess, functioning as the channel through which the divine intercession and response to it finds

---

47 See above.

48 For this ideology, see J. A. Brinkman, "Through a Glass Darkly: Esarhaddon's Retrospects on the Downfall of Babylon," *JAOS* 103 (1983) 35–42, esp. 40–41. Cf. the prophetic word of reconciliation of the "angry gods" (of Babylon) SAA 9 2.5 iii 20 and the prophetic appeal for the exiled gods of Esaggil SAA 9 2.3 ii 24–27.

an expression in human language. Similarly in extispicy, the judicial role of the gods is transferred to the diviner who pronounces the judgement of the council in the terrestrial sphere.[49]

The specific situation behind the concern for Assurbanipal becomes clear from the date of the tablet, 18th of Nisan (I), 650. By this time Assurbanipal, being at war against his brother Šamaš-šumu-ukin, the ruler of Babylon, evidently sought support from the divine council. The intercession on behalf of the king is expressed also in the Dialogue of Assurbanipal and Nabû (SAA 3 13), a text written by the same scribe and deriving from the same situation as the prophecy of Dunnaša-amur[50]. In this text, best characterized as a literary offshoot of prophetic language,[51] Assurbanipal repeatedly pleads with Nabû not to leave him "in the assembly of those who wish him ill" (*ina puḫur ḫaddānūtēšu* line r. 3; cf. lines 6, 22, r. 4) and Nabû asserts: "My pleasant mouth shall ever bless you in the assembly of great gods" (*ina puḫur ilāni rabûti* line 26; cf. line r. 11). Even though the role of the intercessor is assumed here by Nabû, Assurbanipal utters his prayers in temples of Ištar/Mullissu (lines 3, 12, 13–17), and the reason for Nabû's intercession is that Assurbanipal "sat in the lap of the Queen of Nineveh" in his childhood (line r. 7), "grasps the feet of the Queen of Nineveh" and "sits next to Urkittu" (lines r. 2–3). Hence, it is the intimate relationship of the king with the goddess that ultimately counts before the divine council.

A prayer related to similar circumstances is included in Assurbanipal's inscription concerning the war against Teumman, the king of Elam, two and a half years earlier in the month of Ab (V), 653.[52] According to this inscription, Assurbanipal was worshipping Ištar in Arbela, when he heard about the assault of the Elamites. Upon these news, he uttered a pious prayer, pleading with the goddess for help. The following passage of the prayer again stresses the importance of the intercession of Ištar (lines v 37–40):

> *umma atti Bēlet bēlēti ilat qabli bēlet tāḫāzi mālikat ilāni abbēša / ša ina maḫar Aššūr abi bānîki damiqtī taqbê / ina niš ēnēšu ebbi ihšuḫanni ana šarrūti*

49 Cassin, "Note sur le 'puḫru(m)' des dieux," 113; Starr, *The Rituals of the Diviner*, 57–58.

50 A. Livingstone, *Court Poetry and Literary Miscellanea* (SAA 3; Helsinki: Helsinki University Press, 1989), esp. 33–35; cf. Parpola, *Assyrian Prophecies*, lxxi.

51 Pongratz-Leisten, *Herrschaftswissen in Mesopotamien*, 75.

52 Prism B v 16 – vi 9; J. Novotny and J. Jeffers, *The Royal Inscriptions of Ashurbanipal (668–631 BC), Aššur-etel-ilāni (630–627 BC), and Sîn-šarra-iškun (626–612 BC), Kings of Assyria*, Part 1 (RINAP 5/1; University Park, Pa.: Eisenbrauns, 2018), 68–71.

You are the Lady of the Ladies, the Goddess of warfare, the Lady of battle and the counsellor of the gods, your (lit.: her) fathers! / You spoke good words for me before Aššur, the father who made you, / so that he, raising his pure eyes, wished me to be the king.

Ištar appears here in a similar role as Mullissu in the letter of Aššur-ḫamatu'a (SAA 13 139). Her good words for Assurbanipal make the supreme god decide in favor of his kingship. Moreover, Ištar is addressed as the "councellor (*māliktu*) of gods" which presumably refers to her role as the diviner within the divine council and the intermediary of its judgements. Her answer to Assurbanipal is composed as a quotation of prophetic words (lines 46–49):

inhēya šūnuḫūti Ištar išmēma lā tapallaḫ iqbâ / ušarḫiṣanni libbu / ana nīš qātēka ša taššâ ēnāka imlâ dimtu artaši rēmu

Ištar heard my desperate sighs and said to me: "Fear not!". / She made my heart confident, / saying: "Because of the prayer you said with your hand lifted up, your eyes being filled with tears, I have compassion for you".

Intercession of the Goddess in Context of Divine Love

At this turn a slight digression may be allowed. It is worth noting that the divine council is not the only context of manifesting the divine intercession on behalf of the king. The goddess has the same function in divine love poetry and rituals, where there is no divine council but just the divine couple in the intimacy of the ceremonial bedroom where the goddess says a good word on behalf of the king to her beloved.[53] In fact, the purpose and function of the divine love-making seems to have been to establish the kingship and support the king and his family, whereby the role of the goddess is decisive. To quote just one Neo-Assyrian example (BAK 338)[54]:

53 See a fuller treatment in M. Nissinen, "Akkadian Rituals and Poetry of Divine Love," in *Mythology and Mythologies* (ed. R. M. Whiting; Melammu Symposia 2; Helsinki: Neo-Assyrian Text Corpus Project, 2001) 93–136.

54 H. Hunger, *Babylonische und assyrische Kolophone* (AOAT 2; Kevelaer: Botzon & Bercker/Neukirchen-Vluyn: Neukirchener, 1968), esp. 106 (# 338):21–25; cf. e.g., Esarhaddon Uruk B: 16–17; E. Leichty, *The Royal Inscriptions of Esarhaddon, King of Assyria (680–669 BC)* (RINAP 4; Winona Lake, Ind.: Eisenbrauns, 2011), 274: *Aššūr amat damiqtīya liššakin šaptukki* "O Ištar in Uruk, the superior lady, when you happily dwell in your cella, may a favorable word for me, Esarhaddon, king of Assyria, be uttered by your lips"; and the variant Uruk C: 16–17 (ibid., 276): *Nanāya Uruk bēltu ṣīrti ina qereb bīt papāḫi šuāte ḫadiš ina ašābīki yāti Aššur-aḫu-iddina šar māt Aššūr ina maḫar Nabû ḫā'irīki tisqari bānīti* "O Nanaya, the superior lady, when you happily dwell in your cella, may you speak a favorable word for me, Esarhaddon, king of Assyria, before Nabû,

> *[Tašmē]tu bēltu rabītu ḫīrtu naramtaka ṣābitat abbutti ina maḫrīka ina mayyāl taknê [ūmišam] lā naparkâ literriška balāṭī [tākilk]a ul ibâš Nabû*
>
> [Tašme]tu, the Great Lady, your beloved spouse, who intercedes (for me) [daily] before you in the sweet bed, who never ceases demanding you to protect my life. [The one who trusts in] you will not come to shame, oh Nabû.

In older poetry, probably attached to rituals of love, the intercession may have a clearly amatory context, as in the Love Lyrics of Nanaya and Muati, where the goddess, after a flirting description of her beloved, puts the following in his mouth (VAT 17347:14): *šarrum lū dari ina qabēki Abī-ešuḫ lû dar*[*i ina qabêki*] "Let the king live for ever at your command! Let Abi-ešuḫ live for ever [at your command]!"[55]. Similarly in an Old Babylonian hymn it is said of Ištar (AO 4479: 45): *išti Anim ḫāwirīša tēteršaššum dāriam balāṭam arkam* "She kept entreating Anu, her beloved, a long and everlasting life for him".[56] In rituals of divine love, the intercessory function is transferred from the sessions of the divine council into the privacy of the divine bedroom, where the mutual love of the gods makes it even more effective.

The Council of Gods and the Concept of the Divine

In addition to her role as intercessor, the goddess also appears as the convener of the divine council (SAA 9 3.4 ii 33–36)[57]:

> *abat Issār ša Arbail ana Aššūr-aḫu-iddina šar māt Aššūr ilāni abēya ahhēya alkāni ina libbi ad*[*ê*...]
>
> Word of Ištar of Arbela to Esarhaddon, king of Assyria. Come, gods, my fathers and brothers! [*Enter*] the cove[nant ...]

These are introductory words of an oracle delivered on the occasion of the meal of the covenant as a part of the enthronement festival of Esarhaddon (lines iii 1–15). The goddess serves the gods of Assyria and the subordinate states

---

your spouse"; Nabonidus 1 ii 38–39 (S. Langdon, *Die neubabylonischen Königsinschriften* [VAB 4; Leipzig: Hinrichs, 1912], 224): *Nikkal ummu ilāni rabûti ina maḫar Sîn narāmīšu liqbâ banītī* "May Nikkal, the mother of the great gods, speak favorably on my behalf before Sîn, her beloved".

55 W. G. Lambert, "Divine Love-Lyrics from the Reign of Abi-ešuḫ," *MIO* 12 (1966) 41–56, esp. 49, 51.

56 F. Thureau-Dangin, "Un hymne à Ištar de la haute époque babylonienne," *RA* 22 (1925) 169–77, esp. 170–71.

57 See Parpola, *Assyrian Prophecies*, lxxxv n. 48 for further occurrences.

(represented by their earthly rulers) with food and drink, and the meal is accompanied by a prophetic oracle proclaiming that the covenant is made by Ištar on behalf of Esarhaddon. In this case, the divine council is there to witness the treaty of the newly enthroned king with his vassals. Ištar boldly represents it as her treaty, as if it would be something different from the treaty of Aššur read in the king's presence and mentioned in the preceding oracle (SAA 9 3.3 ii 27). This, however, is hardly the case; rather, the attribution of the covenant to two deities reflects a certain concept of God which merges the divine council into a single corpus, the members of which have different functions working for the same goal[58]

This concept of the divine is visible in the prophecy of Bayâ in which no less than three deities speak through the mouth of the prophet (SAA 9 1.4):

> *lā tapallaḫ Aššūr-aḫu-iddina anāku Bēl issīka adabbūbu / gušūrē ša libbīka aḫarrīdi / kî ummaka tušabšûkani 60 ilāni rabûti issīya ittitissū ittaṣarūka / Sîn ina imittīka Šamaš ina šumēlīka 60 ilāni rabûti ina battibattīka izzazzū qabalka irtaksū / ina muḫḫi amēlūti lā tatakkil mutuḫ ēnēka ana ayyāši dugulanni / anāku Issār ša Arbail Aššūr issīka ussallim / ṣeherāka attaṣakka lā tapallaḫ na''idanni / ayyu šū nakru ša idibakkanni anāku qālākūni / urkīūte lū kî pānīūte / anāku Nabû bêl qarṭuppi na''idāni*
>
> Fear not, Esarhaddon! / am Bel, I speak to you! / I watch over the supporting beams of your heart. / When your mother gave birth to you, sixty Great Gods were there with me, protecting you. / Sîn stood at your right side, Šamaš at your left. Sixty Great Gods are still staying around you, they have girded your loins. / Do not trust in humans! Lift up your eyes and contemplate me! / I am Ištar of Arbela. I have reconciled Aššur with you. / I already carried you when you were a baby. Fear not, praise me! / Is there an enemy that has attacked you, while I have kept silent? / The future shall be like the past! / I am Nabû, the Lord of the Stylus. Praise me!

As a matter of fact, even more than the three gods speaking are involved in this oracle. Aššur, the supreme god of Assyria, is explicitely mentioned, and the sixty great gods represent the divine council in its entirety as bestowing their favors upon Esarhaddon. The three divine voices may be taken as a sequence of three different addresses in which each deity speaks for him/herself,[59]

---

58 See ibid., xxiv: "On the allegorical level this corresponds to a meeting of the divine council ... On a deeper, mystical level, the passage describes a process taking place within Aššur himself, with Ištar, the 'heart' of his cosmic body, playing a key role in the process. (...) Thus, while Ištar in the oracle appears as the *primus motor* of the covenant, it was the council in its entirety, that is, within Aššur himself, who concluded it".

59 Thus K. van der Toorn, "Mesopotamian Prophecy between Immanence and Transcendence: A Comparison of Old Babylonian and Neo-Assyrian Prophecy," in *Prophecy in Its Ancient Near*

but the oracle is not a series of unconnected speeches. Instead, each deity adds a specific function to the whole. Bel/Marduk presents himself as the divine father of the king at the head of the council of sixty gods when the king was born. Ištar fulfills her function as the divine intercessor who has reconciled Aššur, i.e., the council in its entirety,[60] with the king. The reconciliation of Esarhaddon with Aššur, intermediated by Ištar, corresponds exactly to the reconciliation of Assurbanipal with Bel upon the intercession of Mullissu in SAA 13 139 (see above), and clearly presents the main subject of the oracle, around which everything else revolves. Nabû, as the keeper of heavenly records and the lord of destiny, sees to it that the future shall be like the past. All this forms a whole which determines the position of the king before the divine council and encompasses his whole life in the past and in the future.

Did the Prophets Stand in the Divine Council?

The Neo-Assyrian documents, like the earlier sources from Mari and Ešnunna, leave no doubt of the significance of the prophetic involvement in the divine council; indeed, proclaiming its decisions appears as an essential function of prophecy and a fundamental reason for prophetic activity. Returning to the verse from the Book of Jeremiah quoted in the beginning, we may now ask whether the Mesopotamian prophets were actually imagined as attending the sessions of the divine council. To be sure, the prophets never play a personal role in the process. They never themselves open their mouth before the council or intercede on behalf of the people. This role belongs to the divine members of the council, whereas the prophets are there to speak its decisions as mouthpieces of the gods. Nevertheless, there is a document from the early Neo-Assyrian period (year 809), a long decree of expenditures for various festivals and ceremonies in Ešarra, the Aššur temple in the city of Assur, that suggests the prophetic participation in the divine council in very specific terms (SAA 12 69:27–31)[61]:

> *nadbāku ša puḫur ilāni / 1 sūt dišpu 5 qa šamnu 4 sât [5 qa šamaššammi k]arkadinnu inašši / 10 emār kurummutu ana kusāpi 5 emār kibtu ana qa[duāti āpiāni inaššiū] / 1 emār 5 sât ša*

Eastern Context: Mesopotamian, Biblical, and Arabian Perspectives (ed. M. Nissinen; SBLSymS 13; Atlanta GA: Society of Biblical Literature, 2000) 70–87, esp. 83.

60 Cf. Parpola, *Assyrian Prophecies*, xxi.

61 L. Kataja and R. Whiting, *Grants, Decrees and Gifts of the Neo Assyrian Period* (SAA 12; Helsinki: Helsinki University Press, 1995), esp. 74.

pān maḫḫâte širāše inašši[ū] / gimir 1 sūt 4 qa dišpu 5 qa šamnu 4 sât 5 qa šamaššammi [*11 emār 5 sât kurummutu*] *5 emār kibtu / mimma anniu* [*nadbāku ša puḫur ilāni*]

The expenditure for the divine council: / [The c]onfectioner tak[es] 1 seah of honey, 5 liters of oil and 4 seahs [5 liters of sesame. / The bakers take] 10 homers of barley for bread and 5 homers of wheat for ga[dūtu]-bread. / The brewers tak[e] 1 homer 5 seahs of barley[62] for the presence of the female prophets. / Total: 1 seah 4 liters of honey, 5 iters of oil, 4 seahs 5 liters of sesame, [11 homers 5 seahs of barley], 5 homers of wheat. / All this [is the expenditure for the divine council].

This passage implies that the divine council was not just an abstract idea but was celebrated ceremonially. According to a recent study of Stefan M. Maul, the celebration of *puḫur ilāni* was one of the high points of the major royal festivities of the month of Shebat (XI) in Ešarra.[63] These festivals are best documented from the time of Assurbanipal but, thanks to this source, they are traceable back to the time of Adad-nirari III (810 – 783). The text also demonstrates that the prophets – or prophetesses (*maḫḫâte*), to be precise – could have an institutional and cultic setting in the temple precisely in these ceremonies. This exciting piece of evidence confirms the conviction that even in Assyria, sitting in the council of God indeed was an essential prerequisite of prophecy – and that much beer was needed to have their task properly fulfilled!

---

62 There is no word for "barley" in the original, but this is what the context and the surrounding passages of the text suggest.

63 S. M. Maul, "Die Frühjahrsfeierlichkeiten in Aššur," in *Wisdom, Gods and Literature*, FS W. G. Lambert (ed. A. R. George and I. L. Finkel; Winona Lake, Ind.: Eisenbrauns, 2000) 389 – 420, esp. 390, 397.

Wisdom as Mediatrix in Sirach 24: Ben Sira, Love Lyrics, and Prophecy[1]

1 The Triple Context of Sirach 24

Within the book of Ben Sira, chapter 24 has a prominent compositional position. Concluding the first major part of the book, which begins with reflections on the origins and essence of Wisdom (Sir 1), it also initiates the second part, which, again, ends with a praise of Wisdom (Sir 51:13–30).[2] The idea of Wisdom in the entire book is dependent on these three structurally emphatic passages, and this gives even chapter 24 a programmatic nature. The chapter is a poetic composition that begins with a lengthy self-praise of Lady Wisdom herself, who claims to have been created before ages and now to abide in Zion (vv. 1–22). The poem continues with a third-person section on Law and Wisdom (vv. 23–29) and ends with first-person reflections of Ben Sira himself who as a teacher of Wisdom pours out instruction "like prophecy" (vv. 30–34).

In its primary context, that is, in the book of Ben Sira, chapter 24 reads like a compendium of Ben Sira's ideology of Wisdom. It brings together the essential concepts of the book: Wisdom, Law, prophecy[3] – and even the temple, which is to be understood as the dwelling-place of Wisdom (vv. 10–11).[4]

Doubtless one of the most researched passages of the book of Ben Sira,[5] chapter 24 has been analyzed from a variety of points of view, such as those

---

1 I wish to express my gratitude to Dr. Marko Marttila, whose presentation on Sir 24 in the Helsinki-Munich-Tartu doctoral colloquium in Helsinki, September 22, 2007 gave me the impetus to study this chapter from the point of view of love lyrics. I would also like to thank Prof. Pancratius C. Beentjes for his valuable comments on my text and Dr. Robert M. Whiting for correcting my English.

2 On the central position and structure of Sir 24, see P. W. Skehan, "Structures in Poems on Wisdom: Proverbs 8 and Sirach 24," *CBQ* 41 (1979) 365–79; id. and A. A. DiLella, *The Wisdom of Ben Sira* (AB 39; New York: Doubleday, 1987), 333–38; J. Marböck, *Weisheit im Wandel: Untersuchungen zur Weisheitstheologie bei Ben Sira: Mit Nachwort und Bibliographie zur Neuauflage* (BZAW 272; Berlin: Walter de Gruyter, 1999 [= 1971]), 41–47; G. Sauer, *Jesus Sirach/Ben Sira* (ATD.A 1; Göttingen: Vandenhoeck & Ruprecht, 2000), 34–35, 179–80.

3 Sauer, *Jesus Sirach/Ben Sira*, 185: "Gesetz, Prophetie und Weisheit finden damit zu einer großen Einheit zusammen."

4 Ibid., 182; A. M. Sinnott, *The Personification of Wisdom* (SOTSMS; Burlington: Ashgate, 2005), 125.

5 Cf. commentaries, the newest being Skehan and DiLella, *The Wisdom of Ben Sira*; Sauer, *Jesus Sirach/Ben Sira*; and J. Schreiner, *Jesus Sirach 1–24* (NEB.AT 38; Würzburg: Echter, 2002).

DOI 10.1515/9783110466546-025

of the Law,[6] creation,[7] theology,[8] education,[9] scriptural interpretation,[10] poetic structure,[11] the personification of Wisdom,[12] the inner-biblical traditions underlying the poem[13] as well as its cultural background.[14] Since this essay began to take shape when I observed similarities between the Song of Songs and Sirach 24 and, by further reflection, found out their bearing on the question of the cultural context, it will focus on the two last mentioned aspects.

As Jessie Rogers has noted, the book of Ben Sira "is permeated with biblical allusions and phrases [...] Ben Sira is most likely to use allusions or paraphrases and he makes imaginative use of metaphors that allow for a variety of free associations with biblical imagery."[15] The second context of Sirach 24 is, thus, the set of texts that in Ben Sira's time enjoyed an authoritative status: "the Law, the prophets, and the other writings" (Sir Prol. 9–10). One of the lasting results of previous scholarship on Sirach 24 is that its most important biblical subtext is to be found in Proverbs 8, where the personified female figure of preexistent Wisdom, created by God before ages, unmistakably serves as the model for Lady

---

6 M. Gilbert, "L'éloge de la Sagesse (*Siracide* 24)," *Revue Théologique de Louvain* 5 (1974) 326–48, esp. 345–48; J. C. H. Lebram, "Jerusalem, Wohnsitz der Weisheit," in *Studies in Hellenistic Religions* (ed. M. J. Vermaseren; EPRO 78; Leiden: Brill, 1979) 103–28, esp. 108–12; Marböck, *Weisheit im Wandel*, 81–96.

7 Gilbert, "L'éloge de la Sagesse," 341–45; J. F., Rogers, "Wisdom and Creation in Sirach 24," *JNES* 22 (1996) 141–56; J. J. Collins, *Jewish Wisdom in Hellenistic Age* (OTL; Louisville, Ky.: Westminster John Knox, 1997), 57–61.

8 J. Marböck, *Gottes Weisheit unter uns: Zur Theologie des Buches Sirach* (HBS 6; Freiburg: Herder, 1995); and id., *Weisheit im Wandel.*

9 F. Ueberschaer, *Weisheit aus der Begegnung: Bildung nach dem Buch Ben Sira* (BZAW 379; Berlin: Walter de Gruyter, 2007), 297–305.

10 G. D. Sheppard, *Wisdom as a Hermeneutical Construct* (BZAW 151; Berlin: Walter de Gruyter, 1980).

11 Skehan, "Structures in Poems on Wisdom."

12 J. E. MacKinlay, *Gendering Wisdom the Host: Biblical Invitations to Eat and Drink* (JSOTS 216; Sheffield: Sheffield Academic Press, 1996), 133–59; Sinnott, *The Personification of Wisdom*, 110–41.

13 Sheppard, *Wisdom as a Hermeneutical Construct*, 19–71; Marböck, *Weisheit im Wandel*, 55–57; Beentjes, P. C., "Ben Sira and the Book of Deuteronomy," in J. Pakkala and M. Nissinen (eds.), *Houses Full of All Good Things: Essays in Memory of Timo Veijola* (PFES 95; Helsinki: The Finnish Exegetical Society and Göttingen: Vandenhoeck & Ruprecht, 2008), 413–33.

14 H. Conzelmann, "Die Mutter der Weisheit," in *Zeit und Geschichte*, FS R. Bultmann (ed. E. Dinkler; Tübingen: Mohr Siebeck, 1964) 225–34; Lebram, "Jerusalem, Wohnsitz der Weisheit," 112–28; Rogers, "Wisdom and Creation in Sirach 24," 144–47.

15 Rogers, "Wisdom and Creation in Sirach 24," 144.

Wisdom in Sirach 24.[16] But Proverbs 8 is not the only source the poem draws from; in fact, scholars have disclosed a dense network of allusions to various biblical texts in Sirach 24 – for instance, to Deuteronomistic literature, several psalms, Gen 1:2, Prov 3:13–26; Job 9:8, and many other texts.[17] Nevertheless, one obvious biblical precedent of Sirach 24 has thus far gone virtually unnoticed. Apart from a few passing references,[18] the Song of Songs has not been compared with the self-praise of Lady Wisdom in Sir 24:1–22 at all, even though – as I hope to be able to demonstrate – the allusions are as apparent as manifold.

The third context of Sirach 24 is the Hellenistic world of the early 2nd century BCE The cultural influences on Sirach 24 have, quite understandably and with good reason, been derived from Hellenistic literature. Since Hans Conzelmann, the aretalogy of Isis has often been regarded as a prototype of the self-praise of Lady Wisdom,[19] but she has been associated with even other goddesses, for instance, Athene[20] and the much older tree goddesses attested in Palestinian iconography.[21] The erotic imagery employed in Sir 24 is in line with the image of Lady Wisdom elsewhere in the biblical tradition; "she is mother, wife, lover, beloved, virgin, and bride."[22] In the absence of goddesses, Lady Wisdom takes their place in early Judaism.[23] However, there has not been any discus-

16 See, e.g., Skehan, "Structures in Poems on Wisdom"; Skehan and DiLella, *The Wisdom of Ben Sira*, 333–38; Marböck, *Weisheit im Wandel*, 55–56.

17 See the works mentioned above, nn. 5–14, esp. Sheppard, *Wisdom as a Hermeneutical Construct*, 19–71.

18 E.g., in ibid., 53–54; and Marböck, *Weisheit im Wandel*, 75. In the Song of Songs scholarship, I am aware only of R. E. Murphy, *The Song of Songs: A Commentary on the Book of Canticles or the Song of Songs* (Minneapolis, MN: Fortress, 1990), 99 n. 387: "Metaphorical imagery, comparable to that of the Song, is used to describe Wisdom in Sir 1:16–20 and 24:13–22"; and Y. Zakovitch, *Das Hohelied* (trans. D. Mach; HThKAT; Freiburg: Herder, 2004), 251 (cf. also 201, 203): "In einem unverkennbar von Hld beeinflussten Abschnitt in Sir vergleicht sich die Weisheit mit einer Palme (Sir 24,14)." I owe this quotation to Dr. Marko Marttila.

19 Conzelmann, "Die Mutter der Weisheit," 228–34, cf. Marböck, *Weisheit im Wandel*, 49–54 (but see id., *Gottes Weisheit unter uns*, 76); Rogers, "Wisdom and Creation in Sirach 24," 146–47; Collins, *Jewish Wisdom in Hellenistic Age*, 50.

20 Lebram, "Jerusalem, Wohnsitz der Weisheit," 124–28.

21 S. Schroer, *Wisdom Has Built Her House: Studies on the Figure of Sophia in the Bible* (trans. L. M. Maloney and W. McDonough; Collegeville, Minn.: Liturgical Press, 2000), esp. 92.

22 Ibid., 143; cf. Job 28, Prov 1–9, Sir 15:2, 51:13–22, Wis 7:21–26. For the likewise multiple image of the goddess Ištar, see S. Parpola, *Assyrian Prophecies* (SAA 9; Helsinki: Helsinki University Press, 1997), xxvi–xxxi.

23 Cf. T. Frymer-Kensky, *In the Wake of the Goddesses: Women, Culture, and the Biblical Transformation of Pagan Myth* (New York: The Free Press, 1992), 183: "These mediating figures did not

sion on the possible Mesopotamian background of the poem, which is quite plausible even in the Hellenistic context.

In this essay, which I gratefully dedicate to my teacher and friend Simo Parpola, I attempt to demonstrate the close affinity of Sirach 24 with the Song of Songs as well as to disclose the underlying ideology of the goddess as mediatrix of divine knowledge, prominent not only in the ancient Near Eastern love lyrics, but also in prophecy.

2 Ben Sira's Allusions to the Song of Songs

As much as the first part of the self-praise of Lady Wisdom (24:1–12) echoes Proverbs 8, the second part (24:13–22) unmistakably draws from the Song of Songs, among other texts. Even the section reflecting Wisdom and Law (24:23–29) and Ben Sira's words about himself (24:30–33) can be associated with the Song of Songs. In what follows, I will survey the allusions of the poem to the Song of Songs, making occasional references even to ancient Near Eastern texts – first and foremost to the Love Lyrics of Nabû and Tašmetu (SAA 3 14), which is the best-preserved representative of love lyrics in the Akkadian language and the closest extrabiblical parallel to the Song of Songs.[24] It is important to note that nothing of the original Hebrew text of Sirach 24 has been preserved, hence verbatim quotations are impossible to identify and retroversions remain speculative at best.[25] Nevertheless, even the Greek text clearly reflects the parallelistic structure of the original Hebrew poem, and the lexical associations are easily observable.

---

disappear because they addressed the great existential dilemma of monotheism, the centrality of humankind, and its sense of inadequacy in the face of the divine power."

24 A. Livingstone, *Court Poetry and Literary Miscellanea* (SAA 3; Helsinki: Helsinki University Press, 1989), 35–37; cf. M. Nissinen, "Love Lyrics of Nabû and Tašmetu: An Assyrian Song of Songs?," in *"Und Mose schrieb dieses Lied auf": Studien zum Alten Testament und zum Alten Orient*, FS O. Loretz (ed. M. Dietrich and I. Kottsieper; AOAT 250; Münster: Ugarit-Verlag, 1998) 585–634, esp. 587–592.

25 For an attempt at a retroversion of the poem, see Skehan, "Structures in Poems on Wisdom," 374.

Sirach 24
(New Revised Standard Version)[26]

1 Wisdom praises herself, and tells of her glory in the midst of her people.
2 In the assembly of the Most High she opens her mouth, and in the presence of his hosts she tells of her glory:
3 I came forth from the mouth of the Most High, and covered the earth like a mist.
4 I dwelt in the highest heavens, and my throne was in a pillar of cloud.
5 Alone I compassed the vault of heaven and traversed the depths of the abyss.
6 Over waves of the sea, over all the earth, and over every people and nation I have held sway.
7 Among all these I sought a resting place; in whose territory should I abide?
8 Then the Creator of all things gave me a command, and my Creator chose the place for my tent. He said, "Make your dwelling in Jacob, and in Israel receive your inheritance."
17 Like the vine I bud forth delights, and my blossoms become glorious and abundant fruit.
19 Come to me, you who desire me, and eat your fill of my fruits.
20 For the memory of me is sweeter than honey, and the possession of me sweeter than the honeycomb.
21 Those who eat of me will hunger for more, and those who drink of me will thirst for more.
22 Whoever obeys me will not be put to shame, and those who work with me will not sin.
23 All this is the book of the covenant of the Most High God, the law that Moses commanded us as an inheritance for the congregations of Jacob.
25 It overflows, like the Pishon, with wisdom, and like the Tigris at the time of the first fruits.
26 It runs over, like the Euphrates, with understanding, and like the Jordan at harvest time.

9 Before the ages, in the beginning, he created me, and for all the ages I shall not cease to be.
10 In the holy tent I ministered before him, and so I was established in Zion.
11 Thus in the beloved city he gave me a restingplace, and in Jerusalem was my domain.
12 I took root in an honored people, in the portion of the Lord, his heritage.
13 I grew tall like a cedar in Lebanon, and like a cypress on the heights of Hermon.
14 I grew tall like a palm tree in En-gedi, and like rosebushes in Jericho; like a fair olive tree in the field, and like a plane tree beside watered I grew tall.
15 Like cassia and camel's thorn I gave forth perfume, and like choice myrrh I spread my fragrance, like galbanum, onycha, and stacte, and like the odor of incense in the tent.
16 Like a terebinth I spread out my branches, and my branches are glorious and graceful.
27 It pours forth instruction like the Nile, like the Gihon at the time of vintage.
28 The first man did not know wisdom fully, nor will the last one fathom her.
29 For her thoughts are more abundant than the sea, and her counsel deeper than the great abyss.
30 As for me, I was like a canal from a river, like a water channel into a garden.
31 I said, "I will water my garden and drench my flower-beds." And lo, my canal became a river, and my river a sea.
32 I will again make instruction shine forth like the dawn, and I will make it clear from far away.
33 I will again pour out teaching like prophecy, and leave it to all future generations.
34 Observe that I have not labored for myself alone, but for all who seek wisdom.

---

26 My own translations of the Greek are not necessarily consistent with this translation.

The image of Lady Wisdom as a fruit-bearing tree is likely to allude to Prov 3:18 where Wisdom is called a tree of life, which, again, leads the thoughts to the Garden of Eden. The rivers surrounding Eden are also mentioned in Sir 24:25 – 27.[27] In addition to these and many other probable subtexts, the Song of Songs provides a parallel for almost every line of Sir 24:13 – 20.

The parallelism of cedar and cypress (Sir 24:13) can be found both in Cant 1:17 and in SAA 3 14:9 – 10; in both cases, however, referring to the interior of the scene of lovemaking. Moreover, in Cant 5:15, the male partner is compared with a cedar, paralleled by the mountains of Lebanon, whereas the "brothers" of the female partner, depicted as an adolescent girl, say of her: "If she is a door, we will panel[28] her with cedar." Lebanon and Hermon appear together in Cant 4:8, and Lebanon is also a common metaphor elsewhere in the Song of Songs (Cant 3:9; 4:11, 15; 7:5).

While the woman of the Song of Songs is associated with a palm tree in Cant 7:8 – 9 and En-Gedi appears as a seat of vineyards (Cant 1:14), the statement of Lady Wisdom about herself in Sir 24:14, "Like a palm tree in En-Gedi I stand out," rather calls to mind what the woman says about her beloved: "Like an apple tree among the trees of the wood, so is my beloved among men" (Cant 2:3). Obviously, Ben Sira does not read this imagery as gender-specific but is free to adapt the originally male image to Lady Wisdom, the focus being on her outstanding quality. Jericho is not mentioned in the Song of Songs, nor does a rose garden (*phyta rhodou*) feature anywhere in the Hebrew Bible. Nevertheless, the garden is one of the basic topoi in ancient Near Eastern love lyrics in general (cf. SAA 3 14 r.17 – 18, 23 – 25),[29] and the woman is equated with a garden in Cant 4:12 – 14, a passage that is likely to have inspired Sirach 24.

The Song of Songs does not know olive trees or plane trees (Sir 24:14), but as a plane tree, Wisdom (according to one branch of the textual tradition[30]) "is lofty beside the water", which not only alludes to Ps 1:3 but also to Cant 4:13, where

---

27 Cf. Rogers, "Wisdom and Creation in Sirach 24," 150; MacKinlay, *Gendering Wisdom the Host*, 140 – 42.

28 Thus J. C. Exum, *Song of Songs: A Commentary* (OTL; Louisville, Ky.: Westminster John Knox, 2005), 244, deriving the verb from *ṣwr* III 'to fashion, shape.'

29 For further evidence, see Nissinen, "Love Lyrics of Nabû and Tašmetu," 618; for the garden imagery in the Song of Songs and its mythological background, see O. Keel, *Das Hohelied* (ZBK.AT 18; Zürich: Theologischer Verlag, 1986), 158 – 62; W. G. Lambert, "Devotion: The Languages of Religion and Love," in *Figurative Language in the Ancient Near East* (ed. M. Mindlin, M. J. Geller, and J. E. Wansbrough; London: School of Oriental and African Studies, 1987) 25 – 39, esp. 27 – 31.

30 Thus GII and Peshitta, cf. Skehan and DiLella, *The Wisdom of Ben Sira*, 330.

pomegranates with choice fruits grow by watering channels.[31] What follows both in Sir 24:15 and in Cant 4:14 is a catalogue of fragrances, of which cinnamon and fragrant cane,[32] as well as myrrh, are common to Sirach and the Song of Songs, whereas the galbanum, onycha and mastic clearly draw from Exod 30:34.[33] In the Song of Songs, the fragrance is poured forth to seduce the male beloved to the garden (cf. Sir 24:19), but in Sir 24:15, Wisdom herself is compared to the odor of incense in the holy tent, the prototype of the temple of Jerusalem which now is her domain (cf. Sir 24:10 – 11). There is nothing in the Song of Songs to compare with incense in a sanctuary, since no cult places are mentioned in this book; but it is all the more interesting to find a rather exact counterpart to this line of Ben Sira in the Love Lyrics of Nabû and Tašmetu, where it is said to the goddess Tašmetu: "Save, sit down in the cella! Let (the scent of) pure juniper fill the sanctuary" (SAA 3 14:8). The image of the savior-goddess in the cella is closely related to that of Lady Wisdom ministering in the holy tent, and Ben Sira's use of this motif is a wonderful example of the adaptation of love poetry in the context of worship, Wisdom assuming the role of the goddess.

Terebinth (*tereminthos* Sir 24:16) is in the Hebrew Bible a tree (*'ēlôn*) that is associated with both love and worship,[34] hence it is a most fitting metaphor for Lady Wisdom's cultic and erotic aspects, echoing even the ancient Palestinian tree goddess.[35] The Song of Songs does not mention this tree, but it does speak about sitting in the shade of a fruit-bearing tree (here a metaphor for the male beloved), enjoying the delights of wine and love (Cant 2:3 – 6). For Tašmetu, "the shade of a sprig of juniper is shelter for my Nabû and my games" (SAA 3 14:11). The goddess is sitting in the sanctuary filled with the odor of juniper in the shade of cedar and cypress – imagery closely akin to the self-praise of Lady Wisdom, who, while sojourning in the temple of Jerusalem, "puts forth delights like the vine" (Sir 24:17). The erotic connotations of fruits, well attested in the Song of Songs and in the ancient Near Eastern love poetry (Cant 4:13, 16; SAA 3 14 r.20, 30),[36] are conspicuous also in Sir 24:17, 19, and Wisdom's invitation to those who yearn for her to come and be filled with her fruits is closely rem-

---

31 For this translation of *šĕlāḥayik*, see Keel, *Das Hohelied*, 162 – 64.

32 I am tempted to ask whether *kinnamōnon kai aspalathos aromatōn* actually translate the Hebrew *qānê wĕ-kinnāmôn* in Cant 4:14.

33 See Sinnott, *The Personification of Wisdom*, 124.

34 Gen 12:6, 13:18, 14:13, 18:1, 35:8; Deut 11:30; Josh 19:33; Judg 4:11, 9:6, 37; Hos 4:13; cf. Gilbert, "L'éloge de la Sagesse," 333 – 34; Skehan and DiLella, *The Wisdom of Ben Sira*, 335.

35 Cf. Schroer, *Wisdom Has Built Her House*, 92.

36 Cf., e.g., Lambert, "Devotion," 27 – 29; Nissinen, "Love Lyrics of Nabû and Tašmetu," 619.

iniscent of Cant 4:16: "Let my beloved come to his garden and eat his choice fruits" (cf. Cant 6:2 and SAA 3 14 r.30: "May her eyes see the plucking of my fruit"). A conscious allusion to the Song of Songs becomes all the more probable when we notice that the fruit metaphor is followed by that of honey and honeycomb in both texts: "I eat my honeycomb with my honey" (Cant 5:1) – "My remembrance is sweeter than honey, inheritance better than the honeycomb" (Sir 24:20). It seems like Lady Wisdom presents herself superior even to the (divine) love praised by the Song of Songs.

The motif of the insatiable hunger and thirst in Sir 24:21 does not find a direct counterpart in the Song of Songs, and the same is true for the assurance of those who obey Wisdom not being put to shame. The Love Lyrics of Nabû and Tašmetu, however, starts with a programmatic expression of trust and devotion to the divine couple, which reads like a positive formulation of the same idea: "May anyone trust in whomever he trusts! As for us, we trust in Nabû, we are devoted to Tašmetu" (SAA 3 14:1–3; cf. Sir 15:4b: "He will trust in her [scil. Wisdom] and not be put to shame").

Verse Sir 24:18 is only to be found in the secondary Greek GII tradition and is missing from the most important manuscripts. Original or not, the verse is worth mentioning here because it depicts Lady Wisdom as "mother of fair love (*tēs agapēseōs tēs kalēs*),of reverence (*phobou*), of knowledge (*gnōseōs*), and of holy hope (*hosias elpidos*)." It would be no surprise to find an ancient Near Eastern goddess, Ištar in particular, praising herself or being praised with similar attributes.

The passages following the self-praise of Lady Wisdom are less filled with allusions to the Song of Songs; however, a few obvious and important cases can be found. The sea (*thalassa*) and the abyss (*abyssos*) certainly allude to Gen 1:2 as well as to Prov 8:24, but a clear echo from Cant 8:6 can also be heard. "Deeper than the sea are her thoughts, her counsels, than the great abyss" (Sir 24:29) reads well together with "Love is strong as death, passion as adamant as Sheol," followed by floods and rivers in Cant 8:7. When Ben Sira, again, reflects his own role as a teacher of wisdom, he compares himself with a watering channel, hence invoking the watercourses of Cant 4:13, and his "pouring out instruction" can be read as echoing the flowing streams from Lebanon in Cant 4:15. The channel metaphor makes Ben Sira the medium of Wisdom,[37] but

---

37 See Sinnott, *The Personification of Wisdom*, 130–32, Ueberschaer, *Weisheit aus der Begegnung*, 303–5.

his self-identification as one of the channels of the garden – in fact, as one part of the garden – implies an intimate affiliation with Wisdom herself.[38]

Apart from chapter 24, motifs and metaphors related to the Song of Songs and ancient Near Eastern love poetry can be found in other parts of the book of Ben Sira as well. In another poem about Wisdom, Sir 14:20 – 15:10, spying at the gates of Wisdom and peeping through her windows (14:22 – 23) is clearly reminiscent of Cant 5:2 – 4, and the erotic connotations of the tree metaphor can, again, be traced in 14:26 – 27.[39] Wisdom provides the one received by her with food and drink (15:3; cf. Cant 4:16 – 5:1; 6:2); he will not be put to shame (15:4; cf. Sir 24:22) but will have an elevated position among his peers (15:5; cf. SAA 3 14 r.26: "Among the counsellors, her [scil. Tašmetu's] throne is foremost").

More distant but still recognizable echoes from the Song of Songs can be heard also in the praise of Lady Wisdom concluding the book of Ben Sira (Sir 51:13 – 22). "Wisdom was my wet nurse; thanks to the one who taught me" (51:17) may be taken as a heavily modified reading of "I would lead you and bring you to the house of my mother, and you would teach me[40]" (Cant 8:2). While this remains somewhat unclear, the source of the seeking-and-finding motif in Sir 51:18 – 21 can quite plausibly be traced to Cant 3:1 – 4 and 5:2 – 6. Rather than repeating either version of the story of the nocturnal yearning of the woman, Ben Sira picks up images such as opening the door of Wisdom with his hand (Sir 51:19; cf. Cant 5:4a)[41] and the bodily thrill caused by the passion for Wisdom (Sir 51:21; cf. Cant 5:4b).

Finally, a series of allusions to the Song of Songs can be found in the praise of Simon the high priest concluding Ben Sira's *laus patrum* (Sir 50:1 – 24).[42] This is important to note because the description of the high priest unmistakably repeats motifs used in Sir 24:1 – 22 of Wisdom herself. He is now the cedar of Lebanon, surrounded by the "sons of Aaron" like the willows growing by the water

---

38 Cf. MacKinlay, *Gendering Wisdom the Host*, 145: "But although in v. 30a Ben Sira likens himself to a small canal which flows from a river, with strong echoes of Wisdom/Torah, in the very next verse this has swollen to become a river itself, in turn to becoming a sea."

39 Note that the Greek text in Sir 14:26 reads *thēsei ta tekna autou en tē skepē autēs* for the Hebrew *way-yāśîm qēnô bĕ-ʿŏpêhā*, toning down the erotic connotations.

40 Thus MT; the Septuagint has *kai eis tamieion tēs syllabousēs me*, probably translating a different (and original?) Hebrew text *wĕ-ʾel ḥădar hôrātî* "and to the chambers of the one who gave me birth."

41 The Greek translation is euphemistic, avoiding the well-known sexual meaning of "hand" as the male organ: *tas kheiras mou ekhepetasa pros hypsos* "I stretched out my hands to heaven."

42 For a thorough analysis of this text, see O. Mulder, *Simon the High Priest in Sirach 50: An Exegetical Study of the Significance of Simon the High Priest as Climax to the Praise of the Fathers in Ben Sira's Concept of the History of Israel* (JSJSup 78; Leiden: Brill, 2003).

(Sir 50:12; cf. 24:13–14, 31). The way Simon "looked forth from the tent, as he came from the house of the veil" (Sir 50:5) inevitably brings to mind the "Lady at the window" motif,[43] the adaptation of which to a male person is fully understandable if the high priest is representing the qualities of Lady Wisdom. A variation of the "Lady at the window" image has also been recognized in Cant 6:10, a verse that corresponds to the astral imagery used of the high priest in Sir 50:6–7: "Who is this that gazes down like the dawn, beautiful as the moon, radiant as the sun, terrifying as the *nidgālôt*."[44] Further images in Sir 50:8–10 that may be inspired by the Song of Songs are the lilies (Cant 2:1–2, 16; 4:5; 5:13; 6:2–3; 7:3), Lebanon (Cant 3:9; 4:8, 11, 15; 5:15; 7:5), the bowl (Cant 7:3); the precious stones (Cant 5:14), and the berries (Cant 7:14) – altogether a cluster of individual motifs fused together by the poet without much regard to their context in the source text. By using this imagery, the function of the high priest is drawn as close as possible to that of Lady Wisdom who, as we learn from Sir 24:10–11, abides in the temple where the high priest is ministering.[45]

The above list of links between the Song of Songs and Ben Sira is far too long and detailed to be purely coincidental. It rather demonstrates that the Song of Songs, among other texts, has served as a subtext for chapter 24 and some other passages. Especially Cant 4:12–5:1 stands out as a source of many motifs in chapter 24 and other pertinent texts in the book of Ben Sira. But this is not the whole truth: as the comparison of Sirach 24 with the Love Lyrics of Nabû and Tašmetu shows, Ben Sira, while doubtless reading the Song of Songs, uses the same reservoir of ancient East Mediterranean erotic-lyric tradition as does the Song of Songs. While the Song of Songs itself represents the genre of love lyrics, leaving the religious and spiritual connotations of love metaphors to the reader's imagination (which does not warrant its definition as "secular" poetry[46]), Ben Sira is free to draw from this reservoir for his own pedagog-

43 I.e., the widespread Near Eastern iconographical motif showing a female figure looking out of a window.

44 For different translations of *'ayummâ kan-nidgālôt*, see Keel, *Das Hohelied*, 210; H.-P. Müller, "Das Hohelied," in *Das Hohelied, Klagelieder, Das Buch Ester* (ed. id., O. Kaiser, and J. A. Loader; ATD 16/2; Göttingen: Vandenhoeck & Ruprecht, 1992) 1–90, esp. 68–69.

45 According to MacKinlay, *Gendering Wisdom the Host*, 138–39, the ministering of Wisdom before the creator expresses "another aspect of Wisdom the mediator between Yahweh and people, between the things heavenly and things earthly. At the same time, it could be an even closer identification with Israel, as she shares the priestly tradition, anticipating her embodiment in Simeon in ch. 50."

46 For the rehabilitation of the religious reading of the Song of Songs, see, e.g., D. M. Carr, *The Erotic Word: Sexuality, Spirituality, and the Bible* (New York: Oxford University Press, 2003), 144–46; M. Nissinen, "Song of Songs and Sacred Marriage," in Nissinen and Uro (eds.), *Sacred Mar-*

ical and theological purposes. His method of reading the Song of Songs is not straightforward allegorization; rather, he "makes imaginative use of metaphors that allow for a variety of free associations with biblical imagery."[47] When utilizing metaphors drawn from the Song of Songs, he does not seem to care overly much about the original context; their use is not gender-specific and does not necessarily mirror the role structure of the Song of Song's lovers.

Quite obviously, Ben Sira reads the Song of Songs as a religious text that formed part of the instruction he poured out "like prophecy" to his students (Sir 24:33). Bringing the figure of Lady Wisdom to the play, Ben Sira can do something the role-casting of the Song of Songs does not allow for: he can make ample use of the theological connotations of love poetry and read erotic verses in a religious context quite as freely as was done overall in the ancient Near East. Just like the Love Lyrics of Nabû and Tašmetu, and unlike the Song of Songs, Ben Sira makes the erotic odors fill the sanctuary without seeing any problem in combining the sacred with the erotic. Since ancient love poetry does not recognize the dichotomy of "sacred" vs. "secular," its religious adaptation does not mean depriving it of its "original" meaning.

3 Wisdom and Prophecy

As free and imaginative as Ben Sira appears to be when he uses the Song of Songs and other texts in constructing his hermeneutical construct of Wisdom,[48] his adaptation of the tradition of love poetry is not wild and uncontrolled. In the case of chapter 24, there is a clear "contextual clue"[49] that can be found when we take a deeper look at Ben Sira's potential world of reference in the Near East. As I attempt to show below, the role Lady Wisdom assumes in chapter 24 is not his own invention but corresponds to an established Near Eastern pattern. Even the issue of prophecy, which at first sight might seem a deviation from the theme in Sir 24:33, firmly belongs to the picture.

---

riages: The Divine-Human Sexual Metaphor from Sumer to Early Christianity (2008) 173–218, esp. 212–15.

47 Rogers, "Wisdom and Creation in Sirach 24," 144.

48 For Wisdom as a hermeneutical construct, see Sheppard, *Wisdom as a Hermeneutical Construct*, 116–19.

49 Cf. the remarks of Beentjes, "Ben Sira and the Book of Deuteronomy," 415 on the necessity of the identification of a contextual clue that supports Ben Sira's use of Scripture in order to avoid an uncontrolled "parallelomania."

To properly understand the role of Lady Wisdom in Sirach 24, we need to return to the beginning of the chapter, where her self-praise is introduced as follows: "In the assembly of the Most High she opens her mouth, in the presence of his host she declares her worth" (Sir 24:2). The *ekklēsia hypsistou* has usually been interpreted as the angelic host (*dynamis*) around God,[50] and this interpretation may well correspond to the Hellenistic Jewish imagination of the heavenly beings. The source of this idea is unmistakably the common Near Eastern concept of the divine council (Akk. *puḫur ilāni*, Ug. *pḫr ilm*), that is, the heavenly court where the gods make decisions about earthly matters and the fate of the people and their rulers.[51] Several traces of the divine council can be found in the Hebrew Bible,[52] and not only there, but even in one of the Dead Sea Scrolls, 4Q491, where we encounter an anonymous speaker who claims to be "in the assembly of gods"(*bĕ-ʿădat ʾēlîm*), "with gods" (*ʿim ʾēlîm*) and "in the holy congregation" (*bĕ-ʿădat qôdeš*).[53] However the Jews might have imagined the heavenly assembly within the context of their monotheistic theology, the concept was alive in Hellenistic Judaism.

As a member of the ancient Near Eastern divine council, the goddess – more often than not Ištar or one of her manifestations – is the "diviner of the gods,"[54] a mediatrix through whom the decisions of the divine council are communicated to the people.[55] A similar pattern functions in the Mesopotamian sacred mar-

---

50 E. g., Skehan and DiLella, *The Wisdom of Ben Sira*, 331; Collins, *Jewish Wisdom in Hellenistic Age*, 50; cf. Marböck, *Weisheit im Wandel*, 58: "Auf jeden Fall steht dahinter die alte Vorstellung von Jahwe, der von himmlischen Mächten oder vom himmlischen Rat umgeben ist."

51 For an overview of the evidence, see H.-D. Neef, *Gottes himmlischer Thronrat: Hintergrund und Bedeutung vom* sôd JHWH *im Alten Testament* (Arbeiten zur Theologie 79; Stuttgart: Calwer, 1994); cf. also M. Nissinen, "Prophets and the Divine Council," in U. Hübner and E. A. Knauf (eds.), *Kein Land für sich allein*, FS M. Weippert (OBO 186; Freiburg Schweiz and Göttingen: Universitätsverlag and Vandenhoeck & Ruprecht, 2002) 1–19 (= pp. 461–77 in this volume).

52 E. g., Ps 82, 89:6–8; Jer 23:18; 1 Kgs 22:19–22; Isa 6:8; Amos 3:7.

53 Frag. 11, lines I, 12, 14, 18. Publication: M. Baillet, *Qumrân Grotte 4: III (4Q482–4Q520)* (DJD 7; Oxford: Clarendon Press, 1982), 26–30.

54 See Nissinen, "Prophets and the Divine Council," 10.

55 Thus, e. g., in the oracle from Ešnunna, where the local manifestation of Ištar speaks as follows: "O king Ibalpiel, thus says Kititum: The secrets of the gods are placed before me. Because you constantly pronounce my name with your mouth, I constantly disclose the secrets of gods to you" (FLP 1674: 1–8; M. deJong Ellis, "The Goddess Kititum Speaks to King Ibalpiel: Oracle Texts from Ishchali," *MARI* 5 [1987] 235–66, esp. 240–41). For further evidence, see Nissinen, "Prophets and the Divine Council," 7–10; B. Pongratz-Leisten, "When the Gods Are Speaking: Toward Defining the Interface between Polytheism and Monotheism," in *Propheten in Mari, Assyrien und Israel* (ed. M. Köckert and M. Nissinen; FRLANT 201; Göttingen: Vandenhoeck & Ruprecht, 2003) 132–68, esp. 155–59.

riage, where the goddess assumes the role of an intercessor for the king and the people and the intermediary between gods and humans.[56] Likewise in Assyrian prophecy, Ištar speaks for the king in the presence of *puḫur ilāni*.[57] In both cases, the goddess is the transmitter of divine love and knowledge, establishing an ideal relationship between the heavenly and earthly domains.[58] More or less direct derivatives of this role of the goddess can be found in both Jewish and early Christian and "Gnostic" literature, where it is often mingled with the Greek concept of *logos*.[59]

It is not difficult to recognize a similar pattern in the role of Lady Wisdom in Sirach 24, where she undeniably appears as a mediatrix.[60] Subordinated to the highest God, she is of divine origin (cf. Sir 1:1; Prov 8:21), and her figure is godlike; in fact, explicit statements about God are here applied to her.[61] At the same time, she is associated with priests and their ministry, and the description of Simon the high priest in Sir 50:5–10 almost equates him with her.[62] On the other hand, Ben Sira identifies himself as a teacher as a rivulet from her stream in Sir 24:30–31. Wisdom "opens her mouth" in the divine assembly, maintaining that she actually came forth "from the mouth" of the Most High. All this makes her an interlocutor and her words divine knowledge to be transmitted "among her own people" (Sir 24:1: *en mesō laou autēs*), which probably refers to the people of Israel.[63]

What, then, is the divine knowledge to be transmitted? This is declared unambiguously in Sir 24:23: "All this" – that is, the preceding words of Lady Wis-

---

56 See M. Nissinen, "Akkadian Rituals and Poetry of Divine Love," in *Mythology and Mythologies: Methodological Approaches to Intercultural Influences* (ed. R. M. Whiting; Melammu Symposia, 2; Helsinki: The Neo-Assyrian Text Corpus Project, 2001) 93–136, esp. 110–13; P. Lapinkivi, *The Sumerian Sacred Marriage in the Light of Comparative Evidence* (SAAS 15; Helsinki: The Neo-Assyrian Text Corpus Project, 2004), 248–52.

57 SAA 9 9:16: "I have ordained life for you in the assembly of all the gods" (Parpola, *Assyrian Prophecies*, 41); more evidence in Nissinen, "Prophets and the Divine Council," 11–17.

58 See Pongratz-Leisten, "When the Gods Are Speaking."

59 For evidence, see Parpola, *Assyrian Prophecies*, xxviii; Schroer, *Wisdom Has Built Her House*, 132–54; for *logos* and Ben Sira, see especially B. Mack, *Logos und Sophia: Untersuchungen zur Weisheitstheologie im hellenistischen Judentum* (StUNT 10; Göttingen: Vandenhoeck & Ruprecht, 1973).

60 Thus, e.g., Lebram, "Jerusalem, Wohnsitz der Weisheit," 117–18; Skehan and DiLella, *The Wisdom of Ben Sira*, 335; cf. Rogers, "Wisdom and Creation in Sirach 24," 153: "Her rule is equated with that of Yahweh. He exercises his dominion in and through the rule of Wisdom."

61 Cf. Sheppard, *Wisdom as a Hermeneutical Construct*, 32–36.

62 Ibid., 55–56.

63 Thus, e.g., Skehan and DiLella, *The Wisdom of Ben Sira*, 331; Collins, *Jewish Wisdom in Hellenistic Age*, 50.

dom – "is the Book of the Covenant of the Most High" (*tauta panta biblos diathēkēs theou hypsistou*). This statement, followed by a quotation from Deut 33:4, probably refers to the five books of the Pentateuch as a whole.[64] It brings Lady Wisdom and the Torah very close to each other, but does not quite equate them; rather, the Torah should be understood as the verbal expression of Wisdom, revealing her essence but not being directly identifiable with her.[65] Lady Wisdom cannot be reduced to the Torah, but the Torah is equal with the word spoken by her "among her people."

In Sir 24:25–27, the Torah is compared with the rivers bringing wisdom (*sophia*), understanding (*synesis*), and learning (*paideia*) – that is, the stream of Wisdom through which she transmits the divine knowledge to people. It is this stream that Ben Sira feels himself a rivulet of, and it is no coincidence that he claims to "pour out instruction like prophecy (*hōs propheteian*)." This certainly implies the divine inspiration of the teacher who, by the will of God, "will be filled with the spirit of understanding" (Sir 39:6). The spirit is to be understood as nothing else but Lady Wisdom herself,[66] and the words of Wisdom as the Torah, whose teaching and interpreting is understood as prophetic activity. Hence, prophecy and teaching of Wisdom, that is, the Law, fulfill essentially the same function. This corresponds to the tendency of Second Temple Judaism, observable in the Hebrew Bible[67] as well as in the Dead Sea Scrolls,[68] to fuse the roles of prophets and scribes (or teachers of wisdom) together as mediators of

---

64 Cf. T. Veijola, "Law and Wisdom: The Deuteronomistic Heritage in Ben Sira's Teaching of the Law," in *Ancient Israel, Judaism, and Christianity in Contemporary Perspective*, FS K.-J. Illman (ed. J. Neusner et al.; Lanham: University Press of America, 2006) 429–48, esp. 434–35.

65 Ueberschaer, *Weisheit aus der Begegnung*, 357–58: "Die Weisheit ist in der Tora erfahrbar. Dabei handelt es sich nicht um eine Gleichsetzung. Vielmehr bleibt die Weisheit für Ben Sira immer umfassender als die Tora, doch sie äußert sich in ihr und findet in ihr eine konkrete Ausdrucksform." Cf. Lebram, "Jerusalem, Wohnsitz der Weisheit," 108–12; Sauer, *Jesus Sirach/Ben Sira*, 184.

66 Cf. Parpola, *Assyrian Prophecies*, xxvi: "Accordingly, Ištar can be viewed as the 'spirit' or the 'breath' of Aššur (= God) – a concept well attested in Neo-Assyrian texts. Going a step further, one can say that Ištar of the prophecies is the spirit of God, who, residing in the heart of the prophet, *spirits* him and speaks through his or her lips" (emphasis original).

67 Cf., e.g., M. H. Floyd, "The Production of Prophetic Books in the Early Second Temple Period," in *Prophets, Prophecy, and Prophetic Texts in Second Temple Judaism* (ed. M. H. Floyd and R. D. Haak; LHBOTS 427; London: T & T Clark, 2006) 276–97.

68 Cf. M. Nissinen, "Transmitting Divine Mysteries: The Prophetic Role of Wisdom Teachers in the Dead Sea Scrolls," in *Scripture in Transition: Essays on Septuagint, Hebrew Bible, and Dead Sea Scrolls in Honour of Raija Sollamo* (ed. A. Voitila and J. Jokiranta; JSJ.S 126; Leiden: Brill, 2008) 513–33 (= pp. 631–49 in this volume).

divine knowledge, second only to Wisdom herself as the mediatrix *par excellence.*[69]

The similarity of the patterns of transmitting divine knowledge in the ancient Near Eastern evidence and in Sirach 24 is summarized in table 1:

Table 1. The Patterns of Transmitting Divine Knowledge in the Ancient Near East and in Sirach 24

Ancient Near East		*Sirach 24*
Divine Council	Source	Assembly of the Most High
|		|
Goddess	Divine mediatrix	Lady Wisdom
|		|
Prophecy	Word	Torah
|		|
Prophet	Human medium	Ben Sira (teacher/prophet)
|		|
King/people	Recipient	People of Israel

4 Ben Sira, Sacred Marriage, and Prophecy

In view of the dense network of intertextual links between the Song of Songs and Ben Sira, there can be no doubt that Ben Sira actually knew the book and utilized its imagery as a part of his hermeneutical construct of Lady Wisdom. Sirach 24 in particular reads like an early commentary of the Song of Songs; in fact, it may not be much later than the canonical composition of the Song of Songs, which most probably dates from the Hellenistic period.[70] This implies that the Song of Songs was regarded by him as an authoritative text and that he interpreted it as a part of "the Law, the prophets, and the other writings" of his ancestors

---

69 P. C. Beentjes, "Prophets and Prophecy in the Book of Ben Sira," in Floyd and Haak (eds.), *Prophets, Prophecy, and Prophetic Texts in Second Temple Judaism*, 135–50, esp. 150: "[...] in two strategic passages (24:33; 39:1) he uses the concept of 'prophecy' in order to describe the sage's – that is to say, his own – function and activities as passing down and interpreting Torah. It is especially here Ben Sira breaks new ground in respect of the notion 'prophecy.'" On prophecy in Ben Sira, see also M. Marttila, "Die Propheten Israels in Ben Sira's 'Lob der Väter,'" in Pakkala and Nissinen (ed.), *Houses Full of All Good Things*, 434–50.

70 For the Hellenistic date, see, e.g., Müller, "Das Hohelied," 3–5; for linguistic arguments in favor of this date, see F. W. Dobbs-Allsopp, "Late Linguistic Features in the Song of Songs," in *Perspectives on the Song of Songs/Perspektiven der Hoheliedauslegung* (ed. A. Hagedorn; BZAW 346; Berlin: Walter de Gruyter, 2005) 27–77.

(cf. Sir Prol. 9–10). Ben Sira had no difficulty in reading the Song of Songs, and love imagery in general, in a religious context. This reading cannot be seen as constrained misuse of love poetry for purposes alien to its original function. Ben Sira rather adheres to the age-old Near Eastern tradition of using erotic imagery to describe the divinehuman relationship, whereby the image of Lady Wisdom as a mediatrix between the heavenly and earthly worlds closely resembles that of the Near Eastern goddesses. This tradition, which we can still call "sacred marriage" despite the infamous connotations of this designation,[71] is known from the Sumerians to Hellenistic times, and its offshoots can be traced in Hellenistic Judaism, especially in texts where the personified female Wisdom plays a role.[72]

One of the principal functions of the goddess in Near Eastern theology is the transmission of divine favors and knowledge to the king and the people. This was believed to happen especially within the contexts of both sacred marriage and prophecy.[73] Accordingly, the role of Lady Wisdom as mediatrix, expressed in Sirach 24 with imagery inspired by love lyrics, also has a prophetic dimension. As Table 1 demonstrates, the pattern of the transmission of the divine word in Sirach 24 is virtually identical to that in the ancient Near East in general. It may be that "personified Wisdom refuses to be obscured by such comparisons";[74] nevertheless, Lady Wisdom clearly brings the function of the goddess back to the picture, while Ben Sira assumes the position of the human medium, or the prophet, in his role as a teacher of Wisdom, a "rivulet from her stream". The prominent position of chapter 24 within the composition of the book gives this idea a special emphasis.

The ancient Near Eastern pattern is an important addition to the Hellenistic evidence (the aretalogies of Isis and other texts) that has hitherto been suggested

---

71 For a new understanding of sacred marriage as a metaphor for a symbolic union of two complementary gendered entities in a religious context, see M. Nissinen and R. Uro, "Sacred Marriages, or the Divine-Human Sexual Metaphor: Introducing the Project," in *Sacred Marriages: The Divine-Human Sexual Metaphor from Sumer to Early Christianity* (ed. iid.; Winona Lake, Ind.: Eisenbrauns, 2008) 1–6. Cf. B. Pongratz-Leisten, "Sacred Marriage and the Transfer of Divine Knowledge: Alliances between the Gods and the King in Ancient Mesopotamia," ibid., 43–73, esp. p. 57, who underlines the communicative aspect of sacred marriage: "By linking the blessing to the 'sexual encounter' between goddess and king, the biological nature of the divine-human interaction is transformed and is now included in the social experience of symbolic universes (*symbolische Sinnwelten*); religion takes on an essential role in constructing reality."

72 See R. Zimmermann, "The Love Triangle of Lady Wisdom: Sacred Marriage in Jewish Wisdom Literature?," in Nissinen and Uro (eds.), *Sacred Marriages*, 243–58.

73 See Pongratz-Leisten, "Sacred Marriage and the Transfer of Divine Knowledge," 43–74.

74 Sinnott, *The Personification of Wisdom*, 111.

to fertilize the soil of the wisdom of Ben Sira. We will probably never be able to identify a single source from whence Ben Sira draws this pattern. What is more important is that the book of Ben Sira, being a product of the Hellenistic-Jewish culture, at the same time forms a part of the ancient Near Eastern heritage of early Judaism.

Part Four: **Prophecy in the Hebrew Bible**

The Historical Dilemma of Biblical Prophetic Studies

Prophetic Studies in Transition

It has been noted since late 1980's at the latest that the study of biblical prophecy and prophetic books is going through a paradigm switch.[1] Indeed, prophetic studies have for quite a while found themselves in a period of transition; they are not the same as they used to be a couple of decades ago. A quick look at the spectrum of today's variety of methodological approaches in biblical studies is enough to demonstrate that traditional historical-critical studies have given way to less historical and non-historical ways of viewing the prophetic books, such as literary and gender approaches or postcolonial studies and ideological criticism. However, as many contributions published in the present volume (including an article by Hans Barstad to which this article originally responded)[2] and other recent collections of essays[3] well demonstrate, even historical-critical

1 Cf. F. E. Deist, "The Prophets: Are We Heading for a Paradigm Switch?," in *Prophet und Prophetenbuch*, FS O. Kaiser (ed. V. Fritz, K.-F. Pohlmann, and H.-C. Schmitt; BZAW 185; Berlin: de Gruyter, 1989) 1–18; O. Loretz, "Die Entstehung des Amos-Buches im Licht der Prophetien aus Māri, Assur, Ishchali und der Ugarit-Texte: Paradigmenwechsel in der Prophetenforschung," *UF* 24 (1992) 179–215.

2 The first draft of this article was presented as a response to Hans Barstad's opening lecture of the Society of Biblical Literature International Meeting in Edinburgh, July 2, 2006; cf. H. M. Barstad, "What Prophets Do: Reflections on Past Reality in the Book of Jeremiah," in *Prophecy in the Book of Jeremiah* (ed. id. and R. G Kratz; BZAW 388; Berlin: de Gruyter, 2009) 10–32.

3 E. g., E. Ben Zvi and M. H. Floyd (eds.), *Writings and Speech in Israelite and Ancient Near Eastern Prophecy* (SBLSymS 10; Atlanta: Society of Biblical Literature, 2000); M. Nissinen (ed.), *Prophecy in Its Ancient Near Eastern Context: Mesopotamian, Biblical, and Arabian Perspectives* (SBLSymS 13; Atlanta: Society of Biblical Literature, 2000); L. L. Grabbe and R. D. Haak (eds.), *'Every City Shall Be Forsaken': Urbanism and Prophecy in Ancient Israel and the Near East* (JSOTS 330; Sheffield, Sheffield Academic Press, 2001); M. Köckert and M. Nissinen (eds.), *Propheten in Mari, Assyrien und Israel* (FRLANT 201; Göttingen: Vandenhoeck & Ruprecht, 2003); I. Fischer, K. Schmid, and H. G. M. Williamson (eds.), *Prophetie in Israel*, GS G. von Rad (Altes Testament und Moderne 11; Münster 2003); L. L. Grabbe and A. O. Bellis (eds.), *The Priests in the Prophets: The Portrayal of Priests, Prophets, and Other Religious Specialists in the Latter Prophets* (JSOTS 408; New York and London, T & T Clark, 2003); E. Ben Zvi (ed.), *Utopia and Dystopia in Prophetic Literature* (PFES 92: Helsinki: The Finnish Exegetical Society, 2006); M. H. Floyd and R. D. Haak (eds.), *Prophets, Prophecy, and Prophetic Texts in Second Temple Judaism* (LHBOTS 427; New York: T & T Clark, 2006); B. E. Kelle and M. B. Moore (eds.), *Is-*

DOI 10.1515/9783110466546-026

studies have by no means lost their relevance in studies of prophecy; nevertheless, it is observable that their focus has turned away from the reconstruction of the life and deeds of historical prophets and directed towards literary processes that resulted in the biblical prophetic books and socioreligious issues related to prophecy and society. The diachronic studies in the prophetic books no longer aim at "the pristine and uncontaminated verse of the author, poet and prophet"[4]; they would rather give to each layer and gloss its own meaning and significance. Even synchronic studies that refrain from reconstructing the literary genesis of the prophetic books are often historically oriented, reading the books against the background of the Second Temple period, that is, the date of the prophetic books in their advanced (but not "final") literary form.[5]

In addition, historical studies are no longer restricted to the biblical text itself, thanks to the increasing attention to the documentation of ancient Near Eastern prophecy, which enables the appreciation of the Hebrew prophecy as another specimen of a wider cultural and socioreligious phenomenon of transmitting allegedly divine words to human recipients. No serious study of prophecy as a historical phenomenon can do without extrabiblical sources, which today are available to every researcher.[6]

Recent methodological innovations as well as the extended corpus of source material have caused fundamental reorientations in the study of prophecy. There was a time when the study of the prophetic books was essentially focused on the reconstruction of the message of each biblical prophet as a historical personality and the original author of the prophetic book ascribed to him, whose work had subsequently been supplemented by later hands. Classical studies of this kind–

---

rael's Prophets and Israel's Past, FS J. H. Hayes (LHBOTS 446; New York and London: T & T Clark, 2006).

4 Thus F. I. Andersen and D. N. Freedman, *Hosea: A New Translation with Introduction and Commentary* (AB 24; Garden City, N.Y. Doubleday, 1980) 60.

5 Cf., e.g., the following works on the book of Hosea, both of which read the book in a postmonarchical setting: E. Ben Zvi, *Hosea* (FOTL 21 A/1; Grand Rapids, Mich.: Eerdmans, 2005); J. M. Trotter, *Reading Hosea in Achaemenid Yehud* (JSOTS 328; Sheffield: Sheffield Academic Press, 2001).

6 The ancient Near Eastern prophetic sources are now available in: M. Nissinen (ed.), with contributions by C.-L. Seow, R. K. Ritner, and H. Craig Melchert, *Prophets and Prophecy in the Ancient Near East* (2nd edition; SBLWAW 41; Atlanta: Society of Biblical Literature, 2019). The two main corpora of ancient Near Eastern documents of prophecy, those deriving from Mari (18th cent. BCE) and Nineveh (7th cent. BCE), are published in J.-M. Durand, *Archives épistolaires de Mari 1/1* (ARM 26/1; Paris: Editions Recherche sur les Civilisations, 1988) and S. Parpola, *Assyrian Prophecies* (SAA 9; Helsinki: Helsinki University Press, 1997).

such as Bernhard Duhm's on Israel's prophets[7]–are the absolute prerequisite of the critical study of biblical prophecy, and the prophetic books are still quite commonly approached through the prophets to whom the texts are traditionally ascribed. However, a brief look at recent introductions to the Hebrew Bible or to the prophetic literature reveals that the prophetic books are introduced primarily as books, whereas the prophets to whom they are attributed tend to become indistinct.[8] This reflects the scholarly conviction that the primary mission of prophetic studies can no longer be to establish the *ipsissima verba* of ancient prophets, since they can hardly be distracted from any written sources, whether biblical or nonbiblical[9]–it is not even to identify the earliest material included in the prophetic texts, as if it were more interesting and valuable by virtue of its alleged "originality". The "author-in-time" model is increasingly being replaced by other models, more or less interested in historical issues–whatever is meant with "history."[10]

What is the aim of prophetic studies, then? There is certainly more than one answer to this question. Since the reliance on objective and value-free questions is gone, the answer depends on each researcher's agenda; the concerns of a theologian, postcolonialist, feminist, or, say, discourse analyst will result in sets of questions that may be equally relevant but different from those implied by the title of this paper which focuses on the historical dilemma of prophetic studies. Biblical studies have many aims, one of them still being a historical one.

---

7 B. Duhm, *Israels Propheten* (Tübingen: Mohr Siebeck, 1916 [^{2}1922]).

8 Cf. the treatments of the prophetic books in E. Zenger et al., *Einleitung in das Alte Testament* (Stuttgart: Kohlhammer, ^{8}2012) 509–699; T. Römer, J.-D. Macchi, and C. Nihan (eds.), *Introduction à l'Ancien Testament* (MdB 49; Geneva: Labor et Fides, ^{2}2009) 313–556. See also U. Becker, "Die Wiederentdeckung des Prophetenbuches: Tendenzen und Aufgaben der gegenwärtigen Prophetenforschung," *BTZ* 21 (2004) 30–60.

9 On the impossibility of reaching the *ipsissima verba* in ancient Near Eastern prophecy, see K. van der Toorn, "From the Oral to the Written: The Case of Old Babylonian Prophecy," in Ben Zvi and Floyd (eds.), *Writings and Speech in Israelite and Ancient Near Eastern Prophecy*, 219–34; and M. Nissinen, "Spoken, Written, Quoted and Invented: Orality and Writtenness in Ancient Near Eastern Prophecy," ibid., 235–71.

10 For a critical review of the "author-in-time" model and viewing the prophets as religious individuals *sui generis*, see C. R. Seitz, *Prophecy and Hermeneutics: Toward a New Introduction to the Prophets* (Studies in Theological Interpretation; Grand Rapids, Mich.: Baker Academic, 2007) 75–92.

Prophecy: A Social Phenomenon or a Literary One?

As an example of a sophisticated discussion reflecting the change of paradigm in prophetic studies, I would like to refer to the debate on the applicability of the category of prophecy to the prophetic figures like Jeremiah. This debate was initiated in 1983 by Graeme Auld.[11] In his article published in the *Journal for the Study of the Old Testament*, Auld analyzed the usage of the word *nābîʾ* and other nouns indicating prophetic roles in the Hebrew Bible, proposing that not only *nābîʾ* but the biblical concept of prophecy in general is a creation of a literary tradition, not historically applicable to a person like Jeremiah. In the following number of *JSOT*, Auld received a positive response from Robert Carroll, according to whom the biblical figures called "prophets" were rather poets and intellectuals who were subsequently transformed into prophetic mediators of the divine word;[12] and a more critical one from Hugh Williamson based on examination of Auld's principal arguments.[13]

The discussion was reinitiated in the same journal in 1990 by Thomas Overholt who turned the focus on the social reality of prophecy as another type of religious intermediation, which is a widely distributed and well documented cross-cultural phenomenon.[14] Biblical prophecy, according to him, conforms to this pattern, hence there were prophets in Israel and Judah, and the biblical figures thus designated were recognized as prophets by their contemporaries. Overholt received a short response from Auld[15] and a more substantial one from Carroll[16] who did not deny that the biblical representation of the prophets conforms

---

11 A. G. Auld, "Prophets through the Looking Glass: Between Writings and Moses," *JSOT* 27 (1983) 3–23.

12 R. P. Carroll, "Poets not Prophets: A Response to 'Prophets through the Looking Glass,'" *JSOT* 27 (1983) 25–31.

13 H. G. M. Williamson, "A Response to A. Graeme Auld," *JSOT* 27 (1983) 33–39. The round of discussion was closed by A. G. Auld, "Prophets through the Looking Glass: A Response to Robert Carroll and Hugh Williamson," *JSOT* 27 (1983) 41–44.

14 T. W. Overholt, "Prophecy in History: The Social Reality of Intermediation," *JSOT* 48 (1990) 3–29; cf. id., *Prophecy in Cross-Cultural Perspective: A Source-Book for Biblical Research* (SBLSBS 17; Atlanta, GA: Society for Biblical Literature, 1986), and *Channels of Prophecy: The Social Dynamics of Prophetic Activity* (Minneapolis, Minn.: Fortress Press, 1989).

15 A. G. Auld, "Prophecy in Books: A Rejoinder," *JSOT* 48 (1990) 31–32.

16 R. P. Carroll, "Whose Prophet? Whose History? Whose Social Reality? Troubling the Interpretive Community Again: Notes towards a Response to T. W. Overholt's Critique," *JSOT* 48 (1990) 33–49.

to the social reality model but questioned its bearing on the definition of the historicity of biblical characters and the differentiation between the character and the character's author. The debate was closed by Overholt's short rejoinder with the title "It Is Difficult to Read",[17] but the issue was taken up once more in *JSOT* by Hans Barstad[18] who shared the scepticism of Auld and Carroll with regard to the historicity of biblical prophetic figures but, like Overholt, defined prophecy as transmission of the divine word[19] and paid attention to the reality of prophetic practice by referring to the corpus of ancient Near Eastern prophetic texts as relevant parallels to biblical prophecy. When compared critically with the Hebrew Bible, these parallels corroborate the view that the biblical prophetic books indeed represent edited collections of originally prophetic sayings.

The above described discussion was found significant enough to be included as a whole in an anthology entitled *The Prophets* (1996),[20] edited by Philip R. Davies who[21], in the introduction to that volume, summarizes the problem as follows: "Is *biblical* prophecy, then, a social phenomenon or a literary one? If both, what is the connection between ancient Israelite/Judaean intermediaries and the biblical prophetic literature?"[22] I find these questions still valid and engaging. In many recent studies, biblical prophecy appears first and foremost as literature created by the Second Temple literate circles,[23] while in others, prophe-

17 T. W. Overholt, "It Is Difficult to Read," *JSOT* 48 (1990) 51–54.

18 H. M. Barstad, "No Prophets? Recent Developments in Biblical Prophetic Research and Ancient Near Eastern Prophecy," *JSOT* 57 (1993) 39–60 (repr. in *The Prophets: A Sheffield Reader* [ed. P. R. Davies; The Biblical Seminar 42; Sheffield: Sheffield Academic Press, 1996] 106–26).

19 This definition builds upon the one formulated by Manfred Weippert in "Aspekte israelitischer Prophetie im Lichte verwandter Erscheinungen des Alten Orients," in *Ad bene et fideliter seminandum*, FS Karlheinz Deller (ed. G. Mauer and U. Magen; AOAT 220; Kevelaer: Butzon & Bercker; Neukirchen-Vluyn: Neukirchener Verlag, 1988) 287–319; cf. id., "Prophetie im Alten Orient," *NBL* 3 (1997) 196–200, esp. 197.

20 Davies (ed.), *The Prophets*, 22–126.

21 To be sure, the author of the introduction is not indicated, but I presume it is written by the editor of the volume.

22 Davies (ed.), *The Prophets*, 14 (emphasis original).

23 E.g., E. Ben Zvi, "Introduction: Writings, Speeches, and the Prophetic Books: Setting an Agenda," in Ben Zvi and Floyd (eds.), *Writings and Speech in Israelite and Ancient Near Eastern Prophecy*, 1–29; id., *Hosea*, 12–20; M. H. Floyd, "Basic Trends in the Form-Critical Study of Prophetic Texts," in *The Changing Face of Form Criticism for the Twenty-First Century* (ed. M. A. Sweeney and E. Ben Zvi; Grand Rapids, Mich.: Eerdmans, 2003) 298–311; id., "The Production of Prophetic Books in the Early Second Temple Period," in id. and R. D. Haak (eds.), *Prophets, Prophecy, and Prophetic Texts in Second Temple Judaism*, 276–97; P. R. Davies, "Amos: Man and Book," in Kelle and Moore (eds.), *Israel's Prophets and Israel's Past*, 113–31; K. van der

cy is examined as a socioreligious phenomenon, often utilizing extrabiblical documents.[24] These two aspects need not be seen as each other's alternatives, and efforts have been made to extend the definition of prophecy to include even the literary enterprises of those who interpret received prophetic texts for their own contemporaries, thus highlighting the social reality of prophecy as a *literary* phenomenon.[25] But the question remains concerning the relationship between the Israelite/Judaean intermediaries and the biblical prophetic literature– or ancient Hebrew prophecy and biblical prophecy, as I would like to rephrase this dichotomy.[26] The paradigm switch, if I interpret it correctly, seems to be leading to a sharpened awareness of both aspects, the literary character of biblical prophecy, and prophecy as a crosscultural phenomenon.

Toorn, *Scribal Culture and the Making of the Hebrew Bible* (Cambridge, Mass.: Harvard University Press, 2007), 173–204.

24 In addition to the works mentioned in n. 9, cf., e.g., L. L. Grabbe, *Priests, Prophets, Diviners, Sages: A Socio-Historical Study of Religious Specialists in Ancient Israel* (Valley Forge, PA: Trinity Press International, 1995), 66–118; H. B. Huffmon, "A Company of Prophets: Mari, Assyria, Israel," in Nissinen (ed.) *Prophecy in Its Ancient Near Eastern Context*, 47–70; K. van der Toorn, "Mesopotamian Prophecy between Immanence and Transcendence: A Comparison of Old Babylonian and Neo-Assyrian Prophecy," ibid., 71–87; M. Nissinen, "The Socioreligious Role of the Neo-Assyrian Prophets," ibid., 89–114 (= pp. 103–126 in this volume); H. B. Huffmon, "The One and the Many: Prophets and Deities in the Ancient Near East," in Köckert and Nissinen (eds.), *Propheten in Mari, Assyrien und Israel*, 116–31; id., "The Oracular Process: Delphi and the Near East," *VT* 57 (2007) 449–60; A. C. Hagedorn, "Looking at Foreigners in Biblical and Greek Prophecy," *VT* 57 (2007) 432–48; A. Lange, "Greek Seers and Israelite-Jewish Prophets," *VT* 57 (2007) 461–82; H. M. Barstad, "Mari and the Hebrew Bible: Some Parallels," *SEÅ* 70 (2005) 21–32; id., "*Sic dicit dominus:* Mari Prophetic Texts and the Hebrew Bible," in *Essays on Ancient Israel in Its Near Eastern Context*, FS N. Na'aman (ed. Y. Amit, E. Ben Zvi, I. Finkelstein, and O. Lipschits; Winona Lake, Ind.: Eisenbrauns, 2006) 21–52.

25 See, e.g., L. L. Grabbe, "Poets, Scribes, or Preachers? The Reality of Prophecy in the Second Temple Period," in *Knowing the End from the Beginning: The Prophetic, the Apocalyptic and their Relationships* (ed. id. and R. D. Haak; JSPSup 46; London: T & T Clark International, 2003) 192–215; M. Nissinen, "How Prophecy Became Literature," *SJOT* 19 (2005) 153–72; A. Lange, "Literary Prophecy and Oracle Collection: A Comparison between Judah and Greece in Persian Times," in: Floyd and Haak (eds.), *Prophets, Prophecy, and Prophetic Texts in Second Temple Judaism*, 248–75.

26 See M. Nissinen, "What Is Prophecy? An Ancient Near Eastern Perspective," in *Inspired Speech: Prophecy in the Ancient Near East*, FS H. B. Huffmon (ed. J. Kaltner and L. Stulman; JSOTS 378; London and New York 2004) 17–37, esp. 28–31 (= pp. 53–73 in this volume).

Who Is Talking Now?

So what can we know about the prophets as historical figures? Hans Barstad attempts to find the way out of the *ipsissima verba* dilemma by going beyond the fact-or-fiction distinction and taking a narrative approach.[27] He takes it for granted that the stories about prophets in the Hebrew Bible do not translate as accurate records of historical factualities (after more than two centuries of critical study, this still needs to be said aloud!). Instead, he reads them as literary universes that in all likelihood present their narrative world in a way that was imaginable to their audiences; in other words, the textual world had to be designed in a way that corresponded to the real and symbolic worlds of the implied readers. In his words: "A fictitious story is a historically untrue story that could have happened but that did not happen."[28] Every text informs something about its time, and there is an element of fact in every fiction. I welcome this approach which, like every other approach, also raises questions.

No historical study can be done without some confidence in the sources as documents of historical factualities. The problem is that the source material is always fragmentary, sometimes helplessly so, and comes to us through several filters that contribute to the picture available to us. Apart from the two substantial corpora of texts from Mari and Assyria, the ancient Near Eastern documentation of prophecy is extremely scattered, and it is more than probable that important aspects of Near Eastern prophecy remain entirely hidden from the eyes of the modern researcher. When it comes to the biblical text, there can be no doubt of the literary and composite character of the biblical prophetic books; the available text critical evidence, even though it is late, testifies to a complicated literary history of these texts that was still going on at the time when the Dead Sea

---

27 H. M. Barstad, "What Prophets Do: Reflections on Past Reality in the Book of Jeremiah," in id. and R. G. Kratz (eds.), *Prophecy in the Book of Jeremiah*, 10–32. Cf. also his reflections on genre in id., "'Fact' versus 'Fiction' and Other Issues in the History Debate, and Their Relevance for the Study of the Old Testament," in *Vergegenwärtigung des Alten Testaments: Beiträge zur biblischen Hermeneutik*, FS R. Smend (ed. C. Bultmann, W. Dietrich, and C. Levin; Göttingen: Vandenhoeck & Ruprecht, 2002) 433–47; id., "Prophecy in the Book of Jeremiah and the Historical Prophet," in *Sense and Sensitivity*, FS R. Carroll (ed. A. G. Hunter and P. R. Davies; JSOTSup 348; Sheffield: Sheffield Academic Press, 2002) 87–100; and id., "Jeremiah as Text: Some Reflections on Genre and Reality in Old Testament Prophetic Research," in *Historie og konstruktion*, FS N. P. Lemche (ed. M. Müller and T. L. Thompson; Forum for Bibelsk Eksegese 14; Copenhagen: Tusculanum, 2005) 11–18.

28 Barstad, "What Prophets Do," 22.

Scrolls were written and the Septuagint was translated.[29] This means that the prophetic and other books of the Hebrew Bible, in all their voluminous appearance, provide us with only a fragmentary documentation of prophecy in the kingdoms of Israel and Judah and in the Persian province of Yehud. Still, both biblical and Near Eastern sources are indispensable evidence for a historian, since they are the only sources informing about prophecy in their time.

The dilemma is this: Who is talking now? If we agree that, for instance, the book of Jeremiah tells us 'a lot about what prophecy was like in ancient Israel',[30] we have to ask again the questions like those posed by Carroll in his debate with Overholt. After the methodological turmoil and the growing attention to the Near Eastern prophetic sources during the past two decades, these questions are still up-to-date–in fact, burning as never before. Two of them, in particular, should be contemplated before saying anything further, because they have a bearing on all that follows from them:

- Which Israel? Does 'ancient Israel' refer to the kingdoms of Israel and Judah that existed before the 6th century BCE or to the Second Temple community?
- Whose prophet? Same problem as before, *mutatum mutandum*; but there are even more alternatives, since we have to make a difference between biblical and modern concepts of prophecy, which are more than one on both sides. "If a *nabî* was a *ro'eh*, what then was a *ro'eh*?"[31] A question simple as this presents the problem in a nutshell, since the answer requires fundamental distinctions to be made with regard to the biblical, religio-historical, as well as the modern presentations of prophecy.

As a corollary of these two root questions, at least the following three immediately suggest themselves:

- Whose history are we dealing with? That of a certain prophet, for instance, Jeremiah, his hangers-on, or certain factions of the Second Temple communities of different times?
- What are the socioreligious prerequisites of the texts under scrutiny? For example, which temple of Jerusalem is it that individual texts in the book of Jeremiah actually speak about–the First, the Second, or an imaginary one? Where are the false prophets to be looked for and why are they false?

29 See, e.g., E. Ulrich, *The Dead Sea Scrolls and the Origins of the Bible* (Studies in the Dead Sea Scrolls and Related Literature; Grand Rapids, Mich., 1999); for a case study, see A. Aejmelaeus, "Lost in Reconstruction? On Hebrew and Greek Reconstructions in 2 Sam 24," *BIOSCS* 40 (2007) 89–106.

30 Barstad, "What Prophets Do," 22.

31 R. P. Carroll, "Whose Prophet? Whose History? Whose Social Reality?," 90.

- What should we do with the gaps and empty spaces that inevitably remain in our historical reconstruction? Whose voices do we not hear or fail to take notice of?

The answers to these questions do make a difference if we want to relate the texts with a social reality of any kind. I do agree with Hans Barstad that even fictitious texts may contain historically true information on ancient societies;[32] in his footsteps, I have myself used Jeremiah 36 as an example of a fiction that is not entirely void of historical information.[33] However, it is far from self-evident which societies we are dealing with when we start examining the book of Jeremiah. Take the three illustrious commentaries of Jeremiah published in 1986, those of Robert Carroll, William McKane and William Holladay, and you will find three different approaches and respective answers to this question: one reading the text as the product of the Second Temple community without even trying to reconstruct the historical prophet,[34] another introducing the idea of a "rolling corpus" that includes words of the prophet that have triggered a long chain of literary interpretations included in the same text,[35] and yet another attempting at a maximalist reading of the book as a document from the time of the prophet himself.[36] So the question, "Who is talking now?," not only applies to the texts but also to their interpreters. Indeed, it is difficult to read.

---

32 Cf. Barstad, "What Prophets Do"; id., "Jeremiah as Text"; id., "'Fact' versus 'Fiction' and Other Issues in the History Debate," 443–45.

33 Nissinen, "How Prophecy Became Literature," 163–64; cf. H.-J. Stipp, "Baruchs Erben: Die Schriftprophetie im Spiegel von Jer 36," in *"Wer darf hinaufsteigen zum Berg JHWHs?": Beiträge zu Prophetie und Poesie des Alten Testaments*, FS S. Ö. Steingrímsson (Arbeiten zu Text und Sprache im Alten Testament 72; St. Ottilien: EOS Verlag, 2002) 145–70; van der Toorn, *Scribal Culture and the Making of the Hebrew Bible*, 184–88.

34 R. P. Carroll, *The Book of Jeremiah: A Commentary* (OTL; London: SCM, 1986).

35 W. McKane, *A Critical and Exegetical Commentary on Jeremiah*, vol. 1: Introduction and Commentary on Jeremiah 1–25 (ICC; Edinburgh: T & T Clark, 1986); cf. id., *A Critical and Exegetical Commentary on Jeremiah*, vol. 2: A Commentary on Jeremiah 26–52 (ICC; Edinburgh: T & T Clark, 1996).

36 W. L. Holladay, *Jeremiah*, vol. 1: *A Commentary on the Book of the Prophet Jeremiah, Chapters 1–25* (Hermeneia; Philadelphia: Fortress Press, 1986); cf. id., *Jeremiah*, vol. 2: *A Commentary on the Book of the Prophet Jeremiah, Chapters 26–52* (Hermeneia; Minneapolis: Fortress Press, 1989).

What Prophecy?

Like every historical reconstruction, even that of ancient prophecy begins with the identification of sources. It is the task of the scholarly community to decide where the evidence can be found and what kind of evidence can be judged as prophetic. This is everything else but a matter of course. There is no unanimity about what prophecy is–not even in the biblical text, not to mention the sources where the whole concept is not inherent; hence we already at the outset have to confront different scholarly positions, sometimes associated with value judgments concerning biblical prophets and extrabiblical soothsayers, or more and less valuable prophecy within the Hebrew Bible. Amos is not by necessity the paragon of true prophecy, but he has been given this elevated position by Western scholarship that has found "his" moral vision superior to anything represented by his co-Israelites, not to mention the notorious Canaanites. Today still, Amos tends to be used as a test case of a prophet *par excellence* in scholarly literature,[37] even though he could as well be considered an anomaly when compared with his Near Eastern or even domestic colleagues (with whom he does not want to be identified anyway, Am 7:7–10!).

The issue between Auld, Carroll, Overholt and others was essentially how much prophecy can actually be found in the Hebrew Bible. This, of course, depends entirely on what the scholarly community wants the word "prophecy" to mean. Prophecy is, ultimately, a scholarly category deeply rooted in Jewish-Christian theology and biblical studies, and its application to nonbiblical sources is no matter of course either.

There is no reason to give up the whole concept of prophecy, if we can come to terms about what kind of activity it is used for, and make the definition flexible enough to allow a degree of variability depending on time and culture. Prophecy remains a useful category especially now that we are able to work cross-culturally to a greater extent than before. Indeed, the recent definitions of prophecy take prophecy as a religio-historical phenomenon documented by various source materials, ancient and modern, the Hebrew Bible being but one of them without any precedence over the others. This is without doubt the result of the growing knowledge of ancient Near Eastern prophetic documents, and it is no coincidence that today's most-quoted definition of prophecy is formulated by

37 The elevated position of Amos can be traced back (at least) to Julius Wellhausen and the 19th century ideal of "ethical monotheism"; see Loretz, "Die Entstehung des Amosbuches," 198–203.

Manfred Weippert, one of the few pioneers of their study.[38] Having its roots in earlier scholarship, the cross-cultural reading of prophecy has established itself during the 1980's hand in hand with the acknowledgement of intermediation being the primary quality of prophecy. Weippert was not the first and only one of the scholars of the 1980's who based his cross-cultural reading of prophecy on the understanding of prophecy as transmission. The names Herbert Huffmon,[39] Robert Wilson,[40] Thomas Overholt[41] and David Petersen[42] from the other side of the Atlantic deserve to be mentioned, too, as representatives of the understanding of prophecy as transmission, while approaching the issue from different perspectives. Sharing the same notion, I fully agree with Overholt that prophecy is a kind of religious intermediation that is cross-culturally distributed and conforms to a describable pattern of communication and social behavior.[43]

The significance of the ancient Near Eastern comparative material to solving the historical dilemma of prophetic studies is beyond any reasonable doubt. It helps to see things that on the basis of the biblical text alone would appear in a distorted light. For instance, it has contributed decisively to dismantling the strict division between prophecy and divination and helped to appreciate prophecy as another, non-inductive, or non-technical, method of the alleged communication with the divine and receiving divine knowledge.[44] The comparative material, ancient and modern, provides the biblical and cross-cultural studies with a model of the prophetic practice, language, roles, and social setting, enabling a view of the biblical text from a distance, as a part of a bigger picture.

---

38 In addition to the works mentioned in n. 19, see especially M. Weippert, "Assyrische Prophetien der Zeit Asarhaddons und Assurbanipals," in *Assyrian Royal Inscriptions: New Horizons in Literary, Ideological and Historical Analysis* (ed. F. M. Fales; Orientis Antiqui Collectio 17; Roma: Istituto per l'Oriente, 1981) 71–115.

39 See, e.g., H. B. Huffmon, "The Origins of Prophecy," in *Magnalia Dei: The Mighty Acts of God: Essays on the Bible and Archaeology in Memory of G. Ernest Wright* (ed. F. M. Cross, W. E. Lemke, and P. D. Miller; Garden City, NY: Doubleday, 1976) 171–86.

40 See especially R. R. Wilson, *Prophecy and Society in Ancient Israel* (Philadelphia: Fortress, 1980).

41 See T. W. Overholt, *Prophecy in Cross-Cultural Perspective*; id., *Channels of Prophecy.*

42 See, e.g., D.L. Petersen, *The Roles of Israel's Prophets* (JSOTSup 17; Sheffield: Shefield Academic Press, 1981).

43 Overholt, "Prophecy in History," 66, 69.

44 Cf. E. Cancik-Kirschbaum, "Prophetismus und Divination: Ein Blick auf die keilschriftlichen Quellen," in Köckert and Nissinen (eds.), *Propheten in Mari, Assyrien und Israel*, 33–53; B. Pongratz-Leisten, "When the Gods Are Speaking: Toward Defining the Interface between Polytheism and Monotheism," ibid., 132–68; Barstad, "Prophecy in the Book of Jeremiah," 87–89.

The danger with the distance is that we may not see the trees from the forest: it is difficult to resist the temptation of sacrificing the particular for the general to keep the picture clean.[45]

When we move from the identification of the sources to their interpretation and reconstruction of historical circumstances, it is important to take heed of the nature of different source materials. The ancient Near Eastern prophetic documents may lend themselves to apologetic defending of the historicity of the biblical prophets, but this approach hardly lets them speak with their own voice. I find the Near Eastern sources helpful in a different vein. They provide a patterned background for biblical prophecy and a sensible analogy of what prophecy may have looked like in Israel, Judah and Yehud, but they also help to recognize the points where the Hebrew Bible takes a course of its own.

One of the basic observations to be made is the diversity of the text types. The Near Eastern documentation of prophecy consists of a plethora of genres from oracles and oracle collections to letters, inscriptions, word-lists, administrative documents and so on, all dealing with prophets and prophetic appearances in more or less immediate past. The Hebrew Bible, on the other hand, is the only context where ancient Hebrew prophecy is documented, apart from a couple of Lachish letters.[46] It is a canonical composition *sui generis* in the ancient Near East, the result of the editorial history of several centuries and, hence, temporally distant from the prophets appearing on its lines. The Hebrew Bible not only documents the prophetic phenomenon in Southern Levant but also the emergence and early development of the concept of prophecy. This fundamental difference of the Hebrew Bible from other Near Eastern documents of prophecy must be recognized, otherwise we fail to understand what we are comparing.

What Is New in the Bible?

The prophetic texts of the Hebrew Bible represent the prophetic phenomenon in their own characteristic way, not only attaching to the ancient Near Eastern prophetic tradition but also drifting apart from it. Prophecy as it appears in the biblical texts ("biblical prophecy") is a literary construct related to the historical phenomenon of prophetic intermediation ("ancient Hebrew prophecy") but not identical with it. Of course, the written documents of prophecy in the ancient

45 Carroll, "Whose Prophet? Whose History? Whose Social Reality?," 90.

46 I.e., Lachish Ostraca 3, 6, and (possibly) 16; see C. L. Seow, in Nissinen, *Prophets and Prophecy in the Ancient Near East*, nos. 139, 140, and 141; H. M. Barstad, "Lachish Ostracon III and Ancient Israelite Prophecy," *ErIsr* 24 (1993) 8* – 12*.

Near East are not identical with the actual phenomenon either, but the literary process behind the Hebrew Bible is significantly different from these documents.

It stands to reason that the Hebrew Bible presents very different challenges to the historical studies of the prophets in comparison with the remaining Near Eastern evidence, especially if we want to know something about the prophets as historical figures. None of the Near Eastern prophetic documents comes even close to, say, the book of Jeremiah, with regard to the extensive literary form, complicated literary history, and the highly developed figure of the prophet, all this constituting a world of its own, set in the late 7th century Judah but created much later. Because of this difference, as Carroll pointed out, the comparative evidence provides a patterned *background* for biblical prophecy but it does not necessarily provide a sophisticated *reading* of biblical prophetic texts.[47] Sometimes it actually may even do so, but this must be judged carefully from case to case.

It would be hopelessly naïve to assume that the letters form Mari or the Assyrian oracles give a full and neutral picture of Mesopotamian prophecy either. They do not, because their ending up in the archives is the result of a procedure no less biased than the editorial history of the Hebrew Bible.[48] The procedures behind the texts are different, however, and should be evaluated accordingly, in awareness of the fact that the available set of sources our knowledge is distracted from, whether biblical or extrabiblical, does not yield a full and authentic picture of the prophetic phenomenon anywhere at any historical moment. Taking this as a starting point, we can rejoice over every new piece of evidence that helps to reconstruct the big picture–and hopefully also become more sensitive to details.

I happily recognize myself among those with the "tendency to stress the factor that the prophetic corpus, similar to the rest of the texts of the Hebrew Bible, represents late literary creations of the Persian, or even Hellenistic, eras."[49] I think this is simply true for the prophetic books as a literary genre. The fact that there was prophecy in the ancient Near East cannot be used as a counterclaim because the comparability of the biblical prophetic literature with ancient Near Eastern documents does not directly support any specific dating. There is at least one answer to the questions, "Which Israel?", "Whose prophet?": we can safely say that, in their present form, the biblical texts dealing with prophecy present the views of the Second Temple communities over several centuries.

---

47 Carroll, "Whose Prophet? Whose History? Whose Social Reality?," 91.
48 Cf. Nissinen, "Spoken, Written, Quoted and Invented," 268–71.
49 Barstad, "What Prophets Do," 31.

It does not follow from this by any logic, however, that the prophetic texts "have no connections whatsoever with prophecy as a historical phenomenon in ancient Israel"[50]–first and foremost because they, even as literature, *are* part of this phenomenon, but also because there are enough good reasons to see a historical relation between these texts and the prophetic phenomenon. The comparative material, as I hope to be able to demonstrate in another context,[51] makes it possible to observe that virtually every single function of prophecy known from Mesopotamia and the West Semitic milieu has a point of reference in the Hebrew Bible.[52] The phenomenon was known in Israel, Judah, and also in Yehud; it is evident that the authors of the biblical texts had an idea of prophecy based on knowledge of prophetic practices. This idea they communicated to their audiences who were supposed to understand the message. This is beyond any reasonable doubt; the issue is rather how they used this knowledge and how they themselves contributed to the history of the prophetic phenomenon. Prophets as presented in the biblical texts do not necessarily conform to the pattern of prophetic intermediation as we know it from the Near Eastern documents. Sometimes we may have to look for analogies for prophets as they appear in the Bible in other sources–Brad Kelle has found them among the Greek orators like Demosthenes.[53] But the question remains, whose prophets and whose audiences are we dealing with. If biblical prophets, who "engage in discourse that is communicative, argumentative public address"[54] can be compared with Greek orators, can the same be said about ancient Israelite, Judaean, or Yehudite prophets who, as I contend, cannot be simply identified with the biblical prophets?

Prophecies were written down and collected in Assyria as well as probably in Israel and Judah. There is reason to believe that the biblical prophetic books–and some other texts, too[55]–partly derive their origin from collections of prophet-

---

50 Ibid.

51 M. Nissinen, "Biblical Prophecy from a Near Eastern Perspective: The Cases of Kingship and Divine Possession," in *Congress Volume Ljubljana 2007* (ed. A. Lemaire; VTSup 133; Leiden: Brill, 2010) 441–68 (= pp. 351–75 in this volume).

52 Cf. also Barstad, "Prophecy in the Book of Jeremiah."

53 B. E. Kelle, "Ancient Israelite Prophets and Greek Political Orators: Analogies for the Prophets and Their Implications for Historical Reconstruction," in Kelle and Moore (eds.), *Israel's Prophets and Israel's Past*, 57–82; cf., from a different perspective, Lange, "Greek Seers and Israelite-Jewish Prophets."

54 Kelle, "Ancient Israelite Prophets and Greek Political Orators," 63.

55 E.g., some psalms; see J. W. Hilber, *Cultic Prophecy in the Psalms* (BZAW 352; Berlin and New York: W. de Gruyter, 2005).

ic words based on oral performances and written down shortly after them.[56] Prophetic books are more than written prophecies, however. They document the transition from writing down oral messages to a literary interpretation on previously written texts, representing a shift from written prophecy to literary prophecy.[57] The literarization of prophecy has been called the proprium of biblical prophecy by Jörg Jeremias,[58] which may slightly overstated; Armin Lange has recently referred to similar phenomena in ancient Greece.[59] In any case, the development of prophecy in the Second Temple period, including the production of prophetic books, the shift of emphasis from oral to scribal prophecy, the authority given to the prophetic tradition, and the emergence of "prophecy by interpretation," is without rival anywhere in the East Mediterranean world. This development makes it an arduous task to acquire knowledge of the Hebrew prophets as historical figures. On the other hand, without this development we would probably not even know that there were prophets in Israel.

Towards an Answer

This article has been a *Problemanzeige* rather than a detailed attempt at answering the questions it has posed. Let me, by way of a conclusion, sketch out a proposal of how the question "Who Is Talking Now?" with a reference to the historical dilemma of prophetic studies, could be given an answer.

First, the question can be understood as referring to contemporary voices. In order to agree what their communication on prophecy is all about, the scholars must understand each others' meanings of the concept of prophecy. The widespread agreement of prophecy as intermediation is very helpful especially when it comes to prophecy as oral activity and a social phenomenon; however, the application of the concept of prophecy to literary activity appears to be more problematic. This can be seen, for instance in the discussions concerning the re-

56 Cf. Nissinen, "How Prophecy Became Literature," 166–69; cf. Barstad, "Prophecy in the Book of Jeremiah," 96–97. Cf. the "memory hypothesis" of K. van der Toorn, attributing a crucial role to "recollections about the prophet that were shared among his followers and admirers" (*Scribal Culture and the Making of the Hebrew Bible*, 195); this model relies strongly on oral transmission of the "Acts and Oracles of Jeremiah."

57 This distinction is introduced by Lange, "Literary Prophecy and Oracle Collection," 249–61.

58 J. Jeremias, "Das Proprium der alttestamentlichen Prophetie," *ThLZ* 119 (1994) 483–94.

59 Lange, "Literary Prophecy and Oracle Collection," 261–73.

lationship of prophecy and apocalypticism[60] or recognizing prophecy in the Dead Sea Scrolls.[61] The meaning of prophecy still depends partly on the speaker, and this has implications for the historical dilemma of prophetic studies.

Secondly, and no less importantly, the question applies to the biblical text and biblical prophecy. There is more than one construct of prophecy in the Hebrew Bible, each one representing the agenda of their creators, who have contributed to the literarization of the prophetic phenomenon; for example, the Deuteronomistic idea of prophecy is clearly distinct from that in Chronicles.[62] The invention of a new genre, the prophetic book, is an important factor in this development, since along with it, the few names we are accustomed to call "classical prophets" became canonized, and the difference between them and contemporary prophetic practices began to grow. Alongside this development, "the Prophets" refers to the canonical writings thus labelled rather than the historical figures whose words these writings are supposed to carry on.[63]

The people that are responsible for the biblical text as we have it, are the first voices to be heard in the biblical text–and they are historical voices, for that matter. If such thing as a "history of prophecy in Israel" can be written,[64] this is what it should rather begin than end with, and I do not mean the chronological order of things but the focus of attention. The historical approach in prophetic studies should not only, or even primarily, be focused on the quest for historical prophets, because prophecy as a historical phenomenon did not die off with them. This necessarily implies that even literary prophecy is consid-

60 See the discussion between J. J. Collins, "Prophecy, Apocalypse and Eschatology: Reflections on the Proposal of Lester Grabbe," and L. L. Grabbe, "Prophetic and Apocalyptic: Time for New Definitions–and New Thinking," in Grabbe and Haak (eds.), *Knowing the End from the Beginning* (2003) 44–52, 107–133.

61 See the essays by Timothy Lim, George Brooke and myself in *Prophecy after the Prophets? The Contribution of the Dead Sea Scrolls to the Understanding of Biblical and Extra-Biblical Prophecy* (ed. K. De Troyer and A. Lange; CBET 52; Leuven: Peeters, 2009); cf. H. M. Barstad, "Prophecy at Qumran?," in *In the Last Days: On Jewish and Christian Apocalyptic and Its Period*, FS B. Otzen (ed. K. Jeppesen, K. Nielsen, and B. Rosendal; Aarhus: Aarhus University Press, 1994) 104–20; M. Nissinen, "Transmitting Divine Mysteries: The Prophetic Role of Wisdom Teachers in the Dead Sea Scrolls," in: A. Voitila and J. Jokiranta (eds.), *Scripture in Transition*, FS R. Sollamo (JSJ.S 126; Leiden: Brill, 2008) (= pp. 631–49 in this volume); A. P. Jassen, "Prophets and Prophecy in the Qumran Community," *AJS Review* 37 (2008) 299–334.

62 See, e.g., W. K. Schniedewind, *The Word of God in Transition: From Prophet to Exegete in the Second Temple Period* (JSOTS 197; Sheffield: Sheffield Academic Press, 1995), esp. 245–49.

63 Thus, e.g., Seitz, "Prophecy and Hermeneutics."

64 This doubt is by no means directed against Joseph Blenkinsopp's important book, *A History of Prophecy in Israel* (rev. and enlarged ed.; Louisville: Westminster John Knox, 1996).

ered a part of the prophetic phenomenon, and that prophecy by interpretation is seen as a continuation of the prophetic process of communication.

Thirdly, it can be assumed that biblical texts include elements of ancient Hebrew prophecy, that is, prophetic intermediation of the oral/aural type, comparable to that documented by ancient Near Eastern texts. No-one denies existence of this kind of prophecy in ancient Israel and Judah, and we are well-advised to remember that it did not cease to exist in the postmonarchical period. The voices of these prophets are, by necessity, to be heard only as an echo within the constructs of biblical prophecy, but it can be heard if we know how to listen to it. The prophetic documentation from the ancient Near East is an indispensable tool in learning to listen to the fragmented voices of the Israelite, Judaean, or Yehudite prophets. But the extrabiblical evidence is not only necessary for understanding ancient Hebrew prophecy as an oral/aural phenomenon, sometimes involving writing as a medium of communication. It also helps to acknowledge the continuity and change between ancient Hebrew prophecy and biblical prophecy.

Comparative studies are of paramount importance in recognizing that the constructors of biblical prophecy have been aware of the prophetic phenomenon, its language, practices, and social dynamics. Evidently, they were familiar with the social and linguistic codes of prophetic intermediation, and this knowledge did not come exclusively from written texts but was based on experience. This made it possible for them to utilize prophecy *both* as a socioreligious pattern *and* as a written text. The book of Jeremiah provides a telling example of how a prophet is moulded out from elements that the audience could easily identify as prophetic, with the result of creating a prophet that virtually ends all prophets.

On the other hand, belonging to the class of literati, the constructors of biblical prophecy also knew prophecy from written texts. The prophetic books mostly hide their literary history by presenting every word as coming from the mouth of the prophet, but Jeremiah 36, again, gives a clear indication of redactional activity. The linguistic and formal proximity of biblical prophecies to ancient Near Eastern prophetic oracles suggests that the authors of the prophetic and other biblical books were well aware of what written prophetic oracle looked like. It is difficult to deny the possibility that they actually utilized written oracles, either by quoting them or imitating their style. This cannot be absolutely proven until we have identical or similar oracles of ascertained archaeological provenance at our disposal; but if the editors of the prophetic books had knowledge of these texts, they may as well have not only imitated but also quoted them. In fact, it may be that the genre of the prophetic book would never have emerged without the existence of written documents of ancient Hebrew prophecy; if this is true, then written prophecy is a prerequisite of literary prophecy.

Since When Do Prophets Write?

Writing Prophets?

Several generations of Bible students have learned in their textbooks that there are two kinds of prophets in the Hebrew Bible: the "writing prophets" responsible for the prophetic books, at least in embryonic form, and other prophets not associated with any kind of writing activity. The former group is often given the title "classical prophets", implying an elevated status among the biblical prophets, while the latter group, consisting of the so-called "pre-classical" prophets and the somewhat amorphous bunch of "cult prophets", "court prophets" and the kind, has enjoyed a considerable lesser degree of admiration.[1] While still well and alive even in some quite recent textbooks and introductions to the Hebrew Bible, the distinction between writing and non-writing prophets has eroded significantly in critical scholarship during the past decades. This development has taken place hand in hand with the growing conviction that the biblical prophetic books are the product of a long scribal process which distances the prophetic figures, however highly appreciated, from the textual product bearing their names.[2] This development, however, has not solved the question of whether "writing prophets" actually existed; that is, whether writing can be seen as be-

1 See, e.g., M. J. de Jong, "Biblical Prophecy – A Scribal Enterprise: The Old Testament Prophecy of Unconditional Judgement Considered as a Literary Phenomenon," *VT* 61 (2011) 39–70, esp. 42–44.

2 For recent contributions, see J.-D. Macchi and T. Römer, "La formation des livres prophétiques: enjeux et débats," in *Les recueils prophétiques de la Bible: Origines, milieux, et contexte proche-oriental* (ed. J.-D. Macchi, C. Nihan, T. Römer, and J. Rückl; Le Monde de la Bible 64; Geneva: Labor et Fides, 2012) 9–27; R. G. Kratz, "Probleme der Prophetenforschung," in *Prophetenstudien: Kleine Schriften II* (ed. id.; FAT 74; Tübingen: Mohr Siebeck, 2011) 3–17; D. Edelman, "From Prophets to Prophetic Books: The Fixing of the Divine Word," in *The Production of Prophecy: Constructing Prophecy and Prophets in Yehud* (ed. ead. and E. Ben Zvi; London: Equinox, 2009) 29–54; E. Ben Zvi, "The Concept of Prophetic Books and Its Historical Setting," ibid., 73–95; K. van der Toorn, *Scribal Culture and the Making of the Hebrew Bible* (Cambridge, Mass.: Harvard University Press, 2007), esp. 173–232; M. H. Floyd, "The Production of Prophetic Books in the Early Second Temple Period," in *Prophets, Prophecy, and Prophetic Texts in Second Temple Judaism* (ed. id. and R. D. Haak; LHBOTS 427; London: T & T Clark, 2006) 276–97; K. Schmid, "Hintere Propheten (Nebiim)," in *Grundinformation Altes Testament: Eine Einführung in Literatur, Religion und Geschichte des Alten Testaments* (ed. J. C. Gertz; UTB 2745; Göttingen: Vandenhoeck & Ruprecht, 2006) 303–401; M. Nissinen, "How Prophecy Became Literature," *SJOT* 19 (2005) 153–72.

DOI 10.1515/9783110466546-027

longing to prophetic activity, independently from the issue of the authorship of the biblical prophetic books. In other words, is there is a historical grain of truth to the idea of "writing prophets"?

Already in ancient texts, the image of a prophet is associated with production of texts, and the idea of a prophetic "book", or scroll, dates back to the Hebrew Bible itself. The act of writing as such is a prerequisite of the production of prophetic books, hence the question remains whether the sources available to us – whether biblical or not – actually imply that prophets were involved in scribal activities leading to the transformation of oral transmission of divine messages into written and/or literary prophecy.[3]

The title of this essay was originally formulated in the past tense: "Since when *did* prophets write?"; however, who would be able to answer such a question on the basis of the very fragmented source material we have at our disposal? The title in the present tense, "Since when *do* prophets write?", implies the continuation, "... in the sources available to us", and this is what makes the question answerable. In this essay, dedicated with much pleasure to Anneli Aejmelaeus, my dear colleague in Helsinki,[4] I will confine myself to the simple question: Is there evidence of "writing prophets" in the ancient Near Eastern sources, including the Hebrew Bible, and if prophets are not caught in the very act of writing, are they otherwise involved in production of texts? Larger issues such as sociology of literacy, the authorship of the biblical prophetic books, the oral/written distinction, and the textualization of prophecy, I leave to be discussed in another contexts.

Ancient Near East

In Neo-Assyrian texts, prophecy appears as an oral phenomenon. The Neo-Assyrian technical term for prophesying is the verb *ragāmu*, which means "to shout",

3 For the distinction of written prophecy (prophetic oracles written down and sometimes compiled in collections) and literary prophecy (reapplication and recontextualizarion of prophetic oracles and creation of prophetic literature), see A. Lange, "Literary Prophecy and Oracle Collection: A Comparison between Judah and Greece in Persian Times," in Floyd and Haak (eds.), *Prophets, Prophecy, and Prophetic Texts in Second Temple Judaism*, 248–75.

4 Anneli Aejmelaeus has herself contributed to the issue of the textual evidence of the emergence of the prophetic books, especially Jeremiah; see "Nebuchadnezzar, My Servant: Redaction History and Textual Development in Jer 27," in *Interpreting Translation*, FS J. Lust (ed. F. García Martínez and M. Vervenne; BETL 192; Leuven: Peeters, 2005) 1–18; id., "Jeremiah at the Turning-Point of History: The Function of Jer xxv 1–14 in the Book of Jeremiah," *VT* 52 (2002) 459–82.

"to proclaim", expressly referring to oral activity; consequently, the Neo-Assyrian prophets bear the designation *raggimu* (male) or *raggintu* (female).[5] The colophons of the prophetic oracles regularly present them as coming "from the mouth" (*ša pî* or *issu pî*) of the prophets mentioned by name.[6]

In some inscriptions, prophecies (together with celestial omens) are referred to as *šipir maḫḫê*, literally "messages ("sendings") of prophets," also equated with *našparti ilāni u Ištar* "messages of the gods and Ištar":

> Favorable omens in the sky and on earth came to me. Oracles of prophets (*šipir mahhê*), messages of the gods and Ištar (*našparti ilāni u Ištar*), were constantly sent to me and they encouraged my heart.[7]

The words *šipru* and *našpartu* both mean "message", and in the Assyrian royal inscriptions, they are used specifically to mean divine messages.[8] One can plausibly think the expression *šipir maḫḫê* to refer to the entire prophetic performance and the subsequent process of communication that eventually may (but need not) have included writing the oracle down; this was demonstrably the case on occasion of Esarhaddon's ascending the throne.

The entire corpus of extant prophetic oracles from Assyria[9] is the product of the work of professional scribes.[10] There is nothing in the Neo-Assyrian texts

---

5 Verb *ragāmu:* SAA 9 6 r. 12; SAA 9 10 s. 2 (?); SAA 10 352:23; SAA 13 37:10; noun *raggimu/raggintu:* SAA 9 3.5 iv 31; SAA 9 6 r. 11 (?); SAA 9 7:1; SAA 9 10 s. 2; SAA 2 6 § 10:116; SAA 7 9 i 23; SAA 10 109:9; SAA 10 294 r. 31; SAA 10 352:23; SAA 13 37:7; SAA 13 144 r. 7; *MSL* 12 6.2:134 see S. Parpola, *Assyrian Prophecies* (SAA 9; Helsinki: Helsinki University Press, 1997), xlv–xlvi; M. J. de Jong, *Isaiah among the Ancient Near Eastern Prophets: A Comparative Study of the Earliest Stages of the Isaiah Tradition and the Neo-Assyrian Prophecies* (VTSup 117; Leiden: Brill, 2007), 291–92; J. Stökl, *Prophecy in the Ancient Near East: A Philological and Sociological Comparison* (CHANE 56; Leiden: Brill, 2012) 111–27.

6 SAA 9 1.1 i 28; 1.2 ii 9; 1.3 ii 13; 1.4 ii 40; 1.5 iii 5; 1.7 v 10; 1.8 v 24; 1.10 vi 31; SAA 9 9 r. 4 (*ša pî*); SAA 9 2.3 ii 28; 2.4 iii 18 (*issu pî*); cf. SAA 2 6 § 10:116 (*ina pî*). See Parpola, *Assyrian Prophecies*, lxiii.

7 Esarhaddon Nin A ii 5–7 (see E. Leichty, *The Royal Inscriptions of Esarhaddon, King of Assyria (680–669 BC)* [RINAP 4; Winona Lake, Ind.: Eisenbrauns, 2011], 14); cf. Esarhaddon Ass A ii 12–26 (see ibid., 121, 124); Assurbanipal T ii 14–17 (see J. Novotny and J. Jeffers, *The Royal Inscriptions of Ashurbanipal (668–631 BC), Aššur-etel-ilāni (630–627 BC), and Sîn-šarra-iškun (626–612 BC), Kings of Assyria*, Part 1 (RINAP 5/1; University Park, Pa.: Eisenbrauns, 2018), 216.

8 See B. Pongratz-Leisten, *Herrschaftswissen in Mesopotamien: Formen der Kommunikation zwischen Gott und König im 2. und 1. Jahrtausend v. Chr.* (SAAS 10; Helsinki: The Neo-Assyrian Text Corpus Project, 1999), esp. 224–26.

9 See the edition in Parpola, *Assyrian Prophecies*; cf. also M. Nissinen, with contributions by C. L. Seow, R. K. Ritner, and H. Craig Melchert, *Prophets and Prophecy in the Ancient Near East* (2nd ed.; SBLWAW 41; Atlanta, Ga.: Society of Biblical Literature, 2019), nos. 68–96.

to suggest that the prophets themselves ever wrote down the oracles they spoke, neither is there any particular reason to believe they did so; the complete silence of the sources rather indicates the opposite. There were, for sure, diviners who were intensively involved with writing and text production, as is demonstrated by the abundance of correspondence of the Neo-Assyrian kings with diviners,[11] but these diviners – haruspices, astrologers, and exorcists – belonged to the class of scholars who were thoroughly versed in traditional omen literature and were expected to write their own reports. Prophets, to all appearances, did not belong to this class, and even though literacy in Mesopotamia may well have been higher than has been expected,[12] there is nothing to suggest that it was required or expected of prophets. Sometimes their words were recorded in writing by others,[13] and there are a few letters reporting prophetic appearances.[14] In most cases, however, the words they spoke were probably not written down at all.

Similar observations can be made when reading the second major corpus of prophetic documents from the 18th century BCE kingdom of Mari.[15] Even in these

---

10 For scribal characteristics of the Neo-Assyrian prophecies, see Parpola, *Assyrian Prophecies*, lv–lxii.

11 See especially S. Parpola, *Letters from Assyrian Scholars to the Kings Esarhaddon and Assurbanipal*, 2 vols. (AOAT 5/1–2; Kevelaer and Neukirchen-Vluyn: Butzon & Bercker and Neukirchener Verlag, 1970/1983; repr. Winona Lake, Ind.: Eisenbrauns, 2007); cf. the later editions by H. Hunger, *Astrological Reports to Assyrian Kings* (SAA 8; Helsinki: Helsinki University Press, 1992); S. Parpola, *Letters from Assyrian and Babylonian Scholars* (SAA 10; Helsinki: Helsinki University Press, 1993); S. W. Cole and P. Machinist, *Letters from Priests to the Kings Esarhaddon and Assurbanipal* (SAA 13; Helsinki: Helsinki University Press, 1998).

12 Cf. D. Charpin, *Reading and Writing in Babylon* (trans. J. M. Todd; Cambridge, Mass.: Harvard University Press, 2010), esp. 53–65.

13 Cf. especially SAA 13 139; see M. Nissinen and S. Parpola, "Marduk's Return and Reconciliation in a Prophetic Letter from Arbela," in in *Verbum et calamus: Semitic and Related Studies in Honour of the Sixtieth Birthday of Professor Tapani Harviainen* (ed. H. Juusola, J. Laulainen, and H. Palva; StudOr 99; Helsinki: Finnish Oriental Society, 2004) 199–219 (= pp. 245–65 in this volume); de Jong, *Isaiah among the Ancient Near Eastern Prophets*, 279–82.

14 E.g., SAA 10 352; 13 37; 13 144; 13 148; 16 59; see M. Nissinen, *References to Prophecy in Neo-Assyrian Sources* (SAAS 7; Helsinki: Helsinki University Press, 1998); id., *Prophets and Prophecy in the Ancient Near East*, nos. 109, 111, 113, 114, and 115; and several references to these texts in de Jong, *Isaiah among the Ancient Near Eastern Prophets*, and Stökl, *Prophecy in the Ancient Near East*.

15 For writing, literacy, and the prophetic process of communication at Mari, see D. Charpin, "Le prophétisme dans le Proche-Orient d'après les archives de Mari," in Macchi et al. (eds.), *Les recueils prophétiques de la Bible*, 31–73; J. M. Sasson, "The Posting of Letters with Divine Messages," in *Florilegium Marianum 2*, FS M. Birot (ed. D. Charpin and J.-M. Durand; Mémoires de NABU 3; Paris: SEPOA, 1994) 299–316.

documents, prophecy appears as an oral phenomenon, and the prophetic performance is referred to using verbs denoting speaking or saying, such as *qabûm* and *dabābum*.[16] There is a profusion of correspondence between the king of Mari and the diviners who, like their Assyrian colleagues a full millennium later, reported their observations and interpretations to the king and who represented a high level of literacy. The prophetic activity at Mari is known to us thanks to some fifty letters reporting, among other things, prophetic words and performances.[17] These letters typically inform the king about prophets who have "come" (*alākum*) or "risen" (*tebûm*), sometimes "gone into frenzy" (*mahûm*), and "said" (*qabûm/dabābum*) divine words that the letter-writers have either experienced themselves or become conversant of by go-betweens.[18] This implies an ecstatic performance involving oral delivery of divine messages, often in a temple context.

The genre of written prophecies is entirely missing from the Mari archives. There is one tablet, though, that can be seen as representing a type of an oracle collection (ARM 26 194), beginning with the words "Speak to Zimri-Lim: Thus the prophet of Šamaš". This is the only letter in the Mari corpus with a prophet as the sender. The letter contains three or four individual prophecies of Šamaš and ends with the exhortation: "Let Zimri-Lim, governor of Šamaš and Adad, listen to what is written on this tablet ...". The tablet, hence, could be characterized as a collection of oracles embedded in a letter.

16 FM 7 38:4, 17; 39:29, 36, 42, 46, 61; A 3760:9; ARM 26 197:9, 20; 198:4; 199:29, 43; 200:21; 206:25; 209:7, 17; 210:10; 214:7; 215:16; 220:24; 221:10, 20; 221bis:27; 233:8; 414:30, 34 (*qabûm*); ARM 26 199:55; 204:5; 206:29; 207: 36–37; 217:27; 219:6, 22; 233:41; 243:8 (*dabābum*). Sometimes the prophetic performance is referred to as "giving an oracle" (*têrtam nadānum*): ARM 26:197:5; 200:6; 206:34 (cf. ARM 26 216:8–9; 217:30–31: *têrtam epēšum*). All three expressions are used in ARM 26 206, suggesting that their meanings virtually overlap. In ARM 26 371: 10, 20, 32, the public proclamation of a prophet of Marduk is described with the Št form of *šanû* "proclaim incessantly".

17 See the editions in J.-M. Durand, *Archives épistolaires de Mari I/1* (ARM 26/1; Paris: Editions Recherche sur les Civilisations, 1988); D. Charpin, F. Joannès, S. Lackenbacher, and B. Lafont, *Archives épistolaires de Mari I/2* (ARM 26/2; Paris: Editions Recherche sur les Civilisations, 1988); J.-M. Durand, *Florilegium Marianum 7: Le culte d'Addu d'Alep et l'affaire d'Alahtum* (Mémoires de NABU 4; Paris: Editions Recherche sur les Civilisations, 2002). See also the translations in J. J. M. Roberts, *The Bible and the Ancient Near East: Collected Essays* (Winona Lake, Ind.: Eisenbrauns, 2002), esp. 157–253; W. Heimpel, *Letters to the King of Mari: A New Translation, with Historical Introduction, Notes, and Commentary* (Mesopotamian Civilizations 12; Winona Lake, Ind.: Eisenbrauns, 2003); Nissinen, *Prophets and Prophecy in the Ancient Near East*, nos. 1–50b.

18 E.g., FM 7 38:4; 7 39:47; ARM 26 197:8; 199:43; 206:6; 210:8; 212:6; 220:10; 221bis:13; 223:5; 414:30; ARM 27 32:9 (*alākum*); A. 3760:6; ARM 26 195:7; 204:5; 209:7, 16; 215:16; 219:5; 237:23 (*tebûm*); ARM 26 213:7; 214:7; 222:6, 13 (*mahûm*); for *qabûm/dabābum*, see above, fn. 15.

What exactly is the role of the prophet as the sender of this letter? Could he have written it himself? That this is not the case becomes evident from another letter (ARM 26 414), in which the official Yasim-El reports the king the following:

> Another matter: Atamrum, prophet of Šamaš, came to me and spoke to me as follows: "Send me a discreet scribe! I will have him write down the message which Šamaš has sent me for the king." This is what he said to me. So I sent Utu-kam and he wrote this tablet. This man brought witnesses and said to me as follows: "Send this tablet quickly and let the king act according to its words." This is what he said to me. I have herewith sent this tablet to my lord.

Dominique Charpin has argued convincingly that the letter sent "herewith" to the king is nothing else but the above-mentioned letter ARM 26 194 containing the message of Šamaš.[19] If this is true, these two letters, one accompanying the other, give us a rare description of how written prophecies came into being. The prophet Atamrum, apparently, could not write himself, so Yasim-El commissioned a professional scribe called Utu-kam to write down the divine message which was then forwarded to the king by Yasim-El, together with another letter containing other reports. This is the only text from Mari connecting a prophet with any kind of writing, and it shows that, even though the prophet himself does not seem to have had scribal skills, he knew how to use written media in transmitting the divine word to its addressee.

Apart from the two main corpora of documentation of prophecy, there are two of texts that associate prophets with writing, both coming from places close to the biblical landscape. The famous prophetic text from Tell Deir 'Alla[20] begins with the words: "The warning of the book (*spr*) of [Balaam, son

19 D. Charpin, "Prophètes et rois dans le Proche-Orient amorrite: Nouvelles données, nouvelles perspectives," in *Florilegium Marianum 6*, FS A. Parrot (ed. id. and J.-M. Durand; Mémoires de NABU 7; Paris: SEPOA, 2002) 7–38, esp. 14–15; cf. id., "Le prophétisme dans le Proche-Orient d'après les archives de Mari," 36.

20 Editio princeps: J. Hoftijzer and G. van der Kooij, *Aramaic Texts from Deir 'Alla* (DMOA 19; Leiden: Brill, 1976); for later editions, see, e.g., H. Weippert and M. Weippert, "Die 'Bileam'-Inschrift von Tell Deir 'Allā," *ZDPV* 98 (1982) 77–103 (= M. Weippert, *Jahwe und die anderen Götter: Studien zur Religionsgeschichte des antiken Israel im syrisch-palästinischem Kontext* [FAT 18; Tübingen, 1997] 131–61); J. A. Hackett, *The Balaam Text from Deir 'Allā* (HSM 31; Chico, Calif.: Scholars Press, 1984); C.-L. Seow in Nissinen, *Prophets and Prophecy in the Ancient Near East*, no. 138; E. Blum, "Die Kombination I der Wandinschrift von Tell Deir 'Alla: Vorschläge zur Rekonstruktion mit historisch-kritischen Anmerkungen," in *Berührungspunkte: Studien zu Sozial- und Religionsgeschichte Israels und seiner Umwelt*, FS R. Albertz (ed. I. Kottsieper, R. Schmitt, and J. Wöhrle; AOAT 350; Münster: Ugarit-Verlag, 2008) 573–601.

of Beo]r,[21] who was a seer of the gods". The text, written in a language akin to Aramaic and Hebrew is dated to the 8th century. It was originally written on the plaster of the wall of a small building. Interestingly, this "writing on a wall" is called a "book" – that is, a scroll – which indicates that the text had been copied on the plaster from another source, perhaps even compiled of originally independent texts. The Deir ʿAlla text, hence, provides compelling evidence of writing and editing prophetic texts just a little before we see the the first biblical "writing" prophets appearing on the other side of the river Jordan.[22] The text does not, however, say anything about who actually and originally wrote it; the title "Book of Balaam" names Balaam as the central character of the text, not as its author or writer.

Finally, an extrabiblical text from the kingdom of Judah should be quoted here, that is, the Lachish Ostracon no. 3. The letter is sent by Hoshaiah to Yaush, the military commander at Lachish, some time before the collapse of Jerusalem in 586 BCE, and it ends with the following lines: "As for the letter of Tobiah the servant of the king, which came to Shallum the son of Jaddua from the prophet, saying: 'Beware!' – your servant has sent it to my lord".[23] The letter refers to a process of communication that involves five different persons and is difficult to reconstruct. Who is to be imagined as the actual writer of the "letter of Tobiah" (*spr ṭbyhw*) that "came to Shallum" (*hbh ʾl šlm*) "from the prophet" (*mʾt hnbʾ*), which "your servant" (that is, Hoshaiah) has sent to his "lord" (that is, Yaush)? Perhaps the royal official Tobiah had become aware of the "Beware!" prophecy and written a report of it that had then been mediated to Hoshaiah, the present letter-writer, by Shallum.[24] In any case, the letter tells about another

---

21 The name is fully preserved on line 4.

22 Cf. E. Blum, "Israels Prophetie im altorientalischen Kontext: Anmerkungen zu neueren religionsgeschichtlichen Thesen," in *"From Ebla to Stellenbosch": Syro-Palestinian Religions and the Hebrew Bible* (ed. I. Cornelius and L. Jonker; ADPV 37; Wiesbaden: Harrassowitz, 2008) 81–115; É. Puech, "Balaʿam and Deir ʿAlla," in *The Prestige of the Pagan Prophet Balaam in Judaism, Early Christianity, and Islam* (ed. G. H. van Kooten and J. T. A. G. M. van Ruiten; TBN 11; Leiden: Brill, 2008) 25–47.

23 Lak (6):1.3 r. 3–5; edition: J. Renz, *Die althebräischen Inschriften, Teil 1: Text und Kommentar* (Handbuch der althebräischen Epigraphik 1; Darmstadt: Wissenschaftliche Buchgesellschaft 1995), esp. 412–19; cf. C.-L. Seow in Nissinen, *Prophets and Prophecy in the Ancient Near East*, no. 139.

24 U. Rüterswörden, "Der Prophet der Lachish-Ostraka," in *Steine – Bilder – Texte: Historische Evidenz außerbiblischer und biblischer Quellen* (ed. C. Hardmeier; Arbeiten zur Bibel und ihrer Geschichte 5; Leipzig: Evangelischer Verlagsanstalt, 2001) 179–92, esp. 187: "Die einleuchtendste Erklärung besteht darin, dass der ספר von Ṭōbyāhû stammt, der wesentliche Inhalt aber – vor allem mit dem Kurzzitat – von dem Propheten'. Cf. also S. B. Parker, "The Lachish

letter, the essential contents of which comprises a prophetic oracle. The letter may have been sent on the prophet's initiative. It does not indicate that the prophet (the only anonymous member in this chain of communication[25]) had written the prophecy down himself, but it may reflect a process of communication similar to that in the case of the prophecy of Atamrum described above (ARM 26 414).

The survey of available evidence leaves empty-handed anyone who wants to find writing prophets in the ancient Near East: not a single source from the entire Near Eastern documentation even remotely alludes to a prophet writing a text her- or himself. The best explanation of the complete silence of the sources is that prophets simply did not belong to the class of literati at Mari or in Assyria, or anywhere in the ancient Near East. On the other hand, there is firm evidence of the connection between the prophetic and scribal practices: prophecies were occasionally, even though not routinely, written down, and, as the letter ARM 26 414 from Mari and the Lachish Ostracon 3 demonstrate, the prophets may sometimes have even initiated the scribal process.

Hebrew Bible

As Michael Floyd fittingly notes, "[t]he Bible's narrative descriptions of prophets hardly ever involve written documents".[26] To be sure, persons designated as prophets are sometimes depicted as writing a text themselves in the Hebrew Bible, but this does not happen very often – only five times, to be precise. In 1 Sam 10:25, Samuel, having told the people the rights and duties of the kingship of the newly elected king Saul, "wrote them in a book (*yiktob bas-sēper*) and laid it up before the Lord".[27] In Jer 32:10–12, Jeremiah buys a field at Anatoth from his cousin and says:

> I signed the deed (lit. "wrote in a book", *wā-'ektob bas-sēper*), sealed it, got witnesses, and weighed the money on scales. Then I took the sealed deed of purchase, containing the

Letters and Official Reactions to Prophecies," in *Uncovering Ancient Stones*, FS H. N. Richardson (ed. L. M. Hopfe; Winona Lake, Ind.: Eisenbrauns, 1994) 65–78.

25 According to an alternative interpretation, Tobiah himself is the prophet; thus Stökl, *Prophecy in the Ancient Near East*, 170. The definitive article in *hnb'* points to this direction, but the title "servant of the king" sounds somewhat strange as a prophetic title.

26 M. H. Floyd, "'Write the Revelation!' (Hab 2:2): Re-imagining the Cultural History of Prophecy," in *Writings and Speech in Israelite and Ancient Near Eastern Prophecy* (ed. E. Ben Zvi and id.; SBLSymS 10; Atlanta, Ga.: Society of Biblical Literature, 2000) 103–43, esp. 103.

27 The translations of the Hebrew Bible follow the NRSV.

terms and conditions, and the open copy; and I gave the deed of purchase to Baruch son of Neriah son of Mahseiah, in the presence of my cousin Hanamel, in the presence of the witnesses who signed the deed of purchase (*hak-kōtĕbîm bĕ-sēper ham-miqnâ*), and in the presence of all the Judeans who were sitting in the court of the guard.

Jeremiah is also said to have written down his oracles against Babylon: "Jeremiah wrote in a scroll (*way-yiktob yirmĕyāhû* ... *'el sēper*) all the disasters that would come on Babylon, all these words that are written concerning Babylon" (Jer 51:60). In Chronicler's report of the reign of Uzziah it reads: "Now the rest of the acts of Uzziah (*wĕ-yeter dibrê 'uzziyyāhû*), from first to last, the prophet Isaiah son of Amoz wrote" (*kātab* 2 Chr 26:22). Finally, Daniel (as far can he can be called a prophet[28]) is once said to have written down (*kātab*) his own dream (Dan 7:1).

Moreover, two prophets are presented as sending a letter without indicating who is thought to have actually written them. Jeremiah 29 includes a letter "that the prophet Jeremiah sent (*šālaḥ*) from Jerusalem to the remaining elders among the exiles, and to the priests, the prophets, and all the people"; and in 2 Chr 21:12–15, king Jehoram of Judah receives a letter from the prophet Elijah (*miktab mē-'ēliyyāhû han-nābî'*). In both cases, the contents of the letter consists of words of Yahweh, hence the letters can also be regarded as oracular accounts.

The documents that are said to have been written by a prophet include two legal documents, two oracular reports, one historical account, and, perhaps, two letters. All these text types are well known from the Near East, but apart from the Bible, we never find a prophet writing such texts. Even the biblical cases are not very conclusive: Samuel is not really acting as a prophet when writing the king's rights,[29] and Jeremiah's "writing" (*kātab*) of the purchase document refers to his signature rather than to writing the whole document – the same verb is used of the witnesses. Daniel, on the other hand, is depicted as belonging to the scribal elite (Dan 1:3–7).

---

28 Daniel is called a prophet in the Dead Sea Scrolls (4QFlor frag. 1, II, 3, 24, 5:3) and the New Testament (Matt 24:15), but not in the Hebrew Bible; however, his image has much in common with biblical prophets, such as Amos and Jeremiah; cf. L. L. Grabbe, "Daniel: Sage, Seer ... and Prophet?," in *Constructs of Prophecy in the Former and Latter Prophets and Other Texts* (ed. id. and M. Nissinen; ANEM 4; Atlanta, Ga.: Society of Biblical Literature, 2011) 87–94.

29 W. Dietrich, "Samuel: Ein Prophet?," in *Prophets and Prophecy in Jewish and Early Christian Literature* (ed. J. Verheyden, K. Zamfir, and T. Nicklas; WUNT.2 286; Tübingen: Mohr Siebeck, 2010) 1–17, esp. 9: "Hier agiert Samuel wieder nicht als Prophet, sondern als Leiter eines Volks-Things, vielleicht auch als Priester, der ein kultisches Los- und Orakelverfahren leitet."

In addition to the texts referring explicitly to a prophet performing the act of writing, in a number of texts a prophet receives the divine command to write; all of them use the verb *kātab:*

> Isa 8:1–2: Then the Lord said to me, Take a large tablet and write on it in common characters, "Belonging to Maher-shalal-hash-baz," and have it attested for me by reliable witnesses, the priest Uriah and Zechariah son of Jeberechiah.
>
> Isa 30:8: Go now, write it before them (*'ittām*) on a tablet (*lûăḥ*), and inscribe it in a book (*sēper*), so that it may be for the time to come as a witness forever.
>
> Ezek 24:1–2: In the ninth year, in the tenth month, on the tenth day of the month, the word of the Lord came to me: Mortal, write down the name of this day, this very day. The king of Babylon has laid siege to Jerusalem this very day.
>
> Ezek 37:15–16: The word of the Lord came to me: Mortal, take a stick (*'ēṣ 'eḥād*) and write on it, "For Judah, and the Israelites associated with it"; then take another stick and write on it, "For Joseph (the stick of Ephraim) and all the house of Israel associated with it.
>
> Hab 2:2: Then the Lord answered me and said: Write the vision; make it plain on tablets (*lūḥôt*), so that a runner may read it. For there is still a vision for the appointed time; it speaks of the end, and does not lie.
>
> Jer 30:2: Thus says the Lord, the God of Israel: Write in a book (*sēper*) all the words that I have spoken to you.
>
> Jer 36:1–2: In the fourth year of King Jehoiakim son of Josiah of Judah, this word came to Jeremiah from the Lord: Take a scroll (*mĕgillat sēper*) and write on it all the words that I have spoken to you against Israel and Judah and all the nations, from the day I spoke to you, from the days of Josiah until today.
>
> Jer 36:27–28: Now, after the king had burned the scroll with the words that Baruch wrote at Jeremiah's dictation, the word of the Lord came to Jeremiah: Take another scroll (*mĕgillâ*) and write on it all the former words that were in the first scroll (…).

Some of these divine commands imply short inscriptions carved on stone (Isa 8:1) or a piece of wood (Ezek 37:16). In these cases, the act of writing, together with the text itself, fulfills a primarily symbolic and magical function rather than that of a prophetic oracle.[30] These texts seem to presuppose that the prophets in question were able to produce texts comprising a few words, and hence "possessing at least basic literacy",[31] but they do not present prophets as producing written prophecies, or even otherwise participating in their creation.

---

30 Cf. R. G. Kratz, "'Siehe ich lege meine Worte in deinen Mund': Die Propheten des Alten Testaments," in *Die Bibel: Entstehung – Botschaft –Wirkung* (ed. R. Feldmeier and H. Spieckermann; Göttingen: Vandenhoeck & Ruprecht, 2004) 24–39 (= id., *Prophetenstudien*, 18–31), quoted from p. 24: "Es handelt sich um eine Symbolhandlung, die Öffentlichkeit herstellt und zugleich magische Bedeutung hat."

31 D. M. Carr, *Writing on the Tablet of the Heart: Origins of Scripture and* Literature (New York: Oxford University Press, 2005), 118.

More to the point are the texts to be inscribed on the tablet and the scroll in Isa 30:8, and on the tablets in Hab 2:2. These texts read like short oracles written down, publicized,[32] and preserved as a testimony for the coming generations. They do not even imply an oral proclamation of the words to be written down; what matters much more is their applicability for reinterpretation by the posterity.[33] The same function is evident in Isa 8:16: "Bind up the testimony (*tĕʿûdâ*), seal the teaching (*tôrâ*) among my disciples"; this is usually interpreted as referring to a small collection of oracles (such as the so-called *Denkschrift* of Isaiah).[34] These three verses have often been interpreted as direct evidence of the prophets Isaiah and Habakkuk taking care of the written documentation of their words. It is important to note, however, that the divine commands to write form part of the literary structure of the oracles themselves, hence it is very difficult to

---

32 The expression "before them" (Isa 30:8) and the reference to the "runner" in Hab 2:2 (actually: "town-crier"; see J. Schaper, "On Writing and Reciting in Jeremiah 36," in *Prophecy in the Book of Jeremiah* [ed. H. M. Barstad and R. G. Kratz; BZAW 388; Berlin: De Gruyter, 2009] 137–47, esp. 143–44) indicate that the texts are meant to be seen or heard by an audience.
33 See M. H. Floyd, "Prophecy and Writing in Habakkuk 2,1–5," *ZAW* 105 (1993) 462–81, esp. 477; W. Zwickel, "Kommunikation und Kommunikationsmöglichkeiten im Alten Israel aufgrund biblischer und ausserbiblischer Texte," in *Bote und Brief: Sprachliche Systeme der Informationsübermittlung im Spannungsfeld von Mündlichkeit und Schriftlichkeit* (ed. A. Wagner; Nordostafrikanisch/Westasiatische Studien 4; Frankfurt a. M.: Peter Lang, 2003) 113–23, esp. 116: "In Jes 30,8; Jer 30,2 (dtr.); Hab 2,2 geht es nicht um eine Niederschrift prophetischen Überlieferung im herkömmlichen Sinne, sondern um ein bewußtes Festhalten als Zeugnis für die Nachwelt. Prophetische Botschaft soll hier um ihrer Überprüfbarkeit willen schriftlich festgehalten werden, nicht um der Wertigkeit als theologischer Text willen. Hinter diesen Texten steht somit schon das dtr. Prophetengesetz Dtn 18,21f." Cf. de Jong, *Isaiah among the Near Eastern Prophets*, 113: "30:8, originally the conclusion of 30:6–8, became a fundamental statement of the necessity of written documentation of the rejected prophetic words, as a part of a literary reworking of the earlier prophetic material [scil. in 30:9–11]". According to R. G. Kratz, "Rewriting Isaiah: The Case of Isaiah 28–31," in *Prophecy and the Prophets in Ancient Israel: Proceedings of the Oxford Old Testament Seminar* (ed. J. Day; LHBOTS 531; New York and London: T & T Clark, 2010) 245–66 (= "Jesaja 28–31 als Fortschreibung," in id., *Prophetenstudien*, 177–97), the command to write in 30:8 corresponds to 8:16 as a part of the *Fortschreibung* of Isaiah 1–12 in Isaiah 28–31.
34 E.g., de Jong, *Isaiah among the Near Eastern Prophets*, 80: "The testimony and teaching (תְּעוּדָה, תּוֹרָה) mentioned in 8:16 are likely to refer to the composition of Isa 6–8 itself". The "testimony and teaching" here is clearly distinct form the text mentioned in 8:1, and it is not indicated who is thought to have actually written the text referred to here. More emphasis is (rightly) given to Isaiah's followers, whether the so-called "disciples" (thus, among many others, Carr, *Writing on the Tablet of the Heart*, 143–45) or the scribes who took care of the formation of the early forms of the book of Isaiah (cf. M. Nissinen, "Das Problem der Prophetenschüler," in J. Pakkala and id. [eds.], *Houses Full of All Good Things*, GS T. Veijola [PFES 95; Helsinki: The Finnish Exegetical Society, 2008] 337–53, esp. 349–51) (= pp. 563–75 in this volume).

know whether they can be read as reports of something that was actually done.[35] At best, they can be read as reflecting a common imagination of what could have taken place in the writers' or readers' real world.

The production of all these texts is presented as imitating a legal procedure: the text is written, read aloud, and notarized in the presence of witnesses and preserved as a binding document and a testimony for the posterity: "As a sealed real estate transaction serves to guarantee proof of title (e.g., Jer 32:9–15), so the written text committed to the prophet's disciples and protected by its seal guarantees the authenticity of the prophecy".[36] Writing, hence, is understood here in the same way as in Jer 32:10 as a part of the legal act, and the text equals to a legally binding document also in that what is written is simultaneously enforced. The identity of the scribe is ancillary to that of the commissioner of the document. In the case of prophetic words, the prophet acts on behalf of the actual divine commissioner of the deed, whether or not he is thought to write it him/herself. The focus is clearly (1) on the written product itself as containing testimony of divine words that transcend the particular moment when they are first uttered (or written); and (2) on the later generations for whom this testimony is meant.

Seen from this perspective, the divine command to write does not need to be understood as literally as the translations suggest, let alone as implying the literacy of the prophets. In fact, the verb *kātab* seems to refer to the whole process of production and authorization of the text, not merely to the physical act of writing.[37] This can be illustrated by the case of Jeremiah's scroll related in Jere-

---

35 This is presupposed by Floyd, "Prophecy and Writing in Habakkuk 2,1–5," 471, who reads Hab 2:1–5 as "the report of an oracular inquiry", that "reflects a complex underlying course of events". It is possible, however, that neither Hab 2:1–5 nor Isa 8:16 and 30:8 are transcriptions of an actual order received by the prophets, but, rather, literary imaginations based on a common practice of textual production; thus de Jong, *Isaiah among the Near Eastern Prophets*, 56, and J. Blenkinsopp, *Isaiah 1–39: A New Translation with Introduction and Commentary* (AB 19; New York: Doubleday, 2000), 415.

36 J. Blenkinsopp, *Opening the Sealed Book: Interpretations of the Book of Isaiah in Late Antiquity* (Grand Rapids, Mich.: Eerdmans, 2006), 13. See also Schaper, "On Writing and Reciting Jeremiah 36," 145; K. Cathcart, "'Law is Paralysed' (Habakkuk 1.4): Habakkuk's Dialogue with God and the Language of Legal Disputation," in Day (ed.), *Prophecy and the Prophets in Ancient Israel*, 339–53.

37 It deserves attention that the verb is never used in Hiph'il in biblical Hebrew, as if there was no need for a causative meaning of the verb. Even in the Dead Sea Scrolls, the Hiph'il form of the verb is attested only once in 4QJub[a] 1:27 (see *DCH* 4:474).

miah 36.[38] God ordered the prophet Jeremiah to take a scroll and write the divine words on it, so "Jeremiah called Baruch son of Neriah, and Baruch wrote on a scroll at Jeremiah's dictation (*mip-pî yirmĕyāhû*) all the words of the Lord that he had spoken to him" (Jer 36:4; cf. 45:1). All this looks a lot like what happened at Mari between Atamrum the prophet of Šamaš, Utu-kam the scribe, Yasim-El the official, and King Zimri-Lim (ARM 26 414).[39] Divine words are mediated by a prophet who commissions a professional scribe; the scribe writes the tablet and takes care of its transportation to the king, but the prophet still appears as its actual author on behalf of the god Šamaš. In both cases, the addressee of the divine message cannot be reached by means of oral communication, hence the prophetic process of communication requires the use of written media as a surrogate for the oral proclamation.

The very act of writing, let alone the individual who is imagined to have physically performed it, is clearly subordinate to the divine actor who is believed to be the actual subject of the message. Still, the person of the prophet is not without significance as the human mediator of the divine word. The Near Eastern texts usually mention the name of the prophet, because there is no divination without the diviner. In the divinatory – or prophetic – process of communication, the identity of the divinely commissioned human mediator must be known in order to be able to become convinced of that the message comes from a reliable

---

38 The recent profusion of literature on Jeremiah 36, highlighting the chapter as documenting and/or reflecting the emergence of prophetic literature from various angles, includes, e.g., J. Ferry, "'Le livre dans le livre': Lecture de Jérémie 36," in Macchi et al. (eds.), *Les recueils prophétiques de la Bible* (2012) 283–306; Schaper, "On Writing and Reciting Jeremiah 36"; M. Leuchter, *The Polemics of Exile in Jeremiah 26–45* (New York: Cambridge University Press, 2008), 82–112; C. Hardmeier, "Zur schriftgestützten Expertentätigkeit Jeremias im Milieu der Jerusalemer Führungseliten (Jeremia 36): Prophetische Literaturbildung und die Neuinterpretation älterer Expertisen in Jeremia 21–23," in *Die Textualisierung der Religion* (ed. J. Schaper; FAT 62; Tübingen: Mohr Siebeck, 2009) 105–49; id., "Schriftgebrauch und Literaturbildung im Milieu der Jerusalemer Führungseliten in spätvorexilischer Zeit (Jeremia 36)," in Kottsieper, Schmitt, and Wöhrle (eds.), *Berührungspunkte*, 267–90; van der Toorn, *Scribal Culture and the Making of the Hebrew Bible*, 184–88; H.-J. Stipp, "Baruchs Erben: Die Schriftprophetie im Spiegel von Jer 36," in *"Wer darf hinaufsteigen zum Berg JHWHs?": Beiträge zu Prophetie und Poesie des Alten Testaments*, FS S. Ö. Steingrímsson (ed. H. Irsigler; Arbeiten zu Text und Sprache im Alten Testament 72; St. Ottilien: EOS-Verlag, 2002) 145–70; H. M. Wahl, "Die Entstehung der Schriftprophetie nach Jer 36," *ZAW* 110 (1998) 365–89.

39 Cf. Schaper, "On Writing and Reciting Jeremiah 36," 141–42, referring to A. Malamat, "New Light from Mari (ARM XXVI) on Biblical Prophecy," in *Storia e tradizioni di Israele*, FS J. A. Soggin (ed. D. Garrone and F. Israel; Brescia: Paideia, 1991) 185–90 (= id., *Mari and the Bible* [SHCANE 12; Leiden: Brill, 1998] 128–33).

source and, in the case of need, to test the trustworthiness of the prophet.[40] The prophets are sometimes bestowed with an individual agency,[41] and a prophet can even be credited with a certain kind of authorship, as in the cases of the prophets Atamrum and Jeremiah.

The scroll of Jeremiah, however, differs from the case of Atamrum in one significant respect. When this scroll had been destroyed by Jehoiakim, God told Jeremiah to take another scroll and write on it. Again, it was Baruch who rewrote the contents of the first scroll: "And many similar words were added (Niph'al: *nôsap*) to them" (Jer 36:32). This signals something that is unheard of elsewhere in ancient Near Eastern sources. Even though Atamrum's letter can be read as a small collection of oracles of Šamaš, and the practice of compiling collections of prophecies is well-known from Assyria, this is the first time we hear of divine words attributed to one and single prophet on a scroll, reedited and supplemented by new material by anonymous scribes.

Evidently, we are witnessing a new development in the history of Near Eastern prophecy: the birth of a prophetic *book*. Depending on how we perceive the textual growth in Jeremiah 36, it is possible that in earlier versions of the story[42] the scope was narrower, focusing on the public reading of the scroll as a substitute to oral delivery rather than to its scribal *Überlieferung*. In its more advanced form available to us, however, Jeremiah 36 presents itself outspokenly as a scribal work, highlighting the agency of Baruch the scribe.[43] Even the whole *book* of Jeremiah, as we know it, refers to itself in 30:2, in 45:1, and especially in 25:13:

> I will bring upon that land all the words that I have uttered against it, everything written in this book, which Jeremiah prophesied (*'et kol-hak-kātûb bas-sēper haz-zê 'ăšer nibbā' yirmĕyāhû*) against all the nations.

---

40 For example, by enclosing the prophet's "hair and fringe" (*šārtum u sissiktum*) in letters reporting the prophets' performances at Mari; see E. J. Hamori, "Gender and the Verification of Prophecy at Mari," *WO* 42 (2012) 1–22.

41 For prophetic agency, see M. Nissinen, "Gender and Prophetic Agency in the Ancient Near East and in Greece," in *Prophets Male and Female: Gender and Prophecy in the Hebrew Bible, the Eastern Mediterranean and the Ancient Near East* (ed. J. Stökl and C. L. Carvalho; Ancient Israel and Its Literature; Atlanta: Society of Biblical Literature, 2013) 27–58.

42 The earliest layer of Jer 36 has been identified in vv. 1–2b, 4–6, 8, 10–30 by Wahl, "Die Entstehung der Schriftprophetie nach Jer 36," 372; in vv. 5–6a, 8a, 14–16, 20–27abα; 28–30 by Stipp, "Baruchs Erben," 157–60; and in vv. 1, 4–5a, 8–14aα; 14b, 15b–16abα; 20–26 by Hardmeier, "Zur schriftgestützten Expertentätigkeit Jeremias," 142–45.

43 So recently Ferry, ""Le livre dans le livre,'" 300–3; Leuchter, *The Polemics of Exile in Jeremiah 26–45*, 101–2.

It is noteworthy that the verb *kātab* is here in passive: the activity of the prophet is not described as writing but as prophesying. Nonetheless, the person of the prophet is not indifferent; on the contrary, it authenticates the prophetic process of communication in which the agency of the prophet is duly acknowledged. Compared to the traditional patterns of prophetic communication, however, the very writtenness of the divine word becomes an unprecedented emphasis. The scroll becomes a medium that not only fulfills the function of keeping records for posterity but also exists as a reference work on its own right, becoming a medium of the divine revelation itself.[44]

Traditionally in the ancient Near East, the written version of a prophetic oracle was understood as a transcript of the original message that existed independently from the written tablet. In Jeremiah, the written product is clearly on its way of claiming the authority of the divine word for itself as the final and definitive account of the divine word. This development goes even further in the book of Ezekiel where the written document is the prerequisite for oral prophecy, not vice versa. This is powerfully illustrated in Ezek 2:9–3:3 where a written scroll is opened in front of the prophet who opens his mouth and God gives him a scroll to eat: "He said to me, Mortal, eat this scroll that I give you and fill your stomach with it. Then I ate it; and in my mouth it was as sweet as honey" (3:3). Here the prophetic process of communication changes at a crucial point; in the words of Joachim Schaper, "God himself is depicted as an author/scribe and as requiring humans to make use of writing in order to further the effectiveness of his own oracles".[45] The prophet and priest Ezekiel may well have been a literate person, but the book of Ezekiel is not interested in his literacy; instead, it presents him as a visionary and proclaimer of a text, in the production of which he himself does not participate. Ezekiel is commissioned by God to speak (3:4), not to write, except for the two above-mentioned cases (24:2; 37:16) where the short inscriptions belong to symbolic-magical actions accompanied by an oral sermon.

Whereas the role of the prophet in the textual production is recognized in the books of Isaiah and Habakkuk and emphasized in the book of Jeremiah, in the book of Ezekiel it fades away in favor of an idealized conception of a di-

44 Cf. H. Najman, "The Symbolic Significance of Writing in Ancient Judaism," in *The Idea of Biblical Interpretation*, FS J. L. Kugel (ed. ead. and J. H. Newman; JSJSup 83; Leiden: Brill, 2004) 139–73, esp. 169; J. Ben-Dov, "Writing as Oracle and as Law: New Contexts for the Book-Find of King Josiah," *JBL* 127 (2008) 223–39, esp. 236.

45 J. Schaper, "Exilic and Post-Exilic Prophecy and the Orality/Literacy Problem," *VT* 55 (2005) 324–42, esp. 333. Cf. E. F. Davis, *Swallowing the Scroll: Textuality and the Dynamics of Discourse in Ezekiel's Prophecy* (JSOTS 78; Sheffield: Almond Press, 1989).

vinely authored text that appears in a written form in the first beginning and serves as the basis of the oral prophetic proclamation.

The prophets Jeremiah and Ezekiel are positioned differently with regard to the written texts; however, both are related to, even though not quite identical with, the Deuteronom(ist)ic concept of the book of Torah (*sēper hat-tôrâ*) and the role of Moses as the prophet who proclaims it. In Deut 31:26–28, the book of Torah appears as a written document, placed next to the ark of the covenant and remaining there as a witness for coming generations:

> Take this book of the law (*sēper hat-tôrâ*) and put it beside the ark of the covenant of the Lord your God; let it remain there as a witness against you. For I know well how rebellious and stubborn you are. If you already have been so rebellious toward the Lord while I am still alive among you, how much more after my death! Assemble to me all the elders of your tribes and your officials, so that I may recite these words in their hearing and call heaven and earth to witness against them.

As a witness for the posterity, the book of Torah is reminiscent of the prophecies mentioned in Isa 30:8 and Hab 2:2.[46] More than these individual prophecies, however, the written text of the Torah is presented a transtemporal focal point of the whole community "created by the shared reading of shared texts and the shared imagination of lasting 'realities' that resulted from this reading."[47] In the Deuteronom(ist)ic imagination, Moses is the model of every true prophet (Deut 18:15–18), and Ezekiel compares to him first and foremost as the proclaimer of a text written by God himself (Exod 32:16; 34:1). According to this ideology, the prophet is a mere proclaimer of Torah without any independent agency or authorship. In the case of Jeremiah, again, the link between Moses and Jeremiah manifests itself in the similar agency of both prophets, even including a role in textual production (cf. Exod 34:27).[48] Both in Ezekiel and in Jeremiah, the text remains the actual site of the divine revelation.

Yet a different idea of the association between prophecy and writing is provided by Chronicles, where the prophets assume an important role as inspired messengers.[49] Chronicles report a significant number of prophetic appearances,

---

46 Cf. Carr, *Writing on the Tablet of the Heart*, 145.

47 E. Ben Zvi, "Imagining Josiah's Book and the Implications of Imagining It in Early Persian Period," in Kottsieper, Schmitt, and Wöhrle (eds.), *Berührungspunkte*, 193–212, esp. 201.

48 See C. R. Seitz, "The Prophet Moses and the Canonical Shape of Jeremiah," *ZAW* 101 (1989) 3–27; cf. Ferry, "Le livre dans le livre," 296–99.

49 Prophets and prophecy in Chronicles has been studied intensively during the recent years; see, e.g., P. C. Beentjes, "Constructs of Prophets and Prophecy in the Book of Chronicles," in Grabbe and Nissinen (eds.), *Constructs of Prophecy in the Former and Latter Prophets and*

most of which are unique to Chronicles and not derived from Samuel–Kings. Many of the Chronicler's prophets are interpreters of historical events involved in text production, notably Elijah who in Chronicles does not perform miracles but sends a letter to King Jehoram (2 Chr 21:12–15), and Jeremiah who "uttered a lament for Josiah" that is said to have been "written in the lamentation" (*kĕtûbîm 'al haq-qînôt* 2 Chr 35:25). It is not indicated whether Elijah and Jeremiah are thought of as having written these texts themselves, but at least in the case of Jeremiah, a reference is made to an existing collection of texts, among which his lamentation can be found.

The Book of Chronicles is written in a world where texts have become important, if not principal, sources of revelation. This is made plain, not only by direct citations and unacknowledged allusions, but also by frequent source references.[50] Many of the Chronicles' source references refer to works of prophets or seers; in most cases, in fact, prophets appear as annalists and record-keepers of the kings of Judah.[51] The most explicit reference is 2 Chr 26:22:

> Now the rest of the acts of Uzziah, from first to last, the prophet Isaiah son of Amoz wrote.

There are six further references to the deeds of the kings written in the records of prophets:

> 1 Chr 29:29: Now the acts of King David, from first to last, are written (*kĕtûbîm*) in the records of (*'al dibrê*) the seer Samuel, and in the records of the prophet Nathan, and in the records of the seer Gad.

Other Texts, 21–40; L. Jonker, "The Chronicler and the Prophets: Who Were His Authoritative Sources?," in *What Was Authoritative for Chronicles?* (ed. E. Ben Zvi and D. Edelman; Winona Lake, Ind.: Eisenbrauns, 2011) 145–64; A. K. Warhurst, "The Chronicler's Use of the Prophets," ibid., 165–81; G. N. Knoppers, "Democratizing Revelation? Prophets, Seers and Visionaries in Chronicles," in Day (ed.), *Prophecy and the Prophets in Ancient Israel*, 391–409; Y. Amit, "The Role of Prophets and Prophecy in the Chronicler's World," in Floyd and Haak (eds.), *Prophets, Prophecy and Prophetic Texts in the Second Temple Period*, 80–101; W. M. Schniedewind, *The Word of God in Transition: From Prophet to Exegete in the Second Temple Period* (JSOTS 197; Sheffield: Sheffield Academic Press, 1995); J. Kegler, "Prophetengestalten im Deuteronomistischen Geschichtswerk und in den Chronikbüchern: Ein Beitrag zur Kompositions- und Redaktionsgeschichte der Chronikbüchern," *ZAW* 105 (1993) 481–97.

50 See, e.g., S. J. Schweitzer, "Judging a Book by Its Citations: Sources and Authority in Chronicles," in Ben Zvi and Edelman (eds.), *What Was Authoritative for Chronicles?* (2001) 37–75.

51 See Schniedewind, *The Word of God in Transition*, 213–30; Beentjes, "Constructs of Prophets and Prophecy in the Book of Chronicles," 37–38.

2 Chr 9:29: Now the rest of the acts of Solomon, from first to last, are they not written in the history of the prophet Nathan, and in the prophecy (*nĕbûʾâ*) of Ahijah the Shilonite, and in the visions (*ḥăzôt*) of the seer Iddo concerning Jeroboam son of Nebat?

2 Chr 12:15: Now the acts of Rehoboam, from first to last, are they not written in the records of the prophet Shemaiah and of the seer Iddo, recorded by genealogy?

2 Chr 13:22: The rest of the acts of Abijah, his behavior and his deeds, are written in the story (*midrāš*) of the prophet Iddo.

2 Chr 32:32: Now the rest of the acts of Hezekiah, and his good deeds, are written in the vision of the prophet Isaiah son of Amoz in the Book of the Kings of Judah and Israel.

2 Chr 33:19: His [Manasseh's] prayer, and how God received his entreaty, all his sin and his faithlessness, the sites on which he built high places and set up the sacred poles and the images, before he humbled himself, these are written in the records of the seers.

Some of these prophets are familiar from Samuel–Kings, but none of these prophets, except for Isaiah who also features in Kings, belong to the "classical" or "writing" prophets of the Hebrew Bible, and the prophetic books known to us – probably apart of some form of Jeremiah[52] – seem not have served as sources of the Chronicles. Nonetheless, it deserves attention that the writings of the prophets are equated with "prophecy" (*nĕbûʾâ*) and "visions" (*ḥăzôt*) in 2 Chr 9:29, hence giving them an inspired status. The world of the Chronicles is emphatically text-centered, and the book "communicates and embodies Torah, without claiming to be Torah",[53] hence presupposing the Deuteronom(ist)ic idea of the Book of Torah as the center of the community. Moreover, in Chronicles, unlike the Deuteronomistic literature, there is a strong connection between the documentation and inspired interpretation of the past, which appears as a specifically prophetic task.[54] Divination, again unlike Samuel–Kings, plays no role in Chronicles, since it seems that "the unfolding of history is itself the omen"[55] to be interpreted.

But does Chronicles assume that the prophets actually wrote their records themselves, especially if we understand the verb *kātab* to refer to the textual production at large and not just the act of writing? According to Gary Knoppers, the

52 See Jonker, "The Chronicler and the Prophets: Who Were His Authoritative Sources?," and Warhurst, "The Chronicler's Use of the Prophets."

53 E. Ben Zvi, "One Size Does Not Fit All: Observations on the Different Ways that Chronicles Dealt with the Authoritative Literature of Its Time," in Ben Zvi and Edelman (eds.), *What Was Authoritative for Chronicles?*, 13–35, esp. 27. Cf. Jonker, "The Chronicler and the Prophets"; E. S. Gerstenberger, "Prophetie in den Chronikbüchern: Jahwes Wort in zweierlei Gestalt," in *Schriftprophetie*, FS J. Jeremias (ed. F. Hartenstein et al.; Neukirchen-Vluyn: Neukirchener Verlag, 2004) 351–67.

54 Cf. Knoppers, "Democratizing Revelation?," 402.

55 Amit, "The Role of Prophets and Prophecy in the Chronicler's World," 90.

prophets "appear as literati, scribes who take a consistent interest in writing about the times in which they lived".[56] This statement is justified in the world of Chronicles which is a text-centered world of literati,[57] and it is not difficult to imagine the authors of Chronicles to create the prophets in their own image. In the Chronicler's source refererences, the prophets truly appear as authors of the inspired interpretation of the past, hence the prophets in Chronicles can be seen as belonging to the class of "writing prophets" – but they do not write prophetic books; instead, they write the past.

One text that does not exactly fit any of the above-discussed patterns remains to be discussed: Jer 51:59 – 64. Here Jeremiah is said to have written a scroll containing prophecies against Babylon, in order to be read publicly by Seraiah the quartermaster and then thrown in the Euphrates. This text presents the prophet Jeremiah as writing a scroll – apparently by himself – and commissioning an official to act in Babylon according to his instructions. The text gives the prophet an agency and authority unheard of in the previously discussed texts. It shares features with Jeremiah 36 and may be dependent on it,[58] but in 51:59 – 64 Jeremiah is not commissioned by God, neither does he need any help in writing the scroll. If the text corresponds to 50:1, then the scroll is probably thought of as containing the words God spoke against Babylon "by (*bĕ-yad*) (MT: the prophet) Jeremiah" in chapters 50 – 51. These words, unlike Jeremiah 36, are not designed to be rewritten, nothing is added to them, and they are not meant to be preserved for posterity; instead, they are used as a sign portenting the destruction of Babylon. The magical and symbolic function of the text written by Jeremiah connects it with the short inscriptions in Isa 8:1 and Ezek 37:16, only this time we have to do with a large scroll containing "all" the words concerning Babylon. The ominous nature of the text, together with the image of Jeremiah as a scribe capable of authoring such a scroll, again, bear a certain resemblance to the image of the prophets in Chronicles, the scribes writing the ominous past.

---

56 G. N. Knoppers, *1 Chronicles 10 – 29: A New Translation with Introduction and Commentary* (AB 12A; New York: Doubleday, 2004), esp. 958.

57 Cf. Ben Zvi, "One Size Does Not Fit All," and id., "Observations on Josiah's Account in Chronicles and Implications for Reconstructing the Worldview of the Chronicler," in *Essays on Ancient Israel in Its Near Eastern Context*, FS N. Na'aman (ed. Y. Amit, E. Ben Zvi, I. Finkelstein, and O. Lipschits; Winona Lake, Ind.: Eisenbrauns, 2006) 89 – 106.

58 Thus, e.g., R. P. Carroll, *The Book of Jeremiah: A Commentary* (OTL; London: SCM, 1986), espp. 856.; B. Gosse, "La malédiction contre Babylone de Jérémie 51,59 – 64 et les redactions du livre de Jérémie," *ZAW* 98 (1986) 383 – 99. According to Gosse, Jer 51:59 – 64 (LXX: 28:59 – 64) is also inspired by Jer 25:1 – 13 which in the LXX is the first oracle against nations.

Conclusion

Since when do prophets write in the ancient Near Eastern sources available to us, including the Hebrew Bible? If the question refers to the act of writing according to the traditional "writing prophets" model, the answer is: probably not before Chronicles and Jer 51:60, whatever their chronological order.[59]

The ancient Near Eastern and biblical sources do connect prophets with writing, and the prophetic agency sometimes implies a role in text production, hence the sources presuppose a connection between prophetic and scribal activities.[60] It is evident that the prophetic process of communication sometimes included written media. However, texts other than Chronicles and, perhaps, Jer 51:60 do not seem to presuppose prophets to represent but a basic literacy, if any. In theory, it would be entirely possible that persons with scribal education could sometimes act as prophets, but this is neither reported nor presupposed by our sources.[61]

In the non-biblical Near Eastern sources, no single prophet can be found writing a text, probably because prophets seem not to have belonged to people of whom literacy was expected. In the Hebrew Bible, prophets do appear a few times as subjects of the verb *kātab* (1 Sam 10:25; Jer 32:10; 51:60; 2 Chr 26:22; Dan 7:1), of which only Jer 51:60 and 2 Chr 26:22 can be seen as implying the idea of a prophet writing a text. The cases where the prophets are explicitly told to *kātab* by God (Isa 8:1; 30:8; Jer 30:2; 36:2, 28; Ezek 24:2; 37:15–16; Hab 2:2) mostly belong to the very wording of the oracle and, hence, to the virtual rather than the factual world. The act of writing is not described except for the case of Jeremiah 36 where the command is fulfilled by employing Baruch the scribe to accomplish the actual writing.

---

59 In fact, I have not put much effort into dating the texts discussed above; it is not impossible that some of them actually postdate Chronicles.

60 Floyd, "The Production of Prophetic Books," 142: "Various types of prophetic activity might entail direct use of writing, whether in a nonacademic setting like the cult or in the context of a scribal school. And conversely, various types of scribal activity, whether in or out of an academic context, could be prophetic in the sense that documents were written and studied in order to discern divine involvement in contemporary human affairs."

61 K. van der Toorn leaves the door open for the possibility that Jeremiah was actually capable of writing; however, "Jeremiah was a spiritual leader, an advisor to the king, a priest whose intercessory prayer was credited with special efficacy – but he was no literary author" ("From the Mouth of the Prophet: The Literary Fixation of Jeremiah's Prophecies in the Context of the Ancient Near East," in *Inspired Speech: Prophecy in the Ancient Near East*, FS H. B. Huffmon [ed. J. Kaltner and L. Stulman; JSOTSup 378; London and New York: T & T Clark, 2004] 191–202, esp. 201).

Indeed, the question arises whether the verb *kātab* should be understood as denoting the whole process of textual production with several individuals participating in it. If "writing" is understood in this broader meaning, there is more evidence of prophets involved in the scribal continuation of the prophetic process of communication; this evidence includes at least the letters of Yasim-El from Mari (ARM 26 414) and the Lachish ostracon nr. 3. Biblical passages such as Isa 8:1; 8:16; 30:8 and Hab 2:2, reflect a procedure that imitates a legal act of writing and notarizing a document in the presence of witnesses, perhaps also reading it out before the public. Prophetic literacy is not an issue here; what matters more is the role of the prophet as a prophet, that is, the intermediary of divine words. All this is makes sense against the Near Eastern scribal practices that sometimes may have accompanied prophetic performances.

The book of Jeremiah goes further in presenting itself as an edited oracle collection on its own right, as "licensed outgrowths of Jeremiah's work".[62] The self-references in Jeremiah presuppose the emergence of a new type of divinatory text, a prophetic book, which marks the transition from written to literary prophecy and, implicitly, highlights the role of scribes in the *Fortschreibung* of prophetic words. The prophet is credited an authorship that surpasses the commissioner-type of agency ascribed to Isaiah or Habakkuk; however, as the role of Baruch the scribe clearly demonstrates, this in no way highlights the literacy of the prophet but, rather, the agency of the scribes in the prophetic process of communication. From now on, the class of literati has assumed the prophetic role, which, in fact, eclipses the issue of the literacy of the prophet.

In the book of Ezekiel, the prophet is deprived of authorship altogether by making him the recipient of the divinely written scroll. Here the prophetic process of communication takes a new, scribal turn whereby the agency of the prophet with regard to writing is understood in a way different from the Near Eastern sources, and also from Jeremiah: the text itself becomes an authority related to the authority of the Torah. In Chronicles, finally, the scribalization of prophecy has reached the point where visions and prophecies are referred to as scribal products, and prophets have become their authors. These books are presented as inspired historywriting, interpreting the omen constituted by the past itself.

62 Leuchter, *The Polemics of Exile*, 107.

Prophets and Prophecy in Joshua–Kings: A Near Eastern Perspective

Prophecy is one of the major literary ingredients of the multilayered narrative in the so-called Deuteronomistic History. Whether the result of a specific redaction (DtrP)[1] or continuing textual growth, stories of prophets span over large textual entities and play a crucial ideological role in the overall design of the work. The significant role given to prophets in the historical narrative raises the question of the relation of the narrative to the historical phenomenon of prophecy and the familiarity of its writers[2] with it. Fictitious as the stories on prophets probably are for the most part, they nevertheless represent the storytellers' imaginative understanding of prophets and prophecy. These imaginative portrayals are likely to be based on the storytellers' knowledge, experience, and appreciation of prophetic activities in their own socioreligious environment.

It is neither my aim to test the historical veracity or accuracy of the image of prophecy in Joshua-Kings, nor to develop a theory of interdependencies between the texts and their editorial history. The purpose of this essay is rather to view the portrayal of prophets and prophecy in Joshua-Kings against the background of the Near Eastern prophetic phenomenon as represented by the available sources, paying attention to commonalities as well as discrepancies between the constructs of prophecy in these different source materials. I will conclude that the biblical narrators, to all appearances, were familiar with the prophetic phenomenon as an ancient tradition not essentially different from that reflected by Near Eastern prophetic sources. However, constructs of prophecy in Joshua–Kings, postdating the destruction of Jerusalem, belong to a very different textual and ideological context. This necessarily causes the biblical portrayal of prophets to diverge from Near Eastern constructs as well.

1 Thus the classic work of W. Dietrich, *Prophetie und Geschichte* (FRLANT 108; Göttingen: Vandenhoeck & Ruprecht, 1972).

2 The complex literary history of Joshua–Kings, or the Deuteronomistic History, has been amply demonstrated; however, it is not my purpose in this essay to adhere to any specific theory concerning its emergence; hence, I am consistently referring to its "writers" assuming that they are many.

DOI 10.1515/9783110466546-028

Prophecy and Divination

In the ancient Near East, prophecy was one of several methods of acquiring divine knowledge and becoming conversant with the will of the gods. Prophecy was probably never the foremost method of divination, but certainly one that at times enjoyed high appreciation by Near Eastern kings. Zimri-Lim of Mari maintained a regular correspondence with diviners, including receiving reports on prophecies addressed to him in different cities,[3] and the same is true for Kings Esarhaddon and Assurbanipal of Assyria,[4] who in their inscriptions juxtapose prophetic oracles (*šipir maḫḫê*) with other kinds of omens.[5]

In the ancient Near Eastern sources, prophecy is much less represented than, say, extispicy or astrology, but in Joshua–Kings, the significance of prophecy clearly exceeds that of other divinatory techniques. This may be explained by the compliance of the writers to the general ban of divination as expressed in Deut 18:9–14, where anyone "who practises divination, or is a soothsayer, or an augur, or a sorcerer, or one who casts spells, or who consults ghosts or spirits, or who seeks oracles from the dead"[6] is declared as abhorrent to YHWH, God of Israel, and the only diviner to be listened to is a prophet like Moses. King Manasseh of Judah is condemned because of allowing such divinatory practices (2 Kgs 21:6), perhaps referring to Mesopotamian kind of methods of divination employed in Jerusalem.

In spite of such a categorical prohibition, however, divination is not absent from Joshua–Kings. On the contrary, it is reported many times without the slightest hesitation, and asking (*drš*) direction from YHWH—in other words, divination—is something the people are expected to do.[7] Joshua, for example, uses lot-casting, not only to find out who had confiscated the *ḥerem* and caused the defeat at

3 J.-M. Durand, *Archives épistolaires de Mari 1/1* (ARM 26/1; Paris: Éditions Recherche sur les Civilisations, 1988); D. Charpin, F. Joannès, S. Lackenbacher, and B. Lafont (eds.), *Archives épistolaires de Mari 1/2* (ARM 26/2; Paris: Éditions Recherche sur les Civilisations, 1988).

4 H. Hunger, *Astrological Reports to Assyrian Kings* (SAA 8; Helsinki: Helsinki University Press, 1992); S. Parpola, *Assyrian Prophecies* (SAA 9; Helsinki: Helsinki University Press, 1997); id., *Letters from Assyrian and Babylonian Scholars* (SAA 10; Helsinki: Helsinki University Press, 1993).

5 Esarhaddon Nin. A ii 3–11; Ass. A ii 12–26; Assurbanipal Prism T ii 7–24; see M. Nissinen, with Contributions by C.-L. Seow, R. K. Ritner, and H. C. Melchert, *Prophets and Prophecy in the Ancient Near East* (2nd edition; SBLWAW 41; Atlanta: Society of Biblical Literature, 2019), nos. 97, 98, and 99. This work is henceforth referred to as SBLWAW 41 in this essay.

6 No translation will do justice to the Hebrew terminology, and the exact point of reference of each diviner listed here is conjectural.

7 See Rannfrid L. Thelle, *Ask God: Divine Consultation in the Literature of the Hebrew Bible* (BBET 30; Frankfurt a. M.: Peter Lang, 2002).

the city of Ai (Josh 7:14–18), but even to divide the promised land to the Israelite tribes and to allot towns to the Levites (Josh 13–21). Gideon ventures to attack the Midianites on the basis of dream interpretation (Judg 7:13–15), and Saul, the first king of the Israelites, is recognized by Samuel by means of lot-casting (1 Sam 10:20–21). The oracle device called ephod appears in somewhat suspicious light when mentioned together with idols of cast metal and the teraphim in Micah's sanctuary (Judg 17:5; 18:11–20), but David's use of it is reported with approval:[8]

> When David learned that Saul was plotting evil against him, he said to the priest Abiathar, "Bring the ephod here." David said, "O Lord, the God of Israel, your servant has heard that Saul seeks to come to Keilah, to destroy the city on my account. And now, will Saul come down as your servant has heard? O Lord, the God of Israel, I beseech you, tell your servant." The LORD said, "He will come down." Then David said, "Will the men of Keilah surrender me and my men into the hand of Saul?" The LORD said, "They will surrender you" (1 Sam 23:9–12; cf. 30:7–8).[9]

Likewise, urim and thummin appear as a legitimate means to find out why YHWH does not answer his inquiry concerning his attempted attack against the Philistines (1 Sam 14:41–42).

Technical methods of divination, such as the ephod or the urim and thummin, are used to answer a binary question that can only be replied "yes" or "no" and, obviously, always require an act of solicitation. Even prophecy is often actively sought for in Samuel-Kings by Judahite and Israelite kings (and even by Ben-Hadad of Damascus, 2 Kgs 8:7–15). Saul, facing the Philistine troops in Gilboa, resorts to the necromancer in En-Dor, but only after having failed to receive an answer from YHWH by means of dreams, urim, and prophets (1 Sam 28:6). Prophecy, hence, is unmistakably understood as another technique of consulting God.[10] There are also cases where an unprovoked divine revelation is confirmed by another divinatory act, using a different method, such as the election of Saul that is first revealed to Samuel by the direct word of God (1 Sam 9:15–17) and

8 See T. Veijola, "David in Keïla: Tradition und Interpretation in 1 Sam 23, 1–13," *RB* 91 (1984) 51–87 (= id., *David: Gesammelte Studien zur Davidüberlieferungen des Alten Testaments* [PFES 52; Helsinki: Finnish Exegetical Society, 1990]). Veijola finds David's oracle consultation possibly "einen der wenigen Züge, die uns von der Religion des historischen David erhalten sind."

9 Henceforth, all biblical quotations in English are according to the NRSV.

10 See E. J. Hamori, "The Prophet and the Necromancer: Women's Divination for Kings," *JBL* 132 (2013) 827–43.

subsequently confirmed by lot-casting (1 Sam 10:20–24).[11] The practice of mantic confirmation is well-known from Near Eastern sources[12] and is also used in order to verify prophetic oracles, especially at Mari, where the prophet's "hair and hem" (*šārtum u sissiktum*) were often taken to cross-check the prophecy through another method of divination, probably extispicy.[13]

Sometimes the consultation of God is based on questions and answers, which resemble technical inquiries, but the answer is not necessarily of the binary type:

> After this David inquired of the Lord, "Shall I go up into any of the cities of Judah?" The Lord said to him, "Go up." David said, "To which shall I go up?" He said, "To Hebron." (2 Sam 2:1)
>
> David inquired of the Lord, "Shall I go up against the Philistines? Will you give them into my hand?" The Lord said to David, "Go up; for I will certainly give the Philistines into your hand." ... When David inquired of the Lord, he said, "You shall not go up; go around to their rear, and come upon them opposite the balsam trees. When you hear the sound of marching in the tops of the balsam trees, then be on the alert; for then the LORD has gone out before you to strike down the army of the Philistines." (2 Sam 5:19, 23)

In both cases the first question allows an answer of the binary type ("Shall I go up?"—"Go up!"/"Do not go up!"), but the second one cannot be answered with a simple "yes" or "no." The method of the inquiry is not revealed to the reader and seems to be indifferent from the point of view of the writer, who either did not care or did not know how technical divination works. The quasi-realistic question-answer pattern is turned into a literary conversation between King Ahab and the anonymous prophet with a special foresight in 1 Kgs 20:13–14:

> Then a certain prophet (*nābîʾ ʾeḥad*) came up to King Ahab of Israel and said, "Thus says the Lord, Have you seen all this great multitude? Look, I will give it into your hand today; and you shall know that I am the Lord." Ahab said, "By whom?" He said, "Thus says the Lord, By the young men who serve the district governors." Then he said, "Who shall begin the battle?" He answered, "You."

---

11 See J. L. Cooley, "The Story of Saul's Election (1 Samuel 9–10) in the Light of Mantic Practice in Ancient Iraq," *JBL* 130 (2011) 247–61. Cooley does not deny that the acts of election in 1 Sam 9–10 may derive from different traditions, but takes it for granted that "an editor chose to weave these traditions together to make what he believed to be a single logical narrative" (249).
12 Ibid., 250–56.
13 See, e.g., J.-M. Durand, "Mari," in *Mythologie et religion des sémites occidentaux*, 2 vols. (ed. G. del Olmo Lete; OLA 162; Leuven: Peeters, 2008) 1:163–631, esp. 514–518; E. J. Hamori, "Gender and the Verification of Prophecy at Mari," *WO* 42 (2012) 1–22.

In the case of the joint attempt of Jehoshaphat of Judah and Ahab of Israel, the question to the four hundred prophets whom the kings are consulting (*drš*), and eventually to Micaiah ben Imlah, is formulated exactly the same way as inquiries addressed to a technical oracle, for instance: "Shall I go to battle against Ramoth-gilead, or shall I refrain?" resulting in the yes-answer: "Go up; for YHWH will give it into the hand of the king" (1 Kgs 22:6, 15). This could suggest that the *nĕbîʾîm* consulted by Jehoshaphat and Ahab are, in fact, to be seen as technical diviners, but this is difficult to reconcile with the prophets "prophesying" (*mitnabbĕʾîm*) by symbolic gestures and shouting, which points toward ecstatic behavior (1 Kgs 22:10–12). The result, hence, is an interesting mixture of features of technical and non-technical divination difficult to find in Near Eastern sources of prophecy,[14] but more common in Greek sources. For instance the Delphic Pythia, known for her hexametric oracles, is also associated with lot-casting[15] and the inquiries addressed to the women prophets of Dodona are formulated in a strictly binary manner.[16] Indeed, Micaiah's assertion, "whatever the Lord says to me, that I will speak" (1 Kgs 22:14), is almost verbatim the same as that of the Pythia in Aeschylus' *Eumenides:* "For as the god doth lead, so do I prophesy."[17]

The fluidity of the boundary between prophecy and technical divination in the narrative world of Joshua–Kings may indicate that even in the writers' real world, the socioreligious boundary of technical/non-technical divination was somewhat less strict than it was at Mari or in Assyria. What may have mattered

---

14 The activity of the group of *nabûs* of the Haneans in ARM 26 216 (SBLWAW 41 26) may actually refer to technical divination; this is suggested by the form of the question posed to them: "Will my lord, when performing [his] ablution rite and [st]aying seven days ou[tside the city walls], [return] safe[ly to the ci]ty [...]?"

15 E.g., Plutarch, *Moralia* 492b; see S. I. Johnston, *Ancient Greek Divination* (Blackwell Ancient Religions; Chichester: Wiley-Blackwell, 2008), esp. 52–55.

16 For the Dodona oracle, see E. Eidinow, *Oracles, Curses, and Risk among the Ancient Greeks* (Oxford: Oxford University Press, 2007). According to Kallisthenes, an oracle was given to the ambassadors of the Spartans by collecting lots in a pot and letting the prophetess make the choice (*FGrH* 124 F 222a and b; the story of Kallisthenes is quoted by Cicero, *De divinatione* 1.34.76 and 2.32.69).

17 Aeschylus, *Eum.* 29–33. The prophecy of Micaiah has also been compared with the oracle of the Pythia to Croesus, king of Lydia (Herodotus 1.46–49) by W. Oswald ("Ahab als Krösus: Anmerkungen zu 1 Kön 22," *ZTK* 105 [2008] 1–14). Oswald concluded, "Beide, Ahab und Krösus, erhalten je ein zweideutiges Orakel, das sie jeweils in ihrem Sinne interpretieren, dessen tatsächlicher Sinn aber eine Unheilsankündigung ist. In beiden Fällen ist es im Übrigen so, dass die Interpretation der Könige ohne Zweifel die nächstliegende ist. Krösus' Annahme, das Orakel müsse das Reich des Kyros meinen, ist ebenso verständlich wie die des Ahab, dass Jhwh ihm Ramot-Gilead in die Hand geben werde" (8–9).

more was the distinction of accepted and prohibited kinds of divination; lot-casting is practised by the narrative characters without hesitation, but astrology and extispicy are never employed in Joshua-Kings and necromancy (1 Samuel 28) appears in a dubious light— even though it eventually works!

The writers of Joshua–Kings appear perfectly on a par with their Near Eastern colleagues in understanding the role of prophecy, as divination in general, as a normal way of acquiring the *Herrschaftswissen* necessary for the kings (or their predecessors) to have their (quasi-)royal functions fulfilled.[18] Prophecy is used as another method of divination, and it is practised especially in connection with kings. However, unlike the Near Eastern sources, the prophets in Joshua–Kings occupy more prominent seats than other diviners.

It is noteworthy that, apart from Deborah in Judg 4:4 and the anonymous prophet in Judg 6:8–10,[19] prophets do not feature at all in the premonarchical settings of Joshua–Judges. Joshua receives divine words akin to prophecies addressed to kings, but this always happens without the mediation of prophets: "Be strong and courageous; do not be frightened or dismayed, for the Lord your God is with you wherever you go" (Josh 1:9, cf. 10:8). Prophets become significant actors only when monarchy is introduced: Samuel, the first king-maker, is not only the last judge but also marks the rise of prophecy as the preferred method of divination in Samuel–Kings. The first kings still keep utilizing divinatory methods, Saul turning to a necromancer (1 Sam 28) and David using the ephod (1 Sam 23:9–12; 30:7–8; cf. 2 Sam 2:1; 5:19, 23), but after them, explicit references to diviners other than prophets become rare. Ahaziah's turning to Baalzebub, the god of Ekron, sounds like a technical inquiry, but it is condemned by the prophecy of Elijah and eventually becomes the reason of Ahaziah's death— not because of the divinatory method, however, but because of turning to a wrong god, "as if there was no God in Israel" (2 Kgs 1).

Prophets and Kings

Prophecy appears in Joshua–Kings predominantly in a royal setting. The divine word is almost without exception addressed to men who already are kings or to whom kingship is promised. The only prophets in Joshua–Kings who do *not* communicate with kings belong to premonarchical contexts: Deborah in Judg 4:4, the

---

18 See B. Pongratz-Leisten, *Herrschaftswissen in Mesopotamien: Formen der Kommunikation zwischen Gott und König im 2. und 1. Jahrtausend v. Chr.* (SAAS 10; Helsinki: The Neo-Assyrian Text Corpus Project, 1999).

19 Cf. Judg 13:6, where the "man of God" is actually an angel.

anonymous prophet speaking to the Israelites in Judg 6:7–10, and the man of God addressing Eli in 1 Sam 2:27–36—even the old prophet from Bethel in 1 Kgs 13:11–32 is indirectly connected with Jeroboam through the man of God's prediction of the destruction of the altar in Bethel. The royal association of prophecy in the narrative world of Joshua–Kings, and probably also in the mental map of the writers of the texts, is reinforced by the absence of prophets in the book of Joshua and their rarity in Judges.

The royal focus of prophecy in Joshua–Kings is perfectly in line with other ancient Near Eastern documents, whether from Mari or from Assyria, in which prophecy mostly fulfills the function of *Herrschaftswissen* and the divine messages transmitted by prophets are almost always addressed to kings or members of the royal family. Unlike Greek texts, in which oracle sites are visited by kings and private individuals alike,[20] the Near Eastern documents are virtually silent about non-royal individuals being addressed by prophets.[21] One might wonder to what extent this corresponds with historical reality; even sparse hints are enough to suggest that prophecy, among other divinatory means, was perceived of as available even to nonroyal persons, as implied by 1 Sam 9:9: "Formerly in Israel, anyone who went to inquire of God would say, 'Come, let us go to the seer.'" In the textual world of the preserved documents from the ancient Near East, however, prophecy is inextricably linked with kingship and royal ideology—and the same holds true for Joshua–Kings, even though the connection between prophecy and ideology is rather more intricate in the Hebrew Bible, thanks to its complicated literary history.

It is most intriguing to find some basic features of ancient Near Eastern royal ideology expressed by David in his "last words" in 2 Sam 23:1–7. The late origin of this text reveals itself in the very fact that the words are designated as an oracle (*nĕʾum*) of David who himself is presented as a prophet through whom the spirit of God speaks (v. 2); this marks the beginning of the prophetic career of David to be continued in later texts, such as the Dead Sea Scrolls,[22] the New Testament (Acts 2:30), and even in the Qur'an.[23] Otherwise, the image emerging from

20 See M. A. Flower, *The Seer in Ancient Greece* (Berkeley, Calif.: University of California Press, 2008).

21 The few exceptions include the scholar Urad-Gula (SAA 10 284 = SBLWAW 41 108) and the recipient of the Lachish Ostracon 3, possibly the official Tobiah (Lak[6]:1.3 = SBLWAW 41 139).

22 See P. W. Flint, "The Prophet David at Qumran," in *Biblical Interpretation at Qumran* (ed. M. Henze; SDSRL; Grand Rapids, Mich.: Eerdmans, 2005) 158–67.

23 See P. M. Wright, "The Qur'anic David," in *Constructs of Prophecy in the Former and Latter Prophets and Other Texts* (ed. L. L. Grabbe and M. Nissinen; ANEM 4; Atlanta, Ga.: Society of Biblical Literature, 2011) 197–206.

the poem of the king "who rules over people justly, ruling in the fear of God" (v. 3), with whom God has made "an everlasting covenant, ordered in all things and secure" (v. 5), and whose godless adversaries "are all like thorns that are thrown away" (v. 6), matches exactly with the image of the ideal Near Eastern king who rules justly, has an exclusive relationship with the divine world, and tramples his enemies underfoot.

Ancient Near Eastern royal prophecies typically consist of divine expressions of support, instruction, warning, and indictment/judgment, but the distribution of these aspects varies according to source materials. It is easy to observe that in the extant prophetic oracles from Assyria, the divine support for the king is the actual *cantus firmus*, while the prophecies quoted in the letters form Mari give more expression to warning,[24] instruction,[25] and indictment/judgment.[26] This does not warrant the conclusion that the other aspects were absent from Assyrian prophecy, since there are traces of them even in the Assyrian sources;[27] it is rather the accident of discovery and preservation that causes the differences between the source materials in this respect.

Prophetic support, instruction, warning, and indictment/judgment can be found in Joshua–Kings as well, again in different proportions. A couple of times the judgment relates to an individual king whose recovery from accident or illness is denied: Ahaziah is condemned to death because he had inquired a wrong god (2 Kgs 1) and Elisha's prophecy concerning the death of Ben-Hadad, the sick king of Damascus, comes true by the hand of his follower, Hazael (2 Kgs 8:7–15).

---

24 E.g., ARM 26 195 (= SBLWAW 41 5); ARM 26 197 (= SBLWAW 41 7); ARM 26 199 (= SBLWAW 41 9); ARM 26 202 (= SBLWAW 41 12); ARM 26 213 (= SBLWAW 41 23); ARM 26 216 (= SBLWAW 41 26); ARM 26 238 (= SBLWAW 41 43).

25 E.g., FM 7 39 (= SBLWAW 41 1); FM 7 38 (= SBLWAW 41 2); ARM 26 194 (= SBLWAW 41 4); ARM 26 199 (= SBLWAW 41 9); ARM 26 204 (= SBLWAW 41 14); ARM 26 205 (= SBLWAW 41 15); ARM 26 195 (= SBLWAW 41 5); ARM 26 206 (= SBLWAW 41 16); ARM 26 215 (= SBLWAW 41 25); ARM 26 217 (= SBLWAW 41 27); ARM 26 220 (= SBLWAW 41 30); ARM 26 221 (= SBLWAW 41 31); ARM 26 221bis (= SBLWAW 41 32); ARM 26 234 (= SBLWAW 41 39).

26 E.g., FM 7 39 (= SBLWAW 41 1); ARM 26 198 (= SBLWAW 41 8); ARM 26 206 (= SBLWAW 41 16); ARM 26 215 (= SBLWAW 41 25); ARM 26 217 (= SBLWAW 41 27); ARM 26 219 (= SBLWAW 41 29); ARM 26 221bis (= SBLWAW 41 32); ARM 26 233 (= SBLWAW 41 38). See the table in J. H. Walton, *Ancient Near Eastern Thought and the Old Testament: Introducing the Conceptual World of the Hebrew Bible* (Grand Rapids, Mich.: Baker Academic, 2006), 245–47.

27 See M. Nissinen, "Das kritische Potential der altorientalischen Prophetic," in *Propheten in Mari, Assyrien und Israel* (ed. M. Köckert and M. Nissinen; FRLANT 201; Göttingen: Vandenhoeck & Ruprecht, 2003) 1–32, esp. 10–14 (= pp. 163–94 in this volume).

It has often been noted that the most significant dissimilarity between biblical and Near Eastern prophecy is the categorical judgment of the prophets of their own king or people in the Hebrew Bible, a feature that may be due to historical circumstances but also to literary developments. This holds true even for Joshua–Kings, where the divine judgment more often than not concerns the offspring of the king. In the extant Near Eastern documents, a divine word predicting the end of the royal dynasty is extremely rare but not totally unheard of. For example, as reported to Esarhaddon concerning a prophecy in Harran, the god Nusku proclaimed that the name and seed of Sennacherib will be destroyed (SAA 16 59).[28] In the Hebrew Bible, the *locus classicus* of such a reversal of a dynastic promise is the prediction of the annihilation of the eradication of the progeny of Jerobeam I by the prophet Ahijah the Shilonite (1 Kgs 14:10 – 11, 14):

> I will bring evil upon the house of Jeroboam. I will cut off from Jeroboam every male, both bond and free, in Israel and will consume the house of Jeroboam, just as one burns up dung until it is all gone. Anyone belonging to Jeroboam who dies in the city, the dogs shall eat; and anyone who dies in the open country, the birds of the air shall eat; for the Lord has spoken. ... Moreover, the Lord will raise up for himself a king over Israel, who shall cut off the house of Jeroboam today, even now!

This prophecy reverses diametrically the dynastic promise pronounced by the prophet Ahijah to Jeroboam, according to which God would build him an enduring house, as he did for David (1 Kgs 11:37 – 39). The prophecy eventually comes true when Baasha kills Jeroboam's son Nadab and becomes king of Israel; according to 2 Kgs 15:29, Baasha "left to the house of Jeroboam not one that breathed, until he had destroyed it, according to the word of the Lord that he spoke by his servant Ahijah the Shilonite— because of the sins of Jeroboam that he committed and that he caused Israel to commit, and because of the anger to which he provoked the Lord, the God of Israel." The principal sin of Jeroboam, of course, was the worship of the golden calves at Bethel and Dan, and since Baasha himself continued this practice, the same judgment is pronounced over him by Jehu, son of Hanani (1 Kgs 16:1 – 3). The third king to receive the very same judgment, this time by Elijah, is Ahab together with his queen Jezebel, with

---

28 For this text, see M. Nissinen, *References to Prophecy in Neo-Assyrian Sources* (SAAS 7; Helsinki: The Neo-Assyrian Text Corpus Project, 1998), 108 – 52, and cf. the discussion on the historical background of the letter in S. W. Holloway, *Aššur is King! Aššur is King! Religion in the Exercise of Power in the Neo-Assyrian Empire* (CHANE 10; Leiden: Brill, 2002), esp. 410 – 12; and M. de Jong, *Isaiah among the Ancient Near Eastern Prophets: A Comparative Study of the Earliest Stages of the Isaiah Tradition and the Neo-Assyrian Prophecies* (VTSup 117; Leiden: Brill, 2007), esp. 271 – 74.

an explicit reference to the fate of Jeroboam and Baasha (1 Kgs 21:20–24; 2 Kgs 9:9–10). Even this prophecy comes true as predicted (1 Kgs 22:37–38; 2 Kgs 9:30–37).

The prophetic judgment in these interconnected texts is the key element of the narrative of the northern kingdom from the beginning (cf. 1 Kgs 12:15) to the end (cf. 2 Kgs 17:21–23). It does not represent any kind of royal ideology of the kingdoms of Israel and Judah, but the ideologies and narrative strategies of the writers of Joshua–Kings, for whom the destruction of the kingdom of Israel was an essential constitutent of their collective memory.

While prophetic judgment plays a crucial role in the narrative of Kings concerning the northern kingdom, it is not such an overwhelming feature of prophecy in Joshua–Kings as it is in the prophetic books of the Hebrew Bible; even other aspects of royal prophecy are well represented in Joshua–Kings. Quite the same way as Zimri-Lim of Mari is warned by prophets,[29] David receives a word of warning from the prophet Gad to leave his stronghold (1 Sam 22:5), and Rehoboam is warned by the man of God called Shemaiah not to wage war against the people of Israel who had made Jeroboam their king (1 Kgs 12:22–24). These prophetic warnings are not condemnatory as such, but they do function within the narrative plots of David's rise to power and the division of Solomon's kingdom.

The divine word pronounced to kings and other leaders of people in Joshua–Kings is, in fact, quite as often supportive as it is condemnatory. The divine promise to deliver enemies into the king's hands is one of the most typical features in ancient Near Eastern prophecy.[30] A similar promise is given directly by God to Joshua (Josh 6:2; 8:1, 18; 10:8), by the prophetess Deborah to Barak (Judg 4:6–7), by the mouth of an angel to Gideon (Judg 6:16; 7:9); and later by an anonymous prophet to Ahab (1 Kgs 20:13), by Elisha to Jehoram and Jehoshaphath (2 Kgs 3:18), and by Isaiah to Hezekiah (2 Kgs 19:6–7); moreover, Jeroboam II is said to have restored the previous borders of the northern kingdom

29 ARM 26 197 (= SBLWAW 41 7): 21–24: "Now protect yourself! Without consulting an oracle do not enter the city!"; ARM 26 213 (= SBLWAW 41 23): 7–19: "Thus says Annunitum: Zimri-Lim, you will be tested in a revolt! Protect yourself! Let your most favored servants whom you love surround you, and make them stay there to protect you! Do not go around on your own!"

30 E.g., Mari: ARM 26 194 (= SBLWAW 41 4); ARM 26 195 (= SBLWAW 41 5); ARM 26 197 (= SBLWAW 41 7); ARM 26 211 (= SBLWAW 41 21); ARM 26 214 (= SBLWAW 41 24); ARM 26 217 (= SBLWAW 41 27); ARM 26 233 (= SBLWAW 41 38); Assyria: SAA 9 1.1 (= SBLWAW 41 68); SAA 9 1.2 (= SBLWAW 41 69); SAA 9 1.6 (= SBLWAW 41 73); SAA 9 1.7 (= SBLWAW 41 74); SAA 9 2.3 (= SBLWAW 41 80); SAA 9 2.5 (= SBLWAW 41 82); SAA 9 3.2 (= SBLWAW 41 86); SAA 9 3.5 (= SBLWAW 41 88); SAA 9 4 (= SBLWAW 41 89); SAA 9 7 (SBLWAW 41 92); SAA 9 8 (SBLWAW 41 93).

according to the word of God pronounced by the prophet Jonah, son of Amittai (2 Kgs 14:25), which also implies a divine promise of military conquest. Personal divine promises concerning the fate of an individual king are given by Isaiah to Hezekiah concerning his recovery form the illness (2 Kgs 20:5–6), as well as by Huldah to Josiah who is said to die in peace—a prediction that, eventually, does not come true (2 Kgs 22:20, cf. 23:29).

Considering the strong link between prophecy and kingship, it is not surprising to find prophecy accompanying ancient Near Eastern kings' way to the throne. Prophets appear to have played a role in the investiture and enthronement of the Assyrian crown princes Esarhaddon and Assurbanipal.[31] The royal succession appears as an emphatically prophetic concern and Esarhaddon received oracles from the mouth of the prophet La-dagil-ili that sound like a dynastic promise: "Your son and grandson will exercise kingship in the lap of Ninurta."[32] In the Old Babylonian sources of prophecy preserved to us, prophets do not appear as actual king-makers. However, some prophecies from that period are best understood as coronation oracles, such as the oracle from Ešnunna to Ibalpiel II[33] and the prophecy of Adad reported to Zimri-Lim of Mari by Nur-Sîn, his representative in Aleppo.[34]

The letter of Nur-Sîn is probably the oldest reference to anointing kings in the Near East, but it says nothing about prophetic involvement in the act of anointing. In Samuel–Kings, a king is anointed four times. Samuel anoints Saul the first king of the Israelites, thus fulfilling their request to have a king (1 Sam 10:1); however, as the first king turns out to be a failure, Samuel repeats the act with David (1 Sam 16:13). In both cases, the spirit of God is bestowed upon the anointed king. David receives the spirit immediately as if belonging to the very act of anointing, and Saul the very same day as he encounters the band of prophets at Gebah (1 Sam 10:10). In the case of Solomon, the act of anointing is technically performed by the priest Zadok, but this is done in the presence of the prophet Nathan who is likewise presented as protagonist of the anointing rit-

---

31 See Parpola, *Assyrian Prophecies*, xxxvi–xliv; Nissinen, *References to Prophecy*, 14–34; de Jong, *Isaiah among Ancient Near Eastern Prophets*, 251–59; K. Šašková, "Esarhaddon's Accession to the Assyrian Throne," in *Shepherds of the Black-Headed People: The Royal Office vis-à-vis Godhead in Ancient Mesopotamia* (ed. ead., L. Pecha, and P. Charvát; Plzeň: Západočeská univerzita, 2010) 147–79.

32 SAA 9 1.10 (= SBLWAW 41 77) vi 27–29; SAA 9 2.3 (= SBLWAW 41 80) ii 13–14.

33 FLP 1674 (= SBLWAW 41 66); see M. deJong Ellis, "The Goddess Kititum Speaks to King Ibalpiel: Oracle Texts from Ishchali," *MARI* 5 (1987) 235–66.

34 FM 7 38 (= SBLWAW 41 2); see J.-G. Heintz, "Des textes sémitiques anciens à la Bible hébraïque: Un comparatisme légitime?" in *Le comparatisme en histoire des religions: Pour un état de la question* (ed. F. Bœspflug and F. Dunand; Paris: Boccard, 1997) 127–56, esp. 146–50.

ual (1 Kgs 1:32–53, esp. v. 34, 39, 45). The fourth case is Jehu to whom Elisha sent one of his "sons" to anoint him king of Israel and to perform the eradication of the progeny of Ahab (2 Kgs 9:6–10). All four biblical cases of anointing a king thus involve a prophet.

The anointing of Solomon and the role of the prophet Nathan therein is part and parcel of the narrative of David's succession which also includes the dynastic promise pronounced to David by Nathan (2 Sam 7:12–16), according to which God will establish the kingdom of David's offspring: "I will be a father to him, and he shall be a son to me. ... Your house and your kingdom shall be made sure forever before me; your throne shall be established forever." Nathan's oracle has plausibly been interpreted as reflecting a common Near Eastern royal ideology.[35] Indeed, the biblical prophet Nathan is quite as actively involved in king-making as his Assyrian colleagues seem to have been, even though Nathan's relationship to David seems rather more intimate than what is known of the Assyrian prophets' connection to their kings.

The function of prophecy in the Succession Narrative is too manifold and multilayered to match anything we know from the ancient Near East; one common feature is interesting, however: the role of the queen mother. We know how crucial the role played by Naqia, Esarhaddon's mother, was in the succession of her husband Sennacherib,[36] and a similarly important role is ascribed to Bathsheba, the mother of Solomon, in the Succession Narrative. Even prophecy is part of the picture in both cases: Naqia demonstrably turned to prophets on behalf of her son[37] and Solomon's kingship is presented as a joint project of Bathsheba and the prophet Nathan in 1 Kgs 1.

Prophets and Cult Places

Prophets and temples coincide in the ancient Near Eastern and Greek sources often enough to warrant the assumption that prophecy was at home in temples and cult places all over the Eastern Mediterranean. This is neither to say that prophecy was exclusively confined to temples, nor that a specific class of "cultic

35 E.g., M. Avioz, *Nathan's Oracle (2 Samuel 7) and Its Interpreters* (Bible in History; Bern: Lang, 2005). Avioz interprets 2 Sam 7 as reflecting the vassal treaty ideology.

36 See S. C. Melville, *The Role of Naqia/Zakutu in Sargonid Politics* (SAAS 9; Helsinki: The Neo-Assyrian Text Corpus Project, 1999); S. Svärd, *Women's Roles in the Neo-Assyrian Era: Female Agency in the Empire* (Saarbrücken: VDM Verlag, 2008), esp. 31–33; Šašková, "Esarhaddon's Accession to the Assyrian Throne," 153–54, 170–71.

37 SAA 9 1.8 (= SBLWAW 41 75); cf. SAA 9 5 (= SBLWAW 41 90).

prophets," as distinct from "court prophets" or "free prophets," should or could be postulated. Anyhow, there is plenty of evidence of temples as venues of prophetic performances. At Mari, prophets are reported to have "arisen" (*tebû*) or "gone into trance" (*maḫû*) in a temple to deliver an oracle:

> Another matter: a prophetess arose in the temple of Annunitum and spoke: "Zimri-Lim, do not go on campaign! Stay in Mari, and I shall continue to answer."[38]
>
> In the temple of Annunitum in the city, Aḫatum, a servant girl of Dagan-Malik, went into trance and spoke: "Zimri-Lim (...)"[39]

Prophetic messages may be transmitted by priests like Aḫum, the priest of the temple of Annunitum,[40] or the Assyrian priests Adad-aḫu-iddina, Aššur-ḫamatu'a, and Nabû-reši-išši,[41] who report what had happened in their temples, including prophetic performances.

In spite of the recurrent appearances of prophets in temples, the affiliation of the prophets with temples at Mari is somewhat unclear.[42] It is not impossible to find prophets participating in cultic practices,[43] but this is not very common either. The Assyrian sources, on the other hand, explicitly mention prophets as belonging to the temple personnel. A Middle-Assyrian provisions list from Kar-Tukulti-Ninurta (ca. eleventh century B.C.E.) lists prophets and prophetesses (*maḫḫû/maḫḫūtu*) together with the *assinnu*s of the Ištar temple as recipients of a ration of barley,[44] and a decree of expenditures for ceremonies in the temple of Ešarra in Assur from 809 B.C.E. mentions prophetesses (*maḫḫūtu*) as recipients of barley as a part of the expenditure for the divine council.[45] One of the

38 ARM 26 237 (SBLWAW 41 42): 21–26; cf. ARM 26 219 (SBLWAW 41 29): 4–5; ARM 26 195 (SBLWAW 41 5): 5–6.

39 ARM 26 214 (SBLWAW 41 42): 5–8; cf. ARM 26 213 (SBLWAW 41 23): 5–7.

40 ARM 26 200 (SBLWAW 41 10) and ARM 26 201 (SBLWAW 41 11).

41 SAA 13 37 (SBLWAW 41 111); SAA 13 139 (SBLWAW 41 112); SAA 13 144 (SBLWAW 41 113).

42 See D. E. Fleming, "Prophets and Temple Personnel in the Mari Archives," in *The Priests in the Prophets: The Portrayal of Priests, Prophets and Other Religious Specialists in the Latter Prophets* (ed. L. L. Grabbe and A. O. Bellis; JSOTS 408; London: T & T Clark 2004) 44–64.

43 FM 3 3 (= SBLWAW 41 52); see J.-M. Durand and M. Guichard, "Les rituels de Mari," in *Florilegium marianum 3*, FS M.-T. Barrelet (ed. D. Charpin and J.-M. Durand; Mémoires de *NABU* 4; Paris: SEPOA, 1997) 19–78, esp. 59–63; M. Nissinen, "Prophetic Madness: Prophecy and Ecstasy in the Ancient Near East and in Greece," in *Raising Up a Faithful Exegete*, FS R. D. Nelson (ed. K. L. Noll and B. Schramm; Winona Lake, Ind.: Eisenbrauns, 2010) 3–29, esp. 9–11.

44 VS 19 1 (= SBLWAW 41 123) i 37–39; see B. Lion, "Les mentions de 'prophètes' dans la seconde moitié du IIe millénaire av. J.-C.," *RA* 94 (2000) 21–32.

45 SAA 12 69 (= SBLWAW 41 110): 27–31; see M. Nissinen, "Prophets and the Divine Council," in *Kein Land für sich allein: Studien zum Kulturkontakt in Kanaan, Israel/Palästina und Ebirnâri für*

preserved Assyrian prophecies from the seventh century B.C.E. is spoken by Issar-beli-da''ini, the votaress (*šēlūtu*) of the king, that is, a person who had been donated by the king to the temple.[46] A poorly preserved fragment of a text sent by another votaress to the king may also be a remnant of a prophetic oracle.[47] In fact, the domicile of several prophets in Arbela implies an affiliation with the prominent temple of Ištar in the same city.[48]

Whatever functions the prophets may have fulfilled in relation to the temples at Mari, they repeatedly appear as advocates of worship, reproaching the king for neglecting his ritual duties[49] and giving orders to him concerning ritual performances such as *pagrā'um* and *kispum* offerings[50] or sacrifices to a commemorative monument (*ḫumūsum*).[51] Similar prophetic orders can also be found on the recently published tenth-ninth century B.C.E. Luwian stele of Hamiyata, king of Mazuwari (Til Barsip), who mentions a prophet ordering the establishment of the statue of the storm-god Tarhunza.[52] In Neo-Assyrian texts, prophets are usually not found expressing ritual demands, except for one case, where Ištar requires offerings from the newly enthroned Esarhaddon.[53] However, even in Assyrian sources, the welfare of the temples appears as a prophetic concern. Two letters of the Assyrian temple officials report prophecies concerning temple

---

Manfred Weippert zum 65. Geburtstag (ed. E.-A. Knauf and U. Hübner; OBO 186; Fribourg: Universitätsverlag; Göttingen: Vandenhoeck & Ruprecht, 2002) 4–19, esp. 16–17 (= pp. 461–77 in this volume).

46 SAA 9 1.7 (= SBLWAW 41 74); see Svärd, *Women's Roles in the Neo-Assyrian Era*, 79–80.

47 SAA 13 148 (= SBLWAW 41 114).

48 See Parpola, *Assyrian Prophecies*, xlvii–lii; de Jong, *Isaiah among Ancient Near Eastern Prophets*, 294–98, M. Nissinen, "City Lofty as Heaven: Arbela and Other Cities in Neo-Assyrian Prophecy," in *"Every City Shall Be Forsaken": Urbanism and Prophecy in Ancient Israel and the Near East* (ed. L. L. Grabbe and R. D. Haak; JSOTS 330; Sheffield: Sheffield Academic Press, 2001) 172–209, esp. 176–83 (= pp. 267–300 in this volume).

49 ARM 26 219 (SBLWAW 41 29): 4–9.

50 ARM 26 220 (SBLWAW 41 30): 20–23; ARM 26 221 (SBLWAW 41 31): 7–17. For these offerings, associated with the cult of the dead, see Durand and Guichard, "Les rituels de Mari," 19–78; J.-M. Durand, "Le *kispum* dans les traditions amorrites," in *Les vivants et leurs morts: Actes du colloque organisé par le Collège de France, Paris, les 14–15 avril 2010* (ed. id., T. Römer, and J. Hutzli; OBO 257; Fribourg: Academic Press; Göttingen: Vandenhoeck & Ruprecht, 2012) 33–52.

51 ARM 26 218 (SBLWAW 41 28: 5–13; for *ḫumūsum*, see Durand and Guichard, "Les rituels de Mari," 33.

52 Tell Ahmar 6 §§ 21–23 (SBLWAW 41 143) (cf. 5 §§ 12–15): "I destroyed for myself the enemies, and the god-inspired (one) said to me: 'Establish Tarhunza of the Army!'" Editio princeps: J. D. Hawkins, "Inscription," in *A New Luwian Stele and the Cult of the Storm-God at Til Barsib-Masuwari* (ed. G. Bunnens; Tell Ahmar 2; Leuven: Peeters, 2006) 11–31, esp. 15, 27–28. For the historical context of this text, see ibid., 85–102.

53 SAA 9 3.5 (SBLWAW 41 88).

property[54] and Assurbanipal in his inscription mentions dreams and prophetic oracles as the source of divine orders to renovate the temple of the Lady of Kidmuri, that is, Ištar of Calah.[55]

While not yielding an accurate picture of the function of prophets in the worship of gods, the ancient Near Eastern sources confirm the close connection between temples and prophets. Prophetic messages, for sure, could be uttered in different environments, but the temples provided a sacred space where divine-human encounters, even prophetic ones, were believed to take place; therefore, temples were an ideal venue for communication with the divine by means of prophecy.[56] The constructs of prophecy in texts from Mari and Assyria present the prophets as sharing the symbolic worlds of both the temple communities and the (implied) authors of the texts and, for their part, contributing to the maintenance of the institutional order and the symbolic universe it was based on.[57]

Maintenance of the institutional order and the symbolic universe is also a major preoccupation of the writers of Joshua–Kings, especially in so far as they are devoted to the Deuteronomic idea of worshiping YHWH, and YHWH alone, in one place only (Deuteronomium 12). When the high priest Hilkiah reports to have recovered the book of the law (*sēper hattôrâ*) in the temple, King Josiah orders him to inquire YHWH concerning the book, which, to all appearances, prohibits sacrifices to gods other than YHWH. Hilkiah, together with four high officials including the scribe Shaphan, go to Huldah, a female prophet who is said to be the wife of Shallum, keeper of the wardrobe, presumably of the temple of Jerusalem (2 Kings 22). The narrative is interesting in many respects. The female gender of the prophet alone is noteworthy. Huldah is the last prophet in Joshua–Kings, Deborah being the first (Judg 4:4), and these are the only female prophets mentioned;[58] if anything, this indicates that the writers

---

54 Adad-aḫu-iddina: SAA 13 37 (SBLWAW 41 111); Nabû-reši-iššši: SAA 13 114 (SBLWAW 41 113).
55 Prism T ii (SBLWAW 41 99): 16–17.
56 Cf. C. Bonnet, "Dove vivono gli dei? Note sulla terminologia fenicio-punica dei luoghi di culto e sui modi di rappresentazione del mondo divino," in *Saturnia Tellus: Definizioni dello spazio consacrato in ambiente etrusco, italoci, fenicio-punico, iberico e celtico* (ed. X. D. Raventós, S. Ribichini, and S. Verger; Roma: Consiglio nazionale delle ricerche, 2008) 673–85, esp. 680.
57 For the machinery and social organization of "universe-maintenance," see P. L. Berger and T. Luckmann, *The Social Construction of Reality: A Treatise in Sociology of Knowledge* (New York, Anchor Books, 1989 [orig. 1966]), 104–28. For the ideological background of the Neo-Assyrian prophetic texts, see Parpola, *Assyrian Prophecies*, xviii–xlviii.
58 Cf. H. G. M. Williamson, "Prophetesses in the Hebrew Bible," in *Prophecy and Prophets in Ancient Israel: Proceedings of the Oxford Old Testament Seminar* (ed. J. Day; LHBOTS 531; London: T & T Clark, 2010) 65–80.

were familiar with the non-gender-specific nature of Near Eastern prophecy and did not hesitate to ascribe a divine word of paramount importance to the mediation of a female prophet who at least indirectly, through her husband, is affiliatied with the temple of Jerusalem. Moreover, the narrative presents an interesting case of interaction of divinatory methods: an authoritative text, itself a medium of the divine word, is being cross-checked with another divinatory medium, prophecy.[59] The prophecy of Huldah does not give any cultic instructions, but it prompts Josiah to effectuate an unprecedented cultic reform, which adds Huldah's name to the inventory of Near Eastern prophets appearing as advocates of legitimate worship.

Even other prophets are given a crucial role in mediating the divine word concerning legitimate and illegitimate worship in Joshua–Kings. First Kings 13 is explicitly connected with the Josiah narrative, reporting the performance of an anonymous prophet (*ʾîš hā-ʾĕlōhîm*) while King Jeroboam of Israel is sacrificing by the altar of the sanctuary of Bethel where he had erected the notorious golden calves: "O altar, altar, thus says the Lord: 'A son shall be born to the house of David, Josiah by name; and he shall sacrifice on you the priests of the high places who offer incense on you, and human bones shall be burned on you'" (1 Kgs 13:1–2). The prophecy is followed by the destruction of the altar as a sign of the illegitimacy of the cult in Bethel; once again, a prophet appears as an advocate of legitimate worship, albeit per *viam negationis*. The man of God and Huldah are placed in two ends of the narrative span, marking the beginning and the end of the phase of royal idolatry in the writers' scheme of the history of Israel.

It is not uncommon to find prophets in cult places or in their vicinity. The book of Joshua does not mention a single prophet but makes Joshua, the successor of Moses, a leader of people who does not need prophetic mediation to receive the divine word but plays the roles of the king, the priest, and the diviner at the same time. He performs divinatory and cultic acts upon God's direct orders, such as lot-casting (see above), circumcision (Josh 5:2–9), and building an altar (8:30–31). Samuel, the first male prophet mentioned by name in Josh-

59 J. Ben-Dov ("Some Precedents for the Religion of the Book: Josiah's Book and Ancient Revelatory Literature," in Grabbe and Nissinen (ed.), *Constructs of Prophecy*, 43–62, esp. 50–51) suggests that *sēper hat-tôrâ* in the oldest, pre-Deuteronomistic version of the story refers to a written oracular document, and its equation with Deuteronomy as a *sēper hab-bĕrît* is due to Deuteronomistic editing. He finds a similar case of double-checking the divine message in the letter of Nur-Sîn to Zimri-Lim (FM 7 39 = SBLWAW 41 1), in which oracles obtained from extispicy (*têrtum*, an Akkadian cognate of *tôrâ*) are immediately elaborated by prophets and reported to the king in a letter.

ua–Kings, is given to be dedicated to God as a little boy (1 Sam 1:24–28), hence having a role akin to that of the above-mentioned votaresses (*šēlūtu*) uttering prophecies in Assyrian temples. It is in the temple of Shiloh where God henceforth is said to reveal his word to Samuel (1 Sam 3:21). Samuel's roles and activities are manifold, and it is difficult to determine whether he should be called a prophet, a priest, or a judge in the first place. He is explicitly identified as a prophet, whether a *nābîʾ* (1 Sam 3:20), a *rōʾê* (1 Sam 9:11, 18–19), or an *ʾîš hā-ʾĕlohîm* (1 Sam 9:6, 10), but he also functions in priestly roles not usually associated with prophetic activities. Such a profusion of different functions of one and the same individual is probably due to textual growth; it has been assumed that Samuel's prophetic role is secondary to his more original priestly function.[60]

While Samuel's close affilitation to the temple of Shiloh, together with his cultic functions, may be due to his priestly past in the history of the narrative itself, there are several other prophets in Samuel-Kings appearing in temple contexts. The band of prophets whose prophetic frenzy Saul shares is located in the "hill of God" (*gibʿat ʾĕlōhîm* 1 Sam 10:5; cf. v. 10). The encounter of the anonymous *ʾîš hā-ʾĕlōhîm* with Eli (1 Sam 2:27–36) only makes sense within the context the temple of Shiloh, all the more because the explicit concern of the prophecy is the proper execution of the priestly office. The legacy of this temple is carried forward by the prophet Ahijah the Shilonite (1 Kgs 11:29–39), who continually lived in Shiloh and was consulted there by Jeroboam as if the ancient temple were still standing (1 Kgs 14:1–18). Even Isaiah seems to be located in the temple of Jerusalem; Hezekiah, when facing the threat from Assyria (2 Kgs 19:1–7; cf. Isa 37:1–7), goes to the temple wearing a sackcloth and sends his representa-

---

60 Recent studies on Samuel explain his different roles in different ways. W. Dietrich ("Samuel: Ein Prophet?" in *Prophets and Prophecy in Jewish and Early Christian Literature* [ed. J. Verheyden, K. Zamfir, and T. Nicklas; WUNT.2 286; Tübingen: Mohr Siebeck, 2010] 1–17) argues that the role of the historical Samuel was that of a judge, whereas his prophetic functions are the result of a literary development. According to M. A. Sweeney ("Samuel's Institutional Identity in the Deuteronomistic History," in Grabbe and Nissinen [ed.], *Constructs of Prophecy*, 165–74), the Deuteronomistic writer uses an earlier Samuel narrative in which he functions as a priest and turns him into a prophet; according to him, Samuel follows the Northern model of priest, where the firstborn functioned in this pre-Levitical role. S. Frolov ("1 Samuel 1–8: The Prophet as Agent Provocateur," in Grabbe and Nissinen [ed.], *Constructs of Prophecy*, 77–85), on the other hand, argues that 1 Samuel 1–8 in its entirety is polemically directed against the Deuteronomic and Deuteronomistic concept of prophecy, Samuel being introduced as an agent provocateur, commissioned by God to cause the people to bring a disaster upon themselves.

tives, also clothed with sackcloth, to Isaiah, as if the prophet was to be found there.[61]

According to 1 Kgs 18:21–40, Elijah slaughtered four hundred prophets of Baal and Asherah after demonstrating YHWH's superiority in a formidable sacrificial performance at an altar specifically constructed for this purpose on Mount Carmel. This account, apart from the Samuel narratives, is the only occasion in ancient Near Eastern literature where a prophet himself performs a sacrificial ritual, but it hardly gives any information concerning the prophets' cultic role. Nevertheless, a connection between prophets and altars in the writer's (and the implied reader's) mind is suggested also by Elijah's mention of the killing of prophets with sword in the same breath as throwing down the altars (1 Kgs 19:10, 14), as if all this was the result of a single act of violence against every type of idolatry.

In the ancient Near East, temples were divinely ordered centers of the mythological universe.[62] Likewise in the Hebrew Bible, the temple of Jerusalem is the focal point of the identity of Israel, the establishment of which appears as a decisive act of the maintenance of the symbolic universe in Joshua–Kings. The prophet Nathan's oracle to King David combines the dynastic promise with the ordinance that David's son will build a temple for YHWH: "He shall build a house for my name, and I will establish the throne of his kingdom for ever. I will be a father to him, and he shall be a son to me" (2 Sam 7:13–14). As we saw earlier, the dynastic promise in Nathan's oracle can be read against a common Near Eastern royal ideology. A further Near Eastern feature in 2 Sam 7 is the expression of the divine initiative in temple-building and its placement in the mouth of a person who is called a prophet; however: "The dissociation of temple building and dynastic promise, as promulgated in 2 Sam 7, is unprecedented in the Ancient Near East."[63]

---

61 According to H. Wildberger, "the situation is purely political; the ministers ... are sent to Isaiah, who is certainly not a temple prophet and is clearly not held in very high regard by the priestly circles at the temple" (*Isaiah 28–39: A Continental Commentary* [trans. T. H. Trapp; Minneapolis: Fortress, 2002], 400). This is consistent with Wildberger's image of the prophet Isaiah as closely related to the court but not to the temple (cf. ibid., 569–72), but not necessarily with Isa 37:1–7//2 Kgs 19:1–7, where the prophet seems to be consulted in the context of a mourning ritual.

62 See B. Pongratz-Leisten, Ina sulmi īrub: *Die kulttopographische und ideologische Programmatik der* akītu-*Prozession in Babylonien und Assyrien im 1. Jahrtausend v. Chr.* (BaF 16; Mainz: Philipp von Zabern, 1994), esp. 20, 36.

63 W. Oswald, "Is There a Prohibition to Build a Temple in 2 Samuel 7?" in *Thinking towards New Horizons: Collected Communications to the XIXth Congress of the International Organization for the Study of the Old Testament, Ljubljana 2007* (ed. M. Augustin and H. M. Niemann; BEA-

The Literary Portrayal of Prophets

We have seen above that prophecy, as presented in Joshua–Kings, is in many ways analogous to the image of prophecy that can be obtained from the ancient Near Eastern sources available to us. Prophecy fulfills the function of the divinatory *Herrschaftswissen* needed by the king and other leaders of the people; it is essentially connected to the kings' politics, warfare, and succession; and it has an affiliation with worship, which sometimes is its principal concern.

On the other hand, the portrayal of prophecy in Joshua–Kings has several features poorly represented or unknown in the extant Near Eastern sources. We have already noted above the fluidity of the boundary between prophecy and technical divination, for which there is very little evidence in the ancient Near East. Moreover, Samuel, immediately after Saul is proclaimed king, gives his farewell speech to the people presenting himself the following way (1 Sam 12:3):

> Here I am; testify against me before the Lord and before his anointed. Whose ox have I taken? Or whose donkey have I taken? Or whom have I defrauded? Whom have I oppressed? Or from whose hand have I taken a bribe to blind my eyes with it? Testify against me and I will restore it to you.

This corresponds in every respect to the ancient Near Eastern ideal of a just king also illustrated when the god Adad says to King Zimri-Lim: "When a wronged man or woman cries out to you, be there and judge their case. This only I have demanded from you."[64] The curious thing with Samuel is that, while having executed his office as a judge the way a just king does, he also acted as a prophet, diviner, and priest. Such a combination of diverse roles within one and the same person is unknown in Near Eastern documents of prophecy.

In Joshua–Kings, there are many other prophets whose portrayal goes beyond the usual socioreligious repertoire of an ancient Near Eastern prophet as we know it from the available sources. Nathan, besides acting in a prophetic role in mediating the divine promise, also functions as the king's closest advisor executing considerable political power.[65] Deborah bears the title "prophetess,"

TAJ 55; Frankfurt a.M.: Lang, 2008) 85–89, esp. 88. For the literary development of theological ideas in 2 Sam 7, see also T. A. Rudnig, "König ohne Tempel: 2 Samuel 7 in Tradition und Redaktion," *VT* 61 (2011) 426–46.

64 FM 7 39 (= SBLWAW 41 1): 53–55; cf. FM 7 38 (= SBLWAW 41 2) r. 6–11.

65 Cf. W. Oswald, *Nathan der Prophet: Eine Untersuchung zu 2 Samuel 7 und 12 und 1 Könige I* (AThANT 94; Zürich: Theologischer Verlag, 2008), 258: "Nathan ist von dem, was historisch plau-

and she actually transmits divine words to Barak (Judg 4:6–9), but she also acts as a judge for the Israelites; one wonders if the combination of her roles as a diviner and a judge actually implies the idea of a divine judgment by means of technical divination performed under the palm tree named after her (Judg 4:4–5).[66]

Furthermore, unlike any prophet in the ancient Near Eastern sources, biblical prophets may perform miraculous deeds. Health, for instance, was an important concern of Near Eastern kings (Esarhaddon in particular[67]), but they usually seem to have consulted magicians and scholars rather than prophets in matters of healing. Neither do prophets perform healing rituals in the sources known to us, even though their presence in such a ritual is mentioned in one Neo-Assyrian text.[68] In the Hebrew Bible, Elijah and Elisha, both designated as "prophets" or "men of God," appear as powerful healers and resuscitators (1 Kgs 17:17–24; 2 Kgs 4:8–37; 5:1–19)—Elisha even after his death (2 Kgs 13:20–21). Isaiah also acts as the healer of King Hezekiah, performing another miracle: he cries to God who lets the shadow retreat ten intervals as a sign of Hezekiah's recovery from his illness (2 Kgs 20:1–11; cf. Isa 38:1–8).

Biblical prophets also sometimes control the weather. Samuel, having finished his farewell speech, calls upon God to send thunder and rain (1 Sam 12:17–18) and Elijah's contest with the prophets of Baal and Asherah, motivated by a draught declared by him, ends with a heavy rain (1 Kgs 18:38–45; cf, 17:1). The narratives on Elijah and Elisha include many other miracles performed by these two persons who in different ways control the forces of nature (2 Kgs 2:14, 19–22; 4:38–41; 6:1–7, 18–20), including a kind of clairvoyance (2 Kgs

---

sibel gemacht werden kann, weit entfernt und kann nicht in die Geschichte der Prophetic der frühen Königszeit eingeordnet werden."

66 K. Spronk ("Deborah, a Prophetess: The Meaning and Background of Judges 4:4–5," in *The Elusive Prophet: The Prophet as a Historical Person, Literary Character and Anonymous Artist* [ed. J. C. de Moor; OTS 45; Leiden: Brill, 2001] 232–42) surmises that the figure of Deborah was originally that of a necromancer similar to the woman of En-Dor in 1 Sam 28. On the other hand, Y. Kupitz and K. Berthelot ("Deborah and the Delphic Pythia: A New Interpretation of Judges 4:4–5," in *Images and Prophecy in the Ancient Eastern Mediterranean* [ed. M. Nissinen and C. E. Carter; FRLANT 233; Göttingen: Vandenhoeck & Ruprecht, 2009] 95–124) find intriguing similarities in the figures of Deborah and the Pythia of Delphi.

67 See, e.g., SAA 10 187; 201; 213; 241; 242; 243; 297; 299; 302; 309; 315; 318–327.

68 Ritual of Ištar and Dumuzi (SBLWAW 41 118), 31–32: "For the frenzied man and woman (*zabbi zabbati*) and for the prophet and prophetess (*maḫḫê u maḫḫûti*) you shall place seven pieces of bread. Then let the sick person recite the following to Ištar: (...)." It is unclear whether the prophecy of Irra-gamil concerning the death of a royal baby in ARM 26 222 (= SBLWAW 41 33) coincided with a healing ritual.

6:8–17) and the multiplication of food (1 Kgs 17:7–16; 2 Kgs 4:1–7, 42–44). No such activities are reported with regard to ancient Near Eastern prophets in the sources at our disposal.

The differences between the biblical and ancient Near Eastern portrayals of prophecy may partly be due to different socioreligious circumstances on the historical scene. The amalgamation of the prophetic role with other socioreligious functions can, at least in theory, be explained by the smallscale and less differentiated structure of the Israelite/Judahite/Yehudite society, allowing an individual to assume a cluster of social roles not to be found in the more differentiated societies of ancient Mesopotamia. While this remains a possibility especially with regard to divinatory functions, it deserves attention that similar differences cannot be observed comparing sources coming from imperial Assyria and the city-state of Mari, despite all dissimilarities in the socioreligious structure of these societies.

The principal reason for the diverse portrayals of prophets is to be sought first and foremost in the difference in their emergence, transmission, and literary function. The information about prophets and prophecy in ancient Near Eastern sources comes from a variety of texts of different types: written oracles, letters, word-lists, ritual texts, administrative documents, and inscriptions, which were written, edited, and deposited in archives relatively soon after the events they describe. They do not usually have a long editorial history behind them; however, they are not neutral accounts either, but represent the interests of the writers and officials who have selected the material to be included in the archives.[69] The Assyrian prophecies, for example, represent an orthodox royal ideology, portraying the prophets accordingly.[70] The narratives, including prophetic performances in Joshua–Kings,[71] primarily function within the literary contexts of this multilay-

69 Cf., e.g., J. M. Sasson, "The Posting of Letters with Divine Messages," in *Florilegium Marianum 2*, FS M. Birot (ed. D. Charpin and J.-M. Durand; Mémoires de NABU 3; Paris: SEPOA, 1994) 299–316; K. van der Toorn, "From the Oral to the Written: The Case of Old Babylonian Prophecy," in *Writings and Speech in Israelite and Ancient Near Eastern Prophecy* (ed. E. Ben Zvi and M. H. Floyd; SBLSymS 10; Atlanta, Ga.: Society of Biblical Literature, 2000) 219–34; D. Charpin, "The Writing, Sending and Reading of Letters in the Amorite World," in *The Babylonian World* (ed. G. Leick; New York: Routledge, 2007) 400–17.

70 See M. Nissinen, "Prophecy as Construct: Ancient and Modern," in *"Thus Speaks Ishtar of Arbela": Prophecy in Israel, Assyria and Egypt in the Neo-Assyrian Period* (ed. R. P. Gordon and H. M. Barstad; Winona Lake, Ind.: Eisenbrauns, 2013) 11–35 (= pp. 3–27 in this volume).

71 For prophets and prophecy in the Deuteronomistic History, see, e.g., W. Dietrich, "Prophetie im deuteronomistischen Geschichtswerk," in *The Future of the Deuteronomistic History* (ed. T. Römer; BETL 147; Leuven: Peeters, 2000) 47–65; Ben Zvi, "The Prophets"; and the articles col-

ered composition scholars call the Deuteronomistic History, serving the narrative and ideological purposes of their multiple editors, and only occasionally informing about historical factualities. Therefore, any comparison between biblical and Near Eastern sources concerns the *constructs* of prophecy represented by the texts and it is to be expected that the construct is dependent on the agenda of the writers of each text, biblical or nonbiblical. It is no wonder that official royal documents from imperial Assyria and the post-586 writers of Joshua–Kings have very distinct views of the function of prophets, resulting in divergent constructs of prophecy. The narratives in Joshua–Kings show what the (post-) Deuteronomistic writers living in the Second Temple communities[72] took for granted with regard to prophets and their activities in the times these literary compositions describe. It is reasonable to assume that a part of the image of the ancient prophets in these writings is based on older documents. This said, it is important to recognize that all this material is reread and adapted to a secondary context, and new layers of redaction have modified the image of the prophets and added new dimensions to their characteristics.

The stories about Elijah and Elisha, for example, belong primarily to their present literary contexts with a complex editorial history.[73] They may contain ancient elements, but they are not first-hand evidence of prophecy in the ninth-cen-

---

lected in *Past, Present, Future: The Deuteronomistic History and the Prophets* (ed. J. C. de Moor and H. F. van Rooy; OTS 44; Leiden, Brill, 2000).

72 Recent thoroughgoing analyses of the emergence of Joshua–Kings include R. G. Kratz, *The Composition of the Narrative Books of the Old Testament* (trans. John Bowden; London: T & T Clark, 2005); J. C. Gertz, "Tora und vordere Propheten" in *Grundinformation Altes Testament* (ed. id.; UTB 2745; Göttingen: Vandenhoeck & Ruprecht, 2006) 187–302, esp. 278–302; T. Römer, *The So-Called Deuteronomistic History: A Sociological, Historical, and Literary Introduction* (London: T & T Clark, 2005).

73 The complicated literary history of the Elijah and Elisha narratives has been analyzed with varying results; for recent contributions, see, e.g., S. Otto, *Jehu, Elia und Elisa: Die Erzählung von der Jehu-Revolution und die Komposition der Elia-Elisa-Erzählungen* (BWANT 152; Stuttgart: Kohlhammer, 2001); J. Keinänen, *Traditions in Collision: A Literary and Redaction-Critical Study on the Elijah Narratives 1 Kings 17–19* (PFES 80: Helsinki: Finnish Exegetical Society and Göttingen: Vandenhoeck & Ruprecht, 2001); B. Lehnart, *Prophet und König im Nordreich Israel: Studien zur sogenannten vorklassischen Prophetie im Nordreich Israel anhand der Samuel-, Elija- und Elischa-Überlieferungen* (VTSup 96; Leiden: Brill, 2003); M. Köckert, "Elia: Literarische und religionsgeschichtliche Probleme in 1Kön 17–18," in *Der Eine Gott und die Götter: Polytheismus und Monotheismus im antiken Israel* (ed. M. Oeming and K. Schmid; AThANT 82; Zürich: Theologischer Verlag, 2003) 111–44; D. Pruin, *Geschichten und Geschichte: Isebel als literarische und historische Gestalt* (OBO 222; Fribourg: Academic Press and Göttingen: Vandenhoeck & Ruprecht, 2006); R. Sauerwein, *Elischa: Eine redaktions- und religionsgeschichtliche Studie* (BZAW 465; Berlin: de Gruyter, 2014).

tury northern kingdom. It is commonly assumed that the narratives are based on older traditions about miracle-workers who have only secondarily been given a prophetic designation.[74] On the other hand, it is noteworthy that "much of the Elijah material belongs to the genre of hagiography, and therefore it can be compared with, among other things, the Life of Anthony the Hermit by Athanasius, the rabbinic traditions about Hanina ben Dosa the Galilean wonder-worker, or the biographical memoir of the Pythagorian sage Apollonius of Tyana written by Philostratus";[75] this may imply a late rather than an early origin of some of the miracle stories in the Elijah-Elisha cycle.

The overwhelmingly positive attitude toward the king in ancient Near Eastern—especially Assyrian—prophecy, and the largely critical stance of the prophets toward the kings in Joshua–Kings both reflect the constructs of prophecy represented by each source material. In Assyria, and also at Mari, the documentation of prophecy derives from the royal archives, and it comes up to every expectation that devastating criticism never ended up in these archives. The Assyrian collections of prophetic oracles in particular are intentionally designed to proclaim the Assyrian state religion and ideology.[76] The present composition of Joshua–Kings, on the other hand, represents the postmonarchichal, or post-586, view of the past kingdoms of Israel and Judah. Also the image of prophecy in this literature has been constructed with the destruction of Jerusalem belonging to the shared memory and this causes ideological subversions of royal prophecy, such as the reversal of the dynastic promise concerning the kingdom of Israel. The basic prophetic function of transmitting the *Herrschaftswissen* to the king remains the same as everywhere in the Near East, but the contents of the message proclaimed by the prophets is oriented toward the end of monarchy.[77]

In sum, the portrayals of prophets in Joshua-Kings bear enough resemblance to the images of ancient Near Eastern prophets known from the sources from Mari and Assyria to warrant the conclusion that the biblical narrators were famil-

74 Gertz, "Tora und die vorderen Propheten," 296: "Wie groß der Umfang der in die Zeit des Elija (Elischa) zurückgehenden Traditionen im Einzelnen auch immer zu bestimmen ist, am Anfang der Traditionsbildung scheint ein Wundertäter und Regenmacher gestanden zu haben, der erst im Zuge der dtr (oder: nach-dtr) Rezeptionsgeschichte zum Paradigma für einen Jhwh-Propheten wurde, dessen Wort in jedem Fall in Erfüllung ging."

75 Blenkinsopp, *A History of Prophecy in Israel: Revised and Enlarged* (Louisville, Ky.: Westminster John Knox, 1996), 59.

76 Cf. Parpola, *Assyrian Prophecies*, xviii – xliv.

77 R. G. Kratz, *Die Propheten Israels* (Munich: Beck, 2003), 35: "Das alles erinnert an die altorientalischen Zustände. Nur, daß das Verhältnis der Propheten zum Königtum in der biblischen Überlieferung von Anfang an gestört und das Ende der Monarchie vorprogrammiert ist."

iar with the phenomenon as an ancient tradition, probably also as a contemporary practice. The prophetic phenomenon was probably not drastically different in Mesopotamia and the southern Levant. As in the Near East, the socioreligious foundation of prophecy in Joshua-Kings consists of the institutions of divination, kingship, and worship. It is evident that prophecy was a significant element in the symbolic world of the writers of the evolving historical narrative that eventually became the literary composition labeled by scholars as the Deuteronomistic History.

However, the biblical portrayal of prophets also often diverge from what is familiar to us from ancient Near Eastern sources. This may partially go back to culture-specific differences in divinatory functions and socioreligious positions of prophets in Israel, Judah, and Yehud, but the primary source of the discrepancies should be sought from the context-specific constructs of prophecy in different literary and ideological contexts.

Das Problem der Prophetenschüler

I

Es ist ein bleibendes Verdienst von Timo Veijola, zu dessen Gedächtnis diese Zeilen in Dankbarkeit verfaßt sind, die entscheidende Rolle der Schriftgelehrten als der vornehmsten Vermittler und Schöpfer der biblischen Tradition hervorgehoben zu haben.[1] Veijola hat in seinen Studien gezeigt, daß die Schriftgelehrten, die zugleich als Exegeten, Pädagogen und Juristen anzusehen sind, sich nicht erst in der hellenistischen Zeit in den Vordergrund drängten. Vielmehr wurzelt die Schriftgelehrtsamkeit schon im Werk der Deuteronomisten, das mit dem Ende des babylonischen Exils nicht abgeschlossen war, sondern bis weit in die Zeit des zweiten Tempels hinein gewirkt und zu der Entstehung des Judentums maßgeblich beigetragen hat.[2] Veijola richtete sein Augenmerk hauptsächlich auf die Tora und die vorderen Propheten, aber es versteht sich von selbst, daß auch die späteren Propheten, d. h. die eigentlichen Prophetenbücher, in denselben Problemkreis gehören. Daß die Deuteronomisten zur Redaktion der Prophetenbücher einen wichtigen Beitrag leisteten, ist seit Jahrzehnten anerkannt, auch wenn der Umfang der deuteronomistischen Redaktion in den einzelnen Prophetenbüchern nach wie vor eine Streitfrage ist und das Deuteronomistische in ihnen verschieden definiert wird.[3]

In den neuesten Studien zu den Prophetenbüchern hat die Rolle, die die Schreiber bei der Gestaltung der Prophetenbücher in der nachmonarchischen Zeit hatten, beträchtlich an Bedeutung gewonnen, und zwar unabhängig davon, ob sie als Angehörige einer deuteronomistischen Schule betrachtet werden.[4] Dazu zählt

---

1 S. die in T. Veijola, *Moses Erben: Studien zur Dekalog, zum Deuteronomismus und zum Schriftgelehrtentum* (BWANT 149; Stuttgart: Kohlhammer, 2000) gesammelten Beiträge, insbesondere „Die Deuteronomisten als Vorgänger der Schriftgelehrten: Ein Beitrag zur Entstehung des Judentums" (ibid., 192–240).

2 Veijola, *Moses Erben*, 238.

3 Vgl. z. B. T. Römer, „L'École deutéronomiste et la formation de la Bible hébraïque," in *The Future of the Deuteronomistic History* (ed. id.; BETL 117; Leuven: Peeters, 2000) 179–93, dort 185–87.

4 O. H. Steck, *Die Prophetenbücher und ihr theologisches Zeugnis: Wege der Nachfrage und Fährten zur Antwort* (Tübingen: Mohr Siebeck, 1996); E. Ben Zvi, „The Urban Center of Jerusalem and the Development of the Literature of the Hebrew Bible," in *Urbanism in Antiquity: From Mesopotamia to Greece* (ed. Walter E. Aufrecht, N. A. Mirau, and S. W. Gauley; JSOTSup 244; Sheffield: Sheffield Academic Press, 1997), 194–209; id., *Micah* (FOTL 21B; Grand Rapids, Mich.: Eerdmans, 2000), 4–6; id., *Hosea* (FOTL 21 A/1; Grand Rapids, Mich.: Eerdmans, 2005), 4–6; M. H. Floyd, „The Production of Prophetic Books in the Early Second Temple Period," in *Prophets, Prophecy, and*

DOI 10.1515/9783110466546-029

auch ein kleiner Artikel von meiner Hand, in dem ich versuche, den Weg vom Prophetenwort zur Literatur umgekehrt von den späten Textzeugen zurück zum gesprochenen Wort zu verfolgen.[5] Dabei sehe ich in den Prophetenbüchern das Ergebnis der literarischen Tätigkeit der nachmonarchischen Zeit, muß aber abschließend auch noch fragen, ob es wirklich nötig war, einen schriftlichen Text zu haben, um die Botschaft der Propheten über Generationen übermitteln zu können, oder ob die Worte der Propheten doch in erster Linie mündlich überliefert worden sind.[6] Damit verbunden ist die Frage, in welchen Kreisen eine solche Überlieferung stattgefunden haben konnte. Da ich dieses Problem damals nur annäherungsweise skizzieren konnte,[7] möchte ich hier den Fragenkreis etwas eingehender behandeln.[8]

Als Ausgangspunkt wähle ich einen interessanten Artikel von James L. Crenshaw.[9] Crenshaw plädiert stark für die mündliche Übermittlung der Prophetenworte in Schülerkreisen. Mit Recht verweist er auf die sehr begrenzte Kunst des Lesens und Schreibens und auf den wesentlich mündlichen Charakter weisheitlicher Lehre im alten Israel und Juda und fragt, ob die Prophetie anders überliefert werden sein kann.[10] Nach dem Beispiel von Schülern, die sich um einen

---

Prophetic Texts in Second Temple Judaism (ed. id. and R. D. Haak; LHBOTS 427; London: T & T Clark, 2006) 276–97; R. G. Kratz, *Die Propheten Israels* (Munich: Beck, 2003), 41–51.

5 M. Nissinen, „How Prophecy Became Literature," *SJOT* 19 (2005) 153–72.

6 Die Rolle der mündlichen Überlieferung neben und hinter dem geschriebenen Wort ist jüngst vor allem von S. Niditch, *Oral World and Written Word: Ancient Israelite Literature* (Library of Ancient Israel; Louisville, Ky.: Westminster John Knox, 1996), zur Diskussion gestellt worden. Auch D. M. Carr, *Writing on the Tablet of the Heart: Origins of Scripture and Literature* (New York: Oxford University Press, 2005), betont die überwiegend orale Lernweise und die Gleichzeitigkeit von mündlicher und schriftlicher Tradition in ostmediterranen Gesellschaften. Zu dieser Symbiose aus der Perspektive der Prophetenbücher, s. E. Ben Zvi, „Introduction: Writings, Speeches, and the Prophetic Books: Setting an Agenda," in *Writings and Speech in Israelite and Ancient Near Eastern Prophecy* (ed. id. und M. H. Floyd; SBLSymS 10; Atlanta, Ga.: Society of Biblical Literature, 2000) 1–29, dort 21–28.

7 Nissinen, „How Prophecy Became Literature," 170–72.

8 Im Januar 2006 hatte ich die Gelegenheit, die hier behandelten Fragen im Rahmen des „souper biblique" des biblischen Instituts an der Universität Fribourg zu diskutieren. Ich möchte an dieser Stelle meinen Kollegen Hans Ulrich Steymans, Othmar Keel und Max Küchler sowie den anderen Anwesenden, die an der anregenden Diskussion teilnahmen, herzlich danken.

9 J. L. Crenshaw, „Transmitting Prophecy across Generations," in: Ben Zvi und Floyd (ed.), *Writings and Speech in Israelite and Ancient Near Eastern Prophecy*, 31–44.

10 Crenshaw, „Transmitting Prophecy across Generations," 42–43: „If writing played a minimal role among the Israelite sages, is it likely that things were different in prophetic circles? Never does a wisdom teacher in Israel advise anyone to consult a written text; instead, young men are urged to observe what transpires before their eyes and to listen eagerly to intelligent people. That is how one aqcuired knowledge."

Lehrer versammelten, postuliert Crenshaw Kreise der Nachfolger der Propheten, die die Botschaft ihres Meisters treu (wenn auch nicht notwendig wortgetreu) bewahrten und überlieferten. Diese Gruppen hätten mit Institutionen wie Hof und Tempel in Austausch gestanden, seien jedoch im wesentlichen unabhängig (self-sustaining), nicht-institutionalisiert gewesen. Es habe sich nicht um literarische Kreise gehandelt; die wenigen Hinweise auf Verschriftung prophetischer Worte seien eher als Einzelfälle zu verstehen. Vielmehr hätte das *traditum* in mündlicher Form bestanden, wie es in der überwiegend nicht-literarischen Kultur im allgemeinen der Fall gewesen sei.[11]

Die Bedeutung der mündlichen Überlieferung über Generationen hinweg ist als ein verbreitetes Phänomen sicher nicht zu unterschätzen. Die Tatsache, daß es jedenfalls schriftliche Prophetenworte gibt, und zwar nicht nur in der Bibel, sondern auch in anderen altorientalischen Quellen, berechtigt jedoch zu der Frage, warum es denn überhaupt nötig wurde, sie aufzuschreiben, und wer dies getan haben soll, wenn die Prophetenschüler sich nicht mit literarischen Unternehmungen beschäftigten.

Die Prophetenschüler als Tradenten der Prophetenworte sind natürlich nicht erst von Crenshaw ins Spiel gebracht worden. Schon lange wurde angenommen, daß zum Beispiel die Worte des Hosea von einem Kreis seiner Schüler bewahrt und nach dem Untergang des Nordreichs in den Süden mitgebracht wurden.[12] Im Unterschied zu der Theorie von Crenshaw denkt man dabei nicht so sehr an die mündliche Überlieferung, sondern eher an einen literarischen Nachlaß, der schon in Buchform existierte und als die Urform des biblischen Hoseabuches diente.

Wollen wir das Bild von einem Propheten als einem von Schülern umgebenen heiligen Mann aufrecht erhalten, verbunden mit der Annahme einer festen, von den Schülern gepflegten mündlichen Tradition, erhebt sich die Frage nach der historischen Beweisfähigkeit dieser Annahme; denn so eindeutig ist die Sache angesichts des indirekten Zeugnisses des in einem langen Redaktionsprozeß entstandenen Textes der hebräischen Bibel nicht. Deswegen soll es das Ziel dieses kleinen Aufsatzes sein, eine Antwort auf die einfache Frage zu geben: Gibt es Beweise für Schülerkreise der Propheten, die die Worte ihres prophetischen Leiters entweder mündlich oder schriftlich bewahrt und überliefert haben?

---

11 Crenshaw, „Transmitting Prophecy across Generations," 35–40.

12 S. J. Jeremias, *Der Prophet Hosea* (ATD 24/1; Göttingen: Vandenhoeck & Ruprecht, 1983), 18–19; vgl. T. Naumann, *Hoseas Erben: Strukturen der Nachinterpretation im Buch Hosea* (BWANT 131; Stuttgart: Kohlhammer, 1991), 164–66, der nicht von Schülern, sondern von einem „Kreis der Gleichgesinnten" spricht.

II

Wäre die Existenz prophetischer Schülerkreise für die Verfasser der Prophetenbücher und anderer Schriften der hebräischen Bibel selbstverständlich gewesen, sollten wir erwarten, daß sich diese Überzeugung mit einiger Klarheit im Bibeltext widerspiegelt. Dies ist aber nicht der Fall. Die Erzählungen über Propheten und ihren Taten in den erzählenden und prophetischen Büchern der hebräischen Bibel wissen erstaunlich wenig darüber zu berichten; vielmehr wird den Lesern und Hörern in der Regel das Bild eines Propheten als einer Einzelfigur vermittelt, der nicht mit einer Schar von Schülern umherwandelt und ihnen seine Lehre in einem geschlossenen Kreis weitergibt, vielmehr in der Öffentlichkeit auftritt.[13]

Als Ausnahme erscheint allerdings der Prophet Elischa, wird doch in den Elischaerzählungen mehrfach berichtet, wie der Prophet mit „Prophetensöhnen" *(bĕnê han-nĕbîʾîm)* umgeht (2 Kön 2:1–18; 4:1–7, 38–41; 5:22; 6:1–7; 9:1–13). Was ist damit gemeint? Im Singular kommt der Ausdruck *ben nābîʾ* nur in Am 7:14 vor in der berühmten Behauptung des Propheten Amos, er sei kein Prophet und auch kein „Prophetensohn", was in diesem Zusammenhang wohl ein Mitglied der Prophetenzunft bedeutet, entweder als eine allgemeine Berufsbezeichnung[14] oder als Hinweis auf eine prophetische Gruppe. An was für eine Sozietät hier aber gedacht ist, bleibt im Dunkel; allerdings können wir beobachten, wie der Verfasser dieser Erzählung implizit den unabhängigen Bauern Amos, der wirklich von Gott berufen ist, von den Propheten unterscheidet, denen auf solche Weise die Eigenschaft des Propheten abgesprochen wird, obwohl die prophetische Tätigkeit ihnen Lebensunterhalt darstellt.[15] So folgenschwer diese Dichotomie für das spätere (akademische) Prophetenideal gewesen ist, hilft sie für unsere Fragestellung nicht weiter.

Wie verhält es sich aber mit dem Schülerkreis um Elischa? Der einzige Beleg von *bĕnê han-nĕbîʾîm* außerhalb der Elischaerzählungen kommt ein wenig früher im ersten Königebuch vor, wo ein anonymer „Prophetensohn" den Tod des Königs Ahab verkündet (1 Kön 20:35–43). Er wird *ʾîš ʾeḥād mib-bĕnê han-nĕbîʾîm* genannt

---

13 Vgl. H. Wildberger, *Jesaja, 1. Teilband: Jesaja 1–12* (BKAT 10/1; Neukirchen-Vluyn: Neukirchener, 1972), 346 über Jesaja: „Wie andere Propheten steht er auf einsamer Höhe, aber sein Wort gilt letztlich immer der *Öffentlichkeit*, dem Volk und dessen verantwortlichen Führern" (Hervorhebung im Original).

14 Vgl. die Berufsbezeichnungen im Nehemiabuch: *ben-ḥarhayâ* „Salbenmischer" (Neh 3:8); *bĕnê hamšōrĕrîm* „Sänger" (Neh 12:28); dieser Gebrauch des Wortes *ben* entspricht dem des akkadischen *māru* (s. *CAD* M/1: 314–15).

15 S. J. Jeremias, *Der Prophet Amos* (ATD 24/2; Göttingen: Vandenhoeck & Ruprecht, 1995), 110.

(vgl. 2 Kön 2:7; 5:22; 9:1), woraus man den Eindruck gewinnt, daß die „Prophetensöhne“ als eine Gruppe vorgestellt werden. Dasselbe ist auch den Elischaerzählungen zu entnehmen. Die *bĕnê han-nĕbîʾîm* agieren oft als Gruppe, sind immer anonym, und es wird deutlich vorausgesetzt, daß Elischa unter ihnen die führende Rolle innehat: die Prophetensöhne beugen sich vor ihm (2 Kön 2:15), er beauftragt einen von ihnen mit der Salbung des Jehu zum König (2 Kön 9:1–3), und sie versammeln sich im Haus des Elischa, wo sie „vor ihm sitzen“ (2 Kön 4:38; 6:1). Was in diesen Versammlungen genau geschieht (außer Speisen, 2 Kön 4:38–41), wird nirgendwo erzählt. Man kann sich vorstellen, daß der Leiter der prophetischen Gruppe den vor ihm Sitzenden etwas von seiner prophetischen Kunst beibringt, aber nichts deutet darauf hin, daß dazu die mündliche oder schriftliche Überlieferung prophetischer Tradition gehört. Die Erzählungen geben nirgends den Eindruck, die „Prophetensöhne“ seien mit der Bewahrung der Worte ihres Meisters Elischa, der auch gar nicht als Rhetoriker vorgestellt ist, befaßt gewesen.

Die historischen Rückschlüsse über die Rolle der „Prophetensöhne“ werden auch dadurch erschwert, daß wir nicht wissen, ob die Elischaerzählungen uns wirklich über Begebenheiten des 9. Jahrhunderts v. Chr. informieren. Als Teil des deuteronomistischen Geschichtswerks erscheinen sie jetzt innerhalb eines viel späteren literarischen Rahmens und können deshalb ein anachronistisches Bild der Prophetie im 9. Jh. vermitteln; selbst Crenshaw hält die Elija- und Elischaerzählungen für Rückprojektionen späterer Vorstellungen über die frühe Prophetie,[16] so daß er die einzigen in der hebräischen Bibel explizit vorkommenden Prophetenschüler als Beweis für seine These entwertet. Demgegenüber hat neuerdings Bernhard Lehnart mit Nachdruck die These vertreten, die *bĕnê han-nĕbîʾîm* selbst seien für die Überlieferung der von den Deuteronomisten übernommenen Elischatradition verantwortlich.[17] Dieses Argument ist mit der Schwierigkeit belastet, daß in den Erzählungen weder ein Hinweis auf mündliche Überlieferung noch auf die literarische Schulung der „Prophetensöhne“ zu finden ist. Das konzentrierte Vorkommen der *bĕnê han-nĕbîʾîm* in der Tradition um Elischa läßt sie als eine eigene, mit Gilgal verbundene soziologische Größe erscheinen,[18] die

---

16 Crenshaw, „Transmitting Prophecy across Generations,“ 36 Anm. 16.

17 B. Lehnart, *Prophet und König im Nordreich Israel: Studien zur sogenannten vorklassischen Prophetie im Nordreich Israel anhand der Samuel-, Elija- und Elischa-Überlieferungen* (VTSup 96; Leiden: Brill, 2003), 439–71. Auch S. Otto, *Jehu, Elia und Elisa: Die Erzählung von der Jehu-Revolution und die Komposition der Elia-Elisa-Erzählungen* (BWANT 152; Stuttgart; Kohlhammer, 2001), hat sich dafür ausgesprochen, daß die ältesten Erzählungen über Elischa in den Kreisen der Elischaschüler entstanden sind und auch die späteren Bearbeitungen prophetischen Kreisen entstammen.

18 Vgl. Lehnart, *Prophet und König im Nordreich Israel*, 450.

möglicherweise phänomenologisch mit der in den Samuel-Saul-Geschichten vorkommenden Gruppenprophetie (1 Sam 10:5–7, 10–12; 19:19–24) zu tun hat, aber nicht allgemein als Vorbild eines prophetischen Schülerkreises im biblischen Israel gelten kann. Wie Lehnart richtig bemerkt, „dürfte der Akzent ihres Wirkens am ehesten im heilenden und exorzistischen Bereich zu suchen sein";[19] ob sich damit eine Textproduktion verbinden läßt, wird man eher bezweifeln müssen.[20] Außerdem hat die Gruppe der *běnê han-nĕbîʾîm* nach Lehnart das Ende des Nordreichs nicht überlebt, was wohl auch das Ende der Kontinuität einer mündlichen Tradition gewesen sein dürfte. Wenn damals schon eine schriftliche Tradition vorlag, wie entstand sie, wer waren die Traditionsträger und wo wurden die Schriften seitdem gepflegt und bewahrt, um sie viel später den Deuteronomisten zugänglich zu machen? Wie auch immer die Antwort lautet, bedurfte es dazu Menschen, die in die schriftliche Kultur hineingewachsen waren.

Außer Elischa ist ein Prophet, der von Schülern umgeben gewesen ist, in der hebräischen Bibel kaum zu finden. Indiziert dies, daß Schülerkreise nicht zu dem Prophetenbild der Tradenten gehörten und auch historisch nicht vorhanden gewesen sind?

III

Daß die Propheten in Gemeinschaften lebten, ist aus dem altorientalischen Befund klar. In Assyrien wie auch in Mari gehörten die Propheten in der Regel zu Tempelgemeinschaften.[21] Dabei handelt es sich nicht um im engeren Sinne prophetische Kreise, sondern um Kultgemeinschaften, in denen die prophetische Tätigkeit mit anderen Kulthandlungen, z. B. mit Musik und Klage, in Verbindung

19 Lehnart, *Prophet und König im Nordreich Israel,* 467.

20 Der Raum mit einer prophetischen Wandinschrift in Deir ʿAlla ist als einen Versammlungsraum von prophetischen Gruppen gedeutet worden (R. Wenning und E. Zenger, „Heiligtum ohne Stadt – Stadt ohne Heiligtum: Anmerkungen zum archäologischen Befund des Tell Dēr ʿAllā," *ZAH* 4 [1991] 171–93; vgl. Lehnart, *Prophet und König im Nordreich Israel,* 467–68), was dafür sprechen würde, daß in solchen Kreisen auch schriftliche Prophetenworte überliefert wurden. Gibt es aber wirklich hier eine Analogie mit den biblischen Erzählungen? In der Bibel haben wir prophetische Gruppen, die sich in einem Raum versammeln aber nichts lesen und schreiben, in Deir ʿAlla gibt es wiederum einen Raum mit einem prophetischen Text ohne Angaben davon, wer den Text verfaßt hat.

21 S. z. B. M. Nissinen, „Das kritische Potential in der altorientalischen Prophetie," in *Propheten in Mari, Assyrien und Israel* (ed. M. Köckert und M. Nissinen; FRLANT 201; Göttingen: Vandenhoeck & Ruprecht, 2003) 1–32, dort 4–14 (= S. 163–94 in dem vorliegenden Band).

steht.[22] Man kann sich leicht vorstellen, daß die Propheten als Mitglieder dieser Gemeinschaften auch ihre prophetische Rolle und die dazugehörenden Fertigkeiten erlernten, aber nichts deutet darauf hin, daß sich solche Schülerkreise um einen einzelnen Charismatiker geschart hätten. Für eine mündliche oder schriftliche Überlieferung der Prophetenworte in diesen Gemeinschaften gibt es im altorientalischen Schrifttum ebensowenig einen Beweis. Wir können allenfalls davon ausgehen, daß die Propheten als Mitglieder der Tempelgemeinschaften mit ihren divinatorischen Methoden, ihrer Sprache und anderen Ausdrucksweisen vertraut gemacht wurden und daß eine Schülerschaft in diesem Sinne gut vorstellbar ist.

Ähnliche Aspekte kommen auch in der hebräischen Bibel vor; was in den uns bekannten altorientalischen Quellen freilich bisher fehlt, sind die Wundertaten, die Elischa und seinen „Prophetensöhnen" in der hebräischen Bibel zugeschrieben werden. Wie es mit der Historizität der „Prophetensöhne" um Elischa und den prophetischen Gruppen in den Samuel- und Saulüberlieferungen auch sei, in den diesbezüglichen biblischen Erzählungen wird eine prophetische Gruppenbildung vorausgesetzt, und zwar in der Nähe von Kultstätten.[23] Die hebräische Bibel hat diese Art von Prophetie als Präludium zu der eigentlichen, durch Einzelfiguren verkörperten Prophetie dargestellt, und in diesem Sinne hat die alttestamentliche Forschung sie mit dem Attribut „vorklassisch" versehen. Interessant dabei ist, daß beinahe alles, was von der Tätigkeit dieser Propheten erzählt wird, gut zu dem paßt, was wir von der altorientalischen Prophetie im allgemeinen wissen: Verbindung mit dem Kult, ein göttlich inspirierter, veränderter Sinneszustand bzw. Ekstase, Musik, Wahrsagen, Zugehörigkeit zu einer Gemeinschaft und eine aus all diesem folgende unkonventionelle gesellschaftliche Rolle, die wohl zu dem Sprichwort „Ist denn auch Saul unter den Propheten?" (1 Sam 10:12; 19:24) Anlaß gegeben hat.[24]

Es sind aber nicht nur die „vorklassischen" Gruppenpropheten, die sich in der hebräischen Bibel prophetisch benehmen—Wahrsagen, Ekstase, seltsames Be-

22 Als erhellendes Beispiel dafür kann das Ištar-Ritual aus Mari dienen; s. J.-M. Durand und M. Guichard, „Les rituels de Mari," in *Florilegium Marianum 3*, FS M.-T. Barrelet (Mémoires de NABU 4; Paris: SEPOA, 1997) 19–78, bes. 52–58.

23 Ähnliches könnte man anhand der riesigen Prophetenscharen vermuten, die als Gegenspieler von Elija und Micha ben Jimla erscheinen (1 Kön 18:19: 450 Propheten des Baal und 400 der Aschera; 1 Kön 22:6: 400 Propheten). Da diese jedoch eher als eine *massa perditionis* falscher Propheten dargestellt werden, ist es schwierig zu Sagen, ob dabei an irgendwelche Gemeinschaftsbildung im konkreten Sinne gedacht worden ist.

24 S. zu der Tätigkeit der Gruppenpropheten Lehnart, *Prophet und König im Nordreich Israel*, 449–54.

nehmen und eine ungewöhnliche soziale Rolle gehören auch zu dem Profil der „großen" Propheten. Selbst das kritische Potential haben die biblischen Propheten mit den altorientalischen gemeinsam. Auch das Verhältnis der Propheten mit dem Kult sollte nicht nur anhand des Amosworts „Ich hasse eure Feste!" (Am 5:21) aufgefaßt werden, steht doch von Jesaja und Ezechiel bis Maleachi und der Chronik der vermeintlich antikultischen Orientierung der biblischen Propheten die fundamentale Verbindung mit dem Tempel gegenüber.

Aus der uns zur Verfügung stehenden altorientalischen Überlieferung gewinnt man den Eindruck, daß die Propheten sogar mehrheitlich Frauen waren und daß Prophetie jedenfalls zu den wenigen Berufen gehörte, die beiden Geschlechtern offen waren. Prophetinnen sind auch in der hebräischen Bibel bekannt, wo vier Prophetinnen namentlich genannt werden—Mirjam (Ex 15:20), Debora (Ri 4:4), Hulda (2 Kön 22:14) und Noadja (Neh 6:14)—während die Prophetin, mit der Jesaja Kinder zeugt (Jes 8:3), namenlos bleibt. Es ist durchaus möglich, daß die Rolle der Frauen in der altisraelitischen Prophetie gewichtiger gewesen ist, als der biblische Text uns zu verstehen gibt.[25] Theoretisch könnten die Prophetinnen ebensogut wie männliche Propheten Leiter der Prophetengemeinschaften gewesen sein; der Hinweis auf „Noadja und die übrigen Propheten" mag die führende Rolle von Prophetinnen in Jerusalem zur Zeit Nehemias andeuten (Neh 6:14). Auch hier spielt aber mündliche oder schriftliche Überlieferung keine Rolle, sondern die Frage nach der gesellschaftlichen Stellung der Prophetie in der Perserzeit.

Das Neue in der biblischen Prophetie ist demnach keine historische Reformation des prophetischen Phänomens von einer primitiven „vorklassischen" zu der geistig wie moralisch überlegenen „klassischen" Prophetie; was von den biblischen Propheten erzählt wird, stimmt meistens mit dem altorientalischen Befund überein. Vielmehr geht es um ein neues, durch Neuinterpretation des Alten entstandenes Verständnis des Verhältnisses von Gott und Israel, wobei der Prophetie eine entscheidende Rolle zugeschrieben ist.[26] Hier geht es offenbar nicht um mündliche Überlieferung alter Prophetenworte, sondern um gelehrte, ausle-

---

25 S. z. B. R. Kessler, „Mirjam und die Propheten der Perserzeit," in *Gott an den Rändern*, FS W. Schottroff (ed. U. Bail and R. Jost; Gütersloh: Gütersloher Verlagshaus, 1996) 64–72, bes. 71; engl. „Miriam and the Prophecy of the Persian Period," in *Prophets and Daniel* (ed. A. Brenner; FCB 8; Sheffield: Sheffield Academic Press, 2001) 77–86; und programmatisch I. Fischer, *Gotteskünderinnen: Zu einer geschlechtsfairen Deutung des Phänomens Prophetie und der Prophetinnen in der hebräischen Bibel* (Stuttgart: Kohlhammer, 2002). Vgl. auch U. Bechmann, „Prophetische Frauen am Zweiten Tempel? Ein Vorschlag, die Töchter Zelofhads (Num 27) als Kultprophetinnen zu verstehen," *BN* 119/120 (2003) 52–62.

26 S. R. G. Kratz, „Das Neue in der Prophetie des Alten Testaments," in *Prophetie in Israel: Beiträge des Symposiums „Das Alte Testament und die Kultur der Moderne,"* GS G. von Rad (ed. I. Fischer, K. Schmid und H. G. M. Williamson; Altes Testament und Moderne 11; Münster: LIT, 2003) 1–22.

gende Tätigkeit, die die vorliegende alte Tradition auf eine neue Grundlage stellt und schriftlich neu kontextualisiert, so daß die Propheten erst jetzt Propheten im biblischen Sinne werden, während das Alte nur in wenigen, dem neuen Kontext untergeordneten Resten identifizierbar ist. Kurzum: die althebräische Prophetie wird zur biblischen Prophetie.[27]

IV

Die altorientalischen schriftlichen Dokumente geben keine direkten Belege dafür, daß die Prophetenorakel auf eine feste mündliche Tradition zurückgehen. Gewiß ist vor allem in den assyrischen Prophetensprüchen Phraseologie anzutreffen, die durchaus zum mündlichen Repertoire der assyrischen Propheten gehört haben kann[28] und die die Propheten zum Beispiel im Kontext der Ištarverehrung gelernt haben. Es gibt auch Verweise auf früher ausgesprochene Orakel.[29] Dies bedeutet nicht, daß diese Orakel als ganze überliefertes Gut darstellten. Vielmehr gelten sie als Dokumente von einzelnen prophetischen Auftritten, die *ad hoc* formuliert und nach Bedarf dem König zur Kenntnis gebracht wurden. Der ganze Prozeß konnte durchweg mündlich vor sich gehen (ohne daß daraus eine mündliche Tradition entstand), aber manchmal bekamen die mündlich gesprochenen Orakel auch eine schriftliche Form, entweder als aufgeschriebene Einzelorakel wie in Assyrien, oder als Zitate in Briefen, wie wir sie aus Mari wie auch aus Assyrien gut kennen. Wenn die verschrifteten Prophetien darüber hinaus archiviert wurden, wurden sie zugleich Teil der literarischen Tradition und Material für *Schreiber*tätigkeit, wie es in

27 Zur Unterscheidung von althebräischer und biblischer Prophetie, s. M. Nissinen, „What Is Prophecy? An Ancient Near Eastern Perspective," in *Inspired Speech: Prophecy in the Ancient Near East*, FS H. B. Huffmon (ed. J. Kaltner and L. Stulman; JSOTS 378; London: T & T Clark, 2004) 17–37, dort 31 (= S. 53–73 in dem vorliegenden Band).

28 Vgl. M. Nissinen, „The Socioreligious Role of the Neo-Assyrian Prophets," in *Prophecy in its Ancient Near Eastern Context: Mesopotamian, Biblical, and Arabian Perspectives* (SBLSymS 13; Atlanta, Ga.: Society of Biblical Literature, 2000) 89–114, 97–98 (= S. 103–26 in dem vorliegenden Band). Dies würde ungefähr dem entsprechen, was R. C. Culley mit mündlich-traditionellem (oral-traditional) Stil meint; s. id., „Orality and Writtenness in the Prophetic Texts," in: Ben Zvi und Floyd (eds.), *Writings and Speech in Israelite and Ancient Near Eastern Prophecy*, 45–64.

29 S. M. Weippert, „'Das Frühere, siehe, ist eingetroffen...': Über Selbstzitate im Prophetenspruch," in *Oracles et prophéties dans l'antiquité: Actes du Colloque de Strasbourg 15–17 Juin 1995* (ed. J.-G. Heintz; Université des sciences humaines de Strasbourg, Travaux du Centre de recherche sur le Proche-Orient et la Grèce antiques 15; Paris: Boccard, 1997) 147–69.

Assyrien nachweislich, wenn auch in geringem Maße, der Fall war.[30] Was in den altorientalischen Quellen interessanterweise fehlt, ist jeder Hinweis auf Memorierung und Überlieferung der prophetischen Worte innerhalb prophetischer Gemeinschaften. Auch das Prophet-Schüler-Modell tritt nirgends in Erscheinung. Obschon die Prophetensprüche ihre Sprache und Ideologie sicher aus einer festen literarisch-kultischen Tradition schöpfen, sind sie offenbar nicht selbst als *traditum* gemeint. Die Wiederverwendung der Prophetensprüchen beginnt erst mit deren Verschriftung und Archivierung.

Auch in der hebräischen Bibel deutet das Werden der Prophetenbücher eher auf einen schriftlichen Wiederverwendungs- und Interpretationsprozeß, d. h. auf Redaktion und Fortschreibung, als auf einen mündlichen Ursprung der Texte hin.[31] Als solche sind die Prophetenbücher Werke der postmonarchischen Gesellschaften und ihr Adressat ist die Gemeinde des zweiten Tempels von Jerusalem. Da sie nachdrücklich und exklusiv als Wort Gottes dargestellt sind, das den Propheten der Vergangenheit zukam, das aber in der Gegenwart oder in der Zukunft in Erfüllung gehen soll (die kanonischen Prophetenbücher sind eschatologische Literatur!), gehört es zu ihrer Textstrategie, jegliche Spuren nachträglicher Überlieferer zu verwischen. Daß die Prophetenbücher nicht von Prophetenschülern schwärmen, mag sich zumindest theoretisch daraus erklären, daß die Prophetenschüler eben dieser Strategie zum Opfer gefallen sind; dasselbe gilt natürlich auch für die Redaktoren, die außer indirekten Andeutungen wie Jer 36:32 nirgends erwähnt werden.

Gibt es solche Hinweise auch auf Prophetenschüler? Es gibt eine wichtige Stelle, wo „Schüler" explizit genannt sind (Jes 8:16 – 18):

> Verschnüre das Zeugnis, versiegle die Weisung im Beisein meiner Schüler (*bě-limmūdāy*)! Ich will auf JHWH warten, der sein Angesicht vor dem Haus Jakob verbirgt, und auf ihn hoffen. Siehe, ich und die Kinder, die mir JHWH gegeben hat, sind Zeichen und Weissagung in Israel von JHWH Zebaoth, der auf dem Berge Zion wohnt.

30 Den prophetischen Kommunikationsprozeß habe ich in „Spoken, Written, Quoted and Invented: Orality and Writtenness in Ancient Near Eastern Prophecy," in Ben Zvi und Floyd (ed.), *Writings and Speech in Israelite and Ancient Near Eastern Prophecy*, 235 – 71 zu skizzieren versucht.

31 Zur Fortschreibung als Schlüssel der Entstehung der Prophetenbücher s. R. G. Kratz, „Die Redaktion der Prophetenbücher," in *Rezeption und Auslegung im Alten Testament und in seinem Umfeld*, FS O. H. Steck (ed. id. und T. Krüger; OBO 153; Freiburg Schweiz und Göttingen: Universitätsverlag und Vandenhoeck & Ruprecht, 1997) 9 – 27, dort 15.

Die *limmūdîm* in Jes 8:16 versteht man zumeist als Schüler des Jesaja.[32] Soll dies der Fall sein, könnte die Stelle den erwünschten historischen Beweis für Prophetenschüler als Vermittler der Prophetenworte erbringen, besonders wenn das Stück in die Zeit des Jesaja datiert werden kann. Wie dem auch sei, verdient es immerhin Beachtung, daß die *limmūdîm* hier nicht Worte ihres Lehrers lernen oder überliefern. Die Schriftrolle wird „unter meinen Schülern" (*bĕ-limmūdāy*), das heißt in ihrer Anwesenheit,[33] versiegelt. Die Schüler dienen nicht als Tradenten, sondern als Zeugen bei der Versiegelung der Rolle.[34] Darüber hinaus stehen die „Kinder" (vgl. Jes 7:3; 8:3) zusammen mit dem Propheten als Zeichen und Omina (*lĕ-'ōtôt û-lĕ-môpĕtîm*) da. Eine in ähnlicher Weise zukunftsorientierte Vorstellung ist auch anderswo im Buch Jesaja (Jes 30:8) und im Buch Habakuk (Hab 2:2–3) zu finden, freilich ohne jeden Hinweis auf Schüler:

> Jes 30:8: So geh nun hin und schreib es vor ihnen nieder auf eine Tafel und zeichne es in einem Buch, daß es bleibe für immer und ewig.
>
> Hab 2:2–3: Schreib auf, was du geschaut hast, deutlich auf eine Tafel, damit man sie geläufig lesen kann! Denn die Schauung wird noch erfüllt werden zu ihrer Zeit und wird endlich frei an den Tag kommen und nicht trügen.

In keiner von diesen drei Stellen ist von einer mündlich zu überliefernden Lehre die Rede, sondern von einer versiegelten Rolle (Jes 8:16) oder einer Schrifttafel (Hab 2:2) oder von beidem (Jes 30:8), also von einem schriftlichen Dokument (einem Prophetenbuch?), das an die kommenden Generationen gerichtet ist, damit sie den Plan Gottes zur gegebenen Zeit lesen, hören und verstehen. Die Perspektive ist ganz und gar die der späteren Leser- und Hörerschaft und mag eher auf die Situation der späteren Tradenten der literarischen Tradition als auf die Schüler des Propheten Jesaja bzw. Habakuk oder die Propheten selbst hindeuten.[35]

---

32 So die meisten Kommentare, z. B. J. Blenkinsopp, *Isaiah 1–39: A New Translation with Introduction and Commentary* (AB 19; New York: Doubleday, 2000), 243–44. Vgl. Carr, *Writing on the Tablet of the Heart,* 143–45.

33 Die Präposition *bĕ* ist mehrdeutig, jedoch läßt sich *bĕ-limmūdāy* eher im rechtlichen Sinne verstehen als Hinweis auf eine wirkliche Versiegelung der Rolle in Anwesenheit der *limmūdîm* (vgl. Jes 8:2 und Rt 4:7 und s. O. Kaiser, *Das Buch des Propheten Jesaja: Kapitel 1–12* [ATD 17; Göttingen: Vandenhoeck & Ruprecht, [5]1981], 190) als als Metapher („in meinen Jüngern") für die Weitergabe der Tradition (so u. a. Wildberger, *Jesaja 1–12,* 344).

34 Vgl. den Maribrief ARM 26 414, wo der Schreiber eine Prophetie in Anwesenheit von Zeugen niederschreibt und dem König übersendet; s. Nissinen, „Spoken, Written, Quoted and Invented," 245–46.

35 Vgl. Steck, *Die Prophetenbücher und ihr theologisches Zeugnis,* 176–77: „Mit Gottesworten begabte Nachkommenschaft Jesajas – wir stehen nicht an, hierin Jesajas Tradentennachkommenschaft zu sehen, womöglich sogar die Traditionspflege in einem bestimmten Schreibermilieu,

Die Vorstellung der versiegelten Rolle setzt möglicherweise schon die Existenz der Prophetenbücher in irgendwelcher Form voraus, was eine Frühdatierung eher unwahrscheinlich macht,[36] obschon man in diesen Stellen auch den Beweis dafür gesehen hat, daß zumindest einige Propheten ihre Worte selbst schriftlich überliefert haben.[37] Bemerkenswert ist auf alle Fälle die Betonung der *Schrift* als Methode der Bewahrung der Prophetie.[38] Der Vorgang ist im Prinzip derselbe wie in Assyrien (abgesehen davon, daß das eschatologische Moment der biblischen Prophetenbücher dort noch fehlt): Prophetenworte, die als besonders wichtig galten, wurden aufgeschrieben und gespeichert, damit das in ihnen dokumentierte Gotteswort als Zeuge des göttlichen Willens auch in späteren Zeiten vorhanden war.

V

Gibt es also einen Beweis für Schülerkreise der Propheten, die die Worte ihres prophetischen Meisters entweder mündlich oder schriftlich bewahrt und überliefert haben? Angesichts des biblischen und altorientalischen Befunds muß die Antwort ein qualifiziertes „Nein" sein. Die Idee der Prophetenschüler als Über-

---

in dem Jahwes Jesaja verliehener Geist weiterhin wirksam ist"; P. D. Miscall, *Isaiah* (Readings; Sheffield: JSOT Press, 1993), 39–40: „Isaiah 'back then' had this knowledge, this teaching and testimony, and handed it on through his 'children and disciples.' These are figures for all who listen to or read Isaiah whether those depicted later in the book are no longer deaf and blind or postexilic readers of the book of Isaiah"; W. Zwickel, „Kommunikation und Kommunikationsmöglichkeiten im alten Israel aufgrund biblischer und außerbiblischer Texte," in *Bote und Brief: Sprachliche Systeme der Informationsübermittlung im Spannungsfeld von Mündlichkeit und Schriftlichkeit* (ed. A. Wagner; Nordostafrikanisch/Westasiatische Studien 4; Frankfurt a. M.: Peter Lang, 2003), 113–23, dort 116: „Prophetische Botschaft soll hier um ihrer Überprüfbarkeit willen schriftlich festgehalten werden, nicht um der Wertigkeit als theologischer Text willen."

36 Ein Text wie Jes 8:16 ist natürlich nicht notwendig als eine ursprüngliche Einheit zu betrachten. Nach U. Becker, *Jesaja: Von der Botschaft zum Buch* (FRLANT 178; Göttingen: Vandenhoeck & Ruprecht, 1997), 144–20, stehen hinter Jes 8:16–18 drei verschiedene Verfasser mit unterschiedlichen editorischen Absichten (Vss. 16*, 17, 18). In V. 16 sei der ursprüngliche Abschluß des jesajanischen Bestandes in 6:18* + 8:1, 3–4 zu sehen, und zwar ohne das Wort *bĕ-limmūdāy*, das später zugefügt sei und das ursprüngliche Gotteswort als Rede Jesajas verstehe. Becker vermutet auch mit Vorsicht, daß „ein (unmittelbarer?) Schüler die Niederschrift vornahm" (S. 121).

37 Vgl. z. B. zu Jes 8:16 Carr, *Writing on the Tablet of the Heart*, 143–45: zu Hab 2:2 M. H. Floyd, „Prophecy and Writing in Habakkuk 2,1–5," *ZAW* 105 (1993) 462–81; R. D. Haak, *Habakkuk* (VTSup 44; Leiden: Brill, 1992), 152.

38 Besonders Hab 2:2 setzt gar kein gesprochenes Orakel voraus; s. Floyd, „Prophecy and Writing in Habakkuk 2,1–5," 477.

lieferer der Prophetenworte ist zwar nicht unmöglich, muß aber als ein heuristisches Modell gelten, das nicht eigentlich bewiesen werden kann.

Die Propheten hatten wohl Gemeinschaften um sich, in denen sie ihre Berufsfähigung erlangten und in die religiöse Tradition hineinwuchsen. Es hat aber nicht den Anschein, daß dabei die Memorierung der Worte eines prophetischen Leiters der Gemeinschaft oder überhaupt die Überlieferung verbaler Lehre eine Rolle spielte. Dies mag mit der traditionellen Natur und Funktion der Prophetie zusammenhängen. Aus den altorientalischen Zeugnissen für Prophetie gewinnt man den Eindruck, daß Prophetien von Hause aus kein mit Weisheitssprüchen, mythischen Erzählungen oder Poesie vergleichbares Traditionsgut waren, das dazu gedacht war, über Generationen hin überliefert zu werden, vielmehr wurden sie als Worte zur Stunde verstanden und gebraucht. Anders verhielt es sich, sobald die Orakel aufgeschrieben und gespeichert wurden, denn dies impliziert schon, daß die betreffende Prophetie eine über die Verkündigungssituation hinausreichende Bedeutung hatte, wie es noch im babylonischen Talmud verstanden worden ist: „Prophetie (*nĕbûʾâ*), die für die späteren Generationen nötig war, wurde niedergeschrieben, und die nicht nötig war, wurde nicht niedergeschrieben" (*b. Meg.* 14a). Dies entspricht völlig der Aussage von Stellen wie Jes 8:16; 30:8 und Hab 2:2, die wegen ihrer nachträglichen Perspektive schwerlich als Beweis für die literarische Tätigkeit der Prophetenschüler gelten können, vielmehr ein Zeugnis für den wachsenden Status des geschriebenen Gotteswortes ablegen.

Von wem wurden aber die Prophetenworte aufgeschrieben und überliefert, wenn nicht von den Prophetenschülern? Crenshaw fragt mit guten Gründen, ob das Überleben der Prophetenworte überhaupt einer institutionellen Unterstützung bedurfte.[39] Meines Erachtens kann diese Frage nur mit einem nachdrücklichen „Ja" beantwortet werden. Der prophetische Kommunikationsprozeß konnte nicht einsetzen ohne einen Widerhall der Gemeinschaft, wenn auch nicht notwendig der ganzen Gemeinschaft.[40] Auch die Propheten, die sich dem Establishment ihrer Gemeinschaft kritisch gegenüberstellten, mußten Anhänger oder Sympathisanten—also in diesem Sinne „Schüler"—haben, die schriftkundig waren und sich darum kümmerten, daß die mündlich verkündeten Worte der Pro-

---

39 Crenshaw, „Transmitting Prophecy across Generations," 40: „Was sponsorship by an institution necessary for the survival of the prophetic oracles?"

40 Dies hat schon R. R. Wilson, *Prophecy and Society in Ancient Israel* (Philadelphia: Fortress Press, 1980), 51 betont: „Intermediaries do not operate in a vacuum. They are integral part of their societies and cannot exist without social guidance and support. This support need not come from the whole society, but it must be present in some form, or the intermediaries will disappear."

pheten verschriftet und irgendwo bewahrt wurden.[41] Wenn mündliche Prophetentraditionen allerdings existierten, müssen ihre Trägergruppen den literarischen Kreisen nahe genug gestanden haben. Andernfalls wären die Prophetenbücher nie entstanden. Denn „Literatur braucht zu ihrer Entstehung einen institutioneilen Rahmen und ein wirksames Interesse."[42]

In der hebräischen Bibel sind die schriftlichen Prophetenworte in einem vollen Sinne *traditum* geworden, und zwar im Gefolge eines schriftlichen Prozesses, dessen Ergebnis die Prophetenbücher sind. Jetzt handelt es sich nicht mehr lediglich um Archivalien, sondern um lebendige Tradition. Einerseits wurde Prophetie zunehmend mit der literarischen Auslegung der schon geschriebenen prophetischen Worte gleichgesetzt,[43] andererseits wurden die prophetischen Schriften zu einem Teil des in der Ausbildung der Führungselite gebrauchten Curriculums.[44] In beiden Fällen gilt es an das zu erinnern, was Timo Veijola über die Sukzessionskette von Mose zu den Propheten bis hin zu den Schriftgelehrten ausgeführt hat: die Propheten gelten als Vorgänger der Schriftgelehrten, die auf dem Lehrstuhl des Urpropheten Mose sitzen.[45] Seither funktioniert das von Crenshaw und anderen vertretene Modell des vorwiegend mündlichen Lernens sehr gut, wie es zum Beispiel im Buch Jesus Sirach in Erscheinung tritt,[46] auch wenn die Schülerkreise sich nunmehr im *bēt midrāš* eines Gelehrten (Sir 51:23) statt im Haus eines Propheten versammelten.

---

41 Vgl. Niditch, *Oral World and Written Word*, 119: „The recording, the keeping of prophetic oracles, and perhaps their subsequent revision in any event comes from a member of the [prophetic] group or a sympathetic outside supporter."

42 C. Levin, *Das Alte Testament* (München: Beck, ^{2}2003), 22; Engl. *The Old Testament: A Brief Introduction* (trans. M. Kohl; Princeton, N.J.: Princeton University Press, 2005), 23.

43 Vgl. L. L. Grabbe, „Poets, Scribes, or Preachers: The Reality of Prophecy in the Second Temple Period," in *Knowing the End from the Beginning: The Prophetic, the Apocalyptic and their Relationships* (ed. id. and R. D. Haak; JSPSup 46; London: T & T Clark, 2003) 192–215, dort 209–10; A. Lange, „Literary Prophecy and Oracle Collection: A Comparison between Judah and Greece in Persian Times," in Floyd and Haak (eds.), *Prophets, Prophecy, and Prophetic Texts in Second Temple Judaism*, 248–75, dort 256–61.

44 Carr, *Writing on the Tablet of the Heart*, 150: „Whatever their origins, they were no longer mere archival records of a prophetic word or scholarly notations of oracles given. Instead, such prophetic words eventually became part of a stream of educational-enculturational oral-written literature used in the formation of (elite) Israelites."

45 S. Veijola, *Moses Erben*, 216–18.

46 Vgl. J. L. Crenshaw, „The Primacy of Listening in Ben Sira's Pedagogy," in *Wisdom, You Are My Sister*, FS R. E. Murphy (ed. M. L. Barré; CBQMS 29; Washington, D.C.: Catholic Biblical Association of America, 1997) 172–87.

The Dubious Image of Prophecy

1 Introduction

What happened to prophecy in the Second Temple period, and why is it so difficult to answer this question? Undoubtedly, the core of the problem is to be found in the nature of the evidence: everything we can tell about prophetic activity in concrete historical terms comes to us through the filter of scribal activity. In their present form, the prophetic books of the Hebrew Bible document primarily how earlier prophecy was chosen, edited, interpreted, and rewritten to serve the ends of the editors and to correspond with their idea of prophecy and its significance.

This inevitably distorts the picture of pre-exilic prophets and their activities, but even the nature of the post-exilic prophecy remains faint in concrete terms. As argued by Michael Floyd,[1] even the prophets of the Second Temple period were dependent on scribes who kept record of their activity at their own discretion. Even if the prophets were able to write their oracles down, the production of prophetic *books*, examined recently by Ehud Ben Zvi,[2] was a matter of a wider communal recognition of their relevance. Therefore, even the books that bear names of post-exilic prophets do not reveal much of the prophetic or visionary activities that may have given the impetus to the production of books named after them. We do not even know to what extent they go back to oral performances. The historical narratives of the Hebrew Bible provide little relief in this respect. The Deuteronomistic history swarms with prophets who, however, are presented from the point of view of the editors as paradigmatic figures of the past.[3]

---

1 M. H. Floyd, "The Production of Prophetic Books in the Early Second Temple Period," in *Prophets, Prophecy, and Prophetic Texts in Second Temple Judaism* (ed. id. and R. D. Haak; LHBOTS 427; London: T & T Clark, 2006) 276–97.

2 See E. Ben Zvi, " Introduction: Writings, Speeches, and the Prophetic Books: Setting an Agenda," in *Writings and Speech in Israelite and Ancient Near Eastern Prophecy* (ed. id. and M. H. Floyd; SBLSymS 10; Atlanta, Ga.: Society of Biblical Literature, 2000) 1–29; id., "The Prophetic Book: A Key Form of Prophetic Literature," in *The Changing Face of Form Criticism for the Twenty-First Century* (ed. id. and M. A. Sweeney; Grand Rapids, Mich.: Eerdmans, 2003) 276–97; id., *Signs of Jonah: Reading and Rereading in Ancient Yehud* (JSOTS 367; New York: T&T Clark, 2003).

3 Cf., e.g., W. Dietrich, "Prophetie im deuteronomistischen Geschichtswerk," in *The Future of the Deuteronomistic History* (ed. T. Römer; BETL 147; Leuven: Peters, 2000) 47–65, who reckons with a pre-Deuteronomistic prophetic narrative from the seventh century, adopted and reused by the Deuteronomistic editors.

DOI 10.1515/9783110466546-030

The Chronicles, as Yairah Amit demonstrates,[4] have a very distinctive understanding of prophecy, whereas Ezra and Nehemiah—the only biblical books that actually *describe* the Second Temple period—are conspicuously silent about prophetic activities during that time. Therefore, conclusions regarding prophecy as a phenomenon of the Second Temple period can only be drawn from indirect evidence.

In this paper, I attempt to illustrate this problem with the help of four texts datable to the Second Temple period. All of them present prophets in a dubious light and demonstrate that the actual prophetic activity, comparable to similar phenomena in the ancient Near East, could be viewed as too precarious to conform to the prophetic ideal cherished by the scribal circles.

2 Prophets of Apostasy (Deuteronomy 13:2–6)

The verses Deut 13:2–6 prohibit the Israelites from listening to any prophet or dreamer who calls on them to follow gods other than their own. Even if the sign or portent offered by such a prophet or dreamer should come true, he must be killed right away, because he has incited people to rebellion against the God of Israel. This passage has a well-known Assyrian counterpart in the Succession Treaty of Esarhaddon which obliges the contracting parties to denounce any "prophet, ecstatic or inquirer of oracles" who has uttered improper words about Assurbanipal, the crown prince designate of Assyria (SAA 26 § 10).[5] These texts have been the object of intensive comparison, the result of which is a general consensus that the points of similarity between them is not coincidental but goes back to the direct or indirect influence of the Assyrian treaty stipulations on Deuteronomy in general.[6]

4 See Yairah Amit, "The Role of Prophecy and Prophets in the Chronicler's World," in Floyd and Haak (eds.), *Prophets, Prophecy, and Prophetic Texts in Second Temple Judaism*, 80–101.

5 S. Parpola and K. Watanabe, *Neo-Assyrian Treaties and Loyalty Oaths* (SAA 2; Helsinki: Helsinki University Press, 1988), 28–58, esp. 33:108–22.

6 The more recent works on Deut 13 include P. E. Dion, "Deuteronomy 13: The Suppression of Alien Religious Propaganda in Israel during the Late Monarchical Era," in *Law and Ideology in Monarchic Israel* (ed. B. Halpern und D. W. Hobson; JSOTSup 124; Sheffield: Sheffield University Press 1991) 147–216; H. M. Barstad, "The Understanding of the Prophets in Deuteronomy" *SJOT* 8 (1994) 236–51; T. Veijola, "Wahrheit und Intoleranz nach Deuteronomium 13," *ZThK* 92 (1995) 287–314; repr. in id., *Moses Erben: Studien zum Dekalog, zum Deuteronomismus und zum Schriftgelehrtentum* (BWANT 8/9; Stuttgart: Kohlhammer, 2000) 109–30; id., "Deuteronomismusforschung zwischen Tradition und Innovation (1)," *TRu* 67 (2002) 273–327, esp. 292–98; B. M. Levinson,"'But You Shall Surely Kill Him': The Text-Critical and Neo-Assyrian Evidence

Exactly how close the relationship between these texts is, has recently been a matter of dispute, however. Some scholars are ready to see Deut 13:2–6 as directly dependent on the treaty of Esarhaddon and, hence, date the verses to the seventh century,[7] while others deny the direct dependence and reckon with a gradual theologization of the Assyrian political ideology, dating the text to exilic or early post-exilic times.[8] As a matter of fact, all points of similarity notwithstanding, it is evident that the verses Deut 13:2–6 do *not* present a translation of any paragraph of the Assyrian treaty,[9] which makes the assumption of direct dependence less than compelling. While the resemblances between Deut 13 and the Succession Treaty of Esarhaddon should be fully recognized, there can be no certainty of the familiarity of the authors of Deut 13 with this particular treaty of Esarhaddon, which happens to be at our disposal, while many, if not most, of the

---

for MT Deut 13:20," in *Bundesdokument und Gesetz: Studien zum Deuteronomium* (HBS 4; Freiburg: Herder, 1995) 37–63; id., "Recovering the Original Meaning of ולא תכסה עליו (Deuteronomy 13:9)," *JBL* 115 (1996) 601–20; id., "Textual Criticism, Assyriology, and the History of Interpretation: Deuteronomy 13:7a as a Test Case in Method," *JBL* 120 (2001) 211–43; M. Nissinen, "Falsche Prophetie in neuassyrischer und deuteronomistischer Darstellung," in *Das Deuteronomium und seine Querbeziehungen* (ed. T. Veijola; PFES 62; Helsinki: Finnische Exegetische Gesellschaft; Göttingen: Vandenhoeck & Ruprecht, 1996) 172–95 (= pp. 419 – 40 in this volume); E. Otto, "Treueid und Gesetz: Die Ursprünge des Deuteronomiums im Horizont neuassyrischen Vertragsrechts," *ZABR* 2 (1996) 1–52; id., "Die Ursprünge der Bundestheologie im Alten Testament und im Alten Orient," *ZABR* 4 (1998) 1–84; id., *Das Deuteronomium: Politische Theologie und Rechtsreform in Juda und Assyrien* (BZAW 284; Berlin: de Gruyter, 1999), esp. 32–90; J. Pakkala, *Intolerant Monolatry in the Deuteronomistic History* (PFES 76; Helsinki: The Finnish Exegetical Society and Göttingen: Vandenhoeck & Ruprecht, 1999), esp. 20 – 50; M. Köckert, "Zum literargeschichtlichen Ort des Prophetengesetzes Dtn 18 zwischen dem Jeremiabuch und Dtn 13," in *Liebe und Gebot: Studien zum Deuteronomium*, FS L. Perlitt (ed. R. G. Kratz and H. Spieckermann; FRLANT 190; Göttingen: Vandenhoeck & Ruprecht 2000) 80 – 100; U. Rüterswörden "Dtn 13 in der neueren Deuteronomiumforschung," in *Congress Volume Basel, 2001* (ed. A. Lemaire; VTSup 92; Leiden: Brill, 2002) 185 – 203; A. Lange, *Vom prophetischen Wort zur prophetischen Tradition: Studien zur Traditions- und Redaktionsgeschichte innerprophetischer Konflikte in der Hebräischen Bibel* (FAT 34; Tübingen: Mohr Siebeck, 2002) 163 – 68.

7 Thus Otto, who reckons with direct literary influence of the Succession Treaty of Esarhaddon on the earliest core of Deuteronomy *(Urdeuteronomium)* in his various publications (e.g., *Deuteronomium*, 32–88); cf. Lange, *Vom prophetischen Wort zur prophetischen Tradition*, 163 – 86. A dating to the time of Josiah has been suggested by Dion ("Deuteronomy 13," 198 – 205), and a preexilic date by Rüterswörden ("Dtn 13 in der neueren Deuteronomiumforschung," 203), without the assumption of a direct dependence of Deut 13 on the Succession Treaty of Esarhaddon.

8 Veijola, "Wahrheit und Intoleranz," 308 – 10; repr. *Moses Erben*, 125 – 27; id., "Deuteronomismusforschung zwischen Tradition und Innovation," 295 – 98; Nissinen, "Falsche Prophetie," 180 – 82; Pakkala, *Intolerant Monolatry*, 47– 50; Köckert, "Zum literargeschichtlichen Ort des Prophetengesetzes," 82– 84.

9 Pakkala, *Intolerant Monolatry*, 43.

Neo-Assyrian treaties have not been found, and not a single copy of a Neo-Babylonian treaty has been preserved. Considering the Assyrian cultural influence on Judah as a whole,[10] and taking for granted that the kings of Judah were bound by treaties with Assyrian and Babylonian kings until the destruction of Jerusalem, it is not to be wondered that the ideology and phraseology of these authoritative political documents have left clear traces in the language of the Hebrew Bible—not only in texts contemporary to these treaties but also in later theological adaptation of the treaty ideology.[11]

On the other hand, there may be stronger dependencies between Deut 13 and other biblical, especially Deuteronomistic texts, Deuteronomy itself included. Matthias Köckert has recently argued, in my view convincingly, for the dependency of Deut 13 on Deut 18.[12] If this is correct, then the general statements on prophecy in Deut 18, rather too vague and theoretical to be tested in a concrete situation, are here applied to a more specific case. It seems evident to me that Deut 13:2–6 presents a commentary on Deut 18:20–22, where it is prescribed that a prophet who speaks in the name of other gods shall die, but, on the other hand, the criterion of true prophecy is that it comes true.[13] These verses seem like individual sentences, one (18:20) dealing with prophets of other gods, the other (18:21–22) with the problem of true prophecy. In sequence, however, they present a pitfall that has probably given the reason for the commentary in Deut 13: What if the word of the prophet who speaks in the name of other gods comes true? Since this is taken as a realistic option, the criterion of acceptable prophecy is moved from the fulfillment of the prophecy to its socio-religious and confessional basis.

There is no programmatic hostility towards prophecy as such in Deut 13. Elsewhere in Deuteronomy, prophecy is acknowledged as a legitimate phenom-

---

10 Cf. S. Parpola, "Assyria's Expansion in the 8th and 7th Centuries and its Long-Term Repercussions in the West," in *Symbiosis, Symbolism, and the Power of the Past: Canaan, Ancient Israel, and Their Neighbors from the Late Bronze Age through Roman Palaestina* (ed. W. G. Dever and S. Gitin; Winona Lake, Ind.; Eisenbrauns, 2003) 99–111.

11 Here I interpret the evidence contrary to Rulerswörden ("Dtn 13 in der neueren Deuteronomiumforschung," 203), who writes: "Es dürfte aber keinem Zweifel unterliegen, dass wir hier zeitlich vor dem Exil liegen. Denn nicht nur die subversive Übernahme der Treueidvorstellung hat nur in die Ära Sinn, in der diese noch in Funktion waren – auch die Konzepte der Sicherung der Dynastie, die sich im Westen darum ranken, haben – komplementär dazu – ihre praktisch-politische Bedeutung, solange es noch eine Dynastie gibt." I would rather argue that the Deuteronomistic theological reinterpretation of the political ideology was possible only when the respective political structures no longer existed.

12 Köckert, "Zum literargeschichtlichen Ort des Prophetengesetzes."

13 Thus also Köckert, "Zum literargeschichtlichen Ort des Prophetengesetzes," 84–85.

enon, and not only that, but elevated above all other forms of divination, most of which are forbidden altogether (Deut 18:9–14). When it comes to the actual manifestations of this respected phenomenon, however, prophecy appears in a more dubious light, since it is not taken for granted that the prophets actually conform to the Deuteronomistic program.[14] The prophets of the past are highly esteemed as the heirs and successors of Moses,[15] but in the contemporary circumstances of the early Second Temple period, prophecy seems to have caused trouble from the point of view of the leaders of the community who were also proponents of the new monolatric program. As long as other nations were acknowledged to have their own gods, the existence of prophets of other gods had to be acknowledged as well. Therefore, the members of the early Second Temple community had to be advised which prophets were by any circumstances not to be listened to. Fantastic as the whole scenario of Deut 13 is, if we look at it as an actually applicable law,[16] it is not purely theoretical reasoning on the limits of prophetic activity but probably motivated by the very fact that there actually were, as there always had been, prophets that spoke in the name of gods other than the God of Israel[17]—or, perhaps, spoke in a way that was interpreted in terms of apostasy regardless of the deity involved.

Being an interpretation of the general rule that the real prophet should be like Moses (Deut 18:15–18), Deut 13 is, more than anything, about loyalty to the Mosaic tradition and its Deuteronomistic guardians. In this respect, it fulfills the same function as its Assyrian counterpart, which is all about faithfulness to king and country. This, in turn, means compliance with the treaty of the king, or, in the context of Deuteronomy, with the covenant of YHWH with Israel.[18] This is what makes Deut 13 and the Succession Treaty of Esarhaddon true parallels demonstrating a historical continuity even without the assumption of coexistence of

---

14 Barstad, "The Understanding of the Prophets in Deuteronomy," 241: "The content of Deuteronomy is accordingly being awarded authority *superior to* that of the prophets. In consequence of this, if in the future there should arise any disagreement between the contents of Deuteronomy (cf. Deut 12,1) and some future prophet, then it is Deuteronomy that represents the revealed word of YHWH, and not the prophet in question."

15 Veijola, *Moses Erben*, 216–18.

16 Pakkala, *Intolerant Monolatry*, 40.

17 Pakkala, *Intolerant Monolatry*, 49: "Since the opponents of the writer included religious professionals like prophets and dreamers, there is every reason to suspect that they were not merely private individuals or a popular 'sect' but represented a serious religious alternative to Yahwe-alone theology or the nomists."

18 According to T. Veijola, "Bundestheologische Redaktion im Deuteronomium," in id. (ed.), *Das Deuteronomium*, 242–76, esp. 245–47; repr. in *Moses Erben*, 155–56), the basic text of Deut 13 is part of the covenant theological redaction of Deuteronomy (DtrB).

the texts or direct literary dependence between them. In both cases, the acceptability of the prophets is dependent on their institutional allegiance, and it is the prophets' potential disloyalty to the ideological constitution of the community that makes the image of prophecy appear as dubious.

3 Noadiah and the Rest of the Prophets (Nehemiah 6:14)

In Ezra–Nehemiah, prophets are mentioned only a few times. Except for the references to Haggai and Zechariah in Ezra 5:1–2 and 6:14, prophets are only mentioned as figures of the past in Ezra's and Nehemiah's penitential prayers (Ezra 9:11; Neh 9:26, 30, 32). There is, however, a passage in the Nehemiah Memoire,[19] in which prophets and prophecy make an interesting appearance: "Remember, my God, Tobiah and Sanballat, for what they have done, and also the prophetess Noadiah and the rest of the prophets who have tried to intimidate me" (Neh 6:14). What had they done, then? In Nehemiah's Memoire, two non-Israelites, Sanballat the Horonite and Tobiah, an Ammonite, play the role of Nehemiah's archenemies, who from the very beginning try to prevent him from doing his mission, because they were "much vexed that someone should have come to promote the interests of the Israelites" (Neh 2:10).[20] Tobiah, thanks to his affinities, is said to have been in league with the high society of Judah, and Nehemiah said to have received frightening letters from him (Neh 6:17–19). Sanballat, for his part, had tried to discourage Nehemiah from rebuilding the city wall of Jerusalem by referring to rumors, according to which Nehemiah is building the wall only to stir up a revolt and to put prophets up to proclaiming him king of Jerusalem (Neh 6:5–7). These rumors, however, are declared to be pure imagination; Nehemiah knew nothing about such prophets (Neh 6:8). Further intimidation

---

19 For theories of the literary history of the Nehemiah Memoire (Neh 1–7*; 11–13*), see, e.g., H. G. M. Williamson, *Ezra, Nehemiah* (WBC 16; Waco, Tex.: Word, 1985), esp. xxiv–xxviii; T. Reinmuth, *Der Bericht Nehemias: Zur literarischen Eigenart, traditionsgeschichtlichen Prägung und innerbiblischen Rezeption des Ich-Berichts Nehemias* (OBO 183; Fribourg and Göttingen: Academic Press Fribourg and Vandenhoeck & Ruprecht, 2002); for the problems with its use as a historical source, cf. D. J. A. Clines, "The Nehemiah Memoire: The Perils of Autobiography," in id., *What Does Eve Do to Help? and Other Readerly Questions to the Old Testament* (JSOTSup 94; Sheffield: JSOT Press, 1990) 124–64; L. L. Grabbe, *Ezra–Nehemiah* (Old Testament Readings; London: Routledge, 1998), esp. 154–56.

20 For the opposition to Nehemiah, see Grabbe, *Ezra–Nehemiah*, 161–67; for the narrator's view of Sanballat's intentions, see Clines, "The Nehemiah Memoire," 144–52.

had been provided by Shemaiah son of Delaiah who had asked Nehemiah to shut himself away with him inside the temple of God *(bêt ʾĕlōhîm)*, otherwise he would have been killed. The word of Shemaiah is presented as a false prophecy *(nĕbûʾâ)*,[21] which Tobiah and Sanbaltat had bribed him to utter (Neh 6:10–13).

The involvement of prophets in proclaiming kings is presumed by the Hebrew Bible,[22] but it is even better documented in extrabiblical sources.[23] We know the Neo-Assyrian pseudoprophecy regarding the kingship of an alleged conspirator (SAA 16 59),[24] the political implications of which are similar with the case of Nehemiah: were the allegations against him true, he would be guilty of high treason against the Persian king, so he had to refute such rumors, whatever the historical truth behind them.[25] The Nehemiah narrative seems to aim at a realistic scenery to which even the political (ab)use of prophecy belongs. Therefore, the allegation that Nehemiah had appointed prophets to proclaim him the king of Judah need not be understood as a mere literary allusion to Sa-

---

21 Reinmuth *(Der Bericht Nehemias,* 200), reckons here with an echo from the Jeremianic polemic against the false prophets (Jer 14:14–15; 23:21, 32; 27:14–15; 29:8–9).

22 I Sam 9–10; 1 Kgs 1:32–40; 2 Kgs 9:1–13; cf. for the present context, J. Blenkinsopp, *Ezra–Nehemiah: A Commentary* (OTL; London: SCM Press, 1989), esp. 269–70.

23 The collection SAA 9 3 consists of prophecies proclaimed on the occasion of the enthronement ceremony of Esarhaddon; cf. S. Parpola, *Assyrian Prophecies* (SAA 9; Helsinki: Helsinki University Press, 1997), lxx. As the letter SAA 10 352 demonstrates, prophecies were uttered even to substitute kings; cf. M. Nissinen, *References to Prophecy in Neo-Assyrian Sources* (SAAS 7; Helsinki: The Neo-Assyrian Text Corpus Project, 1998), esp. 68–77. There is important evidence also from the Old Babylonian period: the oracle of Kititum (Ištar) from Ešnunna (FLP 1674) is most probably connected with the enthronement of King Ibalpiel II (thus M. deJong Ellis, "The Goddess Kititum Speaks to King Ibalpiel: Oracle Texts from Ishchali," *MARI* 5 [1987] 235–66, esp. 250), and the letter of Nur-Sîn, the delegate of Zimri-Lim, king of Mari in Aleppo/Alaḫtum, quotes a prophecy that reads like a paraphrase of a coronation oracle (A. 1968); see J.-M. Durand, *Florilegium Marianum 7: Le Culte d'Addu d'Alep et l'affaire d'Alahtum* (Mémoires de *NABU* 8; Paris: SEPOA, 2002), esp. 134–35; M. Nissinen, "Das kritische Potential in der altorientalischen Prophetie," in *Propheten in Mari, Assyrien und Israel* (ed. M. Köckert and M. Nissinen; FRLANT 201; Göttingen: Vandenhoeck & Ruprecht, 2003) 1–32, esp. 19–22 (= pp. 163–94 in this volume).

24 Nissinen, "Falsche Prophetie," 182–93; id., *References to Prophecy,* 108–53. The newest edition of the text is to be found in M. Luukko and G. Van Buylaere, *The Political Correspondence of Esarhaddon* (SAA 16; Helsinki: Helsinki University Press, 2002), esp. 52–53 (n. 59).

25 Grabbe *(Ezra–Nehemiah,* 50, 165–66) reckons with opponents as well as supporters of Nehemiah in prophetic circles; the accusation that there had been prophets who would have proclaimed him the king of Judah "would have been a difficult charge to make if no such prophecies were known" (p. 165).

muel and Nathan as kingmakers.[26] While the accusation against Nehemiah is presented as a false one, the joint attempts of Shemaiah, Noadiah, and other prophets with Tobiah and Sanballat to intimidate Nehemiah are meant to be taken seriously as an attack of influential people who try to prevent his activity. "The rest of the prophets" *(yeter han-nĕbîʾîm)* plays with "the rest of our enemies" *(yeter ʾōyĕbênû)* in Neh 6:2 and gives the impression that Nehemiah sees the entire guild of the prophets of Jerusalem as his opponents. Whether or not this impression is consistent with the historical fact, this is what the reader of Neh 6 is supposed to imagine.

The sympathies of the scholars have usually been with Nehemiah, which has led to disparaging comments on Shemaiah, Noadiah, and her associates.[27] Seen from the other side, however, Noadiah and her associates could as well be considered "true" prophets who stick to their legitimate tradition and blame Nehemiah for a misuse of prophecy for his own purposes.[28]

The text reckons with prophetic activity in Jerusalem directed against Nehemiah's mission that was not unanimously welcomed by the local population. Even though the reference to Noadiah cannot be understood as a general assessment of prophecy as such,[29] "the rest of the prophets" gives the impression that from the writer's point of view, the prophets of Jerusalem belonged as a group to "those in personal alliance with one who had set himself to oppose all the values for which Nehemiah stood."[30] As a matter of fact, the only prophets that are said to have stood *for* what Nehemiah—or, rather, the authors of Ezra–Nehemiah—stood for, are Haggai and Zechariah, that is, figures of the past.[31]

---

26 Cf. Williamson, *Ezra, Nehemiah*, 256–57.

27 F. C. Fensham, *The Books of Ezra and Nehemiah* (NICOT; Grand Rapids: Eerdmans, 1982), 206: "in the time of Nehemiah a group or visionaries was around, but their spiritual standard was indeed low."

28 For this view, see R. P. Carroll, "Coopting the Prophets: Nehemiah and Noadiah," in *Priests, Prophets and Scribes*, FS J. Blenkinsopp (ed. H. Ulrich, J. W. Wright, R. P. Carroll, and P. R. Davies; JSOTSup 149; Sheffield: Sheffield Academic Press, 1992), 87–99. R. Kessler ("Mirjam und die Propheten der Perserzeit," in *Gott an den Rändern*, FS W. Schottroff [ed. U. Bail and R. Jost; Gülersloh: Gütersloher, 1996] 64–72; ET: "Miriam and the Prophecy of the Persian Period," in *Prophets and Daniel* [ed. A. Brenner; A Feminist Companion to the Bible, Second Series 8; Sheffield: Sheffield Academic Press, 2001] 77–86), postulates an anti-Persian prophetic tradition that emerges from the aspiration for independence derived from the activity of Haggai and Zechariah; for support for this view, see below, n. 35; for criticism, see Reinmuth, *Der Bericht Nehemias*, 201.

29 Lange, *Vom prophetischen Wort zur prophetischen Tradition*, 54–55.

30 Williamson, *Ezra, Nehemiah*, 262.

31 Cf. Carroll, "Coopting the Prophets," 88.

Furthermore, the female sex of Noadiah is an interesting feature that should not be passed without a comment. While prophecy in the ancient Near East was one of the few professions open to both (or all[32]) sexes, and women often appeared as prophets, in the Hebrew Bible female prophets can be counted with the fingers of one hand. It is difficult to know whether this difference between the biblical and extrabiblical records is only coincidental or actually due to different socioreligious circumstances,[33] but it is interesting to note how influential roles the few biblical female prophets assume. Hulda, who was affiliated with the temple of Jerusalem through her husband, is the godmother of Deuteronomy to whom the temple authorities have to go in 2 Kings 22.[34] Miriam, on the other hand, falls into disrepute in her attempt to be equal to Moses as a channel of the divine words (Numbers 12), but this underlines the unrivalled authority of Moses (and probably also the guardians of his heritage) rather than deprives Miriam of her prophetic role.[35]

---

32 See below, n. 53.

33 S. Ackerman ("Why is Miriam Also among the Prophets? [And is Zipporah among the Priests?]," *JBL* 121 [2002] 47–80) argues that during periods of destabilization, women could achieve positions in the Israelite communities that they would otherwise be denied; such a period was at hand during the time of Nehemiah's rebuilding endeavors, whereby "Noadiah is a woman able to gain recognition as a religious functionary because the relatively destabilized religious organization of Jerusalem during her lifetime had room for women prophets in a way that the cult in more stabilized periods did not" (p. 57). The problem with this argument is that we are entirety dependent on the Hebrew Bible in reconstructing the women's religious roles in Israel, Judah, and Yehud, and it is very difficult indeed to know exactly what kind of positions women actually held in religious institutions. Very high positions are, admittedly, unlikely, but the prophetic role did not belong to them. Moreover, when it comes to the prophetess Hulda, I have difficulties in seeing the time of Josiah *before* the reform as a "period of religious disarray" (p. 58). True, the Assyrian hegemony had had a decisive impact on the religio-political status of Judah since the time of Hezekiah, but in the 620s, this slate of affairs had probably established itself well enough. The actual destabilization, however, was just around the corner: Josiah made a muddle of the religious institutions of Judah with his reform, and Assyria fell in 612.

34 For Hulda, see Ackerman, "Why Is Miriam Also among the Prophets?," 57–59; R. J. Weems, "Huldah, the Prophet: Reading a (Deuteronomistic) Woman's Identity," in *A God So Near*, FS P. D. Miller (ed. B. A, Strawn and N. R. Bowen; Winona Lake, Ind.: Eisenbrauns, 2003) 321–39. According to Weems, the interpreting of the newly found scroll's meaning for Judah "establishes Huldah as a true prophet—one who fits the criterion for becoming part of the Deuteronomistic canon" (p. 325).

35 For a substantial treatment on Miriam, see U. Rapp, *Mirjam: Eine feministisch-rhetorische Lektüre der Mirjamtexte in der hebräischen Bibel* (BZAW 317; Berlin: de Gruyter, 2002). Rapp builds on the theory of Rainer Kessler (see above, n. 28), suggesting that the advocacy of Miriam's prophetic role goes back to the same circles of the Persian period that even Noadiah represented (pp. 178–93). A similar argument has been made by I. Fischer, "The Authority of Mir-

The unusual formulation "Noadiah and the rest of the prophets," which rather atypically names the woman but not the men, may be best explained as implying Noadiah's leadership among the prophets. What matters is not so much the gender of the prophet but her position from the point of view of the writers: "prophets are co-opted according to whether they support or oppose a particular position."[36] Noadiah opposes Nehemiah like Miriam opposes Moses, and this is the reason for discrediting her. Moreover, an echo from the purity ideology in Ezra–Nehemiah may be sensed in Noadiah's alliance with the non-Israelites, whose very presence in the sanctuary pollutes it (cf. the case of Tobiah in Neh 13:4–9).[37] Whether Noadiah herself was an Israelite is not indicated, but her banding together with the aliens alone may be seen as a threat to the purity of the land; the concern for purity can be seen also in Nehemiah's resolute refusal to enter the temple in Neh 6:11. It may be farther speculated to what extent the issue of intermarriage contributes to Noadiah's opposition against Nehemiah. Tobiah and Sanballat, with whom she is associated in Neh 6:14, are non-Israelites who are said to have close family ties with the nobles of Jerusalem (Neh 6:17–19), including the family of the priest-administrator Elyashib (Neh 13:28), and who, therefore, can be imagined to have opposed the dissolution of intermarriages.[38] This might have caused opposition especially from the

---

iam: A Feminist Rereading of Numbers 12 Prompted by Jewish Interpretation," in *Exodus to Deuteronomy* (ed. A. Brenner; A Feminist Companion to the Bible, Second Series; Sheffield: Sheffield Academic Press, 2001) 159–73, according to whom the groups "claim to have the ministry of prophecy themselves and, in fact, oppose those who see themselves to be the successors to Moses" (p. 165).

36 Carroll, "Coopting the Prophets," 91.

37 See S. M. Olyan ("Purity Ideology in Ezra–Nehemiah as a Tool to Reconstruct the Community," *JSJ* 35 [2004] 1–16) who, I think, is more sensitive here to the ideology of Ezra–Nehemiah than H. G. M. Williamson ("The Belief System of the Book of Nehemiah," in *The Crisis of Israelite Religion: Transformation of Religious Tradition in Exilic and Post-Exilic Times* [ed. B. Becking and M. C. A. Korpel; OTS 42; Leiden: Brill, 1999] 276–87), who writes on Neh 13:4–13 (pp. 280–81): "There is nothing in the text to suggest that in the case of expulsion of Tobiah Nehemiah was motivated by anything other than a sense of outrage that a former opponent has used his family connections to establish himself in the temple, while his concern for the Levites is very much that of the supportive outsider, seeking to ensure that the cult was adequately financed and administered."

38 For the issue of intermarriage, cf. two recent contributions, one from the point of view of purity – Olyan, "Purity Ideology in Ezra–Nehemiah," 5–8 – and the other emphasizing the influence of the Deuteronomistic (DtrN) opposition to intermarriage on Ezra–Nehemiah – T. Veijola, "The Deuteronomistic Roots of Judaism," in *Sefer Moshe: The Moshe Weinfeld Jubilee Volume: Studies in the Bible and the Ancient Near East, Qumran, and Post-Biblical Judaism* (ed.

women, which would explain Noadiah's leadership among the prophetic opponents of Nehemiah.[39]

Whether or not Neh 6 can be taken as a historically accurate record, prophecy is described in a way that is quite plausible from both biblical and ancient Near Eastern points of view. The royal function of prophecy, its use as a tool in politics, female prophets, as well as the problems of the ideological correctness of the prophets are all features to be found everywhere in prophetic sources. What makes the image of prophecy "dubious," then? In fact, there is neither generic criticism of prophecy as such nor any programmatic juxtaposition of true and false prophecy, even though the *nĕbûʾâ* of Shemaiah is rejected as a bribed pseudoprophecy. Nehemiah's problem is rather that some prophetic circles, instead of supporting his building enterprise, use their influential role as prophets to prevent it, allying themselves with his non-Israelite archenemies. Nothing in Neh 6 suggests that Nehemiah's prophetic opponents represent a deviant or degenerated kind of prophecy. They had only chosen the wrong side. Thus, prophecy is presented as an influential phenomenon that is difficult to control and may serve unwanted purposes.

4 "I Am Not a Prophet" (Zechariah 13:2 – 6)

The most radically polemical attack against prophets in the Hebrew Bible is without doubt Zech 13:2 – 6, which condemns the *nĕbîʾîm* without mercy, associating them with idols, unclean spirit, and lying. The researchers of these verses have often seen the target of this criticism in some kind of pagan, syncretistic, or otherwise degenerated sort of prophecy, but these interpretations succumb to the harsh language of the author who undoubtedly presents the opponents in the worst possible light. It seems reasonable to me to take these verses as a general rejection of prophecy.[40] The density of the intertextual network employed in

C. Cohen, A. Hurvitz, and S. M. Paul; Winona Lake, Ind.: Eisenbrauns, 2004) 459 – 78, esp. 462 – 64.

39 See Carroll, "Coopting the Prophets," 95; Rapp, *Mirjam*, 185 – 88, and cf. the reservations of Reinmuth, *Der Bericht Nehemias*, 201.

40 Thus R. D. Rhea, "Attack on Prophecy: Zechariah 13,1 – 6," *ZAW* 107 (1995) 290 – 93; Lange, *Vom prophetischen Wort zur prophetischen Tradition*, 291 – 306; J. Jeremias, "Gelehrte Prophetie: Beobachtungen zu Joel und Deuterosacharja," in *Vergegenwärtigung des Alten Testaments: Beiträge zur biblischen Hermeneutik*, FS R. Smend (ed. C. Bultmann, W. Dietrich, and C. Levin; Göttingen: Vandenhoeck & Ruprecht, 2002) 97 – 111, esp. 109 – 10, against those who would rather see the criticism targeted at "false" prophets only, e. g.: H. Graf Reventlow, *Die Propheten Haggai, Sacharja und Maleachi* (ATD 25/2; Göttingen: Vandenhoeck & Ruprecht, 1993), 199; C. L. Meyers

these verses[41] testifies to a profound knowledge of scriptures, both prophetic and non-prophetic, that already enjoy an authoritative status. This also gives a hint at the socioreligious context of the text in scribal circles of the Second Temple period,[42] who appear to have no respect at all for actual prophetic activity.

Why this "furious finale" of the eschatological process of purification,[43] which predicts the total extermination of prophets in the ideal eschatological future?[44] Certainly, the whole polemic can be inspired by an interpretation of creatively combined scriptural references in the context of a dualistic worldview. Nevertheless, I find it probable that the text reflects an actual controversy that, in the author's mind, will find a definitive solution in the eschatological future. Who are the opposing parties, then? The author or authors of Zech 13:2–6 make their standpoint clear: by adding their contribution to prophetic literature by means of alluding to and quoting from other authoritative literary sources, they reveal themselves as representing *schriftgelehrte Prophetie*, in which actual prophetic activity had been replaced by interpretation of scriptures, *prophetische Prophetenauslegung*,[45] which had become the only true prophecy.[46]

How about the other side? In Zech 13:2–6 the prophets are given a twofold description, which may indicate that the text originates from (at least) two differ-

---

and E. M. Meyers, *Zechariah 9–14: A New Translation with Introduction and Commentary* (AB 25C; New York: Doubleday, 1993), 402–4.

41 Cf. Lange, *Vom prophetischen Wort zur prophetischen Tradition*, 294–304; for the intertextuality of Zech 9–14 in general, see Meyers and Meyers, *Zechariah 9–14*, 35–45.

42 In dating Zech 9–14, the Persian period (fifth century) seems to prevail in today's scholarship; cf., e.g., A. E. Hill, "Dating Second-Zechariah: A Linguistic Reexamination," *HAR* 6 (1982) 105–34; Reventlow, *Die Propheten Haggai, Sacharja und Maleachi*, 88; Meyers and Meyers, *Zechariah 9–14*, 26–27; D. L. Petersen, *Zechariah 9–14 and Malachi: A Commentary* (OTL; Louisville, Ky.: Westminster/John Knox, 1995), esp. 5; Lange, *Vom prophetischen Wort zur prophetischen Tradition*, 305, but also the dating into the Hellenistic period has proponents, cf. E. Bosshard and R. G. Kratz, "Maleachi im Zwölfprophetenbuch," *BN* 52 (1990) 27–46; O. H. Steck, *Der Abschluß der Prophetie im Alten Testament* (BThSt 17; Neukirehen-Vluyn: Neukirchener, 1991), esp. 43–44.

43 Lange, *Vom prophetischen Wort zur prophetischen Tradition*, 305.

44 Cf. Joel 3:1, where the scenario of the end of prophecy is totally different: every one becomes a prophet; for the difference, see Jeremias, "Gelehrte Prophetie," 108–9.

45 For this term, see O. H. Steck, *Die Prophetenbücher und ihr theologisches Zeugnis: Wege der Nachfrage und Fährten zur Antwort* (Tübingen: Mohr Siebeck, 1996).

46 Jeremias, "Gelehrte Prophetie," 110: "Sach 13 verurteilt also alle Prophetie der eigenen Zeit, weil sie vorgibt, mehr zu wissen als die prophetischen Texte. Es ist demnach für diesen Text alles nötige über Gott und seine Zukunft langst von Propheten gesagt und niedergeschrieben worden. Ein Mehr könnte nur zur Irreführung dienen."

ent hands.[47] In vv. 2–3, the prophets are associated with idolatry and unclean spirit, and they are accused of lying, much in the spirit of Deut 13 and the Jeremianic polemic against false prophets. In these verses, prophesying *(nibbāʾ)* as such, practiced by anyone, is equated with speaking falsely *(dibber šeqer*; cf. Isa 59:3; Jer 9:4; 29:23, etc.) in the name of the Lord. No exceptions to this rule are mentioned, neither are any prophetic practices specified. The accusations thus remain on an ideological and abstract level.

Verses 4–6, again, describe the prophets in more concrete terms: they wear hairy mantels and they have wounds in their bodies. Even these elements can be explained as allusions to scriptures, the hairy mantel to the one worn by Elijah and inherited by Elisha (2 Kgs 1:8; 2:13)—or, possibly, to the goatskins worn by Jacob when he cheated Esau[48]—and the wounds to those the prophets of Baal inflicted on themselves on Mount Carmel (1 Kgs 18:28). These characteristics are often seen as purely rhetorical as the accusations of idolatry, lying, and unclean spirit in the preceding verses; however, they lack the tangibility of physical objects like mantels and wounds, observable by anyone regardless of ideology or religion. Therefore, without denying the intertextual links provided by these features, I am tempted to suggest that the mantel and the wounds have a concrete point of reference in prophetic practices known from the ancient Near East.

Outside the Hebrew Bible, the hairy mantel is known to have been worn by John the Baptist (Mark 1:6 parr.), who cannot be the model of Zech 13:4, but who may adhere to the same prophetic practice scorned by the author of this verse. An early counterpart to the hairy mantel of the prophet may be found in a letter from Mari, ARM 26 199, in which King Zimri-Lim's prime minister Sammetar reports to have given a garment and a nose-ring to a prophetess *(qammatum)* in return for her oracle:[49]

istēn ṣubāt laḫarûm u ṣerretam u ṣerretam [ī]rišma ad[dinš]im

She demanded a *laḫarûm*-garment and a nose-ring, and I ga[ve them to] her.

---

47 The repetitive formula *wĕ-hāyâ bay-yôm hā-hûʾ* (13:2,4) is often interpreted as a marker of textual growth or different sources combined by the editor. Petersen *(Zechariah 9–14 and Malachi,* 124) thinks that 13:2–3 and 4–6 are additions to the preceding seven sayings introduced by the "on that day" formula. Rhea ("Attack on Prophecy") reckons with two or three subsequent redactions (13:1,2 and 3–6 respectively), while M. Kartveit ("Sach 13,2–6: Das Ende der Prophetie – aber welcher?," in *Text and Theology,* FS M. Sæbø [ed. A. Tångberg; Oslo: Verbum, 1994] 143–56) finds four subsequent authors in the vv. 2,3,4, and 5–6, each of whom has a different view on the prophets.

48 Thus Petersen, *Zechariah 9–14 and Malachi,* 127.

49 ARM 26 199:51–52; see J.-M. Durand, *Archives epistolaires de Mari 1/1* (ARM 26; Paris: Éditions Recherche sur les Civilisations, 1988), esp. 247.

The garment is called *laḫarûm*, which is a *hapax legomenon* in Akkadian[50] and is left untranslated by commentators. The only word in Akkadian that I can think of as etymologically related to *laḫarûm* is *laḫru* ("sheep"), equivalent to Hebrew *raḥel*. Thus, *laḫarûm* may be understood as a sheepskin cloak, hairy as the goatskins worn by Jacob.

The wounds, for their part, appear as a feature of the prophetic image in the so-called Middle Babylonian "Righteous Sufferer" text found at Ugarit.[51] This text mentions several kinds of divination, comparing people who "bathe in their blood" to prophets (*maḫḫû*):[52]

> *aḫḫu'ā kīma maḫḫê* [*d*]*āmīšunu ramkū*
>
> My brothers bathe in their [bl]ood like prophets.

This, in addition to the prophets of Baal in 1 Kings 18, is the only explicit reference to prophets wounding themselves that I am aware of, but it should not be forgotten that the prophetic role was both at Mari and in Assyria assumed by the gender-neutral people called *assinnu*, the image of whom as devotees of the goddess Ištar the ritual self-mutilation may have belonged to.[53] This tradition contin-

---

50 Cf. the feminine counterpart TUG.*la-ḫa-ri-tum* in the Old Babylonian document of an outlay of garments (CT 45 36); see *CAD L* 40 and cf. ARM 23 375; 26 366:24. The affix **-ītim/-ītum* is often used for *nisbe* formations; this is probably why Durand translates "un habit à la mode de Lahara," a city in Southeastern Mesopotamia (J.-M. Durand, "Les 'declarations prophetiques' dans les lettres de Mari," in *Prophéties et oracles*, vol. 1: *Dans le Proche-Orient ancien* [Supplément au Cahier Evangile 88; Paris: Cerf, 1994] 8–74, esp. 59). This, however, is not the only use of the affix; see *GAG* §56q, p. 70.

51 J. Nougayrol, "Textes suméro-accadiens des archives et bibliothèques privées d'Ugarit," *Ugaritica* 5 (1968) 1–446, esp. 267–69 n. 162.

52 *Ugaritica* 5 162:11; cf. J. J. M. Roberts, "A New Parallel to I Kings 18:28–29," *JBL* 89 (1970) 76–77; repr. in id., *The Bible and the Ancient Near East: Collected Essays* (Winona Lake, Ind.: Eisenbrauns, 2002) 102–3.

53 The genderless *assinnus* appear as prophets at Mari, two of whom (Šelebum: ARM 26 197; 198; 213, and Ili-ḫaznaya: ARM 26 212) arc known by name. In other texts, *assinnus* are mentioned in the same breath with prophets (VS 19 I i 38, a Middle Assyrian food rations list; *MSL* 12 4.212 and 4.222, Neo-Assyrian lexical lists). Moreover, the sex of three Assyrian prophets, Issar-la-tašiyaṭ (SAA 9 1.1 i 28), Bayâ (SAA 9 1.4 ii 40) and Ilussa-amur (SAA 9 1.5 in 5–6), is not clear – a fact that I find difficult to explain away with the assumption of recurrent misspellings (thus M. Weippert, "'König, fürchte dich nicht!' Assyrische Prophetien im 7. Jahrhundert v. Chr.," *Or* 71 [2002] 1–54, esp. 33–34). For the *assinnu* and the *kurgarrû* in general, see W. Roscoe, "Priests of the Goddess: Gender Transgression in Ancient Religion," *HR* 35 (1996) 195–230, esp. 213–17; M. Nissinen, *Homoeroticism in the Biblical World: A Historical Perspective* (trans. K. Stjerna; Minneapolis, Minn.: Fortress, 1998), esp. 28–36; P. Lapinkivi, *The Sumerian Sacred*

ues in Hellenistic Syria in the activity of the devotees of Cybele, the *galli*,[54] who by and large share the characteristics of the *assinnu*—including the prophetic role—and who are neither temporally nor geographically too distant from the authors of Zech 13:4–6.

The Near Eastern examples of hairy mantels and bodily wounds associated with prophets may be regarded as too random and historically remote to be of any relevance in the present context. Still, one can ask why the author of Zech 13:4–6, without any concrete point of reference, happened to pick up these two characteristics, which in the context of the Hebrew Bible are no less haphazard. Whatever the actual personal experience the writers of these verses might have had of prophets and their activities, they are described here as extremists whose queer appearance is presented not only as shameful and wrong but also as an integral part of prophesying *(nibbā')*.

5 Prophet as a Madman (Hosea 9:7–9)

Did the prophets, then, have any advocates at all in the Second Temple community that may have left traces in the Hebrew Bible? I would like to draw attention to a text that may strike one as surprising. In the verses Hos 9:7–9 we read that the prophet is *'ĕwîl* ("foolish") and *mĕšugga'* ("crazy"), the latter term having approximately the same meaning as one of the Akkadian standard designations of a prophet, *muḫḫûm/maḫḫû*.[55] These are negative words as such and are used in a derogatory way in the Hebrew Bible. The word *'ĕwîl* has a strong concentration in the book of Proverbs where it designates the paradigmatic fool,[56] whereas *mĕšugga'* has a connotation with mental illness or the state of ecstasy.[57] It occurs

Marriage in the Light of Comparative Evidence (SAAS 15; Helsinki: The Neo-Assyrian Text Corpus Project, 2004), esp. 155–66.

54 For the *galli*, see Roscoe, "Priests of the Goddess," 198–206; P. Pachis,"'Γαλλαῖον Κυβέλης ὀλόλυγμα' *(Anthol, Palat*, VI, 173): L'élément orgiastique dans le culte de Cybele," in *Cybele, Attis and Related Cults*, FS M. J. Vermaseren (ed. E. M. Lane; Religions of the Graeco-Roman World 131; Leiden: Brill, 1996) 193–222.

55 Cf. A. Malamat, "Parallels between the New Prophecies from Mari and Biblical Prophecy," *NABU 4* (1989) 61–64, esp. 62; repr. in id., *Mari and the Bible* (SHCANE 12; Leiden: Brill, 1998) 122–27, esp. 123.

56 Prov 1:7; 7:22; 10:8, 10, 14, 21, etc.; outside Proverbs, the word occurs in Isa 19:11; 35:8; Jer 4:22; Hos 9:7; Ps 107:17; Job 5:2, 3.

57 See S. B. Parker, "Possession Trance and Prophecy in Pre-Exilic Israel," *VT* 28 (1978) 271–85, esp. 282–85. Parker concludes that "possession trance was *not* an element of Israelite prophecy, and figures in a history of Israelite prophecy only marginally in discussions of i) the possible

only a few times in the Hebrew Bible. In Deut 28:34 it belongs to a curse ("the sights you see will drive you mad"); in 1 Sam 21:12–15 it is used of David who behaves like a lunatic in front of the king of Gath. The rest of the occurrences are prophetic in nature: in 2 Kgs 9:11 it is used of a companion of Elisha, and in Jer 29:26 of "every madman who sets up as a prophet." In this case, the word is put in the mouth of a prophet who scorns the other prophet;[58] in Hos 7:9, however, *mēšuggaʿ* is combined with a conspicuous sympathy towards the prophet who is persecuted in the house of his God.

Late datings of passages in the book of Hosea are seldom welcomed with undivided enthusiasm; nevertheless, I dare suggest a Second Temple date for this text for the following reasons. First, the vv. 7–9 seem to include various materials inserted between the lines of an original bicolon in vv. 7ab and 9bc:[59]

7a *bāʾû yĕmê hap-pĕquddâ*
7b *bāʾû yĕmê hašillûm*
7c *yēdĕʿû yiśrāʾēl*
7d *ʾĕwīl han-nābîʾ*
7e *mĕšuggaʿ ʾîš hā-rûăḥ*
7f *ʿal rōb ʿăwōnĕkā*
7g *wĕ-rabbâ maśṭēmâ*
8a [*ṣōpê ʾeprayim ʿim ʾĕlōhāy nābîʾ*[60]]
8b *paḥ yāqôš ʿal-kol-dĕrākâw*
8c *maśṭēmâ bĕ-bêt ʾĕlōhâw*
9a *heʿmîqû-šiḥētû kî-mê hag-gibʿâ*
9b *yizkôr ʿăwōnām*
9c *yipqôd ḥaṭṭôʾtām*

---

impact of Phoenician prophecy on Israelite institutions, especially in the Omride court, and ii) the calumny and mockery to which prophets could be subjected" (p. 285). This conclusion requires, however, that the root *nbʾ* is divorced from prophecy (pp. 274–75).

58 R. P. Carroll (*The Book of Jeremiah: A Commentary* [OTL; London: SCM Press, 1986], 565): "The view of Jeremiah as a crazy play-acting prophet is interesting in that it demonstrates the ease with which prophets may abuse each other."

59 W. Schütte, "Hosea 9,7–9: Eine crux interpretum?," *BN* 114/115 (2002) 57–60, presents a very similar outline, without, however, drawing any diachronic consequences from it

60 Despite all efforts to make sense of this line, I am at a loss here; the assumption of a gloss originally written between the lines or in the margin strongly suggests itself. For attempts to translate the line, see P. A. Kruger, "The Prophet 'with' God: The Prophetic Image in Hos 9:7b–8 and the Colometry," *UF* 25 (1993) 219–26; M. A. Klopfenstein, "Hosea 9,7–9: Ein Lese- und Übersetzungsversuch," *ThZ* 57 (2001) 135–39; Schütte, "Hosea 9,7–9."

It seems that the rather unpoetical lines 7c and 9a have first been inserted because of the applicability of the historical reminiscence of Gibeah,[61] and in a later stage of the textual development, the pro-prophetic interpretation in the neatly structured lines 7d–8c (save the possible gloss in 8a), again based on clear parallelisms, has been added. Rather than to the historical prophet Hosea, the *nābî* then, refers to the paradigmatic prophet in the mind of the scribe.[62]

Second, the word *maśṭēmâ* ("hostility") is found only here in the Hebrew Bible; otherwise it is well known from Dead Sea Scrolls[63] and also from *Jubilees*[64] where Mastemah is the name of the leader of evil angels identified with Satan.[65] An ancient attestation of a word that otherwise occurs only in late sources is not impossible, of course, but this kind of distribution of *maśṭēmâ* rather points to its late provenance.

Thirdly, and most importantly, the place where the persecution of the prophet takes place is *bêt ʾĕlōhâw* ("the house of his God"). In the commentaries, this expression is usually understood, either not as the temple but as the *land* of his God, that is, Israel,[66] or as a cultic site not associated with the prophet Hosea but with the Ephraimites.[67] The need for these rather constrained interpretations

61 Cf. Y. Amit, "Epoch and Genre: The Sixth Century and the Growth of Hidden Polemics," in *Judah and Judeans in the Neo-Babylonian Period* (ed O. Lipschitz and J. Blenkinsopp; Winona Lake, Ind.: Eisenbrauns, 2003) 135–51, esp. 146, according to whom the explicit polemic against Gibeah reflects an implicit polemic against "the Jerusalem-based regime that had failed its people."

62 The passage is usually understood as a quotation from the mouth of the people mocking the prophet Hosea; for the most recent argument to this effect, see Klopfenstein, "Hosea 9,7–9." However, S. A. Irvine ("Enmity in the House of God [Hosea 9:7–9]," *JBL* 117 [1998] 645–53) argues, against this *opinio communis*, that these are words of the prophet Hosea denouncing another prophet, translating: "Foolish (are you), O prophet; crazy (are you), O man of the spirit!" I find it difficult, however, to interpret *han-nābîʾ* as a vocative. Francis Landy, on the other hand, thinks that it is the prophet himself who claims to be mad (*Hosea* [Readings: A New Biblical Commentary; Sheffield: Sheffield Academic Press, 1995], 115).

63 In the Dead Sea Scrolls, *malʾak maśṭēmâ* is a definition of Belial (IQM 13:11); for a considerable number of further occurrences, see *DCH* 5:502–3.

64 *Jub.* 10:8–9; 11:5; 17:16; 19:28.

65 Cf. J. W. van Henten, "Mastemah," *DDD*[2] (1999) 553–54.

66 E. g. H. W. Wolff, *Dodekapropheton*, vol 1: *Hosea* (BKAT 14/1; Neukirchen-Vluyn: Neukirchener, [3]1976), 203; J. Jeremias, *Der Prophet Hosea* (ATD 24/1; Göttingen: Vandenhoeck & Ruprecht, 1983), 118 n. 16.

67 According to A. A. Macintosh *(A Critical and Exegetical Commentary on Hosea* [ICC; Edinburgh: T&T Clark, 1997], 355) "'the house of his God' can scarcely refer to the prophet (Hosea) since he would be unlikely so to describe cultic sites with their syncretistic improprieties"; "Ho-

comes from the traditional dating of the text to the prophet Hosea's alleged lifetime, and they become unnecessary if we simply allow *bêt ʾĕlōhîm* to mean what it always means; the temple of Jerusalem,[68] The most natural reading of the text, then, brings us to the Second Temple period and provides a glimpse at the socio-religious concerns of the temple community of Yehud. The personal suffix referring to the prophet indicates that the prophet who identified himself with this temple is not appreciated in his spiritual home. Together with other pro-prophetic passages in Hosea, especially Hos 6:5 and 12:11, which seem to adhere to the Deuteronomistic idea of a succession of prophets, these verses may reflect a socioreligious clash, usually interpreted against an eighth-century setting,[69] but equally applicable to the circumstances of the Second Temple period.[70]

What exactly lies behind the contention that a prophet is persecuted in the temple remains unclear; it is possible but not not self-evident that the verses refer to actual ecstatic performances of a prophet. The undeniably negative tone of the characterization of the prophet as a madman, combined with the obvious sympathy towards his person, give the impression that the frantic behavior of the prophets is not appreciated as such. The words *ʾĕwîl* and *mĕšuggaʿ* describe the prophet's state of mind as an unwanted result of the animosity he has experienced, mirroring the senselessness of his contemporaries.[71] Hence, even this text throws suspicion on the traditional prophetic behavior, which is seen as depriving the prophet of his credibility and competence in the eyes of

---

sea's unequivocal condemnation of such sites (cf. 4.15; 8.11 ff.) renders it unlikely that he would speak (even sarcastically) of them in this way" (p. 356).

68 The compound *bêt ʾĕlōhîm* with or without suffixes, has 95 occurrences in the Hebrew Bible, 77 of which are to be found in Ezra–Nehemiah and Chronicles, where it refers to the temple of Jerusalem in all but two cases (1 Chr 10:10: a temple of the Philistines; 2 Chr 24:5: a temple of King Sennacherib's god). Of the remaining 18 occurrences, the temple of Jerusalem is doubtless meant in Isa 2:3//Mic 4:2; Joel 1:13, 16; Pss 42:5; 52:10; 55:15; 84:11; 135:2; Qoh 4:17; and Dan 1:2, probably even in Josh 9:23. In Judg 18:31 it is used of its predecessor at Shiloh, und in Gen 28; 17,22 of the venue of Jacob's dream. In Judg 9:27 it denotes a temple of the Shechemites, and in Judg 17:5 the private shrine of Micah the Ephraimite.

69 S. L. Cook, "The Lineage Roots of Hosea's Yahwism," in *The Social World of the Hebrew Bible: Twenty-Five Years of the Social Sciences in the Academy* (ed. R. A. Simkins and id.; Semeia 87; Atlanta, Ga.: Society of Biblical Literature, 1999) 145–61, reckons with a clash between two ritual systems, the prophet Hosea's priestly lineage and the contemporary northern state cult.

70 In my own dissertation, I have detected a conflict between the Deuteronomistic editors of the book of Hosea and the contemporary priests of the Second Temple; see M. Nissinen, *Prophetie, Redaktion und Fortschreibung in Hoseabuch: Studien zum Werdegang eines Prophetenbuches im Lichte von Hos 4 und 11* (AOAT 231; Kevelaer: Butzon & Bercker; Neukirchen-Vluyn: Neukirchener, 1991), 208–11.

71 Cf. Landy, *Hosea*, 115.

the author (and, in the same vein, of the modern commentators).[72] Why and when, by and towards whom the hostility was shown in concrete terms, is the subject of another study,

6 Concluding Remarks

As a conclusion to this brief analysis of the four texts dated to the Second Temple period, it appears that prophecy did not cease altogether. However, it is very difficult to draw a trustworthy image of the prophets of the period that covers some three centuries. Dating biblical texts is problematic and our knowledge of socio-religious circumstances of the Second Temple period is insufficient. It is evident, however, that the bloom of literary prophecy, triggered by the continuation of prophecy on the literary level as a kind of scribal divination, eclipsed the traditional, more or less ecstatic manifestations of prophecy. The more scripture represented the true word of God and its interpreters the intermediaries of God, the more dubious the traditional prophetic performance became, especially if there was any doubt about the loyalty of the prophets to the guardians of the scriptural tradition. Some forms of traditional prophetic activity, as attested in the Hebrew Bible as well as in the Near Eastern sources, probably continued to exist, but the texts discussed in this article reveal that they were despised rather than appreciated by the learned circles and were therefore probably driven to the margins of the society.

72 Cf. E. Zenger, "'Durch Menschen zog ich sie …' (Hos 11,4): Beobachtungen zum Verständnis des prophetischen Amts im Hoseabuch," in *Künder des Wortes: Beiträge zur Theologie der Propheten*, FS J. Schreiner (ed. L. Ruppert, P. Weimar, and E. Zenger; Würzburg: Echter, 1982) 183–201, esp. 188; Schütte, "Hosea 9,7–9," 59–60.

(How) Does the Book of Ezekiel Reveal Its Babylonian Context?

The Prophet Ezekiel Prophesying to the Exiles in Babylonia?

The six essays published in *Die Welt des Orients* 45/1 (2015) attempt to read the book of Ezekiel in its Babylonian context, adding importantly to the existing dossier of studies analyzing the text of the book of Ezekiel from an ancient Near Eastern perspective.[1] In this response, it is not my aim to present detailed criticism of these studies which, in my view, all make out good cases of relevant topics. Instead, I would like to add some methodological viewpoints to the general topic of the possibility of reading the book of Ezekiel in its Babylonian context.

It is often assumed as a matter of course that the book of Ezekiel is essentially about "the prophet Ezekiel prophesying to the exiles in Babylonia" – indeed, this sometimes serves as the undisputed starting point for further study on this biblical book. Historically, however, almost every word of this statement can and should be questioned, because it all too easily identifies the *implied* author and audience with *historical* flesh-and-blood ones.[2] As in fictional narra-

1 E.g., O. Keel, *JHWH-Visionen und Siegelkunst: Eine neue Deutung der Majestätschilderungen in Jes 6, Ez 1 und 10 und Sach 4* (SBS 84/85; Stuttgart: Katholisches Bibelwerk, 1977); D. Bodi, *The Book of Ezekiel and the Poem of Erra* (OBO 104; Göttingen: Vandenhoeck & Ruprecht and Fribourg: Academic Press, 1991); id., "Ezekiel," *Zondervan Illustrated Bible Backgrounds Commentary* 4 (ed. J. W. Walton; Grand Rapids, Mich.: Zondervan, 2009) 400 – 517; D. I. Block, "Divine Abandonment: Ezekiel's Adaptation of an Ancient Near Eastern Motif," in *The Book of Ezekiel: Theological and Anthropological Perspectives* (ed. M. S. Odell and J. T. Strong; SBLSymS 9; Atlanta: Society of Biblical Literature, 2000) 15 – 42; J. F. Kutsko, *Between Heaven and Earth: Divine Presence and Absence in the Book of Ezekiel* (Biblical and Judaic Studies 7; Winona Lake, Ind.: Eisenbrauns, 2000); C. Uehlinger and S. Müller Trufaut, "Ezekiel 1: Babylonian Cosmological Scholarship and Iconography: Attempts at Further Refinement," *TZ* 57 (2001) 140 – 71; D. F. Launderville, *Spirit and Reason: The Embodied Character of Ezekiel's Symbolic Thinking* (Waco, Tx.: Baylor University Press, 2007); B. N. Peterson, *Ezekiel in Context: Ezekiel's Message Understood in Its Historical Setting of Covenant Curses and Ancient Near Eastern Mythological Motifs* (PTMS 182; Eugene, Or.: Pickwick, 2012); C. A. Strine, *Sworn Enemies: The Divine Oath, the Book of Ezekiel, and the Polemics of Exile* (BZAW 436; Berlin and Boston: De Gryuter, 2013).

2 For recent discussion on the narratological concept of the implied author launched by W. C. Booth in his *The Rhetoric of Fiction* (Chicago: Chicago University Press, 1983 [orig. 1961]), see id., "Resurrection of the Implied Author: Why Bother?" *A Companion to Narrative*

DOI 10.1515/9783110466546-031

tives, one must distinguish between the author and the narrator.[3] The prophet Ezekiel is the first-person speaker, the narrator of his visions, but this does not automatically make him the author of the book. We cannot assume at the outset that the implied speaker, "the prophet Ezekiel," the implied audience, "the exiles," and the implied setting in "Babylonia" are identical with the historical author, audience, and setting. Instead, we have to ask who, in fact, communicates with whom in this book, and where this communication is supposed to take place. If we attempt to read the text in a historical, cultural, chronological, and geographical context, these questions have to be asked on both the textual and the historical level.

Before further inquiry, we have to decide what we want to know. Not all relevant research questions are specifically historical, hence it is possible to analyze the book of Ezekiel as a textual world of its own, paying attention to the structure, theology, and aesthetics of the chosen version of the book, for instance, the Masoretic Text or the Septuagint, unencumbered by its historical origin, emergence, or context. In practical terms, however, the perception of the symbolic world reflected by the text may be difficult without any historical presumptions and comparison with other source materials. The essays at hand read the book of Ezekiel *in* its Babylonian context, which is an outspokenly historical inquiry. This requires the use of historical methodology, that is, textual criticism, literary and editorial history, and comparison with parallel texts in the Hebrew Bible, as well as extrabiblical ancient Near Eastern evidence.

The Prophet or the Book?

The title of the 2015 theme issue of *Die Welt des Orients* is deliberately formulated as "The Book of Ezekiel in Its Babylonian Context" instead of "The Prophet Ezekiel in His Babylonian Context." In other words, the purpose is defined as contextualizing the *text*, not the *prophet*.

In fact, the latter alternative, contextualizing the prophet Ezekiel, would be a difficult and ultimately impossible task. The prophet Ezekiel is the main character and the implied speaker of the text. There is no way of knowing the person-

Theory (ed. J. Phelan and P. J. Rabinowitz; Oxford: Blackwell, 2005) 75–88 and the theme issue dedicated to the topic of the implied author, *Style* 45 (2011), especially the essay of Dan Shen, "What Is the Implied Author?" (here 80–98).

3 See P. Merenlahti and R. Hakola, "Reconceiving Narrative Criticism," in *Characterization in the Gospels: Reconceiving Narrative Criticism* (ed. D. Rhoads and K. Syreeni; JSNTSup 184; Sheffield; Sheffield Academic Press, 1999) 13–48.

ality of the actual author of the text, completely hidden behind the implied author or, rather, speaker whose voice is the one the audience is supposed to listen to. The book of Ezekiel, including the prophet Ezekiel as its main character, is a thoroughly literary creation that hides its actual authors. The figure of the prophet Ezekiel is "a first-person sympathetic narrator," through whom the reader is supposed to experience "all speech, all action."[4] In other words, "[t]he real Ezekiel is the symbolic Ezekiel, who is more than the historical Ezekiel."[5] The figure of the prophet is already part of the literary construct of the book, which (rather than the historical framework) is the primary context of his identity.[6]

Very often the author of the book of Ezekiel is called "the prophet" without exactly revealing who is being called by this epithet: the implied speaker, the historical author, or both in the same person. The epithet is sometimes used as a shorthand admitting the uncertainty about who the author actually was or how many they were. However, the singular form generates the imagination of a single author, the implied speaker tends to be virtually equated with the historical prophet, and the caveats are already forgotten when conclusions are drawn. Indeed, "[t]he storytelling in the book is so artful that it draws the reader into assuming that what it says about Ezekiel reflects a historical person's real experience."[7] Such a temptation, however, should be resisted in scholarly discourse. A designation like "the prophet" should not be used for the sake of convenience without qualifications, and assumptions concerning the historical the authorship of the book of Ezekiel should not be based on default positions such as claiming the historical authorship for the prophet Ezekiel unless the opposite is proven.

Also, the dating of the book of Ezekiel is very often treated as a preliminary issue, assuming the book to have been written during the "ministry" of the prophet Ezekiel between 593 and 571 BCE and interpreting the whole book's

---

4 C. L. Patton, "Priest, Prophet, and Exile: Ezekiel as a Literary Construct," *Ezekiel's Hierarchical World: Wrestling with a Tiered Reality* (ed. S. L. Cook and C. L. Patton; SBLSymS 31; Atlanta, Ga.: Society of Biblical Literature, 2004) 73–90, esp. 74; cf. K. Schöpflin, *Theologie als Biographie im Ezechielbuch: Ein Beitrag zur Konzeption alttestamentlicher Prophetie* (FAT 36; Tübingen: Mohr Siebeck, 2002), esp. 17–18; M. J. de Jong, "Ezekiel as a Literary Figure and the Quest for the Historical Prophet," in *The Book of Ezekiel and Its Influence* (ed. H. J. de Jonge and J. Tromp; Aldershot: Ashgate, 2007) 1–16.

5 Launderville, *Spirit and Reason*, 11.

6 Cf. H. Liss, "'Describe the Temple to the House of Israel': Preliminary Remarks on the Temple Vision in the Book of Ezekiel and the Question of Fictionality in Priestly Literatures," *Utopia and Dystopia in Prophetic Literature* (ed. E. Ben Zvi; PFES 92; Helsinki: The Finnish Exegetical Society, 2006) 122–43, esp. 123.

7 Patton, "Priest, Prophet, and Exile," 74.

content against the background of the exilic period. If this is taken as a default position, the historical context of the text may be misinterpreted. The available textual witnesses of the book of Ezekiel, like the books of the Hebrew Bible in general, reveal only the latest stages of the complicated process of emergence and transmission, but they show clearly enough that such a process took place and should never be ignored when historical questions are posed to the text.[8] Reconstructing the editorial history of any biblical book is notoriously difficult, but this should not lead to the virtual preference of the Masoretic Text, which does not represent the primary, let alone the "final" form of the text of the book of Ezekiel.[9]

The problem of the editorial process preceding the textual witnesses at our disposal has sometimes been circumvented by way of a synchronic, or holistic, reading of the text, often combined with the assumption of a single author responsible for the overwhelming majority of the text which is interpreted as a rhetorical and structural unity, indeed, a work of art not to be destroyed by the scissors-and-paste approach to the text.[10] This approach typically grows out of the frustration over the ever-varying reconstructions of the emergence of the text. However, the synchronic reading does not make historical questions any easier to cope with. Single authorship, for one thing, does not mean that "the prophet," that is, the implied speaker of the text, is its historical author. Moreover, structure alone, however beautiful, does not prove the single authorship; even editorial activity can follow literary strategies that result in a purposeful structure. Historical questions require historical methodology, and purely

8 See R. Müller, J. Pakkala, and B. ter Haar Romeny, *Evidence of Editing: Growth and Change of Texts in the Hebrew Bible* (SBLRBS 75; Atlanta, Ga.: Society of Biblical Literature, 2014), 9–17; K.-F. Pohlmann, "Synchrone und diachrone Texterschließung im Ezechielbuch," *HeBAI* 1 (2012) 246–70.

9 For text-critical studies on the book of Ezekiel, see J. Lust, "Ezéchiel dans la Septante," *Les Récueils prophétiques de la Bible: Origines, milieu, et contexte proche-oriental* (ed. J.-D. Macchi, C. Nihan, T. Römer, and J. Rückl; Le Monde de la Bible 64; Geneva: Labor et fides, 2012) 337–58; I. E. Lilly, *Two Books of Ezekiel: Papyrus 967 and the Masoretic Text as Variant Literary Editions* (VTSup 150; Leiden: Brill, 2012); A. S. Crane, *Israel's Restoration: A Textual-Comparative Exploration of Ezekiel 36–39* (VTSup 122; Leiden: Brill, 2008).

10 E.g., M. Greenberg, *Ezekiel 1–20: A New Translation with Introduction and Commentary* (AB 22; Garden City, N.Y.: Doubleday, 1983); id., *Ezekiel 21–37: A New Translation with Introduction and Commentary* (AB 22A; Garden City, N.Y.: Doubleday, 1997); D. I. Block, *The Book of Ezekiel: Chapters 1–24* (NICOT; Grand Rapids, Mich.: Eerdmans, 1997); idem, *The Book of Ezekiel: Chapters 25–48* (NICOT; Grand Rapids, Mich.: Eerdmans, 1997); and, most recently, Peterson, *Ezekiel in Context*.

aesthetic criteria based on one textual witness, typically the Masoretic Text, do not warrant historical conclusions.

Audience – Implied or Real?

The beginning of the third millennium has witnessed a considerable increase of attention paid to the Judean communities in Babylonia from early sixth century BCE on. This is due to growing evidence of Judean population in Babylonia. The so-called "Weidner list," that is, a ration list of the Neo-Babylonian royal court from the year 592 BCE mentioning Jehoiachin, the king of Judah, together with 53 other Judeans, was published already in 1939.[11] Names of Hebrew origin can also be found in the archive of the Murašû banking family, dating from the mid-fifth to mid-fourth centuries and published as early as in 1898.[12] The West Semitic onomastic evidence in Neo-Babylonian texts collected by Ran Zadok adds significantly to this corpus.[13]

The newest and most substantial addition to the evidence of Judeans in Babylonia, consisting of ca. 200 administrative records from different museums and private collections, is recently published by Laurie Pearce and Cornelia Wunsch.[14] On the basis of these and previously published samples[15] we know

---

11 E. F. Weidner, "Jojachin, König von Juda, in babylonischen Keilschrifttexten," *Mélanges Syriens*, FS M. R. Dussaud, vol. 2 (BAH 30; Paris: Geuthner, 1939) 923–35.

12 See M. W. Stolper, *Entrepreneurs and Empire: The Murašû Archive, the Murašû Firm, and Persian Rule in Babylonia* (PIHANS 54; Istanbul: Nederlands Historisch-Archeologisch Instituut te Istanbul, 1985); id. and V. Donbaz, *Istanbul Murašû Texts* (PIHANS 79; Istanbul: Nederlands Historisch-Archeologisch Instituut te Istanbul, 1997).

13 E.g., R. Zadok, *The Jews in Babylonia during the Chaldean and Achaemenid Periods According to the Babylonian Sources* (Haifa: University of Haifa, 1979); id., *The Earliest Diaspora: Israelites and Judeans in Pre-Hellenistic Mesopotamia* (PDRI 151; Tel Aviv: The Diaspora Research Institute, Tel Aviv University, 2002); id., "Judeans in Babylonia: Updating the Dossier," *Encounters by the Rivers of Babylon: Scholarly Conversations between Jews, Iranians, and Babylonians in Antiquity* (ed. U. Gabbay and S. Secunda; TSAJ 160; Tübingen: Mohr Siebeck, 2014) 163–216.

14 L. E. Pearce and C. Wunsch, *Documents of Judean Exiles and West Semites in Babylonia in the Collection of David Sofer* (CUSAS 28; Bethesda, Md.: CDL Press, 2014); C. Wunsch, *Judeans by the Waters of Babylon: New Historical Evidence in Cuneiform Sources from Rural Babylonia* (Babylonische Archive 6; Dresden: ISLET-Verlag, forthcoming).

15 F. Joannès and A. Lemaire, "Contrats babyloniens d'époque achéménide du Bit abî Râm avec une épigraphie araméenne," *RA* 90 (1996) 41–60; iid., "Trois tablettes cunéiformes à l'onomastique ouest-sémitique (Collection Sh. Moussaieff)," *Transeuphratène* 17 (1999) 17–34; K. Abraham, "West Semitic and Judean Brides in Cuneiform Sources from the Sixth Century BCE: New Evidence from a Marriage Contract from Al-Yahudu," *AfO* 51 (2005/6) 198–219; ead., "An

that these texts, written between 572 and 477 BCE, yield information on ordinary Judeans, allowing glimpses to their everyday life in places such as Al-Yahudu ("Judahtown"), Bit-Abi-râm ("House of Abraham"), and Alu-ša-Našar ("Town of Našar"). These localities are most probably to be sought in the Nippur region, even though the exact locations are unknown. Altogether, the Judean population attested in the cuneiform documents from the Neo-Babylonian and the Achaemenid periods comprises three kinds of people: upper class at the royal court, traders in different Babylonian cities, and subsistence farmers in the Nippur region. The documents "provide a window into the Judean's full integration into the economic institutions of Babylonian and Achaemenid society."[16] The people of Judean origin appear in the sources running their everyday affairs and businesses over several generations as members of the Babylonian society. They seem to have formed communities composed largely of Judeans, and their status was comparable to other populations with non-Babylonian origin.[17]

The question is whether the existence of these communities is in any way recognizable in the book of Ezekiel. Does the book give any hint at these people as belonging to its implied audience? What does the book of Ezekiel tell about its audience anyway?

Inheritance Division among Judeans in Babylonia from the Early Persian Period," *New Seals and Inscriptions: Hebrew, Idumean, and Cuneiform* (ed. M. Lubetski; HBM 8; Sheffield: Sheffield Phoenix, 2007) 206–21.

16 L. E. Pearce, "Continuity and Normality in Sources Relating to the Judean Exile," *HeBAI* 3 (2014) 163–84, esp. 177.

17 See the discussion in L. E. Pearce, "New Evidence for Judeans in Babylonia," *Judah and Judeans in the Persian Period* (ed. O. Lipschits and M. Oeming; Winona Lake, Ind.: Eisenbrauns, 2006), 399–411; ead., "Sealed Identities," *Opening the Tablet Box*, FS B. R. Foster (ed. S. C. Melville and A. L. Slotsky; CHANE 42; Leiden: Brill, 2010) 301–28; ead., "'Judean': A Special Status in Neo-Babylonian and Achemenid Babylonia," *Judah and Judeans in the Achaemenid Period: Negotiating Identity in an International Context* (ed. O. Lipschits, G. N. Knoppers, and M. Oeming; Winona Lake, Ind.: Eisenbrauns, 2011) 267–77; ead., "Identifying Judeans and Judean Identity," in *Exile and Return: The Babylonian Context* (ed. C. Waerzeggers and J. Stökl; BZAW 478; Berlin: De Gruyter, 2015) 7–32; C. Wunsch, "Glimpses on the Lives of Deportees in Rural Babylonia," *Arameans, Chaldeans, and Arabs in Babylonia and Palestine in the First Millennium B. C.* (ed. A. Berlejung and M. P. Streck; LAOS 3; Wiesbaden: Harrassowitz, 2013) 247–60; C. Waerzeggers, "Locating Contact in the Babylonian Exile: Some Reflections on Tracing Judean-Babylonian Encounters in Cuneiform Texts," in: Gabbay and Secunda, *Encounters by the Rivers of Babylon* (2014) 131–46; J. Stökl, "Schoolboy Ezekiel: Remarks on the Transmission of Learning," *WO* 45 (2015) 50–61; T. Alstola, "Judean Merchants in Babylonia and Their Participation in Long-Distance Trade," *WO* 47 (2017) 25–51.

Apart from his spiritual journeys, Ezekiel is clearly located in the "Land of the Chaldeans," that is, in Babylonia. In the Masoretic Text, his location is specified by two geographical names: "I came to the exiles at Tel-Abib, who lived by the river Chebar" (*wā-ʾābôʾ ʾel-hag-gôlâ Tel ʾĀbib hay-yôšĕbîm ʾel-nĕhar-Kĕbār* 3:15[18]; cf. 1:1–3; 11:24). The exact location of the "river Chebar," also mentioned in 1:1, 3; 3:23; 10:15, 20, 22, and 43:3, is unknown; Babylonian sources mention two canals called Kabaru, one in the vicinity of Nippur and the other perhaps in Babylon-Borsippa region.[19]

In any case, the text locates Ezekiel in a place where his compatriots, the *gôlâ*, can approach him. Elders of Judah (8:1) or Israel (14:1; 20:1) come to visit him to receive the divine word, as does someone who has escaped from Jerusalem to bring the news of the fall of the city (33:21). Sometimes the "people" (*hāʿām*) attend Ezekiel's symbolic actions (24:18–24; 37:16–23) which, to all appearances, are staged in Babylonia. In so far, the text indeed gives the impression that Ezekiel addresses people in Babylonia and "wants to be read as a text conceived of by someone living there."[20]

With regard to its expressly Babylonian setting, it is interesting how conspicuously unspecific the book of Ezekiel is about its audience. The overall accusation throughout the book is that these people are sinful, rebellious, treacherous, and idolatrous, but this really tells nothing about the actual audience of the text. Only very few individuals are mentioned: King Jehoiachin in 1:2,[21] and Jaazaniah son of Azzur and Pelatiah son of Benaiah, who are not among the exiles but officials in Jerusalem where Ezekiel has been brought to by the spirit (11:1, 13). A couple of times, Ezekiel addresses the elders who have come to him for

---

18 Verse 3:15 is syntactically problematic, and *hay-yôšebîm ʾel-nĕhar-Kĕbār* is interpreted as a secondary specification of the location of Tel-Abib (*BHS*; cf., e.g., K.-F. Pohlmann, *Das Buch des Propheten Hesekiel (Ezechiel): Kapitel 1–19* [ATD 22/1; Göttingen: Vandenhoeck & Ruprecht, 1996], 46). LXX translates these words but seems to read an otherwise different Hebrew text here: *kai eisēlthon eis tēn aikhmalōsian meteōros kai periēlthon tous katoikountas epi tou potamou tou Khorab tous ontas ekei*. Instead of the place name Tel-Abib, the Vorlage of the LXX seems to have included forms of the verbs *tlh* (> *meteōros*) and *sbb* (> *perierkhomai*) separated by the conjunction *we-* (*kai*).

19 See D. S. Vanderhooft, "Chebar," *EBR* 5 (2012) 46. One Babylonian text mentions even the place name Al-Nar-Kabari (Joannès and Lemaire, "Contrats babyloniens d'époque achéménide," text 7:5). As L. Pearce notes, "this datum does not confirm the existence of the toponym at a time proximate to Ezekiel's mission, since the text dates to Xerxes 4 (481 B.C.E.)" ("Continuity and Normality in Sources Relating to the Judean Exile," 171); however, if Ezek 3:15 is of later origin, the place name could reflect the existence of Judean settlements in that area.

20 Stökl, "Schoolboy Ezekiel," 51.

21 D. I. Block, "The Tender Cedar Sprig: Ezekiel on Jehoiachin," *HeBAI* 1 (2012) 173–202, finds metaphorical allusions to Jehoiachin also in 17:3–4, 22a and 19:10–14.

advise (14:1–5; 20:1–4), which is reminiscent of the elders of Israel approaching Moses in Exod 18:15.[22] Chapter 13 addresses prophets, both male (13:1–16) and female (13:17–23), but, conspicuously enough, it is not revealed to the reader whether these people were active in Babylonia or in the old country.[23]

The addressees of the divine word mediated by Ezekiel are mostly defined as the "house of Israel" (*bêt yiśrā'ēl:* 3:1, 4, 5, 7, 17; 11:15; 12:9, 27; 17:2; 18:25; 20:27, 30, 39; 24:21; 33:7, 10, 20; 36:22; 37:11; 40:4; 43:10; 44:6); sometimes as "sons of Israel" (*bĕnê yiśrā'ēl:* 2:3); "rebellious house" (*bêt hammĕrî:* 24:3; cf. 12:9; 44:6) "Land of Israel" (*'admat yiśrā'ēl:* 7:2; 12:22; 18:2; 21:7; 33:24), "princes of Israel" (*nĕśî'ê yiśrā'ēl:* 19:1;45:4); "shepherds of Israel" (*rō'ê yiśrā'ēl:* 34:2); "mountains of Israel" (*hārê yiśrā'ēl:* 6:2; 36:1, 4, 6, 8). Sometimes the addressees are expressly located in Judah (33:24: "inhabitants of the waste places in the land of Israel"). Most of the time, however, the reader is, perhaps intentionally, left betwixt-and-between: the divine words do not specifically locate the addressees in any one place, although the Babylonian context of the implied audience is implicit, for instance, in the vision of the dry bones in 37:1–14. The dichotomy of Jerusalem and Babylonia is cast in the very foundation of the symbolic structure of the book, nourishing its theological discourse and triggering ongoing interpretations.[24]

All this leaves the reader asking whether the book of Ezekiel is at all interested in the affairs and whereabouts of the actual Judeans who lived in Babylonia. Reconstructions of the editorial history of the book have, of course, identified a redactional layer with a strong *Golaorientierung*, that is, a tendency of favoring the (first) exilic community as the new true Israel,[25] but these texts consist of future-oriented theological discourse that reveals nothing about the life and work of their flesh-and-blood audience. Moreover, these texts give the impression that quite some time has passed after the catastrophy in Jerusalem

22 Cf. Patton, "Priest, Prophet, and Exile," 84.

23 Schöpflin (*Theologie als Biographie im Ezechielbuch*, 305) wonders whether Ezekiel 13 describes ongoing practices or, rather, gives a theological lesson about the past. E. J. Hamori (*Women's Divination in Biblical Literature: Prophecy, Necromancy, and Other Arts of Knowledge* [The Anchor Yale Reference Library; New Haven: Yale University Press, 2015], 167–83) reads the chapter as "a window onto an inner-Yahwistic conflict" (p. 182).

24 Cf. Schöpflin, *Theologie als Biographie im Ezechielbuch*, 348.

25 Especially K.-F. Pohlmann, *Ezechielstudien: Zur Redaktionsgeschichte des Buches und zur Frage nach den ältesten Texten* (BZAW 180; Berlin and New York: de Gruyter, 1992); id., *Das Buch des Propheten Hesekiel/Ezechiel*; cf. the modification of the theory by A. Klein, *Schriftauslegung im Ezechielbuch: Redaktionsgeschichtliche Untersuchungen zu Ez 34–39* (BZAW 391; Berlin and New York; de Gruyter, 2008).

took place.[26] The unspecific presentation of the audience enables the *Fortschreibung* and rereading of the text across generations, serving the identity policies of different communities in different times.

Babylonia – Historical or Symbolic?

While the book of Ezekiel shows minimal interest in its actual audience, it seems to be even less interested in what the essays in this issue try to figure out, that is, in its Babylonian context. In the book of Ezekiel, the country where the *gôlâ* lives is most often called the "land of the Chaldeans" (*'ereṣ kaśdîm*), which a traditional-theological rather than political-historical designation. The use of the name Babylon (*Bābēl*) is restricted in three contexts: as the place where the king of Judah, i.e., Zedekiah, was brought after the conquest of Jerusalem (12:13–16; 17:12–21; 19:5–9, all dependent on 2 Kgs 24–25); as a part of the title of the king of Babylon, i.e., Nebuchadnezar II (21:24–28; 24:2; 26:7; 29:18–20; 30:10–12, 24–25; 32:11–12), and as the origin of Oholiba's lovers (23:11–27). Otherwise the name Babylon is, as it were, programmatically avoided.

Indeed, since Ezekiel is "not sent to a people of obscure language and foreign tongue, but to the house of Israel" (3:5), the readers of the book of Ezekiel learn nothing about the life, politics, culture, ideology, and religion of the world surrounding the exiles. No actions of the Babylonian king or his officials in their own country are described, and the book is in no way concerned about the everyday realities of the people living in Babylonia, whether Judeans or others. Babylonia is not even included in the nations condemned in the Ezekielian cycle of oracles against nations including Ammonites, Moabites, Philistines, Tyre, Sidon, and Egypt – unless we take some portions of the book (e.g., the Gog oracles in chs. 38–39) to include indirect counterdiscourse against contemporary Babylonian rule or religion.[27]

If the "real" Ezekiel is the symbolic Ezekiel, then the "real" Babylonia is the symbolic Land of the Chaldeans, the site of the "Babylonian captivity." The striking disinterest of the book in the everyday life of its actual (or even implied) audiences arouses the question of the relationship between the book of Ezekiel and the Judean communities in Babylonia. Did Ezekiel's message

---

26 See Klein, *Schriftauslegung im Ezechielbuch*, 402–3; Schöpflin, *Theologie als Biographie im Ezechielbuch*, 353.

27 Cf. C. A. Strine, "*Chaoskampf* against Empire: YHWH's Battle against Gog (Ezek 38–39) as Resistance Literature," in *Divination, Politics, and Ancient Near Eastern Empires* (ed. A. Lenzi and J. Stökl; ANEM 7; Atlanta, Ga.: Society of Biblical Literature, 2014) 87–108.

reach King Jehoiachin and his entourage in the Babylonian royal court? Was the message of the book of Ezekiel later circulated among the Judean communities "tilling the land, marrying and prospering"[28] in places such as Al-Yahudu?[29] Were the Judeans who borrowed money from the bank of the Murašû family moved by its words, feeling themselves belonging to the new true Israel? Or was it only a small circle of literati that was aware of its existence anyway?

The Ezekielian utopia distances itself entirely from such mundane affairs, leaving the reader without answer to such questions. What matters is not the historical reality surrounding the authors of the text; instead, "[i]t replaces reality, taking place in the realm of history, by a reality in the 'realm of the text.'"[30]

Ancient Near Eastern or Specifically Babylonian Influence?

So far, we have found the text of the book of Ezekiel to be rather inconclusive about its historical audience and cultural context. That the historical inquiry nevertheless makes sense, is due to the well-demonstrated presence of ancient Near Eastern motifs – indeed, a mixture of motifs – in the book of Ezekiel.[31] At least the following types of parallel features arise from the essays published in this issue and other recent studies on the topic:

(1) *Iconographic motifs*. Shawn Aster shows how the "glory of God" (*kĕbôd YHWH*) in Ezekiel owes the radiant appearance to the Mesopotamian images of the *melammu*,[32] while Daniel Bodi demonstrates the background of the imagery of Ezekiel 47, especially of the double current flowing from the temple and of the trees of healing growing on the river banks, in Mesopotamian iconography[33]. Christoph Uehlinger argues that the vision in Ezekiel 1 presupposes knowledge of Mesopotamian, sometimes specifically Babylonian, cosmology, astronomy,

28 Wunsch, "Glimpses on the Lives of Deportees in Rural Babylonia," 257.
29 Cf. Pearce, "Continuity and Normality in Sources Relating to the Judean Exile," 181; D. M. Carr, "Reading into the Gap: Refractions of Trauma in Israelite Prophecy," in *Interpreting Exile: Displacement and Deportation in Biblical and Modern Contexts* (ed. B. E. Kelle, F. R. Ames, and J. L. Wright; SBLAIL 10; Atlanta, Ga.: Society of Biblical Literature, 2011) 295–308, esp. 303.
30 Liss, "Describe the Temple to the House of Israel," 143 on Ezekiel 40–48.
31 See above, n. 1.
32 S. S. Aster, "Ezekiel's Adaptation of the Mesopotamian *Melammu*," *WO* 45 (2015) 10–21; cf. already P. Grelot, "GALGAL (Ézéchiel 10,2.6.13 et Daniel 7,9)," *Transeuphratène* 15 (1998) 137–47.
33 D. Bodi, "The Double Current and the Tree of Healing in Ezekiel 47:1–12 in Light of Babylonian Iconography and Texts," *WO* 45 (2015) 22–37.

and theology visible in Mesopotamian texts and iconography from the eighth through the fourth centuries BCE, applying these conceptions to Yhwh theology.[34] Indeed, as Margaret Odell has argued in another context, in the depiction of the glory of God in Ezekiel 1, "Ezekiel tells us that what he sees are appearances (*mar'ê*) and representations (*dĕmût*)" inspired by Mesopotamian iconography.[35]

(2) *Prophecy and divination.* Dale Launderville reads the book of Ezekiel against the background of Assyrian prophecy, arguing that in the vision of the dry bones (Ezek 37:1–14), the functions of Ištar and Ea are claimed to Yhwh, in order to "recontextualize the exiles' understanding of their social and cosmic location," creating a "monotheistic context for understanding the data of experience.").[36] Knowledge of women's participation in Mesopotamian magic and divination in Ezekiel 13:17–23 has recently been suggested by Jonathan Stökl.[37]

(3) *Vocabulary.* The essays pubished in this issue give several convincing cases of words in the book of Ezekiel can be best explained as loans from Akkadian. One of them is *ḥašmal* (1:4, 27; 8:2), which in all likelihood goes back to the Akkadian word for amber, *elmešu*, which, for its part, is possibly a Baltic loanword.[38] Stökl argues for the origin of the word *'eškār* (27:15) in Akkadian *iškaru* 'work, assignment,' as well as of *gallāb* (5:1) in *gallābu* 'barber.[39]' The list can be supplemented by, for instance, by *nādān* (16:33) <*nudunnû* 'gift, dowry'; *dĕrôr* (46:17) <*andurāru* 'manumission'; *sûgar* (19:9) <*sigaru* 'neckstock'; *šāšar* (23:14) <*šaršerru* "red clay, paste, pigment.' Even phrases may be translated

---

34 C. Uehlinger, "Virtual Vision vs. Actual Show: Strategies of Visualization in the Book of Ezekiel," *WO* 45 (2015) 62–98.

35 M. S. Odell, "Ezekiel Saw What He Said He Saw: Genres, Forms, and the Vision of Ezekiel 1," in *The Changing Face of Form Criticism for the Twenty-First Century* (ed. M. A. Sweeney and E. Ben Zvi; Grand Rapids, Mich.: Eerdmans, 2003) 162–76, esp. 176; E. van Wolde, "Ezekiel's Picture of God in Ezekiel 1," in *The God Ezekiel Creates* (ed. P. Joyce and D. Rom-Shiloni; LHBOTS 607; New York: T&T Clark, 2014) 87–106.

36 D. Launderville, "The Threat of Synchretism to Ezekiel's Exilic Audience in the Dry Bones Passage," *WO* 45 (2015) 38–49, esp. 41.

37 See J. Stökl, "The מתנבאות in Ezekiel 13 Reconsidered," *JBL* 132 (2013) 61–76, according to whom the *mitnabbe'ôt* originally mean technical diviners and became (intuitive) prophets only when vv. 22–23 were added to the text.

38 Aster, "Ezekiel's Adaptation of the Mesopotamian *Melammu*," 14 n. 10. For the Baltic origin, see M. Heltzer, "On the Origin of the Near Eastern Archaeological Amber," in *Languages and Cultures in Contact: At the Crossroads of Civilizations in the Syro-Mesopotamian Realm* (ed. K. van Lerberghe and G. Voet; OLA 96/CRRAI, 42; Leuven: Peeters, 1999) 169–76; U. Masing, "Kas *elmešu* = helmes?," in *Aarted tellistes* (ed. M.-L. Tammiste, R. Järv, and K. Salve; Tartu: Kirjastus Ilmamaa, 2011), 189–99 (= *Emakeele Seltsi Aastaraamat* 23 [1977] 23–32).

39 Stökl, "Schoolboy Ezekiel," 56–58.

from Akkadian, such as *mâ ʾămullâ libbātēk* (16:30) "How I am incensed against you" reflecting the idiom *libbāti malû* 'to be angry with.'[40]

(4) *Allusions to Mesopotamian literature.* Apart from linguistic borrowing, the book of Ezekiel shows familiarity with Mesopotamian texts. Daniel Bodi demonstrated more than two decades ago the "literary emulation" of the *Erra Epic* in the book of Ezekiel.[41] Abraham Winitzer argues for intended allusions to *Gilgameš Epic* in the book of Ezekiel, especially in the oracles against Tyre in chapter 28. According to Winiter's intriguing suggestion, the highly enigmatic expression *tuppêkâ û-nĕqābêkâ* (28:13) can be read as reflecting the title of the Epic, *ṭuppi ša naqba īmuru* "He who Saw the Depths."[42]

(5) *Theological patterns.* Many theological and mythological motifs in the book of Ezekiel are interpreted against ancient Near Eastern patterns. The book as a whole reflects variations of the theme of divine presence and absence,[43] which is closely related to the divine alienation—divine reconciliation pattern well known from Mesopotamian sources from different times.[44] The ancient Near Eastern treaty curses have also been regarded as the cultural setting for the theology of the book,[45] and the Akkadian *nasû nadānu* formula has been seen as a counterpart to the Ezekielian "lifted hand" formula.[46] Quite recently, Tova Ganzel and Shalom Holtz have compared the architecture of the temple of Jerusalem as described in the vision of chapters 40–48 with the available evidence of Neo-Babylonian temples, arguing that "[t]he prophet describes a temple whose architecture and organization resemble those of temples contemporary with and geographically most proximate to the prophet's stated time and place."[47]

This short inventory of ancient Near Eastern topics in the book of Ezekiel is neither exhaustive nor indisputable. Taken together, however, the accumulation of Near Eastern features leave no doubt that the book of Ezekiel was written in an environment where such elements of tradition were part and parcel of the in-

---

40 For these examples, see D. S. Vanderhooft, "Ezekiel in and on Babylon," in *Bible et Proche-Orient: Mélanges André Lemaire III* (ed. J. Elayi and J.-M. Durand) = *Transeuphratène* 46 (2014) 99–119, esp. 106–14.

41 Bodi, *The Book of Ezekiel and the Poem of Erra*, 315.

42 A. Winitzer, "Assyriology and Jewish Studies in Tel Aviv: Ezekiel among the Babylonian *literati*," in: Gabbay and Secunda, *Encounters by the Rivers of Babylon* (2014) 163–216.

43 Kutsko, *Between Heaven and Earth*, 154.

44 See Block, "Divine Abandonment."

45 Peterson, *Ezekiel in Context*.

46 Strine, *Sworn Enemies*.

47 T. Ganzel and S. E. Holtz "Ezekiel's Temple in Babylonian Context," *VT* 64 (2014) 211–26, esp. 225.

tellectual milieu. The question to be asked is, of course, to what extent these features are distinctly Babylonian. Geographically, the relevant parallels do not always derive from specifically Babylonian sources but also from Assyria and, for instance, from Mari. Temporally, the time-span of the parallels ranges well over a millennium, rarely suggesting a specific date or location of their cultural transmission.

The familiarity of the authors of the book of Ezekiel with Near Eastern topics and language cannot be restricted to Babylonia in the exilic period (so-called). Mesopotamian traditions were known in the Near East even in Achaemenid and Hellenistic periods, not only in Mesopotamia but even even in Judah, as, for instance, the astrological texts from Qumran demonstrate.[48] Therefore, the Near Eastern themes in the book of Ezekiel could theoretically be adopted anywhere in the Near East. The integration of the Persian province of Yehud into the Achaemenid imperial system[49] included also scribal practices, especially the rise of Aramaic as the *lingua franca*, which may have facilitated the transmission of traditions originally cultivated in the cuneiform culture. It is not excluded that some of the above-mentioned topics were mediated through Aramaic.

What makes Babylonia a plausible site of acculturation of at least the earliest material in the book of Ezekiel is not the conventional notion of "the prophet Ezekiel prophesying to the exiles in Babylonia" but, rather the *terminus post quem* of the book in early sixth century, together with the fact that there were Judean communities in Babylonia. These communities, attested in both Neo-Babylonian and Achaemenid cuneiform records, did not live in a splendid isolation but, while maintaining their Judean identity, were integrated in their Babylonian social and economical, and probably also cultural environment. Whether the actual authors and audiences of this extremely learned book can be sought in Al-Yahudu and other communities known from the Babylonian records, is another question.

The multiple evidence of acculturation indicates the historical authors of the book of Ezekiel were learned persons whose literacy was on a high level. The creation of a literary work such as the book of Ezekiel cannot have come about without scribal education, and therefore, the origin of the book should be sought in highly literate circles. Jonathan Stökl's arguments on the traces of knowledge

48 See, e.g., W. Horowitz and J. Ben-Dov, "The Babylonian Lunar Three in Qumran Calendars," *ZA* 95 (2005) 104–20.

49 See David S. Vanderhooft, "*ʾel medînâ ûmedînâ kiktābāh:* Scribes and Scripts in Yehud and in Achaemenid Transeuphratene," in Lipschits et al. (eds.) *Judah and Judeans in the Persian Period* (2011) 529–44.

of Mesopotamian literary and iconographic tradition[50] make the Babylonian scribal training of at least some authors of the book probable indeed. As Margaret Odell argues, "Ezekiel saw what he said he saw"[51]: the iconographical literacy in at least some parts of the book exceeds superficial observation, requiring interpretative tools that were only available through the knowledge of cuneiform culture. Christoph Uehlinger, too, argues that the author of Ezekiel 1 must have had considerable exposure to Babylonian cosmological scholarship, whether as the result of formal education or another type of interaction.[52] How the connection of the people of Judean descent with the Babylonian scribal schools and their access to texts was established is, unfortunately, difficult to know on the basis of the available evidence.[53] Heuristically, one can surmise with Uehlinger that such an interaction was more easily available to people belonging to Jehoiachin's entourage than to the agricultural communities in the Nippur region.

It is very difficult to identify the *people* with whom the book of Ezekiel communicates, but it is fairly easy to recognize the *texts* it interacts with, such as other prophetic books, the Priestly material in the Pentateuch including Lev 17–26, and Ezra–Nehemiah. The *traditum* in the book of Ezekiel, therefore, is not only Babylonian/Mesopotamian but, at the same time, distinctively Judean.[54] The dense network of intertextual links between the book of Ezekiel and other texts known to us from the Hebrew Bible[55] testifies to an intensive occupation with Hebrew language and literature, presupposing not only continuation of the literary tradition of monarchical Jerusalem, but also a relationship with communities engaged in creation and interpretation of Hebrew texts and identifying themselves as Israel, Yhwh's congregation.

---

50 Stökl, "Schoolboy Ezekiel."

51 Odell, "Ezekiel Saw What He Said He Saw"; cf. P. Kingsley, "Ezekiel by the Grand Canal: Between Jewish and Babylonian Tradition," *JRAS* 3/2 (1992) 339–46.

52 Uehlinger, "Virtual Vision vs. Actual Show"; cf. Uehlinger and Müller Trufaut, "Ezechiel 1."

53 For possible "pathways" between Judeans and Babylonian texts, see Waerzeggers, "Locating Contact in the Babylonian Exile," who is all too modest in characterizing the results of her study in Judean-Babylonian encounters "very much inconclusive" (143).

54 See M. Nevader, "On Reading Ezekiel by the Rivers of Babylon," *WO* 45 (2015) 99–110, esp. 107–110.

55 These have been the object of intensive study for decades; for most recent contributions, see M. A. Sweeney, "Ezekiel's Conceptualization of the Exile in Intertextual Perspective," *HeBAI* 1 (2012) 154–72; D. Rom-Shiloni,"Ezekiel and Jeremiah: What Might Stand Behind the Silence," *HeBAI* 1 (2012) 203–30; R. Müller, "A Prophetic View of the Exile in the Holiness Code: Literary Growth and Tradition History in Leviticus 26," in *The Concept of Exile in Ancient Israel and Its Historical Contexts* (ed. E. Ben Zvi and C. Levin; BZAW 404; Berlin and New York: de Gruyter, 2010) 207–40.

Conclusion

In the virtual reality of the book of Ezekiel, the "real" Ezekiel is the symbolic Ezekiel, and the "real" Babylonia is the symbolic Land of the Chaldeans. The book is minimally interested in the life and physical environment of the flesh-and-blood Judeans who lived in Babylonia. Therefore, it yields minimal information on its authors, audience, and place of writing.

At the same time, the book is permeated with language and motifs deriving from ancient Near Eastern, especially Mesopotamian literary and iconographic traditions. To all appearances, the book emerged in a context of learning, within a community of literati who have been familiar with both Hebrew and Mesopotamian texts and traditions. The familiarity of the authors of the book with both traditions clearly exceeds the superficial, which suggests a high level of scribal training.

Babylonia can be considered the most probable source of the learned tradition used and reflected in the book of Ezekiel in general, but this is not always evident. It is difficult to determine the source and place of learning throughout the process of the emergence of the book of Ezekiel which was an intertextual process involving many other texts known to us from the Hebrew Bible. Within this interdependent textual system, the book of Ezekiel occupies an important position in establishing its version of the ideology of exile, but it is much more difficult to estimate the impact of the book on the Judean communities in Babylonia. If we say that Ezekiel "laid the foundations for the Babylonian community's self-perception as the only people of God," reshaping the "exiles' group identity as early as the beginning of the sixth century,"[56] we would need to define the group whose identity we assume to be at stake.

The biblical intertextual network does not reveal us to what extent the biblical ideology of exile, as represented by the book of Ezekiel and many other biblical texts, was the shared ideology of the Judean communities in Babylonia, and the existing extrabiblical sources from Babylonia provide little help in this respect. What the essays published in the theme issue of *Die Welt des Orients* 45/1 (2015) do make evident, however, is the Mesopotamian seedbed of the Eze-

56 Thus D. Rom-Shiloni in her important article on the comparison of Ezekiel and Ezra–Nehemiah, "From Ezekiel to Ezra–Nehemiah: Shifts of Group Identities within Babylonian Exilic Ideology," in Lipschits et al. (eds.), *Judah and Judeans in the Achaemenid Period* (2011) 127–51, esp. 146, 147; cf. a thorough discussion in ead., *Exclusive Inclusivity: Identity Conflicts between the Exiles and the People who Remained (6th–5th Centuries BCE)* (LHBOTS 543; New York and London: T & T Clark, 2013).

kielian ideology, even though the book itself hides rather than reveals this background. Perhaps unintendedly, the dichotomy of Jerusalem and Babylonia shows itself in the thoroughly Near Eastern subsoil of the exclusively Yahwistic discourse.

The Book of Hosea and the Last Days of the Northern Kingdom: The Methodological Problem

1 How Can We Reach the Eighth Century BCE?

The essays published in this volume demonstrate that the historical reconstruction of the last decades of the Kingdom of Israel is a meaningful enterprise. Some significant problems notwithstanding, it is possible to base such a reconstruction on a number of biblical and Assyrian texts. Whatever took place within the Northern Kingdom during the very last years of its existence is a tricky question, however, because there are hardly any sources where such knowledge could be drawn from. Nadav Na'aman has recently argued that "Hosea is the only available source for discussing the kingdom's internal affairs in the second half of the eighth century BCE; hence the great importance of elucidating the potential contribution of Hosea for the historical investigation."[1] This statement, of course, implies a great deal of confidence in the possibility that significant parts of the Book of Hosea actually date to the late eighth century BCE which, evidently, is no longer a matter of course.

The question of the dating of, not only the Book of Hosea, but also of the prophetic books in general has become a serious and manifold methodological problem.[2] How can the eighth century datings, or any datings predating the oldest manuscript evidence, be methodologically justified? Can the eighth century

---

1 N. Na'aman, "The Book of Hosea as a Source for the Last Days of the Kingdom of Israel," *BZ* 59 (2015): 232–56, esp. 234.

2 For recent discussion, see, e.g., R. G. Kratz, *The Prophets of Israel* (Winona Lake Ind.: Eisenbrauns, 2015); id., "Probleme der Prophetenforschung," in id., *Prophetenstudien: Kleine Schriften II* (FAT 74; Tübingen: Mohr Siebeck, 2011) 3–17; B. E. Kelle, "The Phenomenon of Israelite Prophecy in Contemporary Scholarship," *CurBR* 12 (2014): 275–320; J. Jeremias, "Das Rätsel der Schriftprophetie," *ZAW* 125 (2013): 93–117; D. M. Carr, *The Formation of the Hebrew Bible: A New Reconstruction* (New York: Oxford University Press, 2011), 317–38; E. Blum, "Israels Prophetie im altorientalischen Kontext: Anmerkungen zu neueren religionsgeschichtlichen Thesen," in *"From Ebla to Stellenbosch": Syro-Palestinian Religions and the Hebrew Bible* (ed. I. Cornelius and L. C. Jonker; Wiesbaden: Harrassowitz, 2008): 81–115; H. M. Barstad, "What Prophets Do: Reflections on Past Reality in the Book of Jeremiah," in *Prophecy in the Book of Jeremiah*, ed. id. and R. G. Kratz (BZAW 388; Berlin: de Gruyter, 2009): 10–32; U. Becker, "Die Wiederentdeckung des Prophetenbuches: Tendenzen und Aufgaben der gegenwärtigen Prophetenforschung," *BTZ* 21 (2004): 30–60.

DOI 10.1515/9783110466546-032

be assumed as the date of any part of the Book of Hosea unless the opposite is proven? Can textual growth caused by centuries of transmission be identified in the text available to us so that more or less precise dates could be given to the textual layers thus recognized? Or should one, rather, date the book as a whole – and if so, to which period of time? How can the material in the Book of Hosea be compared to other sources, biblical as well as non-biblical, in a historically responsible way? The view of the Book of Hosea as a historical document depends essentially on the answers given to these methodological questions, which I attempt to address in this chapter.[3]

First of all, in my view, datings of the Book of Hosea or any prophetic book should not be based on default positions preferring the alleged lifetime of the prophet after whom the book is named. Every dating must be argued for, we cannot date texts for the sake of convenience. Any principle of the type "innocent until proven guilty" should not be applied to texts that are neither accused of anything nor in need of being defended. Therefore, the practice of dating Hoseanic passages routinely to the eighth century without an argument to justify it is unacceptable. This practice may emerge from the often unspoken preference of the prophet for the later editors, early datings for late datings, or textual unity for disunity.[4] Preferences like this are, however, difficult to reconcile with the documented evidence of textual transmission. Drawing historical conclusions from the Book of Hosea (or any other book) on the basis of such default positions is likely to introduce errors into the historical record.

How could such errors, then, be avoided? At the very least we must be aware of the nature of our source material. The oldest "hard" evidence of the existence of the Book of Hosea (like any other book of the Hebrew Bible) comes from the

---

3 Cf. my previous musings in, e.g., M. Nissinen, *Ancient Prophecy: Near Eastern, Biblical, and Greek Perspectives* (Oxford: Oxford University Press, 2017), 144–67; id., "Comparing Prophetic Sources: Principles and a Test Case," in *Prophecy and the Prophets in Ancient Israel*, (ed. John Day, London: T&T Clark, 2010): 3–24 (= pp. 377–96 in this volume); id., "The Historical Dilemma of Biblical Prophetic Studies," in Barstad and Kratz (ed.), *Prophecy in the Book of Jeremiah*, 103–20 (= pp. 499–515 in this volume).

4 For a good representation of this view, see F. I. Andersen and D. N. Freedman, *Hosea: A New Translation with Introduction and Commentary* (AB 24; Garden City NY: Doubleday, 1980), 59: "In both cases [scil. the unity of the Book of Hosea and the integrity of the text] our premise and point of departure are conservative, that the book is essentially the work of a single person, and that the text is basically sound. These are hardly ringing affirmations; they are more like defensive desperation. If the opposite were true, if many hands and voices could be found from the book, then we would have the thankless and ultimately fruitless task of apportioning the work among a variety of people whose existence is hypothetical, and whose only distinguishing mark is some obscurity or inconsistency in the text."

Dead Sea Scrolls. Parts of the Book of Hosea have been preserved in three scrolls, that is, 4QXII^{c}, 4QXII^{d} and 4QXII^{g}, all dating to the first half of the first century BCE.[5] This material alone, together with the Old Greek translation of the Book of Hosea which in some cases is arguably translated from a Hebrew text different from the Masoretic text,[6] demonstrates that textual transmission not only preserved ancient texts but also changed them.[7] We may assume that the texts transmitted in the Scrolls often date back several centuries, but the documented evidence of textual growth makes it impossible to believe that any of the available manuscripts provides us with a text that had remained unchanged for such a long time.[8] In the case of Hosea, the documented changes are usually less than dramatic, but they testify to actual scribal interventions to the text that cannot be dismissed either.[9] This is why any dating beyond the age of the extant manuscript material requires a diachronic theory concerning the transmission of the given text through a long period of time. Creating such a theory, however, immediately raises further methodological questions. While extant textual evidence shows that the idea of textual growth is not based on imagination, detecting the early phases of textual transmission on the basis of the text itself without empirical evidence is a matter of ongoing debate.

Diachronic analysis is, of course, the most traditional way of approaching the Book of Hosea in academic biblical studies, and has been practiced by many scholars over the last decades, myself included. Traditionally, the diachronic enterprise has been motivated by the search of the original message of the prophet by way of separating later additions from the original text and

5 See B. Webster, "Chronological Index of the Texts from the Judaean Desert," in *The Texts from the Judaean Desert: Indices and an Introduction to the Discoveries in the Judaean Desert Series* (ed. E. Tov; Oxford: Clarendon Press, 2002): 393, 397. Taken together, these fragments include the following verses at least partially: 1:6–9; 2:1–5, 13–19, 22–25; 3:1–5; 4:1–19; 5:1; 6:3, 8–11; 7:1, 12–16; 8:1; 9:1–4, 9–17; 10:1–14; 11:2–5, 6–11; 12:1–15; 13:1, 3–13, 15; 14:1, 3–6, 9–10; see the convenient translation of the Dead Sea Scrolls material in M. Abegg, P. Flint and E. Ulrich, *The Dead Sea Scrolls Bible* (New York: Harper, 1999), 420–27.

6 For instance, the Greek text of Hos 13:4 must have been translated from a *Vorlage* much longer than the MT but similar to 4QXII^{g}.

7 For 4QXII^{c}, see H. von Weissenberg, "Changing Scripture? Scribal Corrections in MS 4QXII^{c}," in *Changes in Scripture: Rewriting and Interpreting Authoritative Traditions in the Second Temple Period* (ed. ead., J. Pakkala and M. Marttila, BZAW 419; Berlin: de Gruyter, 2011) 247–71.

8 For examples of documented evidence of textual growth, see R. Müller, J. Pakkala and B. ter Haar Romeny, *Evidence of Editing: Growth and Change of Texts in the Hebrew Bible* (SBLRBS 75; Atlanta GA: SBL Press, 2014).

9 Cf. von Weissenberg, "Changing Scripture," 269: "Even the smaller, individual scribal additions and corrections in manuscripts illustrate the minor forms of growth in the texts. They attest to the scribal contribution to the development of the texts that became the Hebrew Bible."

identifying the oldest material, which is often virtually equated with the words once uttered by the prophet Hosea. The ripest fruit carried by this branch of methodology can be found in the work of Jörg Jeremias, according to whom the essential contents of the Book of Hosea date back to the last years of the Northern Kingdom and the time immediately following the catastrophe: "Das Buch Hosea hat seine entscheidende Prägung im untergegangenen Nordreich erhalten."[10] According to Jeremias, the earliest form of the book is essentially the work of his disciples, who had collected and interpreted the prophet's words, whereas the book as we know it was edited and augmented in Judah after the collapse of the Northern Kingdom. A similar line of thought has been followed by many scholars.[11]

Another type of diachronic analysis of the Book of Hosea is not concerned with finding the prophet's message or even the original core of the book but reckon with a complicated process of redaction and/or *Fortschreibung* over a long period of time.[12] These studies have typically identified only scattered remains of material datable to the eighth century BCE, shifting the emphasis from the prophet and his disciples to the scribal circles of the monarchic and postmonarchic periods.

Diachronic studies reconstructing the emergence of the Book of Hosea have done their best to remove the illusionary innocence with regard to the textual transmission and its relation to historical events. Since, however, no two scholars arrive at the same conclusion but the results typically vary from study to

10 Jeremias, "Das Rätsel der Schriftprophetie," 113; cf. many well-known works of Jörg Jeremias, e.g., *Studien zur Theologie des Alten Testaments* (ed. F. Hartenstein and J. Krispenz; FAT 99; Tübingen: Mohr Siebeck, 2015) 269–87 (= "Die Anfänge der Schriftprophetie," 1996) and 311–25 (= "Prophetenwort und Prophetenbuch: Zur Rekonstruktion mündlicher Verkündung der Propheten," 1990); *Hosea und Amos: Studien zu den Anfängen des Dodekapropheton* (FAT 13; Tübingen: Mohr Siebeck, 1996); *Der Prophet Hosea* (ATD 24/1; Göttingen: Vandenhoeck & Ruprecht, 1983).

11 E.g., Na'aman, "The Book of Hosea as a Source," 255–56 dates Hosea's prophecies to the time of Hoshea, the last king of Israel, and the earliest scroll to the time immediately after the Assyrian annexation of the kingdom (720 BCE).

12 E.g., R. Vielhauer, *Das Werden des Buches Hosea: eine redaktionsgeschichtliche Untersuchung* (BZAW 349; Berlin: de Gruyter, 2007); S. Rudnig-Zelt, *Hoseastudien: Redaktionskritische Untersuchungen zur Genese des Hoseabuches* (FRLANT 213; Göttingen: Vandenhoeck & Ruprecht, 2006); H. Pfeiffer, *Das Heiligtum von Bethel im Spiegel des Hoseabuches* (FRLANT 183; Göttingen: Vandenhoeck & Ruprecht, 1999); M. Nissinen, *Prophetie, Redaktion und Fortschreibung im Hoseabuch: Studien zum Werdegang eines Prophetenbuches im Lichte von Hos 4 und* 11 (AOAT 231; Kevelaer: Butzon & Bercker and Neukirchen-Vluyn: Neukirchener Verlag, 1991); G. A. Yee, *Composition and Redaction in the Book of Hosea: a Redaction Critical Investigation* (SBLDS 102; Atlanta Ga. Scholars Press, 1987); cf. R. G. Kratz, "Die Redaktion der Prophetenbücher," in id., *Prophetenstudien*, 32–48.

study, many colleagues have found it difficult to decide on whose analysis is the more reliable one. Therefore, the possibility of unfolding the process of textual growth with a precision that could reveal even relative datings of each individual passage in the book has been seriously questioned. The ever-changing results of diachronic analyses have been found frustrating enough for many scholars to abandon them altogether and to read the texts synchronically, giving up the attempt to reconstruct the hypothetical phases of textual transmission.

Textual growth in prophetic books is not usually denied altogether, although acknowledging its existence often does not go beyond lip-service. Some scholars say they are reading the "final form" of the text; however, there is no such thing as the final form of any biblical book, unless modern editions of the Masoretic text are regarded as such.[13] Of course, any given form of the text can form the basis of an analysis that does not attempt to go historically beyond the textual witness itself. However, if we want to relate the Book of Hosea historically with the last days of the Northern Kingdom, the so-called "final form" readings clearly lead to an impasse.

A synchronic reading of the Book of Hosea does not as such require an eighth-century BCE setting, even though this very often seems to be assumed. A synchronic analysis can take the text as the product of postmonarchical readerships, relating the text of the Book of Hosea to a later historical period when one can suppose the text to have reached more or less the shape known to us from existing textual evidence. Thus, for instance, Ehud Ben Zvi consistently reads the book as the product of the literati of the late Persian period.[14] This way of reading the text neither denies the possibility that some parts of the book indeed have earlier origins, nor enables sorting these parts out. Historical links can be made to the time chosen as the setting of the alleged (re-)readership of the book, but historical connections with the events of the eighth century BCE fall entirely out of scope.

The methodological problem of relating the Book of Hosea to the last days of the Northern Kingdom, thus, consists of the following components:

(1) The oldest manuscript evidence from the Dead Sea Scrolls is enough to demonstrate that textual development and growth took place; however, coming

---

13 Cf., e.g., E. Ulrich, "Our Sharper Focus on the Bible and Theology Thanks to the Dead Sea Scrolls," *CBQ* 66 (2004) 1–24; A. Aejmelaeus, "Licence to Kill? Deut 13:10 and the Prerequisites of Textual Criticism," in *Verbum et calamus: Semitic and Related Studies in Honour of the Sixtieth Birthday of Professor Tapani Harviainen*, ed. H. Juusola, J. Laulainen and H. Palva (StOr 99; Helsinki: Finnish Oriental Society, 2004) 1–22.

14 E. Ben Zvi, *Hosea* (FOTL 21 A/1; Grand Rapids MI: Eerdmans, 2005); cf. J. M. Bos, *Reconsidering the Date and Provenance of the Book of Hosea: The Case of Persia-Period Yehud* (LHBOTS 580; London: Bloomsbury, 2013).

from the first century BCE, it documents only the very latest phases of textual transmission and does not help to date individual passages of the book to older periods.

(2) There are good grounds to assume that the text of the Book of Hosea existed in some form several centuries earlier than the Dead Sea Scrolls. The book is one of the "Twelve Prophets" already in the oldest textual witnesses, but one can assume that the books included in this collection existed as individual scrolls before they were joined together in several phases, and that each phase of transmission is likely to have transformed the text.[15] However, the late date of the earliest textual witnesses makes it impossible simply to equate the extant textual evidence with any earlier form of the text. The Book of Hosea as we know it is already part of a larger composition and the product of a long chain of textual transmission, but no documented evidence is available to help with the reconstruction of this process. This is essentially due to the tendency of the texts themselves to hide rather than to reveal their editorial history.[16]

(3) If we want to establish a direct historical connection from the Book of Hosea to the last days of the Northern Kingdom, we should be able to date at least some parts of Hosea to this period of time. Diachronic studies detecting the oldest parts of the Book of Hosea have yielded exact results, but these have been varying enough to raise suspicions about the viability of even the diachronic methodology. The ever-changing results of ever-greater precision have been seen as pointing towards problems in the method itself. But the task cannot be fulfilled by way of synchronic reading either unless the book as a whole is dated to the 730s–720s, which is not viable for reasons just mentioned.

---

15 For theories concerning the history of redaction of the "Book of the Twelve," see, e.g., J. Wöhrle, *Die frühen Sammlungen des Zwölfprophetenbuches: Entstehung und Komposition* (BZAW 360; Berlin: de Gruyter, 2006); A. Schart, *Die Entstehung des Zwölfprophetenbuches: Neubearbeitungen von Amos im Rahmen schriftenübergreifender Redaktionsprozesse* (BZAW 260; Berlin: de Gruyter, 1998); J. D. Nogalski, *Literary Precursors to the Book of the Twelve* (BZAW 217; Berlin: de Gruyter, 1993); cf. Ben Zvi who finds it impossible to reconstruct redactional processes from the existing text. For two different views of the "Twelve Hypothesis", see E. Ben Zvi and J. D. Nogalski, *Two Sides of a Coin: Juxtaposing Views on Interpreting the Book of the Twelve/The Twelve Prophetic Books* (with an introduction by T. Römer; Analecta Gorgiana 201; Piscataway NJ: Gorgias Press, 2009).

16 According to Ehud Ben Zvi, "the ongoing process of redaction was not bent on promoting, or archiving and analyzing itself; instead its function was to shape a series of texts in which the last, if successful, was meant to supersede and erase the memory of the previous one" ("Is the Twelve Hypothesis Likely from an Ancient Reader's Perspective?" in Ben Zvi and Nogalski, *Two Sides of a Coin*, 46–96, esp. 59).

So have we ended up in a cul-de-sac: if synchronic analysis is not the way to go and the results of diachronic studies are found to be disappointing, what else can we do other than give up entirely on the task of connecting the Book of Hosea with the last days of the Kingdom of Israel? Or is there a historically responsible way of doing this?

2 Historical Echoes from the Eighth Century?

Perhaps we could try circumventing the problems of diachronic methodology by way of looking for clues in the text that seem to point towards an eighth-century date, and, if possible, comparing such clues with the available historical data of the last days of the kingdom of Israel. If they seem to fit this documentary environment, they could be dated to the same period of time. The best candidates for an early date would be passages that do not show clear signs of intertextual influence, and are not to be taken as *Fortschreibung* of earlier texts but rather as belonging to the source materials of an early collection upon which the Book of Hosea has grown.

The fall of Samaria and the subsequent de- and repopulations of the area can indeed be confirmed by Assyrian sources and even by archaeological evidence.[17] The problem is rather how to reconstruct the internal affairs of the kingdom of Israel, of which there is no documentation outside of, or even within, the Hebrew Bible. The following three examples may illustrate the case.

(1) A contemporary reflection of a disturbing political event could perhaps be found in Hos 7:3–7, a highly enigmatic passage that seems to reflect on the murder of a king, perhaps one of the successors of Jeroboam II. Of the last kings of Israel

17 See now the essays collected in *The Last Days of the Kingdom of Israel* (ed. S. Hasegawa, C. Levin, and K. Radner; BZAW 511; Berlin: de Gruyter, 2018). For archaeological evidence of the devastation, see Z. Gal, *Lower Galilee during the Iron Age* (ASOR Dissertation Series 8; Winona Lake Ind.: Eisenbrauns, 1992), 108–109. Cf. A. Faust, "Settlement, Economy, and Demography under Assyrian Rule in the West: The Territories of the Former Kingdom of Israel as a Test Case," *JAOS* 135 (2015) 765–89, who concludes that the Assyrians "did not really care about the fate of the areas they conquered. They carried off whatever they could and their investment was minimal" (782). However, the Assyrians did not just plunder but also, for example, looked after the water supply in Samaria as reported in a letter from the time of Sargon II: S. Parpola, *The Correspondence of Sargon II, Part I: Letters from Assyria and the West* (SAA 1; Helsinki: Helsinki University Press, 1987), no. 255. According to A. Berlejung, "The Assyrians in the West: Assyrianization, Colonialism, Indifference, or Developmental Policy?" in *Congress Volume Helsinki 2010* (ed. M. Nissinen; VTSup 148; Leiden: Brill 2012): 21–60, esp. 48: "[s]uccess was maximal profit with minimal investment."

only Menahem is said to have died peacefully, whereas his predecessors Zechariah and Shallum as well as his followers Pekahiah and Pekah were killed. A rather laconic report of the four coups d'état that took place after Jeroboam II can be found in 2 Kgs 15:8–31, a passage probably based on court chronicles that were used as sources of the Deuteronomistic History.[18] Hos 7:3–7 seems to give a metaphoric account of the day when one of the kings was murdered. The actors "make glad" (7:3) the unsuspecting king and his officials, who get drunk, presumably in the privacy of the royal palace. They become easy prey for the murderers who, compared with a heated oven, just wait "from the kneading of the dough until it is leavened," that is, for the opportunity to "devour their rulers" (7:7). Compared to the account of 2 Kgs, such an event could best be identified with the murder of Pekahiah, committed by his captain (*šālîš*) Pekah, who conspired against him with fifty Gileadites and attacked him in the citadel of the palace (2 Kgs 15:25).[19] This is what I argued in my master's thesis in 1984, and I would still like to agree with myself. The passage is probably neither interpreting a pre-existing text in the Book of Hosea nor is it dependent on another biblical text outside the book, hence it could belong to the material from which the early version of the book is composed.[20] However, I have to admit that the link between Hos 7:3–7 and Pekahiah's murder derives from what is visible through the keyhole provided by 2 Kgs 15:25. The two sources seem to connect nicely, but the connection depends entirely on what we happen to see.

(2) Further echoes from the last days of the Northern Kingdom, either contemporary or slightly later, can be heard in passages of the Book of Hosea that reflect the fall of Samaria. The demise of the Northern Kingdom, or Ephraim (the name may refer to the truncated kingdom in the time of the last king Hoshea[21]), is reflected in several passages that sound like fragments of laments (9:10–17; 11:1–5). Some passages in the Book of Hosea could be imagined to

---

18 For court chronicles as the sources of the Deuteronomistic history, see L. L. Grabbe, *1 & 2 Kings: An Introduction and Study Guide: History and Story in Ancient Israel* (T & T Clark Study Guides to the Old Testament; London: Bloomsbury, 2017), 21–28; cf., e.g., E. Würthwein, *Die Bücher der Könige: 1. Kön. 17–2. Kön. 25* (ATD 11/2; Göttingen: Vandenhoeck & Ruprecht, 1984), 376–84.

19 Pekahiah has not been among the prime suspects in this murder case; see, however, A. A. Macintosh, *A Critical and Exegetical Commentary on Hosea* (ICC; Edinburgh: T&T Clark, 1997), 256.

20 Cf. Vielhauer, *Das Werden des Buches Hosea*, 86–92, according to whom verses 7:5–6 go back to oral words of northern origin and the remaining verses to the oldest written layer (*erste Verschriftung*). Rudnig-Zelt, *Hoseastudien*, 212–30, sees a pre-exilic core in the passage (verses 7:4b, 5b), however, without a reference to the murder of a king.

21 Thus Na'aman, "The Book of Hosea as a Source," 238–39.

go back to contemporary laments; for instance, Hos 10:5–8 could be based on something like the following:[22]

l [‘glwt byt ’wn]	For [the calf of Beth-Awen[23]]
ygwrw škn šmrwn	the inhabitants of Samaria tremble.
ky ’bl ‘lyw ‘mw	Its people mourn for it,
wkmryw ‘lyw ygylw	its priests wail over it
[‘l kbwdw ky glh mmnw]	[over its glory that has departed from it[24]].
gm ’wtw l’šwr ywbl	The thing itself is carried to Assyria
mnḥh lmlky rb	as tribute to the Great King[25].
bšnh ’prym yqḥ	Ephraim has received shame,
wybwš yśr’l m‘ṣtw	and Israel is ashamed for his own counsel.
ndmh šmrwn mlkh	Samaria and its king perish
kqṣp ‘l pny mym	like a splinter on the face of the waters.
[wnšmdw bmwt ’wn ḥṭ’t yśr’l	[The high places of Awen, the sin of Israel, shall be destroyed.
qwṣ wdrdr y‘lh ‘l mzbḥwtm]	Thorn and thistle shall grow up on their altars.][26]
w’mrw lhrym kswnw	They shall say to the mountains: “Cover us!”
wlgb‘wt nplw ‘lynw	and to the hills: “Fall on us!”

22 This reconstruction is based on my analysis in Nissinen, *Prophetie, Redaktion und Fortschreibung*, 309–12; cf. the different reconstructions of Pfeiffer, *Das Heiligtum von Bethel*, 103–17; Vielhauer, *Das Werden des Hoseabuches*, 165–72; M. Köhlmoos, *Bet-El – Erinnerungen an eine Stadt: Perspektiven der alttestamentlichen Bet-El-Überlieferung* (FAT 49; Tübingen: Mohr Siebeck, 2007) 126–31.

23 The peculiar and pejorative expression *‘eglôt Bêt-āwen* (pl. fem.) is probably inspired by the Deuteronomistic polemics against the calf of Bethel, replacing the original name of the object to which the sg. masc. suffixes in the following bicolon refer.

24 This sentence probably serves as a secondary explanation of the masculine suffix in *‘ālâw* “for it/over it,” which is not applicable to *‘eglôt*.

25 Adopting the usual reading *malkî rāb* instead of *melek yāreb* (MT).

26 Verse 8a reads like a later, prosaic theological interpretation of the original lament.

This passage may originally refer to the transportation of a precious item, presumably, a divine statue, to Assyria.[27] It resonates well with the Nimrud Prism of Sargon II, which reads: "[The inhabitants of Sa]maria who agreed [and plotted] with a king [hostile to] me, not to endure servitude and not to bring tribute to Assur and who did battle, I fought against them with the power of great gods, my lords. I counted as spoil 27,280 people together with their chariots and gods in which they trusted" (lines iv 25–32).[28] One could easily imagine laments like the one possibly quoted in Hos 10:5–8* to have been uttered after the fall of Samaria, if not by prophets, then perhaps by professional lamenters similarly to the ones known from Assyrian records.[29]

Prophecy and lament are related performances both in the Hebrew Bible and in the ancient Near Eastern sources,[30] and the literary reflection of the fate of the city of Samaria and the Kingdom of Israel may have been inspired by source texts representing both genres. The Mesopotamian *kalû*'s were not only singers but also scribes who wrote divinatory texts.[31] If this was true also in Samaria (which can only be speculated), this could explain the early textualization of such laments. Laments like Hos 10:5–8* could have belonged to the material comprising the first beginnings of what we know as the Book of Hosea.[32] The

---

27 Cf. Köhlmoos, *Bet-El*, 135–38.

28 See C. J. Gadd, "Inscribed Prisms of Sargon II from Nimrud," *Iraq* 16 (1954): 173–201, esp. 179–80. For other texts of Sargon II related to the conquest of Samaria, see E. Frahm, "Samaria, Hamath, and Assyria's Conquests in the Levant in the Late 720s BCE: The Testimony of Sargon II's Inscriptions," in Hasegawa, Levin, and Radner (eds.), *The Last Days of the Kingdom of Israel*, 55–86.

29 However, the assumed reference to Samarian lamenters in a text from Calah – read as 3 ŠÚ.MEŠ KUR.*Sa-mir-na-a-a* by S. Dalley and J. N. Postgate, *The Tablets from Fort Shalmaneser* (CTN 3; London: British School of Archaeology in Iraq, 1984), no. 121: 6 and, assuming that ŠÚ was used as a logogram for *kalû*, interpreted as a reference to "three Samarian lamentation-priests" by K. L. Younger Jr., "The Deportations of the Israelites," *JBL* 117 (1998) 221 – cannot be used as evidence for the existence of Samarian lamenters, as the passage needs to be read 3-*šú*.MEŠ KUR.*Sa-mir-na-a-a*, meaning "Third Men (of a chariot crew) from Samaria" (pers. comm., Karen Radner).

30 Cf. M. Nissinen, "Biblical Prophecy from a Near Eastern Perspective: The Cases of Divine Kingship and Divine Possession," in *Congress Volume Ljubljana* 2007 (ed. A. Lemaire; VTSup 133; Leiden: Brill, 2010): 441–68, esp. 458–61 (= pp. 351–75 in this volume).

31 See, e.g., F. Rochberg, *In the Path of the Moon: Babylonian Celestial Divination and Its Legacy* (Studies in Ancient Magic and Divination 6; Leiden: Brill, 2010), 247.

32 I am, thus, suggesting an earlier date to this passage than Vielhauer, *Das Werden des Buches Hosea*, 176–77, 227–78, according to whom already the basic layer of Hos 10:1–8 is Deuteronomistic. This is probably true for the *Kultpolemik* in chapter 10 in general, but not necessarily for the source material used by the editors.

later redactors have subsequently used this material as a tool of criticism against past and/or contemporary religious practices referred to with the pejorative designation designation *'āwen* ("iniquity").

(3) My third example is the possible reference to the so-called Syro-Ephraimite war in 734–732 BCE. This war can be reconstructed from biblical texts only (2 Kgs 16:5; 2 Chr 28:5–8; Isa 7:1–9), but, if it actually took place, as scholars usually assume, it may be interpreted as an act of hostility towards Ahaz, the king of Judah, who refused to join the anti-Assyrian alliance.[33] A contemporary echo of it is usually heard in Hos 5:8–14*.[34] The alarm blown in three cities from south to north, Gibeah, Ramah, and Beth-Awen (scil. Bethel) (5:8), as well as the accusation of the princes of Judah acting "like those who remove the landmark" (5:10) give the impression of a Judahite attack to the area of the Kingdom of Israel and refer to Ephraim's resorting to the help of Assyria (5:13). Nothing of this is known from other sources which rather present the Northern Kingdom as attacking Judah, and this is exactly the reason why it could be interpreted as a reference to historical events rather than as interpretation or *Fortschreibung* of an already existing text. Hence, the text could be interpreted as referring to events of the Syro-Ephraimite war unknown from other sources, such as the attack of Judah on Israel and Israel's turning to Assyria for help. The passage is now embedded and reworked in the context of the Book of Hosea, but the old oracle could originate from either Israel or Judah.

Of course, the passage can be interpreted otherwise. Na'aman, for example, dates the counter-attack of Judah to the time of Hoshea, the last king of Israel, when Israel was at its weakest.[35] Ben Zvi, on the other hand, does not see a compelling reason to connect the passage with the historical circumstances of the last days of the kingdom of Israel: "The text as it stands does not lead to such

---

33 See, e.g., N. Na'aman, "Let Other Kingdoms Struggle with the Great Powers — You, Judah, Pay the Tribute and Hope for the Best: The Foreign Policy of the Kings of Judah in the Ninth–Eighth Centuries BCE," in *Isaiah's Vision of Peace in Biblical and Modern International Relations: Swords into Plowshares* (ed. R. Cohen and R. Westbrook; New York: Palgrave MacMillan, 2008) 55–73, esp. 62–64.

34 Thus the majority of scholars following A. Alt, "Hosea 5,8–6,6: ein Krieg und seine Folgen in prophetischer Beleuchtung," *NKZ* 30 (1919) 537–68, repr. in id., *Kleine Schriften zur Geschichte des Volkes Israel*, vol. 2 (Munich: Beck, 1953) 163–87. Even Vielhauer, *Das Werden des Buches Hosea*, 225–26 finds remnants of oral proclamation from the last days of the Northern Kingdom in verses 5:8–11*, whereas the written text in verses 5:8–14 belongs to the late 8th century layer (*erste Ergänzungsschicht*) written from the perspective of Judah. Rudnig-Zelt, *Hoseastudien*, 157–77, reconstructs a complicated editorial process, dating the polemics against Samaria to its latest phases.

35 Na'aman, "The Book of Hosea as a Source," 239–40.

a reading" which is also unknown to ancient readerships who knew about the Syro-Ephraimite war on the basis of biblical texts.[36]

Ben Zvi is right in stressing that the reconstructions of the historical scenery behind passages in the Book of Hosea are based on the assumption that the texts directly reflect the historical prophet's oral speeches and should, therefore, be given a historical setting within his lifetime. "Given that there are only a limited number of political events during that period that are known and potentially relevant, the only question is which one would fit better a particular speech."[37] This easily leads to a chain of circular arguments causing erroneous historical conclusions. On the other hand, if one follows the principal that when writing history, all potential sources should be considered and nothing should be ruled out *a priori*, even secondary sources such as prophetic books deserve to be critically scrutinized.[38] Therefore, the possibility that a given passage in the Book of Hosea actually provides a keyhole view into the historical landscape, however narrow, should not be dismissed at the outset, even though the secondary nature of the evidence should never be forgotten. Individual passages of the Book of Hosea may contain reminiscences of real historical events, but they always appear recontextualized in literary settings created by scribes who may or may not have been aware of the actual historical reference.

Many other texts in the Book of Hosea, most recently collected by Na'aman,[39] could be highlighted to demonstrate the original connection of the text with the fall of Samaria and the last days of the Kingdom of Israel. The problem with using such clues as evidence of events that took place in the 730s–720s BCE is that, however nicely they seem to fit our picture of that period of time, there is always the risk of *potest, ergo* and circular reasoning. For example, the recurrent juxtaposing of Egypt and Assyria (Hos 7:11; 9:3; 11:5, 11; 12:1) undoubtedly makes sense with regard to the political maneuvers of Hoshea, the last king of Israel—provided that they actually took place and 2 Kgs 17:3b–5a is not later historical speculation as suggested by Christoph Levin.[40] The problem is, evidently, that the parallelism of Egypt and Assyria could be used by any subsequent writer reflecting on the event. For later readers, the names can

---

36 Ben Zvi, *Hosea*, 140.

37 Ben Zvi, *Hosea*, 141.

38 See L. L. Grabbe, *Ancient Israel: What Do We Know and How Do We Know It?* (London: T&T Clark 2007), 35–36.

39 Na'aman, "The Book of Hosea as a Source," *passim*.

40 C. Levin, "In Search of the Original Biblical Record of the Assyrian Conquest of Samaria," in Hasegawa, id., and Radner (eds.), *The Last Days of the Kingdom of Israel*, 251–64.

stand for Ptolemaic Egypt and Seleucid Syria.[41] Even Samaria was still there, providing itself continually as a target for theological criticism for circles who considered that the wrong kind of Yahwism was practiced in the north.[42] Therefore—and this is generally the problem with the dating of individual passages in Hosea—even if an eighth-century setting makes sense, it cannot automatically be preferred.

3 Evidence or Reflection of Eighth-Century Events?

I am convinced that the beginnings of the Book of Hosea must be sought from the last days of the Northern Kingdom or shortly thereafter. It is virtually impossible to imagine the emergence of the Book of Hosea without the contemporary experiences of the end of the Northern Kingdom. The fall of Samaria must be considered the decisive event that triggered the emergence of the book, in whatever way this happened over the subsequent centuries. It is usually assumed that the redaction and transmission of the book took place in Judah, not only because of the multiple mentions of Judah, which are often ascribed to a specific redaction, but also because of the harsh criticism of Israel, Ephraim, and Samaria throughout the book.[43] However, this criticism does not need to derive from the eighth century only, since, as Christoph Levin has argued, there was enough reason for it even later when the Samari(t)an society and worship gradually became an issue to the (religious) elite of Jerusalem.[44] The echoes on the last days of the Northern Kingdom in what may have constituted the earliest form of the Book of Hosea were readily available for interpretations of the subsequent generations who likewise reflected their relationship with what took place in the Northern Kingdom.

---

41 Cf. C. Levin, *The Old Testament: A Brief Introduction* (Princeton NJ: Princeton University Press, 2005), 133 with regard to Hos 7:8 – 11.

42 As G. N. Knoppers, *Jews and Samaritans: The Origins and History of Their Early Relations* (Oxford: Oxford University Press, 2013) emphasizes, there was no absolute breakdown of relations between Yehud and Samaria in the first centuries BCE but, rather, a considerable cultural and religious overlap. The debate on the common heritage and religious identity is evidence of the overlap and continuity, not of the breakdown.

43 See, e.g., Jeremias, *Der Prophet Hosea*, 18 – 19 and *passim*.

44 Levin, *The Old Testament*, 129 – 33; cf. the late "Samariapolemik" reconstructed by Rudnig-Zelt, *Hoseastudien*, 271 – 73.

It is, thus, problematic to quote verses of the Book of Hosea as quasi-eyewitness reports of events that took place in the 730s–720s BCE, even if we have good grounds to assume that some material in the book indeed dates back to this historical period. Some passages in Hosea, like the ones discussed above, undeniably give the impression of contemporary experience, indeed making sense when compared to what we know about the last days of the Kingdom of Israel from other sources. However, even these passages rarely reveal historical data that could not even theoretically go back to later reflection. *Potest,* we can say quite often, but we should be careful with the *ergo.*

Without suggesting anything that has not been said and done before, I would like to argue that if any part of the Book of Hosea actually derives from a time not too distant from the last days of the kingdom of Israel (and I do believe this to be the case to some extent), such passages can only be identified by way of the diachronic method and comparative analysis. Individual parts of the Book of Hosea should not be dated randomly but the dating of each passage should be based on a well-argued theory concerning the emergence, growth, and transmission of the text of the Book of Hosea. The methodological problem is how to sort datable passages out from a text that is the product of a process of long textual transmission, and if there is a great deal of uncertainty about this, one should be cautious about making precise contemporary connections between the last days of the Kingdom of Israel and the literary work we call the Book of Hosea. This is why it is so difficult to detect independent historical information in the Book of Hosea that could be *reliably* used as *evidence of* the last days of the Northern Kingdom. Even texts that seem to connect well with historical circumstances known from other sources may go back to subsequent reflection and *Fortschreibung.*

However, the book can be used as a powerful document of the *reflection and interpretation* of this historical event. The event itself is real. The fall of the Northern Kingdom and its capital Samaria is something that can be historically reconstructed from the available sources. It would be nonsensical to deny the connection of the Book of Hosea with this event, but the nature of the connection is evidently more complicated than a simple contemporary eyewitness response. The book and the historical event are rather linked through social memory, which creates an indirect connection between the text and the shared past – not only through remembering but also by way of forgetting.[45]

45 Cf. E. Ben Zvi, "Remembering Hosea: The Prophet Hosea as a Site of Memory in the Persian Period Yehud," in *Poets, Prophets, and Texts in Play: Studies in Biblical Poetry and Prophecy in Honour of Francis Landy,* (ed. id, C.V. Camp, D. M. Gunn, and A.W. Hughes; LHBOTS 597; London:

T & T Clark, 2015) 37–57. For social memory and the collective past, see also G. Cubitt, *History and Memory* (Manchester: Manchester University Press, 2007), 199–249.

Part Five: **Prophecy in the Dead Sea Scrolls**

Transmitting Divine Mysteries: The Prophetic Role of Wisdom Teachers in the Dead Sea Scrolls*

Who May Be Called a Prophet?

The issue of prophecy in the Dead Sea Scrolls has attracted scholarly attention for quite some time. The reasons for this are obvious. The scribes who wrote the Scrolls were deeply involved with the interpretation of Hebrew prophetic scriptures, even creating exegetical literature of a new kind, the pesharim. Some prominent figures, notably King David and the "Teacher of Righteousness," have sometimes been seen as assuming prophetic roles in the Scrolls, and even Josephus tells us that there were people among the Essenes (usually identified with the Qumran community) who "profess to foreknow the future, being educated in sacred books and various purifications and sayings of prophets."[1]

While the emphasis of scholarly work has been laid on the techniques and significance of biblical interpretation in the Dead Sea Scrolls,[2] less attention has been paid to the questions of whether the phenomenon of prophecy actually manifests itself in the Scrolls, and what kind of activity should be labelled as "prophetic." In the recent discussion on these matters it has been asked whether there really were persons within the Qumran community who would either identify themselves as prophets or who would have been regarded as such by others. Hans Barstad, for instance, has reviewed all relevant Dead Sea Scrolls in which prophets (*nābîʾ/nĕbîʾîm*) are mentioned, and comes to the conclusion that little

* I am grateful to Jutta Jokiranta for her comments and her help in writing this article.

1 *Eisin d'en autois hoi kai ta mellonta proginōskein hypiskhnountai, biblois hierais kai diaphorois hagneiais kai prophētōn apophthegmasin empaidotriboumenoi* (*B. J.* 2:159). On Josephus and the Essene prophets, see R. Gray, *Prophetic Figures in Late Second Temple Jewish Palestine: The Evidence from Josephus* (New York: Oxford University Press, 1993), 80–111.

2 A significant amount of literature on biblical interpretation at Qumran has been written between O. Betz, *Offenbarung und Schriftforschung in der Qumransekte* (WUNT 6; Tübingen: Mohr Siebeck, 1960) and the newest collections of essays on the subject, *The Bible at Qumran: Text, Shape, and Interpretation* (ed. P. W. Flint; Studies in the Dead Sea Scrolls and Related Literature; Grand Rapids, Mich.: Eerdmans, 2001) and *Biblical Interpretation at Qumran* (ed. M. Henze; SDSRL; Grand Rapids, Mich.: Eerdmans, 2005). See the bibliography in M. J. Bernstein, "Interpretation of Scripture," in *EDSS* 1 (2000) 376–83.

DOI 10.1515/9783110466546-033

evidence of actual prophetic activities at Qumran can be found in these texts.[3] Only a couple of occurrences may, according to Barstad, be taken as reflecting "prophetic activity of the traditional visionary kind,"[4] and even in these cases it is far from certain that contemporary practices are referred to; only in one passage in the Hodayot (1QH[a] IV, 16), the "prophets of error" (*nby'y kzb*) may be understood as a reference to contemporary prophetic activity, either aural or interpretative.[5] George Brooke, on the other hand, has found enough "prophetic continuities" to conclude that there was a still ongoing prophetic practice at Qumran. This can be inferred from the existence of legislation against false prophets which would make little sense if no actual prophesying took place. On the other hand, the prophetic activity went on in the form of interpretative practices that were regarded as a matter of divine revelation.[6] Both views are derived from the same material, and one of the crucial questions seems to be what kind of activity should be labelled as prophetic. While both scholars use of the word "prophecy" of oral/aural as well as interpretative activity, Barstad clearly sees the former as prophecy *per se*, while Brooke lays more emphasis on the scribal basis of the prophetic activity at Qumran.

A similar problem is at hand when we ask whether figures like the Teacher of Righteousness or King David can be seen as prophets in the Dead Sea Scrolls. Two recent contributions by Peter Flint[7] and Timothy Lim[8] can be quoted as representing different opinions on David. Flint interprets the evidence in favor of the prophetic role of David especially in view of 11Q5 XXVII, 11 (see below), where David is said to have composed his psalms and songs through prophecy; and with regard to the fact that pesharim were written not only on the prophetic books but also on the psalms of David. Lim, while acknowledging that the Psalms were considered prophetic, is reluctant to identify David as prophet: he is never called a prophet in the Dead Sea Scrolls, and the "songs of David"

3 H. M. Barstad, "Prophecy at Qumran?" in *In the Last Days: On Jewish and Christian Apocalyptic and Its Period* (FS Benedikt Otzen; ed. K. Jeppesen, K. Nielsen, and B. Rosendal; Aarhus: Aarhus University Press, 1994), 104–20.

4 I.e., 11Q5 XXII, 14 and 4Q88; Barstad, "Prophecy at Qumran?" 116–17.

5 Barstad, "Prophecy at Qumran?" 117–18.

6 G. J. Brooke, "Prophecy and Prophets in the Dead Sea Scrolls: Looking Backwards and Forwards," in *Prophets, Prophecy and Prophetic Texts in Second Temple Judaism* (ed. M. H. Floyd and R. D. Haak; LHBOTS 427; London: T&T Clark, 2006), 151–65, esp. 158–63.

7 P. W. Flint, "The Prophet David at Qumran," in Henze (ed.), *Biblical Interpretation at Qumran*, 158–67.

8 T. H. Lim, "'All These He Composed through Prophecy,'" in *Prophecy after the Prophets? The Contribution of the Dead Sea Scrolls to the Understanding of Biblical and Extra-Biblical Prophecy* (ed. K. De Troyer and A. Lange; CBET 52; Leuven: Peeters 2009) 61–73.

were treated as a collection distinct from the "books of the prophets." The nature of the prophetic inspiration referred to in 11Q5 XXVII, 11 should be related to the reference to the prophesying of the temple musicians in 2 Chr 25:1–3.[9]

As to question of the prophetic role of the Teacher of Righteousness, George Brooke has given two answers: a qualified "No" and a qualified "Yes."[10] The status and function of the Teacher of Righteousness could well be called prophetic, and he might even have been seen as the eschatological prophet by some. This notwithstanding, he is never called a prophet, and the absence of this label may be a deliberate choice. As much as he would have deserved to be called a prophet, he represented the focal identity of the community and had, hence, a role different from the classical prophets who stood over against their communities.

One of the primary problems in identifying a person as a prophet or recognizing prophetic activity in the Dead Sea Scrolls seems to be the elusive interplay of scholarly language with titles, roles, and functions discernible from the original texts. Calling a person a prophet may happen in accordance with the textual world of the sources, following their idea of what a prophet is, or it may be based on a scholarly definition of prophecy which can be used independently from the vocabulary used in the texts. Accordingly, the role model for a prophet may be found either in the biblical prophets and the sources' own understanding of them, or in a function that a person may fulfill irrespective of whether the label "prophet" is used. In an ideal case, both perspectives are combined. The concept of prophecy has not emerged, and cannot be developed, independently of certain vocabulary denoting people and activities thus defined (*nābîʾ*, *prophētēs*, and related words in different languages), neither can the concept be restricted to the use of this vocabulary and its varying meanings in different texts. The scholarly concept of prophecy needs a textual as well as a theoretical basis. In practical terms, this means a functional definition of prophecy adaptable to different texts and contexts, strict enough to avoid inflation but also broad enough to be used across the boundaries of religions, cultures, and source materials. Rather than charismatic qualities, distinct social roles, the use of specific literary forms, or characteristic features of proclamation (for instance, prediction or social criticism), such a definition today assumes the essential feature of prophecy

---

9 Cf. Barstad, "Prophecy at Qumran?" 117. For divine inspiration and the Levitical singers in 2 Chr 25 :1–3, see W. M. Schniedewind, *The Word of God in Transition: From Prophet to Exegete in the Second Temple Period* (JSOTSup 197; Sheffield: Sheffield Academic Press, 1995), 174–88.
10 G. J. Brooke, "Was the Teacher of Righteousness Considered to be a Prophet?" in De Troyer and Lange (eds.), *Prophecy after the Prophets?*, 77–97. Cf. idem, "Prophecy," in *EDSS* 2 (2000) 695–700, esp. 698–99.

to be the *transmission* of divine messages to human recipients by a person who in this capacity is called a prophet.[11]

A further aspect to be taken into account when mapping the meaning of prophecy in the Dead Sea Scrolls is the historical development of the phenomenon and idea of prophecy in Second Temple Judaism. Recent studies have emphasized the social marginalization (but not the cessation) of oral/aural prophecy of the traditional type,[12] that took place during the Second Temple period along with the emergence of the biblical prophetic books and the growing status of the ancient, "classical" prophetic figures.[13] The increasing superiority of the written to the spoken word led to an intellectualization, or sapientalization, of prophecy, both as a concept and a practice. This gave prophecy a new divinatory context, virtually merging it together with the ideas and practices of scribal, intellectual divination; as George Brooke has put it, "[t]he intellectual transformation of prophetic activity has its setting in a complex matrix of apocalyptic, priestly, scribal and mantological ideas and practices."[14] This, in my view, is

11 For qualifications of this definition, see M. Nissinen, "What Is Prophecy? An Ancient Near Eastern Perspective," in *Inspired Speech: Prophecy in the Ancient Near East*, FS H. B. Huffmon (ed. J. Kaltner & L. Stulman; JSOTSup 378; London: T&T Clark, 2004), 17–37 (= pp. 53–73 in this volume).

12 This has recently been discussed independently by Armin Lange ("Reading the Decline of Prophecy," in *Reading the Present in the Qumran Library: The Perception of the Contemporary by Means of Scriptural Interpretations* [ed. K. De Troyer and A. Lange; SBLSymS 30; Atlanta: Society of Biblical Literature, 2005], 181–91) and myself (M. Nissinen, "The Dubious Image of Prophecy," in Floyd and Haak, eds., *Prophets, Prophecy, and Prophetic Texts in Second Temple Judaism*, 26–41 = pp. 577–96 in this volume).

13 See, e.g., E. Ben Zvi, "The Prophetic Book: A Key Form of Prophetic Literature," in *The Changing Face of Form Criticism for the Twenty-First Century* (ed. E. Ben Zvi and M. A. Sweeney; Grand Rapids, Mich.: Eerdmans, 2003), 276–97; M. H. Floyd, "The Production of Prophetic Books in the Early Second Temple Period," in Floyd and Haak, eds., *Prophets, Prophecy, and Prophetic Texts in Second Temple Judaism*, 276–97.

14 Brooke, "Prophecy and Prophets in the Dead Sea Scrolls," 165; cf. J. C. VanderKam, "The Prophetic-Sapiential Origins of Apocalyptic Thought," in *A Word in Season: Essays in Honor of William McKane* (ed. J. D. Martin and P. R. Davies; JSOTSup 42; Sheffield: JSOT Press, 1986), 163–76 (repr. in idem, *From Revelation to Canon: Studies in the Hebrew Bible and Second Temple Literature* [JSJSup 62; Leiden: Brill, 2000], 241–54); L. L. Grabbe, "Poets, Scribes, or Preachers: The Reality of Prophecy in the Second Temple Period," in *Knowing the End from the Beginning: The Prophetic, the Apocalyptic and their Relationships* (ed. L. L. Grabbe and R. D. Haak; JSPSup 46; London: T&T Clark, 2003), 192–215, esp. 209–10; A. Lange, "Interpretation als Offenbarung: Zum Verhältnis von Schriftauslegung und Offenbarung," in *Wisdom and Apocalypticism in the Dead Sea Scrolls and in the Biblical Tradition* (ed. F. Garcia Martinez; BETL 168; Leuven: Peeters, 2003), 17–33; M. Nissinen, "Pesharim as Divination: Qumran Exegesis, Omen Interpretation and

the landscape against which the issue of prophecy in the Dead Sea Scrolls should be viewed, and where the "prophets" in them can be found.

The purpose of this article is to overcome the difficulties in identification of the prophetic roles in the Dead Sea Scrolls by examining the prophetic vocabulary and functions from the above mentioned two points of view: the function of prophecy as transmission of divine knowledge and the intellectualization of the idea of prophecy in Second Temple Judaism. My treatment of the texts is a synchronic one,[15] which makes it liable to harmonizations and anachronisms; I try to avoid these as much as I can, but the inner development of the idea of prophecy at Qumran must await another, diachronic study.

Prophetic Vocabulary in the Dead Sea Scrolls

Although there is no lack of up-to-date inventories of the occurrences of *nābîʾ* and related vocabulary in the Dead Sea Scrolls,[16] it is necessary for the purposes of this study to review them again, paying special attention to cognate terminology and the idea of the transmission of divine knowledge discernible from the texts.[17]

nbʾ "To Prophesy"

Let us begin with the verb *nbʾ* (ni.), which is rather uncommon in the Dead Sea Scrolls with some ten occurrences altogether, half of which belong to the paraphrase of the book of Ezekiel in the fragments of *Pseudo-Ezekiel* and simply copy the verb from the biblical text with no apparently independent idea of its use.[18] Two further occurrences are more interesting, however. A fragment

---

Literary Prophecy," in De Troyer and Lange (eds.), *Prophecy after the Prophets?*, 43–60 (= pp. 663–80 in this volume).

15 Cf. the diachronic treatment of the prophetic role of the Teacher of Righteousness by Brooke, "Was the Teacher of Righteousness Considered to be a Prophet?"

16 See Barstad, "Prophecy at Qumran?"; Flint, "The Prophet David at Qumran," 161–62; and especially J. E. Bowley, "Prophets and Prophecy at Qumran," in *The Dead Sea Scrolls after Fifty Years: A Comprehensive Assessment* (ed. P. W. Flint and J. C. VanderKam; Leiden: Brill, 1999), 354–78.

17 The most important tool for finding the pertinent texts has been M. G. Abegg et al., *The Dead Sea Scrolls Concordance*, Vol. 1: *The Non-Biblical Texts from Qumran* (Leiden: Brill, 2003).

18 4Q385 2 5–7; 4Q386 1 I, 4.

of 3QIsaiah Pesher,[19] again, uses the verb of the prophet Isaiah (3Q4 3), while in the *Damascus Document*, the verb denotes the activity of false prophets who, in contrast to Moses and the "holy anointed ones" through whom God gave his precepts, "prophesied deceit (*nb'w šqr*) in order to divert Israel from following God" (CD VI, 1; par. 4Q267 2 6–7; 4Q269 4 I, 2).[20] Hence, the verb has both positive and negative connotations: positive when used of an ancient prophet and negative when referring to false prophets, whether ancient or contemporary.

nĕbû'â "Prophecy"

Even more rare but all the more interesting is the derivative of the verb *nb'* denoting "prophecy," *nĕbû'â.*[21] In addition to the best preserved text in the Great Psalms Scroll (11Q5 XXVII, 11, see below), it has only two occurrences, one in a broken context (4Q458 15 2) and another, if the text is correctly reconstructed, as the initial word of the 4QIsaiah Pesher[e] (4Q165 1–2 1) where it replaces the Masoretic word for "vision," *ḥăzôn.*[22]

The word *nĕbû'â* can be found in three verses of the Hebrew Bible. In Neh 6:12, it has a negative connotation, referring to the bribed prediction of Shemaiah son of Delaiah, the purpose of which was to harm Nehemiah. In 2 Chr 9:29, again, the prophecy of Ahijah of Shiloh *(nĕbû'at 'ăḥiyyâ haš-šîlônî)* is paralleled by the chronicles of Nathan the prophet (*dibrê nātān han-nābî'*) and visions of Iddo the seer (*ḥăzôt ye'ddô ha-ḥōzê*) as the source where the acts of Solomon are recorded (literally: "written," *kĕtûbîm*). Here the word *nĕbû'â* seems to refer to a written document, whereas in 2 Chr 15:8, the "prophecy of Oded the prophet" (*han-nĕbû'â 'ōdēd han-nābî'*) means the spoken words just quoted.[23]

19 Whether or not the text, despite its conventional title, is really a pesher, is not our concern here; it is not included in the list of pesharim compiled by Timothy Lim in his *Pesharim* (Companion to the Qumran Scrolls 3; London: Continuum, 2003), 1–6.

20 Translations of Dead Sea Scrolls are from García Martínez, F., and E. J. C. Tigchelaar, *The Dead Sea Scrolls: Study Edition*, 2 vols. (Leiden: Brill, 2000).

21 For this word, see A. Hurvitz, "Can Biblical Texts Be Dated Linguistically? Chronological Perspectives in the Historical Study of Biblical Hebrew," in *Congress Volume Oslo 1998* (ed. M. Sæbø; VTSup 53; Leiden: Brill, 2000), 143–60, esp. 151–52.

22 The word is reconstructed as *hn[b]w'wt* [in J. M. Allegro, *Qumran Cave 4* (DJD V; Oxford: Clarendon Press, 1968), 28.

23 Since *han-nĕbû'â* is not in the construct state, the words "Oded the prophet" may be secondary; see R. B. Dillard, *2 Chronicles* (WBC 15; Waco, Tx.: Word Books, 1987), 114.

Ben Sira knows *nĕbû'â* as practiced by the forefathers of Israel, whereby the word is used of both prophetic activity and of the quality of being a prophet.[24] In 44:3–5, the "seers of all in their prophecies" (*ḥwzy kl bnbw'tm*) are paralleled by eleven other functions such as kings, famous heroes, counsellors, wise scholars versed in scriptures (*ḥkmy šyḥ bsprtm*), teachers, and even composers of psalms (*ḥwqry mzmwr*). This vocabulary is closely reminiscent of Sir 39:1–8 where the study of prophecies[25] is one of the qualities of the ideal scribe.[26] Both Joshua and Samuel are introduced with this word as holders of the prophetic office (46:1, 13), and Samuel is said to have uttered a prophecy after his death from the ground (*wyś' m'rṣ qwlw bnb'w*[.], 46:20).[27]

The overview of the use of *nĕbû'â* in the Hebrew Bible and in Ben Sira reveals a varied range of meanings, not only of the word itself but of the concept of prophecy in Hellenistic Judaism in general. It can be used of false prophesying, but more importantly, it is paralleled with visionary and scribal activities, denoting both spoken and written word. While the word can be used of the prophetic office, the clusters of the functions of learned men in Sir 44:3–5 and 39:1–3 let prophecy appear as an essential aspect of the revelatory wisdom to be learned and interpreted.

All this is of great significance with regard to the most important occurrence of *nĕbû'â* in 11Q5 XXVII, 11, where the following is said of King David:[28]

kwl 'lh dbr bnbw'h 'šr ntn lw mlpny h'lywn

All these he spoke through prophecy which had been given to him before the Most High.

"All these" refers to the four thousand and fifty songs composed by David, to whom God had given "a discerning and enlightened spirit" (line 4: *rwḥ nbwnh w'wrh*). The catalogue of songs on lines 4–10 is framed by the words *rwḥ* and

24 See P. C. Beentjes, "Prophets and Prophecy in the Book of Ben Sira," in Floyd and Haak, eds., *Prophets, Prophecy, and Prophetic Texts in Second Temple Judaism*, 134–50, esp. 137–41; M. Marttila, "Die Propheten Israels in Ben Siras 'Lob der Väter,'" in *Houses Full of All Good Things: Essays in Memory of Timo Veijola* (ed. J. Pakkala and M. Nissinen; PFES 95; Helsinki: Finnish Exegetical Society; Göttingen: Vandenhoech & Ruprecht, 2008) 434–50.

25 I.e., *prophēteia*; the Hebrew text has not been preserved here.

26 Cf. Beentjes, "Prophets and Prophecy in the Book of Ben Sira," 147–48.

27 The Hebrew text of Ben Sira according to P. C. Beentjes, *The Book of Ben Sira in Hebrew: A Text Edition of All Extant Hebrew Manuscripts and a Synopsis of All Parallel Hebrew Ben Sira Texts* (VTSup 68; Leiden: Brill, 2003).

28 See: P. W. Flint, *The Dead Sea Psalms Scrolls and the Book of Psalms* (STDJ 17; Leiden: Brill, 1997); idem, "The Prophet David at Qumran," 162–64; Lim, "'All These He Composed through Prophecy,'" passim.

nĕbû'â, which can be understood as meaning essentially the same thing, hence there is a fundamental unity of prophecy and spirit. Furthermore, while there is no question about these songs being essentially written documents, the verb *dbr* gives the impression of oral activity, not necessarily just speaking but also singing, and the preposition *b* enables *nĕbû'â* to be understood both as the state of being possessed by the spirit or as the quality of being a prophet—which again, ultimately, mean the same thing. The spirit and prophecy have been given to David by God, and therefore, the songs composed by him are not his own work but well out from a divine source. Even though David is not explicitly called a prophet, his prophetic role could not be more clearly expressed. The author of the Great Psalms Scroll may have had reasons not to name David directly as a prophet,[29] but the modern scholar can do it without hesitation, at least if the transmission of divine messages is understood as the primary prophetic function.

nābî' / *nĕbî'â* "Prophet"

While it is important to register the single instance of *nby'h* "prophetess" in the Dead Sea Scrolls (PAM 43.677 6, 2),[30] little consequences can be drawn from the tiny fragment where it appears, apart from noticing the actual existence of the word and that it is followed by the preposition *lĕ*.

The masculine noun *nābî'*, "prophet," on the other hand, is rather common in the Scrolls, where its use is largely inspired by the biblical texts. Quite frequently, the word appears as the tide of a biblical prophet,[31] and this often happens in formulaic phrases such as "as God has said by means of (*byd*) the proph-

29 According to Flint, the Qumran writers were reluctant to do this because of the suspicious overtones of the word *nābî'* ("The Prophet David at Qumran," 166–67), while Lim thinks David is not called a prophet because this title is never attached to him in the Hebrew Bible, and because the prophetic gift attributed to him is akin to that of the Levitical singers in 1 Chr 25:1–3 ("'All These He Composed through Prophecy'").

30 See D. M. Pike and A. C. Skinner, *Qumran Cave 4 XXIII: Unidentified Fragments* (DJD 33; Oxford; Clarendon Press, 2001), 104 and Plate XVIII. Theoretically, the reading *nbw'h* would also be possible, since the letters *yod* and *waw* look much alike in the Dead Sea Scrolls. However, judging from the photograph in DJD 33 Plate XVIII, the middle letter cannot be read as *waw.*

31 E.g., the prophet Habakkuk (1QpHab I, 1); Jeremiah the prophet (4Q385b 16 I, 2, 6); c.f. the mentioning of Samuel as God's prophet who anointed David in Ps 151A and 151B (11Q5 XXVIII, 8 [*nby'w*], 13 [*nby' 'lwhym*].

et Isaiah,"[32] or "as is written in the book of Daniel, the prophet,"[33] followed by a quotation from the book attributed to the prophet in question. The prophet may even be said to have written the word himself, as in CD XIX, 7: "when there comes the word which is written by the hand (*'šr ktwb byd*) of the prophet Zechariah."

In addition to the prophets mentioned by their names, prophets often appear as an anonymous collective, as in the reference to the "kindnesses of your prophets" (*ḥsdy nby'yk*), paralleled by the "deeds of you devoted ones" (*m'śy ḥsydyk*) in 11Q5 XXII, 5–6. The Dead Sea Scrolls adopt the Deuteronomistic phrase "his/your servants the prophets," which implies the idea of a succession of prophets, through whom God has given to the people his precepts[34] or blessings.[35] This succession begins with Moses the law-giver who is also the prototype of a prophet and the first person to hold the prophetic office. The *Rule of the Community* is written "in order to do what is good and just in his presence, as he commanded by the hand of Moses and by the hand of all his servants the prophets" (1QS I, 2–3),[36] and the task of the followers of Moses is not merely to repeat the words of the law but to study the law "wh[i]ch he commanded through the hand of Moses, in order to act in compliance with all that has been revealed from age to age, and according to what the prophets have revealed through his holy spirit" (1QS VIII, 15–16). Teaching this revelation is the responsibility of the teachers who are there to make hidden things known to the community: "And every matter hidden (*nstr*) from Israel but which has been found out by the Interpreter (*hdwrš*),[37] he should not keep hidden from them for fear of a spirit of desertion" (1QS VIII, 11–12).

Prophets are known to prepare the coming of the Messiah in *11QMelchizedeq*, where the pesher of Isa 52:7 says: '"[How] beautiful upon the mountains are the feet [of] the messen[ger who] announces peace, the mess[enger of good who announces salvati]on, [sa]ying to Zion: your God [reigns.'] Its interpretation: The

---

32 CD IV, 13; cf. similar cases in CD III, 21 (Ezekiel); VII, 10 (Isaiah); XIX, 11–12 (Ezekiel); 11Q13 II, 15 (Isaiah).

33 4Q174 1 3 II, 3; cf. 4Q174 1–2 I, 15–16 (Isaiah); 4Q177 II, 2, 13 (Zechariah, Ezekiel); 4Q285 5 1 (Isaiah); 4Q265 2 3 (Isaiah).

34 Cf. 4QpHos[a] (4Q166) II, 5; 4QpsMoses[e] (4Q390) 2 I, 5.

35 4Q292 2 3 4: "... may you bless them [like] you [spoke] to them through all your servants the prophets."

36 Cf. 4Q504 1–2 III, 12–13.

37 This translation assumes that the Interpreter is not just any member of the community but belongs to the "priests who keep the covenant and interpret his (i. e., God's) will," assuming that it is through them the hidden things are revealed "to the multitude of the men of their covenant who freely volunteer together for his truth" (1QS V, 9–10).

mountains [are] the prophet[s...]—And the messenger i[s] the anointed of the spir [it]" (11Q13 II, 15–18). Likewise, according to the ideology of the *Rule of the Community*, the community is to be ruled "by the first directives which the men of the Community began to be taught until the prophet comes, and the Messiahs of Aaron and Israel" (1QS IX, 10–11). The revelation, thus, is entrusted to the acknowledged teachers of the community until it is taken over again by the eschatological prophet whose appearance indicates the beginning of the Messianic time.[38]

The idea of revealing hidden things with an explicit reference to prophecy is to be found in *Pesher Habakkuk*, where the eschatological events that are going to take place to the final generation are to be heard "from the mouth of the Priest whom God has placed wi[thin the Commun]ity, to foretell the fulfillment of all the words of his servants, the prophets, [by] means of whom God has declared all that is going to happen to his people Is[rael]" (1QpHab II, 7–10). Whereas prophets are presented as the followers of Moses, the teachers of the community are commissioned with the task of teaching and instruction which, in a non-canonical psalm from Qumran, are introduced as a prophetic function: "And through his spirit prophets <were given> to you to teach you and show you (*'tkm lhśkyl wllmd*) [...]" (4Q381 69 4). Prophets are doubtless meant also in CD II, 12–13 by the holy spirit-anointed ones (*mšyḥy rwḥ*) and seers of the truth (*ḥwzy 'mt*), by the hand of whom (*byd*) the people have been taught.[39]

Like Moses, the prophets are acknowledged as book-writers. The books of the prophets are juxtapositioned with Torah in the phrase "the book of Moses [and] the book[s of the pr]ophets and David" in 4QMMT (4Q397 14–21 10).[40] Irrespective of whether this should be taken as a reference to the tripartite Hebrew canon[41]—and provided that the text is correctly reconstructed[42]—this phrase

38 It is not my intention here to go any deeper into the discussion on the Qumran messianism; for the "Messiahs of Aaron and Israel," see J. Zimmermann, *Messianische Texte aus Qumran: Königliche, priesterliche und prophetische Messiasvorstellungen in den Schriftfunden von Qumran* (WUNT 2/104; Tübingen: Mohr Siebeck, 1998), 23–45, and for the prophetic aspects of messianology, ibid., 312–417. For the eschatological prophets, see also Bowley, "Prophets and Prophecy at Qumran," 366–70.

39 Cf. Bowley, "Prophets and Prophecy at Qumran," 359.

40 Cf. line 15 without the mentioning of David.

41 This has been refuted by T. H. Lim, "The Alleged Reference to the Tripartite Division of the Hebrew Bible," *RevQ* 20 (2001): 23–37, and E. C. Ulrich, "The Non-Attestation of a Tripartite Canon in 4QMMT," *CBQ* 65 (2003) 202–14.

42 Ulrich, "The Non-Attestation of a Tripartite Canon in 4QMMT," questions the reading "books" before "prophets," because the fragment 4Q397 17 containing the word [ ]*bspr*[ ] is placed here merely because of the contents of the passage, whereas Lim, "The Alleged Reference

makes the succession of Moses and the prophets manifest itself in the form of written texts. This is by no means surprising, but it is important to pay attention to the utmost significance of the writtenness of prophecy, which makes it possible to transmit the prophetic words by means of interpretation to the final generation, as reflected by the exposition of the *Damascus Document* of Amos 5:26–27 and Num 24:13: "The books of law are the Sukkat of the King, as he said: 'I will lift up the fallen Sukkat of David.' The King is the assembly; and the Kiyyune of images <...> are the books of the prophets, whose words Israel despised. And the star is the Interpreter of the law (*dwrš htwrh*), who will come to Damascus, as it is written: 'A star moves out of Jacob, and a scepter arises out of Israel'" (CD VII, 15–20). The Interpreter, according to this text, is placed in continuum with Moses and the prophets, whose books contain the information on the divine plans concerning the final generation, to be revealed to the community by means of interpretation.

The texts discussed so far use the word *nābîʾ* of individual biblical prophets, of the succession of prophets beginning with Moses, and of eschatological figures. As such, the word has a positive and reverent tone. However, as the verb *nbʾ*, also the noun *nābîʾ* has negative connotations, too. Apart from the respectful references to the prophets of the past, named or anonymous, and to the future, eschatological prophet, the word is also used of false prophets. In the *Hodayot*, the people who "search you with a double heart, and are not firmly based in your truth" go to "search for you in the mouth of the prophets of error (*nbyʾy kzb*) attracted by delusion" (1QH[a] XII, 14, 16). One Aramaic text (4Q339) is a list of false prophets (*nbyʾy šqrʾ*) who arose in Israel, containing names of biblical[43] and, possibly, even contemporary figures.[44] The *Temple Scroll* includes versions of the texts of Deuteronomy relevant to the issue of false prophecy, Deut 13:2–6

---

to the Tripartite Division of the Hebrew Bible," 24–25, confirms the restoration. For textual criticism of 4Q397 14–21, see also H. von Weissenberg, *4QMMT: Reevaluating the Text, the Function, and the Meaning of the Epilogue* (STDJ 82; Leiden: Brill, 2009).

43 I.e., Balaam (Num 22–24); the man of Bethel (1 Kgs 13:11–31); Zedekiah (1 Kgs 22:1–28); Zedekiah son of Maaseiah (Jer 29:21–24); Shemaiah the Nehelamite (Jer 29:24–32); and Hananiah son of Azur (Jer 28).

44 If the restoration [*ywḥnn bn šm*]*ʿwn* is correct, there is a reference to John Hyrcanus on line 9; thus E. Qimron, "On the Interpretation of the List of False Prophets," *Tarbiz* 63 (1994) 273–75. Whether or not there is a reference to him, Bowley thinks that the interest of this text was more than antiquarian; "it was likely inspired by the present concerns of the community ("Prophets and Prophecy at Qumran," 365). For this text, see also M. Broshi and A. Yardeni, "On 'Netinim' and False Prophets," in *Solving Riddles and Untying Knots: Biblical, Epigraphic, and Semitic Studies in Honor of Jonas C. Greenfield* (ed. Z. Zevit, S. Gitin and M. Sokoloff; Winona Lake, Ind.: Eisenbrauns, 1995), 29–37.

(11Q19 LIV, 8 – 18) and 18:20 – 22 (11Q19 LXI, 1 – 5), without any further interpretation, whereas the *Apocryphon of Moses* (4Q375) elaborates on the possibility that there is a prophet who preaches apostasy and thus, according to Deut 13:2 – 6, deserves to be killed, but the tribe from which he comes affirms that he is a just man and a trustworthy prophet. In such a situation, the anointed priest shall perform a ritual, probably in order to test the credibility of that prophet.[45]

It is important to pay attention to the fact that the authors of the Dead Sea Scrolls never call their contemporaries as prophets with a respectful tone; the title *nābîʾ* has a positive connotation only with regard to the ancient "classical" prophets, or to the future eschatological prophets (1QS IX, 10 – 11; 11Q13 II, 17–18).[46] It is not self-evident that the false prophets labelled with this title are thought of as contemporary figures either. This largely depends on whether the exegeses of the *Temple Scroll* (11Q19) and the *Apocryphon of Moses* (4Q375) should rather be read as theoretical treatments of eschatological events (cf. CD VI, 1),[47] or whether they can be understood as dealing with a live contemporary issue.[48] If the latter alternative is true, the use of the title "prophet" is twofold: the positive use of the word *nābîʾ* is reserved for the ancient (or future) prophets, while contemporary persons are thus designated only in a pejorative sense.

Prophetic Functions, Past and Present

The above inventory of prophetic vocabulary in the Dead Sea Scrolls yields a rather comprehensive picture of the functions of prophecy as perceived by the authors of the Scrolls and their implied audiences. Everything points to the conclusion that prophecy means essentially transmission of divine words, orders and blessings, that is, God-given revelation on present and future things

---

45 For 4Q375, see G. Brin, "The Laws of the Prophets in the Sect of the Judaean Desert: Studies in 4Q375," *JSP* 16 (1992): 19 – 57; Zimmermann, *Messianische Texte aus Qumran*, 233 – 40.

46 Cf. Flint, "The Prophet David at Qumran," 162; Brooke, "Was the Teacher of Righteousness Considered to be a Prophet?"

47 Thus J. Strugnell, "4QApocryphon of Moses[a]," in *Qumran Cave 4.XIV: Parabiblical Texts, Part 2* (ed. M. Broshi et al.; DJD 19; Oxford: Clarendon Press, 1995), 111 – 19, esp. 119.

48 Thus Brooke, "Prophecy and Prophets in the Dead Sea Scrolls," 159 – 60. For 4Q375, see also G. Brin, *Studies in Biblical Law: From the Hebrew Bible to the Dead Sea Scrolls* (JSOTSup 176; Sheffield: JSOT Press, 1994), 164; idem, "The Laws of the Prophets in the Sect of the Judaean Desert"; cf. the criticism in Zimmermann, *Messianische Texte aus Qumran*, 239 – 40.

which is mediated by Moses and, after him, by the prophets. It is through (*byd*) them God has revealed his will.

Prophecy is thought to be received in a divinely inspired condition, that is, through the holy spirit (1QS VIII, 16; 4Q381 69 4), or in a vision as implied in 11Q5 XXII, 13–14: "Acquire a vision (*ḥzwn*) spoken in your regard, and dreams of prophets (*ḥlmt nby'ym*) requested for you." The state of God-given inspiration is also implied by the term *nĕbûʼâ* (11Q5 XXVII, 11) which can also mean the prophecy itself (4Q165 1–2, 1; cf. Neh 6:12; 2 Chr 9:29; 15:8; Sir 44:3–5) or the status of being a prophet (11Q5 XXVII, 11; cf. Sir 46:1, 13). All this is consistent with the idea and practice of non-inductive (or non-technical) divination as intermediation as we know it from a wide range of ancient Near Eastern sources.[49] Even the false prophets seem to fulfill this function, but they are deprived of a truly prophetic status because they are "attracted by delusion" (1QH[a] XII, 14, 16) and are, therefore, comparable to the false prophets of Deuteronomy who act without divine authorization (11Q19 LIV, 8–18; LXI, 1–5; cf. Deut 13:2–6; 18:20–22).

What about prophetic functions in the communities that produced the Scrolls: was prophecy still alive, or did it belong to the past altogether?[50] This question is highly relevant to the issue of the alleged cessation of prophecy during the Second Temple period discussed in several recent studies.[51] We have just seen that the word *nābîʼ* is of restricted use in the Dead Sea Scrolls and tends to be used in a pejorative tone in cases that have chances to give a glimpse of contemporary concerns of the communities. This, however, does not mean that the principal function of prophecy, the transmission of divine knowledge and revelation, had ceased to exist in the world of the Dead Sea Scrolls. This would be the conclusion if we expected a clone of a biblical prophet to reappear in the Scrolls as a contemporary figure; but in my view, the question is rather how much we allow the concept and the practice of prophecy to be transformed in different sources and circumstances and to be still called prophecy.

---

49 Cf. Nissinen, "What Is Prophecy?" 21–22; E. Cancik-Kirschbaum, "Prophetismus und Divination: Ein Blick auf die keilschriftlichen Quellen," in *Propheten in Mari, Assyrien und Israel* (ed. M. Köckert and M. Nissinen; FRLANT 201; Göttingen: Vandenhoeck & Ruprecht, 2003), 33–53.

50 For this issue, see Brooke, "Prophecy," 697–98.

51 See O. H. Steck, *Der Abschluß der Prophetie im Alten Testament* (Biblisch-theologische Studien 17; Neukirchen-Vluyn: Neukirchener, 1991); F. Greenspahn, "Why Prophecy Ceased?" *JBL* 108 (1989) 37–49; B. D. Sommer, "Did Prophecy Cease? Evaluating a Reevaluation," *JBL* 115 (1996) 31–47; Grabbe, "Poets, Scribes, or Preachers: The Reality of Prophecy in the Second Temple Period"; Nissinen, "The Dubious Image of Prophecy."

The key issue, I think, is intermediation as a divinatory practice.[52] Prophets are essentially intermediaries but not all intermediaries can be called prophets. Who deserves this title is never self-evident but must be judged with regard to the whole ensemble of divinatory ideas and practices in any given socio-religious environment. Sometimes, as in Mesopotamia or probably in the kingdom of Judah, it is possible to make a rather clear-cut distinction between (non-technical) prophetic and (technical) other kinds of divination,[53] but this seems to be no longer the case in Second Temple Judaism where prophecy as a concept began to amalgamate with literary and scribal roles and activities. When literary interpretation of prophecy virtually replaced the oral/aural prophecy as the generally preferred divinatory practice, it took over essential prophetic functions despite the fact that the designation "prophet" was primarily used of figures of the past. Hence, the restricted use of the word "prophet" for contemporary figures in a positive sense begins already in the Hebrew Bible. The literary activity of the scribes who edited the prophetic books and stories about prophets fulfilled the prophetic function of transmitting revelation; however, they did not adopt the title "prophet" but rather used it in a negative way with reference to their contemporaries. A good example of this is the view of prophets and prophecy in the Deuteronomistic literature, where the prophets of old have an elevated position (as in the books of Kings), whereas the actual prophetic activity is looked upon with great suspicion (as in Deuteronomy).[54] This, however, should not deprive the Second Temple scribes of their prophetic role, even though it can be seen as a secondary development where aspects of traditional oral/aural prophecy and scribal or mantic divination merge together.[55]

---

52 For intermediation as the essential prophetic function, see, e.g., D. L. Petersen, "Defining Prophecy and Prophetic Literature," in *Prophecy in Its Ancient Near Eastern Context: Mesopotamian, Biblical, and Arabian Perspectives* (ed. M. Nissinen; SBLSymS 13; Atlanta: Society of Biblical Literature, 2000), 33–44.

53 For this distinction, see, e.g, Cancik-Kirschbaum, "Prophetismus und Divination," 44–47.

54 Cf. the works mentioned above in n. 12 and H. M. Barstad, "The Understanding of the Prophets in Deuteronomy," *SJOT* 8 (1994) 236–51; id., "Some Remarks on Prophets and Prophecy in the 'Deuteronomistic History,'" in Pakkala and Nissinen (eds.), *Houses Full of All Good Things*, 300–15. Interestingly, the Chronicler's view differs from the view of both Deuteronomists and the Dead Sea Scrolls in that the contemporary, "false" prophets do not play a role in Chronicles; see Schniedewind, *The Word of God in Transition*, 247–49.

55 Cf. VanderKam, "The Prophetic-Sapiential Origins of Apocalyptic Thought," 254: "[T]he term prophecy should not be limited to what the few great literary prophets taught or did. Israelite or Judean prophecy was a far broader phenomenon that included not only their efforts but also late prophecy, of course, and an unavoidable mantic element."

From Prophecy to Mystery

The transmissive divinatory function as a living practice is, of course, widely attested in the Dead Sea Scrolls—however, primarily as literary and interpretative pursuit rather than oral/aural activity. To be sure, there are a couple of texts that give the impression of a traditional prophetic oracle based on oral performance; for instance, 4Q410,[56] a highly enigmatic text, seems to present itself as originating from a visionary experience:[57] "And now, I, th[ese things] in the spirit [...] you, and the or[acle] will not fail, [and] not [will be du]mb [...]" (*w'th 'ny 't '[lh] brwḥ* [...]*kh wlw' ykzb ḥm*[*ś' w*]*lw'* [*yḥ*]*ryš*) (4Q410 1 7–8). There is no way of knowing whether or not the text goes back to an actual visionary event, but it is worth noting that, if the fragmentary text is correctly understood, there were people who did not hesitate to make the claim that they have acted "in the spirit" with the result of an oracular utterance (*maśśā'*).[58]

The term *maśśā'* can also be found in *1QMysteries* that predicts what happens to "those born of sin" and says: "This word (*hdbr*) will undoubtedly happen, the prediction (*hmś'*) is truthful" (1Q27 1 I, 8). Again, it is impossible to know whether this actually implies an originally spoken utterance. In any case, it deserves attention that the sinners are presented as people who "do not know the mystery of existence (*rz nḥyh*), nor understand ancient matters" (line 3), and when they have been destroyed, "knowledge (*d't*) will pervade the world" (line 7). The text is not only a good example of the close affinity between wisdom, eschatology and divination,[59] but it also resonates with the famous passage in *Pesher Habakkuk* on the Teacher of Righteousness (lQpHab VII, 1–8):

> And God told Habakkuk to write what was going to happen to <...> the last generation, but he did not let him know the consummation of that era. And as for what he says: "So that

56 The edition of Annette Steudel can be found in S. J. Pfann et al, *Qumran Cave 4 XXVI* (DJD 36; Oxford: Clarendon, 2000), 316–19; here quoted from García Martínez and Tigchelaar, *The Dead Sea Scrolls: Study Edition*, 840–41.

57 Bowley, "Prophets and Prophecy at Qumran," 376: "A text could hardly be more prophetic in form than this."

58 In general, the authors of the Dead Sea Scrolls seem rather reluctant to claim that they have had visionary or auditory experiences; see E. M. Good, "What Did the Jews of Qumran Know about God and how Did They Know It? Revelation and God in the Dead Sea Scrolls," in *The Judaism of Qumran: A Systemic Reading of the Dead Sea Scrolls*, Vol. 2: *World View, Comparing Judaisms* (ed. A. J. Avery-Peck, J. Neusner and B. D. Chilton; HO 57/5; Leiden: Brill, 2001), 3–22, esp. 8.

59 Cf. also 4QMysteries (4Q299–300).

> may run the one who reads it." Its interpretation concerns the Teacher of Righteousness, to whom God has made known all the mysteries of the words of his servants, the prophets (*'šr hwdy'w 'l 't kwl rzy dbry 'bdyw hnby'ym*). "For a vision (*ḥzwn*) has an appointed time, it will have an end and not fail." Its interpretation: the final age will be extended and go beyond all that the prophets say, because the mysteries of God (*rzy 'l*) are wonderful.

Elsewhere in *Pesher Habakkuk*, the words of the Teacher of Righteousness are said to come from the mouth of God (1QpHab II, 2–3), and the "Priest whom God has placed wi[thin the commun]ity" (identical with the Teacher?) is said to be there "to foretell (or: interpret, *lpšwr*) the fulfillment of all the words of his servants, the prophets" (1QpHab II, 8–9). One can indeed agree with George Brooke in his statement that the "exegete comes as close as he can to calling the Teacher a prophet, but he does not take the final actual step."[60] That the pesherist does not take this step should not prevent the modern exegete to acknowledge the genuinely prophetic role of the Teacher of Righteousness. He clearly acts as an intermediary whose utterances are actually words of God. He is also the one who receives a new revelation that, without invalidating the words of the prophets of old,[61] reveals their true meaning for the final generation; but even he may not know *all* the wonderful mysteries of God, since the final age goes beyond all that the prophets say.[62]

That the Teacher of Righteousness, according to *Pesher Habakkuk*, has been revealed the mysteries of the words of the prophets not only reminds of the phraseology of 1Q27 quoted above, but introduces the key term "mystery," *raz* (Heb)/ *rāz* (Aram.), which is crucial in comprehending the function of divination in the world of the Dead Sea Scrolls. In the book of Daniel, *raz* denotes a divine mystery to be revealed to people by means of learned interpretation (Dan 2:18, 19, 27–30, 47; 4:6),[63] and in the Aramaic text of *1 Enoch*, it is used of the knowledge about the final judgment given to Enoch (4QEn^{e} = 4Q204 5 II, 26–27; cf. 106:19). The word is of Persian etymology, but it corresponds to Akkadian *piristu* and *niṣirtu*, both denoting the secret lore and cosmic knowledge kept by gods and revealed to selected individuals, that is, diviners initiated into the scribal lore who possessed the means of revealing the secrets of the gods to the king and the peo-

60 Brooke, "Was the Teacher of Righteousness Considered to be a Prophet?"

61 Cf. S. L. Berrin, *The Pesher Nahum Scroll from Qumran: An Exegetical Study of 4Q169* (STDJ 53; Leiden: Brill, 2004), 12–18.

62 Cf. J. Jokiranta, *Social Identity and Sectarianism in the Qumran Movement* (STDJ 105; Leiden: Brill, 2012) 168–69.

63 For the use of *raz/rāz* in the Book of Daniel and in the Dead Sea Scrolls, see G. K. Beale, *The Use of Daniel in Jewish Apocalyptic Literature and in the Revelation of St. John* (Lanham, Md.: University Press of America, 1984), 12–19.

ple.[64] This was also the role of Daniel, the Jew educated by the Babylonians, who turned out to be ten times wiser than his fellow diviners in Babylonia (Dan 1:20).

Likewise in the Dead Sea Scrolls, *raz* (often paralleled by *d‘t* "knowledge," *'mt* "truth," *ḥkmh* "wisdom," and the like) is the central term for the cosmic, hidden, and divine knowledge. It is typically used in the *Hodayot*, in the *Rule of the Community* and in *4QInstruction* where it is mostly part of the compound *rz nḥyh* "mystery of existence" (cf. above, 1Q27).[65] Using this phrase, "4QInstruction purports, like Daniel and 1 Enoch, to disclose heavenly wisdom that would not be otherwise available."[66] It is the "light of the heart" of those who can observe what is hidden from mankind (1QS XI, 3–9). Even in other texts, *rz* denotes hidden wisdom not understood by those unworthy of it: "for sealed up has been from you [the s]eal of the vision (*[hḥzwn ḥ]tm*) and you have not considered the eternal mysteries (*rzy ‘d*), and knowledge (*bynh*) you have not understood" (4Q300 1 II, 2). Accordingly, the mystery is revealed only to selected people—often through intermediaries like the Teacher of Righteousness or other instructors who adopt a role similar to Mesopotamian scholars or Daniel: they are the ones, conversant with the divine knowledge, who are capable of transmitting it to the community.

The use of "mystery" in the same breath with the prophets, as in *Pesher Habakkuk*, or within an eschatological oracle, as in 1Q27, or in parallel with "vision," as in 4Q300, indicates that the prophetic function of transmitting divine knowledge is understood primarily as the revelation of divine mysteries and their transmission by wisdom teachers.[67] These teachers—whose identity is not the primary concern here—are the ones who reveal the mysteries to the members of the community: "He should lead them with knowledge and in this way teach them the mysteries of wonder and of truth (*rzy pl' w'mt*) in the midst of the men of the Community, so that they walk perfectly, one with another, in all that has been revealed to them" (1QS IX, 18–19).

---

64 See *CAD* P 400–1; *CAD* N/2 277. For the significance of the secret lore in Mesopotamian divination, prophecy and royal ideology, see B. Pongratz-Leisten, *Herrschaftswissen in Mesopotamien: Formen der Kommunikation zwischen Gott und König im 2. und 1. Jahrtausend v. Chr.* (SAAS 10; Helsinki: The Neo-Assyrian Text Corpus Project, 1999), 286–320.

65 1Q26 1 1; 4Q415 6 4; 4Q416 2 I, 5; 2 III, 9, 14, 18; 4Q418 10 1; 43–45 I, 4, 14, 16; 77 2; 123 II, 4; 172 1. For *rz nḥyh* and its interpretations, see M. J. Goff, *The Worldly and Heavenly Wisdom of 4QInstruction* (STDJ 50; Leiden: Brill, 2003), 30–79.

66 Goff, *The Worldly and Heavenly Wisdom of 4QInstruction*, 79.

67 Cf. Brooke, "Prophecy and Prophets in the Dead Sea Scrolls," 162–63; J. C. VanderKam, "Mantic Wisdom in the Dead Sea Scrolls," *DSD* 4 (1997) 336–53; Schniedewind, *The Word of God in Transition*, 241–47.

Especially in the *Hodayot*, the exclusive position of the teachers of wisdom is expressed in a variety of ways in the Dead Sea Scrolls. Their ears have been opened to the mysteries (1QH^a IX, 21), which does not necessarily mean a revelation by audition but rather an intellectual illumination which is likewise perceived as revelation.[68] The knowledge of divine mysteries was, after all not just a matter of learning scholarly skills and scribal techniques but something that was concealed *in* the teacher (1QH^a XIII, 25) and revealed *through him* to the community: "Through me you have enlightened the face of the Many, you have increased them, so that they are uncountable, for you have shown me your wondrous mysteries" (1QH^a XII, 27).

In some key passages, the function of intermediation is expressed with the word *mlyṣ* "mediator, interpreter," as in the *Psalms Pesher*, where the privileged teacher[69] is called "Interpreter of Knowledge" (*mlyṣ d't*) (4Q171 I, 27), or in the *Hodayot*, where it is precisely the "mystery" that the speaker is commissioned to mediate: "But you (i.e., God) have set me like a banner for the elect of justice, like a knowledgeable mediator of secret wonders (*mlyṣ d't brzy pl'*)" (1QH^a X, 13). But even this privileged instructor has a predecessor who has mediated the knowledge to him: "You have opened a spring in the mouth of your servant—to mediate (*lmlyṣ*) these matters to dust such as me" (1QH^a XXIII, 10–12); most probably, this should be taken as referring to Moses and, indirectly, his followers, the prophets. Like the prophets, the teachers of wisdom were not superhuman beings but "dust" as humans in general, but they were chosen through the divine spirit to be the intermediaries of the divine knowledge.[70]

Conclusion

In conclusion, it may be recognized that the divinatory function of prophecy was well taken care of in communities that produced the Dead Sea Scrolls. The an-

---

68 Cf. 1QH^a XX, 13: "You have [op]ened *within me* (*ltwky*) knowledge of the mystery of your wisdom." Revelation, according to Good, "What Did the Jews of Qumran Know about God," 8, "refers to God's disclosure of himself to certain human vessels, informing them of his character and purposes; these disclosures may be preserved in writing or through oral tradition."

69 Cf. J. Jokiranta, "Qumran—The Prototypical Teacher in the Qumran Pesharim: A Social-Identity Approach," in *Ancient Israel: The Old Testament in Its Social Context* (ed. P. F. Esler; Minneapolis: Fortress, 2006), 254–63, esp. 259.

70 Good, "What Did the Jews of Qumran Know about God," 7: "Although human nature as commonly found is too weak or sinful to understand God or his ways, God through his grace can transfer his own knowledge to certain chosen individuals, and these in turn can serve as sources of the knowledge of God."

cient prophetic figures, to whom the title *nābî'* was reserved, had an authoritative status as followers of Moses, the first prophet. But the revelation, based in part in their writings, was now received by the privileged teachers—such as the Teacher of Righteousness—who like the prophets were inspired by the divine spirit and were, therefore, capable of knowing and transmitting the divine mysteries to the community. These teachers were not called prophets, but they certainly had a similar status and function,[71] even though fused into the scholarly and scribal role that was not necessarily part of traditional prophecy but rather belonged to scholarly divination.

In the Dead Sea Scrolls, the role of the prophets is primarily the same as that of Near Eastern prophets in general: transmission of divine words, virtually deprived of other functions. What is different is the emphasis on scriptures and their interpretation based on the knowledge of divine mysteries, which gives them a role comparable with that of the Mesopotamian scholars. This is consistent with what Josephus writes on the Essene prophets whose knowledge of the future was based on their education "in sacred books and various purifications[72] and sayings of prophets." It is noteworthy that even the ancient prophets are not presented in the Dead Sea Scrolls in the way that modern scholars and interpreters of the Bible would like to see them, that is, as oppositional figures and social critics;[73] neither are the teachers of wisdom, their prophetic role notwithstanding, the very image of the ancient prophets as we may have learned to imagine them. Could it be, after all, that the authors of the Dead Sea Scrolls imagined the prophets of old in their own image?

It is with utmost pleasure that I, full of gratitude, dedicate this study to Raija Sollamo, my teacher, friend, and colleague for more than two decades.

---

71 This can be compared with the concept of prophecy in Chronicles: "We may infer from Chronicles that prophecy (divine inspiration for speaking/writing) continued in the post-exilic period, but the prophets themselves (prophetic office) did not" (Schniedewind, *The Word of God in Transition*, 249).

72 On "various purifications" (*diaphorois hagneiais*) and the significance of purity for the study of scriptures, see Gray, *Prophetic Figures in Late Second Temple Jewish Palestine*, 86–92.

73 Cf. Bowley, "Prophets and Prophecy at Qumran," 366: "The prophets of Israel are not presented in their roles as social agitators, advisors to kings, or reformers—the prophets are essentially books, books written by God himself."

Oracles at Qumran? Traces of Inspired Speakers in the Dead Sea Scrolls*

The Persistence of Prophecy in the Dead Sea Scrolls

Prophecy appears in the Dead Sea Scrolls first and foremost as inspired interpretation of sacred texts, that is, as a scribal enterprise.[1] No explicit evidence of oral/aural prophetic performances has been identified so far in the Dead Sea Scrolls, and there are not many texts that could be used as evidence for the continuation of the prophetic phenomenon. However, some recent studies on prophecy in the Dead Sea Scrolls have highlighted the significance of prophecy, not only as a concept related to ancient prophets and the interpretation of authoritative scriptures but also as ongoing practice.

George Brooke has identified five aspects of the continuation of prophecy in the Dead Sea Scrolls: the life in the wilderness as a symbolic prophetic action; the divinatory activities such as lot-casting (1QS V, 3, etc.) and physiognomy (4Q186); the distinction between true and false prophets; the literary interpretation of the biblical prophetic texts; and the eschatological vision of the Qumran community.[2] Samuel Thomas has recognized the prophetic nature of the "mys-

---

* This article is a reworked version of the paper read in the session of the Qumran Section at the Annual Meeting of the Society of Biblical Literature in Baltimore, November 25, 2013. I would like to thank Charlotte Hempel, the chair of the Qumran Section, for accepting my paper, as well as the audience, especially George Brooke, Armin Lange, and Lawrence Schiffman, for very helpful comments. Thanks are also due to Katri Antin, Jutta Jokiranta, and the editors of this volume for reading the manuscript with critical eyes and making valuable suggestions, and to Hanna Vanonen for her help in coping with the manuscripts of Qumran war texts.

1 See, e.g., G. J. Brooke, "Les mystères des prophètes et les oracles d'exégèse: Continuité et discontinuité dans la prophètie à Qumran," in *Comment devient-on prophète? Actes du colloque organisé par le Collège de France, Paris, les 4–5 avril 2011* (ed. J.-M. Durand, T. Römer, and M. Bürki; OBO 265; Fribourg: Academic Press and Göttingen: Vandenhoeck & Ruprecht, 2014) 159–66.

2 G. J. Brooke, "La Prophétie de Qumrân," in *Les recueils prophétiques de la Bible: Origines, milieux, et contexte proche-oriental* (ed. J.-D. Macchi et al.; MdB 64; Geneva: Labor et Fides, 2012) 480–510; see also id., "Prophecy," in *EDSS* 2 (2000) 694–700; id., "Prophecy and Prophets in the Dead Sea Scrolls: Looking Backwards and Forwards," in *Prophets, Prophecy, and Prophetic Texts in Second Temple Judaism* (ed. M. H. Floyd and R. D. Haak; LHBOTS 427; New York and London: T&T Clark, 2006) 151–65.

DOI 10.1515/9783110466546-034

tery" texts and language in the Dead Sea Scrolls,[3] and Alex Jassen has detected the persistence of prophetic activity in the polemics against "lying prophets" in the *Hodayot* (1QH^a XII, 5–17) and the "movers of the boundary" in the *Damascus Document* (CD V, 20–VI, 2), as well as in the traces of a prophetic conflict in the *Temple Scroll* (11Q19 LIV, 8–18); the *Apocryphon of Moses* (4Q375); and the *List of False Prophets* (4Q339).[4]

The texts discussed by Jassen present contemporary prophetic goings-on in an entirely negative light. This raises the question whether prophecy was recognized in any positive sense as a contemporary oracular practice by and within the Qumran movement and its historical environs, and whether this is in any way visible in the Dead Sea Scrolls. I would like to discuss this issue with regard to three texts: the *Vision and Interpretation* (4Q410), the *Mysteries* (1Q27), and the so-called *Self-Glorification Hymn* known to us in no less than four different literary contexts (1QH^a XXVI, 6–14; 4Q427 7 I, 7–13; 4Q471b; 4Q491c). I am not going to make strong claims about the correspondence of the wording of these texts with actually spoken words, since *ipsissima verba* are probably as impossible to identify in the Dead Sea Scrolls as they are in the Hebrew Bible or in Near Eastern texts. I would nevertheless like to discuss the origin of these passages in oral/aural or otherwise oracular[5] activity as a distinct possibility, first and foremost as examples of interpretative processes that may have begun in an oracular performance and subsequently ended up in written form in different kinds of literary contexts—a process so often detected from biblical and ancient Near Eastern sources.

Vision and Interpretation (4Q410)

> 1 [...] which [...] 2 [...] cross over all [...] 3 [...] which are lifted (?), not [...] 4 [...] for you, and curse upon cu[rs]e will cleave [to] you 5 [...] upon you, and you will not have there peace [...] 6 [...] what is good in truth and what is bad in [...] 7 [... a]ll days of eternity. *vacat* And now I with (the help) of the L[ord] in spirit (*brwḥ*) 8 [saw what will come upon t]hem, and it will not lie, the or[acle, and it will] not [be s]ilent 9 [the vision *vacat* Concern-

3 S. I. Thomas, *The "Mysteries" of Qumran: Mystery, Secrecy, and Esotericism in the Dead Sea Scrolls* (SBLEJL 25; Atlanta, Ga.: Society of Biblical Literature, 2009), 188–220.

4 A. P. Jassen, *Mediating the Divine: Prophecy and Revelation in the Dead Sea Scrolls and Second Temple Judaism* (STDJ 68; Leiden: Brill, 2007), 279–308.

5 Since I understand prophecy as one kind of divination, and prophetic activity as one type of oracular activity, the word "oracle" is used in this article of all "verbal communications to humans from the gods or other supernatural beings" (thus J. Bowden, "Oracles," in *OEAGR* 5 [Oxford: Oxford University Press, 2010] 106–8, esp. 106), including prophecies.

ing ...] is the oracle (*hmś'*) and concerning the house of [... is the] vision (*hḥzwn*), f[or] I have [s]een (*r'yty*) 10 [...] and h[e] defied the T[orah of God] 11 [......][6]

The first text, the *Vision and Interpretation* (4Q410), is poorly preserved and has, therefore, not attracted much scholarly attention. It can be grouped together with other visionary texts, some of which are clearly presented as visions of ancient figures such as the *Visions of Amram*$^{a-g}$ ar (4Q543–549), while others may contain reports of contemporary visions. What remains of the *Vision and Interpretation* is very fragmentary and does not yield much information on the circumstances, content, and interpretation of the vision in question.[7] Nevertheless, the largest fragment has luckily preserved a section of the text where, to all appearances, the report of the vision ends (lines 1–7) and is followed after a blank space by a commentary in which the visionary speaks in the first person singular (lines 7–11).

The vision, judging from the concluding lines, is a prophecy of doom: "curse upon cu[rs]e will cleave [to] you – – – you will not have there peace." In the commentary, the first-person speaker explicitly refers to something he (she?) has seen (*r'yty* line 9), refers to the spirit (*rwḥ* line 7) under the influence and authorization of which this has happened, and assures the reader that the oracle will not fail. The vision itself is called either *hmśh* or *hḥzwn* (line 9), and the definite article gives the impression that both words refer to nothing else but the vision described earlier in the same text.

In the words of Alex Jassen, "4QVision and Interpretation provides a tantalizing piece of what was likely a larger visionary text."[8] Moreover, the very fact that a first-person commentary has been added to the vision report strongly suggests that what we have here is not a vision of a legendary ancient seer but an actual oracle that has been received and transmitted by a contemporary person who pleads with his/her audience to heed to its message. That the vision and its interpretation have been preserved in written form indicates that it was indeed not neglected by the community, and that the seer in question had been ac-

6 Translation after the edition of A. Steudel in S. J. Pfann et al., *Qumran Cave 4 XXVI* (DJD 36; Oxford: Clarendon Press 2000), 316–19 + pl. XXI; cf. F. García Martínez and E. J. C. Tigchelaar, *The Dead Sea Scrolls Study Edition*, vol. 2 (Leiden: Brill, 1998), 840–41.

7 A. Lange, "Die Weisheitstexte aus Qumran: Eine Einleitung," in *The Wisdom Texts from Qumran and the Development of Sapiental Thought* (ed. C. Hempel, A. Lange, and H. Lichtenberger; BETL 159; Leuven: Peeters, 2002) 3–30, esp. 6: "Die noch erhaltenen, stark beschädigten vier Frag. von 4QVision and Interpretation lassen nur noch eine kurze Visionsbeschreibung mit anschließender Auslegung (7 ff.) erkennen."

8 Jassen, *Mediating the Divine*, 67 n. 5.

knowledged as a reliable source of divine revelation for the community. But which community should we imagine as the first audience of this text? The manuscript is too poorly preserved to answer this question, hence there is no certainty about its origin in the Qumran community, but a pre- or extra-Qumran origin is likewise possible.[9]

Since we do not know how, when, and by whom the vision was received, it is impossible to know whether it goes back to a public oral performance. Nevertheless, visionary activity as such is oracular activity in the sense of transmission of divine knowledge through an inspired individual. In this sense, if the *Vision and Interpretation* contains a report of an actual vision seen by the I-speaker, it can be read as a specimen of contemporary oracular activity, whether it took place in the Qumran community or elsewhere.

Mysteries (1Q27 I 1–10)

> 1 [...] all [...] 2 [...] mysteries of sin 3 [... all] their wisd[om]. And they do not know the mystery of existence (*rz nḥyh*), nor understand ancient matters. And they do not 4 know what is going to happen to them; and they will not save their souls from the mystery of existence. *vacat*
>
> 5 *And this will be for you the sign* (*wzh lkm h'wt*) that this is going to happen. When those born of sin are locked up, evil will disappear before justice as [da]rkness disappears before 6 light. As smoke vanishes, and n[o] longer exists, so will evil vanish for ever. And justice will be revealed like the sun which regulates 7 the world. And all those who curb the wonderful mysteries will no longer exist. And knowledge will pervade the world, and there will ne [ver] be folly there. 8 *This word will undoubtedly happen* (*nkwn hdbr lbw'*), *the prediction is truthful* (*w'mt hmś'*).
>
> And by this he will show you that it is irrevocable: Do not all 9 nations loathe sin? And yet, it is about by the hands of all them. Does not praise of truth come from the mouth of all nations? 10 And yet, is there perhaps one lip or one tongue which persists with it. – – –[10]

My second example of the possible afterlife of an original oracle is the opening section of *Mysteries* preserved in 1Q27 (partly also in 4Q300, fragment 3). The

9 This is also the case of the *Visions of Amram*; see J. C. Greenfield, M. E. Stone, and E. Eshel, *The Aramaic Levi Document: Edition, Translation, Commentary* (SVTP 19; Leiden: Brill, 2004), 31; H. Tervanotko, *Denying Her Voice: The Figure of Miriam in Ancient Jewish Literature* (JAJSup 23; Göttingen: Vandenhoeck & Ruprecht, 2016).

10 Edition: J. T. Milik in D. Barthélemy and J. T. Milik, *Qumran Cave I* (DJD 1; Oxford: Clarendon Press, 1955), 102–7; translation after García Martínez and Tigchelaar, *The Dead Sea Scrolls Study Edition*, 1:66–69; cf. the translation of Wise, Abegg, Cook, and Gordon in D. W. Parry and E. Tov, *Calendrical and Sapiential Texts* (DSSR 4; Leiden: Brill, 2004), 198–99.

first column of fragment 1 can be divided into three parts. The first part (lines 1–4) constitutes an introductory chapter mentioning an "out-group," that is, people who do not know the "mystery of existence" (the translation of the term *rz nḥyh*, prevalent in *Mysteries* as well as in *Instruction*, is not our concern here). The second part (lines 5–8) is a future-oriented section predicting how "knowledge will pervade the world and there will ne[ver] be folly there"; and the third part (lines 8–12) reads like a wisdom passage in which questions and comments alternate, and which "serves as a proof for the correctness of the prediction preceding it."[11]

This is a carefully designed textual unit, within which the middle section (lines 5–8) stands out as a description of what Matthew Goff calls the "key event" of *Mysteries:* the ultimate transformation of the world and the elimination of the wicked.[12] This is expressed in a quasi-poetic language; it has a certain rhythm and a clear structure based on dualistic dichotomies, but it does not follow the parallelistic pattern. As Torleif Elgvin has recently shown, it alludes to several biblical texts: line 7 rephrases Isa 11:9 and Hab 2:14; line 8 uses language from Deut 13:15 and 17:4; and the whole passage could be read as the implementation of the judgment on the diviners in Isa 47.[13] The content of the passage also bears a certain resemblance to the *Community Rule.*[14]

An important structural feature is that the prediction in the middle section is framed by divinatory terminology. It is introduced with a phrase known from the Hebrew Bible[15] as well as from Luke 2:12: "And this shall be a sign unto you" (*wzh lkm h'wt* line 5), the word *h'wt* explicitly referring to what follows and signaling the ominous nature of the text. At the end of the prediction we read: "This word will definitely happen, and the oracle is truthful" (*nkwn hdbr lbw' w 'mt hdbr* line 8). Such a clear structure, in my view, indicates that it is precisely the preceding passage, rather than an external source, that is referred to with *hdbr* and *hdbr*, again with definite articles like in the *Vision and Interpretation.*

---

11 D. Flusser, "The 'Book of Mysteries' and the High Holy Days Liturgy," in *Judaism of the Second Temple Period*, vol. 1: *Qumran and Apocalypticism* (ed. id. and A. Yadin; Grand Rapids, Mich.: Eerdmans, 2007) 119–39, esp. 125.

12 M. J. Goff, *Discerning Wisdom: The Sapiental Literature of the Dead Sea Scrolls* (VTSup 116; Leiden: Brill, 2007), 86.

13 T. Elgvin, "The Use of Scripture in 1Q/4QMysteries," in *New Perspectives on Old Texts: Proceedings of the Tenth International Symposium of the Orion Center for the Study of the Dead Sea Scrolls and Associated Literature, 9–11 January, 2005* (ed. E. G. Chazon, B. Halpern-Amaru, and R. A. Clements; STDJ 88; Leiden: Brill, 2010) 117–31.

14 See Flusser, "The 'Book of Mysteries'," 128.

15 Exod 3:12; 1 Sam 2:34; 2 Kgs 19:29; 20:9; Isa 37:30; 38:7 (*wzh lk h'wt*); 1 Sam 14:10 (*wzh lnw h'wt*).

These divinatory terms correspond to *h'wt* on line 5, presenting the section explicitly as an oracle.

It deserves attention that the word *mś'* in this meaning[16] is not at all common in the Dead Sea Scrolls. To my knowledge, derived from the DSSEL database, the word appears only here and in the *Vision and Interpretation*, plus in the *Vision of Samuel* (4Q160), a paraphrase of 1 Sam 3:14–17.[17] In 4Q160, *mś'* replaces the Masoretic *mr'h*, "vision," on line 4; on the next line, the text uses the expression *mr'h h'lwhym*, "vision of God," not to be found in the Masoretic Text.[18] Hence, every time the word *mś'* appears in the Dead Sea Scrolls, it is paralleled by another divinatory term: *ḥzwn* (4Q410), *dbr* (1Q27), or *mr'h* (4Q160). The word, thus, presents itself as the outcome of intuitive divination, translatable as "oracle" or "prophecy."

But what kind of divination is this? Elgvin characterizes the author as "a self-conscious writer (or writers) who deliberately plays with biblical phrases, reasoning them in new contexts,"[19] and this is without doubt a correct description of the author(s) of *Mysteries* in general, especially when combined with Goff's notion that *Mysteries* forms new genres by drawing from older sources and traditions in new ways.[20] Furthermore, Thomas has noted that the use of prophetic tropes and motifs is one of the important aspects of the use of mystery language in the Dead Sea Scrolls.[21] My question is whether they are used only with regard to existing authoritative texts or whether there was room for ongoing "sapiential revelation" (to use a term launched by Jassen[22]) that was not of purely scribal nature, but was believed to be received by a contemporary seer such as the one speaking in the *Vision and Interpretation*. In other words: Was the mystery sometimes transmitted *as* a prophetic oracle?

The framing of the oracle in 1Q27 1 I 5–8 strongly suggests that the oracle, designated by words *'wt* and *mś'* is a quotation, perhaps from a contemporary source. The lines read like a biblically inspired oracle recontextualized and em-

16 Other meanings include "burden" or "task"; see M. G. Abegg et al., *The Dead Sea Scrolls Concordance*, vol. 1: *The Non-Biblical Texts from Qumran* (Leiden: Brill, 2003) 489.

17 Cf. 4Q182 2 1, but the text of the fragment is too broken to suggest the meaning of *mś'* with any degree of probability: *m]ś' l'ḥryt hy[my]m* (perhaps translatable as: "...or]acle for the last d[ay]s").

18 See the edition in J. M. Allegro, *Qumrân Cave 4 I: 4Q158–4Q186* (DJDJ 5; Oxford: Clarendon Press, 1968), 9.

19 Elgvin, "The Use of Scripture," 129.

20 M. J. Goff, "Qumran Wisdom Literature and the Problem of Genre," *DSD* 17 (2010) 315–35, esp. 326.

21 See the texts quoted by Thomas, *The "Mysteries" of Qumran*, 207–20.

22 Jassen, *Mediating the Divine*, 241.

bedded in the opening section of *Mysteries* as definitive revelatory knowledge about "what is going to happen." Again, it remains impossible to determine whether or not the oracle can be seen as a written version of an oral performance. The biblical allusions as such do not invalidate this assumption, since even inspired speakers can be thoroughly versed in scriptures.

The present literary context of the oracle does not give any kind of a hint at any proclamation situation, and it is improbable that the Qumran community was its first audience.[23] However, *Mysteries* is clearly written for a group that was self-assured about its elect status, viewing itself as possessing revealed wisdom (*rz nḥyh*) not available to their opponents—probably diviners whose divinatory methods were disqualified.[24]

The Self-Glorification Hymn (4Q491c 1 5–11)

> 5 [... et]ernal; a mighty throne in the congregation of the gods above which none of the kings of the East shall sit, and their nobles no[t ...] silence (?) 6 [...] my glory is in{comparable} and besides me no-one is exalted, nor comes to me, for I reside in [...], in the heavens, and there is no 7 [...] ... I am counted among the gods (*'m 'lym*) and my dwelling is in the holy congregation (*b'dt qwdš*); [my] des[ire] is not according to the flesh, [but] all that is precious to me is in (the) glory (of) 8 [...] the holy [dwel]ling. [W]ho has been considered despicable on my account? And who is comparable to me in glory? Who, like the sailors, will come back and tell? 9 [...] Who bea[rs all] sorrows like me? And who [suffe]rs evil like me? There is no-one. I have been instructed, and there is no teaching comparable 10 [to my teaching ...] And who will attack me when [I] op[en my mouth]? And who can endure the flow of my lips? And who will confront me and retain comparison with my judgment? 11 [... friend of the king (*ydyd hmlk*), companion of the holy ones (*r' lqwdšym*) ... incomparable, f]or among the gods is [my] posi[tion, and] my glory is with the sons of

23 Cf. T. Elgvin, "Priestly Sages?: The Milieus of Origin of 4QMysteries and 4QInstruction," in *Sapiential Perspectives: Wisdom Literature in Light of the Dead Sea Scrolls, Proceedings of the Sixth International Symposium of the Orion Center, 20–22 May, 2001* (ed. J. J. Collins, G. E. Sterling, and R. A. Clements; STDJ 51; Leiden: Brill, 2004) 67–87, esp. 71; Goff, *Discerning Wisdom*, 99–100. Cf. also A. Lange ("In Diskussion mit dem Tempel: Zur Auseinandersetzung zwischen Kohelet und weisheitlichen Kreisen am Jerusalemer Tempel," in *Qohelet in the Context of Wisdom* [ed. A. Schoors; BETL 136; Leuven: Peeters, 1998] 113–59, esp. 157), who derives the origin of *Mysteries* from the temple of Jerusalem.

24 Cf. 4Q299 3 and 4Q300 1; see E. J. C. Tigchelaar, "Your Wisdom and Your Folly: The Case of 1–4QMysteries," in *Wisdom and Apocalypticism in the Dead Sea Scrolls and in the Biblical Tradition* (ed. F. García Martínez; BETL 168; Leuven: Peeters, 2003) 69–88.

> the king (*ky' 'ny' 'm 'lym m'mdy wkbwdy 'm bny hmlk*). To me (belongs) [pure] gold, and to me, the gold of Ophir 12 – – –[25]

The third text under scrutiny is the so-called *Self-Glorification Hymn*, thus designated because of the first-person speaker who presents himself as a member of the congregation of gods. More or less similar versions of this passage can be found in four different manuscripts, and its placement in contexts such different as the *Hodayot* and the *War Scroll* indicates a complicated editorial history, which has been the subject of intensive study for quite some time. It is commonly assumed that these manuscripts represent two recensions of the same work, Recension A (1QH^{a} XXVI, 4Q427, 4Q471b+4Q431) and Recension B (4Q491c), either so that the one derives from the other or that the two recensions share a common source.[26] However, Florentino García Martínez has argued that the relationship between 4Q491c with the other manuscripts is generic rather than genetic.[27] Both ways, the *Self-Glorification Hymn* pops out from its extant contexts in a way that makes it reasonable to assume that it originates independently of the rest of both textual corpora.[28]

Another widely discussed topic is the identity of the speaker of the *Self-Glorification Hymn*. Several figures have been suggested: the archangel Michael;[29] Enoch (cf. *1 En.* 45:3);[30] Menachem the Essene;[31] the Teacher of Righteousness or his disciple;[32] each member of the community for him- or herself;[33] an escha-

---

25 Translation after García Martínez and Tigchelaar, *The Dead Sea Scrolls Study Edition*, 2:980–81; cf. the translation of Wise, Abegg, Cook, and Gordon in D. W. Parry and E. Tov, *Texts Concerned with Religious Law* (DSSR 1; Leiden: Brill, 2004), 254–57.

26 See, e.g., J. Duhaime, *The War Texts: 1QM and Related Manuscripts* (CQS 6; New York: T&T Clark, 2004), 35–40; M. Wise, "מי כמוני באלים: A Study of 4Q491c, 4Q471b, 4Q427 7 and 1QH^{a} 25:35–26:10," *DSD* 7 (2000) 173–219; E. Eshel, "4Q471b: A Self-Glorification Hymn," *RevQ* 17 (1996) 175–203.

27 F. García Martínez, "Old Texts and Modern Mirages: The 'I' of Two Qumran Hymns," in *Qumranica Minora 1: Qumran Origins and Apocalypticism* (ed. E. J. C. Tigchelaar; STDJ 63; Leiden: Brill, 2007) 105–25.

28 Cf. J. J. Collins, *The Scepter and the Star: Messianism in Light of the Dead Sea Scrolls* (Grand Rapids, Mich.: Eerdmans, 1997), 147; similarly E. Schuller, "A Hymn from a Cave Four *Hodayot* Manuscript: 4Q427 7 i + ii," *JBL* 112 (1993) 605–28, esp. 628.

29 Thus the author of the *editio princeps:* M. Baillet, *Qumrân grotte 4 III (4Q482–4Q520)* (DJD 7; Oxford: Clarendon Press, 1982).

30 E. Miller, "The Self-Glorification Hymn Reexamined," *Hen* 31 (2009) 307–24.

31 I. Knohl, *The Messiah before Jesus* (Berkeley: University of California Press, 2000), 80–86.

32 J. Blenkinsopp, *Opening the Sealed Book: Interpretations of the Book of Isaiah in Late Antiquity* (Grand Rapids Mich.: Eerdmans, 2006), 272–82; id., "The Servant of the Lord, the Teacher of

tological priest;[34] or, as has been suggested by Joseph Angel, a priestly member of the Qumran community who shares his heavenly experience with the community in a liturgical context.[35] García Martínez identifies two different speakers: Michael in the context of the *War Scroll*, and the Teacher of Righteousness in the *Hodayot* manuscripts.[36] This is entirely possible if the text has been adopted from an external source and recontextualized in these new contexts.

I would like to add that, without the two masculine epithets in "the friend (*ydyd*) of the king and the companion (*r'*) of the Holy Ones," another good candidate would be Lady Wisdom with whom the speaker shares quite a few characteristics.[37] These include the authoritative teaching; the self-praise (cf. Prov 8:22–31);[38] the position among the divine council (cf. Sir 24);[39] and even the friendship of the king (cf. Wisdom of Solomon). This raises the question whether the original "I" speaker has been masculinized in the process of transmission.

With regard to the topic of this paper, the main question is whether there is any reason to think that the different versions of the *Self-Glorification Hymn* go back to oracular/prophetic activity. I think the suggestion of Paulo Augusto de

---

Righteousness, and the Exalted One of 4Q491c Source," in *Far from Minimal*, FS P. R. Davies (ed. D. Burns and J. W. Rogerson; LHBOTS 484; London and New York: T&T Clark, 2012) 41–51.

33 Wise, "מי כמוני באלים," 216–19.

34 Collins, *The Scepter and the Star*, 147; cf. E. Eshel, "The Identification of the 'Speaker' of the Self-Glorification Hymn," in *The Provo International Conference on the Dead Sea Scrolls: Technological Innovations, New Texts, and Reformulated Issues* (ed. D. W. Parry and E. C. Ulrich; STDJ 30; Leiden: Brill, 1999) 619–35.

35 J. Angel, "The Liturgical-Eschatological Priest of the *Self-Glorification Hymn*," *RevQ* 96 (2010) 585–605. Cf. K. Antin, "Sages in the Divine Council: Transmitting Divine Knowledge in Sirach 24, *1 Enoch* 14–16, Daniel 7, and in Two *Hodayot* Psalms (1QH^{a}12:6–13:6; 20:7–22:42," in *Transgressing Imaginary Boundaries: The Dead Sea Scrolls in the Context of Second Temple Judaism* (ed. M. S. Pajunen and H. Tervanotko; PFES 108; Helsinki: The Finnish Exegetical Society, 2015), 182–209, identifying the speaker in the context of *Hodayot* as the *maśkîl* to whom the *hodayah* is attributed.

36 García Martínez, "Old Texts and Modern Mirages," 336, 339.

37 Cf. J. J. Collins, *Apocalypticism in the Dead Sea Scrolls* (LDSS; London: Continuum, 1997), 147: "[T]here is no parallel for a speech such as we find in 4Q491 by a messianic figure. Neither is there any parallel for such claims by anyone else, with the possible exception of personified Wisdom."

38 Cf. Blenkinsopp, *Opening the Sealed Book*, 274.

39 Cf. M. Nissinen, "Wisdom as Mediatrix in Sirach 24: Ben Sira, Love Lyrics, and Prophecy," in *Of God(s), Trees, Kings, and Scholars*, FS S. Parpola (ed. M. Luukko, S. Svärd, and R. Mattila; StudOr 106; Helsinki: Finnish Oriental Society, 2009) 377–90 (= pp. 479–95 in this volume).

Souza Nogueira[40] and Joseph Angel that the text originates from a ritual context makes sense and hints towards a "process of deification or angelification that accompanies participation in the heavenly liturgy."[41] This experience may have resulted in a performance in which a member of the cultic community assumed a prophetic role and delivered an inspired speech powerful and influential enough to become reinterpreted and recontextualized by the community. The versions of the *Self-Glorification Hymn* testify to the use and significance of the Hymn within the Qumran community, but it is entirely possible that the text, just like the *Vision and Interpretation* and *Mysteries*, derives from pre-Qumranic roots.

The wording of the "original" oracle, the identity of the first speaker, and the context in which it was first uttered can no longer be reconstructed. Originally, the implied speaker, the "I" of the text, may not be identical to the actual speaker who may have uttered the original oracle as an intermediary (as a prophet, that is) of the (semi-)divine speaker. In the process of reinterpretation and recontextualization, the identity of the speaker has become dependent on the context in which the *Self-Glorification Hymn* has been embedded, and may indeed now, as García Martínez suggests, be interpreted as a different figure in different contexts, whoever the speaker has been in earlier versions and contexts of the oracle.

Conclusion

There are no more *ipsissima verba* of prophets in the Dead Sea Scrolls than there are in the Hebrew Bible, and, therefore, there is also no conclusive proof to the assumption that any of the passages discussed above—in fact, any passage in the Dead Sea Scrolls in general—goes back to an oral performance. Nevertheless, as Brooke and Jassen have argued, not only the accusations of false prophecy against some contemporaries but also several other features indicate that there was an ongoing need for prophetic practices and divination. The revelatory encounter with the divine and the transmission of divine knowledge took

40 P. A. de Souza Nogueira, "Ecstatic Worship in the Self-Glorification Hymn (4Q471b, 4Q427, 4Q491c): Implications for the Understanding of an Ancient Jewish and Early Christian Phenomenon," in *Wisdom and Apocalypticism in the Dead Sea Scrolls and in the Biblical Tradition* (ed. F. García Martínez; BETL 168; Leuven: Peeters, 2003) 385–93.
41 Thomas, *The "Mysteries" of Qumran*, 220.

place in "modified modes,"[42] whereby the function of intermediation was probably more important than the method.

The three texts discussed here may be interpreted as an indication of the presence of inspired speakers in the communities that produced these texts: the visionary of the *Vision and Interpretation*; the one who delivered the *mś'* concerning the fate of the false diviners; and the semidivine figure praising himself (originally, perhaps, herself) in the different versions of the *Self-Glorification Hymn*. The performances of these persons took place either in pre-Qumranic communities or in the Qumran community where they followed in the footsteps of the legendary Teacher of Righteousness. Such speakers were not called prophets—in the Dead Sea Scrolls, this designation was reserved in a positive meaning to the prophets of old only.[43] Nevertheless, there seem to have been persons (perhaps including the first-person speaker of the *Hodayot*)[44] who were acknowledged by the community to possess the *rz nḥyh* or some other form of revealed divine knowledge to be transmitted to the community. The scarcity of evidence suggests that such a status was difficult to achieve, and the anonymity indicates that the authority of the speakers was considered subordinate to the authority of the divine knowledge intermediated by them.

I hope to have been able to demonstrate how particularly relevant the interface between wisdom, apocalypticism, and prophecy is to the mapping of the modes of the transmission of revealed knowledge. This requires crossing some boundaries that may turn out to be imaginary altogether; in the words of Elisa Uusimäki and Hanne von Weissenberg, "The search for interconnections between wisdom and prophecy is still in its early stages, but the references in

---

42 Cf. Jassen, *Mediating the Divine*, 329.

43 Cf. M. Nissinen, "Transmitting Divine Mysteries: The Prophetic Role of Wisdom Teachers in the Dead Sea Scrolls," in *Scripture in Transition*, FS R. Sollamo (ed. A. Voitila and J. Jokiranta; JSJSup 126; Leiden: Brill, 2008) 513–33, esp. 521–25 (= pp. 631–49 in this volume). See also G. J. Brooke, "Was the Teacher of Righteousness Considered to Be a Prophet?" in *Prophecy after the Prophets: The Contribution of the Dead Sea Scrolls to the Understanding of Biblical and Extra-Biblical Prophecy* (ed. K. de Troyer and A. Lange; CBET 52; Leuven: Peeters, 2009) 77–97.

44 Thomas, *The "Mysteries" of Qumran*, 208: "According to several passages in the Hodayot, the speaker, like the prophets before him, makes reference to having participated in a heavenly gathering which has resulted his apprehension of the 'mysteries,' which in turn has prepared him to 'illumine the face of many'"; see also Antin, "Sages in the Divine Council."

the texts to predictions and visions call for a reassessment of the relationship of wisdom and prophecy at the turn of the common era."[45]

45 E. Uusimäki and H. von Weissenberg, "Viisaus ja ilmoitus Qumranin viisauskirjallisuudessa" [Wisdom and Revelation in the Wisdom Literature from Qumran], *Teologinen Aikakauskirja* 118 (2013) 235–46, esp. 244 (my translation of the Finnish original).

Pesharim as Divination: Qumran Exegesis, Omen Interpretation and Literary Prophecy*

This essay is written in favor of two arguments concerning a characteristic group of exegetical works among the Dead Sea scrolls, the so-called pesharim: First, that the idea of a pesher is historically and culturally related to divinatory practices in the ancient Near East, especially to the interpretation of omens; and, secondly, that the pesharim should be seen as yet another representative of scribal divination that became the preferred way of interpreting the divine will in Second Temple Judaism. I am not the first one to present these arguments, but I hope to be able to support them with some additional evidence, mainly from Mesopotamia.

It goes beyond my competence to discuss here specialized questions like what exactly is meant by the scholarly category called pesharim,[1] hence I simply quote two definitions, one mainly structural and another more comprehensive. According to Timothy Lim, the pesharim are "scriptural commentaries named after the technical Hebrew term *pesher* (pl. *pesharim)* which characteristically appears in formulae that introduce an exposition of a biblical verse (e.g., 'the interpretation' [Hebrew: *pesher*] of the matter is ...)."[2] This definition identifies the genre by the use of the Hebrew word *pešer,* the most conspicuous structural and functional identifier of the text type in question. It can be supplemented by a content-oriented definition formulated by Shani Berrin, according to whom a pesher is "a form of biblical interpretation peculiar to Qumran, in which biblical poetic/prophetic texts are applied to postbiblical historical/eschatological settings through various literary techniques in order to substantiate a theological conviction pertaining to divine reward and punishment."[3]

* I would like to thank Jonathan Ben-Dov for critical remarks and bibliographical advice, and Robert M. Whiting for improving my English.

1 See, e.g., M. P. Horgan, *Pesharim: Qumran Interpretations of Biblical Books* (CBQMS 8; Washington, D.C.: The Catholic Biblical Association of America, 1979), 229–59; G. J. Brooke, "Qumran Pesher: Toward a Redefinition of a Genre," *RevQ* 10 (1981) 483–503; T. H. Lim, *Pesharim* (Companion to the Qumran Scrolls 3; London: Continuum, 2003); S. L. Berrin, *The Pesher Nahum Scroll from Qumran: An Exegetical Study of 4Q169* (STDJ 53; Leiden: Brill, 2004), 9–18; ead., "Qumran Pesharim," in *Biblical Interpretation at Qumran* (ed. M. Henze; Studies in the Dead Sea Scrolls and Related Literature; Grand Rapids, Mich.: Eerdmans, 2005) 110–33.

2 *Lim, Pesharim,* 13.

3 Berrin, *The Pesher Nahum Scroll from Qumran,* 9–10; ead., "Qumran Pesharim," 110.

DOI 10.1515/9783110466546-035

Furthermore, it has been commonplace to distinguish between two types of pesharim, the continuous pesharim on one hand, consisting of a series of biblical passages and their expositions that follow the biblical texts sequentially; and the so-called thematic pesharim, a diverse group of texts organized according to different principles and using a variety of introductory formulae besides *pešer*. This division is not absolute, though,[4] and, even though the following deliberations are mostly written with the continuous pesharim in mind, they aim to be equally applicable to the thematic pesharim as well.

Broadly speaking, the pesharim can be classified as a representative of the type of texts, the purpose of which is the interpretation of preexisting authoritative sources for contemporary concerns of the given community. Since such literary activity is by no means restricted to Qumran, it is feasible to look for a cultural context, in which the peculiar characteristics of the pesharim could be best understood.

So far, the exegetical methods of the pesharim have mostly been investigated in the context of biblical or rabbinic literature as belonging to the exegetical continuum that begins with inner biblical interpretation and leads to Jewish and Christian exegesis as demonstrated by the Midrashim, the Targums and the New Testament. To a lesser extent, even sources from the surrounding cultures of ancient Palestine have been brought into the discussion. The significance of Mesopotamian dream interpretation for the study of the pesharim has been noted since the seminal study of A. Leo Oppenheim,[5] even though some Qumran scholars have pointed out a difference between the revelatory and exegetical nature of the pesharim and the magical function of the Mesopotamian dream interpretations.[6]

Otherwise, cuneiform literature has not been utilized very extensively in the study of the pesharim. Recently, Armin Lange has done some interesting comparison between the pesharim and related sources from Egypt and Greece.[7] This essay can be understood as a rejoinder to Lange's attempt at understanding

---

4 Cf. G. J. Brooke, "Thematic Commentaries on Prophetic Scriptures," in Henze (ed.), *Biblical Interpretation at Qumran* (2005) 134–57.

5 A. L. Oppenheim, *The Interpretation of Dreams in the Ancient Near East With a Translation of an Assyrian Dream-Book* (Transactions of the American Philosophical Society 46/3; Philadelphia, Pa.: American Philosophical Society, 1956), 217–25; cf, e.g., M. Fishbane, *Biblical Interpretation in Ancient Israel* (Oxford: Clarendon Press, 1985), 455.

6 Berrin, "Qumran Pesharim," 125; cf. Horgan, *Pesharim*, 231.

7 A. Lange, "Interpretation als Offenbarung: Zum Verhältnis von Schriftauslegung und Offenbarung," in *Wisdom and Apocalypticism in the Dead Sea Scrolls and in the Biblical Tradition* (ed. F. García Martínez; BETL 168; Leuven: Peeters, 2003) 17–33.

the pesharim within a broader context of literary culture in the ancient Eastern Mediterranean. I will supplement the evidence with some Mesopotamian sources that have not been discussed so far with respect to the pesharim. I will also discuss the significance of the pesharim for the question of the literarization of prophecy in Second Temple Judaism.

Akkadian *pašāru:* Releasing from Evil

The Hebrew word *pešer* is derived from the common Semitic root *pšr (<*pṯr)* "loosen," "dissolve."[8] Besides Hebrew, the root is attested in Aramaic, Akkadian and Arabic. It has been noted since Oppenheim that the cognate Akkadian verb, *pašāru,* corresponding to the Sumerian búr, firmly belongs to the language of Mesopotamian dream divination. This verb is used, for instance, in the *Assyrian Dream Book*; for example:

> If a man had a bad dream and is depressed, let him recount *(lipšur)* his dream to a reed sprout.[9]

The usual translation of *pašāru* as "recounting" implies an act of recitation of the dream to an object, in this case, to a reed sprout; however, there is more to the verb than verbal recitation. According to Oppenheim, it can be used "to render (a) the reporting of one's dream to another person, (b) the interpreting of an enigmatic dream by that person, and (c) the dispelling or removing of the evil consequences of such a dream by magic means."[10] This brings the verb *pašāru* into to the context of telling, interpreting and "undoing" dreams, corresponding to the therapeutic as well as interpretive aspects of the divinatory process. These aspects would also correspond to the double function of the *Assyrian Dream Book* as a compendium of dream omens on one hand and ritual instructions on the other.[11]

Annette Zgoll, in her comprehensive study on Mesopotamian dreams, has recently clarified the meaning of *pašāru,* demonstrating that it does not actually

8 For this root and words derived from it, see Horgan, *Pesharim,* 231–37.

9 *Assyrian Dream Book* 343:18 (Oppenheim, *Interpretation of Dreams,* 343); translation from *CAD* P 241.

10 Oppenheim, *Interpretation of Dreams,* 219; cf. J.-M. Husser, *Dreams and Dream Narratives in the Biblical World* (trans. J. M. Munro; The Biblical Seminar 63; Sheffield: Sheffield Academic Press, 1999), 29.

11 Cf. S. A. L. Butler, *Mesopotamian Conceptions of Dreams and Dream Rituals* (AOAT 258; Münster: Ugarit-Verlag, 1998), 99–100.

refer to recounting, reciting or any other verbal act, but always has the general meaning "to release, resolve," whereas other verbs, like *qabû* and *manû*, are used for reciting or recounting dreams.[12] In the case quoted above, according to Zgoll, the reed sprout is the vehicle for the act of releasing; this becomes probable indeed when we read the next line: "Let him bum (the reed sprout) in fire. He shall blow (on it) with his mouth, and he is released *(pašir)*,"[13] that is, from his dream. The verb *pašāru* is used when Gilgameš gives an account of his dream to his mother (Gilg i 245 etc.), but even here there is another verb, *zakāru*, that refers to the actual speaking.[14] Hence, *pašāru* refers to a process of releasing a person form a dream rather than to its interpretation.

At first sight, Zgoll's redefinition of the meaning of *pašāru* might seem like an end to the relevance of the Mesopotamian dreams to the study of the Qumran pesharim. This, however, is not the case if we consider the purpose of a pesher against the background of Mesopotamian dream practice—a practice still attested even in the Hellenistic period,[15] and thus without a significant chronological gap between the sources. With respect to the pesharim as eschatological texts preparing their audience for the coming events and reinforcing their identity as those who will endure, they clearly have a therapeutic and apotropaic function. By means of interpretation, the harsh and threatening words of the prophetic base-texts are directed towards the enemies (the Wicked Priest, the Kittim, etc.), hence the community itself—the "in-group"—is released from the evil consequences of the forthcoming eschatological tumult by shifting them on to the "out-group."[16] The difference from Mesopotamian dream divination is that the

---

12 A. Zgoll, *Traum und Welterleben im antiken Mesopotamien: Traumtheorie und Traumpraxis im 3.–1. Jahrtausend v. Chr. als Horizont einer Kulturgeschichte des Träumens* (AOAT 333; Münster: Ugarit-Verlag, 2006), 383–96. The German verb "lösen" is difficult to translate into English properly in this context, because it not only refers to releasing but also to clarifying and unraveling, for example, a mystery or a riddle.

13 *Assyrian Dream Book* 343:19; cf. Zgoll, *Traum und Welterleben*, 392–93.

14 Gilg i 245: *itbēma Gilgameš šunatam ipaššar izzakkaram ana ummīšu;* cf. the translations of Zgoll, *Traum und Welterleben*, 395: "Es erhob sich Gilgameš, um den Traum zu lösen, indem er zu seiner Mutter sprach"; and Oppenheim, *Interpretation of Dreams*, 247: "Gilgamesh arose to report his dreams, he said to his mother: ..."

15 Cf. the dream ritual from the Seleucid period, *SpTU* 2 21; see Butler, *Mesopotamian Conceptions of Dreams and Dream Rituals*, 197 (discussion), 401–5 (text and translation).

16 For the social-identity approach involving the concepts of "in-group" and "outgroup," see J. Jokiranta, "Qumran: The Prototypical Teacher in the Qumran Pesharim: A Social Identity Approach," in *Ancient Israel: The Old Testament in its Social Context* (ed. P. F. Esler; Minneapolis, Minn.: Fortress Press, 2006) 254–63.

act of releasing is an eschatological event yet to happen rather than a ritual that delivers the people from the evil at once.

Pišru—pěšar—pešer

While the semantic field of the verb *pašāru* is very broad and only a small corner of it has to do with interpretative activity,[17] the noun derived from the verb, *pišru,* quite consistently refers to the unfolding of the meaning of omens,[18] although in a way different from the use of *pašāru* in the context of dream interpretation. The word *pišru* is routinely used by Neo-Assyrian scholars who report to the king their astronomical observations and give the explanation of their meaning, using *pišru* as a technical term for quoting omen literature:[19]

> [The moon] was surrounded by a halo, Cancer stood in it. This is its interpretation *(anniu piširšu):* [If the moon] is surrounded by a halo and Cancer stands in it: The king of Akkad will extend the life.[20]

> When Mars, furthermore, retrogrades from the Head of Leo and touches Cancer and Gemini, its interpretation is this *(anniu piširšu):* End of the reign of the king of the Westland.[21]

> In the night of the 10th of Tammuz (IV), the constellation Scorpius approached the moon. Its interpretation is as follows *(akī annî piširšu):* If at the appearance of the moon Scorpius stands by its right horn: in th[at year] locusts will rise and consume the harvest, variant: [The king of] Elam will be killed in that year ...?[22]

As these examples reveal, *pišru* means a verbatim quotation of passages from omen collections, presented as a solution and prognosis for the contemporary situation. Since this pertains to a divinatory activity involving answers to inquiries, it is a procedure different from reporting and explaining (unsolicited) symbolic dreams for therapeutic purposes. This is why Oppenheim would not trans-

---

17 See *CAD* P 241–42 and cf. the criticism of the translations by Zgoll, *Traum und Welterleben,* 396.

18 See *CAD* P 429–30.

19 Cf. Fishbane, *Biblical Interpretation in Ancient Israel,* 455.

20 SAA 8 178:1–4; see H. Hunger, *Astrological Reports to Assyrian Kings* (SAA 8; Helsinki: Helsinki University Press, 1992), 103–4.

21 SAA 10 8 r. 3–7; see S. Parpola, *Letters from Assyrian and Babylonian Scholars* (SAA 10; Helsinki: Helsinki University Press, 1993), 9.

22 SAA 10 364 r. 9–13; see Parpola, *Letters from Assyrian and Babylonian Scholars,* 301.

late it with "interpretation" or "explanation" at all.[23] This difference does not, however, set the idea *of pišru* categorically apart from the use of *pašāru* in dream contexts. In both cases we have to do with the outcome of a divinatory process, the purpose of which is to "solve" or "release" (*pašāru*) and, consequently, understand the meaning of an ominous situation and, eventually, provide relief from the potential threat it constitutes.

Oppenheim quotes "for completeness' sake rather than because the passage is revealing in any way" a passage from a late Sumero-Akkadian vocabulary,[24] which equates the Sumerian me.gal.zu, "to know/understand the nature of something," with the Akkadian phrases *šutta pašāru,* "to release (a person from) a dream," and *qību šakānu,* which is a technical term for giving a prognosis, for example, by a diviner or a physician.[25] It is most fortunate that Oppenheim actually quotes this text, even though his only comment to it is: "implications unknown."[26] This vocabulary entry explicitly associates both kinds of divinatory acts, the dream practice and the prognostication based on an omen, with the understanding of the meaning of a thing. This is what divination is all about: unfolding, proclaiming and explaining meanings of signs that disclose hidden things to those of humankind who deserve this understanding.

The functional similarity of *piširšu* with *pišrô,* the introductory formula in the Qumran pesharim, is unmistakable. The Assyrian evidence points to the use of a *pišru* as a part of the technical vocabulary of scholarly divination that was the privilege of those few who had been initiated into the scribal lore and who possessed the means of revealing the secrets of the gods to the king and the people. This observation can be generalized, asking whether the Dead Sea Scrolls, and the pesharim in particular, demonstrate any affinity with the important socio-religious phenomenon of divination in the ancient Near East.

---

23 Oppenheim, *Interpretation of Dreams,* 220: "The word *pišru* cannot mean here 'interpretation' or 'explanation' on account of the characteristic situation underlying all these letters: the king sends an inquiry concerning the mantic implications of a specific ominous happening, and the scholar provides him with a quotation which he has excerpted from a collection of omina dealing with the pertinent subject matter. This procedure can in no way be considered an 'interpretation,' nor *can pišru* be translated as such." Cf I. Rabinowitz, *"Pēsher/pittārōn:* Its Biblical Meaning and Its Significance in the Qumran Literature," *RevQ* 8 (1973) 219–32.
24 *CT* 18 29–30 iv 13–14; see Oppenheim, *Interpretation of Dreams,* 220.
25 See *CAD* Q 249, where, among others, the following examples are given: "[When] the diviner is about to perform a divination and to make a prognostication *(qība šakāni)* for the king" (*BBR* 11 r. 2); "Without you (scil. Šamaš) the dream interpreter *(šāʾilu)* cannot give a prognostication *(qība lā išakkan)* to the king" (*AMT* 71,1:40).
26 Oppenheim, *Interpretation of Dreams,* 220.

The ancient Near Eastern cultures shared largely similar traditions of divinatory practices and methods as well as the theology of divination and the idea of the role of the diviner.[27] Jewish religion certainly limited the acceptable forms of divination, but even the Jews did not live in splendid isolation in this respect. The Hebrew word *pešer* in the Dead Sea Scrolls may not be a direct translation from the Akkadian *pišru*, but the functional equivalence of the vocabulary based on the root *pšr* is certainly more than a mere linguistic coincidence.[28] In the book of Daniel, the Aramaic equivalent, *pěšar*, features prominently as a technical term for the interpretation of dreams (Dan 2:4–7:11; 4:3, 15, 16; 5:12, 15, 16, 26; 7:16). This term is closely related to the word *rāz*, a word of Persian etymology denoting a divine mystery to be revealed to people by means of learned interpretation (Dan 2:18, 19, 27–30, 47; 4:6).[29] This was precisely the task of the scholars in Mesopotamia in general, and the role of Daniel and his friends in particular; they are found "ten times better than all the magicians and exorcists *(kol ha-ḥarṭummîm hā-aššāpîm)*" in the whole kingdom (Dan 1:20). With regard to the ideological strategy of the Book of Daniel, it is clear that "[t]here is no positive theology of pagan or secular learning here, but rather the assurance that it can be triumphed over."[30] But this triumph does not deprive Daniel and his friends of their learned status.

That Jewish scholarship did not remain unaffected by the Mesopotamian wisdom is, hence, presupposed by the book of Daniel itself: Daniel and his friends are presented as Jews educated by the Babylonians, and we may suppose that such narrative figures had a sufficient degree of credibility in the eyes of the readership. That the Babylonian intellectual heritage indeed survived in Babylonian Jewish circles, the Qumran community included, is also documented by the Babylonian Talmud,[31] Midrashic techniques of biblical interpretation,[32] as

---

27 For an overview of ancient Near Eastern divination, see, e.g., F. H. Cryer, *Divination in Ancient Israel and its Near Eastern Environment: A Socio-Historical Investigation* (JSOTS 142; Sheffield: Sheffield Academic Press, 1994); A. Jeffers, *Magic and Divination in Ancient Palestine and Syria* (SHCANE 7; Leiden: Brill, 1996).

28 Cf. the probable origin of Hebrew *hălākâ* in Akkadian *alaktu* "(oracular) decision"; see T. Abusch, "*Alaktu* and *halakhah:* Oracular Decision, Divine Revelation," *HTR* 80 (1987) 15–42.

29 For the use of *pěšar* and *rāz* in the Book of Daniel and in the Dead Sea Scrolls, see G. K. Beale, *The Use of Daniel in Jewish Apocalyptic Literature and in the Revelation of St. John* (Lanham, Md.: University Press of America, 1984), 12–19.

30 J. E. Goldingay, *Daniel* (WBC 30; Waco, Tx.: Word Books, 1989), 27.

31 See M. J. Geller, "The Survival of Babylonian Wissenschaft in Later Tradition," in *The Heirs of Assyria: Proceedings of the Opening Symposium of the Assyrian and Babylonian Intellectual Heritage Project Held in Tvärminne, Finland, October 8–11, 1998* (Melammu Symposia 1; Helsinki, The Neo-Assyrian Text Corpus Project, 2000), 1–6.

well as by astronomical pseudepigrapha like the *Astronomical Book of Enoch* (4Q208–209)[33] or *The Treatise of Shem,*[34] not to forget the calendrical scrolls from Qumran (4Q320, 4Q321 etc.)[35] and a text like *4QZodiology and Brontology* (4Q318), which demonstrably has Mesopotamian antecedents.[36] The Jews seem to have been well aware of the "pagan" origin and religious implications of astrology in particular,[37] but this, obviously, did not prevent them from learning and practicing such wisdom.

Pesharim and Divination: Omens and Exegesis

As a literary genre, the pesharim do not have exact parallels in the ancient Near Eastern textual sources and seem to be typical of the Qumran community. Nevertheless, when it comes to their structure and function as interpretive literature, they can be compared with several kinds of Near Eastern texts. Armin Lange has highlighted the late Egyptian predictive texts such as the *Demotic Chronicle*, the *Potter's Oracle* and the *Lamb of Bocchoris*, as well as the Greek interpretation of oracles, as relevant representatives of a similar divinatory hermeneutics without reckoning with a literary dependence of the pesharim on these sources.[38] It is also worth the trouble to take a look at some Mesopotamian divinatory texts which, as I believe, help us to locate the pesharim in a wider cul-

32 S. J. Lieberman, "A Mesopotamian Background for the So-Called *Aggadic* 'Measures' of Biblical Hermeneutics?," *HUCA* 58 (1987) 157–225 discusses at length the techniques known as *notariqon* and *gemaṭriah*.

33 See, e.g., J. C. VanderKam, *Enoch and the Growth of an Apocalyptic Tradition* (CBQMS 16; Washington, D.C: Catholic Biblical Association, 1984), 76–109.

34 J. H. Charlesworth, *The Old Testament Pseudepigrapha*, vol. 1: *Apocalyptic Literature and Testaments* (New York: Doubleday, 1983), 473–86; cf. K. Atkinson, "Astrology and History in the Treatise of Shem: Two Astrological Pseudepigrapha and their Relevance for Understanding the Astrological Dead Sea Scrolls," *QC* 14 (2006) 37–55.

35 See, e.g., J. Ben-Dov and W. Horowitz, "The Babylonian Lunar Three in Calendrical Scrolls from Qumran," *ZA* 95 (2005) 104–20.

36 See J. C. Greenfield and M. Sokoloff, "4QZodiology and Brontology ar," *DJD* 36 (2000) 259–74. The predictive part of the text draws, probably indirectly, from the Babylonian astrological series *Enūma Anu Enlil*, tablet 44; see D. Pingree ibid., 271–72.

37 Cf. M. Albani, "Horoscopes in the Qumran Scrolls," in *The Dead Sea Scrolls after Fifty Years: A Comprehensive Assessment*, vol. 2 (ed. P. W. Flint and J. C. VanderKam; Leiden: Brill, 1999) 279–330, esp. 323: "What is certain is that astrology was a subject of interest to them, but it is probable that this interest in the 'wisdom of the Chaldeans' had a critical slant."

38 Lange, "Interpretation als Offenbarung."

tural context and understand their underlying idea of being conversant with divine knowledge by means of interpretation.

It has been noted previously that the structure of the pesharim resembles the structure of the Near Eastern omens.[39] The structure of the continuous pesharim includes first the quotation of the base-text and then the pesher interpretation introduced by the formula *pišrô*.[40] This is reminiscent of the account of a dream and its interpretation, not only in Mesopotamian but also in biblical (e.g., Dan 2:31–45) dream texts. A classical omen, on the other hand, consist of the actual omen (protasis) and its interpretation (apodosis), as in the city omen:

> If there are many crazy men in the city, the city is well;[41]

or in the dream omen:

> If a man (in his dream) eats human meat, he will have great riches;[42]

or in the birth omen:

> If an anomaly's right ear is cropped and inflated with wind: female prophets will seize the land;[43]

or in the astrological omen:

> If the moon and the sun are in opposition: the king of the land will widen his understanding;[44]

---

39 Cf, e.g., Lange, "Interpretation als Offenbarung," 19, 22–30.

40 For the form of the continuous pesharim, see Berrin, "Qumran Pesharim," 111–13.

41 *Šumma ālu* i 87; see, S. M. Freedman, *If a City Is Set on a Height: The Akkadian Omen Series* Šumma ālu ina melê šakin, vol. 1: *Tablets 1–21* (Occasional Publications of the Samuel Noah Kramer Fund 17; Philadelphia, Pa.: University of Pennsylvania Museum, 1998), 32.

42 *Assyrian Dream Book* 315 (K. 6663+8300): 14; see Oppenheim, *Interpretation of Dreams*, 271, 315.

43 *Šumma izbu* xi 7; see E. Leichty, *The Omen Series* Šumma izbu (TCS 4; Locust Valley, N.Y.: Augustin, 1970), 131.

44 SAA 8 186:1–2; see Hunger, *Astrological Reports to Assyrian Kings*, 108.

or in an omen text from Qumran:

> If it in Gemini thunders, (there will be) fear and distress from the foreigners and [...].[45]

In view of their binary structure, the pesharim could be read the same way as the omen collections, consisting of omens (the base-text) and their interpretations (the pesharim). The correspondence between the two text types is not quite exact, though. The omens usually describe an observable circumstance in the world of the interpreter, i. e., the actual omen (protasis), explaining its meaning (apodosis). In the pesharim, on the other hand, the base-text itself seems to serve as the omen to be interpreted. The pesharim are different from the Mesopotamian omen texts in that the interpretation presents a systematic exposition of the base-text.[46] This difference notwithstanding, the binary structure, the use of canonical literature and the role of the interpreter in the pesharim reflect similar dynamics of the divinatory process familiar to us especially from the well-known evidence of the practice of astrology and extispicy.

The idea of omen-based divination is to acquire divine information on contemporary circumstances by systematic observation of god-given signs of different kind, which are interpreted with the help of authoritative literature for the community that needs this knowledge. The role of the diviner—astrologer, haruspex, exorcist, etc.—was that of a mediator of divine knowledge, hence the diviner had to be qualified to reveal secrets of the heavenly world. In practical terms this meant not only education in the scribal lore and profound knowledge of the "proof-texts"— i. e., canonical omen collections—but also recognition by the community which, in the case of Assyria, was demonstrated by membership in the trusted circle of the ruling king. In Neo-Assyrian society, the scholars assumed a key role in the formation and propagation of the Assyrian imperial identity and ideology.[47]

---

45 4Q318 (*4QZodiology and Brontology*) VIII, 9; see Greenfield and Sokoloff, "4QZodiology and Brontology ar," 264.

46 It has recently been pointed out that, rather than consisting of atomistic, disconnected commentaries on individual biblical passages, the pesharim pay attention to the base-text as a whole; see Berrin, *Pesher Nahum Scroll*, 12–18; J. Jokiranta, *Social Identity and Sectarianism in the Qumran Movement* (STDJ 105; Leiden: Brill, 2012. Cf. also G. J. Brooke, "The Pesharim and the Origins of the Dead Sea Scrolls," in *Methods of Investigation of the Dead Sea Scrolls and the Khirbet Qumran Site: Present Realities and Future Prospects* (ed. M. O. Wise et al.; Annals of the New York Academy of Sciences 722; New York: New York Academy of Sciences, 1994) 339–52.

47 Cf. Parpola, *Letters from Assyrian and Babylonian Scholars*, xxiv–xxvii.

This can well be compared with the idea and practice of the pesharim, which are all about acquiring divine knowledge on the eschatological events that the "final generation" was anticipating. The authoritative base-text gives the means and the language of the interpretation, but it also serves itself as the sign to be interpreted. The role of the qualified interpreter, who in many pesharim is called the Teacher of Righteousness (sometimes also the Interpreter of Knowledge, *mēlîṣ daʿat,* 4QpPs[a] I, 27), is functionally similar to that of the Mesopotamian diviner. The Teacher of Righteousness appears as a prototypical character representing the Qumran community as the one to whom the divine mysteries had been revealed and whose interpretations, therefore, were equated with divine knowledge. In the words of Jutta Jokiranta, he serves the group identity of the Qumran community by representing the "in-group" as opposed to the "out-groups," a division omnipresent in the pesharim.[48]

The practice of pesharim—and also of allegorical, typological, and other kinds of scriptural interpretation—implies the idea that the base-text means something other than what it says. The outer appearance of the text (like that of an omen) is obvious to anyone, but its actual meaning is not evident before it is properly interpreted. The meaning can be discerned with the help of certain rules, rituals and techniques available to those few who have learned them, but it is ultimately a matter of divine revelation. This corresponds to the logic of the omen interpretation: an omen—whether a dream, an astrological constellation, the appearance of a sheep liver or a text—is something, the actual meaning of which is decided in heaven and is revealed only to those that are worthy of the revelation.

If the theory of the base-text as a kind of omen interpreted by its pesher is correct, it might lend some support for Shani Berrin's idea of the textual multivalence at Qumran, in other words, that the pesher application would have superseded, but not invalidated, the meaning the original prophet was supposed to transmit to his own community in the past.[49] The very existence of the canonical omen literature relects te idea that an omen was not valid at one historical moment only, but was to be interpreted in any given situation by those who were considered capable of revealing the divine will to their communities. An interpretation once given could be revoked and replaced by a new one:

48 Jokiranta, "The Prototypical Teacher in the Qumran Pesharim," 263 (cf. ead., *Social Identity and Sectarianism in the Qumran Movement,*175–83).

49 Berrin, *Pesher Nahum Scroll,* 12–18

> Its interpretation (*pišru)* will remain the same ... But the interpretation ... which I previously sent to the king, my lord, is no longer valid.[50]

The Assyrian scholars did not interpret their signs with any kind of eschatology in mind. Nevertheless, in a similar vein, the interpretations of the pesharim can be understood as an indispensable update (if not necessarily a replacement) of the information given to the prophet of the past. For the final generation, the Teacher of Righteousness, the prototypical teacher of the community, is the one to whom the mysteries of the prophets have been revealed, hence it is his interpretation that matters for this generation; his position vis-a-vis the earlier prophets could be compared with the relation of the prophet Muhammad to his predecessors Moses and Jesus in Islamic theology.

In addition to the omen literature and practice, two texts deserve to be mentioned here: the *Uruk Prophecy* and the *Dynastic Prophecy.* These are Hellenistic texts that, in spite of their conventional designations, are not actually prophecies but literary predictive texts, referring to past circumstances in the form of a prediction (*vaticinium ex eventu*).[51] Without being omens in a formal sense, these texts can be understood against the background of the omen institution[52] as learned explanations of past events for the purpose of explaining the present. These texts are structured as sequences of historical periods ruled by kings whose rule is described in good or bad terms:

> After him a king will arise, but he as well will not provide justice in the land, he will not give the right decisions for the land. He will subdue the world, and all the world will tremble at the mention of his name.[53]

---

50 SAA 10 363 r. 11–17; see Parpola, *Letters from Assyrian and Babylonian Scholars,* 300.

51 For these texts and their classification as "literary predictive texts," see M. deJong Ellis, "Observations on Mesopotamian Oracles and Prophetic Texts: Literary and Historiographie Considerations," *JCS* 41 (1989) 127–86; cf. M. Nissinen, "Neither Prophecies nor Apocalypses: The Akkadian Literary Predictive Texts," in *Knowing the End from the Beginning: The Prophetic, the Apocalyptic and their Relationships* (ed. L. L. Grabbe and R. D. Haak; JSPSup 46; London: T & T Clark, 2003) 134–48 (= pp. 87–99 in this volume); M. Neujahr, *Predicting the Past in the Ancient Near East: Mantic Historiography in Ancient Mesopotamia, Judah, and the Mediterranean World* (Brown Judaic Studies 354; Providence, R. I.: Brown University, 2012).

52 Cf. deJong Ellis, "Observations on Mesopotamian Oracles and Prophetic Texts," 159.

53 *Uruk Prophecy* r. 9–10; see H. Hunger and S. A. Kaufman, "A New Akkadian Prophecy Text," *JAOS* 95 (1975) 371–75, esp. 372.

Compare this with, e.g., 1QpHab III, 4–6:

> Its interpretation concerns the Kittim, the fear and dread of whom are on all the peoples; all their thoughts are premeditated to do evil, and with cunning and treachery they behave towards all the nations.[54]

The descriptions and the critique of the "arising" kings can be compared with the references of the pesharim to historical circumstances[55] and to some extent also with the actions of the notorious figures on the Qumran eschatological scene known by several nicknames or "sobriquets" like the Wicked Priest, the Man of the Lie, or the Seekers-After-Smooth-Things.[56] There are enough differences between the pesharim and the literary predictive texts to exclude the possibility of any dependence between them: the literary predictive texts have a different structure, they are neither commentaries of preexisting texts, nor do they demonstrate any eschatological concern. What unites the texts is the interpretation of current circumstances by post-event prediction, a hermeneutical tool that enjoyed growing popularity in the (pre)apocalyptic circles of the Hellenistic world.

Pesharim and Prophecy: From Oral/Written to Literary Prophecy

The ancient Near Eastern prophetic sources can also be seen as the result of divinatory practices, albeit of a different kind. The interpretative element does not feature very prominently in the prophetic texts available to us, even though a few examples can be mentioned. In the letters of Mari, we can trace the proverbial saying "beneath straw water runs":

> Now, a prophetess *(qammatum)* of Dagan of Terqa came and spoke to me. She said: "The peacemaking of the man of Eš[nunna] is false: beneath straw water runs! I will gather him

---

54 Translation from F. García Martínez and E. J. C. Tigchelaar, *The Dead Sea Scrolls: Study Edition*, vol. 1 (Leiden: Brill, 1998), 13.

55 For history in the pesharim, see G. J. Brooke, "The Kittim in the Qumran Pesharim," *Images of Empire* (ed. Loveday Alexander; JSOTS 122; Sheffield: Sheffield Academic Press, 1991) 135–59; Lim, *Pesharim*, 64–80.

56 For these, see H. Bengtsson, "What's in a Name? A Study of Sobriquets in the Pesharim" (PhD diss., Uppsala University, 2000).

into the net I knot. I will destroy his city and I will ruin his wealth, which comes from time immemorial."[57]

In addition to this letter to Zimri-Lim, King of Mari, there are two further occurrences of the saying probably referring to one and the same prophetic appearance.[58] The interpretation of this saying, which is claimed to have been recited by a prophetess, is not repeated but in any case is similar in all three cases (King Zimri-Lim should not conclude a treaty with the king of Ešnunna).[59] This probably implies that the interpretation was given by the prophetess herself; hence we might be dealing with ominous words, the meaning of which is disclosed by the divinely inspired prophet. On the other hand, one can ask whether a saying like "beneath straw water runs" is suggestive enough to be understood by its own force.

In an Assyrian prophetic oracle, a more obvious case can be found:

ḫallalatti enguratti! You ask: "What means *ḫallalatti enguratti?*" *ḫallalatti* I will enter Egypt, *enguratti* I will go out![60]

This is without doubt a quotation of ominous words together with their interpretation which here forms part of the actual prophetic oracle. The words *ḫallalatti enguratti* are virtually impossible to translate[61] and seem to be intentionally obscure: why else would the Assyrian king have had to ask what they mean? Even the prophetess does not translate the words but reveals their true meaning, prob-

---

57 ARM 26 197:6–19; see J.-M. Durand, *Archives epistolaires de Mari* 1/1 (ARM 26/1. Paris: Editions Recherche sur les Civilisations, 1988), 424; translation from M. Nissinen, with Contributions by C.-L. Seow, R. K. Ritner, and H. C. Melchert, *Prophets and Prophecy in the Ancient Near East* (2nd edition; SBLWAW 41; Atlanta, Ga.: Society of Biblical Literature, 2019), no. 7.

58 ARM 26 199:41–50 and ARM 26 202:7–13; see Durand, *Archives epistolaires de Mari 1/1*, 426–27, 431; Nissinen, *Prophets and Prophecy in the Ancient Near East*, nos. 9 and 12.

59 Cf. J. M. Sasson, "Water beneath Straw: Adventures of a Prophetic Phrase in the Mari Archives," in *Solving Riddles and Untying Knots*, FS J. C. Greenfield (ed. Z. Zevit, S. Gitin and M. Sokoloff; Winona Lake, Ind.: Eisenbrauns, 1995) 599–608; K. van der Toorn, "From the Oral to the Written: The Case of Old Babylonian Prophecy," in *Writings and Speech in Israelite and Ancient Near Eastern Prophecy* (ed. E. Ben Zvi and M. H. Floyd; SBLSymS 10; Atlanta, Ga.: Society of Biblical Literature, 2000) 219–34, esp. 230–32.

60 SAA 9 7 r. 3–5; see S. Parpola, *Assyrian Prophecies* (SAA 9; Helsinki: Helsinki University Press, 1997), 39; translation from Nissinen, *Prophets and Prophecy in the Ancient Near East*, no. 92.

61 The word *ḫallalatti* may be derived from *ḫallulāja* "centipede," but no certain meaning can be established for *enguratti;* see Parpola, *Assyrian Prophecies*, ad loc.

ably reminding the addressee, Assurbanipal, of the conquest of Egypt by his father, Esarhaddon, in the year 671 BCE.

The going-and-coming topos is used in another Assyrian prophetic text:

> Thus says [the God]: "I have go[ne, I ha]ve come!" Five, six times he s[ai]d this. Then he said: "I have come from the [m]ace. The snake in it I have hauled and cut in pieces." And: "I have crushed the mace." And: "I will crush Elam! Its army shall be levelled to the ground." And: "This is how I will finish off Elam."[62]

This rather curious text, which has no formal parallel anywhere, seems first to give an ominous explanation for the "going and coming" of the god, and then to explain the cryptic words about the mace and the snake with their actual meaning concerning Assurbanipal's war against the Elamites, probably in the year 653 BCE.

These few interpretations of ominous words within prophetic oracles are rather exceptional, and I fail to see any remarkable affinity between them and the pesharim. Ancient Near Eastern prophetic oracles do not usually interpret themselves; this is not even necessary, since they are not omens to be interpreted but messages to be heard and understood, therefore being understandable as such. They may be interpreted by others, however, as is the case of many letters from Mari and Assyria in which the letter writers make suggestions to the king on the basis of prophecies.[63] This is a further step in the prophetic process of communication which, when it goes further, also may involve literary interpretations of written prophecies.[64] This is what, more than anywhere else, happened in the Second Temple community of Yehud, as attested by the emergence of the prophetic books of the Hebrew Bible.[65]

---

62 SAA 9 8; see Parpola, *Assyrian Prophecies*, 40; translation from Nissinen, *Prophets and Prophecy in the Ancient Near East*, no. 93.

63 Cf, e.g., J. M. Sasson, "The Posting of Letters with Divine Messages," in *Florilegium Marianum 2*, FS M. Birot (Mémoires de NABU 3; Paris: SEPOA, 1994) 299–316; Van der Toorn, "From the Oral to the Written," 228–33; M. Nissinen, *References to Prophecy in Neo-Assyrian Sources* (SAAS 7; Helsinki: The Neo-Assyrian Text Corpus Project, 1998), 68–105.

64 Cf. A. Lange, "Literary Prophecy and Oracle Collection: A Comparison between Judah and Greece in Persian Times," in *Prophets, Prophecy, and Prophetic Texts in Second Temple Judaism* (ed. M. H. Floyd and R. D. Haak; LHBOTS 427; London: T & T Clark, 2006) 248–75.

65 Cf., e.g., E. Ben Zvi, "Introduction: Writings, Speeches, and the Prophetic Books— Setting an Agenda," in id. and M. H. Floyd (eds.), *Writings and Speech in Israelite and Ancient Near Eastern Prophecy* (2000) 1–29; id., "The Prophetic Book: A Key Form of Prophetic Literature," in *The Changing Face of Form Criticism for the Twenty-First Century* (ed. id. and M. A. Sweeney; Grand Rapids, Mich.: Eerdmans, 2003) 276–97; M. H. Floyd, "The Production of Prophetic

The transition from proclaiming prophecies and writing them down to the literary interpretation of previously written prophecies is well recognizable from biblical and other texts from the Second Temple period. It caused a major shift of emphasis from prophecy as a primarily oral delivery of divine words by the prophets to contemporary recipients to a learned interpretation of written prophetic words by later scholars and scribes for their own and future generations. Being now in charge of the prophetic tradition transmitted in written form, the scribes also assumed the role of the prophets as their legitimate heirs.[66] This development, labeled variously as "prophecy by interpretation"[67] or as "*prophetische Prophetenauslegung*,"[68] has recently won more recognition than ever[69]—and rightly so, because understanding this development is decisive for comprehending prophecy and its interpretation in the writings of the late Second Temple period, including the Dead Sea Scrolls.

The shift from oral to scribal prophecy also reflects a development in the concept of a prophet from a speaker to a scribe. The proclaimer of the divine word, whose words may or may not be written down and passed on to further recipients, turns into the scholar who, as a successor of the prophets of the ancient days, interprets their words handed down to him in written form. He is the "wise man" who "knows the interpretation (*pešer*) of a thing" (Qoh 8:1) and who assumes the role of the mediator of the divine knowledge. The fulfillment of the mysteries once revealed to the prophet are now disclosed to him, whereby the prophetic process of communication reaches a new, advanced level of interpretation which is possible only through a new act of revelation. The pesharim, to judge from 1QpHab VII, 1–2, present themselves as a prime example of this understanding of prophecy, which can be observed, not only in other texts from Qumran,[70] but throughout the Jewish literature of the late Second Temple Period from Daniel and Ben Sira[71] to Josephus[72] and Philo[73].

Books in the Early Second Temple Period," in id. and R. D. Haak (eds.), *Prophets, Prophecy, and Prophetic Texts in Second Temple Judaism*, 276–97.

66 Cf. Floyd, "The Production of Prophetic Books," 288–90.

67 Thus J. J. Collins, "Jewish Apocalyptic against its Hellenistic Near Eastern Environment," *BASOR* 220 (1975) 27–36.

68 Thus O. H. Steck, *Die Prophetenbücher und ihr theologisches Zeugnis: Wege der Nachfrage und Fährten zur Antwort* (Tübingen: Mohr Siebeck, 1996).

69 See, e.g., the articles collected in Floyd and Haak (eds.), *Prophets, Prophecy, and Prophetic Texts*.

70 See G. J. Brooke, "Prophecy and Prophets in the Dead Sea Scrolls: Looking Backwards and Forwards," in Floyd and Haak (eds.), *Prophets, Prophecy, and Prophetic Texts*, 151–65; Lange, "Interpretation als Offenbarung."

The transition from oral and, eventually, written prophecy to literary prophecy also meant a move from one type of divination to another. The traditional prophetic activity—i.e., oral delivery or otherwise non-inductive mediation of divine messages through necessary go-betweens to contemporary recipients—is certainly to be classified as one form of divination.[74] This activity, well documented from Mari, Assyria and other parts of the Near East, corresponds to the definitions of prophecy as transmission of allegedly divine words to human recipients accepted by most scholars today. This is how we are supposed to envision the role of the biblical prophets as described by the authors of the prophetic books of the Hebrew Bible. The traditional type of prophecy, however, is a phenomenon different from the scholarly interpretation of signs, omens and texts. This is another kind of divination involving scribal skills and pre-existing physical objects as the material for interpretation. This is also the divinatory context of the new revelation required of the scribe for the exegesis of the ancient prophecies. Being the result of the alleged revelation, the interpretation of prophecies was not understood as an intellectual enterprise prompted by the skills of the interpreter but as a divinatory act inspired by God.[75]

The difference between the two types of divination is that traditional prophecy is essentially oral activity allegedly based on a revelatory experience, and prophetic messages may or may not be written down for later use by the community. Literary prophecy, on the other hand, is scribal divination where the text itself serves as the source of revelation and exegesis becomes a revelatory act. While beginnings of the development of prophecy in this direction can

---

71 See P. C. Beentjes, "Prophets and Prophecy in the Book of Ben Sira," in Floyd and Haak (eds.), *Prophets, Prophecy, and Prophetic Texts*, 135–50.

72 See L. H. Feldman, "Prophets and Prophecy in Josephus," in Floyd and Haak (eds.) *Prophets, Prophecy and Prophetic Texts*, 210–39 (= *JTS* 41 [1990] 386–422); L. L. Grabbe, "Thus Spake the Prophet Josephus...: The Jewish Historian on Prophets and Prophecy," ibid., 240–47.

73 See J. R. Levison, "Philo's Personal Experience and the Persistence of Prophecy," ibid., 194–209.

74 Cf., e.g., E. Cancik-Kirschbaum, "Prophetismus und Divination: Ein Blick auf die Keilschriftlichen Quellen," in *Propheten in Mari, Assyrien und Israel* (ed. M. Köckert and M. Nissinen: FRLANT 201; Göttingen: Vandenhoeck & Ruprecht, 2003) 33–53; A. M. Kitz, "Prophecy as Divination," *CBQ* 65 (2003) 22–42.

75 Cf. L. L. Grabbe, "Poets, Scribes, or Preachers: The Reality of Prophecy in the Second Temple Period," in Grabbe and Haak (eds.) *Knowing the End from the Beginning*, 192–215, esp. 209–10.

be observed already in the Hebrew Bible (esp. in Ezekiel),[76] the pesharim of Qumran present themselves as a full-blown representative of scribal divination.

Conclusion

The relation of the pesharim to ancient Near Eastern, especially Mesopotamian, divination is twofold. First, the therapeutic and apotropaic purpose of the Mesopotamian dream practice, implied by the Akkadian verb *pašāru* "to release," can be seen as functionally equivalent to the pesharim, which announce an eschatological release of the final generation by transferring the evil proclaimed by the ancient prophets on the "out-group." Second, the structure of the pesharim resembles the protasis-apodosis structure of classical omens, and the standard introductory formula of the pesharim, *pišrô,* is functionally equivalent to the Akkadian *piširšu,* used by Assyrian scholars in their reports to introduce quotations from omen collections. The idea and practice of the pesharim in general is related to the purpose of omen-based divination to acquire divine information on contemporary circumstances by systematic observation of god-given signs. In the case of pesharim, the base-texts take the role of such signs. The interpretation could only be performed by qualified diviners recognized by the community, which can be compared to the status of the Teacher of Righteousness as the prototypical teacher of the Qumran community.

In addition, the pesharim have the element of post-event prediction in common with the Akkadian literary predictive texts, while there are only a few affinities between the pesharim and the ancient Near Eastern prophetic sources. This notwithstanding, the pesharim contribute to the history of prophecy by providing a prime example of the result of the metamorphosis of prophecy from oral proclamation to literary interpretation in Second Temple Judaism. In other words, they document the shift of emphasis from intuitive to scribal divination, comparable to ancient Near Eastern divinatory scholarship. Rather than an intellectual enterprise, interpretation of prophetic texts was a divinely inspired divinatory act.

---

76 Cf., e.g., J. Schaper, "The Death of the Prophet: The Transition from the Spoken to the Written Word of God in the Book of Ezekiel," in Floyd and Haak (eds.), *Prophets, Prophecy, and Prophetic Texts*, 63–79.

Bibliography

Abegg, M. G., P. Flint and E. Ulrich, *The Dead Sea Scrolls Bible* (New York: Harper, 1999).
Abegg, M. G., et al., *The Dead Sea Scrolls Concordance*, Vol. 1: *The Non-Biblical Texts from Qumran* (Leiden: Brill, 2003).
Abraham, K., "West Semitic and Judean Brides in Cuneiform Sources from the Sixth Century BCE: New Evidence from a Marriage Contract from Al-Yahudu," *AfO* 51 (2005/6) 198–219.
Abraham, K., "An Inheritance Division among Judeans in Babylonia from the Early Persian Period," *New Seals and Inscriptions: Hebrew, Idumean, and Cuneiform* (ed. M. Lubetski; HBM 8; Sheffield: Sheffield Phoenix, 2007) 206–21.
Abusch, T., "*Alaktu* and *halakhah:* Oracular Decision, Divine Revelation," *HTR* 80 (1987) 15–42.
Ackerman, S., "Why is Miriam Also among the Prophets? (And is Zipporah among the Priests?)," *JBL* 121 (2002) 47–80.
Addey, C., "Divine Possession and Divination in the Graeco-Roman World: The Evidence from Iamblichus's *On the Mysteries*," in *Spirit Possession and Trance: New Interdisciplinary Perspectives* (ed. B. E. Schmidt and L. Huskinson; London: Continuum, 2010).
Aejmelaeus, A., "Jeremiah at the Turning-Point of History: The Function of Jer xxv 1–14 in the Book of Jeremiah," *VT* 52 (2002) 459–82.
Aejmelaeus, A., "Licence to Kill? Deut 13:10 and the Prerequisites of Textual Criticism," in *Verbum et Calamus: Semitic and Related Studies in Honour of the Sixtieth Birthday of Professor Tapani Harviainen* (eds. H. Juusola, J. Laulainen and H. Palva; StOr 99: Helsinki: Finnish Oriental Society, 2004) 1–22.
Aejmelaeus, A., "Nebuchadnezzar, My Servant: Redaction History and Textual Development in Jer 27," in *Interpreting Translation*, FS J. Lust (ed. F. García Martínez and M. Vervenne; BETL 192; Leuven: Peters, 2005) 1–18.
Aejmelaeus, A., "Lost in Reconstruction? On Hebrew and Greek Reconstructions in 2 Sam 24," *BIOSCS* 40 (2007) 89–106.
Ahlström, G., *Royal Administration and National Religion in Ancient Palestine* (SHCANE 1; Leiden: Brill, 1982).
Ahmad, A. Y., "The Archive of Aššur-mātu-taqqin," *Al-Rāfidān* 17 (1996) 207–288.
Albani, M., "Horoscopes in the Qumran Scrolls," in *The Dead Sea Scrolls after Fifty Years: A Comprehensive Assessment*, vol. 2 (ed. P. W. Flint and J. C. VanderKam; STDJ 30; Leiden: Brill, 1999) 279–330.
Albertz, R., "Religionsgeschichte Israels statt Theologie des Alten Testaments!" *JBTh* 10 (1995) 3–24.
Albright, W. F., *Yahweh and the Gods of Canaan: A Historical Analysis of Two Contrasting Faiths* (London: Athlone Press, 1968).
Allegro, J. M., *Qumran Cave 4 I: 4Q158–4Q186* (DJD 5; Oxford: Clarendon Press, 1968).
Allen, S. L., *The Splintered Divine: A Study of Ištar, Baal, and Yahweh Divine Names and Divine Multiplicity in the Ancient Near East* (SANER 5; Berlin: de Gruyter, 2015).
Alster, B., "Paradoxical Proverbs and Satire in Sumerian Literature," *JCS* 27 (1975) 201–30.
Alster, B., "Tigris," *DDD*^{2} (1999) 870–71.
Alstola, T., "Judean Merchants in Babylonia and Their Participation in Long-Distance Trade," *WO* 47 (2017) 25–51.

Alt, A., "Hosea 5,8–6,6: ein Krieg und seine Folgen in prophetischer Beleuchtung," *NKZ* 30 (1919) 537–68 (repr. in id., *Kleine Schriften zur Geschichte des Volkes Israel*, vol. 2 [Munich: Beck, 1953]).

Amit, Y., "Epoch and Genre: The Sixth Century and the Growth of Hidden Polemics," in *Judah and Judeans in the Neo-Babylonian Period* (ed O. Lipschitz and J. Blenkinsopp; Winona Lake, Ind.: Eisenbrauns, 2003) 135–51.

Amit, Y., "The Role of Prophecy and Prophets in the Chronicler's World," in *Prophets, Prophecy, and Prophetic Texts in Second Temple Judaism* (ed. id. and R. D. Haak; LHBOTS 427; London: T&T Clark, 2006) 80–101.

Anbar, M., "Aspect moral dans un discours 'prophetique' de Mari," *UF* 7 (1975) 517–18.

Anbar, M., *Les tribus amurrites de Mari* (OBO 108; OBO 162; Fribourg and Göttingen: Academic Press Fribourg and Vandenhoeck & Ruprecht, 1991)

Andersen, F. I. and D. N. Freedman, *Hosea: A New Translation with Introduction and Commentary* (AB 24; Garden City, N.Y.: Doubleday, 1980).

André, G., "Ecstatic Prophecy in the Old Testament," in *Religious Ecstasy: Based on Papers Read at the Symposium on Religious Ecstasy Held at Abo, Finland, on the 26th–28th of August 1981* (ed. N. G. Holm; Stockholm, 1982) 187–200.

Angel, J., "The Liturgical-Eschatological Priest of the *Self-Glorification Hymn*," *RevQ* 96 (2010) 585–605.

Annus, A., "Ninurta and the Son of Man," in *Mythology and Mythologies: Methodological Approaches to Intercultural Influences* (ed. R. M. Whiting; Melammu Symposia 2; Helsinki: The Neo-Assyrian Text Corpus Project, 2001) 7–17.

Annus, A., *The God Ninurta in the Mythology and Royal Ideology of Ancient Mesopotamia* (SAAS 14; Helsinki: Neo-Assyrian Text Corpus Project, 2002).

Annus, A. (ed.), *Divination and the Interpretation of Signs in the Ancient World* (Oriental Institute Seminars 6; Chicago, Ill.: Oriental Institute, 2010).

Anor, N., *Reading the Oil Omens: A Study of Practice and Record of Mesopotamian Lecanomancy* (Jerusalem: Hebrew University, 2010).

Antin, Katri, "Sages in the Divine Council: Transmitting Divine Knowledge in Sirach 24, *1 Enoch* 14–16, Daniel 7, and in Two Hodayot Psalms (1QHa12:6–13:6; 20:7–22:42," in *Transgressing Imaginary Boundaries: The Dead Sea Scrolls in the Context of Second Temple Judaism* (ed. M. S. Pajunen and H. Tervanotko; PFES 108; Helsinki: The Finnish Exegetical Society, 2015), 182–209.

Appleby, R. S., *The Ambivalence of the Sacred: Religion, Violence, and Reconciliation* (Oxford: Rowman & Littlefield, 2000).

Aro, S., "Tabal: Zur Geschichte und materiellen Kultur des zentralanatolischen Hochplateaus von 1200 bis 600 v.Chr." (PhD diss., University of Helsinki, 1998).

Artzi, P., and A. Malamat, "The Correspondence of Šibtu, Queen of Mari in *ARM* X," *Or* 40 (1971) 75–89 (reprinted in A. Malamat, *Mari and the Bible* [SHANE 12; Leiden: Brill, 1998] 175–91).

Assmann, J., *Religion and Cultural Memory: Ten Studies* (trans. R. Livingstone; Stanford, Calif.: Stanford University Press, 2006); trans. of id. *Religion und kulturelles Gedächtnis: Zehn Studien* (Munich: Beck, 32007).

Aster, S. S., "Ezekiel's Adaptation of the Mesopotamian Melammu," *WO* 45 (2015) 10–21.

Atkinson, K., "Astrology and History in the Treatise of Shem: Two Astrological Pseudepigrapha and their Relevance for Understanding the Astrological Dead Sea Scrolls," *QC* 14 (2006) 37–55.

Aufrecht, W. E., *A Corpus of Ammonite Inscriptions* (Lewiston, N.Y.: The Edwin Mellen Press, 1989).

Aufrecht, W. E., N. A. Mirau, and S. W. Gauley (eds.), *Aspects of Urbanism in Antiquity. From Mesopotamia to Crete* (ed. W. E. Aufrecht, N. A. Mirau, and S.W. Gauley; JSOTSup 244; Sheffield: Sheffield Academic Press, 1997).

Auld, A. G., "Prophets through the Looking Glass: Between Writings and Moses," *JSOT* 27 (1983) 3–23.

Auld, A. G., "Prophets through the Looking Glass: A Response to Robert Carroll and Hugh Williamson," *JSOT* 27 (1983) 41–44.

Auld, A. G., "Prophecy in Books: A Rejoinder," *JSOT* 48 (1990) 31–32.

Auld, A. G., "Amos and Apocalyptic: Visions, Prophecy, Revelation," in *Storia e tradizioni di Israele*, FS J. A. Soggin (ed. D. Garrone and F. Israel; Brescia: Paideia, 1991) 1–15.

Aune, D. E., *Revelation 17–22* (WBC 52C; Nashville: Thomas Nelson, 1998).

Aune, D. E., "'Magic' in Early Christianity and Its Ancient Mediterranean Context: A Survey of Some Recent Scholarship," in *Ancient Christianity and "Magic"/Il cristianesimo antico e la "magia"* (ed. T. Nicklas, and T. J. Kraus; Annali di storia dell'esegesi 24/2; Bologna: Edizioni Dehoniane, 2007) 229–94.

Avioz, M., *Nathan's Oracle (2 Samuel 7) and Its Interpreters* (Bible in History; Bern: Lang, 2005).

Bahrani, Z., *The Graven Image: Representation in Babylonia and Assyria* (Philadelphia, Pa.: University of Pennsylvania Press, 2003).

Bahrani, Z., *Rituals of War: The Body and Violence in Mesopotamia* (New York: Zone Books, 2008).

Baillet, M., *Qumrân Grotte 4 III (4Q482–4Q520)* (DJD 7; Oxford: Clarendon Press, 1982).

Baker, H. D., "Bēl-iqīša," *PNA* 1/2 (1999) 315–16.

Baker, H. D., "Kabtīa," *PNA* 2/1 (2000) 594.

Baker, H. D., "Nabû-šarru-uṣur," *PNA* 2/2 (2001) 877.

Baltzer, K., *Deutero-Jesaja* (KAT 10/2; Gütersloh: Gütersloher Verlagshaus, 1999); ET: *Deutero-Isaiah: A Commentary* (Hermeneia; Minneapolis: Fortress, 2001).

Barr, J., *History and Ideology in the Old Testament: Biblical Studies at the End of a Millennium* (Oxford: Oxford University Press, 2000).

Barr, J., "Evaluation, Commitment, and Objectivity in Biblical Theology," in *Reading the Bible in the Global Village* (ed. H. Räisänen; SBLGPBS 6; Atlanta, Ga.: Society of Biblical Literature, 2000) 127–52.

Barstad, H. M., "Lachish Ostracon III and Ancient Israelite Prophecy," *ErIsr* 24 (1993) 8*–12*.

Barstad, H. M., "Prophecy at Qumran?," in *In the Last Days: On Jewish and Christian Apocalyptic and Its Period*, FS B. Otzen (ed. K. Jeppesen, K. Nielsen, and B. Rosendal; Aarhus: Aarhus University Press, 1994) 104–20.

Barstad, H. M., "The Understanding of the Prophets in Deuteronomy," *SJOT* 8 (1994) 236–51.

Barstad, H. M., "No Prophets? Recent Developments in Biblical Prophetic Research and Ancient Near Eastern Prophecy," *JSOT* 57 (1993) 39–60 (repr. in *The Prophets: A Sheffield Reader* [ed. P. R. Davies; The Biblical Seminar 42; Sheffield: Sheffield Academic Press, 1996] 106–26).

Barstad, H. M., "*Comparare necesse est?* Ancient Israelite and Ancient Near Eastern Prophecy in a Comparative Perspective," in *Prophecy in Its Ancient Near Eastern Context: Mesopotamian, Biblical, and Arabian Perspectives* (ed. M. Nissinen; SBLSymS 13; Atlanta, Ga.: Society of Biblical Literature, 2000) 3–11.

Barstad, H. M., "Den gammeltestamentliga profetismen belyst ved paralleller fra Mari," *TTK* 72 (2001) 51–67.

Barstad, H. M., "'Fact' versus 'Fiction' and Other Issues in the History Debate, and Their Relevance for the Study of the Old Testament," in *Vergegenwärtigung des Alten Testaments: Beiträge zur biblischen Hermeneutik*, FS R. Smend (ed. C. Bultmann, W. Dietrich, and C. Levin; Göttingen 2002) 433–47.

Barstad, H. M., "Prophecy in the Book of Jeremiah and the Historical Prophet," in *Sense and Sensitivity*, FS R. Carroll (ed. A. G. Hunter and P. R. Davies; JSOTSup 348; Sheffield: Sheffield Academic Press, 2002) 87–100.

Barstad, H. M., "Jeremiah as Text: Some Reflections on Genre and Reality in Old Testament Prophetic Research," in *Historie og konstruktion*, FS N. P. Lemche (ed. M. Müller and T. L. Thompson; Forum for Bibelsk Eksegese 14; Copenhagen: Tusculanum, 2005) 11–18.

Barstad, H. M., "Mari and the Hebrew Bible: Some Parallels," *SEÅ* 70 (2005) 21–32.

Barstad, H. M., "*Sic dicit dominus:* Mari Prophetic Texts and the Hebrew Bible," *in Essays on Ancient Israel in Its Near Eastern Context*, FS N. Na'aman (ed. Y. Amit, E. Ben Zvi, I. Finkelstein, and O. Lipschits; Winona Lake, Ind.: Eisenbrauns, 2006) 21–52.

Barstad, H. M., "Some Remarks on Prophets and Prophecy in the 'Deuteronomistic History,'" in *Houses Full of All Good Things. Essays in Memory of Veijola* (ed. J. Pakkala and M. Nissinen; PFES 95; Helsinki: Finnish Exegetical Society, 2008) 300–15.

Barstad, H. M., "What Prophets Do: Reflections on Past Reality in the Book of Jeremiah," in *Prophecy in the Book of Jeremiah* (ed. id. and R. G Kratz; BZAW 388; Berlin: de Gruyter, 2009) 10–32.

Barthélemy, D. , and J. T. Milik, *Qumran Cave I* (DJD 1; Oxford: Clarendon Press, 1955).

Barton, J., *Oracles of God: Perceptions of Ancient Prophecy in Israel after the Exile* (London: Darton, Longman & Todd, 1986).

Barton, J., *The Nature of Biblical Criticism* (Louisville: Westminster John Knox, 2007).

Bauer, W., *Griechisch-Deutsches Wörterbuch zu den Schriften des Neuen Testaments und der frühchristlichen Literatur* (ed. K./B. Aland; Berlin/New York: W. de Gruyter, ^{6}1988).

Bauks, M., "'Chaos' als Metapher für die Gefährdung der Weltordnung," in *Das biblische Weltbild und seine altorientalischen Kontexte* (ed. B. Janowski and B. Ego; FAT 32; Tübingen: Mohr Siebeck, 2001) 431–64.

Beal, R. H., "Hittite Military Rituals," in *Ancient Magic and Ritual Power* (ed. M. W. Meyer and P. A. Mirecki; RGRW 129; Leiden: Brill, 1995) 63–76.

Beal, R. H., "Hittite Oracles," in *Magic and Divination in the Ancient World* (SAMD 2; ed. L. Ciralo and J. Seidel; Leiden: Brill, 2002) 57–81.

Beale, G. K., *The Use of Daniel in Jewish Apocalyptic Literature and in the Revelation of St. John* (Lanham, Md.: University Press of America, 1984).

Beard, M., J. North, and S. Price, *Religions of Rome: A Sourcebook* , 2 vols. (Cambridge: Cambridge University Press, 1998).

Beaulieu, P.-A., "The Historical Background of the Uruk Prophecy," in *The Tablet and the Scroll*, FS W. W. Hallo (ed. M. E. Cohen, D. C. Snell, and D. B. Weisberg; Bethesda, Md.: CDL Press, 1993) 41–52.

Bechmann, U., "Prophetische Frauen am Zweiten Tempel? Ein Vorschlag, die Töchter Zelofhads (Num 27) als Kultprophetinnen zu verstehen," *BN* 119/120 (2003) 52–62.

Becker, J., *Gottesfurcht im Alten Testament* (AnBib 25; Rome: Pontifical Biblical Institute Press, 1965).

Becker, U., *Jesaja: Von der Botschaft zum Buch* (FRLANT 178; Göttingen: Vandenhoeck & Ruprecht, 1997).

Becker, U., "Die Wiederentdeckung des Prophetenbuches: Tendenzen und Aufgaben der gegenwärtigen Prophetenforschung," *BTZ* 21 (2004) 30–60.

Beckman, G. M., "The Tongue is a Bridge: Communication between Humans and Gods in Hittite Anatolia," *ArOr* 67 (1999) 519–34.

Beentjes, P. C., *The Book of Ben Sira in Hebrew: A Text Edition of All Extant Hebrew Manuscripts and a Synopsis of All Parallel Hebrew Ben Sira Texts* (VTSup 68; Leiden: Brill, 2003).

Beentjes, P. C., "Prophets and Prophecy in the Book of Ben Sira," in *Prophets, Prophecy, and Prophetic Texts in Second Temple Judaism* (ed. M. H. Foyd and R. D. Haak; LHBOTS 427; New York: T&T Clark, 2006) 135–50.

Beentjes, P. C., "Ben Sira and the Book of Deuteronomy," in in *Houses Full of All Good Things*, FS T. Veijola (ed. J. Pakkala and M. Nissinen; PFES 95; Helsinki: Finnish Exegetical Society and Göttingen: Vandenhoeck & Ruprecht, 2008) 413–33.

Beentjes, P. C., "Constructs of Prophets and Prophecy in the Book of Chronicles," in *Constructs of Prophecy in the Former and Latter Prophets and Other Texts* (ed. L. L. Grabbe and M. Nissinen; ANEM 4; Atlanta, Ga.: Society of Biblical Literature, 2011) 21–40

Beentjes, P. C., "What about Apocalypticism in the Book of Ben Sira," in *Congress Volume Helsinki 2010* (ed. M. Nissinen; VTSup 148; Leiden: Brill, 2012) 207–27.

Begrich. J., "Das priesterliche Heilsorakel," *ZAW* 52 (1934) 81–92; repr. in *Gesammelte Studien zum Alten Testament* (ed. W. Zimmerli; TB 21; Munich: Kaiser, 1964) 217–31.

Ben-Dov, J., "Writing as Oracle and as Law: New Contexts for the Book-Find of King Josiah," *JBL* 127 (2008) 223–39.

Ben-Dov, J., "Some Precedents for the Religion of the Book: Josiah's Book and Ancient Revelatory Literature," in *Constructs of Prophecy in the Former and Latter Prophets and Other Texts* (ed. L. L. Grabbe and M. Nissinen; ANEM 4; Atlanta, Ga.: Society of Biblical Literature, 2011) 43–62

Ben-Dov, J. and W. Horowitz, "The Babylonian Lunar Three in Calendrical Scrolls from Qumran," *ZA* 95 (2005) 104–20.

Ben Zvi, E., "Who Wrote the Speech of Rabshakeh and When?," *JBL* 109 (1990) 79–92.

Ben Zvi, E., "The Urban Center of Jerusalem and the Development of the Literature of the Hebrew Bible," in *Urbanism in Antiquity: From Mesopotamia to Crete* (ed. W. E. Aufrecht, N. A. Mirau, and S. W. Gauley; JSOTSup 244; Sheffield: Sheffield Academic Press, 1997) 194–209.

Ben Zvi, E., "Introduction: Writings, Speeches, and the Prophetic Books: Setting an Agenda," in *Writings and Speech in Israelite and Ancient Near Eastern Prophecy* (ed. id. and M. H. Floyd; SBLSymS 10; Atlanta, Ga.: Society of Biblical Literature, 2000) 1–29.

Ben Zvi, E., *Micah* (FOTL 21B; Grand Rapids, Mich.: Eerdmans, 2000).

Ben Zvi, E., “One Size Does Not Fit All: Observations on the Different Ways that Chronicles Dealt with the Authoritative Literature of Its Time,” in *What Was Authoritative for Chronicles?* (ed. id. and D. Edelman; Winona Lake, Ind.: Eisenbrauns, 2011) 13–35.

Ben Zvi, E., *Signs of Jonah: Reading and Rereading in Ancient Yehud* (JSOTSup 367; New York: T&T Clark, 2003).

Ben Zvi, E., “The Prophetic Book: A Key Form of Prophetic Literature,” in *The Changing Face of Form Criticism for the Twenty-First Century* (ed. id. and M. A. Sweeney; Grand Rapids, Mich.: Eerdmans, 2003) 276–97.

Ben Zvi, E., “‘The Prophets’ – References to Generic Prophets and their Role in the Construction of the Image of ‘Prophets of the Old’ within the Postmonarchic Readership/s of the Book of Kings,” *ZAW* 116 (2004) 555–67.

Ben Zvi, E., *Hosea* (FOTL 21 A/1; Grand Rapids, Mich.: Eerdmans, 2005).

Ben Zvi, E., “Observations on Josiah’s Account in Chronicles and Implications for Reconstructing the Worldview of the Chronicler,” in *Essays on Ancient Israel in Its Near Eastern Context*, FS N. Na’aman (ed. Y. Amit, E. Ben Zvi, I. Finkelstein, and O. Lipschits; Winona Lake: Eerdmans, 2006) 89–106.

Ben Zvi, E., “Imagining Josiah’s Book and the Implications of Imagining It in Early Persian Period,” in *Berührungspunkte: Studien zur Sozial- und Religionsgeschichte Israels und seiner Umwelt*, FS R. Albertz (ed. I. Kottsieper, R. Schmitt, and J. Wöhrle; AOAT 350; Münster: Ugarit-Verlag, 2008) 193–212.

Ben Zvi, E., “The Concept of Prophetic Books and Its Historical Setting,” in *The Production of Prophecy: Constructing Prophecy and Prophets in Yehud* (ed. D. Edelman and id.; London: Equinox, 2009) 73–95.

Ben Zvi, E., “Remembering Hosea: The Prophet Hosea as a Site of Memory in the Persian Period Yehud,” in *Poets, Prophets, and Texts in Play: Studies in Biblical Poetry and Prophecy in Honour of Francis Landy* (ed. id, C.V. Camp, D. M. Gunn, and A.W. Hughes; LHBOTS 597; London: T & T Clark, 2015) 37–57.

Ben Zvi, E. (ed.), *Utopia and Dystopia in Prophetic Literature* (PFES 92: Finnish Exegetical Society, Helsinki 2006).

Ben Zvi, E., and M. H. Floyd (eds.), *Writings and Speech in Israelite and Ancient Near Eastern Prophecy* (SBLSymS 10; Atlanta, Ga.: Society of Biblical Literature, 2000).

Ben Zvi, E., and J. D. Nogalski, *Two Sides of a Coin: Juxtaposing Views on Interpreting the Book of the Twelve/ The Twelve Prophetic Books* (with an introduction by T. Römer; Analecta Gorgiana 201; Piscataway NJ: Gorgias Press, 2009).

Bengisu, R. L., “Lydian Mount Karios,” in *Cybele, Attis and Related Cults*, FS M. J. Vermaseren (ed. E. N. Lane; RGRW 131; Leiden: Brill, 1996).

Bengtsson, H., “What’s in a Name? A Study of Sobriquets in the Pesharim” (PhD diss., Uppsala University, 2000).

Berger, P. L., and T. Luckmann, *The Social Construction of Reality: A Treatise in Sociology of Knowledge* (New York: Anchor Books, 1989 [orig. 1966]).

Berger, P.-R., “Einige Bemerkungen zu Friedrich Ellermeier: Prophetie in Mari und Israel (Herzberg, 1968),” *UF* 1 (1969), 209.

Berlejung, A., *Die Theologie der Bilder: Herstellung und Einweihung von Kultbildern in Mesopotamien und die alttestamentliche Bilderpolemik* (OBO 162; Fribourg and Göttingen: Academic Press Fribourg and Vandenhoeck & Ruprecht, 1998).

Berlejung, A., "The Assyrians in the West: Assyrianization, Colonialism, Indifference, or Developmental Policy?" in *Congress Volume Helsinki 2010* (ed. M. Nissinen; VTSup 148; Leiden: Brill 2012): 21–60.

Berlinerblau, J., *The Secular Bible: Why Nonbelievers Must Take Religion Seriously* (New York: Cambridge University Press, 2005).

Berlinerblau, J., "The Unspeakable in Biblical Scholarship," *SBL Forum* (March 2006); available at http://www.sbl-site.org/publications/article.aspx?articleId=503.

Bernstein, M. J., "Interpretation of Scripture," in *EDSS* 1 (2000) 376–83.

Berrin, S. L., *The Pesher Nahum Scroll from Qumran: An Exegetical Study of 4Q169* (STDJ 53; Leiden: Brill, 2004).

Berrin, S. L., "Qumran Pesharim," in *Biblical Interpretation at Qumran* (ed. M. Henze; SDSRL; Grand Rapids, Mich.: Eerdmans, 2005) 110–33.

Betz, O., *Offenbarung und Schriflforschung in der Qumransekte* (WUNT 6; Tübingen: Mohr Siebeck, 1960).

Bidmead, J., *The* Akītu *Festival: Beligious Continuity and Royal Legitimation in Mesopotamia* (Piscataway, N.Y.: Gorgias, 2002).

Biggs, R. D., "More Babylonian 'Prophecies'," *Iraq* 29 (1967) 117–32.

Biggs, R. D., "Akkadian Oracles and Prophecies," *ANET*[3] (1969) 604–5.

Biggs, R. D., "Mesopotamia," *JCS* 37 (1985) 86–90.

Biggs, R. D., "Babylonian Prophecies, Astrology, and a New Source for 'Prophecy Text B'," in *Language, Literature, and History: Philological and Historical Studies Presented to Erica Reiner* (ed. F. Rochberg-Halton; AOS 67; New Haven, Conn.: American Oriental Society, 1987) 1–14.

Biggs, R. D., "The Babylonian Prophecies," *BCSMS* 23 (1992) 17–20.

Birot, M., *Textes administratifs de la salle 5 du palais (2e partie)* (ARM 12; Paris: Editions Recherche sur les Civilisations, 1964).

Black, J., and A. Green, *Gods, Demons and Symbols of Ancient Mesopotamia: An Illustrated Dictionary* (ill. T. Rickards; London: British Museum Press, 1992).

Blasius, A., and B. U. Schipper (eds.), *Apokalyptik und Ägypten: Eine kritische Analyse der relevanten Texteaus dem griechisch-römischen Ägypten* (OLA 107; Leuven: Peeters, 2002).

Blenkinsopp, J., *Ezra-Nehemiah: A Commentary* (OTL; London: SCM Press, 1989).

Blenkinsopp, J., *Sage, Priest, Prophet: Religious and Intellectual Leadership in Ancient Israel* (Library of Ancient Israel; Louisville, Ky.: Westminster/John Knox Press, 1995).

Blenkinsopp, J., *A History of Prophecy in Israel* (rev. and enlarged ed.; Louisville, Ky.: Westminster/John Knox Press, 1996 [[1]1984]).

Blenkinsopp, J., *Isaiah 1–39: A New Translation with Introduction and Commentary* (AB 19; New York: Doubleday, 2000).

Blenkinsopp, J., *Isaiah 40–55: A New Translation with Introduction and Commentary* (AB 19 A; New York: Doubleday, 2002).

Blenkinsopp, J., *Opening the Sealed Book: Interpretations of the Book of Isaiah in Late Antiquity* (Grand Rapids, Mich.: Eerdmans, 2006).

Blenkinsopp, J., "The Servant of the Lord, the Teacher of Righteousness, and the Exalted One of 4Q491c Source," in *Far from Minimal*, FS P. R. Davies (ed. D. Burns and J. W. Rogerson; LHBOTS 484; London and New York: T&T Clark, 2012) 41–51.

Bloch-Smith, E., "Bible, Archaeology, and the Social Sciences: The Next Generation," in *The Hebrew Bible: New Insights and Scholarship* (ed. F. E. Greenspahn; New York: New York University Press, 2008) 24–42.
Block, D. I., *The Book of Ezekiel: Chapters 1–24* (NICOT; Grand Rapids, Mich.: Eerdmans, 1997).
Block, D. I., *The Book of Ezekiel: Chapters 25–48* (NICOT; Grand Rapids, Mich.: Eerdmans, 1997).
Block, D. I., "Divine Abandonment: Ezekiel's Adaptation of an ancient Near Eastern Motif," in *The Book of Ezekiel: Theological and Anthropological Perspectives* (ed. M. S. Odell and J. T. Strong; SBLSymS 9; Atlanta, Ga.: Society of Biblical Literature, 2000) 15–42.
Block, D. I., "The Tender Cedar Sprig: Ezekiel on Jehoiachin," *HeBAI* 1 (2012) 173–202
Blum, E., "Die Kombination I der Wandinschrift von Tell Deir 'Alla: Vorschläge zur Rekonstruktion mit historisch-kritischen Anmerkungen," in *Berührungspunkte: Studien zu Sozial- und Religionsgeschichte Israels und seiner Umwelt*, FS R. Albertz (ed. I. Kottsieper, R. Schmitt, and J. Wöhrle; AOAT 350; Münster: Ugarit-Verlag, 2008) 573–601.
Blum, E., "Israels Prophetie im altorientalischen Kontext: Anmerkungen zu neueren religionsgeschichtlichen Thesen," in *'From Ebla to Stellenbosch': Syro-Palestinian Religions and the Hebrew Bible* (ed. I. Cornelius and L. Jonker; ADPV 37; Wiesbaden: Harrassowitz, 2008) 81–115
Bodi, D., *The Book of Ezekiel and the Poem of Erra* (OBO 104; Fribourg and Göttingen: Academic Press Fribourg and Vandenhoeck & Ruprecht, 1991).
Bodi, D., "Ezekiel," *Zondervan Illustrated Bible Backgrounds Commentary* 4 (ed. J. W. Walton; Grand Rapids, Mich.: Zondervan, 2009) 400–517
Bodi, D., "The Double Current and the Tree of Healing in Ezekiel 47:1–12 in Light of Babylonian Iconography and Texts," *WO* 45 (2015) 22–37.
Bonnet, C., "Dove vivono gli dei? Note sulla terminologia feniciopunica dei luoghi di culto e sui modi di rappresentazione del mondo divino," in *Saturnia Tellus: Definizioni dello spazio consacrato in ambiente etrusco, italoci, feniciopunico, iberico e celtico* (ed. X. D. Raventós, S. Ribichini, and S. Verger; Roma: Consiglio nazionale delle ricerche, 2008) 673–85.
Booth, W. C., *The Rhetoric of Fiction* (Chicago: Chicago University Press, 1983 [orig. 1961]).
Booth, W. C., "Resurrection of the Implied Author: Why Bother?" *A Companion to Narrative Theory* (ed. J. Phelan and P. J. Rabinowitz; Oxford: Blackwell, 2005) 75–88.
Bordreuil, P., and D. Pardee, "Le combat de *Ba'lu* avec *Yammu* après les textes ougaritiques," *MARI* 7 (1993) 63–70.
Borger, R., *Die Inschriften Asarhaddons, Königs von Assyrien* (AfO.B 9; Graz: Selbstverlag, 1956).
Borger, R., "Gott Marduk und Gott-König Šulgi als Propheten: Zwei Prophetische Texte," *BO* 28 (1971) 3–24.
Bos, J. M., *Reconsidering the Date and Provenance of the Book of Hosea: The Case of Persia-Period Yehud* (LHBOTS 580; London: Bloomsbury, 2013).
Bosshard, E., and R. G. Kratz, "Maleachi im Zwölfprophetenbuch," *BN* 52 (1990) 27–46.
Bowden, H., *Classical Athens and the Delphic Oracle: Divination and Democracy* (Cambridge, UK: Cambridge University Press, 2005).

Bowden, J., "Oracles for Sale," in *Herodotus and His World: Essays from a Conference in Memory of George Forrest* (ed. P. Derow and R. Parker; Oxford: Oxford University Press, 2003) 256–74.

Bowden, J., "Oracles," in *OEAGR* 5 (Oxford: Oxford University Press, 2010) 106–8.

Bowen, N. R., "The Daughters of Your People: Female Prophets in Ezekiel 13:17–23," *JBL* 118 (1999) 417–33.

Bowley, J. E., "Prophets and Prophecy at Qumran," in *The Dead Sea Scrolls after Fifty Years: A Comprehensive Assessment* (ed. P. W. Flint and J. C. VanderKam; Leiden: Brill, 1999) 354–78.

Braaten, C. E., and R. W. Jenson (eds.), *Reclaiming the Bible for the Church* (Edinburgh: T&T Clark, 1996).

Braw, J. D., "Vision as Revision: Ranke and the Beginning of Modern History," *History and Theory* 46.4 (2007) 45–60.

Brin, G., "The Laws of the Prophets in the Sect of the Judaean Desert: Studies in 4Q375," *JSP* 16 (1992) 19–57.

Brin, G., *Studies in Biblical Law: From the Hebrew Bible to the Dead Sea Scrolls* (JSOTSup 176; Sheffield: JSOT Press, 1994).

Brinkman, J. A., "Merodach-Baladan II," in *From the Workshop of the Chicago Assyrian Dictionary*, FS A. L. Oppenheim (ed. R. D. Biggs and J. A. Brinkman; Chicago, Ill.: The Oriental Institute, 1964) 6–53.

Brinkman, J. A., "Through a Glass Darkly: Esarhaddon's Retrospects on the Downfall of Babylon," *JAOS* 103 (1983) 35–42.

Brinkman, J. A., *Prelude to Empire: Babylonian Society and Politics, 747–626 B.C.* (Occasional Publications of the Babylonian Fund 7; Philadelphia, Pa.: Babylonian Fund, University Museum, 1984).

Brison, O., "Jael, *'eshet heber* the Kenite: A Diviner?" *Joshua and Judges* (ed. A. Brenner and G. A. Yee; Texts @ Contexts; Minneapolis: Fortress Press, 2013) 139–60.

Brooke, G. J., "Qumran Pesher: Toward a Redefinition of a Genre," *RevQ* 10 (1981) 483–503.

Brooke, G. J., "The Kittim in the Qumran Pesharim," *Images of Empire* (ed. Loveday Alexander; JSOTSup 122; Sheffield: Sheffield Academic Press, 1991) 135–59.

Brooke, G. J., "The Pesharim and the Origins of the Dead Sea Scrolls," in *Methods of Investigation of the Dead Sea Scrolls and the Khirbet Qumran Site: Present Realities and Future Prospects* (ed. M. O. Wise et al.; Annals of the New York Academy of Sciences 722; New York: New York Academy of Sciences, 1994) 339–52.

Brooke, G. J., "Prophecy," *EDSS* 2 (2000) 695–700.

Brooke, G. J., "Thematic Commentaries on Prophetic Scriptures," in *Biblical Interpretation at Qumran* (ed. M. Henze; SDSRL; Grand Rapids, Mich.: Eerdmans, 2005) 134–57.

Brooke, G. J., "Prophecy and Prophets in the Dead Sea Scrolls: Looking Backwards and Forwards," in *Prophets, Prophecy and Prophetic Texts in Second Temple Judaism* (ed. M. H. Floyd and R. D. Haak; LHBOTS 427; London: T&T Clark, 2006) 151–65.

Brooke, G. J., "Was the Teacher of Righteousness Considered to be a Prophet?," in *Prophecy after the Prophets: The Contribution of the Dead Sea Scrolls to the Understanding of Biblical and Extra-Biblical Prophecy* (ed. K. de Troyer and A. Lange; CBET 52; Leuven: Peeters, 2009) 77–97.

Brooke, G. J., "La Prophétie de Qumrân," in *Les Récueils prophétiques de la Bible: Origines, milieu, et contexte proche-oriental* (ed. J.-D. Macchi, C. Nihan, T. Römer, and J. Rückl; MdB 64; Geneva: Labor et fides, 2012) 480–510.

Brooke, G. J., "Les mystères des prophètes et les oracles d'exégèse: Continuité et discontinuité dans la prophètie à Qumran," in *Comment devient-on prophète? Actes du colloque organisé par le Collège de France, Paris, les 4–5 avril 2011* (ed. J.-M. Durand, T. Römer, and M. Bürki; OBO 265; Fribourg and Göttingen: Academic Press Fribourg and Vandenhoeck & Ruprecht, 2014) 159–66.

Broshi, M. and A. Yardeni, "On 'Netinim' and False Prophets," in *Solving Riddles and Untying Knots*, FS J. C. Greenfield (ed. Z. Zevit, S. Gitin, and M. Sokoloff; Winona Lake, Ind.: Eisenbrauns, 1995) 29–37.

Buis, P., *La notion d'Alliance dans l'Ancien Testament* (LeDiv 88; Paris: Cerf, 1976).

Burkert, W., *Homo necans: Interpretation altgriechischer Opferriten und Mythen* (RVV 32; Berlin and New York: Walter de Gruyter, 1972).

Burkert, W., *Greek Religion* (trans. J. Raffan; Cambridge, Mass.: Harvard University Press, 1985).

Burkert, W., *The Orientalizing Revolution: Near Eastern Influence on Greek Culture in the Early Archaic Age* (trans. id. and M. E. Pinder; Cambridge, Mass.: Harvard University Press, 1992).

Burkert, W., "Olbia and Apollo of Didyma: A New Oracle Text," in *Apollo: Origins and Influences* (ed. J. Solomon; Tucson, Ariz.: The University of Arizona Press, 1994) 49–60.

Burkert, W., "Signs, Commands, and Knowledge: Ancient Divination between Enigma and Epiphany," in *Mantikê: Studies in Ancient Divination* (ed. S. I. Johnston and P. T. Struck; RGRW 155; Leiden: Brill, 2005) 29–49.

Butler, S. A. L., *Mesopotamian Conceptions of Dreams and Dream Rituals* (AOAT 258; Münster: Ugarit-Verlag, 1998).

Byrskog, S., "När gamla texter talar: Om att tolka det förgångna," *STK* 84 (2008) 49–57.

Cagni, L., *L'Epopea di Erra* (Studi Semitici 3; Rome: Istituto di Studi del Vicino Oriente, 1969).

Cancik, H., "Rome as Sacred Landscape: Varro and the End of Republican Religion in Rome," *Visible Religion* 4–5 (1985–86) 250–65.

Cancik-Kirschbaum, E., "Konzeption und Legitimation von Herrschaft in neuassyrischer Zeit: Mythos und Ritual in VS 24, 92," *WO* 26 (1995) 5–20.

Cancik-Kirschbaum, E., "Prophetismus und Divination: Ein Blick auf die keilschriftlichen Quellen," in *Propheten in Mari, Assyrien und Israel* (ed. M. Köckert and M. Nissinen; FRLANT 201; Göttingen, Vandenhoeck & Ruprecht, 2003) 33–53.

Carr, D. M., "Moving Beyond Unity: Synchronic and Diachronic Perspectives on Prophetic Literature," in *Prophetie in Israel: Beiträge des Symposiums 'Das Alte Testament und die Kultur der Moderne'*, FS G. von Rad (ed. I. Fischer, K. Schmid, and H. G. M. Williamson; Altes Testament und Moderne 11; Münster: LIT, 2003) 59–93.

Carr, D. M., *The Erotic Word: Sexuality, Spirituality, and the Bible* (New York: Oxford University Press, 2003).

Carr, D. M., *Writing on the Tablet of the Heart: Origins of Scripture and Literature* (Oxford and New York: Oxford University Press, 2005).

Carr, D. M., "Reading into the Gap: Refractions of Trauma in Israelite Prophecy," in *Interpreting Exile: Displacement and Deportation in Biblical and Modern Contexts* (ed.

B. E. Kelle, F. R. Ames, and J. L. Wright; SBLAIL 10; Atlanta, Ga.: Society of Biblical Literature, 2011) 295–308.

Carr, D. M., *The Formation of the Hebrew Bible: A New Reconstruction* (New York: Oxford University Press, 2011).

Carroll, R. P., *From Chaos to Covenant: Prophecy in the Book of Jeremiah* (New York: Crossroad, 1981).

Carroll, R. P., "Poets not Prophets: A Response to 'Prophets through the Looking Glass,'" *JSOT* 27 (1983) 25–31.

Carroll, R. P., *The Book of Jeremiah: A Commentary* (OTL; London: SCM, 1986).

Carroll, R. P., "Prophecy and Society," in *The World of Ancient Israel: Sociological, Anthropological and Political Perspectives* (ed. R. E. Clements; Cambridge: Cambridge University Press, 1989) 203–25.

Carroll, R. P., "Coopting the Prophets: Nehemiah and Noadiah," in *Priests, Prophets and Scribes*, FS J. Blenkinsopp (ed. E. Ulrich, J. W. Wright, R. P. Carroll, and P. R. Davies; JSOTSup 149, Sheffield: Sheffield Academic Press, 1992) 87–99.

Carroll, R. P., "Clio and Canons: In Search of a Cultural Poetics of the Hebrew Bible," *BibInt 5* (1997) 300–323.

Carroll, R. P., "Poststructuralist Approaches: New Historicism and Postmodernism," in *The Cambridge Companion to Biblical Interpretation* (ed. J. Barton; Cambridge: Cambridge University Press, 1998) 50–66.

Carroll, R. P., "Whose Prophet? Whose History? Whose Social Reality? Troubling the Interpretive Community Again: Notes towards a Response to T. W. Overholt's Critique," *JSOT* 48 (1990) 33–49.

Cassin, E., "Note sur le "puḫru(m)" des dieux," *La voix de l'opposition en Mésopotamie* (Colloque organisé par l'Institut des Hautes Etudes de Belgique, 19 et 20 mars 1973; Bruxelles: Institut des Hautes etudes de Belgique,, 1973) 111–18.

Cathcart, K., "'Law is Paralysed' (Habakkuk 1.4): Habakkuk's Dialogue with God and the Language of Legal Disputation," in *Prophecy and the Prophets in Ancient Israel: Proceedings of the Oxford Old Testament Seminar* (ed. J. Day; LHBOTS 531; New York and London: T & T Clark, 2010) 339–53.

Charlesworth, J. H., *The Old Testament Pseudepigrapha*, vol. 1: *Apocalyptic Literature and Testaments* (New York: Doubleday, 1983).

Charpin, D., "Nouveaux documents du bureau de l'huile à l'époque assyrienne," *MARI* 3 (1984) 83–126.

Charpin, D., "Nouveaux documents du bureau de l'huile (suite)," *MARI* 5 (1987) 597–99.

Charpin, D., "L'*andurârum* à Mari," *MARI* 6 (1990) 253–70.

Charpin, D., "Un traité entre Zimri-Lim de Mari et Ibâl-Ibâlpî El II d'Ešnunna," in *Marchands, Diplomates et Empereurs*, FS P. Garelli, (ed. id. and F. Joannès; Paris: Éditions Recherche sur les Civilisations, 1991) 139–66.

Charpin, D., "Le contexte historique et géographique des prophéties dans les textes retrouvés à Mari," *BCSMS* 23 (1992) 21–31.

Charpin, D., "Prophètes et rois dans le Proche-Orient amorrite," in *Prophètes et rois: Bible et Proche-Orient* (ed. A. Lemaire; Paris: Cerf, 2001) 21–53.

Charpin, D., "Prophètes et rois dans le Proche-Orient amorrite: Nouvelles données, nouvelles perspectives," in *Florilegium Marianum 6*, FS A. Parrot (ed. id./J.-M. Durand; Mémoires de NABU 7; Paris: SEPOA, 2002) 7–38.

Charpin, D., "Histoire politique du Proche-Orient amorrite (2002–1595)," in *Mesopotamien: Die altbabylonische Zeit* (ed. id., D. O. Edzard, and M. Stol; OBO 160/4; Fribourg and Göttingen: Academic Press Fribourg and Vandenhoeck & Ruprecht, 2004) 25–480.

Charpin, D., "The Writing, Sending and Reading of Letters in the Amorite World," in *The Babylonian World* (ed. G. Leick; New York: Routledge, 2007) 400–17.

Charpin, D., *Reading and Writing in Babylon* (trans. J. M. Todd; Cambridge, Mass.: Harvard University Press , 2010).

Charpin, D., "Le prophétisme dans le Proche-Orient d'après les archives de Mari," *Les Récueils prophétiques de la Bible: Origines, milieu, et contexte proche-oriental* (ed. J.-D. Macchi, C. Nihan, T. Römer, and J. Rückl; Le Monde de la Bible 64; Geneva: Labor et fides, 2012) 31–73.

Charpin, D., "Un traité entre Zimri-Lim de Mari et Ibâl-pî-El II d'Ejnunna," in *Marchands, Diplomates et Empereurs*, FS P. Garelli, (ed. id. and F. Joannès; Paris: Éditions Recherche sur les Civilisations, 1991) 139–66.

Charpin, D., and J.-M. Durand, "La prise du pouvoir par Zimri-Lim," *MARI* 4 (1985) 297–343.

Charpin, D., and J.-M. Durand, "'Fils de Sim'al': Les origines tribales des Rois de Mari," *RA* 80 (1986) 141–83.

Charpin, D., and J.-M. Durand, "Des volontaires contre l'Élam," in *Literatur, Politik und Recht in Mesopotamien*, FS C. Wilcke (ed. W. Sallaberger, K. Volk, and A. Zgoll; Orientalia Biblica et Christiana 14; Wiesbaden: Harrassowitz, 2003) 63–76.

Charpin, D., and J.-M. Durand (eds.), *Florilegium marianum 3*, FS M.-T. Barrelet (Mémoires de *NABU* 4; Paris: SEPOA, 1997).

Charpin, D., and J.-M. Durand (eds.), *Florilegium marianum 6*, FS A. Parrot (Mémoires de *NABU* 7; Paris: SEPOA, 2002).

Charpin, D., F. Joannès, S. Lackenbacher, and B. Lafont, *Archives épistolaires de Mari I/2* (ARM 26/2; Paris: Editions Recherche sur les Civilisations, 1988).

Charpin, D., and Ziegler, N., *Florilegum marianum 5: Mari et le Proche-Orient à l'époque amorrite, Essai d'histoire politique* (Mémoires de NABU 6; Paris: SEPOA, 2003).

Chuytin, M., "The Redaction of the Qumranic and the Traditional Book of Psalms as Calendar," *RevQ* 63 (1994) 367–97.

Civil, M., et al., *The Series lū = ša and Related Texts* (MSL 12; Rome: Pontificium Institutum Biblicum, 1969).

Clark, E. A., *History, Theory, Text: Historians and the Linguistic Turn* (Cambridge: Harvard University Press, 2004).

Clarke, E. C., J. M. Dillon, and J. P. Hershbell, *Iamblichus: De mysteriis: Translated with Introduction and Notes* (SBLWGRW 4; Atlanta, Ga.: Society of Biblical Literature, 2003).

Clements, R. E., "Max Weber, Charisma and Biblical Prophecy," in *Prophecy and Prophets: The Diversity of Contemporary Issues in Scholarship* (ed. Y. Gitay; SBLSymS; Atlanta, Ga.: Scholars Press, 1997) 89–108.

Clifford, R. J., "The Roots of Apocalypticism in Near Eastern Myth," in *The Encyclopedia of Apocalypticism*, vol. 1: *The Origins of Apocalypticism in Judaism and Christianity* (ed. J. J. Collins; New York: Continuum, 1998) 3–38.

Clines, D. J. A., "The Nehemiah Memoire: The Perils of Autobiography," in *What Does Eve Do to Help? ami Other Readerly Questions to the Old Testament* (ed. id.; JSOTSup 94; Sheffield: JSOT Press, 1990) 124–64.

Clines, D. J. A., "Metacommenting Amos," in *Of Prophets' Visions and the Wisdom of Sages*, FS R. N. Whybray (ed. H. A. McKay and D. J. A. Clines; JSOTSup 162; Sheffield: JSOT Press, 1993) 142–60.

Clines, D. J. A., *Interested Parties: The Ideology of the Writers and Readers of the Hebrew Bible* (Sheffield: Sheffield Academic Press, 1995).

Clines, D. J. A., *The Bible in the Modern World* (Sheffield: Sheffield Academic Press, 1997).

Clines, D. J. A., "Historical Criticism: Are Its Days Numbered?" *Teologinen Aikakauskirja* 114 (2009) 542–58.

Cogan, M., *Imperialism and Religion: Assyria, Israel and Judah in the Eighth and Seventh Centuries B.C.E.* (SBLMS 19; Missoula, Mt.: Society of Biblical Literature, 1974)

Cogan, M., "Omens and Ideology in the Babylon Inscription of Esarhaddon," in *History, Historiography, and Interpretation: Studies in Biblical and Cuneiform Literatures* (ed. H. Tadmor and M. Weinfeld; Jerusalem: Magnes Press; Leiden: Brill, 1983) 76–87.

Cogan, M., "Judah Under Assyrian Hegemony: A Re-examination of Imperialism and Religion," *JBL* 112 (1993) 403–14.

Cogan, M., and H. Tadmor, "Gyges and Assurbanipal: A Study in Literary Transmission," *Or* 46 (1977) 65–85.

Coggins, R. J., "Prophecy: True and False," in *Of Prophets' Visions and the Wisdom of Sages*, FS R. N. Whybray (ed. H. A. McKay and D. J. A. Clines; JSOTSup 162; Sheffield: Sheffield Academic Press, 1993) 80–94.

Coggins, R. J., *Nippur IV: The Early Neo-Babylonian Governor's Archive from Nippur* (OIP 114; Chicago, Ill.: Oriental Institute, 1996).

Cole, S. W., and P. Machinist, *Letters from Priests to the Kings Esarhaddon and Assurbanipal* (SAA 13; Helsinki: Helsinki University Press, 1998).

Collins, B. J., *Hittites and Their World* (Archaeology and Biblical Studies 7; Atlanta, Ga.: Society of Biblical Literature, 2007).

Collins, J. J., "Jewish Apocalyptic against its Hellenistic Near Eastern Environment," *BASOR* 220 (1975) 27–36.

Collins, J. J., *Apocalypticism in the Dead Sea Scrolls* (LDSS; London: Continuum, 1997).

Collins, J. J., *Jewish Wisdom in Hellenistic Age* (OTL; Louisville, Ky.: Westminster John Knox, 1997).

Collins, J. J., *The Scepter and the Star: Messianism in Light of the Dead Sea Scrolls* (Grand Rapids, Mich.: Eerdmans, 1997).

Collins, J. J., *The Apocalyptic Imagination: An Introduction to Jewish Apocalyptic Literature* (Grand Rapids, Mich.: Eerdmans, ^{2}1998).

Collins, J. J., "Prophecy, Apocalypse and Eschatology: Reflections on the Proposal of Lester Grabbe," in *Knowing the End from the Beginning: The Prophetic, the Apocalyptic and their Relationships* (ed. L. L. Grabbe and R. D. Haak; JSPSup 46; London: T&T Clark International, 2003) 44–52.

Conrad, E. W., "Second Isaiah and the Priestly Oracle of Salvation," *ZAW* 93 (1981) 234–46.

Conrad, E. W., "The 'Fear Not' Oracles in Second Isaiah," *VT* 34 (1984) 129–52.

Conzelmann, H., "Die Mutter der Weisheit," in *Zeit und Geschichte*, FS R. Bultmann (ed. E. Dinkler; Tübingen: Mohr Siebeck, 1964) 225–34.

Cook, S. L., *Prophecy and Apocalypticism: The Postexilic Social Setting* (Minneapolis, Minn.: Fortress Press, 1995).

Cook, S. L., "The Lineage Roots of Hosea's Yahwism," in *The Social World of the Hebrew Bible: Twenty-Five Years of the Social Sciences in the Academy* (ed. R. A. Simkins and S. L. Cook; Semeia 87; Atlanta, Ga.: Society of Biblical Literature, 1999) 145–61

Cooley, J. L., "The Story of Saul's Election (1 Samuel 9–10) in the Light of Mantic Practice in Ancient Iraq," *JBL* 130 (2011) 247–61.

Couey, J. B., "Amos vii 10–17 and Royal Attitudes toward Prophecy in the Ancient Near East," *VT* 53 (2008) 300–14.

Craigie, P. C., *Psalms 1–50* (WBC 19; Waco, Tex.: Word Books, 1983).

Crane, A. S., *Israel's Restoration: A Textual-Comparative Exploration of Ezekiel 36–39* (VTSup 122; Leiden: Brill, 2008).

Crenshaw, J. L., *Prophetic Conflict* (BZAW 124, Berlin: de Gruyter, 1971).

Crenshaw, J. L., "The Primacy of Listening in Ben Sira's Pedagogy," in *Wisdom, You Are My Sister*, FS R. E. Murphy (ed. M. L. Barré; CBQMS 29; Washington, D.C.: Catholic Biblical Association of America, 1997) 172–87.

Crenshaw, J. L., "Transmitting Prophecy across Generations," in *Writings and Speech in Israelite and Ancient Near Eastern Prophecy* (ed. E. Ben Zvi and M. H. Floyd; SBLSymS 10; Atlanta Ga.: Society of Biblical Literature, 2000) 31–44.

Cross, F. M., "Council of Yahweh in Second Isaiah," *JNES* 12 (1952) 274–78.

Crüsemann, F., "Religionsgeschichte oder Theologie? Elementare Überlegungen zu einer falschen Alternative," *JBTh* 10 (1995) 69–77.

Cryer, F. H., "Der Prophet und der Magier: Bemerkungen anhand einer überholten Diskussion," in *Prophetie und geschichtliche Wirklichkeit im alten Israel*, FS S. Herrmann (ed. R. Liwak und S. Wagner; Stuttgart: Kohlhammer, 1991) 79–88

Cryer, F. H., *Divination in Ancient Israel and Its Near Eastern Environment: A Socio-Historical Investigation* (JSOTSup 142; Sheffield: Sheffield Academic Press, 1994).

Cubitt, Geoffrey, *History and Memory* (Manchester: Manchester University Press, 2007).

Culley, R. C., "Orality and Writtenness in the Prophetic Texts," in *Writings and Speech in Israelite and Ancient Near Eastern Prophecy* (ed. E. Ben Zvi and M. H. Floyd; SBLSymS 10; Atlanta Ga.: Society of Biblical Literature, 2000) 45–64.

Dalley, S., *Myths from Mesopotamia: Creation, The Flood, Gilgamesh and Others* (Oxford: Oxford Univ. Press, 1989).

Dalley, S., and J. N. Postgate, *The Tablets from Fort Shalmaneser* (CTN 3; London: British School of Archaeology in Iraq, 1984).

Davies, P. R., *In Search of "Ancient Israel"* (JSOTSup 148; Sheffield: Sheffield Academic Press, 1992).

Davies, P. R., *Whose Bible Is It Anyway?* (Sheffield: Sheffield Academic Press, 1995; London: T&T Clark, ^{2}2004).

Davies, P. R., "Amos: Man and Book," in *Israel's Prophets and Israel's Past*, FS J. H. Hayes (ed. id. and M. B. Moore; LHBOTS 446; New York and London: T&T Clark, 2006) 113–31.

Davies, P. R., *The Origins of Biblical Israel* (LHBOTS 485; London: T&T Clark, 2007).

Davies, P. R., "The History of Ancient Israel and Judah," *ExpTim* 119 (2007) 15–21.

Davies, P. R., *Memories of Ancient Israel: An Introduction to Biblical History—Ancient and Modern* (Louisville: Westminster John Knox, 2008).

Davies, P. R. (ed.), *The Prophets* (BibSem 42; Sheffield: Sheffield Academic Press, 1996).

Davis, E. F., *Swallowing the Scroll: Textuality and the Dynamics of Discourse in Ezekiel's Prophecy* (JSOTSup 78; Sheffield: JSOT Press, 1989).

Day, J., *God's Conflict with the Dragon and the Sea: Echoes of a Canaanite Myth in the Old Testament* (UCOP 35; Cambridge: Cambridge University Press, 1985).

Day, J. (ed.), *In Search of Pre-Exilic Israel* (JSOTSup 406; London: T&T Clark International, 2004).

Deist, F. E., "The Prophets: Are We Heading for a Paradigm Switch?," in *Prophet und Prophetenbuch*, FS O. Kaiser (ed. V. Fritz, K.-F. Pohlmann, and H.-C. Schmitt; BZAW 185; Berlin: De Gruyter, 1989) 1–18.

Deller, K., "STT 366: Deutungsversuch 1982," *Assur* 3 (1983) 139–53.

Del Monte, G. F., *Testi dalla Babylonia Ellenistica*, vol. 1: *Testi Cronografici* (Studi Ellenistici 9; Pisa and Roma: Istituti editoriali e poligrafici intemazionali, 1997).

Dennis, G. W., "The Use of Water as a Medium for Altered States of Consciousness in Early Jewish Mysticism: A Cross-Disciplinary Analysis," *Anthropology of Consciousness* 19 (2008) 84–106.

Derousseaux, L., *La crainte de Dieu dans l'Ancien Testament: Royauté, Alliance, Sagesse dans les royaumes d'Israël et Juda. Recherches d'exégèse et d'histoire sur la racine yâré* (LeDiv 63; Paris: Cerf, 1970).

Devauchelle, D., "Les prophéties en Egypte ancienne," in *Prophéties et oracles*, vol. 2: *En Égypte et en Grèce* (ed. J. Asurmendi, D. Devauchelle, R. Lebrun, A. Motte, and C. Perrot; Supplément au Cahier Evangile 89; Paris: Cerf, 1994) 6–30.

Dever, W. G., *What Did the Biblical Writers Know and When Did They Know It? What Archaeology Can Tell Us about the Reality of Ancient Israel* (Grand Rapids, Mich.: Eerdmans, 2001).

Dieterle, M., *Dodona: Religionsgeschichtliche und historische Untersuchungen zur Entstehung und Entwicklung des Zeus-Heiligtums* (Spudasmata 116; Hildesheim: Olms, 2007).

Dietrich, M., "Prophetenbriefe aus Mari," in *TUAT* 2/1 (1986) 89–93.

Dietrich, M., *Die Aramäer Südbabyloniens in der Sargonidenzeit (700–648)* (AOAT 7; Kevelaer, Germany: Butzon & Bercker; Neukirchen-Vluyn: Neukirchener, 1970).

Dietrich, M., "Prophetie in den Keilschrifttexten," *JARG* 1 (1973) 15–44.

Dietrich, M., and O. Loretz, "Der Vertrag zwischen Šuppiluliuma und Niqmadu," *WO* 3 (1966) 206–45.

Dietrich, M., and O. Loretz, *Mantik in Ugarit: Keilalphabetische Texte der Opferschau, Omensammlungen, Nekromantie* (ALASP 3; Münster: Ugarit-Verlag, 1990).

Dietrich, W., *Prophetie und Geschichte* (FRLANT 108; Göttingen: Vandenhoeck & Ruprecht, 1972).

Dietrich, W., "Prophetie im deuteronomistischen Geschichtswerk," in *The Future of the Deuteronomistic History* (ed. T. Römer; BETL 147; Leuven: Peters, 2000) 47–65.

Dietrich, W., "Samuel: Ein Prophet?," in *Prophets and Prophecy in Jewish and Early Christian Literature* (ed. J. Verheyden, K. Zamfir, and T. Nicklas; WUNT.2 286; Tübingen: Mohr Siebeck, 2010) 1–17 (= *Sacra Scripta* 5 [2007] 11–26).

Dijkstra, M., *Gods voorstelling: Predikatieve expressie van zelfopenbaring in oudoosterse teksten en Deutero-Jesaja* (Dissertationes Neerlandicae, Series Theologica 2; Kampen: Kok, 1980)

Dijkstra, M., "'I Am Neither a Prophet nor a Prophet's Pupil': Amos 7:9–17 as the Presentation of a Prophet like Moses," in *The Elusive Prophet: The Prophet as a Historical Person, Literary Character, and Anonymous Artist* (ed. J. C. de Moor; OTS 45; Leiden: Brill, 2001) 105–28.

Dillard, R. B., *Neo-Babylonian Texts from the John Frederick Lewis Collection of the Free Library of Philadelphia* (PhD diss., Philadelphia, Pa., Dropsie University, 1975).
Dillard, R. B., *2 Chronicles* (WBC 15; Waco, Tex.: Word Books, 1987).
Dion, P.-E., "The 'Fear Not' Formula and Holy War," *CBQ* 32 (1970) 565–70.
Dion, P.-E., "Deuteronomy 13: The Suppression of Alien Religious Propaganda in Israel during the Late Monarchical Era," in *Law and Ideology in Monarchic Israel* (ed. B. Halpern und D. W. Hobson; JSOTSup 124; Sheffield: Sheffield University Press 1991) 147–216.
Dion, P.-E., "Ahaz and Other Willing Servants of Assyria," in *From Babel to Babylon*, FS B. Peckham (ed. J. Rilett Wood, J. E. Harvey, and M. Leuchter; LHBOTS 455; New York and London: T. & T. Clark, 2007) 133–45.
Dobbs-Allsopp, F. W., "Rethinking Historical Criticism," *BibInt* 7 (1999) 235–71.
Dobbs-Allsopp, F. W., "Late Linguistic Features in the Song of Songs," in *Perspectives on the Song of Songs/Perspektiven der Hoheliedauslegung* (ed. A. Hagedorn; BZAW 346; Berlin: De Gruyter, 2005) 27–77.
Donner, H., and W. Röllig, *Kanaanäische und aramäische Inschriften*, 3 vols. (Wiesbaden: Harrassowitz, ^{3}1971–76 [^{2}1966–69/^{1}1962–64]).
Dossin, G., *Lettres de la première dynastie babylonienne II* (TCL 18; Paris: Geuthner, 1934).
Dossin, G., "Une révélation du dieu Dagan à Terqa," *RA* 42 (1948) 125–34.
Dossin, G., "Sur le prophétisme à Mari," in *La divination en Mésopotamie ancienne et dans les régions voisines* (CRRAI 14; Paris: Presses universitaires de France, 1966) 77–86.
Dossin, G., "Une opposition familiale," in: *La voix de l'opposition en Mésopotamie: Colloque organisé par l'institut des Hautes Études de Belgique 19 et 20 mars 1973*, (Bruxelles: Institut des hautes études de Belgique, 1973) 179–188.
Driel, G. van, *The Cult of Aššur* (SSN 13; Assen: van Gorcum, 1969).
Duhaime, J., *The War Texts: 1QM and Related Manuscripts* (CQS 6; New York: T&T Clark, 2004).
Duhm, B., *Die Theologie der Propheten als Grundlage für die innere Entwicklungsgeschichte der israelitischen Tradition* (Bonn: Marcus, 1875).
Duhm, B., *Das Buch Jeremia* (KHC 11; Tübingen: Mohr Siebeck, 1901).
Duhm, B., *Israels Propheten* (Tübingen: Mohr Siebeck, 1916 [^{2}1922]).
Durand, J.-M., "Note à propos de la date d'*ABL* 290," *RA* 75 (1981) 181–85.
Durand, J.-M., "In vino veritas," *RA* 76 (1982) 43–50.
Durand, J.-M., *Textes administratifs des salles 134 et 160 du Palais de Mari* (ARM 21; Paris: Editions Recherche sur les Civilisations, 1983).
Durand, J.-M., "L'Organisation de l'espace dans le palais de Mari: Le témoignage des textes," in *Le système palatial en Orient, en Grèce et à Rome: Actes du colloque de Strasbourg 19–22 Juin 1985, Université des sciences humaines de Strasbourg* (ed. E. Lévy; Travaux du Centre de recherche sur le Proche-Orient et la Grèce antiques 9; Leiden: Brill 1987) 39–110.
Durand, J.-M., *Archives épistolaires de Mari 1/1* (ARM 26/1; Paris: Editions Recherche sur les Civilisations, 1988).
Durand, J.-M., "La cité-état d'Imâr à l'époque des rois de Mari," *MARI* 6 (1990) 39–92.
Durand, J.-M., "Le mythologème du combat entre le dieu de l'orage at la mer en Mésopotamie," *MARI* 7 (1993) 41–61.

Durand, J.-M., Les 'declarations prophetiques' dans les lettres de Mari," in *Prophéties et oracles*, vol. 1: *Dans le Proche-Orient ancien* (ed. B. N. Porter; Supplément au Cahier Evangile 88; Paris: Cerf, 1994) 8–74.

Durand, J.-M., "La religión en Siria durante la época de los reinos amorreos según la documentación de Mari," in *Mitología y religión del Oriente Antiguo*, vol 2/1: *Semitas occidentales (Ebla, Mari)* (ed. id. and P. Mander; Estudios Orientales 8; Sabadell: AUSA, 1995) 125–533.

Durand, J.-M., "La divination par les oiseaux," *MARI* 8 (1997) 273–82.

Durand, J.-M., *Les documents épistolaires du palais de Mari*, vol. 3 (LAPO 18; Paris: Cerf, 2000)

Durand, J.-M., *Florilegium marianum 7: Le culte d'Addu d'Alep et l'affaire d'Alahtum* (Mémoires de *NABU* 8; Paris: SEPOA, 2002).

Durand, J.-M., "Mari," in *Mythologie et religion des sémites occidentaux* , 2 vols. (ed. G. del Olmo Lete; OLA 162; Leuven: Peeters, 2008) 1:163–631.

Durand, J.-M., "La religion à l'époque amorrite d'après les archives de Mari," in Mythologie et religion des sémites occiden taux, Vol. 1: Ebla, Mari (ed. Gregorio del Olmo Lete; OLA 162; Leuven: Peeters, 2008), 163–631.

Durand, J.-M., "Le *kispum* dans les traditions amorrites," in *Les vivants et leurs morts: Actes du colloque organisé par le Collège de France, Paris, les 14–15 avril 2010* (ed. id., T. Römer, and J. Hutzli; OBO 257; Fribourg and Göttingen: Academic Press Fribourg and Vandenhoeck & Ruprecht, 2012) 33–52.

Durand, J.-M., and M. Guichard, "Les rituels de Mari," in *Florilegium marianum 3*, FS M.-T. Barrelet (ed. D. Charpin and J.-M. Durand; Mémoires de *NABU* 4; Paris: SEPOA, 1997) 19–78.

Edelman, D., "From Prophets to Prophetic Books: The Fixing of the Divine Word," in *The Production of Prophecy: Constructing Prophecy and Prophets in Yehud* (ed. ead. and E. Ben Zvi; London: Equinox, 2009) 29–54.

Edelman, D., and E. Ben Zvi (eds.), *The Production of Prophecy: Constructing Prophecy and Prophets in Yehud* (London: Equinox, 2009).

Ego, B., "Die Wasser der Gottesstadt: Zu einem Motiv der Zionstradition und seinen kosmologischen Implikationen," in *Das biblische Weltbild und seine altorientalischen Kontexte* (ed. B. Janowski and B. Ego; FAT 32; Tübingen: Mohr Siebeck, 2001) 361–89.

Eidinow, E., *Oracles, Curses, and Risk among the Ancient Greeks* (Oxford: Oxford University Press, 2007).

Elgvin, T., "Priestly Sages?: The Milieus of Origin of 4QMysteries and 4QInstruction," in *Sapiential Perspectives: Wisdom Literature in Light of the Dead Sea Scrolls, Proceedings of the Sixth International Symposium of the Orion Center, 20–22 May, 2001* (ed. J. J. Collins, G. E. Sterling, and R. A. Clements; STDJ 51; Leiden: Brill, 2004) 67–87.

Elgvin, T., "The Use of Scripture in 1Q/4QMysteries," in *New Perspectives on Old Texts: Proceedings of the Tenth International Symposium of the Orion Center for the Study of the Dead Sea Scrolls and Associated Literature, 9–11 January, 2005* (ed. E. G. Chazon, B. Halpern-Amaru, and R. A. Clements; STDJ 88; Leiden: Brill, 2010) 117–31.

Ellens, R., *The Destructive Power of Religion: Violence in Judaism, Christianity, and Islam,* Vol. 1, *Sacred Scriptures, Ideology, and Violence* (ed. id.; Westport, Conn.: Praeger, 2004).

Ellis, Maria deJong, "A New Fragment of the Tale of the Poor Man of Nippur," *JCS* 26 (1974) 88–89.
Ellis, Maria deJong, "The Goddess Kititum Speaks to King Ibalpiel: Oracle Texts from Ishchali," *MARI* 5 (1987) 235–66.
Ellis, Maria deJong, "Observations on Mesopotamian Oracles and Prophetic Texts: Literary and Historiographic Considerations," *JCS* 41 (1989) 127–86.
Erbil, Y., and A. Mouton, "Water in Ancient Anatolian Religions: An Archaeological and Philological Inquiry on the Hittite Evidence," *JNES* 71 (2012) 53–74.
Eshel, E., "The Identification of the 'Speaker' of the Self-Glorification Hymn," in *The Provo International Conference on the Dead Sea Scrolls: Technological Innovations, New Texts, and Reformulated Issues* (ed. D. W. Parry and E. C. Ulrich; STDJ 30; Leiden: Brill, 1999) 619–35.
Eshel, E., "4Q471b: A Self-Glorification Hymn," *RevQ* 17 (1996) 175–203.
Evans, R. J., *In Defence of History* (London: Granta, 1997).
Ewald, H., *Die Propheten des Alten Bundes: Zweite Ausgabe in drei Bänden*, vol. 1 (Göttingen: Vandenhoeck & Ruprecht, 1867).
McEwan, G. J. P., "A Seleucid Augural Request," *ZA* 70 (1980) 58–69.
McEwan, G. J. P., "Agade after the Gutian Destruction: The Afterlife of a Mesopotamian City," *AfO.B* 19 (1982) 8–15.
Exum, J. C., *Song of Songs: A Commentary* (OTL; Louisville, Ky.: Westminster John Knox, 2005).
Fabry, H.-J., "*sôd:* Der himmlische Thronrat als ekklesiologisches Modell," in *Bausteine biblischer Theologie*, FS G. J. Botterweck (ed. id.; BBB 50; Köln/Bonn: Hanstein, 1977) 99–126.
Fales, F. M., *Censimenti e catasti di epoca neo-assira* (Studi Economici e Tecnologici 2; Roma: Centro per l'Antichità e la Storia dell'arte del Vicino Oriente, 1973).
Fales, F. M., "The Enemy in Assyrian Royal Inscriptions: the 'Moral Judgement,'" in *Mesopotamien und seine Nachbarn: Politische und kulturelle Wechselbeziehungen im Alten Vorderasien vom 4. bis 1. Jahrtausend v. Chr.* (ed. H.-J. Nissen and J. Renger; BBVO 1; Berlin: Reimer, 1982), 425–35.
Fales, F. M., "A Fresh Look at the Nimrud Wine Lists," in *Drinking in Ancient Societies: History and Culture of Drinks in the Ancient Near East* (ed. L. Milano; History of the Ancient Near East, Studies 6; Padova: Sargon srl, 1994) 361–80.
Fales, F. M., "On *Pax Assyriaca* in the 8th–7th Centuries BC and Its Implications," in *Isaiah's Vision of Peace in Biblical and Modern International Relations* (ed. R. Cohen and R. Westbrook; New York: Palgrave Macmillan, 2008) 17–35.
Fales, F. M., *Guerre et paix en Assyrie: Religion et impérialisme* (Paris: Cerf, 2010).
Fales, F. M., and J. N. Postgate, *Imperial Administrative Records, Part I: Palace and Temple Administration* (SAA 7; Helsinki: Helsinki University Press, 1992).
Fales, F. M., and G. B. Lanfranchi, *Lettere dalla corte Assira* (Venezia: Marsilio Editori, 1992).
Fales, F. M., and G. B. Lanfranchi, "The Impact of Oracular Material on the Political Utterances and Political Action in the Royal Inscriptions of the Sargonid Dynasty," in *Oracles et prophéties dans l'antiquité* (ed. J.-G. Heintz; Université des sciences humaines de Strasbourg, Travaux du Centre de recherche sur le Proche-Orient et la Grèce antiques 15; Paris: De Boccard, 1997) 99–114.

Farber, W., *Beschwörungsrituale an Ištar und Dumuzi: Attī Ištar ša harmaša Dumuzi* (Veröffentlichungen der Orientalischen Kommission 30; Wiesbaden: Franz Steiner, 1977).

Farber, W., "Altassyrische *addaḫšu* und *ḫazuannū*, oder von Safran, Fenchel, Zwiebeln und Salat," *ZA* 71 (1991) 234–42.

Faust, A., "Settlement, Economy, and Demography under Assyrian Rule in the West: The Territories of the Former Kingdom of Israel as a Test Case," *JAOS* 135 (2015) 765–89.

Feldman, L. H., "Prophets and Prophecy in Josephus," in *Prophets, Prophecy, and Prophetic Texts in Second Temple Judaism* (ed. M. H. Floyd and R. D. Haak; LHBOTS 427; New York: T&T Clark, 2006) 210–39 (= *JTS* 41 [1990] 386–422).

Fensham, F. C., *The Books of Ezra and Nehemiah* (NICOT; Grand Rapids: Eerdmans, 1982).

Fenton, T. L., "Deuteronomistic Advocacy of the *nābîʾ*: 1 Samuel ix 9 and Questions of Israelite Prophecy," *VT* 47 (1997) 23–42.

Fenton, T. L., "Israelite Prophecy: Characteristics of the First Protest Movement," in *The Elusive Prophet: The Prophet as a Historical Person, Literary Character and Anonymous Artist* (ed. J. C. de Moor; OTS 45; Leiden: Brill, 2001) 129–41.

Ferry, J., "'Le livre dans le livre': Lecture de Jérémie 36," in *Les Récueils prophétiques de la Bible: Origines, milieu, et contexte proche-oriental* (ed. J.-D. Macchi, C. Nihan, T. Römer, and J. Rückl; MdB 64; Geneva: Labor et fides, 2012) 283–306.

Finkelstein, I., "High or Low: Megiddo and Rehov," in *The Bible and Radiocarbon Dating: Archaeology, Text, and Science* (ed. T. E. Levy and T. Higham; London: Equinox, 2005) 302–9.

Fischer, I., Tora für Israel—Tora für die Völker (SBS 164; Stuttgart: Katholisches Bibelwerk, 1995).

Fischer, I., "World Peace and 'Holy War'—Two Sides of the Same Theological Concept: YHWH as Sole Divine Power" (A Canonical and Intertextual Reading of Isaiah 2:1–5, Joel 4:9–21, and Micah 4:1–5)," in *Isaiah's Vision of Peace in Biblical and Modern International Relations. Swords into Plowshares* (eds., Cohen and Westbrook; Houndmills: Palgrave Macmillan), 151–65

Fischer, I., "The Authority of Miriam: A Feminist Rereading of Numbers 12 Prompted by Jewish Interpretation," in *Exodus to Deuteronomy* (ed. A. Brenner; A Feminist Companion to the Bible, Second Series; Sheffield: Sheffield Academic Press, 2001) 159–73.

Fischer, I., *Gotteskünderinnen: Zu einer geschlechtsfairen Deutung des Phänomens Prophetie und der Prophetinnen in der hebräischen Bibel* (Stuttgart: Kohlhammer, 2002).

Fischer, I., K. Schmid, and H. G. M. Williamson (eds.), *Prophetie in Israel: Beiträge des Symposiums 'Das Alte Testament und die Kultur der Moderne'*, FS G. von Rad (Altes Testament und Moderne 11; Münster 2003).

Fishbane, M., *Biblical Interpretation in Ancient Israel* (Oxford: Clarendon Press, 1985).

Fleming, D. E., "*nābû* and *munabbiātu*: Two New Syrian Religious Personnel," *JAOS* 113 (1993) 175–83.

Fleming, D. E., "The Etymological Origins of the Hebrew *nābîʾ*: The One Who Invokes God," *CBQ* 55 (1993) 217–24.

Fleming, D. E., *Time at Emar: The Cultic Calendar and the Rituals from the Diviner's House* (Winona Lake, Ind.: Eisenbrauns, 2000).

Fleming, D. E., "Prophets and Temple Personnel in the Mari Archives," in *The Priests in the Prophets: The Portrayal of Priests, Prophets and Other Religious Specialists in the Latter*

Prophets (ed. L. L. Grabbe and A. O. Bellis; JSOTSup 408; London: T & T Clark 2004) 44–64.

Flint, P. W., *The Dead Sea Psalms Scrolls and the Book of Psalms* (STDJ 17; Leiden: Brill, 1997).

Flint, P. W., "The Prophet David at Qumran," in Biblical Interpretation at Qumran (ed. M. Henze; SDSRL; Grand Rapids, Mich.: Eerdmans, 2005) 158–67.

Flint, P. W. (ed.), *The Bible at Qumran: Text, Shape, and Interpretation* (ed. Peter W. Flint; SDSRL; Grand Rapids, Mich.: Eerdmans, 2001).

Flower, M. A., *The Seer in Ancient Greece* (Berkeley, Calif.: The University of California Press, 2008).

Floyd, M. H., "Prophecy and Writing in Habakkuk 2,1–5," *ZAW* 105 (1993) 462–81.

Floyd, M. H., "'Write the Revelation!' (Hab 2:2): Re-imagining the Cultural History of Prophecy," in *Writings and Speech in Israelite and Ancient Near Eastern Prophecy* (ed. E. Ben Zvi and id.; SBLSymS 10; Atlanta, Ga.: Society of Biblical Literature, 2000) 103–43.

Floyd, M. H., "Basic Trends in the Form-Critical Study of Prophetic Texts," in *The Changing Face of Form Criticism for the Twenty-First Century* (ed. M. A. Sweeney and E. Ben Zvi; Grand Rapids, Mich.: Eerdmans, 2003) 298–311

Floyd, M. H., "The Production of Prophetic Books in the Early Second Temple Period," in *Prophets, Prophecy, and Prophetic Texts in Second Temple Judaism* (ed. id. and R. D. Haak; LHBOTS 427; London: T & T Clark, 2006) 276–97.

Floyd, M. H., and R. D. Haak (eds.), *Prophets, Prophecy, and Prophetic Texts in Second Temple Judaism* (LHBOTS 427; New York: T & T Clark, 2006).

Flusser, D., "The 'Book of Mysteries' and the High Holy Days Liturgy," in *Judaism of the Second Temple Period*, vol. 1: *Qumran and Apocalypticism* (ed. id. and A. Yadin; Grand Rapids, Mich.: Eerdmans, 2007) 119–39.

Fontenrose, J., *Didyma: Apollo's Oracle, Cult, and Companions* (Berkeley, Calif.: University of California Press, 1988).

Foster, R., "The Poem of the Righteous Sufferer," *COS* 1:486–92.

Foucault, M., *The History of Sexuality*, 3 vols. (trans. Robert Hurley; New York: Vintage, 1988–90).

Fox, M., "*Ṭôb* as a Covenant Terminology," *BASOR* 209 (1973) 41–42.

Frahm, E., *Einleitung in die Sanherib-Inschriften* (AfO.B 26; Wien, Institut für Orientalistik, 1997).

Frahm, E., "Hochverrat in Assur," in *Assur-Forschungen: Arbeiten aus der Forschungsstelle "Edition literarischer Keilschrifttexte aus Assur" der Heidelberger Akademie der Wissenschaften* (Ed. S. M. Maul and N. P. Heeßel. Wiesbaden: Harrassowitz, 2010) 89–137.

Frahm, E., "Reading the Tablet, the Exta, and the Body: The Hermeneutics of Cuneiform Signs in Babylonian and Assyrian Text Commentaries and Divinatory Texts," in *Divination and Interpretation of Signs* (ed. A. Annus; Oriental Institute Seminars 6; Chicago: Oriental Institute, 2010) 93–141.

Frahm, E., "Samaria, Hamath, and Assyria's Conquests in the Levant in the Late 720s BCE: The Testimony of Sargon II's Inscriptions," in *The Last Days of the Kingdom of Israel* (eds. Hasegawa, S., C. Levin, and and K. Radner; BZAW 511; Berlin: de Gruyter, 2018) 55–86.

Frame, G., "Some Neo-Babylonian and Persian Documents Involving Boats," *OrAnt* 25 (1986) 29–50.

Frame, G., "Nabonidus, Nabû-šarra-uṣur, and the Eanna Temple," *ZA* 81 (1991) 37–86.

Frame, G., *Babylonia 689–627 B.C.: A Political History* (Uitgaven van het Nederlands Historisch-Archaeologisch Instituut te Istanbul 69; Istanbul: Nederlands Historisch-Archaeologisch Instituut, 1992).

Frame, G., *Rulers of Babylonia from the Second Dynasty of Isin to the End of Assyrian Domination (1157–612 BC)* (RIMB 2; Toronto: University of Toronto Press, 1995).

Frankena, R., "The Vassal-Treaties of Esarhaddon and the Dating of Deuteronomy," *OTS* 14 (1965) 122–54.

Freedman, S. M. [= S. M. Moren], *If a City Is Set on a Height: The Akkadian Omen Series* Šumma ālu ina mēlê šakin, vol. 1: *Tablets 1–21* (Occasional Publications of the Samuel Noah Kramer Fund 17; Philadelphia, Pa.: Samuel Noah Kramer Fund, 1988).

Frei, N., *1968: Jugendrevolte und globaler Protest* (Munich: Deutscher Taschenbuch Verlag, 2008).

Freydank, H., "Zwei Verpflegungstexte aus Kār-Tukultī-Ninurta," *AoF* 1 (1974) 55–89.

Freydank, H., *Mittelassyrische Rechtsurkunden und Verwaltungstexte* (VS 19; Berlin: Akademie-Verlag, 1976).

Fritz, V., *Die Entstehung Israels im 12. und 11. Jahrhundert v. Chr.* (Biblische Enzyklopädie 2; Stuttgart: Kohlhammer, 1996).

Fritz, V., *The City in Ancient Israel* (BibSem 29; Sheffield: Sheffield Academic Press, 1995).

Frolov, S., "1 Samuel 1–8: The Prophet as Agent Provocateur," in Grabbe and Nissinen, *Constructs of Prophecy* (2011) 77–85.

Fronzaroli, P., "Les combats de Haddad dans les textes d'Ébla," *MARI* 8 (1997) 283–290

Frymer-Kensky, T., "The Tribulations of Marduk: The So-Called 'Marduk Ordeal Text,'" *JAOS* 103 (1983) 131–41.

Frymer-Kensky, T., *In the Wake of the Goddesses: Women, Culture, and the Biblical Transformation of Pagan Myth* (New York: The Free Press, 1992).

Fuchs, A., and S. Parpola, *The Correspondence of Sargon II, Part III: Letters from Babylonia and Eastern Provinces* (SAA 15; Helsinki: Helsinki Univ. Press, 2001).

Fuchs, E., "The History of Women in Ancient Israel: Theory, Method, and the Book of Ruth," in *Her Master's Tools? Feminist And Postcolonial Engagements of Historical-Critical Discourse* (ed. Vander Stichele and Penner; SBLGPBS 9; Atlanta, Ga.: Society of Biblical Literature, 2005) 211–31.

Fuhs, H. F., "יָרֵא *jāre'*," *ThWAT* 3 (1982) 869–93.

Fukuyama, F., *Trust: The Social Virtues and the Creation of Prosperity* (London: Hamish Hamilton, 1995).

Gabbay, U., "The Akkadian Word for 'Third Gender': The kalû (gala) Once Again," in *Proceedings of the 51st Rencontre Assyriologique Internationale Held at the Oriental Institute of the University of Chicago, July 18–22, 2005* (ed. R. D. Biggs, J. Myers, and M. T. Roth; Studies in Ancient Oriental Civilizations 62; Chicago, Ill.: The Oriental Institute, 2008) 49–56.

Gadd, C. J., "Inscribed Prisms of Sargon II from Nimrud," *Iraq* 16 (1954) 173–201 and pls. 43–51.

Gafney, W. C., *Daughters of Miriam: Women Prophets in Ancient Israel* (Minneapolis: Fortress Press, 2008).

Gagnon, R. A. J., *The Bible and Homosexual Practice: Texts and Hermeneutics* (Nashville, Tenn.: Abingdon, 2001).
Gal, Z., *Lower Galilee during the Iron Age* (ASOR Dissertation Series 8; Winona Lake Ind.: Eisenbrauns, 1992).
Galter, H. D., "Die Zerstörung Babylons durch Sanherib," in *Studia Orientalia memoriae Jussi Aro dedicata* (ed. H. Halén; StOr 55/5; Helsinki: Finnish Oriental Society, 1984) 161–73.
Galter, H. D., "Probleme historisch-lehrhafter Dichtung in Mesopotamien," in *Keilschriftliche Literaturen: Ausgewählte Vorträge der XXXII. Rencontre Assyriologique International, Münster, 8.–12.7.1985* (K. Hecker and W. Sommerfeld; Berliner Beiträge zum Vorderen Orient 6; Berlin: Reimer, 1986) 71–79.
Galter, H. D., "Hubur," *DDD*^{2} (1999) 430–31.
Galter, H. D., L. D. Levine, and J. E. Reade, "The Colossi of Sennacherib's Palace and Their Inscriptions," *ARRIM* 4 (1986) 28–30.
Ganzel, T., and S. E. Holtz "Ezekiel's Temple in Babylonian Context," *VT* 64 (2014) 211–26.
García Martínez, F., "Old Texts and Modern Mirages: The 'I' of Two Qumran Hymns," in *Qumranica Minora 1: Qumran Origins and Apocalypticism* (ed. E. J. C. Tigchelaar; STDJ 63; Leiden: Brill, 2007) 105–25.
García Martínez, F., and E. J. C. Tigchelaar, *The Dead Sea Scrolls: Study Edition*, 2 vols. (Leiden: Brill, 2000).
Gardiner, A. H., *Late Egyptian Stories* (Bibliotheca Aegyptiana 1; Brussels: La fondation égyptologique reine Élisabeth, 1932).
Geller, M. J., *Forerunners to Udug Hul* (Stuttgart: Steiner Verlag, 1985).
Geller, M. J., "The Survival of Babylonian Wissenschaft in Later Tradition," in *The Heirs of Assyria: Proceedings of the Opening Symposium of the Assyrian and Babylonian Intellectual Heritage Project Held in Tvärminne, Finland, October 8–11, 1998* (Melammu Symposia 1; Helsinki, The Neo-Assyrian Text Corpus Project, 2000).
Geller, M. J., "West Meets East: Early Greek and Babylonian Diagnosis," in *Magic and Rationality in Ancient Near Eastern and Graeco-Roman Medicine* (ed. H. F. J. Horstmanshoff, M. Stol, and C. R. van Tilburg; Studies in Ancient Medicine 27; Leiden: Brill, 2004)
Geller, M. J., "Deconstructing Talmudic Magic," in *Magic and the Classical Tradition* (ed. C. Burnett and W. F. Ryan; Warburg Institute Colloquia 7; London: The Warburg Institute, 2006) 1–18.
Geller, S. A., *Sacred Enigmas: Literary Religion in the Hebrew Bible* (London and New York: Routledge, 1996).
Genière, J. de la, "Klaros: Bilan provisoire de dix campaignes de fouilles," *REA* 100 (1998) 235–56.
George, A. R., *Babylonian Topographical Texts* (OLA 40; Leuven: Peeters, 1992).
George, A. R., *House Most High: The Temples of Ancient Mesopotamia* (Mesopotamian Civilizations 5; Winona Lake, Ind.: Eisenbrauns, 1993a).
Gerardi, P., "Assurbanipal's Elamite Campaigns: A Literary and Political Study" (Dissertation, University of Pennsylvania, 1987).
Gerstenberger, E. S., "Prophetie in den Chronikbüchern: Jahwes Wort in zweierlei Gestalt," in *Schriftprophetie*, FS J. Jeremias (ed. F. Hartenstein et al.; Neukirchen-Vluyn: Neukirchener Verlag, 2004) 351–67.

Gertz, J. C., "Tora und vordere Propheten" in *Grundinformation Altes Testament* (ed. id.; UTB 2745; Göttingen: Vandenhoeck & Ruprecht, 2006) 187–302.
Gilbert, M., "L'éloge de la Sagesse (*Siracide* 24)," *Revue Théologique de Louvain* 5 (1974) 326–48.
Girard, R., *Violence and the Sacred* (Baltimore: Johns Hopkins University Press, 1977).
Glazov, G. Y., *The Bridling of the Tongue and the Opening of the Mouth in Biblical Prophecy* (JSOTSup 311; Sheffield: Sheffield Academic Press, 2001).
Goertz, H.-J., *Umgang mit Geschichte: Eine Einführung in die Geschichtstheorie* (Rowohlts Enzyklopädie; Reinbek bei Hamburg: Rowohlt, 1995)
Goertz, H.-J., *Unsichere Geschichte: Zur Theorie historischer Referentialität* (Stuttgart: Philipp Reclam, 2001), 11–31.
Goetze, A., *Die Pestgebete des Muršiliš* (Kleinasiatische Forschungen 1; Weimar, 1927–30) 218–19.
Goetze, A., "An Old Babylonian Prayer of the Divination Priest," *JCS* 22 (1968) 25–29.
Goff, M. J., *The Worldly and Heavenly Wisdom of 4QInstruction* (STDJ 50; Leiden: Brill; 2003).
Goff, M. J., *Discerning Wisdom: The Sapiental Literature of the Dead Sea Scrolls* (VTSup 116; Leiden: Brill, 2007).
Goff, M. J., "Qumran Wisdom Literature and the Problem of Genre," *DSD* 17 (2010) 315–35.
Goldingay, J. E., *Daniel* (WBC 30; Waco, Tex.: Word Books, 1989).
Goldstein, J. A., "The Historical Setting of the Uruk Prophecy," *JNES* 47 (1988) 43–46.
Gonçalves, F. J., "Les 'prophètes écrivains' étaient-ils des נביאים?," in *The World of the Aramaeans*, vol. 1, FS P.-E. Dion (ed. P. M. M. Daviau, J.W. Wevers, and M. Weigl; JSOTSup 324; Sheffield: JSOT Press, 2001) 144–85.
Good, E. M., "What Did the Jews of Qumran Know about God and how Did They Know It? Revelation and God in the Dead Sea Scrolls," in *The Judaism of Qumran: A Systemic Reading of the Dead Sea Scrolls*, vol. 2: *World View, Comparing Judaisms* (ed. A. J. Avery-Peck, J. Neusner and B. D. Chilton; HO 57.5; Leiden: Brill, 2001) 3–22.
Gordon, R. P., "From Mari to Moses: Prophecy at Mari and in Ancient Israel," in *Of Prophets' Visions and the Wisdom of Sages*, FS R. N. Whybray (ed. H. A. McKay and D. J. A. Clines; JSOTSup162; Sheffield: JSOT Press, 1993) 63–79.
Gosse, B., "La malédiction contre Babylone de Jérémie 51,59–64 et les redactions du livre de Jérémie," *ZAW* 98 (1986) 383–99.
Grabbe, L. L., *Priests, Prophets, Diviners, Sages: A Socio-Historical Study of Religious Specialists in Ancient Israel* (Valley Forge, Pa.: Trinity Press International, 1995).
Grabbe, L. L., *Ezra-Nehemiah* (Old Testament Readings; London: Routledge, 1998).
Grabbe, L. L., "Ancient Near Eastern Prophecy from an Anthropological Perspective," in *Prophecy in Its Ancient Near Eastern Context: Mesopotamian, Biblical, and Arabian Perspectives* (ed. M. Nissinen; SBLSymS 13; Atlanta, Ga.: Society of Biblical Literature, 2000) 13–32.
Grabbe, L. L., "Poets, Scribes, or Preachers? The Reality of Prophecy in the Second Temple Period," in *Knowing the End from the Beginning: The Prophetic, the Apocalyptic and their Relationships* (ed. id. and R. D. Haak; JSPSup 46; London: T&T Clark International, 2003) 192–215.
Grabbe, L. L., "Prophetic and Apocalyptic: Time for New Definitions–and New Thinking," in *Knowing the End from the Beginning: The Prophetic, the Apocalyptic and their*

Relationships (ed. id. and R. D. Haak; JSPSup 46; London: T&T Clark International, 2003) 107–133.

Grabbe, L. L., *A History of the Jews and Judaism in the Second Temple Period*, Vol. 1: *Yehud History of the Persian Province of Judah* (Library of Second Temple Studies 47; London and New York: T & T Clark, 2004).

Grabbe, L. L., "Thus Spake the Prophet Josephus...: The Jewish Historian on Prophets and Prophecy," in *Prophets, Prophecy and Prophetic Texts in Second Temple Judaism* (ed. M. H. Floyd and R. D. Haak; LHBOTS 427; New York: T. & T. Clark, 2006) 240–47.

Grabbe, L. L., *Ancient Israel: What Do We Know and How Do We Know It?* (New York: T&T Clark, 2007).

Grabbe, L. L., "Daniel: Sage, Seer ... and Prophet?," in *Constructs of Prophecy in the Former and Latter Prophets and Other Texts* (ed. id. and M. Nissinen; ANEM 4; Atlanta, Ga.: Society of Biblical Literature, 2011) 87–94.

Grabbe, L. L., "Her Outdoors: An Anthropological Perspective on Female Prophets and Prophecy," in *Prophets Male and Female: Gender and Prophecy in the Hebrew Bible, the Eastern Mediterranean, and the Ancient Near East* (ed. Corrine L. Carvalho and Jonathan Stökl; SBLAIL 15; Atlanta, Ga.: Society of Biblical Literature, 2013) 11–25.

Grabbe, L. L., *1 & 2 Kings: An Introduction and Study Guide: History and Story in Ancient Israel* (T & T Clark Study Guides to the Old Testament; London: Bloomsbury, 2017).

Grabbe, L. L., and A. O. Bellis (eds.), *The Priests in the Prophets: The Portrayal of Priests, Prophets, and Other Religious Specialists in the Latter Prophets* (JSOTSup 408; New York and London, T & T Clark 2003).

Grabbe, L. L., and R. D. Haak (eds.), *'Every City Shall Be Forsaken': Urbanism and Prophecy in Ancient Israel and the Near East* (JSOTSup 330; Sheffield: Sheffield Academic Press, 2001).

Grabbe, L. L., and R. D. Haak (eds.), *Knowing the End from the Beginning: The Prophetic, The Apocalyptic, and their Relationship* (JSPSup 46; London/New York: T&T Clark International, 2003).

Gray, R., *Prophetic Figures in Late Second Temple Jewish Palestine: The Evidence from Josephus* (New York: Oxford University Press, 1993).

Grayson, A. K., "The Walters Art Gallery Sennacherib Inscription," *AfO* 20 (1963) 83–96.

Grayson, A. K., *Babylonian Historical-Literary Texts* (Toronto Semitic Texts and Studies 3; Toronto/Buffalo: University of Toronto Press, 1975).

Grayson, A. K., *Assyrian and Babylonian Chronicles* (TCS 5; Locust Valley, NY: J.J. Augustin, 1975).

Grayson, A. K., "Assyria and Babylonia," *Or* 49 (1980) 140–94.

Grayson, A. K., "Assyria: Sennacherib and Esarhaddon (704–669 B.C.)," *CAH*² 3/2 (²1991) 103–41.

Grayson, A. K., and W. G. Lambert, "Akkadian Prophecies," *JCS* 18 (1964) 7–30.

Greaves, A. M., *Miletos: A History* (London: Routledge, 2002).

Green, T. M., *The City of the Moon God: Religious Traditions of Harran* (RGRW 114; Leiden: Brill, 1992).

Green, T. M., "The Presence of the Goddess in Harran," in *Cybele, Attis and Related Cults*, FS M. J. Vermaseren (ed. E. N. Lane; RGRW 131; Leiden: Brill, 1996) 87–100.

Greenberg, M., *Ezekiel 1–20: A New Translation with Introduction and Commentary* (AB 22; Garden City, N.Y.: Doubleday, 1983).

Greenberg, M., *Ezekiel 21–37: A New Translation with Introduction and Commentary* (AB 22A; Garden City, N.Y.: Doubleday, 1997).
Greenblatt, S, "Towards a Poetic of Culture," in *The New Historicism*, H. Aram Veeser (ed. New York: Routledge, 1989) 1–14.
Greenfield, J. C., M. E. Stone, and E. Eshel, *The Aramaic Levi Document: Edition, Translation, Commentary* (SVTP 19; Leiden: Brill, 2004).
Greenfield, J. C. and M. Sokoloff, "4QZodiology and Brontology ar," *DJD* 36 (2000) 259–74.
Greenspahn, F., "Why Prophecy Ceased?," *JBL* 108 (1989) 37–49.
Grelot, P., "GALGAL (Ézéchiel 10,2.6.13 et Daniel 7,9)," *Transeuphratène* 15 (1998) 137–47.
Gressmann, H., "Die literarische Analyse Deuterojesajas," *ZAW* 34 (1914) 254–97-
Gressmann, H., "Die Aufgaben der alttestamentlichen Forschung," *ZAW* 24 (1930) 1–33.
Griffiths, J. G., "Apocalyptic in the Hellenistic Era," in *Apocalypticism in the Mediterranean World and the Near East: Proceedings of the International Colloquium on Apocalypticism, Uppsala, August 12–17, 1979* (ed. D. Hellholm; Tübingen: Mohr Siebeck, 1983) 273–93.
Grimm, W., and K. Dittert, *Deuterojesaja: Deutung – Wirkung – Gegenwart* (Calwer Bibelkommentare; Stuttgart: Calwer, 1990).
Groneberg, B., "Die sumerisch-akkadische Inanna/Ištar: Hermaphroditos?," *WO* 17 (1986) 25–46.
Gruber, M. I., "Fear, Anxiety and Reverence in Akkadian, Biblical Hebrew and Other North-West Semitic Languages," *VT* 40 (1990) 411–22.
Güterbock, H. G., "Die historische Tradition und ihre literarische Gestaltung bei Babyloniern und Hethitern bis 1200," *ZA* 42 (1934) 1–91.
Guichard, M., *Florilegium Marianum 14: L'Épopée de Zimrī-Lîm* (Mémoires de NABU 16; Paris: SEPOA, 2014).
Guichard, M., and L. Marti, "Purity in Ancient Mesopotamia: The Paleo-Babylonian and Neo-Assyrian Periods," in *Purity and the Forming of Religious Traditions in the Ancient Mediterranean World and Ancient Judaism* (ed. C. Frevel and C. Nihan; Dynamics in the History of Religion 3; Leiden: Brill, 2013) 47–113.
Guinan, A., "The Perils of High Living: Divinatory Rhetoric in *Šumma Alu*," in *DUMU.E$_2$.DUB.BA.A*, FS Å. W. Sjöberg (ed. H. Behrens, D. Loding, and M. T. Roth; Occasional Publications of the Samuel Noah Kramer Fund 11; Philadelphia, Pa.: The University Museum, 1989) 227–35.
Guinan, A., "A Severed Head Laughed: Stories of Divinatory Interpretation," in *Magic and Divination in the Ancient World* (ed. L. Ciraolo and J. Seidel; SAMD 2; Groningen: Styx, 2002) 7–40.
Guinan, A., "Left/Right Symbolism in Mesopotamian Divination," *SAAB* 10 (1996) 5–10.
Gunkel, H., "Einleitungen," in *Die großen Propheten übersetzt und erklärt* (ed. H. Schmidt; SAT II/2; Göttingen: Vandenhoeck & Ruprecht, 1915) xi–lxxii.
Gunkel, H., *Einleitung in die Psalmen: Die Gattungen der religiösen Lyrik Israels* (completed by J. Begrich; Göttingen: Vandenhoeck & Ruprecht, ^{4}1985).
Gurney, O. R., "Hittite Prayers of Mursili II," *AAA* 27 (1940) 26–27.
Gurney, O. R., and P. Hulin, *The Sultantepe Tablets II* (Occasional Publications of the British Institute of Archaeology at Ankara 7; London: The British Institute of Archaeology at Ankara, 1964).
Haak, R. D., *Habakkuk* (VTSup 44; Leiden: Brill, 1992).
Hackett, J. A., *The Balaam Text from Deir ʿAllā* (HSM 31; Chico, Calif.: Scholars Press, 1984).

Hacking, I., *The Social Construction of What?* (Cambridge, Mass.: Harvard University Press, 1999).
Hämeen-Anttila, J., *A Sketch of Neo-Assyrian Grammar* (SAAS 13; Helsinki: The Neo-Assyrian Text Corpus Project, 2000).
Hämeen-Anttila, J., "Arabian Prophecy," in *Prophecy in Its Ancient Near Eastern Context: Mesopotamian, Biblical, and Arabian Perspectives* (ed. M. Nissinen; SBLSymS 13; Atlanta, Ga.: Society of Biblical Literature, 2000) 115–46.
Hagedorn, A. C., "Looking at Foreigners in Biblical and Greek Prophecy," *VT* 57 (2007) 432–48.
Haldar, A., *Associations of Cult Prophets among the Ancient Semites* (Uppsala: Almqvist & Wiksell, 1945).
Hallo, W. W., "Akkadian Apocalypses," *IEJ* 16 (1966) 231–42.
Hallo, W. W., and K. L. Younger (eds.), *The Context of Scripture*, vol. 1: *Canonical Compositions from the Biblical World* (Leiden: Brill, 1997).
Hallo, W. W., and K. L. Younger (eds.), *The Context of Scripture*, vol. 2: *Monumental Inscriptions from the Biblical World* (Leiden: Brill, 2000).
Hallo, W. W., and K. L. Younger (eds.), *The Context of Scripture*, vol. 3: *Archival Documents from the Biblical World* (Leiden: Brill, 2002).
Halton, C., "Allusions to the Stream of Tradition in Neo-Assyrian Oracles," *ANES* 46 (2009) 50–61.
Hamori, E. J., "Gender and the Verification of Prophecy at Mari," *WO* 42 (2012) 1–22.
Hamori, E. J., *Women's Divination in Biblical Literature: Prophecy, Necromancy, and Other Arts of Knowledge* (The Anchor Yale Reference Library; New Haven: Yale University Press, 2015).
Hamori, E. J., "Childless Female Diviners in the Bible and Beyond," in *Prophets Male and Female: Gender and Prophecy in the Hebrew Bible, the Eastern Mediterranean, and the Ancient Near East* (eds. C. L. Carvalho and J. Stökl; SBLAIL 15. Atlanta, Ga.: Society of Biblical Literature, 2013) 161–91.
Hamori, E. J., "The Prophet and the Necromancer: Women's Divination for Kings," *JBL* (2013) 827–43.
Handy, L. K., "The Role of Huldah in Josiah's Cult Reform," *ZAW* 106 1994) 40–53.
Hardmeier, C., "Zur schriftgestützten Expertentätigkeit Jeremias im Milieu der Jerusalemer Führungseliten (Jeremia 36): Prophetische Literaturbildung und die Neuinterpretation älterer Expertisen in Jeremia 21–23," in *Die Textualisierung der Religion* (ed. J. Schaper; FAT 62; Tübingen: Mohr Siebeck, 2009) 105–49.
Hardmeier, C., "Schriftgebrauch und Literaturbildung im Milieu der Jerusalemer Führungseliten in spätvorexilischer Zeit (Jeremia 36)," in *Berührungspunkte: Studien zur Sozial- und Religionsgeschichte Israels und seiner Umwelt*, FS R. Albertz (ed. I. Kottsieper, R. Schmitt, and J. Wöhrle; AOAT 350; Münster: Ugarit-Verlag, 2008) 267–90.
Harner, P. B., "The Salvation Oracle in Second Isaiah," *JBL* 88 (1969) 418–34.
Hasegawa, S., C. Levin, and and K. Radner (ed.), *The Last Days of the Kingdom of Israel* (BZAW 511; Berlin: de Gruyter, 2018).
Hawkins, J. D., "Inscription," in *A New Luwian Stele and the Cult of the Storm-God at Til Barsib-Masuwari* (ed. G. Bunnens; Tell Ahmar 2; Leuven: Peeters, 2006) 11–31.

Hawkins, J. D., "Hattusa: Home to the Thousand Gods of Hatti," in *Capital Cities: Urban Planning and Spiritual Dimensions: Proceedings of the Symposium Held on May 27–29, 1996, Jerusalem, Israel* (ed. J. G. Westenholz; Bible Lands Museum Jerusalem Publications 2; Jerusalem: Bible Lands Museum, 1998) 65–82.

Heacock, A., "Wrongly Framed? The 'David and Jonathan Narrative' and the Writing of Biblical Homosexuality [sic]" *The Bible and Critical Theory* 3/2 (2007) 1–22.

Hecker, K., "Zukunftsdeutungen in akkadischen Texten," *TUAT* 2/1 (1986) 56–82.

Heimpel, W., *Tierbilder in der sumerischen Literatur* (StP 2; Roma: Editrice Pontificio Istituto Biblico, 1968).

Heimpel, W., "Minding an Oath," *NABU* (1999) 41.

Heimpel, W., *Letters to the King of Mari: A New Translation, with Historical Introduction, Notes, and Commentary* (Mesopotamian Civilizations 12; Winona Lake, Ind.: Eisenbrauns, 2003).

Heintz, J.-G., "Oracles prophétiques et 'guerre sainte' selon les archives royales de Mari et l'Ancien Testament," in *Congress Volume: Rome 1968* (VTSup 17; Leiden: Brill, 1969) 112–28.

Heintz, J.-G., "Note sur les origines de l'apocalyptique judaïque à la lumière des 'prophéties akkadiennes'," in *L'Apocalyptique* (ed. F. Raphael *et al.*; Etudes d'histoire des religions 3; Paris: Paul Geuthner, 1977) 71–87.

Heintz, J.-G., "Aux origines d'une expression biblique: *ūmūšu qerbū*, in A.R.M. X/6, 8'?," *VT* 21 (1971) 528–40.

Heintz, J.-G., "Des textes sémitiques anciens à la Bible hébraïque: Un comparatisme légitime?" in *Le comparatisme en histoire des religions* (ed. F. Bœspflug and F. Dunand; Paris: Cerf, 1997) 127–56.

Heintz, J.-G., "La 'fin' des prophètes bibliques? Nouvelles théories et documents sémitiques anciens," in *Oracles et prophéties dans l'antiquité* (ed. id.; Université des sciences humaines de Strasbourg, Travaux du Centre de recherche sur le Proche-Orient et la Grèce antiques 15; Paris: de Boccard, 1997) 195–214.

Heintz, J.-G. (ed.), *Oracles et prophéties dans l'antiquité. Actes du Colloque de Strasbourg, 15–17 Juin 1995* (Université des sciences humaines de Strasbourg, Travaux du Centre de recherche sur le Proche-Orient et la Grèce antiques 15; Paris: de Boccard, 1997).

Heltzer, M., "On the Origin of the Near Eastern Archaeological Amber," in *Languages and Cultures in Contact: At the Crossroads of Civilizations in the Syro-Mesopotamian Realm* (ed. K. van Lerberghe and G. Voet; OLA 96/CRRAI, 42; Leuven: Peeters, 1999) 169–76.

Henten, J. W. van, "Mastemah," *DDD*^{2} (1999) 553–54.

Henz-Piazza, G., *The New Historicism* (GBS; Minneapolis, Minn.: Fortress, 2002).

Henze, M. (ed.), A *Biblical Interpretation at Qumran* (SDSRL; Grand Rapids, Mich.: Eerdmans, 2005).

Herbordt, S., *Neuassyrische Glyptik des 8.–7. Jh. v. Chr. unter besonderer Berücksichtigung der Siegelungen auf Tafeln und Tonverschlüssen* (SAAS 1; Helsinki: The Neo-Assyrian Text Corpus Project, 1992).

Herbordt, S., "Neo- Assyrian Royal and Administrative Seals and their Use," in *Assyrien im Wandel der Zeiten* (ed. H. Waetzoldt and H. Hauptmann; CRRAI 39 = HSAO 6; Heidelberg: Heidelberger Orientverlag, 1997) 279–83.

Hermisson, H.-J., "Kriterien "wahrer" und "falscher" Prophetie im Alten Testament: Zur Auslegung von Jeremia 23,16–22 und Jeremia 28,8–9," *ZThK* 92 (1995) 121–39.

Herrmann, S., *Jeremia* (BKAT 12/2; Neukirchen-Vluyn: Neukirchener Verlag, 1990).
Hilber, J. W., *Cultic Prophecy in the Psalms* (BZAW 352; Berlin and New York: De Gruyter, 2005).
Hill, A. E., "Dating Second-Zechariah: A Linguistic Reexamination," *HAR* 6 (1982) 105–34.
Hodder, I., *Archaeology beyond Dialogue* (Foundations of Archaeological Inquiry; Salt Lake City: University of Utah Press, 2003).
Höffken, P., "Heilszeitherrschererwartung im babylonischen Raum: Überlegungen im Anschluß an W 22 307.7," *WO* 9 (1977) 57–71.
Hölscher, G., *Die Profeten* (Leipzig: Hinrichs, 1914).
Hörig, M., *Dea Syria: Studien zur religiösen Tradition der Fruchtbarkeitsgöttin in Vorderasien* (AOAT 208; Kevelaer Neukirchen-Vluyn: Neukirchener Verlag, 1979).
Hoffner, Jr., H. A., *Letters from the Hittite Kingdom* (SBLWAW 15; Atlanta, Ga.: Society of Biblical Literature, 2009).
Hoftijzer, J., and G. van der Kooij, *Aramaic Texts from Deir 'Alla* (DMOA 19; Leiden: Brill, 1976).
Holladay, W. L., *Jeremiah*, vol. 1: *A Commentary on the Book of the Prophet Jeremiah, Chapters 1–25* (Hermeneia; Philadelphia, Pa.: Fortress, 1986).
Holladay, W. L., *Jeremiah*, vol. 2: *A Commentary on the Book of the Prophet Jeremiah, Chapters 26–52* (Hermeneia; Minneapolis, Minn.: Fortress, 1989).
Holloway, S. W., "Harran: Cultic Geography in the Neo-Assyrian Empire and its Implications for Sennacherib's 'Letter to Hezekiah' in 2 Kings," in *The Pitcher is Broken*, FS G. W. Ahlström (ed. id. and L. K. Handy; JSOTSup 190; Sheffield: Sheffield Academic Press, 1995) 276–314.
Holloway, S. W., *Aššur Is King! Aššur Is King! Religion in the Exercise of Power in the Neo-Assyrian Empire* (CHANE 10; Leiden: Brill, 2002).
Horgan, M. P., *Pesharim: Qumran Interpretations of Biblical Books* (CBQMS 8; Washington, D.C.: The Catholic Biblical Association of America, 1979).
Horowitz, W., and J. Ben-Dov, "The Babylonian Lunar Three in Qumran Calendars," *ZA* 95 (2005) 104–20.
Hossfeld, F.-L. (ed.), "Vorwort," in *Vom Sinai zum Horeb: Stationen alttestamentlicher Glaubensgeschichte* (Würzburg: Echter, 1989).
Hossfeld, F.-L., und I. Meyer, *Prophet gegen Prophet: Eine Analyse der alttestamentlichen Texte zum Thema: Wahre und falsche Prophetie* (BiBe NF 9; Fribourg: Fribourg Academic Press, 1973).
Houston, W., "Was there a Social Crisis in the Eighth Century?," in *In Search of Pre-Exilic Israel* (ed. J. Day; JSOTSup 406; London: T&T Clark International, 2004) 130–49.
Hout, T. van den, *The Purity of Kingship: An Edition of CTH 569 and Related Hittite Oracle Inquiries of Tut aliya IV* (DMOA 25; Leiden, Boston, and Köln: Brill, 1998).
Hout, T. van den, "Bemerkungen zu älteren hethitischen Orakeltexten," in *Kulturgeschichten*, FS V. Haas (ed. T. Richter et al.; Saarbrücken: Saarbrückener Druckerei und Verlag, 2001) 423–40.
Hübner, U., and E. A. Knauf (eds.), *Kein Land für sich allein: Studien zum Kulturkontakt in Kanaan, Israel/Palästina und Ebirnâri für Manfred Weippert zum 65. Geburtstag* (OBO 186; Fribourg and Göttingen: Academic Press Fribourg and Vandenhoeck & Ruprecht, 2002).

Huffmon, H. B., "The Origins of Prophecy," in *Magnalia Dei: The Mighty Acts of God*, FS G. E. Wright (ed. F. M. Cross, W. E. Lemke, and P.D. Miller; Garden City, N.Y.: Doubleday, 1976) 171–86.

Huffmon, H. B., "Ancient Near Eastern Prophecy," *ABD* 5 (1992) 477–82.

Huffmon, H. B., "The Expansion of Prophecy in the Mari Archives: New Texts, New Readings, New Information," in *Prophecy and Prophets: The Diversity of Contemporary Issues in Scholarship* (ed. Y. Gitay; SBL Semeia Studies; Atlanta, Ga.: Society of Biblical Literature, 1997) 7–22.

Huffmon, H. B., "A Company of Prophets: Mari, Assyria, Israel," in *Prophecy in Its Ancient Near Eastern Context: Mesopotamian, Biblical, and Arabian Perspectives* (ed. M. Nissinen; SBLSymS 13; Atlanta, Ga.: Society of Biblical Literature, 2000) 47–70.

Huffmon, H. B., "The one and the Many: Prophets and Deities in the Ancient Near East,"in *Propheten in Mari, Assyrien und Israel* (ed. M. Köckert and M. Nissinen; FRLANT 201; Göttingen: Vandenhoeck & Ruprecht, 2003) 116–31.

Huffmon, H. B., "The *assinnum* as Prophet: Shamans at Mari?" in *Nomades et sédentaires dans le Proche-Orient ancien* (ed. C. Nicolle; Amurru 3; Paris: Éditions Recherche sur les Civilisations, 2004) 241–47.

Huffmon, H. B., "The Oracular Process: Delphi and the Near East," *VT* 57 (2007) 449–60.

Hunger, H., *Babylonische und assyrische Kolophone* (AOAT 2; Kevelaer and Neukirchen-Vluyn: Butzon & Bercker and Neukirchener Verlag, 1968).

Hunger, H., *Astrological Reports to Assyrian Kings* (SAA 8; Helsinki: Helsinki University Press, 1992).

Hunger, H., *Spätbabylonische Texte aus Uruk*, vol. 1 (Ausgrabungen der Deutschen Forschungsgemeinschaft in Uruk-Warka 9; Berlin: Gebr. Mann, 1976).

Hunger, H., and S. A. Kaufman, "A New Akkadian Prophecy Text," *JAOS* 95 (1975) 371–75.

Huntington, S., *The Clash of Civilizations and the Remaking of World Order* (New York: Simon & Schuster 1996).

Hurowitz, V., "Isaiah's Impure Lips and Their Purification in the Light of Akkadian Sources," *HUCA* 60 (1989) 39–89.

Hurowitz, V., "Advice to a Prince: A Message from Ea," *SAAB* 12 (1998) 39–53.

Hurvitz, A., "Can Biblical Texts Be Dated Linguistically? Chronological Perspectives in the Historical Study of Biblical Hebrew," in *Congress Volume, Oslo 1998* (ed. A. Lemaire and M. Sæbø; VTSup 53; Leiden: Brill, 2000) 143–60.

Husser, J.-M., *Dreams and Dream Narratives in the Biblical World* (trans. J. M. Munro; BibSem 63; Sheffield: Sheffield Academic Press, 1999).

Hutter, M., *Religionen in der Umwelt des Alten Testaments I: Babylonier, Syrer, Perser* (Studienbücher Theologie 4/1; Stuttgart: Kohlhammer, 1996).

Iggers, G. G., *Geschichtswissenschaft im 20. Jahrhundert: Ein kritischer Überblick im internationalen Zusammenhang* (Göttingen: Vandenhoeck & Ruprecht, 1993).

Iggers, G. G., *Historiography in the Twentieth Century: From Scientific Objectivity to the Postmodern Challenge* (Hanover, N.H.: Wesleyan University Press, 1997).

Iggers, G. G., and J. M. Powell (eds.), *Leopold von Ranke and the Shaping of the Historical Discipline* (Syracuse, N.Y.: Syracuse University Press, 1990).

Iggers, G. G., "The Crisis of the Rankean Paradigm in the Nineteenth Century" in Leopold von Ranke and the Shaping of the Historical Discipline (ed. id. and J. M. Powell; Syracuse, N.Y.: Syracuse University Press, 1990) 170–79.

Irvine, S. A., "Enmity in the House of God (Hosea 9:7–9)," *JBL* 117 (1998) 645–53.

Ishida, T., *The Royal Dynasties in Ancient Israel: A Study on the Formation and Development of Royal-Dynastic Ideology* (BZAW 142; Berlin and New York: De Gruyter, 1977).

Jacobs, J., "Traces of the Omen Series Šumma izbu in Cicero, *De divinatione*," in *Divination and Interpretation of Signs in the Ancient World* (ed. A. Annus; The Oriental Institute of the University of Chicago Oriental Institute Seminars 6; Chicago: The Oriental Institute, 2010) 317–39.

Jacobsen, T., "Primitive Democracy in Ancient Mesopotamia," *JNES* 2 (1943) 159–72.

Jannot, J.-R., *Religion in Ancient Etruria* (trans. J. Whitehead; Madison, Wisc.: University of Wisconsin Press, 2005).

Janowski, B., *Rettungsgewissheit und Epiphanie des Heils: Das Motiv der Hilfe Gottes "am Morgen" im Alten Orient und im Alten Testament*, vol. 1: *Alter Orient* (WMANT 59; Neukirchen-Vluyn: Neukirchener Verlag, 1989).

Jassen, A. P., *Mediating the Divine: Prophecy and Revelation in the Dead Sea Scrolls and Second Temple Judaism* (STDJ 68; Leiden: Brill, 2007).

Jassen, A. P., "The Presentation of Ancient Prophets as Lawgivers at Qumran," *JBL* 127 (2008) 307–37.

Jassen, A. P., "Prophets and Prophecy in the Qumran Community," *AJS Review* 37 (2008) 299–334.

Jean, C., "Divination and Oracles at the Neo-Assyrian Palave: The Importance of Signs in Royal Ideology," in *Divitation and Interpretation of Signs* (ed. A. Annus; Oriental Institute Seminars 6; Chicago: Oriental Institute, 2010) 267–75.

Jeffers, A., *Magic and Divination in Ancient Palestine and Syria* (SHCANE 8; Leiden: Brill, 1996).

Jenni, S. E., "Dtn 19,16: *sarā* "Falschheit"," in *Mélanges Bibliques et orientaux en l'honneur de M. Henri Cazelles* (ed. A. Caquot und M. Delcor; AOAT 212; Kevelaer/Neukirchen-Vluyn: Neukirchener Verlag, 1981).

Jepsen, A., *NABI: Soziologische Studien zur alttestamentlichen Literatur und Religionsgeschichte* (Munich: Beck'sche Verlagsbuchhandlung, 1934).

Jepsen, A., " אמן 'āman," *TDOT 1* (1974) 292–323.

Jepsen, A., " בטח bāṭaḥ," *TDOT 2* (1975) 88–94.

Jeremias, J., *Der Prophet Hosea* (ATD 24/1; Göttingen: Vandenhoeck & Ruprecht, 1983)

Jeremias, J., "Das Proprium der alttestamentlichen Prophetie," *ThLZ* 119 (1994) 483–94.

Jeremias, J., *Der Prophet Amos* (ATD 24/2; Göttingen: Vandenhoeck & Ruprecht, 1995).

Jeremias, J., *Hosea und Amos: Studien zu den Anfängen des Dodekapropheton* (FAT 13; Tübingen: Mohr Siebeck, 1996).

Jeremias, J., "Gelehrte Prophetie: Beobachtungen zu Joel und Deuterosacharja," in *Vergegenwärtigung des Alten Testaments: Beiträge zur biblischen Hermeneutik*, FS R. Smend (ed. C. Bultmann, W. Dietrich, and C. Levin; Göttingen: Vandenhoeck & Ruprecht, 2002) 97–111.

Jeremias, J., *Die Propheten Joel, Obadja, Jona, Micha* (ATD 24/3; Göttingen: Vandenhoeck & Ruprecht, 2007).

Jeremias, J., "Das Rätsel der Schriftprophetie," *ZAW* 125 (2013): 93–117.

Jeremias, J., *Studien zur Theologie des Alten Testaments* (ed. F. Hartenstein and J. Krispenz; FAT 99; Tübingen: Mohr Siebeck, 2015).

Joannès, F. and A. Lemaire, "Contrats babyloniens d'époque achéménide du Bitabî Râm avec une épigraphie araméenne," *RA* 90 (1996) 41–60.

Joannès, F. and A. Lemaire, "Trois tablettes cunéiformes à l'onomastique ouest-sémitique (Collection Sh. Moussaieff)," *Transeuphratène* 17 (1999) 17–34.

Johag, I., "*ṭwb:* Terminus Technicus in Vertrags- und Bündnisformularen des Alten Orients und des Alten Testaments," in *Bausteine biblischer Theologie*, FS G. J. Botterweck, (ed. H.-J. Fabry; BBB 50; Köln/Bonn: Hanstein, 1977) 3–23.

Johnston, S. I., *Ancient Greek Divination* (Blackwell Ancient Religions; Chichester: Wiley-Blackwell, 2008).

Jokiranta, J., "Qumran: The Prototypical Teacher in the Qumran Pesharim: A Social-Identity Approach," in *Ancient Israel: The Old Testament in Its Social Context* (ed. P. F. Esler; Minneapolis, Minn.: Fortress, 2006) 254–63.

Jokiranta, J., *Social Identity and Sectarianism in the Qumran Movement* (STDJ 105; Leiden: Brill, 2012).

Jong, Matthijs de, "Ezekiel as a Literary Figure and the Quest for the Historical Prophet," *The Book of Ezekiel and Its Influence* (ed. H. J. de Jonge and J. Tromp; Aldershot: Ashgate, 2007) 1–16.

Jong, Matthijs de, *Isaiah among the Ancient Near Eastern Prophets: A Comparative Study of the Earliest Stages of the Isaiah Tradition and the Neo-Assyrian Prophecies* (VTSup 117; Leiden: Brill, 2007).

Jong, Matthijs de, "Biblical Prophecy – A Scribal Enterprise: The Old Testament Prophecy of Unconditional Judgement Considered as a Literary Phenomenon," *VT* 61 (2011) 39–70.

Jonker, L., "The Chronicler and the Prophets: Who Were His Authoritative Sources?," in *What Was Authoritative for Chronicles?* (ed. E. Ben Zvi and D. Edelman; Winona Lake, Ind.: Eisenbrauns, 2011) 145–64.

Jutikkala, E. and K. Pirinen, *A History of Finland* (trans. by Paul Sjöblom; Helsinki: WSOY, 2003).

Kaiser, O., "Traditionsgeschichtliche Untersuchung von Genesis 15," *ZAW* 70 (1958) 107–26.

Kaiser, O., *Das Buch des Propheten Jesaja: Kapitel 1–12* (ATD 17; Göttingen: Vandenhoeck & Ruprecht, [5]1981).

Kaiser, O., *Der Gott des Alten Testaments: Theologie des Alten Testaments*, vol. 1: *Grundlegung* (UTB 1747; Göttingen: Vandenhoeck & Ruprecht, 1993).

Kaiser, O., "Kult und Kultkritik im Alten Testament," in *'Und Mose schrieb dieses Lied auf': Studien zum Alten Testament und zum Alten Orient*, FS Oswald Loretz (ed. M. Dietrich and I. Kottsieper; AOAT 250; Münster: Ugarit-Verlag, 1998) 401–26.

Kalimi, I., "Religionsgeschichte Israels oder Theologie des Alten Testaments: Das jüdische Interesse an der biblischen Theologie," *JBTh* 10 (1995) 45–68.

Kammenhuber, A., *Orakelpraxis, Träume und Vorzeichenschau bei den Hethitern* (Hethitische Texte 7; Heidelberg: Winter, 1976).

McKane, W., *A Critical and Exegetical Commentary on Jeremiah*, vol. 1: Introduction and Commentary on Jeremiah 1–25 (ICC; Edinburgh: T. & T. Clark, 1986).

McKane, W., *A Critical and Exegetical Commentary on Jeremiah*, vol. 2: A Commentary on Jeremiah 26–52 (ICC; Edinburgh: T&T Clark, 1996).

Kartveit, M., ("Sach 13,2–6: Das Ende der Prophetie – aber welcher?," in *Text and Theology*, FS M. Sæbø (ed. A. Tangberg; Oslo: Verbum, 1994) 143–56.

Kasari, P., *Nathan's Promise in 2 Samuel 7 and Related Texts* (PFES 97; Helsinki: The Finnish Exegetical Society,) 2009.

Kataja, L., and R. M. Whiting, *Grants, Decrees, and Gifts of the Neo-Assyrian Period* (SAA 12; Helsinki: Helsinki University Press, 1995).

Kaufman, S. A., *The Akkadian Influences on Aramaic* (AS 19; Chicago, Ill. and London: The University of Chicago Press, 1974).

Kaufman, S. A., "Prediction, Prophecy, and Apocalypse in the Light of New Akkadian Texts," in *Proceedings of the Sixth World Congress of Jewish Studies*, vol. 1 (ed. A. Shinan; Jerusalem: World Union of Jewish Studies, 1977) 221–28.

Keck, L. E., "Will the Historical-Critical Method Survive? Some Observations," in *Orientation by Disorientation: Studies in Literary Criticism and Biblical Literary Criticism*, FS W. A. Beardslee (ed. R. A. Spencer; Pittsburgh: Pickwick, 1980) 115–27.

Keel, O., *JHWH-Visionen und Siegelkunst: Eine neue Deutung der Majestätschilderungen in Jes 6, Ez 1 und 10 und Sach 4* (SBS 84/85; Stuttgart: Katholisches Bibelwerk, 1977).

Keel, O., *Das Böcklein in der Milch seiner Mutter und verwandtes: Im Lichte eines altorientalischen Bildmotivs* (OBO 33; Fribourg and Göttingen: Academic Press Fribourg and Vandenhoeck & Ruprecht, 1980).

Keel, O., *Das Hohelied* (ZBK.AT 18; Zurich: Theologischer Verlag, 1986).

Keel, O., "Altägyptische und biblische Weltbilder, die Anfänge der vorsokratischen Philosophie und das Ἀρχή-Problem in späten biblischen Schriften," in *Das biblische Weltbild und seine altorientalischen Kontexte* (ed. B. Janowski and B. Ego; FAT 32; Tübingen: Mohr Siebeck, 2001) 27–63.

Kegler, J., "Prophetengestalten im Deuteronomistischen Geschichtswerk und in den Chronikbüchern: Ein Beitrag zur Kompositions- und Redaktionsgeschichte der Chronikbüchern," *ZAW* 105 (1993) 481–97.

Keinänen, J., *Traditions in Collision: A Literary and Redaction-Critical Study on the Elijah Narratives 1 Kings 17–19* (PFES 80: Helsinki: Finnish Exegetical Society and Göttingen: Vandenhoeck & Ruprecht, 2001).

Kelle, B. E., "Ancient Israelite Prophets and Greek Political Orators: Analogies for the Prophets and Their Implications for Historical Reconstruction," in *Israel's Prophets and Israel's Past*, FS J. H. Hayes (ed. id. and M. B. Moore; LHBOTS 446; New York and London: T & T Clark, 2006) 57–82.

Kelle, B. E., "The Phenomenon of Israelite Prophecy in Contemporary Scholarship," *CurBR* 12 (2014): 275–320.

Kelle, B. E., and M. B. Moore (eds.), *Israel's Prophets and Israel's Past*, FS J. H. Hayes (LHBOTS 446; New York and London: T & T Clark, 2006).

Kessler, J., "Reconstructing Haggai's Jerusalem: Demographic and Sociological Considerations and the Search for an Adequate Methodological Point of Departure," in *"Every City Shall Be Forsaken": Urbanism and Prophecy in Ancient Israel and the Near East* (ed. L. L. Grabbe and R. D. Haak; JSOTSup 330; Sheffield: JSOT Press 2001) 137–58.

Kessler, K., *The Book of Haggai: Prophecy and Society in Early Persian Yehud* (VTSup 91; Leiden: Brill, 2002).

Kessler, R., "Mirjam und die Propheten der Perserzeit," in *Gott an den Rändern*, FS W. Schottroff (ed. U. Bail and R. Jost; Gütersloh: Gütersloher Verlagshaus, 1996) 64–72.

Kessler, R., *Micha* (HTKAT; Freiburg: Herder, 1999).

Kessler, R., "Zwischen Tempel und Tora: Das Michabuch im Diskurs der Perserzeit," *BZ* 44 (2000) 21–36.

Kessler, R., "Miriam and the Prophecy of the Persian Period," in *Prophets and Daniel* (ed. A. Brenner; FCB 2/8; Sheffield: Sheffield Academic Press, 2001) 77–86.

Kilian, R., "Ps 22 und das priesterliche Heilsorakel," *BZ* 12 (1968) 172–85.

Kimball, C., *When Religion Becomes Evil* (San Francisco: Harper San Francisco, 2002).

Kindt, J., "Omphalos," *Encyclopedia of Ancient History* (ed. R. S. Bagnall et al.; Wiley Blackwell, 2013), 4900–4901.

Kingsbury, E. C., "The Prophets and the Council of Yahweh," *JBL* 83 (1964) 279–86.

Kingsley, P., "Ezekiel by the Grand Canal: Between Jewish and Babylonian Tradition," *JRAS* 3/2 (1992) 339–46.

Kitchen, K. A., *On the Reliability of the Old Testament* (Grand Rapids: Eerdmans, 2003).

Kitz, A. M., "Prophecy as Divination," *CBQ* 65 (2003) 22–42.

Klauber, E. G., *Politisch-religiöse Texte aus der Sargonidenzeit* (Leipzig: Eduard Pfeiffer, 1913).

Klauber, E. G., "Zur Politik und Kultur der Sargonidenzeit," *AJSL* 30 (1914) 233–87.

Klein, A., *Schriftauslegung im Ezechielbuch: Redaktionsgeschichtliche Untersuchungen zu Ez 34–39* (BZAW 391; Berlin and New York: De Gruyter, 2008).

Klengel, H., "Der Wettergott von Halab," *JCS* 19 (1965) 87–93.

Klengel, H., *Geschichte des hethitischen Reiches* (HdO 1/34; Leiden: Brill, 1998).

Klengel, H., "Ḫalab – Mari – Babylon: Aspekte syrisch-mesopotamischer Beziehungen in altbabylonischer Zeit," in *De la Babylonie à la Syrie, en passant par Mari*, FS J.-R. Kupper (ed. Ö. Tunca; Liége: Université de Liège, 1990) 183–95

Klopfenstein, M. A., "Hosea 9,7–9: Ein Lese- und Übersetzungsversuch," *ThZ* 57 (2001) 135–39.

Knauf, E.-A., "From History to Interpretation," in *The Fabric of History: Texts, Artifact and Israel's Past* (ed. D. V. Edelman; JSOTSup 127; Sheffield: Sheffield Academic Press, 1991) 26–64.

Knauf, E.-A., "Vom Prophetinnenwort zum Prophetenbuch: Jesaja 8,3f im Kontext von Jesaja 6,1–8,16," *lectio difficilior* 2/2000 (www.lectio.unibe.ch).

Knauf, E.-A., "The Glorious Days of Manasseh," in *Good Kings and Bad Kings* (ed. L. L. Grabbe; LHBOTS 393; London: T&T Clark, 2005), 164–88.

Knohl, I., *The Messiah before Jesus* (Berkeley, Calif.: University of California Press, 2000).

Knoppers, G. N., *1 Chronicles 10–29: A New Translation with Introduction and Commentary* (AB 12 A; New York: Doubleday, 2004)

Knoppers, G. N., "Democratizing Revelation? Prophets, Seers and Visionaries in Chronicles," in *Prophecy and the Prophets in Ancient Israel: Proceedings of the Oxford Old Testament Seminar* (ed. J. Day; LHBOTS 531; New York and London: T & T Clark, 2010) 391–409.

Knoppers, G. N., *Jews and Samaritans: The Origins and History of Their Early Relations* (Oxford: Oxford University Press, 2013).

Koch, K., "Die Briefe 'prophetischen' Inhalts aus Mari: Bemerkungen zu Gattung und Sitz im Leben," *UF* 4 (1972) 53–77.

Koch, U. S., "Three Strikes and You're Out! A View on Cognitive Theory and the First-Millennium Extispicy Ritual," in *Divination and the Interpretation of Signs in the Ancient World* (ed. A. Annus; Oriental Institute Seminars 6; Chicago: Oriental Institute, 2010) 43–59.

Koch-Westenholz, U., *Mesopotamian Astrology: An Introduction to Babylonian and Assyrian Celestial Divination* (CNI Publications 19; Copenhagen: Museum Tusculanum Press, 1995).

Köckert, M., "Zum literargeschichtlichen Ort des Prophetengesetzes Dtn 18 zwischen dem Jeremiabuch und Dtn 13," in *Liebe und Gebot: Studien zum Deuteronomium*, FS L. Perlitt (ed. R. G. Kratz and H. Spieckermann; FRLANT 190; Göttingen: Vandenhoeck & Ruprecht 2000) 80–100.

Köckert, M., "Die Theophanie des Wettergottes Jahwe in Psalm 18," in *Kulturgeschichten*, FS V. Haas (ed. T. Richter, D. Prechel, and J. Klinger; Saarbrücken: Saarbrücker Druckerei und Verlag, 2001) 209–26.

Köckert, M., "Elia: Literarische und religionsgeschichtliche Probleme in 1Kön 17–18," in *Der Eine Gott und die Götter: Polytheismus und Monotheismus im antiken Israel* (ed. M. Oeming and K. Schmid; AThANT 82; Zurich: Theologischer Verlag, 2003) 111–44.

Köckert, M., and M. Nissinen (eds.), *Propheten in Mari, Assyrien und Israel* (FRLANT 201; Göttingen: Vandenhoeck & Ruprecht, 2003).

Kofoed, J., *Text and History: Historiography and the Study of Biblical Texts* (Winona Lake, Ind.: Eisenbrauns, 2005).

Köhler, L., "Die Offenbarungsformel 'Fürchte dich nicht' im Alten Testament," *SThZ* 36 (1919) 33–39.

Köhler, L., *Deuterojesaja stilkritisch untersucht* (BZAW 37; Gießen: Töpelmann, 1923).

Kolf, M. C. van der, "Prophetes," in *PW* 45 (1957) 797–814.

Koppen, F. van, "Seized by the Royal Order: The Households of Sammêtar and Other Magnates at Mari," in *Florilegium marianum 6*, FS A. Parrot (ed. D. Charpin and J.-M. Durand; Mémoires de *NABU* 7; Paris: SEPOA, 2002) 289–372.

Kowalzig, B., *Singing for the Gods: Performances of Myth and Ritual in Archaic and Classical Greece* (Oxford: Oxford University Press, 2007).

Krämer, H., "προφήτης κτλ. A: Die Wortgruppe in der Profangräzität," *ThWNT* 6 (1959) 783–95.

Kratz, R. G., "Die Redaktion der Prophetenbücher," in *Rezeption und Auslegung im Alten Testament und in seinem Umfeld*, FS O. H. Steck (ed. id. and T. Krüger; OBO 153; Fribourg and Göttingen: Academic Press Fribourg and Vandenhoeck & Ruprecht, 1997) 9–27.

Kratz, R. G., "Das Neue in der Prophetie des Alten Testaments," in *Prophetie in Israel: Beiträge des Symposiums 'Das Alte Testament und die Kultur der Moderne'*, FS G. von Rad (ed. I. Fischer, K. Schmid, and H. G. M. Williamson; Altes Testament und Moderne 11; Münster: LIT, 2003) 1–22.

Kratz, R. G., *Die Propheten Israels* (Munich: Beck, 2003).

Kratz, R. G., *The Composition of the Narrative Books of the Old Testament* (trans. John Bowden; London: T & T Clark, 2005).

Kratz, R. G., "'Siehe ich lege meine Worte in deinen Mund': Die Propheten des Alten Testaments," in *Die Bibel: Entstehung – Botschaft –Wirkung* (ed. R. Feldmeier and H. Spieckermann; Göttingen: Vandenhoeck & Ruprecht, 2004) 24–39 (= id., *Prophetenstudien: Kleine Schriften II* [ed. id.; FAT 74; Tübingen: Mohr Siebeck, 2011] 18–31).

Kratz, R. G., "Rewriting Isaiah: The Case of Isaiah 28–31," in *Prophecy and the Prophets in Ancient Israel: Proceedings of the Oxford Old Testament Seminar* (ed. J. Day;

LHBOTS 531; New York and London: T & T Clark, 2010) 245 – 66 (= "Jesaja 28 – 31 als Fortschreibung," in id., *Prophetenstudien: Kleine Schriften II* [ed. id.; FAT 74; Tübingen: Mohr Siebeck, 2011] 177 – 97).

Kratz, R. G., "Probleme der Prophetenforschung," in *Prophetenstudien: Kleine Schriften II* (ed. id.; FAT 74; Tübingen: Mohr Siebeck, 2011) 3 – 17.

Kratz, R. G., "Die Worte des Amos von Tekoa," in *Propheten in Mari, Assyrien und Israel* (ed. M. Köckert and M. Nissinen; FRLANT 201; Göttingen: Vandenhoeck & Ruprecht, 2003) 54 – 89.

Kruger, P. A., "The Prophet 'with' God: The Prophetic Image in Hos 9:7b–8 and the Colometry," *UF* 25 (1993) 219 – 26.

Krüger, T., "Theoretische und methodische Probleme der Geschichte des alten Israel in der neueren Diskussion," *VF* 53 (2008) 4 – 22.

Küchler, F., "Das priesterliche Orakel in Israel und Juda," in *Abhandlungen zur semitischen Religionsgeschickte und Sprachwissenschaft*, FS W. W. Grafen von Baudissin (ed. W. Frankenberg and F. Küchler; BZAW 33; Gießen: Töpelmann, 1918) 285 – 301.

Kuenen, A., *De Profeten en de Profetie onder Israël: Historisch-dogmatische Studie*, 2 vols. (Leiden: Engels, 1875).

Kupitz, Y., and K. Berthelot, "Deborah and the Delphic Pythia: A New Interpretation of Judges 4:4 – 5," in *Images and Prophecy in the Ancient Eastern Mediterranean* (ed. M. Nissinen and C. E. Carter; FRLANT 233; Göttingen: Vandenhoeck & Ruprecht, 2009) 95 – 124.

Kutsko, J. F., *Between Heaven and Earth: Divine Presence and Absence in the Book of Ezekiel* (Biblical and Judaic Studies 7; Winona Lake, Ind.: Eisenbrauns, 2000).

Kwasman, T., and S. Parpola, *Legal Transactions of the Royal Court of Nineveh, Part I: Tiglath-Pileser III through Esarhaddon* (SAA 6; Helsinki: Helsinki University Press, 1991).

Köhlmoos, M., *Bet-El – Erinnerungen an eine Stadt: Perspektiven der alttestamentlichen Bet-El-Überlieferung* (FAT 49; Tübingen: Mohr Siebeck, 2007) 126 – 31.

Laato, A., *"About Zion I Will not Be Silent": The Book of Isaiah as an Ideological Unity* (CB.OT 44; Stockholm: Almqvist & Wiksell, 1998).

Laato, A., and J. van Ruiten (eds.), *Rewritten Bible Reconsidered: Proceedings of the Conference in Karkku, Finland, August 24 – 26, 2006* (Studies in Rewritten Bible 1; Turku: Åbo Akademi Press; Winona Lake: Eisenbrauns, 2008).

Lafont, B., "Le roi de Mari et les prophètes du dieu Adad," *RA* 78 (1984) 7 – 18.

Lambert, W. G., *Babylonian Wisdom Literature* (Oxford: Clarendon Press, 1960; repr. Winona Lake, Ind., 1996).

Lambert, W. G., "Divine Love-Lyrics from the Reign of Abi-ešuh," *MIO* 12 (1966) 41 – 56.

Lambert, W. G., "History and the Gods: A Review Article," *Or* 39 (1970) 170 – 77.

Lambert, W. G., *The Background of Jewish Apocalyptic* (The Ethel M. Wood Lecture delivered before the University of London on 22 February 1977; London: The Athlone Press, 1978).

Lambert, W. G., "Devotion: The Languages of Religion and Love," in *Figurative Language in the Ancient Near East* (ed. M. Mindlin, M. J. Geller, and J. E. Wansbrough; London: School of Oriental and African Studies, 1987) 25 – 39.

Lambert, W. G., "Esarhaddon's Attempt to Return Marduk to Babylon," in *Ad bene et fideliter seminandum*, FS K. Deller (ed. G. Mauer and U. Magen; AOAT 220; Kevelaer: Butzon & Bercker; Neukirchen–Vluyn: Neukirchener Verlag, 1988) 157 – 74.

Lambert, W. G., *Babylonian Wisdom Literature* (Oxford: Oxford Univ. Press, 1960; repr. Winona Lake, Ind.: Eisenbrauns, 1996).
Lambert, W. G., *Babylonian Oracle Questions* (Winona Lake, Ind.: Eisenbrauns, 2007).
Lampinen, A., "Θεῷ μεμελημένε Φοίβῳ: Oracular Functionaries at Claros and Didyma in the Imperial Period," in *Studies in Ancient Oracle and Divination* (ed. Mika Kajava; Acta Instituti Romani Finlandiae 40; Rome: Institutum Romanum Finlandiae, 2013) 49–88.
Landsberger, B., *Brief des Bischofs von Esagila an König Asarhaddon* (Mededelingen der Koninklijke Nederlandse Akademie van Wetenschappen, afd. Letterkunde, Nieuwe reeks 28/6; Amsterdam: Koninklijke Nederlandse Akademie van Wetenschappen, 1965).
Landy, F., *Hosea* (Readings: A New Biblical Commentary; Sheffield: Sheffield Academic Press, 1995).
Landy, F., "Torah and Anti-Torah: Isaiah 2:2–4 and 1:10–26," *BibInt* 11 (2000) 317–34.
Lanfranchi, G. B., and S. Parpola, *The Correspondence of Sargon II, Part II: Letters from the Northern and Northeastern Provinces* (SAA 5; Helsinki: Helsinki University Press, 1990).
Lang, M., and R. Rollinger, "Im Herzen der Meere und in der Mitte des Meeres: Das Buch Ezechiel und die in assyrischer Zeit fassbaren Vorstellungen von den Grenzen der Welt," in *Interkulturalität in der Alten Welt: Vorderasien, Hellas, Ägypten und die vielfältigen Ebenen des Kontakts* (ed. R. Rollinger et al.; Philippika 34; Wiesbaden: Harrassowitz, 2010) 207–64.
Lange, A., "In Diskussion mit dem Tempel: Zur Auseinandersetzung zwischen Kohelet und weisheitlichen Kreisen am Jerusalemer Tempel," in *Qohelet in the Context of Wisdom* (ed. A. Schoors; BETL 136; Leuven: Peeters, 1998) 113–59.
Lange, A., "Die Weisheitstexte aus Qumran: Eine Einleitung," in *The Wisdom Texts from Qumran and the Development of Sapiental Thought* (ed. C. Hempel, A. Lange, and H. Lichtenberger; BETL 159; Leuven: Peeters, 2002) 3–30.
Lange, A., *Vom prophetischen Wort zur prophetischen Tradition: Studien zur Traditions- und Redaktionsgeschichte innerprophetischer Konflikte in der Hebräischen Bibel* (FAT 34; Tübingen: Mohr Siebeck, 2002) 163–68.
Lange, A., "Interpretation als Offenbarung: Zum Verhältnis von Schriftauslegung und Offenbarung," in *Wisdom and Apocalypticism in the Dead Sea Scrolls and in the Biblical Tradition* (ed. F. García Martínez; BETL 168; Leuven: Peeters, 2003) 17–33.
Lange, A., "Reading the Decline of Prophecy," in *Reading the Present in the Qumran Library: The Perception of the Contemporary by Means of Scriptural Interpretations* (ed. K. de Troyer and A. Lange; SBLSymS 30; Atlanta, Ga.: Society of Biblical Literature, 2005) 181–91.
Lange, A., "Literary Prophecy and Oracle Collection: A Comparison between Judah and Greece in Persian Times," in *Prophets, Prophecy and Prophetic Texts in Second Temple Judaism* (ed. M. H. Floyd and R. D. Haak; LHBOTS 427; New York: T. & T. Clark, 2006) 248–75.
Lange, A., "Greek Seers and Israelite-Jewish Prophets," *VT* 57 (2007) 461–82.
Langdon, S., *Die neubabylonischen Königsinschriften* (VAB 4; Leipzig: Hinrichs, 1912).
Langdon, S., *Sumerian Epic of Paradise: The Flood and the Fall of Man* (PBS 10/1; Philadelphia, Pa.: University of Pennsylvania Museum, 1915).
Lapidus, I. M., "Cities and Societies: A Comparative Study of the Emergence of Urban Civilization in Mesopotamia and Greece," *Journal of Urban History* 21 (1986) 257–92.
Lapinkivi, Pirjo, *The Sumerian Sacred Marriage in the Light of Comparative Evidence* (SAAS 15; Helsinki: The Neo-Assyrian Text Corpus Project, 2004).

Lapsley, J. E., “Body Piercings: The Priestly Body and the ‘Body’ of the Temple in Ezekiel,” *HeBAI* 1 (2012) 231–45.

Larsen, M. T., “Unusual Eponymy-Datings from Mari and Assyria,” *RA* 68 (1974) 14–24.

Larson, J., *Greek Nymphs: Myth, Cult, Lore* (Oxford: Oxford University Press, 2001).

Lau, W., *Schriftgelehrte Prophetie in Jes 56–66* (BZAW 225; Berlin: De Gruyter, 1994).

Lauha, Risto, *Psychophysischer Sprachgebrauch im Alten Testament: Eine struktursemantische Analyse von לב, נפש und רוח*, vol. 1: *Emotionen* (AASF B Diss 35; Helsinki: Academia Scientiarum Fennica, 1983).

Launderville, D. F., *Spirit and Reason: The Embodied Character of Ezekiel’s Symbolic Thinking* (Waco, Tex.: Baylor University Press, 2007).

Launderville, D. F., “The Threat of Synchretism to Ezekiel’s Exilic Audience in the Dry Bones Passage,” *WO* 45 (2015) 38 –49.

Lawrence, J. D., *Washing in Water: Trajectories of Ritual Bathing in the Hebrew Bible and Second Temple Literature* (SBLAB; Atlanta, Ga.: Society of Biblical Literature, 2006).

Lebram, J. C. H., “Jerusalem, Wohnsitz der Weisheit,” in *Studies in Hellenistic Religions* (ed. M. J. Vermaseren; EPRO 78; Leiden: Brill, 1979) 103–28.

Lefèvre-Novaro, D., and A. Mouton, “Aux origins de l’ichthyomancie en Anatolie ancienne: sources archéologiques et textuelles,” *Anatolica* 34 (2008) 7–51.

Lehnart, B., *Prophet und König im Nordreich Israel: Studien zur sogenannten vorklassischen Prophetie im Nordreich Israel anhand der Samuel-, Elija- und Elischa-Überlieferungen* (VTSup 96; Leiden: Brill, 2003).

Leichty, E., *The Omen Series Šumma izbu* (TCS 4; Locust Valley, N.Y.: Augustin, 1970).

Leichty, E., *The Royal Inscriptions of Esarhaddon, King of Assyria (680–669 BC)* (RINAP 4; Winona Lake, Ind.: Eisenbrauns, 2011).

Leick, G., *Sex and Eroticism in Mesopotamian Literature* (London and New York: Routledge, 1994).

Lemaire, A., “Notes d’épigraphie nord-ouest sémitique,” *Syria* 64 (1987) 205–16.

Lemaire, A., “Oracles, politique et littérature dans les royaumes araméens et transjordaniens (IXe–VIIIe s. av. n.è.),” in *Oracles et prophéties dans l’antiquité* (ed. J.-G. Heintz; Université des sciences humaines de Strasbourg, Travaux du Centre de recherche sur le Proche-Orient et la Grèce antiques 15; Paris: De Boccard, 1997) 171–93.

Lemaire, A., “Prophètes et rois dans les inscriptions ouest-sémitiques (IXe–VIe siècle av. J.C.),” in *Prophètes et rois: Bible et Proche-Orient* (ed. id.; LeDiv, hors série; Paris: Cerf, 2001) 85–115

Lemaire, A. (ed.), *Prophètes et rois: Bible et Proche-Orient* (LeDiv, hors série; Paris: Cerf, 2001).

Lemche, N. P., *Early Israel: Anthropological and Historical Studies on the Israelite Society before the Monarchy* (VTSup 37; Leiden: Brill, 1985).

Lemche, N. P., “Warum die Theologie des Alten Testaments einen Irrweg darstellt,” *JBTh* 10 (1995) 79–92.

Lemche, N. P., *The Old Testament between Theology and History: A Critical Survey* (Louisville, Ky.: Westminster John Knox, 2008).

Lenzi, A., *Secrecy and the Gods: Secret Knowledge in Ancient Mesopotamia and Biblical Israel* (SAAS 19; Helsinki: The Neo-Assyrian Text Corpus Project, 2008).

Leuchter, M., *The Polemics of Exile in Jeremiah 26–45* (New York: Cambridge University Press, 2008).

Levin, C., *Die Verheißung des neuen Bundes in ihrem theologiegeschichtlichen Zusammenhang ausgelegt* (FRLANT 137; Göttingen: Vandenhoeck & Ruprecht, 1985).
Levin, C., "Das Amosbuch der Anawim," *ZThK* 94 (1997) 407–36.
Levin, C., *Das Alte Testament* (Munich: Beck, ²2003).
Levin, C., "Das Wort Jahwes an Jeremia: Zur ältesten Redaktion der jeremianischen Sammlung," *ZThK* 101 (2004) 257–80.
Levin, C., *The Old Testament: A Brief Introduction* (Princeton NJ: Princeton University Press, 2005).
Levin, C., "In Search of the Original Biblical Record of the Assyrian Conquest of Samaria," ," in *The Last Days of the Kingdom of Israel* (eds. Hasegawa, S., C. Levin, and and K. Radner; BZAW 511; Berlin: de Gruyter, 2018) 251–64.
Levine, B. A., "The Deir ʿAlla Plaster Inscriptions," in *The Context of Scripture*, vol. 2: *Monumental Inscriptions from the Biblical World* (ed. W. W. Hallo and K. L. Younger; Leiden: Brill, 2000) 140–45.
Levine, L. D.,"Sennacherib's Southern Front: 704–689 B.C.," *JCS* 34 (1982) 28–69.
Levinson, B. M., "'But You Shall Surely Kill Him': The Text-Critical and Neo-Assyrian Evidence for MT Deut 13:20," in *Bundesdokument und Gesetz: Studien zum Deuteronomium* (ed. G. Braulik; HBS 4, Freiburg: Herder, 1995) 37–63.
Levinson, B. M., "Recovering the Original Meaning of ולא תכסה עליו (Deuteronomy 13:9)," *JBL* 115 (1996) 601–20.
Levinson, B. M., "Textual Criticism, Assyriology, and the History of Interpretation: Deuteronomy 13:7a as a Test Case in Method," *JBL* 120 (2001) 211–43.
Levison, J. R., "Philo's Personal Experience and the Persistence of Prophecy," in *Prophets, Prophecy, and Prophetic Texts in Second Temple Judaism* (ed. M. H. Foyd and R. D. Haak; LHBOTS 427; New York: T & T Clark, 2006) 194–209.
Lewis, T. J., "'You Have Heard What the Kings of Assyria Have Done': Disarmament Passages vis-à-vis Assyrian Rhetoric of Intimidation," in *Isaiah's Vision of Peace in Biblical and Modern International Relations: Swords into Plowshares* (ed. R. Cohen and R. Westbrook; Culture and Religion in International Relations; New York: Palgrave MacMillan, 2008) 75–100.
Lewy, H., "Nitokris – Naqîʾa," *JNES* 11 (1952) 264–86.
Lewy, J., *Tablettes cappadociennes, troisième série, première partie* (TCL 19; Paris: Geuthner, 1935).
Lichtheim, M., *Ancient Egyptian Literature: A Book of Readings.* I. *The Old and Middle Kingdoms*, 3 vols. (Berkeley, Calif.: University of California Press, 1973).
Lieberman, S. J., "A Mesopotamian Background for the So-Called Aggadic 'Measures' of Biblical Hermeneutics?," *HUCA* 58 (1987) 157–225.
Lilly, I. E., *Two Books of Ezekiel: Papyrus 967 and the Masoretic Text as Variant Literary Editions* (VTSup 150; Leiden: Brill, 2012).
Lim, T. H., "The Alleged Reference to the Tripartite Division of the Hebrew Bible," *RevQ* 20 (2001) 23–37.
Lim, T. H., *Pesharim* (CQS 3; London: Continuum, 2003).
Lim, T. H., "'All These He Composed through Prophecy,'" in *Prophecy after the Prophets? The Contribution of the Dead Sea Scrolls to the Understanding of Biblical and Extra-Biblical Prophecy* (ed. K. de Troyer and A. Lange; CBET 52; Leuven: Peeters, 2009) 61–73.

Limburg, J.,"Swords to Ploughshares: Text and Contexts," in *Writing and Reading the Scroll of Isaiah. Studies of An Interpretative Tradition,* Vol. 1 (eds. C. C. Broyles and C. A. Evans; VTSup 70; Leiden: Brill, 1997) 279–93.

Lindblom, J., "Zur Frage des kanaanäischen Ursprungs des altisraelitischen Prophetismus," in *Von Ugarit nach Qumran*, FS O. Eissfeldt (ed. J. Hempel and L. Rost; Berlin: Töpelmann, 1958) 89–104.

Lindblom, J., *Profetismen i Israel* (Stockholm: Svenska kyrkans diakonistyrelsen, 1934).

Lindblom, J., *Prophecy in Ancient Israel* (Oxford: Blackwell, 1963, [2]1973).

Lion, B., "Les mentions de 'prophètes' dans la seconde moitié du IIe millémaire av. J.-C.," *RA* 94 (2000) 21–32.

Lipiński, É., *Le poème royal du Psaume LXXXIX 1–5.20–38* (CRB 6; Paris: Gabalda, 1967).

Lipiński, É., *Studies in Aramaic Inscriptions and Onomastics* (OLA 57; Leuven: Peeters, 1994).

Liss, H., "'Describe the Temple to the House of Israel': Preliminary Remarks on the Temple Vision in the Book of Ezekiel and the Question of Fictionality in Priestly Literatures," *Utopia and Dystopia in Prophetic Literature* (ed. E. Ben Zvi; PFES 92; Helsinki: The Finnish Exegetical Society, 2006) 122–43.

Liverani, M., *Studies on the Annals of Ashurnasirpal II*, vol. 2: *Topographical Analysis* (Quaderni di Geografica Storica 4; Rome: Centro Stampa d'Ateneo, 1992).

Livingstone, A., *Mystical and Mythological Explanatory Works of Assyrian and Babylonian Scholars* (Oxford: Clarendon Press, 1986).

Livingstone, A., *Court Poetry and Literary Miscellanea* (SAA 3; Helsinki: Helsinki University Press, 1989).

Lods, A., and G. Dossin, "Une tablette inédite de Mari, intéressante pour l'histoire ancienne du prophetisme sémitique," in *Studies in Old Testament Prophecy*, FS T. H. Robinson (ed. H. H. Rowley; Edinburgh: T & T Clark 1950) 103–10.

Long, B. O., "Social Dimensions of Prophetie Conflict," *Semeia* 21 (1981) 31–53.

Longman, T. I., *Fictional Akkadian Autobiography: A Generic and Comparative Study* (Winona Lake, Ind.: Eisenbrauns, 1991).

Loretz, O., *Die Königspsalmen: Die altorientalisch-kanaanäische Königsideologie in jüdischer Sicht*, vol. 1: *Ps 20, 21, 72, 101 und 144: Mit einem Beitrag von I. Kottsieper zu Papyrus Amherst* (UBL 6; Münster: Ugarit-Verlag, 1988).

Loretz, O., "Die Entstehung des Amos-Buches im Licht der Prophetien aus Māri, Assur, Ishchali und der Ugarit-Texte: Paradigmenwechsel in der Prophetenforschung," *UF* 24 (1992) 179–215.

Loretz, O., "Review of W. W. Hallo and K. L. Younger (eds.), *The Context of Scripture*," *UF* 28 (1996) 791–93.

Loretz, O., "Rechtfertigung aus der Perspektive altorientalischer und alttestamentlicher juristischer Terminologie," *Teologinen Aikakauskirja* 105 (2000) 75–88.

Lucas, E. C., "Daniel: Resolving the Enigma," *VT* 50 (2000) 66–80.

Luckenbill, D. D., *The Annals of Sennacherib* (OIP 2; Chicago, Ill.: University of Chicago Press, 1924).

Lust, J., "Ezéchiel dans la Septante," in *Les Récueils prophétiques de la Bible: Origines, milieu, et contexte proche-oriental* (ed. J.-D. Macchi, C. Nihan, T. Römer, and J. Rückl; MdB 64; Geneva: Labor et fides, 2012) 337–58.

Luukko, M., and G. van Buylaere, *The Political Correspondence of Esarhaddon* (SAA 16; Helsinki: Helsinki University Press, 2002).

Macchi, J.-D., and T. Römer, "La formation des livres prophétiques: enjeux et débats," in *Les recueils prophétiques de la Bible: Origines, milieux, et contexte proche-oriental* (ed. J.-D. Macchi, C. Nihan, T. Römer, and J. Rückl; MdB 64; Geneva: Labor et fides, 2012) 9–27.

Machinist, P., "Assyria and Its Image in First Isaiah," *JAOS* 103 (1983) 719–37.

Macintosh, A. A., *A Critical and Exegetical Commentary on Hosea* (ICC; Edinburgh: T&T Clark, 1997).

Mack, B., *Logos und Sophia: Untersuchungen zur Weisheitstheologie im hellenistischen Judentum* (StUNT 10; Göttingen: Vandenhoeck & Ruprecht, 1973).

MacKinlay, J. E., *Gendering Wisdom the Host: Biblical Invitations to Eat and Drink.* (JSOTSup 216; Sheffield: Sheffield Academic Press, 1996).

Malamat, A., "A Forerunner of Biblical Prophecy: The Mari Documents," in *Ancient Israelite Religion*, FS F. M. Cross (ed. P. D. Miller Jr., P. D. Hanson, and S. D. McBride; Philadelphia, Pa.: Fortress Press, 1987) 33–52.

Malamat, A., "A Mari Prophecy and Nathan's Dynastic Oracle," in *Prophecy,* FS G. Fohrer (ed. J. A. Emerton; BZAW 150. Berlin/New York: De Gruyter, 1980) 68–82.

Malamat, A., "Parallels between the New Prophecies from Man and Biblical Prophecy," *NABU 4* (1989) 61–64; repr. in id., *Mari and the Bible* (SHCANE 12; Leiden: Brill, 1998) 122–27.

Malamat, A., "New Light from Mari (ARM XXVI) on Biblical Prophecy," in *Storia e tradizioni di Israele*, FS J. A. Soggin (ed. D. Garrone and F. Israel; Brescia: Paideia, 1991) 185–90 (= id., *Mari and the Bible* [SHCANE 12; Leiden: Brill, 1998] 128–33).

Malamat, A., "The Cultural Impact of the West (Syria-Palestine) on Mesopotamia in the Old Babylonian Period," *AoF* 24 (1997) 310–19.

Malamat, A., *Mari and the Bible* (SHCANE 12; Leiden: Brill, 1998).

Marböck, J., *Gottes Weisheit unter uns: Zur Theologie des Buches Sirach* (HBS 6; Freiburg: Herder, 1995).

Marböck, J., *Weisheit im Wandel: Untersuchungen zur Weisheitstheologie bei Ben Sira: Mit Nachwort und Bibliographie zur Neuauflage* (BZAW 272; Berlin: De Gruyter, 1999 [= 1971]).

Marinatos, N., "The Role of the Queen in Minoan Prophecy Rituals," in *Images and Prophecy in the Ancient Eastern Mediterranean* (ed. M. Nissinen and C. E. Carter; FRLANT 233; Göttingen: Vandenhoeck & Ruprecht, 2009) 86–94.

Marjanen, A., "Female Prophets among Montanists," in *Prophets Male and Female: Gender and Prophecy in the Hebrew Bible, the Eastern Mediterranean, and the Ancient Near East* (ed. C. L. Carvalho and J. Stökl; SBLAIL 15; Atlanta, Ga.: Society of Biblical Literature, 2013), 127–43.

Marjanen, A., and I. Dunderberg, *Juudaksen evankeliumi* (Helsinki: WSOY, 2006).

Marshall, J. W., "Postcolonialism and the Practice of History," in *Her Master's Tools? Feminist And Postcolonial Engagements of Historical-Critical Discourse* (ed.C. Vander Stichele and T. Penner; SBLGPBS 9; Atlanta, Ga.: Society of Biblical Literature, 2005), 93–108.

Marttila, M., "Die Propheten Israels in Ben Sira's 'Lob der Väter,'" in *Houses Full of All Good Things. Essays in Memory of T. Veijola* (ed. J. Pakkala and M. Nissinen; PFES 95; Helsinki: Finnish Exegetical Society; Göttingen: Vandenhoeck & Ruprecht, 2008) 434–50

Masing, U., "Kas *elmešu* = helmes?," in *Aarted tellistes* (ed. M.-L. Tammiste, R. Järv, and K. Salve; Tartu: Kirjastus Ilmamaa, 2011), 189–99 (= *Emakeele Seltsi Aastaraamat* 23 [1977] 23–32).

Mattila, R., "The Political Status of Elam after 653 B. C. according to *ABL* 839," *SAAB* 1 (1987) 27–30.

Mattila, R., *The King's Magnates: A Study of the Highest Officials of the Neo-Assyrian Empire* (SAAS 11; Helsinki: Neo-Assyrian Text Corpus Project, 2000).

Maul, S. M., *Zukunftsbewältigung: Eine Untersuchung altorientalischen Denkens anhand der babylonisch-assyrischen Löserituale (Namburbi)* (BaF 18; Mainz: Philipp von Zabern, 1994).

Maul, S. M., "Der assyrische König: Hüter der Weltordnung," in, *Priests and Officials in the Ancient Near East: Papers of the Second Colloquium on the Ancient Near East – The City and its Life* (ed. K. Watanabe; Heidelberg: Winter, 1999) 201–14.

Maul, S. M., "Die Frühjahrsfeierlichkeiten in Aššur," in *Wisdom, Gods and Literature*, FS W. G. Lambert (ed. A. R. George and I. L. Finkel; Winona Lake, Ind.: Eisenbrauns, 2000) 389–420.

Maurizio, L. "Anthropology and Spirit Possession: A Reconsideration of the Pythia's Role at Delphi," *JHS* 115 (1995): 69–86.

Mayer, W., "Sargons Feldzug gegen Urartu – 714 v. Chr.: Eine militärhistorische Würdigung," *MDOG* 112 (1980) 13–33.

Mayer, W., "Der babylonische Feldzug Tukulti-Ninurtas I. von Assyrien," *SEL* 5 (1988) 143–61.

Mayer, W., *Politik und Kriegskunst der Assyrer* (ALASP 9; Münster: Ugarit-Verlag, 1995).

Mazar, A., "The Debate over the Chronology of the Iron Age in the Southern Levant: Its History, the Current Situation, and a Suggested Resolution," in *The Bible and Radiocarbon Dating: Archaeology, Text, and Science* (ed. T. E. Levy and T. Higham; London: Equinox, 2005) 15–30.

Melugin, R. F., *The Formation of Isaiah 40–55* (BZAW 141; Berlin and New York: De Gruyter, 1976).

Melville, S. C., *The Role of Naqia/Zakutu in Sargonid Politics* (SAAS 9; Helsinki: Neo-Assyrian Text Corpus Project, 1999).

Menzel, B., *Assyrische Tempel*, vol. 1: *Untersuchungen zu Kult, Administration und Personal* (StPSM 10.1; Rome: Biblical Institute Press, 1981).

Menzel, B., *Assyrische Tempel*, vol. 2: *Anmerkungen, Textbuch, Tabellen und Indices* (StPSM 10.2; Rome: Biblical Institute Press, 1981).

Merendino, R. P., "Literarkritisches, Gattungskritisches und Exegetisches zu Jes 41,8–16," *Bib* 53 (1972) 1–42.

Merenlahti, P., and R. Hakola, "Reconceiving Narrative Criticism," *Characterization in the Gospels: Reconceiving Narrative Criticism* (ed. D. Rhoads and K. Syreeni; JSNTSup 184; Sheffield; Sheffield Academic Press, 1999) 13–48.

Merlo, P., "Profezia neoassira e oracoli di salvezza biblici. Motivazioni, forme e contenuti di un possibile confronto," *Rivista Biblica* 50 (2002) 129–52.

Merlo, P., "āpilum of Mari: A Reappraisal," *UF* 36 (2004): 323–32.

Mettinger, T. N. D., *King and Messiah: The Civil and Sacral Legitimation of the Israelite Kings* (CB.OT 8; Lund: CWK Gleerup, 1976).

Metzler, D., "Mural Crowns in the Ancient Near East and Greece", in *An Obsession with Fortune: Tyche in Greek and Roman Art* (ed. S. B. Matheson; Catalogue for the Exhibition

held at the Yale University Art Gallery, 1 September–31 December, 1994; New Haven, Conn.: Yale University Press, 1994).
Meyer, I., *Jeremia und die falschen Propheten* (OBO 13; Fribourg and Göttingen: Academic Press Fribourg and Vandenhoeck & Ruprecht, 1977).
Meyers, C. L., and E. M. Meyers, *Zechariah 9–14: A New Translation with Introduction and Commentary* (AB 25C; New York: Doubleday, 1993).
Michalowski, P., "Durum and Uruk during the Ur III Period," *Mesopotamia* 12 (1977) 83–96.
Michalowski, P., *Letters from Early Mesopotamia* (SBLWAW 3; Atlanta, Ga.: Scholars Press, 1993).
Middlemas, J., *The Templeless Age: An Introduction to the History, Literature, and Theology of the 'Exile'* (Louisville, Ky.: Westminster John Knox, 2007).
Mieroop, M. van de, *The Ancient Mesopotamian City* (Oxford: Clarendon Press, 1997).
Millard, A., "La prophétie et l'écriture: Israël, Aram, Assyrie," *RHR* 202 (1985) 125–44.
Miller, E., "The Self-Glorification Hymn Reexamined," *Hen* 31 (2009) 307–24.
Miller, P. D., *The Religion of Ancient Israel* (Library of Ancient Israel; London: SPCK; Louisville, Ky.: Westminster John Knox Press, 2000).
Miscall, P. D., *Isaiah* (Readings; Sheffield: JSOT Press, 1993).
Montrose, Louis"Professing the Renaissance: The Poetics and Politics of Culture,"in *The New Historicism* (ed. H. Aram Veeser; New York: Routledge, 1989) 15–36.
Moor, J. C. de, and H. F. van Rooy (eds.) *Past, Present, Future: The Deuteronomistic History and the Prophets* (OTS 44; Leiden, Brill, 2000).
Moran, W. L., "New Evidence from Mari on the History of Prophecy," *Bib* 50 (1969) 15–56.
Mulder, O., *Simon the High Priest in Sirach 50: An Exegetical Study of the Significance of Simon the High Priest as Climax to the Praise of the Fathers in Ben Sira's Concept of the History of Israel* (JSJSup 78; Leiden: Brill, 2003).
Multanen, P., "Nouseeko Lähi-idän kriisi uskonnoista" ["Does the Crisis in the Middle East Arise from Religions?"], in *Vanhan aatamin kuoletus: Herännäiskirjoituksia vuodelta 2004* (ed. U. Karjalainen; Lapua: Herättäjä-yhdistys, 2004), 79–95.
Müller, H.-P., "Das Hohelied," in *Das Hohelied, Klagelieder, Das Buch Ester* (ed. H.-P. Müller, O. Kaiser, and J. A. Loader; ATD 16/2; Göttingen: Vandenhoeck & Ruprecht, 1992) 1–90.
Müller, R., "A Prophetic View of the Exile in the Holiness Code: Literary Growth and Tradition History in Leviticus 26," in *The Concept of Exile in Ancient Israel and Its Historical Contexts* (ed. E. Ben Zvi and C. Levin; BZAW 404; Berlin and New York: De Gruyter, 2010) 207–40.
Müller, R., J. Pakkala, and B. ter Haar Romeny, *Evidence of Editing: Growth and Change of Texts in the Hebrew Bible* (SBLRBS 75; Atlanta, Ga.: Society of Biblical Literature, 2014)
G. Münderlein, *Kriterien wahrer und falscher Prophetie: Entstehung und Bedeutung im Alten Testament* (EHS.T 33; Frankfurt a. M.: Peter Lang, 1974 [^{2}1979]).
Mullen, E. T., Jr., *The Divine Council in Canaanite and Early Hebrew Literature* (HSM 31; Chico, Calif.: Scholars Press, 1980).
Munn, M., "Earth and Water: The Foundations of Sovereignty in Ancient Thought," in *The Nature and Function of Water, Baths, Bathing and Hygiene from Antiquity through Renaissance* (ed. C. Kosso and A. Scott; Technology and Change in History 11; Leiden: Brill, 2009) 191–210.
Murphy, R. E., *The Song of Songs: A Commentary on the Book of Canticles or the Song of Songs* (Minneapolis, Minn.: Fortress, 1990).

Na'aman, N., ., "Let Other Kingdoms Struggle with the Great Powers – You, Judah, Pay the Tribute and Hope for the Best: The Foreign Policy of the Kings of Judah in the Ninth–Eighth Centuries BCE," in *Isaiah's Vision of Peace in Biblical and Modern International Relations: Swords into Plowshares* (ed. R. Cohen and R.Westbrook; New York: Palgrave MacMillan, 2008) 55–73.

Na'aman, N., "The Book of Hosea as a Source for the Last Days of the Kingdom of Israel," *BZ* 59 (2015) 232–56.

Najman, H., "The Symbolic Significance of Writing in Ancient Judaism," in *The Idea of Biblical Interpretation*, FS J. L. Kugel (ed. id. and J. H. Newman; JSJSup 83; Leiden: Brill, 2004) 139–73.

Nakata, I., "Two Remarks on the So-Called Prophetic Texts from Mari," *ASJ* 4 (1982) 143–48.

Nardelli, J.-F., *Homosexuality and Liminality in the Gilgameš and Samuel* (Amsterdam: Hakkert, 2007).

Naumann, T., *Hoseas Erben: Strukturen der Nachinterpretation im Buch* Hosea (BWANT 131; Stuttgart: Kohlhammer, 1991).

Neef, Heinz-Dieter, *Gottes himmlischer Thronrat: Hintergrund und Bedeutung von sôd JHWH im Alten Testament* (Arbeiten zur Theologie 79; Stuttgart: Calwer, 1994).

Nelson, R. D., "Priestly Purity and Prophetic Lunacy: Hosea 1:2–3 and 9:7," in *The Priests in the Prophets: The Portrayal of Priests, Prophets, and Other Religious Specialists in the Latter Prophets* (ed. L. L. Grabbe and A. Ogden Bellis; JSOTSup 408; London: T & T Clark, 2004) 115–33.

Neujahr, M., *Predicting the Past in the Ancient Near East: Mantic Historiography in Ancient Mesopotamia, Judah, and in the Mediterranean World* (Brown Judaic Studies 354; Providence, R. I.: Brown University, 2012).

Nevader, M., "On Reading Ezekiel by the Rivers of Babylon," *WO* 45 (2015) 99–110.

Niehr, H., *Der höchste Gott* (BZAW 190; Berlin: De Gruyter, 1990).

Nielsen, K., *Yahweh as Prosecutor and Judge: A Investigation of the Prophetic Lawsuit (Rîb-Pattern)* (JSOTSup 9; Sheffield: JSOT Press, 1978).

Niesiołowski-Spanò, Ł., "Biblical Prophet Amos: A Simple, Poor Shepherd from Judah?" in *Εὐεργεσίας χάριν*, FS B. Bravo and E. Wipszycka (ed. T. Derda, J. Urbanik, and M. Węcowski; The Journal of Juristic Papyrology, Supplement 1; Warsaw: Sumptibus auctorum, 2002) 211–17.

Niditch, S., *Oral World and Written Word: Ancient Israelite Literature* (Library of Ancient Israel; Louisville, Ky.: Westminster John Knox, 1996).

Nissinen, M., *Prophetie, Redaktion und Fortschreibung im Hoseabuch: Studien zum Werdegang eines Prophetenbuches im Lichte von Hos 4 und 11* (AOAT 231; Kevelaer: Butzon & Bercker; Neukirchen–Vluyn: Neukirchener Verlag, 1991).

Nissinen, M., "Die Relevanz der neuassyrischen Prophetie für die alttestamentliche Forschung," in *Mesopotamica – Ugaritica – Biblica*, FS K. Bergerhof (ed. M. Dietrich and O. Loretz; AOAT 232, Kevelaer, Germany: Butzon & Bercker; Neukirchen-Vluyn: Neukirchener, 1993) 217–58.

Nissinen, M., "Falsche Prophetie in neuassyrischer und deuteronomistischer Darstellung," in *Das Deuteronomium und seine Querbeziehungen* (ed. T. Veijola; PFES 62; Helsinki: Finnische Exegetische Gesellschaft and Göttingen: Vandenhoeck & Ruprecht, 1996) 172–95.

Nissinen, M., *Homoeroticism in the Biblical World: A Historical Perspective* (trans. K. Stjerna; Minneapolis, Minn.: Fortress, 1998).

Nissinen, M., "Love Lyrics of Nabû and Tašmetu: An Assyrian Song of Songs?" in "*Und Mose schrieb dieses Lied auf": Studien zum Alten Testament und zum Alten Orient*, FS O. Loretz (ed. M. Dietrich and I. Kottsieper; AOAT 250; Münster: Ugarit-Verlag, 1998) 585–634.

Nissinen, M., "Prophecy against the King in Neo-Assyrian Sources," in *'Lasset uns Brücken bauen…': Collected Communications to the 15th Congress of the International Organization for the Study of the Old Testament, Cambridge 1995* (ed. K.-D. Schunk and M. Augustin; BEATAJ 42; Frankfurt a. M.: Peter Lang, 1998) 157–70.

Nissinen, M., *References to Prophecy in Neo-Assyrian Sources* (SAAS 7; Helsinki: The Neo-Assyrian Text Corpus Project, 1998).

Nissinen, M., "Spoken, Written, Quoted and Invented: Orality and Writtenness in Ancient Near Eastern Prophecy," in *Writings and Speech in Israelite and Ancient Near Eastern Prophecy* (ed. E. Ben Zvi and M. H. Floyd; SBLSymS 10; Atlanta Ga.: Society of Biblical Literature, 2000) 235–71.

Nissinen, M., "The Socioreligious Role of the Neo-Assyrian Prophets," in *Prophecy in Its Ancient Near Eastern Context: Mesopotamian, Biblical, and Arabian Perspectives* (ed. id.; SBLSymS 13; Atlanta, Ga.: Society of Biblical Literature, 2000) 89–114.

Nissinen, M., "Akkadian Rituals and Poetry of Divine Love," in *Mythology and Mythologies* (ed. R. M. Whiting; Melammu Symposia 2; Helsinki: Neo-Assyrian Text Corpus Project, 2001) 93–136.

Nissinen, M., "City as Lofty as Heaven: Arbela and Other Cities in Neo-Assyrian Prophecy," in L. L. Grabbe and R. D. Haak (eds.), *'Every City Shall Be Forsaken': Urbanism and Prophecy in Ancient Israel and the Near East* (JSOTSup 330; Sheffield: Sheffield Academic Press, 2001) 172–209.

Nissinen, M., "A Prophetic Riot in Seleucid Babylonia," in H. Irsigler (ed.), *'Wer darf hinaufsteigen zum Berg YHWHs?' Beiträge zu Prophetie und Poesie des Alten Testaments, Festschrift für Sigurdur Örn Steingrimsson zum 70. Geburtstag* (Arbeiten zu Text und Sprache im Alten Testament 72; St Ottilien: EOS Verlag, 2002a) 62–74.

Nissinen, M., "Prophets and the Divine Council," in *Kein Land für sich allein: Studien zum Kulturkontakt in Kanaan, Israel/Palästina und Ebirnâri für Manfred Weippert zum 65. Geburtstag* (ed. U. Hübner and E. A. Knauf; OBO 186; Fribourg and Göttingen: Academic Press Fribourg and Vandenhoeck & Ruprecht, 2002) 4–19.

Nissinen, M., "Das kritische Potential in der altorientalischen Prophetie," in *Propheten in Mari, Assyrien und Israel* (ed. M. Köckert and M. Nissinen; FRLANT 201; Göttingen: Vandenhoeck & Ruprecht, 2003) 1–32.

Nissinen, M., "Fear Not: A Study on an Ancient Near Eastern Phrase," in *The Changing Face of Form Criticism for the Twenty-First Century* (ed. M. A. Sweeney and E. Ben Zvi; Grand Rapids, Mich.: Eerdmans, 2003) 122–61

Nissinen, M., "Neither Prophecies nor Apocalypses: The Akkadian Literary Predictive Texts," in *Knowing the End from the Beginning: The Prophetic, the Apocalyptic and their Relationships* (ed. L. L. Grabbe and R. D. Haak; JSPSup 46; London: T & T Clark, 2003) 134–48.

Nissinen, M., "What Is Prophecy? An Ancient Near Eastern Perspective," in *Inspired Speech: Prophecy in the Ancient Near East*, FS H. B. Huffmon (ed. J. Kaltner and L. Stulman; JSOTSup 372; London: T. & T. Clark, 2004) 17–37.

Nissinen, M., "How Prophecy Became Literature," *SJOT* 19 (2005) 153–72.

Nissinen, M., "The Dubious Image of Prophecy", in *Prophets, Prophecy, and Prophetic Texts in Second Temple Judaism* (eds. M. H. Floyd and R. D. Haak; LHBOTS 427; New York / London: T & T Clark, , (2006) 26–41.

Nissinen, M., "Das Problem der Prophetenschüler," in *Houses Full of All Good Things*, GS T. Veijola (ed. J. Pakkala and id.; PFES 95; Helsinki: Finnish Exegetical Society, 2008) 337–53.

Nissinen, M., "Song of Songs and Sacred Marriage," in *Sacred Marriages: The Divine-Human Sexual Metaphor from Sumer to Early Christianity* (ed. id. and R. Uro; Winona Lake, Ind.: Eisenbrauns, 2008) 173–218.

Nissinen, M., "Transmitting Divine Mysteries: The Prophetic Role of Wisdom Teachers in the Dead Sea Scrolls," in *Scripture in Transition: Essays on Septuagint, Hebrew Bible, and Dead Sea Scrolls in Honour of Raija Sollamo* (ed. A. Voitila and J. Jokiranta; JSJSup 126; Leiden: Brill, 2008) 513–33.

Nissinen, M., "Reflections on the 'Historical-Critical' Method: Historical Criticism and Critical Historicism," in *Method Matters*, FS D. L. Petersen (ed. J. M. LeMon and K. H. Richards; SBLRBS 56; Atlanta, Ga.: Society of Biblical Literature, 2009) 479–504.

Nissinen, M., "The Historical Dilemma of Biblical Prophetic Studies," *in Prophecy in the Book of Jeremiah* (ed. H. M. Barstad and R. G Kratz; BZAW 388; Berlin: de Gruyter, 2009) 103–20.

Nissinen, M., "Wisdom as Mediatrix in Sirach 24: Ben Sira, Love Lyrics, and Prophecy," in *Of God(s), Trees, Kings, and Scholars*, FS S. Parpola (ed. M. Luukko, S. Svärd, and R. Mattila; StOr 106; Helsinki: Finnish Oriental Society 2009) 377–90.

Nissinen, M., "Pesharim as Divination: Qumran Exegesis, Omen Interpretation and Literary Prophecy," in *Prophecy after the Prophets: The Contribution of the Dead Sea Scrolls to the Understanding of Biblical and Extra-Biblical Prophecy* (ed. K. de Troyer and A. Lange; CBET 52; Leuven: Peeters, 2009) 43–60.

Nissinen, M., "Biblical Prophecy from a Near Eastern Perspective: The Cases of Kingship and Divine Possession," in *Congress Volume, Ljubljana 2007* (ed. A. Lemaire; VTSup 133; Leiden: Brill, 2010) 441–68.

Nissinen, M., "Prophecy and Omen Divination: Two Sides of the Same Coin," in *Divination and the Interpretation of Signs in the Ancient World* (ed. A. Annus; Oriental Institute Seminars 6; Chicago: Oriental Institute, 2010) 341–51

Nissinen, M., "Comparing Prophetic Sources: Principles and a Test Case," in *Prophecy and the Prophets in Ancient Israel* (ed. J. Day ; LHBOTS 531; London: T&T Clark, 2010): 3–24

Nissinen, M., "Prophetic Madness: Prophecy and Ecstasy in the Ancient Near East and in Greece," in *Raising Up a Faithful Exegete*, FS R. D. Nelson (ed. K. L. Noll and B. Schramm; Winona Lake, Ind.: Eisenbrauns, 2010) 3–29.

Nissinen, M., "Gender and Prophetic Agency in the Ancient Near East and in Greece," in *Prophets Male and Female: Gender and Prophecy in the Hebrew Bible, the Eastern Mediterranean and the Ancient Near East* (ed. J. Stökl and C. L. Carvalho; SBLAIL 15; Atlanta, Ga.: Society of Biblical Literature, 2013) 27–58.

Nissinen, M., "Prophecy as Construct: Ancient and Modern," in *"Thus Speaks Ishtar of Arbela": Prophecy in Israel, Assyria and Egypt in the Neo-Assyrian Period* (ed. R. P. Gordon and H. M. Barstad; Winona Lake, Ind.: Eisenbrauns, 2013) 11–35.

Nissinen, M., *Ancient Prophecy: Near Eastern, Biblical, and Greek Perspectives.* (Oxford: Oxford University Press, 2017).

Nissinen, M., *Prophets and Prophecy in the Ancient Near East*, with contributions by Choon-Leong Seow, Robert K. Ritner, and Craig Melchert. 2nd ed. (SBLWAW 41; Atlanta, Ga.: SBL Press, 2019).

Nissinen, M., "Ištar of Arbela," in *Ancient Arbela: Pre-Islamic History of Erbil* (ed. Raija Mattila, Zidan Bradosty, and Jessica Giraud; Syria Supplement Series; Beirut: Institute Français en Proche-Orient, Forthcoming).

Nissinen, M. (ed.), *Prophecy in Its Ancient Near Eastern Context: Mesopotamian, Biblical, and Arabian Perspectives* (SBLSymS 13; Atlanta, Ga.: Society of Biblical Literature, 2000).

Nissinen, M., and R. Uro, "Sacred Marriages, or the Divine-Human Sexual Metaphor: Introducing the Project," in *Sacred Marriages: The Divine-Human Sexual Metaphor from Sumer to Early Christianity* (ed. iid.; Winona Lake, Ind.: Eisenbrauns, 2008) 1–6.

Nissinen, M., and S. Parpola, "Marduk's Return and Reconciliation in a Prophetic Letter from Arbela," in *Verbum et calamus: Semitic and Related Studies in Honour of the Sixtieth Birthday of Professor Tapani Harviainen* (ed. H. Juusola, J. Laulainen, and H. Palva; StOr 99; Helsinki: Finnish Oriental Society, 2004) 199–219.

Nissinen, M., and M.-C. Perroudon, "Bāia," *PNA* 1/2 (1999) 253.

Noegel, S. B.,"'Sign, Sign, Everywhere a Sign': Script, Power, and Interpretation in the Ancient Near East," in *Divination and Interpretation of Signs in the Ancient World* (ed. A. Annus; Oriental Institute Seminars 6; Chicago: Oriental Institute, 2010) 143–62.

Nogalski, J. D., *Literary Precursors to the Book of the Twelve* (BZAW 217; Berlin: de Gruyter, 1993).

Noort, E., *Untersuchungen zum Gottesbescheid in Mari: Die "Mariprophetie" in der alttestamentlichen Forschung* (AOAT 202; Kevelaer: Butzon & Bercker; Neukirchen–Vluyn: Neukirchener Verlag, 1977).

Nougayrol, J., *PRU IV: Textes accadiens des archives sud* (Mission de Ras Shamra 9; Paris: Imprimerie nationale and Librairie C. Klincksieck, 1956).

Nougayrol, J., "Textes suméro-accadiens des archives et bibliothèques privées d'Ugarit," *Ugaritica* 5 (1968) 1–446.

Novick, P., That Noble Dream: The "Objectivity Question" and the American Historical Profession (Cambridge: Cambridge University Press, 1988).

Novotny, J. R., "Sin-šarru-iškun," *PNA* 3/1 (2002) 1143–45.

Novotny, J. R., *Selected Royal Inscriptions of Assurbanipal: L^3, L^4, LET, Prism I, Prism T, and Related* Texts (SAACT 10; Helsinki: The Neo-Assyrian Text Corpus Project, 2014).

Novotny, J. R., and J. Jeffers, *The Royal Inscriptions of Ashurbanipal (668–631 BC), Aššur-etel-ilāni (630–627 BC), and Sîn-šarra-iškun (626–612 BC), Kings of Assyria*, Part 1 (RINAP 5/1; University Park, Pa.: Eisenbrauns, 2018).

McNutt, P., *Reconstructing the Society of Ancient Israel* (Library of Ancient Israel; Louisville, Ky.: Westminster John Knox Press, 1999).

Odell, M. S., "You Are What You Eat: Ezekiel and the Scroll," *JBL* 117 (1998) 229–48.

Odell, M. S., "Ezekiel Saw What He Said He Saw: Genres, Forms, and the Vision of Ezekiel 1," *The Changing Face of Form Criticism for the Twenty-First Century* (ed. M. A. Sweeney and E. Ben Zvi; Grand Rapids, Mich.: Eerdmans, 2003) 162–76.

Ogden, D., *Magic, Witchcraft and Ghosts in the Greek and Roman Worlds: A Sourcebook* (New York: Oxford University Press, 2002).

Ollenburger, B. C., *Zion, the City of the Great King: A Theological Symbol of the Jerusalem Cult* (JSOTSup 41; Sheffield: Sheffield Academic Press, 1987).

Ollenburger, B. C., "Gerhard von Rad's Theory of Holy War," in *Holy War in Ancient Israel* by G. von Rad (trans. M. J. Dawn; Grand Rapids, Mich.: Eerdmans, 1991), 1–33.

Olyan, S. M., "Purity Ideology in Ezra-Nehemiah as a Tool to Reconstruct the Community," *JSJ* 35 (2004) 1–16.

Oppenheim, A. L., *The Interpretation of Dreams in the Ancient Near East: With a Translation of an Assyrian Dream-Book* (Transactions of the American Philosophical Society 46/3; Philadelphia, Pa.: American Philosophical Society, 1956).

Oppenheim, A. L., *Ancient Mesopotamia: Portrait of a Dead Civilization* (Chicago, Ill. and London: The University of Chicago Press, ²1977).

Oswald, W., "Ahab als Krösus: Anmerkungen zu 1 Kön 22," *ZThK* 105 (2008) 1–14.

Oswald, W., "Is There a Prohibition to Build a Temple in 2 Samuel 7?" in *Thinking towards New Horizons: Collected Communications to the XIXth Congress of the International Organization for the Study of the Old Testament, Ljubljana 2007* (ed. M. Augustin and H. M. Niemann; BEATAJ 55; Frankfurt a.M.: Lang, 2008) 85–89.

Oswald, W., *Nathan der Prophet: Eine Untersuchung zu 2 Samuel 7 und 12 und 1 Könige I* (AThANT 94; Zurich: Theologischer Verlag, 2008).

Otto, E., "Treueid und Gesetz: Die Ursprünge des Deuteronomiums im Horizont neuassyrischen Vertragsrechts," *ZABR* 2 (1996) 1–52.

Otto, E., "Die Ursprünge der Bundestheologie im Alten Testament und im Alten Orient," *ZABR* 4 (1998) 1–84.

Otto, E., *Das Deuteronomium: Politische Theologie und Rechtsreform in Juda und Assyrien* (BZAW 284; Berlin: De Gruyter, 1999).

Otto, E., "Die besiegten Sieger: Von der Macht und Ohnmacht der Ideen in der Geschichte am Beispiel der neuassyrischen Großreichspolitik," *BZ* 43 (1999) 180–203.

Otto, S., *Jehu, Elia und Elisa: Die Erzählung von der Jehu-Revolution und die Komposition der Elia-Elisa-Erzählungen* (BWANT 152; Stuttgart: Kohlhammer, 2001).

Overholt, T. W., *Prophecy in Cross-Cultural Perspective: A Source-Book for Biblical Research* (SBLSBS 17; Atlanta, Ga.: Society for Biblical Literature, 1986).

Overholt, T. W., *Channels of Prophecy: The Social Dynamics of Prophetic Activity* (Minneapolis, Minn.: Fortress, 1989).

Overholt, T. W., "Prophecy in History: The Social Reality of Intermediation," *JSOT* 48 (1990) 3–29.

Overholt, T. W., "It Is Difficult to Read," *JSOT* 48 (1990) 51–54.

Oxford Advanced Learner's Dictionary of Current English (ed. S. Wehmeier; Oxford: Oxford University Press, ⁶2000).

Pachis, P., "'Γαλλαῖον Κυβέλης ὀλόλυγμα' (*Anthol, Palat,* VI, 173): L'élément orgiastique dans le culte de Cybele," in *Cybele, Attis and Related Cults*, FS M. J. Vermaseren (ed. E. M. Lane; RGRW 131; Leiden: Brill, 1996) 193–222.

Pagels, E., and K. L. King, *Reading Judas: The Gospel of Judas and the Shaping of Christianity* (New York: Viking, 2007).

Pakkala, J., *Intolerant Monolatry in the Deuteronomistic History* (PFES 76; Helsinki: The Finnish Exegetical Society and Göttingen: Vandenhoeck & Ruprecht, 1999).

Pakkala, J., S. Munger, and J. Zangenberg, *Kinneret Regional Project: Tel Kinrot Excavations* (Proceedings of the Finnish Institute in the Middle East, Report 2/2004; Vantaa: The Finnish Institute in the Middle East, 2004); available at www.kinneret-excavations.org.

Parke, H. W., and D. E. W. Wormell, *The Delphic Oracle*, vol. 1: *The History* (Oxford: Blackwell, 1956).

Parker, B., "Administrative Tablets from the North-West Palace, Nimrud," *Iraq* 23 (1961) 15–67.

Parker, R., *Miasma: Pollution and Purification in Early Greek Religion* (Oxford: Clarendon Press, 1983).

Parker, S. B., "Possession Trance and Prophecy in Pre-Exilic Israel," *VT* 28 (1978) 271–85.

Parker, S. B., "Official Attitudes toward Prophecy at Mari and in Israel," *VT* 43 (1993) 50–68.

Parker, S. B., "The Lachish Letters and Official Reactions to Prophecies," in *Uncovering Ancient Stones*, FS H. N. Richardson (ed. L. M. Hopfe; Winona Lake, Ind.: Eisenbrauns, 1994) 65–78.

Parker, S. B., "The Beginning of the Reign of God: Psalm 82 as Myth and Liturgy, *RB* 102 (1995) 532–59.

Parker, S. B., *Studies in Scripture and Inscriptions: Comparative Studies on Narratives in Northwest Semitic Inscriptions and the Hebrew Bible* (New York and Oxford: Oxford Univ. Press, 1997).

Parker, S. B., "Council," *DDD*[2] (1999) 204–8.

Parpola, S., *Letters from Assyrian Scholars to the Kings Esarhaddon and Assurbanipal*, vol. 1: *Texts* (AOAT 5/1; Kevelaer and Neukirchen-Vluyn: Butzon & Bercker and Neukirchener Verlag, 1970; repr. Winona Lake, Ind.: Eisenbrauns, 2007).

Parpola, S., *Neo-Assyrian Toponyms* (AOAT 6; Kevelaer: Butzon & Bercker; Neukirchen–Vluyn: Neukirchener Verlag, 1970).

Parpola, S., "The Murderer of Sennacherib," in *Death in Mesopotamia* (ed. B. Alster; Mesopotamia 8 (= CRRAI 26); Copenhagen: Akademisk Forlag, 1980) 171–82.

Parpola, S., *Letters from Assyrian Scholars to the Kings Esarhaddon and Assurbanipal*, vol. 2: *Commentary and Appendices* (AOAT 5/2; Kevelaer and Neukirchen-Vluyn: Butzon & Bercker and Neukirchener Verlag, 1983; repr. Winona Lake, Ind.: Eisenbrauns, 2007).

Parpola, S., "Neo-Assyrian Treaties from the Royal Archives of Nineveh," *JCS* 39 (1987) 161–89.

Parpola, S., *The Correspondence of Sargon II, Part I: Letters from Assyria and the West* (SAA 1; Helsinki: Helsinki University Press, 1987).

Parpola, S., *The Correspondence of Sargon II*, vol. 2: *Letters from the Northern and Northeastern Provinces* (SAA 5; Helsinki: Helsinki University Press,) 1990.

Parpola, S., "The Forlorn Scholar," in *Language, Literature, and History*, FS E. Reiner (ed. F. Rochberg-Halton; AOS 67; New Haven, Conn.: American Oriental Society, 1987) 257–78.

Parpola, S., *Letters from Assyrian and Babylonian Scholars* (SAA 10; Helsinki: Helsinki University Press, 1993).

Parpola, S., "Mesopotamian Astrology and Astronomy as Domains of the Mesopotamian 'Wisdom,'" in *Die Rolle der Astronomie in den Kulturen Mesopotamiens* (ed. H. D. Galter; Grazer Morgenländische Studien 3; Graz, Austria: Universitätsbibliothek, 1993) 47 – 59.

Parpola, S., "The Assyrian Tree of Life: Tracing the Origins of Jewish Monotheism and Greek Philosophy," *JNES* 52 (1993) 161 – 208.

Parpola, S., "The Assyrian Cabinet," in *Vom Alten Orient zum Alten Testament*, FS W. von Soden (ed. M. Dietrich and O. Loretz; AOAT 240; Kevelaer, Germany: Butzon & Bercker; Neukirchen-Vluyn: Neukirchener, 1995) 379 – 401.

Parpola, S., *Assyrian Prophecies* (SAA 9; Helsinki: Helsinki University Press, 1997).

Parpola, S., "Monotheism in Ancient Assyria," in *One God or Many? Concepts of Divinity in the Ancient World* (ed. B. N. Porter; Transactions of the Casco Bay Assyriological Institute 1; Casco Bay, Maine: Casco Bay Assyriological Institute, 2000) 165 – 209.

Parpola, S., "Assyria's Expansion in the 8th and 7th Centuries and its Long-Term Repercussions in the West," in *Symbiosis, Symbolism, and the Power of the Past: Canaan, Ancient Israel, and Their Neighbors from the Late Bronze Age through Roman Palaestina* (ed. W. G. Dever and S. Gitin; Winona Lake, Ind.; Eisenbrauns, 2003) 99 – 111.

Parpola, S., "Cuneiform Texts from Ziyaret Tepe (Tušḫan), 2002 – 2003," *SAAB* 17 (2008) 1 – 113.

Parpola, S., and K. Watanabe, *Neo-Assyrian Treaties and Loyalty Oaths* (SAA 2; Helsinki: Helsinki University Press, 1988).

Parpola, S., and R. M. Whiting (eds.), *Assyria 1995. Proceedings of the 10th Anniversary Symposium of the Neo-Assyrian Text Corpus Project* (Helsinki: The Neo-Assyrian Text Corpus Project, 1997).

Parry, D. W., and E. Tov, *Calendrical and Sapiential Texts* (DSSR 4; Leiden: Brill, 2004).

Parry, D. W., *Texts Concerned with Religious Law* (DSSR 1; Leiden: Brill, 2004).

Patterson, L., *Negotiating the Past: The Historical Understanding of Medieval Literature* (Madison, Wisc.: University of Wisconsin Press, 1987).

Patton, C. L., "Priest, Prophet, and Exile: Ezekiel as a Literary Construct," *Ezekiel's Hierarchical World: Wrestling with a Tiered Reality* (ed. S. L. Cook and C. L. Patton; SBLSymS 31; Atlanta, Ga.: Society of Biblical Literature, 2004) 73 – 90.

Pearce, L. E., "New Evidence for Judeans in Babylonia," in *Judah and Judeans in the Persian Period* (ed. O. Lipschits and M. Oeming; Winona Lake, Ind.: Eisenbrauns, 2006) 399 – 411.

Pearce, L. E., "Sealed Identities," *Opening the Tablet Box, FS B. R. Foster* (ed. S. C. Melville and A. L. Slotsky; CHANE 42; Leiden: Brill, 2010) 301 – 28.

Pearce, L. E., "'Judean': A Special Status in Neo-Babylonian and Achemenid Babylonia," in *Judah and Judeans in the Achaemenid Period: Negotiating Identity in an International Context* (ed. O. Lipschits, G. N. Knoppers, and M. Oeming; Winona Lake, Ind.: Eisenbrauns, 2011) 267 – 77.

Pearce, L. E., "Continuity and Normality in Sources Relating to the Judean Exile," *HeBAI* 3 (2014) 163 – 84.

Pearce, L. E., "Identifying Judeans and Judean Identity," in *Exile and Return: The Babylonian Context* (ed. C. Waerzeggers and J. Stökl; BZAW 478 Berlin: De Gruyter, 2015) 7 – 32.

Pearce, L. E., and C. Wunsch, *Documents of Judean Exiles and West Semites in Babylonia in the Collection of David Sofer* (CUSAS 28; Bethesda, Md.: CDL Press, 2014).

Peled, I., "*assinnu* and *kurgarrû* Revisited," *JNES* 73 (2014) 283 – 97.

Perlitt, L., *Vatke und Wellhausen: Geschichtsphilosophische Voraussetzungen und historiographische Motive für die Darstellung der Religion und Geschichte Israels durch Wilhelm Vatke und Julius Wellhausen* (BZAW 94; Berlin: Töpelmann, 1965).

Perlitt, L., "Mose als Prophet," *EvT* 31 (1971) 588–608 (repr. in id., *Deuteronomium-Studien* [FAT 8; Tübingen: Mohr Siebeck, 1994] 1–19).

Perlitt, L., *Die Propheten Nahum, Habakuk, Zephanja* (ATD 25/1; Göttingen: Vandenhoeck & Ruprecht, 2004), 82–83.

Perroudon, M.-C., "An Angry Goddess," *SAAB* 6 (1993) 41–44.

Pesch, W., "Zur Formgeschichte und Exegese von Lk 12,32," *Bib* 41 (1960) 25–40.

Petersen, D. L., *The Roles of Israel's Prophets* (JSOTSup 17; Sheffield: Shefield Academic Press, 1981).

Petersen, D. L., *Zechariah 9–14 and Malachi: A Commentary* (OTL; Louisville, Ky.: Westminster/John Knox Press, 1995).

Petersen, D. L., "Rethinking the Nature of Prophetic Literature," in *Prophecy and Prophets: The Diversity of Contemporary Issues in Scholarship* (ed. Y. Gitay; SBLSS; Atlanta, Ga.: Scholars Press, 1997) 23–40.

Petersen, D. L., "Defining Prophecy and Prophetic Literature," in *Prophecy in Its Ancient Near Eastern Context: Mesopotamian, Biblical, and Arabian Perspectives* (ed. M. Nissinen; SBLSymS 13, Atlanta Ga.: Society of Biblical Literature, 2000) 33–44.

Peterson, B. N., *Ezekiel in Context: Ezekiel's Message Understood in Its Historical Setting of Covenant Curses and Ancient Near Eastern Mythological Motifs* (PTMS 182; Eugene, Or.: Pickwick, 2012).

Pettinato, G., *Die Ölwahrsagung bei den Babyloniern* (Studi Semitici 21–22; Roma: Istituto di studi del Vicino Oriente, 1966).

Pfann, S. J., et al., *Qumran Cave 4 XXVI* (DJD 36; Oxford: Clarendon Press 2000).

Pfeiffer, H., *Das Heiligtum von Bethel im Spiegel des Hoseabuches* (FRLANT 183; Göttingen: Vandenhoeck & Ruprecht, 1999).

Pfeiffer, R. H., "Akkadian Oracles and Prophecies," *ANET* (1955) 449–52.

Pfoh, E., "Más allá del círculo hermenéutico: El pasado de Israel entre la teologia del Antiguo Testamento y la historia de Palestina," *Revista Bíblica* 69 (2007) 65–82.

Pike, D. M., and A. C. Skinner, *Qumran Cave 4 XXIII: Unidentified Fragments* (DJD 33; Oxford; Clarendon Press, 2001).

Plath, S., *Furcht Gottes: Der Begriff* jāra' *im Alten Testament* (AzTh 2/2; Stuttgart: Calwer, 1963).

Ploeg, J. P. M. van der, "Un petit rouleau de psaumes apocryphes (11QpsAp[a])," in *Das frühe Christentum in seiner Umwelt*, FS K. G. Kuhn (ed. G. Jeremias et al.; Göttingen: Vandenhoeck & Ruprecht, 1971) 128–39.

Pohlmann, K.-F., *Ezechielstudien: Zur Redaktionsgeschichte des Buches und zur Frage nach den ältesten Texten* (BZAW 180; Berlin and New York: De Gruyter, 1992).

Pohlmann, K.-F., *Das Buch des Propheten Hesekiel (Ezechiel): Kapitel 1–19* (ATD 22/1; Göttingen: Vandenhoeck & Ruprecht, 1996).

Pohlmann, K.-F., "Synchrone und diachrone Texterschließung im Ezechielbuch," *HeBAI* 1 (2012) 246–70.

Polley, M. E., "Hebrew Prophecy within the Council of Yahweh, Examined in its Ancient Near Eastern Setting," in *Scripture in Context: Essays in the Comparative Method* (ed.

C. D. Evans, W. W. Hallo, and J. B. White; Pittsburgh Theological Monograph Series 34; Pittsburgh: Pickwick,, 1980) 141–56.

Pongratz-Leisten, B., *Ina šulmi īrub: Die kulttopographische und ideologische Programmatik der* akītu-*Prozession in Babylonien und Assyrien im 1. Jahrtausend v. Chr.* (BaF 16; Mainz: Philipp von Zabern, 1994).

Pongratz-Leisten, B., "The Interplay of Military Strategy and Cultic Practice in Assyrian Politics," in *Assyria 1995: Proceedings of the 10th Anniversary symposium of the Neo-Assyrian Texts Carpus Project, Helsinki September 7–11, 1995* (ed. S. Parpola and R. M. Whiting; Helsinki: The Neo-Assyrian Texts Corpus Project, 1997) 145–52.

Pongratz-Leisten, B., "Toponyme als Ausdruck assyrischen Herrschaftsanspruchs," in Ana šadî Labnāni lū allik: *Beiträge zu altorientalischen und mittelmeerischen Kulturen*, FS W. Röllig (ed. ead., H. Kühne and P. Xella; AOAT 247; Kevelaer: Butzon & Bercker; Neukirchen–Vluyn: Neukirchener Verlag, 1997) 325–43.

Pongratz-Leisten, B., *Herrschaftswissen in Mesopotamien: Formen der Kommunikation zwischen Gott und König im 2. und 1. Jahrtausend v. Chr.* (SAAS 10; Helsinki: The Neo-Assyrian Text Corpus Project, 1999).

Pongratz-Leisten, B., "When the Gods Are Speaking: Toward Defining the Interface between Monotheism and Polytheism," in *Propheten in Mari, Assyrien und Israel* (ed. M. Köckert and M. Nissinen; FRLANT 201; Göttingen: Vandenhoeck & Ruprecht, 2003) 132–68.

Pongratz-Leisten, B., "Sacred Marriage and the Transfer of Divine Knowledge: Alliances between Gods and King in Ancient Mesopotamia," in *Sacred Marriages: The Divine-Human Sexual Metaphor from Sumer to Early Christianity* (ed. M. Nissinen and R. Uro; Winona Lake, Ind.: Eisenbrauns, 2008) 43–74.

Pongratz-Leisten, B., "Akitu," *EBR* 1 (2009) 694–97.

Porter, B. N., *Assyrian Bas-reliefs at the Bowdoin College Museum of Art* (Brunswick, ME: The Bowdoin College Museum of Art, 1989).

Porter, B. N., *Images, Power, and Politics: Figurative Aspects of Esarhaddon's Babylonian Policy* (Philadelphia, Pa.: American Philosophical Society, 1993).

Porter, B. N., "What the Assyrians Thought the Babylonians Thought about the Relative Status of Nabû and Marduk in the Late Assyrian Period," in *Assyria 1995: Proceedings of the 10th Anniversary symposium of the Neo-Assyrian Texts Carpus Project, Helsinki September 7–11, 1995* (ed. S. Parpola and R. M. Whiting; Helsinki: The Neo-Assyrian Texts Corpus Project, 1997) 253–60.

Porter, B. N., "Beds, Sex, and Politics: The Return of Marduk's Bed to Babylon," in *Sex and Gender in the Ancient Near East* (ed. S. Parpola and R. M. Whiting; CRRAI 47; Helsinki: The Neo-Assyrian Text Corpus Project, 2002) 523–35.

Porter, B. N. (ed.), *One God or Many? Concepts of Divinity in the Ancient World* (Transactions of the Casco Bay Assyriological Institute 1; Chebeaque Island, ME: Casco Bay Assyriological Institute, 2000).

Postgate, J. N., *The Tablets from Fort Shalmaneser* (CTN 3; London: British School of Archaeology in Iraq, 1984).

Postgate, J. N., *Early Mesopotamia: Society and Economy at the Dawn of History* (London: Routledge, 1992).

Postgate, J. N., and J. Reade, "Kalhu," *RlA* 5 (1976–80) 303–23.

Provan, I. V., P. Long, and T. Longman, *A Biblical History of Israel* (Louisville, Ky.: Westminster John Knox, 2003).

Pruin, D., *Geschichten und Geschichte: Isebel als literarische und historische Gestalt* (OBO 222; Fribourg and Göttingen: Academic Press Fribourg and Vandenhoeck & Ruprecht, 2006).
Puech, É., "Bala'am and Deir 'Alla," in *The Prestige of the Pagan Prophet Balaam in Judaism, Early Christianity, and Islam* (ed. G. H. van Kooten and J. T. A. G. M. van Ruiten; TBN 11; Leiden: Brill, 2008) 25–47.
Pyysiäinen, I., *Supernatural Agents: Why We Believe in Souls, Gods, and Buddhas* (New York: Oxford University Press, 2009).
Qimron, E., "On the Interpretation of the List of False Prophets," *Tarbiz* 63 (1994) 273–75.
Rabinowitz, I., "*Pēsher/pittārōn:* Its Biblical Meaning and Its Significance in the Qumran Literature," *RevQ* 8 (1973) 219–32.
Rad, G. von, *Der Heilige Krieg im alten Israel* (Zurich: Zwingli, 1951); ET: *Holy War in Ancient Israel* (trans. M. J. Dawn; Grand Rapids, Mich.: Eerdmans, 1991).
Rad, G. von, *Theologie des Alten Testaments*, vol. 1: *Die Theologie der geschichtlichen Überlieferungen Israels* (Munich: Kaiser, ^{2}1958).
Rad, G. von, *Theologie des Alten Testaments*, vol. 2: *Die Theologie der prophetischen Überlieferungen Israels* (Munich: Kaiser, ^{2}1960).
Radner, K., "The Relation Between Format and Content of Neo-Assyrian Texts," in *Niniveh 612 BC: The Glory and Fall of the Assyrian Empire* (ed. R. Matilla; Catalogue of the 10th Anniversary Exhibition of the Neo-Assyrian Text Corpus Project; Helsinki, 1995) 63–78.
Radner, K., *Die neuassyrischen Privatrechtsurkunden als Quelle für Mensch und Umwelt* (SAAS 6; Helsinki: Neo-Assyrian Text Corpus Project, 1997).
Radner, K., "Aššur-hamātū'a," *PNA 1*/1 (1998) 186–87.
Radner, K., "Money in the Neo-Assyrian Empire," in *Trade and Finance in Ancient Mesopotamia* (ed. J. G. Dercksen; MOS Studies 1; Leiden: NINO, 1999) 127–57.
Radner, K., *Die neuassyrischen Texte aus Tall Šēḫ Ḥamad* (Berichte der Ausgrabungen Tall Šēh Ḥamad, 6; Berlin: Dietrich Reimer, 2002).
Radner, K., "The Assyrian King and His Scholars: The Syro-Anatolian and the Egyptian Schools," in *Of God(s), Trees, Kings, and Scholars*, FS S. Parpola (ed. M. Luukko et al.; StOr 106; Helsinki: Finnish Oriental Society, 2009) 221–38.
Räisänen, H., *Moving beyond New Testament Theology? Essays in Conversation with Heikki Räisänen* (ed. T. Penner and C. Vander Stichele; PFES 88; Helsinki: Finnish Exegetical Society, 2005).
Räisänen, H., *Beyond New Testament Theology: A Story and a Programme* (London: SCM, 2000).
Räisänen, H., "Biblical Critics in the Global Village," in *Reading the Bible in the Global Village: Helsinki* (ed. id.; SBLGPBS 6; Atlanta, Ga.: Society of Biblical Literature, 2000) 9–28.
Räisänen, H., "Matthew in Bibliodrama," in *Neutestamentliche Exegese im Dialog: Hermeneutik – Wirkungsgeschichte – Matthäusevangelium*, FS U. Luz (ed. P. Lampe, M. Mayordomo, and M. Sato; Neukirchen-Vluyn: Neukirchener, 2008) 183–95.
Rapp, U., *Mirjam: Eine feministisch-rhetorische Lektüre der Mirjamtexte in der hebräischen Bibel* (BZAW 317; Berlin: De Gruyter, 2002).
Rattue, J., *The Living Stream: Holy Wells in Historical Context* (Woodbridge: Boydell Press, 1995).

Al-Rawi, F. N. H., "Tablets from the Sippar Library I. The 'Weidner Chronicle': A Suppostitious Royal Letter Concerning a Vision," *Iraq* 52 (1990) 1–13.

Reade, J. E., "Kalhu," *RlA* 5 (1976–80) 303–23.

Reade, J. E., *Assyrian Sculpture* (London: The Trustees of the British Museum, 1983).

Reiner, E., *Šurpu: A Collection of Sumerian and Akkadian Incantations* (AfO.B 11; Osnabrück: Biblio, 1970 [= 1956]).

Reinmuth, T., *Der Bericht Nehemias: Zur literarischen Eigenart, traditionsgeschichtlichen Prägung und innerbiblischen Rezeption des Ich-Berichts Nehemias* (OBO 183; Fribourg and Göttingen: Academic Press Fribourg and Vandenhoeck & Ruprecht, 2002).

Renfrew, C., and P. Bahn, *Archaeology: Theories, Methods and Praxis* (London: Thames & Hudson, ^{4}2004).

Renz, J., *Die althebräischen Inschriften, Teil 1: Text und Kommentar* (Handbuch der althebräischen Epigraphik 1; Darmstadt: Wissenschaftliche Buchgesellschaft, 1995).

Reventlow, H. Graf, *Liturgie und prophetisches Ich bei Jeremia* (Gütersloh: Gütersloher Verlagshaus, 1963).

Reventlow, H. Graf, *Die Propheten Haggai, Sacharja und Maleachi* (ATD 25/2; Göttingen: Vandenhoeck & Ruprecht, 1993).

Reynolds, F., *The Babylonian Correspondence of Esarhaddon and Letters to Assurbanipal and Sin-šarru-iškun from Northern and Central Babylonia* (SAA 18; Helsinki: Helsinki University Press, 2003).

Rhea, R. D. , "Attack on Prophecy: Zechanah 13,1–6," *ZAW* 107 (1995) 290–93.

Richardson, S. F. C., "On Seeing and Believing: Liver Divination and the Era of Warring States (II)," in *Divination and Interpretation of Signs in the Ancient World*, (ed. A. Annus; Oriental Institute Seminars 6; Chicago: Oriental Institute, 2010), 225–66.

Ringgren, H., *"gā'al," TDOT* 2 (1975) 350–55.

Ringgren, H., "Akkadian Apocalypses," in *Apocalypticism in the Mediterranean World and the Near East: Proceedings of the International Colloquium on Apocalypticism, Uppsala, August 12–17, 1979* (ed. D. Hellholm; Tübingen: Mohr Siebeck, 1983) 379–86.

Ringgren, H., "Israelite Prophecy: Fact or Fiction," in J. A. Emerton (ed.), *Congress Volume, Jerusalem 1986* (VTSup 40; Leiden: Brill, 1988) 204–10.

Roberts, J. J. M., "A New Parallel to 1 Kings 18:28–29," *JBL* 89 (1970) 76–77; repr. in *The Bible and the Ancient Near East: Collected Essays* (ed. id.; Winona Lake, Ind.: Eisenbrauns, 2002) 102–3.

Roberts, J. J. M., *The Bible and the Ancient Near East: Collected Essays* (Winona Lake, Ind.: Eisenbrauns, 2002).

Robinson, H., "The Council of Yahweh," *JTS* 45 (1944) 151–57.

Robinson, T. H., *Prophecy and the Prophets in Ancient Israel* (London: Duckworth, 1923, ^{2}1953).

Rochberg, F., "'If P, then Q': Form and Reasoning in Babylonian Divination," in *Divination and Interpretation of Signs in the Ancient World* (ed. A. Annus; Oriental Institute Seminars 6; Chicago: Oriental Institute, 2010) 19–27.

Rochberg, F., *The Heavenly Writing: Divination, Horoscopy, and Astronomy in Mesopotamian Culture* (Cambridge: Cambridge University Press, 2004).

Rochberg, F., *In the Path of the Moon: Babylonian Celestial Divination and Its Legacy* (SAMD 6; Leiden: Brill, 2010).

Röllig, W., "Literatur: § 4. Überblick über die akkadische Literatur," *RlA* 7 (1987/90) 48–66.

Römer, T., "L'école deutéronomiste et la formation de la Bible hébraïque," in *The Future of the Deuteronomistic History* (ed. id.; BETL 117; Leuven: Peeters, 2000) 179 – 93.
Römer, T., "From Prophet to Scribe: Jeremiah, Huldah, and the Invention of the Book," *Writing the Bible: Scribes, Scribalism, and Script* (ed. P. R. Davies and T. Römer; BibleWorld; Durham, NC: Acumen, 2013) 86 – 96.
Römer, T., J.-D. Macchi, and C. Nihan (eds.), *Introduction à l'Ancien Testament* (MdB 49; Geneva: Labor et fides, , ^{2}2009).
Römer, W. H. P., *Frauenbriefe über Religion, Politik und Privatleben in Māri: Untersuchungen zu G. Dossin, Archives Royales de Mari X (Paris, 1967)* (AOAT 12; Kevelaer, Germany: Butzon & Bercker; Neukirchen-Vluyn: Neukirchener, 1971).
Rogers, J. F., "Wisdom and Creation in Sirach 24," *JNES* 22 (1996) 141 – 56.
Rollinger, R., *Alexander und die großen Ströme: Die Flußüberquerungen im Lichte altorientalischer Pioniertechniken (Schwimmschläuche, Keleks und Pontonbrücken)* (Classica et Orientalia 7; Wiesbaden: Harrassowitz, 2013).
Rom-Shiloni, D., "From Ezekiel to Ezra-Nehemiah: Shifts of Group Identities within Babylonian Exilic Ideology," in *Judah and Judeans in the Achaemenid Period: Negotiating Identity in an International Context* (ed. O. Lipschits, G. N. Knoppers, and M. Oeming; Winona Lake, Ind.: Eisenbrauns, 2011) 127 – 51.
Rom-Shiloni, D., "Ezekiel and Jeremiah: What Might Stand Behind the Silence," *HeBAI* 1 (2012) 203 – 30.
Rom-Shiloni, D., *Exclusive Inclusivity: Identity Conflicts between the Exiles and the People who Remained (6th–5th Centuries BCE)* (LHBOTS 543; New York and London: T&T Clark, 2013).
Rooke, D. W., "Prophecy," in *The Oxford Handbook of Biblical Studies* (ed. J. W. Rogerson and J. M. Lieu; Oxford: Oxford University Press, 2006) 385 – 96.
Roscoe, W., "Priests of the Goddess: Gender Transgression in Ancient Religion," *HR* 35 (1996) 195 – 230.
Rosenberger, V., *Griechische Orakel: Eine Kulturgeshichte* (Darmstadt: Wissenschaftliche Buchgesellschaft, 2001).
Ross, J. F., "Prophecy in Hamath, Israel, and Mari," *HTR* 63 (1970) 1 – 28.
Routledge, B., "Learning to Love the King: Urbanism and the State in Iron Age Moab," in *Aspects of Urbanism in Antiquity: From Mesopotamia to Crete* (ed. W. E. Aufrecht, N. A. Mirau, and S. W. Gauley; JSOTSup 244; Sheffield: Sheffield Academic Press, 1997) 130 – 44.
Routledge, C., "Temple as the Center in Ancient Egyptian Urbanism," in *Aspects of Urbanism in Antiquity: From Mesopotamia to Crete* (ed. W. E. Aufrecht, N. A. Mirau, and S. W. Gauley; JSOTSup 244; Sheffield: Sheffield Academic Press, 1997) 221 – 35.
Rowlett, L. L., *Joshua and the Rhetoric of Violence: A New Historicist Analysis* (JSOTSup 226; Sheffield: Sheffield Academic Press, 1996).
Rudnig, T. A., "König ohne Tempel: 2 Samuel 7 in Tradition und Redaktion," *VT* 61 (2011) 426 – 46.
Rudnig-Zelt, S., *Hoseastudien: Redaktionskritische Untersuchungenzur Genese des Hoseabuches* (FRLANT 213; Göttingen: Vandenhoeck & Ruprecht, 2006).
Rudolph, W., *Jeremia* (HAT 1/12; Tübingen: Mohr Siebeck, ^{3}1968).

Rüterswörden, U., "Der Prophet der Lachish-Ostraka," in *Steine – Bilder – Texte: Historische Evidenz außerbiblischer und biblischer Quellen* (ed. C. Hardmeier; Arbeiten zur Bibel und ihrer Geschichte 5; Leipzig: Evangelischer Verlagsanstalt, 2001) 179–92.

Rüterswörden, U., "Dtn 13 in der neueren Deuteronomiumforschung," in *Congress Volume: Basel, 2001* (ed. A. Lemaire; VTSup 92; Leiden: Brill, 2002) 185–203

Rüterswörden, U., "Das Böse in der deuteronomistischen Schultheologie," in *Das Deuteronomium 22 und seine Querbeziehungen* (ed. T.Veijola; PFES 62 Helsinki: Finnische Exegetische Gesellschaft un Göttingen:Vandenhoeck & Ruprecht, 1996), 223–41.

Russell, J. M., *The Writing on the Wall: Studies in the Architectural Context of Late Assyrian Palace Inscriptions* (Mesopotamian Civilizations 9; Winona Lake, Ind.: Eisenbrauns, 1999).

Sachs, A. J., and H. Hunger, *Astronomical Diaries and Related Texts from Babylonia*, vol. 1: *Diaries from 652 B.C. to 262 B.C.* (Österreichische Akademie der Wissenschaften, Philosophisch-historische Klasse, Denkschriften 195; Wien: Österreichische Akademie der Wissenschaften, 1988).

Sachs, A. J., and H. Hunger, *Astronomical Diaries and Related Texts from Babylonia*, vol. 2: *Diaries from 261 B.C. to 165 B.C.* (Österreichische Akademie der Wissenschaften, Philosophisch-historische Klasse, Denkschriften 210; Wien: Österreichische Akademie der Wissenschaften, 1989).

Sachs, A. J., and H. Hunger, *Astronomical Diaries and Related Texts from Babylonia*, vol. 3: *Diaries from 164 B.C. to 61 B.C.* (Österreichische Akademie der Wissenschaften, Philologisch-historische Klasse, Denkschriften 247; Wien: Österreichische Akademie der Wissenschaften, 1996).

Sacks, J., *The Dignity of Difference: How to Avoid the Clash of Civilizations* (rev. ed., London and New York: Continuum, 2003).

Sæbø, M., "Old Testament Apocalyptic and its Relation to Prophecy and Wisdom: The View of Gerhard von Rad Reconsidered," in *In the Last Days: On Jewish and Christian Apocalyptic and its Period*, FS B. Otzen (ed. K. Jeppesen, K. Nielsen, and B. Rosendal; Arhus: Aarhus University Press, 1994) 78–91.

Sanders, G. D. R., "The Sacred Spring: Landscape and Traditions," in *Corinth in Context: Comparative Studies on Religion and Society* (ed. S. J. Friesen, D. N. Schowalter, and J. C. Walters; Leiden: Brill, 2010) 365–89.

Sanders, J. A., *The Psalms Scroll of Qumran Cave 11 (11QPs^a)* (DJD 4; Oxford: Clarendon Press, 1965).

Sandmel, S., "Parallelomania," *JBL* 81 (1962) 1–13.

Šašková, K., "Esarhaddon's Accession to the Assyrian Throne," in *Shepherds of the Black-Headed People: The Royal Office vis-à-vis Godhead in Ancient Mesopotamia* (ed. ead., L. Pecha, and P. Charvát; Plzeň: Západočeská univerzita, 2010) 147–79.

Sasson, J. M., "An Apocalyptic Vision from Mari? Speculations on ARM X:9," *MARI* 1 (1982) 151–67.

Sasson, J. M., "Mari Dreams," *JAOS* 103 (1983) 283–93.

Sasson, J. M., "The Posting of Letters with Divine Messages," in *Florilegium Marianum 2*, FS M. Birot (ed. D. Charpin and J.-M. Durand; Mémoires de NABU 3; Paris: SEPOA, 1994) 299–316.

Sasson, J. M., "Mari Apocalypticism Revisited," in *Immigration and Emigration within the Ancient Near East*, FS E. Lipiński (ed. K. van Lerberghe and A. Schoors; OLA 65; Leuven: Peeters, 1995) 285–98.

Sasson, J. M., "Water beneath Straw: Adventures of a Prophetic Phrase in the Mari Archives," in *Solving Riddles and Untying Knots*, FS J. C. Greenfield (ed. Z. Zevit, S. Gitin, and M. Sokoloff; Winona Lake, Ind.: Eisenbrauns, 1995) 599–608.

Sasson, J. M., "About 'Mari and the Bible'," *RA* 92 (1998) 97–123.

Sauer, G., *Jesus Sirach/Ben Sira* (ATD.A 1; Göttingen: Vandenhoeck & Ruprecht, 2000).

Sauerwein, R., *Elischa: Eine redaktions- und religionsgeschichtliche Studie* (BZAW 465; Berlin: de Gruyter, 2014).

Schaper, J., "Exilic and Post-Exilic Prophecy and the Orality/Literacy Problem," *VT* 55 (2005) 324–42.

Schaper, J., "The Death of the Prophet: The Transition from the Spoken to the Written Word of God in the Book of Ezekiel," in *Prophets, Prophecy, and Prophetic Texts in Second Temple Judaism* (ed. M. H. Floyd and R. D. Haak; LHBOTS 427; New York: T& T Clark, 2006) 63–79.

Schaper, J., "On Writing and Reciting in Jeremiah 36," in *Prophecy in the Book of Jeremiah* (ed. H. M. Barstad and R. G. Kratz; BZAW 388; Berlin: De Gruyter, 2009) 137–47.

Schart, A., "Combining Prophetic Oracles in Mari Letters and Jeremiah 36," *JANESCU* 23 (1995) 75–93.

Schart, A., *Die Entstehung des Zwölfprophetenbuches: Neubearbeitung von Amos im Rahmen schriftenübergreifender Redaktionsprozesse* (BZAW 260; Berlin: de Gruyter, 1998).

Schaudig, H., "Sîn-šarru-iškun," *RlA* 12 (2009) 522–24.

Scheuer, B., "Huldah: A Cunning Career Woman?" *Prophecy and Prophets in Stories: Papers Read at the Fifth Meeting of the Edinburgh Prophecy Network* (ed. B. Becking and H. M. Barstad; OTS 65; Leiden: Brill, 2015) 104–23.

Schipper, B. U., "'Apokalyptik,' 'Messianismus,' 'Prophetie': Eine Begriffsbestimmung," in *Apokalyptik und Ägypten: Eine kritische Analyse der relevanten Texteaus dem griechisch-römischen Ägypten* (eds. A. Blasius and B. U. Schipper; OLA 107; Leuven: Peeters, 2002) 21–40.

Schmid, K., "Klassische und nachklassische Deutungen der alttestamentlichen Prophetie," *Zeitschrift für neuere Theologiegeschichte* 3 (1996) 225–50.

Schmid, K., "Hintere Propheten (Nebiim)," in *Grundinformation Altes Testament: Eine Einführung in Literatur, Religion und Geschichte des Alten Testaments* (ed. J. C. Gertz; UTB 2745; Göttingen: Vandenhoeck & Ruprecht, 2006) 303–401.

Schmitt, A., *Prophetischer Gottesbescheid in Mari und Israel* (BWANT 6/14; Stuttgart: Kohlhammer, 1982) 22–23.

Schmitt, H.-C., "Erlösung und Gericht: Jes 43,1–7 und sein literarischer und theologischer Kontext," in *Alttestamentlicher Glaube und biblische Theologie*, FS H.-D. Preuß (ed. J. Hausmann and H.-J. Zobel; Stuttgart: Kohlhammer, 1992) 120–31.

Schniedewind, W. M., *The Word of God in Transition: From Prophet to Exegete in the Second Temple Period* (JSOTSup 197; Sheffield: Sheffield Academic Press, 1995).

Schöpflin, K., *Theologie als Biographie im Ezechielbuch: Ein Beitrag zur Konzeption alttestamentlicher Prophetie* (FAT 36; Tübingen: Mohr Siebeck, 2002).

Schoors, A., *I Am God Your Saviour: A Form-Critical Study of the Main Genres in Is. xl–lv* (VTSup 24; Leiden: Brill, 1973).

Schreiner, J., *Jesus Sirach 1–24* (NEB.AT 38; Würzburg: Echter, 2002).
Schroer, S., *Wisdom Has Built Her House: Studies on the Figure of Sophia in the Bible* (trans. L. M. Maloney and W. McDonough; Collegeville, Minn.: Liturgical Press, 2000).
Schroer, S., "Erich Zenger," in *Wer knackt den Kode: Meilensteine der Bibelforschung* (ed. T. Staubli; Düsseldorf: Patmos, 2009) 127–28.
Schüngel-Straumann, H., "Gott als Mutter in Hosea 11," *ThQ* 166 (1986) 119–34.
Schüssler Fiorenza, E., "Defending the Center, Trivializing the Margins," in *Reading the Bible in the Global Village* (ed. H. Räisänen; SBLGPBS 6; Atlanta, Ga.: Society of Biblical Literature, 2000) 29–48.
Schuller, E., "A Hymn from a Cave Four *Hodayot* Manuscript: 4Q427 7 i + ii," *JBL* 112 (1993) 605–28.
Schütte, W., "Hosea 9,7–9: Eine crux interpretum?," *BN* 114/115 (2002) 57–60.
Schweitzer, S. J., "Judging a Book by Its Citations: Sources and Authority in Chronicles," in *What Was Authoritative for Chronicles?* (ed. E. Ben Zvi and D. Edelman; Winona Lake, Ind.: Eisenbrauns, 2011) 37–75.
Scurlock, J., "Prophecy as a Form of Divination, Divination as a Form of Prophecy," in *Divination and Interpretation of Signs in the Ancient World* (ed. A. Annus; Oriental Institute Seminars 6; Chicago: Oriental Institute, 2010) 277–316.
Segovia, F., *Decolonizing Biblical Studies: A View from the Margins* (Maryknoll, N.Y.: Orbis, 2000).
Seitz, C. R., "The Prophet Moses and the Canonical Shape of Jeremiah," *ZAW* 101 (1989) 3–27.
Seitz, C. R., "Prophecy and Tradition-History: The Achievement of Gerhard von Rad and Beyond," in *Prophetie in Israel: Beiträge des Symposiums 'Das Alte Testament und die Kultur der Moderne'*, FS G. von Rad (ed. I. Fischer, K. Schmid, and H. G. M. Williamson; Altes Testament und Moderne 11; Münster: LIT, 2003) 29–52.
Seitz, C. R., *Prophecy and Hermeneutics: Toward a New Introduction to the Prophets* (Studies in Theological Interpretation; Grand Rapids, Mich.: Baker Academic, 2007) 75–92.
Seligman, A., *The Problem of Trust* (Princeton, N.J.: Princeton University Press, 1997).
Seow, C.-L., "West Semitic Sources," in M. Nissinen, with Contriburtions by C.-L. Seow, R. K. Ritner, and H. C. Melchert, *Prophets and Prophecy in the Ancient Near East* (SBLWAW 41; Atlanta, Ga.: SBL Press, 2019) 251–69.
Seters, J. van, *In Search of History: Historiography in the Ancient World and the Origin of Biblical History* (New Haven, Conn. and London: Yale University Press, 1983).
Seux, M.-J., *Épithètes royales akkadiennes et sumériennes* (Paris: Letouzey et Ané, 1967).
Shen, D., "What Is the Implied Author?," *Style* 45 (2011) 80–98.
Shanks , M., and I. Hodder, "Processual, Postprocessual and Interpretive Archaeologies," in *Interpreting Archaeology: Finding Meaning in the Past* (ed. I. Hodder et al.; London: Routledge) 3–29.
Shaw, I., "Building a Sacred Capital: Akhenaten, El-Amarna and the 'House of the King's Statue,'" in *Capital Cities: Urban Planning and Spiritual Dimensions: Proceedings of the Symposium Held on May 27–29, 1996, Jerusalem, Israel* (ed. J. G. Westenholz; Bible Lands Museum Jerusalem Publications 2; Jerusalem: Bible Lands Museum, 1998) 55–64.
Sheppard, G. D., *Wisdom as a Hermeneutical Construct* (BZAW 151; Berlin: De Gruyter, 1980).
Shupak, N., "Egyptian 'Prophecy' and Biblical Prophecy: Did the Phenomenon of Prophecy, in Biblical Sense, Exist in Ancient Egypt?" *JEOL* 31 (1989–90) 1–40.

Sicre, J. L., *Profetismo en Israel: El profeta, los profetas, el mensaje* (Estella, Spain: Verbo divino, 1992).
Siikala, A.-L., "The Siberian Shaman's Technique of Ecstasy," in *Studies on Shamanism* (ed. ead. and M. Hoppál; Ethnologica Uralica 2; Helsinki: Finnish Anthropological Society; Budapest: Akadémiai Kiadó, 1992) 26–40.
Singer, I., *Hittite Prayers* (SBLWAW 11; Atlanta, Ga.: Society of Biblical Literature, 2002).
Sinnott, A. M., *The Personification of Wisdom* (SOTSMS; Burlington: Ashgate, 2005).
Skehan, P. W., "Structures in Poems on Wisdom: Proverbs 8 and Sirach 24," *CBQ* 41 (1979) 365–79.
Skehan, P. W., and A. A. DiLella, *The Wisdom of Ben Sira* (AB 39; New York: Doubleday, 1987).
Smend, R., "Heinrich Ewalds biblische Theologie: Hinweis auf ein vergessenes Buch," in *Epochen der Bibelkritik: Gesammelte Studien*, vol. 3 (ed. id.; Munich: Kaiser, 1991) 155–67.
Smend, R., *Julius Wellhausen: Ein Bahnbrecher in drei Disziplinen* (Themen 84; Munich: Carl Friedrich von Siemens Stiftung, 2004).
Smend, R., *From Astruc to Zimmerli: Old Testament Scholarship in Three Centuries* (trans. M. Kohl; Tübingen: Mohr Siebeck, 2007).
Smith, M., "On the History of ΑΠΟΚΑΛΥΠΤΩ and ΑΠΟΚΑΛΥΨΙΣ," in Apocalypticism in the Mediterranean World and the Near East: Proceedings of the International Colloquium on Apocalypticism, Uppsala, August 12–17, 1979 (ed. D. Hellholm; Tübingen: Mohr Siebeck, 1983) 9–20.
Smith, M. S., *Untold Stories: The Bible and Ugaritic Studies in the Twentieth Century* (Peabody, Mass.: Hendrickson, 2001).
Smith-Christopher, D. L., *A Biblical Theology of Exile* (Overtures to Biblical Theology; Minneapolis: Fortress, 2002).
Soden, W. von, "Aramäische Wörter in neuassyrischen und neu- and spätbabylonischen Texten: Ein Vorbericht III," *Or* NS 46 (1977) 183–97.
Sollberger, E., *The Business and Administrative Correspondence under the Kings of Ur* (TCS 1; Locust Valley, N.Y.: J.J. Augustin, 1966).
Sommer, B. D., "Did Prophecy Cease? Evaluating a Reevaluation," *JBL* 115 (1996) 31–47.
Sommerfeld, W., *Der Aufstieg Marduks: Die Stellung Marduks in der babylonischen Religion des zweiten Jahrtausends v. Chr.* (AOAT 213; Kevelaer: Butzon & Bercker; Neukirchen-Vluyn: Neukirchener Verlag, 1982).
Souza Nogueira, P. A. de, "Ecstatic Worship in the Self-Glorification Hymn (4Q471b, 4Q427, 4Q491c): Implications for the Understanding of an Ancient Jewish and Early Christian Phenomenon," in *Wisdom and Apocalypticism in the Dead Sea Scrolls and in the Biblical Tradition* (ed. F. García Martínez; BETL 168; Leuven: Peeters, 2003) 385–93.
Spek, R. J. van der, "Assyriology and History: A Comparative Study of War and Empire in Assyria, Athens, and Rome," in *The Tablet and the Scroll*, FS W. W. Hallo (ed. M. E. Cohen, D. C. Snell, and D. B. Weisberg; Bethesda, Md.: CDL Press, 1993) 262–70.
Spek, R. J. van der, *"Ik ben een boodschapper van Nanaia!": Een Babylonische profeet als teken des tijds (133 voor Christus)* (Amsterdam: Vrije Universiteit Amsterdam, 2014).
Spieckermann, H., *Juda unter Assur in der Sargonidenzeit* (FRLANT 129; Göttingen: Vandenhoeck & Ruprecht, 1982).

Spieckermann, H., "Judah Under Assyrian Hegemony: A Re-examination of Imperialism and Religion," *JBL* 112 (1993) 403–14.

Spronk, K., "Deborah, a Prophetess: The Meaning and Background of Judges 4:4–5," in *The Elusive Prophet: The Prophet as a Historical Person, Literary Character and Anonymous Artist* (ed. J. C. de Moor; OTS 45; Leiden: Brill, 2001) 232–42.

Stähli, H.-P., "ירא *jrʾ* fürchten," *THAT* 1 (1971) 765–78.

Starr, I., *The Rituals of the Diviner* (Bibliotheca Mesopotamica 12; Malibu, Calif.: Undena, 1983).

Starr, I., *Queries to the Sungod: Divination and Politics in Sargonid Assyria* (SAA 4; Helsinki: Helsinki University Press, 1990).

Steck, O. H., *Der Abschluß der Prophetie im Alten Testament* (BThSt 17; Neukirchen-Vluyn: Neukirchener, 1991).

Steck, O. H., *Die Prophetenbücher und ihr theologisches Zeugnis: Wege der Nachfrage und Fährten zur Antwort* (Tübingen: Mohr Siebeck, 1996).

Steiner, R. C., "The Aramaic Text in Demotic Script," in *The Context of Scripture*, vol. 1: *Canonical Compositions from the Biblical World* (ed. W. W. Hallo and K. L. Younger; Leiden: Brill, 1997) 309–27.

Stendahl, K., "Dethroning Biblical Imperialism in Theology," in *Reading the Bible in the Global Village* (ed. H. Räisänen; SBLGPBS 6; Atlanta, Ga.: Society of Biblical Literature, 2000) 61–66.

Stichele, C. Vander, and T. Penner, "Mastering the Tools or Retooling the Masters: The Legacy of Historical-Critical Discourse," in *Her Master's Tools? Feminist and Postcolonial Engagements of Historical-Critical Discourse* (ed. iid.; SBLGPBS 9; Atlanta, Ga.: Society of Biblical Literature, 2005) 1–29.

Stipp, H.-J., "Baruchs Erben: Die Schriftprophetie im Spiegel von Jer 36," in *'Wer darf hinaufsteigen zum Berg JHWHs?': Beiträge zu Prophetie und Poesie des Alten Testaments*, FS S. Ö. Steingrímsson (ed. H. Irsigler ; Arbeiten zu Text und Sprache im Alten Testament 72; St. Ottilien: EOS Verlag, 2002) 145–70.

Stjerna, K., "Finnish Sleep-Preachers: An Example of Women's Spiritual Power," *Nova religio* 5 (2001) 102–20.

Stökl, J., "Female Prophets in the Ancient Near East," in *Prophecy and Prophets in Ancient Israel: Proceedings of the Oxford Old Testament Seminar* (ed. J. Day. LHBOTS 531. London: T & T Clark, 2010) 47–61.

Stökl, J., *Prophecy in the Ancient Near East: A Philological and Sociological Comparison* (CHANE 56; Leiden: Brill, 2012).

Stökl, J., "The מתנבאות in Ezekiel 13 Reconsidered," *JBL* 132 (2013) 61–76

Stökl, J., "Gender 'Ambiguity' in Ancient Near Eastern Prophecy: A Reassessment of the Data behind a Popular Theory ," in *Prophets Male and Female: Gender and Prophecy in the Hebrew Bible, the Eastern Mediterranean and the Ancient Near East* (ed. C. L. Carvalho and J. Stökl; SBLAIL 15; Atlanta, Ga.: Society of Biblical Literature, 2013) 59–80.

Stökl, J., "Schoolboy Ezekiel: Remarks on the Transmission of Learning, WO 45 (2015) 50–61.

Stol, M., *Letters from Collections in Philadelphia, Chicago and Berkeley* (AbB 11; Leiden: Brill, 1986).

Stolper, M. W., *Entrepreneurs and Empire: The Murašû Archive, the Murašû Firm, and Persian Rule in Babylonia* (PIHANS 54; Istanbul: Nederlands Historisch-Archeologisch Instituut te Istanbul, 1985).

Stolz, F., *Strukturen und Figuren im Kult von Jerusalem* (BZAW 118; Berlin: De Gruyter, 1970).
Stone, K.,"Homosexuality and the Bible or Queer Reading? A Response to Martti Nissinen," *Theology and Sexuality 7* (2001) 107–18.
Strang, V., *The Meaning of Water* (Oxford: Berg, 2004).
Streck, M., *Assurbanipal und die letzten assyrischen Könige bis zum Untergang Niniveh's*, vol. 2 (VAB 7; Leipzig: Hinrichs, 1916).
Strine, C. A., *Sworn Enemies: The Divine Oath, the Book of Ezekiel, and the Polemics of Exile* (BZAW 436; Berlin and Boston, Mass.: De Gryuter, 2013).
Strine, C. A., "*Chaoskampf* against Empire: YHWH's Battle against Gog (Ezek 38–39) as Resistance Literature," in *Divination, Politics, and Ancient Near Eastern Empires* (ed. A. Lenzi and J. Stökl; ANEM 7; Atlanta, Ga.: Society of Biblical Literature, 2014) 87–108.
Strugnell, J., "4QApocryphon of Moses[a]," in *Qumran Cave 4.XIV: Parabiblical Texts*, vol. 2 (ed. M. Broshi et al.; DJD 19; Oxford: Clarendon Press, 1995) 111–19.
Sugirtharajah, R. S., "Critics, Tools, and the Global Arena," in *Reading the Bible in the Global Village* (ed. H. Räisänen; SBLGPBS 6; Atlanta, Ga.: Society of Biblical Literature, 2000) 49–60.
Svärd, S., *Women's Roles in the Neo-Assyrian Era: Female Agency in the Empire* (Saarbrücken: VDM Verlag Dr. Müller, 2008).
Svärd, S., and M. Nissinen, "(Re)constructing the Image of the Assinnu," in Studying Gender in the Ancient Near East (eds. Saana Svärd and Agnès Garcia Ventura; University Park, Pa.: Eisenbrauns, 2018) 373–411.
Sweeney, M. A., *Isaiah 1–39 with an Introduction to Prophetic Literature* (FOTL 16; Grand Rapids, Mich.: Eerdmans, 1996).
Sweeney, M. A., "Isaiah and Theodicy after the Shoah," in *Strange Fire: Reading the Bible after the Holocaust* (ed. Tod Linafelt; Sheffield: Sheffield Academic Press, 2000), 208–19.
Sweeney, M. A., "King Manasseh of Judah and the Problem of Theodicy in the Deuteronomistic History," in *Good Kings and Bad Kings* (ed. L. L. Grabbe; LHBOTS 393; London: T&T Clark, 2005), 264–78.
Sweeney, M. A., "The Dystopianization of Utopian Prophetic Literature: The Case of Amos 9:11–15," in *Utopia and Dystopia in Prophetic Literature* (ed. E. Ben Zvi; PFES 92; Helsinki: Finnish Exegetical Society, 2006) 175–85.
Sweeney, M. A., "Samuel's Institutional Identity in the Deuteronomistic History," in *Constructs of Prophecy in the Former and Latter Prophets and Other Texts* (ed. L. L. Grabbe and M. Nissinen; ANEM 4; Atlanta, Ga.: Society of Biblical Literature, 2011) 165–74.
Sweeney, M. A., "Ezekiel's Conceptualization of the Exile in Intertextual Perspective," *HeBAI* 1 (2012) 154–72.
Syreeni, K., "Wonderlands: A Beginner's Guide to Three Worlds," *SEÅ* 64 (1999) 33–46.
Tadmor, H., "History and Ideology in the Assyrian Royal Inscriptions," in *Assyrian Royal Inscriptions: New Horizons in Literary, Ideological and Historical Analysis* (ed. F. M. Fales; OAC 17; Roma: Istituto per l'Oriente, 1981) 13–33.
Tadmor, H., "The Aramaization of Assyria: Aspects of Western Impact," in *Mesopotamien und seine Nachbarn: Politische und kulturelle Wechselbeziehungen im Alten Vorderasien vom 4. bis 1. Jahrtausend v.Chr* (ed. H.-J. Nissen and J. Renger; Berliner Beiträge zum Vorderen Orient 1; Berlin: Reimer, 1982) 449–70.

Tadmor, H., B. Landsberger, and S. Parpola, "The Sin of Sargon and Sennacherib's Last Will," *SAAB* 3 (1989) 3–52.

Talmon, S., "The Biblical Concept of Jerusalem," *JES* 8 (1971) 300–16.

Talon, Ph., "Les Textes Prophétiques du premier millénaire en Mésopotamie," *in Prophéties et oracles, vol. 1: Dans le Proche-Orient ancient.* (ed. J. Asurmendi, J.-M. Durand, R. Lebrun, E. Puech, and Ph. Talon; Supplément au Cahier Evangile 88; Paris: Cerf, 1994), 97–114.

Taylor, R., "River Raptures: Containment and Control of Water in Greek and Roman Constructions of Identity," in *The Nature and Function of Water, Baths, Bathing and Hygiene from Antiquity through Renaissance* (ed. C. Kosso and A. Scott; Technology and Change in History 11; Leiden: Brill, 2009) 21–42.

Tedlock, B., "Divination as a Way of Knowing: Embodiment, Visualisation, Narrative, and Interpretation," *Folklore* 112 (2001) 189–97.

Teppo, S., "Sacred Marriage and the Devotees of Ištar," in *Sacred Marriages: The Divine-Human Sexual Metaphor from Sumer to Early Christianity* (ed. M. Nissinen and R. Uro; Winona Lake, Ind.: Eisenbrauns, 2008) 75–92.

Tervanotko, H., *Denying Her Voice: The Figure of Miriam in Ancient Jewish Literature* (JAJSup 23; Göttingen: Vandenhoeck & Ruprecht, 2016).

Tervanotko, H., "Speaking in Dreams: The Figure of Miriam and Prophecy," in *Prophets Male and Female: Gender and Prophecy in the Hebrew Bible, the Eastern Mediterranean and the Ancient Near East* (ed. C. L. Carvalho and J. Stökl; SBLAIL 15; Atlanta: Society of Biblical Literature, 2013) 147–68.

Thelle, R. L., *Ask God: Divine Consultation in the Literature of the Hebrew Bible* (BBET 30; Frankfurt a. M.: Peter Lang, 2002).

Thiel, W., *Die deuteronomistische Redaktion von Jeremia 1–25* (WMANT 41; Neukirchen-Vluyn: Neukirchner Verlag, 1973).

Thomas, J. D., "Jewish Apocalyptic and the Comparative Method," in *Scripture in Context: Essays on the Comparative Method* (ed. C. D. Evans, W. W. Hallo, and J. B. White; PTMS 34; Pittsburgh, Pa.: Pickwick, 1980) 245–62.

Thomas, S. I., *The "Mysteries" of Qumran: Mystery, Secrecy, and Esotericism in the Dead Sea Scrolls* (SBLEJL 25; Atlanta, Ga.: Society of Biblical Literature, 2009).

Thomas, S. M., *The Global Resurgence of Religion and the Transformation of International Relations: The Struggle for the Soul of the Twenty-First Century* (New York: Palgrave MacMillan, 2005).

Thompson, T. L., *Early History of the Israelite People: From the Written and Archaeological Sources* (SHANE 4; Leiden: Brill, 1992).

Thomson de Grummond, N., "Prophets and Priests," in *The Religion of the Etruscans* (ed. N. Thomson de Grummond and E. Simon; Austin, Tex.: University of Texas Press, 2006) 41–42.

Thureau-Dangin, F., *Rituels accadiens* (Paris: Leroux, 1921).

Thureau-Dangin, F., "Un hymne à Ištar de la haute époque babylonienne," *RA* 22 (1925) 169–77.

Tigchelaar, E. J. C., "Your Wisdom and Your Folly: The Case of 1–4QMysteries," in *Wisdom and Apocalypticism in the Dead Sea Scrolls and in the Biblical Tradition* (ed. F. García Martínez; BETL 168; Leuven: Peeters, 2003) 69–88.

Toorn, K. van der, "L'Oracle de victoire comme expression prophétique au Proche-Orient ancien," *RB* 94 (1987) 63–97.
Toorn, K. van der, "*A Prophetic Role-Play Mistaken for an Apocalyptic Vision:* ARM 26/196," *NABU* (1998) 3.
Toorn, K. van der, "Old Babylonian Prophecy between the Oral and the Written," *JNSL* 24 (1998) 55–70.
Toorn, K. van der, "From the Oral to the Written: The Case of Old Babylonian Prophecy," in *Writings and Speech in Israelite and Ancient Near Eastern Prophecy* (ed. E. Ben Zvi and M. H. Floyd; SBLSymS 10; Atlanta, Ga.: Society of Biblical Literature, 2000) 219–34.
Toorn, K. van der, "Mesopotamian Prophecy between Immanence and Transcendence: A Comparison of Old Babylonian and Neo-Assyrian Prophecy," in *Prophecy in Its Ancient Near Eastern Context: Mesopotamian, Biblical, and Arabian Perspectives* (ed. M. Nissinen; SBLSymS 13; Atlanta Ga.: Society of Biblical Literature, 2000) 70–87.
Toorn, K. van der, "Sources in Heaven: Revelation as a Scholarly Construct in Second Temple Judaism," in *Kein Land für sich allein: Studien zum Kulturkontakt in Kanaan, Israel/Palästina und Ebirnâri für Manfred Weippert zum 65. Geburtstag* (ed. U. Hübner and E. A. Knauf; OBO 186; Fribourg and Göttingen: Academic Press Fribourg and Vandenhoeck & Ruprecht, 2002) 265–77.
Toorn, K. van der, "From the Mouth of the Prophet: The Literary Fixation of Jeremiah's Prophecies in the Context of the Ancient Near East," in *Inspired Speech: Prophecy in the Ancient Near East*, FS H. B. Huffmon (ed. J. Kaltner and L. Stulman; JSOTSup 378; London: T & T Clark, 2004) 191–202.
Toorn, K. van der, *Scribal Culture and the Making of the Hebrew Bible* (Cambridge, Mass.: Harvard University Press, 2007).
Toorn, K. van der, *Papyrus Amherst 63* (AOAT 448; Münster: Ugarit-Verlag, 2018).
Trotter, J. M., *Reading Hosea in Achaemenid Yehud* (JSOTSup 328; Sheffield: Sheffield Academic Press, 2001).
Tuchelt, K., *Branchidai—Didyma: Geschichte, Ausgrabung und Wiederentdeckung eines antiken Heiligtums, 1765–1900* (Antike Welt Sondernummer 22 [= Zaberns Bildbände zur Archäologie 3]; Mainz: von Zabern, 1991).
Ueberschaer, F., *Weisheit aus der Begegnung: Bildung nach dem Buch Ben Sira* (BZAW 379; Berlin: De Gruyter, 2007).
Uehlinger, C., "Audienz in der Götterwelt: Anthropomorphismus und Soziomorphismus in der Ikonographie eines altsyrischen Zylindersiegels," *UF* 24 (1992) 339–59.
Uehlinger, C., "Figurative Policy, Propaganda und Prophetie," in *Congress Volume Cambridge 1995* (ed. J. A. Emerton; VTSup 66; Leiden: Brill, 1997) 297–349.
Uehlinger, C., "Neither Eyewitnesses, Nor Windows to the Past, but Valuable Testimony in its Own Right: Remarks on Iconography, Source Criticism and Ancient Data-Processing," in *Understanding the History of Ancient Israel* (ed. H. G. M. Williamson; Proceedings of the British Academy 143; Oxford: Oxford University Press, 2007) 173–228.
Uehlinger, C., "Virtual Vision vs. Actual Show: Strategies of Visualization in the Book of Ezekiel," *WO* 45 (2015) 62–98.
Uehlinger, C., and S. Müller Trufaut, "Ezekiel 1: Babylonian Cosmological Scholarship and Iconography: Attempts at Further Refinement," *ThZ* 57 (2001) 140–71.
Ulrich, E. C., *The Dead Sea Scrolls and the Origins of the Bible* (SDSRL; Grand Rapids, Mich.: Eerdmans, 1999).

Ulrich, E. C., "The Non-Attestation of a Tripartite Canon in 4QMMT," *CBQ* 65 (2003) 202–14.
Ulrich, E. C., "Our Sharper Focus on the Bible and Theology Thanks to the Dead Sea Scrolls," *CBQ* 66 (2004) 1–24.
Ungnad, A., *Babylonische Briefe aus der Zeit der Hammurapi-Dynastie* (VAB 6; Leipzig: Hinrichs, 1914).
Uusimäki, E., and H. von Weissenberg, "Viisaus ja ilmoitus Qumranin viisauskirjallisuudessa," [Wisdom and Revelation in the Wisdom Literature from Qumran] *Teologinen Aikakauskirja* 118 (2013) 235–46.
Vanderhooft, D. S., "*ʾel medînâ ûmedînâ kiktābāh:* Scribes and Scripts in Yehud and in Achaemenid Transeuphratene," in *Judah and Judeans in the Achaemenid Period: Negotiating Identity in an International Context* (ed. O. Lipschits, G. N. Knoppers, and M. Oeming; Winona Lake, Ind.: Eisenbrauns, 2011) 529–44.
Vanderhooft, D. S., "Chebar," *EBR* 5 (2012) 46.
Vanderhooft, D. S., "Ezekiel in and on Babylon," in *Bible et Proche-Orient: Mélanges André Lemaire III* (ed. J. Elayi and J.-M. Durand; Transeuphratène 46; Paris: Gabalda, 2014) 99–119
VanderKam, J. C., *Enoch and the Growth of an Apocalyptic Tradition* (CBQMS 16; Washington, D.C.: Catholic Biblical Association, 1984).
VanderKam, J. C., "The Prophetic-Sapiential Origins of Apocalyptic Thought," in *A Word in Season*, FS W. McKane (ed. J. D. Martin and P. R. Davies; JSOTSup 42; Sheffield: JSOT Press, 1986) 163–76 (repr. in id., *From Revelation to Canon: Studies in the Hebrew Bible and Second Temple Literature* [JSJSup 62; Leiden: Brill, 2000] 241–54)
VanderKam, J. C., "Prophecy and Apocalyptics in the Ancient Near East," *CANE* 3 (1995) 2083–94.
VanderKam, J. C., "Mantic Wisdom in the Dead Sea Scrolls," *DSD* 4 (1997) 336–53.
Varner, G. R., *Sacred Wells: A Study in the History, Meaning, and Mythology of Holy Wells and Waters* (New York: Algora Publishing, ²2009).
Vawter, B., "Were the Prophets *nābîʾs?*," *Bib* 66 (1985) 206–20.
Veeser, H. A. (ed.), *The New Historicism* (New York: Routledge, 1989).
Veijola, T., "Zu Ableitung und Bedeutung von *hēʿîd* I im Hebräischen," *UF* 8 (1976) 343–51.
Veijola, T., *Verheißung in der Krise: Studien zur Literatur und Theologie der Exilszeit anhand des 89. Psalms* (AASF B 220; Helsinki: Academia Scientiarum Fennica, 1982).
Veijola, T.,
"Davidverheißung und Staatsvertrag. Beobachtungen zum Einfluß altorientalischer Staat verträge auf die biblische Sprache am Beispiel von Psalm 89," *ZAW* 95 (1983) 9–31.
Veijola, T., "The Witness in the Clouds: Ps 89:38," *JBL* 197 (1988) 413–17.
Veijola, T., "David in Keïla: Tradition und Interpretation in 1Sam 23, 1–13," *RB* 91 (1984) 51–87 (= id., *David: Gesammelte Studien zur Davidüberlieferungen des Alien Testaments* [PSES 52; Helsinki: Finish Exegetical Society, 1990]).
Veijola, T., "David und Meribaal," in id., *David: Gesammelte Studien zu den Davidüberlieferungen des Alten Testaments* (PFES 52; Helsinki: Finnish Exegetical Society; Göttingen: Vandenhoeck & Ruprecht, 1990) 58–83 (= *RB* 85 [1978] 338–61).
Veijola, T., "Bundestheologische Redaktion im Deuteronomium," in *Das Deuteronomium und seine Querbeziehungen* (ed. T. Veijola; PFES 62; Helsinki: Finnische Exegetische Gesellschaft; Göttingen: Vandenhoeck & Ruprecht, 1996) 242–76; repr. in id.ö, *Moses*

Erben: Studien zum Dekalog, zum Deuteronomismus und zum Schriftgelehrtentum (BWANT 149; Stuttgart: Kohlhammer, 2000) 155–56.

Veijola, T., "Wahrheit und Intoleranz nach Deuteronomium 13," *ZThK* 92 (1995) 287–314; repr. in id., *Moses Erben: Studien zum Dekalog, zum Deuteronomismus und zum Schriftgelehrtentum* (BWANT 8/9; Stuttgart: Kohlhammer, 2000) 109–30.

Veijola, T., *Moses Erben: Studien zum Dekalog, zum Deuteronomismus und zum Schriftgelehrtentum* (BWANT 149; Stuttgart: Kohlhammer, 2000).

Veijola, T., "Text, Wissenschaft und Glaube: Überlegungen eines Alttestamentlers zur Lösung des Grundproblems der biblischen Hermeneutik," *JBTh* 15 (2000) 313–39.

Veijola, T., "Deuteronomismusforschung zwischen Tradition und Innovation (1)," *TRu* 67 (2002) 273–327.

Veijola, T., "The Deuteronomistic Roots of Judaism," in *Sefer Moshe: The Moshe Weinfeld Jubilee Volume: Studies in the Bible and the Ancient Near East, Qumran, and Post-Biblical Judaism* (ed. C. Cohen, A. Hurvitz, and S. M. Paul; Winona Lake, Ind.: Eisenbrauns, 2004) 459–78.

Veijola, T., "Law and Wisdom: The Deuteronomistic Heritage in Ben Sira's Teaching of the Law," in *Ancient Israel, Judaism, and Christianity in Contemporary Perspective*, FS K.-J. Illman (ed. J. Neusner et al.; Lanham, Md.: University Press of America, 2006) 429–48.

Veijola, T., "Depression als menschliche und biblische Erfahrung," in id., *Offenbarung und Anfechtung: Hermeneutisch-theologische Studien zum Alten Testament* (ed. W. Dietrich and M. Marttila; Biblisch-theologische Studien 89; Neukirchen-Vluyn: Neukirchener, 2007) 158–90.

Veijola, T., *Leben nach der Weisung: Exegetisch-historische Studien zum Alten Testament* (ed. W. Dietrich in collaboration with M. Marttila; FRLANT 224; Göttingen: Vandenhoeck & Ruprecht, 2008).

Vera Chamaza, G. W., *Die Omnipotenz Aššurs: Entwicklungen in der Aššur-Theologie unter der Sargoniden Sargon II, Sanherib und Asarhaddon* (AOAT 295; Münster: Ugarit-Verlag, 2002).

Viaggio, S. "Sull'amministrazione del tempio di Ištar Kitītum a Ishjali," *EVO* 29 (2006) 185–217.

Vielhauer, R., *Das Werden des Buches Hosea: eine redaktionsgeschichtliche Untersuchung* (BZAW 349; Berlin: de Gruyter, 2007).

Villard, P., "Les prophéties à l'époque néo-assyrienne," in *Prophètes et Rois: Bible et Proche-Orient* (ed. A. Lemaire; Paris: Cerf, 2001) 55–84.

Volz, P., *Der Prophet Jeremia* (KAT 10; Leipzig and Erlangen: Deichert, 1922).

Wacker, M.-T., "'Religionsgeschichte Israel's' oder ‚Theologie des Alten Testaments' –(k)eine Alternative? Anmerkungen aus feministhischexegetischer Sicht," *JBTh* 10 (1995) 129–55.

Waerzeggers, C., "Locating Contact in the Babylonian Exile: Some Reflections on Tracing Judean-Babylonian Encounters in Cuneiform Texts," in *Encounters by the Rivers of Babylon: Scholarly Conversations between Jews, Iranians, and Babylonians in Antiquity* (ed. U. Gabbay and S. Secunda; TSAJ 160; Tübingen: Mohr Siebeck, 2014) 131–46.

Wagenaar, J., *Judgement and Salvation: The Composition and Redaction of Micah 2–5* (VTSup 85; Leiden: Brill, 2001).

Wagstaff, J. M., "The Origin and Evolution of Towns: 4000 BC to AD 1900," in *The Changing Middle Eastern City* (ed. G. H. Blake and R. I. Lawless; London: Croon Helm, 1980) 11–33.
Wahl, H. M., "Die Entstehung der Schriftprophetie nach Jer 36," *ZAW* 110 (1998) 365–89.
Waldow, H.-E. von, "Anlass und Hintergrund der Verkündigung des Deuterojesaja" (diss.; Univ. of Bonn, 1953).
Walton, J. H., *Ancient Near Eastern Thought and the Old Testament: Introducing the Conceptual World of the Hebrew Bible* (Grand Rapids, Mich.: Baker Academic, 2006).
Wanke, G., *Untersuchungen zur sogenannten Baruchschrift* (BZAW 122; Berlin: De Gruyter, 1971).
Wanke, G., "φοβέω κτλ. B. φόβος und φοβέομαι im Alten Testament," *ThWNT* 9 (1973) 194–201.
Warhurst, A. K., "The Chronicler's Use of the Prophets," in *What Was Authoritative for Chronicles?* (ed. E. Ben Zvi and D. Edelman; Winona Lake, Ind.: Eisenbrauns, 2011) 165–81.
Wasserman, N., and U. Gabbay, "Literatures In Contact: The Balag Úru àm-ma-ir-ra-bi and Its Akkadian Translation UET 6/2, 403," *JCS* 57 (2006) 69–84.
Watanabe, K., *Die adê-Vereidigung anläßlich der Thronfolgeregelung Asarhaddons* (BaM.B 3; Berlin: Mann, 1987).
Waterman, L., *Royal Correspondence of the Assyrian Empire*, vol. 2. (University of Michigan Studies, Humanistic Series 18; Ann Arbor, Mich.: University of Michigan Press, 1930).
Waters, M. W., *A Survey of Neo-Elamite History* (SAAS 12; Helsinki: Neo-Assyrian Text Corpus Project, 2000).
Watts, J. D. W., *Isaiah 34–66* (WBC 25; Waco, Tex.: Word Books, 1987).
Watts, J. D. W. (ed.), *Persia and Torah: The Theory of Imperial Authorization of the Pentateuch* (ed. id.; SBLSymS 17; Atlanta: Ga.: Society of Biblical Literature, 2001).
Webster, B., "Chronological Index of the Texts from the Judaean Desert," in *The Texts from the Judaean Desert: Indices and an Introduction to the Discoveries in the Judaean Desert Series* (ed. E. Tov; Oxford: Clarendon Press, 2002) 351–446.
Weems, R. J., "Huldah, the Prophet: Reading a (Deuteronomistic) Woman's Identity," in *A God So Near*, FS P. D. Miller (ed. B. A. Strawn and N. R. Bowen; Winona Lake, Ind.: Eisenbrauns, 2003) 321–39.
Weidner, E. F., "Assyrische Beschreibungen der Kriegs-Reliefs Aššurbânaplis," *AfO* 8 (1932/33) 175–203.
Weidner, E. F., "Jojachin, König von Juda, in babylonischen Keilschrifttexten," in *Mélanges syriens*, FS R. Dussaud, vol. 2 (Paris: Geuthner, 1939) 923–35.
Weinfeld, M., *Deuteronomy and the Deuteronomic School* (Oxford: Clarendon, 1972).
Weinfeld, M., "Covenant Terminology in the Ancient Near East and its Influence on the West," *JAOS* 93 (1973) 190–99.
Weinfeld, M., "Ancient Near Eastern Patterns in Prophetic Literature," *VT* 27 (1977) 178–195.
Weinfeld, M., "Divine Intervention in War in Ancient Israel and in the Ancient Near East," in *History, Historiography and Interpretation: Studies in Biblical and Cuneiform Literatures* (ed. id. and H. Tadmor; Jerusalem: Magnes, 1983) 121–47.
Weinfeld, M., "Sabbatical Year and Jubilee in the Pentateuchal Laws and their Ancient Near Eastern Background," in *The Law in the Bible and in its Environment* (ed. T. Veijola;

PFES 51; Helsinki and Göttingen: Finnish Exegetical Society and Vandenhoeck & Ruprecht, 1990) 39–62.
Weinfeld, M., *Social Justice in Ancient Israel and in the Ancient Near East* (Publications of the Perry Foundation for Biblical Research in the Hebrew University of Jerusalem; Jerusalem and Minneapolis, Minn.: Fortress Press, 1995).
Weinfeld, M., "Jerusalem: A Political and Spiritual Capital," in *Capital Cities: Urban Planning and Spiritual Dimensions: Proceedings of the Symposium Held on May 27–29, 1996, Jerusalem, Israel* (ed. J. G. Westenholz; Bible Lands Museum Jerusalem Publications 2; Jerusalem: Bible Lands Museum, 1998) 15–40.
Weippert, M., "'Heiliger Krieg' in Israel und Assyrien: Kritische Anmerkungen zu Gerhard von Rads Konzept des 'Heiligen Krieges im alten Israel,'" *ZAW* 84 (1972) 460–93.
Weippert, M., "Assyrische Prophetien der Zeit Asarhaddons und Assurbanipals," in *Assyrian Royal Inscriptions: New Horizons in Literary, Ideological and Historical Analysis* (ed. F. M. Fales; OAC 17; Roma: Istituto per l'Oriente, 1981) 71–115.
Weippert, M., "De herkomst van het heilsorakel voor Israël bij Deutero-Jesaja," *NedTT* 36 (1982) 1–11.
Weippert, M., "Die Bildsprache der neuassyrischen Prophetie," in *Beiträge zur prophetischen Bildsprache in Israel und Assyrien* (ed. H. Weippert, K. Seybold, and M. Weippert; OBO 64; Fribourg and Göttingen: Academic Press Fribourg and Vandenhoeck & Ruprecht, 1985) 55–93.
Weippert, M., "Aspekte israelitischer Prophetie im Lichte verwandter Erscheinungen des Alten Orients," in *Ad bene et fideliter seminandum*, FS Karlheinz Deller (ed. G. Mauer and U. Magen; AOAT 220; Kevelaer: Butzon & Bercker; Neukirchen-Vluyn: Neukirchener Verlag, 1988) 287–319.
Weippert, M., "The Balaam Text from Deir ʿAllā and the Study of the Old Testament," in *The Balaam Text from Deir ʿAlla Re-Evaluated: Proceedings of the International Symposium Held at Leiden, 21–24 August 1989* (DMOA 19; ed. J. Hoftijzer and G. van der Kooij; Leiden: Brill, 1991) 151–84.
Weippert, M., "'Das Frühere, siehe, ist eingetroffen…': Über Selbstzitate im Prophetenspruch," in *Oracles et prophéties dans l'antiquité: Actes du Colloque de Strasbourg 15–17 Juin 1995* (ed. J.-G. Heintz; Université des sciences humaines de Strasbourg, Travaux du Centre de recherche sur le Proche-Orient et la Grèce antiques 15; Paris: Boccard, 1997) 147–69.
Weippert, M., "Prophetie im Alten Orient," *NBL* 3 (1997) 196–200.
Weippert, M., "'Ich bin Jahwe' – 'Ich bin Ištar von Arbela.' Deuterojesaja im Lichte der neuassyrischen Prophetie," in *Prophetie und Psalmen*, FS K. Seybold (ed. B. Huwyler, H.-P. Mathys, and B. Weber; AOAT 280; Münster: Ugarit-Verlag, 2001) 31–59.
Weippert, M., *Jahwe und die anderen Götter* (FAT 18; Tübingen: Mohr Siebeck, 1997).
Weippert, M., "'König, fürchte dich nicht!' Assyrische Prophetie im 7. Jahrhundert v. Chr.," *Or* 71 (2002) 1–54.
Weippert, M., *Götterwort in Menschenmund: Studien zur Prophetie in Assyrien, Israel und Juda* (FRLANT 252; Göttingen: Vandenhoeck & Ruprecht 2014).
Weippert, M., and H. Weippert, "Die "Bileam"-Inschrift von Tell Deir ʿAllā," *ZDPV* 98 (1982) 77–103 (= M. Weippert, *Jahwe und die anderen Götter: Studien zur Religionsgeschichte des antiken Israel im syrisch-palästinischem Kontext* [FAT 18; Tübingen: Mohr Siebeck, 1997] 131–61).

Weissenberg, H. von, *4QMMT: Reevaluating the Text, the Function, and the Meaning of the Epilogue* (STDJ 82; Leiden: Brill, 2009).

Weissenberg, H. von, "Changing Scripture? Scribal Corrections in MS 4QXIIc," in *Changes in Scripture: Rewriting and Interpreting Authoritative Traditions in the Second Temple Period* (ed. ead., J. Pakkala and M. Marttila; BZAW 419; Berlin: de Gruyter, 2011) 247–71.

Weissert, E., "Royal Hunt and Royal Triumph in a Prism Fragment of Ashurbanipal (82–5–22,2)", in *Assyria 1995: Proceedings of the 10th Anniversary symposium of the Neo-Assyrian Texts Carpus Project, Helsinki September 7–11, 1995* (ed. S. Parpola and R. M. Whiting; Helsinki: The Neo-Assyrian Texts Corpus Project, 1997) 339–58.

Wellhausen, J., "Review of B. Duhm's, *Die Theologie der Propheten als Grundlage für die innere Entwicklungsgeschichte der israelitischen Tradition* (Bonn: Marcus, 1875)," in *Jahrbuch für Deutsche Theologie* 21 (1876) 152–58.

Wellhausen, J., *Geschichte Israels*, vol. 1 (Berlin: Reimer, 1878).

Wellhausen, J., *Prolegomena zur Geschichte Israels* (Berlin: Reimer, [3]1886).

Werlitz, J., "Amos und sein Biograph: Zur Entstehung und Intention der Prophetenerzählung Am 7,10–17," *BZ* NF 44 (2000) 233–51.

Westenholz, J. G., *Legends of the Kings of Akkade: The Texts* (Mesopotamian Civilizations 7; Winona Lake, Ind.: Eisenbrauns, 1997).

Westenholz, J. G., "The Theological Foundation of a City, the Capital City and Babylon," in *Capital Cities: Urban Planning and Spiritual Dimensions. Proceedings of the Symposium Held on May 27–29, 1996, Jerusalem, Israel* (ed. id.; Bible Lands Museum Jerusalem Publications 2; Jerusalem: Bible Lands Museum, 1998) 43–54.

Westenholz, J. G., (ed.), *Capital Cities: Urban Planning and Spiritual Dimensions. Proceedings of the Symposium Held on May 27–29, 1996, Jerusalem, Israel* (ed. id.; Bible Lands Museum Jerusalem Publications 2; Jerusalem: Bible Lands Museum, 1998).

Westermann, C., *Grundformen prophetischer Rede* (BEvT 31; Munich: Kaiser, 1960; [5]1978); ET: *Basic Forms of Prophetic Speech* (trans. H. C. White; Louisville, Ky.: Westminster/John Knox, 1991).

Westermann, C., "Das Heilswort bei Deuterojesaja," *EvT* 24 (1964) 355–73 (summarized in id., *Forschung am Alten Testament* [TB 24; Munich: Kaiser, 1964], 117–24).

Westermann, C., *Prophetische Heilsworte im Alten Testament* (FRLANT 145; Göttingen: Vandenhoeck & Ruprecht, 1987) ; ET: *Prophetic Oracles of Salvation in the Old Testament* (trans. K. Crim; Louisville, Ky.: Westminster/John Knox, 1991).

White, H. V., *Metahistory: The Historical Imagination in Nineteenth-Century Europe* (Baltimore, Md.: Johns Hopkins University Press, 1973).

White, H. V., *Tropics of Discourse: Essays in Cultural Criticism* (Baltimore, Md.: Johns Hopkins University Press, 1978).

White, H. V., *The Content of the Form: Narrative Discourse and Historical Representation* (Baltimore, Md.: Johns Hopkins University Press, 1987).

White, H. V., "New Historicism: A Comment," in *The New Historicism* (ed. H. Aram Veeser; New York: Routledge, 1989) 293–302.

Wilcke, C., "*ittātim ašqi aštāl:* Medien in Mari?," *RA* 77 (1983) 93.

Wildberger, H., "'Glauben' im Alten Testament," *ZThK* 65 (1968) 129–59.

Wildberger, H., *Jesaja, 1. Teilband: Jesaja 1–12* (BKAT 10/1; Neukirchen-Vluyn: Neukirchener, 1972).

Wildberger, H., *Isaiah 28–39: A Continental Commentary* (trans. T. H. Trapp; Minneapolis, Minn: Fortress, 2002).
Williamson, H. G. M., "A Response to A. Graeme Auld," *JSOT* 27 (1983) 33–39.
Williamson, H. G. M., *Ezra, Nehemiah* (WBC 16; Waco, Tex.: Word, 1985)
Williamson, H. G. M., "The Prophet and the Plumb-Line: A Redaction-Critical Study of Amos 7," in *The Place Is Too Small for Us: The Israelite Prophets in Recent Scholarship* (ed. R. P. Gordon; Sources for Biblical and Theological Study 5; Winona Lake, Ind.: Eisenbrauns, 1995) 453–77.
Williamson, H. G. M., "The Belief System of the Book of Nehemiah," in *The Crisis of Israelite Religion: Transformation of Religious Tradition in Exilic and Post-Exilic Times* (ed. B. Becking and M. C. A. Korpel; OTS 42; Leiden: Brill, 1999) 276–87.
Williamson, H. G. M., "In Search of the Pre-Exilic Isaiah," in *In Search of Pre-Exilic Israel* (ed. J. Day; JSOTSup 406; London: T&T Clark International, 2004) 181–206.
Williamson, H. G. M., "Prophetesses in the Hebrew Bible," in *Prophecy and Prophets in Ancient Israel: Proceedings of the Oxford Old Testament Seminar* (ed. J. Day; LHBOTS 531; London: T&T Clark, 2010) 65–80.
Willis, J. T., "Isaiah 2:2–5 and the Psalms of Zion," *in Writing and Reading the Scroll of Isaiah Studies of an Interpretive Tradition*, Vol. 1 (eds. C. C. Broyles and C. A. Evans; VTSup 70/1; Leiden: Brill, 2001) 295–316.
Wilson, R. R., *Prophecy and Society in Ancient Israel* (Philadelphia, Pa.: Fortress, 1980).
Wilson, R. R., "Prophet," *HBD* (1996) 884–89.
Winitzer, A., "The Divine Presence and Its Interpretation in Early Mesopotamian Divination," in *Divination and Interpretation of Signs in the Ancient World* (ed. A. Annus; Oriental Institute Seminars 6; Chicago: Oriental Institute, 2010) 177–97.
Winitzer, A., "Assyriology and Jewish Studies in Tel Aviv: Ezekiel among the Babylonian *literati*," in *Encounters by the Rivers of Babylon: Scholarly Conversations between Jews, Iranians, and Babylonians in Antiquity* (ed. U. Gabbay and S. Secunda; TSAJ 160; Tübingen: Mohr Siebeck, 2014) 163–216.
Winter, I. J., "Art in Empire: The Royal Image and the Visual Dimensions of Assyrian Ideology," in *Assyria 1995: Proceedings of the 10th Anniversary Symposium of the Neo-Assyrian Text Corpus Project, Helsinki, September 7–11, 1995* (ed. S. Parpola and R. M. Whiting; Helsinki: The Neo-Assyrian Text Corpus Project, 1997) 359–81.
Winter, U., *Frau und Göttin: Exegetische und ikonographische Studien zum weiblichen Gottesbild im Alten Israel und in dessen Umwelt* (OBO 53; Fribourg and Göttingen: Academic Press Fribourg and Vandenhoeck & Ruprecht, 1983).
Wise, M., "מי כמוני באים": A Study of 4Q491c, 4Q471b, 4Q427 7 and 1QH^{a} 25:35–26:10," *DSD* 7 (2000) 173–219.
Wohl, H., "The Problem of the *mahhû*," *JANESCU* 3 (1970–71) 112–18.
Wolde, E. van, "Ezekiel's Picture of God in Ezekiel 1," in *The God Ezekiel Creates* (ed. P. Joyce and D. Rom-Shiloni; LHBOTS 607; New York: T & T Clark, 2014) 87–106.
Wolff, H. W., *Dodekapropheton*, vol 1: *Hosea* (BKAT 14/1; Neukirchen-Vluyn: Neukirchener, ^{3}1976).
Wright, B. G., "Conflicted Boundaries: Ben Sira, Sage and Seer," in *Congress Volume Helsinki 2010* (ed. M. Nissinen; VTSup 148; Leiden: Brill, 2012) 229–53.

Wright, P. M., "The Qur'anic David," in *Constructs of Prophecy in the Former and Latter Prophets and Other Texts* (ed. L. L. Grabbe and M. Nissinen; ANEM 4; Atlanta, Ga.: Society of Biblical Literature, 2011) 197–206.

Wunsch, C., "Glimpses on the Lives of Deportees in Rural Babylonia," *Arameans, Chaldeans, and Arabs in Babylonia and Palestine in the First Millennium B. C.* (ed. A. Berlejung and M. P. Streck; LAOS 3; Wiesbaden: Harrassowitz, 2013) 247–60.

Wunsch, C., *Judeans by the Waters of Babylon: New Historical Evidence in Cuneiform Sources from Rural Babylonia* (Babylonische Archive 6; Dresden: ISLET-Verlag, [forthcoming]).

Würthwein, E., *Die Bücher der Könige: 1. Kön. 17–2. Kön. 25* (ATD 11/2; Göttingen: Vandenhoeck & Ruprecht, 1984).

Wyatt, S. N., *Myths of Power: A Study of Royal Myth and Ideology in Ugaritic and Biblical Tradition* (UBL 13; Münster: Ugarit-Verlag, 1996).

Wyatt, S. N., "Arms and the King: The Earliest Allusions to the *Chaoskampf* Motif and their Implications for the Interpretation of the Ugaritic and Biblical Traditions," in: "'Und Mose schrieb dieses Lied auf': Studien zum Alten Testament und zum Alten Orient," FS O. Loretz (ed. M. Dietrich and I. Kottsieper; AOAT 250; Münster: Ugartit-Verlag, 1998) 833–882

Wöhrle, J., *Die frühen Sammlungen des Zwölfprophetenbuches: Entstehung und Komposition* (BZAW 360; Berlin: de Gruyter, 2006).

Yee, G., A., *Composition and Redaction in the Book of Hosea: a Redaction Critical Investigation* (SBLDS 102; Atlanta Ga. Scholars Press, 1987).

Younger, K. I. Jr., "The Deportations of the Israelites," *JBL* 117 (1998) 221.

Zadok, R., *The Jews in Babylonia during the Chaldean and Achaemenid Periods According to the Babylonian Sources* (Haifa: University of Haifa, 1979).

Zadok, R., *The Earliest Diaspora: Israelites and Judeans in Pre-Hellenistic Mesopotamia* (PDRI 151; Tel Aviv: The Diaspora Research Institute, Tel Aviv University, 2002).

Zadok, R., "Judeans in Babylonia: Updating the Dossier," in *Encounters by the Rivers of Babylon: Scholarly Conversations between Jews, Iranians, and Babylonians in Antiquity* (ed. U. Gabbay and S. Secunda; TSAJ 160; Tübingen: Mohr Siebeck, 2014) 163–216.

Zagorin, P., "History, the Referent, and Narrative: Reflections on Postmodernism Now," *History and Theory* 38 (1999) 1–24.

Zakovitch, Y., *Das Hohelied* (trans. D. Mach; HTKAT; Freiburg: Herder, 2004).

Zehnder, M., "Observations on the Relationship between David and Jonathan and the Debate on Homosexuality," *WTJ* 69 (2007) 127–74.

Zenger, E., "'Durch Menschen zog ich sie …' (Hos 11,4): Beobachtungen zum Verständnis des prophetischen Amts im Hoseabuch," in *Künder des Wortes: Beiträge zur Theologie der Propheten*, FS J. Schreiner (ed. L. Ruppert, P. Weimar, and E. Zenger; Würzburg: Echter, 1982) 183–201.

Zenger, E., et al. (eds.), *Einleitung in das Alte Testament* (ed. C. Frevel; Stuttgart: Kohlhammer, [8]2012).

Zgoll, A., *Traum und Welterleben im antiken Mesopotamien: Traumtheorie und Traumpraxis im 3.–1. Jahrtausend v. Chr. als Horizont einer Kulturgeschichte des Träumens* (AOAT 333; Münster: Ugarit-Verlag, 2006).

Zimmerli, W., "Ich bin Jahwe," in *Geschichte und Altes Testament*, FS A. Alt (BHT 16; Tübingen: Mohr, 1953) 179–209; repr. in id., *Gottes Offenbarung: Gesammelte Aufsätze* (TB 19; Munich: Kaiser, 1963) 11–40.

Zimmerli, W., *Grundzüge der alttestamentlichen Theologie* (Theologische Wissenschaft 3; Stuttgart: Kohlhammer, [3]1978).

Zimmermann, J., *Messianische Texte aus Qumran: Königliche, priesterliche und prophetische Messiasvorstellungen in den Schriftfunden von Qumran* (WUNT 2/104; Tübingen: Mohr Siebeck, 1998).

Zimmermann, R., "The Love Triangle of Lady Wisdom: Sacred Marriage in Jewish Wisdom Literature?," in *Sacred Marriages: The Divine-Human Sexual Metaphor from Sumer to Early Christianity* (ed. M. Nissinen and R. Uro; Winona Lake, Ind.: Eisenbrauns, 2008) 243–58.

Zobel, H.-J., "Das Gebet um Abwendung der Not und seine Erhörung in den Klageliedern des Alten Testaments und in der Inschrift des Königs Zakir von Hamath," *VT* 21 (1971) 91–99.

Zsolnay, I., "The Misconstrued Role of the assinnu in Ancient Near Eastern Prophecy,"in *Prophets Male and Female: Gender and Prophecy in the Hebrew Bible, the Eastern Mediterranean and the Ancient Near East* (ed. C. L. Carvalho and J. Stökl; SBLAIL 15; Atlanta, Ga.: Society of Biblical Literature, 2013) 81–99.

Zwickel, W., "Kommunikation und Kommunikationsmöglichkeiten im Alten Israel aufgrund biblischer und ausserbiblischer Texte," in *Bote und Brief: Sprachliche Systeme der Informationsübermittlung im Spannungsfeld von Mündlichkeit und Schriftlichkeit* (ed. A. Wagner; Nordostafrikanisch/West-asiatische Studien 4; Frankfurt a. M.: Lang, 2003) 113–23.

Index of Names

Personal Names

Aaron 147
Abi-ešuḫ 474
Abiya 113, 181–184
Abraham 230
Adad-aḫu-iddina 112, 116, 139, 282, 551, 553
Adad-nirari III 138, 477
Addu-duri 115, 116, 131, 133, 149
Ahab 114, 348, 359, 542, 543, 547, 548, 550
Aḫat-abiša 111, 116, 122, 140, 150, 273, 329
Aḫatum 105, 116, 133, 166, 167, 551
Aḫum 116, 131, 134, 149, 166, 167, 551
Ahaziah 114, 358, 544
Ahaz 230, 359, 414, 623
Ahijah the Shilonite 547, 555, 636
Alexander the Great 454
Amaziah 359, 386
Amittai 549
Ammiditana 203
Amos 20, 50, 61, 192, 346, 359, 369, 386, 387, 388, 389, 393, 396, 566
Anthony the Hermit 561
Apollonius of Tyana 561
Arsaces 305
Asa 359
Asaph 365
Aššur-apla-iddina 51
Assurbanipal 10–15, 66, 93, 97, 109, 110, 115, 116–119, 122, 138, 139, 173, 185, 186, 210–215, 218–220, 224–228, 242–246, 249–254, 257, 259, 261–264, 273–276, 278, 284–287, 292, 295, 297, 315, 317, 318, 323, 327, 328, 334, 336, 341, 342, 345, 348, 349, 354, 356, 380, 383, 384, 400–404, 409, 416, 423–427, 432, 434, 436, 454, 457, 470–473, 476, 477, 540, 549, 553, 578, 677
Aššur-bel-kala 291
Aššur-ḫamatu'a 13, 109, 112, 226, 243, 245, 255–258, 261, 274, 470–473, 551
Aššur-mukin-pale'a 208
Assurnasirpal II 286
Aššur-uballiṭ II 160
Atamrum 51, 113, 522, 524, 529, 530
Athanasius 561
Azariah 359
Azzur 603

Baasha 359, 547, 548
Balaam (Bible) 641
Balaam (Deir 'Alla) 67, 367, 464, 465, 522, 523
Barak 146, 365, 548, 558
Baruch 529, 530
Bathsheba 550
Bayâ 107, 111, 142, 149, 226, 273, 296, 366, 385–389, 396, 475, 590
Bel-iqiša 209, 210
Bel-ušezib 14, 15, 114, 115, 121, 122, 140, 149, 209, 238, 260, 283, 290, 357
Benaiah 603
Ben-Hadad 114, 358, 541, 546
Belshazzar 360
Ben-Hadad 114, 358, 541
Ben Sira (Jesus Sirach) 373, 395, 443, 479–480, 486–489, 491, 494–495, 637
Boatman (*mār Mallāḫi*) 301–311

Croesus 355, 543
Cyrus 359, 415

Dagan-malik 133, 134, 551
Daniel 230, 525, 647
David 37, 50, 208, 231, 332, 338, 359, 361, 368, 372, 541, 544, 545, 547, 548, 549, 550, 554, 556, 631, 632, 637, 638
Darius 360

https://doi.org/10.1515/9783110466546-036

Deborah 145, 146, 151, 324, 364, 544, 548, 553, 557, 570
Delaiah 583, 636
Dunnaša-amur 111, 138, 273, 471

Eli 545, 555
Eliezer 359
Elijah 50, 114, 231, 347, 359, 360, 364, 370, 419, 454, 533, 544, 547, 556, 558, 560, 561, 569, 589
Elisha 50, 114, 231, 358, 360, 364, 365, 454, 548, 550, 558, 560, 561, 566, 567, 569, 589, 592
Elyashib 586
Enkidu 169, 454
Esarhaddon 10–15, 66, 93, 97, 103, 104, 107, 114–119, 122, 129, 139–142, 160, 166, 172–174, 185, 186, 208, 210, 220–223, 226, 227, 233, 234, 237–241, 244–247, 251, 254, 258–263, 273–277, 280–283, 286, 287, 289–295, 297–299, 315, 318, 327–329, 334, 335, 337, 341, 345, 347, 354, 356, 357, 359, 362, 380, 383, 384, 388, 401, 409, 423–439, 452, 453, 457, 474–476, 540, 547, 549, 552, 558, 578, 579, 581, 583, 677
Esau 589
Ezekiel 20, 124, 147, 230, 359, 360, 364, 365, 371, 372, 395, 442, 531, 532, 570, 597, 598, 599, 603, 604, 605, 639
Ezra 582

Gad 359
Gašera 181
Gideon 230, 541
Gilgameš 454, 666
Gomer 144
Gyges 215

Habakkuk 360, 368, 527, 531, 537
Hagar 230
Haggai 20, 124, 143, 230, 359, 361, 394, 582, 584
Hamiyata 552
Ḫammi-šagiš 130, 180
Hammurabi (king of Babylon) 115, 133, 135
Hammurabi (king of Kurdâ) 177
Hammurabi (king of Yamḫad) 180
Hananiah 421, 641
Hanina ben Dosa 561
Heman 365
Hannah (Samuel's mother) 151
Hannah (prophet) 129
Hasael 359
Hezekiah 230, 358, 359, 368, 414, 427, 548, 549, 555, 558, 585, 611
Hilkiah 124, 144
Hosea 20, 50, 144, 192, 346, 359, 360, 369, 372, 594, 616
Hoshaiah 523
Hoshea 616, 620, 623, 624
Hulda 144, 145, 151, 324, 549, 553, 554, 570, 585
Humban-haltaš III 213
Humban-nikaš II 213

Ibalpiel II 65–66, 83, 189, 191, 322, 354, 355, 392, 468, 469, 490, 549, 583
Ili-ḫaznaya 107, 113, 116, 135, 366, 590
Ilussa-amur 109, 142, 149, 281, 324, 366, 590
Indabibi 213
Inib-šina 115, 116, 131, 133, 135, 149, 170, 189
Ion 85
Irra-gamil 105, 113, 558
Isaac 230
Isaiah 20, 50, 114, 144, 192, 230, 325, 346, 359, 360, 365, 378, 392, 414, 525, 527, 537, 548, 549, 556, 558, 570, 573, 574, 636, 639
Išḫi-Dagan 190
Išme-Dagan 115, 160, 451, 468
Issar-beli-da''ini 109, 116, 325, 552
Issar-la-tašiyaṭ 107, 109, 111, 142, 273, 323, 366, 590
Itur-Ašdu 149, 187, 188

Jabin 146
Jacob/Israel 230, 333
Jael 146
Jahaziel 230, 359
Jedutum 365

Jehoiachim 359, 360, 438, 530
Jehoiachin 359, 601, 603, 606, 610
Jehoram 358, 359, 525, 548
Jehoshaphath 114, 358, 359, 543, 548
Jehu 359
Jeremiah 20, 50, 114, 124, 230, 346, 347, 359, 360, 364, 368, 378, 392, 421, 438, 525, 528, 529, 530, 531, 532, 533, 535, 536, 537
Jeroboam I 114, 358, 359, 533, 545, 547, 554, 555
Jeroboam II 359, 386, 388, 548, 620
Jesus 372, 674
Jezebel 547
Job 50
Joash 358
Joel 20, 372
John the Baptist 374, 589
John Hyrcanus 641
Jonah 368, 369, 549
Jonathan 37
Josaphat 348
Joseph 209
Josiah 66, 144, 145, 358–360, 368, 392, 533, 549, 553, 554, 579, 585
Joshua 215, 216, 230, 231, 344, 463, 548, 637

Kabtiya 210
Kakka-lidi 116, 133, 148, 149
Kanisan 133, 189, 190
Kibri-Dagan 116, 133, 149

La-dagil-ili 111, 140, 174, 233, 238, 239, 273, 282, 289, 325, 549
Lanasûm 168, 169
Lupaḫum 113, 158, 188, 190, 455

Malachi 570
Malik-Dagan 187
Manasseh 66, 412, 414, 415, 427, 540
Marduk-nadin-aḫḫe 236
Marduk-šumu-uṣur 436
Marduk-šapik-zeri 14, 291
Marduk-šumu-ibni 210
Mar-Issar 116, 139, 149, 247, 293, 294, 380, 437,
Mephibosheth/Meribaal 208, 209
Merodach-Baladan II 89, 260
Micaiah ben Imlah 20, 114, 192, 347, 414, 419, 543, 569
Micah (prophet) 20, 193, 346, 348, 372, 419
Micah the Ephraimite 594
Miriam 146, 147, 151, 324, 364, 570, 585, 586
Moses 71, 146, 147, 151, 205, 215, 216, 218, 230, 231, 342, 344, 372, 394, 531, 554, 576, 581, 586, 636, 639, 641, 643, 648, 649, 674
Mugallu 223, 286
Muhammad 674
Mullissu-abu-uṣri 106, 112, 116, 139, 149, 282
Mullissu-kabtat 138, 220, 323, 324, 325

Nabad 547
Nabopolassar 89
Nabû'a 256
Nabû-bel-šumati 213
[Nabû]-ḫussanni 140, 150, 281, 288
Nabû-nadin-šumi 121, 208, 284
Nabû-reḫtu-uṣur 15, 16, 141, 149, 186, 295, 296, 362, 423, 429–438
Nabû-reši-išši 111, 116, 149, 168, 273, 551, 553,
Nabû-šarru-uṣur 258, 471
Nabû-šumu-ereš 210
Nahum 360
Naqia 116, 117, 122, 150, 222–224, 251, 276, 277, 291, 327–329, 550
Naram-Sîn 215, 216, 435
Naṣib-ilu 207
Nathan 359, 360, 361, 549, 550, 557, 584, 636
Nebuchadnezzar II 359, 360, 605
Nehemiah 143, 231, 359, 394, 582, 583, 584, 585, 586, 587, 636
Nikkal-iddina 211
Niqmadu II 214, 215
Noadiah 143, 151, 325, 359, 570, 584, 585, 586, 587
Nur-Sîn 117, 132, 149, 178–185, 383, 549, 554, 583

Obadiah 360
Oded 359, 636

Paul 371, 374
Pekah 620
Pekahiah 620
Pelathiah 603
Philip 129
Philo 373, 443, 678
Pilinus 305
Plato 76, 77, 85, 373
Pythagoras 561
Pythia of Delphi 84, 146, 355, 370, 445, 447, 450, 543, 558

Qišti-Diritim 113, 116, 452, 465, 467

Rabshakeh 412
Rachel 151
Rebekah 151
Rehoboam 359, 548
Remutti-Allati 111, 116, 274, 298, 299
Rim-Sîn I 130

Šamaš-naṣir 467, 468
Šamaš-šumu-ukin 210–213, 225, 242, 250, 253, 259, 328, 383, 404, 454, 472
Šamaš-upaḫḫir 278
Sammetar 116, 133, 149, 158, 188, 189, 455, 589
Šamši-Adad 180, 182, 468
Samuel 146, 231, 358, 364, 372, 524, 541, 544, 549, 554, 555, 556, 557, 558, 568, 569, 583–584, 637
Sanballat 143, 582, 584
Sargon II 119, 207, 241, 244, 252, 254, 260, 261, 263, 278, 280, 286, 290, 338, 619, 622
Sasî 15, 141, 186, 295, 429, 430–438
Saul 119, 358, 365, 372, 393, 541, 549, 555, 557, 568, 569
Šelebum 105, 107, 116, 135, 170, 171, 366, 590
Seraiah 535
Sennacherib 13, 15, 95, 118, 119, 141, 174, 234–237, 240, 242, 244, 248, 252, 253, 258, 289–293, 295, 327, 358, 362, 412, 427, 430, 434, 547, 550, 594
Shallum (son of Yaddua) 523, 620
Shallum (Huldah's husband) 144, 145, 553
Shallum (king of Israel) 620
Shalmaneser III 277
Shaphan 144, 553
Shemaiah 359
Shemaiah the Nehelamite 583, 584, 641
Šibtu 115, 116, 133, 135, 149, 166, 167, 451, 452, 465
Simon 488
Sîn-balassu-iqbi 211
Sinqiša-amur 9, 109, 111, 140, 240, 273, 324
Sîn-šarra-uṣur 211, 212
Sîn-šarru-iškun 160
Sîn-tabni-uṣur 211, 212, 218
Sisera 146
Socrates 76, 77, 85
Solomon 331, 412, 549, 550, 636
Šulgi 62, 87–90, 93–97, 320
Šumu-iddina 437
Šumu-lešir 156
Šu-nuḫra-Ḫalu 130
Šuppiluliuma 214, 215, 229

Tammaritu II 213, 214
Tašmetu-ereš 105, 111, 273, 323
Teumman 218, 275, 276, 278, 401–403, 472
Thales 441
Tiglath-Pileser III 119
Tobiah 143, 523, 582, 584, 586

Ubaru 260
Urad-Gula 289, 545
Urad-Nanaya 208
Urkittu-šarrat 111, 140, 149, 234, 274, 286, 287, 324, 326
Urtaku 210, 401
Utu-kam 522, 529
Uzziah 386

Wenamon 67, 68, 320, 370

Yarim-Addu 288
Yasim-El 522, 529, 536
Yasmaḫ-Addu 65, 355, 468

Zadok 549
Zakkur 67, 93, 114, 128, 200, 224, 225, 229, 321, 344, 355
Zechariah 20, 124, 143, 394, 462, 582, 584, 620
Zedekiah 114, 358, 359, 605, 641
Zedekiah son of Maaseiah 641
Zephaniah 360
Zerubbabel 230, 359, 361
Zimri-Lim 65, 66, 115, 116, 129, 131, 133, 135, 149, 158, 160, 166–168, 177, 178, 180, 182, 183, 187–191, 219, 288, 354, 355, 382, 383, 451, 455, 465, 467, 468, 521, 529, 540, 548, 549, 551, 554, 557, 583, 676
Zunana 133, 148, 149

Geographical Names

Ai 541
Akkad 14, 15, 106, 139, 215, 239, 270, 282, 293, 294, 380, 444, 667
Alaḫtum (Alalakh) 178–181, 383
Aleppo 117, 132, 177–183, 355, 549, 583
Alu-ša-Našar 602
Al-Yahudu 602, 606, 609
Ammon 356, 427, 605
Anatoth 524
Andarig 355
Aram 360
Arbela 9, 80, 105, 111, 112, 140, 142, 149, 173, 174, 226, 233, 235, 238, 243–245, 258, 261, 267–282, 289, 292, 295, 298, 299, 326, 329, 386, 401, 472, 552
Arwad 427
Asdod 427
Ashkelon 427
Assur 10, 15, 67, 80, 137, 139, 149, 173, 235–240, 244, 247, 254, 256, 258, 259, 261–263, 270, 271, 277, 279–283, 288, 290, 299, 325, 329, 452, 476
Babylon 13, 95, 115, 135, 160, 174, 175, 203, 212, 213, 226, 234–244, 248, 254, 258–262, 270, 271, 288, 289, 291–293, 300, 301, 303–308, 355, 471, 472, 525, 535, 603, 605
Babylonia 66, 139, 210, 211, 213, 227, 234, 235, 237–245, 247, 250, 260, 261, 272, 288–294, 301, 305, 311, 383, 394, 401, 404, 471, 597, 598, 601, 603–605, 609, 611, 647
Beersheba 412
Bethel 145, 358, 386, 545, 547, 554, 623, 641
Bit-Abi-râm 602
Borsippa 239, 270, 301, 303, 304, 306–309, 603
Byblos 67, 355, 370, 427

Calah 10, 111, 140, 149, 155, 173, 234, 235, 240, 244, 270, 274, 279, 280, 284–287, 326, 329, 553, 622
Canaan 146
Carmel 370, 556, 589
Chebar 603
Cimmerians 11, 186, 286, 328
Claros 447–450, 459
Colophon 448, 449
Cutha 210, 239

Damascus 114, 144, 358, 541, 546
Dan 412
Dara-aḫuya 111, 140, 274, 297–299, 325
Delphi 80, 128, 335, 355, 445, 447, 449, 450, 558
Der 239
Didyma 80, 128, 445, 447, 448, 450, 459
Dodona 128, 449, 450, 543
Dur-Šarruken 239, 272, 278, 280

Edom 358, 427
Egypt 68, 147, 186, 269, 278, 297, 307, 342, 412, 436, 456, 605, 624, 625, 664, 676, 677
Ekallatum 185, 236, 467, 468
Ekron 427, 544

Elam 185, 186, 209, 210, 213, 214, 218, 239, 262, 274, 275, 278, 286, 294, 307, 328, 400–403, 457, 472, 667, 677
Ellipi 11, 186, 328
Emar 67, 178,
En-Dor 151, 541, 558
En-Gedi 484
Ephraim 146, 342, 620, 621, 625
Ešnunna 10, 66, 83, 93, 113, 118, 123, 133, 135, 185, 189–191, 322, 354, 355, 392, 455, 465, 467, 468, 470, 471, 476, 490, 549, 583, 676
Euphrates 455, 535

Gaza 427
Gebah 365, 372, 549
Gibeah 593, 623
Gilboa 541
Greece 80, 370, 444, 513, 664

Hamath 67, 156, 224, 344, 355, 361,
Harran 15, 112, 148, 149, 186, 270, 295–297, 300, 430, 434–438, 547
Hazrak 224
Hermon 484

Jericho 484
Jerusalem 19, 49, 66, 71, 80, 124, 143–145, 151, 193, 264, 267, 268, 311, 331, 333, 337, 347, 349, 361, 368, 372, 393, 394, 410–412, 442, 444, 445, 447, 450, 485, 506, 523, 525, 539, 540, 553–556, 561, 564, 570, 572, 580, 582, 584–586, 594, 603–605, 608, 610, 612, 625
Jordan 454, 465, 523
Judah 18, 20, 49, 66, 114, 151, 348, 350, 354, 358, 362–365, 377–381, 386, 389, 394, 400, 412–415, 427, 502, 506, 510, 512, 515, 523, 525, 533, 540, 543, 548, 561, 562, 580, 582, 583, 585, 601, 603–605, 609, 616, 623, 625, 644

Kar-Tukulti-Ninurta 107, 134, 137, 142, 551
Kinneret 33
Kiš 206

Labbanat 259
Lachish 523
Larsa 129, 130, 235
Lebanon 487, 488
Lydia 355, 543

Mannea 274, 286
Mari 48, 54, 60, 65, 68, 69, 78–80, 84, 93, 94, 104–107, 113–120, 123, 124, 127, 128–135, 141, 148, 149–151, 153, 158, 160, 163, 165, 166, 169, 176–180, 182, 183, 185, 187, 190, 191, 200, 219, 288, 315, 318, 319–325, 331, 347, 349, 355, 357–361, 363, 365–367, 370, 372, 374, 377, 378, 382, 389, 424, 435, 450–452, 455, 456, 459, 465–467, 476, 500, 505, 511, 520–522, 524, 529, 536, 540, 542, 543, 545, 546, 548, 549, 551–553, 559, 561, 568, 569, 571, 589, 590, 609, 675–677, 679
Mazuwari 552
Melid 223, 286
Miletus 441, 449
Milqia 174, 277–279, 297
Moab 356, 358, 400, 427, 605

Nineveh 66, 69, 81, 94, 118, 127, 128, 153, 154, 157, 160, 173, 223, 233, 235, 237, 238, 265, 276, 279, 280, 283–287, 296, 298, 320, 348, 355, 360, 377, 391, 401, 437, 457
Nippur 88, 203, 210, 239, 602, 603, 610

Persia 415

Qaṭṭunan 355

Ramah 145, 623
Ramoth-Gilead 348, 358, 543
Raši 213

Saggaratum 187, 188, 355, 455
Samaria 144, 619–626
Shiloh 555
Sidon 605
Sippar 177, 203, 307
Šubria 156, 270, 286

Surmarrati 210
Susa 403, 457

Takkašta 159
Tel-Abib 603
Terqa 80, 132, 148, 149, 158, 183, 188, 355, 467, 468, 675
Tigris 154, 259, 272, 322, 455–457
Tušḫan 14, 153–161, 379, 391
Tuttul 113, 168, 169, 355
Tyre 297, 427, 453, 605, 608

Ugarit 67, 214, 590
Ur 211, 212, 435
Urartu 277, 286
Uruk 9, 150, 228, 229, 234, 235, 238–240, 269, 270, 287, 289, 307, 326, 378, 473

Yehud 151, 384, 389, 396, 413–415, 506, 510, 512, 562, 594, 609, 677

Zabala 130, 149
Zarephath 230
Zion 410, 411, 413, 479

Divine Names

Adad 113, 116, 169, 177, 178–184, 236, 238, 309, 521, 549, 557
Annunitum 80, 105, 113, 131, 133–135, 148, 149, 167, 170, 219, 548, 551
Anu 307, 469, 474
Apollo 80, 84, 128, 445, 447, 449
Asherah 343, 556, 558, 569
Ashtarte 343
Aššur 9–11, 13, 80, 110–112, 137, 149, 172, 226–228, 247, 250, 254, 258, 261, 263, 270, 275, 281–283, 284, 300, 308, 326, 327, 337, 340, 341, 345, 401, 436, 457, 470, 473, 475, 476, 622
Asumûm 465, 466
Athene 481

Baal 370, 371, 453, 556, 558, 569, 589, 590
Baal-Šamayin 67, 344
Bel (see also Marduk) 9, 14, 109–112, 149, 208, 220, 226–229, 236, 242, 246–252, 254, 258–263, 288, 291, 296, 302–307, 327, 429, 430, 433, 434, 470, 471, 475, 476
Belet-ekallim 113, 133, 166, 167
Belial 593
Beltiya 248

Cybele 306, 591

Dagan 80, 113, 117, 132, 133, 148, 149, 159, 169, 177, 187, 188, 190, 200, 467, 468, 675
Dumuzi 136, 367, 558

Ea 113, 184, 259, 283, 451, 465, 466, 607
El 267, 464
Enlil 184, 309, 326

Inanna 130, 149, 270
Itur-Mer 106, 113, 148, 149

Kidmuri, Lady of 149, 240, 286, 287, 553
Kititum 65, 66, 83, 113, 321, 322, 337, 392, 468, 469, 471, 490, 583

Marduk 9, 13, 14, 88–90, 93, 95, 97, 112, 115, 160, 184, 218, 227, 228, 236, 238, 240–244, 245, 247, 248, 256, 258–260, 261, 263–265, 268, 270, 276, 282, 288, 290–293, 300, 304–306, 309, 326, 327, 367, 457, 471, 476, 521
Mastemah 593
Michael (archangel) 658, 659
Milkom 68,
Mullissu 9, 11–13, 108–112, 117, 139, 149, 220, 226–228, 235, 242, 243, 250–252, 254, 262–264, 273, 274, 282, 284, 287, 289, 296, 306, 309, 323, 326, 329, 339, 433, 434, 436, 470–473, 476

Nabû 9, 110, 111, 149, 208, 220, 225, 227, 256, 262, 270, 274, 282, 283, 284, 293, 296, 307, 309, 317, 327, 341, 342, 430, 433, 434, 472, 474–476, 482, 485–489

Nanaya 271, 302–309, 473, 474
Nergal 113, 177
Nikkal 112, 296, 429, 430, 433–436, 474
Ninḫursag 113, 171, 172,
Ninurta 270, 309, 330, 456, 549
Nusku 15, 112, 141, 148, 149, 186, 295–297, 430, 434–438, 547

Šala 236
Šamaš 84, 113, 177, 238, 242, 285, 307, 456, 475, 521, 522, 529, 530, 668
Satan 593
Šatru 278
Sîn 254, 270, 271, 285, 295–297, 300, 302, 303, 306, 401, 435, 436, 437, 456, 474, 475

Tarhunza 68, 552
Tašmetu 111, 323, 474, 482, 485–489
Tišpak 467
Tyche 306

Urkittu 9, 234, 287, 289, 326, 341, 472

Yam 453
YHWH 84, 145–147, 195, 196, 202, 219, 220, 231, 264, 265, 330, 332, 333, 336–339, 342–345, 349, 364, 371, 372–374, 392, 394, 399, 409–412, 415, 422, 423, 426, 440, 442, 453, 461–463, 465, 488, 491, 524–526, 529, 530, 532, 540, 541–544, 547, 553, 554, 556, 557, 572, 581, 589, 606, 640

Zababa 206
Zarpanitu 112, 184, 236, 243, 367
Zeus 84, 449

Index of modern authors

Abegg, Martin 654, 658
Aejmelaeus, Anneli 518
Angel, Joseph 659, 660
Antin, Katri 651
Amit, Yairah 578
Aster, Shawn Selig 606
Auld, Graeme 502, 503

Bahrani, Zainab 16
Barstad, Hans 499, 503, 505, 507, 631, 632
Beentjes, Pancratius 479
Ben-Dov, Jonathan 663
Ben Zvi, Ehud 577, 617, 623, 624
Bodi, Daniel 606, 608
Brooke, George 632, 634, 651, 660
Begrich, Joachim 196–197, 199
Berrin, Shani 663, 673
Bloch-Smith, Elizabeth 46

Carroll, Robert 502, 503, 506, 507
Charpin, Dominique 522
Clines, David 18, 31
Conrad, Edgar 197
Crenshaw, James 564, 565, 567, 576

Davies, Philip R. 503
Del Monte, Giuseppe 301, 308, 311
Dijkstra, Meindert 199
Dobbs-Allsopp, F. W. 35
Dossin, Georges 178
Duhm, Bernhard 7, 22, 23, 501
Durand, Jean-Marie 178, 378

Elgvin, Torleif 368, 655, 656
Ellis, Maria deJong 87, 91, 98, 318, 319, 320, 322
Ewald, Heinrich 21, 22

Flint, Peter 632
Floyd, Michael 395, 577
Fukuyama, Francis 407

Ganzel, Tova 608
García Martínez, Florentino 658, 659
Goff, Matthew 655, 656
Grabbe, Lester 94
Graf, Karl Heinrich 21
Grayson, A. K. 90
Greenblatt, Stephen 30,
Gressmann, Hugo 29, 195, 196, 198, 201
Gruber, Mayer 204
Gunkel, Hermann 196

Hacking, Ian 3, 4, 5
Harner, Philip 199
Harviainen, Tapani 245
Hempel, Charlotte 651
Holladay, William 507
Holloway, Steven 237
Holtz, Shalom 608
Houston, Walter 382
Huffmon, Herbert 53, 122, 184, 509
Hunger, Hermann 301, 302, 311
Hölscher, Gustaf 369

Jansson, Patrik 148
Jassen, Alex 652, 653, 656, 660
Jeremias, Jörg 513, 616
Jokiranta, Jutta 631, 651, 673
Jones, Christopher 449

Kaiser, Otto 200
Keck, Leander 31
Keel, Othmar 564
Kelle, Brad 512
Kimball, Charles 398, 404
Koch, Ulla 82, 83
Kuenen, Abraham 21
Kühler, Max 564
Köckert, Matthias 580
Köhler, Ludwig 196

Lafont, Bernard 178
Lambert, W. G. 90, 96
Lange, Armin 395, 513, 651, 664, 670

https://doi.org/10.1515/9783110466546-037

Launderville, Dale 607
Levin, Christoph 624, 625
Lehnart, Bernhard 567, 568
Lim, Timothy 632, 663
Lods, A. 178
Loretz, Oswald 33

Machinist, Peter 153
Marttila, Marko 479, 481
Mattila, Raija 202
Maul, Stefan M. 477
McKane, William 507
Mieroop, Marc Van De 268
Mullen, Theodore 463
Na'aman, Nadav 613, 623, 624

Noegel, Scott 82
Noort, Ed 319

Odell, Margaret 607, 610
Oppenheim, Leo 664, 665, 668
Overholt, Thomas W. 502, 503, 509

Pajunen, Mika S. 368
Parpola, Simo 9, 12, 13, 18, 33, 103, 153, 201, 202, 209, 302, 309, 311, 316, 323, 378, 429, 482
Petersen, David 48, 58, 509
Pongratz-Leisten, Beate 83, 192, 392
Pyysiäinen, Ilkka 5

Rad, Gerhard von 17, 24; 200, 399, 400
Radner, Karen 159, 296, 622
Ranke, Leopold von 41
Rogers, Jessie 480
Räisänen, Heikki 32

Sacks, Jonathan 406, 407, 409
Sasson, Jack 182
Schiffman, Lawrence 651
Schaper, Joachim 395, 531
Seligman, Adam 407, 408, 409
Spek, Bert van der 301
Soden, Wolfram von 321
Sollamo, Raija 649
Souza Nogueira, Paulo Augusto de 659–660
Steingrímsson, Sigurður Örn 311
Steudel, Annette 645
Steymans, Hans Ulrich 564
Stökl, Jonathan 607, 609

Thomas, Samuel 651, 656
Thomas, Scott 406
Toorn, Karel van der 201, 536

Uehlinger, Christoph 610
Uusimäki, Elisa 661

Vanonen, Hanna 651
Veijola, Timo 17, 32, 331, 563, 576

Weippert, Manfred 57, 122, 165, 199, 201, 263, 316, 317, 332, 333, 464, 509
Weissenberg, Hanne von 661
Wellhausen, Julius 7, 21, 22, 23
Westermann, Claus 197
Whiting, Robert 302, 479, 663
Williamson, Hugh 502
Wilson, Robert 509
Winitzer, Avi 82, 608

Zenger, Erich 19, 20, 25
Zgoll, Annette 665, 666
Zimmerli, Walther 17, 197

Index of Ancient Near Eastern Sources

Texts and sources

4 R 28 104

A. 1121 see FM 7 39
A. 1249 see FM 3 3
A. 1858 183
A. 1968 see FM 7 38
A. 2731 see FM 7 39
A. 3165 see FM 3 2
A. 3760 521
A. 3796 113, 159, 169
A. 4676 104, 113, 169

ABL 202 210
ABL 456 255
ABL 541 209
ABL 1249 (= SAA 13 139) 245, 249
ABL 1274 212

AD 3 -132 B/C 301–11, 383

Amman Citadel Inscription 68, 114, 128

AMT 71 668

AO 4479: 45 474

Assyrian Dream Book 315 665, 671

ARM 9 22 159, 169
ARM 10 80 (= ARM 26 197) 200
ARM 13 114 (= ARM 26 210) 200
ARM 21 333 104, 106, 113, 159, 169
ARM 22 167 104, 113, 169
ARM 22 326 113, 131, 159
ARM 23 446 104, 106, 113, 169
ARM 25 15 113, 159, 169
ARM 25 142 104, 113, 159, 169
ARM 26 194 113, 177, 521, 522, 546, 548
ARM 26 195 113, 546, 548, 551
ARM 26 196 113, 118, 185, 467
ARM 26 197 (=ARM 10 80) 107, 113, 116, 132, 133, 170, 185, 189, 200, 366, 521, 546, 548, 675–676
ARM 26 198 107, 113, 116, 135, 169, 366, 521
ARM 26 199 113, 113, 116, 132, 133, 158, 159, 185, 186, 188, 455, 546, 589
ARM 26 200 116, 116, 131, 186, 521, 551
ARM 26 201 116, 131, 551
ARM 26 202 104, 113, 133, 189–190, 546
ARM 26 203 132
ARM 26 204 116, 132, 546
ARM 26 205 113, 546
ARM 26 206 104, 371, 521, 546
ARM 26 207 83, 116, 118, 185, 450–451
ARM 26 208 113, 113, 116, 185, 451–452, 465–466
ARM 26 209 113, 113, 185, 521
ARM 26 210 113, 133, 135, 185, 200, 521
ARM 26 211 113, 116, 548
ARM 26 212 83, 113, 116, 170, 185, 366, 451, 467
ARM 26 213 105, 107, 113, 116, 135, 170, 366, 370, 546, 548
ARM 26 214 105, 113, 116, 134, 166–167, 370, 521, 548, 551
ARM 26 215 104, 113, 117, 168–169, 521
ARM 26 217 546, 548
ARM 26 216 543, 546
ARM 26 218 171, 552
ARM 26 219 113, 171, 546, 551, 552
ARM 26 220 104, 113, 521, 552
ARM 26 221 104, 113, 521, 546, 552
ARM 26 221bis 104, 521, 546
ARM 26 222 105, 113, 370
ARM 26 223 113, 186, 546
ARM 26 227 104, 113,
ARM 26 229 167
ARM 26 232 113,121, 133, 148
ARM 26 233 113, 187, 521, 548
ARM 26 234 121,

https://doi.org/10.1515/9783110466546-038

ARM 26 235 121,
ARM 26 236 113, 116, 121, 133, 148, 149
ARM 26 237 83, 113, 130, 131, 133, 219, 551
ARM 26 238 113, 121, 133, 546
ARM 26 239 121,
ARM 26 240 83, 113, 121,
ARM 26 243 104, 521
ARM 26 244 118
ARM 26 371 113, 115, 161, 185, 288
ARM 26 414 113, 522, 524, 529, 536, 573
ARM 27 32 104, 113, 521

Assurbanipal's Inscriptions
A ii 12 104
A ii 126–iii 26 103
A ii 95–110 215
A iii 4–10 380
A iv 110–v 35 40 213
A x 6–39 214
B iv 15–79 401
B iv 15–vi 9 400
B iv 80–v 9 401
B v 10–45 402
B v 16—vi 9 472
B v 36–42 263
B v 45–72 402–403
B v 46 202
B v 46–vi 16 103,
B v 49–76 108, 219
B v 73–vi 9 403
B v 87–92 457
B v 95 118
B v 95 [= C vi 127] 104,
B vi 3–4 403
B vii 61–76 213
C ii 27 427
C ix 11–52 213
E² vi 14–25 215
L⁴ ii 29–33 248
T ii 7–24 103,
T ii 16 [= C i 61] 104,
T ii 16–17 553

BAK 338 473–474

BBR 11 668

BWL 38 104
BWL 50 202

CAI 59 (Amman Citadel Inscription) 68, 114, 128, 356

Codex Hammurabi 184

CT 18 29–30 668
CT 38 4 104, 108
CT 45 36 590

CTH 376.A § 7 157
CTH 378.II § 11 157

CTN 1 3 155
CTN 1 6 155
CTN 1 8 155
CTN 1 14 155
CTN 3 121 622
CTN 3 145 155

Cuthaean Legend of Naram-Sîn 202, 215, 216, 219

DA 211 r. 12 104

Deir 'Alla inscription 67, 93, 114, 128, 185, 321, 367, 464, 465, 522, 523, 568

Demotic Chronicle 63, 97, 670

Enūma Anu Enlil 291, 670

Erra Epic 135, 202–204, 608

Esarhaddon's Inscriptions
AsBbE 239, 259
Ass A 14, 103, 104, 233, 519
Babylon 241, 260
Nin A 14, 43, 103, 104, 118, 121, 173, 456, 519
RINAP 4:13 173, 225, 281
RINAP 4:14 283, 299, 321, 424, 456, 519
RINAP 4:18 210
RINAP 4:23 427
RINAP 4:79 254

RINAP 4:85–86 270
RINAP 4:107 238, 259, 348
RINAP 4:108 235, 240, 259
RINAP 4:116 284
RINAP 4:117 277
RINAP 4:121 14, 282, 519
RINAP 4:124 14, 321, 424, 519
RINAP 4:125 204
RINAP 4:128 235
RINAP 4:136–137 239, 292
RINAP 4:155 274
RINAP 4:167 259
RINAP 4:168 259
RINAP 4:169 259
RINAP 4:196 291
RINAP 4:203 291
RINAP 4:212 291
RINAP 4:244 291
RINAP 4:245 241
RINAP 4:274 473

Gilgameš Epic 67, 169, 173, 608, 666

FLP 1674 66, 83, 94, 113, 118, 322, 392, 468–469, 490, 549
FLP 2064 66, 113, 118, 322

FM 3 2 65, 104, 105, 358, 365
FM 3 3 65, 104, 113, 130, 366, 358, 551
FM 7 38 113, 117, 181, 182, 187, 355, 359, 383, 521, 546, 549, 538, 557
FM 7 39 113, 132, 178, 182, 183, 331, 355, 383, 521, 546, 554, 557

HKM 47 157, 159

K 1913 137, 370
K 2001+ 136, 367

KAI 18 (Mesha stele) 356
KAI 202 (Zakkur Stela) 67, 93, 114, 128, 200, 202, 224, 225, 229, 321, 344, 355

KAR 98 277
KAR 214 256
KAR 421 87, 320
KAR 460 67

KBo 1 13 202, 217
KBo 15.28 157

KuT 49 157
KuT 50 157

KTU 1.17 vi 47 267

Lachish Ostraca
3 68, 128, 381, 523, 524, 536, 545
6 68, 128, 510
16 68, 128, 381

Lamb of Bocchoris 97, 670

Law of Ur-Nammu 184

LKA 29d 108

M. 11299 107, 170
M. 11436 113, 159, 169
M. 7160 130

MDP 10 7 104
MDP 18 171 104, 288

MSL 12 4.212 134, 155, 366, 380, 590
MSL 12 4.213 155
MSL 12 4.222 136, 366, 380, 590
MSL 12 5.22 130, 155, 366
MSL 12 6.2 134, 366, 519
MSL 12 101–102 104
MSL 12 102–103 106
MSL 12 132 104
MSL 12 158 104
MSL 12 233 107
MSL 12 226 107, 425
MSL 132:117–18 104
MSL 158:23 104

ND 2789 278
ND 3467 251

OECT 1 21 104
OECT 13 263 66

OIP 114 98 202, 203

Papyrus Amherst 63 68, 307

PBS 7 17 202, 205

Potter's Oracle 97, 670

PRU 4 35–36 202, 215
PRU 36:32 202

RAcc 144 202

RS 17.132 214

SAA 1 146 278
SAA 1 147 278
SAA 1 149 278
SAA 1 188 254
SAA 1 235 252
SAA 1 236 252
SAA 2 3 432
SAA 2 6 15, 103, 104, 104, 107, 349, 423–426, 432, 433, 519, 578
SAA 3 1 110,
SAA 3 2 110,
SAA 3 3 110, 276, 285, 345, 401
SAA 3 7 108, 110, 280, 285
SAA 3 8 269, 271, 298
SAA 3 9 269
SAA 3 10 269, 280
SAA 3 12 110
SAA 3 13 109, 34, 110, 111, 112, 117, 202, 225, 225, 227, 255, 262, 263, 274, 287, 317, 326, 327, 341, 342, 472
SAA 3 14 111, 482, 484, 485, 486, 487
SAA 3 33 241, 260, 290
SAA 3 34 104, 112, 243, 292–293, 367
SAA 3 34–40 273
SAA 3 35 243, 292–293
SAA 3 37 110
SAA 3 38 273
SAA 3 39 110, 276
SAA 3 44–47 110,
SAA 3 44 318
SAA 3 45 318
SAA 3 46 318
SAA 4 139–148 435
SAA 4 143 435
SAA 4 262 242
SAA 5 45 255
SAA 5 218 338
SAA 6 314 438
SAA 7 6 227
SAA 7 9 103, 104, 116, 425, 519
SAA 7 11 227
SAA 8 178 667
SAA 8 186 671
SAA 8 445 256
SAA 9 66, 118, 219, 423
SAA 9 1–9 317
SAA 9 1 107, 111, 140, 142, 202, 220, 221, 222, 223, 233, 246, 248, 252, 279, 283, 298, 317, 323, 331, 384
SAA 9 1.1 195, 204, 220, 221, 273, 274, 323, 324, 341, 366, 519, 590
SAA 9 1.2 111, 220, 222, 273, 274, 275, 298, 324, 343, 344, 519, 548
SAA 9 1.3 11, 111, 116, 274, 298, 325, 326
SAA 9 1.4 111, 142, 149, 195, 220, 226, 227, 262, 263, 273, 274, 285, 296, 298, 324, 327, 366, 386, 388, 475, 519, 590
SAA 9 1.5 108, 142, 149, 281, 283, 324, 326, 366, 519, 590
SAA 9 1.6 111, 220, 222, 274, 279, 280, 283, 284, 326, 329, 455, 548
SAA 9 1.7 109, 116, 116, 141, 223, 325, 519, 548, 552
SAA 9 1.8 111, 116, 122, 195, 220, 222, 225, 251, 273, 274, 298, 327, 328–329, 454, 519, 550
SAA 9 1.9 274, 279, 298, 326
SAA 9 1.10 273, 325, 330, 347, 468, 519, 549
SAA 9 2 140, 223, 226, 233, 288, 317, 323, 331
SAA 9 2.1 116, 174, 220, 221, 223, 234, 235, 281, 283, 288–289, 326, 327
SAA 9 2.2 220, 221, 223, 324, 386, 388
SAA 9 2.3 111, 221, 223, 233, 234, 238, 261, 273, 274, 279, 289, 325, 330, 519, 548, 549, 552
SAA 9 2.4 111, 108, 220, 221, 234, 235, 274, 284, 285, 286, 324, 326, 345, 357, 519

SAA 9 2.5 111, 220, 221, 226, 227, 234, 240, 262, 285, 334, 343, 548
SAA 9 2.6 116, 174, 288, 289
SAA 9 3 111, 118, 172, 273, 282, 317, 327, 331, 359, 583
SAA 9 3.1 282, 283, 327
SAA 9 3.2 186, 283, 327, 328, 548
SAA 9 3.3 111, 221, 224, 283, 337, 340–341, 456, 475
SAA 9 3.4 274, 327, 334, 335, 357, 452, 474
SAA 9 3.5 104, 108, 172, 173, 280–281, 325, 327, 347, 357, 425, 519, 548
SAA 9 4 221, 317, 548
SAA 9 5 116, 173, 223, 274, 278, 290, 326, 327, 357
SAA 9 6 105, 273, 274, 317, 323, 325, 519
SAA 9 7–11 118, 257
SAA 9 7 104, 108, 111, 117, 138, 139, 186, 220, 221, 274, 317, 323, 324, 325, 327, 328, 334, 339, 357, 519, 548, 676
SAA 9 8 186, 328, 548, 677
SAA 9 9 107, 109, 110, 111, 112, 138, 225, 227, 262, 263, 264, 273, 274, 283, 285, 323, 324, 383, 454, 471, 491, 519
SAA 9 10 111, 138, 317, 519
SAA 9 11 317
SAA 10 8 84, 667
SAA 10 12 276
SAA 10 13 295
SAA 10 40–41 247
SAA 10 53 247
SAA 10 61 247
SAA 10 69 247
SAA 10 76 256
SAA 10 98 254
SAA 10 109 14, 103, 104, 115, 122, 138, 140, 209, 238, 260, 284, 291, 357, 425, 519
SAA 10 111 13, 103, 112, 121, 291
SAA 10 171 202, 209
SAA 10 174 297, 436
SAA 10 179 296
SAA 10 188 202
SAA 10 199 437
SAA 10 240 255
SAA 10 252 247
SAA 10 278 202, 208
SAA 10 284 103, 121, 284
SAA 10 285 202
SAA 10 294 103, 287, 519
SAA 10 296 247
SAA 10 298 247
SAA 10 313 434
SAA 10 315 435
SAA 10 316 437
SAA 10 320 202, 208
SAA 10 338 297
SAA 10 352 103, 104, 105, 71, 138, 139, 247, 294, 359, 380, 425, 444, 519, 583
SAA 10 357 247, 307
SAA 10 363 674
SAA 10 364 667
SAA 10 369 272
SAA 11 294 425
SAA 12 69 104, 112, 118, 137, 149, 281, 476, 477, 551
SAA 12 89 275
SAA 13 37 15, 103, 104, 106, 112, 116, 138, 139, 149, 282, 519, 551, 553
SAA 13 43 253, 469
SAA 13 114 553
SAA 13 138–142 257
SAA 13 138 256,
SAA 13 139 13, 109, 112, 227, 242, 245, 252, 256, 257, 264, 470, 473, 476, 551
SAA 13 140 256, 257
SAA 13 144 111, 116, 140, 168, 273, 519, 551
SAA 13 145 273
SAA 13 148 109, 141, 317, 325, 552
SAA 13 161–185 239
SAA 13 190 235
SAA 14 155 247
SAA 15 90 248
SAA 15 104 202, 207
SAA 15 306 202
SAA 16 2 250
SAA 16 28 250
SAA 16 59 15, 103, 112, 141, 148, 149, 191, 275, 295, 296, 362, 423, 429, 430, 431, 433, 434, 436, 437, 438, 440, 547, 583
SAA 16 60 103, 112, 295, 296, 429, 431, 433, 438

SAA 16 61 103, 295, 296, 429, 433
SAA 18 82 237
SAA 21 16 202, 210
SAA 21 20 202, 212, 219
SAA 21 37 211
SAA 21 38 202, 210, 218, 252
SAA 21 50 202, 209, 210, 218
SAA 21 63 202, 213, 214

SBH 8 307

Sennacherib's Inscriptions
T 16 235
T 18 234
T 25–27 235
T 64 235
T 122 234
T 137 236
T 139 234
T 167 236
T 174:10–11 236

SpTU 1 2 90
SpTU 2 21 666

Šumma ālu 104, 136, 671
Šumma izbu 136, 370, 671

T. 82 113, 169

TCL 1 23 202, 206
TCL 10 39 104, 130
TCL 18 80 202, 206
TCL 19 47 202, 206

TCS 1 369 66, 104

TDP 4:3 104

Tell Ahmar 6 (Til Barsip Stele) 68, 128, 552

Ugaritica 5 162 67, 217, 371, 590

VAT 17347:14 474

VS 4 95:11 305
VS 19 1 104, 107, 118, 134, 137, 551

W19900, 1 378

Weidner Chronicle 90
Weidner List 601

YOS 6 18 104, 288, 305
YOS 7 135 104, 305

ZTT 2 156
ZTT 4 156
ZTT 12 161
ZTT 13 161
ZTT 25 15, 153–161, 379, 391

Index of Biblical References

Hebrew Bible

Genesis
1:2 481, 486
6:2 462
6:4 462
12:6 485
13:18 485
14:13 485
15:1 200, 230
21:17 200, 230
26:24 200, 230
35:17 207
35:8 485
43:23 207
46:3 200, 230
50:21 209

Exodus
14 454
14:13 215, 216, 231
14:13–14 200
14:14 345, 409
15:20 143, 146, 324, 570
15:20–21 364
18:15 604
20:18–21 205
20:20 231
28:30 77
30:34 485
32:16 532
34:1 532
34:27 532

Leviticus
8:8 77
17–26 610
20:6 76

Numbers
11:12 342, 344
11:24–30 106, 372
12 151, 585
12:6–8 147
14:9 215, 231
21:34 215, 229
22–24 641

Deuteronomy
1:21 200, 216, 231
1:29 215, 218, 231
3:2 215, 230, 344
3:22 215, 216, 231
4:37 332
7:6–8 332
7:18 200, 231
10:15 332
11:30 485
13 422, 425, 426, 427, 428, 439, 440, 580, 581
13:1–11 310
13:2 423, 426
13:2–6 419, 422, 578, 579, 641, 642, 643
13:3–4 439
13:4 423, 426
13:6 422, 426
13:7 422
13:13–14 422
13:15 655
17:4 422, 655
17:18–20 145
18 580
18:9–14 76, 581
18:15 440
18:15–18 532, 581
18:15–22 71, 145, 394, 419
18:20–22 349, 422, 580, 642, 643
18:21 421
18:21–22 580
20:1 218, 231
20:3 200, 231
28:34 592
31:6 218, 231
31:8 231

https://doi.org/10.1515/9783110466546-039

31:26–28 531–532
32:18 343
33:4 492

Joshua
1:9 544
3 454
5:2–9 554
6:2 548
7:14–18 541
8:1 200, 216, 230, 548
8:18 448
8:30–31 554
9:23 594
10:8 200, 230, 344, 544, 548
10:25 200, 216, 216, 231
11:6 200, 230
13–21 541
19:33 485

Judges
4–5 145
4:4 143, 145, 324, 365, 544, 553, 558, 570
4:5 146, 558
4:6 145
4:6–7 548
4:6–9 558
4:11 485
4:14 145
5:2–31 365
6:7–10 545
6:8–10 544
6:23 230
5:12 146
7:3 200
7:13–15 541
9:6 485
9:27 594
9:37 485
17:5 541, 594
18:11–20 541
18:31 594

Ruth
3:11 207
4:7 573

1 Samuel
1:24–28 555
2:27–36 545, 555
3:14–17 656
3:20 555
3:21 555
9–10 359, 542
9:6 555
9:9 545
9:10
9:11 555
9:12 372
9:15–17 541
9:18–19 555
10:1 549
10:5 365, 555
10:5–7 568
10:6 372
10:9–12 358
10:10 549, 555
10:10–12 568
10:10–13 106
10:12 569
10:20–21 541
10:20–24 542
10:25 524, 536
12:3 557
12:20 231
14:41–42 541
16:1–3 359
16:13 549
17:45–47 345
19:19–24 568
19:20 106,
19:24 569
21:12–15 592
22:5 359, 548
23:9–12 544
23:16–17 200
28 293, 544
28:6 118, 358, 541
30:6 200
30:7–8 544

2 Samuel
2:1 542, 544
5:19 542, 544

5:23 542, 544
7 361, 556
7:4–17 330, 359, 360
7:12 331
7:12–16 550
7:13–14 556
7:14 331
7:16 331
9:7 208, 231
10:12 200
12:1–14 359, 360
12:24 332
23:1–7 545
23:3 546
23:5 338, 546
23:6 546
24:11–19 359

1 Kings
1 550
1:11–31 360
1:32–40 359
1:32–53 550
5:5 412
11:29–39 359, 555
11:37–39 547
12:15 548
12:22–24 359, 548
13 554
13:1–2 554
13:1–10 114
13:11–32 545
14:10–11 362, 547
14:14 547
17:1 556
17:3–5 624
17:7–16 559
17:13 231
17:17–24 558
16.1–3 547
16:1–7 359
16:2–4 362
18 347, 359, 370, 419, 590
18:16–20 114
18:19 569
18:21–40 556
18:28 371, 589
18:29 106
18:38–45 558
18:41 114
19:10 556
19:14 556
19:15–16 359
20:13 548
20:13–14 359, 542
20:22 359
20:35–43 566
20:39–43 359
21:17–24 360
21:17–29 359
21:20–24 548
22 358
22:1–28 114, 348, 419, 641
22:6 543, 569
22:10 106,
22:10–12 543
22:13 348
22:14 543, 570
22:15 543
22:19–22 462, 490
22:19–23 371, 420, 440
22:37–38 548

2 Kings
1 114, 544, 546
1:8 589
2:1–18 566
2:7 567
2:8 454
2:13 589
2:14 454, 558
2:15 567
2:19–22 558
3:18 548
3:9–20 358
4:1–7 559, 566
4:8–37 558
4:38–41 558, 566, 567
4:42–44 559
5:1–19 558
5:22 566, 567
5:26 371
6:1 567
6:1–7 558, 566

6:8–17 558–559
6:16 231
6:17 371
6:18–20 558
8:7–15 114, 358, 541, 546
8:13 359, 360
9:1 567
9:1–3 567
9:1–13 359, 566
9:6–10 550
9:9–10 548
9:11 592
9:30–37 548
13:14–19 358
13:20–21 558
14:25 549
15:8–31 620
15:25 620
15:29 547
16:5 623
16:6 220
17:13 349
17:21–23 548
19–20 114
19:1–7 360, 555, 556
19:1–34 358
19:6–7 548
20:1–7 368
20:1–11 359, 360, 558
20:5–6 549
21:6 540
22 360, 553, 585
22:3–20 144, 358
22:14 143, 324
22:14–20 392
22:20 549
23:2 145
23:29 549
24–25 605

1 Chronicles
10:10 594
17:3–15 359
21:9–19 359
22:13 231
25:1 372
25:1–7 365, 374
25:3 372
25:6 372
25:7 372
28:20 231

2 Chronicles
9:29 534, 636, 643
12:5–8 359
15:1–7 359
15:8 636
16:7–10 359
18 358
19:1–3 359
20:14–17 359
20:15 230
20:17 230
20:37 359
21:12–15 359, 525, 533
24:5 594
25:1–3 633
25:7–10 359
25:15–16 359
26:22 525, 533, 536
28:5–8 623
28:9–11 59
32:20 358
34:19–28 358
34:22 143, 324
35:25 368, 533

Ezra
5:1–2 143, 582
6:14 143, 582
9:11 143, 582

Nehemiah
2:10 582
4:8 218, 231
6 584, 587
6:2 584
6:5–7 582
6:5–9 143
6:8 582
6:10–13 582
6:11 586
6:12 636, 643
6:14 143, 193, 325, 359, 570, 586

6:14–19 582
6:17–19 586
9:26, 143, 582
9:30 143, 582
9:32 143, 582
13:4–9 586
13:4–13 586
13:28 586

Job
1:6 462
2:1 462
9:8 481
5:18 461
15:8 462

Psalms
1:3 484
2 362
2:7 331
15 176
20:8 345
21 362
21:2–8 330
21:5 330
21:9–13 330
24:3–5 176
24:7 281
25:14 462
29:1 462
36:10 442
42:5 594
45 362
46 267, 410
46:5 442
46:4–5 267
46:4–8 267
46:9 411
48 410
52:10 594
55:15 594
66 410
76 410
82 490
82:1 462
82:6 462
84:11 594,
89 338
89:4 332
89:6 462
89:6–8 490
89:7 462
89:8 462
89:5 331
89:27–30 331
89:20 332
89:30 331
89:35–46 337
89:37f 331
89:38 337
97:7 462
110 362
113:3 327
135:2 594

Proverbs
1:7 202
3:13–26 481
3:18 484
8 481, 482
8:21 491
8:24 486
9:10 202
10:11 442
13:14 442
16:22 442
18:4 442

Qoheleth
4:17 594
8:1 678

Song of Songs 480, 481, 482
1:14 484, 485
1:17 484
2:1–2 488
2:16 488
3:1–4 487
3:9 484, 488
4:5 488
4:8 484, 488
4:11 484, 488
4:12–5:1 488
4:13 484, 486, 488

4:15 484, 486, 488
4:16 486
4:16–5:1 487
5:1 486
5:2–6 487
5:14 488
5:15 484, 488
6:2 486, 487
6:10 488
7:3 488
7:5 484, 488
7:8–9 484
7:14 488
8:2 487
8:6 486
8:7 486

Isaiah
1:11–17 20,
2:2–4 397, 399, 409, 410, 411, 412, 415
2:3 594
3:13–15 20,
5:1–2 365
5:8–23 20,
6 371
6:6–7 444
6:8 462, 490
7 114, 360
7:1–9 623
7:3 573
7:4 195, 212, 230
7:9 212, 409
7:10–25 359
7:11 83,
8:1 535, 536
8:1–2 526
8:1–4 144
8:3 143, 325, 570, 573
8:12 195
8:16 527, 536, 573, 574, 575
8:16–18 572, 574
8:18 83,
8:19 76
9:5 331
9:3–4 411
10:1–4 20,
10:24 195, 230
11:9 655
13–23 20,
13:6 368
14:31 368
19:19–25 412
19:20 83,
20:1–6 371
25:10–12 20,
30:8 526, 532, 536, 573, 575
30:15 409
32:9–14 368
34:4 195
34:5–15 20,
37–39 114,
37:1–7 360, 556
37:1–35 358, 555
37:6 195, 230
38:1–8 360, 558
38:7 83,
38:21–22 360
38:22 83
40:1–8 562
40–55 264, 265, 345, 349
40:2 264
40:9 195, 263
41:4 263, 264
41:8–18 332
41:9–11 345
41:10 195, 230, 263
41:13 195, 220, 263
41:14 195, 220, 263
41:17 263
42:6 220, 263
42:8 263
42:15 263
43:1–4 333
43:1–7 264
43:1 195, 220, 263, 264, 345
43:4 263
43:5 195, 263, 345
43:11 220, 333
43:12 220
43:14 264
43:15 220
44:1–2 263
44:1–5 333
44:2 220, 263, 345

44:6 264
44:22–23 264
44:24 220, 263, 264
45:1–7 333, 359
45:3 220
45:5 220, 263, 333
45:6 327
45:7 220, 263
45:18 220, 263
45:21 220, 333
46:3–4 263
46:9 220
47:4 264
48:12–15 333
48:17 220, 263, 264
48:20 264
49:7 264
49:23 220, 263
49:26 220, 264
51:7 195, 263
52:9 264
54:4 195, 263, 345
54:5 264
54:8 264
55:3 332, 333
57:11 202–203
58 20,
59:3 589
61:1 372
66 20,
66:12 342

Jeremiah
1:1 124, 364
1:8 195, 230
2:13 442
6:13–15 419
6:14 347
6:26 368
7:22 20,
9:4 589
9:19 368
10:5 195
16:1–9 371
17:13 442
18:22 462
20:2 347
21 114,
21:1–10 359
22 114,
22:10–19 359
22:24–30 359
23:18 462, 490
23:22 461
22:30 362
23:5–6 95
23:9–32 347
23:13–32 419
23:16–22 371
23:18 420
23:25–32 439
25:13 530
26:20–24 347
27:2–11 359
27:14–17 419
28 419, 421, 641
28:9 349
29 525
29:8–9 419
29:21–24 641
19:15 419
29:21–23 419
29:23 589
29:26 373, 592
30:2 526, 530, 536
30:10 195
32:3–5 359
32:9–15 528
32:10 528, 536
32:10–12 524–525
34:1–7 114, 359
36 114, 360, 528, 530, 535
36:1–2 526
36:2 536
36:4 529
36:11–26 438
36:27–28 526
36:32 530, 572
37:1–10 114
37:3–10 359
37:17–21 114,
38:14–26 359
38:14–28 114, 360
42:11 195, 230

44:29 83
45:1 529, 530
46–51 20
46:27 195
50–51 535
50:1 535
51:59–64 535
51:60 535, 536

Lamentations
2:14 349
3:57 198

Ezekiel
1 371, 606, 610
1:1 603
1:1–3 603
1:3 364, 365, 603
1:22 365
2:2 372
2:6 195, 230
2:9–3:3 531
3:1 604
3:4 531, 604
3:5 604, 605
3:7 604
3:9 195
3:12–15 371
3:15 603
3:17 604
3:23 603
4–6 371
4:3 83
4:9–17 445
6:2 604
7:2 604
8 371
8:1 359, 365, 603
10 371
11 371
11:1 603
11:13 603
11:15 604
11:24 603
12 371
12:9 604
12:13–16 605
12:22 604
13 347, 349, 419, 604
13:1–16 147, 604
13:9 349
13:10–11 349
13:15–16 349
13:17 143
13:17–23 147, 148, 151, 604, 607
14:1 359, 603
14:1–5 604
17:2 604
17:12–21 605
18:2 604
18:10–13 20
18:25 604
19 368
19:5–9 605
20:1 359, 603
20:1–4 604
30:2 368
20:12 83
20:20 83
20:27 604
20:39 604
23:11–27 605
21:11 368
24:1–2 526
24:2 531, 536
24:3 604
24:15–27 371
24:18–24 603
24:21 604
25–32 20
27–28 453
27:4 453
27:25–27 453
33:7 604
33:10 604
33:20 604
33:21 603
33:24 604
33:32 365
34:23 332
36:1–8 604
36:22 604
36:25 444
37:1–14 371, 604, 607

37:11 604
37:15–16 526, 536
37:16 526, 531, 535
37:16–23 603
37:24 332
37:40–48 371
40–48 608
40:4 604
43:3 603
43:10 604
44:6 604
47 606
47:12 443

Daniel
1–6 360
1:2 594
1:3–7 525
1:20 647, 669
2:4–7:11 669
2:18 646, 669
2:19 646, 669
2:27–30 646, 669
2:31–45 671
2:47 646, 669
4:3 669
4:6 646, 669
5:12 669
5:12 669
5:16 669
5:26 669
4:15 669
4:16 669
6:27 202
7:1 525, 536
7:16 669
8:23–25 96
10:12 195, 230
10:19 195, 230
11:3–45 96
12:10 96

Hosea
1 371
1:2–9 144
1:7 345
4:1–3 20
4:1–10 337
4:13 485
5:1 359
5:8–14 623
5:10 623
5:13 623
6:4–6 20,
6:5 594
7:3–7 620
7:9 592
7:11 624
9:3 624
9:7 372
9:7–9 373, 591, 592, 593
9:10–17 621
10:5–8 621, 622
11:1 342
11:1–5 621
11:3 342
11:4 342
11:5 624
11:11 624
12:1 624
12:3 337
12:11 594
13:4 333

Joel
1:5–14 368
1:13 594
2:21 195
2:22 195
3:1 104, 106,
3:1–2 372
3:18 443

Amos
1:1 386, 387, 388
1:1–2:3 20
2:6–8 20
3:3–8 462
3:7 371, 462, 490
4:1–3 20
5:1–3 368
5:2 388
5:7–12 20
5:21 570

5:21–24 20
7:1–9 371
7:7–10 508
7:9 362
7:10–11 359
7:10–17 386, 387, 390
7:14 387, 388
7:14–15 61
7:17 362
8:1–3 371
8:4–8 20,
9:1–4 371

Obadiah
1–15 20

Jonah
2:3–10 368
3 360

Micah
1:8 368
2:1–5 20
2:6–11 347
3:5 158
3:5–8 347
3:5–12 419
3:8 372
3:9–12 20
3:11 158
4:1–5 397, 399, 409, 410, 411, 415
4:2 594
4:3 412
4:4 412
6:4 147
6:6–8 20
7:1–4 20

Habakkuk
1:2–4 368
1:12–17 368
2:1 368
2:2 526, 532, 536, 573, 575
2:2–3 573
2:5–17 20
2:14 655
3 368
3:1 368
3:8 453

Zephaniah
3:16 195, 204

Haggai
2:5 195, 230
2:20–23 359
2:21–23 361

Zechariah
1–6 371
3:1–7 462
6:12–13 95
7:5–10 20
8:13 195, 230
8:15 195, 230
13:1 444
13:2–3 589
13:2–6 72, 373, 587, 588
13:4 374, 589
13:4–6 589, 591
14:8 443

Malachi
1:11 327
1:11–14 117
1:6–2:9 176

Deuterocanonical Works

Wisdom of Solomon 659

Jesus Sirach
Prol 9–10 480, 494
1 479
1:1 491
14:20–15:10 487
14:22–23 487
14:26–27 487
15:3 487
15:4 487
15:5 487
24 479, 480, 481, 482, 483, 491, 493, 494, 659
24:1–12 482

24:1–22 481, 487
24:1–29 479
24:2 490
24:10–11 485, 488
24:13 484, 485, 488
24:13–20 484
24:13–22 482
24:14 484, 488
24:15 485
24:16 485
24:17 485
24:19 485
24:18 486
24:20 486
24:21 486
24:22 487
24:23 491
24:25–27 484, 492
24:29 486
24:30–31 491
24:30–33 482
24:30–34 443, 479
24:31 488
24:33 373, 395, 489
39:1–3 373, 637
39:1–8 637
39:6 396
39:6 373, 492
44:3–5 637, 643
46:1 637, 643
46:13 637
50:1–24 487
50:5 488
50:5–10 491
50:6–7 488
50:8–10 488
50:12 488
51:13–22 487
51:13–30 479
51:17 487
51:18 487
51:19 487
51:21 487
51:23 576

Psalm 151 372, 638

Pseudepigrapha

1 Enoch (see also 4Q204)
45:3 658

Jubilees
10:8–9 593
11:5 593
17:16 593
19:28 593

Pseudo-Philo 147

Testament of Judah
21:9 419

Treatise of Shem 670

New Testament

Matthew
7:15 419
24:11 419
24:15 525
24:24 419

Mark
1:6 374, 589
13:22 419
14:24 335, 453

Luke
2:12 655
4:14–20 372
6:26 410
18:2 204

Acts
2:30 545
13:6 419

1 Corinthians
11:25 335, 453
14:7 374
14:15 374
14:26 374

2 Corinthians
12:1–5 371

Galatians
1:8 440

Ephesians
5:18–20 374

Colossians
3:16 374

2 Peter
2:1 419

1 John
4:1 419
4:1–3 440

Revelation
16:13 419
19:20 419
20:10 419
21:1–4 267
22:1–2 443

Dead Sea Scrolls

CD (*Damascus Document*) II, 12–13 640
CD III, 21 639
CD V, 20 – VI, 2 652
CD VI, 1 636
CD VI, 1 642
CD VI, 13 639
CD VII, 10 639
CD VII, 15–20 640
CD XIX, 7 639
CD XIX, 11–12 639
PAM 43.677 6, 2 638
1Q27 (*Mysteries*) 646, 647, 652, 654, 655, 656, 657, 661
1Q27 1 I, 8 645
1Q27 1 I 5–8 656
1QH[a] (*Hodayot*) 661
1QH[a] IV, 16 632
1QH[a] IX, 21 648
1QH[a] X, 13 648
1QH[a] XII:5–17 652
1QH[a] XII, 14 643, 641
1QH[a] XII, 16 643, 641
1QH[a] XII, 27 648
1QH[a] XIII, 10–12 648
1QH[a] XIII, 25 648
1QH[a] XX, 13 648
1QH[a] XXVI 658
1QH[a] XXVI, 6–14 652
1QM (*War Scroll*) 13:11 593
1QpHab (*Pesher Habakkuk*) I, 1 638
1QpHab II, 2–3 646
1QpHab II, 7–10 640
1QpHab II, 8–9 646
1QpHab III, 4–6 675
1QpHab VII, 1–2 678
1QpHab VII, 1–8 645–646
1QS (*The Rule of the Community*) 642
1QS V, 3 651
1QS I, 2–3 639
1QS VIII, 11–12 639
1QS VIII, 16 643
1QS IX, 10–11 640
1QS IX, 18–19 647
1QS XI, 3–9 647
3Q4 3 (*3QIsaiah Pesher*) 636
4QpHos[a] (4Q166) II, 5 639
4QpPs[a] (4Q171) I, 27 673
4Q165 (*4QIsaiah Pesher[e]*) 1–2 636, 643
4QXII[c] 615
4QXII[d] 615
4QXII[g] 615
4Q160 (*Vision of Samuel*) 656
4Q171 (*Psalms Pesher*) I, 27 648
4Q174 (*4QFlorilegium*) 1, II, 2, 24 525
4Q174 1 3 II, 3 639
4Q177 II, 2, 13 639
4Q182 2 1 656
4Q186 651
4Q204 (*4QEn[e]*) 5 II, 26–27 646
4Q208–209 (*Astronomical Book of Enoch*) 670
4Q265 2 3 639
4Q267 2 6–7 636
4Q269 4 I, 2 636
4Q285 5 1 639
4Q292 2 3 4 639

4Q300 1 II, 2 647
4Q300 frag. 3 654
4Q318 (*4QZodiology and Brontology*) 670
4Q318 VIII, 9 672
4Q320 670
4Q321 670
4Q339 641, 652
4Q375 (*Apocryphon of Moses*) 642, 652
4Q381 69 4 640, 643
4Q385 2 5–7 635
4Q385b 16 I, 2, 6 638
4Q386 1 I, 4 635
4Q390 (*4QpsMoses*[e]) 2 I, 5 639
4Q397 (*4QMMT*) 14–21 10 640
4Q410 (*4QVision and Interpretation*) 646, 652, 653, 654, 656
4Q410 1–7 653
4Q410 7–8 646
4Q410 7–11 653
4Q427 658
4Q427 7 I, 7–13 652
4Q458 15 2 636
4Q471b 652, 661
4Q471b+4Q431 658
4Q491 490
4Q491c 652, 658
4Q491c 1 5–11 657–658
4Q543–4Q549 (*Visions of Amram*) 147, 653
4Q397 14–21 641
11Q5 (*11QPs*[a]) XXII, 5–6 639
11Q5 XXII, 13–14 643
11Q5 XXVII, 4 372
11Q5 XXVII, 9–10 368
11Q5 XXVII, 11 372, 632, 633, 636, 637
11Q5 XXVIII, 4 372
11Q5 XXVIII, 8 638
11Q13 (*11QMelchizedeq*) II, 3 639
11Q13 II, 15–18 640
11Q13 II, 17–18 642
11Q19 (*Temple Scroll*) 642
11Q19 LIV, 8–18 652
11Q19 LIV, 8–18 642, 634
11Q19 LXI, 1–5 642

Rabbinic Sources

B. Bat. 15a 368
b. Meg. 14a 575

Classical sources

Aeschylus
Eumenides
17–19 84,
29–33 543

Aristotle
Metaphysics
1.3 441

Cicero
On Divination
1.1.1–3 76

Apuleius
Apology
42.6 449

Clement of Alexandria
Exhortation to the Greeks
2.11 449

Diodorus Siculus
16.26.1–6 447

Diogenes Laertius
1.27 441

Euripides
Ion
321, 1322 84
93, 419 445
Phoenician Maidens
224 445

Herodotus
1.46–49 543

Iamblichus
On the Mysteries
3.5 (111:7–11) 448
3.11 (124:8–12) 449
3.11 (127:4–9) 448
3.11 (127:11–13) 445

Josephus
The Jewish War
6.285 419

Kallisthenes
FGrH 124 F 222 543

Lucan
6.425 449

Philo of Alexandria
On the Migration of Abraham
34–35 373
Special Laws
1:65 373
4:51 419

Pliny
Natural History
2.228 450
2.232 449

Plato
Ion
534c–d 85
Phaedrus
244a–245a 76
244b 84,

Plutarch
Moralia
3:397a 445
3:435b 445
492b 543
5:433c–d 447

Servius
Commentary on the Aeneid
3.446 450

Sophocles
Antigone
1055 158

Tacitus
Annals
2.54 449

www.ingramcontent.com/pod-product-compliance
Lightning Source LLC
Chambersburg PA
CBHW050300010526
44108CB00040B/1897
9783110764130